Curtis Jackson
9-1-94

357

SERMON

OUTLINES

Sketches of Sermons on the Parables of Christ
Miracles of Christ
Scripture Characters
Christian Missions
Special Occasions

BY

JABEZ BURNS

KREGEL PUBLICATIONS
Grand Rapids, Michigan 49501

LIBRARY OF CONGRESS CATALOG CARD NUMBER 65-23844

ISBN 0-8254-2206-X

This edition of *357 SERMON OUTLINES* by Jabez Burns is a complete and un-
abridged edition of this book formerly published under the titles *CYCLOPEDIA
OF SERMONS* and *CYCLOPEDIA OF SERMON OUTLINES*.

Reprint edition under title *Cyclopedia of Sermons* 1956
First printing under title *Cyclopedia of Sermon Outlines* 1965
First printing under title *357 Sermon Outlines* 1971
Reprinted 1972, 1974, 1977, 1981

Printed in United States of America

PREFACE.

The sketches of Sermons contained in this volume have been prepared at various times, and may be divided into three or four distinct classes.

Those relating to the subject of *Christian Missions* occupy the first pages. For nearly fifty years, men of decided talent and spiritual excellence have been preaching upon this topic in London, and numerous large towns and cities of England, as well as in our own country. From these discourses most of this class of the sketches have been selected and formed; and it is truly delightful to observe how ministers of the Church of England, Wesleyans, Baptists, Presbyterians, and Congregationalists, all enunciate the same great and glorious truths, when advocating the momentous claims of a world which lieth in wickedness. This class of the selections has been made irrespective of the sect or party of the preacher; the end contemplated being an exposition of the missionary spirit from some of the most talented ministers of past and present times. There are also included in this class four sketches on the subject of the conversion of the Jews; and one especially addressed to children, whose exertions in the cause of missions have been of late so strikingly exhibited. Those which are without name, it may be stated, are the productions of the compiler of the volume.

The next class of these sketches comprise a series which were prepared to form a suitable accompaniment to former volumes published by the author, entitled "Sketches on Types and Metaphors," and "On the Parables of Christ." They, however, contain entirely new themes, and, in some instances, characters and incidents not usually found in volumes of printed discourses.

The third class contains sketches of sermons which have been delivered on more public and special occasions than usual. The appropriateness of the subjects may very properly be considered as a matter of personal opinion or taste; and, of course, the reader will employ his own judgment as to the fitness of the topics there presented to the occasions for which they were designed. The great and blessed Teacher regarded this law of appropriateness with peculiar exactness, in suiting his various parables and discourses to the occasions and circumstances of those whom he addressed. Certain it is, that congregations look for subjects expressly bearing on the object contemplated in the service for which they are convened.

The last class of these sketches has been published with a view to the edification of those persons confined in the chamber of affliction; to Christian families when deprived of the public means of grace; and also to aid village worship, in the absence of the usual preaching of the word. To answer these ends they have been studiously condensed, so as not to weary those who may peruse or hear them; and also to be suggestive of trains of thought which might lead to extended profitable meditations. Among the discourses of this class, there will be found subjects of a doctrinal, experimental, and practical character; yet so simple and plain as to be easily understood, and so thoroughly imbued with the spirit and letter of God's word, that they should lead the mind from the uncertainties of human opinion to the utterances of the living oracles, which convey to us the essential truths of salvation.

In conclusion, it should be stated that the volume now put forth by the American publishers, was first issued by the compiler and author in five small and distinct volumes from the English press, the contents of all of which are comprised in these pages.

CONTENTS

CONTENTS

CONTENTS vii

SERMON OUTLINES

I.—CHRIST'S PARABOLICAL MODE OF TEACHING.

"All these things spake Jesus unto the multitude in parables: and without a parable spake he not unto them."—*Matt.* xiii. 34.

In eastern countries, from the earliest ages, instruction has been extensively communicated through the medium of parables. It is the favorite mode of diffusing knowledge among Oriental nations at the present day. One of the earliest parables on scripture record is that of Jotham, in which the trees are represented as seeking to anoint a king over them, Judges ix. 8. Another ancient parable is that of Jehoash, wherein the thistle is described as seeking a matrimonial alliance with the cedar: see 2 Kings xiv. 9. There is also that of Tekoah, 2 Sam. xiv. 5; and that of Nathan, in which he brought the sin of David before his eyes, and caused the indignant monarch to pass sentence upon himself, must be well remembered by all. It is difficult to decide whether Solomon's vivid description of old age and its infirmities, Eccles. xii. 2, is to be viewed as a parable or allegorical description. Our attention, however, at present, is directed to the parables of the Saviour. So greatly did Christ adopt this mode of instruction, that it is affirmed in the text, "without a parable spake he not unto them." The passage does not design to assert absolutely that he never taught in any other way, but that this was the common, almost the unvarying practice of the great Teacher. Let us then,

I. *Establish the truth of the text.* And,

II. *Assign some reasons for the mode of instruction the Saviour adopted.*

I. *Establish the truth of the text.* The Saviour's ministry did not extend much, if any, beyond the period of three years.

There can be no doubt that the chief themes and topics of his instruction, though in a very condensed form, have been transmitted to us in the writings of the evangelists. Now, these parables form a chief, indeed a great proportion of the Saviour's teaching.

(1.) In some cases parables were the basis of other doctrinal and practical addresses, as in the parables of the sower, and many others.

(2.) In other instances the parable constituted the application of the discourse just delivered, as in the parable of the foolish and wise builders, which was the conclusion of his sermon on the mount.

(3.) But from their number and variety, it is obvious to the ordinary reader of the New Testament scriptures, that the Saviour seldom spake to the people without embodying in parabolical costume his divine instructions.

(4.) In some of the Saviour's discourses we have a series of parables, as in the chapter of which the text forms a part. For here we have the parable of the sower—of the wheat and tares—grain of mustard-seed—of the leaven—hidden treasure—of the net—and the pearl of great price. So profusely rich was the Saviour's blessed discourse on this occasion, that we do not marvel that it should be said, "without a parable spake he not unto them." Let us,

II. *Assign some reasons for the mode of instruction which the Saviour adopted.* We might remark that it accorded with the habits and mental characteristics of the people, and that it harmonized with great portions of their Holy Scriptures. But we observe,

1. *That it rendered great and sublime subjects easy to be understood.* Of all themes,

Christ's were the most lofty and exalted. He had to do with subjects difficult of apprehension to the human mind. His topics were spiritual, heavenly, eternal. By parables, he brought these truths down to the capacities of the people. They could not fail to ascertain the mind and design of the speaker, and the import of his subject. Hence the common people, the illiterate, the mass, heard him gladly. No marvel that the peasantry hung on his sacred lips with wonder, reverence, and admiration. Now this should ever be the chief object of the preacher's attention—the people must understand, or how can they possibly profit?

2. *By parables, subjects were rendered pleasing to the mind.* Figurative illustrations, and metaphorical analogies, are gratifying to most minds. Abstract principles, presented in an abstract form, would attract the careful attention of but a few of mankind. But to see these themes clothed in parabolical costume, was sure to delight the great majority of the Saviour's hearers. To interest our hearers, is generally essential to their profit. And the Saviour's hearers were often so charmed, that for hours they listened to him with gladness and delight. On one occasion he wrought a splendid miracle to supply the people with food who had followed him, and hearkened to his discourses until evening had come. Matt. xiv. 14.

3. *By teaching in parables he obtained a more candid hearing from his auditors.* Many of the Saviour's sermons were intended to convey keen rebukes for sin, and faithful warnings to those who were deceiving themselves. In many cases a direct charge would have at once excited their prejudices and wrath. By parables, therefore, the bitter potion was so administered, that those who were condemned by the discourse must have admired the mode in which the reproof was given, or the threatening denounced. Besides, it was thus more difficult to reject the counsel of the Saviour against themselves.

4. *By parables the Saviour often won the attention of his hearers.* Many of the Saviour's parables were adapted to excite and captivate the best emotions of the heart. Such, for instance, as the parable of the joyous shepherd rejoicing over the recovered wanderer from the fold. Such also as the clement lord who so freely forgave the debt of his servant. Such also as the mercy and goodness of the father who so ardently received back again his prodigal son.

5. *The parables of the Saviour were easily remembered and retained.* The natural imagery in which they were clothed was always before them. The fishermen could not forget the parable of the net; nor the housewife those of the leaven—or the lost piece of silver; nor the husbandman those of the vineyard—of the sower—or of the tares. To be benefited by what we hear, it must be retained and stored up in the chambers of the memory.

6. *By parabolical teaching the Saviour showed the great aim of his ministry.* It was not to perplex the ignorant, or to triumph over the partially instructed, or to exhibit himself as an object for learned admiration; but it was evident he desired their improvement—their enlightenment—their spiritual and eternal profit. He showed the deepest concern for their well-being, and made it evident that he labored for their present and everlasting salvation. How desirable to make this manifest in all our discourses. To convince our hearers that we seek only their profit, that they may be saved.

APPLICATION.

1. How sweet and gracious the character of Christ as a teacher.

2. What a model for ministerial imitation.

3. Let us profit by his blessed discourses which are contained in the scriptures of the New Testament.

Here we can listen to the Saviour and receive his life-giving and soul-saving words. And surely the words of his mouth are better unto us than thousands of gold and silver.

II.—THE WISE AND FOOLISH BUILDERS.

"Therefore whosoever heareth these sayings of mine, and doeth them, I will liken him unto a wise man, which built his house upon a rock," &c.—*Matt.* vii. 24–27.

The Redeemer had just finished his inimitable Sermon on the Mount. He had been opening, in a comprehensive and distinct manner, the spiritual nature of his kingdom, and the true practical character of saving religion. His auditory had doubtless listened with fixed attention, but he, knowing their hearts, perceived that many would be satisfied with hearing, without obeying the truths which they had heard.

He therefore concluded his address with the parable of the builders, which could not fail to remind his hearers that the great end of his teaching was the practical improvement of those who listened to his words. Observe,

I. *What is commendable even in the conduct of the foolish builder.*

II. *Those things which he neglected as contrasted with the wise builder.* And,

III. *The final results in reference to both.* Observe,

I. *What is commendable even in the foolish builder.* (1.) He was not a neglecter of religious things altogether.

(2.) He heard the sayings of the great teacher: ver. 26.

(3.) It is clear also that he heard with sufficient attention to understand.

(4.) He was also greatly influenced by what he heard.

(5.) He felt the importance of making provision for the future. Of building a house to protect himself from the inclemency of the approaching season.

(6.) He actually selected a site, commenced the building, and stayed not until it was finished.

(7.) There is nothing said disparagingly respecting the external appearance of the house. He expended sufficient time and toil in its erection.

It is obvious that the foolish builder, in plain terms, heard, understood, was interested, and was greatly influenced by the teaching of the Saviour, and all these were features worthy of commendation. But observe,

II. *Those things which he neglected as contrasted with the wise builder.* He did not,

1. *Duly calculate the trials his house would have to endure.* He thought only of the present and fine weather. He was solicitous only for its present convenience and comfort. Palestine, as a land of hills and brooks, was peculiarly liable to inundations, and hence it was of the utmost importance to select a site sheltered from the storm, and where the base would not suffer from the teeming rain. Many are satisfied with the present forms of religion, they feel their need of nothing more, and they neglect to prepare for times of temptation, afflictions, and death. They reckon not on the solemn concerns of judgment and eternity. He did not,

2. *Select a sure and safe foundation.* The sand, in the dry season, might appear solid and firm; but who that knew its fragile texture, its movable character, would select it for a foundation. The wise builder knew the value of a firm, immovable basis, and selected the hard, unyielding rock. That which wind could not scatter, nor waves remove. The sandy foundation may represent,

(1.) Our own righteousness, in opposition to the sacrifice and righteousness of the Lord Jesus Christ.

(2.) Or the union of our works with those of the Redeemer, as the ground of our hopes.

(3.) Or the mere assumption of the name and forms of religion, without an acquaintance with its spirit and power.

(4.) Or the public profession of religion, without regard to a practical obedience to the Saviour. The rock on which the wise man built, is the Lord Jesus Christ. The elect, precious, sure, and immutable foundation, which God has laid in Zion. To build on this foundation implies,

(1.) A knowledge of Christ's character, person, offices, and work.

(2.) A rejection of all things else as the basis of hope. "God forbid that I should glory," &c. "Yea, doubtless, and I count all things but loss," &c.

(3.) An implicit resting of the soul on Christ for pardon, acceptance, and eternal life. "No man cometh unto the Father but by me." "Other foundation can no man lay," &c.

(4.) Believing, conformity, and obedience to Christ's authority. Not only hearing, but doing the things which he commandeth. Observe,

III. *The results in reference to both builders.* The foolish builder,

1. *Experienced storms which he had not anticipated.* He had thought only of summer, and its sunshine and calm. He had not prudently calculated on approaching winter, with its winds and tempests. But, alas! these all came. "The rain descended," &c. So affliction, death, and judgment, will try every man's work.

2. *He was overwhelmed in ruin which he had not feared.* It is briefly recorded of his house, "that it fell." Its basis was swept away, and nothing was left to sustain it. Hence it became one heap of ruins. Its beauteous form, its elevated walls, its commodious rooms, were all lost in one utter desolation. So must it be with every kind of religion which rests not on Christ Jesus.

3. *The builder perished with the vain fabric he had reared.* Hence it is recorded,

"And great was the fall of it." Infatuated expectations and aerial prospects were all swept away, and the ruin of the builder was entire—irremediable, and eternal. Of the wise builder it is recorded,

1. *That his house also was tried by the storm*, ver. 25. No exemption even to pure, sincere, and evangelical piety, from the trials and afflictions of life, the solemnities of death, or the decisions of the judgment day. "Every man's work shall be tried with fire." "God will judge every man," &c.

2. *But his hopes were fully realized.* His house withstood the fury of the blast. The rains fell, and the winds blew upon his house in vain. "It fell not." Blessed, joyous declaration for the builder. He was sheltered, happy, and secure. His expectations were not cut off, but his soul's desire was granted. "He knew whom he had believed," &c. "An abundant entrance was administered," &c. Learn,

1. The wisdom of experimental true piety.
2. The peculiar character of evangelical religion. Christ the basis.
3. The folly of all other schemes to save the perishing sinner.

III.—THE PARABLE OF THE SOWER.

"And he spake many things unto them in parables, saying, Behold a sower went forth to sow: And when he sowed, some *seeds* fell by the wayside, and the fowls came and devoured them up," &c.—*Matt.* xiii. 3, 9.

THE Saviour had been delivering a series of pious and faithful admonitions, and had also confirmed his divine mission by healing one who had been possessed with a devil, blind, and dumb, chap. xii. 22. The Jews, under a spirit of infatuation and unbelief, attributed his miraculous power to Beelzebub, the prince of devils. He therefore reasoned with them on the gross improbability, that Satan would help to destroy his own kingdom, ver. 25, 26. He then warned them against the fearful sin of blasphemy against the Holy Ghost; and showed how important it was to have the heart in a right state: for only from a good heart, could the treasure of good things be produced, ver. 35.

Some of the Scribes and Pharisees then sought a sign, on which Jesus referred them to that of the prophet Jonah, and declared that the men of Nineveh should rise to condemn that generation. After he had concluded these and other discourses, the same day he went and sat by the sea-side, and, as great multitudes were gathered together to hear him, He addressed to them the parable of the sower. There can be no doubt that he had before his mind the various characters who had listened to his previous discourses, with the different results which had followed his labors. Observe,

I. *The sower.* The Lord Jesus Christ as the great teacher,—the divine apostle of the gospel. Under Christ, all ministers of the blessed word,

(1.) Whom he hath called by his spirit.
(2.) Qualified by graces and talents. And,
(3.) Sent forth by opening for them a sphere of usefulness. "An open and effectual door."

The ministerial sower must be,

(1.) Judicious. Selecting appropriate seasons and places for his work.
(2.) Diligent. Laboring as one who must give an account.
(3.) Persevering. Instant in season, and out of season.
(4.) Devoted. Yielding himself heartily, entirely, and sincerely to these things.

What wisdom, grace, and courage are necessary to the faithful minister of Jesus Christ! Notice,

II. *The seed.* The seed is the word of God. As such,

1. *It is heavenly and divine.* Isaiah lv. 10, 11.
2. *Living and incorruptible.* 1 Peter i. 23.
3. *Powerful and soul-saving.* Rom. i. 16, and x. 17.
4. *And immutable and everlasting.* "But the word of our God shall stand forever." Is. xl. 8. Observe,

III. *The various kinds of ground into which it was cast.* Some fell,

1. *By the wayside.* These were unenlightened hearers. It took no root. And was speedily devoured by the fowls. Satan by his temptations, and the world by its vanities, and the heart with its sinful tendencies, prevented any good resulting from it. Some seed fell,

2. *In stony places.* Where there was only a shallow layer of earth, and beneath which was hard, unimpressible rock. Such are all *superficial* hearers. They listen with eagerness, and seem to receive it with joy; but, alas! "their goodness is but as the morning cloud," &c. Some other events speedily erase the impressions of the word:

and by some offence is taken, and they walk no more in the company of the pious. Some fell,

3. *Among thorns.* Where the ground had not been prepared for the reception of the seed. Indeed, where it was fully pre-occupied. These are *worldly hearers,* whose thoughts and desires are so engrossed with the concerns of the body and time—with earth and earthly things, that they can give no fixed attention to the great realities of the soul and eternity. "The cares of this world," how they harass, and perplex, and disturb! "Deceitful riches," how they be-guile, ensnare, and destroy! Observe, some fell,

4. *Into good ground.* Those whose hearts were prepared and open to receive it. These were the *practical* hearers. They heard to purpose and profit. They heard so as to understand, retain, and yield a return to the sower. Notice of the good ground hearers,

5. *The varied amount of increase yielded.* They all yield fruit, and abundantly. But the difference is striking. Some gave back thirty fold, a fair return. Others sixty, as much more as the former: while others gave a hundred fold, a return, striking and won-derful. Let each hearer strive not only to be fruitful, but to abound therein to the glory of God.

IV. *The practical application to which our attention is directed.* "Who hath ears to hear, let him hear." Let all hearers of the word consider,

1. *The indispensable characteristics of prof-itable hearing.* These should be (1.) Devo-tional preparation. God's blessing should be sought both on our own hearts, and on the ministering of the word.

(2.) Serious watchfulness, that the mind be not dissipated. That all wanderings of heart are avoided.

(3.) With candid attention : desiring to hear the truth with an ingenuous mind.

(4.) In the spirit of believing obedience. To receive it as the word of God, and not as the word of man. To receive it with holy resolution,—to practise what is heard. "Doers of the word, and not hearers only."

(5.) With humble reliance on God's bless-ing. That the word may be spirit and life to the soul. Let all hearers of the word con-sider,

2. *The advantages resulting from the right hearing of the word.* It will be fol-lowed,

(1.) By an increase of divine knowledge. "The entrance of God's word giveth light."

(2.) By its sanctifying influence on the heart. "Sanctify them by thy truth," &c.

(3.) By the gracious consolations it im-parts. Producing peace and joy in the Holy Ghost.

(4.) By its preserving power over the life. Counselling in perplexity. Keeping the feet from sliding from God's paths. Cleansing the way, &c. See Psa. cxix. 9, 11, &c. Acts xx. 32. "I commend you to God, and to the word of his grace, which is able to build you up," &c.

Learn,

(1.) The greatness of the privilege of those who hear the gospel.

(2.) Their individual responsibility for im-proving those privileges.

(3.) And the awful doom of those who hear to no profit. Heb. iii. 4.

IV.—THE PARABLE OF THE WHEAT AND TARES.

"Another parable put he forth unto them, saying, The kingdom of heaven is likened unto a man which sowed good seed in his field,"&c.— *Matt.* xiii. 24, &c.

It is of great importance carefully to ob-serve the Saviour's interpretation of his own parables. For the want of this, the utmost confusion and contradiction have arisen in reference to the one under consideration. Most commentators have interpreted this parable as if it had been descriptive of the Church, and not of the world. The Re-deemer emphatically explains it as referring to the world. He says, in his concise, yet clear elucidation of it, "The field is the world," &c. It is obvious that this should be kept in view throughout the whole para-ble, and in harmony with this declaration must the whole be expounded. Observe the field—the sowers—the fruit—the recommen-dation—the decision, and the consummation. Observe,

I. *The field.* "The field is the world." That is, the whole earth. Including all men, of all ages, and dispensations. The world may be contemplated,

1. *As a field of great extent.* Including the habitable globe. All nations, and peo-ple, and tongues.

2. *As a field densely populated.* Probably

containing a thousand millions of human, immortal beings.

3. *As a field of improvement.* Where men have numerous mercies, and means, and privileges. The light, and the sunshine, and the shower. The early and the latter rain.

4. *As a field of probation.* Where men are candidates on trial for immortality. Stewards who must give an account. Laborers for the day of life, &c.

5. *As a field of peril.* The temptations and snares innumerable. A world under the usurpation of the prince of darkness. Satan's seat. A world of wiles and dangers. Where sin in all its treacherous arts is spread abroad to the imminent risk and peril of souls. "Satan goeth about." Evil in various forms prevailing, &c. Notice,

II. *The sowers.* We are referred,

1. *To the Son of Man.* He sowed the good seed,—the wheat. He made man upright. Created him in his own likeness, &c. Planted within him holy principles, good desires, &c. We are referred,

2. *To Satan as the enemy.* He sowed the tares,—the evil seed. By tares is probably meant darnel, or rye grass, which had a close resemblance to wheat, and was not easily distinguished till near maturity. By this we are to understand the introduction of evil into the hearts of men by the temptations of the devil. Now here we see distinctly purity and good flowing from God, and depravity and evil from the prince of darkness. Notice then,

III. *The fruit :* ver. 26. The field was soon seen to be productive both of wheat and tares, of evil and of good. This has been the condition of the world ever since the fall. In the first family were Cain and Abel, and through all generations there have been the seed of the evil one, as well as the children of God. Everywhere is presented to the eye of the contemplatist the ignorant and the wise,—the vicious and the good,—the vile and the holy—the enemies and the loyal subjects of God. There has been no exception to this in any age, or country, in our world's history. This mixture everywhere prevails. Never forget that the good and holy are of God, but the evil of the devil. The enemy sowed the tares. Why God allowed it, is not for us to determine, but there can be no doubt he will overrule it for the manifestation of his divine glory. Observe,

IV. *The recommendation.* "The servants said, Wilt thou then that we go and gather them up?" ver. 28. This recommendation seems quite natural,—wherefore allow the soil to be cumbered,—the tares to remain? Is it not better and safer for us to separate the evil from the good?

(1.) How often would men advise thus, who only first contemplate the present, and whose minds do not take in the future.

(2.) How often would men advise thus, who only consult their own feelings of indignation against evil.

(3.) How the mass of men have acted thus in making sanguinary laws, by which criminals have been revengefully and hastily thrust out of life, as not fit to live. But does this accord with the wise benevolent administrations of heaven? Let the text answer the question, for notice,

V. *The decision of the proprietor.* But he said, "Nay; lest while ye gather up the tares, ye root up also the wheat with them:" ver. 29. This shows us,

1. *That to discriminate between good and bad men is not always an easy matter.* The best men are so frail, so liable to err and to fall into sin, that probably thousands whom God has accepted, men would have rejected. Some unconverted men have had so many amiable and lovely features, that men would have pronounced them pious, where God has seen no change of heart, and no evangelical reformation of character. To judge of heart and state, is God's prerogative, and let not fallible men invade it.

2. *God has his own purposes to accomplish in allowing the wicked to live.* He thus exhibits his own clemency and long-suffering. He thus gives space for repentance. He thus renders the ungodly excuseless.

3. *He often overrules the actions of evil men for his own glory.* They are often "His sword." His instrumentality for carrying out his designs. At any rate he says, "Let both grow together," &c. Notice then,

VI. *The consummation.* "And in the time of harvest," &c., &c. Observe,

1. *The harvest is the end of the world.* A predicted—certain—and awful event. A day which is approaching—doomsday. The day of the world's conflagration. See 2 Peter iii. 7, &c.

2. *Angels will be the administrators of the divine judgments.* This has often been so.

It will be so then. See Rev. xiv. 15, &c. Matt. xxv. 31. 2 Thess. i. 7, &c.

3. *The doom of the wicked will be fearful.* "Cast into the furnace of fire," &c. ver. 42. Rev. xx. 11, &c.

4. *The destination of the righteous will be glorious.* "Then shall the righteous shine forth," &c. v. 43. Theirs will be a state of exaltation and blessedness forever. He shall say unto them, "Come, ye blessed of my Father," &c. Matt. xxv. 34.

APPLICATION.

"Who hath ears to hear, let him hear," ver. 43.

How instructive and solemn the whole subject. Are we the wheat, or the tares? What is to be our future, our eternal state?

V.—THE PARABLE OF THE GRAIN OF MUSTARD SEED.

"Another parable put he forth unto them, saying, The kingdom of heaven is like to a grain of mustard seed, which a man took, and sowed in his field: which indeed is the least of all seeds; but when it is grown, it is the greatest among herbs, and becometh a tree, so that the birds of the air come and lodge in the branches thereof." —*Matt.* xiii. 31, 32.

THE text contains another of those parables which refer to the vegetable kingdom, and with which the rural auditory of Christ were intimately acquainted. He had led his hearers to contemplate the sower, casting his seed abroad, with the various results arising from the ground on which it fell. He had expatiated on the field which had produced both the wheat and tares, and he now wishes to present unto them an emblem of the origin, progress, and consummation of his spiritual kingdom. He therefore selects the mustard tree, refers to the smallness of its seed, and shows how it analogously describes that gracious administration he had come to set up in the world.

The parable strikingly exhibits the smallness of the origin—the greatness of the progress—and the glorious magnitude of his kingdom. Observe,

I. *The smallness of the origin of the Saviour's kingdom.* "The kingdom of heaven, or the gracious spiritual reign of the Messiah, is like to a grain of mustard seed," "which is indeed the smallest of all seeds," ver. 31, 32.

In how many points of light is this capable of illustration! Look,

1. *At the birthplace of the Saviour.* Bethlehem. Not Jerusalem, Matt. ii. 1, &c.

2. *Consider the parentage of the Saviour.* A carpenter his reputed father. A poor virgin his real mother.

3. *The circumstances of his birth.* How obscure and humiliating—born in a stable— laid in a manger. No room for the King of kings in the inn.

4. *Notice the commencement of his ministry.* At Nazareth. In comparative privacy. No parade or show connected with it.

5. *See the character of his disciples and the officers of his kingdom.* Fishermen. Tax gatherers, &c. None of the rulers or the great. His friends obscure, illiterate, poor.

6. *The paucity of his followers and adherents.* During any period of his life. At his apprehension. At his death. At his resurrection. When he ascended. They all met in an upper room in Jerusalem. Without learning. Wealth or influence. How apposite the metaphor : scarcely discernible as the small grain of mustard! But notice,

II. *The greatness of its progress.* The ideas in the text indicate progress—rapid, increasing progress. Observe,

1. *The rapid extension of the gospel and kingdom of Christ.* In Jerusalem, the city of Christ's death. In Samaria, &c. Through the then known world. So that forty years after Christ's death, the cross of Christ waved in triumph in Corinth, Athens, Antioch, Rome, &c. Myriads had been converted. Of Jews and Gentile idolaters. Of the learned and illiterate. Of the rich and the poor, &c. This progress is the more wondrous if you reflect,

2. *On the difficulties it had surmounted.* The difficulties of inherent depravity in the human heart. The difficulties of old and sacred systems. Of worldly prejudices and interests. Of rulers and pagan authorities. Yet everywhere the word of the Lord grew, and his subjects were multiplied. We may well be led to inquire,

3. *As to the principle of its success.* It was the divine purity and inherent power of truth. The work of the Spirit of the Lord. "Gospel was the power of God." "Weapons were mighty through God." It was the light of heaven chasing away hellish gloom. The energy of *truth* overthrowing the delusion of error. The power of *love* annihilating the elements of wrath and evil. The Omni-

potence of *holiness* overthrowing the principles of moral evil. Consider it,

III. *In its final glorious magnitude.*
"When it is grown, it is the greatest among herbs," &c.

1. *It shall gain the ascendency over all other systems of religion.* Judaism. Every form of idolatry. Mohammedanism. The papacy. They must all decline and pass away. All be destroyed by the brightness and glory of Christ's kingdom.

2. *It shall evangelize all the nations of the earth.* It is adapted to man in his general character. It will meet the moral state and spiritual wants and desires of all countries. It shall take root in every soil, and grow and thrive in every clime. It is to be carried into all the world, and preached to every creature. Hence its trophies shall be gathered out of all nations, and people, and colors, and tongues, Rev. vii. 9, &c.

3. *It shall bless all men, and make all men blessed.* See the resplendent visions of the inspired psalmist: Psa. lxxii. 16, 17. Also Isaiah lx. 21, &c. When God's kingdom is set up and consummated, then his will shall be done on the earth even as it is done in heaven. The fact, and not however the glorious results of the triumphs of Christianity is presented to us in this parable.

APPLICATION.

1. *The subject is fraught with hope to the friends of Christ.* "He must increase." Of his reign and dominion there shall be no end. All opposing elements shall be overthrown. The mountain shall be levelled, the valley exalted, &c.

2. *The subject is matter of gratulation to all benevolent minds.* His kingdom is one of righteousness, and peace, and joy. "Blessings abound where'er he reigns," &c.

3. *It may properly lead to personal inquiry.* Are we with and for Christ? His subjects. His friends. "The soldiers of the sacred Host of God's elect." Are we laboring to diffuse the knowledge of his character, and offices, and work? Does his cause absorb our warmest affections—our most intense and ardent zeal?

4. *The obdurate enemies of the cross must perish.* "His enemies he will clothe with shame," &c.

VI.—THE PARABLE OF THE LEAVEN.

"Another parable spake he unto them: The kingdom of heaven is like unto leaven, which a woman took, and hid in three measures of meal, till the whole was leavened."—*Matt.* xiii. 33.

THIS parable, in its scope and design, seems closely to resemble that of the grain of mustard seed. But while the grain of mustard seed indicates the small commencement and rapid progress of the gospel in the world, is not the parable of the leaven designed to illustrate more directly the workings of grace in the soul? The one may fitly show the progress of the Saviour's kingdom in the world, and the other the establishment of his kingdom in the soul. Let us then consider the parable of the leaven in its personal and spiritual application to religion in the heart. Observe,

I. *That the leaven introduced into the meal was a foreign element.* Something materially different to the meal itself. Something placed in it by a living, active agency. So also of the grace of God. It is not natural to man. It does not belong to his nature. It is very different to it. And before man can possess it, it must be imparted by the living Holy Spirit of God. The new nature is spiritual and from above. It is of divine operation. Light, and love, and mercy from heaven.

II. *Leaven is of a moving, exciting nature.* No sooner is it introduced into the meal, than a moving process commences. It is not needful to dwell on the nature of this chemical action. Now so is it with the grace of God in the soul. The soul is stirred up—quickened. The powers of the mind and the passions of the soul are excited.

(1.) Darkness gives place to light.
(2.) Chaos and confusion to order.
(3.) Insensibility to feeling.
(4.) Listlessness to anxiety.
(5.) Apathy to earnest desire.

The reign of sinful death and gravelike silence is superseded by intense spiritual life and activity.

III. *Leaven is of an assimilating nature.* It communicates its own nature to the meal with which it comes in contact. It does not destroy its identity, but alters its qualities. Just so the grace of God in the soul. It does not annihilate any of the faculties or powers of the soul, nor add any new attributes to the mind. But it gives forth its own characteristics to the soul, and makes it gracious. Now this process of assimilation is,

1. *Holy.* Grace of God is the principle of holiness, and makes the soul holy. It renovates the heart. It extinguishes the love of sin. Destroys the power of sin. Purifies from its defilement.

(1.) It sanctifies the understanding and fills it with divine knowledge.

(2.) It controls the judgment and brings it under the power of the truth.

(3.) It sanctifies the affections and makes them spiritual and heavenly.

(4.) It purifies the conscience and fills it with divine peace.

(5.) It supplies the memory with stores for meditation.

(6.) It subjugates the will to the authority of the Saviour; and through the mind, it influences the body, so that the members are yielded to works of righteousness. This process of assimilation,

2. *Is silent.* It creates no noise or confusion. So the grace of God in the soul operates secretly and silently. It cometh not with observation. It is the still and silent operation of spirit upon spirit. The effects may be heard in groans, in sighs, in supplications, and also in loud prayers and exultant thanksgiving, but the operation itself is necessarily silent. In this respect it resembles the silent falling of the *dew*, or the silent diffusion of the *morning light*, or the silent influence of the *atmosphere* of life. This assimilation,

3. *Is gradual.* First one part is leavened and then another. The whole is silently progressive. So is it with divine grace in the soul. Sin is forgiven at once. Justification and conversion must be instantaneous. But sanctifying grace is necessarily gradual. All the similes of Scripture confirm this view. First there is the babe, then the youth, then the young man, &c. First there is the dawn, then the morning light, afterwards meridian noon. Hence it is likened to the springing forth of the corn. The growing of the plant. The rising of the building. "All we with open face beholding as in a glass," &c.; 2 Cor. iii. 19. So also the numerous directions to "grow in grace," &c. To "press towards the mark," &c. The leaven operates until the assimilation,

4. *Is complete.* "Till the whole was leavened." This is the tendency and design of the grace of God in the soul. It contemplates the perfection of the Christian character. It designs our "meetness for the inheritance of the saints in light." It sanctifies body, soul, and spirit. It seeks as much the bringing on of the top stone as laying the foundation. Such are the beautiful and important instructions this parable conveys to us.

Learn,

1. *The seat of true religion is the heart.* The leaven was hidden in the meal. And God's grace must be in the heart. Correct views of it may be in the head, and appropriate observations in the mouth; but the soul is the seat of saving religion.

2. *The essential character of religion is holiness.* "The grace of God that bringeth salvation," &c. "But thanks be to God that *though* ye were the servants of sin," &c. "If we say we abide in Him, we should also walk as He walked."

3. *True religion is the religion of progress.* How true it is that we cannot be stationary. Either advancing or declining. Think of the commands in reference to spiritual progress. Think of the provisions made for it. Think of the great concerns essentially devolving on it.

4. *True religion develops to its subjects a state of future perfection.* "Beloved, now are we the sons of God," &c. "Now we see through a glass darkly," &c. Let each one adopt the language of the apostle Paul, and also resolve with him to "press towards the mark," &c. Philip. iii. 8–15.

VII.—THE HIDDEN TREASURE.

"Again, the kingdom of heaven is like unto treasure hid in a field; the which, when a man hath found, he hideth, and for joy thereof goeth and selleth all that he hath, and buyeth that field."—*Matt.* xiii. 44.

The kingdom of heaven, or the gospel dispensation, is here likened to a treasure hidden in a field. Probably referring to such cases where people under fear of invasion were in the habit of taking their riches and concealing them in the ground, or else the Saviour may refer to fields containing mines of precious ore; but either sense will accord with the general scope of the parable. Let us consider, then, the gospel as a treasure. As a hidden treasure. As found by the penitent believer. As purchased by

the sacrifice of all. And as producing unspeakable joy. Consider,

I. *The gospel as a treasure.* It is often
so described. "This treasure we have in
earthen vessels," &c.; 2 Cor. iv. 7. The
gospel is,

1. *A treasure of knowledge and truth.*
Celestial wisdom is more precious than gold.
More to be desired than rubies, &c. God's
saving truth is beyond all description invaluable. Hence we are exhorted to "buy
it, and to sell it not." "Yea, doubtless, and
I count all things but loss," &c.; Philip.
iii. 8. The gospel is a treasure,

2. *Of precious promises.* "Exceeding
great and precious promises;" 2 Pet. i. 4.
Promises of pardon. Acceptance. Adop-
tion. Sanctification. All-sufficient grace.
A triumphant death, and eternal glory.
The gospel is a treasure,

3. *Of distinguished blessings.* The Divine favor. Unspeakable peace. Ecstatic
joy. It makes its recipients "heirs of God,
and joint heirs with Christ;" Rom. viii. 17.
It is a treasure,

4. *Of endless life.* "Gift of God is eternal life." "This is the record that God
hath given to us—eternal life." This includes the "crown of life." A "throne."
A "kingdom." An "inheritance, incorruptible," &c. Observe,

II. *This treasure is hidden.* It may be
considered to have been hidden,

1. *In the ancient types and sacrifices.*
These all contained the germs or seeds of
gospel truth. They all referred to the Mes-
siah and the salvation we should obtain.
They pointed to the Lamb of God, &c.
Hidden,

2. *In Old Testament predictions and
promises.* These all testified of Christ, and
referred to his advent, work, offices, sufferings, and glory. They were radiant with
hope and joy to a guilty world. Yet in
their metaphorical costume and figurative
style, the gospel was rather hidden than
fully revealed. It is hidden, even under the
Christian dispensation,

3. *To the prejudiced, worldly, and careless.* Hence, when Christ revealed to the
Jews the character of his kingdom and the
blessings he came to bestow, they were so
prejudiced that they could not discern in
him their long expected Messiah, and they
despised his person and rejected his offered
grace. "He came to his own," &c. So
the worldly and the careless perceive noth-

ing precious or worthy of their attention in
the announcements of the gospel. Worldly
riches, honors, or pleasures conceal the glory
and preciousness of the gospel from the
minds of men. "If our gospel be hid," &c.
In the parable we are directed to consider
the gospel treasure,

III. *As found by the penitent believer.*
Christ revealed himself to the lowly and the
penitent. The pharisees found not the
treasure, but the humble, self-convicted, penitent publican did.

(1.) Observe, the gospel is calculated to
produce this state of mind. To level the
towering self-righteous thoughts of the
mind. To abase and prostrate the sinner in
the dust.

(2.) To such only is the gospel treasure
promised. "Come unto me, all ye that labor," &c.; Matt. xi. 28. "Blessed are the
poor in spirit," &c.; ver. 29. "A broken
and a contrite heart," &c.

(3.) Such only find the treasure. "The
full soul loatheth the honeycomb," &c.
"Others say they are rich and increased in
goods," &c. Others imagine they are whole,
and need not a physician, &c. Hearing,
understanding, believing, is the order appointed for enriching the souls of men with
the treasure of the gospel. But observe,

IV. *This treasure is purchased by the
sacrifice of all.* It is obvious that this does
not imply any *meritorious* acts on the part
of the sinner. The gospel is a system of
grace, excluding all worthiness on the part
of the sinner. But in securing the treasure
of the gospel, it not only cannot be on the
ground of the sinner's merit, but he must,

1. *Be willing to part with all his imaginary excellences to obtain it.* He must feel
and confess that he has nothing to pay with
before he can be forgiven.

"I nothing am, and nothing have,
    My glory's swallowed up in shame."

2. *He must renounce all self-devised
schemes of Divine acceptance.* Not only
merit, but all other methods of reconciliation to God, except by the sacrifice of the
Lord Jesus.

3. *He must abandon all his sins.* "Let
the wicked forsake his way," &c. "When
the wicked turneth away from his wickedness," &c. See Isaiah i. 16, &c.

4. *He must believingly yield himself up
to the Lord.* "I beseech you, brethren, by
the mercies of God," &c.; Rom. xii. 1. God

demands the confidential surrender of the heart; the whole soul, cheerfully and believingly, and in the spirit of self-denial. "They first gave themselves to the Lord," &c. The cross must be taken up, and all forsaken, incompatible with the glory of the Saviour. Notice the finding of this treasure,

V. *Produces unspeakable joy.* The gospel is glad tidings of great joy, &c. Hence the poet exclaims,

"Hark! the glad sound, the Saviour comes,
The Saviour promised long.
Let every heart exult with joy,
And every voice be song."

This joy is real—spiritual—increasing. And tendeth to the celestial joys and rapturous delights of eternal glory.

APPLICATION.

1. How thankful we should be for the gospel.

2. How solicitous to possess its invaluable treasures.

3. How readily part with all for its blessings.

4. And while rejoicing in its possession, how we should recommend it to all impoverished sinners around us.

"To tell to sinners all around,
What a dear Saviour we have found."

5. Let us take care and hide this treasure in our hearts. Hold it fast. Sell it not, &c.

VIII.—SPIRITUAL VEGETATION.

"And he said, So is the kingdom of God, as if a man should cast seed into the ground: and should sleep, and rise night and day, and the seed should spring and grow up, he knoweth not how," &c.—*Mark* iv. 26–29.

THIS beautiful parable may be interpreted and applied either to the origin and progress of Christianity in the world, or to the establishment, growth, and perfection of the grace of God in the soul. Both views contain much that is instructive to the mind, and in both are opened to us the mysteries of the divine kingdom. We purpose, however, to consider it in its application to personal religion. Observe,

I. *That the principle of religion in the heart is divine.* It is as "seed cast into the ground." Not something natural to the heart, or inherent, but something imparted to it. This seed is divine truth. The gospel of the grace of God, heavenly doctrine. Glad tidings of joy from the Lord.

(1.) Notice the seed is spiritual. Not of man, or from men.

(2.) It is pure. The holy word of God.

(3.) It is vital and imperishable. Liveth and abideth forever.

This seed is the germ of true and saving religion. The regenerated soul is born again of it.

II. *That the instrumentality employed in carrying on religion is human.* "As if a man should cast seed," &c. The apostles and disciples were intrusted with the seed of the kingdom, and they were commissioned to bear it to the wide world. God still employs his own servants to do this.

(1.) Generally the ministers of the gospel. It is their special work to preach the word —to sow this seed.

(2.) Oftentimes Christian parents and friends. Who diligently teach their children, and train them up in the knowledge of God's blessed word. "From a child thou hast known the scriptures," &c.

(3.) *Frequently Sabbath-school teachers and tract distributers.* These go forth bearing the truths of the gospel, and from Sabbath to Sabbath casting this precious seed into the ground. All Christians should labor to do this. What useful examples the word of God furnishes. Those who were scattered in the early persecution "went everywhere preaching the word." Acts viii. 4. So also the woman of Samaria, &c.

III. *The operations of divine grace are invisible and mysterious.* "And the seed should spring up, he knoweth not how," Mark iv. 27. Some of the laws of vegetation are known; for instance, it is understood that the seed must be decomposed, or die, and that from it germinateth the new life and fruit. But how and in what exact manner no man knoweth. The process too is invisible. It is hidden in the deep earth from the eye of the observer. So the process of grace in the soul is, in like manner, both mysterious and invisible to the eye of man. See John iii. 8. God alone knoweth the process of its operations, and seeth its influence on the heart and mind of its recipient. The minister soweth the seed, but for some time knows not its action on the mind. The friend, or relative, even in the midst of daily intercourse, may not for a time discern it. Who can tell the emotions of the heart, and the anxieties and desires of the soul, but God alone?

IV. *The process of grace in the soul is gradual and progressive.* "First the blade, then the ear, after that the full corn in the ear." Thus divine truth first enlightens the mind; then convicts the conscience; then produces anxiety, remorse, compunction; then desire. There will be contrition, true penitential sorrow, forsaking of sin, and faith in the Lord Jesus as the only refuge and hope. With this will be produced,

1. *The new nature.* Heavenly. Tender. Infantile. Or in the similitude of the text, "the blade." From this will be exhibited,

2. *The evidences of the spiritual life.* Then "the ear," or as it means, the stalk as well as the ear. Then will follow,

3. *The fruits of the Christian character.* "The full corn in the ear." The exhibition of the graces and virtues of spiritual religion. The fruits of righteousness to the glory of divine grace. Hence the admonitory counsel of the apostle, "And besides this, giving all diligence, add to your faith, virtue," &c. 2 Peter i. 5–8.

V. *The divine tendency of grace in the heart is to perfect maturity.* "But when the fruit is brought forth," that is, when it is manifestly full and ripe. Now the great end of the owner of the soil was the bringing forth of this fruit. So also this was the divine purpose in preparing the seed to be sown. This was also the object of the sower. To this, tended the sunshine, the rains, and the dews. God graciously designs the perfection of the work he begins. "He who hath begun the good work," &c. Maturity of Christian character involves,

(1.) The perfected graces of the Holy Spirit.

(2.) Deadness to the world.

(3.) Spirituality and heavenly-mindedness of soul.

(4.) Entire conformity and resignation to the divine will.

(5.) "Looking and waiting for that blessed hope," &c. Titus ii. 13.

VI. *God takes the mature Christian to the enjoyment of himself in glory.* "But when the fruit is brought forth, immediately he putteth in the sickle, because the harvest is come," ver. 29. When the Christian is meet for heavenly inheritance. When he has borne the fruit of Christian usefulness. Done his generation's work. Answered all the designs of his heavenly Father—He then gives the commission to the angelic convoy, as in the case of Lazarus, to bear him to his celestial home and reward. He falls asleep on earth—he awakes in glory. He dies to all below, and lives in the regions of immortality for evermore. He is not found here, for he has been gathered to the assembly of the first-born; he is now enrolled with the spirits of just men made perfect.

We ask in conclusion,

1. Has this work been begun in your souls? Have you received the grace of God in truth?

2. Are you advancing in Christian holiness, and going onwards towards perfection?

3. Let the heavenly rewards be often contemplated to quicken your souls, and to elevate your desires.

IX.—THE PARABLE OF THE TWO SONS.

"But what think ye? A *certain* man had two sons: and he came to the first, and said, Son, go work to-day in my vineyard. He answered and said, I will not: but afterward he repented, and went," &c.—*Matt.* xxi. 28–31.

MANY of the scribes and Pharisees exhibited the most deep-rooted and inveterate prejudice against the Saviour's teaching and mission. Often they endeavored to catch him in his sayings, that they might have some charge against him. Jesus often, therefore, self-convicted them, and out of their own mouths overwhelmed them with confusion. We have a striking instance of this in the passage connected with this subject. To show their perverseness, the Saviour addressed to them this parable, and by their own confessions he involved them in self-condemnation, ver. 31, 32. Observe,

I. *The reasonable commands of the father.* "A certain man had two sons, and he came to the first, and said, Son, go work to-day in my vineyard," ver. 28. Observe,

1. *The nature of the command.* "To work in the vineyard." Man was intended for labor. He was made for it. Even in paradise, our first parents were called to it. Indolence is pernicious to body, soul, spirit, and reputation. It is a withering blight. Labor is dignified, and productive both of health and enjoyment. Hence the command itself was reasonable and proper. God calls men to the great work of personal religion. To work out their own salvation, &c. To give diligence to make their calling and

election sure. To work while it is called day. Soul work, is all-important, the chief end of life. Observe,

2. *The sphere of labor appointed.* The father's vineyard. A place in which the sons were personally interested. Now God's vineyard is his church. Into this we are to enter by personal piety, and here we are to grow in meetness for heaven. Here we are to improve our graces, employ our talents, do good to men, and glorify God. Has not God a right to specify both the sphere of duty and the labor he demands? Notice,

3. *The manner in which the command was delivered.* And said, "Son, go work to-day," &c. Here was nothing harsh or tyrannical. He speaks with authority, but it is the authority of a parent. He addresses him as his son, and thus conveys the idea of the relationship subsisting between them. As son, he owed his father reverence and cheerful obedience. God is our heavenly Father. We are therefore all his offspring. He is not only the Author of our being, but the source of all our mercies. What reverence, obedience, and grateful love we owe to him. We are not our own but his, for he hath not only created and preserved, but redeemed us. Observe,

4. *The period of labor required.* "Go work to-day." Daytime is working time. There is light for working, and opportunity also. The period allotted for labor. God worked during the six days of the creation of our world. Life is the day for religious working. "Life is the time to serve the Lord." Jesus said, "I must work while it is called day," &c. What a transient period is the day of life. How soon it passes away. How often interrupted and frequently curtailed by sudden and early death. Such were the reasonable requirements of the father, and the claims of God on his creatures. Notice,

II. *The strange and diversified answers of the sons.*

(1.) The first said, "I will not." What disobedience, insolence, and rebellion. A direct and impertinent refusal. What baseness, and fool-hardihood, and filial ingratitude it involved. Surely of this abandoned son there could be no hope.

(2.) The second said, "I go, sir." Here was respect, submission, and promised obedience. How forcibly and beautifully it contrasts with the rebellious rudeness of the other. God demands the reverence and fear of his creatures. Divine things and claims must be treated with seriousness and respect. But observe,

III. *The conduct of the sons which so strangely contrasted with the answers given.*

1. *The rebellious son becomes penitent and obedient.* Such were the publicans and sinners to whom John the Baptist preached. So also the publicans and sinners to whom the Saviour preached. They notoriously despised sacred things. Were abandoned and profligate, yet they repented and obeyed the Baptist, they repented and received salvation from Christ Jesus. How often it has been so. Cavilling skeptics—profane scoffers,—The openly profane have heard and believed the gospel, to the salvation of their souls. The chief of sinners have been brought to Christ. Zaccheus, the taxgatherer. The woman who was a sinner. The dying thief. The Corinthian convert. John Bunyan, the swearing tinker, and myriads of like character and condition.

2. *The courteous son was disobedient and deceiving.* All he did was to be civil and promise fairly. For of him it is said, "He went not." Such were the scribes and Pharisees. They made high pretensions; they professed much, talked much. But, alas! this was all; they said, and did not. It was merely Lord, Lord, in the mouth, but they did not the things which were commanded. They repented not of sin. They believed not in Christ. They were not sincere workers of godliness before the Lord. How fearfully this will apply,

(1.) To many children of religious parents. They attend with them on the means of grace. They are moral, respectful in their religious conversation, they promise fair, but "go not."

(2.) To many who regularly frequent the house of God. They attend, and listen, and seem interested; but they move not in the way of repentance and holiness.

(3.) It is a faithful picture of many professors. All their religion is in name, in show,—in outside appearance. They walk not in Christ's vineyard. They are not spiritual, or useful, trees with leaves without fruit. Ciphers, cumberers of the ground. How fearful this state! How awful their doom!

Learn,

1. The efficacy of the grace of God to save the vilest of sinners.

2. The importance of experimental and practical religion.

X.—THE PARABLE OF THE DEBTORS.

"Therefore is the kingdom of heaven likened unto a certain king, who would take account of his servants. And when he had begun to reckon, one was brought to him, who owed him ten thousand talents," &c.—*Matt.* xviii. 23, 25.

THE religion of the New Testament is evidently one of goodness and mercy. Its very essence is love,—love to God and love to man. How this was exhibited in the life and doctrines of the Lord Jesus Christ! He was embodied goodness,—incarnate mercy. He came to establish an empire of clemency and kindness in our world. He insisted on his disciples cultivating a merciful and forgiving spirit. Out of a conversation with Peter on this subject, the parable before us originated. See ver. 21, 22. The kingdom of heaven, or the great principles of the gospel, are beautifully set forth in the figurative sketch before us. Observe,

I. *The king, and the conduct he adopted.* This monarch is represented as one of great dignity and wealth. It is also to be remarked, that he took exact observation of the state of his affairs, and the accounts of his servants. He was not indolent or neglectful of the concerns of his kingdom. God is doubtless prefigured in the king before us. He is of boundless authority, riches, and glory. All creatures are under his control, and subject to his dominion. He has always an exact knowledge of the state and concerns of all his creatures. His rule is one of exactness, order, and wisdom. Observe,

II. *The indebted servant.* "One was brought unto him who owed him ten thousand talents." This person represented as a servant, doubtless signifies more properly a petty prince, or one employed to collect the revenue in some district of the kingdom. His arrears were fearful, "ten thousand talents." If even of silver, a sum upwards of three millions pounds sterling. It is not said how he came to be so deeply involved in debt. Whether by misfortune, imprudence, or lavish extravagance. He was also entirely insolvent. "He had not to pay his lord." No reference is made even to compounding with him. How exactly does this portray the true state of the sinner. A debtor to God. The debt immense, incalculable. A debt that has been accumulating from the moment of his birth. A debt of which he cannot pay the smallest dividend, utterly insolvent. "Poor, and wretched, and blind, and naked." Without God and without hope in the world. Observe,

III. *The course the king adopted.*
1. *He reasonably demanded payment.* This was his equitable claim. God requires the yielding of loyal obedience to him. The perfect love of the heart, and the willing service of the life.
2. *He justly insisted on his punishment.* "Commanded him to be sold," &c. This was the regal right, the understood terms—the covenant between them. God has a just right to punish. He may justly inflict his displeasure. But,
3. *Moved by compassion he freely forgave him.* "The servant therefore fell down and worshipped him," &c. ver. 26. The debt was not denied, but acknowledged. His claims were not disputed. But his patience and clemency were supplicated; and moved by noble generosity he freely and entirely forgave the debt. What an extraordinary instance of goodness and compassion. How beautifully does it set forth the clemency of God to penitent believing sinners. When brought to feel their utter insolvency. When they cast themselves on the mercy of God in Christ Jesus. When they earnestly plead for pardon. Then God, moved by the graciousness of his nature, freely forgives their sins, blotting them out as a cloud, &c. "There is forgiveness with thee," &c. "He who confesseth and forsaketh shall obtain mercy." And no matter how great the debt, he says, "Come now and let us reason together," &c. Notice,

IV. *The unmerciful spirit the forgiven debtor displayed.* "But the same servant went out and found one of his fellow-servants, who owed him a hundred pence, and he laid hands on him," &c.
(1.) Observe, the debt owed by the fellow-servant was small, "a hundred pence," about three pounds four shillings and seven pence.
(2.) He, too, had nothing to pay with. Lacked the ability to meet the demand.
(3.) He was willing, if time were given, to meet the claim.
(4.) He humbly and earnestly entreated his compassion.
(5.) But the pardoned debtor was inexora-

ble. He acted violently, "seized him by the throat," &c.

(6.) He exercised no forbearance, but at once thrust him into prison, ver. 30. What vile forgetfulness of the clemency which had been shown to him! What want of feeling and sympathy for an unfortunate fellow-creature! Observe, what a picture of man's unmercifulness to man.

V. *The course which the king then adopted.* "So when his fellow-servants saw what was done they were very sorry, and came and told unto their lord all that was done. Then his lord, after that he had called him, said unto him, O thou wicked servant," &c., ver. 31, 32. Here his hard-heartedness was laid before him. His wickedness asserted, and the course of conduct he ought to have pursued, pointed out, ver. 33. The anger of the king was excited, and in his displeasure he reversed his own merciful decision, and consigned him to the tormentors, ver. 34. The conduct of the king as described by Jesus, is the precise mode in which God will deal with the inclement and unmerciful. "So likewise shall my heavenly Father do also unto you, if ye from your hearts forgive not every man his brother their trespasses," v. 35.

Observe, God requires that we should be merciful, even as he is merciful. That our mercy must extend to all our enemies, and that it must be hearty and sincere. He requires this not as the meritorious ground of our acceptance, but as the evidence of our love to him, and as the fruit of his grace within us. That when this is not evinced, he will not accept or save. That an unforgiving spirit alike disqualifies for his kingdom on earth, and his glory in heaven.

XI.—THE PARABLE OF THE NET.

"Again, the kingdom of heaven is like unto a net, that was cast into the sea, and gathered of every kind: which, when it was full, they drew to shore, and sat down, and gathered the good into vessels, but cast the bad away," &c.—*Matt.* xiii. 47, 50.

THE Redeemer's parables were calculated to interest all classes of persons. The laborer, the sower, the shepherd, and the fisherman, all had divine truth brought down to their capacity, and illustrated by the peculiarities of their several employments. In this parable the Saviour represents the king-

dom of heaven as like unto the net which being cast into the sea, incloses within it all kinds of fish, and which when full and brought to shore, the good are separated from the bad. So, says the Great Teacher, shall it be at the end of the world. The angels shall come forth and sever the wicked from among the just, &c., ver. 49, 50. Observe,

I. *The state in which men are by nature.* In the world, represented in the parable by the sea. The world as distinguished from the Church, like the sea is an element of restlessness and peril. A state of imminent danger to the best interests of the soul. In this state all unconverted men are found. Hence as the sea abounds with fishes of every kind, so the world with sinners of all descriptions. Here are all the various grades of moral evil,—from the self-righteous moralist to the vilest profligate, or daring blasphemer.

II. *Observe the only means of extricating men is by the gospel.* This is the net of the parable. Just as the net is adapted to inclose the fish in the sea, so is the gospel to save sinners.

1. *It comes down to their circumstances of moral wretchedness.* It recognizes them as fallen and perishing, and it contemplates their deliverance. It announces their ruin, and proclaims their help. It asserts their disease, and offers the healing balm.

2. *It is adapted to the circumstances of all sinners.* Like a large drag-net, it comprehends in its designs the rescue of all men. It embraces the wide world. It is addressed to every creature. It speaks to man as man, and reveals a Saviour to every perishing sinner. Hence the commission given by Christ to the disciples. Mark xvi. 15.

3. *The gospel exclusively is adapted to save sinners.* It is God's expedient, and replete with his unerring wisdom. It is the power of God to salvation to every one that believeth. Faith cometh by hearing it, and salvation through faith. We know of no other means of men obtaining justification, holiness, and eternal life.

III. *The gospel must be connected with active instrumentality.* Thus the net must be employed. It must be cast into the sea. So the gospel must be preached. How can men hear without a preacher? Observe,

1. *God has appointed the Christian ministry for this end.* He called, qualified, and sent forth the apostles and evangelists to

cast this net into the sea. To preach the gospel. He does so still. He raises up holy, benevolent, and zealous ministers to give themselves earnestly and devotedly to fishing for souls. Jesus says now, as in the days of his flesh, " Follow me, and I will make you fishers of men." Observe,

2. *That preaching the gospel is an arduous, laborious work.* Few occupations involve more toil and fatigue, and self-denial, than that of the fisherman. Such also is the laborious calling of the Christian minister. He must be wholly given to it in heart, and holy desire for the good of souls. Instant in season and out of season. He must sacrifice the love of ease, and the honors and rewards of the world, and bear the cross of his Divine Master. He must tread in the self-denying steps of his blessed Lord. He must not shun to declare the whole counsel of God. He must bear the truth to men under all circumstances and at all hazards. The early preachers of the cross, as well as modern missionaries, hazarded their lives for Christ and his cause. Observe,

IV. *That the gospel cannot possibly be preached in vain.* " The net cast into the sea gathered of every kind," v. 47. Hence the intentions of the fisherman were answered. He did not employ his net in vain. So God has engaged that his word shall not return unto Him void. Isaiah lv. 10, 11. The success of the gospel has been varied. Sometimes multitudes of men have been converted, as on the day of Pentecost. During the ministry of Wesley and Whitfield, and others. But in all ages and countries, where the cross has been lifted up, sinners have been drawn out of the world to Christ. It is so now, both in our own and in heathen lands. It shall be very successfully so, introductory to the millennial reign of the Saviour. See Isaiah lx. 7, 8, &c. Notice,

V. *That all brought into Christ's visible Church are not converted persons.* The net inclosed " of every kind." Not only will the gospel save men of all ranks and ages, and conditions, but it will bring many into the outward kingdom of Christ, who are not regenerated, spiritual persons. Good and bad.

(1.) Many hypocrites, as Judas, Ananias, and Sapphira, &c.

(2.) Many formalists, having only a name to live, &c.

(3.) Many inconsistent. Who run well for a season, but who are hindered, &c. Who make shipwreck, &c.

VI. *That in the day of judgment there will be a complete separation of the righteous and the wicked.* See ver. 48, 49.

(1.) The period certified is when the net is full and brought to shore. When the gospel dispensation is consummated. The end of the world.

(2.) The agency is that of angels, the ministers of the divine judgments. See parable of the wheat and tares, v. 39.

(3.) The scrutiny will be exact. All the good will be gathered out. Every sincere believer will be recognized and exalted. Every hypocrite and unconverted person will be detected. Escape will be impossible.

(4.) The decision to the ungodly will be awful and final. " Cast away." " Cast into the furnace of fire," &c. v. 30. Without hope,—the subjects of weeping and wailing, and gnashing of teeth.

(5.) The salvation of the righteous will be certain. " Happy the people in such a case," &c.

XII.—THE PARABLE OF THE DAY LABORERS.

" For the kingdom of heaven is like unto a man that was a householder, who went out early in the morning to hire laborers into his vineyard. And when he had agreed with the laborers for a penny a day, he sent them into his vineyard," &c. *Matt.* xx. 1, 15.

By some this parable has been supposed to refer to the various periods of life, when persons are converted and enter into the service of the Lord Jesus Christ. And hence those engaged at the eleventh hour are supposed to refer to persons becoming religious in old age, or to a death-bed repentance. It is very obvious that nothing of this kind was intended to be conveyed to us by the Great Teacher. The whole scope of the parable is to show that God, in the exercise of a gracious sovereignty, may dispose of his rewards to those who are late introduced into his vineyard, and whose period of labor is therefore of very short duration. Hence God may give the same spiritual or eternal blessings to the Gentiles last called, as he did to the Jews ; or to the nations who shall be last converted to the faith, as he did to those converted by the apostles and earliest preachers of the gospel. To all he will be faithful in giving the promised rewards, and to some he may justly do this, who have labored but one hour in his service. Observe, however, several very important principles which the parable contains.

I. *The condition, spiritually, in which sinners live.* "Idle,' during the day of life. "Idle," with the powers and facilities of labor. "Idle," though accountable to God, and notwithstanding his high claims upon their service. With death, and judgment, and eternity before them, still idle as to the great work of godliness.

II. *The great design of the Christian ministry is to urge men to a regard to the duties of religion.* Hence they must show men the folly and wickedness of neglecting their souls. That the toils of sin are infinitely more severe and degrading than the service of the Saviour. That Christ's labor is sweet and refreshing, and in bearing his yoke, men find rest to their souls. Men must be urged to the work,

1. *Of solemn consideration.* A review of their past lives, &c. Their present condition. One great reason of men's unconcern about their soul is, they do not consider. Hence the requirement of heaven is, " that they consider their ways." Hence the expostulation. Isaiah i. 2, 3. Then there is the work,

2. *Of sincere repentance.* "Repentance towards God." A repentance involving in it conviction of sin—contrition and sorrow for sin—breaking off from sin, and turning to the Lord with full purpose of heart. An entire change of heart and life in respect of sin. See Isaiah i. 16, &c. Where fruits meet for repentance are brought forth.

3. *Of faith in the Lord Jesus Christ.* Jesus answered and said unto them, "This is the work of God, that ye believe on him whom He hath sent," John vi. 29. Hence the disciples went forth, and preached that men should repent and believe the gospel.

III. *That the Church of God is a sphere of labor and activity.* Hence Christ's disciples are to be working disciples. Men are introduced into the gospel, not only to enjoy its fruits, but to work therein. True religion is eminently practical. It is the devotion of the heart and life to God. It is walking in the way of his commandments. It is doing the will of our Father in heaven. There are works of devotion—works of self-denial—works of benevolence and mercy. These works are fully specified in the word of God.

And for the discharge of them, sufficient grace is provided.

IV. *That God will reckon with his servants, and reward them when the day of labor is past.* Let it not be forgotten that God has a right to all we are, and to all we can do. We never can place the Lord under any obligations by any thing we do for him. But in mercy and goodness to us, he hath promised great and munificent rewards to all his faithful servants. There are rewards in God's service. For in keeping his commands, there is great reward. But the chief rewards of godliness,

1. *Are reserved until after death.* "Be thou faithful unto death," &c. "He that endureth to the end," &c. So in the parable, "when the even was come," ver. 8. The day of life past.

2. *These rewards will be great.* Not merely equitable remuneration. For, alas ! what would that be to unprofitable servants. But according to his rich and overflowing mercy, the infinite bountifulness of his nature, through the immeasurable merits of the Mediator, will he abundantly bless us. These rewards, according to human calculation,

3. *Will not be always proportionate.* Those hired at the eleventh hour will receive the penny. The last converts, as well as the early ones, will be crowned with glory, immortality, and eternal life. None will receive less than they expected, but many infinitely more. The rewards,

4. *Will be eternal.* An eternity of rest after toil. An eternity of peace after the troubles of life. An eternity of joy after grief, and at God's right hand, pleasures for evermore. A crown of glory that fadeth not away.

Learn,

1. *That the sovereignty of God exhibited in this parable, is a sovereignty that inflicts no wrong on any of his creatures.* It is merciful to all, though especially merciful to some.

2. *How necessary to cherish a candid and generous spirit towards others.* We should rejoice in the abundant blessings and privileges which some enjoy. Our eye ought not to be evil, because God is good, ver. 15.

3. *Human conclusions will in many cases be reversed in the last day.* "So the last shall be first, and the first last," &c., ver. 16.

XIII.—PARABLE OF THE LOST SHEEP.

"And he spake this parable unto them, saying, What man of you, having a hundred sheep, if he lose one of them, doth not leave the ninety and nine in the wilderness, and go after that which is lost until he find it?" &c.—*Luke* xv. 3, 7.

THE scribes and Pharisees were exceedingly indignant with Christ, because he ate and drank with publicans and sinners. As the professed Messiah, they expected to have engaged all his attention, and they desired that he would treat the profane and irreligious with the contempt and scorn which they ever displayed towards them. Instead of this, Christ mingled among them, addressed them in his gracious discourses, and received with open arms all who came in penitence and faith to him. To justify this course was the design of the parable which he now delivered to them. Observe, the endangered wanderer—the kindly shepherd —and the joyous exultation. Observe,

I. *The endangered wanderer.* The parable supposes a sheep of the fold to have wandered and been lost, a striking and fit description of man's natural condition. This is most forcibly expressed by the evangelical prophet who says, "all we like sheep have gone astray: we have turned every one to his own way," Isaiah liii. 6. This is a great doctrinal truth,—the fall of man, and the ruin and depravity of the whole species. Prophets, the Lord Jesus, and apostles, all teach and insist on this truth. Man has wandered,

1. *From the authority of God.* Thrown off divine control—said to the Most High, "Depart from us," &c. He is described as despising and contemning Jehovah. Acting as a traitor and rebel against the sovereign authority of God. He would not have the Lord even in his thoughts. He has wandered,

2. *From the family of God.* He was once in league with holy angels. Most probably they were his companions. We know they were his friends. How holy, and happy, the family of man in innocency. But by apostasy man lost his birthright. Became an outcast, &c. His being driven out of Eden was the visible sign of his having wandered from the family of God. Observe,

3. *He has wandered in the way of peril and death.* The tendency of sin is towards death. It is the way of death. Sin, when it is finished, bringeth forth death. The threatened sentence was, "dying thou shalt die." The

wandering sinner is seeking death in the error of his ways. The end of his course is inevitably death. Observe,

4. *The sinner would wander endlessly but for the intervention of divine grace.* This can easily be accounted for, if you remember, there are no desires after God, no holiness in the heart of man by nature. His tendencies are all downward and towards perdition. Satan, who exercises dominion over him, would beguile him, and seduce him away from God and safety. The habit of sinning would greatly increase his love of evil, and his dislike of holy things. Observe then,

II. *The kindly shepherd.* He pities. He seeks. He restores the wanderer. How applicable this to the Saviour.

1. *He compassionated man in his fallen and ruined condition.* Hence the scheme of redemption is ever attributed to the pure compassion of God.

"He saw us ruined by the fall,
And loved us notwithstanding all."

"When we were without strength," &c. See Titus iii. 3, 7. Compassion moved his heart, and induced him to undertake our recovery and salvation.

2. *He actually came to seek the wanderer.* Jesus left heaven, and laid aside his glory, and became a man,—the subject of poverty, and reproach, and suffering, that he might find the wanderer. "This is a faithful saying, and worthy of all acceptation," &c. "The Son of man came to seek and to save that which is lost." For this he lived, and suffered, and died.

"Jesus sought me when a stranger,
Wandering from the fold of God,
He to rescue me from danger,
Interposed his precious blood."

3. *He finds and restores the wanderer.* He did so in the days of his flesh. He does so now by the ministry of the gospel. All the saved and happy spirits received into heaven from our world,—were the sought and found of the Saviour. Are not many of you among the number who can sing, "He restoreth my soul?" We hope most of you have been found by Christ. Among the wanderers found by Christ are sinners of all descriptions, and of all grades of guilt. Some he found in the polluted haunts of profligacy. Others in the mazes of worldliness. Others in the deceitful paths of pleasure. But they

were all in the way which leadeth to death. All would have perished had they not been sought out and found by him. Observe,

III. *The joyous results.* " And when he hath found it, he layeth it on his shoulders, rejoicing," &c.

1. *The shepherd rejoices in the attainment of his gracious purposes.* He highly values the straying sheep. His best feelings are now gratified. Jesus is represented as seeing of the travail of his soul and being satisfied. This was the end of his sorrows and griefs— the joy set before him. In the rescue and elevation of his fallen creatures, his benevolent spirit overflows with rapturous delight.

2. *Angels also rejoice:* ver. 7. They are deeply interested in the destiny of man. They have often been messengers of mercy to our world. They hailed the advent of the Saviour with great joy. They exult in the sinner's conversion, and they bear the souls of the rescued to the habitations of the blessed. Their love to God, their love of holiness, and their love to man, induce them to rejoice in the sinner's salvation.

3. *The restored wanderer also rejoices.* He sings, " I will praise thee," &c. He invites others to hear what God has done for his soul. He goes on his spiritual way rejoicing. He rejoices with joy unspeakable and full of glory.

4. *All spiritual persons acquainted with the sinner's restoration rejoice.* The minister. The parent. The friend. The church. None but the self-righteous and pharisaic envy and repine. And in proportion to the danger and hopelessness of the sinner's state, is the exultation in his being found by Christ. We ask in conclusion,

1. *Are you still wandering?* If so, oh stop! Reflect, and hear the voice of the seeking Saviour.

2. *Are you found and restored?* Give God the praise, and glorify him with your bodies and souls, which are his.

XIV.—THE PRODIGAL SON.

" And he said, A certain man had two sons : and the younger of them said to his father, Father, give me the portion of goods that falleth to me. And he divided unto them his living," &c.—*Luke* xv. 11, 16.

OF all the Saviour's parables, this is one of the most interesting and affecting. It is impossible to read it without being struck with the felicity of its descriptions, and the tenderness and compassion which it breathes throughout. Surely sin was never painted in more striking colors, or human wretchedness in more piteous strains. And where can we find such an instance of the paternal love and compassion, as is presented to us in the conduct of the father? Let us then examine and dilate on the important particulars it presents to our view. Let us look at the prodigal,

I. *In his original circumstances of honor and happiness.* He was in his father's house a partaker of all its comforts and enjoyments. The object of paternal affection, bearing the honored name, and moving in the honored rank of his family. This was man's original state—upright, innocent, and happy. God his Father. Eden his home. The earth his domain. Angels his companions. Bliss his portion. All that divine wisdom and love could provide, he possessed. All that he could really enjoy was provided. An ample portion was his inheritance. See him,

II. *In the arrogance of his presumptuous claim.* What did he really want? Where could he be more dignified or happy? But he seeks to have his portion to himself. He desires to do with it as he pleases. He seeks to throw off parental restraints and control. He deems himself sufficient for the management of his own concerns. What was the original sin but throwing off God's restraints, though reasonable and kind, and really for man's good? He desired to act as he pleased, and to have his powers and possessions at his own disposal. Alas! this claim was foolish, ungrateful, and, as the sequel shows, fatal to his hopes and happiness. Observe him,

III. *In his dissipated wanderings.* His portion awarded him, he flies the paternal roof, escapes the parental jurisdiction, and goes into a far country. Sin is the soul's moral departure from God. Sinning is wandering from his family and throwing off his authority. Every step in the course of transgression is going farther and farther from the Lord.

(1.) This wandering is very gradual and insidious. The moral aberrations are at first small, and only just perceptible. Our first parents gazed on the forbidden tree. Then admired it. Then desired. Then, with the passions on the side of evil, they reasoned and listened to the temptations of the seducer. Then the hand was stretched out.

And last of all the fruit was eaten. This generally is the gradual and insidious course of the sinner. The prodigal would retire at first a day's journey from his home.

(2.) This wandering is increasingly rapid. The habit and love of evil formed, the course is downward and rapid. Respectability and decency are discarded. Conscience becomes seared—self-respect abandoned. The good opinions of others despised. Now enormous sins are easily perpetrated. No fear of God before the eyes. He now runs greedily and hastily to do evil. He can blaspheme—mock at sin. Sit in the scoffer's chair. Be the hearty associate of the vilest of the vile. He is sold, body, soul, and spirit, to do wickedly.

(3.) This wandering is awfully dangerous. It is the way of shame, misery, and death. Its paths lead down to an early grave, and to the depths of hell. Observe the prodigal,

IV. *In his wretchedness and misery ;* ver. 14. "He had spent all." Sin is fearfully expensive. Let the experience of the drunkard, the gambler, and the pleasure taker certify to the truth of this. Every vice except that of avarice is so, and that feeds on the very vitals of its victims. Pride, ambition, profligacy, are all ruinous to the means of those who wander in their dissipated paths. "He spent all." A rich portion was gone—gone rapidly and foolishly. Now comes the moral dearth—famine. The means are exhausted. He begins now to be " in want." The first transgressors were expelled the garden ; they lost every tree, and all the luxuries of Eden, by tasting of the forbidden fruit. Mad experiment ! Ruinous meal ! Profligacy is followed by want, extravagance by misery. This is the history of myriads. Behold him,

V. *In his unalleviated distress.* The proud prodigal becomes a swineherd, the most degrading and miserable of all occupations. What filthy employment Satan gives his vassals to do ! How iniquity degrades and debases ! It is a constantly falling state—men sink lower and lower, until, covered with infamy, their souls commingle with the vile and the lost in the abyss of woe beneath. Even swine's food is not given him ; ver. 16. By husks is meant the fruit of the carob-tree, which was used in feeding swine, and on which the most poor and wretched were compelled to live. Where are his evil associates ? Why not go to the haunts of his former pleasures and

rioting ? Sin is a cruel, hardening thing. Sinners victimize one another. Rob and destroy each other. "The tender mercies of the wicked are cruel." There is no aliment of life and comfort in the region of sin. Ah ! the contrast between the prodigal's state now and when at home in the midst of plenty and comfort. Look at his wan and pallid countenance. Look at his ragged, filthy dress. See him at his cursed employment. For cursed, said one of the Rabbins, "is he that feedeth swine." See him seeking the meanest fare in vain, and what is the conclusion to which we must come ? "The way of transgressors is hard." "It is a hard and bitter thing to sin against the Lord."

XV.—THE PRODIGAL SON.

(SKETCH II.)

" And when he came to himself, he said, How many hired servants of my father have bread enough and to spare, and I perish with hunger ! I will arise and go to my father, and will say unto him, Father, I have sinned against heaven and before thee," &c.—*Luke* xv. 17, 20.

WE have seen in our last discourse the prodigal in his original state of happiness, in his wanderings, and in his utter wretchedness. We have now to contemplate him under the favorable circumstances, which took place at the very crisis of his misery and distress. Far from home. In a degraded service. In utter destitution. Without friends or sympathy in his misfortunes, and exclaiming, "I perish with hunger." But the darkest part of his career is now passed ; his misery drives him to reflection, for observe,

I. *Reason resumes her dominion.* "And when he came to himself." His course had been one of madness, insanity, delirium. Was it not so to throw off the paternal yoke of wisdom and love ? Was it not so to trust to his own inexperience ? Was it not so to go out into a far and unknown region —without object, or counsellor, or guide ? Was it not so to waste a life's substance in a few years ? Was it not so to become the companion of harlots and thieves ? Was it not so to be indifferent to his affairs, till ruin stared him in the face ; Surely all this was evidence of the direst infatuation, the most obvious madness. All sin is madness, the opposite of sound reason, of true wisdom.

(1.) To reject and despise God.

(2.) To prostitute the powers of the soul to evil.

(3). To neglect the great end of life.

(4.) To be indifferent to our own welfare.

(5.) To disregard the certain solemnities of death, judgment, and eternity. But the prodigal came to himself.

(1.) For behold, he stops in his career of vice to consider. He now soliloquizes with himself.

(2.) He now thinks of the home he had despised. "How many hired servants," &c.

(3.) He now perceives distinctly, and confesses frankly his own condition. "I perish with hunger." In these we see the first indications of the return of a good understanding and a sound judgment. Happy sign, when the sinner pauses and begins to consider. Men perish because they do not, they will not consider. Consideration is the herald of repentance and the harbinger of reformation.

Observe,

II. *The resolution which he adopts.* He determines,

1. *On an immediate return to his forsaken home.* "I will arise," &c.; v. 18. It is evident from the very language he employs, that this resolution is the result of deep conviction, and that it is decisive. He goes no longer in the way of sin and death. He has already repented, changed his mind, and changed his position; his face is now set homewards. His eyes are in the right direction; his mind is made up. He resolves to return, and do so at once. How necessary is such a resolution! For the want of it many have wavered and halted until the door of hope has closed. Let such a resolution be formed in connection with earnest prayer, for the Divine help, in firm confidence that God will give grace for its performance. Avoid self-confidence; let the broken and vain resolutions of untold myriads warn you not to trust in yourselves.

2. *He resolves freely to confess his sins.* "And will say, Father, I have sinned," &c.; v. 18. His confession is frank and ingenuous. No attempt at palliation. Not one word in self-defence. Not the least attempt to extenuate. "I have sinned." By my ingratitude of Heaven's disobedience. I have been foolish, base, and wicked. My career has been one of madness, and self-degradation, and infamy. I now see it,

know it, feel it, deplore it, and confess it. I hate myself for it. I am full of self-loathing and self-condemnation. "Against Heaven;" against its goodness and righteous claims. "And before thee." With fool-hardihood and shameless presumption. How striking and full this confession! How the very purpose of it must have relieved his wretched, guilty spirit!

3. *He resolves to be content with any place in his father's dwelling.* "And am no more worthy to be called thy son," &c.; v. 19. He had forfeited by his infamy the family name. He had no claim to be reinstated in his original place, having squandered the portion allotted to him. He is willing to become a servant. Better far to be a servant of his father than the servile herdsman of swine. He would be satisfied with this—deemed himself worthy of nothing better. Such are the feelings of the sin convicted soul. The soul is prostrated in the dust. The least of God's mercies is earnestly desired. Willing to be any thing or to do any thing for the Lord.

III. *The course which he promptly carries out.* "And he arose," &c.; v. 20.

1. *Immediately, without delay.* At once. He did not defer it to another season. His misery, his danger, urged him to action. His feelings were intense, so that at once "He arose," &c. How many have perished for want of immediate action! Their views have been correct, convictions have been experienced, resolutions formed; but then, delay has followed, and these delays have been increased, until the harvest has ended, and until the day has expired, until it has been too late. "To-day, therefore, if ye will hear his voice," &c. "Behold, now is the accepted time," &c.

2. *He persevered in his homeward course.* He resolutely set out, and retraced his steps. He allowed nothing to divert him from his purpose, and though he had wandered far, he stayed not until he drew near to the land he had forsaken. Hindrances to the repentant sinner will be presented. But the course of penitential return must be pursued; the language of the soul must be, "Hinder me not." The ears must be closed, as in the case of Bunyan's Pilgrim, and the cry must be, "Eternal life! eternal life!!"

Happy change! He now enters on the region of hope. But another discourse must open to us his paternal reception.

We ask, in conclusion,

(1.) How many present know the prodigal's repentance, in their own experience?

(2.) Who will now consider his ways, and turn to the Lord with full purpose of heart?

(3.) There must be repentance, or inevitable death.

XVI.—THE PRODIGAL SON.

(SKETCH III.)

"And he arose and came to his father. But when he was yet a great way off, his father saw him, and had compassion, and ran, and fell on his neck, and kissed him: and the son said unto him, Father, I have sinned against heaven, and in thy sight, and am no more worthy to be called thy son," &c.—*Luke* xv. 20, 32.

WE have now to contemplate the most beautiful part of this moral picture. The prodigal is on his way homeward, and we are now to witness the happy results of true repentance, and spiritual reformation of life. He has now arrived in the precincts of the paternal dwelling. His mind full of anxiety —his heart throbbing with the conflicting emotions of shame, penitence, and hope. The Saviour introduces the father to us, as if he had been looking towards the country to which the prodigal had wandered. No doubt his heart had often been moved, and his bowels yearned over his wicked and disobedient child. Observe then, in this part of the parable,

I. *The happy meeting.* In this meeting there is much of minute detail, that must not be overlooked.

1. *The father first saw the prodigal.* He beheld him when yet at a considerable distance. Saw him in his rags and misery; yet saw him returning,—knew him as his rebellious child, but now with his rebellious heart subdued.

God, our gracious Father, sees the first dawn of spiritual light in the sinner's mind. He observes the emotions of the penitent's heart. He witnesses his feet returning towards the way of obedience and life.

2. *The father ran to meet the prodigal.* Does not withdraw himself, nor even wait for the penitent obeisance of his child. Full of love, he hastens to meet him, and thus to inspire him with hope and joy. How affectionate and condescending! Yet, just so God seeks the wandering sinner,—beseeches

him to come to him, and live. Says, "Come now and let us reason," &c. Isaiah i. 18, &c.

3. *The father exhibits the reconciled state of his heart towards him.* "And had compassion, and ran, and fell on his neck," &c. The father was first in this reconciliation. His bosom overflowed with tenderest love. He required nothing to produce it. It was his very nature. He delighted to exhibit it. How free—how full—how spontaneously it flowed. He embraces him. He gives him the token of his pardon and favor, for he kisses him. And now, observe,

4. *The prodigal's confession.* His father's mercy and tender preventing love, did not satisfy the prodigal, or render his repentance and confession the less, but rather the more necessary. His shame would be doubled. His remorse vastly deepened. His sorrow the more intense at having offended, despised, and forsaken such a father. So he said, "Father, I have sinned," &c. The goodness of God generally leadeth to repentance. It is the cross of Christ subdues the heart. The graciousness of the gospel that gives it its saving power. Observe,

II. *The hearty reception.* We have seen him already in the father's arms and bosom. Observe, now, the train of blessings which he receives.

1. *His rags are exchanged for the family costume.* "The best robe is put upon him." God has appointed to those that mourn in Zion, "Beauty for ashes, the oil of joy for mourning, the garment of praise for the spirit of heaviness." Isaiah lxi. 3. See Psalm xxx. 11.

2. *The ring of acceptance is placed on his finger.* This is the sign, and token, and pledge of pardon, and reconciliation. It would remind him both of his wanderings and adoption.

3. *God gives his spirit to testify to the penitent sinner's acceptance. Shoes* are *placed* on his feet. Servants and slaves generally worked barefoot. This showed, therefore, that he was received as a son, and not as a hired servant. The children of God wear the shoes of the preparation of the Gospel of peace. The emblem of filial obedience and love. Notice,

III. *The distinguished banquet.* "And bring hither the fatted calf," &c., v. 23. Here was a festival of joy and gladness. The gospel dispensation is often likened to a feast. It was predicted as such. See

Isaiah xxv. 6, 7. The Saviour compared it also to a feast, Matt. xx. 1, 4. Observe,

1. *The provision was abundant.* The richest and best the family could provide.

2. *The guests were numerous.* The tidings of the returned prodigal were soon spread abroad, and neighbors and friends were invited to share in the joy of the occasion.

3. *The rejoicing was great.* A lost son found, a dead son alive! No marvel at the sound of mirth and gladness being heard afar off. If the finding of a lost piece of money, or recovering a wandering sheep, should give joy,—how much more the restoration of an immortal mind,—Salvation of a deathless being, the recovery of a prodigal child. What joy should the restoration of a fallen sinner produce on earth, when the very angels of God are enraptured and exult on the occasion. The parable concludes,

IV. *With the cold-hearted envy of the elder brother,* v. 25, &c. Here, doubtless, was portrayed the spirit of the Jews in general, in their dislike of the Gentiles, but more especially the envy of the Pharisees, that Christ should receive publicans and sinners. The spirit of the elder brother,

1. *Was base and inhuman.* For the occasion of the joy, was his brother—his younger brother. He refuses him, however, that appellation, and calls him, "Thy son."

2. *It was self-righteous and odious.* He describes himself as faultless. "Neither transgressed I at any time," v. 29. Who can truly say that? Let him who is without sin cast the first stone. He had no consideration for the frailty of man,—no pity for an erring brother. How striking the contrast of the spirit of the father, and of the elder brother! How forcibly, yet sweetly, he replies to his unkind and envious remarks! How he dwells on the interesting character of the occasion! How he defends the joy and gladness which was exhibited! "It was meet that we should make merry for this thy brother,—not only my son, but thy brother was dead,—so reckoned by us, and is alive again,—lives and breathes in our midst; and was lost, and is found."

Learn,

1. *How generous and pure is the benevolence of the gospel.* It is of God, and from him, and resembles his tender and infinite love.

2. *How hateful is an envious self-righteous*

spirit. It is the spirit of the evil one, and therefore from beneath.

3. *Happy they who have repented of sin, and who have been received into the Saviour's family of love.*

XVII.—PARABLE OF THE UNPROFITABLE SERVANT.

"But which of you, having a servant ploughing or feeding cattle, will say unto him by and by, when he is come from the field, Go and sit down to meat? And will not rather say unto him, Make ready wherewith I may sup, and gird thyself, and serve me, till I have eaten and drunken; and afterward thou shalt eat and drink," &c.— *Luke* xvii. 7, 10.

How important it is that we should have correct views of the divine claims upon us, and the spirit in which those claims should be met. We can err as to our duty through ignorance, or as to the manner of performing it, through the pride which is within us. It is clear that God does not require meritorious services from us in order to our acceptance with him, yet he does require the obedient homage of all who are accepted of him. The sacrifice of Christ alone is the ground of our acceptance,—the evidence of it, the fruits of practical godliness. The parable illustrates the nature of the service God requires. The support he affords in it. And the divine independency with respect to it. Observe,

I. *The nature of the service God requires.* It is indicated by the labors of the servants who are described as "ploughing or feeding cattle." That is, doing his work. Attending to his concerns. Now God just requires that we do his bidding. And this he,

1. *Has revealed in his word.* A knowledge of his statutes will make us acquainted with his will and our duty. Personal, social, and public duties, are all revealed here. The duties we owe immediately to him, to his people, and to the world. The whole province of obedience is mapped out in his holy word.

2. *For this he has given us the capacity and powers which are essential.* In his laws he has consulted our abilities and powers. He demands nothing that cannot be fully yielded. He seeks only according to the ability he bestows, and expects a return just in proportion to the talents committed to

our trust. The obedience he claims must possess the following characteristics.

(1.) It must be the obedience of love. Not of terror or constraint. Not servile,—but affectionate. "This is the love of God, that we keep his commandments," &c.

(2.) It must be spiritual. There must be the act, and also the spirit in the action performed. No service will please him which is not spiritual.

(3.) It must have respect to all his commandments. It must be entire,—obeying all his will.

(4.) It must be constant. The habit of the life. The daily course. In all things seeking to please him.

(5.) It must be persevering fidelity unto death. Occupying till he shall come. Working to the end of the day of life. Observe,

II. *The support he gives in it.* This is implied in his sitting down to "eat and drink," v. 7, 8. Notice,

1. *God gives ability for the service.* The daily strength is imparted by him. All our power and sufficiency is of God. We can do all things through Christ, who strengtheneth us.

2. *He provides daily food for the soul.* The bread of life, and the waters of salvation. Grace according to the day. Food to eat,—of which the world knows nothing. The rich and sufficient blessings of the gospel.

3. *He gives satisfaction and peace in the service.* They have great peace who keep thy law, &c. The peace of faithful servants flows as a river. A satisfaction and joy, sweet and unspeakable. The devoted servant of the Lord sings,

"I would not change my blest estate,
For all the world calls good and great."

All proper labor tendeth to profit, but the service of God especially and pre-eminently. "Godliness is profitable," &c. But there is also,

4. *The joy arising from the hope of reward.* Unto the servants of the Lord are given exceeding great and precious promises. Promises of future and eternal glory. His faith often anticipates the glory that shall be revealed, and the crown that fadeth not away. "I know whom I have believed," &c. Notice,

III. *The divine independency with respect to this service.* Doth the master thank "that servant because he did the things that were commanded," &c., ver. 9. Now the force of this will be seen when it is remembered,

1. *That no man can go beyond the divine claims in his obedience.* God claims the entire obedience of body, soul, and spirit. So that works of supererogation are literally impossible.

2. *God's goodness to man is ever beyond the services he receives from him.* So that man must by necessity ever be a debtor to God.

3. *That man's best services are, in consequence of his infirmities, frail and imperfect.* So that he must ever be the subject of the divine forbearance and long-suffering. "For he knoweth our frame, and remembereth that we are dust." It is only through the virtue of the Saviour's mediation, that either the person or obedience of man can be accepted of the Lord. How fitting then that they should say, "We are unprofitable servants: we have done that which was our duty to do," ver. 10.

Learn,

1. *How necessary is humility even to the most exalted saints.* Indeed in proportion to the progress of religion in the soul, will true and unfeigned humility be evinced. Let us avoid a self-righteous complacency, or satisfaction with ourselves. In reference to true grace,

"Whoever says he has enough,
Confesses he has none."

2. *In all our obedience, let us set the glory of God before us.* We must ever aim at this. "Whether we eat or drink," &c.

3. *Those who refuse to obey the Lord must finally perish.* Disobedience, and the divine wrath, are inseparably allied. The soul that sinneth incorrigibly, must surely die. "Then let the wicked forsake his way," &c.

XVIII.—THE GREAT SUPPER.

"Then said he unto them, A certain man made a great supper, and bade many: and sent his servants at supper time to say to them that were bidden, Come; for all things are now ready," &c. —*Luke* xiv. 16, 24.

ONE of the most common representations given of the gospel is that of a feast. This we not only meet with in the writings of the Jewish prophets, but in several of the parables of the Saviour. It is clear that the idea is that of the munificent preparation made to supply all the wants of perishing sinners. The supper to which our present subject refers, is described as a great one. Probably on account of the station and rank of the person who provided it, or on account of the abundance by which it was distinguished, or perhaps especially because of the great number of the guests invited, for he "bade many." In the conduct of those invited, we see exhibited the unbelief of the Jews to whom Christ came, and who first received the invitation of the gospel. But on their unbelief, the offer of salvation was extended to the Gentiles, and all men were bidden to come to the banquet of grace and partake freely. Observe,

I. *The invitation first issued.* Observe,

1. *The time of the invitation.* "At supper time." The evening of the day. At the introduction of the gospel dispensation by the Lord Jesus Christ.

2. *The nature of the invitation.* "Come." Come to the place of the banquet. Come and unite with the guests expected. Come and partake of the provision prepared. It was free, and generous, and direct.

3. *The persons by whom the invitations were sent.* By "his servants." The Lord Jesus as the servant of the Father, invited men. So also did his apostles and disciples by his express directions. Notice,

II. *The rejection of the invitations by the invited guests.* Observe,

1. *The unanimity of their refusals.* "They all with one consent," &c. They seemed to be actuated by the same spirit, and all began to make excuse. How fearfully illustrated in the general rejection of the Saviour by the Jewish nation. "He came unto his own," &c. "Who hath believed our report," &c. Notice,

2. *The various reasons which they assigned.*

(1.) The inspection of new bought property, ver. 18. His heart was so set upon his purchase, that he could not enjoy even a feast till he had seen it. He desired to gaze on the field which he had added to his former possessions. Hence covetousness, or the lust of the eye, was the impediment to the first. "How hardly shall they who have riches enter into the kingdom of heaven."

(2.) *Engrossing business was the next reason assigned.* "I have bought five yoke of oxen, and must go and prove them," Diligence in the management of worldly affairs, is not only blameless but commendable. The apostolic direction is, "Diligent in business, fervent in spirit, serving the Lord." But here it absorbed the whole man,—engrossed all his care and time. He could not spare a few moments for the supper, for the monopoly which worldly traffic had established in his soul.

(3.) *Domestic duties were assigned by a third.* "I have married a wife, and therefore cannot come." A regard to the claims of social life, is praiseworthy. A man should honor, and love, and care for the things of his wife. How beautiful to see domestic life enlightened and blessed by the cheering rays of enlightened affection and courtesy. But the wife is not to be the idol,—not to have the throne,—not to displace Jehovah. If a man love parents, or wife, or children more than Christ, he is not worthy of Christ. The folly, as well as sinfulness of these excuses, will be manifest, if you consider, that surely the man who bought the ground, would not do so, without first seeing it, nor purchase the oxen without first proving them. And the man had not pledged himself to his wife never to be absent from her, even to go to a feast. So that the excuses indicated the folly of the individuals, and showed that they felt no interest in the feast to which they were invited. Notice,

III. *The invitations which were subsequently issued:* ver. 21. "Then the master said, go out quickly into the streets and lanes of the city," &c. Observe,

1. *How extended the commission.* "To the streets," &c. No longer to special persons, but to the mass. Just so when the kingdom of heaven was opened to the perishing Gentiles. To all the world and to every creature.

2. *How benevolent the arrangement.* "Now the poor, and the maimed, and the halt, and the blind," are invited. The necessitous and perishing. The wretched and unfortunate.

3. *How urgent the appeal.* These crowded to the supper, but still the provision was so ample, and the banqueting hall so large, that yet there was room. Then the invitations were still further extended,—unto the "highways, hedges," with this additional injunction, "Compel them to come in." That is, entreat,—persuade,—urge,—constrain,— to induce the wretched to come,—"That my house may be filled." The whole concludes

with the expressed displeasure of the Master of the feast, "that none of those which were first bidden, should taste of his supper." Here is intimated the rejection of the Jewish nation, which has been fearfully ratified by the centuries which have rolled round since that period.

Learn,

1. *That in the gospel, abundant provision is made for the spiritual wants of mankind.*

2. *That the invitations of divine mercy include all ranks and conditions of men.*

3. *That these invitations are free and full, and urgently and sincerely presented by the Lord Jesus Christ.*

4. *That only self-excluders will be refused a place at the feast of salvation.*

5. *That it is the duty and interest of all, immediately and gratefully to obey the invitation and sit down at the gracious banquet.*

XIX.—THE WICKED HUSBANDMEN.

"Hear another parable: There was a certain householder which planted a vineyard, and hedged it round about, and digged a wine-press in it, and built a tower, and let it out to husbandmen, and went into a far country: and when the time of fruit drew near, he sent his servants to the husbandmen, that they might receive the fruit of it," &c.—*Matt.* xxi. 33, 43.

This parable is an exposition of the privileges God had bestowed on the Jewish nation, and their abuse and perversion of blessings thus conferred. In this case we have a beautiful illustration of the importance of parabolical teaching, for by this means the Jews were constrained to convict and pass sentence on themselves, and to have the enormity of their wickedness forcibly and fully presented before them. Observe,

I. *The privileges conferred.* These are likened to the possession of a "vineyard, planted, hedged round about," &c., v. 33. The Jews had a dispensation of light and mercy. They had ordinances,—a priesthood,—the oracles,—the Divine presence, care, protection, and blessing. Every thing needful to their national prosperity,—ecclesiastical purity, and spiritual happiness.

From the Jews, let us turn to ourselves. Think of our national elevation! Religious privileges, ordinances,—the word of God with all the promises and richer blessings of the gospel dispensation. How numerous too are many of our personal mercies. Pious parentage—religious friends, and unnumbered privileges, and blessings. "Line upon line," &c. Observe,

II. *How these privileges were perverted and abused.* Notice,

1. *Their refusal to yield the fruits thereof to the rightful proprietor.* A portion of these fruits they had to yield to the owner; and at the proper time he sent his servants to receive them. This was equitable and reasonable. But these demands they wickedly refused. Has not God a claim upon us? Does he not require a suitable return for the privileges and benefits received? But are these equitable claims duly met? Met gratefully and faithfully? By the constraining mercies of God, do we present ourselves a living sacrifice, which is our reasonable service?

2. *Their evil treatment of the messenger sent to them.* "And the husbandmen took his servants, and beat one, and killed another," &c., ver. 35. These were literal facts in the history of the Jewish nation. Many of their prophets they put to death. Isaiah is said to have been sawn asunder. See Heb. xi. 37, &c. How often has it been the lot of God's faithful servants to be hated and persecuted by those to whom they brought the message of salvation. This was the lot of most of the apostles, and first preachers of the cross of Christ. Of many of the early Protestant Reformers. Of the devoted Puritans, of the self-denying Nonconformists. Of Wesley and Whitfield, and the early Methodist preachers. Of many modern missionaries—Williams and Harris, and others. In our own country, where the persons and property of Christian ministers are protected by law, yet what bitter hatred and scorn are often evinced by the skeptical and profane rejecters of the gospel. Observe,

3. *Their murder of the heir.* "But last of all, he sent unto them his son, saying, They will reverence my son: but when they saw the son, they said, This is the heir, let us kill him," &c., ver. 37, 38. On the part of the proprietor, we see the utmost forbearance, and his solicitude to obtain the tribute which they owed. He risked his own son. He concluded that for him they would have respect, and to him they would yield homage. But they filled up the measure of their iniquity by basely putting him to death. How all this was predictive of the great act of Jewish hardness and infatuation, in cruci-

fying the Lord of glory. See how Peter charges this murder upon them, Acts ii. 23. How glaring and horrible this deed. And yet wilful sin and unbelief is crucifying the Lord afresh, and putting him to an open shame. Who is not then guilty of the death of Christ?

III. *The just punishment which the Jews deemed a righteous retribution.* The Saviour having presented this case, asked them, what will the Lord of the vineyard do unto those husbandmen? They replied, "He will miserably destroy those wicked men," &c., ver. 41. Here they passed a righteous sentence on themselves. A sentence which was put into execution, when the Romans destroyed their city, and when they were cut off from the privileges which for thousands of years they had possessed. In this we have a sure exhibition of God's terrible wrath against all finally impenitent and incorrigible sinners. There can be no escape for those who despise the gospel, and neglect so great salvation.

Then learn,

1. Rightly to estimate and improve your privileges.

2. Earnestly seek to obtain, and retain, the favor of the Lord.

3. And be ever prepared to surrender your accounts, and that with joy, and not with grief.

XX.—THE PEARL OF GREAT PRICE.

"Again, the kingdom of heaven is like unto a merchant man, seeking goodly pearls: who, when he had found one pearl of great price, went and sold all that he had, and bought it."—*Matt.* xiii. 45, 46.

THIS short and beautiful parable is kindred in spirit and meaning to the one which precedes it—on the treasure hid in a field. No doubt, by the pearl, we are to understand the gospel, in its revelation of life eternal. But it will not be a wide departure from the scope of the parable to consider Christ himself as the pearl, with which the gospel enriches all believers. Whatever grandeur, excellency, or preciousness there is in the gospel, it is entirely derived from Christ. The sweetest designation of the gospel is, that it is the gospel of Christ. He is its author, subject, and glory. So that he who receives the gospel, becomes the happy

and rich possessor of this precious pearl. Let us then dwell a little,

I. *On the similitude.* Wherefore may Christ be likened to a pearl.

1. *Pearls are of mysterious formation.* They are peculiar gems, found in the shells of a certain kind of oyster, chiefly in the eastern parts of the world. How applicable to the mysterious production of the humanity of Jesus, and to the mystery of his divine and human natures. The child of the virgin, and the son of God. Creator in our flesh, and the Lord of worlds in the fashion of a man. Mystery of mysteries. "Great is the mystery of godliness," &c.

2. *Pearls are noted for their variety.* In this we have both resemblance and dissimilarity. For there are in the world numerous pearls, but only one Saviour. God has sent many priests, and prophets, and righteous men. He has commissioned apostles and evangelists, &c.; but there is only one divine, eternal, and infinitely glorious Redeemer. His name—his office—his work—his glory is one—the one mediator between God and man.

3. *Pearls are precious and valuable.* Hence the pearl in the text is described as of Great Price! Who shall declare the worth of Jesus? All titles—all similes—all calculations—all conceptions—

"All are too mean to show his worth,
Too mean to set his glories forth."

Think of his inherent dignity, and majesty, and glory. Think of the Father's estimate of him, as his own elect, beloved and only son! Think of the esteem and love of angels, and their intense admiration of Christ; and still the real preciousness of Christ surpasseth knowledge. Observe,

II. *How this pearl is obtained.*

1. *It is diligently sought for.* Hence the Christian is likened to a "merchantman seeking goodly pearls," ver. 45. Here is the spiritual pursuit of the soul after Christ. By the power of truth, the anxiety for salvation has been produced—desire for the Saviour enkindled; and directed by the unerring testimony—the soul inquires for Christ—mourns for Christ—longs intensely for the manifestation of Christ. This seeking is the result of the proclamation of the gospel, and the direct effect of God's truth on the soul.

2. *All is sacrificed for its possession.* "He sold all that he had." Now, no one

can merit the possession of Christ, or the enjoyment of saving grace. Christ is God's gift, and only as such can we receive him. We can only have the wine and milk of the gospel without money, and without price. Yet, in another and equally consistent sense, all must be parted with to enjoy him. All that may be denominated self. Self-righteousness and esteem—self-love—self-seeking; honors, and all worldly vain distinctions. All sinful pleasures and gratifications. All things incompatible with the Saviour's love and favor. The soul itself must be yielded up to Christ. There must be a complete self-consecration. Rom. xii. 1. And thus only can we possess Christ. In losing all, we find Jesus. In renouncing every thing else, we possess the peerless pearl. We would refer,

III. *To the happiness and advantages of those who have found it.* In finding this pearl, they have found a portion for both worlds—riches for time and eternity.

1. *In Christ is all our need.* Think of the soul's wants—and they are all met in the Saviour. Ignorant, in Christ we have knowledge and wisdom. Naked, in Christ we have the robe of salvation. Hungry, he is the bread of life. Guilty, he is our pardon. Unholy, he is our righteousness. Wretched, he is our peace. Perishing, he is our deliverer and portion. To the soul who has found Christ, it may be said, "All are yours."

2. *In Christ is all the Christian's desire.* Every holy and spiritual desire terminates in Christ. Desires after holiness—after peace—after joy—after heaven, are all met in Christ. He sanctifies—he preserves—he delivers—he glorifies.

3. *In Christ is the believer's eternal salvation.* He is the Christian's portion forever—his likeness will be borne forever—his dwelling is an endless home—his glories our ceaseless bliss—his love our endless song. To see him as he is, and be with him, and enjoy him, is eternal life. How great the treasure of having Christ! Rich indeed are all such: "Heirs of God, and joint heirs with Christ." Heirs of God's eternal kingdom and glory!

Then learn,

1. *The wisdom of true religion.* All else is folly—excuseless folly.

2. *The happiness of true believers.* How rich—how exalted—how blessed! By men they may be considered as the refuse of the world, but with these is true dignity and the reality of blessedness.

3. *Urge sinners to seek and to obtain this pearl.* To do so at any rate, at any loss.

4. *How infatuated those who neglect this precious Saviour.* Of those who prefer the world, and the pleasures of sin. Ah! meager portion—wretched choice! A present bauble, and eternal poverty, misery, and despair.

———

XXI.—THE WISE AND FOOLISH VIRGINS.

" Then shall the kingdom of heaven be likened unto ten virgins, who took their lamps, and went forth to meet the bridegroom. And five of them were wise, and five were foolish," &c.—*Matt.* xxv. 1, 13.

IN this most beautiful parable the character of Christ as a bridegroom, and the solemnity of the nuptial ceremony, are very graphically presented before us. This view of the Redeemer is often the subject of scriptural revelation. In the forty-fifth psalm, and other portions of the Old Testament writings, this figure is adopted and sustained. In the parable of the marriage of the king's son, the same idea is held forth. The apostle Paul adopts the same similitude, 2 Cor. xi. 2. And John, in the sublime visions of Patmos, refers to the church as the Lamb's wife. In this parable, however, while the character of Christ as bridegroom, and the consummation of the marriage are clearly the leading events, yet we are especially directed to the character of those who were to grace the wedding with their personal presence. These are the ten virgins with which the parable commences. Let us then consider,

I. *Whom the virgins represent.* Is it not evidently the visible kingdom of Christ, the professed followers and friends of Jesus? The figure employed, that of virgins, is intended to show us the loveliness and purity of the friends of Jesus. In these virgins we look for a holy affection for Christ, and obedience to his authority. A profession of religion involves these two particulars in a pre-eminent degree. That we love Christ, and desire to exhibit that love in cheerful obedience to his sacred commands. All reasonable profession of religion includes of necessity these two things. Observe,

II. *The essential points in which these virgins differed from each other.*

1. *In the appellations given to them.* "Wise and foolish." (1.) The wise. The professions of the wise were valid. They were earnest, sincere. They professed Christ, and maintained that profession in reference to the future. They knew what it involved. That they would be expected to be found ready, prepared for the bridegroom's appearance. They were therefore prudent in making the requisite preparation. They prepared lamps, or torches, as was customary on such occasions. They also provided themselves with oil for any exigency which might occur. Their wisdom, in one word, consisted in preparing and acting for the future.

(2.) The foolish. These had lamps, but no provision of oil for the future. Their religious profession had only reference to the present. The great end was not duly contemplated, nor provision made for it. Wisdom fixes its attention on the most important things, and arranges chiefly and first for them. Not so shortsighted folly, which only gazes on the present uncertain flitting now, and neglects to prepare for the sure and momentous future. A mere profession of religion may do for the flitting years of life, but will not for the realities of death, judgment, and eternity. Notice, we are referred,

III. *To the period which intervened between the coming of the bridegroom.* "The bridegroom tarried." Did not appear so early as was expected. The second coming of Christ was expected by the Christians of the apostolic age. Hence Paul wrote to disabuse the minds of the early Christians as to his near approach. Since then, eighteen centuries have rolled over. So that from the commencement of the Christian dispensation to the second advent, it may be well certified, "that the bridegroom tarried." During this period, "they all slumbered and slept." This evidently refers to the sleep of death. One race and age of the church rose up and died after another. No other interpretation can meet the case clearly, for the same thing is said of both the wise and foolish, and without any blame being attached to it. It is obvious that both the wise and foolish died as they had lived. The one in union with Christ, and waiting ready for him. The other with only a nominal profession. At length the slumbers of the whole are disturbed. For notice,

IV. *The momentous proclamation.* "Behold the bridegroom cometh: go ye out to meet him:" ver. 6. This takes place at midnight, when the day of the world's probation has passed away. At "midnight," before the day of eternity dawns.

(1.) How sublime the announcement! "Behold the bridegroom cometh." In all his grandeur and magnificence. In all his pomp and glory. Cometh as predicted. Cometh to consummate his kingdom.

(2.) How important the command! "Go ye out to meet him." For this they have been long waiting. And now they all wake and startle into life. The slumbers of the world are disturbed. But the dead in Christ rise first. Now,—now is the grand crisis. The day of destiny and doom.

(3.) How active the arrangements! ver. 7. "Then all those virgins arose and trimmed their lamps." What anxiety and care will press on every mind. It is clear that the foolish virgins were not hypocrites, but formalists. They were not deceivers, but self-deceived; for they earnestly attempt to make ready for the bridegroom's appearance. Notice,

V. *The solemn difference now discovered.* (1.) The foolish have no oil. Their mere profession died with them, and now they have no real grace, and therefore cannot join in the nuptial procession. The wise trim their lamps, and go forth as they had *prepared*, as they had *desired*, as they had *expected*. This difference is now first discovered. But discovered when it is too late. "The harvest is past," &c. The means of mercy past. The day of probation ended. They attempt to buy in vain. The wise have no oil,—no grace,—no merit,—no righteousness to benefit others, and therefore their ruin is inevitable.

(2.) The foolish are excluded. The wise enter in with the bridegroom. Now their faith is realized in sight. Now their hope in eternal fruition. Now they are forever with the Lord. But the foolish are excluded. "The door was shut." How terrible that short sentence! The door shut, and that forever. Shut, and they excluded. And their appeals are in vain,—for they cry "Lord, Lord," &c. But the asseveration is heard, "Verily, I know you not," ver. 12. I never recognized you as more than professors: mine ye never were. I cannot approve of you, or own you now. Let solemn preparation be made for eternity. Let the Christian live for that. Prepare for that. Do all things in reference to that. Apply the subject with ver. 13.

XXII.—THE PARABLE OF THE TALENTS.

"For the kingdom of heaven is as a man travelling into a far country, who called his own servants, and delivered unto them his goods. And unto one he gave five talents, to another two, and to another one; to every man according to his several ability; and straightway took his journey," &c.—*Matt.* xxv. 14, 30.

In this extended parable we have presented to us in full, the doctrine of human responsibility, and the connection between the condition of the present and the condition of the future. These subjects are among the essentials of religion. They deserve our solemn consideration, and are adapted to produce those impressions which are favorable to our highest and eternal interests. We shall not attempt any explanation of the drapery of the parable, but make use of it to illustrate the important propositions we shall place before you. Observe,

I. *That God commits certain talents to his creatures:* ver. 14. Of the most important of these we may mention,

1. *Life.* The time and circumstances of our being.

2. *Reason.* The power to judge between right and wrong, that which can apprehend causes and effects, duties and their obligations.

3. *Influence.* Power arising from our rank, or station, or knowledge.

4. *Wealth.* For of money the wise man saith, it answereth all things. The instrumentality by which all benevolent machinery is established and continued.

5. *Religious privileges.* The word. The preached gospel. Sabbaths. Ordinances. Graces. Providences, &c. &c.

II. *That variety both in character and number distinguishes the talents God confers:* ver. 15.—To some he gave five, to others two, and to another one. We see this,

1. *In the nature of the talents conferred.* In one case in addition to the ordinary blessings and privileges of life, there is given profound learning, — to another commanding eloquence,—to a third great energy,—to a fourth the spirit of enterprise, &c. One has wealth, another useful parts, a third influence, &c. There is as great a difference between the talents of men as between one and five.

2. *In the capability for using them.* "To every man according to his several ability," ver. 15. God suits the talents bestowed to the characteristics of the mind, the sphere occupied, and the mental or physical ability possessed. With the talents conferred, there is ability to use them ever given.

III. *That God will require an exact account of the employment of our talents.*

1. *This is the great doctrine of revelation.* It meets us in every part of the sacred volume, Eccl. xi. 13, 14. To this also conscience responds. This is essential to accountability.

2. *God will do this at the day of judgment.* "After a long time the Lord of those servants cometh," &c. "Because he hath appointed a day in the which he will judge the world," &c. Acts xvii. 31.

3. *This account will be demanded from every one.* None too great to evade,—none too small to escape. Every man of every grade, and color, and condition, and age, and tongue. The dead, small and great, will stand before the throne.

IV. *That men will be judged according to the talents bestowed.*

1. *Improvement will be expected from each.* For this the talents were given. And to this every one must answer. Have they been laid out actively and conscientiously, according to the ability and opportunities given?

2. *The improvement expected will be proportionate.*

(1.) To the number of talents. Where much is given, &c.

(2.) To the time of possession.

(3.) To the favorable circumstances under which they have been enjoyed. Fidelity in the use, and consequent thereon, an increase of the talents will be the test. For in all cases faithful use increases the talents given. He who hath been diligent and active, and conscientious, increases the talents bestowed. Daily, more to him is given.

V. *God will reward his faithful servants according to the improvement made.* See this fully borne out in Luke's version of this parable: chap. xix. 16, &c. The man who had gained ten talents, had rule given him over ten cities. The man who had gained five, over five cities. There can be no doubt as to there being degrees of glory among the beatified. "As one star differeth," &c. Besides, faithfulness in God's service, and usefulness to our fellow-men, increases our capacity for bliss. And the capacity in every case will be the rule of the glory conferred. In all cases the reward,

1. *Will be rich and distinguished.* Worthy

of God to give. Such as his greatness and all-sufficiency can bestow. He hath called us to his "eternal kingdom and glory."

2. *Will be satisfying.* Soul filled with intellectual, holy enjoyment. "Joy of our Lord," ver. 23, &c.

3. *It will be eternal.* "Fulness of joy and pleasures for evermore," &c. These shall enter into life eternal.

VI. *God will punish the unfaithful and slothful with his severe displeasure.* He will,

1. *Overthrow his sophistry.* He excuses himself on the ground of his fear and dread, ver. 25. On that very ground Christ shows he should have been concerned anxiously, to improve his talent, ver. 26.

2. *He will expose him to public shame.* The examination is public. Angels are present. The whole human family are present. Before all he will convict and condemn him. The assembled world shall hear the charge, "Thou wicked and slothful servant."

3. *He will consign him to a state of misery.* His portion and crown are given to another, ver. 28. He is then seized by the administrators of divine justice, and cast into outer darkness, &c. v. 30. His doom is one of intense misery and despair.

Learn,

1. *The importance of faithful constancy and diligence in the service of God.* God says to each Christian, "Occupy till I come." Be faithful, &c.

2. *Exemption from flagrant sins will not save us.* There must be fruitfulness, &c.

3. *The ruined individual* was a servant, not a rebel, nor enemy. Oh, reflect and tremble.

XXIII.—THE UNJUST STEWARD.

"And he said unto his disciples, There was a certain rich man, who had a steward: and the same was accused unto him that he had wasted his goods. And he called him, and said unto him, How is it that I hear this of thee? give an account of thy stewardship; for thou mayest be no longer steward," &c.—*Luke* xvi. 1, 8.

IT is obvious that this parable must be read with care, that its design and purport may be correctly ascertained. Jesus here is not extolling the dishonesty of the unjust steward; nor yet does he inculcate, in the conclusion, the possibility that by any meritorious works, we can assure ourselves of final felicity. The whole scope of the parable is to teach wise, prudent forethought. And this is all that was commendable in the unjust steward. He calculated, arranged, and acted for the future. He had wasted his lord's goods. He was unable to toil for his daily food. He was ashamed to beg. He therefore resolved, by favoring to a large extent his lord's debtors, in the settlement of their accounts, to obtain such a share of their good-will, that in the time of necessity he saw approaching, he might be received into their houses. The lord heard of the sagacity and tact of his unfaithful servant; and while he must have detested his dishonesty, he yet admired the skill and prudence he had displayed. Jesus therefore attests that, as a rule, the children of this world are wiser in their generation than the children of light. He concludes by saying, that his disciples should make to themselves friends of the mammon of unrighteousness, that when they failed on earth, they might receive them into everlasting habitations. It is supposed by many that Christ here refers to the benevolent use of wealth in doing good to his poor disciples, who would hail their benefactors with joy to the abodes of the blessed. Then Christ will say to such, "I was hungry and ye gave me meat," &c. The great motto of the parable is,—live in reference to eternity. In doing this,

I. *Keep the eye of your mind constantly fixed upon it.* As the racer on the goal. As the mariner on his port. As the laborer on the end of the day. As the traveller on his home. Daily remember you are on your way to eternity. Soon you will have to do with eternal things. Think of them in the workshop,—in the market,—in the domestic circle,—in secret. On your beds, &c. Let this be one chief subject of meditation and reflection.

II. *Act for eternity.* (1.) Lay a good foundation, by building on the Lord Jesus Christ alone, and resting exclusively on him for pardon, sanctification, and eternal life.

(2.) Labor to grow in meetness for eternity. Cherish the spirit, and graces, and virtues, which will flourish in the celestial regions of glory. Seek for an entire conformity to God's will and likeness. Be heavenly and spiritually minded. Lay up treasure there, &c.

III. Let your conduct have reference to it. In worldly things act as a citizen of the New Jerusalem. As a Christian more especially, let your destination be recognized of all men. Show your pilgrim's staff and costume. Be ever on your way, &c.

III. *Act with that skill and energy which eternal concerns deserve.*

(1.) See how worldly men contrive and toil for earthly gain,—how much more you for eternal riches.

(2.) For what a little they make immense sacrifices,—how grand the object you have before you,—your self-denial and earnest efforts cannot be too great.

(3.) How they persevere and overcome difficulties. Be as intent on your labors, and as strenuous,—determined and unwavering.

(4.) How anxious are they to improve all opportunities. Be you as wise and watchful,—avail yourselves of all means of getting and doing good. Be especially moved to this course by the consideration,

1. *Of the uncertainty of the present.* Your period of probation is exceedingly limited, and its termination may be just at hand. Much may have to be crowded into a few months, or weeks, or days. What diligence and fervor then are necessary.

2. *Of the momentous character of the future.* Eternal things are solid, unchanging realities. Heaven and its glory is eternal. Hell and its woe is eternal. And in eternity there is no reparation of life's woeful mistakes. No available repentance there. No door of hope there. No throne of grace there. No purifying fountain there. Then while we have these, what concern and diligence should be evinced !

IV. *Under all circumstances prefer eternal to temporary good.* Eternal prosperity to evanescent earthly prosperity. Eternal glory to earthly glory. Eternal pleasures to those of sin and sense. Eternal mansions to those of time, having their foundations in the dust. Keep in mind the wisdom of looking at the unseen realities of eternity, in preference to the temporal vanities of time.

APPLICATION.

1. *Commend the conduct of those who are thus wise and prudent in reference to eternal things.*

2. *Encourage them.* Their reward is nearer every day. Soon shall wisdom be justified of her children. Soon shall the wise shine forth in the kingdom of their Father forever.

3. *Urge the worldly to a better choice.*

Why be absorbed with sublunary good ? It is the portion of the beasts of the field. Seek something higher, better, holier,—more suited to your faculties, and more adapted to the immortality of your being.

4. *Press consideration on the thoughtless.* "O that they were wise, that they understood this, that they would consider their latter end."

XXIV.—THE RICH FOOL.

"And he spake a parable unto them, saying, The ground of a certain rich man brought forth plentifully: and he thought within himself, saying, What shall I do, because I have no room where to bestow my fruits ?" &c.—*Luke* xii. 16–21.

THIS parable originated in consequence of an individual applying to Christ, that he would adjudicate between him and one of his brethren in reference to the family inheritance. This would have been a direct departure from the spiritual province the Saviour came to occupy, and therefore he replied, "Man, who made me a judge or a divider among you?" v. 14. And seeing the anxiety of this individual respecting the attainment of an earthly possession, he said, "Take heed and beware of covetousness, for a man's life consisteth not in the abundance of the things which he possesseth ;" ver. 15. This important principle he illustrates by the parable before us. Observe,

I. *The rich man's possessions ;* ver. 16. "The ground of a rich man brought forth plentifully." He was in circumstances of affluence, rich and prosperous. Just in that condition which men are anxious to attain. The sun of prosperity shone upon him. The gales of prosperity filled the canvas of his vessel, and her gallant course was all that heart could desire. This is often the lot of the thoughtless and the ungodly. So that temporal prosperity is never a sure indication either of piety or irreligion. In this respect one event happeneth to all. Observe,

II. *His anxieties.* Some imagine that anxiety is only the lot of the poor and the wretched, and such as have to buffet with the waves of adversity. The very opposite is generally the case. Anxieties are generally found in proportion to the amount of our earthly possessions. Riches and cares are inseparably wedded together. Hence, though rich and prosperous, he exclaims, "What shall I do?" We marvel not that the poor and starving, that the widow and the orphan, that the distressed and unfortunate should thus exclaim, but this is the language of a man of abounding affluence. He knows not how to dispose of his abundance. "I have no room where to bestow my fruits." I am full to overflowing. I cannot keep pace in my hoarding arrangements with the increase of my substance. He surely had forgotten that the fruits of the earth were for the inhabitants of the earth, and that this superabundance was to enable him to give to the poor and needy, and such as were born for adversity. We see, too, that no degree of prosperity can soften or expand a sordid or selfish heart. We see, too, how he speaks as the proprietor, and not as the steward of his possessions. I have no room for *my fruit;* what shall *I* do? He recognizes no superior authority; he refers to no will but his own. How few remember that riches are only given in trust! And that God says to every one, "Occupy till I come." Observe,

III. *His determinations.* "And he said, This will I do; I will pull down my barns and build greater;" v. 19, 20.

1. *He resolves on the means of accumulation.* He will cherish the sordid, grasping feeling. He will add to his already oppressive abundance. Avarice, like the sea and the grave, never says it has enough. Like the horse-leech, it ever cries, "Give, give!"

2. *He forms his arrangements without any reference to the providence of God.* He says, "I will pull down my barns," &c. He reckons on no contingencies. He calculates on no changes. He is as self-confident as he is rich. He thinks he can dispose of events as easily as of riches. He fancies time and years to be as malleable as gold. He does not even say that he will *endeavor* to do these things, but he confidently declares that he will do them.

3. *He reckons on his riches as the joy and portion of his soul.* "And I will say to my soul, Soul, thou hast much goods laid up for many years," &c. His mind was evidently gross and carnal. His affections earthly. His gold was his idol. He evidently was ignorant that mere material things could not satisfy the mental desires of an immaterial spirit. The fruits of the earth would do well enough to meet many physical necessities, but what could they do in meeting the boundless longings of a deathless soul? How would he extract from wealth, light for his understanding, truth for his judgment, peace for his conscience, or solid hopes for his immortal desires and delights? What stupidity! What infatuation! Yet is not this the very spirit of worldliness—seeking the chief good in the creature, and not in the Creator; having the affections on the earth instead of in heaven?

4. *He confidently calculates on an extended existence.* "Thou hast goods laid up for many years;" ver. 19. Many years of plenty and enjoyment are before thee. Be content, satisfied, happy. All things are right and secure; no interruption, no molestation shall affect me. What folly! Did he not know that no man could reckon with certainty as to to-morrow—that the wisest cannot tell what a day will bring forth? That man's breath is in his nostrils—that man is travelling every moment on the margin of the grave? Yet this infatuated scheme of reckoning on long life, how common it is! Men buy and sell, and build, and form plans, as if they held life on a certain and long protracted term of years. Notice,

IV. *His sudden and fatal arrestment.* It might seem that this colloquy with himself had taken place on his bed. During the commencement of the night season. Having finished the process of his purposes and resolves, he now probably thinks of sleep, intending to commence his new improvements on the morrow. But observe,

1. *How he is disturbed by the voice of Deity.* "God said," either by some deep, unmistakable impression on his heart and conscience, or by some sudden infliction of disease. "Thou fool," &c. What an interruption to his castle-building! What an unexpected leveller of his plans! How soon the aspect of the whole scene is changed! Mark,

2. *The sudden termination of his career.* "This night thy soul shall be required of thee." Thy race is run; thy probation ended. Thou art on the verge of the eternal world. This night. How soon—how unexpected—how awful!

3. *The eternal ruin of his soul.* He had lived for time and for earthly ends. His soul and eternal things had been utterly neglected. Alas! how poor is he now! How wretched! How despairing! He thought he was happy and secure. But he

had built upon the sand, and all, by one fell storm, is swept away. And his soul is lost —lost—lost forever. Oh, reflect, be wise, and lay up treasure in heaven, &c.

XXV.—THE BARREN FIG-TREE.

"He spake also this parable: A certain man had a fig-tree planted in his vineyard; and he came and sought fruit thereon, and found none. Then said he unto the dresser of his vineyard, Behold, these three years I come seeking fruit on this fig-tree, and find none; cut it down; why cumbereth it the ground?" &c.—*Luke* xiii. 6–9.

It is probable that Christ designed this parable to be admonitory to the Jews, whose mercies had been so numerous, but whose day of privileges would soon terminate. But the subject is equally applicable to all persons who are favored with the means of religious knowledge and improvement. How important that we should live constantly and deeply impressed with our responsibility to God, for all we enjoy. That we should remember always, that this is a probationary state. That eternity will be to us, in all its enjoyments, or woes, as we sow here. And, therefore, that we should so improve our blessings, that our account may be surrendered with joy, and not with grief. Observe,

I. *The favorable position in which the fig-tree was placed.* In a "vineyard"—not on some neglected waste ground. Not by the way-side. But in a vineyard. Under culture and care. With all the advantages of the vine-dresser's skill, &c. This was the highly favored condition of the Jews for many generations. See Isaiah v. 1, &c. This is the condition of those favored with the privileges and blessings of the gospel dispensation. This is especially the condition of those who are members of the Christian church.

(1.) Who have been professedly brought out of the world into the church.

(2.) Who are favored with the spiritual means and ordinances of the gospel.

(3.) Who are the subjects of the especial and rich promises of the new covenant.

(4.) Unto whom the graces and blessed influences of the Holy Spirit are freely imparted.

(5.) Who are the objects of the Divine care and complacency. We are directed,

II. *To the expectations of the proprietor.* He came seeking fruit; v. 6. This expectation was reasonable. The vine is a fruitful plant. Under cultivation, it is expected to yield a due increase. God expected this from the Jews. He required them to be more wise, and holy, and obedient, than the heathen who surrounded them. God requires this from all favored with the privileges and blessings of the gospel economy. He particularly requires, and expects it from his own professing people—the members of his church. He expects,

1. *Their hearts to yield the fruits of holy graces.* These are specified by the apostle Paul; Gal. v. 22, &c. He expects,

2. *Their lips to yield the fruit of thanksgiving and praise.* The sanctified mouth glorifies God and extols him. Celebrates his praises, &c. From the abundance of the heart the mouth speaketh. And the stream of the lips is to evidence the nature of the fountain within. He expects,

3. *The fruits of obedience in the life.* The fruits of righteousness to the glory of his grace. That to faith will be added virtue, temperance, &c. That the life shall be regulated by the Divine law, and conformed to the Divine mind. Subject to God's gracious and holy authority. That they be servants of righteousness.

4. *The fruits of usefulness, by the employment of their powers and talents, in his service.* That the powers, and gifts, and blessings conferred, will be laid out and improved. True love to God will lead to a desire to serve him, and glorify him in the world. Love to mankind, which is an essential part of religion, will lead to active exertion to save our fellow-creatures. Observe,

III. *The proprietor's disappointment.* "Behold, these three years I come seeking fruit on this fig-tree, and find none;" v. 7. We marvel not at his disappointment. He had sought fruit year after year, and there had been none. It is said that a tree, not yielding fruit for three years, was considered barren. He found no fruit thereon. No fruit of any quality. No fruit. Not one branch or cluster did this tree bear. It might be strong and green, but it was barren. To the Jews this literally applied. To myriads under the gospel dispensation. And to how many, alas! who are professors in the church—the absence of every grace and virtue God seeks and demands. Notice,

IV. *The command the proprietor issues.*

"Cut it down, why cumbereth it the ground?" v. 7.

1. *This sentence was not a hasty one.* There had been three years' care, and labor, and forbearance. God exercised his great long-suffering towards the Jews. So to men in general. So to fruitless professors in the church. To all, God manifests patient and enduring forbearance. Not willing to destroy, but desirous to save. Hence, he waits long to see if they will bear fruit or not.

2. *A sufficient reason is assigned for the order given.* "Why cumbereth it the ground?" It was worthless in itself. It occupied precious ground. It took up the nutritive portions of the soil, that useful fruitful trees required. So was it with the Jews. So is it with all unfruitful professors. Their influence is worse than useless—it is pernicious to others. Notice at this crisis,

V. *The request the vine-dresser presents.* "He said, Lord, let it alone this year also," &c., v. 8. He denies not the allegations of the owner. He vindicates not the final continuance of the tree. But he entreats,

1. *For a short period of suspense of the sentence.* One year. One year only! One round of the seasons. One year's showers and sunshine.

2. *He engages to give it special attention.* "I will dig about it, and dung it," v. 8. I will try and search out the cause, and use all reasonable means to remedy it. He further adds,

3. *His willingness then to obey the order of the proprietor.* This is not only implied, but directly stated. "If it bear fruit, well." Well for the tree, the proprietor, and the vine-dresser; "and if not, then thou shalt cut it down," v. 9.

This pleading for the cumberer has often been verified in the prayers of the parent, the friend, the minister; but it is true in the highest and best sense of the Lord Jesus. He ever lives to intercede. He prayed for his murderers on earth. He mediates for a lost world in heaven. Our being—our privileges—our gracious calls all flow to us through him. Through the virtue of his sacerdotal influence, the axe may have been stayed in its descent—the affliction removed—the life prolonged. But remember, the suspended blow is not pardon—not acceptance—not salvation. Without repentance, faith, fruitfulness, the sentence will be put into fearful execution.

APPLICATION.

1. *Let the subject lead to serious self-examination.* Am I in the vineyard of the Lord a fruitful tree, or a cumberer of the ground?

2. *Let the formalist be awakened to a deep concern for his soul's salvation.*

3. *Let all remember the great end of life, is to glorify God, and finally obtain eternal blessedness.*

XXVI.—RICH MAN AND LAZARUS.

(1st SKETCH.)

"There was a certain rich man, who was clothed in purple and fine linen, and fared sumptuously every day: and there was a certain beggar named Lazarus, who was laid at his gate, full of sores," &c.—*Luke* xvi. 19, 22.

THIS is confessedly the most awful of all the Saviour's parables. It is worthy of notice how repeatedly Christ adverted to the doctrines of future rewards and punishments. No other teacher ever said more concerning death, and judgment, and eternity—concerning heaven and hell, than Jesus. In this parable, as in many others, two individuals are brought before us in contrast, and the contrast is sustained throughout. It begins in time, and is carried out into the future state. The whole is so graphic and forcible that some have supposed it to be the language of narration and not of parable. In either case the great truths presented must be the same, and to these let us with the utmost seriousness of spirit direct our attention. Observe,

I. *The rich man in his affluence and enjoyments.* Most probably he was rich by descent. Owned some magnificent family inheritance. At any rate his means were abundant. He had riches in profusion. At the greatest possible distance from earthly want or dependency. Hence there is reference made,

1. *To his costume.* "Clothed in purple and fine linen," v. 19. Articles of dress of the most costly kind, and such as could be worn only by one of the grandees of the earth.

2. *To his style of living.* Doubtless a splendid mansion the place of his residence. "And he fared sumptuously every day." Hence his hall would be one continued scene of banqueting and gayety. One round of

sensual enjoyments. Luxuriousness the order of every day. Observe,

II. *Lazarus in his poverty.* Here we have the greatest possible contrast before us. For Lazarus,

1. *Was a beggar.* One without any earthly dependency. One whose wants were to be supplied by the precarious generosity of others. No inheritance—no sure provision laid up for a single day. A child of deep need—one evidently born for adversity. He was anxious for the crumbs of the rich man's table.

2. *Without a dwelling.* He was homeless. Had not even a mud-walled cottage for his habitation. For he was laid at the rich man's gate. The mere animals belonging to the mansion fared better than he. Like the Lord of life and glory, he had not where to lay his head. To the piercing cold—to the teeming rain—to the painful frost of night, and to every peril and wretchedness, he was exposed.

3. *He was miserably afflicted in his person.* "Full of sores," &c., ver. 20. Most likely lame and helpless, and distressed with painful and loathsome ulcers. Probably his extreme poverty might result from his diseased condition, being unable to toil for the bread which perisheth. "Moreover the dogs came and licked his sores," ver. 21. We are directed,

III. *To the death of Lazarus.* "And it came to pass, that the beggar died," ver. 22. We marvel not at this, but rather that he had lived, when his misery and destitution are considered. His poverty and afflictions probably hastened his death. He died as he had lived—poor, forlorn, and neglected. But at his death he became the subject,

1. *Of angelic ministration.* Those bright, and holy, and benevolent spirits, the immediate servants of God in heaven, who are ever hearkening to the voice of his word, were sent to watch the dying agonies of the neglected beggar. No earthly hand is near to close his eyes—no earthly bosom to heave with tender sympathy. But angels witness his last struggles, and might be commissioned to administer celestial consolation.

2. *He is conveyed in triumph to glory.* He exchanges earth for heaven,—poverty for celestial riches,—and disease and destitution for ineffable joy and blessedness. How striking, how indescribable the change! God's saint, who had no dwelling on earth, is now a citizen, a prince royal of immortal glory. Of his funeral we have no account —what became of the diseased, worn-out tabernacle, is not stated; but the soul, the deathless part of the beggar, is beatified. We are now directed,

IV. *To the demise of the rich man.* "The rich man also died and was buried," ver. 22. As the beggar had died of destitution, who knows but the rich man had died of repletion? For the one is almost as unfavorable to health and longevity as the other. At any rate,

1. *He died.* Riches, affluence, earthly glory, could not ward off disease, nor prevent the fatal stroke of mortality. In spite of friends and physicians, the enemy of our species directed the fatal dart with unerring precision. Observe, it is recorded,

2. *That he was buried.* Rank and wealth keep up their distinctions after death, in the magnificence of the funeral obsequies—in the marble monument—in the flattering inscription, and eulogy on the deceased. But this is the utmost stretch of earthly distinction, unless some dependent writer immortalizes his name and deeds in song, or on the pages of his country's history. We have now surveyed the leading features in the earthly history of these two individuals. We have seen them pass away from the scenes of time. We look for them, but they are not. Another lord tenants the mansion, and the beggar no longer is seen prostrate at the family gate. Both are gone—for both, after all, were travellers to the same home. Their final state we must reserve for another occasion. We learn,

1. *That piety on earth is often allied with poverty and suffering.*

2. *That earthly prosperity and magnificence are no proofs of the divine favor.*

3. *That whatever be our condition in this world, we are travelling towards another.* Here we have no abiding. This is not the final abode of either rich or poor.

4. *That death is inevitable to all stations and ranks.* How necessary to remember this. To prepare for it, by a life of sanctity and devotedness to the cause of God in the world.

XXVII.—RICH MAN AND LAZARUS.

(2D SKETCH.)

"And in hell he lifted up his eyes, being in torments, and seeth Abraham afar off, and Lazarus in his bosom. And he cried and said, Father Abraham, have mercy on me, and send Lazarus, that he may dip the tip of his finger in water, and cool my tongue; for I am tormented in this flame," &c.—*Luke* xvi. 23–31.

OUR attention has been directed to the rich man and Lazarus in their opposite circumstances of life, and in their decease; and in those particulars were found much weighty matter for serious reflection. Life is important in itself, but how much more in its vast responsibility in connection with eternity. What I am now, may concern both myself and others,—but the all-momentous question is, What shall I be in eternity? What shall be my future condition,—what my endless portion? Poverty or affliction is endurable with the prospect of eternal blessedness, and surely riches and sensual pleasures can have no attraction if they are linked inseparably with endless woes. We have now to follow the rich man and Lazarus into the eternal world. The Saviour has drawn aside the curtain, and we are permitted to behold them in their fixed estates as the inhabitants of eternal things. Notice,

I. *We see Lazarus in the abodes of the blessed.* Angels had conveyed him into "Abraham's bosom." This is a description of heaven having peculiar charms for the Jewish hearer. To be with the father of the faithful, their nation's sire. And in his bosom amid the festivities of the heavenly banquet. As John was in the bosom of Jesus at the eucharistic supper. His condition in Abraham's bosom was one,

(1.) Of repose after the toils of life.

(2.) Of dignity after the humiliating scenes of his earthly adversity.

(3.) Of abundance after want.

(4.) Of bliss after many griefs and sorrows. And this heavenly estate was permanent and eternal.

II. *We are referred to Dives as consigned to the regions of the lost.* "And in hell," &c., v. 23.

It is not said how he came there. Whether any spirits, the administrators of God's vengeance, were employed to drag him thither. One of our sacred poets thus inquires,

> "Will angel hands convey
> Their brother to the bar,
> Or devils drag my soul away,
> To meet its sentence there?"

He then truly adds,

> "I must from God be driven,
> Or with my Saviour dwell;
> Must come at his command to heaven,
> Or else—depart to hell."

His condition is described as one of extreme suffering. "Being in torments," v. 23.

(1.) Torments arising from the awful change he had experienced when death removed him from his wealth and luxuries on earth.

(2.) Torments from unallayed desires. He seeks now even for one drop of water, but in vain. He doubtless has all his innate feelings and established habits, and loves banqueting and ease; but the power of gratification is forever gone.

(3.) Torments from the bitter and despairing anguish of his doomed spirit.

(4.) Torments of keen self-reproach.

(5.) Torments from the direct infliction of the righteous wrath of God.

(6.) Torments from having the world of joy and glory within the range of his distracted vision.

III. *We are reminded of his unavailing prayers.*

1. *For the alleviation of his own agonies.* "Send Lazarus, that he may dip the tip of his finger," v. 24. But to this Abraham replies, that he had all his enjoyments in his lifetime. That he had chosen earth and earthly things for his God and portion, and that now an eternal lease of evil is his inevitable inheritance. He shows, too, how Lazarus now has an inheritance of comfort and blessedness. He also reminds him that there is now no intercommunion between the good and the bad, the saved and the lost. The two worlds are separated with an impassable gulf, v. 26.

2. *For additional means to save his brethren.* He desires Lazarus to be commanded to go to his father's house to "testify unto them," v. 28. Whether from compassion or from dread of his own misery being increased by their presence he presented this prayer, we know not. But this also was in vain, and though he repeated his request it was peremptorily rejected. "They have Moses and the prophets," being deemed a sufficient reason for the refusal of the request. And the solemn declaration, "If they hear not Moses and the prophets," &c., v. 31.

Learn,

1. *How awful it is to die in a carnal, unregenerate state.*

2. *How connected are the concerns of time*

with the realities of eternity. "Whatsoever a man *sows* that shall he also reap."

3. *How all-important is real personal piety.* A new heart, the enjoyment of God's favors, and a title and meetness for eternal glory.

4. *The sufficiency of the means appointed for man's salvation.* Moses and the prophets, and Christ, and the apostles. The sacrifice of Christ, the word, and the Spirit. All things needful are ready and offered.

XXVIII.—THE UNJUST JUDGE.

"And he spake a parable unto them *to this end,* that men ought always *to* pray, and not to faint: saying, There was in a city a judge, who feared not God, neither regarded man," &c.—*Luke* xviii. 1–8.

THE one great purport of this parable is, to urge and vindicate the importance of earnest importunate prayer. The exercise of prayer is confessedly essential to true religion. The hindrances to prayer are many. Hence, many fail in carrying out the exercise and habit of spiritual devotion. Many too are the subjects of depression, and are liable even to distrust God, in reference to answers to prayer. They ask with apprehension, or with little faith—doubting. Now to excite to prayer, and to induce to persevering prayer, is the design of this parable. The success of the widow is to be the ground of our expectation and success. If she persevered and succeeded, under circumstances so very unpropitious, shall not we obtain our suit, with so many favorable things to encourage us? For observe,

1. *The character of the judge to whom she appealed.* He was an unprincipled person, neither fearing God nor regarding man, v. 2. Who had no regard to the divine laws, nor feared the displeasure of Jehovah. And who was so base and abandoned as to have no self-respect, nor caring for the esteem of those around him; for neither did he regard man. The popular favor had no attractions. The popular indignation no influence with him. He was desperate, lost to all sense of right and wrong. One who debased his office, and made self and iniquity the occupants of the judicial seat. Yet with this man, the woman succeeded. If so, think of the being we address in prayer. The Holy One of Israel. The just and true God.

Whose throne is based on righteousness. Whose laws and ways are all pure and just and good. Whose administrations are all wise and equitable and perfect. But more than this, remember the Divine goodness. His infinite immeasurable love. His boundless grace and benignity. His generous desire for the happiness of his intelligent offspring. The evidences too of his bounty and mercy, in the arrangements of providence, especially in the exceeding riches of his grace, in sending his Son to die for our sins, &c. Observe,

II. *The person of the applicant.* "A widow." One without rank, or influence, or wealth. One probably a stranger, without a friend to introduce her, or to plead for her. Yet she succeeded with this judge. Then turn from the widow and her state in reference to the judge, and think of the praying believer and his relation to God, the object of his supplications. God is the friend of the suppliant. He is his gracious father. His merciful Redeemer. Their connection is close and intimate and kind. They are united in covenant and mutual love. God delights in them, and they delight in God. They are one by solemn covenant,—a covenant ratified by the blood of the cross. Surely, then, the Christian shall be heard in his prayers and supplications. Observe,

III. *The engagements God has entered into in reference to prayer.* The unjust judge was wearied out. For the sake of ease and quiet, he granted her request. But God will assuredly regard his people's prayer,

(1.) Because of his titles. He is the revealed hearer and answerer of prayer. As such, he has proclaimed himself to his saints.

(2.) Because of his promises. These are presented in every possible form and variety. He has given these in great number. They are almost beyond enumeration. They are most express and direct and absolute. The honor and glory of God are concerned in their fulfilment. "They are all yea and amen," &c. "Whosoever asketh, receiveth," &c. These are the promises of God, "who cannot lie."

(3.) Because of his arrangements. The laws of his spiritual kingdom are as fixed and unalterable as those of the physical parts of the universe. He has set up the ordinance of prayer, as the medium through which he will be exalted, and his people blessed and saved. It is an appointment full of wisdom and love. We would urge the great object of the parable,

IV. *From the value of the blessings we supplicate.* This widow desired to be avenged of her adversary. That is, to have justice in some secular matter of litigation. Her importunity was manifested to obtain some earthly good. Then how much more importunate should God's people be, for the attainment of the precious blessings of life and salvation. The blessings we seek in prayer,

(1.) Are inexpressibly precious.

(2.) Necessary to our present happiness.

(3.) And essential to eternal salvation. The soul in all its capacities and desires, both for time and eternity, is concerned. How earnestly—how eagerly—how importunately should we seek the blessings of the well-ordered covenant. The conclusion of the parable clearly shows that God will avenge the quarrel of his people. Thus he reckons their enemies as his own, and their ultimate overthrow is certain. His "elect," his chosen believing children, shall not plead in vain. The question also asked, whether, when the Son of man cometh, he shall find faith on the earth,—may refer either to the saints who may be tempted to doubt the approaching advent of their Lord and deliverer, or to the general unbelief of men, as to that great and momentous event.

Learn,

1. The nature of prevalent prayer.

2. The importance of earnest importunity and perseverance.

3. The certainty that acceptable prayer shall be effectual. "Therefore, men ought always to pray, and not to faint."

XXIX.—THE PHARISEE AND PUBLICAN.

"Two men went up into the temple to pray, the one a Pharisee, and the other a publican. The Pharisee stood and prayed thus with himself: God, I thank thee that I am not as other men *are*, extortioners, unjust, adulterers, or even as this publican," &c.—*Luke* xviii. 10, 14.

PRIDE is inherent in the human heart. It was one of the great elements in the first sin. Man would be as God, and therefore he took of the fruit which was to give him knowledge equal to his. The fall of the angelic host most probably originated in the same feeling of self-exaltation. Its general prevalence is obvious to the most superficial observer. In the world we see it without disguise or affected concealment. In the church it often appears under the semblance of humility. There is often the garb of abasement worn by those who manifestly possess the spirit of self-righteous approbation. To guard against this—to see its odiousness—to observe how God despises it —is the end and scope of the parable before us. It is introduced with this emphatic declaration, "And he spake this parable unto certain who trusted in themselves," &c., v. 9. To expose the evil, and to warn them of its consequences. Let us then,

I. *Examine the portrait drawn of the Pharisee.* And,

II. *Observe the description given of the publican.* And,

III. *The divine treatment of both.* Let us then,

I. *Examine the portrait drawn of the Pharisee.*

1. *The Pharisee was a public professor of religion.* One of avowed habits of sanctity, &c. Known and recognized as a religious man.

2. *He belonged to the strictest of all religious sects.* They professed extraordinary piety. Not only did they conform to the letter of the law, but added thereunto numerous acts of devotion and self-denial. In prayers, fasts, alms-giving, &c., they greatly surpassed all other religious parties. In conformity with this profession, we behold,

3. *The Pharisee at his devotions in the temple.* To this place he often repaired. Here he was often seen. His prayers here were constantly presented.

4. *The nature of his worship is described.* You will observe several objectionable, yea odious features in it.

(1.) He abruptly addresses God. "God, I thank thee!" It sounds more like the language of one to his equal than of a creature to his Maker.

(2.) He gives himself credit for a decided superiority over others. "I am not as other men, extortioners, unjust," &c., v. 11. Here is the essence of self-righteousness and self-approbation. Here he vaunts and exalts himself before the Lord. Here he celebrates his superior excellency, and publishes his good deeds. Hence he considers, comparing himself with his fellow-men, to be acceptable worship before God. He also enumerates his religious excellences. His fastings and his giving tithes of all that he possessed. It is probable that, like most of the Pharisees, all this was merely external. That in heart and soul he was rapacious and unjust—"devouring widows' houses," omitting the weightier matters of the law, "judgment, mercy, and faith." See Matt. xxiii. 13, 28.

(3.) He invidiously compares himself with his fellow-worshipper, " or even as this publican." Surely spiritual arrogance and pride could not go beyond this. He dares before the Searcher of hearts to extol himself, and urge his claims upon heaven, by directly depreciating a fellow-creature in the act of worship with himself.

(4.) He pretendedly thanks God for his moral excellences. "God, I thank thee," was in his mouth, but self-gratulation was evidently the emotion of his heart. What hypocrisy and deceit! What infatuated self-delusion! Such is the portrait drawn of the Pharisee. Observe,

II. *The description given of the publican.* He exhibits,

1. *A deep sense of his unworthiness.* "Standing afar off." He felt the sanctity of the place. He was filled with a sense of awe when he contemplated the Being before whom he was approaching. Of the two worshippers, a poet has said,

"One nearer to God's altar trod,
    The other to the altar's God."

"He lifts not up so much as his eyes towards heaven," ver. 13. He is abased in spirit, and prostrate in soul before God. Notice,

2. *The evident compunction of his soul.* "But smote upon his breast." His guilt was his burden—his shame, his grief. He felt the evil of his nature—the vileness of his heart. He was overwhelmed with his baseness. His spirit was ready to sink within him, and his feelings were those of indignation against himself, and loathing of his iniquities.

3. *He confessed his state before God, and sought mercy.* A sinner he acknowledges himself, and he earnestly supplicates Jehovah's mercy. "God, be merciful to me, a sinner," ver. 13. How concise, how direct, how appropriate. How earnest and intense this one request. Yet how comprehensive and all-sufficient. For the divine mercy could pardon and absolve him. Divine

mercy could purify and restore him. Divine mercy could heal and comfort him. Divine mercy could fully and eternally save him. He needed this, and this was all his need. Notice,

III. *The divine treatment of both.* With both God was fully conversant. He saw through the thin guise of the Pharisee, and despised his mockery and parade. He beheld the afflicted, contrite heart of the publican, and looked on him with complacency and delight. He retired "justified." Accepted and approved of God. The mercy he sought, God imparted freely, richly. He retired rejoicing in the compassion of a merciful prayer-hearing God. He sought not the Lord in vain. The Pharisee's self-worship—for prayer it was not—was rejected. He lived only in the region of self-complacency, and God despised his character, and rejected his service. "For every one that exalteth himself shall be abased," &c., v. 14.

Learn,

1. *Man's true state and character.* "A sinner."

2. *His manifest need of mercy.* Sin must be pardoned or punished.

3. *The true way of obtaining mercy.* Believing, contrite prayer in the name of the Lord Jesus Christ.

4. *The hateful, ruinous nature of self-righteousness.*

————◆————

XXX.—THE GOOD SAMARITAN.

"And Jesus answering said, A certain man went down from Jerusalem to Jericho, and fell among thieves, who stripped him of his raiment, and wounded *him*, and departed, leaving *him* half dead: and by chance there came down a certain priest that way; and when he saw him, he passed by on the other side," &c.—*Luke* x. 30–37.

THIS parable was delivered on the occasion of a certain lawyer, standing up with a view to perplex the Saviour. Under a feigned purpose, he asked a very important question—What he should "do to inherit eternal life?" v. 25. Jesus knowing all that was in his heart, and resolving to convict him out of his own mouth, and at the same time to show him the fallaciousness of pharisaic reasoning, replies, that he must do what is written in the law, v. 26. The lawyer then repeats the two great commandments, v. 27. To which Christ answered, "This do, and thou shalt live," v. 28. But anxious to justify himself, he raises the question, as to who should be understood by his neighbor. This question forms the basis of the inimitable parable then delivered. And Jesus answering said, "A certain man went down from Jerusalem to Jericho," &c. Observe in the parable,

I. *The distressed condition of a fellow-creature.* A traveller is on his way from the metropolis of Judea to Jericho, and is surprised and seized by a band of robbers. The distance, though only about sixteen miles, was through an exposed and dangerous country. Some parts of the road were rocky and mountainous, and not inhabited, affording places of retreat for robbers and highwaymen. Our traveller, alone and unprotected, becomes an easy prey to them. They not only take his property, but they strip him of his clothes, and wound him, leaving him only just alive. Prostrate on the ground, with his wounds open, and probably the gore flowing therefrom, he is helpless, and ready to perish.

What a spectacle of distress and misery! What a proof of the cruelty and ferocity of the depraved heart of man! Of what vileness men are capable—in some respects more to be dreaded than the savage beast of prey that roams abroad in the forest.

In this state of suffering and peril the wretched man lays, when we are called to witness,

II. *The embodiment of selfishness in two travellers who are passing by.*

1. *A certain priest.* Of these a great many resided at Jericho, and therefore would often have occasion to pass to Jerusalem. As he drew near, he beheld the wounded man on the other side of the way, and without doing more than gazing on his mangled fellow-being, he hastens on his journey. He neither stops nor speaks to him, but leaves him in his misery and helplessness, without compassion or aid. Next came,

2. *A Levite.* Another of the sacred profession, whose office was to assist the priests in the public services of religion. He, when he came near, just looked on him—saw more fully his condition than the priest had done; but this was all, for he then held on his journey, and administered no help to the almost dying sufferer. How vile and hardhearted were these two men! How they degraded their own humanity, and especially sinned against the offices which they held.

As men they were base enough, but as religionists they were execrable. Under what a spirit of self-delusion and vain hypocrisy they were living. At this juncture, when both priest and Levite had left the man to perish, we are directed,

III. *To see an exhibition of love and mercy where we should not have expected to find it.* "But a certain Samaritan as he journeyed," &c., ver. 33.

The sufferer was a Jew; and between the Jews and the Samaritans a deadly prejudice and hostility existed. Besides, they were reckoned a selfish and unfeeling people. He, therefore, might have passed on with the utmost indifference, without exciting our surprise. But mark how contrariwise he acted.

1. *His eye affected his heart.* "When he saw him, he had compassion," v. 33. He recognized a fellow-creature in distress and suffering, and his soul was melted, and his sympathies aroused.

2. *His feet hastened to him.* He stayed not to gaze at a distance, nor hurried past the scene, but under the genial influence of mercy, he ran to the spot where the sufferer lay.

3. *His hands ministered to him.* "He bound up his wounds," and thus stayed the effusion of blood. He poured in oil and wine to allay the pain, and to heal them. "He set him on his own beast," as he was unable to walk. He watched over him with the utmost care. Travelled gently as the sufferer could bear. He conveyed him to the nearest tavern—commended him especially to the host. He gave him twopence, or about one shilling and threepence of our money, to pay the charge; and he engaged to pay any other expense that might be incurred in ministering to his future wants. Here was genuine kindness, tender compassion, in which all that is lovely and beautiful were combined. We see that from its rise to its termination, it was sincere, and ardent, and self-denying. And it was to an unknown individual, and one of a nation which he abhorred. But self and prejudice were both sacrificed on the altar of humanity, goodness, and mercy. Observe,

IV. *The inevitable conclusion to which the querulous lawyer was forced.* Now says the Great Teacher, "Which of these three was neighbor unto him that fell among thieves?" v. 30. He replied, "He that showed mercy on him," v. 37. Then said Christ to the lawyer, "Go and do thou likewise," v. 37.

(1.) Think of the Samaritan, and admire his spirit.

(2.) Have equally generous feelings towards all thy suffering fellow-creatures.

(3.) Imitate him when such circumstances shall be presented before thine eyes. And the parable says the same to us. The love of our neighbor, which is one of the great essentials of true religion, involves all that the Samaritan felt and did. Nothing less than this is love. And this, beautiful as it was, was nothing more. Never ask with a view of evading duty, who is my neighbor? For remember,

> "Thy neighbor! it is he whom thou
> Hast power to aid and bless ;
> Whose aching heart, or burning brow,
> Thy soothing hand may press.
>
> Where'er thou meet'st a human form,
> Less favored than thine own ;
> Remember, 'tis thy neighbor worm,
> Thy brother, or thy son."

Learn,

1. *The fallacy of that religion which is devoid of mercy and compassion.*

2. *See under what an awful delusion professors of religion may live.* As in the case of the priest and Levite.

3. *Cherish the spirit, and imitate the conduct of the Lord Jesus*—" Who went about doing good."

XXXI.—THE MERCIFUL CREDITOR.

"And Jesus answering said unto him, Simon, I have somewhat to say unto thee. And he saith, Master, say on. There was a certain creditor who had two debtors: the one owed five hundred pence, and the other fifty," &c.—*Luke* vii. 40, 42.

THE supercilious condition of the Pharisees was ever abhorrent to the spirit and feelings of the Lord Jesus. Yet he had to contend with it everywhere. Because he preached to the outcasts and perishing, he was stigmatized as the friend of publicans and sinners. And on the present occasion, because he permitted a penitential heart-broken woman to remain in his presence, and to wash his feet with her contrite tears, his very Messiahship was doubted. For Simon, the Pharisee, whose guest he was, concluded, that if he had been a prophet, he would have known the character of the woman, v. 39, and of course knowing it, would have repulsed her. The Saviour, with his

characteristic wisdom, met these odious prejudices by desiring the attention of his host to the parable under consideration, and draws from him the inference by which his own merciful conduct is fully vindicated. We remark,

I. *That all men are debtors to God.*

(1.) From him all men have received innumerable blessings in trust. That whatever God confers, he confers to be occupied to his glory. That men are not the proprietors of the mercies they enjoy. At best only stewards. Among these mercies are Life,—Health,—Time,—Daily Food,—Reason. Our privileges through the redemption which is in Christ. The gospel. Our Sabbaths, &c. All have been given for our well-being and improvement.

(2.) A due return for their mercies none have rendered. The return has generally been neglect and ingratitude. Disregard to God's claims. Disobedience. Perversion of our blessings, and an abuse of our mercies. Who has been faithful to the claims of God? Who is not a debtor to him?

II. *That men are debtors to God in different degrees.*

1. *There is a difference as to the blessings intrusted.* One has had two talents,—another five,—a third, ten. One much wealth, another little. One many gifts, another few. One has been the child of prosperity,—another has been born for adversity. One has had his lot in the very midst of signal privileges,—another has had few opportunities of improvement.

2. *There is a difference in the degree of moral guilt contracted.* One has been externally proper in his conduct. Like the young ruler who came to Christ. Another has been dissipated and abandoned. In the text one owed fifty pence, the other five hundred. Here was Simon and the woman who was a sinner.

III. *That sinners of all degrees are incompetent to pay what God fully demands.* "And when they had nothing." Now the best as well as the worst have nothing to pay. The most exemplary man is a sinner, and is justly condemned before God. The vilest of mankind are sinners too, but in a greater degree. Neither the one nor the other,

(1.) Can atone for their past sins.

(2.) Nor yield perfect obedience irrespective of divine grace for the future.

(3.) Nor avert the just consequences of

their misdoings. The whole race are insolvent before God. No real merit to present. No inherent rights to plead. No ability to offer. Nothing to pay is the state of one and of all men by nature before God.

IV. *That the only hope of moral debtors is in the mercy of God.* " When they had nothing to pay, he frankly forgave them both." Observe,

1. *God has revealed himself as the God of mercy.* He has passed by and proclaimed his name, &c. He is rich in mercy. Delighteth in mercy. He will surely have mercy on such as seek him.

2. *God has exhibited his mercy in Christ Jesus.* In the Saviour it was embodied, lived, and it offered him up as the sacrifice for man's redemption and eternal life. Christ was the mercy promised to the fathers.

3. *This mercy is published and offered in the gospel.* " Be it known unto you, men and brethren, that through this man is preached unto you forgiveness of sins," &c. The gospel is full of the invitations and promises of mercy to each and every sinner.

4. *By faith in the Lord Jesus this mercy is realized.* He that believeth is justified freely, &c. Fully pardoned. Enjoys the entire remission of his sin. Is accepted of God, and adopted into the divine family. Be it remembered this forgiveness is " frank," gracious in principle, and in the spirit in which it is imparted.

V. *That the sinner who is most forgiven will love the Saviour most.* This we may reasonably conclude to be the rule, and facts bear out the conclusion. See Simon and the woman who had been a sinner, v. 44. See the history of Saul of Tarsus, who fell because he had been a persecutor, &c., he was the chief of sinners. See the case of Bunyan, the converted blasphemer. And John Newton, the skeptical profligate, and many others.

APPLICATION.

1. *Have you been sensible of your guilt before God?*

2. *Have you felt your own insolvency,— that you have nothing to pay with?*

3. *Have you had recourse to the free grace of God in Christ Jesus?*

4. *Have you evinced your gratitude and great love to Christ for his saving mercy?*

5. *The obstinate debtor will be finally and justly punished.*

The poet has beautifully described this penitent woman :

" Drop, drop slow tears !
And bathe those beauteous feet,
Which brought from heaven,
The news and prince of peace.
Cease not wet eyes,
For mercy to entreat :
To cry for vengeance,
Sin doth never cease.
In your deep floods,
Drown all my faults and fears :
Nor let his eye
See sin, but through my tears."

XXXII.—THE GOOD SHEPHERD.

" I am the good shepherd : the good shepherd giveth his life for the sheep. But he that is a hireling, and not the shepherd, whose own the sheep are not, seeth the wolf coming, and leaveth the sheep, and fleeth : and the wolf catcheth them, and scattereth the sheep," &c.—*John* x. 11–18.

OF the various titles which are applied to the Lord Jesus, none are more general or expressive than that of the Shepherd. As such the Hebrew prophets spoke of Christ. Isaiah says of the Messiah, " He shall feed his flock like a shepherd," &c., ch. xl. 11. The Saviour often also adverted to his own work as that of a shepherd. He evidently depicted his own character and mission in the Good Shepherd, who pursued the wanderer and left the ninety-nine sheep in the wilderness. And a great portion of this rich and instructive chapter is thus occupied. The apostle Paul speaks of him as that " Great Shepherd," Heb. xiii. 20. Peter as " the shepherd and bishop of our souls," 1 Pet. ii. 5, and also as the " Chief Shepherd," who shall bestow the crown of glory upon all his faithful servants in the great day of his glorious appearing, ch. v. 4. At present let us take a survey of the parabolical discourse in which Jesus pursues this subject so fully. Let us contemplate,

I. *Christ Jesus as the Shepherd.* The office is so well known as not to require definition or description. Christ is the Shepherd of souls,

1. *By the Father's appointment.* The Father is represented as knowing him as the Shepherd, in distinction from those who are merely hirelings. His mediatorial authority and offices were given to him of the Father. Hence he is styled by Jehovah, " My shepherd, the man that is my fellow," Zech. xiii. 7.

He ever laid great stress on his being sent of the Father, and receiving his mission and power from him.

2. *By his own voluntary choice.* He was ready both to hear and to conform to the Father's will. He was ready to come, as the Father was to send him. Hence both forms of speech are constantly used by the sacred writers, and both with equal truth and propriety. He was so rich in grace, that he freely came to seek and to save that which was lost.

II. *Consider the flock of Christ.* And here we must consider them,

1. *As redeemed.* He came to redeem. And in his precious blood we have redemption, even the forgiveness of sin. They had wandered, were perishing, and self-destroyed. They required to be ransomed out of the hand of the enemy, and to be brought back to God, from whom they had departed. Christ, by his incarnation, life, obedience, and death, effected this great, this wondrous work. Hence they are described as purchased with the blood of the Son of God. Redeemed not with corruptible things, but with the precious blood of the Lord Jesus Christ.

2. *As restored.* Not only must the sheep be redeemed, but restored. Hence the address of the Good Shepherd is, "Return unto me, for I have redeemed you." And in order to their restoration, he pursues the wanderer, and announces to him the tidings of reconciliation. He sends his servants to find out, and bring the wanderers back. By the gracious influences of the truth and love of the gospel, he allures them, and draws them to himself.

3. *As united to him.* Brought near to him. Reconciled. No longer aliens or outcasts, but citizens and friends. In the day of conversion, the soul is graciously united to Christ. Then they are his, and he is theirs. They are the sheep of his pasture, and as their Shepherd he rejoices over them to do them good.

4. *As recognized by him.* "And know my sheep," v. 14. The Lord Jesus knoweth all things, he therefore knoweth them that are his. And as such they are distinguished from others. They bear the mark of their Divine owner. They differ from others by the operation of the good Spirit within them. He knows every one of his. They are described,

5. *As also knowing Christ.* "And am known of mine," v. 14. None belong to him who do not know Christ, who do not know him in his titles, and offices, and grace. They have all tasted and known that the Lord is gracious. This knowledge, in both cases, signifies also approbation. Christ approves of his sheep, and is the Saviour of their choice and delight.

6. *They distinguish the voice of Christ.* "They shall hear my voice," v. 16, 17. The voice of Christ is presented to us in his word. Here he speaks to us, and his words are spirit and life. He speaks to us, too, by his Holy Spirit, the voice of God within us. Now the carnal and careless disregard the Son of God, and despise his word. But the Saviour's disciples, like Mary, sit at his feet, and hear all his gracious words. Whether he speaks in words of authority, or of direction, or comfort, they hear his voice. And they delight to hear it. It is the joy and life of their souls.

7. *They obey the commands of Christ.* This is also evidently implied in the words, hearing his voice. They so hear as to know and understand his will. So as to love his commands. So as heartily and cheerfully to obey him. "This is the love of God, that we keep his commandments," &c.

8. *They imitate his example.* "And they follow me." The eastern shepherd leads, not drives, his flock to the pastures and streams. He goes before, and with pleasing docility they follow after. Jesus has marked the path of holiness by his own blessed and perfect example. In all things he was the great pattern. In self-government, self-denial, and lowliness, and humility. In kindness, goodness, mercy, and pity. In long-suffering and gentleness. In purity of speech and manners. In holiness of heart and conversation. In the devotion of his spirit and communion with God. In one word, in all things, "He hath left us an example that we should follow his steps." Such, then, are the leading characteristics of the sheep of Christ.

APPLICATION.

1. *How interesting and delightful the character of Christ as a shepherd.* How wise, and good, and gentle,—how gracious and kind.

2. *How lovely and beautiful the character of his flock.* A redeemed company of immortal spirits. Called. Justified. Sanctified.

3. *How important the question, Are we*

his sheep? Have we the signs of his people on us? His love within us?

XXXIII.—THE GOOD SHEPHERD.

(2D SKETCH.)

"Verily, verily, I say unto you, He that entereth not by the door into the sheepfold, but climbeth up some other way, the same is a thief and a robber: but he that entereth in by the door is the shepherd of the sheep," &c.—*John* x. 1–18.

WE have previously contemplated Christ Jesus as a shepherd, and noticed his flock, with the distinguishing signs by which they are recognized. Let us now proceed to consider,

III. *The Saviour's fold.* Now the sheepfold is brought before us in the Saviour's address, ver. 1. We remark,

1. *The Saviour's fold is the church.* Here they are collected and united together. All the saints belong to this one fold. For there is only one fold, and one shepherd. However diversified in opinion—in modes of worship, or sectarian designation; they are but one body, of which Christ is the Head—one fold, of which Christ is the Shepherd.

2. *Of the fold, Christ is the only entrance.* He is the only way into the sheepfold, see ver. 1, &c. Hence he says, "I am the door of the sheep," ver. 8, 9. There is no saving acceptance to God, but by the Saviour. No man cometh to the Father, except by him. Christ is the centre of union to all his people. They are all one in Christ Jesus. Faith in him, and a profession of him before men, are the essential qualifications to membership with his church. Any other mode of admission is climbing over, and is the entrance of the thief and robber.

As we are all the children of God by faith, so being his children we belong to the one fold of the Redeemer. We proceed to notice,

IV. *The Saviour's pastures.* The Psalmist sang, "He leadeth me into green pastures." The shepherd not only has his fold for security, but his pastures for the nourishment of his sheep.

1. *There is the word.* Here is rich and ample provision for his people. By it they are nourished and strengthened. It is the living and abiding word. Here there are resources of instruction, peace, and security.

They are to desire the sincere milk of the word, that they may grow thereby. There are,

2. *The ordinances of the gospel.* Preaching of the gospel. Social prayer. The Lord's Supper, &c. In all these there is abundant nourishment for the soul. Here God prepares his feast of fat things. Here the provision of mercy is laid on the family board. Here there is enough and to spare.

3. *Secret prayer and meditation.* By these the soul comes into immediate and gracious connection with God. Here they have food to eat of which the world knows nothing. These are the delectable mountains. The verdant hills ever fresh and green. The fertile valleys yielding the richest pasturage for the soul.

V. *Some of the peculiar and distinguishing characteristics of Christ as the good shepherd.*

A careful, attentive, and faithful shepherd, under ordinary circumstances, would be entitled a good shepherd. But Christ is pre-eminently so,

1. *On account of his unbounded love to the flock.* This love was exhibited in that great act by which their redemption was accomplished, in laying down his life for the sheep. "I am the good shepherd; the good shepherd giveth his life for the sheep," ver. 11. He not only entertained purposes of mercy and grace—not only left heaven and came to earth to collect the scattered wanderers. Not only lived a life of sorrow, grief, and humiliation; but he gave up his sacred life. His soul sorrowed even unto death, in Gethsemane. He was arraigned, buffeted, tried, condemned, and put to death, even the ignominious death of the cross. Herein was love, such as had never before been exhibited.

"See from his head, his hands, his feet,
　　Sorrow and love flow mingled down!
　Did e'er such love and sorrow meet,
　　Or thorns compose so rich a crown?"

Hence every disciple can say, "He loved me and gave himself for me." We refer,

2. *To his especial care of his flock.* He takes especial interest in their preservation. They are in his hand. He is able to keep them. Hence he adds, "Neither shall any pluck them out of my hand," ver. 28. No enemy can destroy them. Their defence is invincible—their security inviolable, for he avers, "They shall never perish." Indi-

viduals, nations, and vast empires have perished—have been blotted out; but his sheep shall never perish. The wisdom, love, and power of the omnipotent Redeemer are all guaranteed for their preservation. Kept by the power of God through faith to salvation. We allude,

3. *To their future and final destination.* "I give unto them eternal life." They are collected, folded, preserved here, and glorified hereafter. Hence the purpose of Christ respecting them is presented in his sacerdotal prayer, "Father, I will that they also whom thou hast given me be with me where I am, that they may behold my glory," John xvii. 24. Now this is the final destiny of the Saviour's sheep. They are called to his eternal kingdom and glory. Think of the love which purposed such a state of exaltation and blessedness. That has prepared such glorious things for those who love him. Let us just glance,

VI. *At the fold of Christ, when perfected in the heavenly state.* He has had his sheep and fold in every age of the world. He had them in the days of his sojourning on earth. But he said, "Other sheep I have which are not of this fold; these also I must bring, and they shall hear my voice; and there shall be one fold and one shepherd," ver. 16. Here, doubtless, he referred to the Gentiles, who should be called to be partakers of his grace, and who should be one in him with the Jews. But there is yet the grand consummation, when all his sheep shall be collected.

(1.) Gathered from all generations.

(2.) Gathered from all nations, and people, and tongues.

(3.) Gathered to the upper and better fold in heaven.

(4.) Gathered to enjoy the celestial pastures. "For the Lamb which is in the midst of the throne shall feed them, and shall lead them unto living fountains of water; and God shall wipe away all tears from their eyes;" Rev. vii. 17.

APPLICATION.

1. *How transcendently excellent and holy the character of our good shepherd.*

2. *How safe, and happy, and blessed his flock.*

3. *How the hope of future perfected bliss should inspire with joy unspeakable and full of glory.*

4. *How futile the malevolent attacks of satanic agents and wicked men.*

5. *How glorious will be the completed fold of the Saviour in heaven.*

XXXIV.—THE MIRACULOUS POWER OF CHRIST.

" Ye men of Israel, hear these words: Jesus of Nazareth, a man approved of God among you by miracles, and wonders, and signs, which God did by him in the midst of you, as ye yourselves also know."—*Acts* ii. 22.

GOD has been pleased in all dispensations to testify to the authenticity of his truth and the validity of his servants, whom he hath sent forth to instruct mankind. Thus Moses was empowered to exhibit the glory of Jehovah and the reality of his own divine commission, by extraordinary deeds and signs which he wrought. Thus Elijah and Elisha, and others of the prophets, gave unequivocal evidence that God was with them and spake by them. We look for the same evidences of the Messiahship of Christ, and the Gospels abound with the narrations of them. By them it was manifest to all unprejudiced minds that he was indeed the Christ the Son of God. Hence he says of the unbelieving Jews, "If I had not done among them works which none other man did, they had not had sin; but now have they both seen and hated both me and my Father;" John xv. 24. Christ, therefore, desired that his character and office should be tested by the works which he performed, and surely no more obvious and certain ordeal could have been proposed. As the miracles of the Saviour were connected with the whole course of his blessed ministry, we anticipate great instruction and profit in giving them our serious and prayerful consideration. Observe,

I. *The description given of the Saviour.*

II. *A declaration of the miraculous works done by him.* Notice then,

I. *The description given of the Saviour.* He is presented to us,

1. *In his human nature.* "A man," &c. The earliest prediction referred to him as the "seed of the woman." He was promised as a " child born," as a "son given." His lineage and birthplace were foretold. At length, in the fulness of the times he came, "made of a woman," the fruit of the virgin's

womb. Essentially in body, soul, and spirit, a man. Yet with this extraordinary difference, that the holy thing born of the virgin was conceived by the overshadowing of the Holy Ghost. He often described himself as a man, and the Son of man. But with the manhood of the Redeemer was essentially and mysteriously allied the Godhead. He was the tabernacle of the fulness of the God. "God was in Christ." He was "God with us." "The brightness of the Father's glory, and express image of his person." "God manifest in the flesh." "God over all, blessed for evermore." But Peter, on this occasion, was anxious to prove that Jesus was the Christ or anointed of God. He is presented to us next,

2. *In his name, &c.* "Jesus of Nazareth." His name, Jesus, was given to him on account of his being the long promised Saviour. "Because he shall save his people," &c. Nazareth was where he chiefly dwelt until he entered on his ministry. Here he was brought up. The place of his residence. Hence he was called a Nazarene. Here, too, he began to open to men the kingdom of heaven. See Luke iv. 16, &c. How precious the name of "Jesus!"

The poet has beautifully said,

"How sweet the name of Jesus sounds
    In a believer's ear;
It soothes his sorrows, heals his wounds,
    And drives away his fear."

We are referred,

3. *To the Divine approval of Christ.* "Approved of God." There were many evidences that God approved of him. The striking circumstances of his baptism, when the Holy Spirit descended, and the voice was heard, "This is my beloved Son," &c. The repetition of the same testimony on the mount of transfiguration. But such also were all the miracles he wrought. All these were the evidences which God gave to his Messiahship. They were all confirmatory of the Divine approbation. God never gave these signs to establish an impostor or false prophet, or to give efficacy to a delusion or lie. Thus Jesus was approved of God by miracles, and wonders, and signs. By the series of wonders which attended his life and ministry. Observe, we have in the text,

II. *A declaration of the miraculous works done by him.* Now these miracles of Christ,

1. *Were numerous.* We cannot state exactly how many, for often they are given to us in general phraseology. As "he healed multitudes," "cast devils out of many," &c. It is clear that he wrought more miracles than all those recorded of Moses and the prophets. His ministry was one glorious scene of signs, and miracles, and wondrous works.

2. *They were strikingly various.* All sorts of diseases and maladies he healed. All kinds of infirmities removed. Evil spirits of all sorts dispossessed. He wrought miracles on all classes and descriptions of persons. His wonders were performed on the sea and on the land, and on the living and on the dead. Those recently afflicted, as Peter's wife's mother, and those who had been bowed with afflictions for many years.

They were performed in the most public places. Never in secret. There were always some to attest them. Often many persons, and sometimes crowds. Some of his miracles were wrought in the presence of his bitterest enemies. His signs were wrought in the light of day, in "the midst" of the Jews, as they themselves knew.

4. *They were wrought by his own inherent divine power, and in his own name.* Moses and the prophets professedly wrought their miracles by a power given at the time, and in the name of the Jehovah of Israel. But Christ exercised supreme authority, and spake, and by his own power wrought the deeds, and wonders, and signs. He said, "I will, be thou whole." He commanded Lazarus to "come forth." He spoke, and rebuked the winds and the sea, &c. And it is evident that this power he could command on any emergency, and thus was illustrated, "The Father loved the Son, and hath given all things into his hands." And again, when he declared, "All power is given unto me, both in heaven and on earth."

5. *His miracles were in harmony with the kingdom of grace and mercy he came to set up.* His were emphatically miracles of love and mercy. He healed, but never inflicted diseases. He blessed, but cursed not. He imparted ease, and comfort, and joy, but never did minister to increase the miseries of men. He came not to blight or to destroy, but to save. "He went about doing good."

6. *His miracles were often connected with spiritual blessings.* Often, when he healed the body, he also forgave the sin, and healed the maladies of the mind. Often, when he expelled demons, he also made the objects

of his miraculous mercy the subjects of his saving grace. Learn,

1. *How glorious is the character of the Saviour.*

2. *How worthy of our admiration, confidence, and supreme affection.*

3. *How terrible will be his wrath to impenitent sinners.*

XXXV.—THE MIRACLE AT THE MARRIAGE OF CANA.

"And the third day there was a marriage in Cana of Galilee ; and the mother of Jesus was there : and both Jesus was called, and his disciples, to the marriage," &c.—*John* ii. 1-11.

MARRIAGE is an institution of God, and which originated in the Divine desire for the perpetual social happiness of man. In various ages of the world, false ascetic principles have been promulgated, and the purity of celibacy proclaimed. This sentiment had no countenance either from the teaching or conduct of the Saviour. His first miracle at Cana, in Galilee, was a distinguished seal of honor on the marriage relationship, and replete with evidences of his Messiahship and glory. It is probable that the nuptial parties might be related to the mother of Jesus, as we find her, in connection with him, a guest on the occasion. Marriage ceremonies, in the East, are conducted with considerable pomp, and connected with feasting and rejoicing. It would appear that on this occasion a considerable number of persons graced the nuptial banquet, and in this joyous company Jesus and his mother were found. Observe,

I. *The lack of wine intimated.* "And when they wanted wine," &c. v. 3. It is probable that this lack of wine originated either in the humble circumstances of the family, or in the more numerous attendance of guests than had been anticipated. At any rate, the wine was exhausted. The mother of Jesus therefore addressed him, and intimated the state in which they were involved. Is it not evident from this, that she knew the power he possessed, and that she expected the putting forth of that power on the present occasion ? To this, Jesus replied, " Woman, what have I to do with thee ? mine hour is not yet come," v. 4. Our translation of this answer appears harsh, and bordering on disrespect. But it is evident

that the gracious Jesus, in his reply to his mother, merely intended to check her eager anxiety. To urge her to wait for results, and the reason he assigned was surely sufficient : " Mine hour is not yet come." His mother, therefore, directed the servants to obey his intimations, and to watch for them, v. 5. Observe,

II. *The Saviour's commands.* Jesus said unto them, " Fill the water-pots with water." These were stone water-pots, capable of holding about two or three firkins, or seven or eight gallons. They were to be filled with water. Hence Christ acted on this occasion as he did when he fed the five thousand. He made a few loaves and fishes the material of his productive energy. So now water is the basis of the miracle he works.

(1.) In this, however, the miracle became more obvious. The servants knew the wine was all gone, and that it was truly water which had been poured into these pots.

(2.) Being filled to the brim with water, it would be plain that there was no room for pouring in wine, and thus making a mixture of the two.

(3.) The same servants drew it forth who poured in the water, so that collusion or imposition was impossible. Observe,

III. *The direction to draw it forth.* At Christ's command it was borne unto the governor of the feast. The governor was unacquainted with the process which had been going on. He knew not either how or whence it was, v. 9.

(1.) He attests his surprise at the quality of the wine. He declares it to be, emphatically, " good wine," the best they had partaken of.

(2.) He expresses his astonishment that this should have been furnished last. Here was a reverse of the ordinary rule—that the richest wine was to be first brought forth, and then afterwards the less fine and luscious, v. 10. Notice,

IV. *The results arising from the miracle thus wrought.*

1. *It manifested forth the Saviour's glory.* It was an express evidence of his power and Godhead. It exhibited the glory of his creative energy. The same power that acted on the original chaos, and brought forth light, and beauty, and order, was now put forth on the water, and converted it into delicious wine.

2. *It produced faith in his Divine mission.* Many of " his disciples believed on him,"

v. 11. They beheld in him the prophet like unto Moses, &c. They beheld in him the sent of the Father, the Son of the Most High God. And they exercised unwavering faith in him. Now what are the lessons we learn from this miracle?

(1.) That the presence of Christ can alone sanctify our festive occasions. That is a questionable assembly in which Jesus cannot be invited, and heartily welcomed as a guest. Every marriage feast should especially be graced by his Divine and condescending presence.

(2.) That in all exigencies our applications may be confidently made to the Saviour. He can do all for us, and be all to us.

(3.) That the blessings which come with his gracious seal upon them, are manifestly best and most precious.

(4.) We must be careful not to turn the grace of God into an argument for wantonness or dissipation. For we have no right to conclude that either the guests on this occasion were partially inebriated, or that he produced a strong intoxicating wine, which would have imperilled their principles of sobriety. His wine was "the best," and surely by this is meant "the richest,"—containing most of the flavor of the grape, and not a highly stimulating fluid, equally opposed to the welfare of the body, as to the happiness and safety of the soul.

(5.) In all things let us seek to exercise faith in the Redeemer, and to do all things to his glory.

XXXVI.—MIRACLES PERFORMED IN GALILEE.

"And Jesus went about all Galilee, teaching in their synagogues, and preaching the gospel of the kingdom, and healing all manner of sickness and all manner of disease among the people: and his fame went throughout all Syria; and they brought unto him all sick people that were taken with divers diseases and torments, and those who were possessed with devils, and those who were lunatic, and those that had the palsy; and he healed them.—*Matt.* iv. 23, 24.

THE blessed Jesus went about doing good. Thus he began the work of his ministry. Thus he continued, until he could say, " I have finished the work which thou gavest me to do." It was necessary that he should establish his claim to the Messiahship, by the signs and wondrous works which he should perform. With miraculous performances he therefore began the publication of the great truths of his kingdom. The idea given of Christ in this striking passage, is that of great diligence. He "went about all Galilee." Itinerating through the whole district—not waiting for the multitudes to come to him, he went forth to seek them, that they might become acquainted with the glad tidings of salvation, and become the subjects of his gracious kingdom. Observe, then,

I. *The Saviour's ministry.*

II. *The confirmation of that ministry.*

III. *The results which accompanied it.* Observe,

I. *The Saviour's ministry.*

1. *It was personal.* He preached and taught. Not by his servants and ambassadors only, but in his own person. Hence it has been quaintly remarked, "that God had only one son, and he made a preacher of him." It was distinctly predicted that he should be a teacher, and proclaim the good news. As the great anti-type of Moses, the people were to hearken to him. "Grace," says the Psalmist—speaking predictively—"is poured into thy lips." Psa. xlv. 2, &c.

2. *It was gracious.* He "preached the gospel of the kingdom." The good news of that spiritual kingdom of love and mercy, which he came to set up in the world. A kingdom of mercy and grace to be established on earth, for the salvation of guilty, perishing sinners. The reign of infinite compassion and pity among a rebellious race of transgressors. A kingdom in which the sceptre was one of mercy, and one which every traitor was invited to come and touch, and live. No news ever reached the ear of man so joyous and blessed, as that of the gospel of the kingdom: "The law was given by Moses, but grace and truth came by Jesus Christ."

3. *His ministry was instructive.* "Teaching in their synagogues." In the places erected for Jewish worship. Here he went, and met with the pious companies who repaired thither, and instructed them in the doctrines of the new dispensation. Opened to their understandings the mysteries of the kingdom of heaven.

4. *His ministry was arduous and aggressive.* "He went about all Galilee." It was his one great concern—his meat and his drink. He labored incessantly—diligently. He worked while it was day. He never

faltered—nor wearied—nor turned aside. And he pushed his doctrines even into the synagogues. He knew that Judaism must be superseded, and therefore he urged the great truths of his kingdom, and endeavored to overturn, by his powerful declarations and arguments, all impeding principles and systems. Yet he did this in the spirit of meekness and love.

II. *The confirmation of his ministry.* "Healing all manner of sickness, and all manner of diseases," &c.

1. *He supernaturally removed diseases.* Not by any system of medicine; but by his word—by the power of his omnific voice. He spake sickness and disease away from those who were afflicted. At his bidding, pain and disorders fled—and health and vigor were bestowed. Thus too does he remove the disease of the soul, and imparts spiritual health to all who come to him.

2. *He expelled devils.* Those who were under the direct power of the devil. In whom evil spirits dwelt bodily. These were cast out by his word. Devils trembled and fled before him.

The human heart in its carnal state is under the power of Satan, and none but Christ can expel the strong one from the soul. He does this in every case where he exerts his converting power. All such are turned from darkness to light, and from the power of Satan to God. He came that he might destroy the works of the devil.

3. *He restored the insane.* Those afflicted with lunacy. A kind of insanity which was supposed to be greatly influenced by the changes of the moon. These were restored to soundness of mind, and the enjoyment of perfect reason. All sin is madness. Men only come to themselves when they repent and believe the gospel, and are made the subjects of the Saviour's renewing grace. And,

4. *He recovered those afflicted with paralysis.* The withered limbs had vitality and action conveyed to them. Hence, at his word the lame leaped as the hart, and the paralytic and apoplectic danced for joy. To the wasted paralyzed powers of the soul Christ imparts strength,—and to the feeble and lame he gives ability to run in the way of his commandments. Observe in reference to Christ's ministry,

III. *The results which accompanied it.* "And his fame went throughout all Syria," &c.

1. *The power and grace of Jesus were celebrated.* The people beheld and experienced his miraculous power, and they talked of it —extolled it, and spread it far and wide. This ought to be done by all who have experienced his saving power. Every converted soul should spread abroad his mighty and gracious doings. "Come all ye that fear God, and I will tell you what the Lord hath done for my soul."

2. *Multitudes were brought to Jesus.* This was the result of his gracious fame being spread abroad. And this will be the effect when the people of God are faithful witnesses for Christ. It is the province of the Christian to bring others to Christ. Just as Philip brought Nathaniel, and as the woman of Samaria brought her neighbors to see the man who had told her all that ever she had done.

3. *Much sickness and misery was removed.* For it would appear that all were healed who came unto him. That no case was too desperate for his Divine skill and power. Hence health and joy were spread abroad, and disease and sorrow blotted out. Just so is it when sinners are brought to experience the healing influences of the grace of the gospel. Then the painful maladies of the mind are healed; and then the joys of salvation fill the believing soul. Blessed are the people who know the joyful sound.

Learn from this subject,

1. *The divine dignity and power of the Lord Jesus.* His miraculous works not only evinced his real Messiahship, but also were bright evidences of his power and Godhead.

2. *The gracious and merciful character of the gospel.*

3. *The necessity of constant faithfulness, and diligence in the Christian ministry.*

And,

4. *That the way to obtain spiritual healing and happiness, is by faith in the Lord Jesus Christ.*

————◆————

XXXVII.—THE RESTORING OF THE PARALYTIC.

"And he entered into a ship, and passed over, and came into his own city. And, behold, they brought to him a man sick of the palsy, lying on a bed: and Jesus seeing their faith, said unto the sick of the palsy: Son, be of good cheer; thy sins be forgiven thee," &c.—*Matt.* ix. 1–8.

THE whole of the circumstances connected with this miracle are truly interesting. The history of it is comprehended in a short paragraph, but it is replete with valuable thoughts and instructive ideas. Jesus had just left the coasts of the Gergesenes, who, on account of their sordid love of the swine which had perished, had besought that Christ would depart from them. He then entered into a ship and came into his own city, Capernaum, where at that time he resided. No sooner is his arrival known, than the diseased paralytic is brought to him, and the cure wrought recorded in the text. Observe,

I. *The condition of the sufferer.*
II. *The faith of the people.*
III. *The cure wrought by the Saviour.*
IV. *The prejudice of the scribes.* And,
V. *The homage of the multitude.* Observe,

I. *The condition of the sufferer.* His disease was the palsy, v. 2—a disease which incapacitated him for labor or enjoyment. A disease rarely if ever cured. In his case it seemed inveterate and confirmed. He was evidently unable to work, confined to his bed, &c. His condition was truly pitiable, deplorable—and, humanly speaking, hopeless. A fit picture of a diseased soul. A soul weakened,—enervated by sin. Yielding no service to God,—incapable of moral action. Without true enjoyment. Beyond the power of human energy to restore. Yet this is the true state of all unregenerate men,—morally diseased and ready to perish. How desirable that men should know and feel it, and earnestly desire the healing of the Saviour's gracious power. Notice,

II. *The faith of the people.* Who they were is not stated. Most likely they were the relatives and friends of the afflicted man. Most likely they had heard of the fame of the Saviour. Had informed the sufferer, and hence the determination of all parties, when Christ drew near, to avail themselves of his restoring power. We see their faith evidenced inasmuch as,

1. *They brought him to Jesus.* They had confidence in Christ's power and willingness to heal.

2. *They overcame the difficulties which presented themselves.* Mark (ii. 1) states, that the house where Christ was, was so surrounded with the multitude, that they could not reach the door. They then ascended and reached the roof of the building, and removed the awning which was spread over the centre court of the house, and let the man down into the very presence of Christ. Here their faith worked a holy resolution, and a determinate mode of action exceedingly worthy of imitation.

3. *They exhibited the love and compassion which faith produceth.* Faith works by love, and here was a display of generous compassion for a fellow-sufferer. Here selfish indifference was trampled on, and a generous spirit of tender kindliness produced. True faith in the Lord Jesus is ever followed by compassion for perishing sinners around us.

III. *The cure wrought by the Saviour.* "And Jesus seeing their faith, said unto the sick of the palsy, Son, be of good cheer; thy sins be forgiven thee," v. 2. Now mark, Christ,

1. *Removes the malady of the mind.* He pardons the guilt of the soul. He removes the malady from within. He does this readily, tenderly, distinctly. It is probable that his affliction had been the direct result of transgression. The Saviour therefore reminded him of that, and removes the moral cause of his suffering. It is not unlikely that the man was in a state of remorse and compunction of soul for his iniquities. Therefore Christ takes away the load of guilt from his soul. Afterwards,

2. *He bids him arise.* Now circulation has begun,—strength is felt, and the helpless sufferer is enabled to stand up. He stands up, the monument of Christ's healing power and wondrous grace.

3. *He directs him to bear his bed and return to his own dwelling.* Not only can the man stand, but he is able to roll up the mattress on which he had been borne, and to carry it, and return to his house. Here was an unquestionable cure, and the evidence such as no unbelief or prejudice could gainsay. But notice,

IV. *The prejudice of the scribes.* Certain of the scribes "said within themselves, this man blasphemeth." These were the unuttered thoughts of their hearts. Yet Christ was fully conversant of them. As the Omniscient Lord, he knew their thoughts. The miracle Christ had wrought was an evidence of the divinity of his mission, and this they might have reasonably inferred. But no,—disliking the person of the Saviour, offended with his lowly appearance and his spiritual doctrines, they blindly reason in their hearts that Christ is an evil person, and was a blasphemer against God, in promising forgiveness of sin. How deplorable is the mind and heart under the influence of prejudice. How it perverts the judgment, and vitiates the passions, and corrupts the whole man. It was the great sin, and the cause of the final ruin of the Jewish nation. But mark,

V. *The homage of the multitude.* "But when the multitude saw it they marvelled, they glorified God," &c., v. 8.

1. *They admitted the miracle.* They saw it, and believed its reality.

2. *They were greatly astonished.* Abundant reason had they for marvelling. Who would not have been filled with wonder and amazement?

3. *They adored God and gave him the glory.* They saw no signs that this was the work of the evil one. They believed it to be what it really was, a display of the great power of God. And in their hearts, and with their voices, they celebrated Jehovah's praise.

Learn,

1. *That sin is the great cause of suffering.* All our pains, and diseases, and death itself, are the result of sin.

2. *Jesus Christ is the one efficient Saviour.*

> " He is able,—he is willing,—
> Doubt no more."

3. *It should be our desire to bring men to Christ.* Parents, friends, &c., should all labor to do this. Our faith and prayers may be effective of much good.

4. *God in Christ must be glorified in all things.* Ours is the benefit, but to God in Christ Jesus, all the honor and homage must be paid.

XXXVIII.—CASTING OUT THE DUMB SPIRIT.

" And one of the multitude answered and said, Master, I have brought unto thee my son, who hath a dumb spirit: and wheresoever he taketh him, he teareth him: and he foameth, and gnasheth with his teeth, and pineth away: and I spake to thy disciples that they should cast him out; and they could not," &c.—*Mark* ix. 17–27.

SATAN seems to have possessed amazing power about the period of Christ's advent and mission upon earth. Hence not only did he reign in the hearts of the children of disobedience, but he also afflicted persons with grievous diseases, and held bodily possession of numbers of individuals. Our subject describes a peculiarly distressing case of this kind, and exhibits the power and compassion of Christ in the deliverance effected. Let us,

I. *Contemplate the sufferer.* The sufferer was a youth, and his afflicted state is thus described,

1. *He was unable to speak.* Hence the spirit possessing him is called a dumb spirit. This was a very serious deprivation. But,

2. *He was liable to violent convulsions.* Hence under the paroxysms of suffering, " he foamed at the mouth," " gnashed with his teeth," and furiously tore and mangled his own person.

3. *His flesh and strength were wearing away.* And he " pineth away," v. 18. We can scarcely conceive of a more distressing spectacle of suffering and misery. How almost hopeless was his condition,—for it is added that he had been thus afflicted from a child, v. 21. But observe,

II. *The person of the applicant.* This was the father of the sufferer. He said, " I have brought unto thee my son," &c., v. 17. He was evidently excited by deep natural affection and tender compassion for his afflicted child. This example of parental love and solicitude is worthy of our imitation. You will observe in the conduct of the father,

1. *The mistake he originally committed.* He went to the disciples for relief instead of to the Saviour. " And I spake to thy disciples that they should cast him out, and they could not," v. 18. How common it is to go to inferior sources for relief. How many go to means, and trust in these instead of the Author of all good,—the God of the means. How commonly we repair to the creature, forgetting the Creator.

2. *He then came to Jesus.* His error is now corrected, and he is in the presence of him unto whom all power is committed both in heaven and on earth. He now says, " Master, I have brought him unto thee," &c., v. 17. Happy they who come with all their burden and sorrows to Jesus."

> " Only Jesus—only Jesus—
> Can do helpless sinners good."

3. *He describes the sufferings of his child.* He details the particulars, and also dwells on the imminent peril of the child. For he says, " And ofttimes it hath cast him into the fire, and into the waters to destroy him," v. 22.

4. *He earnestly appeals for relief.* "But if thou canst do any thing, have compassion on us and help us," ver. 22. Here he makes his case his own. He identifies his child's sufferings with himself. He evidently had some doubts of Christ's power to meet this extreme case. "If thou canst." But he casts all his deep and anxious care on the Saviour's compassion. "Have compassion and help us." Notice,

III. *The conduct of the Saviour.* He had already rebuked the disciples for want of faith, v. 19. He had ordered the child to be brought unto him. He had kindly inquired into the particulars of his sufferings, ver. 21. And now having the case fully before him, and having heard the earnest and tender appeal of the father, he rolls it back with all its responsibility on the father's faith. Jesus said, "If thou canst believe, all things are possible to him that believeth," ver. 23. As if he had said,

1. *In me there is an efficiency of power.* But thy faith must elicit its operation—canst thou lay hold of my strength? If so, it can do all thou needest.

2. *In me there is amplitude of efficacy.* Canst thou draw out the virtue and apply it to thy suffering son? There is virtue enough in me to heal the maladies of a wretched world. Extract it by thy faith, and thy son is healed.

3. *In me there is graciousness of disposition.* Canst thou honor my office, and mission, and work? If so, I will have compassion on thee, and restore thy child. I came to seek and to save that which is lost, and if thou canst but believe, all thou seekest and desirest is fully possible. For all that can be done, faith can do it.

IV. *The humble prayerful faith of the father.* He now felt that the whole weight of the responsibility rested on himself. The heavy load oppressed him. His spirit became intensely anxious. He collected all the confidence of his soul. And,

1. *Affirmed his faith.* "Lord, I believe." I can trust this case to thee. I do believe in thy power and efficacy, and in thy readiness to save my son.

2. *He admitted the lingerings of his unbelief.* Hence he adverts to his unbelief. There was a great inward conflict distressing his spirit. He felt the difficulties of the case,—the lingering fears interposed as he was endeavoring to cast all on the Saviour's help.

3. *He earnestly sued for the Saviour's aid.* "Help thou mine unbelief." I would fain believe, explicitly, heartily, fully. I feel my soul rising with confidence. I dread lest my wickedness should entail on my child his terrible affliction. I must therefore cast my soul on thy tender sympathy and pity. "Help thou mine unbelief," v. 24. Notice,

V. *The miracle the Saviour wrought.* He charged the deaf and dumb spirit to come out, v. 25. The spirit struggled to retain possession, and "cried and rent him sore." It appeared as if the child would perish in the conflict. Hence "he was as one dead," v. 26. But Christ overcame, the spirit was expelled, and "Jesus took the child by the hand and lifted him up, and he arose," v. 27. Triumphant Saviour!—Happy child, and delighted parent!—Learn,

1. *The malevolent character of the devil.* It is his work to curse, and to torture, and to destroy.

2. *The gracious saving power of the Redeemer.* He can deliver, and he delights to do so.

3. *The mighty efficacy of faith.* Faith honors Christ, and Christ will honor and meet the cries of believing, persevering supplication.

4. *What a lesson of parental affection and influence.* Learn to bring your children to the exercise of faith in the Saviour.

XXXIX.—MIRACLE OF THE LOAVES AND FISHES.

"And when it was evening, his disciples came to him, saying, This is a desert place, and the time is now past; send the multitude away, that they may go into the villages, and buy themselves victuals: but Jesus said unto them, They need not depart; give ye them to eat," &c.— Matt. xiv. 15–21.

JESUS had been employed during a long day in teaching and preaching the gospel of the kingdom, and in doing good to the bodies and souls of men. A multitude of persons had been listening to his discourses, and witnessing the miracles he had wrought. They were now in a desert place, and the shades of evening were surrounding them. The disciples under a feeling of concern for the people, urged the Saviour to dismiss them, that they might return to the villages, and buy themselves victuals, ver. 15. To this the Redeemer replied, "it is not needful for them to depart. Give ye them to eat," ver. 16. They then explain to him the small store they possessed: "We have here but five loaves, and two fishes," ver. 17. A quantity quite inadequate to the wants of so large a multitude.

These then were the circumstances in which they were placed. Christ, however, had a glorious purpose in view. He knew how easily he could meet all their necessities. Observe then,

I. *The limited provision in the hands of Christ.* He said in reference to the five loaves, &c., "bring them hither to me," ver. 18. In the hands of the disciples, this provision was utterly incapable of feeding thousands of persons. But how altered is the case when as so many, golden grains of seed,—this provision is in the hands of the Saviour. Those hands that formed the universe—that stretched out the heavens as a curtain. That roll all the planets in their orbits. That guide and rule over all. Notice,

II. *The order enforced.* The multitude were directed to sit down. The other evangelists add—that they sat in companies, fifties and hundreds. Thus there would be no confusion. None would be overlooked. The exact number would be ascertained, and also the whole miraculous process would be better observed by all. Order is described by one, as heaven's first law. It is evident that the Lord was the author of order and peace, and not of confusion. Wise arrangement and beautiful order characterize all the works of God. Sin threw disorder into the world. Sin produces disorder in the soul. The reign of grace in the heart, is the reign of order.

III. *The devotion, &c., exhibited.* Order makes way for devotion. We now behold Jesus,

(1.) Looking up to heaven in the spirit of adoration and love to his heavenly Father.

(2.) He blessed the food. He sanctified it for this miraculous occasion, by holy thanksgiving. Acknowledged God as the bountiful giver, &c.

(3.) And brake. Divided the small loaves into lesser portions.

(4.) And then presented it to his disciples that they might bear it to the people. He thus honored his disciples. He thus presented an emblem of their real office and work, to receive from him the bread of eternal life, and to bear it to the perishing multitudes of mankind. Observe,

IV. *The miracle now wrought.* The disciples bore it to the people. But there would not be a morsel each for them. Here then the Divine power was displayed. In Christ's hands as he brake it, in the disciples' hands as it was borne to the people; or in the baskets as it was carried from company to company, the provision increased and multiplied —there was no lack. Every one of the five thousand men, and all the women and children ate, and ate heartily, and there was more than enough for all. For of the five small loaves, and two fishes, there were twelve baskets full of fragments, ver. 20, 21. Observe,

V. *The striking features of this miracle.*

(1.) It was public. In the face of thousands.

(2.) It was beyond the power of collusion. For a sufficiency of provision for so many thousands could not have been smuggled into their midst.

(3.) It was most palpable. They saw it. They did more, they ate. It removed the sensation of hunger—they were filled.

(4.) The number of the partakers rendered imposition impossible. Doubtless there were all sorts of persons. If any doubt could have been thrown upon it, it would have been done. But they all ate, and they were all living actual exemplifications of the truth of the miracle which had been wrought. Observe,

VI. *The lesson of frugality which is administered to us.* According to another evangelist, Jesus said—"Gather up the fragments, that nothing be lost." Those hands that had borne the miraculously increasing provision, were not to be wasteful, and to neglect the broken pieces that fell to the ground. These were all to be collected, and of these twelve baskets full remained. What lessons of prudence and frugality are thus taught to us.

(1.) How many temporal mercies are wasted in extravagance, while hundreds have scarcely food to eat.

(2.) How many waste their means in profligacy, and bring themselves to want.

(3.) How many waste their talents instead of employing them in the service of God.

(4.) How many waste their time and opportunities of getting, and doing good. To each and all of these how important the admonition—"Gather up the fragments," &c.

APPLICATION.

1. In the multitudes hungering for food, we have a striking representation of the famishing state of mankind in reference to spiritual things.

2. In the compassion and power of Christ, we see the hope of the perishing sinner. Unless Christ pity and help, the wandering sinner must perish.

3. In the disciples bearing the food to the people, we see exhibited the nature and design of the Christian ministry. They are to break unto men the bread of life. They are to communicate to souls the blessings of the gospel, which Christ has intrusted to them.

4. In the abundance of the provision, we see the fulness of the gospel.

Here is—

"Enough for each—enough for all,
 Enough for evermore."

5. In the satisfaction of the multitude, we learn that personal partaking of Christ is essential to our happiness.

We must feed upon Christ by faith. "Except a man eat his flesh and drink his blood," &c. Hearing merely will not do. We must by living faith receive the grace of God into the soul. This gives real and permanent satisfaction. There is no lack to those who fear the Lord. "Blessed are they who hunger and thirst after righteousness, for they shall be filled." Have you listened to Christ's words? Have you waited on Christ in his ordinances? Have you believed on him to the salvation of your souls?

———◆———

XL—THE BETHESDA POOL, ETC.

"Now there is at Jerusalem by the sheep *market* a pool, which is called in the Hebrew tongue Bethesda, having five porches. In these lay a great multitude of impotent folk, of blind, halt, withered, waiting for the moving of the water," &c.— *John* v. 2–9.

MUCH dispute has arisen from the different views taken by critics and expositors as to the leading features of this interesting paragraph. Some have alleged that the 4th verse is not sufficiently authenticated, and therefore dispute what is stated concerning an angel going down to the pool at certain periods to agitate the waters, and impart supernatural qualities to them. Hence also many have been at considerable pains to ex-plain their sanatory virtues, as being probably connected with some mineral spring. We think it safest and wisest to take the testimony literally, as given by the evangelist. It is obvious that the sentiments conveyed are these. That the waters of the pool of Bethesda were periodically affected, and then, and then only, possessed healing properties, and that this was believed to be effected by the agency of an angel sent from God for this merciful purpose. For the convenience of the sick, five porches had been erected, where they could collect together and be in readiness for the moving of the waters. That pool, with its healing virtues, might typify the fountain opened for sin and uncleanness: with these points of difference —that the Bethesda pool was local, and for the benefit of the inhabitants of Jerusalem chiefly; the gospel pool is equally near and accessible to the wide world. The Bethesda pool was only efficacious occasionally; the gospel pool is open at all times, and is ever restorative to the sin sick soul. The Bethesda pool only healed the first who plunged into it; the gospel fountain saves all who believingly apply to it. Well, at this pool at the time to which the next refers, we are called to contemplate,

I. *An afflicted fellow-creature.* His affliction is not specified, but it was manifestly,

1. *Great.* The Saviour beheld him as he lay. For he was unable to walk, or even to rise without help. Probably his disease was paralysis or catalepsy.

2. *It was of long standing.* "Thirty and eight years." More than the ordinary length of a human generation. Think of the protracted sufferings he must have borne.

3. *It was accompanied with great human neglect.* He seemed to be friendless. His relatives probably deceased. Himself obviously in the lowest stage of penury, and therefore none caring for his sorrows, and no friendly hand to help him in, at the troubling of the waters. Hence,

4. *He had been the subject of grievous disappointments.* When Jesus interrogated him he said, "Sir, I have no man, when the water is troubled, to put me into the pool: but while I am coming, another steppeth down before me," v. 7. He had often witnessed the supernatural agitation of the pool. He had often seen others step in and lose their maladies, but had been the subject of repeated disappointments and blighted hopes. Observe,

II. *The important question proposed to him by the Saviour.* "Wilt thou be made whole?" This was evidently the man's g.eat desire,—the one object of his soul's anxiety. The Saviour, however, probably intended to excite his attention, and to draw forth his hopes. With the disease of sin, there is often a spirit of indifference about the cure. Many do not even believe they are sick, but deliriously exclaim that they are rich and in need of nothing, while their true state is disease, wretchedness, and misery.

Ministers are sent to teach men their morally diseased state, and to press the Saviour's question, "Wilt thou be made whole?" The willingness of the sinner to be saved, is the first step in his recovery. Observe,

III. *The merciful mandate pronounced.* "Jesus saith unto him, Rise, take up thy bed, and walk," ver. 8. This command at the first view seems unreasonable,—for the man was infirm,—he had no power to walk,—for many years he could not even rise without aid. But when Christ commands, he gives the power to obey. His commands and promises are inseparably allied with each other. He desires the willingness of the heart, and the ability to perform is ever afforded. When Christ speaks, let us hearken. When he commands, however apparently impossible, in faith endeavor to obey, and all things are possible to him that believeth. So it was in this case,—the man's heart joyously leaped at the Saviour's mandate,—and the result was, "And immediately the man was made whole, and took up his bed and walked," ver. 9.

(1.) Here we have an instantaneous cure.
(2.) A cure effected at the Saviour's bidding. He spake and it was done.
(3.) A cure full of mercy and compassion to the sufferer.
(4.) A cure without money and without price.
(5.) A cure performed-in public.
(6.) A cure indisputable. For, lo, the man stands,—he walks,—he bears the bed or pallet on which he had lain. We leave the cavillings of the envious Jews, who railed at the miracle because it was performed on the Sabbath day. But observe,

IV. *The caution given to the restored man.* Jesus afterwards found him in the temple, and said unto him, "Behold, thou art made whole: sin no more, lest a worse thing come unto thee," v. 14. It is reasonable to infer therefore that his infirmity had been the direct effect of his sin. How many of the diseases of the human system are thus self-procured,—the immediate result of dissipation and vice. Of this the man was reminded, and a holy, circumspect life was enjoined, "Sin no more," &c. How needful this caution to every converted sinner. When we remember the remains of evil within the heart,—the allurements of the world and the temptations of Satan,—all should feel the force of the admonition, and watch and pray that they enter not into temptation. The healed man departed no doubt humbly, gratefully,—and told the Jews that it was Jesus who had made him whole, ver. 15. Let every one who has been healed of the malady of sin, go and do likewise. Go and proclaim to others the wondrous love and power of the Saviour. Let not shame, nor fear, prevent you from confessing and recommending Christ.

XLI.—THE HEALING OF THE NOBLE MAN'S SON.

"So Jesus came again into Cana of Galilee, where he made the water wine. And there was a certain nobleman, whose son was sick at Capernaum. When he heard that Jesus was come out of Judea into Galilee, he went unto him, and besought him that he would come down, and heal his son: for he was at the point of death," &c.—*John* iv. 46–54.

NEITHER rank nor age is exempt from the common calamities of life. Man is an heir of trouble, affliction, and death,—and in these the distinctions of society make no difference. The poor often suppose that theirs is the only condition of sorrow, but it only requires a little examination to discover that men of every grade are born to trouble even as the sparks fly upward. We see these sentiments borne out in the narrative selected for our present meditation. Among the various applicants to Jesus for relief, is the distinguished person before us. In general his followers were the poor and unfortunate,—but here we have a person of rank and affluence among the train of his attendants. Observe,

I. *The person of the applicant.*
II. *The nature of his suit.*
III. *The triumphs of his faith.*
I. *The person of the applicant.*
1. *His rank.* A certain nobleman. Supposed to be connected by birth with Herod

Antipas. His residence seems to have been Capernaum.

2. *His affliction.* Was of a relative kind. His son was sick. Nigh unto death. Most probably an only son. How valuable are all the relationships of life. Hence amid the blessings of domestic life, we should rejoice as those who rejoice not. How slender is the tie which binds us to the objects of our warmest affections.

3. *His extreme solicitude.* Doubtless all that wealth could obtain, or human aid impart, had been done. But the disease yields not, but rather gains strength. The child's life is in imminent peril. He knows not what to do, but at length he hastens to Christ. The distance was about twenty miles. Observe,

II. *The nature of his suit.*

1. *The object of his request.* This is the recovery of his child. He sought of Jesus that he would "heal his son, for he was at the point of death," ver. 47. How beautiful is natural affection! Is it not a beam reflected from the goodness of the Parent of all living?

2. *He seeks that Christ would come down and heal him.* He is anxious that the far-famed physician should visit the dying patient. While the scribes and Pharisees scorned the Redeemer, and treated him with rude disdain, this nobleman would count himself happy in being favored with his gracious presence.

3. *He urges his plea most fervently.* "And besought him," &c. A sense of misery and peril always makes us in earnest. His deepest and tenderest emotions were concerned, and therefore his desires were presented with intensity and ardor. Such should be all our petitions to the Lord. Not that he requires them to induce him to hear and bless us. But because his richest blessings would not be prized, unless eagerly sought for. The fervor of prayer is necessary for us, and not for God. Hence it is the fervent inwrought prayer of the righteous which availeth much. Observe,

III. *The triumphs of his faith.* His faith evidently actuated him,

1. *In undertaking the journey.* He had heard of Christ, perhaps seen those on whom his miraculous power had been exerted. He despairs of human help, but yet believes that the Messiah could restore his child. Without some degree of faith, the journey would not have been undertaken. We see his faith,

2. *In the prayer he addressed to Christ.* He besought him that he would come down and heal his son. Here is no doubt expressed. He neither stumbles at his want of power or willingness. He does honor to both. He disputes neither. He seems to take it for granted that he could do it, and he addresses him as if he believed,

"His love was as great as his power,
And neither knew measure nor end."

3. *In the entreaty he further urged.* Jesus said, "Except ye see signs and wonders, ye will not believe," probably intimating that the Jews were more anxious to behold his wondrous doings, than to hear his doctrine, and receive the truth of his kingdom. Perhaps also intimating that the nobleman was vastly more concerned to have the miracle of healing wrought, than to attend to the great themes and mysteries of the kingdom of heaven. But thus indirectly repulsed, his faith reiterates his plea,—"Sir, come down, ere my child die." There is little hope if thy power is not at once exerted.

"Do not turn away thy face,
Mine's an urgent pressing case."

We see the power of his faith,

4. *In the gracious answer returned.* "Jesus saith unto him, Go thy way: thy son liveth." And it is further added, that the nobleman "believed the word that Jesus had spoken, and he went his way," ver. 50. He is satisfied with the reply. He now perceives the great physician can heal at a distance as well as near. He feels assured that his child is spared, therefore with triumphing faith and joy he repairs back to his home. Before he arrives at his dwelling, his servants meet him with the joyful tidings, "Thy son liveth." And it is discovered that the fever left him, at the very hour that Jesus had spoken the gracious healing word.

Learn,

1. *The divine power of the Son of God.* Well may we exclaim, "A wonderful method of healing he hath." He has power over all sicknesses, and distance affects not his ability to heal. He can do it by the going forth of his will, by the pronouncing of his word. He can do this in reference to all the moral maladies of the soul.

2. *The necessity, and the importance, of living, vigorous faith.* Faith brings us to Christ. Faith gives tone and power to our pleadings. Faith lays hold of Christ's

strength. Extracts his saving virtue. Faith overcomes all obstacles, levels mountains, exalts valleys,

> "Laughs at impossibilities,
> And cries, It shall be done."

3. *The interest we should take in the well-being of our children.* How we should feel for them. Desire their moral restoration to the image of God. Plead with the Lord for them. Persevere in the midst of discouragement, and cease not till Christ saith, "Thy son liveth."

XLII.—THE LEPER CLEANSED.

"And when he was come down from the mountain, great multitudes followed him: and, behold, there came a leper and worshipped him, saying, Lord, if thou wilt, thou canst make me clean."—*Matt.* viii. 1–4.

JESUS had just finished his inimitable sermon on the Mount. On his descent, great multitudes followed him. Many of these probably had heard the wonderful words which had flowed from his lips. Among the throng who surrounded the Saviour, we behold one who was a striking spectacle of affliction and misery. He is a leper, and he approaches Christ with venerable awe—bows before him, and says, "Lord, if thou wilt, thou canst make me clean." To this appeal, Jesus immediately responds, having touched him with his hand, "I will, be thou clean." And the sacred narrator assures us, that immediately his leprosy was cleansed, ver. 3. Observe,

I. *In this leper a striking representation of the sinner.* Leprosy is one of the most fearful maladies to which human nature can be incident. But in all its worst features it only faintly points out the true nature of sin—the moral leprosy of the heart.

1. *Leprosy dwells in the corruption and impurity of the blood.* So sin in the moral defilement of our nature, by the first transgression. Man's nature was originally holy and good—by sin it became contaminated, &c.

2. *Leprosy is fearfully contagious.* So is sin. It creates an atmosphere of disease and death. One sinner destroyeth much good. The spirit—the conversation, and the actions of wicked men are all fraught with contagious evil.

3. *Leprosy is of a spreading nature.* So

is sin—it defileth the whole man. It affects body, soul, and spirit. It leaves no faculty or power unaffected. "From the crown of the head to the sole of the foot." In the natural man there is no soundness, &c.

4. *Leprosy is exceedingly painful and loathsome.* So is sin. Its fruit is shame, and sorrow, and wretchedness. "The way of transgressors is hard." "What fruit had you in those things," &c. Anxiety, distraction, and horror, are the effects of man's naturally diseased state.

5. *The leprosy is incurable by human agency.* God, under the law, prescribed the remedies for this fearful malady. But it is evident that the restoration can only be effected by the finger of God. Such also is the case with respect to sin. God alone can pardon, and renew, and sanctify the heart.

> "In vain we seek for peace with God,
> By methods of our own;
> Jesus! there's nothing but thy blood,
> Can bring us near thy throne."

6. *The leper was excluded from the society of the healthy and pure.* Sin excludes from communion with God, and his people. It cast angels out of heaven—our first parents out of paradise. "For what fellowship hath light with darkness," &c.

7. *Uncured, it terminates in death.* This is James' description of sin—"Sin when it is finished, bringeth forth death." This was the malady of the wretched man who applied to Jesus on this occasion; and sin is the moral disease of human nature. Notice,

II. *That Christ is able to cure both the leprosy of the body, and the moral defilement of the soul.*

(1.) He possesses all power, both in heaven and on earth.

(2.) He did cure both frequently, in the day of his flesh.

(3.) He came into our world especially to do this.

(4.) He does this by his all-gracious word. He speaks, and it is effected. He sent his word and healed them.

(5.) His precious blood is the fountain for sin and uncleanness. "It cleanseth from all sin." "He is able to save to the uttermost, all that come unto God by him." No case too deep-seated and inveterate—none too protracted and universal for his skill and efficacy.

III. *That application to Christ is necessary, to secure the removal of our maladies.*

Hence this leper came to Christ—worshipped him—addressed him in earnest supplication, and exercised faith in his ability to restore him. Here is beautifully portrayed the acceptable manner of the sinner's access to Jesus.

1. *He came to Christ.* To this, Christ invites the weary and afflicted sinner. "Come unto me," &c., Matt. xi. 28. He is revealed in the gospel, that we may come to him. He urgeth our return to him, "Come now, and let us reason together," &c.

2. *He worshipped Christ.* Gave him reverent homage. Called him Lord, &c., ver. 2. Such are the feelings we must cherish in drawing near to the Saviour. His Divine nature, and supreme glory and dominion, entitle him to our profoundest reverence, and most sacred veneration and fear. Besides, we are sinners. Creatures of the dust. Unclean, &c.

3. *He addressed him in earnest supplication.* He felt his misery, and earnestly desired relief. When this feeling is experienced, the soul will long for help, and the prayer will be both contrite, and fervent, and sincere. It is our great privilege to tell our sorrows—confess our sins, and seek the gracious help of Jesus.

4. *He exercised faith in his ability to heal him.* "If thou wilt, thou canst make me clean," ver. 2. Our faith must rest on Christ's all-sufficient power. That he has power on earth to forgive sins. We can do more,—we can rest on his own assurance, that he is as *willing* as he is able. That he wants to save—desires to save, and will in no case cast out the applicant who comes in faith, and seeks his mercy.

IV. *That believing application will assuredly be effectual.* Hence in this case, the Saviour touched the poor leper, and pronounced him clean. And at once the leprosy was cleansed, v. 3. This is the unvarying experience of every penitent believer that ever came to Christ. Faith in Christ, in every instance, secures the desired help, and obtains the longed-for salvation. Not one ever came and believed in vain. The word, the oath, and hence also the glory of God are concerned in the saving of the humble, trusting soul, that pleads for mercy. Jesus directed the recovered leper to "go to the priest, and offer the gift that Moses commanded for a testimony unto them." By this the priest would see the miracle which had been performed. By this his cure would be officially ratified. In this way he was gratefully to honor God. Let the restored sinner go and tell the congregation the great things the Lord hath done for his soul. Unite himself in fellowship with God's people; and cherish a grateful sense of the Lord's goodness and mercy to his soul. Forget it not, that Christ alone cleanses from the defilement of sin; and that faith is essential to the enjoyment of his saving favor.

XLIII.—THE RESTORED DEMONIACS.

"And when he was come to the other side, into the country of the Gergesenes, there met him two possessed with devils, coming out of the tombs, exceeding fierce, so that no man might pass by that way: and behold, they cried out, saying, What have we to do with thee, Jesus, thou Son of God? art thou come hither to torment us before the time?" &c.—*Matt.* viii. 28-34.

It is truly affecting to contemplate the ravages made by sin in our world. What a troop of diseases affect the body! What a host of maladies and griefs distract the mind! The world is truly a valley of tears—a region of sorrow—a howling wilderness. Everywhere is presented to us the effects of moral evil. Everywhere confusion, sorrow, and wretchedness prevail. During the days of Christ's sojourning upon earth, we often meet with a concentration of evils, afflicting the same individual. This is particularly true of those who were possessed of devils. Read the history of anguish and suffering, in the case of the child possessed with a dumb devil. This is also strikingly verified in the cases introduced to us in the text. Christ had just been hushing the raging tempest on the sea of Tiberias, into a calm; but no sooner does he land, than he meets with two unhappy men, who were fearfully possessed with devils. Their condition appeared miserable in the extreme; but happy for them, they excited the compassion of the Saviour, and became the joyous subjects of his restoring power.

I. *Observe the description given of their miserable condition.*

1. *They were under the direct control of evil spirits.* "Possessed with devils." Entirely subject to the power of evil agency. And not as some others, under the control of one, but of many "devils." It would appear that one of these men is the same de-

scribed by the other evangelists, who was possessed by a legion. Mark v. 9.

All unconverted men are influenced and controlled by the spirit of Satan. He dwelleth in the carnal heart, and rules in the children of disobedience. Often too they are influenced by many evil influences,—as pride, worldliness, sensuality, unbelief, &c., &c. What a debased, wretched condition this is.

2. *They were under the influence of violent and terrific phrensy.* Madness fired their souls. So it is written,—they were exceedingly fierce. Not under the rule of reason, but impelled by violent passion. Not regulated by a good understanding, and sound judgment, but by the excited impulses of a disordered nature. Such is the true state of wicked men. In them reason is dethroned, and passion impels them in their varied courses of infatuated transgression.

3. *They were dangerous to others.* "So that no man might pass by that way," ver. 28. How true of those who give themselves to work iniquity. How they imperil the best interests of their friends, and kindred, and shopmates, and companions. How they pollute and injure society. What acts of wrong and violence men perpetrate on their fellow-men. How especially true of the assassin, the duellist—the ambitious warrior, and the murderer. Observe,

4. *They had their abode among the dead.* Hence these demoniacs dwelt among the tombs, ver. 28. Every sinner is dead while he liveth. He moves and acts in the region of death, and his paths are the broad downward way of death and destruction. The other evangelists add, that no man could tame them. That however bound, they burst their bonds asunder. Men have attempted to renew human nature by legislative enactments—by education—by the influence of art, and science, and literature; but all necessarily fail to subdue the power of inward evil, or to cast Satan from the throne of the human heart. Observe,

II. *The homage the evil spirits paid to Christ.* Hence it is recorded that Christ met these unhappy men, and it is worthy of note, that the spirits which held them in this galling bondage,

1. *Recognized the Redeemer.* Hence they gave him his true title, "Jesus, thou Son of the Most High God," ver. 29. How true the declaration of the apostle, "The devils also believe and tremble." They saw in Christ the long-promised Saviour, the Son of God, who should destroy the works of the devil.

2. *They deprecated his interference.* Hence they cried, "What have we to do with thee?" This truly indicated their rebellious nature. We have thrown off thy authority. We glory in our disobedience. We delight in iniquity. Besides, it might include the idea, that they had no place in his merciful mediation. No interest in his work of atonement and reconciliation. Not encircled in the provisions of salvation.

3. *They dreaded his displeasure.* "Art thou come hither to torment us before the time?" Here is a recognition of Christ's authority,—his judicial power, &c. Here is a recognition of the law of retribution. Here is a deep-seated alarm as to a certain period of future punishment. They admit a time of torment, but aver that the period has not yet arrived.

4. *They seek for admission into the herd of swine.* They saw and felt that they could not retain their present dwelling in the miserable demoniacs, so they seek to possess the swine feeding at a distance. Probably they knew that by the destruction of these, the people would become incensed against the Saviour. Jesus, however, gives consent. He suffered them, and they escape from the men, and enter the swine. The sequel is well known. The swine under the fierce influence of these devils, ran violently down a steep place into the sea, and perished in the waters, ver. 32. Observe,

III. *The conduct of the Gadarenes.* On the destruction of the swine, the swineherds fled into the city, and reported all that had taken place, ver. 33. They related how that the miserable men were restored; but that the fierce spirits had entered the swine, and effected their utter destruction. On this "the whole city came and met Jesus." Surely to behold him—to admire—to adore —to praise him! No; but to beseech him that he would depart out of their coasts, ver. 34. Observe,

1. *They preferred their swine to the happiness of their fellow-creatures.* Instead of rejoicing in the deliverance of their fellow-men from satanic power and misery, they grieve over the loss of their filthy swine.

2. *They preferred their swine to the presence and blessings of Christ.* Jesus the healer of human diseases—the world's philanthropist—man's Saviour, was among them; but their sordid minds prefer the

swine, even to the Lord of life and glory. What a true picture of the infatuated influences of sin! How appropriate to men who prefer their iniquities to Christ. The wrathful man his revenge. The arrogant man his pride. The drunken man his cups. The sordid man his wealth. The sensual man his haunts. And each man his selfish ends, and his evil desires. Christ took them at their word, and he entered into a ship, and passed over, and came into his own city, chap. ix. i.

The restored demoniacs are seen clothed, and in their right mind, sitting at the feet of Jesus. They seek to go with Christ, to be near their deliverer; but are sent to show their friends what great things God had done for them. Learn,

1. *The fearful tendency of sin.* To enfetter, to infatuate, and to destroy.

2. *The gracious power of Jesus.* To rescue, and to save.

XLIV.—THE TWO BLIND MEN.

"And as they departed from Jericho, a great multitude followed him. And behold, two blind men sitting by the wayside, when they heard that Jesus passed by, cried out, saying, Have mercy on us, O Lord, *thou* Son of David," &c.— *Matt.* xx. 29–34.

WHEREVER Jesus went, he bare with him both the ability and desire to do good to the children of sorrow and affliction. Like the good shepherd, he was ever seeking the wandering sheep. He was emphatically the minister of the poor and the friend of the wretched. Wherever distress and anguish were presented to his eye or assailed his ear, his generous bosom heaved with goodness, and his sacred hands distributed abroad the blessings of his grace. And it made no difference what was the character of the malady to be removed, or the blessing to be imparted. Fevers, dropsies, palsies, demoniacal possessions, were all alike to him. By his energetic voice, afflictions and diseases of every kind were exiled, and blessings of every variety were bestowed. Our present subject relates to the miracle wrought on behalf of two blind men who sat by the wayside near unto Jericho, begging. Jesus having to pass that way, the beggars lifted up their voice and entreated his mercy. To their supplications he lent a ready ear, and in the fulness of his compassion he granted them the desire of their hearts. Observe,

I. *The condition of these men.*

II. *Their application to Christ.* And,

III. *The cure which he wrought on them.* Observe,

I. *The condition of these men.* Two words fully express their state.

1. *They were blind.* Deprived of the unspeakably precious blessing of sight. A calamity which none can duly understand but those who are the unhappy subjects of it. Many of the joys and pleasures of life are received through the medium of the eyes. The works of God are an unknown blank to the blind. The face of nature and the countenances of friends impart no thrill of gladness to the blind. The luxury of books are not within the province of the blind. Ah, sad deprivation—mournful state! Yet spiritual blindness is the greater calamity of the two. And this is the condition of all unregenerated persons. One of the characteristics of the sinner is, that he is "blind." That he is a child of the night and of darkness. He beholds nothing glorious in the Divine character, works, or word. He sees no beauty in the kingdom of grace. Ignorant of himself, of the Saviour, and of the way of peace. These men were not only blind, but—

2. *Indigent.* Poverty is often the lot of the blind. Hence, these two men depended for their subsistence on the precarious alms of the people who passed by the place where they sat begging. Spiritual poverty is the condition of all who have not obtained the pearl of great price. They may fancy themselves rich and increased in goods, and that they stand in need of nothing; but the truth is, they are poor, and wretched, and naked. In fact, their misery is such that they are ready to perish. Like the famishing prodigal, who exclaimed, "I perish with hunger." Notice,

II. *Their application to Christ.* Here several things deserve particular notice.

1. *The Saviour's opportune visit.* He passed by where they sat, or they might have lived and died in their blindness. They sought not Christ, but he came near to them. Just so in reference to Christ and the gospel. Jesus comes into our world to save sinners. He seeks the perishing sinner. We are found of Christ, and not Christ of us. There was,

2. *The announcement of his approach.* "They heard that Jesus passed by." Doubtless of Christ and his fame they had often

heard before. But now he was near to them, and this was the crisis of hope to those afflicted men. The gospel proclaims to sinners that Christ the Saviour is near to them. In his humanity he is their brother, and in his divinity he is not far from any who seek his grace and desire salvation. See Rom. x. 8–15.

3. *The petition they presented.*

(1.) It was a plea for mercy. They did not claim the Saviour's gracious interference.

(2.) It was a plea for themselves. The removal of their own misery.

(3.) It was a plea of faith. They honored Christ as the Messiah, the Son of God.

(4.) It was most earnest and importunate. In all these features the prayers of the penitent sinner should resemble those of the blind men. Notice,

4. *The difficulties they met with.* "The multitude rebuked them, because they should hold their peace." How inconsiderate and cruel! How unfeeling and base! They ought rather to have felt and sympathized with them, and then joined in their prayer. Sin has transformed man's heart into coldness and stone. It has frozen up the best emotions of the soul. Sinners seeking the Saviour will often meet with similar difficulties. The world will cry to them to hold their peace. Cold and formal professors will do the same, and often friends and kindred, who see no beauty in piety, nor necessity for spiritual anxiety, will do their utmost to hinder them in their fervent efforts to obtain the mercy of Christ. But they cried the more. They reiterated their earnest plea, and did not present it in vain. For observe,

III. *The cure which Christ wrought on them.*

1. *Their cry arrested the Redeemer on the way.* "And Jesus stood still." He could not pass on. The prayer of the wretched held him to the spot. He stood to contemplate their misery. He stood to listen to their cry. He stood to pity their state.

2. *He kindly inquired as to their desire.* "What will ye that I shall do unto you?" ver. 32. They reply, "That our eyes may be opened," v. 33. O yes, this was their one misery, and the removal of this, their one desire. Hope would now begin to dawn upon them. Already was the day breaking.

3. *He compassionately granted their re-*quest. "He touched their eyes." And instantly light breaks in upon them. And now, behold, they see. Marvellous touch— most wondrous act! It is added that "they followed Christ," ver. 34. Doubtless out of love and gratitude. To extol him and celebrate his praise. We would fain conclude that the eyes of their understanding were also opened, and that they became his disciples indeed and of a truth. All sinners sensible of their blindness and misery may thus hopefully apply to the Saviour. "Whosoever calleth upon the name of the Lord shall be saved." Have you felt the evil of your natural state? Have you earnestly sought the Redeemer? Have you, in the midst of affliction, cried the more? Have you obtained your suit? Mark, none but Christ can open the eyes of the mind, or convey peace and salvation to the soul.

XLV.—THE DUMB SPIRIT CAST OUT.

"As they went out, behold, they brought to him a dumb man possessed with a devil. And when the devil was cast out, the dumb spake: and the multitudes marvelled, saying, It was never so seen in Israel."—*Matt.* ix. 32, 33.

IT would appear that the person on whom this miracle was wrought was not deaf, and therefore dumb by nature from his birth, but one whose speech was prevented by an evil spirit dwelling in him. In some of the cases of persons possessed with devils, they were excited to violent ravings, and became dangerous to those around them. In other cases they appeared to have been deprived of the use of their limbs; while in others, as in this case, the organs of hearing or speaking only were affected. It is obvious that this must have been a great calamity, inflicting extreme wretchedness both on the sufferer and his friends. And humanly speaking, the case was hopeless. For by what earthly instrumentality could the demon be expelled, and his miserable victim be rescued from his grasp? Jesus, however, came expressly to free men from Satan's galling yoke, and to open the prison door to such as were bound. We see this beautifully exemplified in the case of the man before us. Observe his malady—his introduction to Christ—and the deliverance effected. Notice,

I. *His malady.* "He was a dumb man

possessed with a devil," ver. 32. As we consider his dumbness to have arisen from the power of the evil spirit, let us advert,

1. *To the spirit that dwelt in him.* An evil spirit had possession of his mind and body. He was the miserable victim of Satanic agency and power. A striking representation of the human heart subject to the wicked control of Satan. And let it be remembered that all men are either under the dominion of God or of the devil. Every heart is the throne of the Holy Spirit or of the Spirit of Evil. And in all unrenewed, unbelieving souls, Satan has his seat. He dwells in them. He bids them go and they go, and come and they come, and do this or that and they do it. His yoke he places on their neck, and his fetters and manacles on their faculties and powers. How debased, ignominious, and wretched is such a state!

2. *He was dumb.* The power of speech is one of the distinguishing features of human beings. Doubtless the inferior creatures can convey their desires, &c., to their own species. But it is reserved for man to possess the high endowment of speech, to enjoy the blessing of conversation. Thus reason sheds abroad her light. Thus mind has intercourse with mind. And thus heart enjoys delightful communion with kindred hearts. Happy when the power of speech is under the rule of enlightened reason, and happier still when the conversation is always seasoned with grace. But there is a spiritual dumbness, as well as that which applies to the organs of natural speech. This is true,

(1.) Of those who disregard the Divine works and word. Who never speak of God. Of his character, works, or ways. They are silent concerning the Divine attributes and glory.

(2.) *Of those who never pray.* Who never speak to God in supplication and intercession. Strangers to the language of devotion.

(3.) Of those who never speak for God. By extolling his goodness or celebrating his mercy. How many, in all these respects, are possessed with a dumb devil. But observe,

II. *He was introduced to Christ.* "They brought him" to Jesus. Here was consideration, kindness, true compassion. Doubtless they commiserated the man, and had faith in the Saviour. The great work devolving on the members of the church of Christ is to bring men to him. It is theirs to feel for the wretched and the perishing, who are without God and without hope in the world. They can well feel and compassionate their state when they remember their own former miserable condition. They know the power and preciousness of Christ. His ability and willingness to save. On them, therefore, it devolves to employ their talents and influence in bringing souls to the Redeemer.

(1.) Parents should labor to do this with their children.

(2.) Teachers with their juvenile charge.

(3.) Christians with all their friends. This is the truest benevolence, the most noble and Godlike charity to others. This man was brought to Christ, into the immediate presence of him before whom devils feared and trembled. Observe,

III. *The deliverance effected.* The details of the cure are not presented. The processes not given. But it is clear that the devil was cast out, &c.

1. *The man was dispossessed.* The malevolent intruding spirit was cast out. Probably by the mere bidding of the Saviour. Hence the poet rapturously sings,

> "Jesus the name high over all,
> In hell, or earth, or sky:
> Angels and men before it fall,
> And devils fear and fly."

Thus Christ also by his converting grace delivers men from the power of the devil and from the dominion of sin.

2. *His mouth was opened.* He now "spoke." The cause was removed, and the evil effect ceased. Would he not speak gratefully and joyously! Would he not exult and glorify Christ! Would he not

> "Tell to those around,
> What a dear Saviour he had found."

Grace opens the mouth in thanksgiving and praise. "He hath put," says the psalmist, "a new song into my mouth," "even praise to our God." Psalm xl. 3. "I will praise thee: for though thou wast angry with me, thine anger is turned away: and behold thou comfortedst me." Isa. xii. 1.

Learn,

1. *The malevolence and power of the prince of darkness.*

2. *The misery of human nature through the entrance of sin into our world.*

3. *The grace and efficacy of the Lord Jesus.*

4. *Our duty to those who are far from Christ, and ignorant of his favor and love.*

5. *The glory which redounds to Christ from his wondrous doings.* Ver. 33.

XLVI.—THE EXPULSION OF THE UNCLEAN SPIRIT.

"And in the synagogue there was a man, who had a spirit of an unclean devil, and cried out with a loud voice, saying, Let *us* alone; what have we to do with thee, *thou* Jesus of Nazareth? art thou come to destroy us? I know thee who thou art: the Holy One of God," &c.—*Luke* iv. 33–37.

On a variety of occasions the Redeemer manifested his divine power over evil spirits who possessed the bodies and souls of men. On several of these occasions the Saviour conversed with the evil spirits he expelled, which completely overthrows the hypothesis that the persons were merely afflicted with diseases which deranged the mind, and that the representations of their having evil spirits were only given in accordance with the superstitions of the age. It seems, too, that the spirits invariably recognized the person of Christ, and confessed his divinity and power. On this occasion Jesus met the unhappy man in the synagogue, and we are directed,

I. *To the confession the unclean spirit made concerning the Redeemer.* He spake and said, "I know thee who thou art, the Holy One of God," ver. 34. Here Christ's righteousness and purity are admitted. So far from treating him as an impostor, or being in league with Beelzebub, they,

1. Declare "*he is the Holy One of God.*"

(1.) "God's Son—God's servant," ver. 34.

(2.) Having God's holy nature and attributes.

(3.) Formed as to his manhood, by the overshadowing of the Holy Ghost.

(4.) Coming into the world to exhibit, in all its complete excellency, God's holy law.

(5.) On the holy mission of redeeming men from sin, and bringing them to the blessedness of personal holiness.

(6.) In the world for the express purpose of setting up a holy kingdom—a kingdom of righteousness, peace, and joy in the Holy Ghost. How numerous the testimonies to Christ's holiness. The testimony of the Father in the voice which spake from heaven. The testimony of Pilate. The testimony of Judas. The testimony of devils—all unite in exhibiting the Saviour as holy, harmless, and undefiled. This confession was,

2. *Bold and public.* "Cried with a loud voice." So that all around might hear the testimony given. And it was most explicit. "I know thee who thou art," verse 34. Observe,

3. *It was deprecatory.* "Let us alone: what have we to do with thee," &c., ver. 34. Mark (ch. i. 24) adds, that the spirit also said, "Art thou come to destroy us?" Here was the language of dread,—of guilty shame. They knew that their time was limited, that their power was circumscribed, and that their hellish rule and dominion was to be overthrown by the Son of God. All this is clearly implied in the deprecatory appeal of the unclean spirit. Observe,

II. *The course the Redeemer adopted.*

1. *He rebuked the unclean spirit.* "Jesus rebuked him, saying, Hold thy peace," ver. 35. He thus exercised his authority over the spirits of the unseen world. He silences his speech though it confessed his Messiahship. Christ seeks not the constrained, terrific acknowledgment of rebellious demons, —but the humble, penitent confession of contrite, believing sinners.

2. *He bade him to come out of the man.* "Come out of him," exclaimed the benevolent Saviour. "Leave thy usurped throne. Thou hast no right to thy dwelling. He is my creature, the object of my care, and the subject of my saving compassion. Thy rule is one of ignorance, disease, wretchedness, and woe. I have come expressly to proclaim liberty to the captives, and the opening of the prison doors to them that are bound." Therefore his mandate of mercy is heard, "Come out of him." Notice,

III. *The results which followed.*

1. *The unclean spirit gives a last struggle to injure his victim.* "And when the devil had thrown him in the midst," &c. Mark adds, "And when the unclean spirit had torn him," ch. i. 26. Full of dire malignity, he essays to do his worst before he leaves his abode. Showing his cruel, insatiable desire to destroy. Luke remarks, in connection with this violent effort of the spirit, "And hurt him not," v. 35. Christ knew the will and power of the demon, so as to overrule and restrain his diabolical designs. He interposed his almighty arm to save the sufferer.

2. *He came out of him.* Expelled by the

high and supreme power of the Son of God. Miraculous, happy deliverance! Glorious emancipation from the unclean, diabolical power of this malignant spirit.

3. *The people gave homage and glory to Christ.* "And they were all amazed and spake among themselves, saying, What a word is this! for with authority and power he commandeth the unclean spirits, and they come out." In this profession, the dominion and power of Christ are distinctly recognized. His word is magnified. And the adoring reverence of the people is given to God's anointed Son.

4. *The fame of Christ was spread abroad.* "And the fame of him went out into every place and country round about." For this miracle was so public, that many witnessed it. It was so palpable, that none could deny it. It was so wonderful that all were astonished. And it was so gracious and merciful, that the benevolent feelings of the multitude were delighted with it. Hence the fame of it was spread abroad in every direction.

APPLICATION.

1. *The unrenewed mind is under the power of the unclean spirit.* Satan in his nature and designs, and works, is emphatically unclean. He is the enemy of purity. He lives in the region of rebellion and impiety. His work is to spread defilement and sin. And observe, he reigns and rules in the hearts of the children of disobedience.

2. *Such who are thus influenced are in circumstances of misery and peril.* It is a wretched, debased condition. It is one of imminent danger. For such are in a state of condemnation, and the wrath of God abideth on them. They are the objects of the Divine disapprobation, and utterly unfit for a heaven of holiness. Reflect on this, you who are under the power and influence of the spirit of evil.

3. *Christ alone has power to save and deliver.* It is his office and especial work. He came expressly to effect this. He has delivered myriads. He delights to save and bless. He rejoices over the spirits who are disenthralled from the satanic yoke.

4. *In the gospel this deliverance is proclaimed unto you.* "God having raised up Jesus, sent him to bless you, turning away every one of you from his iniquities." Acts iii. 26.

"He breaks the power of cancell'd sin,
And sets the prisoner free:
His blood can make the foulest clean;
His blood availed for me."

XLVII.—THE CENTURION'S SERVANT.

"Now, when he had ended all his sayings in the audience of the people, he entered into Capernaum. And a certain centurion's servant, who was dear unto him, was sick, and ready to die," &c.—*Luke* vii. 1–10.

FEW occupations can be more unfavorable to religion than that of a soldier. The whole aspect of war is adverse to the spirit of the gospel, and practice of true religion. War is essentially an evil from beneath, an evil pandering to the worst passions of the human heart. It breathes forth malevolence and revenge: it gloats in human misery and groans. Christianity, like its divine founder, breathes universal good will. It is full of benignity, kindness, and love. It bears in its triumphant course the olive branch of peace, and it rejoices in the happiness of all classes of men. It sings, "Glory to God in the highest, and peace on earth and good will towards men." Yet the army has not been utterly void of pious men. In spite of unfavorable circumstances there have been soldiers, sincere and devoted disciples of Jesus. We have several centurions referred to in the New Testament. And Colonel Gardiner and others, in modern times, have been distinguished for their eminent piety. Our text relates to one of these; one whose strong faith drew forth from Christ the highest encomium. Let us then contemplate,

I. *His character and application to Christ.* It is obvious,

1. *That he was a Gentile.* One who had not always enjoyed the advantages and privileges of the Jewish religion. No doubt of pagan origin, and most likely educated according to the system of pagan idolatry. He was a commander of a hundred men in the Roman army.

2. *He was a Jewish proselyte.* He had been delivered from idolatry and superstition, and had been brought to know, and love, and obey the Jehovah of Israel.

3. *He had been a liberal benefactor of the Jewish religion.* For the elders of the Jews said of him, "He loveth our nation, and he hath built us a synagogue," ver. 5. So that his was not a cold profession, but an ardent

and liberal attachment to the worship of God.

1. *He was a most compassionate master.* His servant is said to have been " dear unto him." No doubt he was a faithful, good servant. Perhaps an old servant. One who ever consulted his master's interests. And had won his confidence, affection, and esteem. How delightful are such instances of reciprocated attachments between servants and masters. But this servant was now sick, grievously afflicted, ready to die. We learn from Matthew, chap. viii. 6, that it was a severe attack of the palsy. The centurion sympathized with his suffering servant. Did not expel him from his home, or leave him to the care of strangers, but commiserating his affliction, he personally labored to obtain for him relief. Beautiful instance of goodness and condescension!

5. *He applied to Jesus on his servant's behalf.* He did so through the Jewish elders.

(1.) " He sent unto him the elders of the Jews." He deemed himself unfit to make the application, and concluded that these officials in the Jewish synagogue would do better.

(2.) He exhibited extraordinary humility. As Jesus was on his way to his house he sent servants unto him, saying, " I am not worthy that thou shouldest enter under my roof," ver. 6. What low thoughts of himself, and what exalted conceptions of the Redeemer! Yet abstractedly considered, how true, and not only true of the centurion, but of every fallen child of man. Yet how rare is this holiness of heart, this humility of spirit.

(3.) He exercised astonishing faith. He believed that dangerous as his servant was, Christ could heal him. He believed he could heal him without coming to him,—without seeing him. He believed that the mandate of Christ was enough. Hence he said, "But say in a word, and my servant shall be healed." Just speak, and it shall be done. Issue thine orders, and the sickness shall depart. He illustrates the working of his faith, by stating, " I am a man of authority, having under me soldiers; and I say unto one, Go, and he goeth," &c., verse 8. Hence he admitted Christ's universal authority and power over the maladies which afflicted mankind, and he believed that the word given was enough. Marvellous faith! especially in one who had been a Gentile

idolater. How it contrasted with the unbelief of the Jews. How true the Divine saying, "The first shall be last, and the last shall be first." In reference to his application to Christ, observe,

II. *The success which attended it.* Notice,

1. *Christ assents to the first requirement.* When the elders besought him to come, " Jesus at once went with them," ver. 6. He did not hesitate nor delay. When the nobleman sought Christ to go and heal his son, he went not, but sent his word, and healed him. When the centurion applies for his servant, he hastens towards his dwelling. Was it because the applicant was a Gentile, or because the sufferer was a servant? He came to save all, but especially the chief of sinners. He came to bless all, but especially the poor and the wretched.

2. *He restored the servant.* It is not said how, whether by an audible command, or by a secret conveyance of his power,—but he did it, and he did it at once and effectually. For it is written, that "they that were sent returned to the house, and found the servant whole that had been sick," ver. 10.

3. *He commended the centurion's faith.* Addressing the people as well as the elders of the Jews, he said, " I have not found so great faith, no, not in Israel," ver. 9. Even the most devout and spiritual of the Jews, favored with the oracles of truth, the descendants of wrestling Jacob and prevailing Israel, had not evinced such entire and implicit faith or confidence in his healing power.

4. *He indicated the salvation of many Gentiles in various parts of the earth, and the exclusion of many highly favored Jews.* Ver. 11, 12.

Learn from the subject,

1. *A lesson of humanity.* Imbibe the kindly spirit of the centurion. Feel for your servants, and seek their temporal and spiritual welfare.

2. *A lesson of faith.* Believe in Christ heartily, fully, implicitly.

XLVIII.—THE RESTORING OF THE BLIND YOUNG MAN.

" And as Jesus passed by, he saw a man who was blind from his birth. And his disciples asked him, saying, Master, who did sin, this man, or his parents, that he was born blind?" &c.— *John* ix. 1-7.

THE case of this blind man is given at very great length by the evangelist, as it was the occasion of much dispute among the Jews. In the account furnished, there are many highly important subjects introduced, each of which would furnish ample matter for a discourse. It may be well for us therefore to attend to some of these, as they are presented before us. Observe,

I. *The state of the sufferer.* He was blind, and had been so from his birth, v. 1.

It is unnecessary to dwell on the calamity of blindness. Its privations and sorrows are manifest to all. This man had been blind from his birth. Hence it was probably the result of some organic defect. He had never beheld the face of nature, or seen the light of the sun. Notice,

II. *The interrogation of the disciples.* And his disciples asked, " Who did sin, this man or his parents, that he was born blind ?" ver. 2. It was the general belief of the Jews, that extraordinary calamities arose invariably from heinous sins. Hence they concluded that those on whom the tower of Siloam fell, were sinners above all men. Hence when they saw the accumulated sorrows and sufferings of Jesus, they deemed him smitten of God and afflicted. In this case they concluded that the parents, or this man, had incurred the displeasure of the Almighty in that he had been born blind. It would seem also from the very reference to the man himself, that they must have believed in the doctrine of the transmigration of souls, or that he could have sinned in his mother's womb. This idea of sin bringing on itself immediate physical suffering is still common—may arise from a superstitious dread which guilt in the mind produces. Notice,

III. *The reply of the Saviour.* He declared that neither the man nor his parents had sinned, especially so as to procure this calamity, ver. 3. But that God had permitted this affliction, that his wondrous works might be made manifest to him. Here is an undoubted reference to the power which he possessed, and which he was about to put forth for his restoration. Now we should learn from this not to judge nor to indulge in evil surmisings respecting those who are destitute or greatly afflicted, or who are the subjects of grievous and distressing calamities. Notice,

IV. *The declaration of Christ concerning his own mission.* "I must work the works of him that sent me while it is day," &c., ver. 3. He now indicates further, that he had been especially sent to do the miraculous and beneficent works of God. That this was his day. The period allotted and appointed for his marvellous doings, and that he must do it now, for night was coming, the night of death, when no man could work. How truly striking and affecting this declaration. If Jesus, who was clothed with miraculous power, thus felt the importance of diligence in his great vocation, how much more should we be constantly impressed with the supreme necessity of prompt and faithful obedience to the claims of God. Observe,

V. *He asserts himself to be the luminary of the world.* "As long as I am in the world, I am the light of the world," ver. 5. He is the great and only sun of the moral system. He the only orb of spiritual day. He the only source of light and blessedness. He creates natural light, and makes the eye to see it and rejoice in it. He makes spiritual light, and causes the soul to enjoy and delight in it. Then observe,

VI. *The miracle he wrought.*

1. *He employed certain means.* Yet how unlikely to benefit the blind man. "He spat on the ground and made clay of the spittle, and anointed the eyes of the blind man with the clay," ver. 6. All this was much more likely to make a seeing man blind, than to give sight to one already blind. But Jesus often used means, and they were generally of an extraordinary character, and, humanly speaking, unlikely to secure the end contemplated. Thus he concealed, in some measure, his overwhelming glory.

2. *He gave certain instructions.* He told the man to go and wash in the pool of Siloam, v. 7. Here was a trial of the blind man's faith and obedience. Thus also the miracle would be wrought before a great number of witnesses. Here also implicit obedience in the use of appointed means would be sanctioned. Notice,

VII. *The happy result.* He went his way as Jesus directed. He washed. And came back, seeing. How obvious that the spirit of Christ's power and mercy went with him. And in the use of Christ's appointed means, he obtained his sight. Herein the glory of Christ was conspicuously displayed. And herein his love and compassion were beautifully set forth. Thus two ancient predictions were accomplished, and the Sa-

viour's profession of the Messiahship fully exemplified. Yet the effects were not such as
we should have anticipated. For we behold,

1. The Jews filled with envy and unbelief, ver. 16–28.

2. His parents were ensnared through the
fear of man, ver. 20–21. But happily,

3. The young man confessed Christ, vindicated his character, and became a believing and honorable disciple, ver. 25–30,
35–38.

———————————◆———————————

XLIX.—THE CURE OF THE DEAF MAN.

"And they bring unto him one that was deaf,
and had an impediment in his speech ; and they
beseech him to put his hand upon him. And
he took him aside from the multitude, and put
his fingers into his ears, and he spit, and touched
his tongue," &c.—*Mark* vii. 32.

NUMEROUS as the Redeemer's miracles
were, yet variety as to the mode of effecting
them, was constantly manifested. To some
he simply spake, and the cure was wrought
—with others, means were employed—and
in the use of these, the miraculous power
was communicated. It was obvious that all
cases and circumstances were alike to Jesus,
and that all power was given unto him, both
in heaven and on earth. We often see, too,
that the benevolent emotions of the people
led them to bring the miserable and the
afflicted to Christ. It was so on the present
occasion. He was now passing through the
midst of the coasts of Decapolis. And they
bring unto him one who was truly an object
of compassion. Observe,

The nature of his affliction. The miracle
performed. And the effects which were
produced.

I. *The nature of his affliction.*

1. *He was deaf.* The sense of hearing is
especially precious. It is one of the main
inlets of knowledge and enjoyment. It is
one of the chief links in social intercourse,
and one of the sweetest bonds of communion
with our fellow-men. The want of this sense
greatly isolates man from his fellow-creatures,
and dries up one of the few streams of happiness which this world affords.

2. *He had an impediment in his speech.*
It was with extreme difficulty he could confer with those around him. Thus his affliction was greatly increased. Yet it was his

mercy that he was not absolutely dumb.
That, though with difficulty, he could have
intercourse with his friends. Notice,

II. *The miracle performed.* Antecedently
to the exertion of the Saviour's miraculous
interference, he was brought to Christ that
he might put his hand upon him, ver. 32.
Then observe,

(1.) Jesus took him aside. Perhaps to
conceal from the multitude the mode of the
miracle, lest they might presumptuously endeavor to imitate him, or it might be, to
avoid ostentation.

(2.) He then put his fingers into his ears,
&c., ver. 33. Obviously to sanctify the use
of means, and to indicate to the afflicted
man, that his Divine power was about to be
directed to the seat of his maladies.

(3.) He acknowledged his Father, and
evinced the deep compassion of his spirit.
And looking up to heaven, he sighed, &c.,
ver. 34. Here we see the pious emotions
of Jesus. The pity of his soul, which produced such commiseration for the afflicted
children of men.

(4.) He pronounced the cure-working
word. "And saith unto him, Ephphatha,
that is, Be opened :" ver. 34. "And straightway his ears were opened, and the string of
his tongue was loosed, and he spake plain,"
ver. 35. Is not this a striking representation of the sinner's state—deaf to the Divine
commandments—whose mouths glorify not
God ; having no communion with the Creator, nor spiritual intercourse with his people?
When such are brought to feel their need,
and to come to Jesus, by his omnific yet
gracious word, he unstops the ears of the
deaf, and he makes the dumb to sing for joy.
Notice,

III. *The effects which were produced.*
Doubtless, in the man, grateful joy. But in
the people,

1. *Wonder and admiration.* Christ charged
them to tell no man,—but their feelings of
astonishment and delight could not be restrained. Hence it is written, " So much
the more a great deal they published it,"
ver. 36.

2. *They extolled and glorified Christ.* For,
astonished, they exclaimed, " He hath done
all things well," v. 37. His works are wondrous, beyond the power of man, and they
are all gracious and benevolent. He curses
not,—he inflicts no woes nor calamities,—
but " maketh the deaf to hear, and the
dumb to speak." Moses, Elijah, and Elisha

wrought miracles of terror and judgment. Jesus, only miracles of love and mercy. "He hath done all things well." How many could have joyously responded to the declaration. How many blind and paralytic, and lame and leprous, had experienced the mighty energy of his arm, and the tender compassions of his soul! And is not this,

(1.) The testimony of all his saints on earth? Do they not all bear witness to the power and grace of the Saviour? Are they not all the trophies of his mercy? The language of each converted soul is, "He hath done all things well."

(2.) This is the testimony of all the redeemed in heaven. All the beatified around the throne extol the wondrous love of Jesus. All their ears were opened to his word, by his power. All their tongues were loosed to sing his praise at his bidding. And through all eternity, with adoring wonder and grateful praise, they will exclaim—"He hath done all things well." We just ask, "What think ye of Christ?"

(1.) Have you ever contemplated his Divine character and glory?

(2.) Have you ever reflected on his mighty works and marvellous doings? How he displayed these during his ministry on earth!

(3.) How grace alone shone in all the miracles he wrought! Did he not do all things well?

(4.) Are you the subjects of his saving favor? Has he removed your spiritual maladies? Enabled you to hear and rejoice in his word,—to bless and glorify his name? Is it not the Christian's duty and delight to spread abroad the fame of the Redeemer? To tell to others that he hath indeed done all things well?

L.—CHRIST'S POWER OVER THE WINDS AND THE SEA.

"And when he was entered into a ship, his disciples followed him. And, behold, there arose a great tempest in the sea, insomuch that the ship was covered with the waves: but he was asleep," &c.—*Matt.* viii. 23–27.

THE way of duty is often the way of trouble and temporal peril. The most devout and ardent affection for Christ, does not exempt from sorrow or tribulation. Hence we often see the most eminent saints passing through floods and storms on their way to the kingdom. Our present subject is intro-

duced by the statement that Christ entered into a ship, and his disciples followed him. It was their duty to follow where he guided —it was surely their safety to be where his presence was afforded. Yet though in the evident path of duty, they were exposed to great apparent danger, from which they were only rescued by the wonder-working arm of the Redeemer. Our attention is directed,

I. *To the fearful tempest.* "And behold, there arose a great tempest in the sea, insomuch that the ship was covered with the waves," ver. 24. Nothing is more awfully sublime than a storm at sea. When the waves roll mountains high. When the winds howl, and when the largest ships are tossed as insignificant fragments on the mighty waters. The psalmist has given a very vivid description of such a scene with its attendant perils: Psa. cvii. 25, 31. On this occasion the vessel was covered with the foaming waves, and destruction seemed at hand. Amidst this scene of grandeur and terror we are directed,

II. *To the slumbering Saviour.* Jesus "was asleep," ver. 24. Wearied and exhausted with the toils of the day, his human nature required the restoring influences of balmy sleep. He had no sin, and no fear. Besides, he had all dominion over heaven, earth, and hell. What a mighty blessing is sleep to the tired and toil-worn frame! Happy those who sleep under the sweet assurance of God's favor, and who can say in the pious language of the psalmist, "I laid me down and slept: I awaked: for the Lord sustained me." Notice,

III. *The anxious and alarmed disciples.* Their danger appeared imminent, and therefore we are not surprised at the manifestation of their fears. Yet there were many circumstances which might have considerably allayed them. They had this especially to cheer them,—that their Lord and Master was with them. Could they imagine that he could perish? And yet he was in the same vessel, and exposed to the same danger. And if he perished not, then their safety was surely guaranteed. But for the moment sense prevailed over faith, and fears overwhelmed them. Ever since sin entered into the world, man has been the victim of fear. Guilt and alarm are wedded to one another. With perfect purity there would be no dread. Had the faith of the disciples been in vigorous exercise, it would have surmounted the highest wave, and have outridden the most terrible storm. Observe,

IV. *Their earnest prayer.* They came to the Saviour and awoke him, "saying, Lord, save us, we perish !" ver. 25. Their prayer indicated great alarm and great anxiety : also, utter self-distrust, and confidence in the power of Christ to deliver them.

(1.) Their alarm was culpable, though natural. Faith would have overcome the timidity of nature.

(2.) Their anxiety was human, though in its intensity unnecessary. To desire to be delivered from danger is in harmony with the law of our being. But under Christ's care and pilotage, we may venture to trust all to him.

(3.) Their utter distrust of themselves was both rational and pious. What could they do amidst the fury of the blast ? How impotent is man, with all his skill and power, and vauntings, when the elements war with him !

(4.) Their confidence in Christ was praiseworthy, and worthy of our imitation. He can deliver,—he will deliver,—he delights to deliver,—he has engaged to deliver. To him we may confidently and hopefully appeal. And on this occasion the Redeemer awoke, and first he chides their unbelieving fears—" Why are ye fearful, O ye of little faith ?" ver. 26. Then, with all the grandeur of his divinity, " He arose," looked upon the angry raging billows. He spake with his omnific voice, rebuking the turbulent elements, and there was a great calm. What a scene for devout, adoring contemplation ! The ease with which the majestic Jesus did this wondrous deed. The instant effects :—immediately, without delay, the elements heard and obeyed their God. And the calm was great, entire ; not only were the winds hushed, and the waves quieted, but the lake became placid and tranquil at once, and the rolling vessel rested in peaceful security and quietness on its placid bosom. Well might they exclaim with marvellous zeal, " What manner of man is this, that even the winds and the sea obey him ?" ver. 27. We have a similar miracle of grace wrought when the Saviour,

1. *Calms the troubled conscience of the anxious sinner.* When the Lord has wrought conviction of sin in the soul. When a sense of guilt raises the billows of the Divine wrath before the eyes of the penitent. When with deep alarm spreading through the soul,

the exclamation is heard,—" Lord, save, or I perish !" Then Jesus, in the majesty of his grace, speaks to the soul and says, Thy sins are forgiven thee, and instantly within the bosom of the believing penitent there is a great calm. When he,

2. *Delivers the believing soul in the day of fear and trouble.* Often the saint of the Lord is tossed on seas of sorrow,—surrounded by tempests of trouble. Job was called to pass through a series of these. So David, and so most of the Lord's people. Times of bitter persecution are such. Times of severe bodily affliction are such. Times of great spiritual conflict and temptation. Then when the soul goes in confidence to the Lord, and exercises faith and hope in his delivering mercy, he rebukes the wind and the waves, and there is a great calm.

3. *There will be the fearful tempest of the Divine wrath at the last day.* With the great scene of the conflagration of the world. When the hills and mountains shall be moved out of their places,—when the sun shall become as sackcloth,—the moon as blood, and the stars appear to fall,—when one fierce flame shall envelop the globe, with all that it contains, then the Christian, relying on Jesus, interested in his death, and leaning on his mighty arm, shall be safe, and be effectually delivered from the destruction in which all the ungodly shall be eternally involved. Learn,

1. The majesty and power of Jesus.

2. The importance of a vigorous faith.

3. The certainty of deliverance to all who trust in his name. Let our prayer be,

"Thou that didst rule the angry hour,
    And tame the tempest's mood,
O send thy Spirit forth in power,
    O'er our dark souls to brood.
Thou that didst bow the billow's pride,
    Thy mandates to fulfil ;—
Speak, speak to passion's raging tide,
    Speak, and say—'Peace ; be still.' "

———

LI.—THE RESTORATION OF THE WITHERED HAND.

" And, behold, there was a man who had his hand withered. And they asked him, saying, Is it lawful to heal on the Sabbath-days ? that they might accuse him. And he said unto them, What man shall there be among you, that shall have one sheep, and if it fall into a pit on the Sabbath-day, will he not lay hold on it, and lift it out ?" &c.—*Matt.* xii. 10–13.

IT is impossible to read the miracles of

Christ without being struck with the vain and hypocritical spirit which the scribes and Pharisees often evinced. When they could not deny the miracles Jesus wrought, they endeavored captiously to wrangle either with the manner or time in which they were wrought. Hence often they are introduced as appealing against the Saviour exerting his almighty arm on the Sabbath-day. Their regard to that, seems to have greatly outweighed their love and compassion to the afflicted and miserable around them. This was the case with the man whose hand was restored on the present occasion. Jesus met their false and hypocritical reasoning by distinctly stating that it was lawful to do well on the Sabbath-day, and illustrates it by the beautiful simile, of delivering a sheep from a pit into which it might have fallen on that day, ver. 11. And if they did not doubt the propriety of this, how much more proper still was it to do good to man, who is of so much more value than a sheep. At present, however, we have to do with the miracle Jesus wrought on the occasion. Observe,

I. *The affliction stated.* It was evidently one of paralysis. The man's hand was withered. It is supposed that the whole arm was affected, and Luke says it was his right hand. Doubtless this would prevent the man from laboring for his daily bread. So that it is probable he was poor and destitute as well as afflicted. These often go together. The lame and the diseased should ever excite our commiseration, and elicit all the help we can afford. When Jesus saw the man, he compassionated his state, and purposed to restore him. Observe then,

II. *The miracle which he wrought.* The Saviour,

1. *Issued a command which it seemed impossible to obey.* "He saith to the man, Stretch forth thine hand," ver. 13. The hand being withered had long since ceased to obey the volitions of the mind, therefore it would appear in vain to give such a direction. But the Saviour's commands ever involve the idea of ability for their performance. Yet here unbelief might have cavilled, only faith would be found ready to obey. But observe,

2. *The man wished to do Christ's bidding, and the power was given.* He did not reason, nor cavil, nor doubt. But when he heard the mandate of the Saviour, his heart rejoiced in it, and he made the effort, and lo, it was stretched out. It is clear that this power was not inherent in him. That he could not have done it, until the Saviour's command had been given. It was the power of God harmonizing with the faith of the man. The ability of the Saviour put forth in the workings of the afflicted man's faith.

3. *The happy result.* "It was restored whole, like as the other," ver. 13. Circulation now was restored,—the living fluid flowed in its wonted channels,—the paralysis was removed, and the hand became whole, —so that in the power of use, and in its appearance, it became like as the other. Observe,

(1.) In this cure we see the gracious disposition of Christ to restore the man. And this the Saviour feels towards all the perishing children of men. He wills not the final ruin of any. He desires the salvation of all men. His love embraces the wide world,— his atoning sacrifice included in its sufficiency and design every creature. In the gospel, Jesus expresses his love, publishes it abroad, and invites all men to partake of it.

(2.) We see the miraculous power of Christ. By his word he healed him. He spake, and it was done. He thus possesses all power to deliver from sin and guilt, and to restore to the image and favor of God. This power extends to all sin and to all sinners. O yes,

"He is able—he is willing—
Doubt no more."

(3.) We see the influence of faith. An apparent impossibility was enjoined. But to faith it was possible. The man had a warrant and he obeyed, and in the willingness to obey, he found the power. Faith has no inherent power,—it derives all its energy from the word it believes,—from the Saviour on whom it relies,—from the power on which it trusts. It is the creature of weakness laying hold on God's strength, and then all things are possible.

(4.) We see an emblem of the converted sinner. Instantly restored, as the instantaneous work of conversion is effected. Perfectly restored as in conversion,—old things pass away, and behold all things become new. Now the man could use his hand and work for his bread, and now the converted soul can labor for the bread that is imperishable, and do the bidding of his God and Saviour. Learn,

(5.) That our inability is not a sufficient excuse for our sin. We are depraved, actually guilty,—true, and more, we cannot change our own hearts, or cleanse our own consciences. But can we hearken to Christ's gospel? Can we be found in the way of his appointed means? Can we come to the fountain opened for sin and uncleanness? Can we endeavor to do Christ's bidding, and believe in his name? If so, his power shall be exerted, and our restoration effected. To devise a remedy we cannot,—but to try Christ's gracious saving plan we are invited, and this being done, our cure is certain. We cannot meritoriously work out our own salvation,—but we can receive it as the free gift of God, through Jesus Christ our Lord. Then let the sinner feel his responsibility, and delay not to come to Christ to be made whole.

> " Remember him who once applied,
>   With trembling for relief—
> 'Lord! I believe,' with tears he cried,
>   'Oh, help mine unbelief!' "

LII.—RECOVERY OF JAIRUS' DAUGHTER.

" While he spake these things unto them, behold, there came a certain ruler, and worshipped him, saying, My daughter is even now dead; but come and lay thy hand upon her, and she shall live. And Jesus arose, and followed him, and *so did* his disciples."—*Matt.* ix. 18.

DEATH is no respecter of persons. He marks as his victims, the rich and the poor, the learned and the illiterate, the young and the old. Our attention is now directed to the case of a young person of twelve years of age, who had been grievously afflicted, until at length, her sufferings terminated in death. Her father was a distinguished man among the Jews, a ruler of the synagogue, whose name was Jairus. This bereavement was the more distressing, as she was his only child. Doubtless, he had resorted to all the means within his power, but they were ineffectual, and at length he comes with intense anxiety, and makes his case known to Jesus. Let us take a survey,

I. *Of the manner of his address to Christ.* And,

II. *The circumstances connected with the miracle Jesus wrought.*

I. *The manner of his address to Christ.* Observe,

1. *He paid him reverential homage.* "Behold there came a certain ruler, and worshipped him," ver. 18. Here was a visible exhibition of his high and sacred regard for the Saviour, and a striking manifestation of his own humility. In all our approaches to Christ, how lowly we should be before him. How reverentially we should bow before him. This is ever essential—ever beautiful, and most interesting as evinced by the ruler on this occasion.

2. *He stated the nature of his grief.* "My daughter is even now dead." He had left her probably in the agonies of dying, and he concluded that by this, the spirit had departed. His was a relative sorrow : and how vulnerable we are in all the relationships of life. How distressing this affliction —the loss of an only child. None left to whom the parental affection could be transferred. Removed, too, just as she was rising into womanhood. Notice,

3. *He expressed extraordinary faith in the Saviour.* "But come and lay thy hand upon her, and she shall live." His faith had brought him to seek the gracious interposition of Christ. And now, though the case was absolutely hopeless—humanly speaking —he avers his belief that Christ could restore her, and that by laying his hand on her. This was a noble manifestation of faith in the power of the Saviour. It admitted Christ to be indeed the Messiah, and Son of the living God. It put the highest honor on his attributes and mission. We do not wonder, therefore, that Christ bestowed high honor on such faith. Notice,

II. *The circumstances connected with the miracle Christ wrought.*

1. *Christ immediately arose and went with him.* Ver. 19. Here was faith acting immediately on the love and power of Christ. He therefore delays not, but at once accompanies the distressed father to his house.

2. *He silences the mourners.* When he came to the ruler's house, and "saw the minstrels and the people making a great noise, he said unto them, Give place," &c., v. 23 and 24. The minstrels were persons employed to play soft and melancholy music, on the decease of persons, and were accompanied in their plaintive strains by others, who gave themselves up to loud and violent expressions of sorrow and lamentation. He demands the cessation of the music and the mourning, and puts them forth from the room where the corpse was.

3. *He declares it to be but a temporary suspension of life.* He said to them, "The maid is not dead, but sleepeth," v. 24. He

did not mean that death had not really taken place—but that her decease should be no more than a temporary sleep. Death is often spoken of as sleep, and sleep is a very striking emblem of it. Those who heard this declaration, "laughed him to scorn," v. 24. They were certain that she was actually dead, and doubtless despised all attempts for her resuscitation.

4. *He raises her by the hand, and behold she lives!* But when the people were put forth, he went in with his three disciples, Peter, James, and John, "and took her by the hand, and the maid arose," v. 25. Mark adds, that Christ, when he took her by the hand, said,—Talitha cumi: that is, "Damsel, I say unto thee, arise!" And thus, by his almighty word, the damsel arose, and Jesus commanded that something should be given her to eat. Mark v. 41–43.

What a display of divine power and glory was this! No wonder that it is recorded, "And the fame thereof went abroad into all that land," v. 26.

Learn,

1. *The mutability of all earthly enjoyments.* Riches, honors, pleasures, friends, are all mutable. How important, then, to avoid creature idolatry. They who have wives, or husbands, or children, should be as though they had none.

2. *The all-sufficiency of Christ.* For every trouble, and in every time of need.

3. *The power of faith.*

"Faith, mighty faith, the promise sees,
    And looks to that alone;
Laughs at impossibilities,
    And cries, It shall be done!"

LIII.—THE RESTORATION OF THE WIDOW'S SON.

"And it came to pass the day after, that he went into a city called Nain; and many of his disciples went with him, and much people. Now when he came nigh to the gate of the city, behold there was a dead man carried out, the only son of his mother, and she was a widow; and much people of the city was with her," &c.—*Luke* vii. 11, 17.

OUR subject introduces us to one of the most affecting scenes the evangelists record. Death is ever solemn, and, to friends and relatives, a distressing event. But some bereavements are much more afflictive than others. The loss of the wife is described as the removal of the desire of our eyes. Hence, how sad and afflicted must Jacob have been, when his beloved Rachel was no more. The loss of an only child is a deep affliction, but even then the parents may condole with each other; and, by mutual sympathy, lessen the grief of both. But our text introduces us to a widow who had lost her only son, and whom she was now following to the house appointed for all living. Happy for that daughter of sorrow, Jesus was passing by—his compassion was excited —his wonder-working arm was employed in giving back to her her only son. Observe in the miracle Jesus wrought on this occasion,

I. *That it was unsolicited.* On other occasions, sometimes the afflicted persons, at other times the friends of the afflicted, came and sought the merciful interposition of Jesus. But on this occasion the funeral train was moving towards the place of sepulchres, ver. 12. The widow was too absorbed in grief to notice any thing which passed by; and though Christ and his disciples drew near, his aid was not sought, his pity not implored.

II. *This miracle was performed in the most public manner.* All Christ's miracles were performed in the presence of competent witnesses. When he raised the ruler's daughter there were three of the disciples present. Often he wrought his miracles when multitudes surrounded him. So on this occasion, the funeral procession was just passing out of one of the public gates of the city. Here was the widowed mother, and also "much people of the city with her," ver. 12. Christ too was attended by his disciples, and much people were also with him, ver. 11. So that in the most public manner possible did Jesus display his almighty power on this occasion.

III. *The manner of its performance was most signal and striking.*

1. *He touched the bier.* He stepped forth towards those who were bearing the corpse, and then stretched forth his wondrous hand, and touched the bier. No doubt some would recognize him, and probably the bearers would be impressed with feelings of reverence and awe. Hence it is added, they "stood still."

2. *He proclaimed the life-giving word.* "And said, Young man, I say unto thee, arise!" ver. 14. And immediately the spirit resumed its former habitation—the heart

began to heave—the blood to circulate—the senses to resume their functions, and at Christ's omnific bidding he "sat up, and began to speak," ver. 15. Here was unquestionable evidence of the reality of the miracle. Here was the dead attesting by a new given being, and by an audible voice, the glory of him who was the resurrection and the life.

IV. *It was a miracle of tenderest compassion.* When Jesus first saw the funeral procession, he beheld the sorrow of the afflicted widow. He saw that the fountains of her soul were broken up. He beheld the tears which suffused her care-worn cheeks. He heard the deep plaints, and the distressing sighs of her burdened spirit. And it may be said of the gentle and affectionate Jesus, that his eye affected his heart. He resolves therefore to interpose his power in giving back to the widow her son from the regions of the dead. Hence, before he exercised his infinite energy, he said,

(1.) Weep not. Let thy tears cease to flow,—for thy adversity and mourning shall be turned into joy and gladness. When he said, Weep not—it implied that the occasion of her grief should be taken away. How significant of Christ's great mission into our world. He came to dry up the tears of a sinful and afflicted world.

" Change, then, O sad one ! grief to exultation,
   Worship and fall before Messiah's knee :
Strong was his arm, the bringer of salvation,
   Strong was the word of God to succor thee."

When he had wrought the miracle,

(2.) He delivered him to his mother, ver. 15. What a gift ! How infinite the power, and how boundless the grace of the donor. No other gift would have met the weeping widow's need, and such a gift as this, none but the anointed Messiah could bestow. What the mother felt, or said, or did, is not revealed. What the young man uttered when he sat up, or what he spake to the Saviour, or to his mother, or to the multitude, is not made known. The miracle, in all its grandeur, has been performed—the widow has received her son brought to life again—and now the curtain falls, and silently closes the august and wondrous scene. But,

V. *The effects on the multitude are declared.*

1. *A spirit of sacred awe pervaded their minds.* "There came a fear on all," ver. 16. They felt they were in the presence of a great and glorious power. That he who could raise the dead must be an extraordinary person. One sent from God—one on whom the Spirit of God eminently rested. The two worlds had been very forcibly connected in the death of the young man, and disconnected in bringing him again to life.

2. *They glorified God.* And they did this by admitting the Messiahship of the Saviour. By confessing that God, according to the sayings of the prophets, had indeed visited the people. Would not the event remind them of the recorded miracles of Moses and Elijah, and would not they see in Christ, him of whom Moses had written, —"A prophet shall the Lord your God raise up unto you of your brethren, like unto me, him shall ye hear ?" Yet we fear that the awe and the confession of Christ's Messiahship were only temporary impressions. We fear that they did not retain the emotions excited, and that they did not adhere to Christ, or follow him as his disciples. Learn,

1. *How brittle and tender are the cords by which the relationships of life are bound together.* And often the young die before the old, the apparently strong and vigorous before the aged and enfeebled. Here was the corpse of the young man, and the aged widow following him to the tomb.

2. *What exalted views we should have of the Lord Jesus.* What majesty and power can be compared to his ? And how evidently do these miracles testify to the divinity of his nature. He called not for the power from on high to do this mighty deed. No; it dwelt inherently in him. He did it not in the name of the Father, but in his own name. He said, "I say unto thee, arise."

3. *How it familiarizes to us the sublime doctrine of the resurrection.* Here we see the power efficient for the mighty work. He who brought this young man back by his word, will, by his almighty fiat, raise again the slumbering millions at the last day.

4. *How it should teach us to cherish tenderness and compassion for the sorrowing.* Let the kind address of Jesus to the widow of Nain, be remembered and imitated. "Weep not." You may not have the power to remove the cause of sorrow as Jesus did, but labor to assuage the griefs of the afflicted and distressed. Labor to sympathize with the suffering, and be it

your earnest desire to convey, on every possible occasion, tender consolation to the bosom heaving with anguish and distress. "Weep with those that weep," and "Bear one another's burdens, and so fulfil the law of Christ." How much misery and suffering might be dried up in our sad and dreary world, if all the disciples of Jesus would tread in the footsteps of the benevolent and merciful Saviour, "who went about doing good."

LIV.—THE DEATH OF LAZARUS, THE FRIEND OF CHRIST.

"These things said he: and after that he saith unto them, Our friend Lazarus sleepeth; but I go, that I may awake him out of sleep."—*John* xi. 11.

FEW families have been more honorably distinguished than the family of Bethany. Two sisters and one brother constituted this godly household: the names of Martha and Mary will be handed down with holy fragrance to the latest posterity. Their brother was also one of the special objects of Christ's affection and esteem, v. 5. Even the most pious families are exposed to sickness, sorrow, and death. Disease invaded this domestic circle. The sickness waxed worse and worse, until death terminated his sufferings. Jesus had delayed his visit, though apprised of the condition of Lazarus, ver. 6, 7, &c. There are two main ideas in the text,

I. *The true character of Christ's disciples.* And,

II. *A beautiful, metaphorical representation of death.*

I. *The true character of Christ's disciples.* They are his friends. Christ called Lazarus his friend. "Our friend." Now Christ thus denominates all his people. Abraham was called the friend of God.—John xv. 14, 15. Now in reference to this character, observe,

1. *That they were not always such.* Not such by *birth* nor education. Once afar off. Alienated. Without God. Enemies, &c.

2. *They became such by accepting the reconciliation offered in the gospel.* Gospel reveals the Divine system of reconciliation. Publishes it. Urges it. We beseech you to be reconciled to God. By faith, the sinner is accepted into God's favor and family. That day the friendship commences.

3. *This friendship is connected with great* *immunities and blessings.* He reveals his will to such: xv. 15. He communes with such. He blesses, keeps, saves, &c. His promises and ordinances are all theirs. "All are yours," &c.

4. *This friendship with Christ will be made manifest.* We shall profess Christ. Entertain Christ. In our houses and hearts. Honor Christ. Obey him. Make his interests ours, &c. Prefer Christ above all things, &c. Extol and recommend him, &c.

5. *Friendship with Christ ever includes affection for his people.* Hence Christ said, Not my friend, but *ours.* A good man will love all good men. The spirit of goodness and love pervades the whole Christian Church. Every believer is within one holy spiritual bond of grace, mercy, and peace. This is the great badge of Christianity. "By this," &c.

II. *The text contains a beautiful, metaphorical representation of death.* "Our friend Lazarus sleepeth." This metaphor was used at a very early period in reference to Moses, "Behold, thou shalt sleep with thy fathers," Deut. xxxi. 16. Thus, too, Job. For now, saith he, "Shall I sleep in the dust, and thou shalt seek me in the morning, but I shall not be," vii. 21. So Daniel speaks, that, "Many of them that sleep in the dust of the earth, shall awake." So the apostle speaks of "those who sleep in Jesus, and whom God will bring with him." So Christ in his resurrection is said to be "the first fruits of them that slept." Now observe,

1. *The striking resemblance between sleep and death.* The eyes closed,—ears sealed,—senses suspended. The breathing, and the warmth of the body, only indicate between the one and the other. How truly it is the image of death.

2. *As sleep is a state of quiescence and repose.* The toil of the day is over,—fatigue past,—activity ceased. So all energy and labor, &c., end with respect to this world with the sleep of death.

3. *As sleep is identified with night.* They that sleep, sleep in the night, &c., and "I must work while it is called day," &c. To die, is to lie down in darkness. See Job x. 21, 22.

4. *As sound sleep is incompatible with suffering.* Weariness, pain, anguish, &c., are all forgotten in sleep. What a merciful cessation! So in death, all suffering of the body ends. All care has left its distracting seat, &c.

5. *As sleep relates only to the repose of the body.* Mind still active. What scenes and events are familiar to us in the dreams and visions of the night season. Now so in death,—the body only is still and torpid. The mind lives, and thinks, and feels,—and who can describe the visions and scenes with which it becomes immediately conversant?

6. *As sleep is but a temporary suspension of the physical powers.* In a few hours the man awakes, and sees and hears, and resumes his activity. So death is not the annihilation of the body, much less of the soul. In the morning of the great day, the dead shall hear the voice of the Son of God, and shall live. What a scene when countless millions shall be aroused by the trumpet's blast, and come forth at the bidding of their God and Judge. I just add, that death to the righteous,

(1.) Is a safe sleep. Their dust is precious with God.

(2.) Hopeful sleep. Lie down in hope, and that hope shall be realized to the full.

(3.) It is but a short sleep. Compared with eternity, even that of Abel will be but as a few moments.

(4.) *For this sleep serious preparation is necessary.* We should think, and reflect, prepare. Fear of God. Faith in Christ. Obedience to the Divine will, are the essential prerequisites.

Learn,

1. *The essential characteristics of true friendship with Christ.* Faith in him, love to him, and communion with him.

2. *The connection between a holy life and a peaceful death.* The righteous sleep in Jesus. Death is the repose of their wearied bodies, and they retire to the grave with a blessed hope of a glorious resurrection.

3. *The grave is the prison of the unconverted.* There they are reserved until the judgment of the great day.

LV.—CHRIST WEEPING AT THE GRAVE OF LAZARUS.

"Jesus wept."—*John* xi. 35.

WE have previously contemplated Lazarus as the friend of Jesus, and have considered his decease under the striking emblem of sleep,—we are now to advance in the narrative, and mingle with his weeping sisters and friends. In verse 32, we have Jesus in the presence of the sisters, and listening to the sorrowful plaint of the affectionate Mary, who had said to him, "Lord, if thou hadst been here, my brother had not died," ver. 32. He was then brought into the midst of the weeping circle, which when he beheld, it is said he groaned in the spirit, and was troubled, and said, Where have ye laid him? They said unto him, "Lord, come and see." He then proceeded with them to the grave of Lazarus, and it is written of him,—Jesus wept. A more pathetic sentence never was inscribed—so short—so simple—yet so comprehensive. A more natural inference could not have been drawn. When the Jews saw the tears of Jesus flowing, they said, "Behold how he loved him."

I. *Let us ascertain the character of the tears of Jesus.* And,

II. *What lessons we are taught by them.*

I. *The character of the tears of Jesus.*

1. *He wept as a man.* We often insist on the divinity of the Lord Jesus. Cannot do so too extensively. It is one of the grand pillars of the Christian system. But it is equally important to remember his *manhood,*—made of a woman, &c. Truly a descendant of Adam and of the seed of Abraham. Thus he had all our sympathies. God made the heart soft, that it might feel. Tender, that it might sympathize. And surely there is enough in the death of any ordinary friend to produce distress of spirit and a stream of tears. It is not weakness, but true manliness, to weep on just and fitting occasions.

2. *He wept as a friend.* He loved Lazarus. He was one of his disciples, &c. With him he had repeated fellowship and communion of soul. The highest, the richest, and the sweetest communion. Death had rent in twain the kindly bond. For love is the bond of perfectness—the cement of hearts—the one atmosphere of united souls. We would feel for a dear friend in *ordinary* trouble. In *ordinary* conflicts. In *ordinary* sufferings. But who shall describe the *agonies* of death. The *turbid* stream of Jordan. The *severe* conflict with the last *enemy,* &c. What a friend is Christ! But he was also the friend of the two sisters. Their griefs therefore were his.

3. *He wept as the Saviour ; the Son of God.* He here beheld the power of sin—

the degradation of man. The irreversible decree with respect even to the good and the pious. But, as the Saviour, he knew also of the infatuation of men in neglecting preparation for dying. The awful scenes which often immediately follow eternal death. The deep-rooted prejudice of the Jews who were about to witness the miracle, &c.

II. *What lessons are we taught by it?*

1. *That even the beloved saints of Christ must die.*

2. *That grief at the death of friends is both a right and sacred feeling.* Religion does not prohibit, it only moderates and sanctifies it. "Sorrow not as them without hope," &c. Here is the greatest example, &c.

3. *That the death of saints is not overlooked by Jesus.* He is the Lord of providence. Lord both of the living and the dead. Whether we live, &c. He orders all things. He doth all things well. He has the keys of death and the grave.

4. *That death itself is subject to our blessed Lord.* "I am the resurrection," &c. See him standing. Behold his countenance. Hear his voice. Watch its influence. How marvellous, &c. Think of the resurrection day. Time is expiring. Earth reeling. The heavens wrapped up as a scroll. Sun darkened. Moon turned to blood. Hearken to the angel's blast. See the descending Saviour. Hear the omnific mandate. The earth bursts with life. Myriads—myriads rise at his bidding. It is the first resurrection. Their vile bodies are like to Christ's glorious body, &c. They ascend with him, and are so forever with the Lord, &c.

5. *That Christ's presence can alone sanctify the bereavements of life.* In sickness, let us seek the especial presence and grace of Christ. Under bereavements, let us be solicitous to have the presence and grace of Christ. He alone can give strength to bear sorrow, to restrain its workings, and make it a blessing. He alone can be all to us when friends and kindred die. And he can be to us more than father or mother, or brother or sister—for the true believer, "He is all, and in all." "The chiefest among ten thousand;" yea, all our salvation, and all our desire.

LVI.—RESURRECTION OF LAZARUS.

"Then said the Jews, Behold how he loved him," &c. — *John* xi. 36–46.

WE have already witnessed the mighty power of Christ, in raising the ruler's daughter from the bed of death,—the widow's son from the bier as they were bearing him to the tomb,—and now we are called to behold the resurrection of Lazarus from the tomb, who had been dead four days. Jesus had borne his testimony to Lazarus as his friend, he had met with and comforted the bereaved and sorrowful sisters, and had announced the truth that he should rise again. He had wept with the mourners at his tomb, and now he stands ready to give the mandate which should recall him to life, and bring him back from the regions of the dead. Observe,

I. *The scene presented.* He "cometh to the grave," ver. 38. In that grave lay the earthly remains of Lazarus. How fit the description of one who likens it to a house, the house appointed for all living. How low and humble,—dug out of the earth. How small and circumscribed,—a few feet in its dimensions. How silent and dreary;—no sound of mirth or activity is heard proceeding from it. How appalling to flesh and blood. Nature could not court it;—who would wish to exchange the splendid sitting-room, or even the social hearth for it? Yet how numerous and how densely populated! The earth may be likened to one great graveyard,—one world of sepulchres. It is a house whose foundations rest on the sin of man,—rebellion dug out its basis, and but for sin, earth would have been as sepulchreless as heaven. Here we behold the ravages of transgression, and the degradation and ruin of our nature. Yet thanks be to God, it is not an eternal prison, for Jesus stands at its margin to raise to life its slumbering tenant. Notice,

II. *The directions given.* (1.) He ordered the removal of the stone from the mouth of the tomb. Martha's doubts seemed now to arise, for she concluded by that period that the body had become putrescent. To this Jesus replied, that if she would believe, as he had already said, she should see the glory of God, ver. 40. The miracles of the Redeemer reflected the Divine glory. They were the demonstrations of the power and goodness of Jehovah. And they attested the Divine mission of the Lord Jesus. The stone was now removed—then,

(2.) Jesus held devotional communion with his Father. With eyes lifted up towards heaven, he said, "Father, I thank thee that thou hast heard me: and I knew that thou hearest me always," &c., ver. 41, 42. Here the oneness of the Son with the Father's mind is beautifully implied. As they were one in nature, so of necessity in purpose and design. Jesus ever prayed in accordance with the will of his Father, and his Father ever delighted to hear and grant his requests. He thus honored the Father by confidential acknowledgment, and holy thanksgiving. Observe,

III. *The power he exerted.* Having thus communed with God, " He cried with a loud voice, Lazarus, come forth!" Observe, though he had prayed to the Father, he does not raise Lazarus in the Father's name, but by his own almighty command. His voice pierced the caverns of the dead, extended to the spirit of the deceased, and imparted life to the slumbering remains of Lazarus. Hence, immediately, " He that was dead came forth, bound hand and foot with grave-clothes: and his face was bound about with a napkin. Jesus saith unto them, Loose him, and let him go," ver. 44. No wonder that the multitude should have been panic-struck by the scene, and that Lazarus should have been left to struggle with his funeral apparel. Let it be remembered, that this was a miracle of indisputable reality. Collusion, or deception, was out of the question. It was effected by the word of Christ. It was one of the Redeemer's most extraordinary miracles,—one of his most stupendous doings on earth. And yet while it produced faith in some who beheld it (ver. 45), yet the chief priests and the Pharisees were more established in their prejudice and envy of Christ, and sought more diligently after this how they might take him and put him to death. How clear that no evidence can meet the exigencies of the mind, spell-bound by prejudice and the love of sin. Learn,

1. *The glory and dominion of Christ.* How true that he hath the keys of hades and death. That he can open, and no man can shut. That his power and authority extend to all beings and to all worlds. He is Lord of all.

2. *Here we have an emblematical representation of the resurrection of the soul dead in sin.* He quickens by his power and word, those who are dead in trespasses and sins.

3. *This gives us a miniature view of the final resurrection.* That voice which awoke Lazarus, shall wake the slumbering multitudes at the last day. The dead shall hear the voice of the Son of God and live.

LVII.—THE TEN LEPERS.

"And Jesus answering said, Were there not ten cleansed? but where *are* the nine?"—*Luke* xvii. 17.

THE human body is exposed to a number of fearful maladies. Sin has sown its seeds of decay and sorrow in every part of the system, and these have produced a harvest of painful and distressing maladies. During the Saviour's sojourn on earth, he exercised his almighty and gracious influence in allaying and restoring from the various ills that flesh is heir to. He went about doing good both to the bodies and souls of men. He healed all manner of diseases, and even brought back again the spirits of the departed, and resuscitated the lifeless clay already committed to the grave. Our text refers to one of his stupendous miracles, and is fraught with varied and important instruction. Notice,

I. *The real condition of the persons referred to.*

II. *Their application to Christ.*

III. *The cure wrought.* And,

IV. *The thanks of the Samaritan and the ingratitude of the nine.*

I. *The original condition of the persons referred to.* They were lepers. Leprosy was an exceedingly distressing disease. It was painful and disgusting to the individual, and contagious and loathsome to others. It was often inflicted as a punishment upon heinous transgressors. Such were incurable by the power of man. Were excluded from society, and not allowed to enter the courts of the Lord's house. What a concentrated calamity. What a condition of hopelessness and sorrow. Yet on this occasion there were ten of such persons associating together. Outcasts from society, unapproachable by friends, and the terror of all who might even behold them afar off. In these lepers, we see exhibited the true condition of sinners. Sin is to the soul all, and more than all, that leprosy is to the body. It defiles, embitters, defies human aid to eradicate. It separates from the society of the holy, and terminates in the horrors of a guilty death. Worse than leprosy, it ends not with the grave,—but exposes its victims to the everlasting misery of the unending death.

II. *Their application to Christ.*

1. *Observe the distance they kept from his person.* "Who stood afar off," ver. 12. That they might not disgust him by the offensiveness of their disease, and according to law, not being allowed to come near any clean person.

2. *The earnestness of their prayer.* "Have mercy on us." Their supplication was short, but expressive and fervent. It was the real sense of their degradation and misery, that made them so anxious for the interposition of the Redeemer.

3. *The unanimity of their application.* Alike diseased, miserable, so they agree in their suit, and they are one in their prayer.

4. *The reverence and faith they evinced.* "Jesus," *i. e.*, Saviour—"Master," one having authority. Authority from God. The Jews denied this, and treated his claims with disbelief and scorn. These poor lepers acknowledged his character both as Son and Lord. Without one ray of believing hope, they had not prayed. Doubtless they had heard of the miracles of Christ, and therefore some measure of faith had come by their hearing, and this they embodied in their cry, "Jesus—Master," &c.

III. *The cure wrought.*

1. *It was in connection with obedience to his will.* He did not instantaneously do it. He commanded them to go to the priests, &c. Now here two points were involved. *Faith* exercised in him. They had called him Jesus. Now he tests their belief of his authority. He *said, go*, &c. They had called him Master. He now tests their submission, &c. As cured lepers only were to go to the priests, it is evident that these were to expect on their arrival there, that they would be free from their malady. The end of this arrangement might be threefold.

(1.) For their own sake. That the priests might attest their real restoration, and thus enable them to return to their friends and society.

(2.) For the priests' sake. That they might see the almighty power of Christ, and not remain in unbelief. And to render them excuseless if they rejected his Messiahship.

(3.) For his own sake. That his credentials, as the anointed and sent of God, might be read and known of all.

2. *The cure itself.* As they went, they were healed. The weakness arising from it gave way to strength. The impurity to cleanness. Internally made sound, externally their flesh would be as that of a little child. It was a radical, universal, and complete cure. A cure resulting from the gracious and divine power of the Son of God. Consider,

IV. *The thanks rendered by the Samaritan, and the ingratitude of the nine.* Observe,

1. *The Samaritan.* Belonging to a class despised by the Jews,—of supposed inferior knowledge, and feelings. One of a degraded class. Yet when he found himself healed, he immediately returned to Christ, and gave the most lively evidences of joyful exultation, ver. 15, 16. His thanks were ardent, humble, and sincere. How beautiful was the scene. Notice,

2. *The nine.* These were Jews. But having obtained the boon, they forgot the donor. Selfishness excluded the best feelings from their souls, and there is a manifest severe reproof, &c., included in the 18th verse.

3. *Observe the commendation of the one.* He said to him, "Arise, go thy way," &c. No doubt but this man was spiritually, as well as physically, healed. Christ's address *exalted* him. *Arise*, &c. He that humbleth himself, &c. His *faith* is *eulogized.* "Thy faith," &c. Faith had taken hold of Christ's free and rich virtue, and thus he was made whole. Christ's favor evidently accompanies him. "Go thy way," &c.

Learn,

1. *The willingness and power of Christ to heal.* He is still the same, &c. He desires, he delights to heal, &c.

2. *The application to be made.* It must be personal, earnest, and believing.

3. *The return he demands of those he saves.* Gratitude,—that God might be glorified. He thus has a new right to us, "Ye are not your own," &c.

4. *The commonness of ingratitude.* Children are often so to parents. Servants to masters. The relieved towards their benefactors. How vile and odious. But have not we all been so to God? How we have forgotten his benefits, &c. *Vows* broken. That deliverance. That restoration to health, &c. Where are the nine? That *sinner* said he would become serious if recovered,—but where is he? That nominal Christian devout,—but where is he? That believer more devoted, but where is he? &c. O Lord, enter not into judgment, &c.

LVIII.—THE HEALING OF MALCHUS'S EAR.

"And, behold, one of them who was with Jesus stretched out *his* hand, and drew his sword, and struck a servant of the high priest, and smote off his ear. Then said Jesus unto him, Put up again thy sword into its place: for all they that take the sword shall perish with the sword," &c.— *Matt.* xxvi. 51–54.

THE ministry of Jesus began with the manifestation of his miraculous power. Miracles also were constantly confirming the doctrines he taught. And his labors on earth, and his wondrous works, only ended together. Our subject introduces us to Christ subsequently to the agony which he endured in the garden. He had now by communion with his Father obtained the victory over that fear which so oppressed him. He had intimated to his disciples that the hour of his suffering was at hand, when, lo! Judas with a great multitude, and the chief priests and elders of the people, came with swords and staves to arrest him. The base and faithless kiss having been given, Jesus said unto him, "Friend, wherefore art thou come?" Then came they and laid their hands on Jesus and took him, ver. 48–50. Then it was that Peter, under the influence of excitement, stretched out his hand and drew his sword, and struck the servant of the High Priest and cut off his ear, &c. Let us contemplate the scene before us, and in doing so observe,

I. *We have a striking instance of unhallowed zeal in a good cause.* Behold the divine and lowly Jesus,—the heavenly teacher,—the true and tender friend of humanity in the hands of violent and unprincipled men. We marvel not that his disciples should burn with indignation at the rudeness manifested towards him. We would admire the soul that deeply felt and tenderly sympathized with the friend of sinners. Jesus had done nothing amiss. His was the cause of righteousness, and purity, and love. Peter therefore was connected with, and acting for, that which was equitable and right. But his errors were manifold.

1. *Jesus knew best what to do, and not Peter.* He was therefore impetuous and rash. He neither sought advice of his Master, nor of his brethren. "Do nothing rashly," is an admonition worthy of the regard of all men. One very wisely advises, "When ye know not what to do, do not then ye know not what." The cause of religion was never really served by precipitancy and rashness.

2. *Peter's spirit was unsuited to the occasion.* Christ had once said to his disciples, "Ye know not what manner of spirit ye are of." How fully did Peter realize this on this occasion. Had Peter forgotten the intimations that Christ had so frequently given of what should come to pass? Had not the Saviour just reiterated that the Son of man should be betrayed, and that the very hour was at hand? ver. 43. Had he not been one of the witnesses of the Saviour's agonizing devotion in the garden? How discordant was the rash and violent spirit of Peter, with the sacred solemnities of the night the Redeemer had spent in the garden. Peter's mind was evidently under the power of carnal and earthly influences.

3. *His weapon was inappropriate to the cause in which he had embarked.* Had he been the servant of an earthly prince or worldly leader, he might have borne an instrument of worldly combat. But Christ's kingdom was spiritual, heavenly, peaceable. He came to *instruct*, but the sword could not aid in that. He came to *convince*, but an earthly sword could not aid in that. He came to *save and bless*, but the sword could help in neither. He came not to *destroy*, and therefore the sword could be of no avail. Persuasion, conversion, consolation, were not within the province of the sword.

4. *His act was in direct opposition to the spirit and life of Jesus.* It was violent and cruel. It was an act which imperilled the life of man. All Christ's acts were good, and gracious, and kind. He never cursed, or injured, or destroyed. He pitied, and saved, and blessed those to whom he came. He came not to condemn and kill, but to save and make alive. How opposite the spirit and act of the disciple to those of the Saviour.

II. *We have the merciful interposition of Jesus on behalf of one of his enemies.* The sword has smitten off the ear of Malchus,— had not the restraining grace of Christ been at hand, it would probably have been his head, and thus murder and bloodshed would have characterized the ministry of Jesus. Christ, however,

1. *Endeavors to allay the irritation which this act was calculated to excite.* Hence he says to Malchus and those round him, "Suffer ye thus far," Luke xxii. 51. Don't retaliate on my overheated servant. Don't

imagine we intend resistance even to your illegal violence.

2. *He reproves and admonishes Peter.* "Put up again thy sword." My cause requires not the use of carnal weapons. They indeed may injure it, but they cannot promote it. And observe, "they that take the sword, shall perish with the sword," ver. 52. Now by this, Christ might signify that men who used the sword would be met with the same weapons, and that the strongest would gain the mastery. And therefore how foolish for Peter to resist an armed multitude. Or, that all who trusted in the sword for defence and safety, should be abandoned by the providence of God, and the sword should prove their ruin. Or, that those who dared to invade God's prerogative in taking away human life, should, in his righteous retributive providence, suffer in like manner. Or, this might be an indirect prediction of the end of Peter, who afterwards was put to a violent death for adherence to the cause of his Master. It is clear that the sword is forbidden in the propagation or defence of the religion of Jesus. And does not the sword here become the emblem of all that is carnal and earthly?—

(1.) All force or coercion.
(2.) All fines and disabilities.
(3.) All secular interference.
(4.) All bigotry, rancor, and sectarianism. All these are unworthy of Christ's cause, and cannot possibly extend his religion. The tongue, the spirit, the temper of religionists, are often of the same unhallowed kind as Peter's sword.

3. *He affirms his perfect ability to obtain all the aid his exigencies require.* "Thinkest thou that I cannot now pray," &c., v. 53. Here he shows that he could have obtained at once by one single request of the Father, twelve legions of angels for his defence and service. In past ages, angels had served the people of God. They encamp constantly around the righteous. They are all ministering spirits, &c. But the empire of the Redeemer was to be based on Divine truth, and the truth itself, in the hands of Jesus, was destined to accomplish all his purposes.

4. *He then heals the ear of the suffering Malchus.* He remedies the evils of Peter's rashness, and kindly interferes to bless one of his suffering enemies. Here was Divine magnanimity,—heavenly generosity,—tenderest goodness. He acts not with, but against the sword, and thus proves himself

the Prince of Peace. Thus he gives a last display of his miraculous power in the midst of his disciples and enemies, and blesses with his healing influence one who had been sent to arrest him.

Learn,

1. *The spirituality of Christ's religion.* A heavenly kingdom set up in the heart of man. Not a worldly hierarchy. Not a secular establishment. Not a carnal institution.

2. *The true spirit in which it should be promoted.* In the spirit of its divine Lord and Founder. In the spirit of enlightened truth. In the spirit of universal love. In the spirit of calm self-denial. In the spirit of long-suffering and meekness. We often best promote it by *passive suffering.* Earthly resistance is incompatible with its true genius. See the early disciples,—they promoted it by suffering. So the Reformers, Puritans, &c. This requires much more grace than does the spirit of aggressive action. Our subject reads a startling lesson,

3. *To persecutors.* How many of the wise and good have erred in fleeing to the sword,—but how fearfully has it returned upon *themselves.* All history exemplifies this. Beware of the spirit, that you may avoid the doom.

LIX.—THE MIRACLES ACCOMPANYING THE CRUCIFIXION.

"Now from the sixth hour there was darkness over all the land unto the ninth hour. And about the ninth hour Jesus cried with a loud voice, saying, Eli, Eli, lama sabachthani? that is to say, 'My God, my God, why hast thou forsaken me,'" &c.—*Matt.* xxvii. 45-51.

THE Redeemer had given ample evidence, by his wondrous deeds, of the truth of his Messiahship. His ministry had been one continued scene of miracles. The work which had been given him to do, was now accomplished, and the time of his departure to the Father had arrived. Of his sufferings and death he had often spoken, and now he was expiring in unutterable agonies on the cross; but to his Messiahship a series of miracles bore testimony in his dying hour. These are detailed by the sacred evangelists, and are left us for our instruction, and the confirmation of our faith and hope in him. The evangelist directs our attention,

I. *To the supernatural darkness.* "Now from the sixth hour to the ninth hour there was darkness over all the land," ver. 45. That is, from twelve to three o'clock. It is clear that this was not the result of an eclipse of the sun, for it was at the time of the Jewish passover, when the moon was at full. It is obvious, too, that this darkness was something more than the sky being overcast; it was evidently dense palpable darkness. Here then was the intervention of the finger of God. This darkness,

1. *Was the fulfilment of prophecy.* Compare Joel ii. 30–32; and Acts ii. 16, &c.

2. *It symbolized the darkness of the Jewish people, and the heinousness of their sin in putting to death the Son of God.* They had scorned God's servants, and persecuted his prophets; but they said in reference to the Son, "This is the heir, let us kill him." It was the filling up of the measure of their nation's iniquity.

3. *It seemed to indicate the termination of the Mosaic dispensation.* That the day of types and shadows and ceremonies was now ended, and that these were all concluded by the darkness which attended the crucifixion of the Son of God. It was the interval between the times of Moses and the prophets, and those of Christ and the Gospel era.

4. *It ratified the divinity of the Messiah's mission and character.* The darkness in Egypt was one of the signs of the divinity of Moses' commission to Pharaoh. And now in the dense and universal darkness which prevailed, was beheld an astounding confirmation of the Messiahship of Jesus,—that great prophet—of whom Moses was but a type. Dr. Young thus describes the scene:

"The sun beheld it—no, the shocking scene
Drove back his chariot; Midnight veiled his face;
Not such as this, not such as nature makes;
A midnight, nature shuddered to behold;
A midnight new! A dread eclipse
(Without opposing spheres) from her
Creator's frown!
Sun, didst thou fly thy Maker's pain? or start
At that enormous load of human guilt,
Which bowed his blessed head, overwhelmed his
  cross,
Made groan the centre—burst earth's marble
  womb
With pangs, strange pangs! delivered of her dead!
Hell howl'd; and heaven that hour let fall a tear.
Heaven wept, that man might smile!
Heaven bled, that man might never die."

II. *There was the rending of the veil of the temple.* "And, behold the veil of the temple was rent in twain," &c., ver. 51.

There were two veils in the temple. One of them separated the holy place from the outer court. The other separated between the holy place, and the holiest of all. It was doubtless the latter which was now rent from the top to the bottom. This veil was of tapestry of extraordinary dimensions and thickness, and its instantaneous severance was beyond the power of ordinary means. It is likely this took place just at the time that the High Priest was ministering before the Lord.

(1.) This veil typified the body of the Redeemer, which inclosed the divinity—the fulness of the Godhead. Now that body was expiring, and that which shadowed it forth was now torn, and ceased to possess its typical position. See Col. i. 20–22. Heb. ix. 7–8.

(2.) It indicated also the abrogation of the Jewish ritual. The holiest of all was now no longer concealed. Its ends and purposes being consummated, and a new and better dispensation having been brought in.

(3.) It also was expressive of the removal of the wall of partition which had separated between the Jews and the Gentile nations. An economy was now instituted which was to bless all men, irrespective of nation or language. Jesus was now expiring without the gate, as the great sacrifice for sin,—the propitiation for the sins of the whole world.

This miracle was wrought in the presence of the highest Jewish authorities, and in the very midst of their sacred place. We now have to contemplate,

III. *The earthquake and the rending of the rocks.* "And the earth did quake and the rocks were rent." A similar scene occurred at the giving of the law, Exodus xix. 18. Psalm xviii. 7–13. It seems also that the prophet Haggai had referred to it in one of his sublime predictions, ii. 6–21. And the apostle Paul expressly alludes to it, Heb.xii.26,27. This was a public attestation of the wicked deed the Jews were perpetrating, and in connection with the rent veil seemed to refer to the establishment of a new dispensation. Did it not also rebuke the stout-hearted obstinacy of the Jews who had rejected, and were now imbruing their hands in the blood of the Messiah, the true Son of God? And was it not also the last, with the exception of his own resurrection, or concluding miracle, which should certify of Christ during his personal mission in our world? It is not certain whether the dead who arose did so now, or at his resurrection; but the latter seems to be the more probable, and therefore they were rather witnesses of his inherent life and immortality, than signs at his death on the cross. How striking and appropriate the exclamation of the astonished centurion, who said, "Truly this was the Son of God." The impression of the whole scene, which was extraordinary and supernatural, wrought conviction on his mind, and led to his pious and reasonable confession.

Learn,

1. *That in the death of Jesus, we have a deep and sacred interest.* He was apprehended, tried, condemned, and put to an open shame and ignominious death for our sins. While wondering at the astounding phenomenon, never forget that he loved you, and gave himself for you.

2. *That continued sin and unbelief is the putting Christ to death again, so far as we can do it.* It is pouring contempt on Jesus, and all the striking attestations God gave of his divinity and glory.

3. *These should be the results in the whole of us :*—Admiration of the person and character of Christ. Adoring confidence and love. And a decided public confession of him before men.

LX.—THE PROUD ABASED AND THE LOWLY EXALTED.

"And all the trees of the field shall know that I the Lord have brought down the high tree, have exalted the low tree, have dried up the green tree, and have made the dry tree to flourish: I the Lord have spoken and have done it."—*Ezek.* xvii. 24.

THE paragraph of which the text is the conclusion, evidently refers to the setting up of the kingdom of the Lord Jesus Christ. The metaphors employed are very striking and beautiful. It has been realized in part by the coming of the gospel reign, but its full accomplishment is reserved for that period when the Saviour's name shall be great from the rising, &c. When all nations shall be blessed in him, and all people shall call him blessed, &c. In doing this, God is represented in our text as acting by a method different to that of worldly policy. Worldly men select and exalt the great and the flourishing, and despise the small and the weak. God, on the other hand, acts the very reverse, &c. We shall consider the text as exemplified,

I. *In the history of his providence.* Look at the antediluvians and Noah. They were the high and green trees,—Noah and family, the low and the dry. No doubt the objects of derision and scorn. A whole world's principles and conduct against them. Yet how fearfully did God fulfil the spirit of the text, in the doom of the old world, and in the preservation of Noah, &c.

(2.) There was *Pharaoh* and the *Israelites.* Pharaoh, the high green tree. Majesty, dignity, power, riches, were his. Degradation, toil, oppression, the lot of the Israelites. Their thraldom seemed irrevocably fixed. No dawning of hope, &c. But God steps forth, and how he brought down the high tree, &c. Let the rolling waters of the Red Sea expound the passage to all future generations.

(3.) There was *Goliath* and *David.* One a prodigy of Herculean size and strength. Clad in his apparently invincible armor. A man of war, &c. The other a youth of pastoral habits, whose life had been spent in tending his father's flock on the mountains of Israel. Hearken to the challenge. See the combat, and how Jehovah teaches the stripling's hands to war, &c.

(4.) There was *Haman* and *Mordecai.* Haman, the highest tree of all the princes of the Persian king. He was to have the homage of the people, and that by the express mandate of the king. Mordecai was the low tree, a private citizen, a Jew of no power or authority. These trees came in collision,—who can doubt the result? Surely the high tree shall overcome, and the low tree be destroyed. The realization seems at hand,—but, mark, *Haman* is executed, and ends his days in infamy,—*Mordecai* is raised next in power and authority to the king. Let these instances suffice to show how, in the history of Divine providence, God has brought down the high tree, &c.

II. *We see it in the history of the Lord Jesus Christ.* A Messiah had been promised from the earliest period of time. He had been held up in prophecy, types, &c. The Jews had expected him for ages. At the time of the advent of Christ, their expectation was most intense and general. But observe, the Jews expected the high green tree. They expected earthly magnificence. They expected worldly power and authority. They expected an earthly kingdom. But Christ fulfilled the sayings of the prophets. Is. liii. 1, &c. In all things he was the opposite of their desires, &c. Hence they killed him. Yet Christ, the low tree, &c., did God exalt, &c. He hath made him to flourish, &c. His name shall endure as long as the sun, &c.

III. *We see it in the triumphs of the apostolic labors.* The great founders of Christ's kingdom go forth to set up Christianity. Look at the persons of the apostles,—plain, illiterate, poor men. Not the high green tree. Not learned, affluent, or influential. Hearken to their message. What is it? Christ crucified. Not a religion of metaphysical subtleties. Not elaborate doctrines or profound dogmas of philosophy. Not a splendid system of pompous ceremony. But the lowly doctrines of the cross. Humility, self-denial, spirituality, &c. And what is the result? *The high tree* of paganism is brought down. *The green tree* of Judaism is dried up. *The low tree* of Christianity is exalted, and flourishes, and blesses every known civilized land, &c. How forcibly is this described—1 Cor. i. 21–29. Look at its illustration,

IV. *In the experience of the haughty, and of the penitential sinner.*

The man of proud heart, exalted self-esteem. He despises God's authority. Full of self-sufficiency,—perhaps of self-righteousness. He may be the very realization of the Pharisees of old. See him lifting himself up as the high tree, boasting of himself as the green tree. I thank thee, O God, &c.

See the low tree of humble penitency. The poor publican self-convicted, self-abhorred. He is the dry tree, nothing to trust in, or to plead. He scarcely lifts up his eyes,—he smites on his breast, and exclaims, God be merciful, &c. Mark the result. God rejects the high tree,—he despises his work,—he brings him low. He beholds with approbation the low tree, &c. He goes down to his house justified.

V. *Look at it in the lives of the high-minded and of the lowly Christian.*

Pride and self-sufficiency are the great temptations of the human heart. *To be something. To do something. To be thought something.* To exalt ourselves. How prone we are to this. Well, what is the result? God knows it will ruin us, if not eradicated. We must be brought low in *mercy* or *judgment.* He blights the worldly prospects. He reverses the dazzling scene. He sends repeated disappointments. Troops of crosses and troubles. Perhaps keen bereavements.

And thus brings down the *high tree,* dries up the green tree, &c. If *these fail,* then he permits such to make shipwreck of faith, &c. Eternal judgment overwhelms them.

But behold the *low tree,* the dry tree. The lowly Christian says, "I am nothing." He lives by faith on the Son of God, &c. He abases himself, &c. He glories in the cross, &c. He makes mention of Christ's righteousness, &c. He dwells in the dust. God *exalts,* blesses, makes fruitful, &c., lifts them up forever.

APPLICATION.

1. *Learn the evil of self-exaltation.* Avoid it. Watch against it. Pray against it.

2. *Be clothed with humility.* What peace, safety, and honor are here.

3. *God must have all the glory.* See the text: also Daniel iv. 34.

LXI.—PAUL'S APOSTOLIC EXPERIENCE.

"But when it pleased God, who separated me from my mother's womb, and called *me* by his grace, to reveal his Son in me, that I might preach him among the heathen; immediately I conferred not with flesh and blood."—*Gal.* i. 15–16.

THE apostle had been greatly honored, by the success of his ministry, in the region of Galatia. To him his converts were devotedly attached. So ardent was their affection, that they would have plucked out their eyes to have served him. At length, however, false teachers crept in among them, and proclaimed an adulterated gospel. They contended for the essentiality of circumcision, and an observance of the Jewish ritual. To give great weight to their teaching, they insinuated that Paul was not a rightly constituted apostle—not fully authorized to preach the gospel of Christ Jesus. The apostle, therefore, had to vindicate his claim to the ministry, and the divinity of his apostolical call. In our text he does this, by referring both to his conversion, and his call to the ministerial work. Let us then notice,

His declaration concerning his conversion.

His divine commission to preach the gospel; and

The course of conduct which he adopted. Notice then,

I. *His declaration concerning his conversion.* Here he specifies three things,

1. *His separation from his mother's womb.*

Now by this he might refer to his natural birth,—recognize the God of his life as the author of his salvation. That he who formed and gave him being, regenerated him and gave him the new life, and the divine nature. But I rather judge that he refers to his separation from the Jewish church. He was in the highest degree a Jew. See Philip. iii. 4, &c. To this church he was ardently attached, even as a filial son to his mother; but it pleased God to separate, &c., at a time when he was zealously laboring for its interests, &c. How striking—how entire that separation!

2. *God called him by his grace.* That call was miraculous. When he was set against Christ and against the gospel. When he was exceeding mad, &c. A savage destroyer, &c. How gracious the interference of the Redeemer. How he expostulates—Saul, Saul! &c. How he softens his heart, &c. How he directs him where to go for instruction, &c. This was a call from enmity to love. From bondage to liberty. From death to life, &c. From hell to heaven.

3. *God revealed his Son in him.* Now to reveal, is to make manifest what was previously hidden. The rising sun reveals the wonders of nature. Now in Paul's case there was a revelation of Christ to him. Christ appeared in the overwhelming light of heaven, &c. He says, "Christ was also seen by him as one born," &c. Now the gospel reveals Christ to us. But Christ was revealed in him. Revealed to the eyes of his understanding,—to his heart. His soul beheld him and received him. Now this is evangelical conversion,—when Christ is revealed in the heart, the hope of glory. He that thus seeth the Son hath eternal life. I just add, that when Christ is revealed in us, he will also be revealed *by us.* We shall show forth Christ. We shall exhibit the resemblance of our spirits to his. Living epistles—read and known, &c. Consider,

II. *His divine commission to preach the gospel.* "That I might preach him among the heathen." Now here you have,

1. *His special work.* "To preach." That is, to publish and proclaim. To announce, and declare, and to offer. He had many other duties—to counsel, to visit, to write; but his great work was to preach. Wherever he went. Wherever providence placed him. From the time of his conversion to his death, he was to preach.

2. *His great theme.* To preach Christ.

To preach Christ is to preach the gospel; for it is the gospel of Christ. And all preaching that is evangelical and saving, is preaching Christ. All doctrines—all blessings—all privileges—all duties—all ordinances—all graces must be preached in close and indissoluble connection with Christ. All that relates to Christ. Christ to all. Christ always. Christ all and in all. How faithfully Paul obeyed his commission. "I am determined," &c. "We preach Christ," &c. "We preach not," &c. "God forbid," &c. "Yea, doubtless," &c.

3. *The appointed sphere of his ministry.* "Among the heathen." He was emphatically the apostle of the Gentiles, as Peter was of the Jews. Not indeed exclusively, but generally: "Unto me who am less," &c. See Acts ix. 15. So that his commission extended to all the Gentile nations of the earth. Hence he appeared as the angel flying, &c. We meet with him in almost every nation and clime of the then known world, &c. It is said that he visited the distant isles of the sea, and on our shores (England) lifted up the cross of the Lord Jesus Christ. This leads us,

III. *To the course of conduct which he adopted.* "Immediately I conferred not," &c.

1. *He did not confer with his Jewish friends.* If so, they would have labored to dissuade him, &c. But he surrendered them all; and though honored and loved by them he forsook them for the sake of the Lord Jesus Christ.

2. *He did not confer with the other apostles of Christ.* Ver. 17. He states this, that he might show he did not receive his commission from men, however high in office, &c. Had he gone to them they would have probably feared, or reasoned on the propriety of a period of probation, that the Christians might have confidence in his character and conversion.

3. *He did not confer with the feelings of his own nature.* His nature would have resisted the work, and fled from it. His nature would have said *ease,*—his call was to *toil;* honor—his call was to reproach; wealth—his call was to poverty; earthly enjoyment—his call was to suffer, and even to death; self—his call was the moral crucifixion, and for Christ to be all and in all. Observe,

4. *The promptitude of his conduct.* "Immediately." With prompt decision. At once, and with all his heart, and soul, and mind, and strength, he went forth, &c.

APPLICATION.

1. *How much to adore in the Saviour.* His condescension and grace to Saul. Wherefore?—for his own sake, and for the sake of the church and the world. See 1 Tim. i. 16.

2. *How much to imitate in the spirit and conduct of the apostle.* In reference to his own calling to love and serve Jesus—he says, "I was not disobedient unto the heavenly vision." He surrendered—he yielded—he cried for mercy. Have you all thus obeyed the call? &c. He did Christ's work cheerfully. Have you followed the course that divine providence has marked out? &c. Give Christ your talents, influence, time, &c. Like Paul, do not confer with flesh and blood;—with those opposed to Christ, and true inward religion. I urge this upon the young. Those who are half-decided, &c. Oh, be prompt, and earnest, and devoted to Jesus.

3. *This revelation of Christ in us is essential to salvation.* Nothing will do instead. "We must be born again." "Except a man be converted," &c.

LXII.—ALL CHRISTIANS SHOULD WORK FOR GOD.

"And to every man his work."—*Mark* xiii. 34.

This portion of Divine truth is equally applicable to us with those to whom it was originally addressed. And it is of the first importance that we should recognize it, feel it, and live and act under its responsibility.

In religion there is much to *learn:* the great mystery of godliness is spread before us, and we should labor to increase daily in the knowledge of the Lord Jesus Christ. Paul said, "Yea, doubtless," &c.

In religion there is much to *enjoy.* Its blessings are rich and overflowing. Hitherto ye have asked nothing, &c. Ask and receive, &c.

In religion there is much to *endure,*—afflictions, temptations, distresses, &c. Through much tribulation, &c.

In religion there is much *to be done.* It is eminently a practical thing. Obedience is the great evidence of true discipleship. "If ye know, &c., happy are ye if *ye do them.*" Now this is the principle.

I. *Every man has a work assigned him of God.*

There is the work of *repentance* and *faith.*

There is the work of *personal* religion. "Work out your own salvation." Give diligence, &c. "Fervent in spirit," &c.

There is the work of *relative* piety,—discharging those religious duties in our various stations. Parents,— children, — masters,—servants. But in addition to these there is the work,

Of spiritual *influence,* or our *generations' work.*

(1.) To some, the work of the *ministry.* To preach and teach Jesus Christ. To warn, &c. To build up the Church, &c. To make full proof of our ministry. A great, solemn, arduous, and momentous work.

(2.) To others, the work of the deaconship. To serve the tables in the Lord's house. The minister's table. The tables of the poor. The Lord's table.

(3.) To all, works of Christian *usefulness.* How large the sphere. How various the modes of Christian activity. How numerous the claims. How affecting the appeals. What room for the devotion of talents—wealth—influence—knowledge, &c.

II. *It should be the earnest desire of the Christian to know his especial work.* To every man *his* work. That to which he is *qualified.* That to which *he is appointed.* That for which *he is responsible.* This may be ascertained,

(1.) By reflection. As to the desires of the soul—impressions, &c.

(2.) By seeking the counsel of friends.

(3.) By asking direction from the Lord. "If any man," &c. "Lord, what wouldst thou have?" &c. "Commit thy way," &c.

III. *When the work is ascertained, we should enter on the discharge of its duties.*

1. *We should do this instantly.* Not confer with flesh and blood. Not consult feelings, or the opinions of others. We should say, "Lord, here am I." "Speak, Lord," &c.

2. *We should do it cheerfully.* With a willing mind and ready spirit. Not grudgingly. Not by constraint, except the constraint of the Saviour's love,—counting it an honor and privilege.

3. *We should do it earnestly.* "Fervent in spirit," &c. With our might. With the heart. Should be our meat, &c. With the *whole* soul.

4. *We should do it constantly.* The Lord's work is continuous. The work of all days, all seasons, all circumstances. Let us not be weary, &c.

5. *We should do it humbly.* Without self-exaltation. Doing all to God's glory. Remembering the greatness and goodness of the Master. Remembering our obligations to him. Remembering the imperfection of our services.

6. *We should do it, relying on the communications of Divine grace.* God's grace alone sufficient. This must be sought, and relied on, and honored. Without Christ we can do nothing.

III. *For our spiritual work each must give an account to God.* This accords with reason, with equity. With the express doctrines of Scripture. Matt. xxv. This should be remembered. Should constantly influence us.

APPLICATION.

1. Are we working for Christ? If so, in what way? To what extent? In what spirit?

2. *How fearful the doom of the slothful!* Matt. xxv. Not an enemy. Not a rebel, but a servant.

3. *How great the rewards of the righteous!* Including dignity, joy, and eternal blessedness.

LXIII.—THE GREAT FEAST.

"And in this mountain shall the Lord of hosts make unto all people a feast of fat things, a feast of wines on the lees, of fat things full of marrow, of wines on the lees well refined. And he will destroy in this mountain the face of the covering cast over all people, and the vail that is spread over all nations," &c.—*Isa.* xxv. 6-8.

THERE can be no doubt that the text has a distinct reference to gospel times and gospel blessings. Indeed it is quite clear that this is one of those rich evangelical passages with which the writings of Isaiah so fully abound. The text is a fine specimen of the eastern imagery with which the sacred scriptures are so beautifully fraught. Let us then, in the spirit of holy inquiring meditation, endeavor to ascertain the import of the theme under consideration. Observe then, the place, —the festival,—and the blessings identified with it. Observe,

I. *The place.* "In this mountain." No doubt referring to Zion. But Zion was typical of the Church of Christ, and therefore we are to understand this mountain to signify the Church or kingdom of the Saviour, represented as a mountain on account,

1. *Of its elevation.* In the world, but distinct from it: raised above it, rising heavenwards. Not of the earth, earthy—but from heaven, and of heaven, heavenly. Hence Christ said of his people, "Ye are not of the world, even as I am not of the world." Sin sinks men into wretchedness and degradation. Grace lifts up, and the Church is midway between earth and heaven. Described as a mountain,

2. *On account of its visibility.* The prominency and visibility of the mountain are manifest to all. The mountain is seen at a distance. With the sun shining upon it, it cannot be hid. Just so the Saviour's Church is to be seen and known. A city on a hill. A *visible* kingdom. A *glorious* building. Satan's kingdom is set up and seen, and Christ's is to confront it—to overthrow it. On account,

3. *Of its stability.* The mountain is ever the symbol of firmness and immovableness. So the Church of Christ is invulnerably secure and immovable. Like Mount Zion, cannot be moved. "On this rock will I build my church," &c. All the efforts of earth and hell have been unable to overthrow it. Observe,

II. *The festival.* Now this feast is to be in the Church,—in the kingdom of grace. As a rich feast, it is to be distinguished for,

1. *Its variety.* The banquet table is strewed with the most varied and choicest dainties from the eastern pasture and vineyard. All spiritual blessings are provided in the gospel feast. Stores for the understanding. For the judgment. For the conscience. For the affections. Every exigency met, every want and holy desire supplied. For,

2. *Its abundance.* Here is plenty. No lack. Enough, and to spare, &c. Enough for each, &c. For,

3. *Its hilarity.* A joyful feast. Such was the feast when the prodigal was received back. Gospel blessings filled with joy, &c.— See Psa. lxiii. 4, 5. See an emblem of it in the case of the Jews in Nehemiah's time. —Neh. viii. 9, &c. It is in the Church we may sing,

" The sorrows of the mind," &c.

The kingdom of God is not meat and drink, &c.

Notice,

III. *The blessings identified with it.*

1. *The entire removal of moral darkness*, ver. 7. "Darkness hath covered the earth," &c. "Ye were sometime dark," &c. The gospel shall remove it. Introduce into day. The mists are dispelled by the power of the rising sun. So shall the Sun of righteousness arise, &c. "All his people shall be taught of the Lord," &c. "Now ye are the children of light and of the day." Gospel knowledge shall be universal, cover the earth, &c.

2. *The complete conquest of death.* Death has been a ravager, a conqueror, &c. A whirlpool, or abyss, swallowing up nations, &c. But death is to be engulfed and swallowed up.

This was the case *in Christ's resurrection.* He overcame death, &c. He has now the keys, &c. He is now the resurrection, &c.

This is the case when the Christian, by faith, triumphs over it. To many, to die would be gain. They are delivered from all fear. They conquer, and cheerfully face it, and have the spiritual conquest over it.

In the great resurrection then shall it be swallowed up, and be no more. Swallowed up in *eternity.* See 1 Cor. xv. 20–26. See also ver. 52, &c.

3. *The public justification of his people.* "The rebuke of his people," &c., ver. 8. Here they have been maligned, reproached, misrepresented, despised. Then they shall be vindicated, confessed, honored. Their *choice.* Their *sincerity.* Their *worth*, shall all be made evident before angels, and men, and devils.

4. *Every source of sorrow shall then be removed.* "God shall wipe away tears," &c. They now sojourn in the valley of tears. They sow in tears. Tears often their meat, &c. But they shall be wiped, &c. God shall do it, and forever.

APPLICATION.

1. *Congratulate the inhabitants of this mountain.* Happy are ye. Rejoice in hope. "For the mouth of the Lord," &c.

2. *Invite strangers, yea all*, &c. It is a feast for all people, &c. Plead, urge, &c.

LXIV.—MESSIAH'S TRIUMPHS.

"His enemies will I clothe with shame: but upon himself shall his crown flourish."—*Psalm* cxxxii. 18.

It is evident, that from the 11th verse of this Psalm, there is a distinct prophecy relative to the Lord Jesus Christ. By comparing this portion of the Psalm with Luke i. 31, &c., and Acts ii. 30, &c., we have the true key to the signification of the Psalmist, and thus we are infallibly delivered from the possibility of error. In all cases, Scripture is the best interpreter of Scripture. It is equally evident, that this prophecy has not yet been fully accomplished. It has been in the course of accomplishment for more than eighteen centuries, and it will finally receive its complete realization in the universal establishment of the reign of the Messiah. Our text contains a twofold declaration,

I. *As to his enemies.* And,

II. *As to his regal triumphs and glory.* Observe the declaration,

I. *As to his enemies.* The enemies of the Redeemer are vast and various. Among these we notice,

(1.) The powers of darkness. The apostate angels leagued under Satan, the prince of the power of the air. Now these are all united in one compact of evil against God, and holiness, and against the happiness of his creatures.

(2.) The wicked rulers of earthly dominions. In all ages there have been such. Pharaoh, king of Egypt. Balak, and the kings of Canaan. Belshazzar and Herod, and the early Roman emperors. Pagan and infidel rulers. All who have lent their influence to tyranny and oppression, and irreligion. The cruel persecutors of the people of God, in all ages and countries.

(3.) Infidel and blasphemous scoffers. Men who have written against the religion of heaven. Porphyry, Julian, and Bolingbroke, and Hume, and Paine, and Hobbes, &c. Men whose intellects and genius have been consecrated to works of evil. Wandering stars. Founts of corruption and death.

(4.) False teachers and antichrists. Corrupters of the truth. The inventors and supporters of worldly systems of religion. Enemies of the cross of Christ. Seducers from the gospel. In this rank we must place all religious impostors and deceivers. From the false Christs of the apostles' days down to Mahomet, and from Mahomet to Joanna Southcot, and Smith, the degraded Mormonite.

(5.) All pagan priests and worshippers of idols. This is a public poring of contempt on God. Every pagan temple,—altar,—sacrifice and ceremony,—are in open war with the kingdom of Jesus.

(6.) All obstinate and unbelieving Jews. They have had the true light. They have in their possession the very oracles which speak of Christ. But they have closed their eyes, and shut their ears, and hardened their hearts. They are still doing over again the work of their fathers, in despising the Messiah, and putting away from them the only Christ.

(7.) All wicked violators of the laws of heaven, and such as are in unbelief. The unconverted in our own land. Those who do not receive the grace of God in faith. All who refuse their allegiance, and love, and obedience to the Saviour. Such are his enemies, and such shall be clothed with shame. See Psalm cix. 29. They are often so,

(1.) In the depths of their mental and moral wretchedness. When their resources fail them, in the day of affliction, or sorrow, or death. It is said that Julian, after a most bitter and persevering opposition to Christ and his cause, exclaimed, gnashing with his teeth and biting the earth, "O Galilean, thou hast overcome!" This is often the end of the ungodly.

(2.) This will be so, by the utter ruin of all the obstinate foes of Jesus. We cannot tell how this will be effected on the nations, &c., which will not bow to Christ, but it is clear such shall be destroyed, and leave this earth ultimately to be the residence and portion of the meek followers of Christ. See Psa. xxxvii. 9 ; xii. 13 ; xxxv. 36. See especially Psa. ii. 6, &c.

(3.) It will be fully realized in the last great day. Then the wicked shall arise to everlasting contempt. Then be disowned, and convicted, and condemned, and punished. 2 Thess. i. 7, &c. Now consider,

II. *The declaration concerning Christ.* "But upon himself shall his crown," &c. Now here,

1. *The monarchical dignity of Christ is assumed.* The kingdom of Christ is everywhere attested. He is King of Zion. King of the whole earth. King of kings. His kingdom is a universal kingdom, &c. A

righteous sceptre is the sceptre of his kingdom. He is the Supreme Governor. He is appointed "Heir of all things." Observe,

2. *His crown is adverted to.* "His crown." Now confining the subject to Christ's spiritual and mediatorial kingdom : Observe,

(1.) His crown was obtained by conflict. He fought for it. He encountered all the hosts of hell. The legion of evil. He gained the conflict,—obtained the victory. See Col. ii. 15. Psa. lxviii. 17, &c.

(2.) By suffering. His kingdom and people he had to redeem by his own blood. This is an important view of Christ's crown. It is vividly described, Phil. ii. 6, &c.; Heb. ii. 10, 11 ; and Rev. iv. 6, &c.

3. *The glory and prosperity of Christ's royal character is affirmed.* "Upon himself," &c. This shall be realized in

(1.) The extension of his dominion. "From the rivers," &c.

(2.) In the multitude of his subjects. As numerous as the dew-drops of the morning. "In him shall all the families," &c.

(3.) In the discomfiture of his enemies, &c. "He will overturn," &c. His enemies shall become his footstool, &c.

(4.) In the felicity of his people. Abundance of peace and joy. Universal harmony and blessedness, &c. Nothing shall vex, &c.

"Blessings abound where'er he reigns," &c.

(5.) In the consummation of his kingdom and glory. All enlightened, sanctified, and saved in him. His soul satisfied. All united in Christ. All blessed in him, and all proclaiming him blessed, &c. Now this declaration of the text is certain. It must be,

From the superior power of good over evil.
From the very essentials of the covenant.
From the affirmations of God's mouth.
From the glory of both the Father and the Son.

APPLICATION.

1. *Does the subject interest you?* Your minds ; hearts, &c.

2. *Does it engage your energies?* Are you with Christ, and against his enemies ?—Interested, devoted, praying, laboring, conflicting. All such shall reign with him, and sit on his throne, &c.

3. *To the enemies of Christ.* Persevere not. O, bow down,—sue for mercy. Kiss the Son, &c.

LXV.—THE PRAISES OF THE LIVING.

"The living, the living, he shall praise thee, as I *do* this day: the father to the children shall make known thy truth."—*Isa.* xxxviii. 19.

THE text is connected with the history of Hezekiah. He was sick, and nigh unto death—indeed the mandate had gone forth: "Set thine house," &c. In answer to humble and fervent prayer, the sentence was reversed, and his life was spared fifteen years. Hezekiah, on his recovery, composed the following pathetic and pious ode, v. 10, &c. Of this holy and edifying Psalm, our text forms a part. Let us enter on the meditation of it in the spirit of the prayer of Moses, the man of God. "So teach us to number," &c. We ask,

I. *For what should the living praise God?*

1. *For life itself.* Life is God's good gift. Life in its origin,—in its progress—exhibits the care and bounty of God. "He made us, and not we," &c. "He holdeth our souls in life."

2. *For life in its privileges.* And who can number these? Privileges of receiving good. Of receiving knowledge, and grace, and happiness. Privilege of doing good—of imitating God,—resembling God. Being godly,—growing in godlikeness. Honoring God, &c. These privileges are countless. Hearing and reading the Word. Meditation and prayer. Repentance and restitution. Faith and obedience.

3. *For life and its hopes.* Hope is the sunshine of life's day. The *favorable* breeze of life's voyage. The *flowery* path of life's journey. The *balm* and sweetness of life's existence. The *solace* of life's sorrows. But then hope also goes beyond life,—it draws the curtain, and beholds in the distance the goodly land. It brings immortality and glory near. It recognizes the conquest over death and the grave. It brings near to us a brighter, happier, and an eternal world. It sings, "Though this the earthly house," &c. "In my Father's house," &c.

II. *In what manner should the living praise God?*

1. *With true gratefulness of heart.* No service is acceptable without the heart. Praise, especially, must be heartwork. The heart must muse until the fire burns. "Bless the Lord, O my *soul*, and all that is *within me*," &c. From the fulness of the heart, &c. Without this, however musically correct, however sweet, &c., it is formality and hypocrisy before God.

2. *Earnestness of spirit.* Not languidly. Not lifelessly; but with fervor of spirit. We are to exult in God. To extol. To magnify, &c. We are to make a joyful noise, &c. The praises of the redeemed are as the sound of many waters, &c. See also Rev. vii. 9, 10, &c.

3. *With cheerful constancy.* We are to bless the Lord at all times. In every thing to give thanks. Praise is suitable to all places and times. In the *sanctuary.* "Enter into his gates," &c. At the *social* service,—Christ sang a hymn at the establishment of the eucharistic supper. In *family worship.* What so proper as that the living family should unite, &c. In the retirements of the closet. On his bed the Psalmist praised God, &c. Hence the poet sweetly sings,

"I'll praise my Maker," &c.

III. *What advantages will arise to the living from praising God?*

1. *It will cheer and elevate the soul.* The praising soul is like the joyous bird on the wing, rising upwards towards the skies. It gives vigor and elasticity to the mind. It tends to remove depression and despondency. The joy of the Lord is our strength.

2. *It will be peculiarly acceptable to God.* Whoso offereth praise, glorifieth God. It is acknowledging God. It is blessing and honoring God. God will approve and smile upon the grateful, praising Christian.

3. *It will recommend religion.* The idea of the world is, that religion is a gloomy system,—necessarily melancholy. (Hume and Bishop Horne.) Sacred cheerfulness and songs of praise, should remove this false delusion. The Christian should sing,

"The sorrows of the mind," &c.

"Thy statutes shall be my songs," &c. "They shall return and come to Zion," &c.

4. *It will tend to meeten the saint for glory.* Heaven is one vast temple of praise, —myriads of the redeemed sing and praise God. Eternity will be too short, &c. Now we must have the spirit of praise while we live, so that, like Simeon, we may die praising him. Praising God when all is right and spiritual, is heaven on earth,—blessedness on the way to glory.

APPLICATION.

1. *Our subject should claim the attention of all present.* We are the living. On us

the exercise of praise devolves. Do you bless God? Have you the true spirit of praise?

2. *Let us praise God for the greatest of all his gifts.* That of his dear Son. "Thanks be to God," &c. "Worthy is the Lamb," &c.

3. *To those who never truly praise God.* Have you no reason why his long-suffering should lead you to it? Praise God that you are living—not dead—not lost. Within the circle of means, and in the region of hope. Praise him for these things, &c. Seek the spirit of praise.

LXVI.—THE FAITH OF THE SAMARITAN.

"And many of the Samaritans of that city believed on him for the saying of the woman, who testified, He told me all that ever I did. So when the Samaritans were come unto him, they besought him that he would tarry with them: and he abode there two days," &c.—*John* iv. 39–42.

Few narratives exceed in interest, and in graphic and beautiful description, the history of the woman of Samaria.

(1.) The previous character of the woman;
(2.) The circumstances under which she met Jesus;
(3.) The nature of the conversation;
(4.) Her prompt faith in the Saviour;
(5.) Her eager desire to tell her neighbors; and,
(6.) The happy results of her zealous endeavors;—are all points on which we could dwell at great length to our instruction and edification. Her simple, plain, and hearty ministry, was greatly blessed and honored to the good of many precious souls. She convinced several by her testimony, ver. 39. She also brought many more to hear and see for themselves, and of these a number made a good confession, ver. 41, 42. Let us try to seize on the more striking parts of this portion of evangelical history. Observe,

I. *Testimony is essential to faith:* ver. 39. There must be something published. Either by the mouth or pen, some word spoken or written. Faith comes by hearing, &c., or reading. The Bereans. See text. Now the testimony must be credible, resting on good and sufficient evidence. Thus this woman testified of what she had *seen* and *heard*. So the apostles testified concerning Christ what they knew, and had seen, and heard. So Christian ministers preach the great facts of the gospel as in the language of the apostle, 1 Cor. xv. 1, &c. No facts are better attested than those of the *life*, *sufferings*, and *resurrection* of Christ—and who, believing these, can refuse to receive him as the Son of God? The testimony of his *disciples*, who had every thing to lose, and nothing to gain, by their profession. The testimony of Jewish *historians*. The testimony of *pagans*. The testimony of the *fruits* of religion in the hearts and lives of thousands.

II. *Sufficiently authenticated testimony demands our belief.* It is egregious folly not to believe when the evidence is sufficient. What would the opposite in reference to Christ involve?

(1.) That myriads of disciples lived and died to give currency to a lie or delusion.

(2.) That even the Jews, who hated Christ, should support this testimony of falsehood.

(3.) That the wisest and best of many nations, for 1800 years, without any advantage, should keep this delusion up by avowing their experience, and exhibiting a Christian profession. Now, the rejection of Christianity and the gospel must involve all this. We demand, therefore, your clear, decided, and hearty belief of the gospel testimony.

III. *Faith in Christ leads to supreme love for, and delight in him.* "They besought him that he would tarry with them," ver. 40.

1. *How interesting the suitors on this occasion.* The newly converted Samaritans. Their love flaming,—their zeal burning. Whence this desire,

(1.) To *hear* more from Christ.
(2.) To *see* more of him.
(3.) To *enjoy* more.
(4.) To be *better grounded* and established.
(5.) To have more *sensible* communion.

Ought not this to be our desire? To have Christ in our *hearts*. In our *families*. In our *schools*. In our *churches*. In our *means*. Christ *really, sensibly, constantly,* yet by his Spirit. Observe,

2. *How condescending was the Saviour.* "He abode two days." A long period, when you think of his *divinity*, and his *great work*. Yet affectionate, earnest prayer, constrained him. And so it ever does. Prayer obtains

and retains Christ. To faithful prayer, he says, " Be it unto thee," &c.

IV. *Christian faith should be reasonably and magnanimously professed.* "Now we believe." Here observe,

1. *Christian faith may be certainly ascertained.* They believed, and knew it. No hesitation. No doubt. "I know whom," &c. Hence the eunuch, "I believe," &c. The chasm is so wide between disbelief and faith. States of mind so different. So contrary.

2. *Christian faith has its grounds and reasons.* "Now we believe, not because of thy saying," that is, not on account of that *merely.* They had *heard, understood, credited,* and felt the truth as it is in Christ Jesus. "For we have *heard* him," &c., and KNOW that this is INDEED, &c., v. 42, now no *doubt,* perfectly satisfied.

3. *Christian faith when thus realized should be declared.* Hence the Christians were called *confessors.* See Rom. x. 9. *Christ Jesus* has set us the *example,* 1 Tim. vi. 13. See Heb. xiii. 13. Christ also speaks on this subject very solemnly. "Whoso *confesseth* me," &c. "Whoso is *ashamed* of me," &c. We should confess,

(1.) From a sense of love and gratitude to Christ.

(2.) From a desire to benefit others. See the woman of Samaria. So all Christians should, in their own way and sphere, teach and preach Jesus Christ.

(3.) For our own happiness. It will strengthen us. Make us magnanimous. Give us courage. Please the Saviour. It may expose us to the infidel's *sneer.* To the worldling's *laugh.* To the reproach of the *profane.* To the persecution of enemies. To the loss of *friends.* To suffering, &c. Yet Christ, *conscience,* and *Christianity,* all demand it.

V. *The Christian confession is one of mercy to the world.* They testified "that Christ was the Saviour of the world," ver. 42. They felt him to be their *Saviour.* They knew him to be the *other.* He had said so again and again. Hear his sermon to Nicodemus, John iii. 14–17. Surely this is enough. But let his servants also speak. *Isaiah,*—"All we like sheep," &c. *The Baptist,*—"Behold the Lamb of God," &c. *Paul,*—"Who gave himself a ransom for all," &c. *John,*—"Who is the propitiation for our sins," &c. "This we know and testify," &c.

IMPROVEMENT.

1. *Learn not to despise any instrumentality, however simple.* Here is a *woman—illiterate,* &c. Remember Naaman and the little girl.

2. *Imitate the spirit and conduct of the Samaritans.* Their spirit in *hearing, believing, constraining* Christ. Their spirit in making an open confession, &c.

3. *Let us glory in Christ as the willing Saviour of all men.* Oh, this is the *brightness and glory* of the gospel.

"Oh, that the world might taste and see,
    The riches of his grace!
The arms of love that compass me,
    Would all mankind embrace."

"Oh, that my Jesus' heavenly charms,
    Might every bosom move;
Fly, sinners, fly, into those arms,
    Of everlasting love!"

"Happy if with my latest breath,
    I may but gasp his name;
Preach him to all, and cry in death,
    Behold, behold, the Lamb."

LXVII.—THE BLESSEDNESS OF THE CHRISTIAN SABBATH.

"The Jews, therefore, because it was the preparation, that the bodies should not remain upon the cross on the Sabbath-day (for that Sabbath-day was an high day), besought Pilate that their legs might be broken, and *that* they might be taken away."—*John* xix. 21.

IT is impossible to reflect on the mixture of superstition and wickedness which distinguished the Jews, in their conduct towards Jesus, without the utmost astonishment and wonder. They adopt the most base methods of conspiracy to ruin him. They bribe one of his disciples to betray him. They suborn false witnesses to swear away his life. They raise a tumultuous clamor for his blood. They prefer Barabbas, a murderer, to Jesus. They reproach him on the way to the cross. They revile him in the midst of his dying agonies; and then, under the influence of superstitious veneration for the rites of Judaism—they go earnestly entreating Pilate, that the death of those who had been crucified should be accelerated by breaking their legs, lest the bodies should remain suspended on the Sabbath, which was, in the parenthetical language of the text, "A high day." What hypocrisy! What infatuated self-delusion! What a picture of the deceitfulness and depravity of the human heart! But we select the text, that we may apply it to the Christian Sabbath, and the devout feelings we should have towards it. The Sabbath in question was especially great to the Jews, because it was the first day of the Paschal feast, and especial ordinances were connected with it. Let us inquire,

I. *When the Christian Sabbath, or Lord's day, may be considered a high day.*

1. *It is so in itself.* It is the day of the Lord's victory and triumph. The day made especially for himself. The day of hope and assurance to our fallen world. All the great and momentous concerns involved in the reality of Christ's Messiahship, &c., are identified with this day. With this, in one sense, began a new era in our world's history.

2. *It is so in the privileges it confers.* Much more than a day of rest from physical toil and secular labor. Day of especial mercies. The more public worship of God. The exercises of prayer and praise. The hearing of the glorious gospel. Fellowship with the saints, etc. Private reading and meditation, etc.

3. *But it is so as being associated with many of our greatest blessings.* In most cases it was on this day that serious reflection commenced. Solemn conviction. Holy resolution. Believing decision. Open profession. Most of our refreshing seasons, and edifying opportunities, etc.

4. *It is so as a beautiful type of heaven.* The apostle Paul speaks of three Sabbaths.

(1.) The original one, on which God rested.

(2.) The spiritual Sabbath, which we experience by faith on Christ. "We who have believed do enter into rest."

(3.) The heavenly one. There remaineth, therefore, a rest, or keeping of the Sabbath, etc. The cessation of toil, and din, and confusion, and anxiety. Its spiritual services. Its holy joys. Its sanctity, communion, etc., all point upward to heaven.

II. *How we may contribute to the rendering it in an especial degree a high day.* By being in the spirit, etc. God has done much, but we may frustrate that. How many myriads do so. How often have we done so? If we would have it a high day, then,

1. *Conclude as early as possible on the previous evening the duties of the week.* I know this is impracticable with many, but not with all. A late Saturday evening of bustle and confusion is very unfavorable. Retiring to bed later than usual, etc. Many, too, who profess religion, have to go to the tavern for their wages. The noise, and company, and filthiness of a tavern are a bad preparation for the Lord's day. If intoxicating drink be indulged in, there must be all the heaviness and stupor, which must unfit for the exercises of religion.

2. *A conscientious devotion of the Lord's day to spiritual things.* Family should be still and orderly. There should be the exclusion of worldly topics of conversation. The putting away mere secular books, etc. The Bible and the book of praise should be the literary companions. There should be no idle gossiping. No wandering about. No feasting or parties. There should be the preparation for public worship. To be there in time. Not disturbing the minister and congregation, etc. The day should end in holy peace and tranquillity.

3. *Especial prayer for the Divine presence and blessing.* How anxious to have right emotions and desires. "O God, my heart," etc. To have right desires. To be in the spirit of prayer, praise, hearing, and meditation. Works of mercy and usefulness. Now all these must be sought of God. Earnest and believing prayer be offered, so that we may mount up as on eagles' wings, etc. Now, consider,

III. *Some reasons which should make us solicitous that the Sabbath should be a high day.*

1. *On account of the value of the Sabbath itself.* How essential it is. How truly precious. What should we do without it. What the church do. What be done for the world, &c. One of God's greatest mercies. Cannot be too highly prized.

2. *The Sabbath materially will influence the following week.* It supplies spiritual food for the mind. It supplies topics for thought. It presents motives, &c. It gives power, &c. How necessary, then, that it should be a high day. The week will generally be as the Sabbath was.

3. *Our Sabbaths are limited in number.* There are not many in a long life, and of course few in a short one. They will soon be gone. I remember those I spent in the sanctuary with my sainted father, and with my dear Christian friends—the last will soon come.

4. *For our Sabbaths we must give an ac-*

count. Desecration of the Sabbath is guilt and folly. Now the non-improvement of them will make bitter work for reflection. God will require an exact account, &c., in the great day.

APPLICATION.

1. *To the non-religious.* Oh, value this day of mercy. Do not despise it. " Hear, and your souls shall live," &c.
2. *To Christian professors.* Be consistent. If it be the Lord's day, let him have its undivided hours, services, &c.

LXVIII.—THE RUINOUS EFFECTS OF SIN.

" Righteousness keepeth *him that is* upright in the way ; but wickedness overthroweth the sinner."—*Proverbs* xiii. 6.

WE are often warned against evil in the word of God, by the most solemn statements as to the awful consequences of sin. It is written, " The way of transgressors is hard." " God is angry with the wicked," &c. " He that being often reproved," &c. " Say ye to the wicked it shall be ill with him," &c. And in the graphic language of the text, " Wickedness overthroweth," &c. Let us,

I. *Explain the character ;* and
II. *Prove and illustrate the declaration.*
I. *Let us explain the character.* " The sinner."

Sin is the transgression of the law, &c. All men while in a state of nature are sinners. " All have sinned," &c. " There is none righteous," &c. Yet there are degrees and classes of sinners.

1. *There are skeptical and scoffing sinners.* Men who profess to disbelieve revelation. Who ridicule religion. Despise the Bible. Mock at piety. Deride the Christian character. Often glory in their shame, &c.
2. *There are profligate sinners.* These are given up to work iniquity. Go to the race course, the gambling-house, the theatre, and you meet with them. Go to the tavern and the house of dissoluteness, and you meet with them there. You hear them belching out oaths and curses and filthy speeches in the streets. They are eager to do evil. They drink it in as the ox, &c. Bear the mark in their forehead, &c.
3. *There are worldly-minded sinners.* These may be decent in their deportment,

but the world is their god. The ledger or day-book their Bible. Their trade their only religion. All their time and toil devoted to gain the dust of the world. They are literally earth-worms. They are grovelling in the dust. Time and the body absorb all. The soul and eternity forgotten.

4. *There are the formal, the procrastinating sinners.* They give some heed to religion, to Sabbaths, ordinances, preaching, religious duties. They have many convictions, desires, religious purposes. Yet they remain the servants of the evil one. They do not strive to enter in, &c. They do not come to the gospel feast. They are incessantly making excuses. Always putting it off, &c. Not far from the kingdom of God. Now, most persons, if not all, are included in one or other of these classes. Will you inquire ? Search yourselves, &c.

Let us,

II. *Prove and illustrate the declaration.*
" Wickedness overthroweth," &c.

Now, wickedness of any kind or degree will do this—just as one leak will sink a ship, or one mortal disease destroy life. So any kind or order of wickedness will condemn the soul. But it is equally true, that as all virtue or goodness has in its wake certain blessings, and certain exemptions from present evils ; so the more wicked, and the more immediate, the more entire, and the more fearful the ruin produced. As proofs and illustrations of the text, observe,

1. *Wickedness often overthrows the health of the sinner.* Go to the hospital, and see how many have ruined their health by their course of life. That drunkard. That glutton. That debauchee. Nine-tenths of the suffering from disease originates in the wickedness of the sinner. Some blame chance. Some God. While the text contains the true solution. " Wickedness," &c.
2. *Wickedness often overthrows the worldly prospects of the sinner.* Certain moral traits are necessary to success, even in worldly things. What youth would expect to prosper who discarded *truth, fidelity, industry* from his vocabulary ? But many whose prospects have been most flattering, have been entirely wrecked by a course of transgression ; and thousands have been brought to want even a morsel of bread through the vices they have pursued.
3. *Wickedness overthrows the character of its victims.* Is there any honor in being designated an infidel, a liar, a swearer, a

drunkard, a gambler, a profligate? "The very name of the wicked shall rot."

4. *Wickedness overthroweth the lives of sinners.* The wicked do not live out half their days. They go to an early grave. Ponder on this! Look abroad! Observe the occurrences of society. How many fearful illustrations. The criminal on the scaffold—the suicide—the murdered—disease. Myriads who are aged at forty. Sin often lights the taper of life at both ends, and of course existence consumes rapidly away.

5. *Wickedness overthrows the final hopes of the sinner.* Wicked men exist extensively by cherishing a false hope. A hope that it will yet be well with them. That they will escape the fearful consequences of their transgression. That though they eat, they will not die. The devices of Satan are numerous in keeping these illusions in the mind; but wickedness overthrows all these delusions. They are as inscriptions written on sand, and the waters of mortality efface them all, and leave a blank of hopelessness and horror. The candle of the wicked not only, his life, but his hope shall be put out. "The wicked is driven away," &c. This is the *last* overthrow. It is often *sudden.* It is always *terrible,* and certainly everlasting.

APPLICATION.

1. *The gospel has special tidings of joy for the sinner.* "This is a faithful saying," &c. Christ will save from sin, and rescue the sinner.

2. *We appeal to the self-interested feelings of all present.* We urge religion—it is your duty; but we urge it, it is your interest, present and eternal.

3. *Warn the incorrigible.*

LXIX.—THE WATERS OF MARAH.

"And the people murmured against Moses, saying, What shall we drink? And he cried unto the Lord: and the Lord shewed him a tree, *which* when he had cast into the waters, the waters were made sweet: there he made for them a statute and an ordinance, and there he proved them."— *Exodus* xv. 24, 25.

How varied and checkered are the scenes of human life. The triumphant song of Moses had just been sung with grateful ecstasy, and its celestial strains had scarcely died away, when we are called to behold a scene of the directly opposite character.

The Israelites travel three days' journey, in the wilderness, without finding water. This was a very great trial. None but those who have traversed the dreary deserts of the East, can duly judge of this great privation. At length they arrive at Marah, and here was an abundance of the fluid which they wanted; but alas! the waters were bitter, and unfit for use, and "the people murmured," etc. Observe,

1. *That in the journey of life, many are the Marahs, or waters of bitterness.* Man's estate has been disturbed and rendered vexatious and sorrowful through the entrance of sin into our world. "Man that is born," etc. The very figure by which the world is represented. A desert. A wilderness, etc. There are,

1. *Personal waters of bitterness.* Our individual troubles and trials. Our temptations, etc. Every heart knows its own bitterness, etc.

2. *Domestic waters of bitterness.* Family afflictions and troubles. Incorrigible children. Afflictions,—separations,—bereavements,etc.

3. *There are church waters of bitterness.* When the people of God are languid, etc. Sion depressed, etc. When her friends forsake her. Her ordinances neglected, etc. See the case of Nehemiah, ii. 1, etc., and Jeremiah, Lam. vi. 1–4.

4. *There are worldly waters of bitterness.* Distresses arising from our connection with it, etc. Losses, etc.

II. *That even God's people are liable to murmur,when they come to these waters of bitterness.*

1. *This is a truth which the history of the church strikingly attests.* The Israelites. Jacob. Elijah. Jonah.

2. *This is a truth which our own experience confirms.* How prone we have been to do so. Yea, sometimes even in the anticipation of sorrow. How unyielding and self-witted we have been.

3. *This is a truth which exhibits the imperfection and influence of the pious.* It shows that self often predominates. That unbelief still exists. Sense, and not faith, triumphs. That patience has not its perfect work. Such murmuring grieves God—is very offensive to him. Attacks his goodness, faithfulness, and wisdom.

III. *That earnest prayer is the only solace amid the bitter waters of life.* "Moses cried," etc.

1. *Now this is the appointed remedy.* "Call upon me," etc. "Is any afflicted," etc.

2. *This throws the burden on the Lord.*

"Cast thy burden," etc. "Casting all your care," etc.

3. *This secures the interposition of the Divine help.* He has said, he will honor prayer. He has always done so. He ever will do so. He did so in the case of the text.

IV. *That faith in the cross of the Lord Jesus, is the great remedy for all the bitterness of life.* The cross is the wood that makes the waters sweet, and faith in the cross secures the blessing to us.

1. *Now in the cross we learn the transcendent love of God to us.* "If God spared not his own Son," etc.

2. *In the cross we see the real desert of our sins.* Behold the misery we had justly incurred. That cross, in all its agonies, was justly ours. We deserved it. Christ bore it for us, etc. What are our afflictions to those of Jesus?

3. *In the cross we have a model of patience and resignation.* Murmurer, go and see Jesus, calm — resigned — meek — pensive, and he left us an example.

4. *In the cross we have the ground of expectation laid, that God will deal mercifully with us.* He will send us help. He will give consolation, etc. He will make our sufferings the road to exaltation and glory —the path to joy and blessedness, etc. "Yea, doubtless, I count all things but loss," etc.

APPLICATION.

1. *Murmuring at the waters of Marah, only increases our own sorrow.* No joy or consolation ever came by murmuring. It displeases God. Darkens the sky. Blights the spirit.

2. *Let us expect these waters, and thus we shall not be disappointed.* There is a needs-be for the sorrows of life, etc.

3. *Let our prayers be earnest, and have reference to the promises of God.*

4. *To the penitential sinner—look at the cross, and thy sorrow shall be turned into joy, &c.*

———◆———

LXX.—SAVING RELIGION, SPIRITUAL IN ITS NATURE.

"Ye also, as lively stones, are built up a spiritual house, an holy priesthood, to offer up spiritual sacrifices, acceptable to God by Jesus Christ." —1 Pet. ii. 5.

To understand the nature of true religion is of the very highest importance, both to our true peace here and permanent felicity hereafter. It is only true religion that can benefit us. That which is spurious must necessarily blight our expectations, and leave us the victims of disappointment and wretchedness. Myriads there are who profess to be religious, but who will never reap any solid advantages therefrom. To ascertain distinctly the character of God's religion, and his only is genuine, we must examine with the utmost care, his blessed Word,—for here all things are revealed which pertain to life and godliness. With a sincere desire to lead you to a clear and satisfactory understanding of this momentous subject, this series of discourses has been undertaken.

Our first topic is fully expressed in the text. Those who are truly religious, are "a spiritual house," &c. We set out, then, with this essential principle, that Saving Religion is Spiritual in its nature; that is, that it pertains to the heart and mind,—has to do with the inward man. Observe, then,

I. *Saving religion is something more than an intellectual principle.* It is an intellectual principle; but it is also much more, and its intellectuality is of a spiritual kind. Knowledge and wisdom are often put for the whole of religion. Religion is described under the similitude of light, and its disciples are said to be of the day, and not of the night. Sin and ignorance, in scripture, are often synonymous. But observe,

A man may *understand* the truths of the Bible intellectually, and not be possessed of Saving Religion. He may read and see the distinct doctrines and precepts of religion. He may be familiar with its divine truths, and yet be entirely a stranger to the life of God in the soul. He may admit the Divine existence, attributes, works, laws, etc. He may admit the great doctrines relating to Christ's person, work, and offices. He may admit the doctrines of repentance, and see the necessity of holiness, etc. His mind may be well stored with great orthodox truths, and his heart yet be unaffected by Divine grace.

II. *Saving religion is more than a regard to the ceremonials of Christianity.* Christianity has its forms and ordinances. They are, however, but few in number, and very simple in their nature. *Hearing* the word preached. *Baptism into Christ.* Remembrance of his death in the *eucharistic* supper. These are fully enjoined in the Divine word. We have both precept and example for duly and fully regarding them.

But to these there may be the most regular and reverential attention, and yet we may be strangers to saving religion. There are many classes of *hearers*, who derive no saving benefit from hearing. Many may yield assent, and give personal attention to ordinances, without at all feeling their bearing on practical religion, or deriving any benefit from them.

III. *Saving religion is something more than morality.* There can be no acceptable religion without morality, but there may be much morality without religion. The young lawyer was clothed with moral loveliness, so that it is said when Christ beheld him, "he loved him." Saul, of Tarsus, as touching the law, was blameless,—yet was truly ignorant of acceptable piety. However excellent morality is, it is not Saving Religion.

Now observe, then, saving religion,

IV. *Is spiritual in its source.* It is the work of the Holy Spirit of God. Man, in his natural state, is *dead*, dead to God—dead in trespasses and sins. How is he raised and made alive? By the Holy Spirit of God. It is the Spirit that quickeneth. Religion is described as a moral creation. But this is effected by the power of God. "We are his workmanship, created in Christ Jesus unto good works." Religion includes a *new birth*, or regeneration. But we must be born of the Spirit, as well as of water. Religion is described as vegetation, but it is *spiritual vegetation*, the implanting of gracious principles in the soul, and their growth to maturity. It is called *circumcision*, but it is not circumcision of the flesh, but circumcision without hands. " Circumcision of the heart, in the spirit, and not in the letter, whose praise is of God, and not of men." So in the text, the believer is a *building*, or temple, but not of material stones, but a spiritual house to the Lord. He is a temple of the Holy Ghost.

V. *Saving religion is not only of the Spirit, but it is the Spirit's work on our hearts and souls.* It is the renewal of the inward man. The enlightenment of the understanding. The subordination of the judgment to the truth. The cleansing of the conscience. The sanctifying of the affections, and bringing the will into perfect obedience to God's gracious authority. Now all this is inward spiritual work, and is beautifully set forth in one of the Old Testament promises, Ezek. xxxvi. 25. And this agrees with the testimony of the Divine Teacher, "The kingdom of God is within you." And with the declaration of Paul, " The kingdom of God is not meat," &c. Hence, also, it is said of the Christian, that the Spirit of Christ dwelleth in him. That it bears witness with his spirit, &c. "That they are new creatures,—all old things having passed away," etc.

VI. *Saving religion is evidenced in its spiritual effects and fruits.* There will be,

1. *Spiritual desires.* "Hungering and thirsting after righteousness," &c. Desires after holiness. Desires after God's favor and love. Desires of a divine and heavenly nature.

2. *Spiritual affections.* The love of spiritual things. The love of God in the soul. Love of Christians for their spiritual excellences. Love of the truth for the truth's sake. Love of prayer. Love of praise. Love of meditation. Love of holiness. There will be,

3. *Spiritual communion.* Those who understand spiritual things will delight in spiritual fellowship. There will be fellowship with God,—communion with the Father, &c. The thoughts and emotions of the soul will ascend to God. "Oh, God! thou art my God," &c. "On thee, O God! my soul is fixed," &c. "My meditation on thee shall be sweet." *Communion* with kindred minds. Delight in uniting in the means of grace, &c. They will sing and feel,

" And if our fellowship below,
In Jesus be so sweet," &c.

4. *Spiritual exercises.* The exercise of reading and hearing, and prayer and praise, will be performed spiritually. "The true circumcision who worship God in spirit," etc., etc. Finally,

5. *The conversation and life will be spiritual.* No fruit can be different to the tree which produces it. Carnal tree, carnal fruit. The conversation and life will be as is the heart. The new man, spiritual in his nature, will have a conversation according with the gospel. His mouth will issue forth a pure and refreshing stream of gracious conversation. His life will yield holy fruit, acceptable to God, etc.

Learn,

1. *Not to be satisfied with the name and mere forms of religion.*

2. *True religion is internal, in the heart.*

3. *Thus it will produce the fruits of holiness to the praise of divine grace.*

4. *All that is essential to spiritual religion the gospel reveals.* The Word of Truth, and the promise of the Holy Spirit to all who believe.

LXXI.—SAVING RELIGION A RELIGION OF FAITH.

"Therefore *it is* of faith that *it might be* by grace; to the end the promise might be sure to all the seed: not to that only which is of the law, but to that also which is of the faith of Abraham; who is the father of us all."—*Rom.* iv. 16.

It is very clear that man must be saved and accepted of God, on the ground of the one, or of the other, of three things. His intrinsic excellency or freedom from guilt. His good deeds by which he atones for his sins. Or as an act of pure mercy on the part of God. Now as to the first mode, both the Bible and the human conscience testify as to man's guilt. "There is none righteous," &c. "All have sinned," &c. As to the second,—man, by his transgression is so unholy, that he can do no good thing without the gracious help of God. Besides, as a sinner, his life is forfeited to the Divine law which he has broken. He cannot then, redeem his own forfeited life. So that we are shut up to the third process, if saved at all, it must be by a pure, free act of God's grace. This is the reasoning of the apostle, of which the text is the conclusion,—therefore it is of faith, &c. Let us consider,

I. *What is meant by faith.*

II. *What connection faith has with saving religion.*

I. *What is meant by faith.*

Faith is the credence given to testimony. The belief of what is declared. So that there must be some declaration or testimony given to us, before we can believe. Hence, "faith cometh by hearing," &c. Now the testimony or declaration, which is the ground of faith, is the gospel. The glad tidings of God's love to our world, in the gift of Jesus Christ. And that Jesus Christ, the Son of God, came into our world to save sinners. That he died for our sins and rose again, &c. That God was in Christ, &c. And that God in Christ is willing and able to save all who come unto him by Christ. Now this is an epitome of the glorious plan of salvation. Now observe,—All this is distinctly revealed in the Holy Scriptures. These scriptures make known these truths to us, and our faith is demanded in them. Faith, then, receives

this testimony of God as true; that is the intellectual part of faith. Faith heartily and joyously rests on this testimony; that is the experimental exemplification of faith. Faith humbly appropriates the blessings of salvation in Christ to its need, and rejoices in them. *That,* in connection with the other acts of faith, introduces into the soul the *enjoyment* of the blessings bestowed. He then can say,—"He loved me, and gave himself for me." Now the warrant for all this is God's word. He has said, he has so loved the world, &c. I am one, &c. He has sent his Son to save *sinners—I am one.* He came to seek—and to save the lost,—*I am one.* He taketh no pleasure in the death of a sinner,—*I am one,* &c. Whoso cometh, he will in nowise cast out,—I came therefore, &c. We add further, it is the *province of faith* to believe *all that God* has spoken. And to expect, and live and feel, as though we already possessed all that he has *promised.* Such, then, is the *faith* which is an essential principle of religion. Notice, then,

II. *What connection this faith has with saving religion.* (1.) It has not any connection with merit. It is the opposite of this. So says our text. So says the united testimony of scripture. So we have shown in the great truths to be believed. Faith *hears* God's love and mercy in the gospel. Faith sees the Lord Jesus as the only sacrifice for sin. Looks to the cross of Christ entirely. Faith receives the gift of God,—comes with an empty hand, &c. Does nothing that can include the least worthiness. We are saved by and through faith, but not *for* it. But observe the connection of faith,

1. *With the commencement of saving religion in the soul.* By the Word of God the sinner has been brought to see and feel his lost and ruined state. That he is naked, and *faith* receives and puts on the *robe* of salvation. That he is *poor,* and faith receives the pearl of great price, and the unsearchable riches of Divine grace. That he is *guilty,* and *faith* looks to the great *surety alone* for acceptance and pardon. *Polluted,* faith at once plunges into the *fountain,* &c. That he is perishing, and faith rolls the soul on the *one great and precious foundation.* That death and hell are before him, and flies into the city of refuge and is safe. Hence, then, you see how faith has to do with the commencement of religion. Observe,

2. *Its connection with the progress of saving religion.* When a sinner is justified,

that is, pardoned and accepted of God, and regenerated, religion then is only begun.

(1.) There is a progressive work of sanctification. The building up of the soul. The growth of the child of God. The perfection of the graces and virtues,—the meridian noon of holiness and bliss. Now faith believes and meditates on that truth of God's word, by which the soul is fed and nourished. "As babes they desire the sincere milk of the word," &c. "Sanctify them by thy truth," &c. "I commend you to God," &c.

(2.) The life of the Christian is one of trouble and trials. But God has engaged to support and keep,—to sanctify all their afflictions. Now faith looks to the promise and realizes the help, etc. Faith casts all the care and burden on the Lord, etc. Faith calls on the Lord in the day of trouble, etc. Faith sings, Although the fig-tree shall not blossom, etc. "We know that all things work," etc.

(3.) The life of the Christian is one of conflict, as well as of trouble. These conflicts have to do with three enemies : the *world*. This both tries to allure and fascinate, and also to terrify. It labors both to beguile and alarm. How do we overcome the world? "This is the victory," etc. Faith recognizes it as an enemy's country. Looks to the better land. Sings, "This is not *my rest*," etc.

"I seek a country out of sight,
A city in the skies!"

Faith lifts the Christian above it. There is the *unsanctified nature* within. Faith crucifies the flesh. Mortifies the deeds of the body. Brings into the soul the cleansing balm, etc., confesses sin, and obtains forgiveness. Then there is our great adversary, the devil. He tempts and harasses the soul. Faith holds fast to the Divine Word. Satan says, God has forsaken thee. Faith says, God has said, "I will never leave," etc. Satan says, We shall never hold out,—we shall fail to persevere. Faith says, God's grace is sufficient,—the Divine strength shall be given. "As our day is," etc. Satan says, we shall perish after all. Faith says, that Christ's promise runs thus : "My sheep shall never perish," etc. Thus faith is the shield by which we quench all the fiery darts of the devil. Now remember all the appointed means for the *security* and happiness of the Christian life, faith receives and applies, etc. Observe its connection,

3. *With the conclusion of the Christian life, and eternal glory.* The spiritual race is run throughout by faith,—the Christian perseveres till he touches the goal. The sick chamber is irradiated by faith. It supports when the constitution gives way. When pain, etc., indicate the taking down of the tabernacle, etc. "We know," etc. Faith produces resignation to the Divine will. "To live is Christ," etc. Either to wait, as Job said, "I will wait," etc. Or as good old Simeon, "Now, Lord, lettest thou thy servant," etc. And at length the Christian *dies in faith.* Having served God and his generation, he falls asleep in Jesus. Hence as earth recedes,—now faith is lost in the visions of the beatified. The racer is welcomed,—the warrior crowned,—and an abundant entrance given, etc.

Learn,

1. *The inestimable worth of faith.* Have we faith ? Do we credit implicitly the testimony of God ? etc. Do we rest on Christ only ? Do we live the life of faith ? Looking not at the things which are seen, &c.

2. *We see the fearful nature of unbelief.* It disbelieves God's word. Despises God's mercy. Rejects God's Son. Refuses God's pardon. And hence keeps the soul under Divine condemnation and Divine wrath, and then sinks the spirit into the endless darkness of eternal despair.

3. *Call upon all to believe the gospel and live.*

LXXII.—SAVING RELIGION A RELIGION OF LOVE.

"And we have known and believed the love that God hath to us. God is love ; and he that dwelleth in love dwelleth in God, and God in him."—1 *John* iv. 16.

THERE are two peculiar modes of expression in the text, which are in harmony with other passages of Holy Writ, and which will first demand our attention. It is said of the character described, that "he dwelleth in God." Moses in the 90th Psalm, exclaims, "Lord, thou hast been our dwelling-place," &c. The same idea is enlarged upon in the 91st Psalm, v. 1, and 9. It evidently signifies making God the rest, and the chief good of the soul. To trust all *to* him, and to seek all *from* him. Then it is added, "God dwelleth in him." Thus God delights in his people. He is their portion, and they are his portion. Paul speaks of this, 2 Cor.

vi. 16 ; and Romans viii. 9, so ver. 12. Now these two things are essential to saving religion : our dwelling in God, and God dwelling in us. So says the apostle Paul, "That Christ dwelleth in us, except we be reprobates," *i. e.*, disapproved persons. Having explained these parts of the text, we now proceed to that, which is the great subject of our present discourse. Let us consider,

I. *The objects and nature of Christian love :* And,

II. *Its essentiality to saving religion.* Observe,

I. *The objects and nature of Christian love.* We refer,

(1.) *To God.* God is the supreme object of our love. No age, or dispensation, or circumstance, can affect the great commandment, "Thou shalt love the Lord thy God," &c. He is to be the first, the highest object of our affections. Our love to God must be,

(1.) *Filial.* We are his offspring. He is our Father.

(2.) *Reverential.* He is Jehovah, "Lord God, the high and lofty one," &c.

(3.) *Confidential.* Love which trusts in him, relies on him, &c.

(4.) *Grateful.* Our benefactor—our Redeemer. "We love him," &c.

(5.) *Of delight.* Delighting in God—joying in God—blessing God, and being blessed in him. Our love must refer,

2. *To God's people.* The love of the brethren : and it must embrace,

(1.) *All of them.* However different in sentiment, or form of worship. If they love the Lord Jesus Christ in sincerity.

(2.) Not in the *same degree.* This is impossible. Those we have seen—those who are most like Christ. Most lovely, &c. There are Christians who are so repulsive, that it is difficult to love them—*to* others you are *drawn* sweetly and almost *irresistibly.*

(3.) They are to loved *unfeignedly*, in heart. Not merely in pretence or profession.

(4.) *Manifestly.* We are to show forth our love to them. By our kindness of *speech* —by kindness of *spirit*, and of action : Prefer their *company.* "I am a companion of all them," &c. By *praying* for them. Praying for all saints. By doing them all the good in our power. "Do good, and communicate," &c.

(5.) Without respect of persons. Not having men's persons in admiration. Not preferring the rich, and despising the poor. Respect of persons is sinful : and this is a great snare. Then our love,

3. *Must embrace all men.* Our neighbors as ourselves. Even our enemies—those who despise or hate us. Now this love is not the love of complacency or delight, but of deep pity and compassion. Ready to return good for evil—blessings for cursing. "If thine enemy hunger, feed him," &c. Such then are the objects and nature of Christian love. Now we remark,

II. *Its essentiality to saving religion.* It is so,

1. *As love is the very atmosphere of religion.* "Dwelleth in love." The air of the kingdom of heaven is love—pure, spiritual love. It is made so, by the Holy Spirit pervading it ; and the spiritual soul can only live in it, and cannot live in any other.

2. *It is the chief element of the new nature, produced in regeneration.* Born of God,—born from above. Partakers of the Divine nature. Now the old nature is malevolent, its partakers are hateful, and haters of one another.

3. *It is one of the especial fruits of the Holy Spirit.* "But the fruit of the Spirit is 'love.'" Gal. v. 22 : The first and most immediate effect of his divine influence. Now where the spirit of God dwells, there will be his fruits.

4. *It is the necessary badge of Christian discipleship.* "By this shall all men know," &c. Not by,

(1.) Identity of religious features :

(2.) Not by exact agreement of religious phraseology. For Peter complains of Paul : 2 Peter iii. 15, &c.

(3.) Not by uniformity in religious worship, but by loving one another. Christ would have his religion known all the world over, as a *religion of love.*

4. *It is the great New Testament commandment.* The eleventh commandment. "A new commandment give I unto you," &c. See how Christ dwells on it. Emphasizes and reiterates it. See John xiii. 34, see also xv. 12–17.

5. *It is one of the chief features of our resemblance to Christ.* Many things in Christ above our imitation, but here he expects conformity. We are to be imbued with this spirit of our Lord. No other points of likeness can be sufficient, without this.

6. *It is indispensable to fellowship with*

God. If we dwell in the darkness of envy or hatred, then we can have no fellowship with God. If we pray with these elements in our hearts, God will not hear us. The spirit of benignity and love must dwell in us, or God will have no communion with us.

7. *It is the leading element in true happiness.* It is the soul's real bliss. We may say so of *knowledge,* for that is the region of light to the understanding, or intellectual part of man. So also of righteousness, there must be integrity in order to peace. " If ye know," &c. But love is the religion of ecstasy and rapture to the whole soul. Here it finds satisfaction in its kindred region of gladness and delight.

8. *It is the great prerequisite for heaven.* A soul without love, is not only unfit for heaven, but could not enjoy it.

(1.) *The God* of heaven is love.

(2.) *The throne* of heaven rests upon immutable, eternal love.

(3.) *The Lamb* in the midst, &c., is the Saviour who loved, &c.

(4.) *The songs* of heaven all relate to the marvellous love of the Redeemer.

(5.) *The society* of heaven is one of pure unmixed love.

(6.) *The streams* are all flowing with love.

(7.) The absolute *satisfaction,*—the plenitude of bliss is, bathing in the eternal ocean of love.

8. The *law* of heaven which binds God to all the beatified, and all the glorified to one another, is the great Divine law of love. One word more cannot be necessary to show you that—saving religion is therefore a religion of love! We ask in conclusion,

1. *Have you this love to God?* This reverential, grateful feeling towards God? Is it your desire to obey him, please him, and glorify him?

2. *Have you this love to his people, and towards all men?*

3. *This love and happiness are inseparable.*

4. *Want of it and misery are equally so.*

5. A world where it exists not—where selfishness, and hate, and wrath, mark all its inhabitants, is *hell.*

6. Let Christians *cultivate* it. Cherish it —exhibit it; and thus honor.God, and recommend religion.

7. *To the inquiring contrite penitent, God will shed abroad his love in their hearts.*

LXXIII.—SAVING RELIGION A RELIGION OF OBEDIENCE.

" He that hath my commandments, and keepeth them, he it is that loveth me: and he that loveth me shall be loved of my Father, and I will love him, and will manifest myself to him." —*John* xiv. 21.

THERE has been much dispute in the Christian Church, whether salvation is of works or faith. Some have taught a system of mere morality, and have said, that by our own righteousness we are to be saved. Others have taught a system of mere faith, and have said, that faith without works is sufficient. Both of these views are diametrically opposed to the gospel system, as taught by Christ and his apostles. Faith and works are both essential, but in their proper places. Inverted in their position, they are valueless.

Hence in reference to pardon and justification, it is by faith only. " Through this man (Christ Jesus), is preached," &c. " Believe on the Lord Jesus Christ," &c.

Good works are to be the evidences of the genuineness of our faith. Hence James asks, " What doth it profit," &c., ii. 14, &c. Then we see, that in reference to pardon and acceptance with God, it is—faith alone. But that it is productive of good works.

Hence *faith* is the *root*—obedience the fruit.

Faith the *soul* of religion—obedience the body, in which it becomes palpable.

Faith *enters* the Divine family,—obedience shows that we are the children of the family.

Faith receives the kingdom of God— obedience acts with the loyalty of good subjects. Hence Christ declares in the text. Also, ver. 23–24, and chap. xv. 10 and 14. The principle, therefore, of the text is sufficiently established. It is only necessary, then, that we define and specify the nature of that obedience, which is essential to saving religion.

I. *It must be evangelical.* Not self-righteous obedience,—not the mere strivings of the carnal heart,—not the mere respectable morality which will do for the world; but the obedience of the *renewed heart*—the workings of *faith*—the fruit of God's Holy Spirit within us. Not so much *us,* as God working within us. " Nevertheless, I live, yet not I, but Christ liveth in me," &c. " What I am, I am by Christ's grace; and what I do, I do by his grace strengthening me." It is also evangelical, in opposition to *legal* obedience. In legal obedience there is a striving to *obey*, to be saved—to do and *live;* but here in evangelical obedience, I obey, because I am saved—I do, because I *live.* It is essential, therefore, that our obedience be evangelical.

II. *It must be affectionate.* The obedience of love. "He it is that loveth me." "This is the love of God," &c. "If ye love me," &c.

1. *There is slavish* obedience, and this is invariably irksome, galling. Look at the toiling Hebrew in Egypt. The driven Negro.

2. There is the obedience of the mere *hireling.* Theirs is often performed cheerfully, but the eye is ever on the *wages*—on the *reward.* There is no ardent joy, or love to the service. But Christian obedience is *affectionate.* Look at that affectionate child, he heard his father's commands, with delight he hastens to obey. He is happy in obeying! Now this is the reason why God must have first the heart, and then the obedience will be the obedience of love. Rom. vi. 17.

III. *It must be unquestioning.* We must ascertain clearly the will of God, and then do it. Do it without murmuring, or debating, or questioning the propriety of what God demands. Philip. ii. 14, 15. We may not always see the design and fitness; but we should remember our ignorance, and who it is that commands.

It is not customary for servants to question the orders of their masters; or for children to question the orders of parents. How much less, then, should believers question the commands of God. "Thus, saith the Lord" should be ever sufficient. Like Samuel, we should say, "Speak, Lord," &c. Our eyes should be up to the Lord—our ears attent—our feet ready. Like the angels, "Ever hearkening to the voice of his word."

IV. *It should be uniform.* God is to be obeyed at all times. Seasons or days cannot alter his claims, they are ever obligatory. If times could have affected his claims or our duties, then there never had been any need for suffering, for Christ's sake. When friends smile it is not so difficult, but if they frown, hate, revile, or injure. If they forbid, there is the language of the apostles, "We ought to obey God, rather than man." Christian obedience must be the habit of the soul—the golden thread running through the web of life. It must be the walk of the Christian in this the house of his pilgrimage.

V. *It must be universal.* Have respect to all God's bidding. There are things prohibited, and they must be abandoned—avoided. There are positive injunctions, they must be practised. There are positive *institutions* in religion. Profession—faith and *baptism.* Profession of discipleship in the Lord's Supper. Now, both moral and positive institutions must be obeyed. True obedience is only bounded by the divine word. A beautiful picture of this is presented in the record concerning Zacharias and Elizabeth. Luke i. 6. I add,

VI. *It must be persevering.* "He that endureth to the end," &c. "Be thou faithful," &c. "Press toward the mark," &c. The Galatians ran well, but at length were hindered. Of some of Christ's disciples, it is said, "They walked no more with him." Of others—"They made shipwreck." Peter speaks of those who had returned as the dog to its vomit, and the swine that was washed, &c. Hence the exhortations of the apostles. 2 Pet. i. 5–10; chap. iii. 14–17. These then are the great features of that obedience which is essential to salvation. In order to this obedience,

(1.) Seek a filial and willing spirit. Ask of God not only to write his law on your hearts, etc., but to give you the spirit that will delight to do all his commandments.

(2.) Have recourse constantly to the Saviour's grace. Of yourselves you cannot thus obey God. His grace is indispensable. His grace is provided. His grace in answer to prayer will be freely and effectually communicated.

(3.) Rely for acceptance on the great sacrifice. Our souls and services are only acceptable to God through Christ Jesus. All must be laid on that altar, which sanctifies both the worship and the offering. Besides, our infirmities are so numerous that confession of sin, repentance and faith in the Saviour's blood, is constantly necessary. "If we say that we have no sin," &c. Our congregation consists of only two classes.

1. *The obedient, who realize in their experience the text.* To these I read one great and glorious promise. Rev. xxii. 14. "Blessed are they who do his commandments, that they may have right to the tree of life, and may enter in through the gates into the city."

2. *The disobedient.* To these we say, "Turn ye, turn ye, for why will ye die?" "Let the wicked forsake," &c. If not, if you will resolutely set God at defiance, then hearken. Rom. ii. 8, &c.

LXXIV.—SAVING RELIGION A RELIGION OF SELF-DENIAL.

"And when he had called the people *unto him* with his disciples also, he said unto them, Whosoever will come after me, let him deny himself, and take up his cross, and follow me."—*Mark* viii. 34.

THE Lord Jesus not only came to reveal the way of salvation, but also to exhibit all the great features of acceptable piety in his own example. In his discourses we have the great doctrines and precepts of Christianity presented to us. In his life we have these doctrines and precepts exemplified. Thus in the character of Christ, we have exhibited the true spirit of saving religion. In his condescension and conduct, a clear model for Christian imitation. Now this is expressed very distinctly in the text, and more at large, Matt. xvi. 24. Christ's disciples must follow in his steps. They must go after him. Hence he says, "My sheep hear my voice," &c. If we say that we have received him, we must walk also as he walked. True saints are described as "Following the Lamb, whithersoever he goeth." The true Christian "sets the Lord ever before him." "He looks to Jesus, the author and finisher of his faith." Now the Saviour connects this with the spirit and practice of self-denial. The man who is willing to be his disciple, must deny himself, &c. Now it is superfluous to say that the Christian must renounce a course of iniquity—this is too obvious to need proof, or even assertion. But he must be willing to forego even lawful things for Christ's sake. The very essence of self-denial is—to be given up to the will of God, to yield yourselves to *do* it, and *suffer* it, for Christ's sake. Observe,

I. *We must deny our own wisdom, and submit ourselves to the wisdom of God.* Look at this in two or three respects.

1. *In the commencement of a religious course.* The way and principle of our acceptance with God, is very different to the notions of the human mind. We think that we can devise the best plan of returning to God; and the innate conviction is, that we

must do *something*—or have some *recommendation*—some ground of *acceptance* in ourselves. This was the great stumbling-block of the scribes and Pharisees. They would not admit that they were blind and poor, &c. Now this *self* must be denounced, prostrated, crushed, before we can enjoy the divine mercy ; the soul must be dying of hunger, before it is fed. It must be *stripped*, before it is clothed. It must be *perishing*, before the hand of Christ is stretched forth to save. When they had *nothing* to pay, &c. How many are kept out of the kingdom of Christ, because they will not become as little children, and thus enter in the spirit of self-denial.

2. *In the direction of our steps the same truth applies.* Man must be self-guided, or guided of God. How often we think we are sufficient. That we have all the skill, tact, and experience requisite. Lot thought so when he chose the well-watered plains of Sodom. Solomon thought so, and hence made shipwreck. Now the great truth of revelation is—that it is not in *man* that *walks*, &c. Hence this self-wisdom must be renounced. We must commit our way unto the Lord, &c. Our prayer will be, "O Lord, teach me thy paths." "Thou shalt guide me by thy counsel," &c. "Lead me in a plain path," &c. "In all your ways, acknowledge him," &c. To do this *implicitly*, at all *times*, and in all circumstances, is one great exemplification of self-denial.

3. *In reference to extrication from troubles.* Often the Christian is placed in strait and difficult circumstances. Just as the *Israelites* on their approach to the *Red Sea. Jacob* when going to meet Esau. *Daniel* when exposed to the devouring lions. *Peter* in prison. Now in all these cases, God's wisdom directed. They did not trust in themselves. They did not rely on their own understandings. God counselled, and they obeyed. God directed, and they followed. Now this is one great evidence of true self-denial. To renounce our own *wisdom*, and to give ourselves up to the wisdom and will of God.

II. *There must be the utter rejection of all self-righteousness, and entire reliance on the mediation of Christ.* Self ever abased, and Christ ever exalted. To trust to his mediation for every blessing. Not only when we *first come* to God for pardon, but ever afterwards.

(1.) However exemplary to attribute it to

God's grace. "By the grace of God I am what I am,"

(2.) However spiritual to trace it up to the divine influence.

(3.) However useful to give the undivided glory to God.

(4.) In all our services to keep the eye of faith on the mediation of Christ. In *praise*, however fervent. In *prayer*, however earnest and believing. In *duties*, however constant. In the profession of Christ, however consistent. "God forbid that I should glory," &c. "Christ is all, and in all."

III. *In subordinating all self-seeking to the will and pleasure of God.* There are many things that may be laudably desired, and preferred in *themselves*. For instance,

(1.) Mediocrity of condition, rather than adversity. Jacob sought this : so Agar, "Give me neither poverty," &c. But self-denial bows sweetly to God, if it is his will that adversity be our lot.

(2.) Peace rather than opposition and persecution. It is said of the primitive churches, that they had rest, &c. Now it is desirable to have our *privileges*, &c. But self-denial shrinks not from opposition, and odium, and suffering for Christ's sake. Takes up the cross, and cheerfully bears it.

(3.) Health rather than sickness. It is natural and proper to seek health, &c. But self-denial says, in reference to affliction, "The cup which my Father," &c. Now true self-denial *chooses* not—*dictates* not ; but ever seeks to utter the submissive words of Jesus—"Not my will, but thine be done." It can sing with the poet,

"Good when he gives," &c.

Self-denial includes,

IV. *The crucifixion of self, for the good of others.* A man who is a stranger to the spirit of self-denial will stand for all his *own rights*. He will say, I may do this and that. I will only be bound by the great lines of right and wrong. Now what says self-denial, "All things are lawful, but all things are not expedient." Now see this fully illustrated, Rom. xiv. 1. The great principle is laid down, ver. 1. Our duty, ver. 13. This duty applied, 14, 15. Then its general application, ver. 21. The uniform spirit of self-denial is further inculcated, chap. xv. 1, 2. Now I would apply this to *dress*, which others might think *worldly*. To customs in meats or drinks, which others might think *perileus*. And the true principle is, to fore-

go even lawful things for the good of others, 1 Cor. viii. 9. We ought to prefer the salvation of our brethren to all other considerations. Now this is one of the great pillars of the temperance reformation ; it induced me, more than ten years ago, cheerfully to abstain from every inebriating fluid, &c. It is well worthy of the pious consideration of all the people of God.

V. *It involves the putting of ourselves, and all we are and have, at the Lord's disposal.* See v. 35. Christ may call us to great sacrifices and toils. To the loss of liberty, goods, life. Now self-denial would place body, soul, and spirit at the Lord's disposal. Surrendering all to him. Live and die for him. I can scarcely dwell on this, as we have so long basked in the sunshine of prosperity, and have such Christian mercies and privileges. But are we ready to suffer for Christ's sake ? To count not our own lives dear, &c.? Who can answer ? I need not dwell on self-denial being essential to saving religion, the text is decisive. Besides,

(1.) Without it there is no likeness to Christ.

(2.) No assurance of glory. "If we suffer," &c. These then are the *great terms of acceptable piety*. But forget not,

1. Sufficient grace is given.

2. Eternal glory is promised.

LXXV.—SAVING RELIGION A RELIGION OF PRAYER.

"Continuing instant in prayer."—*Rom.* xii. 12.

ALL religions, whether true or false, recognize the duty of prayer. The Mahommedan often approaches God in the name of the Great Prophet. The Pagan bows down to his idol, supplicating good, and deprecating evil. The wild Indian utters his desires to the unseen Great Spirit. Hence it may be said that the religious emotions of the mind, those emotions which are natural to it, lead men, under all circumstances, to the exercise of prayer. Prayer formed one of the leading elements of patriarchal religion. Prayer was a chief exercise under the Mosaic economy,—the tabernacle was for devotion as well as sacrifices,—and the temple was to be a house of prayer for all nations. In the religion of the New Testament this stands prominently out. Jesus was emphatically a man of prayer. When he taught the people, he instructed them how to pray. When he wrought miracles, he sanctified them by prayer. When he was baptized, he prayed. When he was transfigured, he prayed. In his agony in the garden, he prayed more earnestly. When he hung on the cross, his dying breath he spent in prayer. And now exalted on high, seated at the right hand of the Father, he ever liveth to make intercession for us. No proof more can be necessary that saving religion is essentially a religion of prayer. But we ask,

I. *What is prayer?*

II. *What must be its distinguishing features?*

III. *And how instant prayer is to be sustained?*

I. *What is prayer?* Prayer is the presenting of the desires to God. Now this may be done,

1. *Without words.* When the longings of the soul silently, yet earnestly, ascend to God. When the heart ejaculates its wishes, without words, as Nehemiah did when in the presence of the Persian monarch. But while we may pray without audible words, we cannot pray without the heart. The desires must be those of the inward soul. The fervent emotions of the Spirit. And when this is wanting, it is not prayer. Or prayer,

2. *May be expressed in words.* This is the most usual form of prayer. Generally from the fulness of the heart the mouth uttereth. And in praying with words, there may be either words, extemporally conceived and expressed, or they may be in the words of scripture remembered by us, and appropriated as suited to our necessities. Thus many of the prayers of David. Thus the Lord's prayer. Thus the prayers of the apostles in their epistles. And when persons from want of the gift of prayer, or from timidity and fear, cannot thus pray, there can be no reason why they may not use printed forms of prayer, and thus piously make known their requests to God. But it should be the desire of every Christian to have the gift of prayer, that they may be independent of all forms of prayer, and may at all times, and under all circumstances, approach the throne of the *heavenly grace.* Now in prayer, we may appropriately include,

(1.) The adoration and blessing of God.

(2.) Thanksgiving for former mercies,— *with confession* of our sins.

(3.) Deprecation of evil.

(4.) Supplication for the various mercies we need. And,

(5.) Intercession for the Divine blessing to rest on all men. With,

(6.) Pleading; that is, urging our requests, and using the Divine promises, and the mediation of the Lord Jesus, as the ground of our expectation, that our prayers may be answered. Observe,

II. *What must be its distinguishing features?*

1. *Sincerity.* In order to this we must feel our wants,—pray from an inward sense of our need and dependance : there can be no prayer without this. And without this, the service is hypocrisy, or at best a mere formal service. How needful and important to guard against this. "This people draw nigh to me with their mouths, and honor me," &c.

2. *Simplicity.* Not to imagine that we must clothe our desires in words of elegance or grandeur. Remember that the mind can do nothing in this way *equal* to the mind of the lofty Being we *approach.* We should rather study child-like simplicity. How beautifully so, is the Lord's prayer. "Our Father," &c.

3. *Humility.* We must have due thoughts of our own insignificance and unworthiness. If ever we should be bowed down as in dust and ashes, it is in prayer. Think of the majesty and glory of God. The grandeur of his throne. The purity of his nature,—and then look at our pollution and guilt. It is to the lowly that God looks,—with the contrite God dwells. "Though the Lord be high," &c.

4. *Believing confidence.* "He who cometh to God," &c. This is especially insisted on, that we have faith in God when we approach him in prayer. Let us just refer to a few passages of the Divine word on this vital subject : Jas. i. 5, 6. Matt. xxi. 22. Matt. xi. 24. Now our faith in prayer must have respect to two things,

(1.) *God's promise.* And (2.) Christ's mediation. Belief in what God has spoken, and what Christ has done, and is doing for us. Look at the first of these,—Luke xi. 9 & 13. John xiii. 13 & 16–23, &c. Hence the exhortation of the apostle : "Let us come boldly," &c.

5. *With expectation.* That is, we are to pray and watch thereunto. Look for what we have asked. So does the petitioner for the reply of his sovereign. So does the

beggar for the alms he seeks. So should the Christian for the blessings he has sought. Look for the returns of prayer,

6. *With reverential submission.* Deferring all to God's wisdom and love. Leaving the *mode and time* to him who cannot err, bowing to that kindness and love which cannot falter or change. To that faithfulness that endureth through all generations. But the text calls us to *instant* prayer ; that is, to constant persevering prayer. Therefore we ask,

III. *How is it to be sustained?* How are we to be *instant* in prayer? To pray always. "To pray without ceasing," &c.

1. *By continuing to cherish a sense of our entire dependance on God.* Nothing can be more true than this. But we must recognize it—feel it—cherish it. Endeavor to realize it every moment.

2. *By daily intimacy with the Divine word.* We cannot read the scriptures without the flame of devotion being kept alive. If we read the scriptures in the spirit of lowliness, we shall catch the devotional feeling of its sacred writers.

3. *By duly regarding the means of grace.* The public means of grace,—the domestic, —the secret.

4. *By seeking from God the spirit of prayer.* The fire on the altar must never go out. If so, then we must be constantly bringing down the reviving Spirit of God into our souls.

APPLICATION.

1. *How greatly is the spirit of prayer undervalued by numbers of the professing Church.* Hence a speech, a sermon, or meeting, will attract them. But the meeting for devotion is slightly estimated and greatly neglected.

2. *How essentially prayer is connected with every part of experimental and practical religion.* If we would grow in knowledge, we must pray. In grace, pray. In joy. In vigor. In holy maturity. In usefulness. In fitness for life, or meetness for glory.

3. *We call upon the prayerless now to commence a life of prayer.* Seek the Divine mercy. Seek a heart to pray. Seek to enjoy the blessedness of prayer, and seek it this hour in the sanctuary of God.

LXXVI.—THE PRE-EMINENCE OF CHARITY.

"And now abideth faith, hope, charity, these three ; but the greatest of these *is* charity."— 1 *Cor.* xiii. 13.

THE apostle has been largely treating of the various gifts, ordinary and extraordinary, which God had dispensed to the Corinthian Church, ch. xii. v. 4. He then shows the mutual dependancy of the various members of the church on each other, and the spiritual harmony which should subsist between them. He concludes this statement with an exhortation, that they should covet earnestly the best gifts, but annexes to that advice the most beautiful exhibition of Christian charity, which, he affirms, is yet a more excellent way. The superior excellency of charity is then presented over knowledge, over almsgiving, and over faith, even of the most miraculous description, ver. 2. The sum and conclusion of the whole is given thus:— "And now abideth," &c. Let us then,

Define its nature.

Show its supreme pre-eminence. And,

Urge to its acquisition and exercise.

I. *Define its nature.* I need not say that by charity is meant love, and so the text should have been rendered. Now this charity or love must not be confounded with the emotions of mere animal affection or human sympathy. Nor with natural kindness and generosity. Nor with mere amiableness of spirit and temper. Nor indeed with any characteristic of the human heart which may be evinced by man in his unregenerate condition. It is the sacred fire of celestial love, enkindled in the heart by the Holy Ghost, given unto us. It is the spiritual emotion of the new nature, and as such necessarily involves supreme love to God and delight in him. I need not dwell on the infinite and eternal claims he has on our most ardent affection. "We love him because," &c. But the text doubtless contemplates love chiefly in reference to mankind, and wherever love to God reigns, love to man will also be exhibited. The two are inseparable. Now what does it comprise? *Esteem* for man as one of our species. *Affection* for man, as of our kindred. *A benevolent* sympathy with man, as our fellow-heir of misery, trouble, and death. *An intense* desire for his well-being, and a generous readiness to help him and do him good. Now this love has many striking attributes and antagonistical principles. Among its attributes the apostle specifies,

1. *Kindness.* This is its breath. Its language. Its temper. Its conduct.

2. *It is long-suffering.* Bears and forbears. Not hasty and impetuous. Not easily provoked.

3. *It is ingenuous and unsuspecting.* Is not given to surmisings. "Thinketh no evil," &c.

4. *It weepeth over sin and sinners.* "Rejoiceth not in iniquity," &c. It delighteth in goodness wherever it beholds it. Its chief antagonistical principles are,

(1.) *Pride.* Pride treats men with haughtiness and contempt. "Charity vaunteth not itself," &c. "Doth not behave," &c.

(2.) *Selfishness.* Selfishness isolates man. Makes him the centre and end of all his actions. "Charity seeketh not her own," &c. Selfishness is the rankest and vilest idolatry of which man can be guilty, and the most malevolent and withering feeling which can curse and blight the soul.

(3.) *Prejudice.* Prejudging the character or principles of men. How it has separated nations ; divided the church ; alienated friends ; and prevented the free and heavenly flow of gospel charity in the world. Such then is the nature, and such the attributes, and such the antagonistical principles of charity.

II. *Show its supreme pre-eminence.* We assert its pre-eminence over gifts, knowledge, faith, hope, and all other moral elements in the world. Now this is manifest if you consider,

1. *It is the essential nature of God.* It is not so much a perfection of the Deity as his nature. God is love. Pure, unmixed, infinite, changeless, everlasting love. All we know of God proves it. His name. His works. His providence. His wondrous act of sending forth his Son, &c. Paradise. Even the fallen earth. Heaven. Yea— hell itself.

2. *It is the great bond of all unions in the universe.* I begin with the highest and most sublime. (1.) *God in our flesh.* God in the person of Jesus Christ. Was not this incarnate love? The embodiment of Jehovah's goodness. (2.) The union of God and the regenerated spirit. "He that dwelleth in God," &c. (3.) The union of all holy, believing souls, with each other. It is this charity which is the bond of perfectness. (4.) The union of angelic hosts with the human family. The love of Christ has secured their friendship, &c. So that burning with the seraphic flame they are all ministering spirits, &c. Now the absence of love has been the great cause of all the divisions, alienations, strifes, &c.

3. *Love will introduce and constitute the grandeur of the millennial age.* I know it will be a millennium of knowledge,—of holiness,—of peace,—and Divine glory. But its essential grandeur will be, that it will be the golden age of love. Then will be realized the song—"Glory to God," &c. The law of the world will be the law of love, and nothing shall disturb, or vex, or destroy, in all God's holy mountain. Every man will reflect the likeness of God, and every man's heart will overflow with fervent and unfeigned love to his fellow-man.

4. *Love is of eternal endurance, and will form the chief bliss of the beatified forever.* Names, creeds, and sectarian distinctions, which have been so many denominational niches of exclusiveness, will be swept away forever. The *knowledge* of the earth will become invisible before the blaze of heaven's glory, as the radiant stars are seen not when the sun shineth in his splendor. Faith will be ratified in sight and realization, and hope in the fountain of ineffable blessedness ;— but love will still hold her dignified position, and be as essential to the enjoyment of heaven as it was to the happiness of earth. The spark will then not be lost, but become a flame. The drop not absorbed, but swollen and increased to a river ; and flow on, and on, and on, to all eternity.

III. *Urge to its acquisition and exercise.* Now I urge it,

1. *For its own sake.* It has no compeer in regard to intrinsic excellency. It is the brightest gem in the crown of the Redeemer. It is the light, and joy, and glory of heaven.

2. *For your own sake.* If you would have the first fruits of heaven on earth, love will impart them. If you want perfect bliss and enduring joy, love will insure them. If you want both the badge and spirit of a Christian, love will confer them. If you would dwell in God and God in you, and thus obtain a perfect meetness for glory, love will infallibly secure it.

3. *For the Church's sake.* The church wants higher exhibitions of purity—more of the spirit of self-denial,—more of the devotedness of enlarged generosity,—more of the meekness of the Redeemer's lovely dis-

position. But all these would follow if the church were baptized into the spirit of intense and celestial love. Thus she would put on her beautiful garments, and become the joy of the earth and the reflection of heaven.

4. *For the world's sake.* "The world which lieth," &c. Oh, what does it want? More *light*,—but love will diffuse it. More *liberty*,—nothing but love will melt down the fetters and chains of oppression and slavery, and own every man an equal, a friend, a brother. We want the annihilation of crimes, and the restoration of the more debased orders of mankind. Physical restraints, prisons, tortures, and a scaffold, are almost powerless,—nothing but love will restore men to the emotions of humanity, goodness, and mercy. We *want wars* to cease unto the ends of the earth, but love alone shall be the radiant rainbow, spanning in its celestial embrace all the nations of the earth, so that the hellish profession of arms shall be abolished, and men shall not learn war any more. I urge it,

5. *For Christ's sake.* All the true followers of Jesus are identified with his cause and concerned for his glory. This world was created by him and for him. He was offered a sacrifice for its guilt, and he is to exercise his sway of grace over it from the rivers to the ends of the earth. "He shall see of the travail of his soul," &c. But he will accomplish this by the agency of men, and the instrumentality of means. But love alone will provide the men, fit them for their work, and render the agency of heaven, under the Holy Spirit, successful. Read with me, 2 Cor. v. 13–15. Love is the great qualification of the preacher at home, and the missionary abroad,—of the tract distributer, and especially of the Sabbath-school teacher. Love will thrust men into the vineyard, and sustain them in their toils. Nothing is wanted but a pure church, burning with love to evangelize the world, and hasten the period when the jubilee anthem shall be sung. Halleluia, &c. for the kingdom of this world, &c.

APPLICATION.

1. *Have we this love in our hearts?* Does it live, and glow, and burn within us? Is it influential on our hearts, spirits, conversation, lives? Is it evident to men, and does it reflect the image of the ever-blessed God?

2. *All our duties and obligations should be moved by this power.* All other motives are necessarily inferior, and should be subordinate.

3. *It is the duty, interest, and happiness of the sinner to receive and love the Lord Jesus.** Finally, let the genuine fruit of love be seen in our liberality on this interesting and momentous occasion, &c. Love to the dear children who are the germs of the next generation. To be blessings or curses to society. The friends or the enemies of Jesus. The ornaments or adversaries of the Christian church.

LXXVII.—JUDE'S PRAYER FOR THE SAINTS.

"Mercy unto you, and peace, and love, be multiplied."—*Jude* 2.

Our text is the benevolent Christian desire of the apostle Jude, who was a son of Alpheus and a brother of James. You will remember that it was this servant of Christ who presented that interesting question to the Redeemer:—"Lord, how is it that thou wilt manifest?" &c. It is supposed that he wrote this epistle about the 65th or 66th year of the Christian era. It has been usual to denominate this a catholic epistle, as it seems to have been addressed to the saints of Christ in general, and not to any particular class or congregation of believers. Hence it is inscribed "To them that are sanctified," &c. Our present meditation has to do immediately with the benevolent salutation with which it commences. "Mercy," &c. Observe, the text contains three distinct objects of the apostle's desire.

I. *Mercy.*

II. *Peace.*

III. *Love.* And that they all might be multiplied.

I. *He desires for them mercy.* Now this desire may include both the exercise of mercy towards them, and the exhibition of mercy by them. Indeed one is supposed ever to flow from the other. Divine mercy unto you. Observe,

(1.) They were already the subjects of mercy. Mercy had called and sanctified them. And yet,

(2.) They still required its communica-

* Preached on a Sabbath-school anniversary.

tion,—and for this the apostle prays. Now they need it,

1. *In its sustaining and preserving power.* "Hold thou me up," &c. "Kept by the power of God," &c. In perils. In difficulties. In weakness, &c. All their hope and safety is in God's mercy.

2. *In its restraining influence.* The restraints of Divine grace are of the highest moment. Numberless are the sins of the best,—but how many more would have been their apostasies, but for the restraining grace of God. God often keeps his people out of the way of evil. Preserves them from the edge of the precipice. Keeps from falling into the sins which do so easily beset us, &c. David blessed God who had kept him from evil.

3. *In its supplying bounty.* All our blessings are the streams of Divine mercy. So the apostle knew of the need of the saints of God, and this need in all its variety can only be met by mercy. All temporal, all spiritual, and all eternal good proceeds from the Divine mercy.

4. *In its restoring and sanctifying efficiency.* Infirmities and sins pertain to the holiest and the best. How often evil is contracted. Spots on our garments. Spirit cleaves to the dust, &c. Feet slide, &c. Now it is mercy that must restore and sanctify. Forgive our sins, and heal our diseases.

5. *In its accepting condescension.* "We labor whether present or absent," &c. Now our acceptance is all of mercy. Abstract justice never could accept. Nor abstract purity. But God beholds us in mercy,— and thus in Christ Jesus we are accepted of him. So also our services and obedience.

6. *In its crowning glory.* Mercy must lay the foundation, rear the structure, and bring on the head-stone. Mercy to finish the work of grace, and mercy to bestow the rewards of glory. Eternal life is the crowning mercy. "The Lord grant that he may find mercy," &c.

II. *Peace.* Here we may include,

1. *Divine peace within us.* This is ever the fruit of mercy. When God has forgiven, &c., in mercy, then he sheds his peace abroad in the soul. Being justified by faith, we have peace, &c. The storm is allayed. The waves are still, and behold in the soul the peace of heaven. Harmony and joy prevail where strife and confusion reigned. The dove hovers where the vulture only dwelt. The lamb lies down where the lion roamed abroad.

2. *Sacred peace reigneth over us.* Being under the control of peace—subjects of the Prince of peace. Breathing the spirit of peace. Striving for peace. Not the victims of confusion, but peace. Not the slaves of strife, but the sons of peace. When this exists, there will be a pacific spirit towards all men. The mind, and heart, and tongue, and character, will be all pacific. Peace *exemplified.* Peace *makers,* &c. He desireth in the salutation.

III. *Love.* "And love be multiplied."

1. *The love of God towards us.* Doubtless there are degrees of this. Some are more beloved of God than others. God admires and delights in some more than others. We see this in all ages. Hence Enoch and Abraham, and Moses and David. Hence Christ's regards were special towards John, and James, and Peter. He desires that God may delight in you. That his love may be of the highest degree. Of the most copious abundance. Incessant in its manifestation. Transforming and satisfying. That God might rest in his love, &c.

2. *The love of saints towards God.* Ah! here is the great and lamentable deficiency.

> "Our love to Him so faint, so cold,
> His love to us so great."

Now, love to God is the very essence of Christianity. The very life of piety. The very soul of religion. It should be ardent, increasing, supreme, constant, and ever flowing with admiration and delight. He requires that we love him with all our heart, &c. How we should desire and pray.

> "Come, Holy Spirit, heavenly dove,
> With all thy quick'ning powers,
> And shed abroad a Saviour's love,
> And that shall kindle ours."

3. *The love of believers towards one another, and towards all men.* The evidence of our love to God is to be seen in the unfeigned love we have to one another. Often this love is feeble when it ought to be fervent. Often contracted when it ought to be expanded. Often selfish when it ought to be liberal, &c. It ought to be towards all saints, and *in deed* and *in truth.* So also it should include all men. The ignorant and perishing. Our enemies, and the enemies of the Redeemer.

Let the subject,

1. *Lead to self-examination.* How do we stand in reference to mercy, peace, and love?

2. *We should be concerned for their increase.*

3. *Labor to increase it* by faith and prayer, and devotedness to God.

LXXVIII.—THE CHARGE AGAINST THE CHURCH AT EPHESUS.

"Nevertheless I have *somewhat* against thee, because thou hast left thy first love."—*Rev.* ii. 4.

THE text is addressed to the Church of Christ at Ephesus. Ephesus was a celebrated city of Ionia, in Asia Minor, forty-five miles S. E. of Smyrna, built on the side of a hill on the river Cayster, and about five miles from the sea. It was the principal mart as well as the metropolis of the proconsular Asia, and was greatly renowned on account of its magnificent temple erected to Diana. The great apostle of the Gentiles visited this city when on his way to Jerusalem. Acts xviii. 19. He afterwards paid a second visit to it, and faithfully labored in the gospel of Christ for the space of two years. Here the gospel effected mighty changes in the hearts and lives of many of the Ephesians. See Acts xix. 19, &c. To the church established here the apostle addressed one of his most rich and interesting epistles, about five years after he had preached the gospel unto them. It was about thirty years after this that the beloved and holy John was expressly directed to make known to them the will of God, of which our text forms a part. Fervent religion had declined, a spirit of formalism prevailed, and hence the threatenings with which the address concludes. Long since has that threatening been put in execution. It is described now as being a mere heap of stones, and a few mud cottages, without one Christian residing in it. Not only is the Church of Christ extinct, but the once far-famed city of Ephesus is no more. Happy, if only the Christians of Ephesus could be included in the charge of the text—we fear its truths are applicable to some here—yea, to some in every Christian congregation.

Let us then,

I. *Examine the charge made.*

II. *The counsel given.* And,

III. *The threatening appended.*

I. *The charge made.* Observe, it is not licentiousness of conduct, corruption of doctrine, neglect of discipline. It is not the apostasy of the members of the church of Ephesus, but it is the declension of their spiritual affection—the loss of their first love.

(1.) Now, vital religion consists very essentially in love to Jesus Christ. Hence the Saviour's address to Peter. Hence the malediction, "If any man love not," &c. Hence the declaration, "God is love," &c.

(2.) Now, the first love of the Christian is usually very fervent and intense. *"First love."* How ardent. How glowing. How cheerful. How self-denying. How influential. See it evinced in the spiritual and grateful conversation. See it in the earnest reading of the Word. See it in the early and regular attendance in the sanctuary. See it in the liberality and zeal for the cause of Christ. See it in the love of devotion and meditation in the closet, &c. Observe, then,

(3.) The loss of this *first* love. Not of all love. Not of esteem and confidence, &c., but this *first* love. How the picture I have drawn is reversed! Conversation less religious. Bible more neglected—prayer less regarded—ordinances less prized—liberality less exhibited—ministers less esteemed—the world, &c., more in favor, &c. Religion now more of duty, less of privilege—more of service, less of pleasure—more of constraint, less of choice. Ah, what says the Bible—the closet—the pew—but more, the conscience?

II. *The counsel given.*

1. *Meditative remembrance.* Remember from whence, &c. Look back to your high, and holy, and blessed standing. Think of the period when ye were the inhabitants of the rock—elevated, distinguished, happy. A bright prospect of glory. And now in the desert, yea, in the maze—depressed, gloomy, &c. Remember and ponder well the subject.

2. *Repentance.* Change your minds. Return to your first views and feelings respecting your souls and Christ Jesus. Regret the change. Sorrow over the deterioration. Mourn over your backslidings, confess your sins. "Return unto the Lord," &c.

3. *A re-performance of first duties.* Begin as at first. Be diligent, lively, persevering, prayerful as at first. For Christ, and his love, and his gospel, and salvation are now equally as precious. Now, mark,

III. *The threatening appended.* This counsel neglected, God declares what he will do. "Remove the candlestick," &c. It is said that this admonition had a good effect. That they were awakened to fresh zeal, &c., but afterwards fell into the corruption which overspread the Christian world. The threatening is the extinction of the church. Christ forsaking it, &c. Then Ichabod, &c. Now, this will equally apply to individual members. Christ will have the intense, fervent love of his people, or he will abandon his residence. Think of this, and remember how David prayed against it. "Cast me not," &c. If he departs, nothing will be left but dreariness, discomfort, despondency, apostasy, and ruin. "If thou forsake him, he will cast thee off forever." Let the subject then lead,

1. *To personal self-examination.* Does it address me? Am I the person? Oh, do this faithfully. In the light of God's word. With prayer for the Holy Spirit's assistance, &c. "O Lord, search me," &c.

2. *To a reconsecration of ourselves to God.* This is oftentimes necessary. Our condition is perilous. Temptations very numerous, &c.

3. *Let it urge to constant vigilance.* Be vigilant, &c. Let me urge this on young converts, &c. Live near to God. Cleave to the Lord. Give diligence, &c. Watch your lips. Be particular in your associates. Guard against the world. Trust not your own hearts. Exercise constant faith in Christ and earnest prayer, &c. Wait on the Lord, &c.

4. *Some never have loved Jesus Christ.* How ungrateful, base, dangerous. O reflect, repel, believe, &c.

LXXIX.—GOD'S PRESENCE THE SECURITY OF THE CHURCH.

"God *is* in the midst of her: she shall not be moved: God shall help her, *and that* right early."
—*Psalm* xlvi. 5.

THE penning of this psalm, and the occurrence on which it was written, are alike unknown. But its spirit and meaning cannot be misunderstood. It is the triumphant song of the church of God in the midst of enemies, perils, and revolutions. The language is very graphic, the similes bold, and the spirit noble, enterprising, and exulting.

You are aware, I presume, it was one of Luther's favorite psalms. In his day, amidst the changes and commotions which surrounded him, he used to say, "Let us sing the forty-sixth psalm," &c. The text is applicable to the church of God in all ages, and never more so than at the present crisis.

All ecclesiastical communities are in a state of excited activity. Abroad in the distant East, the ancient churches of those countries are in extreme commotion. In general the spirit of inquiry is arousing the myriads who had sunken down into the quiescence of popery. Our missionary stations are attacked not only by pagan priests, but by those of the Roman hierarchy. At home, the gross and superstitious spirit of the Tractarians has threatened the overthrow of godliness in the Episcopal communion. It is quite clear that human authority in matters of religion was never more feeble in its power; and the day is coming when all systems of religion will be brought to a fiery ordeal, and none but the spiritual and the pure shall come forth without loss and ruin. But of the true church we may confidently exclaim, "God is in the midst of her," &c.

Observe then,

I. *The church to which the text will apply.* And,

II. *The declaration concerning it.*

I. *The church to which the text will apply.* Of course we believe there is only one true church of God; and we equally believe that *no* section in the world has a right to that *title* exclusively. We say exclusively. Many may claim it. For instance, the Romish church does so most boldly. The Church of England, &c. But we believe the true church to consist of all true believers, in the Lord Jesus Christ, in every part of the world. We believe there are such in all religious communities. That no religious denomination has every mark of a true church. Excellences and defects exists everywhere, and in every sect. But in the midst of all there is a true catholic church, constituted of all who love the Lord Jesus, &c. And it is to this true spiritual church, the text refers.

The church is an ark of many compartments. A house, having many rooms. A garden with many beds. An army of many regiments. A tree of many branches. A body of many members. A building of many stones. A city of many streets. A kingdom of many towns. A flock of many sheep. The converted, regenerated, God-fearing, and God-serving of all communities, belong to the true church of God.

II. *The declaration concerning it.* The first relates,

1. *To the Divine presence.* The church is of Divine formation, and God dwells in it. He says, "This is my rest;" "Mine eyes and my heart," &c. Wherever his people meet, &c. He is so,

(1.) *By the power of his truth.* The church is the depository and garrison of the truth. The truth is the reflection of God's mind—the utterance of his heart. The diffusion of his effulgent light. Hence there is as much of God, as of pure unadulterated truth. He is present,

(2.) *In the recognition of his ordinances.* God's ordinances are all symbolical of certain blessings and privileges. *Preaching* is the publishing of the glad news, and he is with the preaching of the gospel alway, &c. *Baptism* is the emblem of our regeneration, our spiritual death and resurrection with Christ, and he is there to accept the consecrated offering of body and spirit to his service. The *Lord's Supper* is the reflexion of the Paschal meal, and the symbol of the celestial banquet, and he is there to bless the provision of his house, &c. *Prayer* is the drawing nigh to God, and to such he is pledged to draw nigh.

(3.) *By the residence of his Spirit.* John xiv. 16, &c., xv. 28. The Spirit is the life, and strength, and joy of the church,—its light, and hope, and glory. The other declaration relates,

2. *To the permanency of the church.* "She shall never be moved." Mark,—particular sects in their visible forms, &c., may decay and perish. The true church may be persecuted and oppressed, as in Egypt and Babylon. The early Christian church—the spiritual church in the valleys of Piedmont—in France, &c. The primitive church in this kingdom. The missionary church in Tahiti, &c. Apostasies may exterminate churches from certain localities. As of the churches in the East, &c. Speculations and controversies may disturb and separate the members of the churches from each other; but still the true church of the living God shall never be moved. Never razed—blotted out—destroyed. For this would,

(1.) *Falsify predictions.* The stability, and permanency, and progress, and glory of the church in the earth are the subject of prophetic testimony—"The mountain of the

Lord's house," &c. "Her converts are to outnumber the drops of the dew," &c. All nations are to flow into her, &c. See Isa. lx. 18. "The kingdoms of this world," etc.

(2.) *It would violate promises.* Rich—numerous — express — repeated -- precious promises. God has engaged "to watch it every moment." "To keep it day and night." To be its wall of fire and glory. To bless her friends, and confound her enemies.

(3.) *It would blight Messiah's expectations.* He has redeemed it—called it—chosen it—washed it—prays for it. Its glory—its joy—its prosperity are *his*. His *desire*. His *reward*. Isa. liii. 10.

(4.) *It would disappoint the hopes of the redeemed.* God's people have ever identified their best interests with the church. They have lived—labored—suffered and died for this—untold myriads in heaven—countless thousands on earth. The kingdom must come—truth shall triumph—the church shall be glorified.

APPLICATION.

1. *Are we members of the true church?* What an honor—privilege.

2. *Are we identified with its interests?* "If I forget," etc. "Pray for the peace," etc.

3. *It is our duty to labor, hope, and rejoice, &c.*

LXXX.—THE CHRISTIAN A NEW CREATURE.

(A New Year's Sketch.)

"Therefore if any man *be* in Christ he is a new creature: old things are passed away; behold, all things are become new."—2 *Cor.* v. 17.

It is evident from Scripture that man does not come into the world a religious being. Neither is religion a something which takes possession of him as a matter of course. Nor is it necessarily imparted by parental instruction and example. The heart of man naturally is opposed to God. Far from God—unlike God. So that religion is a great and manifest revolution in the soul. The overthrow of Satan's empire, and the establishment of the kingdom of God in the heart. It is being engrafted into Christ. It is the renovation of all the moral powers. It is the recovery of the lost, and it is life from the dead. Our text is exceedingly graphic and forcible. "If any be in Christ," &c. Observe then,

I. *The new moral creation.* And,

II. *Its unmistakable evidences.*

I. *The new moral creation.* This is partly described, Eph. ii. 10. Now in the moral creation there are several resemblances to the Divine mode of operation in the creation of the world.

1. *It is effected by his word.* "He spake," &c. "By the word of the Lord," &c. So is it in the new creation. He effects the conversion of the soul by his word. "The law of the Lord is perfect, converting the soul." Hence the children of God are born again of the incorruptible seed, even of the Word of God. Hence the apostle says, "Our word came not unto you," &c. "Ye shall know the truth," &c. The Divine word is the sword of the spirit by which he wounds, and it is the healing balm by which peace is whispered to the soul. As in the old creation,

2. *The first production is light.* The first mandate that disturbed the silence of untold ages was, "Let there be light!" So it is in the new creation. The work of grace begins by the opening of the eyes of the understanding. A sight of our sin, and misery, and peril, and helplessness. And then a sight of God's love, Christ's merits, and the way of salvation by faith in his name. Ye who were sometime darkness, are now *light,* &c. Children of the *day,* &c. As in the old creation,

3. *It is holy and good.* All God's works reflected his glory and declared his praise. "The heavens," &c. So this more especially. It is the renewal of the mind in the Divine likeness. A new heart is given, and a holy spirit. There is now order instead of confusion and chaos,—beauty instead of deformity,—righteousness instead of sin,—goodness instead of enmity and malevolence. There is the loveliness, docility, and sweetness of the little child. Now observe,

II. *The unmistakable evidences of this new creation.* Now the evidences are not equally striking and sudden. Some are moral and gentle by nature and habit. Then the process is exceedingly gradual, and almost imperceptible. Others profligate and abandoned, and the change is sudden and deeply marked. We may see this difference in Lydia and Saul. Still the evidences of conversion are represented in the text as being,

1. *Palpable.* Old things depart,—chaos, darkness, &c., pass away. Light, and order, and beauty, are introduced. The desert and the thorn pass away. The garden and the fig-tree appear. The valley of dry bones passes away. The living army, the host of God's elect, appear. The corpse, and its corruption, and its putrescence, pass away, and the living man appears.

2. *Universal.* "Old things." The whole of them, and all things become new. This change extends the mind and its faculties,—all are *renewed.* To the heart, and its passions, all are changed. To the spirit, and its emotions, all are renovated. Then the change will be indicated in the conversation and daily walk. "All things," &c. It is a change,

3. *Most admirable.* Hence the exclamation, Behold! It is worthy of the gaze and attention of all intellectual beings. God beholds, and promises his work to be good. The Saviour beholds, and sees of the travail of his soul, &c. The Spirit beholds, and takes up his abode in the hallowed temple of the new-born Spirit. Angels behold, and there is joy, &c. The pious behold, and glorify God in them and over them. But let us enlarge on some points of this new creation.

(1.) There will be *new* habits. Who were his companions? Where did he spend his time? What was his reading? What the end of his life? Now, behold, they are all new.

(2.) There will be new *dispositions.* Formerly disposed to pride. Now to humility. To vanity and praise of men,—now the honor of God. Formerly avaricious,—now liberal. Formerly selfish,—now good and generous. "All things," &c.

(3.) There will be new tempers. Some do think that religion will change every thing but the temper. If the temper be not changed, there is no religion. It is a delusion—a great, egregious fallacy. There is that *angry* temper. There is that *wrathful* temper. There is that *sullen* temper. There is that *ungovernable,* &c. Are these evidence of religion? What a libel! What a farce! What a cheat! It is the religion of the devil of darkness and of perdition. Such Christians are a byword to scoffers—a curse to their families—a stumbling-block to inquirers, and a reproach to religion. No! my text is true. "All things," &c. There will be meekness. There will be mercy. There will be the lovely and the good reflected. There will be self-govern-ment.

(4.) There will be *new* purposes and de-signs. The natural man liveth to himself. He seeketh his own, &c. The new man seeks to glorify God. He desires and pur-poses to please him. Whatsoever he does, &c. He liveth to the Lord, &c.

(5.) New expectations and hopes. Ask the careless about his destiny, &c. He is like a man in the dark. Or a mariner whose vessel is driven hither, &c. All is involved in perplexing uncertainty. The new crea-ture is the subject of a Divine hope. Begot-ten again to a lively hope. He is looking for that blessed hope, &c. And this hope maketh not ashamed, &c. Finally,—new pleasures and joys. Those of old were the pleasures of sense, and sin—sensual, short-lived, followed by remorse and bitterness. Like the crackling of thorns, &c. The Christian's pleasures are spiritual, heavenly, and divine. They are often unspeakable and full of glory. Yet they are but the drops from the eternal source. " For in thy presence," &c.

APPLICATION.

1. To whom does the text apply? How exalted, blessed, and happy.

2. Who will seek this state on this day? It is attainable. Now, by all. On gracious terms. " To as many as received him," &c.

3. This state is essential to eternal life. " Except a man be born again," &c.

LXXXI.—THE SENTENCE OF DEATH.

(*A New Year's Sketch.*)

"Therefore thus saith the Lord: Behold, I wilt cast thee from off the face of the earth: this year thou shalt die, because thou hast taught re-bellion against the Lord."—*Jer.* xxviii. 16.

THE book of human destiny is in the keeping of Jehovah, and no man, however wise, can tell what to-morrow will bring forth. Ignorance of the future is one of the evidences of God's goodness to us, and care over us. To see clearly the page of our onward history, would often incapacitate alike for present duty and enjoyment. Yet we may indulge a little in probable conjec-ture. Supposing that book were handed to

you, and you were allowed to peruse the records of the year on which you have en-tered. *One* would find that the record would be dark and ominous—a year's trou-bles, and bereavements, and sorrows. *An-other* would find that it would be a year of moral deterioration, and that his downward path would be rapid and fearful. *Another,* that continued procrastination had driven away the striving Spirit, and that conscience would become callous and seared. *Another,* that his winding-sheet and shroud were already woven, the wood of his coffin dry and ready, and he would see written in char-acters of terrific solemnity—" This year shalt thou die." The text was spoken to a wicked, false prophet (see v. 15), and was carried into execution on the seventh month, ver. 17.

I reminded you before, that in a congre-gation of this size, the annual mortality would be from ten to twelve persons. So that it would be next to a miracle if the text should not be realized in the history of many present. Ought not the question to arise in every mind, " Lord, is it I?" Does the text belong to me? It is not for the preacher to say to whom it is applicable. But let us just consider,

I. *The grounds of probability of the text being realized in us.* And,

II. *The influence which even this proba-bility should exert upon us.*

I. *The grounds of probability of the text being realized in us.*

1. *From the precarious tenure on which life is suspended.* No marvel that men should die. The wonder is, that we should live. So many operations necessary to pre-serve life. Seeds of mortality sown in our mortal bodies. Often breathe the atmo-sphere of sickness and mortality.

" Our life contains a thousand springs,
    And dies if one be gone :
Strange that a harp of thousand strings,
    Should keep in tune so long."

One violent spasm might stop the heart. One fit of coughing may prevent respiration, or break a blood-vessel. One little obstacle cause the blood to rush to the head and suffuse the brain. One small wound fester, inflame, and kill. One cold introduce the seeds of insidious consumption or fearful fever. Just think of these things, and do not wonder that we say, " This year you may die."

2. *From the events of the past.* How many died last year, who bade fair to live. Not only the aged and infirm, and afflicted and delicate,—but the hale and robust, and vigorous and active, and young. Many with bright prospects. In important stations. Ministers, philanthropists, statesmen, &c. Many of the most likely for life. Now such have been all past years, and this therefore will no doubt be the same, and form no exception to the rule.

3. *From the previous indications which afflictions have given you.* Some of you have suffered great afflictions during the past year. Had narrow hair-breadth escapes. Many loud warnings. Now these are designed to be subject-matter for serious reflection. They proclaim your mortality, and remind you that this year *you may* die. To many this probability is increased,

4. *From the evidences of old age and decay.* What says that feebleness—that paralyzed trembling—that hesitation of gait—dimness of sight—and other infirmities of the senses? Others may go before you, the sun may go down at noon-day, but it must at evening. The night is surely approaching, which to you must be the night of death.

II. *The influence which this probability of death should exert upon us.*

1. *Should it not lead to solemn inquiry?* We ask,

(1.) What is death? The extinction of animal life. The cessation of existence on the earth. The separation of body and soul. The return of the body to the dust.

(2.) From what does it remove us? From the world in which we live. From the society of friends, &c. From the Christian sanctuary and the means of grace. From the field of hope. From the sphere of gospel mercy.

(3.) To what does death introduce us? Into the immediate presence of God. And thence to heaven or hell,—glory or perdition. To the society of the beatified, or to the company and regions of the lost.

2. *Should it not lead us to reflection?* Two questions of importance.

(1.) Am I fit to die? Is sin forgiven? Have I a new heart? Have I a title to eternal life?

(2.) Am I preparing to die? There is an evangelical fitness, and a spiritual readiness. Both necessary. Are my worldly affairs in an orderly, settled state? Do I often think of death? Pray in reference to it? Watch, that I may not be surprised? Be ye therefore ready, &c.

2. *Should it not lead us to activity?* When there is much to be done, and a small amount of time for doing it, activity is especially important! Two passages :— "Whatsoever thy hand findeth," &c. "I must work while it is day," &c. What claims are there on me? Family—Church of Christ—The world! My talents, time, and wealth, are God's, &c. It is the Christian's glory to die in the field of labor. Working for God and eternity, &c. Surely no time for idleness and trifling.

APPLICATION.

1. *To the unconverted.* How awful if you should die, &c. I beseech you, consider,—repent. Flee to Christ. Do so this very evening. Delay not—for behold, the Judge may be even at the door.

2. *To the young of this congregation.* Do not think the text is of no importance to you. This year may be your last. Several young persons have died from our midst the last year. Religion will make you fit for life and ready for death.

3. *To those who fear God.* If the text should be realized in your experience, that passage will be fulfilled—"Better is the day of a man's death," &c. Then it will be farewell trials, sorrows, enemies, temptations, sins. Welcome purity,—glory, the rapturous vision, eternal life. Oh, think of the subject, and exemplify as well as utter the wish—"Let me die the death of the righteous," &c.

LXXXII.—REMEMBRANCE OF CHRIST.

"We will remember thy love."—*Solomon's Song,* i. 4.

A GREAT deal is said in the Scriptures concerning the love of the Lord Jesus Christ. Indeed, it may be said to be the very essence and glory of the gospel. Take it away, and we have no good news for the sinner—no glad tidings for a perishing world. Take it away, and all before us is dark, and dreary, and hopeless—and all above us, awful and appalling. Take it away, and you leave man without a remedy for his guilt, misery, and condemnation. Everywhere, however, this subject animates the sacred writers.

The patriarchs advert to this. Abraham saw the day of Christ and rejoiced, and was glad. David never was so exhilarated as when he was writing the things concerning the King,—then, indeed, his tongue was as the pen, &c. How Isaiah and most of the prophets testified of Christ, time will not allow me to detail. Our text is the language of the Church, figuratively described in this book as the spouse of the Redeemer, who exclaims—"We will remember," &c. We ask,

I. What are the peculiarities of Christ's love that we will remember.

II. The nature of the remembrance we will maintain. And,

III. The influence which this remembrance will exert.

I. *What are the peculiarities of Christ's love, that we will remember.* We ought affectionately to remember the love of friends and benefactors. The love of parents, especially the love of our pious and devoted mothers. It is base and ungrateful to forget ordinary exhibitions of kindness and love. If so, how striking does the love of the Lord Jesus stand out towards us in the gospel !

1. *In the eternity of its origin.* The love of Christ is seen on the cross—in the garden during his whole life : but they were the flowing streams—where was the fountain ? Go back to paradise, and you find it not there. No! before all time it existed in his purposes,—in his resolves,—in his designs,—which then comprehended the salvation of our race. See Eph. i. 4. "I have loved thee with an everlasting love," &c.

2. *In the freeness of its nature.* Was the love of Christ a mere drop—a mere ray ? Oh, no! it was a stream deep and wide, and overflowing. The winds of the heavens are not more free. The waves of the sea, &c. It was the spontaneous tide of his own goodness setting in on our world, and rolling its billows of mercy on our desolated earth.

3. *In the worthlessness of its objects.* Men seek for fitness, and worth, and excellency, in the object of their affections. We love the beautiful, the intelligent, the good, the amiable! Had the love of Christ been thus regulated, it never would have fixed its regards on sinful men. Instead of beauty, there was the disgusting loathsomeness of depravity. Instead of intelligence, there was gross ignorance. Instead of goodness, there was enmity and unholiness. Instead of the amiable, there was the carnal—the malevolent—the diabolical. Yet on beings so unlovely, did he set his heart's affections, &c.

4. *In the sacrifices of its communication.* To love an unlovely object is surprising; but to do so at much inconvenience, loss, and suffering, is still more marvellous. Yet so did Christ. To render his love available he must remove the difficulties, take away the obstacles, pay the penalty. The objects, &c., were enslaved—he must redeem. They were guilty—he must atone. They were polluted —he must cleanse. Satan held them in fetters—he must burst the bonds. Deity in his holy nature, was bound to punish—he must become the surety. They were carnal, and haters of God—he must renew and change the heart. He did all this. He descended from heaven. Became a child, &c. Man of sorrows,—poor,—persecuted, condemned, crucified, &c. Laid down his life.

"See there, my Lord, upon the tree," &c.

5. *In the graciousness of its application.* We have been speaking of the love of Christ for us ; but see it also manifested to us, in the overtures of the gospel. Suing for a place in our souls. Overcoming our enmity, —captivating our hearts, &c. How gentle, tender, condescending, the love of Christ to us.

6. *In its unchangeable constancy.* His love is not only intense, but abiding. Eternal as to the past, and perpetual as to the future. Often fervent affection is fickle, and speedily cools. Christ's is immutable. And think of its constancy in the midst of our changes, and departures, and sins. All this is wondrous. Well may we say—"We will remember," &c.

II. *The nature of the remembrance.*

1. *It should be affectionate and reciprocal.* We love him, &c. We should remember to exhibit ours. To testify our grateful feelings, &c.

2. *It should be practical.* A religion that influences our conversation and spiritual condition. If any man love me, he will keep my words. "If ye love me," &c.

3. *It should be reflective.* Christ's love to us and in us, should be reflected to those around us. If Christ so loved us, we should also love another. Love to his people, &c. Love to the wretched, &c. Love to the world. Love to our enemies. Oh, remember to *reflect it.* Be so many mirrors of the love of Christ. "By this shall all," &c.

4. *It should be abiding.* A subject never to be forgotten. Daily, hourly remembrance. But there are especial seasons. In the closet. In reading the Word. In the sanctuary. Especially at the Lord's table. May it be in the dying hour, then it will be in the day of judgment and through all eternity.

III. *The influence the remembrance of Christ's love will exert.*

1. *It will destroy the love of sin.*

2. *It will moderate the love of self.* "I am crucified," &c.

3. *It will wean from the love of the world.*

4. *It will transform into the lovely image of Christ.* Feel, and think, and speak, and labor as did Christ.

APPLICATION.

1. Some do remember Christ's love.

2. Some care nothing for it.

3. We trust there are some desirous of loving him.

LXXXIII.—FAULTS REMEMBERED.

"Then spake the chief butler unto Pharaoh, saying, I do remember my faults this day."— *Gen.* xli. 9.

ALL persons who are familiar with the history of Joseph, will remember the consequence of his interpreting the dreams of the chief butler and baker. And how he applied to the chief butler that he would employ his influence on his behalf, Gen. xl. 12, &c. Full of gratitude to the Hebrew youth, no doubt he promised to intercede for him, and most probably intended to fulfil the promise. But with the return of his own prosperity he forgot the prisoner: hence it is written, ver. 23. At length, divine providence, which was watching over the interests of Joseph, caused Pharaoh, the Egyptian monarch, to dream, &c. The magicians, &c., could not interpret, &c., ver. 8. It was thus that the chief butler was reminded of his youthful fellow-prisoner, and he exclaimed—"I do remember," &c. We observe,

I. *The best men have their faults.* By faults, we mean things that are wrong, morally so. There is not a just man on earth, —that doeth good and sinneth not. There are none really, perfectly righteous—no, not one. But even very excellent persons have their faults. If you look at it as a matter of

history. How we are reminded of this in the lives of Noah, Abraham, Jacob, Moses, Aaron, David, Peter. The beloved John, &c.

1. *Some have faults of temper.* Irritable, —soon angry or morose, and a tendency to sullenness.

2. *Some have faults of spirit.* In one, pride is not annihilated. In another, vanity. In a third, pettishness. Jealousy is the plague of some, and envy the torment of others.

3. *Others have faults of the tongue.* Talkativeness. Jesting. Speaking of others. Censoriousness, and sometimes backbiting. A man who offends not in tongue is a perfect man.

4. *In others there are faults of character.* Instability,—frequent relapses into evil. Formality. Worldliness. An uneven, checkered Christian course. The faults which distinguish even the good, include,

(1.) Faults against God in serious reverential love, or obedience.

(2.) Faults against our own souls in negligence of the means,—living at a distance from God. Neglect of self-cultivation, &c.

(3.) Faults against mankind. In unkindness, want of sympathy, mercy, goodness, &c.

II. *We are apt to be ignorant of our faults.* We know a great deal about others. We see the faults of this or that person; but, alas! our own are often buried in selfish ignorance.

(1.) This arises from too great an estimation of ourselves. Often warned against this. Great peril in this.

(2.) From want of self-examination. Without this we cannot know ourselves. Examine, &c. Prove your own selves.

(3.) From being absorbed in the affairs of this life. We know much of our business affairs. Much of the world, &c., but how really little of ourselves, and especially of our faults.

III. *God sometimes brings the faults of men into striking remembrance.* Thus in the text. Thus also in the case of Joseph's brethren, Gen. xlii. 21. Thus also in the case of Belshazzar, Dan. v. 1–7. Thus the woman of Samaria, by the conversation of Christ. This is one great design of the ministry of the Word. Hear what is said of it, Heb. iv. 12. So the preaching of Paul before Felix. Peter's sermon on the day of Pentecost. So it has often been. It is a mercy when this revelation is made in this world. For in the great day, God will bring every work, &c.

IV. *When faults are remembered they should be confessed and forsaken.* Confession always to God. This he requires. "He that confesseth," &c. "If we confess," &c. And in many cases confession to men. If we have injured, &c., it is our duty and privilege. It is the way of comfort and real dignity. Nothing ignoble in it. Thus the butler. Sincere confession will be accompanied by reformation. The abandonment of the sin, restitution to our fellowmen. This is much neglected, yet an essential of acceptable saving religion. I notice,

V. *Faults confessed and forsaken shall assuredly be forgiven.* This is the peculiar doctrine of the gospel. The law knew nothing of it. And forgiveness thus comes to us through the merits of the Lord Jesus Christ. Not for the sake of the confession and amendment. God pardons sin for his name's sake. But the blessing of forgiveness is certain to every one who comes to him through his Son.

APPLICATION.

1. *Let the subject lead to serious self-examination.* How many faults lie forgotten. Oh, explore! bring them to the light, confess, and seek mercy.

2. *Unconfessed faults will meet us at the last day.* When the books are opened, &c.

LXXXIV.—IGNORANCE OF THE HEATHEN, AND THE CONDUCT OF GOD TOWARDS THEM.

BY THE REV. GREVILLE EWING, M.A., OF GLASGOW.*

"And the times of this ignorance God winked at; but now commandeth all men everywhere to repent: because he hath appointed a day in the which he will judge the world in righteousness by that man whom he hath ordained; whereof he hath given assurance unto all men, in that he hath raised him from the dead."—*Acts* xvii. 30, 31.

THE words of our text, which were so well suited to introduce the doctrines of the gospel to a heathen audience, may serve also to explain the motives of those who attempt to propagate those doctrines throughout the

* From a sermon preached before the London Missionary Society, at Tottenham Court Chapel, May 12th, 1803.

world; and, by the blessing of God, which we earnestly implore, a serious consideration of them may, at this time, animate and confirm our zeal in prosecuting the important object of our institution, as a Missionary Society.

In discoursing from them we shall consider,

I. *The ignorance of the heathen.*

II. *The divine procedure with regard to it.*

III. *The reason of this procedure.*

IV. *The evidence by which this reason is confirmed.*

I. *Let us consider the ignorance of the heathen.*

The charge of ignorance which the apostle brought home to his audience at Athens, is by no means to be understood as confined to them. He speaks in general of the ignorance of the nations, and of times, or ages, during which that ignorance had been permitted to reign. It is a truth which divine revelation and universal history unite in attesting,

1. *That wherever men have not been blessed with the Holy Scriptures, they have, time immemorial, been grossly mistaken with respect to the character of God, the situation of man, the way of salvation, and the hopes and fears of a future state.* These mistakes undoubtedly originate in that alienation of the heart from God, which followed as a consequence of the first transgression. Having offended the Almighty, fallen man did not like to retain him in his knowledge; yet the fear of punishment, and probably the example of those whom God separated from the beginning for his service, prevented a total dereliction of worship. But it is not by the idolatry alone of the heathen that their ignorance is betrayed.

2. *It is rendered at least equally conspicuous by that vain and deceitful philosophy, those "oppositions of science falsely so called," which in countries not blessed with the gospel (and in other countries also), have been extolled as the utmost efforts of human understanding.* What else do we learn from the jarring systems of the Epicureans and Stoics, with whom the apostle, at Athens, was called to contend?

3. Further. *The ignorance of the heathen appears not only in the positive errors which they hold, but in their indifference, insensibility, and prejudice with regard to all things spiritual; while they are wholly occupied with worldly pursuits and sensual indul-*

gence. The superstition they have been accustomed to, they cherish with bigoted attachment; but they are unwilling to give ear to any thing else of a religious kind. In them are verified the words of the apostle, "The natural man receiveth not the things of the Spirit of God, for they are foolishness unto him; neither can he know them, because they are spiritually discerned," 1 Cor. ii. 14.

II. *Let us consider the divine procedure with regard to the ignorance of the heathen.*

"The times of this ignorance God winked at, but now commandeth all men everywhere to repent." The word rendered "winked at," intimates nothing respecting the merits of the case; but seems simply to signify, the suspension of decisive measures, either in way of remedy, or of punishment. Thus, in Leviticus xx. 4, a similar phrase, which the Septuagint renders by the same word as that in the original of our text, is used to express the non-execution of punishment—"If the people of the land do any ways *hide their eyes* from the man, when he giveth of his seed unto Molech, and *kill him not.*" Again. In Deut. xxii. 1, it supposes the non-application of a remedy—"Thou shalt not see thy brother's ox or his sheep go astray, and *hide thyself from them:* thou shalt in any case *bring them again* unto thy brother." In our text, both uses of the word may be included. The apostle speaks of the divine forbearance towards the heathen, during the ages which preceded the gospel dispensation; neither cutting them off in their ignorance, nor yet immediately applying the effectual remedy. His words may be illustrated by a parallel passage in Acts xiv. 16, 17—"Who in times past suffered all nations to walk in their own ways. Nevertheless he left not himself without witness, in that he did good, and gave us rain from heaven, and fruitful seasons, filling our hearts with food and gladness."

III. *Let us consider the reason of this procedure respecting the ignorance of the heathen.*

1. *Perhaps heathen ignorance was permitted to continue so long, that the necessity of divine revelation might experimentally appear.* "For after that in the wisdom of God the world by wisdom knew not God, it pleased God by the foolishness of preaching to save them that believe," 1 Cor. i. 21.

2. *God did not approve of it.* From the very beginning, a preparation was going on

for removing that ignorance, by the blessed dispensation which now obtains.

IV. *Let us consider the evidence by which the reason for commanding men to repent is confirmed.*

"He hath appointed a day in which he will judge the world in righteousness by that man whom he hath ordained; whereof he hath given assurance unto all men, in that he hath raised him from the dead."

1. *The proof that God hath appointed a day of judgment to be executed by a man, is the resurrection of that man from the dead.* This proof is held out to all men; for it forms an essential part of the gospel which is preached to all. "I delivered unto you first of all," says the apostle to the Corinthians, "that which I also received, how that Christ died for our sins according to the Scriptures; and that he was buried, and that he rose again the third day according to the Scriptures," 1 Cor. xv. 3, 4. These truths are intimately connected with the future judgment.

2. *The fact that Christ rose from the dead, is well fitted to excite universal attention.* The bare possibility of a resurrection from the dead, is a most interesting discovery to the human race. How much more, then, to hear that such an event has actually happened, and happened to one who is said to have "died for our sins," and to have promised his disciples a share of his glory!

3. *This fact is supported by evidence universally intelligible and convincing.* It depends not on vague tradition, on popular prejudice, or natural peculiarities; we have an authentic history of it, published in the Holy Scriptures, containing the plain, consistent testimony of credible witnesses, who little expected what they saw; who, nevertheless, could not be deceived; who had no possible motive to deceive others; and whose success in preaching the gospel is a manifest token of the divine favor sealing their veracity.

4. *This fact naturally confirms us in the belief of a future judgment, and of such a judgment as the gospel foretells.* It is an example of future life, of the reversal of iniquitous human decisions, and of victory to the righteous over every foe. It establishes the whole doctrine of atonement, the necessity and reasonableness of which are implied, even in the rites of pagan worship. It declares the man Christ Jesus to be the Son of God with power. It shows the acceptance

of his sacrifice, and his ability "to save them to the uttermost that come unto God by him." When it is once admitted, that "Christ both died and rose and revived," it cannot be thought incredible that he should be "Lord both of the dead and living," Rom. xiv. 9; that now he should be exalted to govern the universe, and to judge the quick and the dead at the great day.

The proof, then, which God hath given to all men of the judgment of the world, though not admitted by all, is sufficient for the conviction of all, and leaves those who reject it, without excuse: it is a striking, an apposite, an unanswerable proof. That judgment, again, is a most powerful reason at once for publishing and obeying the command to repent. That command is the grand display of divine mercy to perishing men; and, however great and prevalent and long borne with their ignorance hath been, it is the revealed will of God, that now, at last, it should be effectually removed.

LXXXV.—THE MORAL DIGNITY OF THE MISSIONARY ENTERPRISE.

BY REV. F. WAYLAND, BOSTON.[*]

"The field is the world."—*Matt.* xiii. 38.

To show that the Missionary cause combines within itself the elements of all that is sublime in human purpose; nay, combines them in a loftier perfection than any other enterprise which was ever linked with the destinies of man, will be our design. In prosecuting it, we shall direct your attention to the *grandeur of the object; the arduousness of its execution;* and *the nature of the means on which we rely for success.*

I. *The grandeur of the object.*

In the most enlarged sense of the term, "The field is the world!" Our design is radically to affect the temporal and eternal interests of the whole race of man.

1. We have surveyed this field *statistically,* and find that, of the eight hundred millions who inhabit our globe, but two hundred millions have *any* knowledge of the religion of Jesus Christ. Of these, we are willing to allow that but one half are his

[*] From a sermon delivered before the Boston "Baptist Foreign Mission Society," October 25, 1823.

real disciples; and that, therefore, there are seven of the eight hundred millions to whom the gospel must be sent.

2. *We have surveyed this field geographically.*

We have looked upon our own continent (America), and have seen that, with the exception of a narrow strip of thinly settled country, from the Gulf of St. Lawrence to the mouth of the Mississippi, the whole of this new world lieth in wickedness. Hordes of ruthless savages roam the wilderness of the west; and men, almost as ignorant of the spirit of the gospel, are struggling for independence in the south.

We have looked over Europe, and behold there one nation putting forth her energies in the cause of evangelizing the world. We have looked for another such nation, but it is not to be found. A few others are beginning to awake: most of them, however, yet slumber.

We have looked over Africa, and have seen that upon one little portion, reclaimed from brutal idolatry by missionaries, the Sun of righteousness has shined. It is a land of Goshen, where they have light in their dwellings. Upon all the remainder of this vast continent, there broods a moral darkness, impervious as that which once veiled her own Egypt, on that prolonged and fearful night, when no man knew his brother: see Exod. x. 21–23.

We have looked upon Asia, and have seen its northern nations, though under the government of a Christian prince, scarcely nominally Christian. On the west, it is spellbound by Mohammedan delusion. To the south, from the Persian Gulf to the Sea of Kamschatka, including also its numberless islands—except where, here and there, a Syrian church, or a missionary station, twinkles amidst the gloom—the whole of this immense portion of the human race is sitting in the region and shadow of death.

3. *We have also made an estimate of the miseries of this world.* We have seen how, in many places, the human mind, shackled by ignorance, and enfeebled by vice, has dwindled almost to the standard of a brute. Our indignation has kindled at hearing of men, immortal as ourselves, bowing down and worshipping a wandering beggar, or paying adoration to reptiles and to stones. Not only is intellect everywhere under the dominion of idolatry prostrated; beyond the boundaries of Christendom, on every side,

"the dark places of the earth are full of the habitations of cruelty," Psa. lxxiv. 20.

4. *We have considered these beings as immortal, and candidates for an eternity of happiness or misery.* And we cannot avoid the belief, that they are exposed to eternal misery. To settle the question concerning their future destiny, it would only seem necessary to ask, What would be the character of that future state, in which those principles of heart, which the whole history of the heathen develops, were suffered to operate in their unrestrained malignity?

The object of the missionary enterprise embraces every child of Adam; it is vast as the race to whom its operations are of necessity limited. It would confer upon every individual on earth, all that intellectual or moral cultivation can bestow.

II. *The missionary undertaking is arduous enough to call into action the noblest energies of man.*

Its arduousness is explained in one word— "The field is the world!" Our object is to effect an entire moral revolution in the whole human race.

1. *Its arduousness then results, of necessity, from its magnitude.* This mighty revolution is to be effected not in a family, a tribe, or a nation; but in a world which "lieth in wickedness."

2. *We shall frequently interfere with the more sordid interests of men; and we expect them to increase the difficulties of our undertaking.* We have to assault systems, venerable for their antiquity, and interwoven with every thing that is proud in a nation's history.

3. *This enterprise requires consummate wisdom in the missionary who goes abroad, as well as in those who manage the concerns of a society at home.* He who goes forth unprotected to preach Christ to despotic or badly governed nations, must be "wise as serpents, and harmless as doves." With undeviating firmness upon every thing essential, he must combine the most yielding facility upon all that is unimportant. Great abilities are also required in him who conducts the mission at home. The missionary undertaking calls for perseverance: a perseverance of that character, which, having once formed its purpose, never wavers from it till death. This undertaking calls for self-denial of the highest and holiest character. Hence you see, this undertaking requires courage. But, above all, the missionary un-

dertaking requires faith, in its holiest and sublimest exercise.

III. *Let us consider the means by which the moral revolution is to be effected.*

It is, in a word, by the preaching of Jesus Christ, and him crucified. It is, by going forth and telling the lost children of men, that "God so loved the world, that he gave his only-begotten Son, that whosoever believeth in him should not perish, but have everlasting life," John iii. 16; and by all the eloquence of such an appeal, to entreat them, for Christ's sake, to be reconciled unto God. This is the lever by which we believe the moral universe is to be raised; this is the instrument by which a sinful world is to be regenerated. Consider,

1. *The commanding simplicity of this means, devised by Omniscience, to effect a purpose so glorious.* This world is to be restored to more than it lost by the fall, by the simple annunciation of the love of God in Christ Jesus. Here we behold means apparently the weakest, employed to effect the most magnificent of purposes.

2. *Contemplate the benevolence of these means.* In practice, the precepts of the gospel may be summed up in the simple command, "Thou shalt love the Lord thy God with all thy heart, and with all thy soul, and with all thy mind; and thy neighbor as thyself," Matt. xxii. 37, 39.

3. *Consider the efficacy of these means.* The reasons which teach us to rely upon them with confidence, may be thus briefly stated—

(1.) We see that all which is really terrific in the misery of man, results from the disease of his moral nature. If this can be healed, man may be restored to happiness. Now the gospel of Jesus Christ is the remedy devised by Omniscience, especially for this purpose; and, therefore, we do certainly know that it will inevitably succeed.

(2.) It is easy to be seen, that the universal obedience to the command, "Thou shalt love the Lord thy God with all thy heart, and with all thy soul, and with all thy mind; and thy neighbor as thyself," would make this world a heaven.

(3.) The preaching of the cross of Christ is a remedy for the miseries of the fall which has been tested by the experience of eighteen hundred years; and has never, in a single instance, failed. Its efficacy has been proved by human beings of all ages, from the lisping babe, to the sinner a hundred years old.

All climates have witnessed its power. From the ice-bound cliffs of Greenland, to the banks of the voluptuous Ganges, the simple story of Christ crucified, has "turned men from darkness to light, and from the power of Satan unto God," Acts xxvi. 18.

(4.) We know, from the word of the living God, that it will be successful, until this whole world has been redeemed from the effects of man's first disobedience—"For the earth shall be filled with the knowledge of the glory of the Lord, as the waters cover the sea," Hab. ii. 14.

APPLICATION.

Blessed be God, this is a work in which every one of us is permitted to do something. None so poor, none so weak, none so insignificant, but a place of action is assigned him ; and the cause expects every man to do his duty. We observe, then—

1. You may assist in it by your prayers.

2. You may assist by your personal exertions. This cause requires a vigorous, persevering, universal, and systematic effort.

3. You may assist by your pecuniary contributions.

———

LXXXVI.—PAUL PREACHING AT ATHENS.

"Now while Paul waited for them at Athens, his spirit was stirred in him, when he saw the city wholly given to idolatry," etc.—*Acts* xvii. 16–23.

PAUL had been driven out of Thessalonica by a rude mob of the baser sort; and from thence he had repaired to Berea, where the people gave him a fair and candid hearing. For "these were more noble than those in Thessalonica, in that they received the word with all readiness of mind, and searched the Scriptures daily, whether those things were so," Acts xvii. 11 ; the result was, "many of them believed," verse 12. But the persecuting Jews of Thessalonica pursued the apostle to Berea, and there also stirred up the people. It was deemed prudent, therefore, for Paul to leave Berea; and the brethren conducted him to Athens : here he waited until he should be joined by Silas and Timothy. Thus waiting, our text refers to the feelings and conduct of the apostle, "Now while Paul waited for them," &c. Observe,

I. *The description given of the city of Athens.*

It may be well briefly to refer to its history. Athens was the most celebrated city of Greece. It was distinguished for the military talent, the learning, the eloquence, the luxury, and the politeness of its inhabitants. It was founded about 1,600 years before the Christian era ; and was called Athens in honor of Minerva, who was chiefly worshipped there, and to whom the city was dedicated. No city of antiquity was so celebrated for its warriors, statesmen, philosophers, sculptors, and poets. Here was the celebrated Acropolis, the glory of Grecian art : within this was deposited all that was most interesting in painting, sculpture, and architecture. Here, also, was the Parthenon, or Virgin temple of Minerva, 217 feet in length, 98 in breadth : within which was a statue of Minerva, a masterpiece of art, of ivory, 39 feet in height ; and entirely covered with pure gold, to the value of £120,000 sterling. Besides these, outside the walls, were the temples of Theseus and Jupiter Olympius. Three quarters of a mile to the north of the town, was the academy where Plato taught. Here, also, was the Lyceum, where Aristotle diffused the light of science. In addition to these was the Areopagus. This was an open building on an eminence, in the centre of the city, and was the court of the supreme judges of Athens, where they met to dispense justice, and enforce laws. Here the judges held their court at midnight, that they might be less liable to distraction from surrounding objects.

Now, within this highly-educated city, the people were "wholly given to idolatry,"—full of idols. On every side there were victims, temples, and altars. Among these, there was one peculiar monument, or altar, which bore this strange inscription, "To the Unknown God." It is affirmed, on good historical testimony, that 600 years before Christ, the city was afflicted with a grievous pestilence. Epimenides took a number of sheep to the Areopagus, and then let them go whither they would ; at the place where they halted, they were sacrificed, and the altar was erected "To the Unknown God." Such, then, is a brief description of this celebrated city. Notice,

II. *The feelings which a survey of this city produced on the mind of the apostle.* "His spirit was stirred in him." His soul was agitated, greatly excited.

1. *It was stirred in him with jealousy for the Divine glory.* Every idol and altar was a public dishonor to the true God. Here senseless statues had possession, and received the homage of the thousands of this celebrated city.

2. *It was stirred in him with compassionate indignation for human nature.* The feelings of compassion and indignation are quite in accordance with each other : indignation against the evil, and compassion for the sinner. Here human nature presented a singular appearance : intellectual, yet ignorant; civilized, yea, polished, yet immersed in the senseless stupidity of idolatry. Behold those lofty minds of Athens, those master-spirits of their times and country, yet bowing to idols.

3. *It was stirred up with intense anxiety for their welfare and salvation.* Athens, after all, was the seat of Satan. Its people were spell-bound. As an idolatrous city, it was exposed to the displeasure and indignation of heaven. The soul of the apostle was filled with deepest solicitude for this dark, wicked, and infatuated people. See Deut. v. 7, &c.; xxvii. 15, &c. "Confounded be all they that serve graven images, that boast themselves of idols," Psa. xcvii. 7. Notice,

III. *The course which the apostle adopted.* "He disputed in the synagogue with the Jews." That is, he reasoned, &c.; endeavored, by statement and argument, to convince the people they were wrong. He did this with the Jews, who had a synagogue; with the devout or religious people, and in the market-place; and he did this daily. Observe,

1. *The apostle stood alone as a Christian minister, an apostle of the Nazarene.* The people were all idolatrous, except a few Jewish proselytes.

2. *The apostle grappled with the established errors of the place.* He did not say, I will be passive, and allow all to do as they please : he could not do this. Hence, we see all controversies and disputations are not wrong. Christ disputed and argued with the Jews, &c. So also the apostles; and so must we, with all the God-dishonoring enemies of truth.

3. *He made this his occupation, it was his daily work.* He was to be the light of Athens during his residence in it.

4. *He did this publicly.* "In the synagogue, and in the market." Wherever he could meet with a concourse of people, he felt for them, and argued with them, &c., concerning idolatry, and concerning the true God. Notice, then,

IV. *The opponents the apostle had to encounter.* We have previously referred to the intellectual celebrity of Athens; and, therefore, he had not to contend with a rude and maddened rabble, or bigoted Jews; but with highly cultivated minds, men of profound philosophical research. Certain of these philosophers, of two of the leading sects, encountered him.

1. *The Epicureans.* Epicurus, the founder of that sect, flourished about 300 years before Christ. He represented the world as being formed by a fortuitous concourse of atoms, which met and united, and formed all things. He denied the doctrine of providence, or that the gods exercise any care about human beings. His principal sentiment was, that pleasure was the chief good. He evidently intended more the pleasures of the mind than of the body. His followers, however, were given to indolence, effeminacy, and voluptuousness. Epicurus was a wonderful man for the age and country in which he lived, and was greatly admired for his endowments and virtues. He died in the seventy-second year of his age.

2. *The Stoics.* This was a sect of philosophers, of whom Zeno was the founder. They were so called, because he taught his disciples in an open portico, where he used to walk, and deliver his instructions. He taught, that there was only one Supreme Being; and that all things happened by *fatal necessity.* He held, that happiness consisted in obtaining a total insensibility to pain; and that a good man is always alike joyful, even under the greatest torture. Zeno lived until he was ninety-six years old, and died 264 years before Christ. Now, philosophers of these sects encountered Paul, "because he preached unto them Jesus, and the resurrection," ver. 18. How great a contrast between the Master of Paul, and the founders of these sects! How different his spirit, his maxims, his gospel, his life, his benefits! How strange to them the doctrine of the resurrection! In the soul's immortality many of the heathen philosophers believed; but a single conjecture is not to be found in the writings of all the pagans in the world, on the subject of the resurrection. This is one of the grand and glorious truths confined to the volume of eternal truth, and fully brought to light in the gospel.

V. *The spirit which the Athenians evinced.*

And here there is every thing to commend, for although Paul had come in direct collision with the tenets and the opinions of their distinguished philosophers, yet, with candor and respect, they gave the apostle an opportunity of stating fully and clearly the doctrines which he held. "May we know what this new doctrine, whereof thou speakest, is?" So they took him to the Areopagus, the seat of judicature, the highest and most dignified place within the city, and where thousands might hearken to the statements the apostle might make. Here, within one of the most celebrated tribunals of the world, had the apostle Paul to stand, to declare among these Gentiles, "the unsearchable riches of Christ." Observe,

VI. *The discourse which the apostle delivered.*

Doubtless, we have but the analysis presented to our view.

1. *He refers to their superstitious veneration for idols.* "I perceive," &c. Surely they could not be denominated an irreligious people, a reckless people; no, they carried their superstitious regards to the greatest possible extent. The city was full of temples, of idols, and altars. To these they added one "To the Unknown God." How aptly did this exhibit their true and real character and condition. To them the true God was unknown: they had learning, art, science, philosophy, &c.; yet they were without God.

2. *The apostle gave a striking representation of the true Jehovah.* "Whom therefore ye ignorantly worship, him declare I unto you."

(1.) He declares him as the Creator of all things.

(2.) He declares his universal dominion and authority. "Lord of heaven and earth."

(3.) He declares the immensity of his nature. "Dwelleth not in temples made with hands." That is, cannot be confined, not limited.

(4.) He declares his self-existence, and sufficiency. He is not to be served, or "worshipped with men's hands." See also Psa. l. 7, &c.

(5.) He declares him the Fountain and Author of all life. "Giveth to all life, and breath, and all things." Holds in his hands the breath of lives.

(6.) He declares him the universal parent of all men. "Hath made of one blood," &c.

(7.) He declares him to be the Disposer and Ruler of all events. "Hath determined the times before appointed," &c.

(8.) He declares unto them his omnipresence. He is "not far from every one of us."

(9.) He declares him the source of all our bounties. "In him we live, and move, and have our being."

(10.) He declares his spirituality, ver. 29.

(11.) He declares the forbearance and long-suffering of God, ver. 30. Did not punish, &c.

(12.) He declared the necessity of universal repentance. "But now commandeth all men everywhere to repent."

(13.) He declared the righteous judgment of all by Christ Jesus. "Whom God hath raised up," &c., ver. 31.

Notice,

VII. *The effects which were produced.*

1. *Some mocked.* Derided, as though he had spoken folly.

2. *Some deferred judgment, and agreed to hear again.*

3. *Some were converted.* "Howbeit certain men clave unto him, and believed"—one of the judges, several men, and Damaris.

APPLICATION.

Learn,

1. *The corruption and blindness of the human mind.* To give honor, &c., to stocks and stones—to idols.

2. *The insufficiency of the light of nature in matters of religion.* What can any nation or people have, that they had not? They had sun, moon, and stars. All the works of Deity were around them, &c. Yet by "wisdom they knew not God;" nay, all their science and literature were ineffectual here. Their poets and philosophers were all strangers to God. So it is with the heathen nations to this day.

3. *There is idolatry of heart, as well as of worship.* If Paul visited *this* metropolis, no such statues would arrest his eye, &c. But every one who refuses God's authority, has a something enthroned, and that is their idol; and the love and service of that is idolatry.

4. *God demands the supreme homage of the mind, and affections of the heart.* "Thou shalt have no other gods before me," Exod. xx. 3. "Thou shalt love the Lord thy God with all thy heart," &c., Matt. xxii. 37.

5. *How thankful we should be for the*

gospel. How precious, how invaluable. It will make you wise, holy, and happy. Receive it cordially.

6. *Deeply feel for the perishing heathen.* And let your compassionate solicitude lead you to zealous efforts for their salvation.

LXXXVII.—CONTEMPLATION OF HEATHEN IDOLATRY AN EXCITEMENT TO MISSIONARY ZEAL.

BY REV. RALPH WARDLAW, D. D.*

" Now when Paul waited for them at Athens, his spirit was stirred in him, when he saw the city wholly given to idolatry."—*Acts* xvii. 16.

ATHENS stood pre-eminent, indeed, for the multitude of its deities; but, alas! it stood not alone. It was not a *city* merely that Paul had to contemplate as given to idolatry; but, with the exception of one little spot favored of heaven as "the place which Jehovah had chosen, to put his name there," it was a *whole world.* And now, when eighteen centuries have passed away, does not the same heart-moving spectacle still, to a vast extent, present itself to the view? How very few, comparatively, of the tribes of our fallen and revolted race, have as yet "turned from their idols to serve the living and true God!" How immense the proportion of them that are still going astray after their dumb idols, even as they are led! It is true,—and let us record it with the liveliest feelings of delight and adoration,— the proportion is lessening. The true God is making his name glorious among the heathen. The idols he is abolishing. "The gods that made not the heavens and the earth, are perishing from off the earth, and from under these heavens." The object of these annual meetings is to keep alive a missionary spirit, and to rouse it to still warmer and more active energy. It will not be found, I trust, unsuitable to this design, if we endeavor to show, with humble dependence upon the Divine blessing, how the survey of these idolatries is calculated to produce *indignant grief for the dishonor done by them to God ; amazement at human weakness and folly ; abhorrence of human impiety ; and compassion for human wretchedness.*

* From a sermon, preached before the "London Missionary Society," at Surrey Chapel, May 13, 1818.

I. *The contemplation of heathen idolatries should excite indignant grief for the dishonor done to God.*

This, I have no doubt, was the feeling which first stirred the spirit of the devout apostle of the Gentiles, when, looking around him, he contemplated the endless multiplicity of false deities, "the gods many, and lords many" of the Athenians, and, as he himself afterwards expresses it, "beheld their devotions."—In the altar inscribed "To THE UNKNOWN GOD," Acts xvii. 23, he had seen a melancholy acknowledgment of their ignorance. The only true God was the only God unknown. All the fabled deities were there, of heaven, and earth, and hell; but the one living God, whose peculiar honors were thus usurped and alienated and abused, was not to be found. Not that Paul could have been gratified in his having a place amidst such a collection of falsehood, impurity, and folly. It would have been a vile affront to his infinite Majesty, to have been so associated, even if he had been placed at the head of their pantheon, and made their Jupiter Olympius. For, indeed, this Olympian Jove, the "mighty thunderer," the "father of gods and men," the "best and the greatest," was, in the actions ascribed to him by his deluded worshippers, the foulest and most infamous of the whole fabled fraternity.

Paul could not contemplate the prostrate honors of the infinite God with an unmoved and tranquil heart. He could not behold this world, which ought to have been one great temple to the exclusive worship of Jehovah, "whose he was, and whom he served," crowded with rival deities, the offspring of the depraved fancy of apostate creatures, with which the very thought of bringing Him, even for an instant, into comparison, makes the heart thrill and shudder with detestation.

II. *The contemplation of heathen idolatry may well fill us with amazement at the weakness and folly of the human mind.*

Search the annals of our world, in every age and in every country, I question if you will find a more affecting and humbling exemplification of human imbecility, than that which is afforded by the history of idolatry. It is such, indeed, as we hardly know how to believe,—to be set down amidst the likenesses "to corruptible man, and to birds, and fourfooted beasts, and creeping things," Rom. i. 23, which form the immense museum of heathen mythology, one might be tempted to fancy, that some satirical defamer of our nature had been exhausting an inventive imagination to slander and to vilify it.

When Paul saw the wonderful results of human wisdom, and power, and skill, in the arts and sciences, in philosophy and literature, which existed in Athens in such profusion and splendor; when he beheld a people raised to the very pinnacle of eminence for all that was great and excellent in human attainments; and then viewed the same people, sunk in the abyss of ignorance and stupidity as to all that related to the higher concerns of God and of eternity, how striking, how affecting the contrast! Can we wonder that his "spirit was stirred in him?"

III. *Paul's spirit was stirred in him, and the contemplation of heathen idolatry should stir ours, with abhorrence of human impiety.*

Idolatry, like infidelity, has not been so much an error of the head as of the heart. Here it had its origin; here it still has "its power, and its seat, and its great authority." The head has been the dupe of the heart: the folly has sprung from the corruption; the infatuation of the judgment, from the depravation of the affections. The veil has not been upon the evidences themselves of the existence and perfections of God, but upon the hearts of his fallen creatures. The wretched votaries of idolatry are described as "walking in the vanity of their minds; having their understandings darkened; being alienated from the life of God, through the ignorance that is in them, because of the blindness (or, rather, because of the hardness, or callousness*) of their hearts," Ephes. iv. 17, 18. To this source, even to the "carnal mind," which "is enmity against God," the philosophy of the Bible teaches us to trace the whole system, in all its varieties, of pagan idolatry: "They did not like to retain God in their knowledge," Rom. i. 28.

The origin of idolatry, then, is to be found in the alienation of the heart from God; the unsuitableness of his character, to the depraved propensities of his fallen creatures, and the consequent desire to have a god "such a one as themselves, who will approve their sins." This view of the matter accords well with the characters of their "gods many, and lords many," 1 Cor. viii. 5, and with the nature of the worship with

which they honored them. The worship of their gods is such as might have been expected from their characters. Well are their superstitions denominated "abominable idolatries," 1 Pet. iv. 3. They consist, not merely of the most senseless fooleries and the wildest extravagancies, but of the most disgusting impurities; the most licentious acts of intemperance, and the most iron-hearted cruelties.

IV. *The contemplation of heathen idolatry ought to inspire compassion for human wretchedness.*

I speak not at all, at present, of the wants and miseries of a savage life, destitute of the arts and sciences, and of the comforts and refinements of civilized society; because such miseries, and such wants, were evils unfelt at Athens. The mere man of the world would have looked on that far-famed city, as the emporium of all that was fitted to give dignity and happiness to men. But, in the midst of all this, the eye of the Christian philanthropist could not fail to discern a most melancholy want—a want, sufficient to throw a darkening shade over all the splendors of Athenian glory. The inhabitants of Athens, like those of Ephesus, were, in the eye of the "ambassador of Christ," without God, and having no hope in the world.

Do not your hearts bleed for them? When you think of the depth of their ignorance, and the enormity of their guilt; of their vain sacrifices, and their fruitless ablutions; their painful penances, their self-inflicted tortures and death; when you behold them with suppliant earnestness, crying for protection and deliverance to a thing which cannot help—falling down to the stock of a tree; when you see them with an importunity worthy of a more rational service, repeating their cry from morning till noon, and from noon till evening; and, in the bitterness and frenzy of disappointed eagerness, "cutting themselves with lancets, till the blood gushed out upon them,"—and "there is neither voice, nor any to answer, nor any that regardeth," see 1 Kings xviii. 26–29; when you see them steeling their hearts against the meltings of nature, stopping their ears to the pleadings of parental love, and "giving their first-born for their transgression, the fruit of their body for the sin of their soul" (Micah vi. 1); when you see them the wretched victims of a delusive hope, the dupes of a merciless and degrad-

* πορωσιν—porosin.

ing superstition, devoting themselves to voluntary destruction — crushed beneath the ponderous wheel, or "sinking in the devouring flood, or more devouring flame"—oh! does not a pang of pity go through your very souls for them? Are not your spirits stirred within you? Do not your bowels yearn over your kindred—over those, who are "bone of your bone, and flesh of your flesh,"—for "God hath made of one blood all nations of men, for to dwell on all the face of the earth," Acts xvii. 26.

And, finally, without dwelling on the many particulars of wretchedness, which are suggested to our minds by such a description of personal and social character as we read in the beginning of the Epistle to the Romans, I think, my brethren, of your miserable fellow-men in reference to an eternal world! I must now hasten to a close, by drawing from the subject some further practical improvement.

1. *All the sentiments and feelings which have been illustrated, ought to be principles of active and zealous exertion.*

2. *Let me, from this subject, endeavor to impress your minds with the necessity and value of Divine revelation.*

3. *The feelings expressed in the text, imply the opposite emotions of delight, in witnessing the contrary scene.*

If the spirit be "stirred" with indignant grief for the affront put upon the true God by the "abominable idolatries" of the heathen, it cannot fail to be stirred with exulting joy, when his alienated honors are restored; when the apostate sons of men "turn to God from idols, to serve the living and true God, and to wait for his Son from heaven," 1 Thess. i. 10.

4. *The guilt of idolatry, it is to be feared, attaches to many who little imagine that they are at all chargeable with any thing of the kind.* Yes; there are many who may even, in contemplating the idolatries of the heathen, condemn, and wonder, and pity, without at all reflecting on the possibility of their being themselves in the same condemnation. You are not worshiping the host of heaven; you are not adoring deified men; you are not falling down to stocks and stones; you are not making to yourselves graven images, likenesses of things in heaven above, or in the earth beneath, or in the waters under the earth; and you conclude you are not idolaters. But what is the spirit of idolatry? Is it not the alienation of the heart from God? Is it not the withholding from him, and the giving to other objects, whatever they may be, that homage, and those affections, to which he alone is entitled? Every man's idol is that on which his heart is supremely set; and every heart in which JEHOVAH is not enthroned, is an idol's temple.

————————

LXXXVIII.—THE RECOLLECTION OF THE MISERIES OF A PAGAN CONDITION, A MOTIVE TO ZEAL IN THE MISSIONARY CAUSE.*

BY REV. GEORGE CLAYTON.

"Wherefore remember,—that at that time ye were without Christ."—*Ephes.* ii. 11, 12.

ASSEMBLED as we are from all parts of the British empire, and indeed from all quarters of the globe; drawn together by one common object, and that the grandest which man can propose, or Deity achieve; urged forward by an impulse which, I trust, without presumption, may be pronounced similar, in some humble measure, to that which brought Jesus from the skies, and apostles and martyrs to the stake; it will be salutary to remember what we ourselves once were, in order that our motives may be invigorated, our resolutions confirmed, and our compassions awakened, in favor of those who are still "without God, and without hope in the world;" and whom we are determined, by the assistance and blessing of the Most High, to place on an equal footing with ourselves, in all the light and liberty and joy of which Christianity is the parent and the source.

Let us consider,

I. *The affecting condition which the text describes:* "At that time ye were without Christ."

II. *The duty of cherishing a distinct and constant remembrance of it.*

III. *The practical effects which ought to flow from such remembrance.*

I. *The affecting condition described:* "At that time ye were without Christ."

It is quite clear that the reference in the text is to a state of unenlightened, unregenerated paganism, in which the Ephesians had been long immersed, and from which they had recently been delivered by the free and sovereign love of God, quickening them from

* Preached before the London Missionary Society, at Surrey Chapel, May 9th, 1821.

a moral and spiritual death, and raising them "to sit together in heavenly places in Christ Jesus." In allusion to this period of heathenish darkness, the apostle says, "Remember, that at that time ye were without Christ;" and this short, but comprehensive delineation, contains in itself a finished picture of human wretchedness. We can conceive of no worse predicament for a rational, immortal, sinful, perishing being, than to be without Christ. Let us, then, trace the bearing and influence of this mournful deficiency upon the nature of man.

1. *Upon his understanding.*

And truly, my brethren, I know of nothing more deeply affecting than to contemplate the human intellect left to itself, and toiling, in its entangled march, through all the trackless labyrinths of speculative uncertainty; to behold a mind once adorned with the likeness of God, but now void of knowledge, spending its strength, wasting its energies, and wearing out its courage, in the anxious pursuit of that which satisfieth not; in spite of all that is intense in application, and profound in investigation, "ever learning, and never able to come to the knowledge of the truth," 2 Tim. vii. 7; panting towards the goal, but never reaching it; bewildered, deceived, disappointed, and "in endless mazes lost;" this is, and must ever be the case, so long as men are without Christ.

2. *Consider this subject as it affects the conscience.*

"The whole world is guilty before God," Rom. iii. 19. Guilt is the parent of uneasiness; and though the cause may not be generally understood, the effect is manifest and undeniable. The apostle Paul expressly asserts the operation of conscience, even in minds unenlightened by Christian revelation : " their conscience also bearing witness, and their thoughts the mean while accusing or else excusing one another," Rom. ii. 15. You have, in these words, a representation of the mental process which is the true cause of that inward disquietude which racks and convulses the moral world. Oh, there is a deep and festering wound in the conscience of every sinner, which no balm can reach, but the Balm of Gilead ; no hand can heal, but that of the Physician who is there.

3. *As it affects the character.*

Where Christ is not, morality sheds but a dim, a feeble, and often a delusive ray. The fact, in its application to this part of the subject, is so fully established, and so perfectly ascertained, as to form an argument altogether irresistible. What were the Ephesians, the Corinthians, the Romans, the Cretans, so long as they were without Christ ? " Earthly, sensual, devilish," James iii. 15. " Serving divers lusts and pleasures—hateful and hating one another"—" always liars, evil beasts, slow bellies," Titus iii. 3 ; i. 12. What is now the state of morals in unenlightened Africa ? in unregenerated India? Why, blood toucheth blood ; rapine and cruelty, oppression and violence, injustice and deceit, and all the hideous brood of unnatural abominations, exist and triumph.

4. *As it relates to the happiness of man in the present life.*

Without Christ, you leave man as a sufferer under all the unmitigated weight of trouble ; you leave him to grapple, unaided and unsustained, with the fierce and uncontrollable calamities of life, destitute of any alternative but a morbid sullenness of resentment, or an irritability which goads and chafes itself to death.

5. *We must, in justice to our subject, trace its operation on the civil and religious institutions of human society.*

All countries have found it expedient to form laws and governments for the safe and beneficial regulations of social intercourse ; but, without that benign and salutary influence of Christianity, when has this object been secured ?

Nor are the religious institutions of unenlightened nations in any degree better than their civil ordinances. The whole system of idolatrous worship, intended as it is to placate an offended Deity, only serves to offend him the more highly, and to leave the conscience really more heavily burdened, and more foully stained, instead of affording it relief. The various modes of propitiation resorted to, are alike impious and vain. The ablutions and the penances—the blood of bulls and goats—the immolation of human victims,—all proclaim the truth of the statement I have made ; while they confess their own inadequacy to take away sin, or to satisfy the conscience.

6. *We must consider the relation of our subject to the immortal destiny of man.*

To live without Christ is dreadful; but, oh ! what must it be to die without him ? There is so much of overpowering solemnity in this view of the subject, that one is at a loss how to approach it. To all men " it is appointed once to die;" and all men need consolation (if ever) in a dying hour. But, alas! if, when the veil of the flesh is rent asunder, the mind can see no brightness beyond it, no solid ground of hope, no certain assurance of blessedness, the gloomy veil will be covered with a tenfold obscurity, and darkened with irremediable sadness.

II. *The duty of cherishing a distinct and constant remembrance of this condition.*

1. *The light of reason, and the custom of mankind, are sufficient to show that we should cherish the grateful remembrance of eminent deliverances.*

All men have agreed in preserving the memory of the founders of states, the benefactors of their country, the heroes of the age. Hence pillars, statues, temples, trophies, and monuments, have been reared, as so many commemorative ensigns.

2. *The express direction of Holy Scripture.*

On the Jewish church such recollection was frequently and solemnly inculcated. Exod. xiii. 3, "And Moses said unto the people, Remember this day, in which ye came out from Egypt, out of the house of bondage; for by strength of hand the Lord brought you from this place." See also Deut. v. 15.

3. *We may appeal to the impulse of good feeling in every mind that is rightly, by which I mean religiously constituted.*

It will be found consonant to every dictate of ingenuous sensibility, that we should keep in abiding recollection the state of degradation and misery from which Divine grace has rescued us, whether individually, in our religious connections, or in our national character. That man is chargeable with a brutish negligence, and must carry a heart of adamant in his bosom, who can erase from his mind the recollection of so great a benefit.

III. *The practical effects which should flow from this remembrance.*

1. *This recollection should be productive of deep humiliation and self-abasement.*

What pride studies to forget, humility delights to remember; whenever we are tempted to grow vain of our high distinctions, let us check the risings of self-esteem, and self-admiration, by considering what we once were—untutored barbarians, savage idolaters, fast bound in the fetters of a mental and moral slavery; yet, with maniac infatuation, dancing in our chains.

2. *This recollection should excite sentiments* of the liveliest gratitude, for the happy change which has taken place in our condition.

3. *This recollection should endear to us our native land, which the religion of Jesus has hallowed and blessed.*

From what a depth of abasement has Jesus Christ raised us!

"I would not change my native land,
For rich Peru and all her gold:
A nobler prize lies in my hand
Than East or Western Indies hold."

The lines are fallen to us in pleasant places; yea, we have a goodly heritage!

4. *This recollection should engage us to demean ourselves in a manner answerable to the great change which, through the favor of God, has taken place in our moral situation.*

"The darkness is past, and the true light now shineth," 1 John ii. 8. As the "children of the light, and of the day," much is expected of us; let us, then, labor to profit to the utmost by the privileges we enjoy. In a word, let us cultivate personal piety, family religion, and social usefulness.

5. *This recollection should excite in our bosoms the tenderest compassion for those nations who are yet without Christ, deeply plunged in all the miseries of which we have been hearing.* It should generate pity for human souls, immortal souls, laboring under the infelicities of an unchristianized state.

Finally, *This recollection will supply the amplest justification of missionary efforts, and urge us forward in the prosecution of missionary labors.*

There is no objection brought against this species of active benevolence, which the case before us does not refute and annihilate. The attempt to convert the heathen is rational, scriptural, and must by God's blessing be effectual. "Go ye, into all the world, and preach the gospel to every creature," Mark xvi. 15. Go, reveal "the mystery which was kept secret since the world began, but now is made manifest, and by the Scriptures of the prophets, according to the commandment of the everlasting God, made known to all nations for the obedience of faith," Rom. xvi. 25, 26.

LXXXIX.—THE CERTAIN INCREASE OF THE GLORY AND KINGDOM OF JESUS.

BY REV. JOHN RYLAND, D.D., BRISTOL.

"He must increase."—*John* iii. 30.

It was not subject of regret to that burning and shining light, that his Lord should so greatly outshine him; he was willing to be concealed, or withdrawn, that the Saviour might shine forth with greater splendor. He had no wish that the manifestation of the Redeemer's glory should be delayed, that he himself might have the more time to shine, and that his disciples might rejoice in his light for a longer season. He was glad to recommend them to a more excellent teacher. He rejoiced greatly in the increasing discovery of the Divine glories of Jesus, and wished to direct every eye to behold "the Lamb of God." And, verily, this is the best and noblest ground of joy to all the friends of God and man. All other lights that have shined in the church, have soon arrived at their zenith, and have then declined and disappeared out of our hemisphere; but He who is eminently "the light of the world," John viii. 12, *must still increase,* till this whole benighted globe is illuminated with his brightness; and he will be the light and glory of the upper world forever.

I. *It is proposed to consider the nature of that increase, which the Baptist confidently expected should attend his blessed Lord.*

Doubtless, he principally refers to the manifestation of his spiritual glory, and to the establishment of his kingdom of grace. He could not intend an increase of wordly greatness, pomp, and power; for we know by the subsequent history of the life of Christ, that he never possessed these objects of human ambition, while he abode on earth. They are things he never aspired after while here below, nor was it designed that he should attain them.

1. *It was announced, that "he must increase;"* and, lo! in the midst of poverty and reproach, of apparent weakness, and of cruel sufferings, Jesus exhibited an *increasing* display of Godlike fortitude and resolution; of spotless purity and rectitude ; of infinite zeal for his Father's honor ; and of the riches of grace and compassion for wretched ruined man. "He was numbered with transgressors" himself, that he might justify the ungodly, and make them associates with angels, and inheritors of celestial glory.

2. *On these transactions all the future increase of his kingdom absolutely depended.* But now the purchase of redemption has been completed, what shall prevent the Saviour from receiving his full reward? When his last sufferings were approaching, he said to Andrew and Philip, "The hour is come that the Son

of man should be glorified. Verily, verily, I say unto you, except a corn of wheat fall into the ground and die, it abideth alone : but if it die, it bringeth forth much fruit," John xii. 23, 24.

3. *Well then might John the Baptist affirm, " He must increase," when he foresaw that his shameful death would be followed by so glorious a resurrection ;* when he, who " was made a little lower than the angels, for the suffering of death," should be " crowned with glory and honor;" and after "he had by himself purged our sins, sat down on the right hand of the Majesty on high ; being made so much better than the angels, as he hath by inheritance obtained a more excellent name than they," Heb. i. 3, 4.

4. *And how much more did the transactions of Pentecost justify this blessed prediction.* Then was so copious an effusion of the Spirit bestowed on the apostles, that they, who had lately hid themselves in secret chambers for fear of the Jews, were filled with courage and boldness, to testify to all the house of Israel, that the same Jesus whom they had crucified, was assuredly the Lord Messiah, Acts ii.

5. *The extensive donations of the Father to his incarnate Son had been long since recorded by David and Isaiah.* " Ask of me, and I shall give thee the heathen for thine inheritance, and the uttermost parts of the earth for thy possession."—" It is a light thing that thou shouldest be my servant, to raise up the tribes of Jacob, and to restore the preserved of Israel : I will also give thee for a light to the Gentiles, that thou mayest be my salvation unto the end of the earth," Psa. ii. 8 ; Isa. xlix. 6.

6. *That though the church below has not been always increasing in numbers, the church above is continually increasing.* The gates of the New Jerusalem, which are never shut day nor night, are perpetually admitting some happy spirit, transported from a state of imperfection and conflict, to the perfection of holiness and bliss.

II. *Let me proceed to lay before you some considerations which may confirm our faith in the assured expectation that he must increase.*

(1.) I may briefly remark, before I specify the positive grounds of this conclusion, that it was not founded upon the prospect of his employing a military force to propagate his religion with the sword.

(2.) Nor was this expectation built upon

the rank and influence of his adherents.

(3.) Nor is it on the multitude of Christ's genuine followers, in any period of time already past, that we ground our hope of his future increase.

(4.) We are far from building our hopes upon any flattering promises of worldly gain, and sensual indulgences, by which our Master would draw followers after him.

1. *Because he is the Son of God, in the highest and most absolute sense, and therefore heir of all things.* For, as John the Baptist observes, ver. 35, "The Father loveth the Son, and hath given all things into his hand."

2. *We are persuaded, therefore, that he must increase, because he hath all power to overcome every enemy that opposeth his blessed reign.* But "it hath pleased the Father that in him should all fulness dwell," Col. i. 19 ; and out of his fulness have all his people received, and grace for grace. Still shall his cause be carried on ; nor will the blessed Spirit grow weary of his beloved work, in taking of the things of Christ, and revealing them to the souls of men.

3. *He must increase, for the decrees of heaven ascertain the great event.* God, that cannot lie, promised before the world began that eternal life should be imparted through him, to an innumerable multitude, who were chosen in him, and predestinated to the adoption of sons.

4. *A great part of Scripture consists of promises of the increase of the Messiah's kingdom, and it is evident that the season of their chief accomplishment is yet future.* See Isa. xl. ; lx.

5. *We conclude that Jesus must increase, since this world and all others were "made by him, and for him."* This earth especially had been made in vain, or had been used only as a place of punishment, had not the kingdom of grace been erected here by the glorious Immanuel. But here he has determined that "Mercy shall be built up forever"—not at the expense of righteousness, God forbid ! but that "grace might reign through righteousness unto eternal life by Jesus Christ our Lord," Rom. v. 21. What inferences further shall we draw, my Christian brethren, from these premises ?

(1.) Have they not abundant ground for joy and gratitude, who are decidedly on Christ's side ? You, my dear brethren, were once aliens from the commonwealth of Israel ; you were once enemies in your minds to the King of Zion !

(2.) How shall we all, my Christian friends, and especially we, my honored fathers and brethren, who have been called unto the ministry of the word, be excited to activity and resolution in our Redeemer's cause ? "He must increase ;" and so he shall, whether we are faithful or not. But oh ! what an honor, what a pleasure, will it be, to be employed as instruments in promoting his blessed kingdom !

(3.) Brethren ! seek the increase of Christ's kingdom in your own souls. Let it be our daily prayer, "Thy kingdom come, thy will be done," in us, and by us.

(4.) And oh ! let us seek the increase of his kingdom all around us, by the conversion of souls to God, by their being "turned from darkness to light, and from the power of Satan," to subjection to the Redeemer.

(5.) Nor let us confine our efforts, and much less our ardent prayers, to the increase of true godliness at home.

Finally,

Let all my hearers examine, whether they are yet the genuine subjects of Christ's kingdom. There can be no neutrality in this case : if we are not for him, we are against him. And oh ! how awful will be the lot of them that oppose his government, and despise his grace !

XC.—THE CHARACTER OF CHRIST'S CONQUESTS.

" Gird thy sword upon thy thigh, O most mighty, with thy glory and thy majesty. And in thy majesty ride prosperously because of truth and meekness and righteousness: and thy right hand shall teach thee terrible things. Thine arrows are sharp in the heart of the king's enemies; whereby the people fall under thee."— *Psa.* xlv. 3–5.

THIS striking and beautiful psalm evidently refers to the Messiah. It is impossible, without doing the greatest violence to the glorious truths it contains, to apply it either to Solomon, or to any other earthly sovereign. This is evidently a poetical epithalamium, or song of congratulation, before the marriage of some celebrated monarch. The strain exactly agrees with such compositions. Three subjects are intro-

duced : 1, *The splendor of the bridegroom ;*
2, *The beauty of the bride ;* 3, *The happy
results arising from the union.* The glory
of the bridegroom occupies the chief part of
the psalm. He is praised for the comeliness of his person,—the gracefulness of his
address,—his triumphant military exploits,
—his righteous administration,—the lustre
of his renown,—and the magnificence of his
court. The bride is celebrated for her high
birth, her transcendent beauty, her splendid
and costly apparel, and her dignified attendants. The results arising from the union
are these. The marriage is to produce a
race of princes, who are to possess authority
and dominion to the ends of the earth. The
name, too, of the king is to live through posterity, and his renown to be as lasting as
time itself.

Such is the beauty and richness of the
psalm before us. It can apply to none but
Jesus, who is " King of kings, and Lord of
lords," and to whom the apostle applies the
sixth verse, where he says, " But unto the
Son he saith, Thy throne, O God, is forever
and ever," etc., Heb. i. 8. The psalmist
was, doubtless, inspired to set forth the marriage of the Son of God with his redeemed
church. A subject largely illustrated in the
parables of the New Testament, and sustained in every part of the Divine word.
That part which we have selected for our
present contemplation, relates to the character of the bridegroom as a kingly conqueror, and shows the ardent interest the
church takes in his triumphant career. Thus
she says, " Gird thy sword," etc., Psa. xlv.
3, etc. Consider the *Person*, the *Cause*,
the *Weapons*, and the *Triumphs of the
Saviour.*

I. *The person of the Messiah.*

" He is a king." Distinguished for his
glory, majesty, and might.

1. *His glory is that of supreme Deity.*
" The glory of the only-begotten," &c.,
John i. 14. Glory underived, supreme, universal, everlasting. As the sun is the glory
of the solar system, so Christ is the glory
of the heaven of heavens.

2. *His majesty is that which involves the
highest degree of royal authority.* Hence
his throne is above every other. By him
all principalities exist. By him kings reign,
and princes decree justice, Prov. viii. 15.
" King of kings." King of the whole earth ;
of the whole universe.

3. *Most mighty.* Powerful in the highest

degree. Yet this is but a feeble illustration
of his boundless power. One in whom power
is concentrated ; who has it in all its infinite
and uncontrollable plenitude. So much so,
that what is impossible to the most powerful
of the angelic hosts, yea, impossible to all
created powers, is easily effected by the
mere volition of his almighty mind. In creation, " He spake, and it was done," Psa.
xiii. 9. In the days of his flesh, his word
cured diseases, hushed tempests, expelled
devils, and raised the dead.

II. *The cause of Messiah.*

His cause, or kingdom, is the very transcript of his own personal attributes and
glory. His spiritual empire is based on the
moral perfections of his own holy and blessed
mind. Hence, the great end of redemption
is, to bring our fallen world to reflect the
glory of his moral excellence.

1. *It is the cause of truth.* Sin began in
falsehood,—the whole empire of Satan is
based upon this. Departure from the truth
was the ruin of our world. Our first parents
abode not in the truth. Hence Christ, in
destroying the works of the devil, razes his
fallacies, annihilates that which is tinsel, and
presents God's truth for the reception of his
lapsed and wretched creatures. Truth here,
however, may be taken in its largest latitude : for reality, substance, knowledge.
Christ is the truth of the gospel system.
Truth, as it respects God, and man, and
eternity.

2. *It is the cause of meekness.* And here
we see its resemblance to its Author : Christ
was eminently the meek one : " I am meek
and lowly in heart," Matt. xi. 29. But the
term meekness is to be taken in its most enlarged sense, for lowliness and humility.
The cause of sin is the cause of pride and
self-exaltation. To this Satan aspired. To
this the first human transgressors aspired.
This fills the carnal heart. It is the mental
delusion of every sinner. Christ's kingdom
is essentially connected with human abasement ; prostration of the sinner. It covers
the contrite with the garment of humility ;
brings man to a right estimate of himself
and his deserts, and thus fits him to be a
vessel of mercy.

3. *The cause of righteousness.* Christ is
" THE LORD OUR RIGHTEOUSNESS," Jer. xxiii.
6. He came to set up a righteous dominion.
Sin is unrighteousness,—robs God,—it is the
refusal of Jehovah's claims, &c. This is the
depravity of the spirit of man in its natural

state. Christ's kingdom is a righteous kingdom. He came to turn men from their iniquities. He came to fulfil the prophecies and promises. To put God's laws into their hearts, &c. To give a right spirit,—so that they should walk in his statutes and ordinances to do them. By the gospel men are made righteous, and they work righteousness. Every kind of righteousness is included in the essential constitution of the kingdom of Christ. A right heart and life towards God, and also towards all mankind.

III. *The weapons which, as a warrior, he wields.*

These are the sword and bow. In the sublime visions of the Apocalypse, Christ is represented with both of these weapons, Rev. i. 16, "And out of his mouth went a sharp two-edged sword." See also Rev. vi. 2, "And I saw, and behold a white horse: and he that sat on him had a bow; and a crown was given unto him: and he went forth conquering and to conquer." The divine word is fitly represented by these weapons. Our text supposes Christ in a chariot of war, going forth into the midst of his enemies, using his two-edged sword, and directing his arrows in every direction. The word, or gospel, of Christ is both the sword and arrow. It slays, it pierces, it severs in two; or, like the arrow, it enters the vital part, produces anguish, bitterness, and death to sin. See Heb. iv. 12, "For the word of God is quick and powerful, and sharper than any two-edged sword, piercing even to the dividing asunder of soul and spirit," &c.

Two ends have to be effected,

1. *Conviction of sin.* A sense of it,—a desire for its removal, &c.

2. *The soul healed.* Comforted, and filled with joy and peace. Messiah's weapons produce both these effects: "The power of God to salvation," Rom. i. 16. Every way effectual: "Mighty through God to the pulling down of the strongholds" of sin and Satan, see 2 Cor. x.

IV. *The triumphs which Messiah achieves.* In the phraseology of the text,

1. *He rides prosperously.* As a man of war, he advances in his course. His holy crusade is successful: this is the promise, that "the pleasure of the Lord shall prosper in his hand," Isa. liii. 10. God has pronounced the mandate and fixed the decree, that to him every knee should bow. He therefore says, "Sit thou on my right hand,

until I make thine enemies thy footstool," Psa. cx. 1.

2. *His right hand accomplishes wonderful things.* For so the word was originally rendered in our old Bibles. The history of Christianity is a history of the wonderful things which the right hand of Jesus has accomplished. It was wonderful that his cause lived in the midst of the opposition of earth and hell. Jews and pagans all labored at exterminating it. But Christ's right hand sustained it; and, like the vessel on the lake of Galilee, it survived the storm; or, like the burning bush on Horeb's summit, it lived in the midst of flame. But it was more wonderful that this "stone cut out of the mountain" should overthrow all its opponents,—silence all adversaries,—triumph over all opposition,—and succeed everywhere in spite of earth and hell. His right hand effected wondrous things everywhere, where the gospel chariot won its widening way.

3. *His enemies, subjugated, fell under him.* Not by their destruction,—not as the victims of wrath and vengeance,—but as subdued in heart and converted in life, so as to be the devoted disciples of the Nazarene. Look at the three thousand Jews, Acts ii. 41; at Saul of Tarsus; at the jailer of Philippi, &c. Look to your own personal history, you, who have felt his conquering love, resisted no longer, hated no longer; but were compelled, by the force of truth and the power of grace, to exclaim, in the words of the poet,

"I yield, I yield, I can hold out no more;
But sink, by dying love compelled,
And own thee Conqueror."

Such are the triumphs the conquering Jesus obtains. We ask, by way of

APPLICATION.

1. Do you thus personally know the Saviour? Have you felt the power, the saving power of the gospel? Are you numbered with his loyal subjects, his devoted friends?

2. Are you fully committed to his cause? Do you consider his cause yours? is his glory your first consideration? Do you pray for this—live for this—labor for this? Will this apply to each and all of you? Let us consider the text,

3. As God's voice. He speaks and looks with intense interest and delight on the Church. Oh, yes! and the bride, too, longs for the blissful consummation. Do we, all

and each? This, then, be our prayer: "Blessed be the Lord God of Israel, who only doeth wondrous things. And blessed be his glorious name forever; and let the whole earth be filled with his glory; Amen, and Amen," Psa. lxxii. 18, 19.

XCI.—MESSIAH'S FINAL TRIUMPH.

"I will overturn, overturn, overturn it; and it shall be no more, until he come whose right it is; and I will give it him."—*Ezek.* xxi. 27.

THE prophecy of the text has reference to the removal of the crown from the head of Zedekiah, and the vacancy in the royal line of David, which should not be filled up until the sceptre should be given into Christ's hands, whose true right it should be to reign. Now, all this was literally fulfilled, for the kingdom of Judah ceased not until Christ appeared, who was the root and offspring of David, and King of kings, and Lord of lords. But there is another version of the text which may be taken, and which is in perfect unison with the spirit of prophecy; that Jehovah has given universal empire to Jesus; that it is Christ's right to reign; and that God will overturn every obstacle and impediment until it be accomplished. Let these three topics, then, now engage our attention.

I. *Jehovah has given universal empire to Jesus.*

A few citations from the oracles of truth will establish this. Psa. lxxii. 8–11; ii. 8; lxxxix. 27; Dan. vii. 14; Zech. ix. 10; Phil. ii. 10; Acts ii. 32, &c. It is evident from these truths that Christ's dominion is to embrace the whole world—every empire, kingdom, continent, and island. All people of every language, and color, and tongue. His kingdom is to swallow up every other; and the kingdom that will not serve him is to utterly perish. This blissful consummation was beheld in prophetic vision by John, Rev. xi. 15. With this state of things will be associated universal righteousness, universal knowledge, universal peace, universal bliss. We notice,

II. *That it is Christ's right thus to reign.* "Whose right it is." Now, this right of Jesus to reign supremely and universally is founded,

1. *On his creative property in all things.* The apostle says, Col. i. 16, "All things were made by him, and for him." By his

power, and for his glory. Satan is a usurper—the world is alienated from its rightful Lord. But the right of Christ remains unaffected, and that right he will demand and obtain.

2. *On his supreme authority as universal Lord.* He is Lord of all, King of kings, &c. His majesty and glory fill the heavens. His claims are as great as the universe. As such, he has a right surely to the earth—to the whole earth. This authority is seen in controlling all events, in upholding all things, &c. In his infinite out-goings of benevolence and love.

3. *He has a redeeming right.* He became incarnate, he descended into it, he brought the light of heaven into it, he gave his own life for it, he is the proprietor, &c. Here, then, is a right, ratified with his precious blood. And he redeemed it expressly that he might reign over it. That he might be King, and King alone, that the diadem might encircle his own brow. And thus, in the extension of his kingdom, he is receiving his joy and reward. He was willingly lifted up, that he might draw all men unto him, see John xii. 32.

III. *God will overturn every obstacle until this be effected.* "I will overturn," &c. Now, in effecting this glorious purpose, the works of the devil must be destroyed, and the empire of sin totally overthrown. Ignorance must give place to light, error to truth, sin to holiness. Satan must be driven from his strongholds; and thus Jesus will enlarge his empire, and extend his domains. There are, however, four mighty impediments, which must be overthrown—entirely overturned.

1. *Paganism, and all its multifarious rites.* The idolatry of paganism, the superstitions of paganism, the cruelty of paganism. The very atmosphere of paganism is the smoke of the bottomless pit. Paganism, whether of the intellectual and metaphysical kind of the Hindoos, or of the rude and illiterate kind of the untutored tribes, must be overturned. Every pagan idol must be cast "to the moles and to the bats," &c. Every altar razed, and every temple desolated, see Isa. ii. 18–20.

2. *Mohammedanism in all its earthly gratifications.* Mohammedanism is a splendid admixture of adulterated truth and vulgar error. This must be overturned. The false prophet must be denounced and forsaken; the crescent must wane, and retire

into oblivion before the power of the cross.

3. *Judaism, with its obsolete rites.* A system originally of God, but which consisted of types and shadows, which have long ago been ratified in Jesus, the great Substitute and Antitype. Eighteen hundred years ago that system lost its vitality; and Ichabod has been for ages written upon its rites and services and people—the glory has departed. The Jews are like persons who at eventide are looking for the rising sun; but every vestige of that shadowy economy must pass away, and all the relics of the scattered tribes be collected into the fold of Christ, see Rom. xi. 25.

4. *Antichristian Rome.* The papal hierarchy is evidently that Man of sin to which the apostle alludes, who must be destroyed. This is evidently the mystical Babylon whose overthrow is certain. This is to be as a millstone thrown into the depths of the sea, Rev. xviii. 20. Every thing that exalteth itself against God, or attempts the division of Christ's merits, must be consumed before the brightness of Messiah's countenance, and the power of his truth. But you ask, How will God overturn, &c.? Doubtless his providence will subserve the purposes of his grace. He may cause science and commerce to open a passage for the message of truth. He may even overrule war, and may allow the military hero to pioneer the ambassador of peace. But he will do it by the power of the gospel of truth. The doctrines of the cross are to effect it. "We preach Christ crucified," &c., 1 Cor. i. 23. "Not by might, nor by power," &c. The spiritual sword is the word of God. He did this by the gospel in primitive times. In bigoted Jerusalem, in idolatrous Athens, in lascivious Corinth, in imperial Rome, and in these, then rude islands of the sea. He is doing so now. Look at the islands of the South Sea; look at Central Africa; look on the shores of continental India; look into the interior of Burmah: in one word, that which converts a blaspheming Briton will save a Hindoo idolater, or savage American Indian.

APPLICATION.

1. Are your sympathies and affections on the side of Jesus? Does the subject inspire, inspirit you? Has it your affections, prayers, influence, and help?

2. How necessary is devoted, concentrated effort. What has to be achieved? make

the calculation. We spoke of Pagans, write down 482 millions; Mohammedans, 140 millions; Jews, 3 millions; then add, as disciples of Papal Rome, 80 millions: total 705 millions. Is it not hopeless? No—read the text. God has spoken it, &c.

3. Secure a personal interest in the gracious administration of Jesus.

XCII.—CHRIST'S COLLECTED FLOCK.

BY REV. TIMOTHY DWIGHT, D. D. LL. D.[*]

"And other sheep I have, which are not of this fold: them also I must bring, and they shall hear my voice; and there shall be one fold, and one shepherd."—*John* x. 16.

In the text, after having displayed in his previous observations, a tenderness never exhibited by any other inhabitant of this world, Christ proceeds to inform us, that he had other sheep, besides those of which he had been speaking; that he must bring, or collect, them; and that the two flocks should constitute one—be sheltered by one fold, and led by one shepherd.

"Other sheep," says our Saviour, "I have." Other disciples, besides those of the Jewish nation, and the present age, I have belonging to my family. They exist among the Gentiles in this age; and will exist in every future period. "The gospel of the kingdom," which is to be preached in all nations, will everywhere find those who will cordially receive and obey its dictates: those, who in the exercise of a living and affectionate confidence, will hereafter give themselves up to me, and become mine. They are now mine, and were given to me from the beginning. "Them I must bring." To collect them from every part of the world is one of the greatest duties of my office; a part of the glorious work which my Father gave me to do, and I shall not leave it unaccomplished. "They shall hear my voice." When I call, they will know and acknowledge me as their Shepherd, and cheerfully obey the summons. "There shall be one fold:" a single church—a single assembly of my disciples; one in name; one in their character, their life, and their destination; and I, the good, the only Shep-

* From a sermon before the American Board of Commissioners for Foreign Missions, delivered in Boston, Sept. 16, 1813.

herd, will lead them. "They shall hunger no more, neither thirst any more; neither shall the sun light on them, nor any heat. For the Lamb which is in the midst of the throne shall feed them, and shall lead them unto living fountains of waters," Rev. vii. 16.

"Other sheep," saith our Saviour, "I have, which are not of this fold." The sheep which Christ then had were *Jews:* inhabitants of a single country, and living at that single period. Nay, they were a little flock gathered out of these. His other sheep, as he has taught us in his word, are a great multitude, which no man could number, of all nations, and kindreds, and people, and tongues; born in every future period; gathered out of every distant land, Rev. vii. 9. "Them also I must bring, and they shall hear my voice." He who took such effectual care of the little flock which followed him during his ministry, because it was their "Father's good pleasure to give them the kingdom," will be easily believed, when he informs us, that he must and will bring into his fold a multitude, by their number and character of such immeasurable importance. For this very end, he hath "ascended far above all heavens, that he might fill all things." For this very end, he is constituted Head over all things unto his church. This is the third great division of his employment as Mediator. The first, to teach the will of God for our salvation; the second, to expiate our sins; the third is to gather us into his heavenly kingdom.

I. *What things are to be done for the completion of this end?* I observe,

1. *The views of mankind concerning religious subjects, are to be extensively changed.*

It will not be questioned, that truth is invariably an object of the Divine complacency; and error of the Divine reprobation. As God rejoices in his works, so it is impossible that he should not be pleased with truth; which is only a declaration of the state of those works, of his agency in accomplishing them, and of his character displayed in that agency. Error, which falsifies all these things, must, with equal evidence, be odious to him. As little can it be questioned, that truth is the instrument through which we are sanctified, and made free from the bondage of corruption.

2. *A mighty change, also, must be wrought in the disposition of men.*

Whenever mankind shall be brought into the fold of Christ, will succeed that love to God, and to man, which is the fulfilling of the law; that repentance towards God, and that faith in the Redeemer, which are the primary obedience of the gospel. In the train of these great evangelical attributes, will follow the meek and lowly virtues of Christianity, which so extensively occupied the instructions, and so beautifully adorned the life of the Saviour : "Love, joy, peace, long-suffering, gentleness, goodness, faith, meekness, temperance," Gal. v. 22, 23; all, glorious fruits of the Spirit of grace—natives of heaven ; and though for a time pilgrims in this world, yet destined to return to heaven again.

3. *The change will not be less in the conduct of men.*

Permit me, then, to observe, that the private conduct of men will experience a mighty and wonderful revolution. Truth, at the same time, will resume her empire over the tongue, the pen, and the press. Honesty also will control the dealings of men. In the same manner, will unkindness vanish from the habitations of mankind. The stranger will everywhere find a home, and the wanderer an asylum. Uncharitableness, also, between those who profess the religion of the Redeemer, will be found no more. Nor will the *public* conduct of mankind be less extensively inverted. On the bench, will be seen those, and those only, who shake their hands from holding bribes; stop their ears from hearing evil ; and close their eyes from seeing blood. At the bar of justice, prisoners will cease to be found : the deserted jail will crumble into dust; and the gibbet will be known only in the tales of other times. Wars, also, will be no more.

Then religion will resume her proper station, and no longer be subordinated to pleasure, gain, and glory; to frantic scrambles about place and power, and the aggrandizement of wretches, who steal into office by flattery and falsehood, in order to riot on peculation. From heaven will she descend, clothed with a cloud ; and a rainbow upon her head, her face as it were the sun, and her feet pillars of fire : in her hand she will hold a little book ; and that book will be opened to the eyes of all nations of men, see Rev. x. 1, 2 : on its pages they will read, in lines of light, "Now is come salvation and strength, and the kingdom of our God, and the power of his Christ. God himself will dwell among the great family of Adam, and be their God; and they shall be his people."

II. *In what manner are these things to be done?*

I answer, they are to be accomplished, not by miracles, but by means. St. Paul has, in the most express and decisive terms, given us the law of procedure, by which the kingdom of God is to be established in every part of the habitable world. "How shall they call on him in whom they have not believed? and how shall they believe in him of whom they have not heard? and how shall they hear without a preacher? So then, faith cometh by hearing, and hearing by the word of God," Rom. x. 14–17.

(1.) Permit me to add, that those by whom these mighty things are to be done, are themselves to exhibit the spirit of the gospel as the great controlling principle of their conduct. Common sense has proverbially declared, and all experience uniformly proved, that precept without example is vain. To the intended objects of this beneficence, it would be worse than in vain. From men, who do not practice what they teach, instructions would be received, as the Mexicans received them from the Spaniards, only with contempt and indignation.

(2.) The process of this mighty work is, in this respect also, exactly marked out by St. Paul. "Salvation has come unto the Gentiles to provoke the Jews to jealousy;" or, as in the Greek, To excite them to emulation, Rom. xi. 11.

(3.) The casting away of the Jews is the reconciling of the world: the receiving of them will be to that same world life from the dead.

(4.) It is hardly necessary to observe, that the measures which will produce these mighty effects upon the Jews, will have a similar efficacy wherever they are employed.

III. *By whom are these things to be done?*

This question admits but of one answer—on this subject there can be no debate: the time for doubt is past, the work is begun. Missionaries, already in great numbers, run to and fro, and knowledge is even now greatly increased. "The gospel of the kingdom" is already preached in Greenland, in Labrador, in Tartary, in Hindostan, in China, in New Holland, in the Isles of the Pacific Ocean, and the Caribbean Sea; in Southern America, and in the African deserts. The voice of salvation, the song of praise to Jehovah, echoes already from the sides of Taurus, and trembles over the waves of the Ganges. The Bible has travelled round the globe.

In such an enterprise, all who engage in it must be united: if Christians do not unite their hearts and their hands, they will effectuate nothing. Solitary efforts will here be fruitless; divided efforts will be equally fruitless; clashing efforts will destroy each other. Learn,

1. *The work to which you are summoned is the work of God.* My brethren, it is the chief work of God which has been announced to mankind; it is the end of this earthly creation; it is the end of this earthly providence; it is the glorious end of redemption.

2. *The present is the proper time for this glorious undertaking.* It is the proper time, as it is marked out by the spirit of prophecy.

3. *The necessity of this work irresistibly demands every practicable effort.*

"The whole world," says St. John, speaking of his own time, "lieth in wickedness," 1 John v. 19. Lieth—for such is the indication of the original—as a man slain lies weltering in his blood. How extensively is this strong picture a portrait of the world at this moment!

4. *The day in which these blessings are to be ushered in has arrived.* The day in which the mighty work will be seen in its full completion is at hand. We must labor, that those who come after us may enter into our labors. We must sow, and in due time both we and our successors, if we sow bountifully, shall reap a Divine harvest. With every faithful endeavor of ours, the Spirit of grace will co-operate. "As the earth bringeth forth her bud, and as the garden causeth the things that are sown in it to spring forth; so the Lord God will cause righteousness and praise to spring forth before all the nations," Isa. lxi. 11.

XCIII.—PRAYER FOR THE COMING OF GOD'S KINGDOM.*

BY REV. J. E. BEAUMONT, M. A.

"Thy kingdom come."—*Matt.* vi. 10.

MAN is a selfish being since his fall. So much does selfishness cleave to human na-

* From a sermon delivered on behalf of the Wesleyan Missionary Society, in Southwark Chapel, London, April 27th, 1838.

ture, that many philosophers have affirmed, that every human action is the product of self-love. This principle is so inwoven with our nature, so intwined with the very essence of our being, that it can only be subverted by a principle mightier than itself; and no principle mightier than itself has ever been found, except the principle that the gospel makes known—the principle of love : love to God, love to Christ. The gospel is the antidote to selfishness : its doctrines are all against selfishness ; its facts are all opposed to selfishness ; its precepts are all antagonists to selfishness ; its very prayers are opposed to selfishness.

What a difference there is between the man that prays and the man that never prays ; between the infidel and the believer ! The infidel would environ and smother and crush what we call, what we *believe,* what we *feel,* to be the truth. Yes, he accuses us by our folly, our fanaticism, and our enthusiasm, of turning the world upside down. He scoffs, raves, and ridicules our grand, benevolent, majestic, heaven-planned enterprise. But how is it with the Christian—with the believer—with him to whom the kingdom of God has come with power ? He longs for the diffusion of it ; he prays that this kingdom may stretch far and wide. Observe,

I. *The kingdom itself here referred to.*

The phrase *" kingdom of God"* is, like some other New Testament phrases, employed with some variety of signification—all the varieties, however, having a common relation. Sometimes the expression, " kingdom of God," implies the subjects of Christ's sceptre—the aggregate, the multitude of the " called, and faithful, and chosen ;"—that part of them that are on earth : then it is called the kingdom of Christ in the world. At other times, that part which has arrived already in *heaven :* and then it is called the kingdom of *glory.* In the passage before us, we are to understand that dominion, that holy dominion, which God is setting up in the human heart, in the human world, in and by the Messias : a kingdom of which all time, since its early dawn, hath been the duration, of which mankind are the subjects, of which salvation is the object, of which the glory of the Triune God is the end.

1. *This kingdom is not a worldly kingdom.* And yet the Jews, among whom the Saviour dwelt when he was manifest in the flesh, expected such a kingdom at the hands

of the Messias ; and the apostles themselves were not free from this misleading, master delusion.

2. *This kingdom is constituted in the very person of the King himself.* Christ, like others, has waded to his empire through blood ; but he has waded to his empire through no blood but the blood of his own heart. He fell himself to exalt us.

3. *This kingdom is a peaceable kingdom.* It is a beneficent institution. Its attributes are righteousness, peace, benevolence, integrity, purity, justice, charity.

4. *This kingdom admits of unlimited extension, of indefinite diffusion.* This kingdom shall spread and grow : it shall go out in this direction, and go forth in that ; it shall traverse that region, and pass over the other ; it shall go " from sea to sea, and from the river unto the ends of the earth,—men shall be blessed in him : all nations shall call him blessed," Psa. lxxii. 8, 17. The prophet Isaiah says, " The earth shall be full." Full ! What is the meaning of *full ?* " The earth shall be full." What ! FULL ? Yes, *full ;* that is the word :—" The earth shall be full of the knowledge of the Lord, as the waters cover the sea," Isa. xi. 9.

5. *This kingdom of Christ will be of long duration.* Not like earthly kingdoms, which rise up, run forward, gain the zenith, and then decline, and their names pass away, and their memory is blotted out ; not like these shall be the kingdom of Christ. This kingdom " lasts ; like the sun, it shall stand."

6. *The brightness of this kingdom is perpetually increasing.* Oh ! I rejoice to think —I think it, I believe it—that there is not an hour in any day, in which some straggling rebel is not coming in to Christ, kissing his sceptre, and devoting himself to his service. The number of Christ's subjects is continually increasing ; there is already a multitude before the throne that never can be withdrawn ; and the successes that are going on upon earth are swelling that continually accumulating amount of the first-born that is in heaven. Let us point out,

II. *Some grounds on which the pious may look and pray for the diffusion of this kingdom.* Some of the grounds on which they may expect its universal diffusion.

I. *We are warranted in such an expectation, I may say, from all analogy.* Why does the moon spread her horns ? Why, it is to fill them. Why does the sun rise above the horizon ? It is that he may go on his march upward and onward till he gains his meridian altitude, and pours his vertical glory on the world below. Why is the corn deposited in the soil ? It is that it may unwrap, that it may unfold itself—that, of that single seed, there may come a tree, the branches of which are for a lodgment of the birds, and a shadow for the beasts of the earth. Why does the rill steal silently from under the sod, wend its way among the grass and the pebbles, following its course onward and onward, enlarging its channel, rendering the fissure wider and wider for itself,—till, at last, that little rill becomes a mighty river, bearing on its bosom the riches of a nation, and feeding with its irrigations a nation's agriculture ?

When shall the kingdom of Christ have no boundaries ? Shall it always be in a state of minority ? Shall Satan usurp all ? Why, it is impossible that it should remain so. Christ MUST reign. Take it in the vigorous language of the apostle, in that passage in his first epistle to the Corinthians, where he says, xv. 25, " He must reign, till he hath put all enemies under his feet."

2. Again, *We are led to the same conclusion from the symbolical events of Jewish history.* Look, for a moment, at Egypt, and see the contest that went on between Moses and Aaron, and the magicians of Egypt. Moses was triumphant. So, in the contest between light and darkness, between truth and falsehood, between revelation and idolatry—light, truth, and revelation, shall win the day. So with respect to Dagon and the ark of the Lord. The idol being brought in juxtaposition with the ark of God, the ark retained its place, but the idol fell down prostrate, and was broken in pieces, 1 Sam. v. ; and so, surely, every other idol shall be prostrated before our Immanuel. Passing from individual cases, take the general case —I mean, the contest about the land of Canaan ; and as sure as the children of Israel took possession of that land according to the promise of God to their fathers, so surely the last stronghold of idolatry shall yield to the sceptre of Christ, and the whole earth shall be filled with his glory.

3. *I might say, that moral proportion requires that the kingdom of God should become thus glorious.* Christ must " see of the travail of his soul ;" and oh ! how millennially must his kingdom come, before his philanthropic heart shall say, " Enough ! enough !

that is all I look for : stop ! stop ! I shed my blood for no more !" We know that Jesus Christ, by the grace of God, tasted death for every man, Heb. ii. 9 ; and, having poured out his soul as an offering for the whole race, vast indeed must be his triumphs before he can say, "Enough ! that is all : that completes the whole !"

4. *When we think of the energy which is employed in the diffusion of this kingdom,* our hopes rise, and our expectations rise.

III. *Point out some of the encouraging intimations which we have of the coming of this kingdom of Christ.*

1. *Look at the facilities which there are for it.* There never were such facilities since the apostles' time. We have colonies, great flourishing colonies, all over the globe, which are so many focal points whence the light is to radiate in every direction beyond them. We have swift-winged messengers to carry our missionaries and our Bibles to more distant lands ; and, of all the ships that have left our shores, none surely have ever left them with more interest than those which have gone forth, manned with missionaries, and freighted with Bibles : shiploads of instrumentality with which to put back the frontier of idolatry.

2. *Besides the facilities for effort, there is, I think, rather more union of effort than there has been for ages.*

3. Then, again, *the success of effort* is also a most encouraging circumstance.

APPLICATION.

1. I cannot suppose that all, in this immense assembly, are yet the real, voluntary subjects and followers of the Lord Jesus Christ :—to that part of the congregation, therefore, I address myself. You, my fellow-sinners, are not far from the kingdom of Christ : yes, you are not far from it : you have heard the gospel. Oh ! that this night the kingdom of God may come to you.

2. You who are the subjects of the kingdom of Christ, bear with me while I address one word to you. You have grace—seek for more grace : the reality and the experience of grace are one thing—the abundance of its communications is another. Oh, that great grace may rest on you all ! Amen.

XCIV.—LOVE TO CHRIST THE ONLY TRUE MOTIVE TO MISSIONARY EXERTION.

BY REV. LEGH RICHMOND, M. A.*

"He saith to him again the second time, Simon, son of Jonas, lovest thou me? He saith unto him, Yea, Lord: thou knowest that I love thee. He saith unto him, Feed my sheep."—*John* xxi. 16.

LOVE to Christ, in his person and offices, is inseparably connected with love to his people, and anxiety for the salvation of sinners. He who loveth God will love his brother also, 1 John iv. 21. It will be the prayer and desire of his heart, as it was of Paul's, that Israel may be saved. Hence, in a special manner, spring the solicitude and unwearied diligence of the pastoral office. That holy zeal for the increase of the Redeemer's kingdom, which is so essential a characteristic of the new creature, carries the man of God, whom love has devoted to this peculiar service, through dangers without number, that he may seek and save them that are ready to perish. He knows that the sheep of Christ must be fed. They are a flock purchased with blood. But they are "scattered upon the mountains, and no man gathereth them," Nahum iii. 18. The love of God is shed abroad in his own heart by the Holy Ghost, which is given unto him. Therefore, the shepherd cannot slumber. Awake to the call of love and duty, he hears his Master's voice, and flies to execute his commands.

I propose to consider,

I. *The nature and design of the commission.*

As Peter had thrice denied his Master, so Christ, in the most solemn yet affectionate manner, questioned him three times, whether indeed he loved him. "Simon, son of Jonas, lovest thou me?" The lately fallen, but now recovered sinner, loved much, because much had been forgiven him. He earnestly appealed to his Lord's omniscience, as a testimony to the sincerity and ardor of his love. "Yea, Lord, thou knowest that I love thee. —Lord, thou knowest all things; thou knowest that I love thee." On each repetition of these questions and replies, Jesus deliberately committed that most important charge to his care, as a means of proving the integrity of his profession, "Feed my sheep." It ap-

* From a sermon, delivered before the Society for Missions to Africa and to the East, May 23, 1809.

pears, therefore, that the words of Christ, in this memorable passage, exhibit very clearly the principles, duty, character, and conduct of the faithful shepherd of souls; and especially of the Christian Missionary.

1. *The Christian's love to Christ is his great motive to exertion.* The life which he lives in the flesh, he lives by the faith of the Son of God, who loved him, and gave himself for him, Gal. ii. 20.

2. *The commandment of Christ, to feed his flock, declares the nature and object of his labors.*

3. *The example of Christ himself, in his life and death, is the model and pattern for his imitation.* Thus enlightened, and warmed by the animating beams of the Sun of Righteousness, he lives to the glory of God, and finds by happy experience, that "His service is perfect freedom."

Henceforward, the life of this apostle was a continual comment upon the Redeemer's precept. We find him faithful and diligent in his office; with an unconquerable zeal endeavoring to instruct the ignorant, bring back the wandering, strengthen the weak, confirm the strong, reclaim the vicious, and turn many to righteousness. He took all opportunities of declaring the glad tidings of salvation to perishing sinners. With holy patience and perseverance he endured all conflicts and trials, surmounted every difficulty and opposition, so that he might plant and propagate the Christian faith.

II. *The application of the commandment to feed the sheep of Christ, as it respects the heathen nations at present, and our exertions in order to their conversion.*

1. *Who are comprehended under this term, sheep?* "Ye my flock, the flock of my pasture, are men, and I am your God, saith the Lord God," Ezekiel xxxiv. 31. The flock committed to the apostle's care, consisted of yet unconverted Jews and unconverted heathen, who should, through preaching of the word, become disciples, and believe in the name of Christ. But this promise, said St. Peter to the Jews, "is unto you, and to your children, and to all that are afar off, even as many as the Lord our God shall call," Acts ii. 39. And again, addressing the Gentiles afterwards, at Joppa, "God is no respecter of persons; but in every nation, he that feareth him, and worketh righteousness, is accepted with him," Acts x. 34, 35.

2. *Why ought these sheep to be thus fed?* The positive injunctions of Christ to his apos-

tles, as to the propagation of the truth, give the most direct and unanswerable reply to this question; and in no instance is the appeal made so powerfully to the Christian's affections, as in that related in the text: "Lovest thou me?"—"Feed my sheep."

But, taking the question in another point of view, I should say, when speaking of the heathen, that they ought to be taught the word of life, because we have no warrant whatsoever from the Scriptures for concluding that they will be saved without the knowledge of Christ.

3. *We are next led to consider, when is this great duty of sending missionaries among the heathen to be undertaken?*

To this inquiry, I would unequivocally answer, Now! "Behold, *now* is the accepted time; behold, *now* is the day of salvation," 2 Cor. vi. 2. Go *now*, and proclaim Christ as a light to the Gentiles, and a salvation unto the end of the earth. Of late years, a great increase of gospel light and knowledge has been diffused throughout this country in particular. Protestants have not at the present period of time, as our forefathers had, to contend with the papists, almost for very existence. The growing attention of serious Christians, to the fulfilment of prophecy, as it concerns the downfall of popery, the restoration of the Jews, the conversion of the Gentiles, and the approach of the millennium, all of which are intimately connected with missionary plans, seem to mark the present as a signal period for exertion. I would not here omit to notice that happy consummation of the wishes of the pious and humane in the abolition of the slave-trade.

4. *The next subject of inquiry is, By whom ought the sheep of Christ among the heathen to be fed?*

Evidently, by those who themselves know the joyful sound. The visible churches of Christ are, by their principle and constitution, missionary bodies, from whose bosom holy emissaries should continually come forth to propagate the faith of Christ among the heathen. Is it asked, By whom, individually and personally, are the sheep of Christ to be fed among the heathen? Who shall be your missionaries?—The shepherds, whom you set apart to this honorable labor of feeding and nourishing souls for Christ, must be men who love Christ for the salvation which he hath wrought in their own souls—men who feel in themselves the working of the Spirit of Christ, mortifying the works of the flesh and their earthly members, and drawing up their minds to high and heavenly things. They must be men, not of warmth and zeal alone, but of solidity, patience, and perseverance; men who, like their Lord, can endure the contradiction of sinners, Heb. xii. 3.

5. *Wherewith ought the sheep of Christ to be fed? With the declaration of what truths are we to labor for the conversion of the heathen?*

In answer to this question, there must be one reply,—preach Christ, as a free, full, perfect, and all-sufficient Saviour, to the greatest of sinners. The sheep of Christ, whether at home or abroad, will hear and know their own good Shepherd's voice, and none other. Proclaim, as from the housetop, that "God commendeth his love towards us, in that, while we were yet sinners, Christ died for us," Rom. v. 8; and thus accomplished that wonder of men and angels, "that God might be just, and yet the justifier of him which believeth in Jesus," Rom. iii. 26. Preach to them, the blood of Christ —its atoning and its cleansing power; preach to them, the perfect righteousness of Christ, as alone acceptable in the sight of God; preach to them, free justification by faith in what Christ suffered, and what Christ fulfilled in their stead; unfold to them, the mysteries of the covenant of peace, made in heaven for man; and the unsearchable riches of Christ, so freely therein provided for man's redemption;—set before them the purity of the Divine law—contrast it with the heinousness of their sins, and the pollution of their nature. Hence prove to them, that "Except a man be born of water and of the Spirit, he cannot enter into the kingdom of God," John iii. 3.

Johannes, the Mahikander Indian, at one of the meetings which the Brethren held for pastoral conversation and inquiry into the state of the congregations, related the occasion of his conversion in the following manner, in consequence of their speaking with one another about the method of preaching to the heathen.

"Brethren, I have been a heathen, and have grown old amongst them; therefore, I know very well how it is with the heathen, and how they think. A preacher once came to us, desiring to instruct us, and began by proving to us that there was a God. On which we said to him: 'Well, and dost thou think we are ignorant of that? Now, go back again to the place from whence thou camest.'

"Then another preacher came, and began to instruct us, saying, 'You must not steal, nor drink too much, nor lie, nor lead wicked lives.' We answered him : 'Fool that thou art! Dost thou think that we do not know that? Go and learn it first thyself, and teach the people whom thou belongest to, not to do those things ; for who are greater drunkards, or thieves, or liars, than thine own people ?' Thus we sent him away also.

"Some time after this, Christian Henry, one of the Brethren, came to me into my hut, and sat down by me. The contents of his discourse to me were nearly these : 'I am come to thee in the name of the Lord of heaven and earth. He sends me to acquaint thee, that he would gladly save thee, and make thee happy, and deliver thee from the miserable state in which thou liest at present. To this end he became a man, gave his life a ransom for man, and shed his blood for man. All that believe in the name of this Jesus obtain the forgiveness of sin. To all them that receive him by faith, he giveth power to become the sons of God. The Holy Spirit dwelleth in their hearts ; and they are made free, through the blood of Christ, from the slavery and dominion of sin. And though thou art the chief of sinners, yet, if thou prayest to the Father in his name, and believest in him as a sacrifice for thy sins, thou shalt be heard, and saved ; and he will give thee a crown of life, and thou shalt live with him in heaven forever.'

"When he had finished his discourse, he lay down upon a board in my hut, fatigued by his journey, and fell into a sound sleep. I thought within myself: 'What manner of man is this? There he lies, and sleeps so sweetly. I might kill him, and throw him out into the forest,—and who would regard it? But he is unconcerned. This cannot be a bad man: he fears no evil, not even from us, who are so savage ; but sleeps comfortably, and places his life in our hands.'

"However, I could not forget his words ; they constantly recurred to my mind. Even though I went to sleep, yet I dreamed of the blood which Christ had shed for us. I thought, 'This is very strange, and quite different from what I have ever heard.' So I went and interpreted Christian Henry's words to the other Indians.

"Thus, through the grace of God, an awakening took place among us. I tell you, therefore, brethren," said he, "preach to the heathen, Christ and his blood, his sufferings and death, if you would have your words to gain entrance amongst them ; if you would wish to produce a blessing among them."*

APPLICATION.

I beseech you to hear me, while I propose a few considerations to your attention.

1. Consider the state of the world, its empires, nations, kindreds, and tribes.

2. Again, consider the state of the Church ; and, if you love Christ, feed his sheep.

3. Consider, also, what the Church shall be in the days to come.

4. Again, consider your own privileges ; and, if you love Christ, feed his sheep.

Are you Christians? How came this? Did no man cross the seas, to teach your forefathers wisdom? Did no missionary brave the perils of a journey among your heathen ancestors, because he loved the sheep of Christ? Yea, brethren, through a blessing on missionary exertions, Christ visited Britain. He had a fold here ; and he sent some faithful shepherd to gather the scattered sheep into it. Go, then, and feed the sheep of Christ, as you yourselves have been fed.

XCV.—NO CESSATION OF THE GREAT WORK.

"Why should the work cease ?"—*Neh.* vi. 3.

NEHEMIAH was engaged in building the dilapidated walls of Zion. To this work he was called of God, and for its execution he was qualified from on high. But, during its progress, he had to contend with many difficulties. He had to encounter hostile foes ; he had to resist the craft of secret opponents ; and he had to contend with the formality of professed friends. He was possessed with a most magnanimous spirit, and he nobly persevered.

To some solicitations to discuss the engagements on which he had entered, he replied, "I am doing a great work, so that I cannot come down." And then said, in the

* Loskiel's "History of the Mission of the United Brethren among the Indians in North America."

language of the text, " Why should the work cease ?"

As Christians, we are connected with a greater work than that of Nehemiah—the work of building the spiritual temple of God, and the evangelization of the world. This work is God's work of saving men, and extending his glorious kingdom in the world—the work of true and vital religion ; and which is designed to overthrow the kingdom of darkness, and fill the whole earth with the Divine glory.

Now, this work has been set up in our world from the announcement of the first promise of mercy to our fallen parents. It has been identified with all ages and dispensations. Like a golden thread, it ran through all the families of the pious antediluvians, and through all the godly tribes of Israel. It was exhibited among all the patriotic and devout, during the long line of prophets. It burst forth with peculiar energy during the labors of the Baptist. It shone with meridian splendor in Judea, during the labors of the Redeemer. It went forth with irresistible power in the apostolic age ; and has been handed down to us, and is living and blessing men wherever the evangelical truths of the gospel are known. In reference to this work we intend to apply the text, and ask—" Why should the work cease ?" We shall,

I. *Assign some reasons why this work should not cease.*

II. *Show the interest and concern we should manifest in it.*

I. *Assign some reasons why this work should not cease.*

1. *Because of its moral grandeur.* Every work of God is grand in itself. Every department is so ; but not all in equal degree. The work of saving souls is the most exalted and the greatest of all the Divine works. As such, it occupies a pre-eminence in the sacred volume. As such, God is represented as being especially interested in it. It is the work of God's arm, and the work of his heart. He spoke the universe into being ; but to save men there were councils, covenants, dispensations, promises, oaths, blood ! This work deeply interests and powerfully agitates the three worlds. It is a work which includes all time, and equally all eternity : surely such a work should not cease !

2. *Because of its gracious character.* We might assent to the cessation of displays of mere power. We should rejoice in the cessation of exhibitions of judgment and wrath. We hail the subsiding of the waters of the deluge ; we hail the termination of the plagues of Egypt ; we hail the ceasing of the storm, the rumblings of the earthquake, the descent of the fiery lava. We rejoice when the sword of war finds its peaceful scabbard. But the work of God is one of grace—of favor to guilty man—compassion to the ungodly—mercy to the wretched. This work announces eyesight to the blind, health to the diseased, liberty to the captive, riches to the poor, joy to the mourner, salvation to the lost, heaven to the guilty. The emblem of this work is the rainbow, spanning our world with its arch of peace and mercy. So long as there is one unsaved sinner this work should not cease.

3. *Because of its elevating influences.* This work is one of emphatic exaltation. It humanizes the savage ; intellectualizes the ignorant ; purifies the unholy ; and subordinates the animal man to mind, and to moral power. It ennobles its possessor, it lifts up " out of the mire and clay," &c. It transforms the thorn into a fig-tree, the lion to a lamb, the vulture into a dove, the sinner into a saint, the curse into a blessing. It is this work that has exalted our little sea-girt isle to be the glory of all lands, and the spiritual Goshen of the world.

4. *Because as this work progresses the work of hell and Satan declines.* If this work of light cease, darkness will prevail. If this work of truth cease, error will abound. If this work of liberty cease, tyranny and oppression and slavery will be extended. If this work of purity cease, corruption and profligacy will triumph. If this work of heaven cease, then death and hell will have the accursed ascendency.

5. *Because of its comprehensive and benevolent designs.* The religion of the cross is destined to be the religion of the world.

(1.) It is adapted to the world, and nowhere does it refuse to thrive. It is for man—man everywhere—in every condition, and of every color and tongue.

(2.) It is sent to the world : not to this city or country alone, but for the world. " Go ye into all the world, and preach the gospel to every creature," Mark xvi. 15. It is to be preached among all nations, &c.

(3.) It is to be succeeded by the setting up of the reign of universal righteousness, peace, and blessedness. As yet, little has been done for the great mass of our species. As yet, how much has to be done in our world! Read the annals of savage ferocity, gross idolatry, and pagan cruelty in distant lands; and the fearful accounts of crime, ignorance, and irreligion at home. Do we not, then, deprecate the idea that "the work should cease?" If we desire its continuance and progress, notice,

II. *The interest and concern we should manifest in this work.*

It may be said this is the work of truth, and must live; of God, and must prevail; of holiness, and must spread: so it is. But there are certain things connected with it worthy of especial observation.

1. *That though it is a Divine work, yet it is connected with human instrumentality.* God could carry on this work by miraculous power; but it is not his will to do so. He has set up an instrumentality for the accomplishment of the object. That instrumentality is his *church.* (1.) The church, by its ministers, deacons, and members. (2.) The church in its ordinances, means, and influence. (3.) The church, by its example, truth, and compassion.—By these the work is to be sustained, perpetuated, diffused. God will effect his counsels by, and through, and not without these. Then the church must know its duty, feel its responsibility, and discharge its energies rightly, if the work is not to cease.

2. *Though the work must progress generally, it may cease partially.* This work once flourished in Jerusalem, in Ephesus, in Corinth, in Antioch, in Rome, &c. It once flourished in Italy, Arabia, and Samaria. How fearfully has it ceased in many of these places—ceased for ages upon ages! So we see it, in reference to towns and churches in our own land. How many sanctuaries, scattered through the land, in which the pure doctrines of the cross were once proclaimed; where our puritan fathers lived and labored—where crowded auditories of holy men were being trained for immortality: but another gospel now echoes from those pulpits. The congregation, in most instances, have been scattered, and "Ichabod" written on their walls—the glory is departed.

We doubt not the general progress of the truth, but locally and partially it may cease. Then our concern and labor must be that the work cease not in our own churches and neighborhoods, or we lose the power of con-

veying the tidings of salvation to the distant heathen. And however great the obligations to send the gospel abroad—*Home* must not be forgotten. It must be our anxiety, labor, and prayer, that both in this, and other lands, the work may not cease.

3. *That the work may flourish around us, it is indispensable that it should prosper within us.* The real prosperity of a church is the true spiritual prosperity of each member. If each one is religiously advancing, then the work is going on. It will give us the interest, the desire, and the power of usefulness. By the spiritual prosperity of each, the whole have a moral influence which the world cannot resist: let each be truly the Lord's, and every one will labor for the general work.

(1.) There will be no apathy in the church, for a sleeping church cannot awaken the world.

(2.) There will be no formalism in the church, for a formal church cannot spiritualize a locality.

(3.) There will be no indolence in the church, for an idle church cannot do God's arduous and difficult work.

(4.) There will be no covetousness in the church; for covetousness is the freezing of the waters—the icebergs that interrupt the vessel of mercy on her voyage of salvation.

4. *That the work may not cease, a spirit of glowing zeal and activity must animate every department of the church.* Zeal and diligence and self-denial, like that of Nehemiah. Let those who occupy the temples of Zion as her watchmen, "Cry aloud," &c. "Preach the word; be instant in season, out of season; reprove, rebuke, exhort with all long-suffering and doctrine," 2 Tim. iv. 2. Let them immolate their entire selves on the altar of the Saviour's service. Let those who are the spiritual judges in Israel —who serve tables, and assist in the oversight and rule in the church—be men of uncompromising fidelity, burning ardor, and Christian affection. Let fathers and mothers in Israel cherish a praying and fervid spirit of consecratedness to the institutions of religion; cherish a delightful attachment to those means which will extend the kingdom of the Lord Jesus, both at home and abroad.

Let every member be a worker—"Labor" must be the watchword of Zion; "Activity" her motto; "Zeal" her spirit; "Truth" her ammunition; and clad in the habiliments of "love," she must go forth with her illustrious Head " conquering, and to conquer," Rev. vi. 2.

APPLICATION.

1. Who are for the work going on? More and more—more than ever, &c. Who are ready—willing—able? " Who will come to the help of the Lord?" &c., Judg. v. 23.

2. Think of your obligations to God and his people. Let gratitude, filial piety, &c. If the work had ceased forty years ago, you would have been unenlightened, unsaved, &c. How much you owe to the work!

3. Think of the day in which we live. Unprecedented for activity, and liberal and benevolent institutions. Then shall the work cease in this day? in this country? in Christ's church? Oh no! The vote, the declaration, the vow is — " It shall not cease!"

Finally—What are you doing that the work may not cease? Review your exertions and influence for the last twelve months. In what sphere? to what extent? Put it down on paper : compare it with the labors of prophets, apostles, &c. With those of your forefathers. With those of some around you. Ask, " If all did just so much and no more, would it succeed, or cease?" Do this with the light of eternal things surrounding you—with the day of judgment in prospect; and so do it, as God will do it, when he shall examine every one of you, and render to all " according to their works," Rev. xx. 13.

XCVI. — THE QUESTION OF CHRISTIAN MISSIONS STATED AND EXPLAINED.

BY REV. R. WINTER HAMILTON, D. D.*

" I am come to send fire on the earth ; and what will I, if it be already kindled? But I have a baptism to be baptized with ; and how am I straitened till it be accomplished!"—*Luke* xii. 49, 50.

THE impassioned exclamations of the Redeemer, prefixed to this discourse, admirably agree to our design. There is a good in his religion worthy of any hazard and any expense. The exclamations are conceived un-

* From a sermon in reference to the persecutions in the West India Colonies, delivered in August, 1824.

der this impression of the case. He contemplates nothing but the evolution of that good, by the propagation of that religion.

Missions, we avow, may " bring fire on the earth ;" so did the incarnation of Christ ; and what would he but that it should kindle? Missions will assuredly task the spirit of exertion and self-devotement to the utmost ; but so did the ends of the Saviour's work. For the acquisition of those ends he was impetuous to yield to the ineffable exertions and sacrifices demanded of him ; and, as he approached the awful scene of sore amazement and heaviness, of sorrow unto death (Mark xiv. 33, 34), of the cup and of the cross, he " set his face steadfastly" to it ; and was mysteriously constrained for the catastrophe! That cannot be fanatical in the disciple, which is heroic in the Master ; nor extravagant in the servant, which is magnanimous in the Lord.

I. *The mission of Christ was undertaken for the most important ends.*

There must have been some prospective benefit to draw forth such breathings, and to awaken such desires. A prospective benefit which awaited the close of his sojourn on earth, and had been made conditional on his death. It was not impatience of suffering ; it was not regret that he had interposed, which imbued his mind with those anxieties, and wrung from it those importunities. He longed " to cease from his works," because upon his death alone could he realize the conception of his mind, and grasp the purpose of his heart. He, therefore, anticipated the agony of the garden, as one looking for a spoil ; and waited for the darkness that came over the land, when he was crucified, "more than they who wait for the morning." Let us produce some of these ends.

1. *To present an atonement to the Divine government for the sin of man.*

What an end was this! To make peace between God and man! To bind heaven and earth in amity! Instead of casting down the glorious high throne of the everlasting King under the feet of man, to capacitate man to draw nigh to its footstool here, and to entitle him to sit down amidst its splendors hereafter—a throne of grace, accessible now ; a throne of glory, inheritable forever!

———" Jesus' blood, through earth and skies, Mercy, free, boundless mercy, cries!"

2. *To overthrow the rebellious power which had usurped the dominion of this world.*

Four thousand years witnessed the preparation and muster for this struggle ; and at last he appeared. " Of the people there was none with me," Isa. lxiii. 3. It was not a combat to be shared—his single arm must win it. Nor was it a combat whose grapple was for mortal eye, whose shock was for mortal ear. He returned from it with his trophies. He had stained all his raiment.— His fury, it upheld him, Isa. lxiii. 3–5. He had destroyed the works of the devil: "that through death he might destroy him that had the power of death, that is the devil," Heb. ii. 14. And we may chant as we " walk about" the cross, and " go round about it," He hath " spoiled principalities and powers, he made a show of them openly, triumphing over them in it," Col. ii. 15.

3. *The redemption of innumerable multitudes of our race from the consequences of their apostasy.*

Redemption may sometimes be used much in the same sense as atonement, but its stricter meaning will not suffer this use. As atonement associates itself with the idea of government, it must have a *general* aspect ; as redemption identifies itself with that of purchase, it must have a particular one. Redemption is of persons, not of blessings ; and may be considered that application of the atonement which purchases us as " the church of the Lord." What an end is again proposed in this redemption ! What is a soul ? What is the multitude of these souls ? What is their rescue from sin, death, and hell ? " None can by any means redeem his brother, nor give to God a ransom for him ; for the redemption of their soul is precious, and it ceaseth forever," Psa. xlix. 7, 8.

4. *The formal assumption and complete discharge of his mediatorial characters.*

One of the most distinguished of these is his priesthood. Some have asserted that he could not be a priest until he died. At least, until then he reminds us more of a victim. If a priest, in any acceptation, he was never seen engaged in his highest rites, or arrayed in his costliest vestments. An inspired writer has decided, " if he were on earth, he should not be a priest," Heb. viii. 4. But now he ministers in " the holiest of all." His empire, as King, is founded in death. His sword did not flesh itself in his foes, but clave his own heart. His march to dominion was not cut through his enemies, but he waded to it in his own blood.

5. *The effusion of his Spirit as essential to the promotion of his cause, and accumulation of his church.* All power in heaven and earth was, for the first time, wielded by him, to stamp the missionary law with indelible authority.

With these ends we are zealously determined that our missions shall coincide. We would dislodge the crude and monstrous conceptions of the Divine government which invariably obtain in the absence of Christianity, by the exhibition of the atonement. We would expose the foul usurpation, which has for so long a period arrogantly held and fiercely tyrannized over our nature.

We would proclaim the redemption of souls. The missionary is the herald of universal deliverance. We would exalt the Lord Jesus in all the mediatorial offices, with which he is invested for the salvation of man. We would remember, through all the steps of this work, that the Holy Spirit alone can endue our agents with power, and crown their labors with success.

II. *These ends could alone be prosecuted at a most painful expense.*

By " sending fire on the earth," the Saviour appears to intend some evils, which would accompany the propagation of his religion ; evils not chargeable upon its constitution, but yet contingent upon its progress. He anticipated these, and forewarned his followers of them.

1. *We cannot conceal the fact, that Christianity may affect political systems.*

He who " rebuked kings" for the sake of his ancient church, will never long endure any state of things unfavorable to his people, or prejudicial to his cause. He " will overturn, overturn, overturn it ; until he come whose right it is," Ezek. xxi. 27. Kings and kingdoms are very little matters, in comparison with his glory, and nothing in opposition to it.

2. *It is further admitted that Christianity must produce a variety of innovations.*

Christianity went forth with the torch of extermination. It rendered its " anger with fury" against all that resisted it ; and its " rebuke with flames of fire," Isa. lxvi. 15. It, by the very process of fire, transformed all things into itself. The interested and bigoted beheld the conversion with alarm. All was yielded to the flame. Nothing was proof against its intensity, nothing sufficient to check its progress. We may easily conceive of the inconvenience of such an innovating principle. What excitement of new ideas! What disturbance of immemorial customs! The mind of some bewildered! the craft of more in danger! "No small stir about that way!" "These that have turned the world upside down!" Acts xix. 23 ; xvii. 6.

3. *Very unnatural divisions in society have apparently been fomented by Christianity.*

When it is really understood and truly felt, it constitutes the very balm of life. By it "shall all the families of the earth be blessed," Gen. xxviii. 14. But yet, in its course, many of these ties are severed. The converted child, once folded in the kindest embrace, now finds his parents more cruel than the sea-monster ; and becomes a stranger with his brethren, and an alien unto his mother's children.

4. *Christianity must be viewed in connection with those persecutions which it has experienced.*

Persecution will always endeavor to disguise itself under forms of piety, or enactments of law, or impositions of necessity. He, therefore, whose name, faith, and church, were to be the very lures and marks to this persecuting rage, openly declared that he " came to send fire on the earth." He knew that the fire thus kindled, would prove the ordeal to his followers,—" try every man's work of what sort it is." He announced it from the first that none might think it " strange concerning the fiery trial."

5. *Christianity has drawn forth some acts, on the part of its adversaries, which have more effectually exposed the depravity of human nature than any other occasion could have admitted.*

The doctrine of the cross can never be understood with indifference. No man can comprehend it, and be neutral. It elicits our inner man, it defines emotions which were vague, and bodies forth conceptions which were immature. It is a "sign which shall be spoken against;—that the thoughts of many hearts may be revealed." It has a point to repel, as well as one to attract. It is a stumbling-block and foolishness. The offence of the cross cannot cease.

6. *The religion of Jesus Christ has very frequently been perverted to designs most estranged from its character, and abhorrent to its spirit.*

The most successful antagonists of this religion are they who plead its authority, and retain its name. The anti-christian power grew insensibly out of it. " That wicked," " That man of sin," is revealed from his nativity, 2 Thess. ii. 3, 8. And to what more general abuses has Christianity been desecrated! What hypocrisy has it served to favor! What ambition to desolate! What sensuality to riot! What avarice to grab! What superstition to dote! What bigotry to hoodwink! What despotism to oppress! On its stock, what earthly scions have been grafted! what infernal fruits have been plucked! Hence all the tricks of priestly jugglers—all the plots of wily statesmen—all the persecutions of blood-thirsty monarchs! The religion of Christ has ever been pretext and screen! In this additional manner the Son of God " sent fire on the earth."

7. *The augmentation of moral responsibility has necessarily attended the establishment of Christianity.*

Every hearer of the gospel, from the moment " the kingdom of God" comes nigh to him, enters a far more critical probation, and must abide by a far more fearful issue. The " sweet savor of Christ" is to them who perish, " the savor of death unto death," 2 Cor. ii. 15, 16. They must, if disobedient, await " a sorer punishment."

III. *The importance of these ends justified the vast expense necessary to their acquisition.*

That certain evils, or disadvantages, when intrinsically considered, are contingent on the progress of the gospel we have allowed ; but never would the Saviour have " sent fire on the earth," and even willed it to kindle, had he not been persuaded that all which was intended by the figure, would be absorbed in a glorious and infinite superabundance of blessings. Whatever be the evils, then, arising out of the constitution of Christianity, or attendant on its progress, we think " our light affliction, which is but for a moment, worketh for us a far more exceeding and eternal weight of glory," 2 Cor. iv. 17. They are more apparent than real, more contingent than fundamental, and infinitely countervailed. And, as figured by that " fire sent on the earth," so far from reflecting on the character and religion of Christ, they illustrate the majesty of the one, and the stability of the other. In the first place, the Saviour treats those disadvantages as diminutive : " I am come to send fire on the earth." But when he alludes to these sufferings, he cannot regard them so indifferently. He therefore put them into contrast and opposition: "But I have a baptism to be baptized with." As to the fire, he heeds it not: "What will I, if it be already kindled?" But as to the baptism it engrosses him: "How am I straitened till it be accomplished!" The oracle which foretold that his soul should be made "an offering for sin," also announced, "He shall see of the travail of his soul, and shall be satisfied," Isa. liii. 10, 11. That satisfaction must pervade the vast capacity of his mind, must answer the long suspense of his ambition, and must ascend the infinite scale of his desert. This was "the joy which was set before him," and in whose prospect "he endured the cross, despising the shame," Heb. xii. 2. We ask not what vesture can be too splendid for the form, that the purple mockery insulted; what diadem too glorious for the brow, the thorny coronet lacerated;—but what must be the delight, most exquisite and boundless, which reconciles him to all his endurances and conflicts: which prompts him to bear his crucifixion-wounds, as the scars of his noblest triumph, and centres of his brightest glory!

APPLICATION.

1. Here, then, we find an apology for our warmest zeal and firmest courage, in extending Christianity. We but imbibe the spirit and follow the steps of our Exampler.

2. And here, too, we learn that this unconquerable temper, this inexpressible ardor, is of the first importance in every department of missions. Nothing half-hearted should be betrayed in our institutions at home, or efforts abroad.

3. In this spirit of unshrinking courage, and unabating ardor, let us proceed. We carry the commission of him who "came to send fire on the earth." We may blow the flame, we may spread the conflagration; what will he, if it be already kindled? All must yield to the gospel of Christ, or be consumed by its progress.

XCVII.—THE FIELDS WHITE TO HARVEST.

BY REV. DANIEL WILSON, D. D.,

BISHOP OF CALCUTTA.*

"Say not ye, There are yet four months, and then cometh harvest? behold, I say unto you, Lift up your eyes, and look on the fields; for they are white already to harvest. And he that reapeth receiveth wages, and gathereth fruit unto life eternal: that both he that soweth and he that reapeth may rejoice together."—*John* iv. 35, 36.

THE text was spoken when the disciples, during the absence of the Samaritan woman, had urged to partake of the provisions which they had procured. Our Lord, in reply to their solicitations, described his ardent zeal for the salvation of souls, which the prospect of instructing the Samaritans had excited, as supplying the want of bodily food: "My meat is to do the will of him that sent me, and to finish his work," ver. 34. And then he addressed them in the words of the text, with the design of leading their minds from the natural harvest, which was still four months distant, and of which they had probably been discoursing as they passed through the fields, just springing with the tender blade, to a spiritual harvest, which was already ripe for the sickle; and to excite them, after his example, to that activity in teaching and saving mankind, which the husbandman manifests when the corn is ready for the garner.

The spirit of the passage, then, is obviously to animate the reaper to enter into the harvest, from the consideration of the ripeness of the whitening grain. And it will therefore afford me an occasion of bringing before you various motives to redoubled efforts in the cause of missions, now that opportunities of diffusing the gospel are opening upon us from every quarter. In considering this subject, as represented by the striking image of my text, we must look first at the aspect of the fields; and, secondly, at the encouragements held out to the reaper.

I. *We must look at the aspect of the fields.*

When our Lord uttered these words, he had immediate respect to the Samaritans. It wanted, at that time, four months to the harvest of the earth. But, if the disciples would "lift up their eyes, and look on the fields," across which the inhabitants of Sychar were hastening at the tidings of the woman, and whom our Saviour probably

* Preached on behalf of the Church Missionary Society, 1817.

pointed at with his finger when he spake, they would behold a spiritual harvest, not merely shooting up its early blade, but now ripe for their labor; they would see people coming with eagerness, to hear and receive the doctrine of salvation.

Our Lord had respect also, in this language, to the general state of the Jewish nation, and of the world. The time of God's mercy was then near. The faith of the pious servants of God among the Jews, had welcomed the "Consolation of Israel." The general expectation of the people was fixed on his character and doctrine. But the whole civilized world was also, in a considerable measure, in a like state. Thus things were ripening for the harvest; and the apostles were soon to go forth as reapers into that vastly more extensive field of labor.

The spirit of our Lord's address, however, is applicable generally to all periods of the church, when the providence of God concurs with his grace, to present remarkable opportunities for diffusing the gospel. For when facilities are afforded for disseminating Divine truth; when these facilities are embraced with suitable activity on the part of the spiritual church; and when, above all, a disposition to inquire into Christianity appears among the heathen nations, then the fields may be said to stand loaded with corn, demanding the hand of the reaper. For, if you cast your eye over the different parts of the heathen world, you will find,

1. *That in most places there is evidently a preparation in the minds of both Pagans and Mohammedans for receiving the servants of Christ.*

In the vast continent of India—the most promising scene for missionary labor—we are credibly informed by those who have been eye-witnesses of what they relate, that the native mind is obviously opening to receive the gospel.

In Persia, on the one side of India; and in China on the other—opportunities have offered for extending the knowledge of the word of God.

If, from hence, we pass to the countless islands of the Southern Ocean, it is peculiarly animating to read the accounts of what the providence and grace of God are effecting in those newly-discovered regions. In some of them, large bodies of men have renounced their idols; and received the doctrine of salvation.

The immense territory of New Holland also, and the neighboring islands of New Zealand—the latter under our own Society —are opening to the Christian teacher.

I will not detain you by particularizing what is doing in the two American continents, and the West Indies; but I will merely stop, and ask whether this rapid view, which we have taken, be not highly encouraging to redoubled exertion? But it may here be asked,

2. *What are the peculiar advantages which pious and zealous Christians in Britain enjoy for extending the gospel?*

Here, then, I would first inquire, whether the circumstance of so large a part of the heathen world being subject to the British sceptre, or bordering on its possessions, be not, in itself, a remarkable advantage to our cause. Where can you look, from 100 degrees in the remote West, to Norfolk Island, in the East; or from the Shetlands in the North, to 33 degrees south of the Line: that is, over 270 degrees of longitude, and 94 of latitude, or nearly 20,000 miles, by 6 or 7,000, without seeing parts of that dominion which God has intrusted to this Protestant country? Why is it that such large and important additions have been made to its territory during the last few years—additions which would, of themselves, constitute a great empire?

3. *But the disposition among the heathen to receive the gospel, and the facilities which we possess for diffusing it, would be insufficient, unless the activity of the spiritual church were awake to improve the occasion.* This is, then, the third point, which marks the present period, and contributes to make up the aspect of the ripened field.

By the spiritual church, I mean the invisible and mystical body of true Christians in this country, who hold Christ as the Head, are vitally united to him by his Spirit, and obey his laws; though they may differ in minor points of doctrine and discipline. This body is diligently occupying the post assigned to it. Christians, of almost every class, are exerting their efforts to seize the golden opportunity. Various Societies have been formed—correspondence opened with suitable persons abroad—information circulated at home—appeals made to the public conscience—and missionary stations selected and occupied in heathen countries.

II. *Encouragements held out to the reapers.*

These encouragements, then, we shall now

proceed further to consider, after we have first explained the nature of the labor with which they are connected. The labor of the spiritual reaper consists in preaching the gospel of Christ to perishing sinners; and in achieving those services, and enduring those privations, which, in a heathen country, are inseparable from so arduous an employment.

His main duty is, to set before men the doctrine of the cross of Christ, in all its bearings. This is the appointed means of gathering in the spiritual harvest.

But, great as is the toil of such devoted servants of Christ, the encouragement held out to them is more than commensurate.— " He that reapeth receiveth wages, and gathereth fruit to life eternal : that both he that soweth and he that reapeth may rejoice together."

1. *The important good, which the Christian missionary effects, is, that he gathers fruit to life eternal.*

And what an inspiring motive is this! If the earthly harvest-man is animated by the thought, that he is collecting the blessing of the year, and gathering fruit for the support of temporal life; how much more will the spiritual reaper be cheered by the reflection, that every soul which he is the means of turning from the error of his ways, is fruit gathered to life eternal! But this is not all.

2. *The abundant reward which awaits him, when the toil is finished, is a further incentive to persevering labor.*

" He that reapeth receiveth wages,"—not indeed of merit,—for he is, at last, but an unprofitable servant : all that he has done, which has been good, has come from the grace of God,—but of Divine mercy; wages that his Lord has engaged to give after the harvest is over, which will bear a proportion to the measure of the work done, and to which he is encouraged to look forward, to support and animate him when ready, through sloth and self-indulgence, to faint under his toil; that thus, like Moses, he may endure, " having respect unto the recompense of the reward." Great is his reward in heaven. When he rests from his labors, his works do follow him, Rev. xiv. 13.

His wages are sure. All who have joined in the work shall partake of the reward. They may differ from one another in abilities, and education, and cast of mind; in opinion on smaller matters, in the extent of the stations allotted them, and in the success granted to their labors : but they shall all hear, at last, those blessed words, " Well done ! good and faithful servant : thou hast been faithful over a few things, I will make thee ruler over many things : enter thou into the joy of thy Lord," Matt. xxv. 21. With this joy the reaper's reward is connected ; for, together with his wages, he shall have a peculiar satisfaction and triumph. " He that soweth and he that reapeth shall rejoice together."

(1.) This common joy *began* when the holy apostles, having finished their labors, were taken to receive their reward. Then the patriarchs and prophets, who had been sowing for so many ages, joined them in the strain of triumph, at the gathering in of the first evangelical harvest.

(2.) This joy has been *increasing*, as the several sowers and reapers, in different ages of the New Testament church, have been taken to their eternal rest.

(3.) It will be *completed* when all the church shall meet before the throne; when the mystery of Christ shall be finished ; when God shall have accomplished the number of his elect, and have hastened his kingdom.

APPLICATION.

If such, then, be the encouragement to us to enter on those fields which we have seen to be white for harvest, it remains only, in drawing to conclusion, that, according to the command of our Saviour, we " lift up our eyes, and look on the fields," and apply ourselves without delay to the work.

1. " Behold, I say unto you, Lift up your eyes, and look on the fields"—shows the necessity of rousing men from their torpor, and directing them to the actual state of mankind.

2. And shall not these emotions of surprise and pleasure lead you to redoubled exertion ? Will you not enter into the fields ? Did ever such an exuberant crop wave over the lands ? Was ever our Protestant church invited to such a scene of labor ? And, surely, that church, the glory of the Reformation, will not be backward in such a crisis !

3. But for these ends we must be led, as our Saviour in another and similar passage instructs us, to fervent prayer to the Lord of the harvest, who is so abundantly able to prosper our endeavor. He can send forth

the laborers. He can qualify them for the work. He can sustain them under their fatigue, cheer them when they faint, grant them success, and bestow on them their reward. He can do all this for us; while, without this mighty aid, our utmost efforts must fail.

4. Nor is it a slight recommendation of the measures to which your attention is now called, that zealous exertions in the behalf of missions, accompanied with the spirit of prayer—of habitual, fervent supplication to God, for our own and all other Societies engaged in this great design—will also have the happy effect of materially furthering our own salvation. No one can touch this sacred cause, much less engage in it with a spirit of prayer, but it will promote his individual piety !

XCVIII.—THE TRIUMPHS OF THE GOSPEL.

"Now thanks be unto God, who always causeth us to triumph in Christ."—2 Cor. ii. 14.

OUR text evidently refers to the triumphant entry of heroes into their native kingdoms, or chief cities, after the attainment of some splendid victory. On such occasions the spectacle was of the most imposing kind. The conqueror, either led on horseback, or seated in a triumphal car, was met by the great, the illustrious, and the fair; and conducted through the gates with unusual magnificence and rejoicing. In some cases, deposed monarchs, or captains and great men taken in battle, were dragged at the conqueror's chariot; and often the spoils taken from the foe were exhibited to the admiring gaze of countless thousands.

Whole volumes have been written on these pageant scenes; and historians have vied with each other in setting them forth with all the adornments of a gaudy rhetoric, or vivid, glowing eloquence.

Now, the apostle compares the success of himself and fellow apostles to ancient conquerors; and, in the language of impassioned ardor, exclaims, "Now thanks be unto God," etc. Consider, in reference to the gospel, the achievements obtained; contrast them with the victories of the warrior; and then urge to a holy and pious exultation in God. "Now thanks be unto God, who always causeth us to triumph in Christ." In reference to a preached gospel observe,

I. *The victories achieved.*

Triumph implies conflict, and supposes its successful termination. By the preaching of the gospel by the apostle,

1. *The gospel triumphed over the prejudices of Judaism.* The Jews had a Divine system of religion—a system from God; attested by miracles; identified with heavenly interpositions; established by prophets; and diffusing a holy light and heavenly halo around their nation. To this system they were devotedly attached; indeed, to it they had an idolatrous veneration. Abraham was the father of their nation; Moses their lawgiver; Samuel and Isaiah their prophets; David their poet; Solomon their legislator; the Oracles their directory. But they gave a temporal explanation to the writings of their seers, and expected a Messiah of worldly dignity and warlike prowess. They were looking for secular blessings, and an earthly kingdom. Hence their moral unpreparedness for the Son of God—their dislike, hatred, oppression, persecution, and putting him to death.

All thinking persons know the power of prejudice, and especially when it is associated with blighted hopes and keen disappointments. This was the case with the Jews; yet, even over this barrier, which seemed impassable, did the gospel triumph: three thousand of these prejudiced Jews were enlightened, converted, and saved under one discourse. Oh! think of such a multitude being disarmed, overcome, and added to the kingdom of Jesus, even in the city of his death. And of these, untold thousands were afterwards the humble, adoring disciples of the cross.

2. *The gospel triumphed over the various and multifarious systems of Paganism.* The gentile world had its systems of religion and philosophy. Many of these were ancient; established by law, and sanctified by custom. In some instances, human industry was identified with their temples and worship. Most of these systems pandered to the vices of the people; and were so decorated by art, and so connected with the pleasures of sense, that they presented many attractions to the mass of the people:—But the gospel triumphed over these.

At Ephesus, a holy host was rescued from the worship of Diana; and in Athens, crowded with altars, in Corinth, in Antioch, and in Rome, the churches of the Messiah were founded and established, and men were turned from dumb idols to the service of the pure and living God.

3. *The gospel triumphed over the corruptions and lives of mankind.* The gospel not only encountered error and idolatry, but depravity and sin—depraved hearts and corrupt lives. Interwoven with the systems of Pagan religion and philosophy were the most disgusting and odious vices—vices which were unblushingly practised, and so horrible, that the apostle only feebly hints at them in the first chapter of his epistle to the Romans. Now, if it were something great and glorious for the gospel to triumph over the darkness of the understanding, and the errors of the judgment, how much more over the passions of the heart, and the corruptions of the life. Read 1 Cor. vi. 9, etc.

4. *The gospel triumphed over the love of self and the world.* In the early ages of Christianity, men had more to do than to change their religion, and alter their creed. They had to do this by the most comprehensive self-denial, and often the sacrifice of all things. They had to set at defiance human laws, and oppose themselves to fines, confiscations, imprisonment, and even death! A converted wife had to lose the affections and support of her Pagan husband, and perhaps endure the scorn of her own offspring. In fact, all was to be forsaken for Christ and his kingdom; yet the natural attachment to the enjoyments of this world, the still closer attachment to friends, and the innate love of life, were all too feeble to stay the triumphs of the cross; and despite these fearful obstacles, the apostle could exclaim, "Now thanks be unto God," etc. Let us,

II. *Contrast these triumphs with the victories of ancient warriors.* Do this,

1. *In the agents sent forth.* Contrast an ambitious, worldly, cruel hero, with the humble, spiritual, and benevolent apostles of Jesus. Pride, lust, and cruelty, are the traits in the one; meekness, virtue, and philanthropy, the features in the others. Do this,

2. *In the weapons employed.* In the one case the sword, the arrow, the spear, the battering-ram; in the other, the torch of truth, the message of mercy, and moral suasion. The one appears with his implements of death, and his garments died in blood; in the others, "How beautiful upon the mountains," etc., Isaiah lii. 7. See the warrior, with the instruments of death, on the battle-

field; and then see Paul on Mars' Hill, with the truth of heaven and the gospel of mercy.

3. *In the results that followed.* The warrior may be traced as to his work of woe, by the footsteps of blood, by the groanings of the wounded; by the putrescence of the air, tainted with the slain; by the desolated country, the sacked city, the burning dwellings, the frenzied widows, and desolated orphans. Over the field of the warrior is the vulture hovering for his prey, or the marauding wild beast snuffing his food. The triumphs of the cross are succeeded by the diffusion of knowledge, the communication of joy, the extension of civilization, the prosperity of commerce, domestic felicity, and the true blessedness of the world.

"Blessings abound where'er he reigns," etc.

Human warfare degrades, blights, curses, and enkindles hell upon earth. The triumph of the gospel elevates, sanctifies, blesses, and brings down the reign of heaven to earth. Surely, then, we may proceed,

III. *To urge to a holy and devout exultation in God.* "Now thanks be unto God," etc. Observe,

1. *The object of our exultation*—"God." The Author of the Christian system. It is "The glorious gospel of the blessed God," 1 Tim. i. 11,—full of God; and, therefore, all its efficiency redounds to his glory.

2. *The nature of the exultation.* "Now thanks be unto God, who always causeth us to triumph in Christ." The highest, most earnest thanks, etc.: the ascriptions of the lip, the homage of the mind, the gratitude of the heart, and the service of the life—all and each of these, we must express: "Now thanks be unto God," etc.

3. *The extent of this exultation.*

(1.) As to persons. The whole church, every believer: ministers, deacons, members.

(2.) As to duration. Thanks now, and through all time; and thanks in heaven, and through all eternity.

APPLICATION.

1. The gospel yet triumphs—at home and abroad. How cheering the reports from the servants of Jesus in India, Burmah, Africa, New Zealand, the West Indies, etc.

2. To these triumphs many here are infinitely indebted. To the influence of religion you owe your respectability in life, your preservation from ten thousand perils, and blessings and enjoyments beyond enumeration.

3. To extend these triumphs should be the design and effort of all. Every Christian should possess the missionary spirit, and employ his influence in extending the gospel of our Lord Jesus Christ. The church of Christ, in its collective character, should be one united and catholic missionary association.

XCIX.—THE SPIRITUAL TEMPLE ERECTED BY THE HANDS OF GENTILES.

BY REV. JAMES BODEN, OF SHEFFIELD.*

"And they that are far off shall come and build in the temple of the Lord."—*Zech.* vi. 15.

I SHALL not detain your attention by attempting any critical remarks on the important contents of this chapter. I think I may venture to assume, that in the person of Joshua, and the building of the temple, this context contains a very clear prediction and type of one infinitely greater than the Jewish high priest, or the material temple of God. This text unquestionably refers to the times of the gospel: and under this dispensation of grace, we observe,

I. *God has determined on the erection of a spiritual temple.* And that,

II. *In the execution of this design, he will employ such as have been strangers, and foreigners, and afar off.*

I. *God has determined on the erection of a spiritual temple.*

1. *This temple is the gospel Church.* The church of God is represented, by the prophets and apostles, as a sacred building, of which the temple at Jerusalem, built a thousand years before the Christian era, was a striking type, or figure. Isaiah, under the inspiration of heaven, and wrapt into future times, says, "And it shall come to pass in the last days, that the mountain of the LORD's house shall be established in the tops of the mountains, and shall be exalted above the hills; and all nations shall flow unto it," Isa. ii. 2. The apostle adopts the same language, and perpetuates the same illustration. "Ye are built upon the foundation of the apostles and prophets, Jesus Christ himself being the chief corner-stone; in whom all the building fitly framed to-

* From a sermon preached before the London Missionary Society, at the Tabernacle, Moorfields, May 10th, 1815.

gether groweth unto an holy temple in the Lord: in whom ye are also builded together for a habitation of God through the Spirit," Eph. ii. 20–22.

2. *This temple is the peculiar residence of the Almighty.* But here a difficulty seems to arise. Will "the high and lofty One that inhabiteth eternity, whose name is Holy," whom "the heaven, and heaven of heavens cannot contain;" will God, in very deed, dwell with men on the earth? He will; for he hath said, "I will dwell in them, and walk in them; and I will be their God, and they shall be my people," 2 Cor. vi. 16; and "where two or three are met together in my name, there am I in the midst of them to bless them," Matt. xviii. 20. "The Lord hath chosen Zion; he hath desired it for his habitation. This is my rest forever: here will I dwell; for I have desired it."

3. *The gospel temple is of large extent.* Ezekiel's prophetic temple by its immense dimensions, greater than the whole city of Jerusalem, prefigured the universal and truly catholic church, which was to be collected at that period, when the knowledge of the Lord shall cover the earth, "and all flesh shall see the salvation of God."

4. *Extraordinary magnificence and beauty distinguish the dwelling of God.* Solomon's temple was the most superb and finished material structure the sun ever saw; but the grandeur of the Jewish sanctuary was only a shadow of the celestial glory of the Christian temple. The church of the living God is purified with the blood of the Lamb, covered with the magnificent righteousness of her Redeemer, and adorned with those heavenly graces and good works, which are ornaments after the style of the upper world. Her glory is not indeed appreciated by the rules of worldly wisdom. No; her symmetry and beautiful proportions are confusion; and those splendors of holiness with which God has invested her, are deformity to the carnal eye. But soon the reproach of Zion shall be rolled away forever. Then God will proclaim, "Arise, shine; for thy light is come, and the glory of the Lord is risen upon thee. For, behold, the darkness shall cover the earth, and gross darkness the people: but the Lord shall arise upon thee, and his glory shall be seen upon thee. And the Gentiles shall come to the light, and kings to the brightness of thy rising," Isa. l. 1–3.

5. *The plan of this temple was formed by infinite wisdom.* The first master-builders

in the Christian Church plainly asserted and proved, that the gospel which was preached by them, was not after the corrupt taste of man; neither did they receive it of men; neither were they taught it, but by the revelation of Jesus Christ, Gal. i. 12. The Christian temple is a spiritual edifice, composed of living stones, prepared, collected, and united according to his purpose, "who worketh all things after the counsel of his own will;—wherein he hath abounded towards us in all wisdom and prudence," Eph. i. 8, 11.

6. *This sacred temple is reared under the immediate agency of God the Saviour.* Jehovah incarnate claims the Church as his own house, and as the erection of his own hand. It is the language of prophecy, "The Lord shall build up Zion," Psa. cii. 16. It is the assertion of our Saviour, "Upon this rock I will build my Church," Matt. xvi. 18. Christ builds his Church, not by his instruction and example merely;—so the apostles were laborers with God;—but by his omnipresent energy, and by the efficient power of his Holy Spirit.

7. *The temple of the Lord is placed on a sure foundation.* The foundation answers to the extent, the grandeur, and the elevation of the superstructure. To provide the foundation, God claims as his own exclusive act: "Behold, I lay in Zion for a foundation a stone, a tried stone, a precious corner-stone, a sure foundation," Isa. xxviii. 16. This scripture is quoted by Peter, and applied to the Lord Jesus Christ, whom he calls, "a living stone, disallowed indeed of men, but chosen of God, and precious," 1 Pet. ii. 4.

8. *The completion of this temple is reserved for the world of glory.* The trenches are dug, the corner-stone is laid, and we see the basement already rising to view; yet much, very much, still remains to be done. But the plummet is in the hands of our divine Zerubbabel: "His hands have laid the foundations of this house; his hands also shall finish it;—and he shall bring forth the head-stone thereof with shoutings, crying, Grace, grace unto it," Zech. iv. 9, 7.

II. *In the execution of this design, God will employ such as have been strangers, and afar off.*

1. *By those afar off, are to be understood the Gentile nations,* as contradistinguished from the community of Israel. The admission of the Gentiles to this honorable work was plainly intimated at the erection of the first and second temple in Jerusalem. Solomon was zealously assisted in his great undertaking by Hiram, king of Tyre, and his subjects, the Sidonians; and all the Gentile strangers in the land of Israel were put in a state of requisition on the memorable occasion.

2. *The first stones in the gospel temple were laid by the hands of Jewish master-builders.* Christ himself, a greater than Solomon, and the true Zerubbabel, was of the seed of Abraham, according to the flesh. The apostles were all Jews; and on account of their eminent services at the commencement of the gospel era, the Church is represented as having "twelve foundations, and in them the names of the twelve apostles of the Lamb," Rev. xxi. 14.

3. *The incorporation of the Jews with the Christian Church, is to be accomplished by Gentile instrumentality.*

APPLICATION.

1. In consequence of this promise, you are met here this day. Were you not once numbered with those who are afar off, though now brought nigh?

2. The extension of this temple to all nations, is to crown your exertions, and those of your gentile fellow-laborers. Can any doubt be entertained whether God designs to make Missionary Societies engines to move the world? How far have the concentric circles already extended from this centre? Are they not extending every year?

3. Have we not lately heard that some who were afar off, dwelling even on the extreme verge of humanity, are already enrolled among the builders? I trust, before many years have elapsed, your sight and your souls will be cheered, your zeal and your exertions will be excited, under missionary sermons, by Hottentot, Hindoo, or Chinese ministers of the gospel.

I will only add, let the bounties of Providence; the necessities of a perishing world; and, above all, the dying love of Jesus, constrain your hearts, and direct your contributions. Amen.

C. — ENCOURAGEMENT TO PERSEVERANCE IN MISSIONARY EXERTIONS.

BY REV. JOHN HYATT.*

" As the rain cometh down, and the snow from heaven, and returneth not thither, but watereth the earth and maketh it bring forth and bud, that it may give seed to the sower, and bread to the eater : so shall my word be that goeth forth out of my mouth : it shall not return unto me void, but it shall accomplish that which I please, and it shall prosper in the thing whereto I sent it."— *Isaiah* lv. 10, 11.

HOPE of success imparts energy to the mind, whilst it has to contend with opposition and difficulties, in the pursuit of any grand object. If a man of enterprise possess assurance that he shall succeed, nothing can intimidate and compel him to relinquish his pursuit ; assurance of success in the issue makes him bold and fearless in the face of a thousand opponents and dangers.

My Christian brethren, the object that has long engaged your attention, and called forth your energies, is infinitely important. In its pursuit, your faith and patience have been exercised ; yet you have not despaired of success—nor will you despair. While you expect that the labors of your missionaries, amongst the idolatrous Gentiles, will be crowned with the blessing of Almighty God, you do not expect " a new thing in the earth."

The gospel of Jesus, preached by feeble men, has made the brazen front of superstition blush ; it has riveted the eye of philosophers to the Redeemer's cross ; it has demolished idols and their temples, and taught idolaters to worship " the only true God" in an acceptable manner.

The analogy between the rain in the natural world, and the word of God in the moral world, is the doctrine of the text. We propose to consider four things, in which they are analogous.

I. *Both exhibit the sovereignty of Jehovah.* Two things exhibit the sovereignty of Jehovah in the rain that cometh down from heaven.

1. *The time of its descent.* The earth is not watered with rain by chance. All the works of the infinite Creator are constantly subject to his control ; the different elements which he hath created, are all under a law which they cannot possibly violate. He

From a sermon, preached before the London Missionary Society, at Tottenham Court Chapel, May, 11, 1815.

" giveth rain, and fruitful seasons." He " prepareth rain for the earth," Psa. cxlvii. 8. Every shower of rain depends upon his sovereign pleasure. None but God can raise the clouds—none but he can discharge their contents.

The time when God sends his word to any of the human race, displays his sovereignty. He gave his word to the Jews, and preserved it amongst them for ages ; whilst he left the Gentiles in gross darkness, and gave them up to abominable idolatry.

2. *The place upon which the rain descends,* exhibits the sovereignty of the Supreme Being. The clouds, whose contents water the earth, are not driven by chance ; they steer their course according to the will of God : they are, indeed, driven by the wind ; but the wind is controlled by the Almighty Creator, " who maketh the clouds his chariot, who walketh upon the wings of the wind," Psa. civ. 3.

The sovereignty of Jehovah is displayed in the place to which he sends his word. He sends it to one place, and not to another. One part of the moral world is fertilized by the influence of the gospel, and another remains waste. One part is a garden, producing abundance of the fruits of righteousness ; another is a wilderness, abounding with noxious weeds and thistles.

II. *Both the rain in the natural world, and the word of God in the moral world, are efficient in their influence.*

The great and glorious Governor of the universe doeth nothing in vain : all his works praise him. He gathereth the waters into clouds—conducts them by the wind to the place of their destiny—discharges their contents, and waters the earth, " Nor lets the drops descend in vain." God employs the rain as a means to an end ; and whatever means he employs must be efficient to produce the end he designs. We are not astonished at the efficiency of the rain, when we consider the power by which it is employed.

God sends not the gospel to any place in vain : " It shall prosper in the thing whereto I sent it," is his positive and merciful declaration. Both the rain in the natural world, and the gospel in the moral world, *must* be efficient in their influence. The efficiency of both is promised, and the promises of Jehovah shall assuredly be accomplished. The promises of God insure the continuance, the promulgation, and the success of his word in the world, till time shall expire. The gospel must prosper, and effect what its eternal Author hath purposed. Its success cannot possibly be prevented. "Many shall run to and fro, and knowledge shall be increased," Dan. xii. 4. The way of God shall "be known upon earth; his saving health among all nations."

III. *Both the rain in the natural world, and the word of God in the moral world, are advantageous in their effects.*

The rain promotes vegetation; it causeth "the earth to bring forth and bud." It is the means of producing much that is ornamental, to delight man; and much that is essential to his support. The earth produces innumerable blessings for our use; not one of which could be produced without rain. We enjoy the fruits of the rain in the bread we eat, the beverage we drink, and the clothing we wear.

The effects which are produced by the gospel are both ornamental and useful. When the word of God, accompanied by the influence of the Holy Ghost, savingly operates upon any part of the moral world, how beautiful is its face!—how advantageous are its effects! The gospel transforms mankind, that were counterparts of Satan, into the lovely image of the Son of God. Odiousness is exchanged for beauty; injuriousness gives place to utility; the hateful fruits of the flesh, are supplanted by the admirable fruits of the Spirit. The wilderness is turned into a blooming paradise. The indolent, become industrious; the revengeful, become kind and affectionate; the licentious, become chaste; the proud, become humble; the covetous, become liberal; and the worshippers of dumb idols, worship the God of heaven and earth in spirit and in truth. The gospel binds mankind in fraternal bonds, and they live together in peace and harmony.

IV. *The effects of the rain in the natural world, and of the gospel in the moral world, display the glory of the Divine perfections.*

The beautiful scenery of nature displays the glory of the eternal Creator. Impressions of his infinite perfections appear upon every bud—every blossom—every blade of grass—every ear of corn. In every part of the vegetable world, the glory of illimitable power, infinite wisdom, and boundless goodness shines. The glory of God is visible in every thing that is produced by the rain,

"from the cedar that is in Lebanon, even to the hyssop that springeth out of the wall."

"Nature with open volume stands,
    And spreads her Maker's praise abroad;
  And every labor of his hands,
    Shows something worthy of a God."

Infinitely more of the Divine glory is seen upon the face of the moral world, transformed by the influence of the gospel. How effulgent is the glory that shines in the marvellous change that is produced in the mind of man in regeneration, and in the various fruits of holiness that adorn his life. The glory of Jehovah shines in the existence of an angel; but that glory is eclipsed, when a sinner, saved by grace, united to Christ, and devoted to the pursuit of holiness and heaven,—is placed at his side.

APPLICATION.

1. The gospel cannot be preached altogether in vain. Wherever the Almighty designs to send it, he designs to produce the most glorious effects by its instrumentality.

2. The extent of the success of the gospel is determined. "It shall," saith Jehovah, "accomplish that which I please, and it shall prosper in the thing whereto I sent it."

3. When the word of God is widely diffusing, we may reasonably encourage hope, that much good will be done.

4. The genuine influence of Christianity will produce an ardent concern for the salvation of the heathen. What Christian can place before his imagination, hundreds of millions of the human family, enslaved by Satan, and paying senseless adoration to images, and not feel pity and compassion excited in his bosom towards them?

5. We live at an eventful period: the history of the present age will be read by millions that are unborn, with joyful astonishment.

6. We shall shortly quit this world. We all must die; but the cause of missions will live and flourish. It is the cause, of all others, most dear to God. It is the cause which a gracious Providence hath fostered in all ages. It is the cause whose success a race of holy prophets foretold and anticipated. It is the cause for which a noble army of martyrs cheerfully consented to expire in flames. It is the cause for which the Son of God agonized and died. It is the cause that will bring the largest revenue of glory to the triune Jehovah—*and must pros-*

per! "O Lord, I beseech thee, send now prosperity!" What individual is there in this vast assembly that is not disposed to add a hearty—*Amen!*

CI.—MARY'S MEMORIAL.

BY REV. W. MOORHOUSE, OF HUDDERSFIELD.*

"And Jesus said, Let her alone; why trouble ye her? she hath wrought a good work on me." —*Mark* xiv. 6.

WE presume not to say, that this text is the most pertinent of all others upon the present occasion; yet, it is hoped, it will appear, in the sequel, not so foreign to the subject of our missionary meeting as some might imagine. The design in bringing it forward, is to urge the force of an amiable example of love and zeal in the weaker sex, and to animate all our hearts in the work before us. Oh, that I might be so happy as to advance any thing upon the subject, which might give this sermon a right to the title of Mary's memorial!

With a view, in some small degree, to accomplish this end, there are four things included in the text to which we must attend.

I. *The probable motives.*

II. *A few obvious circumstances which attended this good work.*

III. *The object upon whom it terminated.*

IV. *The testimony of the impartial, infallible, Judge.*—"She hath wrought a good work on me."

I. *The probable motives of the good work.*

I call them probable, not because they are altogether doubtful, but because they are not expressed; and we should always speak cautiously where there is not sufficient authority to be positive. However, let it be remembered by all, that there is one thing, which, in every age, in every nation, in every individual, is essential to a good work in the sense of our text.

1. *A new heart.* That Mary was blessed with this best of blessings we have sufficient reason to conclude from what Jesus said of her in another place, "One thing is needful: and Mary hath chosen that good part, which shall not be taken away from her," Luke x. 42.

2. *The second probable motive of the good*

* Preached before the Missionary Society, at Surrey Chapel, May 10, 1797.

work spoken of in the text is love. Love, that native of the celestial world, which is like the impulsive cause of all mechanical motion. Love, that tender exotic, so little known in this dark, disordered world, moved all the powers of Mary's expanded soul in this good work. The strength and effects of this passion are incredible! What is too hard for love to do, or endure, for the beloved object! Without love, what is zeal but wildfire! devotion, only splendid hypocrisy! My dear hearers, it is owing to a deficiency in this, that the heathen world has been so long and so shamefully neglected by those called Christians.

3. *Gratitude was a motive, not less probable in Mary's good work than the foregoing.* If any were to ask, what gratitude is? my answer should be, it is a pleasing sensation of the mind, excited by the soul being pressed with an inexpressible sense of high obligation to an object, for favors received. Mary knew Christ—for what end he was come into this lower world : she knew what he had done, and what he would do for her. How shall she show her thankful sense of benefits and blessings so great, so undeserved? Like Abigail laying her present at David's feet, she brings forth the best she had in this world; and, with her whole heart, bestowed it upon him whom her soul loved, and to whom she had such transcendent obligations.

II. *We now come to take notice of a few obvious circumstances which attended this good work.*

1. *It was public.* Have any of you, my friends, been ashamed of being active in promoting the missionary business? Be ashamed of your shame; and, from this day, cast away your cowardice, and consider it as a peculiar honor to appear the zealous supporters of such a cause.

2. *It was liberal, nay, profuse.* The passage tells us, the ointment was very costly. I trust you will excuse me for not giving you a particular description of all the articles which constituted the odoriferous composition. Let us, for the present, be content with Judas' estimate : he said " it might have been sold for more than three hundred pence," Mark xiv. 5. The usual way of calculating the value of different coins, gives the Roman penny at rather more than sevenpence halfpenny, sterling; according to this calculation, the ointment was worth near ten pounds : perhaps a great part of her living;

as much, or more, for her to give, than if some rich Jew had given ten thousand guineas.

3. *It was performed in due time.* Had Mary brought her box when Christ had got into heaven, though it had been ten times the value, it would not have availed—she would have lost all. Many good works lose nine-tenths of their value by being too late. The apostolic rule is, "That they which have believed in God might be careful to maintain good works," Titus iii. 8. Critics frequently render it, "to *go before* in good works." We have but too few; but here is one instance:—Mary goes before, or is in due time in her labor of love.

4. *Mary made her little temporalities answer the greatest and the noblest ends.* It is said, Psa. cxv. 16, that the Creator "hath given the earth to the children of men." For what purposes are we to suppose that property is given to all, or any of us? To ornament mortal, dying bodies? To feed the follies of fancy—to foster the pride of the heart; or, to amuse the possessor with counting over his gold, and feasting his eyes by gazing upon it? Oh, no! God gives the good things of this world for the noblest ends; and those ends are specified both in the Old and New Testaments. "Honor the Lord with thy substance, and with the firstfruits of all thine increase," Prov. iii. 9. This brings us to the general proposition.

III. *The object upon whom this good work terminated.* On this our text is very express: "She hath wrought a good work on me."

Too many religious and generous acts terminate in self; and the end they are intended to answer is, to gain a little of that airy bubble, "the honor that cometh of men." Remember Mary's object—it was to make Christ "a sweet-smelling savor;" and, as she is said to anoint him for his burial, it is probable that she intended it to signify that even in the grave his body should breathe a sweet odor, without seeing the least taint of corruption. Here learn the true and laudable object of all well-intended missions, viz., to make known to a perishing world the efficiency and glory of the sacrifice of the Lord Jesus Christ;—the very same which Paul had in view when he went forth into the dark regions of the gentile nations, as will abundantly appear from the following passage: "For we preach not ourselves, but Christ Jesus the Lord; and ourselves your servants for Jesus' sake," 2 Cor. iv. 5.

Actions terminate on Jesus Christ, though mediately, when they are calculated to increase his family; and, of course, the universal sacrifice of praise and thanksgiving ought daily to be presented unto him. The prophetic pen informs us, "Daily shall he be praised;" and if any ask, By whom? the same author tells us, "All nations shall call him blessed," Psa. xxii. 15, 17. This brings us to the last proposition.

IV. *The testimony of the impartial and infallible Judge who speaks in our text.* "She hath wrought a good work on me."

It gives me pleasure to say, the Judge is impartial and infallible; and that he is such, all must admit who believe revelation. An earthly judge may be impartial, but not infallible; nor does the latter unavoidably secure the former; but in Mary's Judge, "the Judge of all the earth," both meet, and forever abide. He sees all motives, and will pronounce just judgment in all cases, temporal or spiritual, between man and man, or between man and God. This is well on various accounts, especially two, upon each of which I would beg leave a moment to dwell.

1. *It is well, because there are so many bad actions in this world which at first sight appear good, by which men of great penetration have been deceived.*

2. *This necessity will appear still greater, by considering how many good actions have appeared the very reverse in the eyes of spectators.*

The judgment formed upon Mary's good work, by some of the company, may serve as one striking instance. Some may judge you sincere, but pity your weakness; others may ascribe it to your pride and vanity, declaring it all a whim—enthusiastic zeal: a work for which you have no Divine authority, etc. Care not for any or all of these reflections. Your Judge liveth; and, we trust, as he is perfectly acquainted with your work, so he will, in due time, say of it, "Ye have wrought a good work for me."

APPLICATION.

1. Suffer me, in the name of the Lord, to entreat all, Look well to your motives! You see it is love to Christ, more than the ointment, which makes the work good and honorable. Dread self-seeking as a deadly enemy, which will taint and spoil the whole.

2. Let all see that Christ puts a high value upon small matters done to him and

his followers. When love and gratitude give energy to their abilities, a cup of cold water shall not lose its reward, Mark ix. 41.

3. Again. We learn, from this passage, that carnal, ungodly men, think all is lost that is laid out for Christ's honor and interest in the world.

4. Once more. We take it for granted, that most of those present are ready to say, the conversion of the heathen is a very desirable object.

Think, oh! think, how inconsistent, how awful, how dreadful, to appear anxious for the conversion of infidels, and yourselves in an unconverted state—your own souls in danger of everlasting perdition! Suppose you saw a man exerting all his power to assist his neighbor, whose house was on fire; and, at the same moment, his own was in flames, and his family in the utmost hazard; and yet he takes no thought for them, nor makes any attempt for their relief. What would you think of him? You might commend his good-will to his neighbor, but all would condemn his shameful negligence to his dearest relatives!

———————

CII.—THE CHARACTER AND WORK OF THE MESSIAH.

BY THE HON. AND REV. G. T. NOEL, M. A.*

VICAR OF RAINHAM, KENT.

"Behold, my servant shall deal prudently. He shall be exalted and extolled, and be very high. As many were astonished at thee; (his visage was so marred more than any man, and his form more than the sons of men :) so shall he sprinkle many nations; the kings shall shut their mouths at him: for that which had not been told them shall they see; and that which they had not heard shall they consider."—*Isaiah* lii. 13–15.

THREE subjects principally claim our attention in this prophetic record :—The introduction of Christianity into the world, by the mysterious sufferings of its Divine Founder; its complete diffusion over the earth; and the process by which that diffusion will apparently be accomplished. Each of these points is full of momentous interest. Let us, then, briefly advert to—

I. *The introduction of Christianity into*

* From a sermon, preached at St. Bride's, Fleet-street, May 3, 1819, before the Church Missionary Society.

the world, by the mysterious sufferings of its Divine Founder.

" Behold, my servant !—Many were astonished at thee : his visage was so marred more than any man, and his form more than the sons of men."

This " astonishment of many" evidently refers to the inconsistency apparent, between the high pretensions and the depressed condition of this Servant of God. He had been foretold as " the Desire of all nations," Hag. ii. 7.; the Shiloh, unto whom should be the gathering of the people, Gen. xlix. 10 ; the Ruler, who should come forth from Judah, to sit upon the throne of David ; upon whose shoulders the government should be laid— and as, emphatically, the " Wonderful" and the " Counsellor," Isa. ix. 6, 7. A sordid and earthly interpretation had enshrined these promises in the hearts of the Jewish nation. The Jewish patriot hailed, in expectation, the brilliant hour in which the Messiah should break to shivers the chains which held his country in subjection to the Roman yoke ; while the man of narrow and selfish ambition, rejoiced in the vision which gleamed before his eyes, when the descendants of Abraham should hold dominion over the prostrate nations of the world.

When, therefore, the Saviour of the world appeared in the lowly garb of the son of the carpenter of Nazareth ; when he shunned every effort for personal aggrandizement ; when he resisted every popular movement to advance his regal claims ; when he put forth his power only to heal the diseased and to comfort the wretched ; when, with a humility which knew no parallel, and with a sympathy which evinced no exclusion, he constantly mingled with the meanest and most despised of his countrymen ;—then the mortified expectations of the Jewish rulers burst with tremendous efficacy on his devoted head.

The evidence in favor of his high claims was speedily examined, and as speedily rejected. That evidence was indeed strong, and clear, and palpable. His character was unimpeached ; his benevolence was diffusive ; his power was undeniable. " Never man spake like this man;" and, " It was never so seen in Israel," John vii. 46 ; Matt. ix. 33. The accents of his lips had more than once controlled the swellings of the deep, and startled the inhabitants of the dead. " He saved others !" was the testimony extorted from his enemies at his dying hour. But the union, in his destiny, of power and of suffering—of dignity and contempt—of riches to others and of poverty to himself —was the source of astonishment to many. In this destiny, the exhibition of every moral beauty was blended with the exhibition of every form of terror and distress. Angels looked on, and wondered, and adored.

In truth, the plan of Christianity, with its introduction into the world, is far above the calculations of human sagacity. It proved, accordingly, "to the Jews a stumbling-block, and to the Greeks foolishness;" nevertheless, to him who believeth it has ever proved, and it will still prove to be, "Christ the power of God, and the wisdom of God," 1 Cor. i. 23, 24. Let us notice,

II. *The declaration of the prophet with regard to the universal diffusion of the religion of Christ on the earth.* "My servant shall deal prudently. He shall be exalted, and extolled, and be very high."

1. The expression, "*He shall deal prudently,*" is, in the margin, translated, "*He shall prosper;*" and thus the whole clause is declarative of the same truth—the triumph and success of the Son of God. If many were astonished at his humiliation, a far greater number shall be astonished at his exaltation.

2. *This grand and glorious achievement he effected by means that came not within the range of mortal discernment.* It was by death that he conquered Death. It was by a perfect obedience in action and in suffering, that he became the second Adam—the spiritual Head of a new and happier race. He "was delivered for our offences, and raised again for our justification," Rom. iv. 25; and thus revived from the dead, he shortly "divided the spoil with the strong.' He planted his religion on the earth, opposed by hostile scorn, and relentless malice, and despotic power. In a few years, the banner of the cross waved upon the conquered fortresses of Paganism, and enlisted under its folds the great and mighty of the earth. Yet no earthly weapon had been raised in its defence. The cause of Christ achieved its victories by its own inherent power. It was resistless by its truth, and by the silent operation of the Spirit of truth. Its adherents were, indeed, strong; but it was in faith, and purity, and charity. Thus the Servant of God prospered, and was extolled, and became very high.

3. *But his reign on the earth is yet very limited, and his conquests incomplete.* "There remaineth yet much land to be possessed." Five-sixths of the millions of the human race are still the prey of idolatry or of imposture; and the ancient people of God are still the outcasts from his favor, and the victims of unbelief. It stands recorded in characters, which no lapse of years can ever erase : "It is a light thing that thou shouldest be my servant to raise up the tribes of Jacob, and to restore the preserved of Israel : I will also give thee for a light to the Gentiles, that thou mayest be my salvation unto the end of the earth," Isa. xlix. 6. We proceed to inquire,

III. *What we may gather from this prophetic account respecting the process by which the kingdom of the Messiah shall thus be fully and finally established.*

Now, it is declared, "As many were astonished at thee : so shall he sprinkle many nations ; the kings shall shut their mouths at him : for that which had not been told them shall they see ; and that which they had not heard shall they consider." This passage of Scripture is pregnant with information, as to the PROCESS by which Christianity shall advance to her sacred and ultmate dominion. We are led to infer,

1. *That there shall be a wide dispersion of Divine knowledge over heathen and Mohammedan nations;* for men cannot see or consider that which is not first presented to their notice. If, then, they shall see and consider that which in former times had not been told them, it follows, that a wide dissemination of Divine knowledge shall take place in the earth. Connect together missionary exertions and the translations of the Scriptures and the education of the young,—connect these with the growing and heavenly sympathy which is dilating itself in the human heart ; and say, whether or not, a mighty machinery is at work, directed by God himself, and impelled by the very movements of the Almighty Hand ! Let us turn again to the prophetic record : "That which had not been told them shall they see ; and that which they had not heard shall they consider." That is,

2. *The nations shall fix their anxious attention on the truths declared to them.* And let me ask, Is there no symptom of the approaching reign of Christ, of this very character, now before our eyes ? If the servants of God are becoming active in the cause of

their adorable Lord, is no corresponding emotion manifesting itself on the part of the heathen? If the fertilizing dews be beginning to fall from heaven, are there no thirsty lands panting for the shower? Surely, the reports from pagan nations are of the most cheering kind. On every hand there is, more or less, a shaking of old opinions. The kingdom of Satan is dividing against itself.—Nor shall success be long unseen; for mark again the encouraging statement of the prophet, "The kings shall shut their mouths at him,"—

3. *Impressed with holy awe, they shall assume the attitude of abasement and submission.* I apprehend, that the expression, "the kings shall shut their mouths at him," implies, the submission of whole nations, here represented by kings; for, as the reception of Christianity on the part of the rulers of a country, requires the overthrow of every system of religious polity previously established; such a reception publicly made, implies, more or less, the submission of the mass of the people. Enlightened by the Divine Spirit, they shall at length "behold the Lamb of God," slain to take away "the sins of the world." They shall recognize his righteous claims; they shall receive his law; they shall trust in his grace; they shall bow to his sway. But who can adequately unfold his ultimate and glorious triumph, when

4. *He shall forgive their iniquities and sanctify their hearts.* For, "He shall sprinkle many nations;" that is, in allusion to the aspersions under the law, by which the people were sanctified, the Son of God shall apply to the souls of regenerated multitudes, the blood of his great atonement, and the sacred influences of his Holy Spirit. "Then a nation shall be born in a day." Then the conquests of the Redeemer shall be visible and splendid. Thus shall adoring millions be washed in the blood of Jesus, and shall be presented holy unto the Lord. "Men shall be blessed in him : all nations shall call him blessed," Psa. lxxii. 17.

APPLICATION.

Let me then—1. Suggest to you, in special allusion to the success of our missionary cause, the importance of conducting all our measures in a spirit of prayer.

2. Let us be diligent in the cultivation of personal godliness. Let us, in very deed and spirit, each draw nearer daily to heaven, while laboring to do the work of heaven in the world!

3. Let us cherish a warmer sentiment of gratitude for the gift of the gospel. What a theme is here for gratitude! what an argument for praise! "Who made thee to differ from another? and what hast thou that thou didst not receive?" 1 Cor. iv. 7. Oh! let it be our care to value and improve our mercies. May the blessing never be withdrawn! May the light never be extinguished!

4. But, once more, in reference to this great cause, it seems to be of essential importance, that we cherish a spirit of Christian union and mutual charity. Oh! it is reserved for the glory of the latter days, to merge minuter differences in those grand questions which are the heart and life-blood of the Christian cause—dear to one church as to another, because dear to God, and essential to the repose of man. Then "Ephraim shall not vex Judah, and Judah shall not vex Ephraim," Isa. xi. 13. And truly, it has been pleasant, during the progress of these few last years, to watch the orient beams of this blessed "unity of the spirit, in the bond of peace;" and to hail them as the harbingers of a brighter day.

Let us solemnly and deliberately cultivate a spirit of tenderness and compassion towards the heathen. Let their actual situation often rest on our remembrance, and have a place in our prayers.

CIII.—HINDERANCES TO THE SPREAD OF THE GOSPEL.

BY REV. LEONARD WOODS, D. D.[*]

"For Zion's sake will I not hold my peace, and for Jerusalem's sake I will not rest, until the righteousness thereof go forth as brightness, and the salvation thereof as a lamp that burneth. And the Gentiles shall see thy righteousness, and all kings thy glory."—*Isaiah* lxii. 1, 2.

SUCH was the love which the evangelical prophet felt for Jerusalem, and such his desire that its glory might be extended. It was a desire which gave him no rest; but prompted him to incessant labor and prayer for the accomplishment of its object. Desires similar to this have been felt, and simi-

[*] From a sermon delivered before the American Board of Commissioners for Foreign Missions, New Haven, Connecticut, Oct. 5, 1831.

lar efforts made, by the faithful servants of God, from age to age, for the propagation of the Christian religion. Since the commencement of the present century, the spread of Christianity has been a subject of growing interest to the friends of religion. Good men have been excited in an unusual degree, to unite their efforts and prayers for the enlargement of the church. The God of heaven has shown, by the promises of his word, and the dispensations of his providence, that he regards this object with the highest favor; and that it is his unalterable purpose, that "the earth shall be filled with his glory." It would certainly be reasonable to expect that the cause of Christianity, thus aided and supported, would soon prevail through the world; that the reign of righteousness and peace would speedily be extended "from the rising of the sun unto the going down thereof." And it becomes a subject of serious inquiry, Why this is not the case? Why has not this blessed cause, which is eminently the cause of God, become universally triumphant?

Our particular inquiry is, What obstacles to the conversion of the world are found among those, who, in different ways, are enlisted in the cause of foreign missions?

I. *The defect of our Christian character, or the want of a higher degree of holiness.*

Before Him who searcheth the heart, "and knoweth all things," and in whose sight "the heavens are not. clean;" we must, every one of us, be filled with shame and self-abhorrence, and penitently cry out, Behold! I am vile; what shall I answer?

That this imperfection of our Christian character must prove a great hinderance to the success of the cause we are endeavoring to promote, appears from the very nature of that cause. It is the cause of holiness. It is the inward, invisible machinery (if I may so call it), which gives efficiency to the external means. It is the spiritual, devout, fervent action of a purified heart, which exerts the most certain and powerful influence in promoting the salvation of men. Who can estimate the amount of good which twelve men, possessing the character of the twelve apostles, might accomplish at the present day?

II. *This unhappy effect must result in a still higher degree, from the direct indulgence of affections which are selfish and earthly.*

Selfish, earthly affections aim at a selfish,

earthly interest. But the spread of the gospel through the world is a benevolent and spiritual interest. These two interests are directly opposite to each other; and the dispositions and efforts which are suited to the one are not suited to the other. If worldly and selfish passions prevail in any considerable degree, they will have a visible influence.

III. *The advancement of Christ's kingdom is essentially hindered by division and strife among his followers.*

The cause of missions must be promoted by the *united* exertions of ministers and Christians. There is, on the contrary, too often displayed a clashing of influence. The efforts actually made for the cause of Christ by one part, will be more or less resisted, and their good effect prevented, by the counter efforts of another part.

IV. *We may hinder the cause of missions by the unnecessary excitement of popular prejudice.*

The missionary enterprise must fail of success, without the cordial affection and support of the Christian community. It essentially needs the aid of their efforts, contributions, and prayers. Now, if those who are instructed with the sacred interests of missions, are chargeable with any misconduct, or any manifest indiscretion; such misconduct or indiscretion proclaimed, as it will be, in the ears of the public, may cool the affections, excite prejudices, and prevent the contributions and prayers of thousands.

V. *We hinder the spread of the gospel, so far as we fall short in our duty in regard to the benevolent use of property.*

Just in proportion to the magnitude and excellence of the object, should be our liberality in contributing of our substance for its promotion.

Brethren, suffer me to speak freely. The Christian community has of late years been waking up, in a measure, to better views in regard to the proper value and use of money; and many examples have been exhibited of a very honorable liberality in contributing to benevolent objects. But is not the prevailing, practical sentiment still very far below the right standard? Can it be that men of wealth make the cause of Christ their great object, when they generally give it so small a proportion of their substance? The only remaining obstacle to the spread of the gospel which I shall mention, is,

VI. *The want of a proper feeling and acknowledgment of our dependence on God for the success of our efforts.*

There is nothing which stands in more direct opposition to the truth, than the spirit of pride and self-dependence. For whatever importance we may attach to our own efforts in the work of evangelizing the world, and whatever good we may expect from the faithful labors of missionaries; yet all success comes from God. In the most favorable circumstances, therefore, nothing can be effectually done to bring men into the kingdom of Christ, except by the special operation of God.

APPLICATION.

1. We have now seen what are the obstacles to the accomplishment of the great and excellent work we have undertaken. Let us keep these obstacles out of the way, and the religion of Christ will soon make rapid progress.

Finally. Let us never forget that it is owing to the grace of God, that the cause of Christianity, with so many obstacles in its way, has made such progress in the world. Is it not rather a matter of wonder, that this light of the world has not been totally extinguished, than that it does not shine more brightly? Is it not a miracle of Divine power, that religion maintains a place in the world, and is making any progress, when there is so much to oppose it, even among its friends? Let, then, the pride of man be abased; let every high thought be brought low, and let God alone be exalted.

CIV.—THE FULNESS OF THE TIMES.

BY REV. JOHN HEY, OF BRISTOL.*

"That in the dispenstaion of the fulness of times he might gather together in one all things in Christ, both which are in heaven, and which are on earth; even in him."—*Eph.* i. 10.

In the discussion of this subject, our thoughts will be employed, firstly, in meditating on the important period specified in the text; and, secondly, on that glorious work which will be accomplished during the same.

* From a sermon, preached at the Tabernacle, September 23, 1795, before the London Missionary Society.

I. *The important period specified in the text.*

The apostle calls it, "The dispensation of the fulness of times;" by which he intends, a marvellous season of grace, which has not yet taken place—at least, in the fullest sense of the words. To discover the import, strength, and beauty of these expressions, we must fix our attention,

1. *On the times referred to.* The Bible speaks of various times: such as, times appointed, times predicted, "times or the seasons, which the Father hath put in his own power," Acts i. 7.

(1.) We read of times of ignorance. Our world has been most awfully afflicted with times of mental obscurity: "Darkness shall cover the earth, and gross darkness the people," Isa. lx. 2.

(2.) A time of error and general defection from the primitive faith. The author of the second Epistle to the Thessalonians, describes this event in the predictive language of "falling away," 2 Thes. ii. 3. This almost universal declension had a surprising effect on the professors of Christianity, and produced an astonishing alteration both in the state and the appearance of things; for from this alarming apostasy resulted—

(3.) A time of awful superstition. The most ridiculous, not to say blasphemous modes of worship, were now invented; an almost endless train of contemptible, unmeaning, and useless ceremonies, were introduced into the pretended worship of God.

(4.) A time of tremendous persecution began under the reign of the papal beast. This persecution raged with unabating fury for several ages.

(5.) The time of the glorious Reformation. This was a time of joy and prosperity to the Church of God. Truth now began to shine in its native lustre and beauty.

(6.) We are now brought to that period referred to in the text. We have glanced at times of almost every description: times of ignorance, defection, superstition, persecution, light, and reformation; at length we are arrived at the period called "the fulness of times!" God, "who worketh all things after the counsel of his own will," hath, in his unerring wisdom, given permission to new and false prophets—sin and hell, popes and devils—to exert their utmost rage and influence in opposition to his cause and interest in the world. And now, to confound these mighty adversaries of his Church, he will bring on, in the end of those times, a dispensation of incomparable glory. This is styled in our text, "The dispensation of the fulness of times." This thought introduces the subsequent part of the subject:

II. *That glorious work which will be accomplished during this wonderful dispensation.*

The nature of this work is expressed under the idea of gathering "together in one all things in Christ," &c.; viz., to incorporate in one body, or unite in one complete system, all things in heaven and on earth. This presupposes that a disunion and disagreement have taken place between the various ranks of beings which God hath made. Several considerations unite to corroborate this idea. But, notwithstanding these awful breaches, the Lord Jehovah will fulfil his gracious purpose, to "gather together in one all things in Christ, both which are in heaven and which are on earth."

(1.) When the apostle asserts, that God will "gather together in one all things in Christ," he means, that all things in creation, together with every event of Divine Providence and effect of sovereign grace, are, and will be, so connected, as to compose one grand system of universal economy; in which all the perfections of Deity will shine forth with ineffable splendor and glory.

(2.) The inhabitants of different climes, customs, colors, habits, and pursuits, both in Christian and Pagan lands, shall be united in one large society under the genial influence of gospel grace, so that "there shall be one fold, and one shepherd," John x. 16.

(3.) These words may signify further, that human and angelic intelligences will be associated in harmony and love. Our adorable Immanuel has informed us, that the time will come, when the millions of redeemed men shall be as the angels of God in heaven, Matt. xxii. 30. The grand instrument by which this amazing work will be accomplished, is the glorious gospel of God our Saviour. All things are to be gathered together in Christ, even in him; viz., in his name, through his mediation, and by his power. The great commission with which the heralds of salvation are invested, is to go and preach repentance and remission of sins, in Immanuel's name, among all nations. To inform them, "that God was (and still is) in Christ, reconciling the world unto himself, not imputing their trespasses unto them," 2 Cor. v. 19.

There are weighty reasons to be assigned, why this important work will be effected by the instrumentality of the gospel of Christ.

1. *It is superior to all other systems.* The superiority of the Christian system appears,

(1.) In the excellency of its doctrines. They are remarkably perspicuous, simple, and plain; though, at the same time, inconceivably sublime.

(2.) In the glory of its promises. It insures to all who embrace it, inviolable security, strong consolation, and ample support under all the trials of the present state. It promises hope and joy in death; and beyond the grave, "an inheritance, incorruptible and undefiled, and that fadeth not away," 1 Pet. i. 4.

(3.) In the purity of its precepts. The threatenings contained in the Bible render it a fit instrument for converting the heathen.

2. *The success which has heretofore attended the preaching of the gospel, evinces it to be the proper instrument for the conversion of mankind.*

3. *Our expectations, as to the spread and prevalence of the gospel, are greatly encouraged by the promises which the Divine Father has made to his incarnate Son.* "Ask of me, and I shall give thee the heathen for thine inheritance, and the uttermost parts of the earth for thy possession." "It is a light thing that thou shouldest be my servant to raise up the tribes of Jacob, and to restore the preserved of Israel: I will also give thee for a light to the Gentiles, that thou mayest be my salvation unto the end of the earth," Psa. ii. 8; Isa. xlix. 6. Can everlasting veracity fail to accomplish such promises as these? No! "Till heaven and earth pass, one jot or one tittle shall in no wise pass from the law, till all be fulfilled," Matt. v. 18.

APPLICATION.

1. From a review of what has passed under our notice at this time, we may derive encouragement as to our present momentous undertaking. That Arm which stands engaged to bring salvation to the heathen, is omnipotent. He that hath promised to gather the outcasts of the people is Jehovah, and his designs cannot fail. "He is the Rock, his work is perfect," Deut. xxxii. 4.

2. But with all this encouragement, let us not forget our province, as to a vigorous,

diligent, and persevering use of means. The means are now before us; and that important plan, by which our active endeavors will be regulated, is now formed.

3. In order to animate our minds and stimulate our efforts, we ought to contemplate the delightful effects which will result from our united exertions, when succeeded by the blessing of God!

What a pleasing change now takes place! How different the aspect of those countries where the gospel hath come with invincible energy. The seed of life is sown—heavenly dews descend upon it—it takes root—springs forth, and produces "some thirty, and some sixty, and some an hundred fold," Mark. iv. 8.

CV.—IMPREGNABLE SECURITY OF ISRAEL, AND GOD'S WONDROUS DOINGS ON THEIR BEHALF.

"Surely there is no enchantment against Jacob, neither is there any divination against Israel: according to this time it shall be said of Jacob and of Israel, What hath God wrought!"—*Numbers* xxiii. 23.

BALAK, king of the Moabites, anxious to rid himself of the children of Israel, whose tents were now pitched in the plains around him, sent for Balaam, that he might curse them. It is evident that the spirit of true prophecy rested on this individual; but influenced by the love of sordid gain, he lent himself to Balak, and endeavored to do his bidding. God placed a variety of hinderances in his way, that he might return to the path of rectitude, and not attempt the execution of Balak's commission. But, blinded by avarice, he went on and on, until God allowed his own infatuations to have the ascendency, so that he became the miserable victim of his own worldliness. But though willing to do Balak's work, yet, when the time came, he was impelled, by the Spirit of God, to predict of Israel the most glorious things. Instead of declaring evil, he proclaimed the enrapturing prophecy recorded in Numb. xxiii. 8, &c.

A second attempt elicited the declaration in verses 18–24: the conclusion of which is the subject of our present discourse. How true is the text of Israel of old! No evil spirit of enchantment could affect them. No spirit of divination injure them. The magicians of Egypt could mimic Moses, but only in adding to the misery of the Egyptians: but neither earth nor hell can injure those who "trust in the Lord: he is their help and their shield," Psa. cxv. 9. Applying our text to the children of God, consider,

I. *The truth affirmed.* "Surely there is no enchantment against Jacob," &c.

II. *The exclamation uttered.*

I. *The truth affirmed.* "Surely there is no enchantment," &c. We enter not into the discussion, how far men may have had power from Satan to "enchant," to "divine," or to "curse" others. But we abide by the text, that there is no such thing against the cause and people of God. Hell is opposed to the cause of God; and united with it are the wicked powers of earth. They have the disposition, the will, the purpose, and may make the attempt to injure the church; but their efforts must fail—their plots must be frustrated—their attacks must be powerless.

Yet sometimes they have been able to harass, and vex, and torture the people of God. Sometimes, they have apparently succeeded and triumphed; but really and eventually they must be frustrated. "For surely there is no enchantment," &c. Now, the certainty of this may be inferred,

1. *Because the counsels of God are more than sufficient to baffle the designs and plots of hell.*

We would not array human skill and tact against the wiles and stratagems of the devil. But the security of the church depends on the counsels of God: on the infinite wisdom of the Most High. He knows how to frustrate the devices of evil, and how to deliver those who trust in his name. His eyes are open to the thoughts and plots of the wicked; and hell has no covering before Him. Hence, he is the Watcher and Keeper of Israel, and neither slumbers nor sleeps, Psa. cxxi. 4.

2. *Because the power of Jehovah is ever effectual in thwarting the attacks of the enemies of his people.*

Divine wisdom or omniscience is united with resistless power. His mandate gave being to the universe: "He spake, and it was done: he commanded, and it stood fast," Psa. xxxiii. 9. The volition of his own mind and will, would overwhelm the fallen spirits with confusion and terror. All created power is mere impotency before him: how, then, can the powers of evil ruin the church, and overthrow the cause of the Eternal?

3. *Because Divine goodness is more than*

enough to counteract the malevolence of our foes.

The wisdom and power of God are combined with immeasurable love. The institutions of the church are those of God's heart. His people are as the apple of his eye, Deut. xxxii. 10. "Behold, I have graven thee on the palms of my hands," Isa. xlix. 16. He has covenanted with them, to sustain, to keep, to preserve, to deliver, to glorify them. "Surely there is no enchantment against Jacob, neither is there any divination against Israel."

4. *The resources of God are more than adequate to render all the means of the church's enemies abortive.*

The enemy can combine various elements of evil—the wrath and power of fallen legions, craft and subtilty; the wealth and influence of the world, the fascinations of earth, &c.; and all these have successively been employed. But all resources are Jehovah's: the angels of his presence, the stars of heaven, the sun and the moon; storms, and winds, and tempest; earthquakes, pestilence, and famine; locusts, and even flies, can effect his bidding. "Surely the wrath of man shall praise thee: the remainder of wrath shalt thou restrain," Psa. lxxvi. 10. On these grounds, we may well say, "Surely there is no enchantment," &c.

II. *The exclamation uttered.*—"According to this time it shall be said of Jacob and of Israel," &c.

1. *What is to be said?* "What hath God wrought!" All deliverances are to be traced up to God. Agents are to be observed, but God only praised: God alone is to have the glory, as he has had the real work of delivering his people. This is to keep up our dependence on God. This is to inspire with adoration and praise. This is to keep human nature in its right place.

Not what Moses did in Egypt, or Joshua, or Gideon, or David, or the apostles, or the first martyrs, or the reformers, or Wesley, or Whitfield; but "What hath God wrought!" There is a tendency to lose sight of God, or to make God secondary; but it ought ever to be—"What God hath wrought!"

2. *Who are to say it?* Sometimes even enemies have said it. Balaam was forced to see it, and in the text to speak it.

(1.) It should be said especially by the ministers of the gospel: they are to draw attention to the doings of Jehovah; they are to extol the Lord, to celebrate the works of his hand, to speak of the glory of his kingdom, and talk of his power, Psa. cxlv. 10, &c.

(2.) It should be said by all the pious. Parents to their children—teachers to their pupils—Christians to one another. Thus the psalmist (lxxvii. 11), "I will remember the works of the Lord," &c.; and thus the prophet Isaiah exclaims (xii. 4, &c.), "Praise the Lord," &c.

3. *When should it be said?*

(1.) It should be said in times of depression, as the means of consolation. However low, or destitute, or afflicted, yet so it has often been—that God has "remembered us in our low estate: for his mercy endureth forever," Psa. cxxxvi. 23.

(2.) In times of great exertion, as an incitement to perseverance. Hope cheers, and renews with vigor for the toil. Never forget that the success is certain. Your efforts must avail,—"Surely," &c.

(3.) In times of great success, to give tone to our exultations. We then have former days brought to our remembrance. Thus reminded of God's doings of old, with grateful, rapturous joy we exclaim, "What hath God wrought!"

(4.) It will be reiterated in the world of the beatified forever. There they will see, in one beautiful series, the doings of God—behold the golden chain entire. There the philosophy of Providence will be elucidated, and its harmony with redemption made clear as with letters of light.

APPLICATION.

1. Our text may apply to many as to their Christian experience before God. "Remember all the way which the Lord thy God led thee," &c., Deut. viii. 2.

2. The text is appropriate to Christian missions. What enemies, difficulties, and discouragements have been overcome and surmounted. Well may we exclaim, "What hath God wrought!" Let India—the islands of the South Sea—the deserts of Africa—the West Indies—New Zealand, &c., all testify.

3. Let God ever be exalted for the blessings we enjoy; and for all the good done in us, and by us.

CVI.—THE LIGHT OF THE GENTILES.

BY' REV. W. B. COLLYER, D. D.*

"A light to lighten the Gentiles."—*Luke* ii. 32.

WE shall endeavor to explain the import of the text, and to apply its testimony to missionary exertions. In explaining its import, we shall discover that the character of Jesus is represented under the image of "Light;" that the subjects of his influences are "the Gentiles;" and that the result of these things taken together, or, in other words, his manifestation to the world, is universal illumination—for he rises upon the nations to lighten them. In applying this testimony to missionary exertions, we shall find that it explains the principles upon which they are founded; and evinces that they proceed from nature, reason, humanity, patriotism, and religion. We shall be induced to examine the encouragements which this testimony affords; and shall find that they arise from revelation, from experience, and from existing circumstances. This is the ground on which we wish to prove that missionary societies are worthy your countenance and support, by showing that the work is of God, and that the heart and the understanding alike pay homage to its excellence.

I. *We shall endeavor to explain the import of the text*, "A light to lighten the Gentiles." Observe,

1. *The character of Jesus is exhibited under the image of "light."* A more appropriate and more beautiful symbol could not have been selected, whether it be applied to the Saviour himself, or to his influence on the world. In both these cases it is employed in the text, and in both of them it will be necessary to examine the figure. Light is the most glorious of all the creatures of God; and is, therefore, a singularly appropriate image in reference to the uncreated glory of the Son of God. If, therefore, light convey to the mind an idea of glory, it is a fit emblem of Him, "by whom all things were created, that are in heaven, and that are in earth, visible and invisible, whether they be thrones, or dominions, or principalities, or powers: all things were created by him, and for him: and he is before all things, and by him all things consist," Col. i. 16.

(1.) Among the properties of light, are

* Preached before the Missionary Society, at Surrey Chapel, May 9, 1810.

penetration and universality. It is said of the sun, "His going forth is from the end of the heaven, and his circuit unto the ends of it: and there is nothing hid from the heat thereof," Psa. xix. 6. Light would have been an inappropriate image, in reference to Christ, had he not intended to illuminate the world. Not to a district, nor to an empire, nor to one quarter of the globe, does that glorious boon of heaven—light—confine its influences. It visits all in their turn—it burns within the torrid zone, and reaches the dark and distant poles: it proceeds with gradual, yet inconceivable speed, in its restless career, till it has enlightened the whole.

(2.) Light is a source of comfort. "Truly the light is sweet, and a pleasant thing it is for the eyes to behold the sun," Eccl. xi. 7.

(3.) Another quality of light is purity. It is this which renders it a fit emblem of Deity; and which induced the apostle John to say, "God is light, and in him is no darkness at all," 1 John i. 5.

2. *The subjects of his influences,* "*The Gentiles.*" The original word signifies no more than *nations*, literally, both in the Old and New Testaments. The confinement of the oracles of truth to the Jewish people, caused nations and heathen, or people who knew not the true God, to be considered synonymous. Our English word heathen, is derived from the word employed in the text: so that the object of missionary societies is one of the express objects of the incarnation of our Lord; and the subjects of his influences, promised in the text, are those who have excited, at this time, your Christian sympathy.

3. *The result of the manifestation of Christ to the world, will be universal illumination.* He rises upon the nations "to lighten" them. The state of mankind, considered as destitute of this light, is a state of most deplorable darkness. We include in this figurative expression, the absence of knowledge and of comfort. They that live "without God," of necessity live "without hope." The text proposes a remedy as wide as the disease, and promises deliverance from this state of darkness and misery, while it preaches Christ as "a light to lighten the Gentiles."

II. *To apply its testimony to missionary exertions, of which we have not entirely lost sight in the exposition.*

1. *Let us examine the principles on which they are founded.* These are of the highest

order; and from them the great effects may be anticipated.

(1.) They are founded in nature. As man is a compound being, his actions are generally the result of many principles, bearing, at the same time, upon one point. This is the fact relative to the exertions this day examined; and it is at present our business to analyze and to arrange these, that by viewing them separately we may be able to appreciate them as a whole. It is a principle of nature, that the same cause should produce the same effects. Whoever sincerely loves the Saviour, will feel a proportionate attachment to his laws, his people, and his interests. He cannot sit down indifferent to the last, any more than he can consent to break the first.

(2.) Missionary exertions are founded on the purest principles of reason. It is consistent with right reason to connect means with the end. This society has been charged with enthusiasm in what? That they expect the universal diffusion of religious knowledge? No such thing! This point is so generally admitted, that it appears impossible to hold the Bible, and to doubt the fact. In what, then, consists their enthusiasm? That they have embodied their faith in the adoption of those means which have received the sanction of all ages; and, having done so, that they wait not without hope, but with patient and chastened expectation, the success of their labors, and the fulfilment of the Divine promise. But, it is objected, that right reason always employs means proportionate to the end. What means could be deemed proportionate to such an end? Nothing less than Omniscience could draw a plan completely adequate to such a design; and nothing less than Omnipotence could execute it. The first has been done, and the last is gradually performing by the Deity himself. In the mean while he employs, for the execution of all his purposes, human instruments; and we shall hereafter prove, that the means adopted by this society are of his own ordination.

(3.) Missionary exertions are founded on the purest principles of humanity. We have described the world as in a state of deplorable ignorance and pollution. The consequences are bitter and inevitable. The empire of sin, must be an empire broken up by the ploughshare of calamity. The tyranny of moral evil is felt in the riot of wide-wasting sorrow, and the victories of unsparing death.

(4.) Missionary exertions are founded on the purest principles of patriotism. What lover of his country does not desire to see her the leader of this great work—the reformation of mankind, and the subversion of depravity? When God gave Jerusalem to desolation, it was not while she was "very zealous," or, in modern language, very enthusiastic "for the Lord of hosts;" but when she ceased to feel an interest in his cause, and when she sunk into the most criminal indifference. Religious lethargy precedes national ruin; patriotism, therefore, calls for the support of religious zeal.

(5.) Missionary exertions are founded on the purest principles of religion. Religion adopts and influences all the springs of action which we have named, and all the properties of the human mind of every description. Religion directs the will, mollifies the passions, regulates the affections. Religion fosters the feelings of nature, guides the researches of reason, elicits the charities of humanity, kindles the fire of patriotism, while her own honor is singularly concerned in this great cause. As her name has been borrowed by ambition and superstition, it is time for her to discover herself in her native majesty. When the Druid slew a man and a brother in the consecrated circle, he called his murderous act a religious rite. The wretched Indian, who lays himself down to be crushed to death under the car of some idol, thinks he is paying homage to religion. But real religion urges the use of all the means which reason points out, and stimulates all the sympathies which nature, or humanity, or patriotism acknowledge.

2. *The considerations by which we are encouraged.*

(1.) Missionary exertions are encouraged by revelation. We will not at this time, in making our appeal "to the law and to the testimony," recapitulate those sublime predictions, and those numerous promises, which relate to the final triumph of Jesus over all his adversaries, and the universal extension of his kingdom—passages which have been so largely produced, and so ably discussed on these occasions. One shall suffice: "The kingdoms of this world are become the kingdoms of our Lord, and of his Christ; and he shall reign forever and ever." Rev. xi. 15.

(2.) Missionary exertions are encouraged

by experience. The lapse of years lays the adversaries of Christianity dead at its foot; while it has acquired vigor from that which impairs every thing earthly, and received evidences from the destroying hand which sweeps into oblivion every record of this world.

(3.) Missionary exertions are encouraged, further, by existing circumstances,—by the existing circumstances of the society. We are not ashamed to appeal to its influence at home and abroad; and to call upon its adversaries to examine what it has actually effected. But what have you done abroad? Is there occasion to ask this question? Look at our reports, and the publication of our transactions. Is it nothing to maintain missionaries in so many remote parts of the world? Is it nothing to acquire languages, not reduced to any grammatical standard, so as to address the heathen in their own tongues? Is it nothing to have their children catechized weekly, and instructed in the fundamental principles of Christianity? Is it nothing to receive Hottentots into Christian Britain, to instruct professors in their own principles? Is it nothing to translate the scriptures into languages which never before conveyed the word of truth to those who speak them? This, and more than this, the society has effected.

(4.) Missionary exertions are further encouraged by the existing circumstances of the world. If we feel the curse in a more sensible degree, the more vigorous should be our exertions to disseminate that which shall destroy the curse. In this single quarter of the globe, amidst the ruin that has marked the progress of ambition, and the calamities attending a state of warfare, protracted almost beyond precedent in any age, the spirit of religion is cultivated, the worship of God is maintained, and peace finds a refuge still from the persecutions of overweening power, and of cruel oppression.

While England is spared, Europe cherishes the fond hope of future deliverance from her present chains; and, with still more animated expectation, fixes her eyes upon this country, as the storehouse of spiritual communications, whence her future supplies are to be drawn. Support missionary exertions, and realize her dream of approaching happiness! Moreover, the awful and impressive features of the present times, correspond with those which distinguished the appearance of our Lord. "For thus saith the Lord of hosts: Yet once, it is a little while, and I will shake the heavens, and the earth, and the sea, and the dry land; and I will shake all nations, and the desire of all nations shall come," Hag. ii. 6. If this prophecy was partially fulfilled at the birth of Christ, it remains to be more completely accomplished now: for he is not as yet revealed as "the Desire of all nations;" and we hope, not without reason, that these dreadful convulsions announce his approach.

APPLICATION.

1. Such are the encouragements to missionary exertions. Nor ought we to be disheartened at the narrowness of our means, when contrasted with the immensity of our design.

2. Let the disciple of the tender and compassionate Jesus, in this assembly, calmly behold the progress of moral evil, the parent of calamity, without making one effort to arrest it in its furious and malignant course, if he can. Let him exult in his personal advantages, and see others perishing for want of them unmoved! Let him say, with benevolent John, "We know that we are of God, and the whole world lieth in wickedness;" but not in his compassionate tone, and with his bowels of tenderness—if he can. Let him, with selfish appetite, sit down to a board covered with religious plenty—to the elements, the pledges of his Master's death—without sending one morsel to the poor heathen, or affording them the crumbs which fall from this table—if he can. Let him contemplate the spirit and purpose of his Master, and withhold his hand from the work—if he can. And then will we, at the second appearance of our Lord, tell, before heaven and earth, that we pleaded a cause for which Jesus shed the last drop of his heart's blood—and pleaded in vain!

———————

CVII.—GROUNDS OF THE MISSIONARY WORK.

BY REV. C. D. GRIFFIN, D. D.*

"And Jesus came and spake unto them, saying, All power is given unto me in heaven and in earth. Go ye therefore, and teach all nations, baptizing them in the name of the Father, and

* From a sermon, preached September 14, 1826, before the American Board of Missions, at Middletown, Connecticut.

of the Son, and of the Holy Ghost: teaching them to observe all things whatsoever I have commanded you: and, lo, I am with you alway, even unto the end of the world."—*Matt.* xxviii. 18–20.

I RISE to advocate the cause of missions to the heathen and to plead for a dying world. My sole object is to enforce the claims of five hundred millions of perishing men, by some plain and simple arguments which have affected my own mind: and I have chosen this text because it contains some of the arguments, and suggests the rest. Both the authority of Christ, and his personal reward, are here distinctly brought to bear on the subject. For his "obedience unto death" he received the inheritance, including "the heathen" and "the uttermost parts of the earth," Psa. ii. 8; and the authority to manage the whole estate. This authority he employed in sending forth missionaries to disciple all nations, and to bring to him the unnumbered millions promised for his seed. My argument, then, is founded,

I. *On the authority of Christ.*

The injunction in the text was not addressed to the eleven exclusively, but to them as depositaries of the Divine commands: and, through them, to the whole body of ministers in every age. This appears from the promise subjoined, "Lo, I am with you alway, even unto the end of the world!" Indeed, the eleven were expressly commanded to transmit to their successors all the injunctions which they themselves received, one of which was to disciple all nations. "Go ye therefore, and teach all nations,—teaching them to observe all things whatsoever I have commanded you." This command is now sounding in the ears of the ministers and churches of the nineteenth century.

II. *The example of Christ and his apostles.*

The Saviour of the world sent out a band of missionaries, and charged them "to preach the gospel to every creature;—and they went forth and preached everywhere" that man should repent, Mark xvi. 15, 20. No one objection can be raised against missions, at the present day, which will not equally lie against Christ and his apostles. The attempt is no more presumptuous now, than then; the prospect is no more discouraging; the difficulties are no greater; the power that is engaged to give success is the same, for the promise remains unchanged, "Lo, I am with you alway, even unto the end of the world." My argument is founded,

III. *In what we owe to the heathen.*

Is the gospel no blessing to you? And would it not be an equal blessing to them? And are we not bound to extend to others all the happiness in our power? To say that Pagans can be as happy without the gospel as with it, is to say that the gospel is no blessing to men; and then you do not believe that it came from God? If the gospel would be no blessing to the heathen, why do you preach or support it at home?

IV. *The sacrifices of the missionaries themselves, and the debt of gratitude which we owe them.*

To see interesting youths, with the spirits of martyrs, offering themselves to die under an Indian or an African sun; for the love of Christ, tearing themselves from parents and brothers and sisters, to see them no more; taking an eternal leave of the scenes and companions of their youth; abandoning their native shore, and their native tongue, to bear the tidings of a precious Saviour to distant nations. To see delicate young females, who have been dandled in the lap of parental tenderness, with a heroism which nothing but Christian principles could support, tearing themselves, for the last time, from the arms of trembling mothers and speechless sisters, to encounter the dangers of the seas, and the still greater dangers of a torrid clime, in order to support their husbands by their smiles and prayers in a foreign land, among darkened Pagans. This is a scene which makes selfishness blush and hang its head; which shames all the ordinary piety which is couched in ease at home, trembling at self-denials. I beseech you to follow these precious youths with your prayers, and your tenderest concern. They have gone in the service of our Father's family—they sacrifice all for us. Shall we not follow them, with the interest of brothers and sisters, through the groves of India, and forests of America? and when we hear of their trials, their dangers, their escapes, their successes, shall we not feel as though we were receiving accounts from our near kindred? When they tell us of the triumphs of Hindoo converts; or send to our ears the young hosannahs of Syrian or Sandwich children; shall we not mingle our songs with theirs, and join in the joy, as though they were bone of our bone and flesh of our flesh? Yes, dear missionaries, we will remember you, and all the sacrifices you have made, till these hearts shall cease to beat. God Almighty go with you, and keep you in the hollow of his hand, till we meet you in heaven.

V. *Foreign missions are likely to prove the most glorious means of grace to us at home.*

While you are feeling for pagan souls, and sending your sons to them, I firmly believe that your prayers and bounty will return into your own bosoms. Such confidence I have in God, for I have heard him say, "He that watereth shall be watered also himself," Prov. xi. 25. I believe that while you are anxious to raise heathen nations from death, you will be enabled to shake off your grave-clothes yourselves; that while you are seeking to draw forth Indian children from their sepulchres, and present them alive to their rejoicing parents, your own children will start into life by your side; that while the love of distant nations glows in our hearts, it will melt us all down into love to each other, and burn up all our jealousies and strifes. Some of these effects I seem already to discern. God grant that they may increase, until the joy of America shall respond to that of Asia, and in one burst of praise rise united to heaven. May your charities return into your own bosom, and that of your children, for days and years, and an eternity to come!

VI. *All the wealth of the world was given to Christ as a recompense for redeeming our souls; and shall the ingratitude of man withhold from him his hire?*

It will not always be thus. The time will come, when "Holiness unto the Lord" shall be written on all the possessions of men,—on the very "bells of the horses;" and when "the pots in the Lord's house," (those used for culinary purposes, in the families of the priests), "shall," in point of holiness, "be like the bowls before the altar," which received the blood of the victims until it was sprinkled; and when "every pot in Jerusalem and in Judah shall be holiness unto the Lord of hosts," Zech. xiv. 20, 21. The common vessels used to dress our food, instead of being regarded as instruments of luxury or display, like our Bibles and psalm-books, shall be all for God. Men will write "Holiness unto the Lord" on every shilling, and on every foot of ground. They will no longer labor to hoard, but to do good. That will be such a generation as has not yet appeared. A few scattered individuals have approached

towards this character: but the mass of mankind, in every age, have held their property as their own, and not as a sacred deposit.

VII. *These exertions are necessary to bring to Christ the seed and the kingdom, the victory and the triumph, promised him as his reward.*

This world belongs to Christ. No other being has a right to erect an interest on this ground. And yet, after the lapse of eighteen centuries, two-thirds of the earth remain in Pagan, or Mohammedan darkness. Ought so great a part of a world which Christ has redeemed and owns, to continue in the hands of his enemy? If the suffrages of nations were to be collected, what would a redeemed race say? To whom would they assign a world given to Christ for redeeming them? Would they assign it to his enemy, who has despoiled it of its Eden, and covered it with briers and thorns, and turned it into a great charnel-house? or, would they give it to him who came to rescue it from the hands of destroying devils, and died to save their souls? What is the vote of a redeemed race on this subject? If human instrumentality is wanted to drive the usurper from his seat, shall not a whole race rise up to the effort?

APPLICATION.

1. And now, my beloved brethren, I invite you to go with me, and look for a moment over the interesting scene which is opening on earth. For many years the Christian world had been sunk in a profound slumber in regard to this duty; but for the last four-and-thirty years they have been waking up. He who has "engraven Zion on the palms of his hands," who never wants means to fulfil his promises, has sent his heavenly influence to rouse the Christian world.

2. We owe the sincerest gratitude to God for giving us our existence in such a day as this. "Many prophets and kings have desired to see those things which ye see, and have not seen them; and to hear those things which ye hear, and have not heard them," Luke x. 24. One spirit has seized the Christian world, to send the gospel, with a great company of its publishers, to all the nations of the earth. Missionary and Bible societies, those stupendous monuments of Christian charity, have risen so rapidly, and in so great numbers throughout Europe and America, that

in contemplating them, we are "like them that dream."

3. My soul is enlarged, and stands erect as I look down the declivity of years, and see the changes which these young Davids, under God, will make in all the earth. Countless millions are shortly to awake from the darkness and sleep of a hundred ages, to hail the day which will never go down. I see the darkness rolling upon itself and passing away from a thousand lands. I see a cloudless day following, and laying itself over all the earth. I see the nations coming up from the neighborhood of the brutes, to the dignity of the sons of God,—from the stye in which they had wallowed, to the purity of the Divine image. I see the meekness of the gospel assuaging their ferocious passions, melting down a million contending units in one, silencing the clamor of arms, and swelling into life a thousand budding charities which had died under the long winter. I hear the voice of their joy—it swells from the valleys, and echoes from the hills. I already hear, on the eastern breeze, the songs of new-born nations. I already catch, on the western gale, the praise of a thousand islands. I ascend the Alps, and see the darkness retiring from the Papal world. I ascend the Andes, and see South America, and all the islands of the Pacific, one altar. I ascend the mountains of Thibet, and hear from the plains of China, and from the jungle and pagoda of Hindoostan, the praises of the living God. I see all Asia bowing before Him, who, eighteen centuries ago, hung in the midst of them on Calvary. I traverse oceans, and hear from every floating Bethel the songs of the redeemed.

"The dwellers in the vales, and on the rocks,
   Shout to each other; and the mountain-tops
From distant mountains, catch the flying joy ;
   Till, nation after nation taught the strain,
   Earth rolls the rapturous hosanna round."

Come that blessed day! Let my eyes once behold the sight, and then give this worthless body to the worms.

———◆———

CVIII.—THE SACRIFICE AND TRIUMPH OF CHRIST.

BY REV. W. ATHERTON.*

* From a sermon delivered in Great Queen-street Chapel, April 28, 1833, in aid of the funds of the Wesleyan Missionary Society.

"But this man, after he had offered one sacrifice for sins, forever sat down on the right hand of God; from henceforth expecting till his enemies be made his footstool."—*Heb.* x. 12, 13.

THE apostle is showing, in this chapter, the superiority of the sacrifice and priesthood of Jesus Christ, when compared with those sacrifices which were offered, and those priests that gave attendance, at the Jewish altar ; and on which things the Hebrew Christians had trusted for acceptance with God. He shows their great superiority by a variety of arguments. The first argument is drawn from the priesthood of the people. "Every high priest taken from among men is ordained for men in things pertaining to God, that he may offer both gifts and sacrifices for sin," Heb. v. 1.; but the Christian's High Priest, is "the Lord from heaven"—"God over all, blessed for evermore." The Jewish high priests, in their official ministrations, had first to offer sacrifices for their own sins, which was a tacit confession that they were sinners. The Christian's High Priest, however, was without sin; he knew no sin, had no sin of his own to atone for, and was perfectly fitted to make atonement for the sins of others.

Another argument he draws from the sacrifices themselves : they offered the blood of bulls, and of goats, and of lambs, which could not take away sin. Our High Priest offered himself a Lamb without blemish ; he poured out the price of our redemption for us, which is emphatically called "the blood of Christ !"

He draws another argument from the multiplicity of their sacrifices, which were repeated, and offered year by year continually ; proving that they could "never make the comers thereunto perfect." "But this man, because he continueth ever, hath an unchangeable priesthood," Heb. vii. 24. It was so full of dignity, so full of merit, so teeming with virtue ; it was stamped with such an infinite desert, that such a sacrifice once offered was enough. The Jewish high priests, in humble reverence, and in readiness to serve, stood within the veil, offering the same sacrifices : "But this man, after he had offered one sacrifice for sins, forever sat down on the right hand of God." This one sacrifice of Christ, stands opposed to the multiplicity of sacrifices that were offered under the law.

1. *This God-man offered one sacrifice for*

sin. That was the sacrifice of himself, which we may consider as implying surrender.

1. *He offered his body.* The prophet says of him: "I gave my back to the smiters, and my cheeks to them that plucked off the hair: I hid not my face from shame and spitting," Isa. l. 6: "they gave me gall for my meat; and in my thirst they gave me vinegar to drink," Psa. lxix. 21; so that in Isa. liii. 14, we read, "his visage was so marred more than any man, and his form more than the sons of men." These were sufferings of no common kind.

2. *But, in suffering, he offered his mind.* The sufferings of our Redeemer's soul must be considered as the soul of his sufferings. These he anticipated at a distance, when he said, "I have a baptism, to be baptized with; and how am I straitened till it be accomplished!" Luke xii. 50. We must, however, go into the garden of Gethsemane to witness this sacrifice offered. What must have been the agony of his mind, when, in the bloom and prime of health, supported by conscious innocence, raised above the natural fear of death, with the prospect of an abundant entrance into the kingdom of heaven—what must have been the agony of his mind, when even the vital fluid, interrupted in its natural course of circulation, was forced through the coats of the veins, the vessels, and integuments, and bathed his body in a sweat of blood!

3. *He offered in sacrifice his glory*—by which we understand how glory will follow up the shame. Now, our Redeemer's feelings were not blunted and stoical; he was alive to his reputation; his sense of indignity, and shame, and dishonor, were exquisite—nay, they were delicately fine; and when they called him an enemy to civil government, and a deceiver of the people; when they said, "He is mad," "a glutton and a wine-bibber;" when they said he had a devil—that he was not fit to live; he must have felt the indignity with great acuteness.

4. *He offered in sacrifice the consolations of heaven's protection.*

This he did when he cried, "My God, my God, why hast thou forsaken me?" Matt. xxvii. 46. Now the dogs of hell opened their mouths on him; the strong bulls of Bashan beset him around; now earth and hell are allowed to do their worst; and such is that worst, as to lead him to cry to God, Why hast thou abandoned me—why hast thou forsaken me?

5. *He offered in sacrifice his life.* Life is dear to every creature: "Greater love hath no man than this, that a man lay down his life for his friend," John xv. 13; but while we were yet enemies, Christ died for us, Rom. v. 8.

6. *He offered in sacrifice his will.* Suffering can never be loved for its own sake; and shame and death are terrible foes. The Redeemer prayed that the cup of suffering might pass from him, Matt. xxvi. 42; yet he gave his person into the hands of those who put it to torture: he voluntarily resigned himself to that train of overwhelming and distressing ideas, that threw his mind into an agony that bathed him in a bloody sweat: he gave up the consolation of heaven's protection. Perhaps it may be asked,

II. *For what purpose did he offer this sacrifice?*

Whenever we think, or read about the sufferings of Christ, we are immediately directed to sin:—"Christ died for our sins," 1 Cor. xv. 3. He suffered once for sin—"the just for the unjust, that he might bring us to God." "Who his own self bare our sins in his own body on the tree." "He was wounded for our transgressions, he was bruised for our iniquities," 1 Pet. iii. 18; ii. 24; Isa. liii. 5. This Man offered himself a sacrifice for sin,

1. *To avert the consequences of it.* Jesus Christ paid the penalty, that he might deliver the sinner from the consequences of his sins; and every sinner that accepts of the sacrifice of Christ by faith, the finger of God's mercy, dipped in the blood of his Son, writes that sinner as one over whom the second death shall never have power.

2. *He died that he might remove the presence of sin, by doing away the love of it;* by cleansing the guilty in the "Fountain opened for sin and for uncleanness,"—rendering the person "without spot or wrinkle, or any such thing,"—that he might so renew the nature of man, so endear the principles of grace to him, that he might deny "ungodliness and worldly lusts," and live above the practices of sin.

3. *He offered himself a sacrifice to overcome the forfeiture of sin.* Sin had forfeited the image, the love, the protection of God. Through sin, man had lost every spark of happiness in life, and comfort in death, and every title to glory; yet, by the sacrifice of Christ, we receive all that we lost in the transgression. We are now directed,

III. *To the exaltation of our Redeemer.*

1. *This was through the medium of his resurrection.* That Jesus Christ died on the cross, was attested by the water and the blood that flowed after the insertion of the spear, anatomically demonstrating that the heart had been pierced. And that he " rose again, according to the Scriptures," we have conclusive evidence.

2. *And he has now " sat down at the right hand of God."* God is a great and invisible Spirit, with whom literally there can be neither standing nor recumbency. We must, therefore, understand this phrase figuratively; and it is (1) expressive of rest. The Jewish high priest, when he entered within the veil, never sat down ; his work was not done ; he had to return, and to come back and " offer oftentimes the same sacrifices," if his life were spared. " But this man, after he had offered one sacrifice for sins, forever sat down on the right hand of God." But this expression " sat down," intimates (2) his being honored. When we read, that Jesus Christ is at the right hand of God, we understand he is raised to the highest honor— he is raised " above all principalities and powers ;" having done his work to the perfect satisfaction of his Father, it has pleased God to give " him a name which is above every name ; that at the name of Jesus every knee should bow ;—and that every tongue should confess that Jesus Christ is Lord, to the glory of God the Father," Phil. ii. 10, 11.

This phrase is expressive (3) of power, of authority, and of dominion. The right hand is employed as an emblem of power, Exod. xv. 6 ; Psa. xvii. 7, etc. Now, when our Redeemer is placed at the right hand of God, we understand him as invested with power : he is now the ruler of all things, the governor of all worlds. There he shall remain, until, according to the promise of the Father to him, " Sit thou at my right hand, until I make thine enemies thy footstool," Psa. cx. 1.

IV. *The purposes of his will shall be fulfilled.*

Of the adversaries of Jesus Christ we observe,

1. *That Satan is the most subtle, ancient, and formidable.* But, my brethren, this adversary shall be the footstool of the woman's all-conquering seed that was given to " bruise his head." Another adversary of Jesus Christ is—

2. *Error.* Error may be said to be a hydra with many heads. The first head which presents itself in this hydra has the face of a beast, by which we understand the errors of popery—so decided an enemy to Christ, that that system, in the New Testament, is called Anti-Christ. Another of these errors has the face of the false prophet, by which we may understand the delusions, impurities, and abominations of Mohammedanism.

The next has the face of a dragon, by which we understand the cruel, the impure, the licentious, the hellish abominations of Paganism, or Heathenism. Paganism gives to the mind the falsest idea of God ; or extinguishes the idea of the Supreme Being from the human mind. Heathenism substitutes, in the place of the great Jehovah, idols and devils—worships them by the impurest rites, propitiates them by the bloodiest sacrifices. Paganism presents the most delusive prospect of happiness and of safety.

Now, these are enemies to Christ, because he is light and truth ; these are false as hell, and dark as the chambers of death. These systems degrade God's creatures, rob the Redeemer, murder the souls of men; and as such they must come down: by the general diffusion of knowledge, by the spread of the Scriptures, by the propagation of the gospel, by the piety and by the influence of God's people, these systems shall be overturned.

3. *Another enemy is to be found in wicked, unconverted men.* But these enemies shall be the footstool of the " Lion of the tribe of Judah." Upon unconverted men, Jesus Christ will employ his gospel and his word on their understandings, and his Spirit on their consciences, and his providence on their circumstances and their bodies; and these weapons shall be " mighty through God to the pulling down of strongholds." By these weapons some shall see their error —shall discover their wickedness—shall perceive their danger, and tremble at it—shall let the weapons of their rebellion drop out of their hands—shall crawl like guilty worms to the footstool of Christ's mercy—shall cordially embrace, with arms of faith, the despised Nazarene ; they shall give him their hearts, and affections, and lives, in devotional obedience ; and they shall joyfully suffer for his sake.

4. *Another enemy of Christ is death.* He is said to be the last enemy that shall be destroyed, 1 Cor. xv. 26.

5. All these enemies have been made by one worse than the devil himself, and that enemy is *sin*.

To destroy sin the Son of God was manifested—for this purpose he offered himself a sacrifice for sin—for this purpose he has commanded his gospel to be preached to every creature—for this purpose he is, at this moment, seated at the right hand of God, invested with all power, with all energy, to employ whatever instrument or agent he thinks proper, and to give a blessing to those means that they may be effectual.

APPLICATION.

1. Here we discover, brethren, the character of sinners. They are said to be enemies of Christ.

2. We learn, again, that these enemies of Christ, these unconverted persons must be his footstool, whether at home or broad. Are any of you unconverted? Are any of you in a state of hostility of mind to the blessed Jesus? Remember, you must come down. Will you be subdued by justice, or by mercy? Will you be conquered by the sceptre of his grace; or will you be broken in pieces by the iron rod of his wrath?

Finally. We see the duty of the people to extend by conquest the triumphs of the Redeemer,—the empire of the Saviour: to bring home his rebel outcasts, that they may be saved from sin and Satan's snare.

Yes; the kingdom of hell is shaking— the gates of perdition tremble. Let us not rest, but take up a bold and manful stand in our own places, until we join in that blessed acclamation—"The kingdoms of this world are become the kingdoms of our Lord and of his Christ; and he shall reign forever and ever. Alleluia: for the Lord God omnipotent reigneth!" Rev. xi. 15; xix. 6. Yes! and he will reign till he has subdued all to the obedience of faith; till death and sin are dead, and God shall be all in all!

CIX.—GOSPEL HARVEST, AND CHRISTIAN'S DUTY.

BY REV. THOMAS DE WITT, D. D., NEW YORK.*

"Then saith he unto his disciples, The harvest truly is plenteous, but the laborers are few; pray ye therefore the Lord of the harvest, that he will send forth laborers into his harvest."— *Matt.* ix. 37, 38.

* Preached at Boston, October 7, 1830, before the American Board of Foreign Missions.

THE words of our text were spoken by Jesus to his disciples, as he contemplated the multitudes destitute of the means of religious instruction. "He was moved with compassion on them because they fainted, and were scattered abroad as sheep having no shepherd," ver. 36. The compassion that dwelt in the heart of Jesus is not foreign to the hearts of his people, for they are of one spirit with him. The text presents, firstly, an argument for missionary efforts. "The harvest truly is plenteous, but the laborers are few." And, secondly, urges a duty in relation to them. "Pray ye therefore the Lord of the harvest," etc.

I. *An argument for missionary efforts.* "The harvest truly is plenteous, but the laborers are few." This harvest will be gathered when the Christian religion shall universally prevail.

1. *It is great, in view of the field which it will cover.*

"The field is the world," Matt. xiii. 38. As yet Christianity has extended its influence to but a small part of the earth; and where that influence has been found, it has been partial in its character. Here and there a spot has appeared in some degree verdant, amid a surrounding wide-spread arid desert. But this desert, in all its extent, will be cultivated and rendered fruitful. All obstacles will be overcome, and the whole earth exhibit the triumphs of truth. Benighted, degraded, and oppressed Africa, shall become enlightened, elevated, and disenthralled. The wall of China (like that of Jericho) shall fall at the sound of the gospel. The castes of the Hindoos shall be broken; and one bond, in the faith and service of Christ, shall unite them. The heathen shall everywhere "cast their idols to the moles and to the bats," and worship "the only true God, and Jesus Christ, whom he hath sent." The worship of the false prophet shall cease; and the pure light and peaceful influence of Christianity shall spread over the regions where now Mohammedanism exerts its sway. The isles shall receive the law of the Lord; all the perversions of the religion of Jesus shall be removed, and the truth be received in love, and exhibit its fruits wherever professed! Then shall be realized

"Scenes surpassing fable,
Yet true!—scenes of accomplish'd bliss!"

2. *The harvest is great, in view of its many blessings.*

The religion of Christ blesses the life which now is, and prepares for happiness in the life to come. It exalts the intellectual character of man;—it restores that balance and harmony in the intellectual and moral powers of man, which are so important in the proper cultivation of both;—it corrects those prejudices, and subdues those corruptions, which prevent the investigation and reception of truth.

Take the map of the world, and select those countries where Paganism, Mohammedanism, and Popery, bear sway, and let the following inquiries receive an answer: Are knowledge and intellectual cultivation generally diffused? Are civil and religious liberty enjoyed? Is the female character elevated and respected? Are the duties of domestic life discharged, and its delights mutually participated? Do purity and peace pervade the community? The negative to these inquiries appears in full view. If we take the contrast, and mark the countries where the Bible has shed its influence, we discover the blessings adverted to, all following in the train.

But the religion of Christ sustains its distinguishing and commanding value, as a revelation of truth and grace, and as the great instrument of our deliverance from everlasting death. The truths peculiar to it respect man's fallen and ruined state; redemption through the atoning merits of the Divine Saviour; the regenerating and sanctifying influence of the Holy Spirit in restoring to that holiness, "without which no man shall see the Lord," Heb. xii. 14. These truths, and others immediately connected with them, constitute the vitality of the religion of the gospel.

3. *The harvest must appear great in view of the instrumentality it requires.*

The great result is to be accomplished by the faithful use of those means which God has, in his wisdom and goodness, appointed. As in the natural world, means must be used in preparation for harvest; and as, ordinarily, the product will correspond to the skill and diligence with which the means are employed; so also, in the spiritual world, means are equally necessary; and a like correspondence in the product will exist. "It pleased God, by the foolishness of preaching, to save them that believed," 1 Cor. i. 21.

As we look farther, through the heathen world, how large and waste is the field!

while, in parts remote from each other, a solitary laborer is found. The regularly ordained missionaries from different Christian denominations among the six hundred millions of heathen, in different parts of the world, as far as ascertained, amount to about six hundred and fifty. They are, in some cases, aided by assistants and native teachers. Still, how emphatically is the harvest great, and the laborers few; while some parts of the field are already white for the harvest.

4. *The harvest is great, in view of the means and prospects furnished by Providence.*

God, in advancing his kingdom on earth, prepares the way in arranging the events of his providence. He raises up instruments qualified for his work; and often opens the way before them, as they go forth crying, "Prepare ye the way of the Lord; make straight in the desert a highway for our God," Isa. xl. 3. The Bible Society multiplies copies of the Scriptures, in the various languages of the world, and supplies the place of the gift of tongues. It is needless to specify the various forms of Christian charity, which, commencing with infancy, lays the basis of a scriptural and religious education, and follows man in every course and state of life; and seeks to apply the best relief of sin, and want, and woe. The efforts of the present day for arresting and turning back that fell destroyer, intemperance, which has annually slain its thousands and tens of thousands, and which has interposed such formidable obstacles to the success of the gospel, are of incalculable worth.

The spirit of missions, which characterizes the present period, commenced with the revival of religion in the churches. Domestic and foreign missions have grown and strengthened in connection with the power of religion. The era of foreign efforts is identified with the prosperity of religion at home.

The events which have recently transpired mark the present as an interesting crisis in the history of the world. The Christian will, with care, study the page of prophecy, and the movements of Providence, and mark the light which they mutually shed on each other.

II. *The text urges our duty in relation to missionary efforts:* "Pray ye the Lord of the harvest, that he will send forth laborers into his harvest." The discharge of the duty enjoined by our Saviour supposes,

1. *That we cherish a deep and constant sense of our dependence upon Divine grace.*

The private Christian, in the divine life, is "clothed with humility;" lives a life of faith in the Son of God; and seeks continued supplies of the grace and help of the Spirit. So the Christian Church should always be found in the attitude of "leaning on her Beloved," Sol. Song, viii. 5; and should realize that all her springs are in God.

2. *This duty requires habitual and fervent remembrance in our private devotions.*

Love to the Redeemer's cause is not a transient emotion in the Christian's heart; but it is a fixed principle, and growing habit of soul. He "prefers Jerusalem above his chief joy." He should then be frequent, fervent, importunate, and persevering, in his intercession.

3. *This duty requires union in Christians.*

Addressing his assembled disciples, Jesus said, "Pray ye," Matt. vi. 9. The true disciples of Jesus are united in spirit and service. The words of our Saviour's prayer are memorable: "That they all may be one; as thou, Father, art in me, and I in thee, that they also may be one in us: that the world may believe that thou hast sent me," John xvii. 21. What Christian can be reluctant to engage in a service so delightful and animating, as united prayer for the coming of Christ's kingdom on earth?

4. *This duty requires the use of all proper means for suitably training laborers for the missionary field.*

In our favored churches, where the Spirit's influence is enjoyed, let the subject of foreign missions be presented in just prominence. In our theological seminaries, let a careful inquiry and deep interest be cultivated and cherished among their members, who shall soon go forth to preside in the churches of our own land, to give a tone to their sentiments and feelings, or else to enter themselves upon the glorious work.

5. *This duty requires that all the churches of Christ should systematically and efficiently aid in the promotion of the cause of missions.*

It cannot be necessary to argue the duty of professed Christians to give their prayers, their property, and labors, to this cause. The Christian judgment needs not be convinced, but the Christian conscience needs to be awakened, and the heart affected. Christians should learn to give, not from the impulse of momentary excitement, but from the deliberate conviction of duty, in the discharge of which the heart seeks its highest joy. Systematically, I say, because it is to be regretted that so many churches so readily relax their efforts, until some new impulse be given, which soon spends itself. These are like the mountain streams, fed by sudden showers, which soon pass away.

APPLICATION.

Let every pastor present the claims of this cause prominently before his people, and feel that its prosperity is identified with the success of his labors at home. Let information be generally extended, and every means to excite interest, and combine effort, be employed. While in opposing the march of truth, various errors and conflicting interests combine, let the Church of God arise in her strength, and in unbroken columns march onward, under the banners of her great Captain, from victory to victory. While the enemy opposes and rages, we remember, "They that be with us are more than they that be with them," 2 Kings vi. 16. God's truth is great, and must finally triumph.

———◆———

CX.—THE FUTURE PROSPERITY OF THE CHURCH THE EFFECTS OF DIVINE INFLUENCE.

BY REV. ROBERT JACK, OF MANCHESTER.*

"He shall cause them that come of Jacob to take root: Israel shall blossom and bud, and fill the face of the world with fruit."—*Isaiah* xxvii. 6.

THE text is supposed to have had its literal accomplishment when Jerusalem was delivered from the destroying army of Sennacherib. But the grace of which it speaks did not terminate in that great temporal deliverance. It is understood, by Christian interpreters, to extend to the times of the gospel; and to lay a foundation for our hope of nobler blessings, and of better days. The posterity of Jacob were a highly-favored people, and were distinguished from the other nations of the earth by the most honorable appellations, and by the most exalted privileges. After, however, many vicissitudes, for dis-

* Preached before the Missionary Society, at the Tabernacle, May 13, 1807.

owning and rejecting the Messiah when he came, they were disinherited by the offended God of their fathers, deprived of all their peculiar privileges, expelled from the land of promise, and are become miserable wanderers among the nations. What shall we say, then, to these things? Is there no Israel now to be found, among whom God's name is great? Yea, verily, though Israel, according to the flesh, be no more the people of God, still there is "a royal priesthood, an holy nation, a peculiar people," a true circumcision, "which worship God in the spirit, and rejoice in Christ Jesus, and have no confidence in the flesh," Phil. iii. 3. Many sinners of the Gentiles, "who sometime were far off, are made nigh by the blood of Christ," Eph. ii. 13; and have become, through faith, the spiritual children of Abraham—the true Israel of God. Such, the Scriptures assure us, are "Israelites indeed," John i. 47; though Abraham be ignorant of them, and Israel, according to the flesh, acknowledge them not, Isa. lxiii. 16; for "if ye be Christ's, then are ye Abraham's seed, and heirs according to the promise," Gal. iii. 29.

There is a period, however, announced in ancient prophecy, a happy period, when "Israel shall be a blessing in the midst of the land," Isa. xix. 24. Converted to the faith of Christ, and restored to their own land, we have ground to believe that they shall be incorporated with the Christian church in one spiritual society, of which Israel according to the flesh was a figure. No remaining distinction shall then subsist betwixt Jew and Gentile, Barbarian and Scythian, bond and free. They shall all be one in Christ Jesus, Col. iii. 11. No longer shall they regard each other as "strangers and foreigners, but fellow-citizens with the saints, and of the household of God," Eph. ii. 19.

The text may be considered as a promise of prosperity to the church; first, in respect of number; secondly, in respect of spiritual vigor; thirdly, in respect of beauty; fourthly, in respect of fruitfulness; fifthly, in respect of joy; and, lastly, in respect of stability, and in respect of extent. These particulars, in dependence upon Divine aid, we now propose to illustrate.

I. *The promise relates to the prosperity of the church in respect of number.*

Under the ancient dispensation, the spiritual Israel were comparatively few. The walls of the church then inclosed but a small portion of the earth. "Salvation," at that time, was only "of the Jews," John iv. 22; and the joyful sound was never heard beyond the precincts of the promised land. But, at the commencement of the Christian dispensation, the wall of partition was broken down, and the boundaries of the church were greatly enlarged. Even among the Jews, multitudes were made "a willing people." New creatures were hourly born in Zion, and came forth to "newness of life," numerous, or rather innumerable, as the drops of dew "from the womb of the morning." Yea, what shall we say? By the diligence of the apostles, the sound of the gospel soon went "into all the earth, and their words unto the ends of the world," Rom. x. 18. And the Gentiles received the word gladly.

II. *The promise relates to the prosperity of the church in respect of spiritual vigor.*

Others remain in a state of spiritual death. They are, as the Scripture emphatically expresses it, dead while they live, 1 Tim. v. 6. But concerning them "that come of Jacob," it is here asserted, that they shall take root. They are not like the tender herb, which springeth up in a night, and withereth in a night; for "the righteous," it is promised, "shall flourish like the palm-tree : he shall grow like the cedar in Lebanon," Psa. xcii. 12. The reason is plain—the root to which they are united by a living faith, is firm and immovable. Though the branches may be violently shaken, and their blossoms blighted by the rude blasts of corruption and temptation, yet "the root of the righteous shall not be moved," Prov. xii. 3.

And may not all this be expected to be more completely realized in the case of those who shall live in the happy period to which the promise in the text particularly refers. "He shall come down," it is promised, "like rain upon the mown grass; as showers that water the earth," Psa. lxxii. 6. "And many people shall go and say, Come ye, and let us go up to the mountain of the Lord, to the house of the God of Jacob; and he will teach us of his ways, and we will walk in his paths : for out of Zion shall go forth the law, and the word of the Lord from Jerusalem," Isa. ii. 3. May it not be supposed, therefore, that believers shall make rapid progress, amidst all this extraordinary cultivation?

III. *The promise relates to the prosperity of the church in respect of beauty.*

Christ himself, "the branch of the Lord, *is* beautiful and glorious," Isa. iv. 2 ; and believers in Christ are made comely through his comeliness put upon them, Ezek. xvi. 14. How beautiful are the trees of the field when adorned with the leaves of spring ! Thus beautiful are the spiritual children of Jacob. We cannot contemplate but with wonder and delight, the transforming energy of the gospel in the days of the apostles. The believers not only increased in number, but flourished in grace. How beautiful must the daughters of Zion have appeared, when their knowledge was sound and spiritual, when their faith was firm, their repentance deep, their hope steadfast, their zeal fervent, their love abounding; when the gentleness of Christ spread an amiable lustre around them; when humility, as a veil, at once clothed and adorned them ; "when the peace of God, which passeth all understanding," kept "their hearts and minds through Christ Jesus," Phil. iv. 7 ; and when patience under suffering had its perfect work in them.

The beauty of believers, evidently, is of an internal nature, for "the king's daughter is all glorious within," Psa. xlv. 13 ; and with this the greatest beauty of external form is not worthy to be compared. "Solomon, in all his glory," was not so elegantly arrayed as "the lilies of the field ;" and yet, what is the beauty of the fairest flower, to that of a saint adorned with the robe of the Redeemer's righteousness, and decked out with the fair flowers of implanted grace ? There can be no doubt that the gospel still produces the same happy effects in all by whom it is truly believed. Wherever "the incorruptible seed" of the word, is sown by the hand of the Spirit, it changes the unkindly soil of the human heart, and restores, in some degree, the moral beauty of our nature. And how much more may this be expected to take place at that happy period, when God "shall cause them that come of Jacob to take root, and when Israel shall blossom and bud." How delightful the prospect, that a time shall arrive when "pure and undefiled religion" shall universally prevail ; when love to God and to man, when truth and righteousness and peace shall be generally and powerfully diffused ; and when the evils shall cease with which men, by the indulgence of their guilty passions, have been grieved and tormented.

IV. *The promise relates to the prosperity of the church in respect of fruitfulness.*

Believers are denominated in Scripture, "trees of righteousness," Isa. lxi. 3, to intimate that they should "bring forth fruit unto God." It is not enough that they are covered with the leaves of a holy profession; and blossom with the flowers of pious resolutions, and good endeavors. It is necessary, also, that in their season they be "filled with the fruits of righteousness, which are by Jesus Christ unto the glory and praise of God," Phil. i. 11. Among the branches ingrafted into Christ, there is, indeed, a considerable variety. Some are slender, and others strong ; some more, and others less, productive. All, it is true, bear good fruit: but even in this respect a variety is less or more observable. They flourish not all in the same way. Some are eminent for one virtue, and some for another ; neither is any of them equally fruitful at all times. Such fruits, however, as they do at any time produce, are of excellent quality. Nor are their fruits more distinguished by their perfection of excellence, than they are often by their greatness of number. They abound "in every good word and work."

V. *The promise relates to the prosperity of the church in respect of joy.*

It is when the dews of heaven "drop upon the pastures of the wilderness," that it is said, "the little hills rejoice on every side." It is when "the valleys also are covered over with corn, that they shout for joy, and they also sing," Psa. lxv. 12, 13. The abundant joy of New Testament times, especially of the times referred to in the passage before us, is often spoken of in Scripture. "Behold," saith the Lord, "I create Jerusalem a rejoicing, and her people a joy. And I will rejoice in Jerusalem, and joy in my people : and the voice of weeping shall be no more heard in her, nor the voice of crying,—for as the days of a tree are the days of my people, and mine elect shall long enjoy the work of their hands. Violence shall no more be heard in thy land, wasting nor destruction within thy borders ; but thou shalt call thy walls Salvation, and thy gates Praise," Isa. lxv. 18, 19, 22 ; lx. 18.

VI. *The promise relates to the prosperity of the church in respect of stability.*

It is here promised, that the Lord "shall cause them that come of Jacob to take root." The vicissitudes which take place in human affairs, teach us the vanity of the world, and the perishing nature of all that seems most durable in this region of shadows. When we read the history of nations, what do we read but the history of incessant revolution, one dominion erecting itself upon the ruins of another? Those kingdoms and empires which seemed established on the firmest foundations, have long since crumbled down, and have left not a wreck behind. Sunk beneath the weight of years, the most venerable institutions have, at length, mouldered into dust. The church of God, however, has been like mount Zion, which cannot be moved, but abideth forever,—built upon "the Rock of Ages," the emissaries of hell, after all their malicious attacks, have found themselves utterly unable to prevail against her. "Thine eyes shall see Jerusalem a quiet habitation, a tabernacle that shall not be taken down; not one of the stakes thereof shall ever be removed, neither shall any of the cords thereof be broken," Isa. xxxiii. 20.

VII. *The promise relates to the prosperity of the church in respect of extent.*

We have already seen that the promise relates to the prosperity of the church in respect of *number*. We have, also, seen that this number shall be exceeding great. It follows, of course, that the boundaries of the visible church must be enlarged; and, indeed, the text leads us to expect that her walls shall encompass the whole habitable world. "His name shall endure forever: his name shall be continued as long as the sun: and men shall be blessed in him: all nations shall call him blessed. He shall have dominion also from sea to sea, and from the river unto the ends of the earth. They that dwell in the wilderness shall bow down before him,—all nations shall serve him," Psa. lxxii. 17, 8, 11. He "will say to the north, Give up; and to the south, Keep not back; bring my sons from far, and my daughters from the ends of the earth; even every one that is called by my name," Isa. xliii. 6, 7.

From the manner in which it is expressed, it is evident that in all the happy events to which it refers, the agency of God shall be signally conspicuous. Mark the phraseology—"He shall *cause* them that come of Jacob to take root." In his works of providence and grace, God frequently sees it meet to employ secondary causes as the instruments of his operation; yet here, efficacy depends entirely on his superintending influence. It is his hand which sustains the great chain of causes and effects; and his agency which pervades and animates the worlds of nature and of grace. It is "not by might, nor by power, but by my spirit, saith the Lord of hosts," Zech. iv. 6.

APPLICATION.

1. What gratitude ought we to feel, that we have been favored with the gospel! "Through the tender mercy of our God; whereby the day-spring from on high hath visited us, to give light to them that sat in darkness and in the shadow of death, to guide our feet into the way of peace," Luke i. 78, 79.

2. How little reason have Christians to complain that they have no prospect of seeing, in their day, the happy period to which the text refers. Have they not heaven in prospect? There they shall enjoy happiness, boundless as their largest wishes, and lasting as their immortal souls!

3. What powerful encouragement does this subject afford to missionary exertions! We have seen that the Scriptures abound with promises of great prosperity to the church in the latter days; and we know that higher security cannot, in the nature of things, be given, than a Divine promise. "The heavens and the earth may pass away," but one word which the mouth of the Lord hath spoken, cannot fail of accomplishment.

4. How careful ought we to be, to attend to the state of our own souls in the sight of God. Have we the greatest reason to be thankful that "to us is the word of this salvation sent?" And should we not be earnestly concerned to improve it to our own salvation? How apt we are to undervalue our privileges, because we have never known what it is to be deprived of them! May God make us "wise unto salvation through faith which is in Christ Jesus;" and may we, at last, reap the fruit of this heavenly wisdom, in "receiving the end of our faith, even the salvation of our souls!" Amen and Amen.

————◆————

CXI.—HAPPY INFLUENCE OF FOREIGN MISSIONS ON THE CHURCH.

BY THE REV. DAVID ABEEL.

"Spare not, lengthen thy cords, and strengthen thy stakes."—*Isa.* liv. 2.

THE text is a command given to the church,—in other words, a duty enjoined upon Christians. The only way to ascertain both its precise meaning, and the best mode of its accomplishment, is to consult the preceding and following verses. " Enlarge the place of thy tent, and 'let them stretch forth the curtains of thine habitations : spare not, lengthen thy cords, and strengthen thy stakes ; for thou shalt break forth on the right hand and on the left; and thy seed shall inherit the Gentiles, and make the desolate cities to be inhabited."

The whole passage, then, refers to the conversion of the Gentiles, or heathen ; and furnishes the following important suggestion, that *there is no system of means so well calculated to give expansion and stability to the church of Christ* (not merely to lengthen her cords, but also to strengthen her stakes), *as foreign missionary operation.*

The direct benefits of missionary exertions upon the heathen, and their reflex action upon the churches which put forth these exertions, are both to be considered in estimating the efficacy of these means. It is a question of great interest, and one which cannot be too freely discussed, nor too quickly determined, whether, for the good of the world, the main energies of the church ought to be expended upon countries nominally Christian and comparatively limited ; or upon the more extensive and populous regions, now shrouded in pagan darkness and Mohammedan delusion ? The decision of this question would indicate to many a mind, now vacillating and distressed ; it would assure the confidence of the doubtful ; it would recall his distracted attention, and concentrate his divided efforts ; it would send forth streams of vital influence through those appropriate channels, which, for aught we know, are now empty and dry.

There are several reasons which are supposed by many to favor the opinion, that Christian exertion is less productive among pagan nations than at home.

(1.) *There are preliminary barriers which oppose the efforts of the missionary, and which do not exist in Christian lands.*

Of these, the most important are strange languages, and strong prejudices. That these are real obstacles, ignorance alone will deny. There is, perhaps, nothing more trying to a sensitive heart, than to be surrounded by crowds of deluded and dying men, between whom and yourself there is no medium of intellectual communication. An ocean rolling between could not more effectually separate you from the objects of your compassion. In some countries, the difficulties of acquiring languages yield to nothing but the most persevering labor. This, however, is not everywhere the case. Perhaps no two languages are equally difficult of attainment. There are places where even transient traders and travellers pick up the native tongue, and soon become eloquent in its employment. As the number of missionaries increase, the difficulties of languages are reduced, and the facilities for their acquisition multiplied. Nay, missionaries not merely abbreviate the term of pupilage to their successors ; but furnish them with useful labor, even during their necessary studies. There are daily services to be performed at every station, which cannot be dispensed with, and which do not demand the employment of the tongue. And these services are generally proportioned, in number and variety, to the efficiency of men engaged.

Another preliminary obstacle mentioned to the successful efforts of the missionary, is prejudice. In a few prominent heathen countries of the world, this barrier appears almost impregnable. China, Japan, and Cochin China, have marshalled their forces on their frontiers, and bade defiance to foreign aggression. But, even to these countries, there are points of attack which they cannot guard. The gospel is gaining access to China through numerous channels ; and, sooner or later, every barrier shall be undermined, and a highway through every part of this empire be prepared for the servants of the Lord.

In almost every land, where missionary efforts have been continued for any considerable time, prejudices have invariably yielded ; and, generally, when they begin to subside, they rapidly disappear, and seldom return.

(2.) Another reason for which, it is believed, Christian effort is more profitable at home than abroad, is the systematic and stubborn opposition which the gospel meets from the established forms of civil government and pagan superstition. How far such opposition will be exerted where the Romish religion has loaded the cause of Christianity with its own opprobrium, we can only conjecture. Experiment has proved, that these obstacles scarcely ever prevent the introduction of the gospel, or greatly arrest its progress in any country.

(3.) A third reason, which may be supposed to operate against the comparative advantages of foreign missionary labor, is the risk and waste of life which it involves. If there be, as there doubtless is, a difference in the mortality of ministers in pagan and Christian nations, the reasons are obvious—the number of missionaries is so limited, that they labor harder, and suffer more, than their brethren at home; and thus far, they have occupied the most unhealthful positions, often under the greatest disadvantages. When missionaries are sent forth in sufficient numbers to supply the stations now possessed, and to occupy the far more extensive and important countries of Northern India, and all the higher divisions of Asia and Europe, the scale will turn; and health and life will probably be enjoyed to as great a degree and protracted a limit in the unevangelical world, as within the present boundaries of Christendom.

This, however, is but one view of the subject. There are arguments which favor the opposite opinion. There are arguments which give a high degree of probability to the conclusion, that the direct results of gospel efforts are greater in pagan than in Christian lands. Among the reasons for such an opinion, is that one which induces almost all ministers of the sanctuary to exchange the sphere of their labor at home; and which would, if they were consistent with their principles, send great numbers of them abroad. The souls to be saved are much more numerous—much more needy. Another reason is, the means of usefulness are both more various and extensively operative.

A further reason, which shows the superior influence of foreign labor, is the activity of native converts. Notwithstanding all that has been uttered by foes, and feared by friends, of the comparative fruitlessness of foreign missions, if the number of converts, in Christian and heathen lands, were divided by the proportion of gospel-ministers allotted to each sphere of labor, it is probable Christians at home would never again put the question, Where are the fruits of foreign missions?

If in connection with the number of souls actually saved, we estimate the instrumentality prepared, not only for present, but for future operation, we believe but few could hesitate in ascribing the greatest influence upon the church and the world, to foreign missionary exertion. And even if it could be showed that Christian efforts among the heathen are not as productive as at home, even then the chief argument which supports the doctrine presented in the text remains untouched.

2. *We believe that foreign missions are the best means of lengthening the cords and strengthening the stakes of the church*, because they establish an action and reaction between themselves and the churches, which is most powerful and advantageous to both parties. This may be demonstrated by several facts.

I. *Missionary labor increases the piety and energy of the churches.*

The missionary spirit includes among its essential endowments, faith, prayer, self-denial, deadness to the world, charity, beneficence, heavenly-mindedness, a willingness to submit to sufferings and hazards, and a supreme regard for the glory of God. If such be the spirit which disposes and prepares men to engage in the work of converting the heathen, it is not difficult to perceive how the churches are benefited by missionary labor.

1. *There is the stimulus of example*, than which nothing is more influential. Hold up to the churches those with whom they are under equal obligations, but who have far exceeded them in the "work of faith, and labor of love," and you bring a motive to bear upon them which piety cannot resist.

2. *It operates through sympathy.* We are brethren. Our work, our aim, our strongest desires, our highest honor, our dearest interests, our eternal recompense are the same. Just so far as we are sanctified, what one feels, and attempts, and accomplishes, must powerfully interest and actuate another.

3. *There is the duty and blessedness of necessary co-operation.* We must labor together. Missionaries are "the messengers of the churches." The churches must send them forth, sustain them with their prayers and contributions, and supply the increasing demand for men, which the opening field requires. The energy of the one increases the energy of the other. The missionary prepares work for the churches, and throws the obligation of its performance upon them; and can the churches remain inactive, when urged to exertion by such a fearful responsibility?

4. Again. *It diverts the mind from those unimportant points of doctrinal difference, and metaphysical distinction, and abstruce*

speculation, which squander the time, and pervert the talents, and ruin the souls of thousands.

5. *It operates, too, through the influence of its own greatness.* It expands the mind, liberalizes the soul, elevates the aim; arouses faculties and feelings which nothing else could have addressed ; and produces efforts and results which no other object could command.

These are some of the invaluable effects of missions upon the churches. But where are your facts? say they who regard this doctrine as a mere splendid theory. Such facts we are capable of furnishing.

(1.) Nothing more powerfully arrests the attention of youth and children, than missionary narratives. By these means they are taught how much they differ from the heathen ; and how they ought to pray, and contribute, and labor for their salvation.

(2.) Much has been attributed to the reaction of missions, as a means of producing our revivals, and improving all our home institutions. How much the education, and tract, and Bible societies owe to the strong appeals we furnish them, let the burden of their reports, and especially the eloquence of their agents, attest.

These are some of the channels through which the richest blessings are poured into the churches from missionary stations.

II. *Missionary operations not only increase the piety and energy of the churches, but greatly assist in supplying their domestic destitution.*

Our former position being admitted, this is its legitimate consequence. If every Christian could be brought to employ all his talents, it would require but a small proportion of the present number—perhaps only the reduced proportion of Gideon's army—to accomplish a greater amount of good than is now effected.

(1.) We have referred to the influence of foreign missions upon the young. Many a converted youth has had his attention directed to the ministry through the reading of missionary journals.

(2.) The reaction of missions upon the domestic interests of individual denominations, is instructive.

(3.) When we speak of the vigor which missionary exertions throw into our domestic institutions, we refer to a very natural operation. That man who has courage to attempt a great enterprise, despises the difficulties of a small one. The energy produced by the one, overlooks all the appalling trifles of the other.

III. *The church, through missionary efforts, places herself in the best, and, indeed, in the only position for receiving the most abundant spiritual blessings.*

1. *These efforts have a direct tendency to remove the most serious obstructions to piety and efficiency.*

Where the work of evangelizing the world is carried on with energy, it indicates and produces self-denial and liberality. We need not stop to show that nothing is more repugnant to eminent holiness, or usefulness, than a selfish parsimonious spirit. It is abhorrent in the eyes of a holy God. "For the iniquity of his covetousness," said Jehovah, "was I wroth, and smote him," Isa. lvii. 17.

2. *It secures to us those promises which are connected with enlarged exertions.*

"The liberal soul shall be made fat; and he that watereth shall be watered also himself," Prov. xi. 25. "If thou draw out thy soul to the hungry, and satisfy the afflicted soul, then shall thy light rise in· obscurity, and thy darkness be as the noon-day : and the Lord shall guide thee continually, and satisfy thy soul in drought, and make fat thy bones : and thou shalt be like a watered garden, and like a spring of water, whose waters fail not," Isa. lviii. 10, 11.

IV. *It must encourage and enable the church still more to extend her limits, and thus to return to the heathen world the full influence of her improved condition.*

This consequence is certain. It would be a dictate of selfish policy, if it were only a secular interest. Missionary effort is its own reward.

We have seen that it not only demands large resources, but supplies the resources it demands. There is, however, a nobler principle for this enlarged policy, than personal recompense. Confidence is gathered from success, and energy from action. Nothing so effectually convinces the church of the impotence of her own might, and the necessity and adequacy of her Redeemer's promised aid, as the effort to restore a rebellious world to its God. It is the most stupendous enterprise, in which mortals have an agency. It taxes the utmost strength; and then makes demands upon faith, which infinitude alone can meet.

APPLICATION.

1. This subject teaches that lengthening

the cords of the church, is strengthening her stakes. The two are inseparable; and they who confine themselves within their own limits, and labor first and exclusively to improve their domestic interests, without obeying the injunction and following the order of the text, will probably accomplish as little at home as they attempt abroad.

2. Our only authority for preaching the gospel—the promises and predictions of the word of God—the purchase of the Saviour's death—the triumph of his oppressed church —the highest glory of his mediatorial reign, —all demand the universal diffusion and dominion of Christianity.

3. Church of the living God, awake! Thy slumbers, oh, how guilty, how cruel! Thy husband—thy Redeemer—bids thee awake: and what he says to all, he says to each— awake!

CXII.—THE CHRISTIAN WARFARE.

"For the weapons of our warfare are not carnal, but mighty through God to the pulling down of strongholds."—2 Cor. x. 4.

THIS world was created by Christ, and for him. He, therefore, is its rightful Lord and Ruler. He is the one blessed and glorious Potentate, unto whom all homage and tribute should be paid. Sin introduced anarchy and rebellion into our world. Man revolted from God, allied himself to Satan, the usurper, and placed himself in an attitude of defiance to the Most High. God could have easily overthrown his rebellious creatures; he could have destroyed them with "the breath of his mouth," and "the brightness of his presence." But "in wrath hath he remembered mercy." He adopted an expedient of grace by which his banished ones might not be expelled from him. The rebel now has the offer of life—now he may return to God, and be forgiven. The preaching of the gospel is that instrumentality which God employs for restoring men to his favor. "Through the ignorance that is in them," men place themselves in opposition to the gospel, Eph. iv. 18. They refuse to hear it, or do not believe it. They cavil at its doctrines, or refuse to obey its precepts. In one word, they dislike Christ's kingdom; and say with the servants in the parable, "We will not have this man to reign over us," Luke xix. 14. Now, to subdue these is

the great end of the Christian ministry. Graciously to conquer these is the design of the preaching of the cross; and the text refers to the character of our weapons and the success of our efforts. "The weapons of our warfare," etc. Notice,

I. *The warfare referred to.*

"Our warfare." Now, our warfare is distinguished from all other scenes of conflict:—

1. *It is Divine, and not diabolical.* War is the general result of hellish passion, and sin. See Jas. iv. 1, 2. Most wars originate from beneath. This is a divine and heavenly warfare. The Son of the ever-blessed God is the "Captain of our salvation."

2. *This is a holy, and not an unrighteous war.* Wars generally arise from avarice, or ambition, or revenge; and are generally wicked and abominable in the sight of God. This war, on the other hand, is based on righteousness. It is the cause of truth, and justice, and equity. It is the cause of holiness against sin. Of obedience against rebellion. Of the reign of God, against the usurpation of the prince of darkness.

3. *It is a benevolent, and not a carnal war.* War aims at spreading misery, devastation, and death. War is one of those insatiable monsters, that has often spread terror, and misery, and woe, through the length and breadth of our world. Peace, comfort, health, and felicity, are exiled by its terrific influence. Our war is one of compassion, of tenderest goodness, and sweetest mercy. Paradoxical as it may appear, our banners bear the symbol of a Lamb. And this is the inscription, "Glory to God in the highest, and on earth peace, good-will towards men," Luke ii. 14. It produces real and abiding blessings, and spreads comfort and felicity in its triumphal course. It offers health, and peace, and life.

4. *It is a blessed and not an accursed war.* It bears along with it every national, domestic, and personal blessing. It strews its flowers of gladness all around. "The wilderness and the solitary place shall be glad for them; and the desert shall rejoice, and blossom as the rose," Isa. xxxv. 1. Contrast those countries where it has extended its conquests, and those where Satan the usurper still reigns. In the one, is intelligence; in the other, ignorance. In the one, civilization; in the other, barbarism. In the one, domestic comfort; in the other, family despotism. In the one, man sinks to the

level of the brute; in the other, he rises almost to an equality with angels. Notice,

II. *The strongholds in which sinners intrench themselves in their opposition to God.* Of these, we notice,

1. *The stronghold of ignorance.* Satan blinds his votaries. Ignorance is essential to the duration of his kingdom. It is the kingdom of darkness. Error is the main pillar on which it rests. Now, men do not know the true state of things. They will not consider the great question. They will not come to the light. This is criminal ignorance—wilful closing the eyes against the light of heaven.

2. *The stronghold of prejudice.* This is the general result of ignorance. Hence, how readily persons seize hold of the most trifling objections to religion. Any foolish thing will satisfy them, if it be against God's holy word and truth. Sometimes this prejudice is against doctrines, or duties, or against the people of God. It is often, however, deadly and fatal.

3. *The stronghold of pride.* This is a common barrier to the salvation of the soul. Sin commenced with it. It is one of the last things to be given up, yet it is incompatible with the spirit of the gospel. "God resisteth the proud, and giveth grace to the humble," 1 Pet. v. 5. Sinners must be abased. Men must confess their iniquity. They must repent, and receive the kingdom of God as a little child, Mark x. 15. They must become nothing, and "Christ be all in all." Thus the gospel was foolishness to the Greeks.

4. *The stronghold of Mammon.* Love of this present world. A desire to gain the riches of time. Setting the affections on things on the earth. This was the stronghold of Balaam, the false prophet—he preferred gain to godliness, Numb. xxii., &c. This was the stronghold of Gehazi, the servant of Elisha, 2 Kings v. 20, &c. Of the young man who came to Christ, Matt. xix. 22. Of Judas, Matt. xxvi. 15. Of Demas, 2 Tim. iv. 10. Of Simon Magus, Acts xviii. 18. Of Ananias and Sapphira, v. 1–10.

5. *The stronghold of unbelief.* The rejection of the truth. Not crediting the gospel. Men do not believe their state so evil and dangerous. They will not believe "that all have sinned," Rom. ii. 23; and that "the wicked shall be turned into hell," Psa. ix. 17. They will not believe in the requirements of the gospel, "repentance towards God, and faith in our Lord Jesus Christ," Acts xx. 21. Neither do they believe the threatenings of the word of God. Unbelief is a gross attack upon the truth of God, and continually throws back the offer of grace and salvation. These are some of the strongholds. Observe,

III. *The weapons by which they are to be overthrown.* Now, the weapons are described, negatively, as "not carnal;" and then, positively, in their efficiency, "mighty through God." Observe, carnal weapons are disowned. Among these we notice,

1. *The sword.* This was the weapon by which Mohammedanism was extended. This was the weapon Peter drew forth to defend the Saviour in the garden. This has too often been employed by the intolerant, and the dominant sects of the professed churches of Christ. This may make slaves, hypocrites, and formalists.

2. *Temporal reward is a carnal weapon.* The multitude followed Christ because of the loaves and fishes. Men have been known to purchase proselytes in this way. Is not this calculated to extend cupidity and deceit?

3. *Sophistry and specious reasonings are carnal weapons.* This was one of the chief weapons of the ancient schools of philosophers. They reasoned, and philosophized, and had their profound mysteries, &c. But "my speech and my preaching was not with enticing words of man's wisdom, but in demonstration of the Spirit and of power: that your faith should not stand in the wisdom of men, but in the power of God. Howbeit we speak wisdom among them that are perfect: yet not the wisdom of this world, nor of the princes of this world, that come to naught: but we speak the wisdom of God in a mystery, even the hidden wisdom, which God ordained before the world unto our glory," 1 Cor. ii. 4–7.

Now, carnal weapons we totally disown and reprobate, in all matters of conscience and religion. Observe, our weapons are the truths of the gospel. The "sword of the Spirit, which is the word of God;" and this used plainly, simply, yet earnestly, is effective to the overthrow and "pulling down of the strongholds" of sin and Satan. The stronghold of ignorance is overthrown by the gospel of truth. The stronghold of prejudice is to be met by the simple facts and statements of the gospel. The stronghold of pride is to be overthrown by the revealed and exalted glories of another world. The stronghold of Mammon, by offering the riches of eternity. The stronghold of unbelief, by the persuasive statements of the evidences of Christianity. The gospel can do all this. It is mighty to produce all these momentous and glorious effects. It is God's own instrument. It is full of the wisdom and power of God. It is that by which the Spirit carries on and perpetuates the kingdom of Christ. Numerous are the evidences of its blissful triumphs. They have existed in all ages, in all countries, and in all ranks and classes of mankind. Many of you are evidences of it—"ye are our epistles, written in our hearts, known and read of all men," 2 Cor. iii. 2.

APPLICATION.

Learn,
1. The only means we are to employ for the extension of Christianity. We repudiate all carnal weapons—the sword and bayonet instrumentality, &c. We must avoid intolerance, bigotry, and coercion. The truth is to convert the world, and lift it up to a holy state of divine exaltation and bliss. And the truth must be preached in love.
2. These means must be faithfully and perseveringly employed. We are responsible to God, and to our dying fellow-men, for an earnest devotedness to the eternal interests of our perishing race.
3. The means we employ are Divine, and must ultimately and universally prevail.

CXIII.—THE GLORY AND PROSPERITY OF THE CHURCH.

BY REV. W. HANNAH, D. D.*

"I will be as the dew unto Israel: he shall grow as the lily, and cast forth his roots as Lebanon. They that dwell under his shadow shall return; they shall revive as the corn, and grow as the vine: the scent thereof shall be as the wine of Lebanon."—Hosea xiv. 5, 7.

OUR text represents three things: first, the influence which God promises to his Church; secondly, the prosperity which his Church shall enjoy in consequence of that

* From a sermon in aid of the funds of the Wesleyan Methodist Society, preached in Lambeth Chapel, London, April 26, 1833.

influence; and, thirdly, the subsequent extension of the Church in the world around it. Let us observe,

I. *That spiritual influence which Almighty God here promises to his Church.*

"I will be as the dew unto Israel,"—a metaphor drawn from the oriental dews, which, in many respects, were remarkable; and which presented to the minds of the people in that country a very forcible view of that influence which was thus suggested. It is,

1. *A copious influence.* Oriental dews abound during the dry season, often supplying the place of rain, penetrating the sources of vegetable life, and being pre-eminently remarkable for copiousness and plenteousness—a circumstance of the utmost importance to the prosperity of those countries; and exceedingly adapted, therefore, for the expression of this promise. It is,

2. *A refreshing and renovating influence which is promised here.* The dews descending abundantly on those eastern countries, reached the very sources of vegetable life, spread a new balm and beauty over the whole scene, caused all things to revive, and flourish in new vigor. We are reminded of "times of refreshing from the presence of the Lord," Acts iii. 19: an expression which, in our own day, particularly suggests this as something which shall refresh, strengthen, and invigorate that which is thirsty and faint. There you look for the influences which God has promised to bestow. They are not only copious enough to fill all your capacities; but are so refreshing as to change your own spiritual state, and give beauty, and glow, and glory to that which before was desert. It is, also,

3. *A fertilizing influence which God promises here.* The design of all dew is to promote a greater measure of fertility. It is encouraging to know, that all the influence which God bestows, leads to the production of a spiritual and practical effort more eminently to advance the diffusion of his glory. If the Spirit descend copiously from on high, it is that converts may "spring up as among the grass, as willows by the water-courses," Isa. xliv. 4. If the Spirit descend, then will "the wilderness be a fruitful field, and the fruitful field be counted for a forest," Isa. xxxii. 15. All things flourish in new life, and in new fruitfulness.

4. *It is silent and instantaneous, yet most mighty in its operations.* Silence is the en-

ergy of God. Look around you at this season of the year. A short time since, all was the dreariness and desolation of winter: a mighty change is now transpiring all around us; every thing begins to wear the hue of beauty, thus proving a mighty change in the vegetable world. What has accomplished it? Has there been aught very noisy? aught very instantaneous? aught to strike men's senses, or to attract especial observation? Nothing of the kind—God has sent forth his own silent and pervading influence; he has penetrated the veil; he has changed the whole scene by his own silent energy; and he has given new life, and new beauty, and new glory. And may we not justly expect that he will proceed in the same way to pour out his influence on his church?

II. *Our text has reference to the prosperity which the church shall enjoy in consequence of this influence.*

And here the prophet, alluding to a tree, has drawn a beautiful representation of that sort of prosperity which we ought most earnestly to covet.

1. *There is the fair promise of future fruit.* "I will be as the dew unto Israel," —more literally, "I will be as blossom on the lily,"—as a tree refreshed by the influence of spring; he shall put forth new blossoms, like the lily, so fair, so lovely: he shall yield promise of most encouraging and renovated life, and more abundant fertility.

2. *But a growing stability in the life of God is a second part of this prosperity.* "He shall cast forth"—he shall strike—"his roots like Lebanon." The allusion is to the cedars of Lebanon, remarkable for striking their roots deep, rising to an eminent height, becoming a monument of permanence and strength. If the prophet had mentioned the blossom merely, it might be thought he had mentioned what was very pleasing and very fair; but he passes to the growing stability of it. That church, thus flourishing in its new blossoms, shall, at the same time, strike deep its roots—take further hold of the soul—shall be more entirely rooted in "the truth as it is in Jesus."

3. *An enlargement of existing members of the church in Divine grace*, is a thorough proof of this prosperity. "His branches shall spread,"—his branches shall go forward, increasing in size—becoming more capable of leaf, and of fruit too. I cannot think that this applies to the accession of new members, so much as to the enlarge-

ment of members already existing—their growth in the spiritual life. We sometimes love to select for contemplation, seasons when Christians have attained, by the power of God, a more eminent degree of Divine grace; when we may see them rising into their proper magnitude, conveying to us the lovely representation of what Christian men ought to be.

4. *This prosperity discovers itself in the church's spirituality.* "His beauty shall be as the olive-tree, and his smell as Lebanon." When we speak of the fruits of Christian piety, we may not improperly distribute them into three classes: fruits of special devotedness to God; fruits of personal purity and circumspection; and fruits of practical charity, fruits of doing good to others. These fruits abound amidst the influence of God, when he pours forth the dew of his blessing. Another mark of this prosperity is,

5. *The healing influence which a prosperous church diffuses;* thus blooming, and taking new root, and enlarging her branches, and sustaining new fruit. The description closes with saying, "His smell shall be as Lebanon;"—the fragrant influence shall spread itself from him as from the odoriferous plants and shrubs on Mount Lebanon. There shall be something inviting and healing in that influence which this prosperous church possesses. How fragrant is the influence of holy tempers, when all the man's dispositions are involved with the influence he has received from on high! How fragrant are holy words, when a person's conversation is with grace, and abundantly filled with that holy unction which descended from heaven! How fragrant are holy actions! It follows,

III. *That there shall be an extension of the church.*

1. *By an accession of new members.* "They that dwell under his shadow shall return," an expression somewhat ambiguous of meaning. The fact, doubtless, is, that many shall turn from their manifold wanderings, to dwell under the shadow of this prosperous church. The prophet may have had three classes of persons on his mind; at least, we may apply the expression to three classes.

The *first* constitutes the apostates from the truth.

The *second* class may comprehend those who are indifferent and careless. While the church is neglected these persons lay disregarded.

The *third* class embraces the distant pagans, whom the prophet seems more especially to have had in view. These neglect the church of the living God, when it is destitute of his blessing; but when it flourishes, then they, of every class and of every name, are ready to return to "dwell under its shadow," and the blessing of its protection. You have reason to expect this will be the case, if God shall prosper us by his own presence.

2. *There shall be an increase of life in these new members of the church:*—"They shall revive as the corn." New life is given to them. At first, they appear naked and unpromising as the corn; they decayed and died like that corn; but, by the blessing of the God of grace, as well as of the God of providence, they revive; they live again as that corn; and, in connection with the living church, they possess its living influence. "They shall grow as the vine," another Scripture emblem of fertility, reviving in newness of life; they shall yield divine fruit, fruit correspondent to that of the true church of God; they shall flourish yet more and more, in all that shall bring glory to God and benefit to man.

3. *They shall present an acceptable memorial to the God whom they have chosen.* "And the scent thereof shall be as Lebanon;" or rather, "The memorial thereof shall be as the wine of Lebanon," used in libation, poured forth as an acceptable offering upon the altar of God. These converts to the flourishing churches, growing in number and abounding in spiritual life, shall bring their offering as a memorial, and pour it forth on the altar. It shall be a memorial of themselves, presented as a libation to God; it shall be a memorial of their service, yielded without reserve, to him who has called them to glory and to virtue; it shall be the memorial of their gifts—they yield to him what they have, as well as what they are: and each new memorial, poured forth on the altar of God, shall come up with acceptance in his sight. His dew gave the prosperity, which, spreading itself into this extension of blessings and hopes, shall be presented again back to God, holy and acceptable in his sight!

APPLICATION.

1. We learn, from this subject, to repose our entire trust in God for the prosperity of the church. It is only when he becomes "as the dew unto Israel," that Israel prospers. Paul may plant, and Apollos may water; but God alone can give the increase, 1 Cor. iii. 6.

3. The usual order of God's proceedings, when he pours forth his blessings, is to give increased grace to his church. What does the revival of religion properly mean? Unquestionably, it properly and strictly means, something which re-lives in the church: the parched and withered field revives, lives again, when it is visited with the plentiful shower; long languishing and decaying, it lives again when the right appliances are used.

In conclusion. Let us learn to cherish the confident hope that God, even our God, will not forsake us. We may look east and west, and north and south, no human effort is able to withstand him who is God. Let a Christian man go forth, not in his own weakness, but relying on God's power; let him go forth, filled with the spirit of prayer, and faith, and zeal; let him go forth, testifying his Lord and Saviour with the Holy Ghost sent down from heaven, and we care not what class of people he may visit: be they ever so degraded, they shall be raised; be they ever so barbarous, they shall be renewed; be they ever so prejudiced, they shall be conquered; be they ever so alienated, they shall be restored. Let us go forward, trusting in God; let us trust in his blessing, and we shall find that barbarian, Scythian, bond, and free—every country, and people, and tongue—shall be ready to yield to an influence so especially proceeding from God —shall turn to a flourishing church; and present the Christian memorial on their altar. And the cross of our Lord Jesus Christ shall bring salvation to all!

CXIV.—DIFFUSION OF CHRISTIANITY DEPENDENT ON THE EXERTIONS OF CHRISTIANS.

BY REV. HENRY GREY, A. M., EDINBURGH.*

"And a vision appeared to Paul in the night: There stood a man of Macedonia, and prayed him, saying, Come over into Macedonia, and help us." —*Acts* xvi. 9.

THE request presented to the apostle, in this striking vision, conveys in it an expres-

* Preached in Lady Glenorchy's Chapel, before the Edinburgh Missionary Society, April 2, 1818.

sive indication of the dependence of man on the assistance of his fellows, and of the obligation under which we are consequently laid to help one another. This dependence, and this obligation, may be traced through human life, in all the variety of its circumstances ; but is particularly deserving of our consideration, in reference to our spiritual and eternal interests. God has appointed, that the knowledge of religion, and the blessings of salvation, should be communicated to others, through the instrumentality of those who have previously been blessed with them ; and he has thus imposed on those who know him, a duty peculiarly honorable and important. We may add, that their success, in discharging this high duty, usually bears some proportion to their fidelity ; and that the actual extension of the knowledge and blessings of salvation seems, in a great degree, to correspond with the activity, zeal, and perseverance exerted in the propagation of them.

I. *We begin with some general observations.*

1. *It cannot be doubted, that those grand arrangements of providence, which determine the general condition and circumstances of the human race, were designed, by infinite wisdom, to call into exercise the moral principles and feelings of man.* God has assigned to each class of beings its appropriate character and relations ; and that dependence of man on his fellows, which requires the exercise of mutual sympathy, and reciprocal kind offices, forms a grand law of human nature, and gives rise to many important duties, and many peculiar enjoyments. The neglect of the obligations imposed by this law, is the source of a large portion of human wretchedness ; a cordial compliance with its demands would go far to restore man to his proper rank as a moral agent ; and adorn his character with some graces of singular excellence, which, we think, are unknown to those higher intelligences who are exempt from suffering and sin.

2. *This grand law of mutual dependence may be traced in operation, through all the different orders of society and departments of life.* And in proportion as any state advances in civilization—in proportion as labor is divided, and art perfected, and human life replenished with accommodations and comforts—the dependence of man on his fellows becomes more and more conspicuous. The blessings of religion are the gifts of sov-

ereign mercy, flowing from the bosom of infinite love ; but, in dispensing them, God is pleased to make use of human agency. We remark,

3. *That true religion is neither the invention of human genius, nor the deduction of human reason ; but is founded on the actual circumstances of mankind, and on those positive discoveries which God has made of his character and will.* God has appointed that the great facts on which it rests, should be made known, from generation to generation, by an unbroken succession of living witnesses.

4. *The obligation under which we lie to help one another in our spiritual concerns, extends through all the various circumstances of life, and is particularly interwoven with its most interesting relations.* This is the highest department of a parent's duty. But to look beyond the family circle. Is it not the duty of every one to help his neighbor in this important concern ? Consider,

II. *The dependence of man on man, and the consequent obligation of mutual assistance,* with a more particular reference to those nations destitute of the gospel.

1. I ask, *Whether the necessities of the nations destitute of the gospel, do not furnish a powerful claim on all the help we can possibly afford them ?* Of their melancholy condition, in a moral view, little need be said to convince those who acknowledge the justness of the representations which the word of God gives us, of the present circumstances of the human race. Those characters of ignorance, guilt, and sin, which it attributes universally to fallen man, are most distinctly traced in those portions of mankind whom God has left most entirely to themselves.

2. I ask, *Whether the means with which you are furnished of supplying the necessities of the nations, do not impose peculiar obligations?* The God of love has made a provision for the recovery of fallen man, and you are acquainted with it. He has declared, that he "is in Christ reconciling the world unto himself, not imputing their trespasses unto them," 2 Cor. v. 19 ; and to you has this word of reconciliation been committed. A remedy is prepared of sovereign efficacy to cure the moral maladies of man, and raise his soul to eternal life ; and you are intrusted with this remedy. Can you suppose it lawful to withhold it from the millions who are incessantly dying for want of it ?

3. I ask, *Whether the declared will and purpose of God do not place beyond all doubt, our obligation to impart the gospel to the heathen ?* Look into the Bible, and say, Was it for you only the Saviour died ? for you only the Holy Ghost was promised ? for you only the gates of heaven were opened ? No ; he "gave himself a ransom for all, to be testified in due time," 1 Tim. ii. 6. The world is the ample theatre on which his grace is to be displayed.

The character of the gospel corresponds with its design. It is simple and spiritual, having nothing in it of a local or limited nature : its blessings are such as all may enjoy ; its services all may perform ; its precepts all may obey.

APPLICATION.

1. Would that I may have conveyed any due sense of the necessities of the nations, or of your obligations to help them !

2. These nations might have been our benefactors, had God willed it ; and, more faithful to their privileges and to the claims of brotherhood than we have been, might have sent us their apostles, their ministers of reconciliation, their ambassadors of peace.

3. It was not a seraph from the throne, but a man of Macedonia, who stood before Paul, and prayed him, "Come over, and help us." Many men, the men of many lands, approach you with this prayer. Christ asks of those who love him, obedience to his commands, the fulfilment of his declarations. He pleads by his cross and intercession ; by the consolations of a throne of grace ; by all your peaceful joys, and happy privileges ; by the blessed hope of immortality,—he entreats you to be fellow-workers with him in fulfilling the purposes of his love, and in communicating to "the Gentiles the unsearchable riches of Christ !"

CXV.—THE INFLUENCE OF CHRISTIAN TRUTH.

BY REV. JOSHUA BATES, D. D.*

"The truth shall make you free."—*John* viii. 32.

THAT Christianity, believed and regarded, has a tendency to exalt the character and

* From a sermon, preached in Northampton, Massachusetts, September 21, 1825, at the Sixteenth Annual Meeting of the American Board of Commissioners for Foreign Missions.

increase the happiness of mankind, is a doctrine clearly implied in our text. "Then said Jesus to those Jews which believed in him, If ye continue in my word, then are ye my disciples indeed ; and ye shall know the truth, and the truth shall make you free." Without repeating the whole context, or giving a disquisition on the metaphorical language which runs through it, I shall be justified in calling your attention, at once, to the doctrine already stated ; and leading you to consider at large, the *influence of Christianity on the character and happiness of mankind.*

I. *Let us consider the influence of Christianity on the character and happiness of man, viewed simply as an intellectual being.*

If we can prove, that Christianity encourages a spirit of free inquiry and philosophical investigation—that it tends to enlarge the sphere of human knowledge, and promote intellectual improvement—the inference will follow, that it elevates the character, and adds to the happiness of mankind. This must be a 'mitted, or stupidity is a blessing ; and unrestrained indulgence of passion, a duty. I know much has been said in praise of ignorance ; and even genius, with all her inventions and acquisitions, has been charged with the crime of entailing mischief and misery on the world. But experience satisfactorily confutes the presumptuous charge. The happiness of ignorance and stupidity is only negative ; it is the appropriate happiness of the brute, not of man—not of beings endowed with intellectual foresight, and capable of anticipation.

Whatever, therefore, tends to promote intellectual improvement, and advance the cause of science, must elevate the character and increase the felicity of man ; must give to the individuals, who are brought under its influence, increased susceptibility of enjoyment, and additional power of rendering others happy. Now such, we contend, is the natural tendency of Christianity. Its very spirit is liberty—not only liberty of action, but liberty of thought, liberty of inquiry. It challenges investigation—it awakens curiosity—it dignifies truth.

For further proof and illustration of our position, let us appeal to facts. Where has science prevailed ? By whom has literature been refined ? In what ages and countries has philosophy—sound, salutary philosophy —been most successfully cultivated ? A reference to history, and a view of the civilized world, will furnish an answer to these inquiries, at once proving and illustrating our doctrine.

Talents, sanctified by Divine grace, and moved by Christian motives, constitutes a mind like Newton's—consistent, splendid, happy ; and leads to such investigations as he made, which, like the orbs of heaven, whose tracks he followed and whose laws he revealed, will continue to enlighten and guide all future generations. Let us consider,

II. *The influence of Christianity on the character and happiness of man, viewed more particularly as a moral being.*

The discussion of this topic we commence with the broad position, that in proportion as man feels and regards his moral relations, other circumstances being equal, will be his power of enjoying and communicating happiness.

I point you, with confidence in the result, to those Christian countries, where no arbitrary restraints are imposed on free inquiry; and to those individuals who receive the Bible as the word of God, yield a willing submission to its authority, and abide by its decisions, without gainsaying ; who have imbibed the spirit of the gospel, and received its peculiar truths in love ; who, in the very language of inspiration, have been "born again, not of corruptible seed, but of incorruptible, by the word of God," 1 Pet. i. 23 ; and are, therefore, sincere, experimental, practical Christians. Let the appeal be made here; and let facts decide the question, if in the minds of any it remains a question, What is the moral tendency of Christianity ? Let us consider,

III. *The influence of Christianity on the character and happiness of man, viewed as a member of civil society, and a subject of civil government.*

Christianity exalts the character and promotes the happiness of mankind, by giving at once the blessings of social order and civil liberty. Standing on the history of the world, I can establish this position. Nothing like civil liberty, united with social order and security, now exists in any country beyond the limits of Christian influence. And within these limits, the degree of settled liberty may be pretty accurately measured by the purity and extent of this influence.

It has gradually modified and improved the law of nations, leading them to admit in theory, and begin to feel in practice, that they are moral persons, bound by moral obligation, to observe, in their intercourse with each other, the great Christian law of love. Especially, has it improved that portion of international law, which relates to war—softening its rigor, mitigating its horrors, and thus preparing the way for that mighty and glorious change, which it is destined to effect, when " they shall beat their swords into ploughshares, and their spears into pruning hooks,"—when " nation shall not lift up sword against nation, neither shall learn war any more," Isa. ii. 4.

APPLICATION.

1. In making an application of the subject of this discourse, I have little to say ; for the lessons of gratitude, and consolation, and duty, which it suggests, are exceedingly obvious ; and they must already have been presented to every reflecting mind, and impressed on every pious and benevolent heart. How obvious, my Christian brethren, is the inference, that we are under peculiar obligations of gratitude, to our God and Redeemer, for our distinguished Christian privileges. We live in Immanuel's land ! To us Christianity has come, in all her simplicity and splendor, in all her beauty and glory. We have the Bible in our hands ; we may learn its truths, and obey its injunctions without fear or restraint.

2. Again. How obvious is the lesson of consolation and joy, which flows from our subject, in connection with the prophetic assurance of the future triumphs of the gospel. If Christianity, in its limited operations, has done so much to meliorate the condition of mankind, what must be its effects, when its influence shall have become universal and unrestrained ; reaching all lands, purifying all hearts, and controlling the counsels of all nations!

3. Finally. How obvious is the inference from our doctrine, that it is the duty of every Christian to aid the cause of Christian missions. The wretched state of the heathen, of Jews, of Mohammedans, and even of multitudes nominally Christian, must awaken the tenderest sympathies, excite the most ardent and importunate prayers, and rouse all the energies of the renewed soul.

My brethren, we have placed before us the strongest motives to induce us vigorously to engage in this cause of love. The sub-

limity of the enterprise, the certainty of ultimate success, the signs of the times, and,
what is paramount to all other considerations,
the command, the last command, of our
blessed Redeemer, urges to active exertion
and persevering effort in this cause !

CXVI.—THE UNSEARCHABLE RICHES OF CHRIST.

BY REV. MELVILLE HORNE.*

"Unto me, who am less than the least of all
saints, is this grace given, that I should preach
among the Gentiles the unsearchable riches of
Christ."—*Ephes.* iii. 8.

In pleading the cause of missions, it oc-
curs to me, that I cannot do better than call
your attention to the animated words I have
read to you.

I. " *The unsearchable riches of Christ.*"

(1.) They are riches of heavenly knowledge.

(2.) Riches of redeeming love.

(3.) Riches of pardoning mercy.

(4.) Riches of sanctifying grace.

(5.) Riches of consolation and hope.

(6.) Riches of immortality and glory.

(7.) All of them "riches of Christ;" and
all of them "unsearchable."

II. *Among whom are they to be preached ?*

1. Paul's commission, and that of the
other apostles, was to "preach the gospel to
every creature," Mark xvi. 15; and *to bring
all nations to the obedience of the faith.*

2. *St. Paul thoroughly understood that
the gospel he preached was emphatically the
gospel of the Gentiles.*

As such the angels announced it to the
shepherds—"Behold, I bring you good tidings of great joy, which shall be to *all* people," Luke ii. 10. Agreeably to this idea,
at the birth of Jesus, they proclaimed, not
peace in Judea, but "peace on earth."

3. *The manner in which St. Paul speaks
of the calling of the Gentiles is highly worthy
of observation.*

He calls it a mystery—"the mystery of
Christ—revealed unto the holy apostles and
prophets by the Spirit; that the Gentiles
should be fellow-heirs, and of the same body;
—to the intent that now unto the princi-

* Preached before the London Missionary Society, at St. Saviour's Church, Southwark, May
12, 1797.

palities and powers in heavenly places might
be known by the Church the manifold wisdom of God, according to the eternal purpose which he purposed in Christ Jesus our
Lord," Eph. iii. 4, 6, 10, 11.

III. *I proceed to observe on the dignified
idea St. Paul had of the apostolic mission.*
—"Unto me is this grace given." Let us
cast our eye,

1. *On the labors and sufferings of the mission:* "I think that God hath set forth us
the apostles last as those appointed unto
death: for we are made a spectacle to the
world, and to angels, and to men," 1 Cor.
iv. 9. Again, "We are troubled on every
side, yet not distressed: we are perplexed,
but not in despair; persecuted, but not forsaken; cast down, but not destroyed; always bearing about in the body the dying
of the Lord Jesus." "In all things approving ourselves as the ministers of God, in much
patience, in afflictions, in necessities, in distresses, in stripes, in imprisonments, in tu-
mults, in labors, in watchings, in fastings," 2
Cor. iv. 8–10; vi. 4, 5. All his crosses and
losses he accounted as nothing, so that he
might communicate to miserable men "the
unsearchable riches of Christ."

2. *But let us not dismiss this part of the
subject without further inquiry into the
grounds of St. Paul's triumph.*—" Unto me
is this grace given, that I should preach
among the Gentiles the unsearchable riches
of Christ." And is it not a high honor to
be made a "steward of the mysteries of God,"
a dispenser of "the unsearchable riches of
Christ?" If dignity be derived from the greatness of the power we serve, what more can
be wished than to be the ambassador of God,
the servant of the King of righteousness and
peace? If the royal David deemed it an
honor to be a door-keeper in the house of
his God (Psa. lxxxiv. 10), well might St.
Paul glory in the honorable dispensation of
life and peace to mankind.

IV. *The forcible admonition given to ministers and missionaries, to think humbly and
soberly of themselves as they ought to think.*

"Unto me, who am less than the least of
all saints." What! Paul, the miraculous
convert of Jesus Christ! Paul, the teacher
of the Gentiles, and "not a whit behind the
very chiefest apostles," 2 Cor. xi. 5. Paul,
who had been caught up into the third
heaven, seen the visions of the Almighty,
and heard unspeakable words, 2 Cor. xii. 2,
4 ; who had "suffered the loss of all things,"

and accounted the loss of all as nothing—who had labored, and suffered, and done more good than all the apostles—who had founded more churches, than many ministers have converted souls—is this man the least! yea "less than the least of all saints!" Wonderful humility! Blessed gospel, which is capable of producing this lovely temper in the proud heart of Saul the persecutor!

Mark, brethren, upon what point St. Paul makes this comparison of himself to turn. It is not riches, learning, power; nor does it turn upon ministerial talent, labor, or success. No; whatever distinctions, real or artificial, prevail among men, they all vanish in the presence of that grand and everlasting distinction which God makes between the man that feareth him, and the man that feareth him not, Mal. iii. 18. The point of honor is true holiness. It is not to preach Christ, but to love him; it is not to convert others, but to be converted ourselves to the image of his holiness, which constitutes our honor and felicity in time, and in eternity.

1. *When the Lord will make a man a chosen vessel, eminently serviceable in the church, it is the method of his grace to humble that man in the dust, and to remove from him every ground of vain-glory.* This is necessary to secure all the glory to the Lord, to whom alone it is justly due. It is, also, necessary to bring the souls of his saints to an absolute dependence on the Lord's wisdom, grace, and power, for all good to themselves and others. And, in the last place, it is of the utmost importance to our own safety and comfort, lest we should be lifted up with pride even by the graces bestowed upon us, and the important services we are enabled to perform.

2. *That it is impossible a missionary should engage in his work in a better spirit than of that humility of which St. Paul is the example.* The man who is brought to see himself as "the chief of sinners," and "the least of all saints," is happily freed from all confidence in the flesh. His talents, labors, sufferings, and success are with him of no account. He goes out of himself to live in Christ—for Christ, and upon Christ. He receives, from the Redeemer, "grace to help in every time of need." Feeling that he is nothing, he also feels that "Christ is all, and in all."

APPLICATION.

1. Let us, then, every day place our dear missionaries under the shadow of the Rock of Israel. The Lord requires it; and the missionaries claim it at our hands. We subscribe money; they give their lives. We preach missionary sermons to polite congregations; they compass sea and land, and feel the extremities of hunger, thirst, cold, and weariness, in preaching to stupid heathen, who, it may be, will some day reward their love with a shower of stones, or a volley of spears.

2. "The harvest truly is plenteous, but the laborers are few: pray ye, therefore, the Lord of the harvest, that he would send forth laborers into his harvest," Luke x. 2. And may we, who are ministers of the word, who have it in charge to dispense "the unsearchable riches of Christ," and who glory to call ourselves God's ambassadors—may we be made to feel the attractions of this calling! "Now unto the King eternal, immortal, invisible, the only wise God, be honor and glory forever and ever! Amen." 1 Tim. i. 17.

CXVII.—JESUS CHRIST'S INSTRUCTIONS TO THE SEVENTY DISCIPLES.

BY THE REV. H. HUNTER, D. D.*

"After these things the Lord appointed other seventy also, and sent them two and two before his face into every city and place, whither he himself would come. Therefore said he unto them, The harvest truly is great, but the laborers are few: pray ye therefore the Lord of the harvest, that he would send forth laborers into his harvest. Go your ways: behold, I send you forth as lambs among wolves. Carry neither purse, nor scrip, nor shoes: and salute no man by the way," etc.—*Luke* x. 1–20.

AT the time when our blessed Lord sent out the seventy, by two and two, he was preparing to follow them in the last circuit which he made through Galilee, being within the last six months of his abode upon earth. What he addressed to them on that memorable occasion, may, with the change of a few circumstances, serve to admonish, warn, and instruct us all; and especially those whom we are sending out in his name, on a progress much more extensive, but precisely with the same view. I trust all will listen to them, therefore, with that attention,

* Delivered at Zion Chapel, on the designation of the first missionaries to the Islands of the South Sea, July 29, 1796.

deference, and humility, which are due, not to the words of a mere man like themselves, but of Him who spake as never man spake.

I. *Christ sent out the seventy by pairs,* seeming to say, with Joseph to his brethren, "See that ye fall not out by the way," Gen. xlv. 24.

The little district of Galilee was thus parcelled out into thirty-five subdivisions; and thereby the labor and danger were diminished, by being equalized. Besides, each missionary was thus provided with a known and tried friend, embarked in the same cause with himself, whose conversation would relieve the tediousness of the way, mutual confidence would be inspired to the discharge of their important trust, and credit would be secured to a message delivered under the concurring testimony of two witnesses.

II. *Our blessed Lord fairly and faithfully warned the seventy of the difficulty and danger of the charge which they were undertaking.*

The labor and difficulty he represents under the idea of an ample harvest, to be reaped by the hands of a few laborers. The harvest-field is a scene of more than ordinary exertion, toil, and fatigue, even when laborers are abundant; it calls for unremitting application through the whole day, and frequently through the night—it demands emulous yet friendly energy.

The danger of the enterprise is represented in the character here given of human nature: "Behold, I send you forth as lambs among wolves." "Beware of men," Mat. x. 17. Mortifying view of human nature! and, alas! it is not the exaggerated account of a discontented, irritable cynic, inflamed with hatred against mankind; but a true representation of the case from one who knew it well, and who bitterly deplored that depravity which he was constrained to expose. Man a wolf to man!—to his brother—his benefactor! Man a victim to the fury of him whom he sought to save!

III. *Our Lord cautions his missionaries against an over-curious and minute regard to accommodation, preparatory to their entering on their mission, and while employed in executing the business of it.*

Observe, he would inculcate on them an unbounded confidence in the care of Providence, and perfect contentment with such provision as the hospitality of those whom they visited might, from time to time, supply. They are enjoined to disregard some particulars which most men would deem essentially necessary to a journey: "Carry neither purse, nor scrip, nor shoes." An anxious solicitude about conveniences, much more about fantastical gratification and indulgence, betrays a mind unsubdued to the authority, and uninfluenced by the example, of the Lord Jesus. It betrays the sickly appetite of a spoiled child, which must be tempted and pampered with delicacies; not the manly spirit of the intrepid youth, who cares not how hard he lies, and how coarsely he fares, provided he gets forward. "I have learned in whatsoever state I am, therewith to be content. I know both how to be abased, and I know how to abound; everywhere and in all things I am instructed both to be full and to be hungry, both to abound and to suffer need," Phil. iv. 11, 12.

IV. *Our Lord recommends to the disciples undivided, undeviating attention to what was specially committed to them.*

This is plainly implied in the injunction, "Salute no man by the way." And this is by no means an encouragement to practice rudeness and incivility; for the gospel inculcates not only the weightier matters— "Whatsoever things are true, whatsoever things are honest, whatsoever things are just, and whatsoever things are pure," but those also, which "are lovely and of good report," Phil. iv. 8; and ordains that "all things be done decently and in order," 1 Cor. xiv. 40. But the salutations of the East were and are formal, tedious, and ceremonious; and custom sanctioned them so far, as to suspend and interrupt the most serious and necessary business. It became needful, therefore, on urgent occasions, to dispense with the customary laws of decorum.

"The King's business requireth haste." When a dark world is to be enlightened; when the "dead in trespasses and sins" are to be quickened into "newness of life," let the servant of Jesus Christ give his whole heart to it, "Let the dead bury their dead," Matt. viii. 22.

V. *Our Lord's instructions to the seventy respecting their work, and the manner in which they were to perform it.*

This consists of three articles: they were to proclaim peace wherever they went; they were to "heal the sick;" and to announce the immediate approach of the kingdom of God. What a copious return for the lodging and refreshments of a day! And it is thus that the great God acknowledges and remunerates the little services which men render him in the person of his ministers. "Say, peace be to this house," verse 5.

"Heal the sick." The seventy were endowed with miraculous powers of healing. They had this supernatural seal affixed to their commission; and thus an effectual door was opened for them to the hearts of those to whom their message was addressed. We pretend not to send you forth armed with such power as this.

But "say unto them, The kingdom of God is come nigh unto you." This prepared the inhabitants of Galilee for the personal visit of the Saviour of the world; thus was his approach announced in "every city and place, whither he himself would come;" and thus are these, our missionary brethren, to "go forth," I trust, in the spirit and power of Elias, in the spirit and power of John Baptist; as "a voice crying in the wilderness, Prepare ye the way of the Lord, make straight in the desert a highway for our God," Isa. xl. 3. A finger pointing out—a tongue proclaiming, "Behold the Lamb of God which taketh away the sin of the world," John i. 29.

VI. *Christ encourages his disciples with the assurance, that he should consider the reception which they met with, as given to himself.*

Every instance of neglect or insult which should be offered to them, as disrespectful to him, and consequently to God; and every expression of kindness and benevolence to them, as a personal favor. "He that heareth you heareth me; and he that despiseth you despiseth me; and he that despiseth me despiseth him that sent me," Luke x. 16.

VII. *Our Lord instructs his disciples to keep their hearts with all diligence, from the emotions of self-gratulation and complacency in the hour of success.*

To the full extent of his promise, and beyond it, his presence and power had accompanied them. This they joyfully acknowledged on their return, "saying, Lord, even the devils are subject unto us, through thy name," ver. 17. But even this was surpassed by a still dearer, and more deeply interesting consideration: "Notwithstanding, in this rejoice not, that the spirits are subject unto you; but rather rejoice because your names are written in heaven," ver. 20. Hereby their great, their eternal all was effectually secured.

To conclude. Let every professed Christian consider himself specially commissioned to declare and to live "the truth as it is in Jesus," in the ears, and before the eyes of a careless and unbelieving world!

CXVIII.—INSUFFICIENCY OF MERE HUMAN EFFORTS TO EVANGELIZE THE HEATHEN WORLD.

BY REV. T. S. CRISP.*

"Not by might, nor by power, but by my Spirit, saith the Lord of hosts. Who art thou, O great mountain? before Zerubbabel thou shalt become a plain."—*Zech.* iv. 6, 7.

WE are endeavoring to rear a temple for God, by spreading the gospel, and building up the church of Christ in the heathen world. Our cause is great, our difficulties many; but God is all-sufficient. We notice,

I. *The conversion of the heathen world is a vast and difficult undertaking.*

Many considerations may be adduced in proof of this position. Let us select a few which are obvious to every one.

1. *Reflect on the object aimed at.* It is no other than the conversion of souls to God. This object is so momentous that, under any circumstances, it is worthy of every effort by which it can be rendered attainable. Compare it with any thing else: with the conquests of ambition, or the nobler triumphs of liberty; the splendor of great achievements, or the benefit of useful discoveries; the treasures which art and labor amass, and the luxuries which these treasures purchase; the blessings of peace, the sweets of friendship, and the most refined endearments of social life: great and alluring as these objects are, the conversion of souls is still greater. Nay, the conversion of one single soul outweighs them all.

2. *Look at the dimensions of the field on which we have entered, in seeking the conversion of the heathen.* "The field," said the Saviour, "is the world," Matt. xiii. 38. The whole world was before the apostles when they commenced their labors: not a spot could they visit, beyond the borders of the promised land, which the tidings of mercy, and the Spirit of life accompanying these tidings, had ever entered.

* From a sermon preached in the Wesleyan Chapel, Great Queen-street, Lincoln's Inn Fields, at the Annual Meeting of the Baptist Missionary Society, June 20, 1821.

3. *Think on the obstacles arising to this undertaking from the degraded state of the heathen world.* Various are the forms which idolatry assumes; but each presents some peculiar character of evil. It is difficult to say which proves the greatest barrier to the reception of the truth—the grossness of some, or the refined sensuality of others. We know not on which to look with the greatest pain : the mind of an idolater, sunk to the lowest point of intellectual debasement, his ideas few, confined within a narrow space, and as grovelling as they are few; or the faculties, acute and polished, capable of taking a large and lofty range, while the mind thus elevated is only rendered the more enslaved, in proportion to the force with which it embraces the delusions and abominations of heathenism.

Idolatry, thus produced and nourished, becomes like an enemy intrenched within an impregnable fortress. All the strong, evil passions are on its side; from them it receives its character and complexion. Corruption is on its side; for it is the source from which it sprang. A guilty conscience is on its side; for, while the principles of idolatry are such as palliate the guilt of sin, its rites are calculated to soften down whatever yet remains of misgiving and uneasiness in the conscience. And though mere frivolous ceremonies can never impart solid peace, yet they lull and stupefy; and, in this deadly repose, the soul is unwilling to be roused and disturbed. The senses and appetites are on its side; for pomp and parade, rioting and mirth, festivals and shows, licentious indulgence, and secret abominations, suit the depravity of the fleshly mind. "Wherein they think it strange that ye run not with them to the same excess of riot," 1 Pet. iv. 4. This is the element in which the carnal mind delights to live and to revel. Oh! with what force, and to what a depth must that religion strike its roots, on which forbidden fruits is seen to grow so luxuriantly. How, then, shall the overthrow of this mighty evil be brought about? This leads to the second general remark, that,

II. *It is vain to attempt it by human power and might.* "Not by might, nor by power," said the Lord to Zerubbabel. Let it, then, be observed,

1. *That human power, in itself, is quite insufficient to effect this object.* Whatever the skill and energy of man may produce, they can never bring about a great moral renovation in the world. The force of human authority has made men hypocrites, but not believers. The power of the sword has been effectual in destroying the faithful; but this weapon of death has never become the instrument of life, by raising up others in their place. Human laws have exerted their energy, and have produced abject, hollow, constrained submission, not the voluntary homage of the heart. Armies have gone forth to demolish the works of man; but armies cannot "build the temple of the Lord of hosts." Great is the power of persuasion : nothing greater than the force of mind over mind. But what was the effect of this before the gospel came? "The world by wisdom knew not God," 1 Cor. i. 21. Among the celebrated nations of antiquity, the human intellect had reached its highest elevation, and was enlarged to the greatest dimensions. Yet all that was effected by the majesty of eloquence, and the charms of poetic fiction, by the researches of philosophy, and the strength of moral reasoning, was an exchange of the barbarism of rude idolatry, for a system of theology as licentious as it was complicated.

Has any system of morals, invented and propagated by the power of man, been attended with efficacy in subduing the corruptions of the heart? Where has such a spectacle ever presented itself? One system, indeed, there was, which did operate with mighty force. Mohammed tried what could be effected by might and by power. And did he succeed? He succeeded to the utmost in leaving to posterity a lasting, awful monument of what human power alone can do. It could give an air of sanctity to gross sensuality. It could stupefy and intoxicate the mind, laying prostrate its intellectual faculties, and brutalizing all the feelings of the heart. It could reduce man to the most odious vassalage by which the mind has ever been fettered; while it exalted a mortal to a dreadful eminence, from which he looked down on whole regions, overspread with blasphemous and infernal delusions, more deadly in their effects than the ravages of the locust, the horrors of war, or the desolations of the plague. But where is the spot, however contracted, over which the same kind of power has spread spiritual life and moral liberty, peace of conscience, and purity of heart? Nowhere : nor can these blessings ever be seen, where no higher power is at work than that of man.

2. *In effecting this object, God will not make a display of human power and might.* In establishing his spiritual kingdom among mankind, how frequently has God chosen " the weak things of the world to confound the things which are mighty !" 1 Cor. i. 27. A nation is selected for the purpose of stripping Satan of his glory, and trampling him in the dust. And what is this nation ? Their progenitor was a wanderer in a strange land. They themselves were oppressed by tyrants, and hated by surrounding nations : they passed through a long and bitter captivity : they were sometimes brought so low that their state became almost hopeless. Yet, while the greatest monarchies rise and fall, this people are preserved, that from them may spring " the Desire of all nations." He comes !—but he is clothed in all the feebleness of a mortal body. He is the subject of want and sorrow, of opposition and cruelty, to which he voluntarily yields. He is betrayed and deserted, derided and crucified. And, in his crucifixion, he passes through that overwhelming desolation of mind, which even exceeds the sufferings of the body. Yet, in the midst of all this, what is he doing ? He is contending, single-handed, against all the powers of darkness—bringing glory to God—spreading peace through the earth—raising the guilty from hell to heaven—and reconciling Divine justice and mercy, in the pardon of the rebellious.

Survey the history of the church, from that period down to the times in which we live, and the truth of the language of the text will receive abundant confirmation. I refer to the Reformation from Popery. This was brought about by the instrumentality of one agent principally—the immortal Luther. It is indeed true, that the way was, in some measure, prepared for that emancipation of the mind which then took place. The writings of such men as Wycliffe had diffused some light through the regions of popish darkness. But where was the man to be found to put a finish to the great enterprise of chasing away the shades of night ? How, then, is the great object we are aiming at, to be effected ? We can cheerfully answer this question by observing, that though it is " not by might, nor by power," yet,

III. *It is by the Spirit of the Lord of hosts.*

This is a part of the subject on which it is pleasant to expatiate. If there be any thing which is as delightful as it is certain, it is that the things which are impossible with men, are possible with God, Matt. xix. 26 ; and where men must confess the inadequacy of their efforts, the power of the Spirit is there seen to shine and triumph.

The following considerations will show that all the good now going forward among the heathen, must be traced to the influence of the Spirit of God.

1. *The great work of converting and purifying souls belongs peculiarly to him.* He exerts an influence, which, in the Old Testament, is brought forward under the image of pouring " water upon him that is thirsty, and floods upon the dry ground," Isa. xliv. 3. For all the holy animation and vigor, all the activity and fruitfulness, which belong to the renewed soul, proceed from him. In the gospel economy, his office is distinctly stated. To him is ascribed the first awakening of the soul—for we are " born of the Spirit," John iii. 4.

2. *The instrument employed for thus converting the heathen world, is peculiarly his own.* The closed eye admits not the light —the callous heart receives not the truth ; yet it is the " word of God" only, which works effectually in the soul. It is by " the Truth" alone, that we are sanctified. " For our gospel came not unto you in word only, but also in power, and in the Holy Ghost," 1 Thess. i. 5.

3. *It is the peculiar office of the Spirit to honor the Lord Jesus Christ.* It is the office of the Spirit to reveal the Saviour effectually to the heart ; for " He shall receive of mine," said Christ, " and shall show it unto you," John xvi. 14. And why does he thus employ his influence, to show forth the power and love, the glories and grace, of the Redeemer ? Why does he give the Cross such mighty attractions, rendering this the object around which all the affections and hopes of redeemed sinners rally as their centre ? Because it is thus that Christ is honored ; for, says the Saviour, " He shall glorify me." In attempting an improvement of the subject on which we are now dwelling, observe,

(1.) That it shows the principle which ought to pervade the exertions of missionary societies : a principle of dependence and humility, a willingness to ascribe all the glory to him, to whom alone it belongs.

(2.) This subject affords encouragement

under difficulties. Let us silence every objection which carnal reason would suggest; and excite ourselves to fresh, unwearied ardor, by continually looking up to the strong for strength. "Our sufficiency is of God," 2 Cor. iii. 5.

(3.) This subject is calculated to give elevation to our hopes. Whatever God's purposes may be, it is as certain that they will be accomplished, as that they have been formed. "The residue of the Spirit" is with him, who is "the head over all things to the Church;" and that which remains to be given is equal to that which remains to be done.

(4.) This subject teaches us in what way every one may effectually promote the interests of missionary societies. The question which Saul addressed to Christ on the road to Damascus, is one which every genuine friend to the cause of the Redeemer will seriously and honestly ask—"Lord, what wilt thou have me to do?" Acts ix. 6. If the mind be devoted to God, there will be no difficulty in finding an answer to such an inquiry.

───────◆───────

CXIX.—THE UNIVERSAL GREATNESS AND GLORY OF GOD'S NAME.

BY REV. B. W. MATTHIAS, M.A.,* OF TRINITY COLLEGE, DUBLIN.

"For from the rising of the sun even unto the going down of the same, my name shall be great among the Gentiles; and in every place incense shall be offered unto my name, and a pure offering: for my name shall be great among the heathen, saith the Lord of hosts."—Mal. i. 11.

THE prophet Malachi lived at a period when the Jewish nation had sunk into a deplorable state of immorality and impiety. The people had forgotten the lesson which their captivity seems to have taught them for a time; as they had previously forgotten that which was intended for them by the dispersion of the ten tribes belonging to their original family. Acknowledging God in their profession, they appear, at this particular period, to have in every other respect denied him.

The eternal God expostulates with the people by his prophet, and reminds them of

* From a sermon, preached at St. Bride's Church, Fleet-street, May 1, 1820, before the Church Missionary Society.

the special kindness which he had bestowed on Jacob their ancestor, and the privileges which he had granted to him beyond those bestowed on Esau; and, marking the little effect which these things had on them, he declares that he had no pleasure in them, and would receive no offering at their hands, ver. 10. But "from the rising of the sun even unto the going down of the same," Jehovah declares, "my name shall be great among the Gentiles; and in every place incense shall be offered unto my name, and a pure offering." As though he had said, "You refuse to bring me offerings? Know, that pure offerings shall be presented to me, and in abundance—not from one solitary nation, consisting of comparatively but few individuals, but from all people on the face of the earth—from the rising of the sun even unto the going down of the same! In all the vast extent of my lower creation, I shall be celebrated and honored; my name shall be great; and my creatures, influenced by my Spirit, shall be found willing to present, not the maimed, the blind, and the lame,—but the incense of prayer and thanksgiving; and the pure offering of a heart cleansed by my Spirit, and washed from its stains in the blood of my Son." In this prediction, we shall consider,

I. *The subject brought before us.*

It is, that the name of the Lord shall be great among the heathen; and that, in every place, incense shall be offered to his name, and a pure offering. The first thing stated here is, that,

1. *The name of Jehovah shall be great.* "My name shall be great among the Gentiles." Melancholy, in every respect, is the view of the heathen world! Whether we consider its present corruptions, or its future prospects, its state is most awful! And all arises from this—that they know not God. But they *shall* know him!—and so know him, that his "name shall be great."

(1.) They shall know him as the only "living and true God," 1 Thes. i. 9; and that all the idols which they have worshipped, are but vanities and lies, and things that cannot profit, Jer. ii. 11.

(2.) Jehovah shall be further known among the heathen, not only as "the living and true God," but as a *Holy God*, a God of rectitude and purity—the very reverse of their present deities! What are the characteristics of these gods? Abomination! What, frequently, is their worship? Abomination! How miserably, then, is the human mind degraded, when its god and its worship are both abominable! Into what a wretched state of degradation, I say, must a human being be plunged, when the god whom he worships, and the worship which he offers, are all defilement and all impurity!

(3.) They shall likewise know him to be a gracious God, as well as holy (Psa. lxxxvi. 16; cxi. 4, &c.) What must be the state of mind of that creature, who approaches his god in the morning, trembling and agitated, with an earnest cry, "Do not kill me!" To such a man, can we not make known "the Father of mercies, and the God of all comfort?" 2 Cor. i. 3. And even, on the common feelings of humanity alone, can we stand by unmoved, while the goodness of our God is thus unknown to three-fourths of his intelligent creatures? Can you remain inactive, when you may, by his blessing, rescue them from the thraldom of such a bondage, and make them acquainted with him, whose nature and whose name are Love? 1 John iv. 8, 10, &c.

(4.) Jehovah shall be known among the heathen, in the only character in which man can know him with safety and comfort—he shall be known as God the Saviour, 2 Cor. v. 19. Towards the close of the forty-fifth chapter of the prophecies of Isaiah, the inspired writer, when speaking of the idolatry of mankind, and the character under which God shall be known among them, "a just God and a Saviour;" adds, "Look unto me, and be ye saved, all the ends of the earth: for I am God, and there is none else."

When we speak of his being known under the character of "God the Saviour," how many delightful reflections burst on the mind! He shall be known, to use the words of him who knew him best, and, therefore, could best describe him—his beloved Son—he shall be known as that God, who of his own mere mercy "so loved the world, that he gave his only-begotten Son, that whosoever believeth in him should not perish, but have everlasting life," John iii. 16. When he is thus known among them, his name shall be great and honored.

2. *And what shall be this honor?* "In every place incense shall be offered unto my name, and a pure offering."

(1.) Incense shall be offered, in every place, to the name of the Lord. The import of the expression in the next, that incense shall be offered to his name, is—that prayer shall be made. But, in considering this point, let us advert to the connection. The sacrifices preceded; and the prayer, externally exhibited by the incense, was afterwards offered. This is calculated to teach us a most important lesson. It is this: that *that* prayer only is efficacious in the sight of heaven—that *that* prayer only comes up before God as incense, which is connected with and dependent on the merits of the Great Atonement. In the view of this atonement it is that David says, "Let my prayers be set forth before thee as incense; and the lifting up of my hands as the evening sacrifice," Psa. cxli. 2.

(2.) It is added—"and a pure offering; for my name shall be great among the heathen, saith the Lord of hosts." The apostle Peter describes Christians as a "holy priesthood, to offer up spiritual sacrifices, acceptable to God by Jesus Christ," 1 Pet. ii. 5. Such a holy priesthood shall the heathen become, under the powerful influences of the grace of the Holy Spirit; and such sacrifices shall they offer!

But what are these offerings? David says, "The sacrifices of God are a broken spirit: a broken and a contrite heart, O God, thou wilt not despise," Psa. li. 17. Through the knowledge of the gospel, the heathen shall be broken down under a sense of their guilt, corruption, and misery. They shall come to God, not to plead their own merits, but, smiting on their breasts, like the publican in the temple (Luke xviii. 13), they shall offer the acceptable sacrifice of "a broken heart," and "a contrite spirit!" St. Paul speaks of another offering—"I beseech you therefore, brethren, by the mercies of God, that ye present your bodies"—yourselves, not the bodies of animals—"a living sacrifice, holy, acceptable unto God, which is your reasonable service" (Rom. xii. 1). This sacrifice also shall the heathen present: they shall offer unto the Lord, themselves, their souls and bodies, to be a reasonable, holy, and lively sacrifice unto him. Believing in Christ, as the Saviour who redeemed them to God by his blood, Rev. v. 9; and knowing themselves to be part of his "purchased possession," Eph. i. 14, they shall feel that "they are not their own, but are bought with a price;" and shall therefore glorify God in their bodies, and in their spirits, which are God's, 1 Cor. vi. 19, 20.

Finally. Praise and thanksgiving to God,

and every exercise of Christian benevolence towards man, are parts of that pure offering, which shall be presented to the eternal God. In the last chapter of St. Paul's Epistle to the Hebrews, the apostle dwells on this subject. Speaking of Jesus, he says, "By him let us offer the sacrifice of praise to God continually, that is, the fruit of our lips, giving thanks to his name. But," he adds, "to do good and to communicate, forget not: for with such sacrifices God is well pleased." The sacrifice of a devoted heart, the sacrifice of a grateful tongue, expressing itself in praise and thanksgiving, and the sacrifice of a benevolent soul consecrated to the service of God and of human kind— these are well-pleasing sacrifices: these are the blessed offerings which the now perishing heathen shall be enabled to present to the Most High God. Let us now consider,

II. *What ground we have to conclude that this prediction shall be accomplished.*

He makes the assertion at the beginning, and he repeats it at the end of the verse, to assure us of its certainty :—" For from the rising of the sun even unto the going down of the same, my name shall be great among the Gentiles; and in every place incense shall be offered unto my name, and a pure offering : for my name shall be great among the heathen, saith the Lord of hosts." We may argue the accomplishment of this promise,

1. *From the truth of the eternal God.* "God is not a man, that he should lie; neither the son of man, that he should repent : hath he said, and shall he not do it ? or hath he spoken, and shall he not make it good ?" Numb. xxiii. 19. "Ask of me," Jehovah says to the Saviour, "a 1 I will give thee the heathen for thine inheritance, and the uttermost parts of the earth for thy possession," Ps. ii. 8. Has not the Redeemer claimed this inheritance ? We may infer the accomplishment of this promise,

2. *From the power as well as the truth of God.* It has been said, that there are insuperable difficulties in the way of converting the heathen—that it is an idle thing to look forward to such an event—that you must first civilize them ; and, till you have conferred that benefit on them, you cannot make them Christians. But what says matter of fact ? Preach the gospel to them, as they can be brought to comprehend it : that will be the most powerful of all instru-

ments in civilizing them. Let the great work in the South Sea Islands bear witness! Let the rapid improvement of the liberated negroes in Sierra Leone testify ! Let the elevation to social enjoyments of even Hottentots, and Greenlanders, and Esquimaux, point out the path to civilization ! The grace of the gospel tempers the soul of even savage man, and fits it to seek after whatever may exalt human nature.

3. *The zeal which God has for his own glory,* presents another and a most forcible argument in proof that this promise shall be accomplished.

Having now offered such evidence as naturally presents itself, in proof that this glorious prediction shall be accomplished, it becomes us to bring the subject home to ourselves, and to consider,

III. *The line of conduct these truths devolve upon us.*

It pleases God to work by second causes; and, if this great prediction is to be accomplished, means must be used for that end. It is, therefore, one of the first duties incumbent on Christians, in order that this prediction may be accomplished,

1. *That those of them who are qualified for the work, should proclaim the truth as it is in Jesus, to the perishing heathen.*

2. *You should advance the cause of missions by your influence.* Your time and talents will be most nobly employed, in exciting in others a feeling and interest in the cause of the heathen.

3. *You should advance the cause of missions by the pecuniary means which God has given you.* The silver and the gold are his, Hag. ii. 8 : a portion of them has, through his providence, fallen to you; and it is but right, therefore, that you should use them for his glory and the good of his creatures.

4. *But prayer and supplication are still more important than the silver and the gold.* Oh, bear ever in mind, what it is that supports the hands of missionaries in the important and difficult work in which they are engaged—it is that grace and influence which God has promised to bestow on them.

APPLICATION.

1. Christian friends,—ere we part, permit me to ask you, or, rather, let each one ask himself, What am I doing ? or, How am I affected in this cause ?

2. Much, undoubtedly, has been done, of

late years, by the Christian world; much has been done by Great Britain; and much has been done by the Society, on behalf of which I am now pleading. But look to the world, and let me ask you, Has enough been done?—No! not one thousandth part of what should have been done!

3. In this labor of love, Christians, we must abound more and more. If ever, then, you prayed for the cause of Christ among the heathen before, pray more earnestly now; if ever you have used influence for the advancement of his glory before, use more now; if ever you have contributed before, contribute more now—that you may hasten the accomplishment of this Divine prediction, "For from the rising of the sun even unto the going down of the same, my name shall be great among the Gentiles; and in every place incense shall be offered unto my name, and a pure offering : for my name shall be great among the heathen, saith the Lord of hosts!"

CXX.—THE WILDERNESS MADE GLAD.

BY REV. JAMES FOOTE, M. A.*

"The wilderness and the solitary place shall be glad for them; and the desert shall rejoice and blossom as the rose."—*Isa.* xxxv. 1.

In prosecuting the idea suggested in the text, we shall, in dependence on Divine aid, take a view of some of the features of a desert, in which it resembles those of the heathen world; endeavoring, as we proceed, to show how, in the latter case, these features would be changed, or improved, by the introduction of the gospel.

I. *A desert may be considered as barren and uncivilized.*

So, in general, are heathen countries. But, instead of unfruitfulness and barbarism, Christianity would introduce culture, civilization, and every thing which, in connection with these, tends to promote the substantial comforts of life. The Bible and the plough go together—they are gradually penetrating into the inmost recesses of its deserts, where already the eye is occasionally refreshed by cultivated spots, like so many fruitful islands

* Preached before the London Missionary Society, at the Tabernacle, May 12, 1819.

rising from the bosom of the ocean. A wilderness may be considered,

II. *As a place of dreary solitude.*

It is here called, "the solitary place." But the gospel would introduce the endearments of society ; or, at all events, sweeten solitude itself. When we take a view of many parts of the heathen world, the want of human beings, the awful solitariness is most obvious. How numerous, how vast, and how beautiful, the tracts of country, both in the old and new world, where not even one rational creature exists to rejoice in the bounty, or to celebrate the praises of the Creator ! And where there are some inhabitants, they are often so thinly scattered, that the solitude is thereby only rendered the more sensible. Can this be a desirable state of existence ? It is also worthy of notice, that among even the more numerous tribes of savages, social enjoyment is but small. They are strangers to the more delicate pleasures of domestic life, and to the enlivening flow of sentiment. They have, indeed, their feasts; but these are seasons of diabolical rather than of human mirth. Then their extravagant madness often ends in scenes of rioting and blood; and it is always preceded by corresponding depression of spirits. Their habitual character, undoubtedly, is retiredness, melancholy, and taciturnity. On the other hand, true religion gives birth to those feelings which prompt man with confidence to seek man; while, at the same time, it enlarges the mind, and furnishes many rational and enlivening topics on which men delight to speak out of the abundance of the heart. I observe,

III. *That a wilderness may be considered as a place of inhumanity and cruelty.*

And that such are heathen countries, Scripture declares in these words : "The dark places of the earth are full of the habitations of cruelty," Psa. lxxiv. 20. How common in heathen lands has been, and still is, the exposure of female infants ! A missionary in South America once reproved a married woman, of good character according to the standard of character prevalent there, for following this custom. The defence she made proved at least, in the most convincing manner, the cruelty under which her whole sex there groaned. "I wish to God, father," said she with tears, "I wish to God that my mother had, by my death, prevented the distresses I endure, and have yet to endure as long as I live. Can human nature endure such tyranny? What kindness can we show our female children equal to that of relieving them from such oppression, more bitter a thousand times than death? I say again, Would to God that my mother had put *me* under ground the moment I was born!"

An excellent author, speaking of the Jaina, in Mysore, says, that "in a quarrel among the Brahmins, on account of some difference of religious sentiment, the party which obtained the victory, caused the priests of Jaina to be ground to death in oil-mills." He further observes, that at Tonoru, where this cruelty took place, though certain animals are very numerous and very hurtful, it is reckoned a very grievous sin to destroy any of them. Thus the very persons who shudder at the thought of a mischievous animal being killed, applaud the Brahmins for having ground the Jainas to death in oil-mills!

IV. *When we hear of a wilderness, we think of a place of comfortless sorrow.*

The promise that the wilderness shall be gladdened and made to rejoice, implies that it is previously the seat of sorrow and mourning. Assuredly the heathen world is a wilderness of comfortless sorrow, as it contains not within itself the means of soothing the sad distress with which it is filled. But such a wilderness would be gladdened by the gospel, which would bring home to the afflicted and the dying "the peace of God, which passeth all understanding," to "keep their hearts and minds, through Christ Jesus;" and through him, also, the powerful consolations of the Holy Spirit, the Comforter. Thus the promise would be fulfilled, "When the poor and needy seek water, and there is none, and their tongue faileth for thirst, I the Lord will hear them, I the God of Israel will not forsake them," Isa. xli. 17.

Lastly. *Like a wilderness, the heathen world is a place of awful danger.*

"I was in perils," said the apostle Paul, "in the wilderness," 2 Cor. xi. 26. "Where there is no vision the people perish," Prov. xxix. 18. We may hope that there are a few exceptions, in some way which we cannot comprehend; but most certainly, the general rule is, "Where there is no vision the people perish!" Those who have the gospel offered to them, and yet reject it, perish with a more aggravated condemnation than those who never had any such offer; but this does not render the state of the heathen safer than it would otherwise have been; for, in the words of the apostle Paul, "As many as have sinned without law shall also perish without law," Rom. ii. 12. A perilous wilderness, then, well represents the spiritual danger of the heathen world.

The subject may be applied in reference both to those in Christian, and to those in heathen countries.

1. *Let us improve it as furnishing ourselves with ground of gratitude and admonition.* How thankful ought we to be, when we contrast our own happy situation with the state of those who "sit in darkness, and in the region and shadow of death!" How thankful should we be, when we compare our present state with that of our heathen forefathers; for, in superstition and cruelty, the ancient Britons seem to have been equal to any savage tribe now on the face of the earth. Many are the advantages of a civil, political, and local nature which we enjoy; but it is the light of revelation which either gives them birth, or enables us fully to avail ourselves of them. "Blessed is the people that know the joyful sound," Psa. lxxxix. 15. "Blessed are your eyes, for they see: and your ears, for they hear," Matt. xiii. 16. But while we make this general acknowledgment of the goodness of the Lord, in thus visiting our land with the gospel of his grace,

2. *It becomes us to consider whether we have personally embraced it.* It is an observation peculiarly worthy of the wise man, that God "hath set the world in the heart," Eccl. iii. 11. Now, what is that world in the heart originally, but a moral "wilderness"—"a solitary place"—"a desert?" It bears no fruit to the glory of God; it knows not communion with its Maker; it is a stranger to every pure and substantial joy. But whenever the truth is received in the love of it, the result is "righteousness, peace, and joy, in the Holy Ghost." Let us ask ourselves, If the gospel be to us the chief source of gladness and rejoicing?

3. *Let us improve the subject in reference to the heathen, whose sad state we are now assembled to commiserate.* We have been often told, but we are not yet sufficiently impressed by the consideration, that not

one-fifth part of the human race have yet been made acquainted with the gospel. Endeavor, then, if you can, to form some conception of the aggregate of misery which exists among the destitute multitude. Think, oh think! of the unmitigated woe, and awful danger of "the waste, howling wilderness!"

While, however, the glory of this work is the Lord's, he condescends to employ human instruments; nay, according to his wise determination, such instruments are necessary. The ministry of reconciliation is committed to ambassadors, who are to beseech sinners to be reconciled to God, 2 Cor. v. 20. "How shall" heathen "believe in him of whom they have not heard? and how shall they hear without a preacher? and how shall they preach, except they be sent?" Rom. x. 14, 15. Hence the necessity for missionaries.

5. *But it is necessary for the Christian public to remember that the means of support must be furnished.* I am not disputing with those who are opposers of this work, but am taking it for granted that your appearance here declares you to be its friends. We are not entitled to dictate. Only be it remembered by us all, "He which soweth sparingly shall reap also sparingly; and he which soweth bountifully shall reap also bountifully," 2 Cor. ix. 6.

6. *Already, he who is to be crowned Lord of all has gained some of his most signal triumphs, in modern times, through this instrumentality.* Consider these triumphs as pledging thee to similar exertions; and then, at last, it shall be seen that thou wast honored to bear a conspicuous part in the full accomplishment of this delightful prophecy—"The wilderness and the solitary place shall be glad for them, and the desert shall rejoice and blossom as the rose!" Amen.

CXXI.—MEANS OF THE WORLD'S CONVERSION.

BY REV. CHARLES HALL,

One of the Secretaries of the American Home Missionary Society, New York.

"After those days, saith the Lord, I will put my law in their inward parts, and write it in their hearts; and will be their God, and they shall be my people. And they shall teach no more every man his neighbor and every man his brother, saying, Know the Lord: for they shall all know me, from the least of them unto the greatest of them, saith the Lord."—*Jer.* xxxi. 33, 34.

THE happy period predicted in this passage has been the desire and the expectation of the church in every age. It has been the burden of prophecy and of prayer. Thousands of the noblest spirits that ever walked the earth, as they beheld this consummation in distant prospect, have kindled into rapture; and, to hasten its approach, have tasked their utmost energies. The delay of this wished-for redemption of the world has ever been a subject of the church's lamentation. As we look backward over her history, we see her, in every period, prostrate before God, and crying, "Thy kingdom come!" while a long line of patriarchs, prophets, and saints, moving in sad procession, lift their tearful eyes, and stretch out their supplicating hands, saying, Why do thy chariot-wheels so long delay?

Who is there among us, having any sympathy with Christ, that has not shared in this feeling, and uttered this cry? How is it possible for a Christian to look out upon the world—to contemplate our race groveling in sensuality, and ravening with malevolence, until earth groans with suffering, and heaven weeps in pity—and not pray that the days of darkness may be shortened? Who has not often inquired, with inexpressible desire, for some more expeditious mode of evangelizing the earth? Who has not asked, If there be not, in the resources of Omnipotence, some more potent means than have ever yet been employed, to bring men back to God?

Such passages of inspiration as our text are adapted to quiet our impatient solicitude, not only by furnishing an assurance of the ultimate accomplishment of our highest hopes; but also by intimating the *mode* in which God's wisdom will operate to produce the glorious result.

I. *Let us inquire what instrument will be employed to bring about the blessed condition of the human family predicted in the text.*

This instrument is Divine truth, most expressively called in the text, Knowledge of the Lord: that is, the exhibition of the Divine character, more than any other truth, before all consciences, is to be the mighty engine, by which heaven will work out the moral revolution of the world. Do any, at first view, imagine that this is a means too simple to accomplish so vast a result? But what is it to "know the Lord?" or, rather, what is it not? All moral truth, every conceivable motive to goodness, is involved in knowing him—in a *true* idea of the holy Lord God. To know the Lord—to have the true conception of the REAL GOD—is the most perfect law which a man can have before his conscience. What is the moral law itself, but God's character—a catalogue of his perfections, written out in the form of precepts? The soul that knows what God is, sees intuitively what itself ought to be. He has only to present himself, as he is, forever before the mental view, in order to keep men under perpetual admonition of right and wrong.

You see, at once, why paganism is a system of wretchedness, even for the life that now is; and why Christianity restrains and blesses even those whom it does not convert, by continually holding up before them at least some dim portraiture of the true God. The power of the Divine character and example, as a persuasive to virtue, and preventive of sin, is immeasurably great. Such a conception as that of a perfect, almighty Being—the Upholder and Governor of all things, is the grandest of which the mind is capable. The idea of a present God, a real, living, all-knowing, all-pervading Spirit, having an infinite aversion to sin, and love of goodness, is a thought that bows down the soul in utter abasement, and sways over it an infinite authority. In proportion to the clearness with which this idea is apprehended by men, are they brought under the control of moral motives. It is, therefore, with a most beautiful propriety, that the Scriptures use the phrase, "knowledge of the Lord," as a comprehensive term for all truth and goodness. To know him, is to know his character, his government, his rights, his claims on us, and our duties to him. It is to know his plan of mercy,—his Son, and his Spirit—his pardoning and sanctifying grace. Let us now ask,

II. *By what methods and agency is this grand instrument to be applied to the renovation of the world?* How is this knowledge of the Lord to be spread all over the earth, and to be brought in contact with every human heart?

In reply to this deeply-interesting inquiry, we remark, that the Holy Scriptures, all along, throughout the whole line of promise and prophecy, speak in such a way as to imply two different and distinct eras under the new dispensation; and they very plainly teach, that the truth will be spread in a different manner in each of these eras. One of these is spoken of as coming after a certain state of things. Thus, in the text, "After those days, saith the Lord, I will put my law in their inward parts," etc. When the period thus indicated shall arrive, we are taught to expect a larger measure of the Divine influence—a measure quite above and beyond that which now accompanies the preaching of the gospel. This special influence will probably differ in degree, rather than in kind, from that which is ordinarily enjoyed. It will act more directly and more efficiently on the hearts of men. It will not be independent of all use of means; but there will be in it so much of God—the effects will be so speedy and so great, that means will be comparatively unobservable. Thus, in the text, this great moral revolution is ascribed to an immediate agency of God himself. The Lord saith, "I will PUT MY LAW in their inward parts, and WRITE IT in their hearts."

Other expressions, denoting sovereign acts of the Deity, are also employed: such as "pouring out my spirit upon all flesh," Joel ii. 8. "He shall come down like rain on the mown grass: as showers that water the earth."—"Truth shall spring out of the earth; and righteousness shall look down from heaven," Psa. lxxii. 6; lxxxv. 11. Such, then, is the way in which the knowledge of the Lord will be diffused in the latter day. God will, by his providence and Spirit, with amazing rapidity and grandeur, accomplish the renovation of the world. We know not how soon this happy period shall arrive, but come it surely will. The day is on the wing, when the empire of sin in this world shall be overthrown, and the crash of its fall shall reverberate afar through the dominions of God.

But ere that time arrives, there is another era—an era in which the truth is to be spread mainly through the instrumentality of the church. It is in *this* period that we are placed. The time has not yet come, in which God will specially interpose for the immediate triumph of holiness. He observes, and requires his people to observe, an established connection between means and ends. For all the good he will bestow,

"Thus saith the Lord God; I will yet for this be inquired of by the house of Israel, to do it for them," Ezek. xxxvi. 37. They shall reap only as they sow. If they desire his kingdom to come, they must deny themselves, and labor for that object. If they wish men to be saved, they must place truth before them, and press its claims upon the conscience. The language of the text teaches this—In that day, saith the Lord, "they shall teach no more every man his neighbor and every man his brother," etc. Observe, it shall *then* be no longer needful —implying, that *till* then it *is* needful to *teach* men, individually, to know the Lord. Here, then, we have the mode in which God wills that the great instrumentality for converting the world shall now be applied: it is by the direct efforts of his people to spread the truth. For the present, the command of God leaves this great work in the hands of his people. "Go ye therefore, and teach all nations," etc., Matt. xxviii. 19, 20. "Go ye into all the world, and preach the gospel to every creature," Mark xvi. 15. "How shall they believe in him of whom they have not heard? and how shall they hear without a preacher? and how shall they preach, except they be sent?" Rom. x. 14.

In this stage of the church's history at least, it is evidently the Divine arrangement that men shall be themselves the instruments of saving their own race. That this is the way to do a great work, we learn from the analogies of the natural world. How are the coral isles of the ocean made? Not by being upheaved by some great convulsion, from the bosom of the deep; but by the ceaseless labors of little insects, each of which works in its own place, and adds its mite to the accumulated mass. It stops not to form combinations and lay plans, but labors in its sphere. How is the huge globe watered, and made productive? Not by great seas, but by little streams, or, rather, by single drops of rain and dew, each refreshing a single leaf, or blade of grass. How is bread produced for the millions of mankind? Each stalk of corn becomes responsible for a limited number of grains. And, in the moral world, we see the same results produced in the same way. How is it that vice is propagated? How are drunkards, gamblers, and infidels made? Not by wholesale, but by individual contact. One corrupt heart infects some other heart: one polluted soul taints some other soul with the infection of its own depravity; and thus recruits are ever multiplied for the host of Satan. Let it be so in the work of salvation. Let each Christian labor to rescue his neighbor and his brother, and how soon will the world "be filled with the knowledge of the Lord!" Nor will such benevolence be restricted to its own immediate circle. A genuine concern for the salvation of *one* soul, is of the nature of the most enlarged philanthropy. Thus it has ever been. The men who have done the greatest good in the world, and most command our veneration for the sublimity of their benevolence, have begun their career of well-doing by blessing their own immediate circle. Some of our most devoted missionaries, were first missionaries in their own families and in their own villages. Thus it was with Martyn, and Brainerd, and Gordon Hall—this was the spirit of Harlan Page. Thus it has been with some beloved living examples. Ere they went abroad to foreign fields, they were living epistles among us, known and read of all with whom they came in contact. This is what must abound, ere the world will be converted—personal holiness, as the vital principle; personal labor, as the mode of effort; and individual persons, as the subjects.

APPLICATION.

From this subject we learn,

1. The true remedy for all our social and political evils. It is, by spreading the knowledge of the Lord. We must "teach every man his neighbor and every man his brother." Every Christian must bring the power of the character and law of God to bear upon some one or more consciences. Then, private friendship, truth, and righteousness, and public faith, and the majesty of law, will reign in our land! the Sabbath will be honored; the Holy Spirit will dwell among us; God will be our God, and we shall be his people.

2. We also learn the excellence of those methods of doing good, which exercise the conscience on questions of personal duty. Hence the excellence of all those forms of effort in which teaching is employed: the mother amid her children—the teacher of a Sabbath-school, or Bible-class—the faithful distributer of tracts—and, pre-eminently, the pastor and the missionary.

3. Finally. This subject illustrates the

mode in which revivals of religion may be promoted. A revival that shall penetrate the *mass* of the community, must be carried into it by the *living agents*, who are accustomed to mingle *with* the mass; and who will go hither and thither, attaching themselves to individuals.

Henceforth, let our course be the simple plan, not to wait for others, but each one do the *first good thing that offers*, and then the next—and the next; and thus proceed, filling up our lives with a succession of individual acts of usefulness.

CXXII.—THE ONLY REMEDY FOR A WORLD'S GUILT AND MISERY.

"The cross of our Lord Jesus Christ."—*Gal.* vi. 14.

In all systems there are greater and lesser principles—truths vital, or essential; and truths minor, or of less importance. So it is in religion.

Natural religion has, as its essential principles, the existence, the wisdom, and power of God. Revealed religion is based on the Divine authenticity of the Scriptures. Evangelical religion holds forth, as its leading truth, the doctrine of the cross of the Lord Jesus Christ. It is to this subject our text calls our attention; and which is identified with the avowal of the apostle, "God forbid that I should glory, save in the cross of our Lord Jesus Christ," Gal. vi. 14. Let us look at the cross of Christ in several lights.

I. *As connected with certain facts.*

These facts have to do with the death of the Lord Jesus. Observe, the hatred of the Jews towards him. See the tide of persecution rising until the waves go over his head; and, at length, he is arrested—tried—falsely accused—and deemed worthy of death. But the Jews cannot execute the sentence on him, inasmuch as they are now tributary to the Romans, for the sceptre has departed from Judah, and the lawgiver from between his feet, Gen. xlix. 10. Christ is, therefore, delivered to the Romans; and at their tribunal he is pronounced innocent: thus his righteousness is vindicated by the pagan ruler. At length, they prevail with Pilate to put him to death; and by this means the death of Christ is attested to mankind. Thus one of the main facts of the gospel is established, so as to set at de-

fiance the cavillings of skeptics to the end of the world.

Then follows, too, the manner of his death —crucifixion, a Roman punishment of the most barbarous and debasing character. Thus Christ's humiliation was the deeper; and hence the exclamation, "Who humbled himself, and became obedient unto death," &c., Phil. ii. 8. To this cross, Christ was nailed—on it he was suspended for several hours—and from it he gave his Spirit into the hands of his Father. Such are the facts: solemn—affecting—important

II. *In the cross of the Lord Jesus Christ we see the vivid illustration of Old Testament Scriptures.*

Here the ancient ordinance of the passover, having answered the end of a commemorative institution of the delivery of the Israelites, meets with its antitype—Jesus "the Lamb of God," stretched on the ignominious cross! Here prophecies which referred to the abasement of the Messiah, the violence of his enemies, his being "numbered with transgressors," his meekness under the grossest provocations, are all fulfilled. Had Isaiah been a spectator, instead of a prophet, living 700 years before the event, could he have been more clear and explicit? See Isa. lii. 14; liii. 7, &c. It is equally true as striking, that priests, Levites, and prophets all contributed, by type, and sacrifice, and mediation, to the interest which attaches to the cross.

III. *In connection with the cross of the Lord Jesus Christ the most astounding phenomena are presented for contemplation.* On no other occasion did events of so marvellous a character occur.

(1.) There was the supernatural darkness. "Now from the sixth hour there was darkness over all the land unto the ninth hour," Matt. xxvii. 45. A darkness so palpable, that it is said, the stars appeared; and this was for three hours, from the sixth to the ninth hour—from twelve till three o'clock. At a time when an eclipse of the sun was impossible; for it was at the time of the passover, when the moon was full, and opposite to the sun. Then,

(2.) As the high priest ministered in the holy place, "the veil of the temple," which divided the holy from the holy of holies, "was rent in twain, from the top to the bottom."

(3.) "The earth did quake, and rocks rent; and the graves were opened." Now, here was the finger of Deity pointing to the sublimity of the event which was to affect the destination of myriads, and universal nature bowed and did homage to the mandate of Jehovah.

IV. *In the cross of the Lord Jesus Christ the doctrine of the atonement is exhibited to the world.*

(1.) Either the Sufferer was innocent or guilty. Even Pilate attests his innocency, and washes his hands, as far as may be, from the guilt of his death, Matt. xxvii. 24.

(2.) His life was either taken from him, or he delivered it up. He had declared that he had power to lay it down, and he had power to take it again, John x. 18. He laid it down. "And Jesus cried with a loud voice, and gave up the ghost." He could have left the cross and saved himself.

(3.) He died for himself, or for others. He had done nothing worthy of death, Luke xxiii. 22. "He came to seek and to save that which was lost," xix. 10. As the good Shepherd, he laid down his life for the sheep. As the "Lamb of God," he was offered for the sin of the world.

(4.) He died either merely as an example, or substitute! It is evident it was both. In his own spirit, meekness—patience—clemency—devotion. But in his sorrows, Divine desertion—horror of soul—intense agony of spirit. "My God, my God, why hast thou forsaken me?" If a martyr only, thousands have had more joy, more ecstasy, &c., than the Prince of martyrs. How shall we solve the enigma? It is here: "He was wounded for our transgressions, he was bruised for our iniquities," Isa. liii. 5. It is here: "For thus it is written, and thus it behooved Christ to suffer," Luke xxiv. 46. It is here: "When we were yet without strength, in due time Christ died for the ungodly," Rom. v. 6. It is here: "Christ also hath once suffered for sins, the just for the unjust, that he might bring us to God," 1 Pet. iii. 18. It is here: "He is the propitiation for our sins, and not for ours only, but also for the sins of the whole world," 1 John ii. 2. It is here: "For ye are not redeemed with corruptible things,—but with the precious blood of Christ, as of a lamb without blemish, and without spot," 1 Pet. i. 18, 19. Finally, "Having made peace through the blood of his cross," &c., Col. i. 19, &c.

"See there, my Lord upon the tree!
I hear—I feel, he died for me!"

V. *In the cross we see the awful nature of sin, and the infinite tenderness of Divine compassion.*

God determined to punish sin, as it deserved; and to save the sinner, as he desired. He did both in the cross of Christ. He called to a guilty world to behold the infinite evil of iniquity. To see his hatred, his utter abhorrence of it. Its essential, irreconcilable contrariety to his nature, perfections, and laws, so that his own Son—his coequal self—his fellow—if he interposed for the guilty, this well-beloved Son must bear the falling shower of descending wrath. The sword must fall, and either the sinner or the Saviour must receive it. The flood—the destruction of Sodom, &c., had exhibited the evil of sin. But on the cross it is written in characters of blood; and that blood the blood of Christ, and that finger the finger of his Father.

What love to the guilty! "Herein is love, not that we loved God, but that he loved us, and sent his Son to be the propitiation for our sins," 1 John iv. 10. "God so loved the world, that he gave his only-begotten Son, that whosoever believeth in him should not perish, but have everlasting life," John iii. 16. We mistake the subject, if we conceive Christ appeasing and overcoming the dislike of the Father to us; for Jesus was the gift of God, and the evidence of his love to our world. "God so loved the world," &c.

VI. *The cross of the Lord Jesus Christ is that which is to affect the moral destinies of our world.*

(1.) Placed on the summit of Calvary, that it might not be concealed. Without the gate of Jerusalem, to signify the whole wide world's interest in it.

(2.) It is to be the spiritual magnet by which men are to be brought to Christ. "And I, if I be lifted up from the earth, will draw all men unto me," John xii. 32.

(3.) It is to be borne by the Christian missionary, not in the form of a crucifix, but as the grand element of the gospel; and wherever it goes it saves or it destroys—it kills or makes alive. It elevates to the Divine favor and heirship to glory; or it writes, on the brow of the unbeliever, his condemnation and everlasting woe.

(4.) Look at the church of God—the spiritual, universal, catholic church, including all saints, &c., they are distinct and separate from the world. They are saved, holy, &c. In each instance the change has been effected by the power of the cross. There is not an exception. Whether the convert be an idolatrous Brahmin—a savage New Zealander—a debased Hottentot—or an intellectual European,—the power of the change, was the power of the cross.

(5.) Contemplate the ranks of the beatified. An innumerable company of every nation, "From the east, and from the west, from the north, and from the south,"—and every one justified, sanctified, and glorified, by the influence of the cross. These have all "washed their robes, and made them white in the blood of the Lamb: therefore are they before the throne of God," Rev. vii. 14.

1. In conclusion. Let me say to the sinner, the cross is your only hope. And the radiance of the cross is sufficient to light and lead any, and every sinner to God. Oh! despise it not, reject it not; fly to the shelter of the cross.

2. To the Christian—the cross is your only boast. "Thanks be to God, which always causes us to triumph in Christ," 2 Cor. ii. 14. Self is abased—services disowned, as the basis of acceptance—righteousness disclaimed—an arm of flesh rejected. Say, with St. Paul, "Yea, doubtless, and I count all things but loss for the excellency of the knowledge of Christ Jesus my Lord," Phil. iii. 8. "God forbid that I should glory save in the cross of our Lord Jesus Christ, by whom the world is crucified unto me, and I unto the world," Gal. vi. 14.

Finally. The cross is the great theme of ministerial discourse. There are other doctrines to be taught; but, then, they are in connection with the cross. There are promises to be declared, but they are the promises of the cross. There are blessings to be offered, but they are the blessings of the cross. There are duties, but such only can be performed in the strength and grace of the cross. There are privileges, but they are the purchase of the cross. There is holiness, but it is the washing of the blood of the cross. There is heaven, but it is a heaven in the centre of which is elevated the cross. "The Lamb which is in the midst of the throne" will be celebrated in the songs of the redeemed forever and ever!

CXXIII.—THE GUILT OF NEGLECTING THE SOULS OF OUR BRETHREN.

BY REV. JOHN SUMMERFIELD, A. M.,

Of the Methodist Episcopal Church, United States.

"We are verily guilty concerning our brother, in that we saw the anguish of his soul, when he besought us, and we would not hear; therefore is this distress come upon us."—*Gen.* xlii. 21.

THIS subject affords a fine opportunity to discourse on the nature and power of conscience—the candle of the Lord. It is not necessary to inquire whether it ever be altogether silenced. *Sleep* and death, however, are two things. See the frozen snake —bring it to the fire! "There is no peace, saith my God, to the wicked," Isa. lvii. 21; they are always subject to bondage through fear of death.

Johnson said, Infidels are of two classes— fools and wretches: if they refuse to think, it is madness; if they do think, it is misery! Why did Felix tremble? Why were the joints of Belshazzar's loins loosed, and why smote his knees one against the other? Dan. v. 6. Why not interpret the handwriting favorably—as the record of his greatness? &c. Herod, though a Sadducee, thought that John the Baptist was risen again: his conscience was too much for his creed. The light will break in through some chink or other. M. de Staël said, "It was in the power of adversity to make every man superstitious in spite of himself;" rather say, Revive the conviction of a Deity.

See the text—comment on it. What similarity of circumstances was there in the situation of these men, that brought Joseph to mind?—famine!—strange land!—governor treated them roughly!—put three days in hold!—they feel they need pity! *Conscience* says, "*You* cannot look for it, for you showed none."

"Blessed are the merciful: for they shall obtain mercy," Matt. v. 7. We only knew the *fact* before, but now we hear of the entreaties which Joseph made—his tears!— his cry, O Judah, O Reuben, waxed fainter and fainter, till it died on the ear—and they sat down to eat and drink. *Wretches!*

You, my friends, are now indulging vengeance on them in their situation—but expend it not *all* on them! Some nearer you —I mean not your neighbors, but *you.* Have you never enjoyed yourselves when the cry of distress has been heard? Yet I mean something higher than this! While you sit down to eat and drink in spiritual privileges, what millions are in more pitiable circumstances? "We are verily guilty concerning our brother;" and I hope to bring this matter home, and convict every one of you!

(Thank God, "The Jews have no dealings with the Samaritans," is not a text often preached on in modern times. Bunyan said, "Master Prejudice fell down and broke his leg; I would," said he, "that he had broken his neck too.")

Mr. Ward said, "I have attended many missionary meetings in England, yet in all you indulge too much in congratulation; if you had seen the wide-spread fields of heathenism as I have seen, etc. *Nothing* comparatively is done; not enough to wipe off the reproach for long neglect." "We are verily guilty concerning our brother." We proceed, then, to notice,

I. *The sources from whence these convictions are to be derived.*

II. *What influence this ought to have on us.*

I. *The sources from whence these convictions are to be derived.*

We cannot condemn a criminal till we convict him. I arraign this whole audience! I charge them with guilt. Consider, then,

1. *The relation of the sufferers—our brethren!* This was the sting in the text—our *brother:* not a stranger, though then our conduct was merciless! Nabal. I hope there are none of his descendants here this morning; you cannot use *his* words in reference to any of the human race. God "hath made of one blood all nations of men for to dwell on all the face of the earth," Acts xvii. 26; all are *your* brethren. See the Hindoo, African, Esquimaux: each says, "Am not I thy brother?" I catechize thee, "Art not thou his brother by infirmities?" His follies and his crimes have stamped him man!

2. *The wretchedness of their state.* Joseph's state was nothing compared with those who address us. You say, however, "Joseph besought them; but the heathen do not beseech us; they are satisfied with their condition." The more pitiable! See the maniac: in his wild ravings he fancies himself a king: is he therefore to be less compassionated? I have seen the infant play with the ensigns of its mother's death. "Precious babe!" said I, "ignorant of thy loss!" So here: their "lack of knowledge" prevents them from being sensible to their condition.

But you say, "Joseph's brethren saw the anguish of his soul." True: and here I feel the disadvantage of my position. If you could but see what a missionary sees! Could I but lead you, not to heathen sensualities— to name which would be a shame—but to their cruelties! Could I show you the devotee lying on sharp spikes, or casting himself under the ponderous car of Juggernaut; could I fix your eyes on children leaving their aged parents to expire on the damp banks of their idol river, or parents casting their children to the crocodiles of the Ganges, or sons lighting the funeral pile of their mothers, you would not keep from me even a ring on your finger.

Philosophers sneer when we talk of the dreadful state of the East; and many Christians concede too much to them. I do not say, God cannot save a heathen; the *influence* of the *fact* of the gospel extends further than the *Revelation*. In reference to infants, this is certain, and Scripture itself assures us that "in every nation he that feareth God, and worketh righteousness, is accepted with him," Acts x. 35. Yet, after all, without a preparedness there can be no heaven; and Mr. Ward said he had not found any thing resembling real holiness among all the heathen with whom he had been conversant. Idolatry is not merely a weakness, as some say; it is a regular system of sensuality and crime. It originates in the vices men love, and hates the virtues which God approves. Do the Scriptures talk lightly of it? It not only tolerates vices, but hallows them; cruelties and crimes are sanctified. It is iniquity personified; yea, the devil deified, and hell incarnated! You inquire, "May there not be with God a secret method of saving the heathen?" I answer, if secret, we know nothing about it, and have nothing to do with it. If revealed, where? The Scriptures say, "Neither is there salvation in any other: for there is none other name under heaven given among men, whereby we must be saved," but the name of Jesus, Acts iv. 12. The heathen feel their guilt; yet they know nothing of the "fountain opened to the house of David and to the inhabitants of Jerusalem for sin and for uncleanness," Zech. xiii. 1. But we shall discover still further evidences of our guilt by considering,

3. *Our orders to succor them.* This succor is not optional with us. It is commanded in every injunction to benevolence and beneficence; and this must, of course, include the highest kinds of them. "Freely ye have received, freely give," is the Divine requisition, Matt. x. 8.

The goodness of the Master is often impugned, because of the wickedness of those servants who neglect or violate the command. (The brute on the seventh day.) One is rich and the other poor. Does God love the rich more? No; but only makes him his almoner: but if the rich hoard it up, shall the Master be condemned? Now, our Saviour said, "Go ye into all the world, and preach the gospel to every creature," Mark xvi. 15. Had the command been acted upon ever since it was given, the earth would now be "full of the knowledge of the Lord, as the waters cover the sea." "But if the gospel be so valuable," say some, "why has it spread so little?" I reply by another interrogatory, Has God no attribute but his *power?* We know that God will be able to justify himself, but we never shall be able to justify ourselves. "We are verily guilty concerning our brother." Another evidence of our guilt will appear when we consider,

4. *The possibility of affording them succor.* "Withhold not good from them to whom it is due, when *it is in the power of thine hand to do it,*" Prov. iii. 27. Our duty to the heathen is based on no impossibilities. Our inability is moral, yea, wilful. We make a difference between the means and the end; the end is his, the means are ours. There is a difference, also, between means and miracles. Miracles have ceased, because they are no longer necessary. Without them the Indian castes have been broken. Without them the Hottentot has been elevated and Christianized, though some said, the swine would receive the gospel as soon. Look, too, at the South Sea islands: long we endured sneers; but now behold language and laws, schools and churches, virtue and piety rising on the ruins of barbarism. If miracles were necessary, we should not have been so guilty; for we could not have furnished the gift of tongues. Yet we could teach them their native language. I repeat, then, that means are ours, and results are God's. If you knew a village perishing by

a disease, and you had an infallible remedy, and yet should withhold it, would you not be verily guilty concerning your brethren? If you see the unsuspecting traveller crossing a rotten bridge, and you warn him not, can you be innocent?

5. *Consider the facilities we have in this cause of compassion.* "If the prophet had bid thee do some great thing, wouldest thou not have done it? how much rather, then, when he saith to thee, Wash, and be clean?" 2 Kings v. 13. Our duty is to commence missionary exertions, whatever may be the peril. But have you gone forth at a peradventure *if* the heathen were salvable! No; you knew God's word; you knew "God so loved the world, that he gave his only-begotten Son, that whosoever believeth in him should not perish, but have everlasting life," John iii. 16. You knew his intention was that *all* should know him, "from the least of them to the greatest of them," Jer. xxxi. 34. Have we, then, ever done any thing magnificent enough to do justice to the declaration of his word? No!

(1.) *Providence* has favored us also. Governments have been favorable to civil liberty. Thus missionaries have not met with the sufferings we might have reckoned on. Not one out of the whole has been put to death!

(2.) The *grace* of God has been with us also. If no result had taken place, still our duty would have been to go. But God has blessed our labors. See the number of converts; your missions, though once feeble, have become strong, which leads me to observe,

6. *That even the efforts we have made in this work furnish evidence of our guilt.* What is our zeal? what the number of missionary societies? what think you of *one* preacher for a whole county? But see:

All missionary societies furnish but six hundred,* and there are six hundred millions perishing.

Are you now convicted? Is there no heart here that says, "I ought to have gone out in this work." Does not another exclaim, "I have not preached often enough on the subject:" and is not the language of a third, "I have prayed too little." And methinks I hear from a fourth, "I have given nothing as I ought! so little." And a fifth confesses, "I could have influenced others, though I could not do much myself."

---

* In the year 1821.

Ah! my brethren, we are all guilty—verily guilty concerning our brother.

II. *What influence should these convictions produce?* If sincere, they will produce four results:

1. *The depravity of human nature will be acknowledged.* This is denied by many, but there is no need *now* to go to Newgate to prove it. If man were not alienated from the life of God, he could not be thus alienated from his brother. You are proof of this degeneracy—the royal law has been broken.

2. *Deep and godly sorrow will be felt.* As in the valley of Hadadrimmon, you will retire in secret and mourn apart, Zech. xii. 11. Ah! brethren, we cannot mourn too deeply over this fatal negligence.

3. *It will lead us to apply to the mercy of God.* "Deliver me from bloodguiltiness, O God, thou God of my salvation; and my tongue shall sing aloud of thy righteousness," Psa. i. 14. The encouragement is, "With the Lord there is mercy, and with him is plenteous redemption," Psa. cxxx. 7. "If we confess our sins, he is faithful and just to forgive us our sins, and to cleanse us from all unrighteousness."

4. *It will awaken zeal.* A sense of Divine forgiveness will not make you forgive yourselves; you will be up and doing. It will operate, not as an opiate, but as a cordial. The inquiry will be, "Lord, what wouldest thou have me to do?"

But if this effect be not produced, I say, as Mordecai to Esther, "If thou altogether holdest thy peace at this time, then shall there enlargement and deliverance arise from another quarter; but thou and thy father's house shall be destroyed," Esth. iv. 14. So here—if you will not labor, the work will go on still, but you will be cursed!

Saurin would finish every sermon with reference to death; and Jesus said, "I must work the works of him that sent me, while it is day: the night cometh, when no man can work," John ix. 4. Life, then, is the only season in which you can serve your generation. Wesley would be willing to come down again, be despised again, and persecuted again, for the opportunities you now possess for making known the Saviour!

This may be the *last* collection—a dying grant.

What says your own welfare? I am ashamed to call on selfishness, yet God himself meets our weakness. The ark with Obed-Edom. Contrast this with the conduct of the Jews when they returned from Babylon, and neglected to build the house of the Lord. The penury they dreaded came on like an armed man. Hear the reproving language of the prophet to these idle professors: "Ye have sown much, and bring in little; ye eat, but ye have not enough; ye drink, but ye are not filled with drink; ye clothe you, but there is none warm; and he that earneth wages earneth wages to put it into a bag with holes.—Ye looked for much, and lo, it came to little; and when ye brought it home, I did blow upon it. Why? saith the Lord of hosts. Because of mine house that is waste, and ye run every man unto his own house. Therefore the heaven over you is stayed from dew, and the earth is stayed from her fruit. And I called for a drought upon the land, and upon the mountains, and upon the corn, and upon the new wine, and upon the oil, and upon that which the ground bringeth forth, and upon men, and upon cattle, and upon all the labor of the hands," Hag. i. 6, 9–11.

Public-spirited men, though not the richest, are generally the most successful. At least, when the ear hears them, then it blesses them; and when the eye sees them, it gives witness to them, Job xxix. 11. Yea, and devout men carry them, like Stephen, to their burial, and make great lamentation over them, Acts viii. 2.

What says your own experience? Have you lost by any thing done for God?

It has been said there are three principles in religion: fear, hope, love, and love the strongest! True; and no love like that a sinner feels to a redeeming God!

What encouragement more than from past success! even *one sinner!*

I am not sorry that these applications are so frequent—these godly vexations. Do you wish exemption from them? Are you now complaining that God is answering the prayer you have so often offered, "Thy kingdom come?"

Determine what to give, with reference to a conscience near you; eternal judgment before you; and the grace of him who, "though he was rich, yet for your sakes became poor, that ye through his poverty might be rich!"

CXXIV.—THE DUTY OF PECUNIARY CON-
TRIBUTIONS TO RELIGIOUS PURPOSES.

BY THE REV. JOHN BROWN, OF BIGGAR, NORTH
BRITAIN.*

"Who is willing to consecrate his service this
day unto the Lord?"—1 *Chron.* xxix. 5.

WE are met to promote an object, the
magnitude of which cannot be exaggerated;
and in comparison of which, the erection of
the temple itself shrinks into insignificance.
At the command of Messiah our Prince, we
are assembled to unite our deliberations, and
contributions, and prayers, for the erection
of a spiritual temple, in which not one favored people only, but "every kindred, and
tongue, and people, and nation," may present spiritual sacrifices to "the God and Father of our Lord and Saviour Jesus Christ;"
and it is he who now, by the voice of one of
the humblest of his ministers, proclaims,
"Who is willing to consecrate his service
this day unto the Lord?" The voice is on
earth, the Speaker is in heaven. "The Lord
is in his holy temple: let all the earth keep
silence before him," Hab. ii. 20.

My object in the following discourse, is to
illustrate and recommend the duty of pecuniary contributions to religious purposes.
But, instead of discussing this subject in a
general way, I wish to show that "whatsoever things were written aforetime (of the
liberality of David and his people) were written for our learning," Rom. xv. 4; and from
the passage of Scripture connected with our
text, to collect some instructions respecting
the manner in which this duty ought to be
performed, and some arguments calculated
to enforce it. Consider,

I. *The instructions in reference to the manner in which the duty of pecuniary contributions to religious purposes should be performed,* suggested by this portion of sacred
writ. We are taught by this passage of
Scripture,

1. *That in contributing of our substance
to the service of God, we should consider ourselves as performing a religious duty.*

It is a service—an act of duty; and as a
service consecrated to God, it is an act of religious duty. There are too many, even
among those who bear the Christian name,
who look on pecuniary contributions to pious
purposes as a matter not of obligation, but of
convenience. They consider it as discretiona-

* Preached before the London Missionary Society, at Tottenham Court Chapel, May 10, 1821.

ry to give or not to give. To withhold they
scarcely account a fault; to contribute they
view as a kind of supererogatory virtue. This
mode of thinking is utterly unreasonable and
unscriptural. Reason plainly teaches us that
we are bound to devote our property, and
every thing else, to the great purposes of our
being—the honor of God, and the happiness
of mankind. Christianity connects every
thing with Divinity—Whether we eat, or
drink, or whatsoever we do, we are to do all
to the glory of God; "giving thanks always
for all things unto God and the Father in
the name of our Lord Jesus Christ," 1 Cor.
x. 31; Eph. v. 20. The whole of the moral
as well as of the strictly religious duties is
described, as presenting our "bodies a living
sacrifice, holy, acceptable unto God," Rom.
xii. 1; 1 Pet. ii. 5; and acts of beneficence,
and almsgiving are, in particular, represented
as "*sacrifices*"—religious services. This passage teaches us,

2. *That in pecuniary oblations to religious purposes, we should give only what is
really our own property.*

"Moreover," said the Israelitish monarch,
"because I have set my affection to the
house of my God, I have of my own proper
good, of gold and silver, which I have given
to the house of my God," 1 Chron. xxix. 3.
The claims of generosity, even of the noblest
kind of generosity, must never be allowed to
encroach on the inviolable rights of justice.
"For I the Lord love judgment, I hate robbery for burnt-offering," Isa. lxi. 8. However much we may deny ourselves, in order
to increase our pious donations (it is scarcely
possible for us to exceed in this way), let us
never, in the slightest degree, trench on the
property of another. A third lesson respecting the duty of pecuniary contribution, suggested by this passage, is,

3. *That our donations should be liberal.*

The donations of David and his people astonish us by their magnitude. In addition
to the immense sums which he had amassed
during his reign for the building of the temple, he, on the occasion referred to in the
text, devoted to this pious purpose what is
equivalent to about eighteen millions of our
money, and his peoples' joint contributions
considerably exceeded thirty millions.

(1.) From the circumstance of the tenth
of the income of the Israelites being appropriated, by express Divine law, to pious purposes, it is surely a fair conclusion, that
among the middle and higher classes, in all

ordinary cases, Christians should not devote a less proportion of their worldly substance to the service of God. The liberal genius of the dispensation under which we live, manifested in rather fixing general principles, than in laying down particular rules, has certainly not produced in us its appropriate and intended effect, if it be used as a cloak for our avarice, pleaded as an apology for our parsimony; instead of being felt as an appeal to Christian honor, a stimulus to Christian liberality.

(2.) Another means of arriving at something like a general principle for determining what constitutes a liberal donation, in particular circumstances, is, reflection on the portion of our substance which we expend on what may be termed the comforts, the luxuries, the superfluities of life.

(3.) A circumstance which must be taken into consideration, in forming a judgment of what is a liberal donation in common cases (and this is the question we are chiefly interested in), is the degree in which God has prospered us. This is proposed by the apostle to the Corinthians as the measure of their alms-giving, "Let every one of you lay by him in store, as God hath prospered him," 1 Cor. xvi. 2. This passage further teaches us that we should,

4. *Present our pecuniary oblations from proper motives.*

In consequence of the decidedly spiritual character of the religion of the Bible, mere external action is accounted of but little value. It is only as it embodies right principle, that it assumes the form of acceptable duty. Donations for religious purposes, however liberal, if they spring from unworthy motives, cannot be pleasing to God. It is no uncommon thing to give to a religious institution from the mere force of custom—from an easiness of temper, which cannot resist solicitation—from the fear of censure—from the love of praise—from a dim, indistinct expectation that such an employment of property may have a favorable influence on the final destiny. In every such case, I need scarcely say, the donation, as a piece of religious service, cannot be acceptable to God; and as a piece of moral discipline, must be not only useless, but hurtful. They who give from such motives, can have no reward of our Father which is in heaven. The motives by which we ought to be actuated, in making pecuniary donations, are chiefly—submission to the Divine authority, regard

for the Divine honor, and sympathy for the woes miseries of our fellow-men. We are taught by this passage,

5. *That our pecuniary contributions to religious purposes should be yielded in the exercise of proper dispositions.*

In performing religious and moral duties we must pay attention to the manner, as well as the motive of action, though the shortest and surest way of securing the former property, is to secure the purity of the latter. Every duty has a set of appropriate tempers, in which it ought to be performed. Cheerfulness, humility, and gratitude, are those which should peculiarly characterize our donations for religious purposes. All these tempers were admirably exemplified by David, and his pious nobles. They gave cheerfully. "Then the people rejoiced, for that they offered willingly, because with perfect heart, they offered willingly to the Lord. As for me," says David, "in the uprightness of mine heart I have willingly offered all these things," 1 Chron. xxix. 9, 17. "God loveth a cheerful giver," 2 Cor. ix. 7. David and his people gave also in the spirit of humility. "Who am I, and what is my people, that we should be able to offer so willingly after this sort," ver. 14. Closely allied with humility is gratitude. "Now, therefore, our God," says David, "we thank thee, and praise thy glorious name," ver. 13.

6. *A sixth lesson, in reference to the duty of pecuniary contribution, taught by this passage, is, that we ought to connect prayer with our donations.*

The great object to which our donations are devoted, is one which no donations of themselves, however munificent, can accomplish. David added prayer to the liberal donations of himself and people, knowing that "except the Lord build the house, they labor in vain that build it," Psa. cxxvii. 1. "O Lord God of Abraham, of Isaac, and of Israel our fathers," said he, "give unto Solomon my son, a perfect heart, to keep thy commandments, thy testimonies, and thy statutes, and to do all these things, and to build the palace, for the which I have made provision," verses 18, 19. While we lay our humble offerings on his altar, let our ardent supplications rise before his throne. "Ye that make mention of the Lord, keep not silence, and give him no rest, till he establish, and till he make Jerusalem a praise in the earth," Isa. lxii. 6, 7. The last lesson, in reference to the duty of pecuniary contribution, taught us by this passage, is,

7. *That we should not only give ourselves, but use all our influence to induce others to give.*

We are to "consider one another to provoke unto love and to good works," Heb. x. 24. David did so; he not only presented a most princely offering himself, but he urged all his nobles to follow his example. "Who then is willing to consecrate his service this day unto the Lord?" Influence is a talent of odigious value, it multiplies a man's power of doing good indefinitely.

II. *The arguments calculated to urge us to the performance of the duty of pecuniary contribution, in the manner now explained, suggested by the passage under consideration.*

These are chiefly derived from the magnitude, the design, and the Divine appointment of the work to which our offerings are devoted, the inadequacy of the immediate agents, the pleasantness of the duty, the religious relations of property, and the short and uncertain duration of human life.

1. *The magnitude of the work to which our pecuniary contributions are devoted, furnishes a powerful argument for liberality.*

"The work is great," said David to the congregation of Israel. To erect an edifice so costly and magnificent as the temple of Jerusalem, was, no doubt, a great enterprise for such people as the Israelites, and called for the co-operation of all. But the work to which we are called on to contribute is immeasurably greater; it is nothing short of the Christianization of the whole world. A second argument for liberality in our pecuniary contributions, suggested by the passage, is to be found in,

2. *The design of the work to which they are devoted.*

The temple of Jerusalem was intended to promote the honor of Jehovah, and the welfare of the Israelitish people; and we find David urging its object as a motive to stimulate the liberality of the nobles. "The palace is not for man, but for the Lord God." The design of that great work to which we are this day called on to yield our support, may be viewed in a twofold aspect—in reference to God, and in reference to mankind; and in both, it furnishes us with invincible arguments for cheerful and liberal donations.

3. *The Divine appointment of the work,* to which our pecuniary contributions are devoted, should operate as a motive to cheerful liberality.

The building of the temple was expressly commanded by God. Jehovah said to David, "Thou shalt not build a house to my name, —but Solomon thy son, he shall build my house and my courts," 1 Chron. xxviii. 3, 6. This command, when connected with the circumstance that the donations of the Israelites were necessary to its being obeyed, was certainly a powerful motive to liberality. The diffusion of Christianity throughout the world, is plainly the will of heaven. This is intimated in the very nature of that religion. In "the Scriptures of the prophets," we have "the commandment of the everlasting God," that "the mystery, which was kept secret since the world began, but which is now made manifest,—should be made known to all nations for the obedience of faith," Rom. xvi. 25, 26. "I will declare the decree: Ask of me, and I shall give thee the heathen for thine inheritance, and the uttermost parts of the earth for thy possession." "All the ends of the world shall remember and turn unto the Lord; and all the kindreds of the nations shall worship before thee," Psa. ii. 8; xxii. 27. "All power," said the Saviour, "is given unto me in heaven and in earth. Go ye therefore, and teach all nations, baptizing them in the name of the Father, and of the Son, and of the Holy Ghost," Matt. xxviii. 18, 19.

4. *The inadequacy of the direct agents to the accomplishment of the work to which our contributions are devoted, is another argument to liberality suggested by the passage.*

"Solomon my son," says David, "is tender, and the work is great." I insist that without the support, the liberal support of the Christian public, all the admirably adapted agency will be utterly inadequate. The machinery is complete, but there must be the power to put it and to keep it in motion. Another consideration suggested by the passage, calculated to enforce the duty of pecuniary contribution, is,

5. *Its pleasantness, as exemplified in the experience of David and his people.*

"The people rejoiced for that they offered willingly, and David the king also rejoiced with great joy." Wherever the duty is performed from right principles, and with right dispositions, it is productive of pleasure. In this case the maxim holds true: "In keeping of God's commandments there is great reward;" and the words of the Lord Jesus are verified, " It is more blessed to give than to receive."

6. *The religious relations of property, as stated in the context, furnish another argument for liberality in our contributions to religious purposes.*

It is God who gives us whatever property we possess. It is " a good gift," which, like every other, " is from above, and cometh down from the Father of lights," Jas. i. 17. If we have inherited a fortune, it is by the arrangement of his providence that it has come into our possession. But this is not all. God is not only the Giver of wealth, but, in strict correctness of speech, he is its Proprietor. He can never cease to be the Proprietor of the universe, for it can never cease to be true, that he is the Creator of the universe. He gives us wealth, not in property, but in trust. Our wealth, if honestly acquired, is our own, in reference to other men; but in reference to God, it is not our own. " The silver is mine and the gold is mine, ·· ·th the Lord of hosts," Hag. ii. 8.

7. *Finally. The short and uncertain duration of human life is suggested in the context as a motive to liberality in our contributions to religious purposes.*

" We are strangers before thee," says David, " and sojourners, as were all our fathers: our days on the earth are as a shadow, and there is no abiding." The period for exertion is extremely limited. Yet a little while, and our property shall have passed to others, and over its destination we shall have no longer any control. " Your fathers, where are they? and the prophets, do they live forever?" Zech. i. 5. Many of those, who, at the earlier celebration of this our British annual festival of Christian benevolence, took a part in the solemn, joyful services, are gathered to the congregation of the dead. Let us cheerfully give a portion, a liberal portion, of that wealth to our God, the whole of which, ere long, we must surrender into the hands of his dread messenger. Solomon says, " Whatsoever thy hand findeth to do, do it with thy might; for there is no work, nor device, nor knowledge, nor wisdom, in the grave, whither thou goest," Eccl. ix. 10.

It is our consolation and joy that the progress of the work does not depend on the inferior agents—whose days are as a shadow, and have no abiding; but on the supreme Agent, who " is the same yesterday, and to-day, and forever," Heb. xiii. 8. " Thou art the same, and thy years shall have no end," Psa. cii. 27. And he will raise successive generations to carry forward his glorious designs. " A seed shall serve him." " One generation shall praise thy works to another, and shall declare thy mighty acts," Psa. xxii. 30; cxlv. 4. The magnificent structure shall continue to extend and advance, till it reach its destined dimensions; and then, " He shall bring forth the headstone thereof," amid the plaudits of all the innocent and restored intelligences in the universe of God; and it shall stand through eternity, the fairest monument of the power, and wisdom, and holiness, and love of the Divine Author. As it rises, and extends under our hands, let us raise the first notes of that anthem, which, on its completion shall peal through the universe, loud as the thunder of heaven, sweet as the music of angels, crying, "*Grace, Grace* unto it !" Zech. iv. 7.

CXXV.—HOLY GRIEF FOR GOD'S VIOLATED LAW.

BY REV. THOMAS ADKINS, OF SOUTHAMPTON.[*]

"Rivers of waters run down mine eyes, because they keep not thy law."—*Psa.* cxix. 136.

THERE is an eloquence in tears. They speak the language of nature, and they find their way to the heart. They tell us of human suffering; and in terms which, though silent, are most forcible.

There is scarcely, in nature, a more touching spectacle than to see a man weep; especially one of exalted intellect, of tried fortitude, and of enlarged benevolence. We readily believe that this natural expression of sorrow, proceeding from such a source, must be produced by causes at least proportioned to the effect, and we sympathize with both the one and the other. Such a spectacle is now presented to our view. It is a man in tears; and that man a saint, a hero, and a king. A man whose intellect, naturally of the highest order, had been carried to the utmost limits of human capacity, by sedulous culture and by Divine inspiration; whose undaunted courage had been tried, in a single-handed contest, with the monsters of

[*] From a sermon, preached on behalf of the London Missionary Society.

the woods, and with the gigantic defier of the armies of Israel; whose regal authority could levy a contribution on the resources of an empire, to minister to his enjoyments and to enhance his splendor. But he weeps; and the deep-seated spring of his grief pours forth torrents of tears. He weeps, not for himself, but for others; and they are the wicked, that "keep not the law." Observe,

I. *The affecting subject by which the sorrow of a holy man is excited.* It is the transgression of the Divine law. And hence it will be necessary,

1. *To inquire into the nature and extent of the law, the violation of which is deplored.*

"Of law, then," to use the language of the judicious Hooker, "there can be no less acknowledged, than that her seat is the bosom of God, her voice the harmony of the world; all things in heaven and earth do her homage, the very least as feeling her care, and the greatest as not exempt from her power; both angels and men, and creatures of what condition soever, though each in a different sort and name, yet all, with one uniform consent, admiring her as the mother of their peace and joy."

The law of the sacred Scriptures is only those principles on which the Deity proceeds in legislating over the moral universe, receiving that peculiar modification by which they are adapted to the nature of incarnate intelligences placed in a state of trial. It is a moral law, as it proceeds from the Moral Governor of the world; as it is suited to the nature of moral agents; and as those sanctions are moral by which the observance of its precepts is enforced.

This law, however, from its very character, is capable of being violated. As a moral law, obedience to it must be the result of motives, and consequently voluntary; and the power to obey, involves the possibility to transgress.

Such is the law which was impressed on the conscience of man in a state of primeval perfection; and by the violation of which he offended his God, and lost his paradise. Such is the law which subsequently was republished, by the audible voice of the Deity, from the bleak and barren Mount Sinai; and which, amplified to a fuller extent, and animated with more evangelical motives, appears in all its excellence in the completed canon of inspiration. The heathen, it is admitted, do not enjoy the noontide clearness of Divine revelation: night—moral night—spreads her sable canopy over them, under which storms and darkness lower. But the reflected beams of a traditional religion flicker around their path; the operations of nature and of conscience, as the constellations in the starry heavens, shed upon them a dim religious light; and all combine to reveal to man his prescribed path of duty, and to the transgressor his criminality and danger. Such is the law which the heathen possess; the transgression of which we shall now proceed to contemplate and to deplore.

(1.) This violation is deep-seated in its origin. They are *haters of God.* "The carnal mind is enmity against God," Rom. viii. 7. "What!" says the pious and learned Howe, "to be haters of God—the most excellent and all-comprehending Good! Be astonished, O ye heavens, at this, and be horribly afraid!—be ye very desolate!"

(2.) This transgression is no less flagrant in its modes, than it is deep-seated in its origin. At once, for an illustration and a proof of this fact, transport yourselves in imagination to the fields of Hindoostan. See the thirty millions of her deities personified in one, the Moloch of India, the horrible Juggernaut, whose throne is the bleached bones of his victims; whose worshippers are like demons; whose libations are human blood; and whose music is the fiendish laugh of disgusting obscenity, mingled with the din of confusion, and the groan of despair. Well might the unearthly Henry Martyn exclaim, when he beheld this spectacle, "I shuddered, as standing in the neighborhood of hell."

(3.) This violation is, likewise, universal in its extent. The universality of human transgression is a fact as true as it is appalling. The excellent Mr. Ward, whose sphere of observation was as extensive as his power of discrimination was acute, said, "I never found one that appeared to fear God, and to work righteousness."

II. *Consider the particular sources from whence this sorrow takes its rise.*

1. *This sorrow arises, primarily, from the recognized relationship of one common nature, existing between ourselves and the subjects of this defection.*

The poorest savage, that either toils in chains, or roams through his native woods, may say to us in the unsophisticated language of nature, by his hopes and fears, his joys and sorrows, the beaming of his intelligence, and the aspirations of his desire—Am not I thy brother?

> * * * * "Pierce his vein,
> Take of the crimson stream meandering there,
> And catechise it well; apply the glass,
> Search it, and prove now if it be not blood
> Congenial with thine own; and, if it be,
> What edge of subtlety canst thou suppose
> Keen enough, wise and skilful as thou art,
> To cut the link of brotherhood, by which
> One common Maker bound him to mankind."

2. *This sorrow proceeds, still further, from a due estimate of the importance of man, considered as an intellectual and immortal agent.*

"The redemption of their soul is precious, and it ceases forever," Psa. xlix. 8. Viewed in this light, the missionary cause loses the character of insignificance, which would seem to attach to a combination of a few feeble mortals and the collection of a few scattered sums, and arises to a majesty which, whilst it catches and reflects the rays of the Divine glory and throws the shadow of its protection over distant lands, buries the remote effects of its operations in the profoundest depths of eternity.

3. *This sorrow is still further increased by contemplating the imminent danger to which the subjects of this transgression are exposed.*

In considering the future probable condition of the heathen, it may be premised, that, in the equitable administration of the government of the universe, all beings will be dealt with according to their moral and natural capacities, and the circumstances in which they are placed; that punishment, if awarded, will be in proportion to crime—crime to violated responsibility—and responsibility to possessed or attainable means of knowledge. Were we, therefore, to take the lowest ground of concession—the mere *possibility* of the final perdition of the heathen—it would be easy to construct upon it an argument for strenuous exertion on their behalf; but when the evidence of their danger accumulates to a fearful magnitude, should not our zeal keep pace with our fears? As they pass along, they lift to us an imploring eye, to transmit to them the only revealed remedy to mitigate their present misery, and avert their future doom.

4. *This sorrow is augmented to the greatest degree by the dishonor which is cast by transgressors upon the perfections of the Most High.*

A prevailing desire for the advancement of the Divine glory, in all the possible forms of its manifestation, is the distinguishing characteristic of a holy soul. Hence, the Psalmist breathed out the fervor of his soul in that memorable prayer, a prayer which comprehends all that even he could desire— "Let the whole earth be filled with his glory! Amen, and Amen," Psa. lxxii. 19. Who can forbear to weep, when he beholds this globe, built by the hand of the Deity, and hung round with the mementoes of his goodness, designed to be a vast temple, resounding with awful voices, and filled with holy inspirations, now desecrated to purposes equally pernicious and vile; replete with foul images and filthy rites of idolatry; with daring acts of rebellion, and with sights and sounds of woe? Consider,

III. *The exalted character by which this sorrow is distinguished.*

1. *It is the fruit of Divine influence, and a collateral evidence of real religion in the heart.*

When the Spirit of God enters into the heart, he provides the elements of a benevolence the most exalted and refined.

2. *It assimilates to the temper displayed by the holiest of men.*

Thus, the sweet singer of Israel, amidst the cares of government and the splendors of royalty, found time and inclination to pour rivers of waters from his eyes over the wicked that kept not the law. Thus, the pathetic Jeremiah could exclaim (ix. 1), "Oh that my head were waters, and mine eyes a fountain of tears, that I might weep day and night for the slain of the daughter of my people!" And thus the apostle to the Gentiles, possessing as he did the most heroic resolution, the most lofty superiority to all the modes of intimidation and danger, a spirit that rose with its difficulties, and exulted in the midst of the most dismaying objects, yet combined the deepest sensibility with the sternest purpose, and melted into more than feminine tenderness, when he reflected on the moral condition of his fellow-men: "Of whom," says he, "I have told you often, and now tell you even weeping, that they are the enemies of the cross of Christ," Phil. iii. 18.

3. *It accords with the spirit evinced by the higher intelligences of the universe.*

The man who identifies himself with the best interests of human nature; who, overstepping the limits of country and of clime, embraces in his affections the whole family of man, acquires an angelic character ; and is only inferior to an angel, as his capacities are more limited and his nature less pure.

4. *It is in harmony with the principles embodied in the glorious work of redemption.*

That work, in all parts, from its commencement to its close, proceeds on the principle of the most exalted benevolence. There we see the eternal Father sparing not his own Son, that he might spare us. There we see the benign Spirit, to whom every form of moral contamination is essentially abhorrent, taking up his abode in the desolate dwelling of the human breast, to enlighten what is ignorant, to elevate what is low ; and though often grieved and insulted, yet neither deserting his residence, nor transferring his love, till he places the selected object of his compassion, with all his foes vanquished and his stains washed away, in the cloudless lustre of the eternal throne. But " oh for a pencil dipped in living light," to trace the lineaments of the Son of God. In him all the elements of goodness were found, yet so blended as to form one perfect and translucent whole. If, however, there was one attribute of his character which prevailed over the rest, it was compassion to the souls of men. Compassion breathed in his spirit, beat in his heart, beamed in his eyes, and lived in his life. He became the weeping Babe in the manger of Bethlehem, the weary Traveller in the journey of life, the agonizing Sufferer in the garden of Gethsemane ; and when the last scene of terror and of death arrived, he bared his bosom to the stroke. Nor did he stop till, by the mysterious oblation on the cross, he had harmonized all the attributes of the Divine nature in one triumphant display of mercy ; and had opened a medium by which compassion, without measure and without restraint, might descend to the vilest of the vile.

IV. *The appropriate modes in which this sorrow should be expressed.*

1. *One of the first and most effectual means by which this feeling is to be indicated, is by fervent and persevering prayer on behalf of the heathen.*

2. *Another mode in which this spirit is to evince itself, is by contributing pecuniary support to the missionary cause.*

There are some considerations arising from the nature of this subject that may serve yet further to enforce its claims. Remember that you possess that gospel which is an effectual remedy for the violation of the law. You possess that which alone can mitigate the present misery of the heathen, and avert their future doom ; which takes the burden from conscience, the bitterness from sorrow, and the sting from death—transforming that eternity, which they now contemplate with trembling horror or vain hope, into a boundless prospect of glory and of joy. Remember—that you can communicate these blessings to them without impoverishing yourselves ; for such is the plenitude of the gospel, that there may be universal participation without individual diminution—each may have all.

I would remind you that the stability of your expectations is equal to the goodness of your cause ; and that the same voice that commands your activity guarantees its success. This world, that was the scene of the Saviour's sufferings, shall be no less the theatre of his triumph and his joy. " His name shall endure forever : his name shall be continued as long as the sun : and men shall be blessed in him : all nations shall call him blessed !" Psa. lxxii. 17.

CXXVI.—THE KINGDOM OF CHRIST.

" Thou sawest till that a stone was cut out without hands, which smote the image upon its feet that were of iron and clay, and brake them to pieces," &c.—*Dan.* ii. 34, 35.

SOME of the most striking and magnificent revelations God ever gave in dreams and visions of the night, were those of king Nebuchadnezzar. It pleased God to select this distinguished and wonderful individual, by causing the most remarkable and striking scenes to pass before his mind during the hours of sleep. The signification of the dream referred to in our text, put the power of the soothsayers, at the time, to utter defiance ; but unto Daniel, the beloved of God, was given the spirit of interpretation.

The king saw a splendid image of a human being, mighty and great ; and which was particularly distinguished by the materials of which it was composed. The head was of gold, the breast and arms of silver, the other parts of the image were of brass, and the feet were partly of iron, and partly of clay. During the time the mind of Nebuchadnezzar was occupied by this imposing scene, he beheld rising up, a small stone cut out of the mountain without hands; that is, the agency by which it was brought out seemed to be invisible. He observed until this stone came in contact with the image, and smote it to powder, and scattered it before the winds of heaven; and the stone grew until it became a large mountain, and filled the whole earth.

It may be requisite for us, first, to refer to this image, and its literal signification; and then to see what this stone was intended to represent. By the head of gold was meant the Chaldean empire then existing; an empire which extended its influence through Egypt, Phœnicia, Palestine, &c., and on account of its immense wealth and opulence was compared to a head of gold. You perceive the breast and arms of this image were of silver—these had reference to the Mede and Persian kingdom. The two arms represented the two kingdoms of the Medes and Persians, which were united under Cyrus. Though these were very opulent and splendid, yet they were but as silver when compared to the Chaldean head of gold. The thighs of this image were represented as brass—this referred to the Grecian empire, founded by Alexander the Great, an empire which extended its influence through the greater part of the then known world. The feet are described as of iron and clay— here is a reference to the Roman empire, an empire as regards luxury, magnificence, and splendor, vastly inferior to the preceding empires; but as superior in strength, physical power, and endurance, as iron is of greater utility and of more essential worth than gold. The Roman empire is described as having two legs. It has been supposed, by some persons, that the two legs were intended to represent the eastern and western divisions of the Roman empire; while others have thought, it pointed to its secular and ecclesiastical power. And, then, observe this image as it regards the legs and feet: it is described as consisting partly of iron, and partly of clay, to show the great inequality of the various parts of the empire. Some parts should be strong, so strong as to appear to be impregnable as iron; while others should be powerless, and seem to possess internal weakness, like clay. Bishop Newton has shown, in his interest-

ing work on the Prophecies, that every sentence of God, in reference to this prediction, was entirely fulfilled to the very letter; and that the ten kingdoms into which the Roman empire was ultimately divided, were represented by the ten toes of the two feet of this image: so particularly and minutely were the predictions of God verified, in reference to this distinguished empire. As it respects the "stone cut out of the mountain without hands," and which smote the image and filled the whole earth, there is no difficulty of interpretation, this is clearly the kingdom of Jesus Christ. The spiritual empire of the Son of God—that empire of truth and righteousness which will extend its influence until the Saviour will overturn, overturn, and overturn, by which he shall possess universal dominion, whose right it is to reign, Ezek. xxi. 27. We invite your attention to several particulars connected with this kingdom, as presented to us in the striking and symbolical language of the text.

I. *It is evident from this representation that the kingdom of Jesus Christ is spiritual in its nature.*

There is something very graphic and important in the words, "a stone cut out of the mountain without hands." That is, the empire of God's Son is not an empire arising from the ruins of preceding empires; not an empire to be founded and supported by martial power or conquests. It is not to be a worldly establishment, or to have secular dominion. When Pilate asked the Saviour, he confessed that he was a King, but said, "My kingdom is not of this world," John xviii. 36. The throne which Christ erects, is a throne within the heart—the kingdom of God is within you. The laws of this kingdom are spiritual—the requirements of this kingdom are spiritual—all the arrangements, blessings, and ordinances of this kingdom are spiritual; they are especially adapted to the soul, and are intended to bring human beings into a state of loyal affection to Jesus Christ, and to a state of holy obedience and spiritual adherence to him.

II. *That the kingdom of Christ is unimposing in its nature.*

"A stone cut out of the mountain,"— mark, a stone, a simple stone, doubtless a small stone. We marvel not that Nebuchadnezzar should wish to know what that little stone signified. In this stone we see how strikingly is predicted to us the origin of the kingdom of Christ in the world. We find even the Monarch in one of the lowest conditions of life—born in a stable, and laid in a manger. When Christ came on his holy and divine mission, he had no illustrious individuals associated with him, or following in his train. His ministers were plain men, mostly fishermen—men without any temporal distinction whatever. He had nothing in his own person to attract the gaze of the human eye. A stranger to external pomp,—the reputed son of a carpenter. He wrought miracles, blessed the people, and delivered his doctrines to the world; and, contrary to all the opinions then existing, he pronounced the poor to be rich, the sorrowful to be blessed, and the persecuted happy, Matt. v. 3, &c. In Christ, and his cause, all was unimposing; and not one element of worldly grandeur existed to meet the carnal desires of the Jewish nation.

III. *The kingdom of Christ is represented as being progressive in its character.*

The "stone cut out of the mountain without hands," while observed by the king, increased; and it became greater and greater, and higher and higher, until it rose to a mighty mountain, every thing else being insignificant when compared with it; and, at length, it filled the whole earth. But in its progress to this consummation it came in contact with the image, and smote it, and ground it to powder. What a splendid representation of the progress of the Saviour's empire! It was originally a small stone cut out of the mountain without hands; but it grew mightily, and greatly prevailed. "And the stone that smote the image became a great mountain, and filled the whole earth."

IV. *This kingdom is to be triumphant in its achievements.*

It was predicted that the stone should smite the image, and the image was smitten. What victory more triumphant, what conquest more absolute, and what prediction more verified! Something might be gathered from the facts of past times, what shall be the result of every thing which sets itself up against God's anointed Son! Surely, as it is written, they shall be broken in pieces; this stone shall break in pieces every such image and power, that shall be arrayed against the progress and triumph of the empire of truth in the world. This stone shall come in contact with every established form

of false religion in the world,—with paganism, and its thousand rites; with Judaism, which the gospel has superseded. This stone shall come in contact with idolatry, that hydra-headed monster; and with another splendid image, Mohammedanism, which Providence has allowed to be set up and exist for centuries, and which has yet scarcely felt the power of Christian influence. Yet that foul image is doomed to fall; in connection with the papal superstitions, and all the multifarious rites of heathenism; whether they may resemble the head of gold, the breast of silver, the thighs of brass, or the feet and toes of iron and clay. Christianity refuses to coalesce with any of the systems and forms of religion men have invented, or set up in our world.

V. *That this kingdom will be universal in its extent.*

This stone must fill the whole earth. Not be as Judaism was, the religion of one land; but the religion of the world. All obstacles are to be removed, and universal power and dominion are to be given into the Saviour's hands, so that

"Jesus shall reign where'er the sun
Does his successive journeys run;
His kingdom stretch from shore to shore,
Till suns shall rise and set no more."

VI. *This kingdom is to be everlasting in its duration.*

In the 44th verse of this chapter it is stated, that this kingdom shall be forever; that is, it will be the last and closing dispensation connected with our world's duration. This kingdom is not like the Chaldean, to be succeeded by the Mede and Persian; the Mede and Persian by the Grecian; or the Grecian by the Roman. When this kingdom shall have attained all its achievements, the Saviour shall reign over all nations and people and tongues. Then shall all proclaim his praise, and rejoice in his dominion, which shall be an everlasting dominion, Psa. cxlv. 13.

In conclusion, observe,

1. The kingdom of Christ is associated with human agency. It is to be promulgated by means and instrumentality. He calls us to spread that gospel which we have received; and he will hold all his people responsible in this matter.

2. To extend this empire is the duty of every individual Christian. I should be satisfied to make this the test of a man's religion; because, if the love of Christ dwell

in his heart and soul, he will ardently desire Christ's cause to be extended. "There remaineth yet very much land to be possessed," Josh. xiii. 1.

3. Personal effort, in our respective spheres, is also necessary. The increase of godliness in our own land. The salvation of our families, and perishing neighbors at home. How much is yet to be done!

4. The enemies of the gospel will be crushed to pieces by the triumphant Saviour. The precious chief corner-stone, which will be a sure and stable foundation to the believer, will grind to powder the proud rejecter of God's Anointed. To all will the gospel be the savor of life unto life, or of death unto death, 2 Cor. ii. 16.

Finally. How glorious will be the day when this stone shall become a mountain, and fill the whole earth! When all the splendid visions of prophecy shall be realized! When peace and concord, righteousness and truth, love and mercy, holiness and knowledge, shall beautify our world! When the tabernacle of God shall be with men; and when one song shall resound from shore to shore, and from the rising to the setting of the sun. Hallelujah! Hallelujah! for "the kingdoms of this world are become the kingdoms of our Lord, and of his Christ; and he shall reign forever and ever," Rev. xi. 15. Amen. Even so, come Lord Jesus, come quickly!

CXXVII.—THE SPIRIT OF THE LORD THE BUILDER OF HIS SPIRITUAL TEMPLE.

BY JUSTIN EDWARDS, D. D.

"Not by might, nor by power, but by my Spirit, saith the Lord of hosts."—*Zech.* iv. 6.

THIS was spoken by the angel of the Lord, concerning the building of the second temple. It is the explanation of a vision, which was seen by the prophet Zechariah, the object of which was to show him, and through him, to make known to the people, a truth which it was of great importance that they should clearly understand, and deeply feel : viz., that while they must, themselves, make strenuous and persevering exertions to build the temple, their dependence for success must be placed, not upon themselves, or upon creatures, but upon the Spirit of the Lord. This is a truth of universal application, with regard to every good

work; and of fundamental importance to all people. For this reason God takes a variety of ways to make it known, and to impress it upon the hearts of men. And for this same reason, I invite your attention to it at this time. This temple is the church; that holy, spiritual building, which is "built upon the foundation of the apostles and prophets, Jesus Christ himself being the chief corner-stone," Eph. ii. 20. It is to be composed of all true believers who shall ever have lived, from the first moment of creation, to the last moment of time. They may not belong to the same denomination; or spend life on the same side of the wall which they have set up; but if they believe on the Son of God, and are so joined to him as to be "one spirit," they shall form a part of his spiritual temple. Europeans, Asiatics, Africans, Indians—all, of every age and color, and out of "every kindred, and tongue, and people, and nation," who believe on the Lord Jesus Christ, shall thus be "builded together for an habitation of God through the Spirit," Eph. ii. 22.

I. *From the greatness of the work which it was necessary to perform, in order to lay the foundation, it appears that the Spirit of the Lord must be the builder of this spiritual temple.*

It was a work which none but God himself could perform. Nor could he even do it, in the wisest and best way, though he was almighty, and had all creation at his disposal, in less than four thousand years.

The physical creation he could complete, and in the wisest and best way, in a single week. "He spake, and it was done; he commanded, and it stood fast," Psa. xxxiii. 9. But to prepare the way, even to lay the foundation, of this eternal habitation for himself, he must operate throughout the kingdoms of nature, providence, and grace, for thousands and thousands of years.—Nor is this all. He, who "was in the beginning with God," "and was God," must himself leave the glory which he had before the creation : take upon him "the form of a servant;" and labor, and "become obedient unto death, even the death of the cross," Phil. ii. 8. And as under its awful, crushing weight, "he bowed his head, and gave up the ghost," the sun turned away, the rocks broke asunder, and the dead started from their graves, to adore him that liveth, but *was* dead, that *they* might live for evermore, Rev. i. 18.

II. *From the foundation itself.*

This foundation is the Son of God—" the brightness of his Father's glory, and the express image of his person," Heb. i. 3 ; in whom "dwelleth all the fulness of the Godhead bodily," Col. ii. 9. "By him were all things created, that are in heaven, and that are in earth, visible and invisible, whether they be thrones, or dominions, or principalities, or powers : all things were created by him, and for him : and he is before all things, and by him all things consist ;"— and he "is over all, God blessed forever," Col. i. 16 ; Rom. ix. 5. To him the Father saith, and he knows, " Thy throne, O God, is forever and ever : a sceptre of righteousness is the sceptre of thy kingdom," Psa. xlv. 6 ; Heb. i. 8. Such is the foundation of this temple—" God manifest in the flesh," 1 Tim. iii. 16. "Behold I lay in Zion for a foundation, a stone, a tried stone, a precious corner-stone, a sure foundation," Isa. xxviii. 16. "For other foundation can no man lay than that is laid, which is Jesus Christ,— the true God, and eternal life," 1 Cor. iii. 11 ; 1 John v. 20.

III. *From the materials out of which the temple is to be made.*

These, as they are in their natural state, universally ; and as they would be, without the Spirit and grace of God, eternally, are described by him, as walking "according to the course of this world, according to the prince of the power of the air, the spirit that now worketh in the children of disobedience : among whom also we all had our conversation in times past in the lusts of our flesh, fulfilling the desires of the flesh and of the mind ; and were by nature the children of wrath, even as others," Eph. ii. 22, 23. And who can take these materials and make them alive, and fill them with "love, joy, peace, long-suffering, gentleness, goodness, meekness, faith, and temperance" (Gal. v. 22, 23), but he who "spake, and it was done ;" who "commanded, and it stood fast ?" Can you do it ? Can any man do it ? Let him make the experiment. And to make it under the most favorable circumstances, let him be a parent, and try it upon his own child. Let him renounce all dependence on God, and the influences of his Spirit, and then take that child, who is now an enemy to his Maker, and, if he can, create him "anew in Christ Jesus unto good works," and cause him to glow like a seraph in the Divine service. No ; not an infidel parent on earth can do this ; and not a Christian parent will dare to attempt it. All the dedications of children to God in baptism ; all the prayers and tears of pious parents while wrestling with God for their salvation, are a standing testimony that the work must be done, not by might, nor by power, but by the Spirit of God. Even children, to be alive unto God, "must be born again ;" "not of blood, nor of the will of the flesh, nor of the will of man, but of God," John iii. 7 ; i. 13. Does any one still doubt ? Let him try the experiment upon *himself.*

Has any one ever done this, of himself merely—by his own unaided wisdom, righteousness, and strength, without the Spirit and grace of God ? Who is he ? When, or where ? Go through creation, and ask every soul that has "passed from death unto life," Who made you to differ ? How were you saved ? And they will all answer, "By grace were we saved through faith ; and that not of ourselves, it was the gift of God," Eph. ii. 8. That God must be the Builder of this glorious edifice, is, if possible, still more plain,

IV. *From the object for which it is to be created.*

The object for which this spiritual temple is to be erected is, to show angels, "principalities, and powers, in heavenly places,— *the manifold wisdom of God,*" Eph. iii. 10. Oh the exceeding riches of his grace in *his kindness towards men, through Jesus Christ :* an object which is infinite ; and which, as it unfolds with ever-increasing brightness, will call forth, from multitudes which no man can number, in louder and louder strains, Alleluias to God and the Lamb, forever and ever. Who can accomplish this but God himself ? Can an angel do it ? Can a superangelic creature ? Can any creature, however exalted, show, by his productions, the manifold wisdom of God ? No man, or angel, or superangelic creature, can conceive a thousandth part of the riches of that grace, which, at such a sacrifice, has opened an eternity of bliss to a world infinitely undeserving.

But suppose he could conceive, and could display all the riches of that grace, he could not be the builder of this temple ; for Jehovah will not give his glory to another, Isa. xlii. 8. And the object of this temple is, not that any creature may display, but that God may display the exceeding riches of his grace, and his manifold wisdom. Of course, no creature can build it : for no creature can display wisdom which he does not possess ; and no building can display more wisdom than is possessed by the builder. But this building is to display more, infinitely more, than is possessed by all creatures in the universe.

(1.) In conclusion. If the Spirit of the Lord is the builder of this temple, no one will ever become a part of it, without being prepared for it by him.

(2.) As the Spirit of the Lord is the builder of this temple, his materials will all be perfectly prepared. However unsightly, or dark, or distant, and totally unfit to form a part of such an edifice, "God, who commanded the light to shine out of darkness," will shine down, not only upon them, and around them, but "into their hearts, to give them the light of the knowledge of the glory of God in the face of Jesus Christ," 2 Cor. iv. 6. And they shall not only see light, but themselves become light in the Lord, Eph. v. 8.

(3.) As the Spirit of the Lord is the builder of this temple, any individual to whom he is made known, and who is in a state of probation, may himself become a part of it. Wherever he may live, and under whatever circumstances he may be placed ; however long he may have been in rebellion against God, and however deeply he may have sunk in degradation and guilt ; he may, nevertheless, be transformed into the Divine image, and live.

(4.) As the Spirit of the Lord is the builder of this temple, we see what each one must do, in order to be prepared for it. He must become acquainted with the Holy Spirit, and must look to him for what he needs. He must attend to his communications—must understand, believe, and obey them. They will thus be spirit and life to his soul.

(5.) As the Spirit of the Lord is the builder of this temple, and he operates by the truth, we see the reason why a knowledge of the Spirit and of his truth, should be communicated, in the least possible time, to all people. All people need this knowledge. They are in imminent danger of perishing eternally without it. It is suited to their condition, and adapted to meet their wants. Nothing else will do it. We have this remedy ! freely we have received, and freely we are bound to give. God commands,

"Go ye into all the world, and preach the gospel to every creature," Mark xvi. 15.

(6.) We see, in view of this subject, that the missionary of the cross is engaged in a great and glorious work. Men may, if they will, view him with pity or contempt—as a wild enthusiast, or blind fanatic. God views him as a co-worker with himself, in preparing his own eternal habitation.

(7.) As the Spirit of the Lord is the author and finisher of this work, all are bound to be instant, sincere, fervent, and persevering, not only in labors, but in supplication to him, that their efforts, and the efforts of others, may not be in vain in the Lord. Without his influence, though you put a Bible into every family, and preach the gospel to every creature, not a blind eye will be opened, not a deaf ear be unstopped, nor a hard heart will be softened, nor a distant soul be brought nigh by the blood of Jesus. Not a living soul will ever shine in that living temple ; but all be cold, motionless, and dead.

(8.) As the Spirit of the Lord is the builder of this temple, it will be completed. For four thousand years he was preparing to lay the foundation ; and that is now done. For six thousand years he has been preparing the materials, and taking them on to the spot. And has HE begun, and will he not make an end ? Shall any of his enemies ever taunt him, and say, "He began to build, and was not able to finish ?" No. Let difficulties accumulate till they fill the whole earth, and rise up to heaven. "Who art thou, O great mountain ? before Zerubbabel thou shalt become a plain ; and he shall bring forth the head-stone thereof with shoutings, crying, GRACE, GRACE UNTO IT," Zech. iv. 7.

CXXVIII.—NATURE AND IMPORTANCE OF CHRISTIAN ZEAL.

"And your zeal hath provoked very many."— *2 Cor.* ix. 2.

THE apostle is pleading the cause of Christian liberality. He exhibits a delightful instance of this in the case of the Macedonian Church. Their liberality is described as abounding to the extent of their power— beyond their power : their contributions were urged upon the apostles, yea, urged with much entreaty. But you say, doubt-less they were rich : but if so, they could only do according to their ability. But the truth is, they were poor, in great trials, and yet they were ensamples of liberality to all the other churches. The apostle commends the liberality of the Corinthians in the verse preceding our text, and then states the influ-ence of their zeal on others. If the main-tenance of Christianity in our own souls, and its diffusion in our own churches, be greatly dependent on the spirit of zeal, how much more the dissemination of the gospel among the perishing heathen, where obstacles of an almost insuperable kind seem to im-pede the advancement of the kingdom of Christ !

I. *Let us, then, consider the nature of Christian zeal.*

The word is derived from the Greek, zelos, the root of which, zeo, signifies to boil, to be hot, etc. Therefore, when applied to the mind, it signifies fervor—an impassioned, ardent state of mind. It is the opposite of listlessness, apathy, and coldness.

1. *Christian zeal is spiritual in its origin.*

It is not natural for man to be religiously zealous. A man may be so in sin, as was Manasseh ; a zealous Pharisee, as Saul of Tarsus. Or a man may have sectarian zeal, and be an ardent bigot ; or superstitious zeal, as the devotees of idolatry. But, un-less a man have the Spirit of God, he can-not have the zeal of the Christian. This flame must be enkindled by the fire of the Holy Ghost. It must descend from heaven on the altar of our souls.

2. *It is intellectual in its character.*

The Jews had a zeal, but it was not " according to knowledge ; so, the apostle Paul was a zealous persecutor, but he did it ignorantly, etc., 1 Tim. i. 13. Now, Chris-tian zeal is not like the fire and smoke which issue from the volcano ; but like the burning rays of the noontide sun—bright, clear, and glorious. A Christian has a rea-son for his zeal, as well as his hope. It is associated with a why and a wherefore. A principle based on sanctified reason.

3. *It is modest and humble in its preten-sions.*

There is a zeal of show, and glare, and pretension. A zeal, which only aims at the exaltation of its possessor, like that of Jehu of old, when he said to Jehonadab, " Come with me, and see my zeal for the Lord," 2 Kings x. 16, etc. It is essential to this

kind of zeal that it must be seen and be applauded, or it will expire. The Pharisees were clad in this. Peter, in his early pro-fession, was characterized by it. " Though all men shall be offended because of thee, yet will I never be offended," Matt. xxvi. 33. How different afterwards—" Simon, son of Jonas, lovest thou me ?" " Yea, Lord, thou knowest that I love thee," John xxi. 16. Christian zeal is diffident and retiring, seek-ing to exalt Christ only.

4. *It is consistent and enduring in its in-fluence.*

The Galatians were zealous, but they ran well only for a time, Gal. iii. The zeal of many is merely spasmodic—a disease, and not health. Or, in many cases, it is like the flaming forth of the eccentric comet, attract-ing general attention, and then passing away. But Christian zeal is the healthy action of the heart, indicating vigor of spirit. It is like the morning light, " that shineth more and more unto the perfect day," Prov. iv. 18.

5. *It is diligent and active in its efforts.*

A man may have a creed in which zeal is an item. Zealous profession—zealous de-sires—zealous principles and intentions—zealous prayers. But let us see these carried out—carried out " in works of faith and la-bors of love." Christian zeal toils and la-bors, etc. Zeal is embodied. It has an ear to hearken to God's commands ; feet to run in the way of usefulness ; the hand to work, and the "houlder to bear burdens ; and a spirit of noble activity and enterprise in the things of God.

6. *It is kind and affectionate in its spirit.*
Christian zeal is not the fire of wrath to hate, of anger to curse, or of presumption to an-athematize ; but of heaven to warm and to bless. It is always in company with the chief of the graces, " charity ;" and there-fore " envieth not," and " thinketh no evil," 1 Cor. xiii. It does not dwell on Sinai, but in Zion. It does not love the tempest, and the thunderings and earthquake ; but the calm serenity of Tabor or Olivet. It has the eagle's eye, and soars upwards ; but the nature and gentleness of the dove. It has the power of the ox, and the courage of the lion ; but the nature of the lamb. It hates sin, but yearns over the sinner ; it denounces vice, but tries to rescue its victim. It de-plores the misery of the world, and ardently prays and labors for its removal. It ascends, and brings the live coal from the celestial

altar, and with it labors to provoke others to love and good works. Consider,

II. *The spheres in which it may be exercised.* These are numberless, but they may be compressed in two.

1. *In securing all the good within its power.*

Zealous in attaining the gifts and graces of the Spirit of God. In seeking knowledge —spiritual power —— conformity to Christ, and meetness for the Divine glory. It must be exercised in mortifying sin—self-denial—growth in grace, etc. All that is included in spiritual, practical, and experimental religion.

2. *In communicating all possible good to others.*

Exerting a beneficial influence on society. Imitating Christ, "who went about doing good." Removing ignorance, reclaiming the vicious, exhorting the careless, reproving the wicked, guiding the inquirer, and comforting the afflicted. This is its motto—"Let us do good unto all men," etc. What a sphere is the missionary field, where untold millions are "living without God, and without hope in the world!" Where the avenues of death are eternally crowded with deathless beings, who are hurrying, in a state of ignorance and pollution, into the eternal world!

III. *The principles on which it should be cultivated.*

1. *It is an essential characteristic of true religion.*

The poet has well said,

> "Religion, without zeal and love,
>   Is but an empty name."

Look over the record of the saints, the excellent of the earth: Noah, Abraham, Jacob, Moses, Caleb, and Joshua; Samuel, David, Elijah, Isaiah, the Baptist, Paul, the early Christians, the Corinthians, etc. It is the spiritual heat of the new life. The sustaining principle in labors, etc.

2. *It is a distinguishing trait in the most excellent order of beings.*

"Who maketh his angels spirits, and his ministers a flame of fire," Heb. i. 7. Seraphim are described as burning ones—they are all ardor, intensity, etc. But I refer Christians especially to the world's Redeemer.

"And he saw that there was no man, and wondered that there was no intercessor: therefore his arm brought salvation unto him; and his righteousness it sustained him.

For he put on righteousness as a breastplate, and an helmet of salvation upon his head; and he put on the garments of vengeance for clothing, and was clad with zeal as a cloak," Isa. lix. 16, 17. He enters on his incarnate state. At twelve years of age, he exclaimed, "Wist ye not that I must be about my Father's business?" He commences his life of sorrow, etc. He sees the tempest before him—the whole was palpable to him, yet he exclaims, "I have a baptism to be baptized with, and how am I straitened till it be accomplished," Luke xii. 50. He crowds a long life of labors into the limits of three years. He then treads the winepress alone—stands in the fearful gap—and ends his toils and sufferings and life together.

3. *It is essential to the triumphs of the church.*

We believe in the final overthrow of sin, and Satan's kingdom. In the millennial glory of the church of Christ. But can it be without zeal on the part of Christians. Three things are essential: the diffusion of unmixed truth—the maintenance of evangelical purity—and the cultivation of intense zeal. Think of the difficulties; of the opposition; of the warring elements, etc.; and say, can we dispense with zeal? Political parties cannot—commerce cannot—science cannot—the cause of freedom cannot,—much less religion.

APPLICATION.

1. Let me urge you to seek after the attainment of this Christian principle. Let me provoke you to zeal. Look at the zeal of Pagans, Mohammedans. Look at the zeal of the worldly. Look at the zeal of the Romish church. Look at the zeal of the infidel.

2. Think of the magnitude of the objects you contemplate. Your designs have to do with the everlasting interests of your own souls, etc.; of those around you; and all the unenlightened heathen—you act for eternity.

3. Think of the limited period of your opportunities. Where are the first friends of the gospel in this island? Where the Puritans? Where are our friends? "Your fathers, where are they?" Go to the graveyard, there lie their sleeping remains; their record is on high—though dead they yet speak to us. Remember, "Whatsoever thy hand findeth to do, do it with thy might; for there is no work, nor device, nor knowledge, nor wisdom, in the grave, whither

thou goest," Eccl. ix. 10. Think of the zeal of those who consecrate themselves to the missionary work. What self-denial they endure, and what sacrifices they make! What enjoyments they surrender! What trials they encounter! What sufferings they sustain! A true missionary must hazard his life for Christ, and for the souls of the heathen. Then let our zeal at home sustain, and cheer, and encourage them; yea, let our "zeal provoke very many."

CXXIX.—JESUS THE TRUE MESSIAH.

BY REV. ANDREW FULLER.*

"Sacrifice and offering thou didst not desire; mine ears hast thou opened: burnt-offering and sin-offering hast thou not required. Then said I, Lo, I come: in the volume of the book it is written of me, I delight to do thy will, O my God: yea, thy law is within my heart."—*Psa.* xl. 6-8.

No Christian can doubt whether the passage relates to the Messiah, seeing it is expressly applied to him in the New Testament, Heb. x. 5-10; and, if a Jew should raise an objection, he will find it difficult, if not impossible, to give a fair exposition of it on any other principle. Who else, with propriety, could use the language here used? Certainly, David could not. Whether the Messiah, therefore, be already come, as we believe, or be yet to come, as the body of the Jewish nation believes, it must be of his coming that the prophet speaks. The question at issue between them and us, is not whether the Scriptures predict and characterize the Messiah: but, whether these predictions and characters be fulfilled in Jesus?

That we may be able to judge of this question, let it be observed, that there are three characters held up in the passage I have read, as distinguishing the Messiah's coming: viz., that the sacrifices and ceremonies of the Mosaic law would, from thence, be superseded; that the great body of Scripture prophecy would be accomplished; and that the will of God would be perfectly fulfilled. Let us calmly and candidly try the question at issue by these characters.

I. *It is intimated that whenever the Messiah should come the sacrifices and ceremonies of the Mosaic law were to be superseded by him.*

* Preached in the Jews' Chapel, Church-street, Spitalfields, 1809.

"Sacrifice and offering thou didst not desire;—then said I, Lo, I come." I am aware that modern Jewish writers contend for the perpetuity of the ceremonial, as well as of the moral law; but in this they are opposed both by Scripture and by fact. As to Scripture, it is not confined to the passage I have read, nor to a few others. It is common for the sacred writers of the Old Testament to speak of sacrifices and ceremonies in a depreciating strain, such as would not, I presume, have been used, had they been regarded for their own sake, or designed to continue always. Such is the language of the following passages: see 1 Sam. xv. 22; Psa. l. 7-15; li. 16, 17; Isa. i. 11, 12; Jer. vii. 21-23; Dan. ix. 27.

Is it not, then, in perfect harmony with the tenor of these Scriptures, that Messiah, when described as coming into the world, should say, "Sacrifice and offering thou didst not desire; mine ears hast thou opened: burnt-offering and sin-offering hast thou not required. Then said I, Lo, I come?"—plainly intimating that he would come to accomplish that which could not be accomplished by sacrifices and offerings; and that, as these were but the scaffolding of his temple, when that should be reared, these should, of course, be taken down. See also Jer. xxxi. 31-34; Heb. viii. 13; x. 17, 18.

II. *It is suggested that whenever Messiah should come, the great body of Scripture prophecy should be accomplished in him.* "In the volume of the book it is written of me." That the prophetic writings abound in predictions of the Messiah, no Jew will deny; the only question is, are they fulfilled in Jesus?

In trying the question, whether the prophecies be fulfilled in Jesus? it will be necessary, for the sake of perspicuity, to class them under different heads, such as time, place, family, etc.

1. *The time when Messiah should come is clearly marked out in prophecy.* It was said by Jacob, when blessing the tribes, "The sceptre shall not depart from Judah, nor a lawgiver from between his feet, until Shiloh come; and unto him shall the gathering of the people be," Gen. xlix. 10. All this was true in respect of Jesus. Till he came, though the ten tribes were scattered, Judah continued a people, and retained the government. But soon after his death, they were dispersed among the nations, and have been so ever since. "Kings and princes,"

says one of your own writers, "we have none!"

If, therefore, Shiloh be not come, he can never come within the limits of time marked out by this prophecy. Again; it is clearly intimated in the prophecy of Haggai, for the encouragement of the builders of the second temple, that the Messiah should come during the standing of that temple; and that the honor that should be done it by his presence, would more than balance its inferiority in other respects to the first. "For thus saith the Lord of hosts: Yet once, it is a little while, and I will shake the heavens, and the earth, and the sea, and the dry land; and I will shake all nations, and the desire of all nations shall come: and I will fill this house with glory, saith the Lord of hosts. The silver is mine, and the gold is mine, saith the Lord of hosts. The glory of this latter house shall be greater than of the former, saith the Lord of hosts," Hag. ii. 6–9. All this was literally fulfilled in Jesus. But soon after his death, the second temple was reduced to ashes. If, therefore, Jesus was not the Messiah, it is impossible that this prophecy should ever be accomplished.

Again. The prophet Daniel was informed by the angel Gabriel as follows, Dan. ix. 20–27. Whether Christian writers agree as to the exact time when these seventy sabbatical weeks, or four hundred and ninety years, began, or not, thus much is certain, that they must have been fulfilled about the time that Jesus appeared and suffered, or they never can be fulfilled. Such was the effect of this, and other prophecies, upon the minds of the Jewish nation, that about that time there was a general expectation of the Messiah's appearance.

2. *The place where Messiah should be born, and where he should principally impart his doctrine, is determined.* "But thou, Bethlehem Ephratah, though thou be little among the thousands of Judah, yet out of thee shall he come forth unto me that is to be ruler in Israel; whose goings forth have been from of old, from everlasting," Micah v. 2. Speaking of Galilee of the nations in connection with the birth of the child, whose name should be called "the mighty God," it is said, "The people that walked in darkness have seen a great light: they that dwell in the land of the shadow of death, upon them hath the light shined," Isa. ix. 2. These prophecies were literally and manifestly ful-

filled in Jesus; and it is scarcely credible that they can be fulfilled in any other.

3. *The house, or family, from whom Messiah should descend, is clearly ascertained.* So much is said of his descending from David, that I need not refer to particular proofs; and the rather, as no Jew will deny it. The genealogies of Matthew and Luke, whatever varieties there are between them, agree in tracing his pedigree to David. And though, in both, it is traced in the name of Joseph, yet this appears to be only in conformity to the Jewish custom, of tracing no pedigree in the name of a female. The father of Joseph, as mentioned by Luke, seems to have been his father by marriage only; so that it was, in reality, Mary's pedigree that is traced by Luke, though under her husband's name; and this being the natural line of descent, and that of Matthew the legal one, by which, as King, he would have inherited the crown, there is no inconsistency between them.

4. *The kind of miracles that Messiah should perform is specified.* Isaiah, speaking of the coming of God to save his people, says, "Then the eyes of the blind shall be opened, and the ears of the deaf shall be unstopped. Then shall the lame leap as an hart, and the tongue of the dumb sing: for in the wilderness shall waters break out, and streams in the desert," Isa. xxxv. 5, 6. That such miracles were performed by Jesus, his enemies themselves bear witness, in that they ascribed them to his connection with Beelzebub, Luke xi. 15. When his Messiahship was questioned, he could say, in the presence of many witnesses, "The blind receive their sight, and the lame walk, the lepers are cleansed, and the deaf hear, the dead are raised up, and the poor have the gospel preached unto them," Matt. xi. 5.

5. *It was predicted of the Messiah, that he should as a king be distinguished by his lowliness,* entering into Jerusalem, not in a chariot of state, but in a much humbler style. "Rejoice greatly, O daughter of Zion; shout, O daughter of Jerusalem: behold thy King cometh unto thee: he is just, and having salvation; lowly, and riding upon an ass, and upon a colt, the foal of an ass," Zech. ix. 9. To fulfil this prophecy, it was necessary that the Messiah should descend from parents in low circumstances; and that the leading people of the land should not accompany him. Had they believed in him, and introduced him as a king,

SKETCH CXXIX

it must have been in another fashion. But it was reserved for the common people and the children to fulfil the prophet's words, by shouting, "Hosanna to the Son of David. Blessed is he that cometh in the name of the Lord; Hosanna in the highest," Matt. xxi. 9.

6. *It is predicted of the Messiah, that he should suffer and die by the hands of wicked men.* "Thus saith the Lord, the Redeemer of Israel, and his Holy One, to him whom man despiseth, to him whom the nation abhorreth. As many were astonished at thee; his visage was so marred more than any man, and his form more than the sons of men: so shall he sprinkle many nations," etc., Isa. xlix. 7; lii. 14, 15; liii.; Dan. ix. 26.

7. *It was foretold that the Messiah, after being cut off out of the land of the living, and laid in the grave, should rise from the dead.* Nothing less can be implied by all the promises made to him as the reward of his sufferings; for if he had continued under the power of death, how should he have seen his seed, or prolonged his days? If his kingdom had been that of a mortal man, how could it continue as long as the sun and moon? How was he to "see of the travail of his soul and be satisfied," unless he survived that travail? But more than this, it is foretold that he should rise from the dead at so early a period as not to see corruption. The argument of Peter, from this passage, has never been answered. David said, "Thou wilt not suffer thine Holy One to see corruption," Psa. xvi. 10: but David did see corruption; he refers to Him, therefore, of whom it is witnessed that he saw no corruption.

Lastly. *It was foretold that the great body of the Jewish nation would not believe in him; and that he would set up his kingdom among the Gentiles.* Such is evidently the meaning of the prophet's complaint, "Who hath believed our report?" and of the Messiah's words, in another part of the same prophecies,—"Then I said, I have labored in vain; I have spent my strength for nought, and in vain; yet surely my judgment is with the Lord, and my work with my God!" etc., Isa. liii. 1; xlix. 4, 6.

III. *It is declared that when the Messiah should come, the will of God would be perfectly fulfilled by him.*

"I delight to do thy will, O my God: yea, thy law is within my heart," Psa. xl. 8.

Agreeably to this, the Messiah is denominated God's servant, whom he would uphold; in whom he would be glorified; and who should bring Jacob again to him," Isa. xlii. 1, etc. The will of God sometimes denotes what he approves, and sometimes what he appoints. The first is the rule of our conduct, the last of his own; and both we affirm to have been fulfilled by Jesus.

(1.) In respect of the Divine precepts, his whole life was in perfect conformity to them. All his actions were governed by love.

(2.) But it was not merely to fulfil the Divine precepts that the Messiah was to come; but to execute his purpose in saving lost sinners. Even his obedience to the law was subservient to this, or he could not have been "the Lord our righteousness." He was God's servant, to raise up the tribes of Jacob, to give light to the Gentiles, and to be his salvation to the end of the earth. In accomplishing this, it behooved him to endure the penalty, as well as obey the precepts of the law. His soul must be made an offering for sin; he must be cut off out of the land of the living—cut off, but not for himself; and this that he might "make reconciliation for iniquity, and bring in everlasting righteousness," Dan. ıx. 24.

I have lately looked into some of the modern Jewish writings. It would be going beyond my limits to attempt an answer to many of their objections to the gospel; but I will touch upon a few which struck me in course of reading. They find many things spoken in prophecy of the reign of Messiah, which are not as yet fulfilled in Jesus; such as the cessation of wars, the restoration of the Jewish nation, etc.; and argue from hence, that Jesus is not the Messiah. But it is not said that these effects should immediately follow on his appearing. On the contrary, there was to be an increase of his government; yea, a continued increase. Jesus may be the Messiah, and his reign may be begun; while yet, seeing it is not ended, there may be many things at present unfulfilled.

But they object, that the doctrine taught by Jesus was not of a pacific tendency—that, on the contrary, it was, by his own confession, adapted to produce division and discord. "Think not that I am come to send peace on earth: I came not to send peace, but a sword. For I am come to set a man at variance against his father, and the daughter against her mother, and the daughter-in-law against her mother-in-law. And a man's foes shall be they of his own household," Matt. x. 34–36.

(3.) They further object, with their fathers, that Jesus pretended to be the Son of God, and so was guilty of blasphemy. But, if he were the Messiah, he was the Son of God. Did not God, in the second psalm, address him as his Son; and are not the kings and judges of the earth admonished to submit to him under that character?

(4.) Some of the precepts of Jesus are objected to, as being impracticable; and Christians accused of hypocrisy for pretending to respect them, while none of them act up to them; that is, when they are smitten on one cheek, they do not offer the other. But this is perverseness. Jesus did not mean it literally; nor did he so exemplify it when smitten before Pilate. Nor do the Jews so understand their own commandments. If they do, however, it will follow that they break the sixth commandment in every malefactor whose execution they promote, and even in the killing of animals for food. The manifest design of the precept is to prohibit all private retaliation and revenge; and to teach us, that we ought rather to suffer insult, than to "render evil for evil."

But I shall conclude with a few words to professing Christians. I can perceive, by what I have seen of the Jewish writings, how much they avail themselves of our disorders and divisions to justify their unbelief. "Let every one that nameth the name of Christ depart from iniquity." Let us beware of valuing ourselves in the name, while we are destitute of the thing. We may yield a sort of assent to the doctrine just delivered, while yet it brings forth no good fruit in us. These are the things that rivet Jews in their unbelief. "He that winneth souls is wise," Prov. xi. 30. I hope all the measures that are taken for the conversion of the Jews, will be of a winning nature. If they be malignant and abusive, they must not be opposed with the same weapons.

CXXX.—APOSTOLIC BENEVOLENCE.

BY REV. EDWARD WILLIAMS, D. D.*

"Brethren, my heart's desire and prayer to God for Israel is, that they might be saved. For

* Preached in the Jews' Chapel, Church-street, Spitalfields, 1811.

I bear them record, that they have a zeal of God, but not according to knowledge. For they being ignorant of God's righteousness, and going about to establish their own righteousness, have not submitted themselves unto the righteousness of God. For Christ is the end of the law for righteousness to every one that believeth."—Rom. x. 1–4.

HERE, my Christian friends, we have a pattern highly worthy of our imitation. And with a view to recommend it, I call your attention to reflect with me on,

I. *The proper nature of that benevolence which was exemplified by the apostle Paul, and which is now recommended to your notice.*

It was not a transitory flash of light, without heat; it was not a weak wish, devoid of energetic efforts; it was not a selfish desire to acquire fame, or to increase a party; nor was it hasty and abrupt, liable to be shaken with every blast of opposition, either from those whose best interests it sought, or from others who took wrong views of the subject. But the temper of mind now recommended had the following characters:

1. *It was deeply seated in the heart.* A benevolence which is not a rooted principle, will finally die away. Love, benevolent love, is the very essence of all real religion, and of all true virtue.

2. *It was the effect of knowledge.* The wise king of Israel observes, "That the soul be without knowledge, it is not good," Prov. xix. 2. No specific truth can be loved, while we remain ignorant of its character. Conviction is the fruit of knowledge; and so is all acceptable devotion. When the mind is divinely enlightened, and consequently well informed, the religious tenets we contemplate appear in their due proportion and importance.

And thus, my brethren, let it be our constant endeavor to possess more Divine light, that all our efforts may be strengthened by knowledge, derived from the Spirit and word of God, and directed by that wisdom which is from above.

3. *It was an operative principle, manifesting itself in substantial acts of kindness.* This principle, resembling its Divine Author, not only partakes of goodness, but also imparts it. Christian benevolence cannot manifest bitterness and wrath, envy and strife. The kindness exercised is like that of a faithful shepherd to a wandering sheep; like that of a firm friend in a season of adversity; or like that of a loving parent interested for the welfare of his child.

4. *It was a disinterested and self-denying principle.* As this is the proper nature of Christian benevolence, so it is an eminent part of its excellence. It stands directly opposite to that odious vice called selfishness. It is indeed perfectly consistent with some regard to ourselves, but it does not rest there. A man without real religion, would fain bring every ray to centre in himself, as the common focus; but benevolence moves in a contrary direction—love and kindness diffuse themselves as from a radiant point, to enlighten and to cheer every capable object. Selfishness is a vortex in which every thing within its power is ingulfed; but benevolence expands itself, like circling waves.

5. *It was a patient and persevering principle.* It was not only kind, as exemplified by Paul, but it "suffered long," it was not weary in well-doing; it coped with unparalleled difficulties, and surmounted stupendous obstacles. He endured all things for the elect's sake, that they also might obtain eternal salvation, which he knew could be obtained only in Christ Jesus, 2 Tim. ii. 10. We come now to consider,

II. *The peculiar objects of that benevolence which was exemplified by Paul, and which is now recommended for imitation.*

Though in its aim it was unbounded, and the Gentile world was Paul's peculiar province, while his brethren in the apostleship labored professedly among the Jews; yet his kinsmen, however disaffected to him, had the warmest affections of his heart. "I say the truth in Christ, I lie not, my conscience also bearing me witness in the Holy Ghost, that I have great heaviness and continual sorrow in my heart. For I could wish that myself were accursed," or excommunicated "from Christ (*i. e.* the Christian assembly), for my brethren, my kinsmen according to the flesh," Rom. ix. 1–3.

1. *The persons he had peculiarly in view were the Israelites, or Jews.* Of these none were excepted; his loving heart included them all : the learned and the ignorant, the rich and the poor, the old and the young.

2. *Their highest, their eternal welfare.* "My heart's desire and prayer to God for Israel is, that they might be saved." Paul had thoroughly learned, that all men, through sin, are become obnoxious to the curse denounced on transgressors by the righteous law of God; and that if Christ be rejected, "there is none other name under heaven given among men whereby they can be saved," Acts iv. 12. Heaven or hell must be the final receptacle of all mankind. Paul felt the momentous influence of such considerations.

III. *The powerful obstacles which the benevolence of Paul, when directed to the Jews, had to encounter.*

1. *The prejudices of education.* God had revealed himself to Abraham, Isaac, and Jacob, their ancestors, and especially to Moses and the prophets, in a very signal manner. They were strenuous in maintaining that the Jewish religion was a temple, while the Christian was a needless appendage to it; or, rather, an insulting and injurious altar against altar. But Paul, on the contrary, was fully convinced that Judaism, in its Divine institution, was but a porch, leading to the Christian temple; and that all the Levitical and Mosaic institutions were but shadows of better things.

2. *Another powerful opposition arose from their zeal and jealousy for the peculiarities of their profession,* which is common to all religious parties prior to impartial examination. Witness the Egyptians, in favor of their idols; the Philistines in favor of Dagon; the Ephesians for their Diana; the Romans for their demi-gods; and the Mohammedans for their pretended prophet. In fact, a strong and resolute adherence to the religion in which we are brought up, is no certain test of either truth or falsehood.

These principles, common to all mankind, while governed by example and selfish interests, at the expense of reason, of reflection, and of truth; in connection with higher pretensions—pretensions, indeed, well established—of a revelation from heaven contained in the Hebrew Scripture; may fully account for that zeal and jealousy with which Paul had to contend. "For I bear them record," says he, "that they have a zeal of God." Not only a zeal which is common to all devotees, whatever be the object of their worship; but a zeal which has the true God for its object, strengthened by a revelation of his will, contained in writings committed to their care. But then, he was constrained to add, that their zeal was "not according to knowledge." This leads me to notice another obstacle.

3. *Their ignorance of God's righteousness.* "For," says the apostle, "they being ignorant of God's righteousness," went "about to establish their own righteousness." If this

were commonly indicative of the character of the Jews about eighteen hundred years ago, it is but too applicable to those of the present day until they embrace the gospel.

4. *A mind not religiously submissive.* "They have not," says the apostle, "submitted themselves to the righteousness of God." Submission to God is essential to all true religion. But prejudice, false zeal, and ignorance of God's righteousness, are decided enemies to this humble temper of mind. Pride, a want of submissive resignation to the will of God, was the condemnation of the devil; and will ever prove, when unsubdued, the condemnation of men. Until the spirit of humility be felt, enmity and opposition to the truth will prevail.

5. *False notions of the Messiah.* "For Christ," says Paul, "is the end of the law for righteousness to every one that believeth." The Jews looked for a deliverer very different from the one whom we preach. They expected—and their descendants of the present day fatally imitate them—they expected a deliverer of a temporal and splendid aspect; one whose office it would be to rescue the seed of Abraham from civil bondage; one who would not set aside Levitical services, but restore them to their pristine form.

6. *The supposed incompatibility between the religion of Moses and that of Jesus.* The Jews did not perceive how the Messiah could be "the end of the law to every one that believeth." Had they not been ignorant of this principle, a principle, however, which is abundantly implied in their own Scriptures, they would have seen that no other Messiah but one resembling Jesus, could possibly do them any essential service.

7. *Many cities of refuge, or, more properly, unauthorized subterfuges.* These are provided by men, and not by the institution of God. They are imaginary modes of obtaining the remission of sin. Such as pleading relation to Abraham, repeating prayers, being punctual in the observance of ceremonies, paying implicit submission to the rules of their pretended guardians, and the traditions of the ancients.

8. *The fear of man and the rod of discipline.* The inspired Solomon tells us, that "the fear of man bringeth a snare: but whoso putteth his trust in the Lord shall be safe," Prov. xxix. 25. These two things are contrasted, and they cannot consist together. No one can put his trust in the Lord aright,

but as he is delivered from the fear of man. Odious names, anathemas, exclusion, from the communion of the body, and from all temporal favors, to be treated as excommunicated persons, to be stripped of all religion (according to the principles of their education), and to be deprived of all common civility,—form a snare of no small power. But the fear of the Lord, if real, though but in small degree, would break the snare, and bid defiance to the fear of man and the puny rod of human authority, when unsupported by the will of God.

What sacrifices the apostle Paul was called to make in maintaining his profession, and preaching the gospel of the grace of God! Yet he could aver, "None of these things move me," Acts xx. 24.

IV. *The manner in which the benevolence recommended ought to be directed and exercised in present circumstances.*

1. *Let your benevolence be exercised in a manner consistent with liberty.* This, I know, is your avowed principle; and on this principle you have acted. But it is proper that others also should know it.

2. *Treat the poor Jews, on all occasions, as you would wish to be treated, supposing yourselves in their circumstances.* This comprehends both benevolence and justice. Keeping this sacred rule in view, you will seek their attention by conciliatory means, by the meekness of wisdom, by an ardent wish for their improvement, ever tempered with candor and justice.

3. *Let every effort of benevolence be in subservience to their eternal welfare.* In some cases, owing to peculiar circumstances, they may need temporal aid; but the greatest need is that of their immortal souls. Let, therefore, your "doctrine drop as the rain, and your speech distil as the dew" upon their minds.

4. *Let prayer be united with benevolent commiseration.* "My heart's desire and prayer to God," says Paul, "for Israel is, that they might be saved." If he does not save them, they are lost forever. "Except the Lord build the house, they labor in vain that build it: except the Lord keep the city, the watchman waketh but in vain," Psa. cxxvii. 1.

5. *Let intelligent zeal, and vigorous exertion, accompany your prayers.* I have endeavored to show that Christian benevolence is an operative principle. But, like every other principle, it requires continually to be

excited and strengthened. In the present imperfect state of our existence, we are apt to lose sight of our best privileges and greatest obligations.

I have endeavored to point out to you particular objects of your benevolent exertions, after the example of one whose character you deservedly revere. Paul, to manifest the purity of his love to souls, devoted his time, his talents, his incessant and unparalleled labors for their salvation. And a man who did this continually to the day of his death, would have thought little of silver and gold, if possessed of it, to accomplish his god-like design. But what has Paul done, compared with his Lord and ours? "For ye know the grace of our Lord Jesus Christ, that though he was rich, yet for our sakes he became poor, that we through his poverty might be rich," 2 Cor. viii. 9,—rich in grace and glory. He gave himself, his body and soul, to humiliation, to labors, to poverty, to insult, to excruciating pain, and an ignominious death, "for us men, and for our salvation."

> "This was compassion like a God,
>   That, when the Saviour knew
> The price of pardon was his blood,
>   His pity ne'er withdrew."

CXXXI.—THE GLORY OF ISRAEL.

BY REV. WILLIAM BENGO COLLYER, D. D.*

"The glory of thy people Israel."—*Luke* ii. 32.

I AM well aware that the text, unsupported by other authority, will have no weight, in the present discussion, with some part of this numerous auditory. It is of moment that we should settle the basis of our reasoning, by determining the parts of the Scripture, which will be respectively regarded as a standard of truth. The former part of the subject must deduce its evidences from Moses and the prophets: these every Jew, who deserves the name, admits to contain a revelation of the will of God. The latter part of our engagement, may, perhaps, be better established by an appeal to the New Testament; not that Christians reject the old covenant, but that it seems right to stimu-

* Delivered at the Jews' Chapel, Spitalfields, before the London Society for Promoting Christianity amongst the Jews.

late them to acts of benevolence towards the remnant of Israel, by the principles of their most holy religion; and by demonstrating that our attentions to his "brethren after the flesh" are strictly in conformity to the spirit of our Master. Simeon announced Jesus, the reputed son of Joseph, as the Messiah, by declaring him "the glory of his people Israel."

I. *We are to establish the fact, in addressing the descendants of Israel.*

1. *The nature of the fact advanced is to be established.*

The Messiah was to be "the glory of his people Israel." The evidences of this fact are to be brought from the Old Testament. The prophet Isaiah, the clearness of whose predictions is rivalled only by the sublimity of his language, kindles into more than ordinary fire, when he contemplates the restoration of Israel under the Messiah. He says, "In that day there shall be a root of Jesse, which shall stand for an ensign of the people; to it shall the Gentiles seek: and his rest shall be glorious," Isa. xi. 10. When the prophet Haggai, in speaking of the second temple, writes—"The glory of this latter house shall be greater than of the former, saith the Lord of hosts," Hag. ii. 9; he explains himself as referring to the splendor which it should derive from the Messiah. "For thus saith the Lord of hosts: Yet once, it is a little while, and I will shake the heavens, and the earth, and the sea, and the dry land; and I will shake all nations, and the desire of all nations shall come: and I will fill this house (that is, the second temple) with glory, saith the Lord of hosts," Hag. ii. 6, 7. Again, in respect of the latter day glory, Zechariah writes — "Thus speaketh the Lord of hosts, saying, Behold the man whose name is The *Branch*; and he shall grow up out of his place, and he shall build the temple of the Lord: even He shall build the temple of the Lord; and he shall bear the glory, and shall sit and rule upon his throne; and he shall be a priest upon his throne: and the counsel of peace shall be between them both," Zech. vi. 12, 13. These predictions, and a variety of others too numerous to produce, correspond with the testimony of the text—that the Messiah is to be the "glory of his people Israel."

2. *That the glory predicted was not confined to a temporal splendor.*

Here, as it appears to us, is the root of the

mistake of the Jews. In saying, that the glory predicted was not confined to a temporal splendor, it becomes my duty to justify this assumption by the testimony of the prophets. In order to do this, I must direct your attention to predictions which seem to have been altogether forgotten, or, to say the least, disregarded by the Jews when they formed their estimate of the character of Jesus Christ: they did not take into the account, that he was to suffer as well as to reign; and that humiliation was to precede his glory. Yet so was it predicted respecting the promised Messiah; and the prophecies, which relate to his depression, are as explicit and as ample as those which describe his triumphs. If this be true, it will follow that the indignity offered to the Messiah was as essential to the evidence of his character, and to the establishment of his claims, as any future glory can be. See Isaiah liii. &c. The next remark which I have to make, will explain why I have said, that the glory of the Messiah was not confined to a temporal splendor; for, it is certain, the existence of the Jewish nation, as such, depended upon the Messiah; and this also constitutes a powerful argument in favor of Jesus of Nazareth as the Messiah. We observe,

3. *The Jews lost their distinction as a nation, and their privilege as the people of God, with their rejection of Christ.*

A reference to history would prove all providence bowed to subserve the scheme of redemption; and the obscure carpenter's son, born at Bethlehem, bred at Nazareth, crucified on Calvary, is the Being for whom, and by whom, the world was created; and whose mission opens and terminates the period of the existence of the universe. As to the sentiment advanced,—we find certain individuals occupying a place of importance in the volume of inspiration, till they separated their interest from the line of the Messiah, and then punished with merited oblivion. The uncertainty attending the ten tribes of Israel, appears to arise from the formal renunciation of their interest in the Messiah. "What portion have we in David? neither have we inheritance in the son of Jesse: to your tents, O Israel: now see to thine own house, David!" was their cry, 1 Kings xii. 16. The house of David was protected according to the Divine promise, and because of its connection with the Messiah; while it is to this day a disputed point, as

well with Jews as Gentiles, whether even a remnant of the ten tribes, excepting that which returned with Judah and Benjamin from captivity, exists. It is most certain, that from the time of the rejection of Jesus of Nazareth by the Jews, they ceased to be a nation. "His blood be upon us and upon our children!" was their imprecation, Matt. xxvii. 25. Upon them and upon their children has it rested to the present hour. "Therefore it is come to pass, that as he cried, and they would not hear; so they cried, and I would not hear, saith the Lord of hosts: but I scattered them with a whirlwind among all the nations whom they knew not," Zech. vii. 13, 14.

4. *Their restoration is predicted in connection with the Messiah.*

I cannot withhold from you the affecting language of the prophet Zechariah, and it shall be in the place of many passages, which might be produced from the Old Testament to establish the position advanced. "And I will pour upon the house of David, and upon the inhabitants of Jerusalem, the spirit of grace and of supplications: and they shall look upon me whom they have pierced, and they shall mourn for him, as one mourneth for his only son, and shall be in bitterness for him, as one that is in bitterness for his first-born," Zech. xii. 10. Two things are apparent here: there must be, on the part of Israel, a deep and unfeigned sorrow for the wrongs done to the Messiah; and, in connection with the homage which they shall be induced to pay to their injured Saviour, is their restoration to their pristine dignity. It follows, that so long as they reject Christ, they are the authors of their own ignominy; and that he is waiting to manifest himself, "The glory of his people Israel."

II. *The claims of this Society upon your cordial support: and in so doing we shall endeavor to point out your duty, as Christians.*

(1.) This Institution deserves your patronage from its spirit. It is not the tool of a party. It moves not in a narrow, sectarian circle. It is open to all "those who love our Lord Jesus Christ in sincerity." It proceeds upon the broad basis of universal co-operation, among good men of every denomination.

(2.) As the spirit of the Society recommends it to your benevolent patronage, so especially does its object. "The lost sheep of the house of Israel" are sought by its measures; and Jesus commanded his disciples to go first to them, Matt. x. 6. As Christians, we are bound to pay a particular regard to the Jewish nation.

1. *Gratitude to them for the oracles of truth.*

They were the ark in which God deposited his law and his ordinances: and to the care which they took of the inspired records do we owe the accuracy, extent, and variety of our knowledge of inspiration.

2. *Love to Christ and to the first preachers of the gospel, ought to teach us to love the Jewish nation.*

The hatred of mankind exercised towards that afflicted people, can be accounted for only on the ground of their own imprecation. Their own desire is accomplished, and the blood of Jesus pursues them everywhere —the rejection of the Messiah is visited upon them in every nation under heaven.

3. *Faith in the Divine promises should stimulate our efforts.*

The restoration of the Jews is the subject of many animated predictions both in the Old and in the New Testaments. Now, if the fall of them be the riches of the world, and the diminishing of them the riches of the Gentiles; how much more their fulness?

4. *Concern for their condition—connected with a sense of our obligations and our happiness.*

Should we not pity the branches, which, because of unbelief, were cut off? and should we not recollect that we occupy their place in the living Vine? They perish through unbelief—and we stand by faith: let us not be "high-minded, but fear," Rom. xi. 20. Shall we not, exulting as we do in our privileges, remember those who once possessed, but who have sadly forfeited them? especially when we know "that blindness (only) in part is happened unto Israel, until the fulness of the Gentiles be come in; and so all Israel shall be saved," Rom. xi. 25. Then the "light to lighten the Gentiles," shall also be "the glory of his people Israel."

CXXXII.—OBLIGATIONS OF CHRISTIANS TO LABOR FOR THE CONVERSION OF THE JEWS.

BY REV. EARL GIBBEE, D. D.[*]

" I will bring thy seed from the east, and gather thee from the west; I will say to the north, Give up: and to the south, Keep not back: bring my sons from far, and my daughters from the ends of the earth."—*Isa.* xliii. 5, 6.

This prophecy looks far beyond the deliverance of the Jews from their former captivity. It evidently points to that great and glorious deliverance which still awaits them. A deliverance that will eclipse, and infinitely outshine, their former deliverances from Egypt and from Babylon. In applying the passage before us to the recall and conversion of the Jews, I would direct your attention to the following particulars.

I. *Our obligations, as Christians, to engage in this work.*

II. *Our encouragement to proceed and persevere in it.*

III. *The glorious consequences that will probably result from it.*

And may the Lord God of Israel, the God of Abraham, the God of Isaac, and the God of Jacob, look down from heaven and visit us! May he graciously be pleased to animate our hearts, and to strengthen our hands, in this work and labor of love!

I. *Our obligations, as Christians, to engage in this work.*

It would not be difficult to show that many are our obligations to seek the salvation of the Jews; but I shall content myself with stating only a few.

1. *Gratitude for the inestimable benefits which we have derived from them.*

Should it be asked, What advantage or benefit have we derived from the Jews? we answer, "Much, every way: and chiefly because that unto them were committed the oracles of God," Rom. iii. 2. They were intrusted with that invaluable treasure, which was to enrich the Church of God through every succeeding age. To them "pertained the adoption," into which we are admitted; "the covenants," with the privileges of which we are favored; "the promises," of which we are made partakers; and "of whom," let it never be forgotten by

[*] Preached at the Church of Kettering, Northamptonshire, before the Bedford Auxiliary Society for promoting Christianity amongst the Jews.

Christians, "as concerning the flesh Jesus Christ came, who is over all, God blessed forever," Rom. ix. 4, 5.

Here let us pause, and contemplate the immensity of the debt which we owe to this despised and outcast people; and let us remember that most of this debt remains to this day unpaid. Ought we not to be ashamed of our culpable neglect? Ought we not to feel a portion at least of the apostle's spirit, who could wish himself cut off and separated from Christ, for his brethren and for his kinsmen's sake, Rom. ix. 3. Surely the Jews have claims upon us far beyond any heathen nation; and yet for the heathen have we chiefly employed our labors.

2. *As a reparation of the cruel wrongs and injuries which we have inflicted upon them.*

It would be a shocking, as it would be endless, to recount the terrible oppressions which this unhappy people have suffered in every age of their dispersion. Dreadful as have been the persecutions which the Church of God hath experienced in former times, I apprehend they have been far exceeded by the persecutions which even Christian nations have inflicted on the Jews. Every Christian country is deep in this guilt, and every Christian country requires a national expiation of it. And let us not fondly suppose, that England is, in this respect, less criminal than other nations. No; the pages of our history are stained with our cruelty and injustice. How often has this miserable people been fined and pillaged by the former governments of this land! How often have they been compelled to redeem their lives at the expense of all their treasures! Did our monarchs want money to carry on their wars? The Jews were sure to be the first objects of their rapacity. Judah's wickedness is no exculpation of England's sin. Rather, have we not reason to fear, that the Lord may have a controversy with us, both for our past and present oppressions of his ancient people? Have we nothing to dread in the prospect of the day, which the prophet emphatically calls, "the day of the Lord's vengeance, the year of recompences for the controversy of Zion?" Isa. xxxiv. 8. Is it nothing to us, that that great and notable day of the Lord is at hand, when Jerusalem shall become "a cup of trembling," and "a burdensome stone," to all the nations that have afflicted her? Zech. xii. 2. Would we

avert from us the indignation of the Lord, and escape his threatened judgments? Let us undo the bands of wickedness. Let us turn to Israel with compassion, and with repentance.

3. *From an ardent desire to promote the glory of God.*

An earnest desire to promote the glory of God is a prominent feature in the character of a true Christian; and we may reasonably doubt the profession of those who do not feel the constant influence of this principle. My brethren, the conversion of the Jews is indisputably an object most intimately connected with the glory of God, and with the honor of Christ. I am fully persuaded, that we can never expect any particular enlargement of the Redeemer's kingdom till the veil be removed from Israel. If, therefore, we would indeed promote the glory of God, and extend the triumphs of the Redeemer, let us turn our attention primarily to the Jews—let us gladly spend and be spent for them. Having thus stated our obligations to engage in this work, let us consider,

II. *Our encouragement to proceed and persevere in it.*

To some, the attempt to convert the Jews may appear visionary; to others, it may appear inexpedient; but they, who are acquainted with their Bibles, must know that it is not hopeless. We are encouraged to attempt this work,—

1. *From the testimony of prophecy.*

The restoration of the whole house of Israel is so plainly and expressly foretold in Scripture, that it may properly be called an article of our faith. "Thus saith the Lord God: Behold, I will take the children of Israel from among the heathen, whither they be gone, and will gather them on every side, and bring them into their own land.— Moreover, I will make a covenant of peace with them; it shall be an everlasting covenant; and I will place them, and multiply them, and will set my sanctuary in the midst of them for evermore. My tabernacle also shall be with them: yea, I will be their God, and they shall be my people," Ezek. xxxvii. 21, 26, 27. See also Hosea iii. 4, 5; Zeph. iii. 14, 15. We are also encouraged to proceed,

2. *From the very great attention which has already been excited among the Jews.*

Arduous as is the work in which we are engaged, and unpromising as it may to many appear; yet we can confidently declare, that our Society hath hitherto no reason to repent of its laudable efforts ; on the contrary, its exertions have already produced very striking effects. A spirit of inquiry has been stirred up among the Jews ; which is, of itself, a most favorable circumstance : for, if the Jews can only be brought diligently to search and study their own Scriptures, we may reasonably hope that the most important consequences will result from their inquiries. Not a few of the Jews have already been brought to abjure their errors, and openly to confess Jesus of Nazareth, as their Messiah and Redeemer. Several others have evinced an earnest desire to know more of the Friend and Saviour of sinners. Another ground of encouragement may be drawn,

3. *From the present signs of the times.*

That a day will come, when both the house of Judah and of Israel shall be brought home to the fold of Christ, is a truth grounded on the express promise of God : and many reasons may be assigned which induce us to think that this day is at hand. Of late years, the attention of Christians has been very remarkably turned to the study of prophecy ; and especially to those prophetic parts of Scripture which directly treat of the conversion of the heathen, of the restoration of the Jews, and of the glories of the millennial era. The strenuous exertions which are making, on every side, to diffuse the knowledge of the gospel of peace, are the surest pledges of the approaching triumph of our Redeemer. Already do the mists of heathen darkness begin to be dissipated ; already do the benign rays of the Sun of righteousness begin to illumine those regions of the earth, which have long "sat in darkness and in the shadow of death." Every thing is preparing for the solemn inauguration of Christ, as King and Lord of all : when both Jew and Gentile shall be given to him "for an inheritance, and the uttermost parts of the earth for a possession," Psa. ii. 8.

III. *The glorious consequences that will result from the conversion of the Jews.* Great will be its consequences both to the world and to the church of God. Consider,

1. *Its glorious consequences to the world.*

Among other blessings, which will result to the world at large from this grand event, we are particularly taught to expect, from the sure word of prophecy, that there will be a universal diffusion of religious knowledge, and a universal enjoyment of uninterrupted peace. "Nation shall not lift up sword against nation, neither shall they learn war any more," Isa. ii. 4. When the Lord shall bring again the captivity of Israel, the whole face of the earth will be changed : it will be the commencement of a new and blessed era to all nations. See Jer. xxxi. 34 ; Psa. lxxii. 7, 8, 10, 11.

2. *Its glorious consequences to the church of God.*

Inexpressibly magnificent is the description of the happiness and glory of the church, in that day when "the Lord shall bring again Zion," Isa. lii. 8. The conversion of the Jews shall be the means of bringing in the whole fulness of the Gentiles. Then shall the name of Christ be known "from the rising of the sun even unto the going down of the same :" his praises shall be heard and celebrated in the uttermost parts of the earth. See Isa. lx. 1, 3, 5.

(1.) To God's covenant with Abraham and with his seed, you owe all that you are, and all that you hope to be. You that are the younger brother of your Father's house, have risen to your present pre-eminence on the ruin of your elder brother.

(2.) My brethren, when Christ sent forth his apostles to preach the gospel of the kingdom, he particularly charged them to "begin at Jerusalem." Let me not be misunderstood, when I humbly hint, that in our attempts to convert the heathen, we should follow this rule, and begin at Jerusalem too. Did Christ command his apostles to "go rather to the lost sheep of the house of Israel," Matt. x. 6 ; and shall we seek them last ? Oh, no ! we will remember that as we "have now obtained mercy through their unbelief," so it is the Divine appointment that "through our mercy they also may obtain mercy," Rom. xi. 30, 31.

CXXXIII.—THE VISION OF THE CHURCH OF CHRIST.

"And there appeared a great wonder in heaven ; a woman clothed with the sun, and the moon under her feet, and upon her head a crown of twelve stars."—*Rev.* xii. 1.

MANY of the prophecies of this highly figurative book are deeply mysterious ; and some of the hieroglyphics employed by the sacred writer are extremely difficult of interpretation. Now, these observations apply to the latter part of the prophecy we have selected for our present consideration. The views of expositors have widely varied, and have even been directly opposed to each other. By the Child brought forth, some have referred it to the Messiah; others, to Constantine. By the dragon, some have understood Pagan Rome; others, Mystical Babylon, or Papal Rome. The text, however, is of clear and evident interpretation, and to that we shall confine our attention. The whole subject is that of magnificent and striking metaphor,—representing the church of God in her divine glory, spiritual and celestial character, and ministerial dignity. Observe,

I. *The figurative representation of the church.*

It is represented under the similitude of a woman. This metaphor is frequently exhibited both in the Old and New Testament scriptures: see Psa. xlv. 10, 11, 13, 14; Isa. lxii. 5; Jer. iii. 14. Thus, also, in the parable of the marriage of the king's son, the bride is evidently the church. Also, in all those representations where Christ is styled the Bridegroom and the Husband of the church. See John iii. 29; Eph. v. 24, 32; Rev. xxi. 9. Weakness, dependence, and fruitfulness, are the chief ideas associated with the metaphor of the church being likened to a woman. Observe,

II. *Her Divine glory.*

"Clothed with the sun." Christ is evidently intended by this magnificent figure. He is the "Sun of righteousness." He proclaimed himself as "the Light of the world," John viii. 12. Christ may be thus represented on account,

1. *Of his greatness.*

Christ is "Most High."—"The Prince of the kings of the earth," Rev. i. 5. "King of kings, and Lord of lords," 1 Tim. vi. 15; "Lord of glory,"—possessed of all the attributes and perfections of Deity. "Over all, God blessed forever," Rom. ix. 5. Infinitely greater than angels, or seraphim, or cherubim.

2. *On account of his oneness.*

Hosts of stars, but only one sun, the centre of the solar system. So but one Messiah—one Mediator—one "only-begotten Son of God." Without fellow or compeer in his mediatorial work, etc.

3. *As the Fountain of light.*

The rays of the sun illumine our world, and make day. So Christ is "the Dayspring," and the great Source of mental and moral light to mankind. He is the true Light—the Light of heaven, and the Light of the earth: his beams make spiritual day in the soul.

4. *For his fertilizing influences.*

Where his rays are not, there frigid winter reigns; there are everlasting mountains of ice; there sterility and barrenness sway their enduring sceptre. The sun softens, fertilizes, gives vegetating power to nature, makes the earth to appear as "the garden of the Lord." So with the influence of Christ on the hearts of men. Where he shines not, is pagan gloom, heathen night, with all its attendant vices and misery! No moral verdure: selfish apathy, cruelty, death. When he shines, goodness, purity, and joy reign, etc.

5. *For his magnificence and glory.*

We cannot do justice to this view of the natural sun. How radiant his light, how grand his rising, how overwhelming his meridian altitude, how gorgeous his setting, how resplendent his circuit, how mighty his attraction, how universal his influence! Now, these things we say of the creature, the natural sun; and what shall we say of the Orb of celestial day? Filling heaven and earth with his glory; exercising his almighty power over all worlds; seated on the throne of the universe; attracting to himself all that is holy on earth and in heaven; and the great Source of all light and joy, and bliss and glory, to angels and men. Now, the church is clothed with this Sun—he surrounds her, overshadows her, throws upon her all his light, and purity, and glory. If she has life, beauty, light, and fertility, he is the Source of the whole,—she owes all to him; and without him would be impotence, and could do nothing.

II. *Her spiritual and celestial character.*

These are indicated by her being in heaven, and having the moon under her feet. The church of God is of heavenly origin,—often called "the kingdom of heaven." Her spirit, principles, aims, and destinies, are all heavenly. She is the "Jerusalem which is above," etc., Gal. iv. 26. But her spiritual character is exhibited in having the moon under her feet. By this,

1. *May be represented her superiority over the Jewish dispensation.*

That was a subordinate economy, borrowing all its light and glory from the Christian, of which its sacrifices and offerings were all typical, "the shadow of good things to come," Heb. x. 1. It was a dispensation of ever-varying rites and ceremonies. Nothing appeared fixed or permanent. This dispensation is obsolete—it has passed away. The Christian church may, therefore, be represented as standing above it—having it under her feet. But, perhaps,

2. *The world may be more especially intended.*

She may be the emblem of the world in the dimness of its light, whether of science, art, philosophy, etc., as compared with the light of the gospel; or, on account of its variableness—ever changing. The pomp and glory of the world are always passing away. Kingdoms, states, etc., exemplify this —Babylon, Tyre, Egypt, all confirm this. Its laws and customs are all transitory. Now, the church of Christ is not of the world—it is elevated above it: called out, separated from, and superior to it. It tramples its honors, distinctions, riches, and gaudy scenes under its feet. She forsakes it, as represented in the Song of Solomon, "leaning on her Beloved." She has the victory over it. "This is the victory which overcometh the world, even our faith," 1 John v. 4. "By whom the world is crucified unto me, and I unto the world," Gal. vi. 14. Observe,

IV. *Her ministerial dignity.* "Upon her head a crown of twelve stars."

By the stars are evidently meant the twelve apostles, as representing the whole body of the faithful ministers of Jesus Christ. We find the same titles given to the seven angels, or messengers of the Asiatic churches, Rev. i. 20. Now, the metaphor teaches us the radiant character of the Christian ministry—they are to shine, in their respective spheres, in the gifts and graces of the Holy Spirit. The metaphor also indicates their connection with the Sun of righteousness. He is the great source of their light, and the centre of union and order to the whole. This figure also exhibits the diversity of talents and gifts which they possess, "as one star differeth from another star in glory."

No, these stars are a crown to the church —they are to exercise rule and order and government in the church. They are to enforce the doctrines and laws of Jesus Christ; and thus the church is resplendent when she shines forth in the dignity of gospel truth and holiness. Observe,

1. *The true character of the church of Christ.*

Spiritual, heavenly; clothed with the magnificence of her Lord; raised above the world; and dignified in the radiant purity of her holy ministry. Take away any of these distinctions, and her glory departs. Without the Sun she becomes dark and frigid. Without her spiritual and celestial elevation, she becomes a mere earthly hierarchy. Without a holy, radiant ministry, she becomes formal and uninfluential.

2. *The honor and happiness of those identified with her.* Her citizens are truly great and glorious.

3. *Her final triumphs are matters of Divine certainty.*

To her the world shall bow. Her "dominion shall be from sea to sea, and from the river unto the ends of the earth," Psa. lxxii. 8.

CXXXIV.—CHRISTIANITY A SYSTEM OF TRUTH AND PEACE.

"Therefore love the truth and peace."—*Zech.* viii. 19.

TRUTH and peace are very important elements of moral worth and power in the world. They are essential to man's moral elevation and real welfare. Are characteristics in the blessed Deity; and leading principles of true religion. And when the religion of the cross shall be universal, they will be the great pillars of the Redeemer's millennial kingdom and glory. Consider their nature; our duty with respect to them; and the reasons on which that duty is grounded.

I. *The nature of truth and peace.*

1. *Truth.* This signifies,

(1.) Veracity—the opposite of falsehood. Hence, we often read of speaking the truth, etc. "I speak the truth in Christ, I lie not," 1 Tim. ii. 7.

(2.) *Sincerity*—the opposite of dissimulation. "Worship God in spirit and in truth," John iv. 24. Paul prays that the Philippians may be sincere, etc., Phil. i. 10.

(3.) It is put for the testimony of the gospel. "Grace and truth." "Who hath bewitched you," etc., Gal. iii. 1.

(4.) It is put for the pure doctrines of Christianity, in opposition to error. "I have no greater joy," etc. See also 2 Thess. ii. 10; 2 Tim. iii. 8; iv. 4.

(5.) For the experimental knowledge of the gospel, or religious experience, in opposition to the form of godliness. "Ye shall know the truth," etc., John viii. 32. Hence, the Spirit guides into all truth, John xvi. 13, etc.

(6.) For the Lord Jesus Christ, "He is the way, the truth, and the life," John xiv. 6. The Prince of truth.

2. *Peace* is the opposite of war, strife, perturbation, and contention, etc. Gospel peace implies,

(1.) A pacific state of mind towards God. No longer enemies, etc., but reconciled to God, etc., Rom. v. 10.

(2.) The peace God imparted to the soul. "Peace be unto you," Luke xxiv. 36. "The peace of God, which passeth all understanding, shall keep your hearts and minds through Christ Jesus," Phil. iv. 7.

(3.) A peaceable spirit towards our fellowmen. "The fruit of the Spirit is peace," etc., Gal. v. 22. "Follow peace with all men," Heb. xii. 14.

II. *Our duty to love the truth and peace.*

1. *What does this imply?*

(1.) That we understand them. Many are ignorant of them. It implies that we have heard, pondered, and understood their nature—that we have chosen them!

(2.) Received the truth. Had its principles implanted, etc. Welcomed peace; given them a residence in our hearts, etc.

(3.) That we delight in them, cultivate them, grow in them, give them their right prominence.

2. *How will love to truth and peace be evidenced?*

(1.) There will be the exhibition of them in our character and lives; words, conduct, profession, etc.

(2.) There will be the earnest maintenance and defence of them—cannot be indifferent; and "earnestly contend for the faith," etc., Jude 3. Witnesses for them—"Truth and Peace," motto. Support them—denying ourselves, etc. Buy them at any price, nor sell at any offer.

(3.) We shall diffuse them. By effort, by prayer, "O send out," etc.

III. *Notice the reasons on which this duty is grounded.*

1. *On account of their intrinsic excellence.* Truth is one of the brightest jewels in the crown of Deity. One of the pillars of the moral world, the girdle of the Christian warrior. It 'ike the light of heaven, etc.

Peace is the very element of enjoyment—the sunshine, the repose of the soul, the atmosphere of heaven, the mind of God.

2. *On account of our Christian profession.* We are called to "love the truth and peace," it is a main part of our religion. If we do not, who ought, and will?

3. *Our love to Christ and his church.* He died for their establishment in the hearts of his people; and for their embodiment in his kingdom. His church cannot be pure or prosperous without them.

4. *Our compassion to the world.* The world is apostate; deceived, dark, and wretched. *Truth* only can extricate and exalt it. *Peace* only can bless it, and make it happy.

Observe, in carrying out the spirit of the text,

1. *The order prescribed. Truth,* and then *Peace.* This order must not be inverted—one is the basis, the other the superstructure; one the life, the other the spirit; one the principle, the other the emotion of the Christian character.

2. *Some love truth and not peace.* Hence they are bitter, intolerant, bigoted; to whom the words of Christ are strikingly applicable. "Ye know not what manner of spirit ye are of," Luke ix. 55.

3. *Some appear to love peace and not truth.* These live under the influence of a false and morbid liberality. Hence they are ready to sacrifice any thing for what they denominate *peace:* such *peace* is valueless, harmonizes with sinful compromising—gratifies the flesh, and is acceptable to Satan.

4. *Truth and peace must go together:* they constitute the very essence of the gospel; and, when universally diffused, will introduce the world's millennial purity and bliss.

CXXXV.—THE WILLING CHURCH.

"Thy people shall be willing in the day of thy power, in the beauties of holiness from the womb of the morning: thou hast the dew of thy youth." —*Psa.* cx. 3.

THIS psalm contains one beautiful and continuous prophecy of the person, work, and kingdom of the Messiah. The text evidently refers to Christ subsequent to his resurrection. It begins with the authoritative yet gracious mandate of Jehovah, "Sit thou on my right hand, until I make thine enemies thy footstool." This seems to be a direct reply to Christ's sacerdotal prayer—"Jesus lifted up his eyes to heaven, and said, Father, the hour is come; glorify thy Son, that thy Son also may glorify thee," John xvii. 1. "I have glorified thee on the earth," &c., ver. 4. God replies to the prayers of his Son,—"Thy engagements have been faithfully executed, thy humiliation is past, thy sufferings are over; thou hast redeemed a fallen world to thyself: thou hast a right to reign."

The prophecy then reveals the means by which his kingdom is to be set up, and his triumph effected:—"The Lord shall send the rod of his strength." Here is a manifest reference to the gospel. It coincides with the apostle's description, "The power of God unto salvation," Rom. i. 16. It is to be sent "out of Zion." The gospel is to be first preached at Jerusalem, and to go forth from thence to all the nations. "Thus it was written, and thus it behooved Christ to suffer," &c., Luke xxiv. 46.

Then the immediate results of preaching the gospel are brought before us. "Rule thou"—or, thou shalt rule—"in the midst of thine enemies." And so it was in the city of Christ's death, his kingdom was set up. In the city where dwelt Pilate, the high priests, the council, the soldiers, and the people, he began his gracious triumphs. Then follows our text. "Thy people"—those who are subjugated by the power of thy gospel, who bow down before the sceptre of thy grace, they "shall be willing;" or, "they shall be volunteers;" or, as in the margin of some Bibles, "A people of willingness." They shall devote themselves to thy cause. They shall be thy cheerful, and faithful, and uncompromising followers and friends. And "in the beauties of holiness," or arrayed in holy vestments, they shall appear as a "holy nation," a "royal priesthood;" clothed in the garments of salvation, they shall adorn their profession, and show forth thy praise. Also, in point of number, they shall appear as the dew-drops of the morning; and that, too, in thy youth, or in the beginning of thy conquests, or as soon as thy dominion is established in the world. How literally was all this accomplished. The first converts, clothed in the habiliments of gospel purity, gave themselves fully to the Lord; and by two sermons of the apostle Peter, on the opening of the kingdom of heaven, five thousand souls were converted, and everywhere the "word of the Lord ran and was glorified." Such we conceive to be the spirit and mean-ing of the text. Now, we cannot dwell on all the points which the text contains. For instance, in fully elucidating the text, we might dwell on the beauty and propriety of the figure, wherein the gospel dispensation is likened to a "day"—to "Christ's day"— the "day of Christ's power;" that is, of his royal authority, of his right to reign and rule, and sway over all the earth, the sceptre of his truth and love. But we wish to confine ourselves to two things:

I. *To the devotedness of the Church.*

II. *The connection between such devotedness and the spread of the gospel and kingdom of Christ.*

I. *To the devotedness of the Church.*

I do not pass over the holy vestments of the people of God as of minor importance; but because we are now speaking only of the spiritual members of Christ's body, we only design our remarks to bear on those who are renewed in their minds, and who are professedly partakers of the Divine nature, and in heart and conversation are holy to the Lord. Such, in reality, are the Church of Christ, and such only. These are "Christ's people," and these are the cheerful volunteers and consecrated followers of the Lamb. Observe, then,

1. *The extent of the willingness, or the devotedness of the Church.*

It clearly involves the devotedness of themselves—their hearts, souls, minds, and bodies. "I beseech you, brethren, by the mercies of God, that ye present your bodies," &c., Rom. xii. 1. It is to give our approbation, our esteem, and our love to Christ. It is to give him our desires, our joys, and our delights; our thoughts, our admiration, and our praise; our conversation, and loyal obedience to his commands. It is to place his interests and claims first and highest. It is to speak and act, to eat and drink, to move and live, so as to glorify him. It is to recognize his will as our only rule—his commands as our one directory. Now, is this beyond Christ's claims? And when this, all this, is yielded, çan any thing else be withheld? Can talents, however splendid? Can powers, however mighty? Can influence, however extensive? Can wealth, however ample? If we have given Christ our souls, our entire selves, without reservation, shall we not be ready for health or sickness, for riches or poverty, for freedom or bonds, for life or death; for any thing to suffer or do, which he requireth of us? We see that devotedness to this extent, yea, and beyond all we can say or even conjecture, was yielded by the early disciples, the first churches of Christ. Consider,

2. *The principle of such devotedness.*

This is one simple element—not miraculous influences, or gifts; but the indwelling, operative love of Christ. The language of the apostle was the language of every disciple. Wherefore do we abandon the faith of our fathers? Wherefore become the followers of the slandered malefactor? &c. Wherefore give up ease and wealth, liberty and life? "The love of Christ constraineth us," 2 Cor. v. 14. It has claims which these have not, and bears us away above all these things. It fills, it captivates, it absorbs our souls. Love so divine, so heavenly, so expensive to its Author, so inexpressibly precious, constrains us. It expands; it causeth us to appear as fools to the world,—as beside ourselves. Oh, yes! This is the principle of true devotedness. Nothing else will accomplish this; this has done it; it cannot fail to do it. This is the hallowed fire which burns up the dross of selfishness; this the hallowed flame, which changes all into its own nature and element. This is the deep and rapid stream which fills the channel of the soul, and sweeps all before it, and bears the man onward to the ocean of eternal love. The Christian exclaims, "I love him, I love his cause, and his gospel, his people, and the whole world, because he first loved me, and because his love is shed abroad in my heart," &c. Consider,

3. *How this devotedness is to be sustained.*

I need not say it will be tried. Our hearts will try and resist, or be indolent. The world will try it, by its fascinations, its maxims; and Satan, too, will try it, and, if possible, suspend or weaken it. Formalists, too, will say, "Be not righteous overmuch; be prudent—be moderate!" All these will try it. How is it to be sustained? By faith and hope in the glories of a blissful immortality. Was it not that which sustained the devotedness of Moses, of the prophets, of the apostles, of the early Christians? The apostle, while looking on the retrospect, exclaimed, "I have fought a good fight, I have finished my course, I have kept the faith: henceforth there is laid up for me a crown of righteousness, which the Lord, the righteous judge, shall give me at that day: and not to me only, but unto all them also that love his appearing," 2 Tim. iv. 7. The primitive saints were so indifferent to the world, because they were seeking a better country; to their homes, because they had titles to heavenly mansions; to their friends, because they had their chief Friend in heaven; to riches, because of the grandeur of their estate in glory; to life, because of the better resurrection to immortality beyond the grave. Oh! this devotedness may and will be sustained by keeping the eye of faith on the goal, on the prize, on heaven, and walking as on the precincts of eternity every day.

4. *By whom should this devotedness be evinced?*

By every minister of Jesus Christ; by every elder and deacon; by every sabbath-school teacher, and tract distributer; by every parent; by all the young men of Christ's sacred army;—yea, in one word, by every Christian! This devotedness must be the rule and spirit of the Church—of the whole Church of the Redeemer; and then, and not till then, will the truth spread generally, and mightily prevail. But we pass on to notice,

II. *The connection between such devotedness, and the spread of the gospel and kingdom of Christ.*

1. *The instrumentality for spreading the gospel, and extending the kingdom of Christ, is committed to the Church.*

The world can only be evangelized by the truth. The gospel must be preached in all the world, and to every creature, Mark xvi. 15. "For whosoever shall call upon the name of the Lord shall be saved," Rom. x. 13; Acts ii. 21. Now, the Church has the gospel in trust for the benefit of the world. Bearing this standard, they are to extend Christ's dominions, and give to him a people out of every nation. This is the work of the Church in her collective capacity, and of each member. "Ye are the salt of the earth."—"Ye are the light of the world," Matt. v. 13, 14.

2. *In proportion to the Church's devotedness will the cause of Christ prevail.*

Look at the apostolic age. Look at the three earliest centuries. Look at the reformation in our land, in the days of Wesley and Whitefield. Look at churches where there is this devotedness in our own day, and the results are invariably the same. Means are established in the kingdom of grace, as in the kingdom of nature. If our brethren had not gone to India, &c., we should not have had converted Brahmins now preaching, &c. And if the churches had not felt, and devoted their property, too, the missionaries had not gone. Look at the dark ages, when the Church was corrupt and faithless, and see the results. Look at churches where there is coldness, avarice, and self; and see what is their condition!

3. *This devotedness of the Church is indispensably necessary to this end, and nothing else is so necessary as this.*

When we look at the world, and see what is requisite for its salvation, where do we begin? With God; with the sacrifice of Christ; with the Holy Spirit; with the gospel. Can you believe any supposable blame rests here? Is there as much piety in our churches—as much zeal—as much love—as much liberality, as God demands? Is the talent and wealth of Christ's professing people given to him? No; not a tithe of it; not so much as God demanded for the Jewish priesthood. Oh, how unlike the first disciples! We are not willing, not fully, not cheerfully, not entirely. If the Church be not faithful in this matter, who shall accomplish this end? Eminent holiness is all-important; but can it exist without this devotedness? We remark,

1. *Let the unwillingness of the church be the subject of solemn reflection.*

I do not say of prayer so much, because the great defect is not there. Christians pray (I do not say enough), but much better than they act. Do not pray less, but act more in accordance with your prayers. Pray not less, but differently; so as not to lay the blame with God. Do not speak and pray as though you wanted souls to be saved, and that God was reluctant; that you desired the gospel to be sent everywhere, but that God did not. Do not pray as if you would arouse Jehovah, but yourselves. Be willing, and every thing shall be effected. Be willing, and every church shall thrust out her sons into the harvest. Be willing, and the converts of our churches, both at home and abroad, shall be as the dew-drops of the morning.

2. *To the unconverted the gospel of the kingdom of Jesus is now come.*

Jesus seeks your return to loyal obedience. He asks your heart's affection, your spirit's devotedness, and your live's obedience. He asks all on the ground of his love to you. Will you bow to the sceptre of his grace?

His arms and heart are both open to receive you—

"Oh that my Jesus' heavenly charms
Might every bosom move;
Fly, sinners, fly into those arms
Of everlasting love!"

CXXXVI.—THE HERALDS OF MERCY.

"How beautiful upon the mountains are the feet of him that bringeth glad tidings, that publisheth peace; that bringeth good tidings of good, that publisheth salvation; that saith unto Zion, Thy God reigneth."—*Isa.* lii. 7.

This beautiful prophecy evidently refers to the proclamation of the gospel; and is thus quoted by the apostle, Rom. x. 15. It is the expression of that joy and delight which the human mind experiences in the annunciation of truths and blessings so rich and glorious, as those which form the sum and substance of Christianity. Our text has been realized in the experience of myriads; and is now strikingly appropriate to the messengers of salvation, as they visit the regions of Pagan superstition and cruelty. Consider,

I. *The representation of the gospel given.*
II. *The character of its ministry.*
III. *Our obligation to labor for its diffusion.*

I. *The representation of the gospel given.*

1. *Glad tidings, or tidings of good.* The gospel does not announce that which is ordinarily good. It loses sight of the inferior blessings which relate to the body and time, although these are generally found in its train; and refers us to that which is pre-eminently good—supremely good—eternally good. The good the gospel announces includes,

(1.) The enjoyment of God's favor and love. By sin this is forfeited. In guilt we are heirs only of wrath, and are condemned already, John iii. 18. Sin exposes to death; the gospel reveals to us the Divine mediation, by which it may be blotted out. It announces remission of sins in the name of Jesus Christ. "Being justified freely," &c. Rom. iii. 24, 25. It calls the sinner, "Repent ye therefore, and be converted, that your sins may be blotted out," Acts iii. 19. It points to Jesus and his atoning death. "In whom we have redemption through his blood, the forgiveness of sins, according to the riches of his grace," Eph. i. 7 ; Col. i. 14. With the forgiveness of sin is connected God's favor, and the rich communications of his love.

(2.) The restoration of the Divine image. Sin defiles the soul; it mars its beauty, impairs its health and vigor. It perverts its powers, and deranges all its dignified energies and attributes. The gospel directs to the means of purity. It refers to the "blood of Jesus Christ," which "cleanseth us from all sin," 1 John i. 7. To the Spirit of God, which renews the mind, and by which the sinfulness of the heart is subdued, &c. To the Divine word, by which the mind is led to the sanctifying knowledge of "the truth as it is in Jesus." Hence the gospel is both the charter of mercy, and the renovator of the heart—for it both brings salvation, and teaches men to deny ungodliness, Titus ii. 11, 12.

(3.) The offer of eternal life. Man is destined to endless being. His guilt exposes to endless punishment. "The wages of sin is death; but the gift of God is eternal life through Jesus Christ our Lord," Rom. vi. 23. It opens to men the gates of everlasting felicity.

2. *It publishes peace.* The cessation of hostilities on the part of God towards the sinner, and the gracious terms on which he makes peace with him. And this comports with the essential character of the gospel, which delivers from the power and works of the devil, and which brings into holy harmony with the will of God, all the passions and feelings of the soul. This peace is the peace of God in us, as well as towards us; and our hearts are swayed, by his word and Spirit, into absolute obedience and love. But peace often signifies every good; and, with the acceptance of the gospel, every good is received and enjoyed :—all the graces of the Spirit; all the plenitude of Divine love; all the regards of a benign Providence; all spiritual blessings in heavenly places in Christ Jesus, Rom. viii. 32.

3. *It affirms the reign of God.* God reigneth; not Baal, nor Ashtoreth, nor Juggernaut. Not the sun, or the moon, &c. But Jehovah—the Creator of the world— the Ruler of the universe. He reigneth in the exercise of wisdom, almightiness, benevolence, purity, and mercy. What a contrast to the senseless idols of heathen lands ! His reign is coeval with time, and shall be universal and eternal !

II. *The character of its ministry.* "How beautiful upon the mountains are the feet of him," &c. Observe,

1. *This ministry is human.* Not angelic: angels are deeply interested; they hailed the advent of the Messiah, and rejoice in its success, &c.; but they do not constitute its ministry. This celestial treasure is put into "earthen vessels, that the excellency of the power may be of God, and not of us," 2 Cor. iv. 7. God sanctifies and calls men to go forth in this embassy of mercy and love.

2. *This ministry is benevolent.* It is emphatically an offer of goodness—a message of mercy—an exhibition of love. The subject is the benevolence of God; the design is benevolent—human happiness; the spirit is to be such—love of Christ, and love to souls constrain. A messenger will produce little effect unless his heart overflows with it.

3. *This ministry is active and diligent.* "Feet upon the mountains," &c.—following the benighted wanderer—seeking the lost. Oh, see the field of effort, and the extent of labor. "Go ye into all the world, and preach the gospel to every creature," Mark xvi. 15.

4. *A ministry which should command attention.* The attention of men is demanded. "How beautiful," &c. Observe, and attend, and hearken. Here are depths of love. Here are subjects of sublime grandeur. Here are concerns of great importance. Here are facts and truths in which we are eternally interested. To attention to this we are called, and for it we are responsible; and what shall the end of those be who obey not the gospel ? "Who hath ears to hear, let him hear !" Matt. xiii. 9.

III. *Our obligations to labor for its diffusion.*

1. *There is the obligation arising from our possession of it.* We have it for ourselves, and next for the world. Monopoly is iniquitous to our dying race, &c.

2. *Obligation of gratefulness.* To God, who sent it to us. To the memories of the missionaries, who introduced it. To our martyred reformers, who rescued it from corruption. To our immediate predecessors, from whom we received it.

3. *Obligation of the Divine command.* Our Divine Saviour is now reiterating, "Go ye therefore, and teach all nations," Matt. xxviii. 19. It is his royal will—his divine mandate. To refuse or neglect, is disloyalty and rebellion.

APPLICATION.

1. Rejoice in the glad tidings of the gospel. Make it your boast, &c. Glory in it —secure its consolations.

2. Value and support its ministry. Do so with your influence, your prayers, and your lives.

3. Be solicitous for its consummation. Oh, think of the universal reign of goodness, and peace, and joy, throughout our world; and hasten it on by an ardent love and strong faith, and by increasing toil in the great vineyard of the Saviour!

CXXXVII.—WHAT CHILDREN SHOULD DO FOR CHRIST'S CAUSE AMONG THE DYING HEATHEN.

"And the children crying in the temple, and saying, Hosanna to the Son of David."—*Matt.* xxi. 15.

IT is not well to overlook the influence of children, or to neglect them in making our efforts for the universal diffusion of the gospel. Samuel ministered before the Lord when a little child, 1 Sam. ii. 18. The captive little maid of Israel directed the leprous Naaman, her master, to the prophet Elisha, who was the instrument in the hands of God of recovering him of his leprosy, 2 Kings v. 3. Josiah very early gave himself to the Lord, and did good service in the cause of pure religion in the land, 2 Kings xxii. 1, 2. And on the interesting occasion to which the text refers, the children mingled their songs of joy with those of the multitude, who did homage to Christ; and cried in the temple, saying, "Hosanna to the Son of David." Let us,

I. *Ascertain what is requisite in children if they would promote the cause of Jesus.*

1. *That they should have a correct knowledge of the state of the heathen.*

This is necessary to give correct views of their condition, and also to excite emotions of compassion for their miseries. This knowledge is given in some portions of God's blessed word : "The dark places of the earth are full of the habitations of cruelty," Psa. lxxiv. 20, &c.; and they are amply supplied by the accounts furnished by modern missionaries.

2. *That they should have just views of the gospel as adapted to save them.*

If the heathen are dark, miserable, and perishing, how can they be rescued? We reply, By the communication of the gospel, which enlightens the eyes, pronounces blessings on the miserable, and offers everlasting life, through Jesus Christ, to all who believe. See Acts xxvi. 16–18. It is indispensable,

3. *That they should have right conceptions of the value of immortal souls.*

Human life is precious; but how much more the soul that will never die—the soul that will think, and feel, be wretched or happy forever!—be exalted to heaven, or consigned to hell!—dwell with angels, or be the companion of devils through all eternity! See Mark viii. 36 ; ix. 44–50.

4. *That they should experimentally know the love of the Lord Jesus Christ.*

If we are ignorant of this love, how can we truly feel for those who are without God and without Christ, and "without hope in the world?" The love of Christ must produce true pity for the dying heathen. When we love Jesus we shall have his spirit, and we shall ardently long that all men may know and love him too. "God is love," 1 John iv. 8. "The love of Christ constraineth us," &c., 2 Cor. v. 14, 15.

II. *What children may do for carrying on the blessed cause of Jesus in the world.*

1. *They can contribute of their means.*

Most children have halfpence and presents given to them. Now, they can lay by a part of these to enable missionaries to go and preach, and to provide teachers, and books, and schools for those who are "perishing for lack of knowledge." A hundred children, giving only a halfpenny a week, would raise nearly eleven pounds a year for this good work.

2. *They can collect from others.*

They can respectfully lend missionary tracts and quarterly papers, and seek of their friends to assist them in this benevolent undertaking. I know a school where about fifty children have given and collected as much as sixty pounds in one year to send missionaries and teachers to Orissa, in India.

3. *They can pray for God's blessing to attend their efforts and give success.*

Every night and morning, when they kneel down to pray for themselves and friends at home, they should think of the heathen, and pray that God would send out to them his light and his truth. And children, who fear God, should meet and converse, and read and pray together, in reference to this blessed and holy cause. See Psa. lxxii. 15; lxxiv. 22; 1 Thes. iii. 1.

4. *Some children might seek gifts and talents for missionary work.*

All the missionaries at present laboring will soon die. Others must supply their places; and therefore pious children, who love the heathen, should ask God to raise up laborers for his vineyard, and, if it be his will, to qualify and send them. See Isa. vi. 8. And now,

III. *What should induce children thus to feel and work in the cause of Christ.*

1. *Gratitude to God for his goodness to them.*

How he has distinguished them! Given them their existence in a land of gospel light and religious mercies. Given them pious parents, pastors, teachers, and friends who love them. Given them Sabbath-schools, books, &c.

2. *From the remembrance that good men once came as missionaries to this country.*

The people of this country were once savages, and gross idolaters. But the servants of Jesus came and brought the gospel to them, and by it they were civilized and saved. Now, ought we not to do the same to those countries which are still ignorant of Jesus Christ and everlasting life?

3. *Because God has commanded it.*

He has ordered that the gospel must be preached in all the world, and to every creature. Now, to keep the gospel to ourselves would be disobeying God, and be extremely cruel to the pagan nations of the earth.

4. *Because we shall have an increase of happiness by thus doing good to others.*

In doing good, we always get good. In doing good, we always increase our own happiness. And besides, if we do good from love to God and love to men, the Lord Jesus Christ will reward us at the last day. The poor heathen may not be able to reward us, but we shall be recompensed at the resurrection of the just, Matt. xxv. 21.

APPLICATION.

1. How many children have given their hearts to the Lord Jesus Christ? Let this be the first concern of each and all of you.

2. How many are laboring for the poor benighted people in pagan lands! Oh! feel for them, and try to help them. Think of the poor children without schools, without ministers and good books, and without any knowledge of the blessed Redeemer.

3. How many will now enroll themselves under the missionary banners of King Jesus? —from this day, serving Christ personally, and also praying, and giving, and laboring for the welfare of the millions who know not God, nor Jesus Christ, whom he hath sent! John xvii. 3.

———•———

CXXXVIII.—EZEKIEL'S VISION OF DRY BONES.

BY REV. J. WEITBRECHT, MISSIONARY AT BURDWAN.*

"The hand of the Lord was upon me, and carried me out in the Spirit of the Lord, and set me down in the midst of the valley which was full of bones, and caused me to pass by them round about: and behold, there were very many in the open valley; and lo, they were very dry. And he said unto me, Son of man, can these bones live? And I answered, O Lord God, thou knowest." &c.—*Ezek.* xxxvii. 1-6.

THIS remarkable vision which the prophet Ezekiel relates was shown to him at a peculiar time, and under peculiar circumstances, which it is proper to point out, in order to render the meaning of it more clear and intelligible. He lived with the remnant of his brethren, far away from the land of his fathers, in Chaldea, a captive and an exile. The Jews had lost their political existence as a nation—king Nebuchadnezzar having transported those who survived the sword of the Chaldeans to his own land, to people its uninhabited parts. They had also lost their religious constitution and ordinances, for their temple was destroyed, and the beautiful service of Jehovah was abolished.

Thus this unfortunate nation suffered for their unfaithfulness to God and their propensity to idolatry, and appeared on the point of being entirely annihilated—struck out, as it were, from the list of nations, and, what must have been more painful to those who still preserved a sense of religion, their very *name* appeared to have been wiped out from the remembrance of the Lord. In their sadness and desolation, they uttered the mournful complaint which the prophet records: "Our bones are dried, and our hope is lost: we are cut off for our parts," Ezek. xxxviii. 11. As a nation, as a religious society, and likewise in reference to their spiritual state, they looked upon themselves as dead in the sight of God and of

* From a sermon, preached in the Church of St. John, Upper Holloway, May 29, 1842.

their fellow-creatures; so entirely deprived of life and energy, and all hope of recovery, as to resemble a body in the grave, of which nothing remains but the dry bones, disjointed and broken. Ah, my hearers! how sad is the state of a sinner, who, after repeated and fruitless invitations of Divine mercy, is at last forsaken by God, and left to feel all the consequences of his rebellion! Considering their situation as it then was, their cries of despondency, and almost despair, were not ungrounded.

But hopeless as their case was in the eyes of man, it was different in the eyes of God: and to assure them that he had still a time of gracious visitation in reserve for them—to revive them as a nation, and more especially to create a new spiritual life and energy among them—the prophet Ezekiel was shown the vision of a valley, strewed all over with dead bones, which, by the breath of the Almighty, were to become reunited to bodies, and endowed with life, so as to constitute, after this miraculous resurrection, "an exceeding great army."

It is not my intention to unfold this impressive scene in its exclusive application to the Jewish Church. We shall recognize in it a striking resemblance to the heathen world at large—and to this subject I desire to direct your particular attention; but we shall find, likewise, that the vision points out the real state of a great portion of the Christian world, so far as formal religion, in its spiritually lifeless and dead aspect, is still prevailing among us. And my earnest prayer to the Lord and Giver of life is, that this feeble testimony to the truth may, in more than one respect, resemble that of the prophet, who, in obedience to the Divine command, prophesied to dead bones; but whose prophecy became, by the manifestation of the Spirit, instrumental to their revival. We will consider,

I. *The appearance of the valley.*

II. *The divine command given to the prophet.*

III. *The effect produced by his prophesying.*

I. *The vision of the valley.*

Ezekiel relates the scene he witnessed in a very lively and interesting manner. "The hand of the Lord was upon me, and carried me out in the Spirit of the Lord, and set me down in the midst of the valley which was full of bones."

(1.) Considering what this earth, a perfect masterpiece of God's creation, was intended for, when first it came from his skilful and omnipotent hand—viz., a dwelling-place for immortal beings—we can form some idea how ill it has answered the end proposed. The workmanship, indeed, was perfect—"God saw every thing that he had made, and, behold, it was *very good*," Gen. i. 31; but man caused the confusion, and defiled it by his transgression. The earth has now become a place of suffering and distress. What with the ravages of war, which in almost every age has devoured its millions, the scourges of pestilence, and the diseases of every description, which, like a deadly atmosphere, have followed the commission of crime and sin in their train, this world has been turned into a *Tophet*, a valley of dead bones, a charnel-house, and a grave, where the dead are cast away from the sight of the living. *We* are walking upon the dust of the departed, and ere long shall be ourselves numbered among them.

(2.) But the vision points out *spiritual death* in a more prominent manner. It is very desirable that we should obtain a correct view of the real state of man. We must hear what the Searcher of hearts says, and then we find at once that the vision which was shown to the prophet is a true and faithful picture of the fallen beings who people this world. A valley of dead bones it presents to this day. Sinners are dead in the sight of God, because they have lost the true life—the life of holiness, the life of love, the life of immortality, with which a merciful Creator had endowed the being he made in his likeness.

The prophet was greatly struck by the *immense number* of dead bones: the valley was strewed over and covered with them. And what else can this fearful sight point out, but the *universal* desolation which sin and apostasy have caused in this world? "Behold there were very many in the open valley." The whole human family has been poisoned by the venom of "the old Serpent." "Wherefore, as by one man sin entered into the world, and death by sin; and so death passed upon all men, for that all have sinned," Rom. v. 12.

I can speak from experience, dear friends, as to the millions of human beings in India. Moral and spiritual death is indeed reigning among *them*. Often, when I saw the masses moving before me, did the thought strike my mind—"Oh, what are these creatures doing in the world, leading little more than an animal life; for the gratification of their bodily wants and desires is all they care for; —and yet they belong to the same family whose original destiny was heaven and immortality!"

Another remark of the prophet, as he was gazing at the scene before him, was, "And, lo, the bones were *very dry*." The moisture which they had derived from the circulation of the blood, while the body was alive and covered with skin and flesh, was dried up; every sign of vitality had disappeared. What does this signify?—*hopeless ruin*—a condition irremediable and forlorn. So lifeless and dry, so entirely past recovery, or, as we should call it, reanimation, in a *spiritual* point of view, is the condition of those who have fallen from God and eternal life, into the death of sin and ignorance! As a branch cut off from the tree withers, and its sap is dried up, so lifeless and senseless to every thing divine and spiritual is the natural man, and especially the dark soul of the idolatrous heathen. Consider,

II. *The command to prophesy.*

There are two things which deserve our particular notice in this passage: first, the command to prophesy; and, secondly, the agency by which the thing prophesied was to be accomplished. A most wonderful operation was about to be performed; the millions of dead bones were to be united to bodies, and endowed with life and energy. The address, of itself, was not likely to produce this effect; but the Lord engaged to accompany it by the power of his Spirit.

A wise and merciful God has so decreed it, that his sovereign power of awakening and converting sinners is to be manifested in the use of means which he has appointed. The work is not intrusted to angelic beings; but sinners are made the instruments of converting sinners: the man who has been enlightened from above is commissioned as the most suitable agent for prophesying, *i. e.*, bearing testimony to the love and mercy of God, and thereby to become a fellow-worker with God, in his wonderful operation upon the heart of man.

Here, then, you perceive the importance of the ministry of the gospel. The prophet had to address a host of dead bones in the valley. This might have appeared to *him* a hopeless task. To speak to one who has no life, no mind, no perception, no understanding of Divine things!—a person

of a skeptical and philosophizing disposition would have been apt to rebel against such a command. But the prophet was obedient: though he could not perceive what his agency was to avail, he believed that God could raise the dead; and the very giving of such a command satisfied him that he WOULD accomplish the thing. Now, in this light we consider the preaching of the gospel to the most hopeless sinners. The gospel is a message of mercy to fallen man, of whatever race, language, or complexion he may be. As in Adam all are fallen, so in Christ are all to be raised up again, 1 Cor. xv. 22.

What is the grand subject of our ministry?—nothing more or less than a Divine declaration to fallen dying sinners, that God, by the power of his grace, *will* cause the dead to live. While we use the means, God works effectually through *our* instrumentality: therefore, what *He* has commanded *we* must do, and what *He* has promised *we* must expect. And here I may mention one encouraging fact: throughout the length and breadth of our Indian empire the impression has gained ground among the natives, that the Christian religion will eventually supersede their idolatrous worship. The Brahmins, who are the most bitter opposers of the labors of the Missionaries, cannot help acknowledging that this will be the case. They feel convinced of it, being acute enough to discern the superior beauty and adaptation of the gospel to man's spiritual wants: they are aware of the approaching fall of idolatry, from the success we have already met with, in the conversion of Hindoos of all castes: and, what is very remarkable, they feel sure of it from a certain prophecy in their own books, foretelling that the present religious system will be destroyed at the end of this age, by a foreign nation. And often have I heard the declaration from the mouth of the haughty Brahmin, "We know that you will eventually succeed in destroying our religion; for it will be nothing less than a proof of the truth of our Shasters."

III. *The effect of the prophesying.*

"So, as I prophesied," etc. Here we see the result of the prophet's ministry. An unexpected, an astonishing change took place among the bones: they were formed into natural bodies, according to their original creation.

The spiritual import of this part of the vision is obvious, and confirms our previous views. The Lord has committed a glorious power to his church:—oh, what could not be effected, if we all did but truly appreciate it! When her ministers go forth upon his command, declaring his word faithfully, not adding thereto nor diminishing aught from it, it *will* effect the thing for which he sent it.

The shaking of the dry bones signifies the awakening of sinners; this is the first great act in a sinner's conversion. When the arrows of the word touch the heart, a concern is manifested. A sinner who effectually receives the word, though he were before dead and insensible to Divine things, will be moved, and tremble with fear, in listening to the message of the Almighty.

After this, the bones were covered with flesh and sinews. Here we recognize a further progress; the body is preparing for a new and active life; all the different parts which are necessary for constituting such a body are one by one joined and prepared for exercise. Here we have a significant description of the wise and wonderful process by which the faculties of the human mind are raised, drawn out from sin and error, and brought into the obedience of the gospel.

Though the bodies were formed into their natural state, the prophet perceived that there was no breath in them. The Lord commanded him again to prophesy;—"Prophesy, son of man, and say to the wind, Thus saith the Lord God, Come from the four winds, O breath, and breathe upon these slain, that they may live. So I prophesied as he commanded me, and the breath came into them; and they lived and stood up upon their feet, an exceeding great army." You all understand the meaning of this, my hearers; this breath bestowed with the prophesying signifies the *Spirit of God*, who is alone the creator of spiritual life.

This earth, degraded as it has been by the Fall, is not to resemble forever a valley of dead bones; they must be, they will be "made alive." Look at this field, my hearers! Do you not hear a sound at a distance? Is there not a shaking of bones perceptible in every part of the world?

Now, before the prophet prophesied, the dead bones could not be raised to life; and without the knowledge of the gospel NO sinner can be converted. God always works through means and instruments, in the spiritual as well as in the natural world; though the display of power in conversion is his own prerogative. Difficulties should never deter us in this holy work; the success depends on and is secured by Him who "inhabiteth eternity," before whom the "nations are as a drop of a bucket."

Should not every Christian consider himself bound, by the love of Jesus, to do more for his glory; and strengthen the hands of his brethren who labor in foreign lands, until in every heathen town and village the Redeemer is adored, and souls rejoice in his salvation?

When the Almighty is about to do an important work, he raises up instruments by which it is to be performed. A century ago, the thought of preaching the gospel to the heathen scarcely entered the mind of any Christian in England. What has the Lord wrought among us since!

Oh, let us work while it is day—work and pray, that we may, in the day of his appearance, be among the great army who shall grace his triumph; and that we may become instrumental in gathering to the host of the redeemed many who shall rejoice in his salvation!

CXXXIX.—THE UNIVERSAL REIGN OF CHRIST.

"And the seventh angel sounded; and there were great voices in heaven, saying, The kingdoms of this world are become the kingdoms of our Lord, and of his Christ; and he shall reign forever and ever."—*Rev.* xi. 15.

THIS world was made by and for Christ. He was the Logos by whom all things were made, whether they be things in heaven, or things on earth, Col. i. 16, 17. He made it to be the theatre of his goodness—the place of the especial manifestations of his power, and wisdom, and love. By the introduction of sin it became rebellious, and revolted from its rightful owner. Satan, the usurper, established his tyrannical and wicked dominion over it; and under his hellish control it has been the scene of crime, and pollution, and woe, and death; and one immense yawning passage has been opened from it to the horrible regions of despair and of everlasting woe. But Divine mercy has appeared on its behalf; a system of renovation has been set up; and its ultimate destiny is one of universal righteousness, peace, and glory.

The text prophetically anticipates the period when angelic voices shall make the courts of heaven to reverberate with loud hallelujahs, and when the burden of the song shall be—" The kingdoms of this world have become the kingdoms of our Lord, and of his Christ; and he shall reign forever and ever."

I. Briefly glance at the present condition of the kingdoms of this world.

II. What the statement of the text involves.

III. The certainty of its realization.

IV. The claims which this subject has upon the friends of the Saviour.

I. Let us briefly glance at the present condition of the kingdoms of the world.

1. Many of these kingdoms are totally enveloped in Pagan darkness and superstition.

Idolatry of the grossest description prevails. Imaginary deities of gold, silver, iron, brass, wood, and clay, are adored and worshipped. Animals and vegetables are deified. Demon vengeance is deprecated, and demon mercy supplicated. Some of these kingdoms have a moral darkness resting on them, as dense and fearful as that of Egypt.

2. Many of these kingdoms are in a state of servile debasement to the power of the false prophet.

Mohammed is their only Saviour—the Koran their only polar star—delusion their only solace. There waves the crescent, not the cross. There triumphs impurity, commingled with superstitious rites, not Christian intelligence and purity.

3. Many of these kingdoms are spell-bound by the influence of corrupt forms of religion.

How true this is of Papal nations, where Antichrist reigns, and where the "Mother of harlots" sways her corrupt influence without let or hinderance. The picture is little brighter in reference to the gross superstitions of the Greek Church, and her pompous array of unmeaning ceremonies.

4. In the most enlightened nations, where a purer form of Christianity prevails, practical iniquity abounds.

Look at so-called Christian Britain, which is the literal Goshen of religious privileges; yet, what profanity! what intemperance! what sensuality! what contempt of God! what disregard of sabbaths and ordinances! what infidelity! what crime, and moral degradation and misery! How few are really walking in the narrow path of spiritual purity; and how densely crowded the broad way of death! Not more than two hundred millions of the human race know any thing correctly of God, or Divine revelation; while from six to eight hundred millions are perishing for lack of scriptural knowledge. We proceed to show,

II. What the statement of the text involves.

1. The universal diffusion of Divine knowledge.

That the beams of gospel-day shall illumine every nation, and people, and tongue; that all men shall know the Lord, from the least of them unto the greatest of them, Jer. xxxi. 34; and that the darkness of ignorance and error shall be banished from the face of the wide earth.

2. That all false systems of religion shall be overthrown.

That the idols of the heathen shall be given "to the moles and to the bats," Isa. ii. 20; that, from Juggernaut to the smallest household god, they shall all be abandoned and abhorred; that the long reign of Polytheism shall come to an entire, universal, and eternal end.

3. Corrupt forms of Christianity shall be annihilated.

That Antichrist shall fall to rise no more; that the clay of human inventions shall be separated from the gold and the silver; that the wood, hay, and stubble, shall be consumed by the mouth of the Lord; and that the one foundation of hope only shall be known, even Jesus Christ.

4. The universal surrender of every heart to love and obey the Lord Jesus Christ.

Religion is ever personal; and it is only when all the persons of a kingdom are pious, that such a kingdom, in reality, becomes the kingdom of Christ; so that all men, of all kingdoms, must personally know and believe in Jesus Christ, before the sublime and holy consummation of the text can be fully accomplished. Observe, then,

III. The certainty of its realization. This cannot be reasonably doubted, when you consider,

1. That all kingdoms are in reality the right of the Lord Jesus.—His right as their Creator, their Governor, and Benefactor; but expressly by their redemption through his infinitely precious blood.

2. The terms of the Divine covenant assure it. Jesus is to see of the travail of his soul until he is satisfied, Isa. liii. 11. All flesh are to see his salvation, Luke iii. 6.

"And men shall be blessed in him : all nations shall call him blessed," Psa. lxxii. 17.

3. *We are directed, on the highest authority, to pray and labor for it.* "Thy kingdom come!" Matt. vi. 10. "Prayer also shall be made for him continually, and daily shall he be praised," Psa. lxxii. 15. "And this gospel of she kingdom shall be preached in all the world for a witness unto all nations, and then shall the end come," Matt. xxiv. 14, etc. "The glory of the Lord shall be revealed, and all flesh shall see it together," Isa. xl. 5. "He shall have dominion also from sea to sea, and from the river unto the ends of the earth," Psa. lxxii. 8. We reason,

4. *From the achievements of the past.* Greater difficulties do not impede the course of Divine truth ; viler hearts do not remain to be converted and sanctified. The untold myriads of the saved of past generations, as the first fruits, indicate with certainty the general harvest of the universal family of man. Now, these, with the promises of the eternal and unchangeable Jehovah, place the subject beyond all doubt and disputation.

IV. *The claims which this subject has upon all the friends of the Saviour.*

1. *It demands their solemn consideration.* A world to be saved ! An all-sufficient Saviour—a universal gospel—an efficient Spirit—a God delighting in the exercise of his clemency and love.

2. *It demands our fervent prayers.* O pray for the heathen ! Pray that Providence may open effectual doors of usefulness, and afford facilities for Christian missions, etc. That God would raise up more laborers, and send them forth into his vineyard. That God would smile on the efforts employed; especially that he would shower down the gracious influences of his Spirit on the Church.

3. *It demands our individual influence.* Plead for missions—collect for missions—give to missions ; and do all these heartily and liberally, and with persevering constancy and devotedness of heart.

4. *It demands a revival of pure religion in the churches at home.* We want more light, and more purity, and more moral power, and more of the mind of our Divine Master : more zeal for God's glory, and more pity for a dying world. Who will enter on this hallowed crusade ? Who will rally round the standard of mercy ? Who will labor for Christ and for souls ? "Who will consecrate himself this day unto the Lord ?" O think of the final issue—the universal triumph of truth, and love, and mercy ! O anticipate the day when the song shall be sung, "The kingdoms of this world are become the kingdoms of our Lord, and of his Christ; and he shall reign forever and ever." Amen.

CXL.—HISTORY OF CAIN, AS A BEACON.

"But unto Cain, and to his offering he had not respect. And Cain was very wroth, and his countenance fell."—*Gen.* iv. 5, &c.

THE depravity of the human heart was soon evidenced in the life and conduct of Cain. The leprosy of sin was rapidly conveyed from our first parents to their posterity, and Cain was an awful living monument of the entrance of sin into our world. We have a desire to exhibit his history as a *Beacon* to warn you of his career and misery. The Bible abounds with many such, and it is for all—but especially the young—to observe and be admonished by the course of evil and woe which such have pursued.

Observe in reference to Cain,

I. *That he was the first-born of the family of man.*

Who can describe the anxiety and wonder which his birth would produce ? The birth of every child is both an interesting and momentous event; but the first, how especially so ! The *first infant* ever beheld, or that ever gazed on the light of the world. How delighted would be his parents. Adam in witnessing the first of his posterity—and that child a *son.* The first heir that entered on the domain of this world. His *mother* was in rapturous ecstasy. She thought she had obtained the promised seed, &c. I cannot attempt to describe the impression his appearance would make ! How lovely—how promising the beginning of his career ! Of noble, and we may conclude, pious parentage. The first object of parental love, care, and instruction, &c.

II. *He was a worshipper of the true God.* We cannot say any thing of the history of his childhood or youth. He had doubtless reached the period of manhood, when he brought his offering to the Lord. Here was a distinct recognition of certain cardinal religious principles

(1.) Proprietorship of God.

(2.) Bounty of God in his gifts.

(3.) Our rightful and grateful homage to the Most High.

Now all these were right. Nothing wrong in the offering, and probably not in the mode adopted. But it was evidently defective, in wanting the spirit of faith in the worshipper. No doubt religious knowledge had been imparted. The promised Messiah revealed. A reference to him as the only acceptable way to God, distinctly made known.

To this Abel had reference in his worship. See Hebrews xi. 3. Here then was the marked distinction—the fearful failure. And this is ever the momentous line of demarcation. In reading the Word or hearing the Gospel. In prayer, &c. " With faith," &c. So that Cain's offering would have done for an innocent person, but was unsuited to a sinner ; and therefore, God rejected the offering and the worshipper.

III. *Cain was distinguished for his industrious labor.*

" A tiller," &c., verse 2.

Labor is honorable. Even Adam in Paradise was called to it. Gen. ii. 15. It is healthy. It tends to the vigor of the body, whose bones, muscles, &c., are all improved by it. It is one of the best preventions of temptation. Satan may tempt the industrious, but the idle tempt him. It is equally favorable to the mind's elevation, and moral improvement; indolence produces effeminacy, weakness, and mental prostration, &c. It is the real wealth of a community, and the foundation of a nation's greatness. What do the idle administer to the real welfare of a country? &c. Every man who labors is a producer, and worthy of honor, respect, and kindness.

IV. *Cain was the subject of the foul and deadly passion of envy.*

See 1 John iii. 12.

Envy is a passion which would not see excellency in another; or sees it with hatred and pain. This was the deadly spirit of Cain.

God had respect to Abel and his offering, but not to Cain. His pride was wounded—his spirit mortified—his soul angry. Well may it be asked, who can stand before Envy? It is the spirit of deadly hate; and none can say what dire crimes it may not perpetrate. How horrid is this passion! How it eats, and corrodes, and gnaws the soul! How it darkens the mind—inflames

the passions. Like an eruption of some volcano, &c. From this you are ready to hear,

V. *That Cain was a murderer.*

He envied—hated—and then slew his brother. One of the most horrid of all murders. The first. That of a brother—that of a younger brother,—of a saint. How cruel and wicked! His crime was connected with *lying*—recreant *misanthropy*, &c., ver. 9.

VI. *Cain was an accursed vagabond.*

Verses 10, 11.

Abhorred and execrated by men. The subject of excessive toil, ver. 12. The victim of inward anguish, &c., ver. 13. A wanderer ; with a hell in his bosom, &c. The *mark*, we presume, was not perceivable, but a sign from God that he would fulfil his word. Hence,

VII. *Cain was the subject of the divine mercy and long-suffering.*

Not put to death, but allowed to live. Spared to reflect, and if it might be, repent. His final moral state is not declared. We dare not guess, &c. God was both just and merciful.

Learn,—

1. The fearful depravity of the human heart.

2. The awful progress of sin.

3. The necessity of faith in the great sacrifice, so as to obtain the renewal of the heart, &c.

CXLI.—ABEL, AS AN EXAMPLE.

" And Abel, he also brought of the firstlings of his flock and of the fat thereof. And the Lord had respect unto Abel and to his offering."— *Gen.* iv. 4.

" By faith Abel offered unto God a more excellent sacrifice than Cain, by which he obtained witness that he was righteous, God testifying of his gifts; and by it he being dead yet speaketh." —*Heb.* xi. 4.

REFER to the previous history, and discourse, &c., on Cain.

We now have to contemplate a character, in whom the contrast is most striking and delightful.

Abel was the second person born into our world. Eve who had been so disappointed in reference to Cain, the first son, called her second *Abel*,—which signifies a Vapor, or vanity. A name peculiarly striking—as though predicted of his transitory earthly career. But his character was distinguished for moral excellences. He shines forth among the illustrious Old Testament saints, who formed a resplendent galaxy of holy lights, in the early period of the history of the world. Observe,

I. *He is the first person described as offering sacrifice to God.* See text.

We are referred to the probable if not certain origin of sacrifices, and to the skins, &c., mentioned. Chap. iii. 21. Unreasonable to suppose the animals slain merely to supply clothing, and certainly not for *food*, —no doubt for sacrifice. Abel, therefore, offered such a sacrifice. A *lamb*. Afterwards the great Annual Sacrifice. It was expressive,

(1.) Of his guilt.

(2.) Of his demerit; or, just desert of death.

(3.) Of his faith in the promised Saviour, as the evidence of God's love and mercy. See Heb. xi. 4. Observe,

II. *Abel is the first of whom God's gracious acceptance is declared.*

We presume our first parents were so; but there is no public record—no testimony. But there is that of Abel. See Heb. xi. 4. Now God gave testimony of his favor by various signs; sometimes,

(1.) By an audible voice.

(2.) By visions of the night.

(3.) By fire from heaven.

(4.) By inward peace.

Now the two last would be the mode, we presume, in which God would show his respect. See the offering. The victim—the death—the confession and expression of faith—the descending fire, &c. Or the passing by of the Divine glory. As a sequel of this,—the peace and real happiness of Abel. How honored—how blessed! How secure to have the respect of God!

III. *Abel was the first who was persecuted and martyred for religion.*

How terrible the history of religious persecution! Here was its rise, the commencement, &c. In Abel's own family. His brother. With deadly hate; even to death. Slain on account of his faith and religion. The first in the noble company of the martyrs. As such,

IV. *Abel was the first who tasted of the bitterness of death.*

Death had been *threatened*, *deserved*. Had been seen in the inferior creatures, their dying struggles and decomposition. But as yet, there was no *tomb*. Abel first entered the house appointed for all living. The great, solemn, and momentous change he first experienced. See our first parents beholding the mangled, pallid corpse. How sad and awful the spectacle! Since then, every house and family has been invaded. The first of millions upon millions. Still it was the first, &c.

V. *Abel was the first to be received into the heavenly state.*

First to pay the penalty of sin. First to enjoy the blessing of immortality. The first human redeemed being, who passed through the gates into the celestial city. The first to enjoy the martyr's crown, and to dwell with God. The first of a multitude, which no man can number. How grand the spectacle to angels, to receive their first companion from earth. Smitten by the agent of Satan—welcomed by the hosts of glory. His mortal remains on earth fulfilling the curse—mingling with the dust. The happy spirit in heaven, &c. Let the subject,

1. *Lead us to see the importance of right religion.*

It must be *revealed*. God's own. It must be *personal*. It must be *accepted*.

2. *That true religion may involve us in suffering.*

World hate you, &c. "Through much tribulation," &c. It may be, *death*. "Whoso will be my disciple," &c.

3. *That true religion will be amply and eternally recompensed.*

God's smile here. Eternal life hereafter, &c.

CXLII.—NOAH, AN EXAMPLE AND BEACON.

"But Noah found grace in the eyes of the Lord. These are the generations of Noah: Noah was a just man and perfect in his generations, and Noah walked with God."—*Gen.* vi. 8, 9.

No life was more eventful in itself, or can be more instructive and edifying to us, in Old Testament history, than that of Noah. Indeed, a series of discourses could be delivered on the various phases presented to us, in the life and times of this illustrious individual. We can only select, therefore, a few of the more prominent points, to illustrate the two aspects of his character, as announced in the notice of this evening's subject.

His career was most marvellous and interesting; and we wonder that persons can give their time and minds to mere fiction, when such astonishing incidents and truthful realities are extensively overlooked.

Let us, then, notice,

I. *The more striking features in his godly character.* And,

II. *The points of his moral weakness and defection.*

I. *The more striking features in his godly character.*

Here it will be requisite to consider, as the basis of the whole,

1. *His faith.* Heb. xi. 7.

No religion without this. We must first *know*, and *come*, and *trust* in God. No works or state of mind pleasing to God, without this.

In connection with this, observe,

2. *His reverential fear.*

A knowledge of God will lead to sacred awe — adoring reverence — devout circumspection. This is the beginning of *wisdom*. Often put for the *sum* of *religion*. The very safeguard of the mind. He was distinguished,

3. *For practical righteousness.*

" A just man." Truthfulness, equity, integrity, are essentially involved in this word.

4. *He was eminently pious.*

" Perfect," &c. Symmetry of parts. A due harmony of graces and virtues. Religion shone—stood out—decided and preeminent.

5. *He was distinguished for his peculiar devotion.*

" He walked with God," &c. So it is said of Enoch. Elevated. Spiritual, &c. Had fellowship. Communion.

6. *He was a preacher of righteousness.*

His subjects, human depravity, guilt, peril. He warned the Old World. He did so, no doubt, verbally. But especially by his conduct—building the Ark,—preparing for the future.

7. *He displayed all these excellences in the midst of general profligacy and sin.*

Remarkably holy in corrupt times. Deep, universal corruption : Chap. vi. 5. The cause of this, verse 4. Warn the young, &c. Bad influences of wretched associates, &c. Domestic irreligion. National vice. The corruption had become universal. Only

this family exempt, &c. Provision was made for Noah's security and deliverance. He survived. Became heir of the New World. Worshipped and sacrificed to God : Chap. viii. 18, &c. Covenant made with him. Animal food given. The bow given as a sign, &c. How exalted, excellent, and blessed was Noah. So far he stands out as an example,—a moral sun. But now we are called to see and be warned by the spots on its moral disk.

Hence, observe,

II. *The points of his moral weakness and defection.*

Noah's sin described : chap. ix. 20. The sin was evidently,

1. *The result of unwatchfulness.*

He was vigilant and circumspect in the Old World—careless in the New. He feared and cleaved to God amid general profligacy and sin ; when he was no longer surrounded with scenes of iniquity, he fell. Maintained his integrity so long, and then became ensnared.

2. *The sin was gross.*

It was drunkenness. Public, palpable drunkenness. So the word of God avers in the plainest terms.

3. *It was the occasion of sin and misery to his family.*

Not the cause, but the occasion. Yet even thus it was to be deplored. Think of Ham and the curse. I fear it has been perverted by many as an excuse for using intoxicating drinks, and a plea for drinking. Yet justice to Noah demands that we should consider it a sin of *surprise*. It might have been the first time that he had ever tasted wine. His sin was *not repeated ;* and doubtless he repented, and found mercy.

Learn,—

From the whole,

1. *The fidelity of the sacred writers.*

Here Noah's excellences and sins are both declared. One to excite emulation, the other watchfulness. " Let him that thinketh," &c. Be sober, be vigilant, &c.

2. *The possibility of religion in the worst circumstances.*

3. *Religion the only refuge from the Divine displeasure.*

CXLIII.—GOD'S INVITATION TO ENTER THE ARK.

"And the Lord said unto Noah, Come thou and all thy house into the ark; for thee have I seen righteous before me in this generation."—*Gen.* vii. 1.

THE text is connected with one of the most fearful judgments with which God ever visited the world. It relates to the deluge.—A visitation of the Divine displeasure, which occurred when the world had existed about 2,000 years. It was a most terrific judgment,—universal, except in reference to one family. It had been long predicted. Was slow in its execution; for the long-suffering of God waited, &c. At length it was *literally* fulfilled. The patience of God is now yielding to retributive justice. The Judge is at the door; and he speaks to Noah, in the text, and says—"Come thou and all thy house."

Observe, in the spiritual application of the subject,

I. *The sinner's imminent peril.*

II. *The sinner's only remedy.* And,

III. *The sinner's especial duty.*

I. *The sinner's imminent peril.*

His peril,

1. *Arises from his guilt and rebellion against God.*

Sin is the violation of the Divine law. Punishment and sin are necessarily connected—they are linked together by the justice of God. Law is powerless, without penalties, &c.

2. *This peril is that of everlasting death.*

"The soul that sinneth shall die." It is exclusion from God, &c. From heaven—from all bliss—and from all hope.

3. *To this peril all unconverted men are exposed.*

No degree of moral excellence. No amiableness or station will exempt. The profligate and the Pharisee—the philosopher and the savage, are alike amenable to God.

4. *This peril is most imminent.*

Life measures our probation,—death ends it; and man's breath is in his nostrils, &c. He is living to-day—a corpse, probably, to-morrow. In the midst of life, we are in death, &c.

II. *Observe the sinner's only remedy.*

The ark was the remedy provided for the repentant, believing antediluvians. Christ Jesus is the ark for a perishing world.

1. *Both originated in the Divine goodness and compassion.*

God was the deviser and architect of the ark. He also contrived the plan of salvation, and sent his only Son, &c. "This we know and testify," &c.

2. *Both were adapted for man's deliverance.*

The ark for the antediluvians,—Christ for our fallen race.

He is our Brother, having our nature.

He is Divine, being equal with God.

He is both, in one mysterious unity; and, therefore, can efficiently mediate between the two parties.

(1.) He is *able* to save. (2.) Efficacious in saving all who apply to him. (3.) Ready to save.

3. *God's free invitation is sent to all.*

Noah preached for one hundred and twenty years, &c. If any had believed, they would have been saved with Noah, &c. Now the gospel is sent to a world of sinners. "Go ye," &c. "This gospel of the kingdom," &c. "Thus it was written," &c. "Come unto me," &c.

Observe,

III. *The sinner's especial duty.*

"Come thou," &c.

1. *He must believe what is said of his danger and remedy.*

"Believest thou this?"

2. *He must come to God's ark.*

Not make an ark.—Or repair to one of man's invention; but come to God's ark.

3. *He must enter into it.*

Be personally and experimentally in Christ. Not only *near*, but really within. "Baptized into Christ." "If any man," &c. I knew a man *in* Christ, &c.

4. *He must labor to bring his relatives with him.*

"All thy house." Abraham, Jacob, Joshua, and David, endeavored to do this. We ask, (1.) Who are in the ark? (2.) Who will come? (3.) Refusers must perish.

CXLIV.—FORMALISM AND PROCRASTINATION ILLUSTRATED IN TERAH.

"And the days of Terah were two hundred and five years: and Terah died in Haran."—*Gen.* xi. 32.

OUR text records a fact in the history of the father of Abram. Terah had dwelt in Ur of the Chaldees, and like those around him, was given up to idolatry. At this time Terah with Abram and Lot, and their wives, left their country and kinsmen, to go towards the land of promise.

Now Haran was midway towards Canaan. Here Terah halted,—here he remained,—here Abram left him,—and the text says, here Terah died. Now, the text, purely incidental as it may seem, and probably to most appearing of little moment, furnishes valuable thoughts for serious and profitable meditation.

Observe,

I. *Terah's original state fitly represents the natural condition of the unconverted sinner.*

He dwelt among idolaters. He was a worshipper of strange gods. Now that which has the supremacy of affection, and for which we make the greatest sacrifice, is our god. Hence, the Apostle John urges on Christians, the caution: " Little children," &c.

The *covetous* idolize wealth.
The *worldly* his business.
The *sensualist* his pleasures.
'The *selfish* themselves.
The *intellectual* often science, or literature, or heroes.
The *ambitious* fame ; or some their friends, or relatives, or pursuits. If God is not on the throne of the heart, and some other object be there, it is *idolatry.* This world, in all its unconverted territory, is one vast territory of idolatry. Like Athens of old, full of altars and gods.

II. *God calls men to the love and service of himself.*

He now commandeth all men everywhere to repent. To forsake the way of evil and peril, and to turn unto him. " Repent ye and be converted," &c. One very applicable passage, 2 Cor. vi. 17, &c. Just as he called Terah. Now he often calls sinners,

(1.) By providential visitations. Reverse of fortune. Afflictions. Bereavements, &c. Or, by want of happiness in the enjoyment of every thing, &c.

(2.) By the admonitions of conscience. A deep inward sense of the evil of sin, and importance of a change of heart and life.

(3.) By the preaching of the gospel. This is God's direct, loud, and gracious call. Here is mercy, pity, expostulation, entreaty, &c.

III. *Many persons rest in mere external reformation, or outward profession.*

Terah seems to have heard the call of Je-

hovah. He bowed to it. He obeyed it. He proceeded some length in the right way. Just so do many who hear the gospel. They pay reverential respect to it. They admit its divinity and excellency, &c. They are moved by it. They enter on a course of obedience to it. Feel sorrow for sin. Desirous of holiness. Necessity for a change of life. They cease to *swear*—or to *drink*—or break the *sabbath*—or mix with the *profane.* They are *outwardly moral.* They *attend* public worshp, *support* religion ; —perhaps *unite* with the church.

Now all this is in the right direction, and good, so far as it goes. But it is *Haran ;* only half way towards religion. No *inward* change. No *newness* of life. Christ said, " Verily, verily," &c. " The kingdom of God is not meat," &c. Now they rest and settle here. How sad, and necessarily wretched, this is ! No doubt Terah was satisfied ; or perhaps intended to proceed at some future time, but did not.

For we notice,

IV. *That men generally die as they live.*

I say generally. Some few exceptions to this. In the dying *thief* we have one. We now and then meet with an isolated case ; but the rule is, *men die as they live.*

Look at the profligate ! Look at the worldly ! Look at the formal ! as fearful illustrations of this. Especially is this the case with those *midway* towards the better land. They are respected and self-satisfied, and hence self-secure. As the foolish virgins. Such, of necessity, do not enter the promised land. They are *self-excluded.* As they live and as they die, they must forever remain.

Then the subject,—

1. *Should lead us to self-investigation.*

Have we obeyed God fully, as Abram did ? See the contrast between the parent and the child ! How often is it the case ; or the *reverse,*—the parent on the way to glory, and the children, at best, in Haran.

2. *The necessity of inward spiritual religion.*

The mere external will not do. There must be something more, and better than this.

3. *Call on all to secure a title and meetness for the land of promise.*

CXLV.—LEADING FEATURES IN ABRAHAM'S HISTORY.

"By faith Abraham, when he was called to go out into a place which he should after receive for an inheritance, obeyed ; and he went out, not knowing whither he went. By faith he sojourned in the land of promise, as *in* a strange country, dwelling in tabernacles with Isaac and Jacob, the heirs with him of the same promise : for he looked for a city which hath foundations, whose builder and maker *is* God."—*Heb.* xi. 8–10.

AFTER God had frustrated the Babel builders, and confused their speech, sacred history refers us to the origin of distinct nations, and refers us to God choosing Abraham to be the father of the Jewish nation, and one whom he engaged to bless, and make a blessing. To this eventful period the text refers. See Gen. xii. 1, &c. Thus Abraham acted through the influence of faith. He believed God. He forsook all for God. He went where God directed. He considered himself but as a stranger. And finally he looked for a more fixed and abiding habitation.

I. *Abraham believed God.*

For this, he holds a most eminent and exalted station in the sacred pages of truth. So much so, that he has the honored appellation—"Father of the faithful." His confidence in God was so full, and entire, and unshaken, that he was styled—"the Friend of God."

Now, as faith is the foundation of every holy work ; in proportion as this is strong and vigorous, will every virtue thrive, and flourish, and bear fruit. Like gold, it is the most precious of all metals ; but we are enriched according to the abundance we possess of it. Weak faith is valuable ; but strong faith gives glory to God. Weak faith will walk safely on the calm lake ; but strong faith will not sink in the tempest or the storm. How desirable it is to believe God ! all God says, and at all times. Faith has an eagle's wing and an eagle's eye. It can rise to the greatest possible elevation. It can gaze on God. It has a lion's courage, amidst confusion and persecution,—even when the sea roars and the earth shakes, it sits with firm security, and sings defiance to the gates of hell.

II. *Abraham forsook all for God.*

His own country—his father's house. Now in this,

1. *He gave up what he possessed for that which was promised.*

He had an interest in his father's house, and his own country. These were in lands, in possessions, and doubtless were far from being despicable. He left, however, his own land, and his father's house, for that which was named in the promise.

2. *He gave up the present for the future.*

Present subsistence and present patrimony, for some good to be hereafter bestowed. Now in these we see the nature of the demands religion makes. Abandonment of our carnal possessions and pleasures for those God promises. To give up the society of the world for the church. To resign present profits for future advantages. To lose sight of earth and time, for heaven and eternity. Abraham became as isolated from the world, to be united to God. A true picture of spiritual religion. We cannot enjoy the world and God. Nor love both—nor serve both. We may use the world, but it cannot be prominent, and God be glorified.

III. *He went where God directed.*

True religion has,

1. *An ear to listen to God.*

"Speak, Lord, for thy servant," &c. God spake to Abraham, and he reverentially heard the will of God propounded to him.

2. *Feet of cheerful obedience.*

Having heard and understood, he "obeyed." Acted as God directed. Walked as he chalked out the way. God said this is the way, and Abraham walked in it.

3. *Unsuspectingly surrendered all into the Lord's hands.*

"Not knowing," &c. God knew, and this was his comfort, &c. It is not necessary for a passenger to understand navigation to reach the port, &c., in safety. Or a child to know the way, when the father holds its hand. Or the patient anatomy and medicine, when the skilful physician is present.

IV. *Abraham considered himself a stranger.*

As such he acted and lived. He conducted himself as a dying man, in a dying world. He knew this was not his *rest*, or *home*, or *portion ;* and this is precisely the spirit we should feel and cherish. A little reflection might convince every one of the propriety of this. This world is merely a land of passage, probably 1,000,000,000 are ever crowding its surface, but they are all moving. "One generation passeth," &c. Some are just leaving it, others just entering ; but all are moving. Human life, as a river, is ever emptying its countless drops into the ocean of eternity.

V. *He looked for a more fixed and abiding habitation.*

Here he recognized his own immortality. He associated with his future existence, a union with kindred spirits. He beheld above not a desert, but a *city*,—the city of God—the New Jerusalem—the palace of Jehovah. He saw its foundations were *firm*; yea, firmer than rock. The very being, and purposes, and perfections of God sustaining it. Its grandeur was worthy of its *artificer*. "Builder and maker God." He looked for it by faith, and daily hope, and constant prayer. He reckoned upon it as his own. He lived in reference to it; and daily felt himself getting near and nearer to it.

APPLICATION.

1. *Have we obeyed God, and given up the sinful pursuits of the present world?*

2. *Are we living by faith or by sight?*

Abandoning present temporal gain, for future spiritual and eternal glory.

3. *Urge all to set out.*

4. *Believers to persevere, &c.*

CXLVI.—ABRAM'S JOURNEYINGS.

"And Abram passed through the land unto the place of Sichem, unto the plain of Moreh: and the Canaanite *was* then in the land: and the Lord appeared unto Abram, and said, Unto thy seed will I give this land: and there builded he an altar unto the Lord, who appeared unto him. And he removed from thence unto a mountain on the east of Beth-el, and pitched his tent, *having* Beth-el on the west, and Hai on the east: and there he builded an altar unto the Lord, and called upon the name of the Lord. And Abram journeyed, going on still toward the south."—*Gen.* xii. 6–9.

EVERY event in the striking history of Abram may well interest the devout reader of the Divine word. He occupies so great a space among the condensed biographies of Old Testament history. His call was so remarkable. His faith and obedience so signal. His devotion to God so eminent. His character so honored, that we may well linger and meditate on the various circumstances of his eventful life. In the 1st verse, we have a Divine call to Abram, to go forth from his country, &c. In verses 2d and 3d the Divine promises made on this occasion. In verses 4th and 5th we have Abram entering on his course, &c. Then follows the text. Observe,

I. *His journeyings.*

II. *His piety.* And,

III. *His blessings.*

I. *Abram's journeyings.*

Observe,

1. *They began by forsaking his native land.*

Doubtless attached to it. The family inheritance, and friends, and kindred all there. But he had to leave *all*, &c. So the penitential believer is to forsake all for Christ. His love of the world—its maxims, society, &c. "Come out," &c. Ye are not of the world, &c. As Matthew, &c.

2. *They were distinguished by various changes.*

He was to look to God for direction. He was to have no choice, &c. *Three* changes are described in the text. He was to have no fixed abode, &c. This fitly describes the varied states of the Christian traveller. Never in precisely the same state, perhaps two days together. Now on the mountain-top, then valley. Now in the fruitful plain, then the arid desert, &c. No rest here. No continuing city, &c. His journeyings,

3. *Were connected with various trials.*

In one case, the text says, the Canaanite was in the land. The idolatrous, scoffing, hating Canaanite. How symbolical of the unsubdued evil of our hearts! Foes without; but the worst, by far, within. The most insidious, deceitful, and dangerous. Hence, also his various removals would try faith, and hope, and patience. So the Christian's spiritual pilgrimage, &c. These journeyings,

4. *Were long and continued.*

The text describes his "Going on still," &c. How graphically it sets forth the Christian's course:—*Tried*, but going on still. *Tempted*, &c. *Persecuted*, &c. *Weary*, &c. *Discouraged*, but going on still. In *duty;* in *labor;* in *suffering*, going on still, and towards the balmy south—towards the better land. But observe,

II. *His piety.*

Now the evidences of this in the text, are,

1. *His uniform obedience.*

He obeyed God. Without reasoning, or questioning, or hesitation, or delay, or reluctance. He believed and obeyed; and did so heartily and cheerfully, &c.: with constancy and perseverance.

2. *His devotional spirit.*

"He called on the name of the Lord." He lived in union and communion with God. He asked of God all he required. Sought every thing at his hands, &c. Was anxious for nothing. How essential this prayerful spirit.

Then observe,

3. *He publicly honored and worshipped God.*

Verse 7. He reared an altar to the Lord, in the face of the idolatrous Canaanite. So verse 8. He avowed his religion. Publicly exhibited it. And as the head of a large household he employed his influence for the pious good of those around him. Hear God's testimony; chap. xviii. 19. What an illustrious example! How worthy of our imitation, &c.

Notice then,

III. *His blessings.*

Here we notice,

1. *Special revelations of the Divine favor.*

"God appeared," &c., ver. 7. Abram was so distinguished and honored, as to be called, the "Friend of God." God favored him with especial manifestations and communion, &c. But such is the Christian's privilege. "How is it that thou," &c. John xiv. 22, &c. 2 Cor. vi. 17, &c.

2. *Constant guidance and protection.*

God led him. Directed him. He said, "Walk before me," &c.: chap. xvii. 1; xv. 1. What more could he desire or need, &c. Yet, thus the Christian has the Spirit of God, who guides his people, &c. "Never leaves nor forsakes," &c. "The Lord God is a sun," &c.

3. *Great and precious promises.*

Verses 2 and 7. Now, these promises were clear, and great, and often *renewed.* Not only referred to the earthly Canaan, but evidently to the heavenly rest. See Heb. xi. 8–16. Now, so are blessed all the followers of the Lord Jesus. Great and precious promises are given, &c. Including all we need for time and eternity, &c.

APPLICATION.

1. *Encourage those who have set out on this heavenly pilgrimage.*

Be steadfast. Go forward. Still look before and above, &c.

2. *Invite others to join with you.*

"We are journeying," &c.

3. *The safety and happiness of the people of God.*

They may sing,

"How happy is the pilgrim's lot," &c.

"I would not change my blest estate, For all the world calls good or great," &c.

CXLVII.—ELIEZUR'S APPEAL, IMPROVED.

"And he said unto them, Hinder me not, seeing the Lord hath prospered my way; send me away, that I may go to my master."—*Gen.* xxiv. 56.

THE incidents of this chapter are exceedingly striking. Abraham is deeply concerned that his son Isaac should not take a wife from the ungodly Canaanites; and, therefore, he commissions his eldest servant —a kind of steward of the family—to go unto his own country, and from his own kindred, to select him a help-meet and fellow sojourner, in the valley of tears. Having been sworn to execute his official trust with fidelity, he enters upon the journey, and at length reaches the city of Nahor, verse 10. He then devoutly asks direction and favor from God, verse 12. Immediately we see the kind hand of Jehovah, and the direct interposition of his providence, verse 15, &c.

At length, the whole of the preliminaries are settled—Rebekah is consulted, and the final arrangements made for her returning with him. They now suggest a few days' delay before the journey is commenced— our text is the reply to this: "And he said," &c. How truly faithful and praiseworthy his conduct! What piety to God, and what conscientious devotedness to man. Many lessons are deducible from it; but I desire to accommodate the text and the language of the Christian minister, when pleading the cause of his Divine master, with the church.

Let us look,

I. *At the Christian minister's way.*

II. *When God may be said to prosper it.*

III. *The hindrances which they deprecate in the execution of their work.*

Let us look,

I. *At the Christian minister's way.*

The way or work of the Christian minister, is variously represented. It is called a Stewardship. It is service; and he is a laborer for, and with God. It is described as fishing for men. Building. Instructing. It is likened to the paternal relationship, &c.

1. *It is a way of Divine appointment.*

Eph. iv. 11. The Christian minister is

called, and qualified, and sent forth by the Lord. God gives him the desire for usefulness,—ability to be useful—and his help in the use of the means to effect it.

2. *It is a way of great responsibility.*

A Christian is responsible. A Christian parent or master, much more so. A Christian deacon, more still. A Christian minister, most of all.

Doddridge sings:

> "'Tis not a cause of small import
> The pastor's care demands;
> But what might fill an angel's heart,
> And filled a Saviour's hands."

I only add,

3. *It is a way of numerous difficulties.*

Many enemies. Much opposition. Our own hearts, &c., often present the very greatest. It is a work in which heaven, and earth, and hell are concerned; and the influences in constant and in vigorous action.

II. *When it may be said that God prospers it.*

"Seeing the Lord hath prospered my way."

1. *When Divine providence opens a suitable sphere of usefulness.*

How important to be in our right place. To have our pastoral heritage chosen by the Lord. To hear the Divine voice saying, This is the way, walk thou in it. A persuasion of this, is of the utmost importance to the comfort, and hope of the minister.

2. *When God gives a minister favor in the eyes of the people.*

That is, when he is acceptable to them. When the majority approve of his labors. So many things necessary to this. Matter and manner, &c.; voice, and appearance, and spirit; and an almost endless number of little things.

3. *When the word is listened to with interest and attention.*

How delightful when persons give heed, &c. When they evidently receive the truth, as the thirsty soul, of the flowing stream. For there must be the spirit of hearing, intent and joyous, if the word profit. It is said of those in Samaria—"That they gave heed to the things," &c.

4. *When souls are converted to God.*

The ignorant enlightened. The hard impressed. The thoughtless become serious. When souls are "turned from darkness," &c. Snatched as brands from the burning. This is God giving testimony to the word of his grace. When it is said, "This and that man are born," &c.

5. *When the disciples of Christ are edified and trained for immortality.*

Growing in grace, &c. Contending earnestly for the faith, &c. Of one mind, striving for the gospel. Minding the same things—working by the same rule, &c. The graces brightening,—the virtues vigorous—character ripening—the practical path more and more radiant. When the various characteristics are suitably blessed, &c. "Happy is the people," &c. Now we notice,

III. *The hindrances deprecated.*

"Hinder me not," &c.

There are just as many ways of hindering as helping. We can only refer to a few. The minister may be hindered,

1. *By inattention to Christian ordinances.*

This hinders in a variety of ways. It chills others. It impedes inquirers. It damps the ardor of the minister. It frustrates the great end of the means. Ordinances and means nothing, without the people. Apply it to a family meal, where several are absent, and the rest know not why.

2. *Formality of spirit hinders.*

Where there seems no impression. No emotion. No spirit. All decent and orderly, but cold and motionless as statues. Devotion evidently neglected. Little zeal, &c.

3. *Inadequate supply of pecuniary means hinder.*

No movement in the Church, but is necessarily connected with pecuniary aid. Schools. Tracts. Missions. Poor and sick. Chapel. Minister. Now it is the duty and honor of the people to provide for these. To be ready to communicate. As stewards of the Lord's money, to give him a portion back, of what he has lent them.

4. *Neglect of prayer for the minister hinders.*

"Brethren, pray for us," &c.

What is the logical deduction? If you do not, the word may not run, &c. Praying earnestly for the minister, will give you a deep interest in his ministry. This will lead you to feel, and sympathize with him. This will prepare you most effectually for hearing, and sanctifying what you have heard. This will hold up his hands,— strengthen his knees—cheer his heart—animate his spirit. With what comfort, and joy, and confidence he will preach, when he knows he is borne up by the people, that united prayers have ascended to God for him. Need you wonder that the minister should say, " Hinder me not ?" &c.

The world will try to hinder.

Disbelievers will do so.

Scorners and the notorious wicked.

The self-righteous, &c. Satan. Our own infirmities, &c. But your profession, your religious spirit will rather tend to aid, and support, and cheer us.

APPLICATION.

1. *Let the subject lead to serious examination.*

Have I hindered my minister, and retarded the gospel ?

2. *Let it lead to a reconsecration of yourselves to God.*

If not hindered, yet perhaps held much aid back. Time, influence, &c.

3. *Who will be trophies for Christ.*

Who will yield to Christ ? Receive him ? Give up all for him, &c.

CXLVIII.—ESAU, AS A BEACON.

"Then Jacob gave Esau bread and pottage of lentiles ; and he did eat and drink, and rose up, and went his way ; thus Esau despised his birthright."—*Gen.* xxv. 34.

FEW characters have been more misunderstood, and therefore more misrepresented than Esau. He has been introduced as a striking monument of the Divine eternal disapprobation. One of the branded reprobates of the world. He has ever been placed in contrast with Jacob, and those who have delighted in the doctrine of eternal unconditional decrees—and have ever pointed to him as one of the outcasts from the favor of heaven, and hope of salvation. Now did we read, and thus exposed Esau's character, we should hold him up as deserving your commiseration, as an object of intense pity ; but as being no moral Beacon at all. If he did, as he was irresistibly necessitated to do, then, I am at a loss to understand his responsibility—and therefore, his sinfulness. But if he could have done otherwise, and did not —then may I appeal to you, and warn you by his example.

Now this misrepresentation has arisen chiefly from a passage—Rom. ix. 3, &c. " Jacob have I loved, but Esau have I hated." Now observe, where it is thus written—Mal. i. 1, &c. ; and it is evident that,

It applies to their posterity.

Jacob was to be selected as the progenitor of the Messiah.

Esau's natural disposition seems equally excellent, and in some things, more noble, &c. But Jacob placed a high value on Divine things, and was a man of piety and devotedness to God.

Now this was the great cardinal sin of Esau, he despised divine things. See Heb. xii. 16. He preferred earthly and carnal things to the things of God ; and this was his own sin and just condemnation.

Now just observe what,

I. *Esau despised.*

His birthright,—which included distinguished privileges and blessings.

1. *A double portion of the paternal estate.*

2. *Family rule and authority.*

3. *The priestly office.*

Here then, by an arrangement of God, wealth, honor, and religious influence were combined ; and especially bestowed on the first born.

Observe,

II. *That for which he sold his birthright.*

A meal of pottage. Something good in itself. Of great importance to Esau at the time ; yet *valueless*, compared with what he disposed of. Is it not manifest,

It was a *rash* bargain.

A *carnal* bargain.

An exceedingly *foolish* bargain. Then worst of all, it was

An *irretrievable* bargain. He could not reverse it, or prevent the consequences. Now, to whom does Esau stand forth as a *Beacon ?* To all who barter away the blessings of salvation, for any, or every consideration the world can present. " What shall it profit," &c. But it will especially apply to the following characters :

To the *miser,* who sells his soul for gold.

To the *ambitious,* who sell it for fame.

To the *vain,* who sell it for show and decoration.

To the *sensual,* who sell it for carnal delights and pleasures.

To the *drunkard,* who sells it for intoxicating excitement.

To the *worldly*, who sells it for earthly advantages.

Alas! how many sell all hope of salvation for the veriest trifles; and thus act a more foolish part than even Esau.

Now, observe, yours is a worse bargain than Esau's; for there are not merely present distinctions, but *spiritual blessings.* You hinder a love of knowledge—pardon—peace —hope, &c.

There are *eternal blessings.* Relate not only to time, but to eternity—eternal salvation. The everlasting loss of your souls. If lost—you are eternally lost.

Now, let the subject lead you,

1. *To seek divine wisdom.*

A due and reasonable estimate of things. A rational value. One formed by the right rule of sanctified reason.

2. *Let divine things have both the preference and pre-eminence.*

First in time. First in intense regard. First in constant practical estimation.

3. *Let me warn all who are treading in the steps of Esau.*

Both the vicious and the virtuous.

Both the repulsive and amiable.

Both the profligate and the reputable.

" One thing is needful." Real practical religion. Faith in Christ. A new nature; and a holy diligence to secure the blessings of eternal life.

CXLIX.—JACOB'S PIOUS EXCLAMATION AT BETHEL.

(*A Chapel Opening Sketch.*)

" And he was afraid, and said, How dreadful is this place! this is none other but the house of God, and this is the gate of heaven."—*Gen.* xxviii. 17.

THERE can be no doubt that man was designed to render religious homage to his Creator. The faculties with which he is endowed, indicate that he was formed for the lofty purposes of contemplation and worship. Such homage our first parents would render in Paradise. After the fall, there was evidently introduced a new element in their worship—the offering of animal sacrifices, which reminded man of his guilt and desert, and which also pointed to the Lamb of God, which was typically, and

in the Divine purpose, slain from the foundation of the world.

For upwards of 2,000 years, the rural altar of stone was connected with the dwellings of the people of God; and here, under the direction of the head of the family, who was priest of the domestic circle, sacrifices were presented, and Jehovah worshipped. Hence it is recorded of Abraham, wherever he sojourned, that he reared an altar to the Lord.

In after ages, the Tabernacle was constructed according to the pattern which God gave to Moses on the Mount; and here he received the services of his people, and revealed his glory. The Tabernacle, which though a costly and magnificent tent, was chiefly adapted to Israel in their wanderings, was superseded by a temple, which for ages remained as the dwelling-place of Jehovah, and the glory of his people Israel. But Jesus not only abolished the ceremonial rites of Judaism, but he came to set up a heavenly kingdom, which should recognize distinctly, the spiritual worship of God. So that now, "wherever two or three," &c. Now it is recorded, that " God is a Spirit," &c.

Our text, though connected with the history of Jacob, may lead us to profitable reflections, on the devotion of this house to the worship of God.

With the narrative connected with the text, you are all familiar. His journey— his fatigue—his solitary condition—his reclining on his mother earth—his vision— and hence his exclamation; ver. 16.

Observe two things,

I. *The place described.* And,

II. *The emotions expressed.*

I. *The place described.*

" The House of God," and " the Gate of Heaven."

1. *The house of God.*

Why may an erection like this be styled the house of God?

(1.) As it bears the inscription of his name. Jacob called the place of his vision, Bethel, *i. e.*, House of God. Not the house of Baal, nor Belus, nor Ashtaroth—but the House of God. The universe is his. He has written his name on the broad arch of heaven—on the face of universal nature. But the Christian sanctuary is the especial property of God. Here his name is peculiarly recorded,—not only as the God of nature and providence, but as the God of grace.

Here is inscribed, "His new best name of love."

2. *As it is reared and devoted to his glory.*

His being and attributes are here acknowledged. His authority recognized. Here intelligent beings exhibit their knowledge of him—their confidence in him—their love for him—their obedience to him. Thus in an especial manner is the Christian sanctuary dedicated to his glory.

It is so also,

3. *As it is the depository of his truth.*

In the Ark of the Covenant, the law of God was sacredly treasured. Here we have (1.) The whole of the lively oracles, the whole canon of the Divine Scriptures—the completed infallible testimony of God to man. We have it,

(2.) In our own tongue, &c.; and for every worshipper. Hence as in the Archives the ancient writings were deposited —so God's house is the hallowed depository of the records of saving and eternal truth.

4. *As it is the residence of his family.*

Here he dwells in the midst of his children. Here is the family table. Here they wait on him,—have constant audience and access. Here he meets with them. Is in the very midst, &c. As it is,

5. *For the manifestation of his Son.*

Christ as the predicted Messiah, was set forth in all the sacrifices of Jewish altars, &c. He was typified both by the Tabernacle and Temple, &c. So in the Christian sanctuary, Christ is emphatically manifested. In the word read. In the gospel preached. In the praises celebrated. As the medium of access to God in every service. Here his Cross is lifted up, and his glory displayed.

6. *As it is the object of God's special regards.*

The history of his Church in all ages attests this. His numerous promises and gracious declarations. He hath chosen Zion, &c. "Mine eyes and mine heart," &c. But observe,

It is the gate of heaven.

Here several ideas are suggested.

1. *It is connected with the entrance of the pathway to heaven.*

As Jacob's sleeping spot was at the foot of the ladder, which reached to heaven. Though distant from heaven, yet it was close to the pathway opened to it. So here, generally the first thoughts of heaven are conceived—first desires excited—first resolutions formed—first prayers offered—first blessings enjoyed. It is,

2. *In immediate union and harmony with heaven.*

Heavenly beings descend. Angels on the ladder, &c. "Are they not all ministering spirits," &c. "There is joy in the presence of the angels," &c. So in the house of God we have communion with heaven. Like a little heaven, &c. The act of worship is, to lift the heart to heaven, &c. Praises offered, as in heaven. Meditation and communion, as in heaven.

3. *As distinguished by heavenly blessings*

"Every good gift," &c. Wisdom—peace —love—gentleness—joy—hope. So that here are the days of heaven on earth. Often come to the gate and behold, by faith, the glories of heaven.

4. *From which the Christian is introduced into heaven.*

He is born in God's house. Reared and educated in it. Trained and meetened in it. He dwells in it all the days, &c. Then he passes upwards. Goes out of the holy place, into the holiest of all. Passes through the vail of the death-smitten body, into the regions of immortality and eternal life. So as the gate is to the mansion, the house of God is to the heavenly world. Such is the description given : "House of God, and the gate of heaven." Notice,

II. *The emotions expressed.*

1. *Adoring surprise.*

"Surely the Lord," &c.; ver. 16. Is it not amazing that God should thus bow down and visit his worshipping people ? Think of his infinite majesty,—unsullied purity ! The worship he receives from perfect and holy beings, &c., in the celestial temple. "Will God in very deed ?" &c. The high and lofty one, &c.

2. *Reverential fear.*

"How dreadful," &c. God is to be feared, &c. To be had in reverence. "Fear before him," &c. Shall we not fear, when we think of his omniscience ? Eyes, as of fire—seeing all, &c. So pure, &c. Then our own infirmities, depravity, guilt, &c. Then there was,

3. *Devout consecration.*

Ver. 18. The oil is typical of the spirit of God. God's spirit really consecrates by his presence, &c. This we are to solicit by prayer, in reference to this house, &c. "If ye being evil," &c. "Whatsoever two or three," &c.

There is,

4. *Grateful remembrance.*

He seeks to perpetuate the scene. To rear a monument, &c. Vers. 18, 19. So should we. "We will not forget," &c. "If I forget," &c. They ought to be dear indeed to us, &c.

"My soul shall pray for Zion still," &c.

Evince it, by seeking its peace, and laboring for its prosperity. Give it our warmest emotions,—our most active efforts. Seek the good of Zion, always.

APPLICATION.

Learn,

1. *The estimate in which we should hold the Christian sanctuary.*

While we avoid all that is superstitious, &c., yet remember it is the house of God. We should keep our feet, &c. Seek for Divine grace to prepare us for its services. Value its privileges. Let us seek,

2. *That the Christian sanctuary may be to us the gate of Heaven.*

How many have found it so! Have you? May this be so to thousands, &c.

3. *That which is essential to the true consecration of the Christian sanctuary.*

"The Divine presence." Let this be sought, &c., cherished. Absence deprecated, &c.

4. *That wherever God manifests himself, is the house of God.*

In the open air, as in the case of the text. On the top of the mountain—glen—ocean—room—cathedral, &c. Christian catholicity rejoices in this,—prays for the whole of his assemblies. Let us cherish this spirit, and glorify God, and thus honor the gospel of the Lord Jesus Christ.

CL.—JACOB'S MONUMENTAL PILLAR.

"And Jacob arose up early in the morning, and he took the stone that he had put for his pillows, and set it up for a pillar, and poured oil upon the top of it," &c.—*Gen.* xxviii. 18, 19.

OUR text is connected with one of the most remarkable incidents in the life of Jacob. He was now an exile from his father's house. On his way to Padan-aram. Alone on this journey, he is overtaken by night. He fixes upon the spot where to rest until the morning. The: God visited him by a most remarkable vision. He dreamed, &c.; ver. 12. Here both the ways of providence and the purposes of grace were unfolded to him. A direct promise, full of comfort, was given to him; vers. 14, 15, &c.

Then Jacob awoke, and exclaimed: "Surely the Lord," &c., ver. 16, &c. He then performs the acts to which our text refers, &c.

Observe,

I. *What Jacob did.*

II. *How he did it.* And,

III. *The reasons on which his conduct was grounded.*

I. *What Jacob did.*

In one word; he erected a monumental pillar, and piously devoted it to celebrate God's goodness towards him.

Observe,

1. *The stone on which he reclined was the material of the pillar.*

A hard pillow for the weary traveller; yet to tired, exhausted nature it was welcome and sweet. But how it had been hallowed by the visions of the night. No ordinary stone. And now it was to be erected to commemorate the events of that season. We read of such erections often in the Divine word—Genesis xxxi. 45; xxxv. 14; Joshua iv. 4; 1 Sam. vii. 12. So Egypt and the cities and plains of Greece are full of such monuments. Our Museum is crowded with entire or portions of such pillars. Some to celebrate battles, triumphs, and other illustrious events.

2. *The pillar was consecrated with oil.*

This was a kind of religious act. Person and things were thus devoted to God. This stone was to celebrate a religious event, and hence, with oil, it is set apart to the divine service: Exodus xl. 9.

3. *He called the pillar and spot on which it rested, Bethel.*

The House of God,—where God had met, and revealed himself, in mercy, to his dependent creature. Where promises had been given,—vows made,—services performed,—engagements realized. How often has God hallowed places, and spots, and times, and circumstances, by his blessing.

Now, notice in reference to this act,

II. *How Jacob did it.*

1. *He did it early.*

"Early in the morning." With the vision still bright—the emotions deep, &c. He did not hesitate, nor delay. He did it *first.* God's things should always be first. "Seek ye first," &c. First in life it should be,

" Remember now thy Creator," &c. " Wilt thou not from this time, cry unto me," &c. Religious things should be *first* in importance; and always first every day. Especially have the entire of the first day of the week.

2. *He did it solemnly.*

How reverential and awe-struck he evidently was. " How dreadful," &c., verse 17. Here was a service in our world, and earth; yet the things of time were forgotten. God and spiritual things were in the ascendant. Should it not always be so in our religious exercises?

3. *It was done spiritually.*

Here were symbols and forms of services, —but there was the inward reality. Not merely signs—but the substance. Not merely forms—but the soul engaged. The pillar presented that to which all the rest only referred—his heart's homage! God demands this in all our worship and duties, that they be spiritual services, &c. "God is a spirit," &c. "We are the true circumcision," &c.

III. *The reasons on which the conduct of Jacob was grounded.*

Now these reasons respected the past, the present, and the future.

1. *The reasons respected the past.*

It was to be an abiding record of God's providential goodness and gracious revelations to him. He had been guided, protected, blessed,—he had both his faith and hope in God strengthened. Then grateful love demanded that those things should be remembered. Have we no such past reasons for rearing monumental pillars of grateful remembrance? No deliverances,—no preservations, — no interpositions, — no spiritual blessings? &c. Ah! has not our path been strewed with them? But I fear we have not rendered again, &c.

2. *Another reason referred to the present.*

It was intended to evince the state of mind he felt. His love—his gratitude—his confidence—his resolutions—his vows, &c. This pillar should testify what he then felt and did; and from this he could easily judge as to his spiritual state in future. God and conscience demands this from us. "I beseech you, brethren, by the mercies of God," &c.

3. *Another reason referred to the future.*

He had had visions which referred to the future. The ministering angels—the smiling God—the blessed and gracious engagements of Jehovah. He would have need to remember these in after life. In sorrows—

in trials—in perils, &c. How sweet to think of the pillar, and the scenes of it. How often might he visit Bethel, with comfort and delight. So the illustrious periods in our history should be remembered, and applied, and improved. This would ever be profitable to our souls—be honorable to our religious character, and especially please God.

APPLICATION.

1. *How God has honored man, by his intercourse with him.*

Think of the greatness of God, and then look at insignificant man; and how appropriate the exclamation of the Psalmist: " What is man," &c.

2. *The most marvellous of all these visits of love and mercy, was in the person of the Lord Jesus Christ.*

" Ye know the grace of our Lord Jesus Christ," &c. This is the most sublime and mysterious visitation to our world. That in which we are most deeply concerned,—to which all others referred. Here is the ladder,—the one way,—the covenant of mercy, &c. The church is now Bethel—the house of God. Believers have this manifestation of love and goodness.

3. *The personal interest we should have in it.*

Has it led us to a grateful devotedness to his service and glory? Have we become the Lord's? &c. Have recorded vows been kept? Holy purposes realized, and happy seasons profitably and gratefully improved?

CLI.—ESAU AND JACOB'S RECONCILIATION.

"And Esau ran to meet him, and embraced him, and fell on his neck, and kissed him: and they wept."—*Gen.* xxxiii. 4.

DIFFERENCES and strifes seem the necessary fruit of our depraved nature. No marvel that men quarrel with one another, when they rebel against God, their best Friend. No sooner is human nature corrupted at the fountain, than the stream becomes polluted.

It does not appear that Adam and Eve had their love to each other increased, by their mutual transgression. In the case of Adam, it is evident that he wished to throw upon her the chief odium of the sin. We see this spirit still more manifest in the history of Cain and Abel. Envy, anger, hatred, and at length murder, occupying the breast of the first-born into our world. Alas! from that day to this, strifes, and divisions, and animosities, have distracted the families of men.

Our subject refers to Jacob and Esau; and here we see the same unlovely spirit predominant. From the careless reading of Scripture, we believe that much too high an estimate has been formed of Jacob, while great injustice has been done to Esau. A careful reader of the narrative will find very much to blame in Jacob, and not a few things to commend in Esau. But some never read, without the idea being ever present and pre-eminent, that Jacob was the elect of God, and therefore all excellency; and that Esau was the reprobated of heaven, and therefore all vileness. Our subject is calculated to rectify such gross and erroneous conclusions.

Observe,

I. *It is evident that Jacob was under the influence of considerable alarm and dread.*

See chap. xxxii. 7.

Now whence did this arise? Doubtless, from the belief, that Esau was his enemy; and one of a formidable and dangerous character. But was there no cause for this state of mind in Esau, towards Jacob? To find out that, we must go back and review the circumstances that then occurred. See chapter xxvii. 1. Observe the plot to deceive Isaac, and to take Esau's blessing. Mark, Jacob hesitates, lest there should be a discovery; verse 11. The scheme however succeeds. Jacob wickedly lies, ver. 18; and repeats it, ver. 24. Esau grievously laments his loss; ver. 34. He also became incensed against his brother; ver. 41.

Now it may be said, that it was God's wish that Jacob should supplant Esau; but if God designed Jacob to have the blessing, he could have effected it without falsehood and deceit,—it is little less than blasphemy to unite the holy Deity with a line of conduct so palpably wicked.

Here then was the ground of Jacob's fears. He knew he had wronged Esau, and had given occasion for the anger, which still burned within his bosom.

II. *Jacob, under this dread, had recourse to God for direction and help.*

The haste he made to obtain the blessing, and the sins of that part of his life, had

doubtless long been effaced by the mercy of God; but the remembrance of them still affected him. Well, how does he act? Does he now employ stratagem? Or, does he meet the wrath of Esau with the spirit of resistance? No. Read chap. xxxii. 9, &c. How humble, devout, and grateful was this address! What faith too! How he pleads the promises of God; ver. 12. How wise and pious this line of procedure! He acknowledges God—seeks his protecting care, &c. Commits his way to the Lord. Honors God. How many differences would be settled, if men would take them to God, in prayer.

III. *He adopts a courteous and conciliatory course of action.*

Having obtained the assurance of God's favor, in prayer, during the eventful night at Peniel, he now arranges his family. At the remotest distance from danger, is Rachel and Joseph. And now observe the spirit under which he acted.

1. *In the homage he paid to his brother.*

He bowed himself seven times, &c. He assumed no superiority. He did not even act as his equal; but gave him reverence as his junior, and inferior. How beautiful to see this self-abasement in one whom God had so visibly honored.

2. *He had with him a present of reconciliation.*

Verses 8, 9, 10.

We cannot tell which most to admire, the liberality of Jacob, or the generosity of Esau. Both parties were sincere, and acted with true greatness and nobility of mind.

Notice,

IV. *The unexpected affectionate meeting.*

"And Esau ran," &c.

1. *The injured was the first to run and forgive.*

His heart softened—his spirit relented. The power of love constrained him.

2. *Jacob also wept.*

No doubt tears of joy, and gratitude to God, and of overflowing affection for his brother. Surely in this we see the finger of God,—God made their hearts soft, &c.

APPLICATION.

I. *How important to avoid offences.*

To avoid giving or taking offence.

2. *How deplorable are hatred and strife.*

Anywhere. Among any class. Especially among friends. Relations and Christians.

3. *How desirable is reconciliation.*
Matt. v. 23 ; vi. 14, 15, &c.

4. *What a beautiful example, as to the spirit in which we should labor to effect it.*

5. *How necessary that the sinner's strife should cease against God, and that he should be reconciled to him.*

CLII.—JOSEPH'S PATHETIC APPEAL TO PHARAOH'S BUTLER.

"But think on me when it shall be well with thee, and show kindness, I pray thee, unto me, and make mention of me unto Pharaoh, and bring me out of this house."—*Gen.* xl. 14.

OUR text is the affecting language of Joseph to the chief butler, whose dream he had just interpreted. Let us look at the scene before us. It is an Egyptian prison. We behold in it three persons,—two of the servants of Pharaoh, the chief butler and baker : verse 1, &c. The other is an interesting youth, of a different nation. Who is he, and what has he done ? That youth is Joseph, the son of the godly Jacob. He was the special object of paternal affection. A few years before, and he was clad in the coat of many colors. He is the object of God's providential complacency. His dreams indicate his future greatness. But he becomes the subject of fraternal envy. His own brethren conspire against him. They even contemplate his destruction. But Providence overrules, and he is sold into Egypt. Here he is falsely and wickedly accused by a person of influence, and he is thrown into prison. In prison, God was with him : chap. xxxix. 21. And now the clouds are breaking—the day of hope begins to dawn. His fellow-prisoners dream, and he interprets ; and this lays the first step towards his future advancement. Having given a most cheering interpretation to the chief butler, he addresses him in the language of the text.
We observe,

I. *The uncertain and precarious tenure on which our earthly enjoyments are held.*

Here are three individuals, who had previously been basking in the sunshine of prosperity, now dwelling in the same prison. Joseph, torn from the home of his childhood, had been mourned over as dead. The two servants of Pharaoh, who, doubtless,

considered that their mountain would not be moved. Who have not in some way, and to some extent, had a similar experience ?

How many have been brought down from affluence to poverty !

From health to sickness !

From the enjoyment of friends, to distressing bereavements !

What earthly good is certain ? Alas, nothing ! "For the fashion of this world passeth away." The changing sky—the fluctuating sea—the veering wind—the alternate seasons—all are symbols of man's changing state.

II. *Affectionate sympathy is most consoling to the afflicted and distressed.*

The want of this deepens the anguish—embitters the cup—darkens the scene. To suffer unpitied—to die unlamented—involves the idea of concentrated calamity. Sympathy may not remove our pain ; lessen our pangs ; annihilate one groan ; but it cheers and invigorates the sufferer. I will tell you what it is like. It is the sunbeam entering through the grating into the dungeon, delighting the eye of the captive. It is the sweet breeze entering the window of the sick-room, which enables the patient to breathe more freely. It is the draught from the cooling spring, to the wearied way-worn scorched traveller. It is more than these,—it is the balm of goodness, poured into the wound of sorrow, which softens, and heals, and comforts.

III. *We ought to cherish the feelings of affectionate sympathy towards our friends, in suffering and adversity.*

We should do so,

Because God has formed us with the emotions necessary.

Because it is an essential part of all acceptable religion, "Thou shalt love thy neighbor," &c.

Because it is a leading characteristic of the Christian religion.

It is the love of God in the soul.—It is the love of Christ constraining.—It is the Spirit of God influencing. Mercy, compassion, pity, are indispensable in New Testament piety. "Be pitiful," &c. "As the elect of God, put on bowels," &c. "He that dwelleth in God, dwelleth in love."

Because we may soon require the sympathy of others. Your mountain may now be strong—circumstances good—health sound —domestic hearth cheerful. But the reverses of Providence may be coming. The east wind, the black clouds, the teeming rain, &c.

IV. *There are special seasons when this sympathetic remembrance should be cherished.*

It should be the habit—the state of the heart. But sometimes more intense, &c.

1. *When at the throne of grace.*

The spirit of prayer has descended upon you,—the fire is burning brightly on the altar of your hearts. You are touching the hem of the Saviour's priestly robe, and the virtue is communicated. You have power with God, and you have access to the riches of the Divine grace. Oh, then, think of the sorrowful, the distressed, the afflicted! Touching the sceptre of the Divine mercy, should transmute all your feelings into mercifulness. Oh! then, pray largely, affectionately, powerfully, for those in adversity.

2. *When at the table of the Lord.*

Feasting at Christ's hallowed board. Favored by the presence of the King of kings. At the sacred banquet. Having audience with the Lord. *Think of those who are deprived.* Be with them in spirit. Seek God's blessing, &c. Think of those you would wish to be there. How many relatives, friends, children, &c.

V. *This spirit has often been exemplified in the history of the pious.*

There was Moses, and the Israelites in Egypt.

There was Ruth and Naomi.

There was Onesiphorus and Paul.

But let us pause. There was Jesus, and our miserable race. It was well with him; yet when he saw us in guilt and peril, oh, amazing love! he flew, &c.

> "This was compassion like a God,
> That when the Saviour knew
> The price of pardon was his blood,
> His pity ne'er withdrew."

After his sojourn of sorrows, he ascended; it is well with him *now*, &c. No more poverty, persecutions, tears, cries, sufferings, &c. But does he forget his people—his tried and tempted ones?

> "Our fellow-sufferer yet retains
> A fellow feeling of our pains;
> And still remembers in the skies
> His tears, and agonies, and cries.
>
> In every pang that rends the heart,
> The Man of Sorrows has a part;
> He sympathizes with our grief,
> And to the sufferer sends relief."

APPLICATION.

Let the subject lead us,

1. *To exemplify the spirit of the text.*

Self must be crucified,—kindness cherished.

2. *Let our text especially have a spiritual bearing.*

To the spiritual concerns of our fellow-creatures. Charity to the soul, is the soul of charity.

3. *Let us rejoice in the affectionate remembrance of Jesus, and reciprocate it.*

At his table we profess to do so.

CLIII.—PHARAOH'S IMPIOUS INTERROGATION.

"And Pharaoh said, Who is the Lord, that I should obey his voice to let Israel go? I know not the Lord, neither will I let Israel go."—*Exodus* v. 2.

THE text was the language of the pagan impious Pharaoh, a person whose history and character are fully presented to us in the Divine word.

Moses, as the servant of the Most High, is commanded to bear to the Egyptian monarch the Divine will respecting Israel. Moses delivers God's message, ver. 1, and to this the proud monarch replies: "Who is the Lord," &c. Here see the infatuation and wickedness of the king,—an infatuation which he cherished, until God visited him with fearful plagues, and which, at length, ended only in his utter and total ruin. But the spirit of the text is often felt, where the words would not be used. All ungodliness sets Jehovah at defiance, and carries out the rebellious feeling felt and expressed by Pharaoh.

In thus applying the subject, observe,

I. *God has spoken to mankind.*

His voice has been heard.

1. *He has spoken significantly by his works.*

"The heavens declare," &c. Rom. i. 20. Here the existence, majesty, power, and wisdom of God are all declared.

2. *He has spoken continually by his good providence.*

The admirable provision made for all creatures, &c. Hear Paul's address to the inhabitants of Lystra: Acts xiv. 15, 17.

3. *God hath spoken awfully by his judgments.*

How terrible his voice to the antediluvians—Pharoah, &c. By war—by pestilence—by famine—by earthquakes, &c.

4. *God has spoken distinctly in his word.*

By the ancient prophets—by his *own* Son. Hear the Apostle; Heb. i. 1, &c. The Saviour also instituted the Christian ministry, to convey the words of God to all the world, &c. Now God's voice has thus come to you. He has spoken to instruct you—to reveal his will—to induce consideration—to produce conviction—to lead you to repentance and salvation.

Consider,

II. *Why, and how you should hear.*

1. *Why you should hear his voice.*

(1.) Because of his *right* in you and over you. He is God—your God. Creator. Lawgiver, &c.

(2.) Because of his *condescension* to you. It is infinite condescension on the part of Deity to stoop and speak to you. How angels hearken! How seraphim listen!

(3.) Because of the *design* of his speaking. For your present and eternal welfare. It is the voice of love and mercy. Nothing but pure, free compassion, constrains him, &c. But we inquire,

2. *How we should hear his voice.*

With profound reverence and awe. When God speaks, let all the earth keep silence.

With sacred and holy attention.

With solicitous anxiety to understand his will.

With a holy desire to be obedient to his authority. "All the words, &c., we will do." Have you thus heard the voice of God?

III. *The impiety and folly of refusing to hear the voice of God.*

But who are guilty of it?

The self-deceived skeptic.

The infatuated sensualist.

The engrossed worldling.

Every impenitent unbelieving sinner.

Now observe,

The pride of the heart leads to this. Unbelief leads to it. Inconsideration tends to it. But mark the folly and misery of such a spirit and practice.

1. *It is flagrant contempt of God.*

2. *It is open rebellion against his authority.*

3. *It must be eventually ruinous to the sinner.*

Who hath hardened himself against God?

&c. See Heb. ii. 1; iii. 7, &c. There can be no escape—no alternative, &c. "He who being often reproved," &c. Let Pharaoh, Belshazzar, and myriads of the disobedient lost, admonish you, &c.

APPLICATION.

1. *To-night God again speaks to you.*

"O, earth," &c. "Hear, and your soul shall live," &c.

2. *Do not despise the Divine word.*

Nor procrastinate, &c.

3. *To the voice of final judgment all, all must hearken.*

"And I saw a great white throne," &c. "The dead shall hear his voice," &c.

CLIV.—THE BLOOD OF THE PASSOVER.

"And the blood shall be to you for a token upon the houses where ye are: and when I see the blood, I will pass over you, and the plague shall not be upon you to destroy you, when I smite the land of Egypt."—*Exodus* xii. 13.

THE last of the plagues which God inflicted on the land of Egypt, was the most awful and terrific. Time after time had Pharaoh, though penitential and humbled at the time, risen again to hardness, and reckless despair of the God of Israel. But now the last and most terrible of the judgments of heaven, is to be brought on Pharaoh and the land. The narrative is given; chap. xii. 29, 30. Oh, think of that ghastly, terrible scene! God had provided for the safety of the children of Israel,—thus, that the blood of the Paschal Lamb was to be sprinkled, &c. See verse 7.

Now this remarkable and gracious provision is instructive in itself; but it was designed also to prefigure the great scheme of human redemption, by Christ Jesus. The apostle says, "Christ our passover is sacrificed for us."

Look,

I. *At the blood referred to.*

II. *The Divine observance of it.* And,

III. *The deliverance enjoyed by it.*

Look,

I. *At the blood referred to.*

Now, here are several interesting particulars. Observe,

1. *It was to be the blood of a lamb.*

The lamb was the leading type among the various sacrifices which referred to the Saviour. He is the Lamb of God, so often referred to. " Behold," &c. The meekness and innocency of the lamb, represents the gentleness and goodness of Jesus.

The lamb was to be without blemish, &c.; verse 5. God would have no maimed or inferior offering. See Mal. i. 12, &c. See the application to Christ. Heb. ix. 14; 1 Peter i. 19. This was essential to Christ's atonement.

It was to be its *blood;* that is, its life. The lamb must be taken, bound, slain, &c. No deliverance without its blood. Observe,

2. *This blood was to be sprinkled according to divine instruction.*

One of the figures by which man is represented, is that of a House. " Whose house are ye," says the Apostle. A temple—a palace. Now it is implied that the house is in peril. Such were the dwellings in Egypt, on account of the threatened visit of the destroying angel. We are so, on account of our sins, &c. Now, the blood was to be particularly applied as God had directed. See verse 21, &c.

This application of the blood on the house, was to teach us the necessity of a *personal* interest in the blood of Christ. No national or family condition can save us. We must be personally saved; for we are personally guilty, &c.

And the manner of application must be observed. As the bitter hyssop was to be dipped, &c. So, by true repentance for sin and godly hatred of it, we must come to the blood of Jesus for pardon and eternal life.

The extensive application of it, as given, verse 7; seems to indicate the power of Christ's atoning sacrifice, as being efficacious to the whole soul,—to the understanding, judgment, will, conscience, heart, &c. The whole soul needs it, and it must be applied to every part. Then observe in reference to the sprinkled blood.

II. *The Divine observance of it.*

" And when I see the blood," &c. Now with respect to you,

God sees the guilt of man.

God sees the punishment due.

He cannot justly remit the penalty, for it is right, &c. " Without shedding," &c.

But he provides the remedy. Substitutes the blood of the lamb; and thus is gracious to the guilty, &c.

Now, mark well,

1. *God does not look at the sinner, but at the blood.*

If he observed, and marked iniquity,

who could stand? Not one who had the least stain upon him. One sin would cry for judgment. So that God looks at the blood of atonement, and not at the imperfect state of the best of his creatures.

2. *God does not look at the application even of his own means.*

It is not the listening to his own word. It is not the humbling of the soul. It is not the repentance. It is not the faith in itself. No, he *looks* at the *blood* only. Here is all the efficacy—all the virtue, &c.

3. *In beholding the blood, God is satisfied.*

His justice is met. His law magnified. His truth vindicated. His greatness upheld; and at the same time, his goodness and love pre-eminently exalted. See the whole as stated by the Apostle. Rom. iii. 20–26.

Observe, then,

III. *The deliverance enjoyed.*

" I will pass over you," &c. So it was with Israel in Egypt. Now both in reference to Israel and to us, the deliverance is twofold.

1. *Deliverance from the destroying angel.*

The house escaped the judgment. In your case, man is delivered from the curse of the law. He is justified freely, &c. No condemnation. All peril is gone. All wrath removed. All danger passed by. But,

2. *There was deliverance from their Egyptian state.*

It was then they became free. Yoke broken. Liberty obtained. Egypt forsaken. So they journeyed on towards the land of promise. So in reference to believers. Faith in Christ's blood, obtains spiritual freedom. " Translated," &c. " Made free," &c. Now children, &c., of God, and heirs of eternal life. Candidates for immortality, &c. Now observe, how all this was divinely arranged, and infallibly carried out. It was God's work, and redounded to his glory. So the whole scheme of the sinner's salvation.

APPLICATION.

1. *There is deliverance from sin and wrath.*

2. *That deliverance is through the blood of Christ.*

We must trust to nothing else. This the one foundation.

3. *A personal interest in it is essential.*

4. *The happiness of the delivered.*

5. *It is the will of God that all may be saved.*

Christ is the Lamb of God for the world.

CLV.—THE PERSONS WHO KEPT THE PASSOVER, TYPES OF THOSE WHO SHOULD SIT DOWN AT THE TABLE OF THE LORD.

"And the Lord said unto Moses and Aaron, This is the ordinance of the passover: There shall no stranger eat thereof," &c.—*Exodus* xii. 43, and verse 47.

In the previous discourse, we showed the peculiar and interesting character of the Passover, and its typical representation of our redemption by Christ Jesus. We wish now to call your attention to the persons who were to eat of the Passover; and you observe that the answer is contained, both negatively and positively, in the two passages I have read to you.

Now in this it was remarkably typical of the persons who ought to celebrate the death of the Lord Jesus, in the ordinance of the supper; and as such we shall apply it.

In doing so, let us,

I. *Consider those divinely excluded from the Lord's table, and the grounds of it.*

II. *Those for whom it is provided, and the duty and manner of observing it.*

I. *Those divinely excluded from the Lord's table, and the grounds of it.*

Now in the text it is said, "There shall no stranger," &c. Now the exclusion of the stranger was evidently grounded on several reasons, each of which will apply to the Lord's Supper.

1. *Want of knowledge.*

No service can be pleasing to God which is performed in ignorance. So far from ignorance being the mother of devotion, it is the spoiler of devotion. It blights and destroys it. God is to be served intelligibly. Not only in spirit, but in truth. And the Israelites were instructed to state the whole grounds of the service to their children. See chap. xii. 26. Now ignorance of Christ and the doctrines of the gospel equally disqualify. We must know Christ before we can eat worthily, &c. Hence, a want of spiritual knowledge must exclude from the table of the Lord.

2. *Want of faith.*

A knowledge of Christ when truly experienced leads to faith in him; and this faith is essential to pleasing God in any duty, and was ever so. "Without faith," &c. All the ancients served God in faith. See a reference to the Passover: Heb. xi. 28.

Now the stranger to God and religion has no faith; and therefore it is a mockery for him to sit down at a religious ordinance.

3. *Want of personal interest in the thing signified.*

Religious services suppose always, that the spirit and heart are concerned—that there is a personal interest in it. This is the very essence of all acceptable worship.

Now it was a deliverance for the Israelites, and they only were concerned; therefore, they only could feel an interest in it. Now, so, deliverance from sin by Christ, is only available to the believer. No unbeliever, as such, can be interested in it. The unbeliever must perish. He has no lot nor part in the matter; therefore, he is appropriately excluded from the Passover in the one case, and the Lord's Supper in the other. Now the stranger to the way of life, by ignorance—the stranger to Jesus, by unbelief—and the stranger to personal religion, in a carnal state, are excluded from the ordinance of the Supper.

Then notice,

II. *Those for whom it is provided, and the duty and manner of observing it.*

Verse 47. "All the congregation of Israel shall keep (or do) it." Now observe here,

1. *It is for the Lord's people.*

For Israel under the law, and the disciples of Christ under the gospel. In the setting up of the ordinance, Christ administered it to his disciples. Matt. xviii. 26. Then afterwards, when Christ's kingdom was set up, and the Holy Ghost poured out, and the first church established, it is said, "Then they that gladly received his word," &c. Acts ii. 41. Hence, they had become disciples. See also Acts xx. 7.

Now Christ's disciples are such as know and believe in him, and have an interest in his love and mercy.

2. *It is for the congregation of the Lord's people.*

Verse 47, "The congregation." The assembly.

Now, congregation, or assembly, is the very idea contained in the word church. So that the Lord's Supper is for the church, for all disciples; but to be observed congregationally. Hence the private administration of the Lord's Supper has no precedent in the Scriptures: and is evidently a corruption of primitive Christianity. A thing done, to set forth the idea of sacramental efficacy. Now no such *idea* was connected with the

Passover. They knew it was but the *sign*—it did not deliver, but God; and this was only a significant memorial of it. So in the Lord's Supper, there is no saving efficacy. That is all in Christ, in the flesh and blood; and the Supper *shows* it forth, or exhibits it to the mind.

3. *It is obligatory on the congregation of Israel.*

"Shall keep it."

In the case of the Passover, it was pre-eminently enjoined. The authority of God given to it. Hear the announcement of it; verses 3 and 14. So also the Lord's Supper. It is clear Jesus enjoined it on all the twelve, &c. It is clear, also, that the first Christian church so understood it. Acts ii. 1, 2, &c. So the statement of the Apostle Paul evidently involves the idea, that it is to be a perpetual ordinance in Christ's church, till his second coming. 1 Cor. xi. 23–26.

All ancient church history shows that this was an ordinance kept up by the early Christians; and also, that it was kept weekly. On the Lord's day, they commemorated the two great facts in the history of redemption—the death and resurrection of Christ Jesus.

4. *It was to be observed by the congregation, just in the manner God had appointed.*

The Passover was to be observed at the exact time. By the precise persons, with the peculiar services. No addition—no alteration. How equally so, the Supper of the Lord! It is to be the standing ordinance of the church. It is to be for all Christ's disciples. The elements are to be preserved, both bread and wine; and the end kept in view, to *show* forth Christ's death—to keep up a memorial of it, and our faith in it; and grateful love for it, till Christ come again. Even the posture is important, &c.

APPLICATION.

1. *Let Christians feel and act up to their duty and privileges.*

2. *Expect from it and in it, spiritual growth and comfort.*

3. *Let sinners come to Christ, and then to his table.*

CLVI.—PHARAOH'S UTTER DESTRUCTION.

"The enemy said, I will pursue, I will overtake, I will divide the spoil; my lust shall be satisfied upon them; I will draw my sword, my hand shall destroy them," &c.—*Exodus* xv. 9, 10.

THE history of Pharaoh is deeply interesting and admonitory. He is introduced to us as a cunning and wary politician; Exod. i. 9, &c. Then as a cruel and heartless oppressor; ver. 11, 12. Then as a relentless murderer; ver. 15. In this war of extermination against man, we find God frustrating his schemes, and defeating his projects; ver. 20, last clause.

This Pharaoh died, but his successor seems equally as infatuated and tyrannical. To him Moses was sent. Before him wrought his miracles. To the request of Moses to let Israel go, he impiously inquired, "Who is the Lord," &c. Miracle after miracle was wrought, &c., but still Pharaoh remained infatuated and desperate; and occasionally relenting, and then hardening his heart. Then came the plagues in awful succession, until he was anxious that Israel should go. The Israelites are now on their way, when Pharaoh repents of his concession, and resolves to overtake, &c.; chap. xiv. 5.

We now see them pursuing, &c. God interposes by the pillar of cloud. Light to the Israelites—dark to the Egyptians, &c.; ver. 20. The sea divided, &c. Then came the fearful catastrophe which is thus sublimely described, verse 23, &c.

Now in the song of Moses, the event is thus described; "The enemy said, I will pursue," &c.

I. *The infatuated spirit of the enemies of Israel.* And,

II. *Their signal overthrow and ruin.*

I. *The infatuated spirit of the enemies of Israel.*

Observe the spirit of the enemy was characterized,

1. *By great ambition.*

It was the love of power and dominion. To hold human beings as property, is the vilest display of ambition. It is to rob God; for all souls are his, &c. This spirit is displayed in warlike kings, in extending their dominions.

Hence, what scenes of horror and bloodshed have been exhibited by nations making aggressive wars, and enlarging their territory, &c.

2. *Great arrogance and pride.*

Observe how self is exalted. " I will pursue, I will overtake, I will divide," &c. What self-confidence,—what boasting,—what assumption, &c.

This spirit distinguished the fallen angels, —was the cause of the overthrow of our first parents, and was the occasion of their ruin. Pride goeth before destruction, &c. God abhorreth the proud, &c.

It was a spirit,

3. *Of insatiable avarice.*

"We will divide the spoil," &c. Had not Pharaoh enough, without sharing the spoils of emancipated slaves? An avaricious spirit can never have enough. It unceasingly cries give, give! It is like the sea, though all the rivers run, &c. Like the grave, &c. What a cursed spirit it is. Well has it been said, that nature is content with little, grace with less, but the lust of avarice not even with all things.

We see in this spirit,

4. *Reckless malevolence and cruelty.*

"My lust shall be satisfied." "I will draw my sword," &c. What indifference to human life. What thirsting for blood! Ambition and avarice render the mind cold, and the heart callous. Tears, wailings, groans, mangled bodies, and the flowing blood of mankind, allay not the fires of human malevolence and lust.

We see in this spirit,

5. *Presumptuous confidence and security.*

The whole text exhibits this. I will do —not endeavor—no peradventure. Contingency and doubt have no place. How foolish for the man who puts on the armor, to boast. Race not always to the swift, &c. Numbers, power, discipline, armaments, do not secure success, &c. Then this presumption is more glaring after the signs, &c., they had seen in Egypt. The lice, the flies, the hail, the frogs, the Nile of blood—the darkness—the death of the first-born, &c. Yet with these events fresh before them, the enemy says, "We will pursue," &c.

II. *Their signal overthrow and ruin.*

"Thou didst blow," &c., verse 10. Observe,

1. *A part of their purpose was accomplished.*

"They did pursue," &c. Followed till they overtook. No doubt vaunting, full of self-confidence, &c.; certain of conquest. But mark, on the point of supposed triumph,

2. *Ruin overtook them.*

Now respecting their overthrow, &c., observe several particulars.

(1.) It was sudden and unexpected. The Israelites pass through the divided heaps of the water; the chasm still is open, they enter, &c., and then the sea rolls its billows over them, and they sink like lead in the mighty waters. The judgments of heaven often overtake men,—as a whirlwind, or as travail of a woman with child—or as a thief, &c. "The wicked are driven away," &c. Death and hell ride upon horses, &c.

(2.) It was universal.

All who entered, &c., perished; verse 4, &c. Fearful type of the ruin of all impenitent sinners, &c. Mal. iv. 1.

(3.) It was total and irrevocable.

Sank to rise no more. Not partial, &c., they had had drops of the Divine vengeance; now they have the tremendous storm.

(4.) It was retributive.

The desert of their sin. Much like their sin. I will pursue. God *pursued.* I will overtake. God *overtook.* I will divide the spoil. God scattered their chariots and treasures. My lust shall be satisfied. God's wrath avenged, &c. I will destroy, &c. God utterly destroyed them, &c. How often has God thus punished, &c. The inhabitants of Sodom, they bounded in unnatural lusts, and God consumed them. Adonibezek and Ham. Rich man, &c. So it shall be of all men.

APPLICATION.

1. *How great and glorious a being is God.*

How to be desired as a friend—how feared as an enemy.

2. *The subject is a mirror for persecutors and oppressors.*

God feels for the oppressed, &c. He will punish the proud, and the arrogant, and the unfeeling.

3. *How necessary is a mediator between such a God, and guilty sinners.*

Our God is a consuming fire. How terrible! We are guilty—deserve to die. Christ is the day's-man, &c. Here is hope and salvation.

4. *How important to have a name and place with God's people.*

CLVII.—THE HANDS OF MOSES HELD UP.

"And it came to pass, when Moses held up his hand, that Israel prevailed; and when he laid down his hand, Amalek prevailed," &c.—*Exodus* xvii. 11, 12.

GOD was pleased to employ various means, under an inferior dispensation, for the punishment of the wicked.

In some cases he sent famine—in others, fire from heaven—in others, pestilence; and in others, war.

The Amalekites, as a wicked nation, had filled up the cup of their iniquity. They now exhibited their hatred to God's people, by making war against them; ver. 8. Moses adopted means for the defence of the Israelites; ver. 9. Our subject exhibits the moral power which he employed on the occasion. Observe, in the moral use of this event,

I. *The cause of God is opposed by bitter and violent enemies.*

These enemies, in the case of the text, were the Amalekites; in our case they comprise,

1. *The powers of darkness.*

Satan and his host. Enemies full of hate, and envy, and revenge. Fierce, restless, combined, powerful, and persevering. Numerous, as our poet says,

"They throng the air, and darken heaven,
And crowd this lower world."

Satan is the leader, the captain, who is described as a roaring lion, &c. We read of his wiles, and of his fiery darts.

2. *The wicked of our world.*

Every man is for or against God, and the truth. Hence, all infidels and deniers of the truth. All scoffers and profligates. All corrupters of the pure doctrines of the Gospel. All formalists, who hate spiritual religion, &c.

Now, the spirit and influence of all these is against God, and his cause, and people. With these, therefore, we have to maintain a spiritual and continued conflict. Observe,

II. *The direct means by which our warfare must be conducted.*

Moses, in this case, stood on the top of the hill, and lifted up the rod, &c.; ver. 9. See Psalm cx. 1, 2.

1. *Let us consider the rod of Moses, as typical of the word of divine truth.*

Hence, Paul says, the gospel is the "power of God," &c. The rod of Moses was the symbol of authority and power. It had wrought, in his hand, many marvellous works. It is called the "Rod of God." Exodus iv. 20.

Having smote the waters of the Nile, they became blood. It had been stretched over the waters of the Red Sea, when they, too, divided, &c. It had smitten the rock, and waters gushed forth, &c. God's word is one of majesty and power. It kills, or makes alive. How terrific its threatenings! How glorious its promises! How it slays the wicked, and saves the righteous!

Now, this *is the only weapon to be employed in Christ's cause.* He sent his apostles forth with this. Hence, the "weapons of our warfare are not carnal," etc. No sword—or statutes—or fines. No earthly power—no coercive means to make people good, etc.

Observe,

2. *The spirit in which it is to be employed.*

Moses, in the spirit of believing devotion, held up the rod, etc. Just so, must the word be preached. The full, pure word, in the spirit of prayer. The apostle says, "Take the sword of the spirit, which is the word of God," and then he adds directly, "praying always, with all prayer."

(1.) The word should be *read* in this spirit. Hence, David, "Open thou mine eyes that I may behold," etc.

(2.) Should be *studied* in a devotional spirit. That we may be preserved from error and confusion. That we may see the truth in all its fulness and harmony.

(3.) It must be *preached* in this spirit. Not expecting it should edify and save, on account of our style of composition, or mode of address, or order of arrangement; but on account of its inherent life and power, and the blessing of God. Prayer and the word must not be separated, etc. And believing prayer may be encouraged from,

(1.) Nature of the word. God's truth; and, therefore, adapted, etc.

(2.) From its numberless trophies. What has it not achieved!

(3.) From the promises of God concerning it. One shall suffice; Isa. lv. 10, 11.

Notice,

III. *The essential aid the Church of God may afford in the accomplishment of this warfare.*

See ver. 12. "And Aaron and Hur stayed up his hands," etc.

(1.) Observe, this aid was *necessary.* Moses was not sufficient. His hands fell down, and then the enemy prevailed.

(2.) Observe, this aid was cheerfully *afforded*. No unwillingness. Their hearts were identified with Moses and his work.

(3.) This aid was *efficient*. "His hands were steady," etc.

Now, all Christians in the Church are called to imitate Aaron and Hur.

(1.) Sunday-school teachers hold up the hands of the ministry, by rearing the young, and bringing them to the house of God, etc.

(2.) Tract distributers, etc.

(3.) The Temperance laborers, as John the Baptist, prepare the way for the gospel of the kingdom.

(4.) The liberal man, who deviseth liberal things, etc.

(5.) The active member, who exhorts and invites, etc.

(6.) The spiritually-minded, who exhibit the beauties of holiness—who are lovely and attractive, etc.

(7.) The fervent devotional believer, who holds up the ministry and cause always, before the throne of God, etc.

Learn,

1. *The true position of the Church of God, in a state of conflict.*

2. *Our great encouragement.*

God's presence and blessing. His great promises, etc.

Observe,

3. *Our individual duty.*

Are we working for God, and souls, and eternity?

4. *The enemies of God must perish, &c.*

The triumphs of truth and the Cross are certain; but still always in connection with the agency God has set up, and has promised to bless.

CLVIII.—JOSHUA AND CALEB'S ENCOURAGING DECLARATION.

"If the Lord delight in us, then he will bring us into this land, and give it us."—*Num.* xiv. 8.

OUR text is connected with a striking event in the history of the Israelites. Twelve spies were sent to report on the land which God had promised them. See chap. xiii. 17, &c. Ten of these spies reported unfavorably: ver. 32. This report spread dismay in the camp of Israel: chap. xiv. 1. Then Moses and Aaron fell on their faces before all the assembly, &c.: ver. 5. Joshua and Caleb had brought a good report, &c.:

xiii. 30. And now they endeavor to cheer and comfort the hearts of the people, &c.

Let us lose sight of the Israelites, and direct our thoughts to the universal family of God; and look beyond Canaan to the heavenly land.

Our text contains,

I. *A supposition.*

"If the Lord delight in us," &c.

II. *An inference.*

"Then he will bring us into this land," &c.

I. *The text contains a supposition.*

"If the Lord delight in us," &c. Prov. viii.; xxx.

God delights in his Son, &c. He delights in holy angels, &c. But have we reason to suppose that he delights in his saints?

1. *We might conclude, indeed, that he could not delight in them.*

When we reflect,

(1.) On their nothingness and vanity. "Man at his best estate," &c.

(2.) At their guilt and rebellion. Not one, but is a sinner.

(3.) At their pollution, and want of conformity to his likeness. And more especially when we reflect on his greatness, independency, and purity.

2. *But there are the most satisfactory evidences that he does delight in his people.*

(1.) Observe the names by which he distinguishes them. He calls them his jewels—inheritance—treasure—diadem—crown and portion. See the very term in the text. Prov. xi. 20.

(2.) Observe the declarations he has made respecting them. "He that toucheth you, toucheth the apple of mine eye." He has engaged his constant presence—his unremitting care—his ceaseless goodness—his tender mercy—his gracious interpositions—his richest gifts—his greatest blessings.

(3.) Observe what he has done for them. Favored them—sustained them—redeemed them—given his Son—Spirit—promises.

(4.) What he has provided for them. All needful grace. "The Lord God is a sun," &c. "My God shall supply," &c. "Eye hath not seen," &c.

(5.) Eternal life, and unceasing glory.

"His saints are precious in his sight,
He views his children with delight," &c.

Notice, then,

II. *The inference.*

"Then he will bring us into this land," &c.

Observe here,

1. *The land specified.*

It is the land afar off. The good land. The heavenly Canaan. The region of immortality. We shall not live here always. Need this rest, &c.

"There is a land of pure delight," &c.

2. *This land is God's gift.*

Not the result of merit—free gift of God. It is given in promise—given in Christ. Purchased inheritance.

3. *To this land God must bring his saints.*

Difficulties, enemies, and dangers intervene. He will guide to it. Keep—safely conduct, and at length, put his people into it, as he did Israel. "Fear not, little flock," &c. "Let not your heart be troubled," &c. Rev. ii. 10 and 26 ; iii. 5 and 12. Oh, yes ; the inference is satisfactory, and most conclusive. Let,

(1.) Christians expect it, and live in reference to it.

(2.) Invite others to go with you, to the better land.

————◆————

CLIX.—CHARACTER OF CALEB.

"But my servant Caleb, because he had another spirit with him, and hath followed me fully, him will I bring into the land whereinto he went ; and his seed shall possess it."—*Num.* xiv. 24.

OF more than six hundred thousand Israelites brought out of Egypt by the outstretched hand of God, only two entered the land of promise. These two were Caleb and Joshua. All the rest were *called, chosen, delivered, guided*, miraculously preserved, &c., and yet they perished in the wilderness. Some for murmuring—some for envy—many for idolatry, &c.

Among those who were not permitted to enter, were Aaron and Moses. Moses the meekest man, "who was faithful," &c.; yet he grieved God by his rashness, and giving way to his own spirit, &c.

The text has to do, with sending twelve spies, &c. Their return—and their discouraging testimony ; by which God was dishonored. Then Caleb is presented in contrast. "But," &c. Let us consider,

I. *His character.*
II. *His spirit.*
III. *His course.* And,
IV. *His reward.*

Let us consider,

I. *His character.*

"God's servant ;" which includes,

1. *Knowledge of God.*
2. *Choice, or consent to God's claims.*
3. *Obedience to the Divine commands.*

It is a very high distinction. Angels are such. Jesus became such. All good men are such. It involves,

Lowliness and reverence.

Waiting and docility.

Constancy and uniformity.

II. *His spirit.*

Another spirit to that of the other spies. Every good man has another spirit, to that possessed by the men of the world. To that he had *once*. A new creature, &c. Now so of Caleb. The spirit of the other spies was evil, &c.

(1.) Theirs was a servile—his a noble spirit.

(2.) Theirs was cowardly—his courageous. How often is Christian magnanimity seen in peril !

(3.) Theirs was distrustful—his believing.

(4.) Theirs selfish—his self-denying.

(5.) Theirs languid—his fervent and zealous.

All these are still essential in the character of the godly.

Observe,

III. *His course.*

He "followed" the Lord, and "fully."

1. *He set God before him.*

Looked to him by faith. Obeyed him. Lived as in his sight. Did all things to his glory.

2. *He advanced in the Divine life.*

He followed—went on—progressed. It is a journey, &c. He was not stationary, much less declined.

3. *He followed God at all times.*

In season and out, &c. Never turned aside. Never veered with the rebellious spies, &c. Loyal and devoted always.

4. *He followed the Lord with all his heart.*

"Fully." With an undivided heart. With all his soul. To the utmost of his ability.

5. *He did so to the end.*

Faithful to death ;—continued steadfast, &c.

IV. *His reward.*

It was that of,

1. *Public distinction.*

God promises his blessing. Holds him up to honor and distinction, &c. Records his excellences on the annals of holy renown.

2. *He insures to him the possession of the goodly land.*

"Him will I bring," &c. See Joshua xiv. 6, &c.

3. *He blesses his seed, for his sake.*

Now, in all ages, religion has been personal; yet there are precious relative blessings, always in its train. These especially will be experienced, when we follow the Lord fully, consistently : hearty devotedness, even the unconverted must admire. This will tell on our children, &c. Recommend religion. Honor God, &c. Caleb we hold up as an *Example.* Lofty—pure—steady—constant—persevering.

APPLICATION.

1. Then study it.

2. Imitate it.

3. And thus secure the glorious and eternal reward.

CLX.—THE PLAGUE STAYED.

"And he stood between the dead and the living; and the plague was stayed."—*Num.* xvi. 48.

NEVER did the depravity of human nature appear more deep and striking, than in the history of the Israelites. Their history is one continuous record of God's goodness, and man's sinfulness. It cannot be read, without yielding both instruction and admonition.

Before pronouncing on them our unhesitating sentence, perhaps we had better examine our own hearts and lives; for human nature is much the same in all ages, and countries, and classes of men. The text refers to God's displeasure on three flagrant offenders; ver. 1, &c. They were the victims of God's severe wrath; ver. 31, &c. Surely this would lead to reverence, and submission, and fear. So far from that, they wickedly murmur against the servants of God; ver. 41. God now, in a most signal manner, sent the plague, etc. Moses and Aaron propitiate Deity, &c.; and the text states the happy results which followed.

Observe,

I. *The evil.*

II. *The punishment.* And,

III. *The remedy.*

I. *The evil.*

Murmuring against God. Dissatisfaction with God—his government, etc. Now this is the essence of all *sin.* Holiness is harmony—agreement with God. Sin, disagreement and murmuring. So it was with the first sin, and every sin since. This leads to irreverence, complaining, and audacious presumption. How these abound !

(1.) In profane swearing,—horrid imprecations.

(2.) In Sabbath profanation. Counted as no sin.

(3.) In gross intemperance.

(4.) In general profligacy.

(5.) In skepticism. Denying God's government, &c.

(6.) In recklessness—amidst divine judgments.

What a sight for a holy God to behold ! I come back to the first idea :—All sin is contrariety to God—dissatisfaction with God ; and hence, rebellion against his government.

Notice,

II. *The punishment.*

It was,

1. *Divine.*

God did it. No magistrate. No human pain or penalty. God immediately did it. Often sin mediately is its own punishment; but sometimes direct, &c.

2. *It was by the plague.*

We do not know precisely what it was. Some sudden disease, which swept all before it. It was however, evidently,

(1.) Fatal. Destroyed life.

(2.) Speedily so. Like a blast of wind, &c.

(3.) Incurably so. No one knew of a remedy.

How analogous is the nature and effect of sin !

(1.) Sin is the disease of the soul.

(2.) It is deadly in three senses—temporal, spiritual, and eternal.

(3.) There is for it, no human remedy. All human skill, &c., failed.

III. *The remedy.*

1. *In itself not apparently adapted.*

Doubtless, the air was charged with death. But the incense was not possibly adapted to decompose, and change, and purify.

2. *It was connected with pious intercession.*

In which there was confession of sin. Admission of the justice of God ; and the divine mercy was implored. It was a direct appeal to God.

3. *It was intercession, grounded on sacrifice.*

By the Priest, in view of the victims presented to God.

4. *It was efficient.*

Completely at once.

Let us turn now to the great remedy for sin. It is,

(1.) Not what human philosophy would have recommended. It is essentially connected with,

(2.) The priestly work of Christ. His obedience — sacrifice — resurrection—ascension—intercession.

(3.) It is *effectual.* The curse removed —wrath averted—mercy published—life offered. None need now *die*—no not one. The connecting links between a guilty world, and the remedy, is on God's part, the preaching of the word. On our part, believing the word so preached;—by which repentance, humiliation of soul, and devotedness to God, are secured. Learn,—

1. The extreme evil of sin.

2. The riches of the grace of God.

3. The immediate duty of the sinner; to call earnestly on the Lord.

CLXI.—BALAAM'S DECLARATION OF ISRAEL'S SECURITY.

"Surely there is no enchantment against Jacob, neither is there any divination against Israel: according to this time it shall be said of Jacob and of Israel, What hath God wrought!"— *Num.* xxiii. 23.

BALAK, the king of the Moabites, anxious to rid himself of the children of Israel, whose tents were now pitched in the plains around him; sent for Balaam, that he might curse them.

It is evident that the spirit of true prophecy rested on Balaam; but influenced by a love of sordid gain, he lent himself to Balak, and engaged to do his bidding. God placed a variety of hindrances in his way, that he might return to the path of rectitude, and not attempt the execution of Balak's commission. But blinded by avarice, he went on and on, until God allowed his infatuation to have the ascendency, so that he became the miserable victim of his own worldliness. But though willing to do Balak's work—

yet when the time came to curse Israel—he was influenced by the Spirit of God, to predict the most glorious things. Instead of declaring evil, he pronounced the following enrapturing prophecy; chap. xxiii. 8, &c. A second attempt elicited the following declaration; ver. 18, &c. The conclusion of which is the subject of our present discourse. How true is the text, of Israel of old. No evil spirit of enchantment could affect them. No spirit of divination injure them. The magicians of Egypt could mimic Moses, but only in adding to the misery of the Egyptians; but neither earth nor hell can injure those who trust in the Lord; "for he is their help and shield."

Applying our text to the church of God in general, consider,

I. *The important truth affirmed.*

"Surely there is no enchantment," &c.

II. *The triumphant exclamation uttered.*

"What hath God wrought!"

I. *The important truth affirmed.*

"Surely there is no enchantment," &c.

We enter not into the discussion how far men may have had power from Satan to enchant, to divine, or curse others. But we abide by the text, that there is no such thing against the cause and people of God. Hell is opposed to the cause of God, and united with it, are the wicked powers of earth— they have the disposition, the will, the purpose, and may make the attempt to injure the church; but their efforts must fail— their plots must be frustrated—their attacks must be powerless. Yet sometimes they have been allowed to harass, and vex, and torture the people of God. Sometimes they have apparently succeeded and triumphed; but really and eventually, they must be frustrated. "For surely," &c. Now the certainty of this may be inferred,

1. *Because the counsels of God are more than sufficient to baffle the designs and plots of hell.*

We would not array human skill and tact, against the wiles and stratagems of the devil. But the security of the church depends on the counsels of God—on the influence and wisdom of the Most High. He knows how to frustrate the devices of evil; and how to deliver those who trust in his name. His eyes are open to the thoughts and plots of the wicked, and hell has no covering before him. Hence, he is the watcher and keeper of Israel, and he neither slumbers nor sleeps.

2. Because the power of Jehovah is ever effectual in resisting the attacks of the enemies of his people.

Divine wisdom and omniscience is united with resistless power. His mandate gave being to the universe. "He spake," &c. The volition of his mind and will, would overwhelm the fallen spirits with confusion and terror. All created power is mere impotency before him. How then can the power of evil ruin the church, and overthrow the cause of the eternal?

3. Because divine goodness is more than enough to counteract the malevolence of the church's foes.

The wisdom and power of God are combined with immeasurable love. The interests of the church are those of God's heart. His people are as the apple of his eye. He bears them on the palms of his hands, &c. He has covenanted with them to sustain, to keep, to preserve, to deliver, to glorify. "Surely then," &c.

4. The resources of God are more than adequate to render all the means of the church's enemies abortive.

The enemy can combine various elements of evil. The craft, subtlety, wrath, and power of fallen legions,—the wealth and influence of the world—the fashions of earth, &c. And all these have successively been employed. But all resources are Jehovah's. The angels of his presence—the stars of heaven—the sun and the moon—storms, and winds, and tempests, earthquakes, pestilence, and famine. Locusts, and even lice and flies, can effect his bidding. He often makes the wrath of man to praise him. On these grounds we may say, "Surely this is no enchantment," &c.

II. *The exclamation uttered.*

"According to this time it shall be said," &c.

Observe,

1. *What is to be said.*

"What hath God wrought!" All deliverances, &c., are to be traced up to God. Agency may be observed, but God only praised. God alone is to have the glory, as he has had the real work of delivering his people.

This is to keep up our dependence on God.

This is to inspire with admiration and praise.

This is to keep human nature in its right place.

Not what Moses did in Egypt, or Joshua, or Gideon, or David, or the Apostles, or the first martyrs, or the Reformers, or Wesley, or Whitefield; but what God hath wrought! There is a tendency to lose sight of God, or to make God secondary. But it ought ever to be, "What hath God wrought!"

2. *Who are to say it.*

Sometimes even enemies have said it. Balak was forced to see it, and the covetous Prophet to speak it.

(1.) But it should be said, especially by the ministers of the gospel. They are to draw attention to the doings of Jehovah. They are to extol the Lord—to celebrate the works of his hand—to speak of the glory of his kingdom—and talk of his power; Ps. ix. 9, &c.

(2.) It should be said by all the pious. Parents to their children. Teachers to their pupils. Christians to one another. Thus the Psalmist, lxxvii. 11, &c. Isa. xii. 4, &c.

3. *When it should be said.*

(1.) It should be said in times of depression as the means of encouragement. However low, or persecuted, or afflicted, yet so it has often been; but God has remembered his people, "for his mercy," &c.

(2.) In times of great exertion, as an incitement to perseverance. Hope cheers and renews with vigor, for the toil. Now, never forget, that the success is certain. Your efforts must avail. Surely, &c.

(3.) In times of great success, to give tone to our exultings. We then have former days brought to our remembrance—thus reminded of God's doings of old. With grateful exclamations of joy, we should exclaim, "What hath God wrought!"

(4.) It will be reiterated in the world of the beatified forever. Then they will see in one beautiful series, the doings of God. Behold the golden chain entire. Then the philosophy of providence will be elucidated, and its harmony with redemption made clear as with letters of light.

APPLICATION.

1. *Our text may apply to many, as to their Christian experience before God.*

Remember all the way God hath led you, &c. What great things he hath done for you.

2. *May it not apply to this Christian Church and congregation?*

What hath God wrought here, for you, in you, by you? &c.

3. Let God ever be exalted by his Church and people for the blessings they enjoy, and all the good done in them, and by them.

CLXII.—THE PRAYER OF MOSES TO GO OVER TO THE GOOD LAND.

"And I besought the Lord at that time, saying, O Lord God, thou hast begun to show thy servant thy greatness, and thy mighty hand: for what God is there in heaven or in earth, that can do according to thy works, and according to thy might? I pray thee, let me go over, and see the good land that is beyond Jordan, that goodly mountain, and Lebanon," &c.—*Deut.* iii. 23–27.

AMONG the pre-eminently exalted saints of olden times, stands Moses. He was distinguished for great energy of character, noble generosity and self-denial, and amazing fortitude and magnanimity. He was in the highest sense of the term, a patriot—a lover of his own people. He was called of God to the most illustrious services,—endowed with the most amazing gifts; and he had the signal honor of being Israel's emancipator, lawgiver, and leader. He was remarkable for his reverence for God, implicit obedience, and profound humility. His spirit was most benignant and meek. Selfishness seemed to have had no lodgment in his heart; nor ambition in his mind. He was ready to live and toil, suffer and conflict for the good of Israel, and the glory of God.

Besides, he was most emphatically a man of a devotional spirit. He had remarkable power with God; and an invincible faith in the divine energy and goodness. He stands forth as the head of one of the great religious dispensations of the world—as a most celebrated prophet, and very striking type of the Lord Jesus Christ. Yet he was but a man; and as such, he had his frailties and sins.

Our text presents this *orb of Judaism* under a partial eclipse, and gives us a very peculiar view of the divine character and procedure.

Observe,

I. *The prayer of Moses.*

II. *The grounds of its partial rejection.*

And,

III. *The divine alternative which was substituted.*

I. *The prayer of Moses.*

Observe,

1. *His sublime ascription.*

"O Lord God," &c.; ver. 24. Here are several weighty particulars :

(1.) Here is the acknowledgment of the divine self-existence and supremacy. The one living God. The Jehovah of Israel, &c. No other being to be addressed or worshipped. See chap. vi. 4. Exod. xx. 3. He alone is God. See the Psalmist's comparison; Ps. cxv. 1–8.

(2.) The greatness and power of God are affirmed. Now God is not only comparatively great, but *essentially* so. Greater than the universe, &c. It is said, that greatness is to be ascribed unto God. See 1 Chron. xvi. 25; xxix. 11. Ps. xcv. 3; civ. 1. It is said, power belongs to the Lord. We read of his voice being "powerful," the "thunder of his power." He is clothed with strength, &c. We are referred,

(3.) To the pre-eminency of his works. All things are of him, and by him, and for him. Think of their variety, extent, grandeur, harmony, design! One boundless whole! from the grain of sand to the largest star—from the imperceptible animalcule to the blazing seraph. See Neh. ix. 6. Job xxxviii. 4, &c. Psalm xix. 1. "The works of the Lord are great," &c. Then notice in this prayer,

2. *The desire expressed.*

"I pray thee, let me go over," &c.; ver. 25. Observe,

It was personal. It referred to himself.

It was most important. "Let me go over," &c. It was a *promised* land. Prepared also for them. It was a rich and great donation. Exceedingly desirable, when contrasted, &c., with the desert. "Good land," &c. See Exod. iii. 8.

It was what he might reasonably expect. He was the object of God's love and favor, &c. He had been so faithful on the whole in God's service, &c. He had been toiling on in the desert, &c.

Then notice in reference to the prayer,

II. *The grounds of its partial rejection.*

He states,

1. *God's refusal to hear.*

This was not contradictory of God being the hearer or answerer of prayer; but we must ask according to his will. Where there is not an implicit promise, this should never be forgotten.

2. *Grounds of the refusal.*

These were connected with Israel's sins. See Numbers xx. 1–12.

3. *God greatly honored Moses, in the manner of the refusal.*

" Let it suffice thee," &c. Leave the matter with me. I cannot grant thy request; yet, "Speak no more." Hence, the prevalency of prayer was admitted, and the devotional power of Moses conceded. See another instance of this kind : Exodus xxxii. 10; in the case of Abraham pleading for Sodom, God heard, and conceded every point. He gave over asking, before God gave over giving. Then notice,

III. *The divine alternative which was substituted.*

1. *A part of his request was conceded.*

" Get thee up unto the top of Pisgah," &c., verse 27. He wished to see it. God allowed him this privilege; and told him how and where he might behold it. See chap. xxxiv. 1, &c.

2. *He granted him a better inheritance.*

He took him to himself. The mind, the spirit of Moses did not die, but was released from the mortal tabernacle, &c. He still lived, and liveth on. For God is the God of the living, &c. He appeared in his refulgent glory, to greet the *Messiah,* when he was transfigured on the mountain. It is said that his death was next to a translation; chapter xxxiv. 5; may be rendered by the "mouth of the Lord." Hence the beautiful fancy of the Rabbins, that God extracted his soul with a kiss. Thus, one sings :

" Like Moses to thyself convey—
And kiss my raptur'd soul away."

Surely this was better than yielding to his prayer—even as heaven is better than earth.

Learn,

1. *To cherish august and reverential views of God.*

Avoid levity, and undue familiarity in prayer. God's nature and perfect works should lead to this.

2. *Let your desires and hopes be fixed on the celestial land.*

All here is poor and fading—evanescent and dying. One vast sepulchre, &c. A better land promised. Christ has redeemed us,—called us to it,—leading us on to its possession. Set your hearts and souls on it, and on Christ Jesus, as the only way to it.

3. *Let all the future events of life be left to the Lord.*

People may err even in desiring to go to heaven. Wait till the Master calls. Let the present be occupied in "living to the Lord," &c. Think of Christ's prayer : "I pray not that thou shouldest take them out of the world," &c.

4. *A word to those who never think of heaven at all.*

Be wise; and now begin an evangelical preparation for heaven, by faith in the Lord Jesus, and devotedness to him.

CLXIII.—SAMSON, BOTH AN EXAMPLE AND BEACON.

" And the woman bare a son, and called his name Samson : and the child grew, and the Lord blessed him. And the Spirit of the Lord began to move him at times in the camp of Dan between Zorah and Eshtaol."—*Judges* xiii. 24, 25.

THE history of Samson is one of the most difficult biographies of the Old Testament. Yet this difficulty arises chiefly from our incorrect mode of judging and concluding of human character. For instance : a man may be unconverted, and yet there may be evinced many traits of moral excellency. He may be truthful, sober, honest; yea, generous and benevolent. We meet with such in every-day life,—and such have existed in all ages.

On the other hand, a man may be really converted, and yet his life may be singularly checkered and uneven—there may be glaring relapses, and numerous infirmities. Now we presume, that Samson is of the latter class. A good man, laden with infirmities.

Let us look at those moral features,

I. *Which hold him up as an example.*

Let us, however, first glance at some general things in his life. His birth was foretold, &c. See the remarkable account; chap. xiii. 1, &c.

He was an instrument of divine providence, for special purposes. In some things, he has been supposed to be a type of the Lord Jesus.

(1.) In overcoming the lion, &c.

(2.) Especially in bearing away the gates of Gaza; typifying the resurrection of the Son of God.

Amazing physical strength was that with which he was especially endowed. We have no evidence of his being distinguished either for great mental or moral power. His excellency may be summed up in one brief sentence, "Public consecratedness to God." He lived, and labored, and suffered, as a public servant of God. As such he was,

(1.) A Nazarite from the birth.

(2.) An entire abstainer from all intoxicating drinks.

(3.) A great sufferer for Israel's sake. Blinded, in prison, &c.

(4.) A voluntary sacrifice on the altar of his country, and religion.

He was also evidently candid, generous, and noble-hearted. As such he is worthy to be an example; in these two things especially:

Personal devotedness. Public usefulness.

Let me urge these on all professing Christians.

But look at him,

II. *As a Beacon.*

1. *He was the victim of sensual passions.*

Neither watchful nor vigilant, — apparently without self-government. Hence, mark all the woes of his life.

2. *His irreligious marriage.*

His bosom companion one of the Philistines, whom he was raised up to punish. No more foolish or wicked a thing can Christians scarcely do, than marry with unbelievers. It must result in evil. It cannot be truly happy, or really prosperous.

3. *See him with his head afterwards in the lap of pleasure.*

Himself on the verge of ruin. Sporting with peril. All who live in pleasure are dead, &c. How many of the young are often seen thus; and how many are daily ruined.

4. *See him bereft of sight, and toiling in the prison.*

Dark, degraded. The victim of slavery, even in the prime of manhood. How often this the result of sensuality and profligacy. Our city asylums are full of such cases. Mental, and often moral blindness, is the result; yet let us HOPE that his adversity and sufferings were sanctified.

As an instrument of God's vengeance on the Philistines, and as a punishment of idolatry, the last scene of Samson's life and doings, are brought before us; chap. xvi. 23. No doubt, a splendid temple. Thousands of spectators. The grandees of the nation, &c. ver. 27. It was to exalt Dagon, ver. 23; and expose Samson to universal contempt. Look at Samson led in. He seeks a resting place. The spirit of the Lord comes upon him. The God of the Philistines is to be shamed, and his worshippers destroyed; ver. 28.

All is silent, as the eager multitudes wait for the sport of their victim.

He prays to God.

Grasps the pillars.

Puts forth his strength; and the house fell, &c.

Samson, thus dying, partially recovers his renown.

God is glorified. Idolatry signally punished. But from Samson, the instrument of God's providence in ancient times—we turn,

To Jesus, the perfect model of all holiness and loveliness. The great deliverer, &c. Mighty to save.

Who died for us; and in dying, redeemed us and a rebellious world, to himself, &c.

(1.) To Him let the sinner repair for mercy and salvation.

(2.) To Him let the believer look for help &c., in every hour of need.

(3.) To-night, at his table, we celebrate his dying victory, &c.

CLXIV.—SAMSON'S RIDDLE IMPROVED.

"And he said unto them, Out of the eater came forth meat, and out of the strong came forth sweetness. And they could not in three days expound the riddle."—*Judges* xiv. 14.

THERE is considerable difficulty in deciding the moral class to which some persons belong. Many are decidedly the enemies of God and religion, beyond doubt. So many are especially decided in their love to God and holiness. But some are occasionally exhibiting tenderness towards good and evil —towards holiness, and then sin—towards heaven, and then hell.

These remarks most forcibly apply to Samson. There are many points in his character, which would induce us rather to place him with the ungodly; but there are others which constrain us to give him a place, though not an exalted one, with the Old Testament saints.

His conception and birth, &c., took place under peculiar circumstances. He was the instrument of divine providence. The champion of Israel. The subject of God's holy spirit; and above all, we find him ranked among an illustrious class of holy heroes, in

Heb. xi. 32. The texts refers to one of his wondrous achievements. See verses 5, 6, 8, 9 to 14.

Now we design to attempt a spiritual improvement of the text, and,

I. *We refer to sin and its entrance into our world.*

Sin is indeed a lion—a destroyer. The lion of hell, the destroyer of man. Who can tell its awfully mischievous effects upon our world. Paradise lost,—hell opened,—death rampant,—misery almost universal. Yet out of this eater came forth meat, &c. Sin, in itself, is an evil—an unmitigated evil, &c. But God in his redeeming goodness has overruled it, for the most glorious purposes.

1. *Man is placed in a more safe and gracious connection with God.*

It was then, obey and live—transgress and die. He had his own stocks of righteousness. His own strength, &c. No place for repentance. Now it is, believe in the Redeemer, come to the fulness of his grace. Rely on him. And now, "If any man sin, we have an advocate." "If we confess," &c.

2. *We have a more glorious exhibition of the divine character.*

Adam knew God; as wise and holy, and great and good. We know him as merciful and gracious, of abundant compassion, &c. "Here the whole Deity is known," &c.

3. *Man's nature is more greatly exalted.*

Sin debased it, cursed it, &c. In redemption, God has thrown a glory round it unspeakably resplendent. He has made it the shrine of his divinity. He tabernacled in it, &c. Thus the Son of God has become our relative and brother—the son of man, &c.

4. *Our destination is higher and more glorious.*

If man had retained his original purity, he would have had, as a servant, perfected bliss in Paradise, or a translation to glory. But sin has been overruled, so that God elevates man to a station of sonship; and places him within the inner circle of the world of glory. He was made but a little lower than the angels; but now he is infinitely *higher;* and is destined to sit with Christ on the throne of his glory. "Thus out of the eater," &c.

II. *Look at the opposition with which the cause of God and truth has had to contend, in every age of the world.*

Persecution has been the lot of the righteous. The burning bush, the emblem of the suffering church.

Now the opposition and sufferings of the church, however evil in their objects, have been overruled, and have,

1. *Displayed the power and excellency of godliness.*

It is in the fire, that the pure metal is known from the dross and counterfeit. Hence all the graces and virtues of the righteous have been manifest. As Joseph, in prison, &c. So also the love of God has been exhibited in supporting and sustaining the bush in flames, and yet unconsumed. The vessel on the foaming billows, yet riding out the storm.

2. *Opposition, &c., has tended to produce a higher kind of religion, and also to extend it.*

The moral heroes of the world have been made such by the peril and opposition of their times. See the Old Testament worthies,—Daniel, the Baptist, and the Apostles,—the early Christians—the Reformers—the Puritans. Also opposition has extended religion. Look at the case of the apostolic churches. Believers scattered by it. Thus the seeds of Christianity were wafted to the ends of the world, &c. Thus the persecution on the Continent drove German and French Protestants to Britain. Thus the Puritan fathers were driven to the shores of America. Time would fail to illustrate how, "Out of the eater," &c.

I would dwell a little on the literary opposition to the gospel. From the earliest ages, men have written against religion. All sorts of objections raised, &c. Now, this may have led some to disbelief; but it has drawn forth the talent of the church. Hence, all our books in defence of new and revealed religion—so that the enemy has been the occasion of bulwarks being raised, against which the gates of hell shall not prevail. Hence, look at the writings of Celsus, of the second century, of Gibbon, Hume, Bolingbroke, Hobbes, Paine, &c. Then look at the countless volumes of Origen, Justin Martyr, Tertullian, and the ancient Fathers; and in modern times, Luther, Leslie, Bishop Watson, Stackhouse, Addison, Jenyns, Butler, Chalmers, &c.; which must not only satisfy all candid inquirers, but establish the faith of intelligent persons to the end of the world. Hence, "Out of the eater," &c.

III. *Look at the troubles and afflictions of the Christian life.*

"It is through much tribulation," &c.

Many are the afflictions of the righteous, &c. Now these are not joyous, &c. Look at one immersed in poverty. Another the subject of constant disappointment. A third, incessant crosses. A fourth, repeated bereavements. A fifth, domestic ungodliness. A sixth, bodily afflictions, and others, terrific temptations, &c. Who can bear up? &c. What a host of evils, &c. Yes, but "Out of this eater," &c.

1. *The troubles and afflictions of life are essential to the exercise and growth of many graces.*

Meekness, patience, &c. Rom. v. 3.

2. *They conform us to Christ.*

"If we suffer," &c. "If any man will be my disciple," &c.

3. *They wean from the world.*

If it were all joy and sunshine, we should cling to the earth, and to life. How often this is seen in the afflictions which immediately precede death, &c. How they loosen the bonds of attachment! "Now they desire a better country," &c. "Our light afflictions," &c. "It was good for me," &c. Heb. xii. 11.

IV. *We appeal to death itself.*

Death is the king of terrors, &c. A roaring lion. An insatiable devourer. The dread of every living thing, &c. Yet this terrific evil, yieldeth meat and sweetness to the Christian.

1. *It terminates the trials and sorrows of life.*

2. *It bringeth us to our best and final home.*

It is the deep valley, from which we ascend to the throne of glory. The river, through which we cross to Canaan. The gate of eternal life. To die, everlasting gain, &c. Think of the triumphs of the dying believer, &c. "O, death," &c.

APPLICATION.

1. *Now remember, that meat and the sweetness, come through the grace of God.*

That grace must be realized by faith, &c.

2. *Is the text in accordance with our experience?*

Do we realize it, and rejoice in it? &c.

3. *It should lead us to glorify God.*

4. *It should reconcile us to the adversities and trials of life, and even to death itself.*

CLXV.—ORPAH AND RUTH CONTRASTED.

"And Orpah kissed her mother-in-law; but Ruth clave unto her."—*Ruth* i. 14.

SOMETIMES a very small and apparently insignificant action, gives the most clear indication as to the true character of the individual. This was especially the case in reference to the two persons introduced in our text. For we shall find that the distinction here presented to us was kept up; and decided the character and destiny of both. But, not only shall we be instructed as to the real principles of both Orpah and Ruth, by considering the text, but we shall find that they are significant representatives of two great classes of persons in our world.

We have a large number of persons who possess the spirit of both; and therefore it is to this extended mode of applying the text, that we shall especially invite your attention.

Observe,

I. *The narrative which precedes the incidents of the text.*

II. *The circumstances as therein stated.*

III. *The subsequent history of both.*

I. *The narrative which precedes the incidents of the text.*

Observe, one of the leading characters in this history was Naomi, the widow of Elimelech. She was now returning to Bethlehem, in her native land. Not only had she been bereaved of her husband, but also of her two sons, who had been the husbands of Orpah and Ruth.

On her resolving to return to her native land, she affectionately stated this to her daughters-in-law; ver. 6: and commenced her journey; ver. 7. They accompanied her, however, a portion of her way back towards the land of Judah. At length the time of separation arrived, when she thus urged on her two companions to return. "And Naomi said unto her two daughters-in-law, Go, return each to her mother's house; the Lord deal kindly with you, as ye have dealt with me," &c.; ver. 8. Doubtless, there was much heartfelt affection existing between them; and, hence it is written: "And they lifted up their voice, and wept again; and Orpah kissed her mother-in-law; but Ruth clave unto her."

Such, then, is the introductory narrative to the text.

Notice, then,

II. *The circumstances as therein stated.*

And here observe,

1. *The conduct of Orpah.*

"She kissed her mother-in-law." We have no reason to doubt her high esteem, and sincere love for her. It is equally evident, that her disposition was kind, and her spirit amiable. She was not indifferent to her mother-in-law's interest—not unconcerned about her journey. She wept at their separation. She showed a most commendable degree both of attention and courtesy; and her parting greeting was, doubtless, warm and sincere; but she preferred her own idolatrous land; see verse 15. She kissed Naomi, and then separated finally from her. It is clear also, that she hastened back, not waiting for Ruth to accompany her. She left Ruth in fond affection, cleaving to Naomi. She esteemed and loved Naomi; but she preferred "her own people, and her gods," ver. 15.

And here Orpah must be considered the type of that large class, who are distinguished—

For many moral qualities.

For much that is courteous and kind.

For reverence for divine things.

For a certain amount of love for the church of Christ, and the society of his people.

For attendance on ordinances, &c.

For the support and patronage of religious and benevolent institutions, which they display.

But yet, who never come out of the world,—never give up the sinful idols of the heart,—never forsake the region of rebellion and unbelief; and while they go far in company with the pious, and give the kiss of esteem and courteous respect—never become the decided adherents of the cross, or pilgrims to the better land.

Notice,

2. *The opposite course pursued by Ruth.*

"She clave unto her." She held fast by Naomi—could not leave her,—resisted all her entreaties to do so. Affirmed her resolve in the most powerful terms. "Entreat me not to leave thee, or to return from following after thee: for whither thou goest I will go," &c.; ver. 16. She so earnestly importuned, that Naomi was constrained to allow her to accompany her; and so they went on together, till they came to Bethlehem; ver. 19.

Now, just observe, Ruth forsook her country—her home, and her friends. She did so most piously: for there can be no doubt, that so much was expressed when she said— "Thy God shall be my God." She preferred her worshippers to her own country's idolaters, for she said, "Thy people shall be my people." She acted evidently by faith; for there appeared nothing to tempt or allure her. Her mother-in-law was a poor widow, yet she clave to her, and returned with her to the land of God's people.

In this, Ruth was a type of all who are led by divine grace—

To abandon the service of sin.

To forsake the world for the church.

To give their hearts and lives to God.

To set out with holy decision and ardor, towards the better land.

And who persevere, however great the sacrifices, in the course they have chosen. Such did Ruth; so do all true penitent believers.

Now notice,

III. *The subsequent history of both.*

And observe,

1. *As to Orpah.*

Of her, sacred history is silent. Doubtless, she lived and died in her own country, and among her own people. Lived and died in the service of idols. Her mind unimproved,—her condition unchanged.

Then turn we,

2. *To Ruth.*

Her career was most eventful. She was evidently the subject of providential direction and care. She became the object of respect and esteem among the people to whom she came. She became the wife of Boaz— an illustrious servant of God. She was the mother of Obed, the grandfather of king David; and thus became distinguished, by raising seed, from whom sprang the Messiah —the world's Redeemer.

Here, then, temporal rewards, substance and honor, and religious blessings, were granted to Ruth, who forsook the land of Moab, and clave unto Naomi. A true representation of the benefits of simple and sincere piety. "Godliness is profitable," &c. "Seek ye first the kingdom of God," &c. "Whoso loseth his life," &c.

In conclusion—

1. Address, and warn those who cherish the spirit of Orpah.

2. Recommend the decision of Ruth.

CLXVI.—RUTH'S PIOUS DECISION.

"Thy people shall be my people, and thy God my God."—*Ruth* i. 16.

A MORE beautiful and affecting narrative was never penned, than is recorded by the inspired historian, in the Book of Ruth.

A famine drove Elimelech and his wife Naomi, and their two sons, into the country of Moab. Elimelech dies there; so also his two sons. Here are three widows: Naomi, and Orpah, and Ruth. The young widows belong to the land of Moab. Naomi, however, resolves to return to her own country.

These two daughters-in-law accompany Naomi a part of the way towards the land of Judah. She then entreats them to return back again; and affectingly prays for them: verses 8, 9. Orpah returned back to her home: ver. 14, &c.; but Ruth would not leave her: ver. 15.

Our purpose is to urge upon you to adopt Ruth's choice,—and evidence Ruth's decision.

I. *Adopt Ruth's choice.*

1. *Choose the God of Israel for your God.*

(1.) He has revealed himself as the God of love, &c.

(2.) He has visited us in our flesh.

(3.) He has redeemed us by his Son.

(4) He invites us in the gospel.

2. *Choose the people of God for your companions.*

(1.) You are social beings, and will associate with some persons.

(2.) Wicked and worldly companions will imperil your salvation. This is obvious, from the power of association. From all observation.

(3.) God's people are the best companions. They are the wisest,—most truly affectionate; therefore, most profitable.

They will counsel you.

They will pray for you.

They will watch over you.

They will sympathize with you.

II. *Adopt Ruth's decision.*

1. *There is need of decision.*

(1.) The world will allure.

(2.) Satan tempt.

(3.) Your hearts lean to evil.

(4.) The backslidings of others will affect you. As when Orpah went back.

2. *What kind of decision is essential.*

(1.) It should be earnest.—The decision of the heart and soul.

(2.) Prayerful. — Seeking the grace of God.

(3.) Humble,—Renouncing all self, &c.

(4.) Believing.—Looking for salvation to Christ only.

(5.) Present.—"Behold, now is the accepted time," &c.

APPLICATION.

1. *Some have made this choice.*

You may well rejoice and exult in it.

2. *Some are halting.*

How strange indeed to hesitate between God's service, and that of sin and death!

3. *Some are deciding.*

Blessed are ye, &c.

4. *Some will not.*

Your ruin is inevitable.

CLXVII.—AGAG'S EXCLAMATION CONSIDERED.

"Then said Samuel, Bring ye hither to me Agag the king of the Amalekites. And Agag came unto him delicately. And Agag said, Surely the bitterness of death is past."—1 *Sam.* xv. 32.

THE words of the text we design to consider as a motto for our discourse, quite independently of their original use or application. No subject can be more proper for our meditation than that of death. For, is it not a subject applicable to all? A subject, solemn in itself—but also one most amazingly forgotten! It is, evidently, one of Satan's chief efforts to keep out of sight from men their own mortality. Hence, the great majority of mankind endeavor to evade the subject of death; or only give it a very occasional or evanescent consideration. But every now and then, events occur in society, which forces it on our attention.

Some instance of sudden death. Perhaps, of some minister in the pulpit—some senator in the house—some judge on the bench—or some crowned head in the palace. And thus the subject of mortality stands out, and calls forth a nation's considerations and reflections.

Let us, then, on the present occasion,

I. *Offer some remarks on the subject of death.*

II. *On that which constitutes its bitterness.*

And,

III. *How the bitterness of death may be removed.*

I. *Some general observations concerning death.*

We may view death,

1. *In its origin, as the result of sin.*

The threatening of death was annexed to the Divine law—as given to our first parents in paradise. " The day thou eatest, &c., dying thou shalt die." So life, from that hour, was a passage to the region of the grave. This doctrine is explicitly stated—Rom. v. 12 ; 1 Cor. xv. 21.

2. *In its universal certainty, in reference to our race.*

All ages have verified this.—All countries.—All classes, and degrees, and conditions of men. No exemption in this war,—" the living know," &c. Only exceptions, Enoch and Elijah. Every house is the residence of mortals,—from the hovel of the peasant, to the palace of the monarch. Moral or spiritual excellences avail not, in preventing the stroke of death. Consider death,

3. *In the uncertainty as to the time, and manner, of its approach.*

We must meet the king of terrors ; but when, and how, and where, we know not. The future is wisely concealed from our knowledge. God reserves the times and seasons in his own power.

But let us notice,

II. *What constitutes its bitterness.*

This arises often,

1. *From its general painful train of precursors.*

Death, as a monarch, generally sends his heralds and harbingers before him. He has a variety of fierce diseases, which go to attack the citadel of the human body. And often this is the season of distressing bitterness—extreme suffering—sometimes, awful agonies—racking tortures—burning fevers—incessant restlessness—overwhelming suffocations—days of suffering—nights of excessive weariness. This is often a cup of bitterness, which language is utterly unable to describe.

It often arises,

2. *From its distressing separations.*

It removes us from those we love. From dear friends and kindred. Often those who are apparently dependent on us. The close ties of devoted attachment. If we died in groups, &c.; emigrated in companies to the better land, it would appear desirable ; but no, the cup must be drank alone,—the journey trodden alone,—the conflict maintained alone ; and, hence, the bitterness of death.

3. *From the actual fears and pains of dying.*

It may be often, that the act of dying is only just falling asleep. But sometimes the agonies of death are distressing; the struggles fearful. Then its very indefiniteness makes it awful. It is a something which has never been described—of which we have had no experience. And, hence, the dread mystery in which it is involved.

4. *From its immediate and awful consequences.*

(1.) The body and the grave.

(2.) It conveys us into eternity. The region to us of unknown darkness. The world of spirits. It brings us into direct contact with God. It fixes our condition, and seals our doom forever.

Thus, these are the chief elements which constitute the bitterness of death.

We ask, then,

III. *How the bitterness of death may be taken away.*

I remark,

1. *Of the happy dead, this is a certified fact.*

" Blessed are the dead," &c. " To die is gain," &c. O yes ; the storm is over—the conflict is past—the sorrow is over—and every tear is wiped away. But the bitterness of death may be taken away, even before the act of death is experienced.

Now this is what the religion of the Lord Jesus can alone effect; and this vital Christianity does, by—

(1.) Extracting from death its fearful sting: 1 Cor. xv. 56. Here death has its poison from sin, and its condemnation from the law broken. Now, destroy sin, and the poison is gone. Destroy sin, and the law is silent. In Christ there is life for the guilty, condemned sinner. And by faith in him, we pass from death to life ; and from condemnation by the law, to justification by the rich and free grace of God.

(2.) By the grace it supplies. We have spoken of pains, agonies, &c. ; but Christianity provides a sustaining portion. A cordial. An invigorating balm. Christ's strength and peace are given, and thus the cup is resignedly, and even cheerfully, drank.

(3.) By the hopes which it inspires. It lifts up the head and directs the eye to the blessed future—the celestial Canaan—the heavenly world of life and glory—the better land. It points to heaven, as our final home. There is our Father, Saviour. The holy and elite of the universe. Many of our friends, and all the rest who are pious, will join us there. How bright these hopes! How ecstatic! "Thou shalt see the king in his beauty," &c.

(4.) From the Saviour's presence, which it actually secures. Christ will be with you on the tempestuous billows of death—as with Peter. He will sustain, when flesh and heart fail, &c. He will hail the racer. Crown the warrior. Receive his saints to himself, &c.

Now in conclusion, remember,

1. *We must all die.*

2. *Death has an essential and awful bitterness.*

3. *Only religion provides an antidote.*

4. *How do you stand—how feel ?*

Out of Christ, all is terrible,—beyond the power of words to express.

CLXVIII.—GOD'S CHOICE OF DAVID.

"And he sent, and brought him in. Now he was ruddy, and withal of a beautiful countenance, and goodly to look to. And the Lord said, Arise, anoint him: for this is he," &c.—1 Sam. xvi. 12, 13.

THE doctrine of the Divine sovereignty has, perhaps, been more perverted than that of any other great truth of revelation. It has often been confounded with arbitrariness—with partiality—and has even been supposed to be akin to mere caprice. The sovereignty of God is his essential right to act, without consulting his creatures, or making known the cause, or end of his proceedings. But it must ever be remembered, that in doing so, God cannot act unworthily of his infinite wisdom or goodness. That he never can be partial, or be a respecter of persons. And that where he does not reveal his reasons for the course he adopts, still that course is based on the essential and eternal principles of righteousness and equity.

We are led to these remarks by the subject which our text introduces to our notice: the choice of David to be king of Israel. The whole narrative is very beautiful.

Observe,

I. *The occasion of David's being chosen.*

This was the rejection of Saul. Saul had been anointed by divine command; but he had been unfaithful, and God rejected him. See chap. xv. 9–11. God took from him his holy Spirit—left him to his infatuated course—and finally he perished by his own sword.

Here we see three steps in the way of ruin :—

Disobedience ;

The withdrawal of the Divine Spirit ; and then,

A ruinous and awful end.

Observe,

II. *The circumstances connected with David's election to the kingdom.*

And here you will observe,

1. *That Samuel was the agent employed.*

He had anointed Saul. He had been his devoted counsellor and friend. Made known to him the Divine will. He had warned him, &c. But God calls him to abandon the infatuated monarch, and to seek a successor, v. 1.

Observe,

2. *Sacrifice was made the medium of the election.*

Verse 2. Samuel goes to Bethlehem, and calls the elders of the city. An important question is proposed, ver. 4 ; and a satisfactory answer is given, ver. 5. He then invites to the holy service, ver. 5.

Here David was a signal type of Christ—chosen in connection with sacrifice. Christ also had to suffer as a sacrifice, before he could begin his royal administration on earth. Heb. ii. 9, 10.

3. *Human sagacity was rejected, in the choice made.*

Samuel was now an aged man—full of years and experience—eminently wise and discriminating, and therefore well adapted to judge of the fitness of the person for the throne of Israel. But observe, how he utterly failed, ver. 6. Then the Lord reminds and admonishes the venerable prophet, that God's process of judging is the opposite of that of men, ver. 7.

Now this must be peculiar to God, for none else can do so. How shallow is man's knowledge of character, and how liable to be deceived! How many rich, exalted, and talented of the world, God rejects! and how many illiterate and poor are chosen of the Lord!

4. *God himself declares the object of his choice.*

Verse 7. The chosen one is absent. He is keeping his flock. In the way of honorable and useful industry. He is sent for; and though the youngest of the family, yet God says, "Arise," &c. Verse 12.

Notice,

III. *The anointing of David, God's chosen.* Verse 12.

The sacred writer narrates the personal appearance of David. Ruddy, beautiful, and of commanding, graceful mien. There is often a close connection between the face and the mind. God intended that the countenance should be the title-page of the soul. It often is so. Vice stamps its ugly impressions on the face; and so do real inward worth and true piety. Now, in reference to the anointing of David, observe,

I. *The anointing was by God's command.*

It was God's own choice; and he bids Samuel to do his command, in setting him apart for the royal office, ver. 12. It is said, he did it in the midst of his brethren. Probably, as some critics read, rather "from the midst of his brethren"—selected out. And by many, it is supposed, it was a private service.

2. *He was anointed with oil.*

This oil was prepared in a peculiar and divinely appointed manner; Exodus xxx. 22.

Now this oil was to be preserved for the purpose of anointing persons and things—devoted to the service of the Lord. It was emblematical of the virtues and graces requisite for the office to which the person was set apart.

3. *The Spirit of God was imparted to him.* Verse 13.

Probably, by the Spirit of the Lord, a meetness of wisdom and energy for the office was imparted. By this, too, the Divine favor was enjoyed and realized, and the providential blessing of Jehovah indicated. This was the grand essential qualification for the office, and its onerous and responsible duties.

Learn, from the subject,

I. *The importance of being found in the way of religious duty.*

God saw David's heart, and he chose him for the high station. But David remained a faithful, diligent, humble shepherd, till God called him to the throne itself.

2. *Divine qualification is necessary for important offices.*

External dedication may be proper; but how essential the inward operation of the Divine Spirit. He alone can make men fit for the duties of life. He is the source of knowledge, wisdom, and power.

3. *Learn the high privileges and exalted station, to which men are invited in the gospel.*

God calls men to be kings and priests, &c. He anoints, and gives his Holy Spirit to all who believe. 2 Cor. i. 21.

CLXIX.—DAVID AND GOLIATH.

"Then said David to the Philistine, Thou comest to me with a sword, and with a spear, and with a shield; but I come to thee in the name of the Lord of hosts, the God of the armies of Israel, whom thou hast defied. This day will the Lord deliver thee into mine hand; and I will smite thee, and take thine head from thee; and I will give the carcases of the host of the Philistines this day unto the fowls of the air, and to the wild beasts of the earth; that all the earth may know that there is a God in Israel. And all this assembly shall know that the Lord saveth not with sword and spear: for the battle is the Lord's, and he will give you into our hands," &c.—1 Sam. xvii. 45-51.

VERY shortly after David had been anointed king, he had an opportunity of displaying both the moral energy of his mind, and the physical power of his arm.

The Philistines waged incessant war with Israel; and it appears at this time, that they gathered their armies together on a mountain, within sight of the camp of Israel. Here they defied Israel and their God.

One of the Philistines was most prominent in this work of defiance, and offered to settle the national contest by single combat. But dismay seized the camp of Israel, on account of the extraordinary size and fearful aspect of this daring Philistine.

At length, David was sent with provision to the camp of Israel. He heard of the proud vauntings of the Philistine; verse 22. He saw, too, the panic of the Israelites, and he inquired, What should be done for the man who should kill him? Eliab, his eldest brother, ridiculed David's purpose; ver.

28; and others also joined in the contempt put on David; ver. 30.

At length, the wishes of David were related to Saul, and the king endeavored to dissuade him from his purpose; when he related to him the achievements of his youthful life, ver. 34. He also expressed his trust in God; ver. 37. And then David was equipped for the conflict; ver. 38. But afterwards, he put aside the weapons of war, and he took his staff, &c.; ver. 41. The Philistines eyed him with contempt, and their champion declared he would give his flesh to the fowls of heaven; ver. 44. Then said David to the Philistine, &c.; ver. 45.

Observe,

I. *The enemy David had to encounter.*

His name was Goliath, and he was a native of Gath. It is said, when the Anakims were routed out of Canaan, several fled to Gath.

Goliath was distinguished for his height. He was upwards of ten feet high. His coat of mail, weighed above two hundred pounds. The staff of his spear is described, ver. 7. The head of it weighed eighteen pounds: so that, he was a terrific enemy—apparently too invulnerable. Besides, with his spear and sword, he would appear beyond the power of an earthly arm to touch him. There can be no doubt, that his spirit and fierceness were in keeping with his size and appearance.

Notice, then,

II. *The conflict.*

1. *How David was armed for it.*

He had no defensive armor. No offensive; except his staff, his sling, and bag of five stones; ver. 40. How apparently unfit for any perilous contest, much more for to conflict with the daring Philistine. A youth, a shepherd—without warlike weapon; and the monstrous giant, with his complete armor, and deadly weapons of war. Observe,

2. *The language of holy defiance and prediction David employed.*

Ver. 46.

Now, you will see here, that God both begins and ends the language of David. Nothing of self-vaunting.—No self-trusting. "This day will the Lord;" ver. 46. Then at the end of the address—"That all the earth may know," &c.

There can be no doubt that the spirit of God in David, showed him both his duty, and intimated the victory he should gain.

So that his soul was encircled by God; and on God his soul relied entirely, for a final triumph. In verse 47, he expresses his faith, not in his sling, nor in his dexterity—but in God; and refers all to the will of God, who can save without the spear, or the sword—for the battle is his.

3. *The mode of attack which David adopted.*

Ver. 48.

See the vaunting Philistine coming forth to meet the stripling! See David hastening his steps towards the formidable giant! He runs, takes the stone from his bag; and then, with all the power he possesses, he slings it at the head of Goliath; and behold, it smote him in the forehead, and he fell to the earth. And thus the victory, as he had predicted, was achieved.

Observe,

III. *The subsequent course which David adopted.*

The Philistine lies dead on the ground, and David has no sword—so he takes the monstrous sword of Goliath, and draws it from its sheath, and cuts off his head therewith, ver. 50, 51. Observe, this was succeeded by the total route of the Philistines —they fled. Israel pursued, and the victory was signal and entire. The head of the Philistine is taken to Jerusalem, and David lays aside his armor in his tent.

APPLICATION.

Learn,

1. *How vain are power and might, when arrayed against God.*

Here was a man that could have done any thing within human possibility, if earthly might could prevail. But, alas! what is man at best? What his ingenuity—his courage—his weapons—his warlike prowess! &c.

2. *That God can effect his purposes by apparently most unlikely means.*

So he did by David, in this case. So he has often done. "For the battle is his." All events are under his control. And he can save by few or many—by sword or sling.

3. *The subject may remind us of the opposition which all God's people meet with from Satan, &c.*

He defies God and his people. He vaunts, intimidates, threatens, tempts, &c.; sometimes almost overwhelms. Yet he is but a creature; mighty, but not invincible before the power of God.

4. *See the spirit in which we should resist the evil one.*

In the name of the Lord. In his strength. With the sword of the divine word, and in the spirit of prayer: and so the victory shall certainly be ours.

CLXX.—DAVID'S POPULARITY AND PERIL.

"And Saul took him that day, and would let him go no more home to his father's house," &c. —1 *Sam.* xviii. 2–16.

DAVID, after his victory over Goliath, was introduced to Saul, the king; and high and distinguished honors were heaped upon him.

The flock upon the mountains, and the shepherd's crook, must now be abandoned; and a long and illustrious public course is before him. But, just in proportion to his public honors, will be his enemies and his perils.

The extended passage we have read, will give us ample evidence of both.

Observe, then,

I. *The happy and prosperous scenes which opened upon David.*

Now among these, is to be noticed,

1. *The patronage of Saul.*

Saul took him from the sheepfold to the palace. Did not allow him to remain in obscurity any longer.

Now this was one of the essential steps to the future elevation of David. He found favor in the eyes of Saul, the king; ver. 2.

Then observe,

2. *The friendship and affection of Jonathan.*

Verse 1.

Now, this friendship is one of the most beautiful instances on record. It was most intense—constant—faithful—devoted—lasted till his death. Never cooled, nor relaxed; yet he might have looked on David with coldness, and even suspicion. But generous love filled his whole soul; vers. 3 and 4. Then observe,

3. *The popular acclamations of the people.*

See ver. 5, middle clause.

The people were delighted with him. He was the subject of their plaudits; and the air resounded with the songs of which he was the hero: ver. 6, 7.

Now such were David's early prosperous scenes. To many they would have been ruinous, would have produced arrogance or ostentation; but not so in the case of David. But now we must look for a reverse of fortune. He has been lifted up to the top of the mount of earthly popularity. He is basking in the sunshine of prosperity; but behold, the heavens lower—the clouds gather—a storm is at hand!

Notice, then,

II. *The perils to which he was exposed.*

And here notice, singularly enough, that his perils began,

1. *With his patron, the king.*

Verse 8.

Not with some rival courtier. Not one of the king's family—but with the king himself. He was wroth, at the laudings of the people. David had been exalted higher than himself, and he could not bear it.

Notice,

2. *The tide of David's prosperity, were the elements of his danger.*

The song that wafted David's renown, contained the very blighting poison, which was to be the sorrow and danger of his spirit, for years to come. How we should watch even the gale of prosperity, and the beams of popular favor. Even these may be the occasion of our greatest distresses.

3. *The great element of David's peril, was the envy of Saul.*

Verse 9.

How expressive is that verse. He fixed an evil eye on David. He could not look on him with pleasure. His heart malignant to overflowing, gave his eye the expression of hate and envy. Who can number the evils which have arisen from jealousy and envy? They have been the main ingredients of our world's disasters and crimes— they are the seeds of wrath and bloodshed,— the leading elements in the character of Satan, and fallen spirits of perdition.

Observe,

4. *The manifestation of the peril itself.*

Verse 10.

God's good spirit had forsaken Saul. God had given him up to the evil spirit of his own depraved nature. See chap. xvi. 14. Under this spirit he affected to prophesy, or to sing holy strains as aforetime. David was to aid him with his harp. While doing so, the deadly weapon was thrown at him; ver. 11.

Here then, the life of David was exposed to the greatest danger; but God, in his preserving providence, delivered him.

Notice,

III. *The spirit which David displayed under the circumstances narrated.*

And here there is much to delight us throughout.

1. *He was not over-elated by the prosperity he had enjoyed.*

Verse 5.

Amidst the breezes of popular favor, he acted, "wisely," that is, prudently, discreetly. Popularity is a dangerous atmosphere to breathe. It often intoxicates. Makes men vain, &c.

But David had good sense, and grace enough to ballast his spirit; and with modest wisdom, he bore the honors which were thrust upon him.

2. *He was preserved from an evil spirit, in his perils.*

See how he acts now the scene is reversed. Does he resent the evil? Does he return evil for evil? Does he reflect the evil spirit of Saul in any degree? No: he still behaved himself "wisely;" ver. 14. He did so in every step he took,—in all his ways. And the secret of this prudence is at once revealed—"The Lord was with him:" The Spirit of God was in him, and influenced him; and regulated his heart and steps;—and thus, both in prosperity and adversity, his soul was preserved.

Learn,—

1. *How mutable are all earthly things.*

This is a world of change—nothing abiding, &c. Learn,

2. *Not to make earthly things your chief good.*

In the day of prosperity you may rejoice; but let it be with trembling. Rejoice as though you rejoiced not, &c.

3. *To trust in the Lord, in the days of evil.*

How inadequate we are for our defence— God alone can shield us, &c. "Who can harm you?" &c.

4. *To seek aid from God's gracious Spirit, at all times.*

We cannot serve God, and preserve our souls, without divine help. It is only by the Spirit of God within us, that we can walk uprightly, and glorify God. God's Spirit must guide, influence, and sustain us.

CLXXI.—JONATHAN'S FRIENDSHIP TO DAVID.

"And Jonathan Saul's son arose, and went to David into the wood, and strengthened his hand in God."—1 *Sam.* xxiii. 16.

How sorely tried was David. Troubles and perils followed him from his youth up. His conflicts with the lion and the bear, were but preludes of that continued warfare, which God in his providence would call him to wage.

His passage from the sheepfold to the throne, was one of suffering and dangers. And when the crown was on his head, it often seemed to tremble—through treachery at home, and rebellion abroad.

Our text alludes to an event in his early history. David had been anointed by Samuel, and Saul's envy and hatred had been fearfully exerted; and he tried various expedients to take his life; ver. 13, &c.

Observe in the text,

I. *David's peril and trouble from Saul.*

And,

II. *His comfort and encouragement from Jonathan.*

I. *David's peril and trouble from Saul.*

1. *Saul was an envious enemy.*

Envy is one of the vilest, deadliest passions of the soul. It was Satan's feeling, when he beheld our first parents in Paradise. Cain's feeling towards Abel. The feeling of Joseph's brethren. The feeling of the Jews towards Christ. One of the basest, of the depraved heart.

2. *Saul was a powerful enemy.*

Had royal authority. Imperial power. Servants. Armies, &c.

3. *He was an unwearied persevering enemy.*

Hence, his various expedients.—His renewed efforts, &c.

4. *He was a mortal enemy.*

Sought his life,—desired to destroy him, &c. Need not marvel at David's anxiety and distress—his moanings and fears. "I shall one day fall," &c. "My soul is cast down," &c. Yet there were hopeful signs —for,

5. *He was a restrained enemy.*

Under God's control. The Lord was indeed David's shield and buckler, &c. God observed both Saul and David; restraining the one, and protecting the other, &c.

Then observe,

II. *His comfort and encouragement from Jonathan.*

How strange the scene! The father—the enemy; the son—the friend. One palace contained both.

Now let us see in Jonathan, all the essential and lofty principles of the most exalted friendship.

Observe, it was founded,

1. *In the approbation of his mind, and the sincere love of his heart.*

Chapter xviii. 1.

Here was the right basis—the essential element, &c. It cannot exist without this. There may be admiration — reverence — esteem; but not real friendship, without deep affection.

2. *It was noble and disinterested.*

Here David might have been viewed as a rival. A youth of an obscure family, would displace him in the succession. Yet all these he despised,—he preferred David to the whole.

3. *It was open and generous.*

Not afraid, nor ashamed. See how he acted: chapter xviii. 3 and 4.

4. *It was constant and self-denying.*

It did not vary with circumstances—nor change with the altered appearances of things. When David was in favor, and out, —in prosperity, or in adversity. He toiled, and planned, and advocated David's cause. Chap. xix. 1, 2, 3; xx. 4. He exposed his life, &c. Chap. xx. 30, &c.

5. *It was sanctified by religious principle.*

No doubt this was its grand elastic principle,—its glorious feature. Hence the text —"Strengthened his hands in God." Recognized God in his providence—covenants, &c. Gave him religious consolation. Here was the best evidence, of the best friendship. How needful it was in David's case. How often equally so, in ours.

6. *It was persevering and effectual.*

Jonathan had his heart's desire; and lived and died a true friend; and the covenant of their love was not broken. He was the instrument, in the hands of God, of securing his life, &c. All true friendship does not thus prove effectual. Here it was signally so, &c.

Observe,

7. *Jonathan's friendship was most fully reciprocated.*

David's heart was eminently fitted for it. Warm, generous—it fully valued—deeply prized—and constantly returned the gush of generous love.

At length, death separated these united hearts, and David expresses the deep anguish of his spirit, in one of the finest elegies ever composed. 2. Samuel i. 25, &c.

Learn,—

1. *The character of true friendship.*

Kindness of spirit—oneness of heart— mutual esteem—delight—confidence—reciprocity. Enduring as the granite—refreshing as the dew—genial as the light—and sweet as the air.

2. *What a contrast to most confederacies, called by that name.*

Confederacies of sin—and pleasure—and vanity—and flattery—and affection—and evanescence, &c.

3. *How supereminent the friendship of Jesus, to his people. No friendship like his.*

———◆———

CLXXII.—DAVID AND NABAL.

" And there was a man in Maon, whose possessions were in Carmel; and the man was very great, and he had three thousand sheep, and a thousand goats; and he was shearing his sheep in Carmel. Now the name of the man was Nabal; and the name of his wife Abigail: and she was a woman of good understanding, and of a beautiful countenance," &c.—1 Sam. xxv. 2, 3.

THE whole of this chapter is full of rich, striking, and most instructive incident. It presents a list of remarkable portraits. There is the churlish Nabal,—the beautiful and prudent Abigail,—the noble-hearted David, the wise and considerate servants; and then in, and through, with the whole, the hand of divine providence, working and overruling all for his own glory, and the purposes of his holy and blessed will. Now let us look,

1. *At Nabal, and the spirit he displayed.*

He is described to us,

1. *By his worldly possessions.*

Verse 2. He was very great, *i. e.*, in worldly riches and dignity. The account is given of these. But we cannot judge men by their condition. He may be rich, and avaricious—wealthy, and yet really poor. On the other hand; a man may be poor, and yet both great and happy.

2. *He was avaricious in his spirit.*

Verse 5, &c.

David's request of Nabal, was most reasonable. He might have satisfied the wants of his men, by taking his substance, in the way of levy; but he did not do so. But observe his reply; verses 10, 11. Then observe,

3. *He was churlish in his temper.*

Verse 3.

His reply to the young men evidenced it; ver. 10. It was a morose and bitter reply. His wife also knew his temper and stated it; ver. 25. How wretched is a bad temper, and a cold heartless disposition. Yet such was Nabal; and such is the portrait drawn of him.

Then observe,

II. *The generous and noble conduct of David.*

He solicits, what he might have taken by force,—solicits it in a kind, courteous spirit. The unkind refusal excited his displeasure, and he was disposed to adopt a summary mode of punishment, on the avaricious churl; ver. 13. But a quick intimation of this is given to Abigail; ver. 14. And the course she adopted, at once turned the tide of affairs with David; and hence, the noble sentiments which he uttered; ver. 32, 33. How worthy of David as a man—as a warrior—as a saint.

But let us now just look, more fully,

III. *At the character and spirit of Abigail.*

It is said of her,

1. *That she was beautiful, and wise.*

Verse 3.

Both desirable qualities—but not always united. Happily so in this case. An intellectual soul beaming through a lovely face. One the reflection of the other. It does not appear that she was either proud or vain, but beautiful and wise. We see in Abigail,

2. *Her prudential arrangements.*

The messenger reports to her, the conduct of Nabal; ver. 14–17. Observe how active she was; ver. 18. No time to be lost. See her generosity; ver. 18. Observe her discretion, in not telling Nabal; ver. 19. Now here was both talent and tact—wisdom and understanding.

Then look at,

3. *Her effective appeal to David.*

Nothing more appropriate and beautiful, can possibly be conceived. Observe,

(1.) Her modesty; ver. 23.

(2.) Her respectful mode of address; ver. 23.

(3.) Her timely, yet properly adjusted severity, on her husband's conduct; ver. 25.

(4.) Her pious recognition of God; ver. 26.

(5.) Her kind and hearty offer, of her rich generosity; ver. 28.

(6.) Her expressed admiration of David's character and office; ver. 28.

(7.) Her reference to true magnanimity, as being worthy of David; ver. 30, 31. Need I refer,

(8.) To the effectiveness of her intellectual and holy eloquence; ver. 32. She obtains her suit, ver. 35; and returns in peace.

But observe,

IV. *The fearful end of Nabal.*

Verse 36.

Though avaricious and churlish, yet he could be profligate on himself. Hence, the expensive feast. Then his mirth and revelry, and his extreme drunkenness—too drunk to be talked to,—a disgusting sot. But on the morrow, his wife communicated the events of the previous day. The startling intelligence, produced inward melancholy and stupor,—the result of the power of avarice, at the gifts bestowed—or mortification, that David should have been so honored—or ·alarm at the peril, into which his folly had placed him. And ten days after, God visited him, and he died; thus died as he lived, the worthless, sordid, churlish Nabal. No one misses him from the earth. No heart moans. No eye weeps. To his wife, and servants, and all, his death must have been a blessing. To himself, a terrible and everlasting curse.

The only wonder in the history is, how Abigail should have been united to such a churl. Was it a parents' match? Or had she been tempted by his earthly greatness? Or was it one of those strange acts of weakness, into which even the wisest sometimes fall? It certainly was a union that neither reason nor religion could have sanctioned; and only fraught with discomfort and sorrow, to all concerned.

Learn,

1. The value of a generous spirit.

2. The importance of a good temper.

3. The pre-eminence of a wise and understanding mind.

4. The potency of soft words.

5. To recognize the overruling providence of God.

6. To be warned by the awful end of the ungodly.

CLXXIII.—DAVID'S RESTORING, AND DANCING BEFORE THE ARK.

"And it was told to king David, saying, The Lord hath blessed the house of Obed-edom, and all that pertaineth unto him, because of the ark of God. So David went and brought up the ark of God from the house of Obed-edom into the city of David with gladness," &c.—2 Sam. vi. 12–14.

THE ark of the Lord had been in Kirjath-jearim, in almost unknown privacy, for seventy years. David resolved to remove it to the tabernacle in Jerusalem, and therefore made arrangements to effect it. God had prescribed a definite way for bearing it, which was by the staves of the priests; but David had sent a new cart, on which it was placed.

On its way, Uzzah touched it, and died for the irreverent act, by the ark of God; ver. 6, 7. David was terror-struck and feared to proceed further; so the ark remained in the house of Obed-edom for three months. This house was honored and blessed of God, during the stay of the ark; and on David being informed of this, he went and brought up the ark to the city, with great gladness and exultation. Observe,

I. The course David adopted.

II. The persecution he met with. And,

III. The resolution he averred.

I. The course David adopted.

It was the removal of the ark, which constituted the great subject of the whole scene. The ark was the appointed symbol of the divine presence and glory. The most hallowed of the furniture of the tabernacle. A reference to it is given—Exodus xxxvii. 1, &c. See Heb. ix. 3, &c.

Now, in the removing of the ark, he had reference to the glory of the tabernacle—which was vain, without the symbol of the divine presence. Here, then, zeal for the divine honor was conspicuous in the conduct of David.

But observe, in removing the ark,

1. He offered sacrifice to the Lord.

Verse 13.

He might do so, that God's grace might be obtained on this eventful occasion; or to acknowledge their error and sin, in their former mode of removing it; or as a general act of worship, and agreeable with the Levitical dispensation. The guilt and unworthiness of man—the honor and justice of God—and a hope in the predicted Messiah, seemed to be connected with all sacrifices.

Then observe,

2. He exhibited the most lively emotions of joy.

He danced before the Lord, &c.; ver. 14.

Here the joy of his heart broke forth in the actions of the body; and he leaped, and danced, and praised God. The whole of this scene was connected with sacred music; ver. 15. Observe, it was a religious act. Nothing in it carnal or worldly, the result of overflowing gratitude to God, and joy in his service. Nothing but a high and fervid state of devout feeling, would have warranted it. See Ps. cl. 14.

Notice in reference to David,

II. The persecution he met with.

Verse 16.

Here we observe a cold spectator, who felt no interest in the event, gazing on the excited conduct of the king. And soon we witness its manifestation. David had feasted the people; again sacrificed to the Lord; and then he goes down to bless his household. He wished to impart the blessedness of his own soul, to his own family circle. He approaches his dwelling, and the proud and irreligious Michal, the daughter of Saul, meets him, and says, "How glorious was the king of Israel," &c.; ver. 20. How astonished must have been the king, by the biting and wicked irony of his ungodly wife.

In this persecution of David, observe,

1. It was persecution for his religious zeal.

Zeal in religion, has always been persecuted. It was so in the case of the disciples, on the day of Pentecost. "These men are drunk," &c. It was so with Paul, when delivering his earnest address before Festus: "Thou art beside thyself," &c. It was so with Whitefield, Wesley, &c. It it so with all very intent and earnest hearts now. Men cannot bear to see fervor in piety. They do not object to it in pleasure taking. In business, &c. They admire it in the warrior, &c.—in the politician—in science. In one word; in any thing, but not in religion. Then they call it wildness, fanaticism, &c.

2. It was a persecution from a near relative.

His own wife. Often a man's foes are those of his own household. In the first family, there was Cain hating Abel. In Noah's family, the profane Ham. In Abraham's, the mocking Ishmael. In Isaac's, the reckless Esau. And now in David's, the bitter Michal. Christ said this should be so in the Christian Church. See Mark xiii. 12.

Notice,

III. *The resolution David averred.*

Observe, he does not make any apology for his conduct. He had been doing it to God. His heart was upright before him. But he vindicates it as a religious act, by saying, "It was before the Lord," &c.; ver. 21. And he reminds her, it was before that Lord who had rejected her father, and who had chosen him to be ruler over the people. A reply, which doubtless, satisfied to the full, the haughty daughter of the rejected monarch. Then he avers,

1. *His resolution still to honor God, in the way she had scorned.*

He was not to be bantered out of an earnest service of the Lord. He would still persevere, notwithstanding all her taunts. He averred his steadfastness in the course he had adopted.

2. *He determined to excel in the ardent service of the Lord.*

Verse 22.

What she deemed vile, he considered dignifying; therefore he would still not only proceed, but go further. And as to his servants despising him, he considered, in religious worship, all distinctions ceased; and he would not shrink from the liveliest exhibitions of piety, in their presence;—and he further states, that so far from the maid servant's sympathizing with her, in her bitter revilings, that of them even, he would be had in honor.

How correct David was in his views, and how God approved of his spirit, we learn from the visitation of Michal, by which she was deprived of the greatest honor a Jewish woman could desire. God has said, "Him that honoreth me, will I honor," &c.

Learn,

1. That ardent zeal is most desirable in the service of God.

2. That in matters of religion we must only look for the Divine approbation.

3. That we must expect persecution from those who are strangers to divine things.

4. That these will often be found among our friends and kindred.

5. That God will reward both now and hereafter, his devoted people.

6. That revilers and persecutors are justly abhorred by the Lord.

CLXXIV.—DAVID'S ADDRESS TO THE LORD.

"Then went king David in, and sat before the Lord, and said, Who am I, O Lord God? and what is my house, that thou hast brought me hitherto? And this was yet a small thing in thy sight, O Lord God; but thou hast spoken also of thy servant's house for a great while to come," &c.—2 Sam. vii. 18–29.

THE occasion of this very interesting and instructive passage, is to be found in the commencement of the chapter. David at this time enjoyed peace round about; ver. 1. His heart was set on rearing a house for the Lord; and he piously expresses it; ver. 2. Only, as yet, had there been a movable tent for the Lord's worship.

Nathan encouraged him to do what was in his heart, and assured him of the Lord's gracious presence; ver. 3. But, that night, God revealed to the prophet his holy will, and gave him a message to David. In this God rehearses his dealings with the king, and gives promises of love and mercy to his seed. But he defers the erection of a house for his name, till after his death; and that Solomon should have that honor.

David had answered the designs of divine providence in his labors; but Solomon, the great type of the Messiah, whose hands were not stained with blood, was to erect the house of peace, for the Lord of Hosts! All this was fully stated to David, and then follow the pious sentiments contained in the paragraph we have read.

In looking at it, let us notice,

I. *The course David adopted.*

Observe here,

1. *The place to which he repaired.*

"Before the Lord!" He went into the tabernacle where the ark of God was, and where God revealed himself by the symbol of his glory. How important to go and worship God in his public sanctuaries! but the time now is, when every spot may be holy ground. In every place God may be found; but *then*, the tabernacle was the especial place of communion with God; ver. 18.

Notice,

2. *The object David had in view.*

It is clear that he went to reflect, to meditate, to bless God, and to pray. All acts of spiritual worship. One word may include the whole—"Communion with God." All worship is designed for this—should effect this; or, else it is in vain. Notice,

3. *The posture he assumed.*

"He sat before the Lord," ver. 18.

This is the only instance in Scripture, where worship is represented as being offered while sitting. Standing, kneeling, and being prostrate, are the usual postures, which the godly have used in the worship of the Lord. But the posture of the body is of secondary moment. "God is a spirit," &c. Yet, perhaps this arose from the mingled character of David's service. Had it been praise, or prayer only, he would probably have knelt or stood. But his soul was to meditate, and to talk with God; therefore, he sat before the Lord.

II. *The sentiments David expressed.*

They were sentiments evidently,

1. *Of lowliness and humility, respecting himself.*

Verse 18.

He refers to his utter insignificancy, and to the lowliness of his father's house. No evidence of self-elevation,—no exalting himself before the Lord. His soul was evidently clothed with humility. He refers,

2. *To God's providential goodness towards him.*

Verses 18, 19.

God had brought him, &c. All the steps of his advancement had been of God; even to that time. "Hitherto." He refers also to the great things God had done for him; ver. 21; and also the things he had revealed to him; ver. 21. How countless were those! Who could estimate them—or enumerate them? Utterly impossible! He expresses his mind, how different this was to man's mode of acting; ver. 19. That God's ways are infinitely higher and better than the ways of men.

3. *He refers to God's supreme greatness and glory.*

Verse 22. No being like to God. Infinitely great! So his name—and works—and word declare. Most high and most blessed! How futile and contemptible the idols of the heathen! All other objects of divine truth and worship, are lighter than vanity.

4. *He speaks of God's great doings for Israel.*

Verses 23, 24. He had distinguished them above all nations. He had redeemed them. He had made them his peculiar people. He had done great and terrible things for them. He had confirmed his doings, and had become their God, before all nations.

5. *He states his entire submission to the divine will.*

Verse 25. He refers to the divine engagements. He approves of it. He pleads it with God. So let it be. Do as thou hast said. Both as it concerned himself, and his house in future. Let it be so. The will of the Lord be done.

Then notice,

III. *The prayers he presents.*

1. *The first refers to the glory of the divine name.*

Verse 26. "Let thy name be magnified," &c. Be thou exalted,—display thy glory, proclaim thy name! How in accordance with Christ's prayer, which he taught his disciples,—"Hallowed be thy name." This is to be the first object—the leading object—the great object. That God may be exalted and magnified.

2. *He refers to God's goodness to his house.*

Verse 27. David felt for his family—his successors. That God's gracious promise might be fulfilled; and that the throne and the kingdom might be blessed of Jehovah.

3. *He seeks the perpetual blessing of God on his seed.*

Verse 29. He repeats the perpetuity of the Divine mercy, in this one verse. Doubtless, the eye of his faith here, had reference to Christ the Messiah, and his spiritual seed. He looked beyond Solomon to Christ. Beyond Salem to the gospel kingdom. Beyond national prosperity to the extension of the spiritual empire of the Messiah. Hence, the last Psalm he composed, fully confirms this view; Psalm lxxii. 17, &c.

4. *In all this, he pleads the truth and goodness of God.*

Verse 28. Now these are the two main pillars of believing prayer. God is true. He will fulfil his word. He will not, cannot lie, nor change. Besides he is good, he will delight to do it. His goodness is unfailing, and his mercy endureth forever. Then how delightful to plead them! How effectual the prayer must be, resting on the truth and goodness of the Lord. "For thou, O Lord, hast spoken it;" verse 29.

This, then, is ever enough. For shall he say and not do it? The world shall fail and pass away, but not one jot or tittle of his word can ever fail.

Learn,

1. *The condescension of God in allowing men to have audience with him.*

2. *The humility befitting all worship of the Lord.*

3. *The gratitude with which our services should be presented.*

Recollections of the Lord's goodness to us, should inspire this.

4. *The public spirit we should cherish in matters of religion.*

That God's name be exalted, and his kingdom enlarged and perfected.

5. *The necessity for prayer in reference to the Church of God.*

6. *The strong grounds of faith and hope the word of God presents to us.*

"Truth and goodness."

7. *The final and universal diffusion of the divine glory.*

"His kingdom shall come," &c. "All nations shall be blessed in him."

CLXXV.—DAVID'S LAMENTATION OVER ABSALOM.

"And the king was much moved, and went up to the chamber over the gate, and wept: and as he went, thus he said, O my son Absalom! my son, my son Absalom! would God that I had died for thee, O Absalom, my son, my son!"—2 *Sam.* xviii. 53.

No life could probably be more checkered than that of David. Light and shade—joy and sorrow—prosperity and affliction—peace and war, were alternately in his career—from his youth up to his dying hour.

His trials were very numerous, and most distressing. They were personal, domestic, and national. They related to his soul, his kingdom, and to the cause of God. He had to contend with Philistines—with Saul—with national dissensions—with treacherous friends, and with domestic rebellion. His heaviest trial, too, came on when he was advanced in years; and this, too, the severest of them all. It was the unnatural rebellion of his son Absalom. This rebellion began by the son insinuating the injustice of his father's administrations; chap. xv. 4. He thus stole the hearts of the people, and at length he app..ared in direct rebellion, and endeavored to chase his father from the

throne, and to seize the kingdom. It was in this wicked conflict that Absalom perished: see chap. xviii. 6. The afflictive event is thus described, in reference to David; ver. 24, to the text.

Let us look at the expressive grief of David,

I. *As that of a father, over a deceased son.*

In the ordinary course of providence, we expect parents to die, and children to survive. Often, however, parents have to mourn the loss of their children. This is distressing, when they are in infancy ; though then there are many consolatory considerations, by which the bitterness of grief may be allayed. But when they rise to maturity—when they are likely to be distinguished in the world—when intellectual and talented—how increased is the sorrow.

Now, Absalom was all this. He was of extraordinary commanding appearance. He was evidently very dear, and much loved by the king ; therefore, David's grief was natural on the ground of parental affection. But,

II. *Consider it as grief greatly heightened, by the suddenness and manner of his removal.*

In ordinary cases, there is the gradual wasting of the system by disease—the afflictive premonitions. Thus the mind is prepared—the event looked for. But Absalom was removed *suddenly:* as well as usual early in the morning, gay, and lively, and inspirited ; in the evening, a corpse,—died too, by the hand of violence ; ver. 9–14.

Here then were fresh elements of distress to the afflicted David.

But notice,

III. *He died in a state of open rebellion to his noble and afflicted parent.*

David had experienced a life of conflict and sorrow ; and where should he have comfort, and joy, and solace, but in the bosom of his own family ? Here he might have been expected to have had the hearty affection of his own children.

Rebellion is a heinous crime under any circumstance. It involves many in sin and peril. It is productive of the direst calamities. But rebellion against a good king—the anointed of God ; and that king a father. David's generous spirit and delicate heart would feel all these things, and hence the bitterness of his grief.

IV. *His son had died in a state of manifest unfitness for eternity.*

This was the darkest feature of the whole history. If there were no hereafter—no

God to meet—no judgment seat—no retribution, then death, a few years earlier or later, would be as nothing; but after death, then the judgment,—the solemn truth is, as the tree leans, it will fall; as it falls, it lies.

The death of the wicked is, therefore, the beginning of everlasting sorrows—of eternal despair. The loss of Absalom's affection was great—the loss of his life great; but the loss of his soul the greatest calamity of all. David wept, as a parent over a deceased son,—as a king, over a rebellious subject,—as a saint, over a ruined soul. It was especially in the last sense, he might well exclaim, "Would God I had died in thy stead."

The subject is replete with great practical lessons.

Learn,—

1. *The doctrine of personal responsibility should teach us submission under the most distressing bereavements.*

All souls are individually accountable to God. Parents have not to answer, in the stead of their children. Parents cannot impart grace. Life is in the hands of God. He will not only do right, but what is really best; therefore, to God should we bow, in submission to his will.

The subject should,

2. *Lead parents to be devoutly concerned for the salvation of their children.*

Means are ours, though results are not. Hence how important to treat our children as accountable, immortal beings. To labor for their spiritual welfare, by example, by teaching, by prayer, &c. To see to it, that they shall have no just cause to blame us, for their eternal ruin.

3. *Let children here see the awful results of opposition to parental authority.*

There is a tradition respecting what is referred to, ver. 18, that all passers-by continued to throw a stone on the heap, to testify their abhorrence of Absalom's rebellion. There is no hope of rebellious wicked children. One of the greatest sins, is the base ungrateful conduct of children, to their parents. So great, that under the law, it was deemed a sin worthy of death. Let me press the subject on all young persons present. "Honor thy father," &c. Exod. xx. 12: which is the first commandment with promise.

4. *Let me now address all who are in a state of rebellion against Christ, the King of kings.*

How base is this! How ruinous it must be! The end of rejecting Christ, is necessarily death — eternal death! Who are guilty of this? Let me press repentance, and forsaking of the evil. Return to him by prayer, and penitential sorrow, and faith in his word and thus obtain mercy.

———————

CLXXVI.—THE ALTAR BUILT, AND THE PLAGUE STAYED.

"And Araunah looked, and saw the king and his servants coming on towards him: and Araunah went out and bowed himself before the king on his face upon the ground. And Araunah said, Wherefore is my lord the king come to his servant? And David said, To buy the threshing-floor of thee, to build an altar unto the Lord, that the plague may be stayed from the people," &c.—2 Sam. xxiv. 20-25.

WE are often prone to wonder at the astounding effects which little causes produce. Hence, unbelief asks, Why so fearful the result of our first parents eating of the forbidden fruit? Now, that *act* was disobedience —direct, wilful and daring transgression against the authority of heaven.

In the case before us, we have a national calamity traceable to the sin of David; and that sin, apparently of minor magnitude. He had just numbered the people—taken the statistics of the nation. It may be well here to show the necessity of comparing verse 1, and 1 Chron. xxi. 1. This was a temptation of the evil one, and David was ensnared. But what evil was there in it?

It was the result of pride and vain-glory.

It was to see the army he could raise, and to which he was induced to trust, instead of God.

It was ingratitude for past deliverances, &c.; and hence the wrath of God was kindled.

David soon became conscious of his guilt; ver. 10. Jehovah sent him a prophet, to announce his will; ver. 11, &c. David's choice, &c.; ver. 14.

Observe then, in the subject of the text,

I. *A fearful evil.*

II. *A divine remedy.*

III. *A generous proposal.* And,

IV. *A noble and self-sacrificing spirit.*

I. *A fearful evil.*

The evil,

1. *Was the plague.*

Some fearful disease, swiftly mortal; for in nine hours at most, some think 70,000 died. How awful! and beyond the power of human skill to deliver. Sudden, terrible, fatal!

2. *An angel was the messenger employed.* Verse 16.

He was now ready to fulfil his commission in Jerusalem, but God stayed him; ver. 16.

3. *David beheld the angel, and interceded for the people.*

A beautiful instance of lofty and conscientious feeling, &c. How generous and magnanimous, &c.; ver. 17.

Notice,

II. *The divine remedy.*

Verse 18.

An altar must be built—sacrifice offered, &c.

Now in this,

1. *Human guilt was acknowledged.*

2. *God was glorified.*

Both his justice and wrath in punishing, and his great mercy, &c. in staying his judgments.

3. *No doubt the typical end of sacrifices would be realized.*

Looking onward to the coming of the Lamb of God, &c. For both the sin, and the evil, and the remedy, may direct us to the great subject of the atonement, for a perishing world, &c. Besides, this *altar* finely symbolizes the erection of houses for the worship of God. For through the divine agency of gospel truth, by these the plague of the world is to be removed. By these,

Ignorance is to be displaced by knowledge.

Profligacy, by moral order.

Irreligion, by godliness.

Unbelief and death, by the bestowment of salvation and eternal life.

I presume, not one place of worship for God was ever raised in vain. And in some, *hundreds* have been converted to God.

Notice,

III. *A generous proposal.*

The altar was to be erected at a *given* spot. Nothing in religion left to fancy, &c.; verse 18. To Araunah, David states the case clearly and fully; ver. 19, &c.

Then came the proposal of Araunah; ver. 22.

(1.) Now this offer was beyond what David had stated; "Oxen," &c.

(2.) It was prompt, and the result of generous and pious resolution.

(3.) It was pressed on David; verse 23.

(4.) It was followed with prayer; ver. 23.

How pious and noble! A finer specimen of godly liberality never was exhibited. The act—the manner—the spirit—the prayer!

But observe, we are called to see,

IV. *A noble and self-sacrificing spirit.*

Araunah did well, yet David did even better; verse 24. Selfishness or formality would have accepted it. David desired the offering,

1. *To be his own.*

The guilt had been his, &c.; so the repentance—so the fruit.

2. *He valued his religion more than his wealth.*

So he paid the full worth for the place, &c. Now this act of David's is the opposite of two classes of persons in our day.

(1.) Those who wish others to pay for their religion.

(2.) Those who wish to have religion without cost. But I will not enlarge.

Learn,—

1. The frailty even of good men. As David in this case, when he numbered the people.

2. The necessary results of sin,—misery and ruin.

3. The only way of averting it. By repentance, and coming to the one sacrifice, on the only perpetual altar, reared for our world's guilt.

4. The fruit of a sanctified heart. Holy zeal, and liberality in the cause of God.

CLXXVII.—THE COST AND SELF-SACRIFICE OF RELIGION.

"And the king said unto Araunah, Nay; but I will surely buy it of thee at a price: neither will I offer burnt-offerings unto the Lord my God of that which doth cost me nothing. So David bought the threshing-floor and the oxen for fifty shekels of silver."—2 *Sam.* xxiv. 24.

THE text is found connected with a variety of interesting circumstances. David had grieved God, by numbering the people. The divine wrath had been displayed,—the plague had broken out. David was deeply afflicted, &c., on account of it; ver. 10. He prays; and the word of the Lord came early next morning; verse 11. He had probably spent the night in distress of soul. Three things were proposed to the sinning monarch; ver. 12, &c. He resolves to fall into the hands of God, &c.; ver. 14.

The pestilence rages. An angel is the instrument:—70,000 died, &c. God, in the midst of wrath, remembered mercy, &c.; ver. 18. Sacrifice was to be presented—specific directions were given. David promptly obeyed; ver. 19. A generous scene of altercation takes place; ver. 21. David's pious and self-sacrificing decision is expressed in the text. Our subject then is—Acceptable religion is a religion of self-sacrifice—a religion of cost; and the cost must be personally paid.

Now, in illustrating this idea, I invite you to contemplate the subject,

I. *In reference to the spiritual expansion of the intellectual powers.*

Theology, or the divine science of religion, is one of boundless extent. The greatness—number—variety, and importance of the subjects. God,—his works—his government—his will. Man; his nature—character—condition—peril—salvation. The Lord Jesus Christ—the gospel—eternal life! Now, to understand these, there must be reading, study, reflection. A course of divine training. Religious education. We may be Christians without much knowledge, but it is our honor, glory, and felicity to abound in knowledge. The cost must be paid, in the attainment of all knowledge. The astronomer pays it. The man of literature. So the Christian. We,

II. *Apply the subject to the spiritual cultivation of the moral nature.*

The soul before conversion is like the barren heath, or desert, arid, &c. It must be cultivated — ploughed — sown — tilled, &c. Much labor, &c., is necessary.

Evil habits to be abandoned.

Holy habits to be formed.

Virtues to be grafted in.

Graces to be cherished.

Hence, the duties, the toils, and spiritual efforts necessary. Hence, the exhortations:—"Be diligent," &c. "Giving all diligence," &c. "Fervent in spirit," &c. "Work out your salvation," &c.

We apply the subject,

III. *To the influence of self-denial, in adorning the Christian profession.*

Self-denial is not the abandoning of sin, &c., but the surrendering even of what might be lawfully retained. Hence, the case of eating flesh, &c., as given by the apostle; Rom. xiv. 1. Now our habits—costume—conversation—spirit, &c., must all be sacrificed, if God's glory, and the good of others,

demand it. Our will sacrificed, that God's may be done.

We apply the subject,

IV. *To the importance of usefulness in the cause of the Lord Jesus Christ.*

Is not this one great end of conversion? "I will bless thee, and make thee a blessing," &c. First, the heart must be given to Christ: then life—talents—gifts—influence—time—wealth. Now, if we will be useful, the cost must be paid—the law of self-sacrifice must rule us, &c. Ease, sordidness, &c., must all be cast off. The Apostle Paul says —"Brethren, I beseech you by the mercies of God," &c. Now these cases are illustrative of the subject.

I wish to add some additional thoughts:—Not only must the cost be paid, but paid,

(1.) In the right spirit. Not in the spirit of ostentation for display; of self-righteousness, for merit; of backwardness and grudgingly; but in humble, cheerful, grateful love to Christ. Felt to be a privilege, as well as duty. Need no force nor threatening. Not the whip, but the curb. As David in the text. "Freely we have received," &c. In the language of the poet,—

> "Had I a thousand hearts to give,
> Lord, they should all be thine," &c.

(2.) Observe, this cost paid in the service of religion, is not equal to the demands of sin. Look at the sacrifice the worldly, the proud, the sensual make. What money! What time! What energies! What peace! The way of transgressors is hard, and the end ruin.

(3.) To pay this cost in the service of Christ, grace is both necessary and provided. It cannot be done, but with the help of divine grace. "Without me," &c. "My grace is sufficient," &c. Grace must inspire the desire, purpose, motive. Give the ability and elasticity.

Now the grace of God is provided abundantly. It was found so by Abraham, Moses, David, Daniel, Paul.

Our subject then should,

1. *Lead to examination.*

What has religion done for us? What have we done for it? What has it *cost* us? Have you the inward sense of God's full favor? "Do you walk in the light?" &c. Have you the testimony that you please God?

2. *It condemns two classes of persons.*

Those who wish others to pay for their

religion, and those who wish to have a cost-less religion. Not so David.

Forget not,

3. *That true religion is its own present reward.*

Peace, and hope, and joy now, and then hereafter the glories of a blissful eternity. Let the spirit of the text ever dwell in you, &c.

4. *Address the sinner.*

Who is indifferent to religion altogether. "Godliness is profitable unto all things," &c.

CLXXVIII.—DAVID'S ADDRESS TO SOLOMON, ON BUILDING THE TEMPLE.

"Of the gold, the silver, and the brass, and the iron, there is no number. Arise, therefore, and be doing, and the Lord be with thee."—1 *Chron.* xxii. 16.

OUR text is the address of David, king of Israel, to his son and successor, Solomon. David had purposed to erect a house for Jehovah's worship; but on account of the wars which had distinguished his reign, God transferred the honor to Solomon; verse 6. But though he could not carry out all the desires of his heart in that matter, yet he prepared the way for the erection, and that in a most liberal and devoted manner. See ver. 14, &c. He concludes this description by the urgent appeal of the text: "Arise, therefore," &c. Observe,

I. *The sublime object contemplated.*

II. *The earnest appeal addressed.* And,

III. *The pious prayer presented.*

I. *The sublime object contemplated.*

It was the building of a temple, for God's honor and praise. Its history, the costliness of its materials, its amazing extent, the labor experienced in its erection, and the end for which it was reared, show how great and sublime that object was.

But that dispensation was only a shadowy and typical one. Solomon was an eminent type of the Lord Jesus. His reign, of the gospel dispensation; and his temple, of the church of the Redeemer. What, therefore, is the object to which our ardent and devout attention is now called? It is the erection of the church of the Lord Jesus. The building up of a spiritual temple, for the sacerdotal ministrations of the great High Priest of our profession.

Now, look at this object, in connection,

1. *With the materials employed.*

In the case of Solomon's temple, there were precious stones, and silver, and gold. In this, the materials are living human beings; intellectual, thinking, immortal spirits. 1 Pet. ii. 5, and Eph. ii. 19, &c.

Now, the forming of these materials into a temple for God, involves all that is majestic, and grand, and momentous! It includes the calling of men from darkness to light, &c. Their conversion, regeneration, and holiness. Their consecration to the highest and purest service. Their moral dignity—spiritual blessedness—and eternal glory.

Look at it,

2. *In connection with the well-being of our world.*

Through the entrance of sin, the earth has been cursed, and become the dominion of Satan, and the territory of the kingdom of darkness. Pollution, misery, and woe, becloud its horizon, and curse its inhabitants. Oppression, suffering, and crime, despair and death, stalk in fearful steps, through our world.

Now, as the temple of the Lord Jesus rises up, darkness gives place to light.

Sin gives place to holiness.

Pollution to purity.

Oppression to freedom.

Suffering to enjoyment.

And death, to life and immortality.

The wilderness blossoms as the rose, and becomes as the fruitful field, yea, even as the garden of the Lord. Heaven is brought down to earth, and paradise is regained and restored.

Look at it,

3. *In connection with the Redeemer's glory.*

He came to bruise the head of Satan—to destroy the works of the devil—to set up his own spiritual empire, &c. And in the joys of the redeemed, and the acclamations and songs of his people, to receive a revenue of honor and glory. Now, in the erection of his spiritual temple, this is secured. Here he witnesses the travail of his soul,—here he sees the purchase of his blood,—here he beholds the triumphs of his grace—the trophies of his truth—the monuments of his love—and the completion of his temple will swell the Saviour's spirit with ecstasy he hath not yet known, and fill the universe with songs of acclamation and praise, which ear hath never yet heard. From myriads—

as countless as the stars of heaven, or as the drops of the morning dew—shall be sung, "Worthy is the Lamb," &c. Rev. v. 12. Notice,

II. *The earnest appeal addressed.*

"Arise, therefore, and be doing."

Now, this appeal involves this great truth,

1. *That the temple of the Saviour is to be reared by human instrumentality.*

This was true of Solomon's temple; and equally so of the church of the Lord Jesus. All the dispensations of religion have been so connected. The Patriarchal—Mosaic—and Prophetical, &c. To prepare the way of Christ and the gospel, was committed to John the Baptist.

Now, the institutions of the Christian dispensation are committed to the Redeemer's church. There is not now a successive priesthood. Jesus is the great High Priest of our profession, &c.; and all believers are priests unto God.

In the ranks of agency, first stands forth the Christian ministry; then the Evangelists and Deacons of the church; but immediately united with these, the whole body of believers.

All Christians are to shine, &c.

All are to be as salt.

All are to testify for Christ, &c.

All to witness for the truth.

All to labor in the cause of love and mercy.

Every Christian is to be the Lord's, in all his powers, and energies, and talents, and influence,—the Lord's entirely, and forever.

2. *To the duties of this instrumentality, the church should be actively excited.*

"Arise, therefore," &c. Even the servants of God are liable to fall into a state of apathy and formalism. The things of time and sense absorb their attention—earthly cares interfere,—the indolence of our nature—temptations of the enemy, &c. Now, nothing can meet these deadly influences, but a spirit of holy and heavenly excitement.

The excitement of holy love.

The excitement of burning zeal.

The excitement of spiritual devotion.

The church must be awake, and lively, and intensely concerned, or the work of the Redeemer's cause will not, indeed cannot, be carried on. Hence, we are to "consider one another, and provoke one another to love and good works," &c.

3. *The spirit of active excitement must ever be associated with holy labor and effort.*

Now, the working part is the real department to which we are called. It is well to contemplate the scenes of joy and glory prophecy depicts. It is well to be accurately acquainted with the instrumentality needful. It is well to devise and set up the essential apparatus; to determine, and purpose, and aver our resolutions. But all will be of no practical avail, without the toil and the doing. "And be doing."

It is the preaching, and the praying, and the teaching of the young,—and the distribution of tracts,—and the exhortation,—and the laying out of our means, &c., by which the great work of religion must be carried on. The church must be a *diligent, faithful, working church.*

And this doing must be discriminate,—in our proper and legitimate sphere.

And cheerful,—with a ready heart and willing spirit.

And earnest,—with all our hearts.

And constant and persevering,—not weary in well-doing.

And united,—as one army,—or as the drops in the wave. "Striving together."

Observe,

III. *The pious prayer presented.*

"And the Lord be with thee."

Now observe,

1. *The object of the prayer.*

The presence of the Lord. All, without this, will be inefficient. Even the wisdom of Solomon, in connection with royal influence and rule, are vain without this. This should ever be impressed on our minds. We need many things,—men and money, &c.; sanctified intellects and eloquent tongues, and burden-bearing shoulders; but with all, and above all, the Lord's presence. "Not by might," &c. "Paul planteth," &c. "Let no man glory in men," &c.

2. *The certainty of its realization.*

The Lord will be with his people.

We have abundant promises.

We have countless instances.

The whole history of the church, &c. The delight God has in his people, &c.

APPLICATION.

1. Are we interested in the great object?

2. Are we laboring for God, and the church, and souls? Is there not a necessity for the exhortation? "Arise," &c.

3. Do we rely on the presence and blessing of God?

4. Can we offer the prayer of the text, for all who are laboring in the cause of God?

CLXXIX.—DAVID'S DEATH-BED.

"Now the days of David drew nigh that he should die: and he charged Solomon his son, saying, I go the way of all the earth: be thou strong therefore, and show thyself a man," &c.—1 *Kings* ii. 1–4.

DEATH is the earthly end of all flesh, whether rich or poor, high or low, monarchs or subjects, holy or vile. The living know that they must die. However extended the earthly thread, it must break. However long the day of life, the evening will come. However numerous the sands in the hour-glass, the last will run out.

David, in all respects, was a memorable man; both as a saint, a prophet, and king. He was raised from obscurity, to great earthly power and magnificence. From handling the shepherd's crook, to swaying the sceptre of Israel.

After a series of most wondrous events, he draws near to the confines of eternity. We now visit him on his sick-bed, and in his dying chamber.

Let us reverently tread the sacred apartment, gaze on the dying king, and hear the words which proceed from his expiring lips.

Observe,

I. *His conscious reference to his approaching dissolution.*

"I go the way of all the earth:" verse 2. That is, the way of death. All around us remind us of death. The expiring day—the returning winter—the falling trees. All animals return to the earth—those that live for an hour, a day, or a hundred years. Man is equally included in this category of death. Formed of dust, to the dust he must return. Every act of respiration is a temporary dying. The breathing out the animal life.

This way is that of all the earth.

No one exempted from death.

No mode of life.

No rank or station.

All, all must die, &c. The antediluvians lived nearly a thousand years. Noah 950 years. Abraham 175 years. Jacob about

147 years. Joseph 110 years. But Moses, in the desert, speaks of the days of man as threescore years and ten, or at most fourscore years.

David had lived about seventy years; but in point of events, and toils, and labors, his life probably had in it more than that of Methuselah itself. He was conscious that he was near the end of the way of life. How wise and proper often to ponder on this! How vain to dream of putting it off, by not making it the subject of meditation! It ought to be remembered, and laid to heart.

Notice,

II. *The dying counsels he tenders.*

Observe,

1. *To whom the counsels are given.*

Verse 1.

To Solomon. His son. His very much beloved son. The wisest, and perhaps best of his sons. His successor. At this time, very young. It is said, Solomon was not more than twenty years of age. What need of counsel! as a young man, a prince; and also as heir to the throne of Israel.

Notice,

2. *The counsel itself.*

Here there are several very important particulars.

(1.) He counsels him to manly strength. He would have need of this. Doubtless, is meant, mental power—strength of mind. Not to be the subject of youthly effeminacy; but to display the mind and spirit of a man. Strength of mind is obtained by mental effort and cultivation. By pursuing great objects—by seeking the invigorating blessing of the Most High. Strong, manly minds are essential to great and arduous pursuits.

(2.) He counsels him to keep God's charge.

To recognize God.

To bow to his authority.

To hearken to his commandments. Four words are used here:—

1. Walk in God's *ways.* The ways of his ordinances. Ways of worship and reverence for God. Ways of godliness.

2. To keep his *statutes.* The very enjoinments of God on his people. To make the Jewish code his study, and act in conformity with them.

3. His *commandments.* The great moral law—the essential rule of right, &c.

4. His *testimonies.* What God had testi-

fied to Moses and the Prophets up to this time, and which were the Scriptures of that day. Then observe,

3. *The spirit in which God's counsel is to be obeyed.*

"In truth." Not feignedly; but with godly sincerity.

"With all the heart." With voluntary heartedness. With earnestness of spirit.

"With all the soul." In which the mental powers and moral faculties would unitedly serve God. In which the whole soul should be consecrated to religion.

Such then, were the counsels given. Consider,

III. *The motives by which they were enforced.*

Now these motives are twofold.

1. *Personal prosperity.*

Verse 3.

To be prosperous in all he did, and wherever he was. How extensive this promise! Yet it is just what we need. What God has engaged to do for his people. Psalm i. 3 ; cxxviii. 2 ; Isa. iii. 10. The declaration of Paul to Timothy, "Godliness is profitable," &c.

2. *A continued succession on the throne of Israel.*

Now this would deeply interest Solomon as a king, and as concerned for the prosperity of the nation. But it was strictly conditional ; and if the conditions were violated, the promise was forfeited. Personal piety secures personal blessings. National piety, national blessings.

David on his death-bed was concerned for both.—For Solomon's right-heartedness, and the religious character of the kingdom. And thus, he spoke as he was moved by the Spirit of God within him.

How beautiful this counsel, as a saint.

How affectionate as a parent.

How patriotic as a king. Learn,—

1. *What alone can give dignity and lustre to a dying hour.*

True religion. This is alike necessary for the monarch as the peasant. How true the lines :—

> "'Tis religion must supply
> Solid comforts when we die."

2. *The good man is alike useful in death as in life.*

Living, he lives to the Lord : dying, he dies to the Lord. How desirable such a death ! "Let me die," &c.

3. *Highly favored are they who have been interested in the dying counsels and prayers of the godly.*

4. *The connection between duty and safety.*

Precept and promise are linked together. Religion and peace—piety and bliss—devotion and God—holiness and heaven.

CLXXX.—SAUL'S SUICIDE.

"Then said Saul unto his armor-bearer, Draw thy sword, and thrust me through therewith ; lest these uncircumcised come and thrust me through, and abuse me. But his armor-bearer would not ; for he was sore afraid. Therefore, Saul took a sword, and fell upon it."—1 Sam. xxxi. 4.

THE history of Saul resembles that of many a gallant vessel, that left its harbor with flying colors, every sail filled with the favorable breeze, amid the admiring exultations of a crowd of spectators ; but which has finally foundered at sea, or been dashed to pieces on the rocks and breakers.

The commencement of Saul's career was bright and hopeful. In his form and person he was noble and manly. He was selected from among all his compeers, to wear the first diadem in Israel. He was anointed by the excellent and devoted Samuel. He entered on his reign with the approbation and heartiest wishes of his people ; and it is evident too, that he enjoyed the special favor of God.

But his pathway was darkened by disobedience to the Lord. He exalted his own authority above that of Jehovah, and was cast off from the divine complacency. He wandered further and further from the path of integrity, and was, at length, destined in the providence of God, to yield his crown and kingdom to another.

His days became embittered by the most deadly envy, and he fell a prey to wretchedness and melancholy. His last end was awfully miserable. He forsook the counsels of heaven, and betook himself to witchcraft for direction. In an encounter with the Philistines, his army fled, &c. ; see ver. 1, 2. And at length he called his armor-bearer to destroy him ; on whose refusal, it is said, "Therefore Saul took a sword," &c. Our subject is suicide.

Let us consider,

Its nature.

The evils comprised in it.

.The means of preventing it.

I. *The nature of this sin.*

It is the taking away our own life. Self-murder is of two kinds :—

1. *Mediate or indirect.*

Where a person withholds from himself what is essential to life.

Where by gluttony or excessive food, disease is produced.

By drunkenness, which impairs health, and brings myriads to a premature grave.

Where by debauchery and sensual excesses, the life is abridged.

Where persons madly expose their lives to imminent risk and peril.

2. *Immediate and direct.*

When a person at once snaps asunder the brittle thread. By the pistol, or the razor —the rope, or the poison, or the water. Saul fell upon his sword. Judas hanged himself, &c.

II. *The evils comprised in it.*

I observe,

1. *It is a sin against the prerogative of God.*

God is the author and arbiter of life. "In his hand is the breath," &c. "He killeth," &c. Infidels have jested with this sentiment. Hume wrote of it in a most flippant style, and merely represents it, as directing a few ounces of blood in a different channel.

God has said—"Thou shalt not kill." None doubt the application of this to others; but, who disputes that it must necessarily include ourselves? I am God's creature, and not mine own.

2. *It is a sin against my friends.*

Every man has his connections. Some, whose interests are bound up with his. These cords of relationship and love, I have no right rudely to sever; I am one of several parties, and should not trample on their rights and affections. Think when this is perpetrated by a father—husband—wife—mother—child—sister! &c. What misery is inflicted! What sorrow entailed! What woe produced! It is a rude and cruel assault on society.

3. *It is a cruel and debasing attack on human nature.*

Man is the highest and most dignified of earthly creatures. Read the history of his creation. Think how God has magnified him. What his Son has done for him. Go to Eden—go to Calvary—go to the holiest of all; and then reflect, on the wicked barbarity of self-destruction.

4. *It is impious and presumptuous interference with the most solemn concerns.*

Life, how precious! Time, how important! Death, how solemn! Eternity, how momentous! One view of this sin is peculiarly awful,—there can be no repentance for it, or deliverance from its guilt and curse. It is a plunge into the abyss, where there is no gospel—no Saviour—no hope. It is destruction of body and soul forever. Of course, I do not include in these remarks, those who are *insane*, and thus unaccountable—except, the insanity has been self-produced.

Notice,

III. *The means of preventing it.*

Here I premise,

(1.) The love of life is much stronger in some, than others.

(2.) The temptation more powerful in some cases than others. But if we would avoid the evil, the causes must be avoided. Let us look at some of the most common.

1. *Pride and worldly ambition.*

So in Saul. Ahithophel. 2 Sam. xvii. 23. This was the case with many of the ancients, and some modern statesmen, &c.

2. *The sorrow of the world.*

Losses, &c. Earthly prospects ruined. Sudden transition from riches to poverty. Speculations in trade, &c. Could not bear to live without wealth, &c.

3. *Remorse and guilty anguish.*

Judas. Matt. xxvii. 3.

Look at the gamester! also,

That ruined female!

That abandoned drunkard!

That forsaken spendthrift!

4. *Despair of God's mercy.*

Influence of temptations, and influence of false doctrines. False views of divine sovereignty—of divine decrees, &c.

Then learn,

1. How necessary it is to fear God.

2. To avoid the paths of the destroyer.

3. To seek God's mercy in the gospel.

4. To live usefully, and thus really enjoy life.

5. To act in all things, in reference to eternity.

6. To repel temptation, by prayer for divine help.

CLXXXI.—BARZILLAI.

"And Barzillai said unto the king, How long have I to live, that I should go up with the king unto Jerusalem? I am this day fourscore years old," &c.—2 *Sam.* xix. 34–37.

DURING the period of Absalom's rebellion, when David was in great straits, Barzillai exhibited his attachment to his sovereign, and provided the king with sustenance, &c. Verse 32, &c.

David was anxious to show his gratitude for the loyal and generous conduct his faithful subject had displayed, and therefore invited him to go with him to Jerusalem; ver. 33. To this evidence of royal favor, he replied in my text; ver. 34, &c. Now there are several striking features in the character of Barzillai, which deserve our careful consideration.

I. *We see in him, life protracted to old age.*

Ages before this, they lived much longer. Moses was 120 years old, &c. Jacob lived 147 years. Abraham 175 years; and the Antediluvians many hundreds of years. But now, we find life greatly abridged. Moses had stated this; Ps. xc. 10. So that Barzillai at eighty, is styled a very old man; ver. 32. Remarkable that the human machine should keep in motion so long. No watch, nor engine can do this, &c.

"Our life contains a thousand springs,
And dies, if one be gone," &c.

Not many attain the age of eighty. How few; not perhaps one now present. No: "Sixteen's as mortal as fourscore; and yet fourscore years are as a shadow."

II. *We see in Barzillai a beautiful exhibition of weanedness from the world.*

Worldly glory had nothing to allure, nor worldly pleasures to attract; ver. 35. He had wisely withdrawn from the fascinations of life, and gayeties of the world. How odious is old age, when thirsting after the sensual scenes of life. How beautiful the character in our text.

III. *Barzillai exhibited great contentment with his state and circumstances.*

Here is nothing morose—nothing of petulance, or impatience. He evidently was composed and happy, in the lot in which providence had placed him. He was aware of his own infirmities, and yet without complaint or murmuring, was resigned to his condition.

IV. *Barzillai evidently contemplated his own mortality.*

Hence, he asks, "How long have I to live?" He knew he had lived long, and that few sands remained. His sun was going down, &c. His journey ending. And he thought of it, and spake about it. How wise—how profitable—how essential,

(1.) To be familiar with death.

(2.) To be expecting it.

(3.) To live for it.

(4.) Evangelically ready for it. Having a title and meetness for the life to come.

How proper for us to ask the same question, "How long," &c. Would it not produce sobriety of mind—seriousness of spirit —indifference to the world—anxiety to be useful, &c. Observe,

V. *Barzillai was an example of politeness and modesty.*

In old age persons are often harsh and self-important. Often look with undue complacency on what they say and do. But Barzillai exhibited great politeness. "Why should the king recompense," &c.; ver. 36. "I will go a little way," &c. He had no high thoughts of himself. How beautiful is humility in all, especially in the aged.

VI. *Barzillai was not unmindful of the concerns of his son.*

"But behold thy servant Chimham," &c. I have no objection that he should have the king's honors and favors, &c.

Now, all parents should be anxious for the future welfare of their children,—should obtain for them honest callings, and useful stations in life. Their wisdom, experience, and influence, should be exerted to secure this for them.

VII. *Barzillai was anxious to be placed in the sepulchre of his parents.*

How beautifully he refers to the grave of his father and mother; ver. 37. He had not forgotten them, even in old age. Probably long since dead, &c.; yet he thinks of them with respect and love, and desires to dwell with them in the house appointed for all living. What a fine old man! Who can fail to admire the portrait thus drawn!

In conclusion, let me ask,

1. *How much of his spirit do you possess?*

Of deadness to the pleasures of the world? &c. Indifference to worldly greatness? &c. Contentedness with your lot?

2. *Do you often think of your mortality?*

"How long have I to live?"

3. *Can you contemplate the event calmly and with hope?*

Are you dying daily?

4. *Let us be anxious for our successors.*

Live so, that we shall leave the impress of our feet in the world. Make it better by our influence. Seek an enduring remembrance by our benevolence and usefulness. Live in the history of the Church of Christ, after the grave has encompassed us.

CLXXXII.—ELIJAH'S TRANSLATION.

"And Elisha saw it, and he cried, My father, my father, the chariot of Israel, and the horsemen thereof. And he saw him no more: and he took hold of his own clothes, and rent them in two pieces."—2 *Kings* ii. 12.

ELIJAH was one of the most illustrious of Old Testament saints. He was pre-eminently distinguished for his stern and austere mode of life—his unswerving fidelity—noble moral heroism—prayerful and believing spirit. He was largely endowed with the spirit of miracles and prophecy. He began his public ministry 914 years, and he finished it about 896 years before Christ; so that, his labors seem to be comprised within about eighteen years. Of his parentage, &c., Scripture is silent. Notwithstanding the distinguished characteristics of Elijah, he was but a man, and as such, had his moral infirmities. He failed in that for which he was most celebrated—courage; and hence, in fear, he fled, and sought death in the bitterness of his soul. His ministry was rather that of terror; and it does not appear to have been signally successful. But to his *removal*, we have now particularly to refer. He had with him a devoted contemporary, and one who was to be his successor. We see them together on the day of his exit from earth. Both knew the wondrous event, as well also as the sons of the prophets; ver. 3. Elijah seemed anxious to be alone, and entreats Elisha to leave him; verses 2, 4, and 6. A splendid miracle is then performed; ver. 8. An affectionate question presented; ver. 9. A pious answer given; ver. 10. The grand scene now takes place, and the exclamation of the text is uttered; ver. 12.

Observe,

I. *What Elisha beheld.*

II. *What he exclaimed.* And,

III. *What he received.*

I. *What he beheld.*

1. *The termination of a saint's career and labors on earth.*

This must be the case with all. The day will end—the probation terminate.

2. *A distinguished honor and felicity, conferred on a faithful servant.*

All such shall be honored and rewarded. Many are so in the circumstances of their death. In having,

(1.) Ecstasy; or,

(2.) Peace.

"The last end of that man is peace." But in this case there was something extraordinary; not death, but a Translation. Only one such instance previously, and none since. World's three grand epochs, are seen connected with

Enoch—Elijah—and the Lord Jesus.

This event taught two great doctrines: The soul's immortality; and the body's final resurrection, &c. He beheld,

3. *Earth and heaven in marvellous communion.*

Doubtless the messengers were angels. The form assumed horses and chariots. See the same symbolical reference; chap. vi. 12, &c. Ps. lxviii. 15–17. The commission is given, and is executed with promptness and delight. Let me turn to the dying moments of the beggar Lazarus. He died, and was carried by angels, &c. The highway to glory we imagine is crowded by descending angels, and attending saints.

II. *What he exclaimed.*

"My father," &c. Observe,

1. *The title he gave the prophet.*

"Father," so they were often designated. As a term of reverence, &c. As a father, he instructed, prayed for, reproved. Gave the example, the care of a father. Paul adopts it; 1 Thess. ii. 11. He was so to Elisha and the nation. A public blessing, &c. He repeats it, indicating his great reverence and deep love.

2. *His reference to the celestial convoy.*

Here was surprise and astonishment. The sublime scene. "The chariot of Israel." Of Israel's God! For Israel's prophet! As Israel's defence. Or the exclamation might refer to Elijah, as being, by his ministry, a defence to the nation, and now removed. The chariot and horsemen are going. Israel is bereaved. Hence his grief, &c. Rent his clothes, &c.

Notice,

III. *What he received.*

1. *The official costume of the prophet.*

The *mantle*,—the sign of his office—by which miracles had been performed; ver. 13. He took it not to worship it, but to wear it. God provides successors to his public servants. What was better in this case,

2. *He imparted to him a double measure of the spirit of Elijah.*

Verses 9, 10.

How vain the mantle without the spirit! He had both. So ought the vaunted successors of the apostles; or give up their absurd pretensions. He soon works a miracle; verse 14. Of Elisha it is said, he wrought twice the number of miracles that Elijah had done.

APPLICATION.

Learn,

1. *What ministers and people should expect.*

The removal of the best and most talented of the Lord's servants. They should live and labor in reference to it.

2. *What they who labor should anticipate.*

The better world, &c.

3. *What should cheer the Church.*

The raising up of Elishas, &c.

4. *What such should seek.*

A double portion of the spirit of their predecessors. The world and the times increasingly need more of the spirit of piety, zeal, and devotedness.

No man should be content with the measure of knowledge, or the amount of influence possessed by his predecessors.

Every age should be in moral advance of the past, as every age has had, in reality, the benefit of those which have preceded it.

Progression should be the rule; and thus all should forget the things which are behind, and press forward to those things which are before.

The mental and spiritual career of the Church should be higher and higher, until the days of heaven should be enjoyed on the earth.

All this would be attained, if every pious servant of God sought and obtained a double portion of the spirit of holiness and zeal, which was enjoyed by their predecessors. There can be no doubt that divine knowledge is increasing, and spiritual truth progressing in the earth.

To meet this more elevated phase of the Church and the world, the teachers of mankind must be richly endowed with the spirit of sanctified emulation.

The great desire to be useful and efficient, in the spheres to which we have been called by divine providence, should ever inspire the prayer—"Let a double portion of thy spirit be upon me."

Forget not, that in proportion as we possess the blessed spirit, we shall be fitted for exerting a hallowed influence on mankind—extending the empire of Jesus—and glorifying our Father in heaven.

———◆———

CLXXXIII.—ELISHA, AND THE WOMAN OF SHUNEM.

"And it fell on a day, that Elisha passed to Shunem, where was a great woman; and she constrained him to eat bread. And so it was, that as oft as he passed by, he turned in thither to eat bread. And she said unto her husband, Behold, now, I perceive that this is an holy man of God, which passeth by us continually," &c.— *2 Kings* iv. 8–13.

MAN is a creature of boundless desires. Hence, when these desires are directed to earthly things, it is impossible that they should meet with perfect satisfaction.

The man who craves for power and dominion is never contented with what he has; and like Alexander the Great, if he conquers one world, would still desire another.

A man who thirsts for earthly distinctions, never reaches the pinnacle of popularity which perfectly satisfies him.

The covetous man, who seeks the acquisition of wealth, never feels that he has plenty; but would ever be gathering more and more.

The man of pleasure finds that earthly gratifications, like salt water, only increases his desires, and inflames his appetites. God alone can satisfy the longings of the soul. He is an infinite good. Hence the Psalmist prays, "Oh, satisfy us early with thy goodness," &c. "Delight thyself in the Lord," &c. "The Lord is my portion," &c.

How beautifully these remarks are illustrated, in the history of the woman of Shunem.

Let us read and expound the narrative; ver. 8, &c.

I. *True piety will lead to a generous and hospitable treatment of God's servants.*

Here was Elisha, God's servant, on his religious journeys, passing and repassing through the village of Shunem. An excellent woman observes it,—invites him to be her guest,—considers his wants. "Constrained" him. Her heart was in the work. It was from a true and noble generosity.

It was repeated.

It was permanent.

It was considerate, and connected with sacrifice; ver. 9.

It was plain, and unostentatious. Real, solid kindness, and not that of mere glitter and show. Observe how this spirit of the woman of Shunem accords,

(1.) With Scripture examples. See the instance of Abraham and the angels: Gen. xviii. 1–8.

The case of Abraham's servant, who received the cordial invitation from Laban, "Come thou blessed of the Lord," &c.

We see, too, the kindly regard paid to the Saviour, by the holy and happy family at Bethany.

The case of Lydia, too, who opened her house, &c., for the Apostles at Corinth. See also 2 Tim. i. 16.

It accords,

(2.) With Scripture exhortations.

"Be not unmindful to entertain strangers," &c.

"Given to hospitality."

"Do good unto all men," &c. One of the many qualifications required in those who should receive the pecuniary aid of the Church, was of this kind: 1 Tim. v. 9.

"Be ready to every good work."

II. *Unfeigned gratitude is one of the essential features of godliness.*

Gratitude to God, and also gratitude to men. The two must be united. There may be gratitude to men, without gratitude to God; but there never is gratitude to God, without gratitude to men. Ingratitude is a base feeling. One of the grossest signs of our depravity. The inferior creatures evidence their gratitude for favors conferred; so that an ungrateful man sinks lower than the brute. Religion cherishes this principle. It elevates it. Makes it manifestly more tender, and fervent, and sincere. See how it glowed in the prophet's heart; ver. 13. Hence, we learn that gratitude will endeavor to return the kindness bestowed. Love begets love,—gratitude produces the fruits of gratitude.

III. *Religion leads to contentment with our present position.*

Verse 13.

The woman of Shunem has no inordinate desires—no ambitious projects.

Her mercies equal her wants.

She prefers a secluded, to a showy life.

Her own dwelling to a palace.

Mediocrity to affluence.

Her own plain people, to the society of the rich and the great.

What wisdom there was in this!

What solid piety! Let us see,

What might she have gained by removal?

Riches—honors—pleasures. What lost?

(1.) Her humble independency.

(2.) Her sweet retirements.

(3.) Her friendly societies.

(4.) Most of all, her peace and satisfaction of mind.

Her snares and anxieties would have been increased. See the case of Lot; Gen. xiii. 5. Two passages are illustrated, Prov. xxx. 8, &c., and "Be content with," &c. Let me add another, "Godliness with contentment," &c.

Now, how may this spirit be produced?

Reflect how little you really need.

How uncertain the lease of life.

How superior are spiritual enjoyments.

How infinitely to be desired, the blessings of heaven. "Set your affections," &c.

APPLICATION.

We address the subject,

1. *To the discontented and unhappy.*

Seek satisfaction in religion.

2. *To the people of God who may mourn and be fretful.*

Contemplate the woman of Shunem, &c. Seek her spirit, and follow in her steps.

CLXXXIV.—THE UNBELIEVING LORD.

"Then a lord on whose hand the king leaned answered the man of God, and said, Behold, if the Lord would make windows in heaven, might this thing be? And he said, Behold, thou shalt see it with thine eyes, but shalt not eat thereof." —2 *Kings* vii. 2.

ONE of the greatest scourges of our race has been war. In itself, it is a fearful evil, an unmitigated woe. It is the harbinger of many sorrows,—death and hell follow in its train. Where war triumphs, desolation reigns; and misery and want prevail. It has been the occasion of the greatest atrocities, and it has transformed even the lovelier sex of our race into living monstrosities.

Our text relates to the siege of Samaria; chap. vi. 25. Then follows an account of the woes which succeeded.

We see, in the sequel, the wrath of the king towards Elisha, instead of being indignant with his own sins. How men quarrel with any thing rather than the evil of their souls, and the idol of their hearts! At length, deliverance draws near, Elisha is the message-bearer of the glad tidings; ver. 1.

To these, one of the lords, leaning on the arm of the king, ventured to express his unbelief; to which Elisha replied, " Behold, thou shalt see it," &c.

Observe,

I. *All events are under the Divine control.*

God ruleth in the heavens above, and on the earth beneath. In all the ordinary arrangements of the world, he ruleth. His power and wisdom are in constant exercise. In all the extraordinary events, he is working by his Almighty arm. All events on a grand scale! All those on the smallest. His government is universal—taking in all. It is minute, including every event.

(1.) Observe, a recognition of this is highly important.

(2.) To live under the influence of this, is one part of true religion.

(3.) Where this is the case, there will be waiting upon God, and resignation to his will.

II. *There is no misery or calamity which God cannot avert, or overrule for good.*

This necessarily follows the last proposition. See it, when Pharaoh pursues the Israelites. Humanly speaking, there was no hope. But how God delivered Israel, and destroyed Pharaoh, &c. Look at the case in the text. There seemed no ray of hope for the people of Samaria; and observe how God opened an effectual door of deliverance; ver. 3, &c.

The spoils and plenty of their besiegers enriched them. They were relieved from the camp of their enemies.

When we think of the knowledge of Jehovah—

His irresistible power!

His numbered resources!

Then we may conclude, that there is no misery which he cannot remove.

Observe,

III. *The folly and wickedness of unbelief in reference to the doings of Jehovah.*

It is foolish for a worm of the earth to dictate to God. To limit his working hand. To pronounce what he can, or cannot perform. A child might laugh at the discoveries of Newton. A savage might despise the reasonings of Bacon. But neither of these equal in infatuation, the mind which ventures to set bounds to the arrangements and workings of God.

But unbelief is wicked.—It despises God. —It gives the lie to God.

God spake by Elisha in the text; and a creature of the dust throws back the declaration, with unbelieving derision. Now, think of the pride and presumption of such a course! And yet, alas, how common!

Thus all skeptics treat the Word of God, and revealed religion. Disputing and denying God's ability to declare his mind, &c.

Thus all presumptuous sinners treat the threatenings of future punishment.

Thus all rejecters of the gospel treat the overtures of dying love.

Thus all unbelievers treat the promises, when they despond in the day of trial and affliction, &c.

Unbelief under the gospel is a denial of the love of God—a rejection of the grace, that gave the Lord Jesus to death, &c.

IV. *Unbelievers are often overwhelmed with irresistible evidence.*

So it was with the inhabitants of the old world, when the flood came.

So with the unbelieving Jews in the wilderness.

So with the unbelieving lord.

So often with sinners in this life, when overwhelmed with remorse.

So it shall be at the day of judgment, with all the ungodly. They shall see and hear what they have refused to believe.

So with the lost in perdition, through all eternity.

V. *The convictions produced by the judgments of God, bring no relief to the unbelieving.*

" Thine eyes shall see, but thou shalt not eat;" v. 18, &c.

This is just emblematical of the state of the lost.—They shall see Christ, but have no interest in him.—They shall see heaven, but have no right to its glories.—They shall behold the tree of life and the rivers of pleasure, but shall not have access thereto, or enjoy the light or joy of the blessedness they behold.

APPLICATION.

1. *How evil and disastrous is unbelief.*
It now prevents the salvation of the soul.
It keeps men from the cross of Christ. It
keeps men in a state of guilt, and misery,
and condemnation—beneath the curse and
wrath of God.

2. *How sweet the message of mercy.*
To the slaves of satanic war and besiege-
ment. To the starving sinner, it offers deliverance and plenty. Let the message be
heartily embraced. Receive it with all gladness, and enjoy the blessedness it declares.

3. *From these blessings none are excluded,
but those who unbelievingly exclude themselves.*
"Ye will not come unto me," &c.

CLXXXV.—HAZAEL'S EXCLAMATION.

"And Hazael said, But what, is thy servant a
dog, that he should do this great thing? And
Elisha answered, The Lord hath showed me that
thou shalt be king over Syria."—2 *Kings,* viii. 13.

BEN-HADAD, king of Syria, was sick, and
anxious to know the result of his affliction,
sent Hazael to visit Elisha, and seek prophetical information from him. Doubtless,
this confidence in Elisha might, in part,
have resulted from the miraculous restoration of Naaman, the chief captain of Ben-
hadad's army. So Hazael went, &c.; ver. 9.

Now, the answer was evidently this: The
disease itself is not of a mortal kind, and
that disease shall not prove fatal; yet he
shall surely die, &c.

The prophet then fixed his eyes steadfastly
on Hazael, until Hazael was overwhelmed
with the gaze; and then Elisha, the man of
God, wept; ver. 11. Hazael then said, Why
weepest, &c. And Elisha replied: ver. 12.
As a man and a patriot, &c., he wept. Then
follows the exclamation of surprise and indignant horror: "Is thy servant a dog,"
&c. Now such is the history.

I intend to ground on the text several
weighty propositions, of a practical character.

I. *That men are extensively ignorant of
the evil of their own hearts.*
So the prophet affirms. "The heart is
deceitful," &c. "Who can know it?" &c.

This ignorance is almost universal. Self-love
leads to undue self-estimation. We can
imagine others to be wicked, &c.; but most
men think more highly of themselves, &c.
In the natural heart are the seeds and germs
of every sin; and these produce all manner
of evil, if left to the influence of the temptations, &c., of Satan. What does Christ say?
Matt. xv. 19. The Word of God describes
the heart as froward—full of evil imaginings
—full of hypocrisy—proud—hard—impenitent—perverse—rebellious—stony, &c.

Now, this ignorance is extensively maintained through viewing ourselves in a
worldly mirror, and not by the Word of
God.

Observe, how men call evil things by false
names. Pride, is a good spirit; revenge,
noble-mindedness; profligacy, generous living, or merely given to pleasure; infidelity,
freethinking, &c., &c.

II. *That the most awful courses of vice,
often have small beginnings.*
The way of sin is wide and downward;
but few think of this.

The leprosy commences with a small pim-
ple, or spot.

Hatred, is murder in the germ.

Unbelief, the precursor of mature infidelity, and rejection of God, and his Word.

The very first transgression commenced
by gazing on the forbidden fruit—and then
hearing the seductive statements of Satan—
then desiring—then receiving—and finally
eating.

III. *That men would have been overwhelmed with horror at one period of their
history, could they have foreseen the crimes of
which they have afterwards been guilty.*
Would it not have been so with

Eve, if she had seen the evil, and woe,
and misery, she would entail on her posterity.

Cain, when he first felt unhappy at the
excellency of Abel.

Noah, in his purity, amid the depravity
of the antediluvians, &c.

Lot, when his righteous soul was vexed,
&c., that he should commit drunkenness and
incest, and repeat them.

David, who was so good, and pure, and
gentle, and generous, that he should fall into the heinous sin of cool and deliberate
murder, after he had yielded to the lusts of
the flesh.

Solomon, the wise, and excellent, and
highly favored of heaven, that he should be

deceived and ensnared, when he was old. Read 1 Kings xi. 4 to 8.

And *Peter* warned, resolved, protesting, &c., then denying Christ with oaths.

Now these are beacons, and show how men have fallen into awful evil, who would have been overwhelmed with the idea of their after sins. How many cases might be added.

That *infidel*, was once a regular hearer of God's word—perhaps a Sabbath-school teacher. Began to keep company with the irreligious. Then was found in the way of sinners—then in the seat of the scorner, &c.

That *drunkard*, once sober, &c., then took the glass. The desire stole his heart, it became necessary, then essential.

That *convict*, once honest, &c.; but he betrayed confidence,—purloined, &c.; till, at length, he became a swindler—a robber —a felon.

That *prostitute* was once chaste and lovely, but threw off the robe of modesty, and went down step by step, until she walks on the street; the scorn of the vile, and the wreck of her former self.

That *murderer* would have shuddered at the idea of blood, but sin hardened him. By yielding, he became the pliant tool of the Devil, until, at length, he could stain his hands with the fearful crimson of human blood.

That *man*, in agony on the bed of death, and on the verge of hell—often resolved, desired, prayed, vowed, &c. But deferred, procrastinated, &c., until he exclaimed, "The harvest is past," &c.

IV. *That our safety and happiness can only be insured by adhering to the way of godliness.*

The way of holiness and heaven are the very opposite of sin, and it is only by walking in the very opposite, that we are secure, &c. There is only one absolutely sure path, —the fear, love, and service of God.

Preserved, and guided, and sustained, by the grace of God.

To trust to ourselves, is the way of deception and ruin.

God will keep and sanctify those who come to him, and seek with humility his divine aid.

V. *Genuine goodness will weep over the errors and crimes of men.*

What a beautiful instance the text presents—Elisha wept, &c. Wherefore? Why, doubtless, for these reasons:—

1. *For the honor of his God.*

All sin dishonors God—insults, grieves him. One wept because men did not keep God's law.

Now this should affect us on the same account. The swearer—the Sabbath-breaker, &c. He wept, doubtless,

2. *On account of his fellow-men.*

Iniquity injures men, as well as offends God. One sinner destroyeth much good. What misery does a drunkard spread! A robber—a murderer! Their friends, their parents, and sisters, &c. Society violated and oppressed.

3. *For his own sake.*

He would remember that Hazael was a man—a brother—an immortal being—accountable to God, &c. His soul precious. His salvation infinitely important.

Now, thus we should feel; however ignorant, vile, brutalized; yet that the sinner is a man, &c. We are often excited, and use harsh words. What would Christ say, if he were in our midst? What he once said, —"He that is without sin," &c. Such, after all, are their own worst enemies.

Learn,—

1. The depravity of human nature.
2. The necessity of renewing grace.
3. The efficiency of Christ's blood to save.

———◆———

CLXXXVI.—THE HUMILIATION OF THE PRINCES, AND THE KING, PLEASING TO GOD.

"And when the Lord saw that they humbled themselves, the word of the Lord came to Shemaiah, saying, They have humbled themselves; therefore, I will not destroy them, but I will grant them some deliverance; and my wrath shall not be poured out upon Jerusalem by the hand of Shishak."—2 *Chron.* xii. 7.

THE text is connected with an historical event, of considerable importance, in the history of Judah.

Rehoboam forsook the law of God, &c.; ver. 1.

The kingdom was invaded. All the fenced cities taken, with the metropolitan city of Jerusalem itself.

Then Shemaiah the prophet, was sent to Rehoboam and to the princes of Judah, to state the reason of their degraded and wretched condition; ver. 5.

This declaration produced the desired effect—a spirit of general humiliation was evinced; "And when the Lord saw that they humbled themselves," &c.

Now, there are certain great principles involved in the text. Principles which have to do with God's moral government, and with the responsibility of his creatures. These principles are applicable to all persons and ages.

We remark, then,

I. *That the rejection of God must ever be productive of consequences the most disastrous.*

In itself, this is a most heinous sin. To forsake the law of the Lord—to reject his authority, &c. This sin is sometimes specially great.

(1.) When committed by those who have had pious ancestors.

(2.) By those who have once professed religion.

(3.) By those to whom the goodness of God has been largely displayed.

All these circumstances were connected with the case of Rehoboam. Is it not the case with many here?

Now, need we marvel that God should be displeased and punish such delinquency.

He did so in our first parents.

He did so in the apostasies of Israel.

He did so in the instance of the text.

He will do so in the case of all who utterly forsake him. "If thou forsake him," &c. "If any man draw back," &c.

II. *That genuine humiliation is the only remedy that will avert these consequences.*

Now there are several branches of genuine humiliation.

It includes,

(1.) A conviction of the evil of our doings.

(2.) An admission and hearty confession before God.

(3.) Deep and intense sorrow of heart, on account of it.

(4.) A turning from the evil of our doings.

(5.) Earnest prayer and supplication to God.

(6.) Faith in the divine mercy and goodness.

Now, these are the genuine features of evangelical humiliation. As in the text, God will behold these, "When the Lord saw," &c. He sees all things; but delights to behold the penitence of the contrite, &c. Hence, it is written, "To that man will I look," &c.

I notice,

III. *That God will not destroy those* who *humble themselves penitentially before him.*

Now this may be fairly deduced,

1. *From the nature of God.*

He desires not to destroy. Judgment is his strange work. Vengeance creeps, while mercy flies. He never destroys, until his forbearance has been exhausted, &c. Now, when the evil ceases, and the sinner is contrite—then God's nature must dispose him to pity and forgiveness.

2. *From the engagements of God.*

He said to Cain—"If thou doest well," &c.

To the Israelites over and over again— "Behold, I set before you this day, a blessing and curse," &c. "Let the wicked man forsake his way," &c. "When the wicked turneth from his wickedness," &c. "Whoso cometh to me," &c.

3. *From the examples left on record.*

How often, when the Jews repented, did he turn aside his anger, &c.

When Manassah repented, &c.

So also in the case of Nebuchadnezzar.

So also in the case of Nineveh. See Jonah iii. 5, 6, &c.

We see the same disposition of God portrayed in the parable of the Prodigal Son, and the Publican.

It has been exemplified in the history of numbers present.

Now from this subject, we learn,—

1. *The gracious character of God.*

A God of goodness, mercy, and compassion. Full of pity, clemency, and long-suffering.

Surely this should enkindle in us emotions of love to him. He claims these. He desires these. Contemplate this God as the object of our unbelief and ingratitude, &c., and how heinous is sin, and how depraved the heart of man!

2. *We learn that the destruction of the incorrigible is certain.*

Either the impenitent sinner must be destroyed, or God's law dishonored, and his truth falsified. These are impossible. His eternal honor and glory demand the destruction of the impenitent. How awful the word *destroy!* Not extinguish being—but destroy the hopes and happiness of the soul —and inflict the vengeance of eternal fire.

3. *In Christ, and through his sacrifice, every penitential sinner shall be saved.*

He is the refuge,—The ark,—The way to God.

Put your suit in his hands. Your souls on his merits. Your sins on his head; and by confession, &c., obtain everlasting life.

CLXXXVII.—THE EVIL OF REHOBOAM'S CHARACTER.

"And he did evil, because he prepared not his heart to seek the Lord."—2 *Chron.* xii. 14.

Our text refers to king Rehoboam. On his accession to the throne, he gave evidence of a desire to walk in the steps of David and Solomon: chap. xi. 16, 17. But after this, he forsook the law of the Lord; chap. xii. 1.

Our text accounts for his wickedness, by stating the main ingredients in his apostasy from God. "He did evil, because he prepared not his heart," &c.

Let us inquire,—

What it is to seek the Lord. What preparation of heart is necessary;—and, The evil of neglecting to do so.

I. *What it is to seek the Lord.*

1. *It signifies to seek reconciliation with him.*

Naturally men are not only morally distant, but opposed—against God. Hence, they are described as rebels, enemies—haters of God, &c. The carnal mind is enmity, &c. One corrupt element of dislike and opposition.

Now, to seek the Lord, is to cease opposition. To give up this strife. To sue for mercy. To yield to his love; and become one with him in Christ, our divine and appointed meeting-place, &c. It signifies,

2. *To live in the habit of earnest prayer.*

The Lord says, "Seek ye my face," &c. Hence, it thus is synonymous with waiting on the Lord, or inquiring of God, &c. Hence, David said, "Early will I seek thee." We read of a generation who seek the Lord. Hence, also the direction—"Seek, and ye shall find." It is,

3. *To seek to please and glorify God in all things.*

Now, this is the great end of religion. To seek his pleasure and favor in all we do. "Whether we live," &c. "To labor, whether present or absent, to be accepted," &c. To glorify God in our bodies and souls. Enoch had this testimony before his translation, &c.

Now, we must first be reconciled,—then live in habitual prayer—and *thus* we shall be led to seek his glory in all things.

II. *What preparation of heart is necessary in seeking the Lord?*

Now, here we must guard against mistake. Not self-effected reformation. Not self-produced purification, &c.

We obtain these from God, in and by his grace. But, in seeking the Lord,

1. *The heart must be fully concerned.*

All seeking will not do. Religion must begin with the heart. It is the renewal of the heart, &c. It is heart, not lip work. A broken and a contrite heart. When we seek him with the whole heart, we find him. Mere wishes, or feeble desires, or a regard to services, will not be sufficient.

2. *The heart must be brought under discipline, or prepared,*

(1.) By solemn consideration. The heart is naturally inconsiderate.

(2.) By self-humiliation. The heart is naturally proud and lifted up. It must be abased—humbled in the dust, &c.

(3.) By self-renunciation. Heart trusts in itself, &c. Leans to itself, &c. This must be given up. Heart loathed, abhorred, &c.

(4.) By firm and decided resolution. There must be a crisis. A grand turning-point. "I will arise," &c., said the prodigal. And in respect of habitual prayer and devotedness to God—there must be,

(5.) Repeated meditation and self-examination. So as to know ourselves, and to go to God with just views of our own state. Observe,

III. *The evil of neglecting to prepare our hearts, &c.*

1. *Without this preparation we shall not find God.*

There may be external reformation, or Christian profession—but God will not be found. We may go to the means of grace, to the baptistry, to the table of the Lord—but God will not be found.

2. *Not finding God will be attended with the most serious results.*

Observe the following,—

(1.) We shall wander further from God. Every act is toward, or from him. The distance is lessening or widening every day.

(2.) Our moral condition will wax worse and worse. The mists of darkness will thicken over the understanding. Error will more firmly enslave the judgment—the will become more obstinate in evil—the passions more enlisted in the love and service of sin—the conscience more defiled—the whole man more devoted to evil; and thus more meet for destruction, &c.

(3.) Our ruin will be inevitable. On the grounds of God's holiness. On the ground of his unchangeableness. On the ground of his truth and divine glory. We must seek him, or die! Call on him, or perish!

APPLICATION.

1. *To those who have sought and found the Lord.*

What a source of joy and thankfulness. You can say, In the day of my misery and ruin I called, and he heard me, &c.

2. *To those whose hearts are not prepared.*

You ask, and have not. You seek, and find not. You wait, and step not into the pool, &c. Then learn from past failures; and make it heart-work, &c. "Strive to enter in," &c.

3. *To those who have never sought the Lord, &c.*

Can you do without him? He is your life, &c., now. But what will you do in the day of sickness, and death, and judgment? &c.

CLXXXVIII. — ANCIENT WORSHIP, AND OPEN AIR PREACHING.

"And Ezra opened the book in the sight of all the people (for he was above all the people); and when he opened it, all the people stood up: And Ezra blessed the Lord, the great God. And all the people answered, Amen, Amen, with lifting up their hands: and they bowed their heads, and worshipped the Lord with their faces to the ground. Also Jeshua, and Bani, and Sherebiah, Jamin, Akkub, Shabbethai, Hodijah, Maaseiah, Kelita, Azariah, Jozabad, Hanan, Pelaiah, and the Levites, caused the people to understand the law: and the people stood in their place. So they read in the book in the law of God distinctly, and gave the sense, and caused them to understand the reading."—*Neh.* viii. 5–8.

OUR subject is the narrative of the earliest instance of preaching with which we are acquainted.

The subject is connected with Ezra's collecting the people together to hear the Word of the Lord.

This congregation was in the open air; ver. 1. The congregation was both men and women, &c.; ver. 2. All that could understand, &c. The service was a protract-

ed one,—from morning till mid-day, &c.; verse 3.

Ezra was exalted above the people, in a pulpit of wood, &c. Literally, "a tower of wood." It was a very large one, it held fourteen persons. Then our text proceeds to describe the order of worship which followed; in which, observe,

The Book. The Worshippers; and the Sermon.

I. *The book.*

It was the book of the law. As such, it was,

1. *A divine book.*

Composed by Jehovah. Written by his command. Exhibiting his will. Revealing his claims, &c.

2. *An ancient book.*

The first book the world ever had.

3. *A wonderful book.*

God for its Author,—Truth its matter,—Salvation its object and end.

4. *An invaluable book.*

Book of books! Oracles of saving truth. The only chart of life—the only guide to heaven.

Yet the book referred to in the text was small and imperfect. We have it complete. The Psalms—the Prophets—the Gospels—the Epistles, &c.

Yet their book was scarce, many had never seen it before. Belonged to the house of God. So the Bible used to be chained in our churches. Now, how plentiful! and, therefore, cheap. All may have it. How we should prize, and love the Word of God, &c.

This book was opened and read to the people. The reading of the Scriptures forms one important part of Divine service. Observe,

II. *The worship.*

Here was,

1. *Adoring praise.*

Ezra "Blessed the Lord," &c.; ver. 6. Exalted his name. Adored his majesty. Praised his goodness. How often this is urged,—"To enter his gates with praise," &c.

Here was,

2. *Humble invocation.*

"Lifting up their hands," &c. Expressive of dependence on God. Expecting, and silently seeking his blessing. Observe, too, the great prostration and humility: "Bowed their heads," &c.

We cannot be too lowly, or too self-abased,

before God. Dust and ashes, &c. There was,

3. *Sincerity and harmony of spirit.*

"And all the people answered, Amen." They understood, they felt, they agreed with the service; they said, "So be it;" and they repeated it,—Amen and amen.

There should be fervor and sincerity in our worship. All should enter into the spirit of it, and give the believing amen.

Notice,

III. *The sermon.*

It was not textual. Not one of mere propositions.—Not an essay.—Not an oration; but, an exposition.

1. *They read in the book of the law, distinctly.*

With solemn precision. With due regard to the sense. To the close of the paragraph. It was "distinctly" read. With clear voice;—well articulated;—and with correct pronunciation.

2. *They gave the sense.*

Explained what it signified. Made its meaning obvious. Did not mystify; nor lose the word in a heap of learned terms; but made the Word to shine forth. Held it before the people, till they saw its meaning.

3. *They caused them to understand it.*

Not the learned merely,—not the quick, &c.; but, all the people. The unlearned and the dull.

No end answered without this. The word must be understood, if it is to benefit. Paul, Luther, Manton, Wesley, Whitefield, all aimed at this.

Plain words—varied forms of illustration —occasional repetitions—earnest mode of address, to secure attention, &c. All needful; that the people should be made to understand.

Such is the account of this memorable sermon! &c.

Let me add a few miscellaneous observations on the things necessary to your profiting by the public worship of God.

1. Be in your places in time, so as to be composed.

2. Seek preparation of heart from the Lord.

3. Have a copy of the Scriptures to refer to; and read with the minister.

4. Labor to understand.

5. Return home to pray and meditate.

6. Forget not the end of the whole—the salvation of your souls.

CLXXXIX.—THE KING'S QUESTION TO ESTHER, IMPROVED.

"And the king said unto Esther, at the banquet of wine, What is thy petition? and it shall be granted thee: and what is thy request? even to the half of the kingdom it shall be performed."—*Esther* v. 6.

THE Book of Esther contains a most vivid and instructive exhibition of the providence of God, in the deliverance of the Jews from impending ruin.

The wicked Haman seeks the destruction of God's people. Obtains a decree for its execution; and there seems no way of escape for them, from it. God, however, by a series of wonderful events, works for their rescue.

Esther, a beautiful Jewess, is chosen queen of the Persian monarch. Through her influence, her countrymen are finally delivered; and their ferocious persecutor perishes on the gibbet.

It was death, by the law, for any one to venture into the king's presence, without the royal invitation: chap. iv. 11. Mordecai urged on Esther the solemn duty she had to discharge: verses 13, 14. Esther then resolves to risk her life in this service: 15, 16, &c. God directed her steps, &c., chap. v. 1. The sceptre is stretched out.—She found favor. Obtained the gracious and munificent promise of the king—as given in the text. The sequel you will find in the concluding chapters of this book.

Let us, however, now turn aside from the Persian king, and contemplate,

I. *The Divine Majesty.*

Think of his,

1. *Regal glory.*

King of kings! Prince of the kings of the earth! His dominion universal—supreme—everlasting. "He ruleth over all." "Doeth according to his mind," &c.

2. *Think of his greatness and glory.*

Not surrounded by the tinsel of worldly magnificence; but dwelling in high, eternal, cloudless light. "Inhabiting eternity!" Seraphim and Cherubim his guard and attendants. No being clad with flesh, &c., could see his face, and live.

3. *Think of his spotless purity.*

Just, and holy, and true! Pure. Heavens, as it were, unclean in his sight.

4. *Think of the throne on which he is seated.*

Not on the throne of dominion merely— but the throne of grace: Rev. iv. 2, 3.

From Esther, we will now turn,

II. *To the anxious sinner.*

(1.) Conscious of his guilt.

(2.) Exposed to death.

(3.) Trembling for his safety. Yet, without mercy from the Divine throne, there is no escape. For the decree is gone forth—the soul that sinneth shall die—condemned already.

What shall he do?

1. *Humble himself before God.*

Chapter iv. 16.

2. *Resolve to venture on the King's clemency.*

" If I perish, I perish." Can only do so, if I am rejected.

3. *Be found in the way of access to him.*

Chap. v. 1, &c. In the closet. House of God. Reading the word.

We now turn from the reception of Esther,

III. *To the acceptance of the humble believer.*

1. *God looks with mercy on the contrite.*

" The king saw Esther," &c. " To that man," &c.

2. *The sceptre of mercy is extended.*

Verse 2. God's free, reconciled love in the gospel. He invites, beseeches sinners to come to him.

3. *Saving faith is exercised.*

" So Esther drew near," &c.: verse 3. " Let us draw near," &c. " Come boldly," &c.

4. *Munificent promises are given.*

See ver. 3, &c., in relation to Esther. John xiv. 13, 14 ; xv. 7–16 ; xvi. 23, &c. Thus, to believing prayer, the key of earth and heaven is given. " All things are possible," &c. " All are yours," &c.

Learn,—

1. How God is glorified by the exhibition of his grace.

2. How precious is Christ, as our way to the Father.

3. How effectual are faith and earnest prayer.

4. How rich and happy, and secure, are God's people.

HISTORY OF JOB.

CXC.—HIS MORAL EXCELLENCES AND PROSPERITY.

[NO. I.]

" There was a man, in the land of Uz, whose name was Job; and that man was perfect and upright, and one that feared God and eschewed evil," &c.—*Job* i. 1–3.

FEW parts of the word of God have exercised the controversial powers of theologians more than the Book of Job.

It has been disputed whether we are to consider it a real narrative, or a poetical allegory.

Then, the writer of the bool has also been elaborately discussed, as well as the country and age in which Job lived.

It would not be profitable to give even a summary of these controversies ; and to do this in a condensed form, would occupy several discourses. We purpose, therefore, rather to give what we believe to be the truth as to the illustrious person under consideration.

Observe, then,

I. *The person introduced to us in the text.*

That the text is a real narrative, is manifest from the other scriptural references to him. In Ezek. xiv. 14. So also James v. 11. The very phraseology of the text, and the minuteness of the detail, seem to settle this beyond successful disputation.

The name itself is significant, as it means " sorrowful."

1. *The place of his residence was the land of Uz.*

The learned Gesenius supposes that the Hebrew word signifies a light sandy soil, and that it lay in the northern part of Arabia-deserta, a place between Palestine and the Euphrates. Dr. Goode supposes it was in Arabia Petrea, on the southwestern coast of the Dead Sea. The belief of the Arabians coincides with that of Gesenius.

2. *The time when Job flourished.*

Here, again, we meet with a great diversity of opinion.

It seems clear that he lived before the commencement of the Mosaic dispensation, as there is no reference in the whole book to any of the rites of that economy. It seems equally probable that he lived before the children of Israel went to sojourn in Egypt. Whether he was contemporary with Terah, the father of Abraham, or lived between the ages of Abraham and Jacob, it is difficult to determine. At any rate, we may presume that he existed about 1800 years before Christ, or about 600 years after the deluge.

The question may arise as to the author of the book.

Bishop Lowth, Magee, and Professor Lee believe he wrote it himself. Lightfoot and others ascribe it to Elihu. Kenicott, Michaelis, and Goode, ascribe it to Moses; Luther, Grotius, and others, to Solomon. Bishop Warburton attributes it to Ezra.

From the fact that Job lived 140 years after his trials—and from the sacred learning and talents he possessed, it is most probable that he was inspired to record the incidents of his life, for the benefit of succeeding generations.

It is not improbable, as Moses spent forty years in various parts of Arabia, that he then met with it, and that it was received by him and the Israelites, as the first written of the Oracles of God.

Do not forget, then, that we have reason to believe that this is the most ancient book in the world, being more than 3,500 years old.

We now proceed to notice,

II. *His worldly riches and prosperity.*

Now his substance did not include either land or houses; as the head of Arabic tribes only claimed the right of pasturage, and a temporary dwelling, and moved from place to place. His wealth therefore consisted of cattle, of which a summary is given; ver. 3. It has been supposed that, at a moderate estimate, Job was worth from thirty to forty thousand pounds sterling; an immense sum for that early age of the world.

In earthly magnificence and riches, he was the greatest of all the men of the East.

Job's wealth was evidently given him from the Lord, and did not elate him with arrogance and pride. And observe, he had a family to be co-sharers, &c.; ver. 2. Notice,

III. *His moral and religious worth.*

As rich in virtues and graces, as in the abundance of his earthly possessions.

I. *He feared God.*

Thus exhibiting true wisdom, and the main element of godliness. He had right conceptions of the divine majesty, glory, works, and perfection. He knew his holiness, and therefore he stood in awe—manifested reverence, and sacred veneration. Had

abasing views of himself, and knew the disparity between himself and God, and therefore cherished a holy vigilance and watchfulness, as being ever in the divine presence.

2. *He was perfect and upright.*

Now the term perfect is not to be understood in its most absolute sense. For thus only is it to be ascribed to God,—nor yet as involving entire innocence, for thus it applies to sinless angels and our first parents, when they came from the hands of their Creator. But the term signifies,

Sincere,—without guile or hypocrisy—or complete in all its parts.

A child is a perfect human being, though not mature. So Job was true, and really godly, and had the various graces which are necessary to acceptable piety. But he was also *upright.* He had one aim and purpose, and was guided by undeviating integrity of heart and life.

3. *He eschewed evil.*

Departed from it. Fled from it. Avoided it. Cultivated personal holiness of life. It is evident he knew the evil of sin. Hated and abhorred it—and practically turned from it.

Now, these were the principles and practice of God's servant Job. We see these all borne out in the conduct of his life.

As a father, he was intensely concerned for the piety and welfare of his family; ver. 4.

As a magistrate or judge, he was distinguished for stern and impartial integrity. Chap. xxiv. 7, 10, and 17.

As a philanthropist or benevolent man; chap. xxix. 11.

As an humble man, he did not walk with vanity.

As free from a profane, envious, and uncharitable spirit; chap. xxxi. 29, 30.

Such was the character of Job.

APPLICATION.

1. *What a portrait of moral excellence and beauty.*

Let us gaze upon it, and admire it, and pray for grace to resemble it. "Be followers of them," &c.

2. *We see the compatibility of riches with piety.*

It is possible, but rare. Grace can do it; but yet even with grace, it is difficult.

Job did not trust in his riches. He employed them for the good of the poor, and to the glory of God. It is not well to desire riches. Having food and raiment, &c. Nature requires little, grace less, and sin is satisfied with nothing.

3. *Job's piety was connected with faith in the promised Messiah.*

Hence, he said, "I know that my Redeemer liveth," &c. This was the root of all his moral excellency; and thus only can we be acceptable to God.

CXCI.—FAMILY FESTIVITIES.

[NO. II.]

"And his sons went and feasted in their houses, every one his day; and sent and called for their three sisters to eat and to drink with them," &c.— *Job* i. 4, 5.

WE have contemplated Job in his earthly dignity, and in his moral excellence. We have seen the integrity and piety of his soul towards God, and his equity and benevolence towards his fellow-men.

Our text brings him before us in his domestic relationship, and shows us how he acted as the head of his family. And here we behold the same exhibition of godly excellences.

That must indeed be a singular religion which does not sanctify the paternal character, and which does not exert its holy influence on the social circle.

Observe,

I. *The festivities described.*

II. *The line of conduct which Job adopted.*

I. *The festivities described.*

It is evident that his sons were now arrived at maturity, and had their separate establishments, or dwellings. The feasts described were most probably their birth-day banquets. "Every one his day." And on these natal occasions the whole circle of the brethren and sisters were collected to rejoice.

Now, we may remark here, that all feasts are not in themselves sinful. We are often referred to such in Scripture, without any condemnation.

The blessings of the gospel are likened to a feast, &c.

We are authorized, in the day of prosperity, to rejoice.

It is evident that these feasts were distinguished by fraternal kindness and affection. "How good and pleasant a thing it is," &c. How such should cherish the spirit of love and gentleness, &c.

How often envy, and bickerings, and strife are found in the same family. Jacob's family—David's family, &c.

Yet it is evident, that even in these feasts there was considerable moral peril. Job acknowledges this, was keenly alive to it. Solomon has said, "It is better to go to the house of mourning," &c.

Joy often terminates in levity. Mirthfulness in folly. And feasting in dissipation.

Feasting is not favorable to watchfulness, or to prayer; and is opposed to the spirit of self-denial.

Observe,

II. *The line of conduct which Job adopted.*

Notice,

1. *He evinced a lively interest in their spiritual welfare.*

Some only care for the health of the bodies of their children—for their worldly advantage. He recognized them as immortal responsible beings. He was concerned for their souls. Can a godly parent feel otherwise? Dear friends, do you feel thus?

2. *He offered up sacrifices on their behalf.*

And he did so for their sanctification.

Now in these sacrifices, guilt was acknowledged—punishment deprecated—and faith in God's mercy exercised. These sacrifices had respect doubtless to the Lamb of God, who was promised to take away the sin of the world.

Now in these sacrifices, observe,

(1.) The time. "Early." Religion and the soul should be first.

(2.) Their number. A sacrifice for each of his sons. Each required one. He loved and cared for the salvation of each and all.

(3.) The design. He feared they might have sinned and cursed God, or have fallen into profanity of speech; and that they might have forgotten God in their mirth. Observe here the inefficiency of animal sacrifices; for,

(4.) He did this continually. Thus these sacrifices were merely typical, and required often to be presented. See Heb. x. 1–14.

Now what are the great practical uses of this part of Job's history?

1. *We have a beautiful exhibition of relative piety.*

Job like Joshua resolved, &c. His family was a congregation for God. He had his altar—his sacrifices—he acted as head and priest. Brethren, do you resemble the pious patriarch in these things?

2. *We have an interesting view of constancy in religion.*

Doubtless Job began early; but now his sons were mature,—yet the bond subsisted. He was still their father. His love, and care, and exertions did not cease. His offerings —prayers—influence, &c. What a fine picture! Job—his sons—the altar—the victims —the fire is laid—the offering presented— the smoke ascends—the fire falls—and then they retire impressed, and instructed, and comforted, to their respective avocations. And this scene is repeated again and again. Job wearies not in God's service, or in pious concern for his children. How different to this is the feeble, flickering, irregular services of the many, who profess to serve God.

One word to induce imitation of it, on all heads of families present :—

Look at it as a duty.

Look at it as a privilege. To be the instrument of good to the souls of your children.

Look at the enjoyment it must yield, through life—on the death-bed—at the day of judgment.

Finally,—

We invite the guilty to the great sacrifice of the Lord Jesus, offered for sin. He is the one and only offering. He is the sacrifice for all. Come to him by faith and penitential supplication; and consecrate yourselves to him.

CXCII.—THE WONDERFUL CONVOCATION.

[NO. III.]

"Now there was a day when the sons of God came to present themselves before the Lord, and Satan came also among them. And the Lord said unto Satan, Whence comest thou? Then Satan answered the Lord, and said, From going to and fro in the earth, and from walking up and down in it," &c.—*Job* i. 6–12.

WHAT a wonderful book is the Bible! How profound its mysteries! How vast its discoveries! How varied its themes! How instructive its narratives! How unsurpassingly sublime many of its descriptions and scenes!

Men of the mightiest genius have been overwhelmed with their own insufficiency to do full justice to the Scriptures.

Few parts are more difficult and perplexing, than the portion selected for our present consideration.

It is a drama in miniature; and the personages are the most distinguished and magnificent that can engage our attention.

First of all is Jehovah, in solemn convocation. He sits on the throne of his holiness. He exercises universal dominion. Angels are his ministering attendants. There, are the *Sons of God*—evidently the angels of his presence, come in their united ranks to do him homage. It is a day of especial audience. A royal court day, when the shining orders of cherubim and seraphim have more immediate communion with their divine Lord.

It is probable, too, that they come to notify their obedience to the divine behests, and to hear the will of God, that they might again fly to do his commands.

And now the mystery increases. *Satan*, the accuser, the fallen angel, the leader of the apostate legions—he also appears. The Lord may require the presence of this fallen spirit, as a proof of his subordination to his own will and authority.

God then addresses him; ver. 7. And he replies, in perfect keeping with his own character,—"Doth Job serve God for naught?" Here he insinuates that Job is a mere hireling, &c. Thus he becomes the accuser of Job! See Zech. iii. 1, 2. Rev. xii. 7–10.

Job's condition is described by Satan as one of invulnerable security; ver. 10, &c.

Then he vents forth the utmost malice and envy of his fallen spirit; ver. 11. He then adds, "But, put forth thine hand," &c.

The Lord accepts the challenge—gives a royal license to the devil, to bring Job into circumstances of adversity; ver. 12.

Thus the drama terminates. The sons of God wing their way to do God's command. Satan retires to exert his hellish influence on the circumstances and family of Job.

Let us, then, ground certain important and instructive propositions, on the subject thus introduced to you.

I. *God is at the head of all authority, dominion, and power.*

All creatures both in heaven and earth are subject to him. "He doeth as he will," &c. All laws are his. All government, &c., emanates from him. Of him it is said— "By whom are all things, and for whom are all things." The drop of water, and the grain of sand, and the lightning, and the thunder; all do his will. All creatures, from the insect to the leviathan. Man is is his creature, &c. All the angels of heaven are subject to him.

How great and .glorious is Jehovah of hosts ! A God greatly to be feared, and had in reverence by all his saints.

II. *Holy angels are especial servants of Jehovah.*

They are called sons. They are holy, wise, and blessed intelligences. Doubtless, they are employed according to his perfect and wise authority. "Bless ye the Lord, all ye his angels, &c., that do his will, hearkening to the voice of his word," &c.

The Scriptures reveal many of their mighty and marvellous doings, both as messengers of terror and of mercy. To the saints, they are friends, guards, and ministering spirits. "The angels of the Lord," &c. "Are they not all ministering spirits," &c.

III. *Satan is the restless, subtle, and malevolent enemy of the saints.*

Verse 7.

How this agrees with that New Testament declaration—"Your adversary the the devil goeth about," &c.

He sees the goodness and piety of the saints, and hates it.

He beholds their felicity, and labors to destroy it.

He delights in diffusing sorrow, and sin, and woe in the earth. Envy, pride, and cruelty, are his essential attributes. But, mark ; he is a creature, and his power bounded by God's supreme authority.

IV. *God's permissive providence allows Satan to distress and afflict the saints.*

Many of the chastisements of the saints are directly from God. He may do it immediately and directly. At other times he permits it. So in this instance. God allows Satan to attack, and tempt, and invade the peaceful province of Job. God never does moral evil. He never tempts to it. He has explicitly averred this. "He is the Father of lights," &c. Author of good, and not evil. Jas. i. 13.

But he may permit evil to arise,—he may allow Satan to tempt, &c.; but still, God is at the helm of affairs, and his love and his care are never withdrawn from his saints.

V. *Satan enunciated a great and important truth in reference to God's people.*

"Doth Job fear God for naught;" vers. 9, 10.

His insinuation was envious and false— but the declaration is true.

1. *The service of God is well remunerated.*

Job did not serve God for naught, nor any other saint. God is a good master. He rewards all his servants. "Godliness with contentment," &c. "Godliness is profitable," &c. "Seek ye first," &c.

God's service has a reward *in* it. "In keeping his commands, there is great reward." There is also freedom, and peace, and joy.

Then there is also a reward *with* it. Every pious act exalts and improves the soul, and conforms it to the image of God.

Besides, there is also a reward following it. "Be thou faithful," &c.

2. *The persons, families, and possessions of the pious are under God's special protection.*

"Hast thou not made an hedge," &c., ver. 10 ; or fence, or palisading, &c. Yes, the providence of God surrounds and environs all his saints. They are in his hands. The very hairs of their head are numbered. "All things work together," &c. "Who is he that shall harm," &c. "If God be for us," &c.

3. *God's blessing is the joyful portion of all his people.*

"Thou hast blessed," &c., ver. 10. This just agrees with the declaration of Balaam. "The Lord hath blessed," &c. So David said, "Thy blessing is on thy people."

This is often seen in reference to their temporal concerns. Always in their spiritual things.

APPLICATION.

1. *How signally great and blessed are the people of God.*

Objects of God's complacent regard. His constant love, and his unfailing care. "Happy art thou, O Israel," &c.

2. *To dwell in the families of the pious is no small privilege.*

The children of such, and the servants of such, are favored beyond others. The hedge surrounds them. As a privilege it may be abused and perverted. Oh, rightly value it, &c.

3. *It must be well with those who serve God.*

Enemies they may have ; and trials and sorrows may befall them ; but still it is written : "Say ye unto the righteous, it shall be well with him." Seek this character, and maintain it.

CXCIII.—JOB'S CALAMITIES.

[NO. IV.]

"And the Lord said unto Satan, Behold, all that he hath is in thy power; only upon himself put not forth thine hand. So Satan went forth from the presence of the Lord. And there was a day when his sons and his daughters were eating and drinking wine in their eldest brother's house," &c.—*Job* i. 12–22.

How wise and good are those divine arrangements, by which our future ills and sorrows are concealed from us. Sufficient for the day, is the evil thereof. Job was, doubtless, ignorant of the counsel that had been held concerning him. In the integrity of his heart, he was walking before God. In the enjoyment of prosperity, he was rejoicing in the Lord. He adored and extolled the providence that supplied all his need, &c. He was imagining in his heart that he should die in his nest, and that the mountain of his prosperity would not be moved.

But the permission has been given to the arch and vile accuser, and a series of the most distressing calamities are now awaiting him. To these our attention must now be directed. Observe,

The afflictions to which Job was subjected;—and,

The spirit he displayed under them.

I. *The afflictions to which Job was subjected.*

Now, his afflictions comprised,

1. *The loss of his property.*

The Sabeans invaded his possessions, and stole his oxen; verses 14, 15. Then his sheep are destroyed by fire, &c. Verse 16. Most probably by lightning.

Then the Chaldeans, in their warlike bands, rush forth and seize his camels.

Thus the inventory of his prosperity as given, ver. 3, is now only a record of his adversity.

It seems that all his worldly possessions thus perished before him. Small losses affect us—great ones very deeply—but the wreck of all, is truly affecting.

2. *The destruction of servants.*

Observe, the Sabeans slay those who were laboring with the oxen; verse 15.

The lightning destroyed those tending the sheep.

The Chaldeans slew all those who were with the camels.

Now this was the second stroke, and would deeply afflict the spirit of Job. A merciful man regardeth the life of his beast; how much more the lives of his fellow-beings.

The sudden removal of one would distress him, how much more the death of nearly the whole. But the heaviest stroke has now to fall.

3. *In the sudden bereavement of his children.*

Verses 18, 19.

Here, by one stroke, his family are removed from the earth. His sons and his daughters every one; and all at once. At a time when he would have least chosen it; in the midst of their feasting. Before he had joined them, as was his wont and custom, to sanctify them by prayer and burnt-offerings, &c.

Ye bereaved parents who have sorrowed so much over one, and that one, perhaps, an infant,—look at Job's loss! The whole—when reared to man and woman's estate—the joy of his heart—the hope of his life—his dearest treasure; and all buried in one calamitous grave together.

Before we pass over Job's afflictions; observe,

(1.) How suddenly they came. No premonitions. Nothing to indicate a change in his condition, &c. No twilight; but from noon to night. No preparatory steps; but at once he is cast from the highest pinnacle of prosperity, into the lowest depth of adversity and sorrow.

(2.) How continuous! No interval of repose. No season for reflection, &c. But one messenger hastens after another. The first finishes his tale of woe, and then comes the second, and afterwards the third, and finally the fourth. How amazed and overwhelmed must the servant of God have been.

(3.) How entire was his calamity. The lovely scene, a desert. The domestic circle, a heap of ruins. His gallant vessel wrecked, so that not a vestige of it remained before his gaze.

And yet all was not lost. He still remained. His life—his health—his reason; and better than all—his hope in God. These were yet preserved.

Friends, in your losses and trials, see what is left, and let not present grief blind your eyes, as to the good you still enjoy.

Now let us ascertain,

II. *The spirit Job displayed under his afflictions.*

1. *His grief was intense.*

Behold the evidences :—He arose and rent his mantle. His outward flowing garment. He shaved his head, and fell prostrate on the ground.

The ornaments of the person and the hair were removed; and the dust of the earth became his mournful bed. See Gen. xxxvii. 34.

Now, grief under calamities is natural, proper; and has been sanctified by the tears of the Lord Jesus. Brutality or stoicism, will only attempt to dispense with it.

2. *His humility was profound.*

He sought the earth, as one of her children. He confesses his original poverty. "Naked," &c.; ver. 21. "We brought nothing into this world," &c. How dependent is man! &c. Think of this, ye lovers and hoarders of wealth! Your bargains, and houses, and lands, &c., must all be left. You will soon be as poor as the poorest. "Naked," &c. Oh, use it well, I pray you, as stewards, &c.

3. *His piety was decided.*

He fell down and "worshipped." Did not forget religious duty—did not neglect God's claims. Gave Jehovah homage in the darkest hour of his calamity. Was not sullen, nor driven to despair; but his habits of communion and prayer were still maintained.

4. *His resignation was entire.*

He acknowledges God's proprietorship over all things. All are God's—all from God. He confesses God's indubitable right to resume his own. "He gave, and he taketh," &c. And then the climax of his resigned and godly submission, he kisses the hand that has brought his sorrows, and exclaims— "Blessed be the name of the Lord." As if he had said,—"He is wise, and faithful, and good, and kind." He cannot err,—he will not do wrong,—"Blessed be the name," &c.

Job maintained his integrity; and like the pure gold, perished not in the heated furnace of trial.

Observe, then,

1. *Satan is confounded.*

Here is piety, he cannot destroy. A character, he cannot deface.

2. *Job is honored.*

He has been weighed, and is not found wanting, &c. He has been tried, and stood the ordeal. He has been winnowed, and he is found good grain. His principles were sound. His heart right. His practice sincere, and his conscience upright before God.

3. *God is glorified.*

His spirit was in Job,—his grace and power. Job's excellences were not natural, but supernatural. Not of earth, but of heaven.

Hearers, have you piety of this kind? Does it support in, and reconcile you, to trouble? If so, hold it fast, &c. If not, seek it, &c.

————◆————

CXCIV.—JOB'S PERSONAL AFFLICTIONS.

[NO. V.]

" Again there was a day when the sons of God came to present themselves before the Lord, and Satan came also among them to present himself before the Lord. And the Lord said unto Satan, From whence comest thou," &c.—*Job* ii. 1–10.

GOD'S way is often in the sea, and his footsteps in the great deep. It is not for us to dictate to him, or to say, What doest thou?

To us it appears strange that God should have permitted Satan to bring adversity on his servant Job; for he knew from the beginning, the integrity of his heart, and the perfection of his character. How applicable the words of the Saviour, "What I do, thou knowest not now," &c.

We have seen, however, how Job retained his uprightness in the furnace of trial, and how he came forth as gold. Surely, now Satan would be confused; and wickedness, abashed, would hide its head! Instead of this, we see the assault renewed.

Observe, another day of solemn convocation is held; v. 1. Satan again appears, and he confesses that he is still wandering abroad, &c.; ver. 2. Then God appeals again as to the holiness of Job, and especially to his stability under the late trial of his faith. Satan does not reiterate his former accusation, but dwells on the value of life; and affirms, for that, men will part with all, &c.; ver. 4.

Various interpretations have been given of this passage. The obvious sense is—that life is, of all things, the most precious; and to secure that, all else will be sacrificed,—therefore, if God put his life in jeopardy, he will abandon his profession of godliness; ver. 5. Then follows the mysterious permission; ver. 6.

Observe,

The nature of Job's personal affliction; and,

The spirit and conduct he exhibited under it.

I. *The nature of Job's personal affliction.*

Now, observe, by what this affliction was preceded,—the wreck of property—the loss of servants—and the sudden bereavement of his children.

Into the depths of this sorrow he had been suddenly plunged, and in those depths he still remained.

His second trial was the suffering of his own person.

1. *Observe the nature of the disease.*

Verse 7.

Critics say, that the boil or ulcer is in the singular in the original: not many, but one wide extended leprous spot. Head enlarged, —countenance hideous and ghastly,—the limbs swelled—the body disfigured. The whole system burning as with fire—the breath like the smoke of a furnace—and foul and disgusting withal. His seat the ground, in the midst of the ashes he had strewn upon his head.

His presence is dreaded, from the contagious character of his affliction. No hand can help him. He is in horror, and an amazement to himself.

He takes a potsherd, a piece of broken earthenware, and scrapes himself withal; ver. 8. Pain, loathsomeness, and of course expected dissolution, and that under circumstances of the most extraordinary kind.

Oh, behold this embodiment of suffering! This object of satanic hate—this child of sorrow and affliction. Think of the distress of inferior afflictions, when mitigated by remaining mercies—when ameliorated by the kindness of friends—when not universal, &c.

2. *The domestic aggravation of his affliction.*

"Then said his wife," &c. Ver. 9.

Various have been the criticisms on this speech. The Chaldee version gives the name of his wife. And Dinah his wife, &c. And some suppose that this was Dinah, the daughter of Jacob. The seventy, or the translators of the Septuagint, put into her mouth a long address. (See Barnes's Notes on Job.)

Others have rendered her speech the very opposite of our translation. "Bless God," &c. This is totally opposed to the drift of

Job's reply, &c. Dr. Goode renders it— "And yet dost thou hold fast thine integrity, blessing God and dying." Noyes renders it—" Renounce God and die." Her language is calculated to vex his righteous soul, and also to be a temptation to him.

Here, as in the first transgression, Satan assaults Job through his wife. How anxious we should be, that we may not be a source of temptation to one another.

Observe, then,

II. *The spirit and conduct which Job exhibited.*

1. *He rejects the advice, and reproves the impiety of his wife.*

"Thou speakest as one of the foolish," &c.; ver. 10.

Sin and folly are ever joined in the Scriptures. The word foolish means in the text impious, wicked—a most godless and presumptuous address. How often this spirit is seen in the afflictions of the wicked,—Restless, fretted, angry, wrathful, blasphemous, &c. Sometimes the wicked throw off all restraint, and give vent to oaths and imprecations even in their dying moments.

2. *He vindicates the supremacy and sovereignty of God.*

Verse 10.

God is here recognized as the source of all good. "Shall we receive good," &c. This is a pious sentiment. Nature and sin never use this kind of language. Carnal men speak of the weather and crops,—their trade and fortune,—their diligence and tact. God is not in all their thoughts.

God is here recognized also as the source of evil. "Shall we not receive evil?" Observe, he does not mean moral evil, but penal: the evil of adversity, suffering and affliction, &c. Several passages beautifully express this. Isa. xlv. 7: Amos iii. 6: Jer. xxxv. 17.

Now, it is necessary to keep this in mind. It is one essential element of submission, &c. Observe,

3. *The pious triumph of Job, in his affliction.*

He did not curse God, as Satan said he would do. He kept himself from that transgression. He honored God in the emotions of his heart, and in the utterances of his lip. He submitted to God. He hearkened to the rod. He kissed the hand, &c. Happy, had he continued to hold fast this spirit of resignation, &c.

Hereafter, we shall have to contemplate

his weakness, and to discover that even Job was only perfect in his generation.

Learn,—

1. *The various and distressing afflictions to which we are exposed.*

Man is vulnerable at every pore! What diseases of body! What afflictions of mind! What domestic troubles! What fearful temptations! What moral conflicts!

2. *The sufficiency of divine grace, under the heaviest calamities.*

"Fear not, worm Jacob," &c. "I will uphold," &c. "My grace is sufficient," &c. "When thou passest through the waters," &c. "In six troubles," &c.

3. *The importance of submission and patience.*

Jas. v. 7 to 11.

4. *The afflictions of the righteous are not signs of God's anger, and are limited to the present life.*

Hence the address of father Abraham to Dives—"Son, remember," &c. "The sufferings of the present time," &c. "Though weeping endure," &c.

Sinner, I ask thee, whose lot is best—that of the prosperous wicked, or the afflicted righteous?

CXCV.—JOB AND HIS THREE FRIENDS.

[NO. VI.]

" Now when Job's three friends heard of all this evil that was come upon him, they came every one from his own place; Eliphaz the Temanite, and Bildad the Shuhite, and Zophar the Naamathite: for they had made an appointment together to come to mourn with him and to comfort him," &c.—*Job* ii. 11–13.

WHO can describe the value of true friendship? It is the union of hearts, in the bonds of goodness and love. It is essential to it, that there should be kindredness of spirit, and harmony of feeling.

The best friendships are based upon moral principle, and are sanctified by mutual and constant prayer. Friendship of this elevated and excellent kind, is precious at all times. It is so in health and in prosperity. Our joys are sweeter and more rapturous, when others rejoice with us. But friendship, like the stars of heaven, is most radiant in the dark night of sorrow, and adversity, and affliction.

Exalted friendship is a sacred thing, and is as rare as it is sacred.

There are many who are *called* friends, who are enemies in disguise—wolves in sheep's clothing. There are many pretended friends, but they only flutter around you, when the candle of your prosperity shines brightly. They love the atmosphere of your dwellings, &c., so long as it is summer, and the air is warm; but they retire into their secrecies in the time of cold and winter.

There are many real, but unsafe friends. Persons, who for want of discretion, imperil your comfort and reputation. Many a man has been ruined by injudicious friends.

Some real friends are deficient in tenderness of feeling, and gentleness of spirit: Hence, they cannot minister to the afflicted soul and the wounded heart. Job's friends seem to have been of the last description.

Let us however, look,—

At the excellent characteristics by which they were distinguished.

At their signal defects; and,

The unhappy influence which they exerted on Job.

I. *At the excellent characteristics by which they were distinguished.*

Job's three friends were Eliphaz, who is conjectured to have been the son of Teman, grandson of Esau. Bildad the Shuhite, probably the descendant of one of Abraham's sons by Keturah; and Zophar the Naamathite, a supposed descendant from some branch of Abraham's family.

They were distinguished, evidently,

1. *By great intelligence and religious knowledge.*

Their speeches were full of wisdom, and were expressed in the most sublime strains. They evinced a great knowledge of God, and his government, and his works. They had lofty views of holiness, and moral rectitude of action. Even in this late era of the world's history, it would be difficult to supply many instances of such profound and varied knowledge, as these men displayed.

Let us take an extract from each of their addresses,—

See Eliphaz's description of the vision with which God had favored him; chap. iv. 12.

Bildad's address is peculiarly sublime; chap. xxv. 1 to 6. One short passage from Zophar; chap. xi. 7.

They were characterized,

2. *By their high moral excellences.*

They were men who had the most profound veneration for God—had just views of man's depraved state and worthlessness before him—were evidently clothed with the spirit of lowliness and humility. They also, doubtless, sincerely desired to glorify God. They were characterized,

3. *By their honest and sincere regard for Job.*

They heard of his afflictions, and did not tarry away—did not forget or overlook him —came in friendly concert to visit him. They came, it is expressly said, to *mourn* with him, and also to *comfort* him. They evinced their sincerity, &c.; ver. 12, 13; that is, during portions of each day, they came and sat with him, &c. They did not rashly break in upon his silent grief, &c.; ver. 13.

Such are the excellences by which they were distinguished. Let us, then,

II. *Notice their signal defects.*

1. *Their minds were under the influence of evil surmisings.*

The idea flashed across their minds that there must have been some extreme cause for Job's calamity; and that cause must have been some moral defect or secret sin, which Job had concealed,—that his character, which had been so dignified and holy, was not the result of inward sincerity.

Now, no one can, perhaps, help such ideas crossing the mind, any more than they can help black clouds darkening the sky above them; but they can help cherishing them. These hard thoughts need not dwell and lodge within us.

It is a breach of the law of charity; "For it thinketh no evil." It is contrary to the divine command,—for evil surmisings are placed in the same catalogue with envy, pride, strife, &c.

2. *They were deficient in tenderness to Job's afflictive condition.*

Though they uttered many truths, yet they were not soft emollients, calculated to mitigate his sufferings; but like keen astringents, which searched and gave additional pain to his distressing wounds. Hence he was led to exclaim—"Miserable comforters are ye all." "Physicians of no value." His spirit required soothing, and his bleeding heart wanted the solace of the holy oil of kindness; but many of their remarks were keen and biting, and even in the highest degree reproachful.

3. *They were not perfectly sound in their theological deductions.*

They all reasoned as if the righteous ought to expect uninterrupted sunshine. That God's providence would preserve them from calamities. See this in chap. v. 23–27, &c.

Now these may be viewed as general truths; but there are many exceptions. Look at Abel,—look at the Israelites in Egypt,—look at David, &c.,—look at Jeremiah,—look at the list of martyrs, &c. Nay, more; suffering is a part of God's paternal discipline, and thus is a sign of love, and not of anger.

This was the great error of Job's friends; and this error in judgment led to the most unhappy effects. It injured Job and displeased God.

Such were the great defects of Job's friends.

Elihu was evidently less reprehensible than the three we have adverted to; yet he was not entirely free from the error of the others.

Observe, then,

III. *The unhappy influence which they exerted on the mind of Job.*

Their addresses,

1. *Led Job to bitter recrimination.*

He retorted their speeches upon themselves. His words and spirit towards them was evidently the reflection of their own. He lost the spirit of equanimity and quietude, so essential to his support, &c.

Their addresses,

2. *Induced Job to adopt an improper style of self-defence.*

They sank him below his real worth. They insinuated concerning his hypocrisy and secret sins. He knew the integrity of his heart, but was induced to say too much in his own defence. How perilous to speak of our own excellences.

Their speeches,

3. *Caused him to use expressions which reflected on God himself.*

Chapter vii. 11, 15, 19, &c.

There are several instances of this in the defence Job set up, which must have been offensive to the majesty of heaven.

But let us not forget that Job only thus erred occasionally—that there were many truly penitent and humble exclamations, which gave the brightest evidences of his lofty piety. See chap. ix. 1 to 4. Notice, also,

His most touching appeals for the pity of his friends, and his abiding confidence in God; chap. xix. 17–26.

Learn,—

1. *The true office of friendship, and the attributes necessary to a right discharge of it.*

"A friend loveth at all times," &c. Kindness, tenderness, and sympathy, are its essential elements.

Learn,

2. *The importance of a charitable spirit and tongue.*

Even·in reference to the graces, the Apostle said,—"The greatest of these is Charity." Better to err in excess of love, than in deficiency. Avoid a censorious conversation. Some are very guilty of it. Seem to delight in speaking of the defects of Christians. Now this is unamiable—very self-righteous and presumptuous—and very displeasing to God. Remember,

3. *There is a friend that sticketh closer than a brother.*

That friend is Jesus, &c. Oh, seek his friendship! Cultivate it—delight in it, &c.

He cannot err in judgment.

He never fails in affection; nor is deficient in sympathy. "The same yesterday," &c. Happy those who can say of him— "He is my beloved, and he is my friend."

CXCVI.—JOB'S WEARINESS OF LIFE.

[NO. VII.]

"My soul is weary of my life."—*Job* x. 1.

IT is of great importance that we should obtain a correct view of the character and spirit of Job. As to his original rectitude and sincerity God has testified most distinctly; chap. i. 8, &c.

His afflictions were of the most distressing kind; and his friends drew the most erroneous inferences from them. They concluded that he was suffering on account of his sins—no doubt, secret sins. Job knew the integrity of his heart, and therefore was goaded and distracted by their insinuations. In this state of mind, he was betrayed into many unjustifiable expressions. He reflected on the government of God; and he even wished and prayed for the extinction of his life. Thus in Job we see a good man—but yet only a man at best.

Let us consider,

I. *The various circumstances under which the sentiment of the text has been expressed.*

II. *The evil the sentiment contains.* And,

III. *The means by which the evil may be remedied.*

I. *The various circumstances under which the sentiment of the text has been expressed.*

The Scriptures furnish several striking incidents illustrative of this part of the subject.

We see it,

1. *As the result of apostasy and despair, as in king Saul.*

How fearful his case! How bright and exalted at one time his career! But he became disobedient, and apostatized from God, —then he became utterly wretched, and at length was weary of his life. See 1 Sam. xxviii. 15; and xxxi. 3. So also the case of Judas; Matt. xxvii. 3, 4.

2. *As the result of mortified pride, as in the case of Ahithophel.*

See 2 Sam. xvii. 23; also Jonah iv. 2.

How often has a similar spirit led to the like result, both in ancient and modern times. Political disgrace,—reverse of circumstances,—some public dishonor, &c.

3. *As the result of sudden fear and despondency.*

The case of Elijah. 1 Kings xix. 1–4.

Here we see the mind suddenly overcome, and sinking under the influence of fear and despondency. Sometimes we see it in,

4. *Its sanctified aspect,—as in the case of David and Paul.*

"Oh, that I had wings," &c. Anxious to enter on the heavenly rest—the port of life. So the apostle: "I have a desire to depart," &c. But this desire was held in abeyance to the divine will, and to his usefulness in the church. "Nevertheless to abide," &c.

Let us,

II. *Consider the evil which this state of mind involves.*

Of course we do not refer to the last instance, but where, as in the text, the soul exclaims—"My soul is weary," &c.

1. *It is a sin against the author of our life.*

He gave it—sustains it—it is in his hand. He knows *best* what to do with it, and will do the *best.* It is his prerogative, and not ours, &c.

2. *It is a sin against the divine bounty and goodness.*

It contains the essential element of discontent. Has not much mercy distinguished our lives? &c. How rich the blessings! how few compared the sorrows, &c. "Wherefore should a living man complain," &c.

3. *It is a sin against our own souls.*

Life is given for the most important ends, and the most momentous purposes. Never too long for these. Think of its duties, and responsibilities, and results—and then, can we be "weary?" &c.

4. *It is a sin against those around us.*

We are not to live to ourselves—others are bound up with us. Families—friends—the church of Christ—the world. Passion, temper, pique, &c., should not warp or poison our spirits. It is selfish inconsideration.

III. *The means by which the evil may be removed.*

1. *By an active attention to the duties of life.*

These are sufficiently numerous and onerous, to keep us occupied. The diligent and energetic have no time to sit and mope, and exclaim—"My soul is weary," &c. To such, time ever flies,—years appear as dreams. Life seems too short, &c. Diligence in our callings, and useful activity in our spheres, are the very best preventives to dulness and melancholy.

2. *By cherishing lowly and correct views of ourselves.*

Who are we? What our true character —deserts? Creatures, sinners, exposed to wrath and eternal misery! shall we quarrel with the good God—our merciful, long-suffering Redeemer? Should it not be as with Job, in his happier hours: "I will wait all the days," &c.

3. *An earnest and constant preparation for the life to come.*

Think of the future world. Its holiness, services, &c. How much is needful to a complete meetness. Instead of expressing the language of the text, we should often pray—"Oh, spare me, that I may recover my strength, before I go hence," &c.

Learn,—

1. *The evil of fretfulness and impatience.*

How liable we are to sin in our haste and impetuosity. In patience possess ye your souls.

2. *The great need of preserving and sanctifying grace.*

How weak and frail are the very best.

3. *The importance of living for eternity.*

CXCVII.—ELIPHAZ'S IMPORTANT INTERROGATION.

[NO. VIII.]

"Are the consolations of God small with thee?"—*Job* xv. 11.

To Job the question was one of peculiar moment; and there is no class of subjects so invariably seasonable, as those which relate to the comfort of God's people.

So truly is this life a scene of sorrow—so truly is man born to trouble, that distress and grief are ever casting their darkening shadows over the pathway of mankind.

Perhaps, if I were to ask each one in the presence of God, Are you entirely free from trouble, are you full of joy? There are few could answer in the affirmative. Some root of bitterness—some withering gourd—some crook in the lot, would be the experience of most.

Let us enter, then, on this important subject, and press on you the inquiry of the text: "Are the consolations," &c.

We observe,

That the Christian stands in need of consolation.

That in God abundant consolation is provided; and,

Account why, notwithstanding this, the consolations of God's people are sometimes small.

I. *That the Christian stands in need of consolation.*

Now this is evident, if you consider,

1. *The character of the world in which he is placed.*

It is a wilderness. Dreary desert. An enemy's country. The seat of Satan. So that Christ said, "In the world ye shall have tribulation." No going through it without. The testimony and experience of all the good, in every age, establishes this.

2. *The enemies with whom he has to contend.*

The Christian's life is a warfare. Enemies without, and fears within. Flesh and blood. The unslain foes of the heart, and principalities and powers, &c. "Your adversary the devil," &c. "Simon, Simon, Satan desireth to have thee."

3. *The afflictions and troubles of life.*

They are various, many, and often severe. Personal—domestic—in the church—in the world—losses and crosses—bereavements, &c.

4. *Inward despondency and weakness.*

"O God, my soul is cast down," &c. Often hope seems to have fled. Faith scarcely appears as a grain of mustard seed. Desires dead—mind oppressed, &c. Oh, this is a state of extreme trial: the Psalmist experienced it, when he exclaimed, "Has the Lord forgotten to be gracious? Is his mercy clean gone forever?"

Now we remark,

II. *That in God there is abundant consolation.*

He is styled the God of comfort—the God of consolation. As he is the source of light, so he is also of all peace and joy.

1. *There is consolation in God's name.*

His name as proclaimed to Moses. Ex. xxxiv. 6.

2. *There is consolation in his nature.*

God is love. Pure,—unbounded,—infinite and eternal love! Not wrath—not vengeance, &c.

3. *There is consolation in his relationship to us.*

He is our God, &c. Our Creator—preserver—Redeemer. But he is our Father, by adoption and grace. "I will be a Father," &c. He allows us to say, "Our Father," &c.

4. *There is consolation in his promises.*

"Whereby are given to us exceeding great," &c. Promises suited to all classes, ages, states, trials, &c.

5. *There is consolation in his providences.*

His government has especial reference to his own children. They are the objects of express and peculiar kindness. They are his delight—his treasure—his jewels. God is ever caring for them. All things work together for their good.

6. *There is consolation in the provisions he has made for them.*

Provisions of grace here—unsearchable riches of grace. Provisions of glory hereafter—eternal glory, &c. So that all things pertaining to present and eternal happiness are prepared for those who love him; so that "eye hath not seen, nor ear heard," &c.

Let us, then,

III. *Assign some reasons why, notwithstanding this, the consolations of God's people are sometimes small.*

It is clear that there can be no reason connected with God, neither as to his will or ability. He is ever ready, and ever able to comfort.

1. *It often arises from the imperfection of our nature.*

It is so connected with frailty and weakness. There must be a connection between moral debility and imperfect enjoyment. Entire holiness would be entire bliss. So that our imperfect state is one of the great reasons of our imperfect, or interrupted enjoyments.

It arises often,

2. *From our weak graces.*

There is consolation in God; but faith is too dim, and hope too languid to receive it. "If ye have not," &c. "Ask and receive," &c. There may be clouds and darkness, and strong faith only can pierce through them. There may be a tempest, and rough sea, &c.; so that faith and a strong confidence can only walk thereon.

3. *From neglect of the appointed means.*

God will console in the way of his appointments—in the sanctuary—in the closet—in meditation, &c.—At his table. But, alas! how often we are absent. God is true and faithful, but we are not.

4. *From depending on other sources.*

God's consolations are in himself. He may make creatures and ordinances the channels, but he is the great and only fountain. How often we rely on the instrument—on the minister—on the friend—on the ordinance, &c.; but God is not recognized or honored.

5. *From not honoring the only way of access to him.*

He demands that all must be by and through Christ. Jesus in his divine offices and work must be honored—and always, and in every thing.

6. *From neglecting his Holy Spirit.*

We need the mediation of Christ in heaven; but we equally need the Holy Spirit in our hearts. His presence must be sought and cherished. We must live, and walk, and serve God, in the spirit. Have we not often neglected, slighted, and grieved? &c.

APPLICATION.

1. Learn where true consolation is to be found. "In God."

2. Learn how it is to be obtained. By faith, and through Christ Jesus our Lord.

3. Learn to what our despondings and griefs are chiefly traceable. Our weaknesses and sins.

CXCVIII.—JOB'S FAITH, AND CONFIDENT
EXPECTATION.

[NO. IX.]

"For I know that my Redeemer liveth, and
that he shall stand at the latter day upon the
earth."—*Job* xix. 25.

THE condition of Job when he uttered the
text was one of extraordinary and unparalleled
adversity and sorrow. As the mariner, tossed on the heaving billows amid the darkness
of the night, at length hails with delight
the first streak of the morning light—so
Job, in the very depths of his afflictions, is
sustained by the hope of a blissful and triumphant deliverance.

The text is the appeal from the surmises
and insinuations of his mistaken friends, to
the inward confidence and experience of his
own soul.

The text is, confessedly, one of the most
difficult passages in the Old Testament records.

A certain explanation has been generally
given and received, which cannot well be
borne out by the text itself. Our translators have supplied several words, which are
in *italics*. Without looking at the subject,
however, critically, observe,

The object of Job's confidence.

And,

The blessings he hopefully anticipated.

I. *The object of Job's confidence.*

"The Redeemer." The term is derived
from Goel—the individual who had the right
under the law,

(1.) To redeem the inheritance : Levit.
xxv. 25, &c.

(2.) To avenge the death of his brother.
Goel is styled, the avenger of blood.

(3.) To vindicate the character, or advocate the rights of another.

Now Jesus, the Messiah, is in each of
these senses, the Redeemer.

1. We had *forfeited life* and the Divine
favor,—lost heaven. He came to restore it
to us. "I am come," &c. "This is the
record," &c.

2. We had been destroyed by the hellish
adversary. For this purpose was the Son
of God manifested, that he might destroy,
&c. Death and the grave were the allies
of Satan. He hath abolished death, &c.
Conquered the grave, &c. "I am he that
liveth," &c. He will finally bind Satan, and
confine him to the place prepared for him,
and his fallen angels.

1. *Christ is our vindicator and advocate.*
He pardons—he justifieth—he pleads our
cause. "If any man sin," &c. "He ever
liveth," &c. He will vindicate his saints
before an assembled world. Job spake of
him,

2. *As living.*
Events seemed to say, that the object of
his hope had failed. Job realized him as
living—the source of all life—the ever self-
existent God ; not like the gods of the
heathen, &c. Job speaks of him,

3. *As his Redeemer.*
"My." How sweet and rich this word.
It is the golden link. *A*, or *the* Redeemer,
alters the whole. It must be *my* Redeemer.
Mine by gift—mine by application and
choice, &c. Job refers to his,

4. *Experience on this subject.*
"I know." I have a clear understanding
of it—an inward assurance. I know, not I
think, or I hope ; but I know. It is holy,
divine assurance. I would add three or four
things respecting this Redeemer :—

His power. "Mighty to save," &c. All
powerful.

His merit. Influence exhaustless ; the
virtue of his blood all efficacious.

His love and compassion. "Ye know the
grace of our Lord Jesus Christ," &c.

His unswerving fidelity. Faithful to his
work—to his Father—and to his saints.

II. *The blessings he hopefully anticipated.*
Observe, however,

1. *He calculated on the certainty of his
own mortality.*
He probably thought his earthly career
would soon end. "If I wait the grave," &c.
At any rate he was aware of the certainty
of death. Worms would feed upon him.
The whole frame be decomposed, and mingle with the dust of the earth. "Dust thou
art," &c.

2. *He believed in the resurrection of his
body.*
"Yet in my flesh," &c. One of the most
profoundly deep and sublime truths, is that
of the resurrection of the dead. "If a man
die, shall he live again," &c. He would not
behold God in his sepulchred state ; but re-
clothed with the flesh which worms had
destroyed ; yet that flesh how marvellously
changed ! "Sown in corruption, in dishonor, in weakness, a mortal body," &c.
1 Cor. xv. 42.

3. *He expected this resurrection to be effected by his Redeemer.*

Evidently the weight of the text rests here. His God or Redeemer would bring him forth from his dusty bed. Resuscitate —restore—glorify, &c. How this harmonizes with the exclamation of Christ: "I am the resurrection and the life," &c.

4. *He expected this event in connection with Christ's second advent.*

"And shall stand at the latter day," &c.

His faith might take in the first advent of the Messiah to redeem the world; but his final hope rested on the second glorious appearance of the Lord from heaven.

This doctrine had been taught before the days of Job. Jude 14, &c. This is distinctly revealed in the New Testament oracles. 2 Thess. i. 7; see especially Philip. iii. 20, &c.

5. *He expected, in his resurrection body, to have the vision of the Redeemer.*

"Whom I shall see," &c. "Blessed are the pure in heart," &c. "Beloved, now," &c. "We shall be like him," &c. Who would not wish to see some of the illustrious of mankind, &c.; but especially to see Jesus, the Creator, Ruler, and Redeemer of the world.

APPLICATION.

1. *Is your experience like that of Job's?*

Do you know scripturally and experimentally that Christ is your Redeemer? That he liveth, &c.

2. *Is this great truth your consolation, and hope, and joy?*

Life is ebbing—death is approaching. How affecting the destiny and the change, which is to pass over you.

The gospel reveals a glorious resurrection. I urge the attainment of the hope, on each and all. This will be to you—light in darkness—peace in trouble—joy in affliction—life in death.

———◆———

CXCIX.—JOB'S COMPASSION AND GRIEF FOR THE POOR.

[NO. X.]

"Did not I weep for him that was in trouble? was not my soul grieved for the poor?"—*Job* xxx. 25.

ONE of the most pathetic appeals ever made, is the one of which our text is a part.

The holy Patriarch is roused by the suspicions and insinuations of his mistaken friends, and gives the detail by which he had been influenced, and the practice which, as a man of God, he had ever pursued. And what a dignified, eloquent self-defence it is! He now pathetically refers to the change he has experienced; ver. 8–16. But he still remembers, with satisfaction, the course he had pursued; for in the text he says, "Did not I weep," &c.

Let us see, then,

What the declaration involves; and

The principles on which it should be imitated.

I. *What the declaration of the text involves.*

There are two parts. We take the latter first.

1. *Grief for the poor.*

In all ages and countries there have been poor. Many are such by their *own* improvidence—would be so though all around were in prosperity.

Indolence is one cause.

Extravagance another.

Want of ordinary prudence.

But there are many *necessarily* poor. Born so—reared so—never can emerge from it—*live* so—*die* so.

Two things not to be forgotten :—

(1.) God has to do with our external condition. See 1 Sam. ii. 7.

(2.) The poor shall never cease out of the land. Ye have the poor always with you. Now we may justly grieve,

1. *For the condition of the poor.*

It is one on which men invariably look down. It is considered an estate of inferiority. Now this is galling to the feelings of the poor. For the feelings of these, at any rate, are often as tender and susceptible as those of others.

2. *We should grieve for the privations of the poor.*

And how numerous are these! Insufficient food,—scanty fare,—miserable dwellings. Often in inclement weather, little fire.

Then look at the higher privations! Few mental enjoyments.

Few interesting volumes to peruse.

No instructive society.

No domestic scenes of hilarity and gladness.

We should grieve,

3. *For the toils of the poor.*

They literally fulfil the curse—"By the sweat of their brow," &c. Labor itself, however, is a curse, which the hand of industry, and the divine favor, turn into a blessing. Constant, and even hard labor, when it is *remunerated*, is agreeable. But, alas! in our country, how sad the details of the fact; and how shamefully true is this of female labor. But look at the ordinary toils of the poor. Rising early, laboring late. Many in toil of the most unpleasant kind. The miner—the mariner—even the laborer in all weathers, &c. We should grieve,

4. *For the temptations of the poor.*

Extreme poverty is, doubtless, one chief cause of crime. Look at that starving *boy*, he sees the tempting morsel, and longs, and steals. Once initiated, he goes on from bad to worse, &c.

Look at that *interesting girl*—half-starved, half-fed; she goes out; a desire for food and dress excite her mind—and she sees, that by the prostitution of her person, she can get what she wants—and she does it—and then becomes a living pestilence.

Look at that *toiling man*—his miserable hearth, &c. He wants pleasure and excitement,—he takes his pence, and goes to the well-lighted, warm, cheerful tavern, and drinks; and afterwards becomes the devotee of alcohol—the worshipper of Bacchus, &c.

You see the poor bitter, envious, violent, &c. Do you wonder at it?

I add one temptation more, that is—to *neglect religion*. To be absent from the means of grace, &c. Swallowed up in the things of the body, &c. But the text has another part,

6. *Sympathy for those in trouble.*

"Did not I weep," &c. The poor have sometimes additional sorrows, to those of poverty. Trouble.

Of absolute distress. The failure of the usual means.

Of afflictions. Sickness, &c. I appeal to the ladies on the troubles of their own sex, amidst the pains and perils of maternity.

Of bereavements. Houses of mourning, &c. Should we not weep, &c.; that is, feel for and sympathize with them? Job said, he did so. See xxix. 11, &c.

Let us then consider,

II. *The principles on which this conduct should be imitated.*

1. *On the grounds of our common humanity.*

They are our brethren and sisters, &c. "The rich and the poor meet together," &c. "God hath made of one blood," &c.

2. *On the grounds of God's authority and conduct.*

He provides of his abundance, &c. He has given repeated orders, &c. Declared his curse shall rest on the despisers and reproachers of the poor. Proverbs xix. 17; and xxviii. 27.

3. *In imitation of the example of our Lord.*

He came to visit the poor—To preach to the poor—To bless the poor, &c. He himself was so, in the deepest degree, &c.

4. *From the real delight and enjoyment this spirit produces.*

The man who remembers and grieves for the poor is *blessed*. "It is more blessed to give," &c. It reacts—pleases God—will ensure his smile, etc. Reward, etc.

APPLICATION.

1. Let the subject engage your attention and practice.

2. Be anxious both for their physical and mental welfare.

3. Act as stewards who must give an account.

4. Be discriminating in your benefactions.

5. There is spiritual poverty—which is the worst kind of all. The rich may be afflicted with this. How distressing, when both kinds of poverty meet, etc.

6. The gospel meets both kinds of poverty. Removes the one, and sweetens and sanctifies the other, etc.

CC.—ELIHU'S ADDRESS TO JOB.

[NO. XI.]

"Behold, in this thou art not just: I will answer thee, that God is greater than man," &c.— *Job* xxxiii. 12, 13.

You have all read of the afflictions of Job. How deep, complicated, continued. How property was destroyed. How of his children he was bereaved. How of health he was deprived; and last, how of hypocrisy he was both suspected and even charged.

His three friends, Eliphaz, Bildad, and Zophar, entirely mistook his case; and hence, instead of pouring healing balm into his wounded heart, they only aggravated his sufferings by unkind and bitter speeches.

At length, another person is introduced to

us. A young man, but of extraordinary wisdom and knowledge. This was Elihu. He did not unite with the three others in bitter charges of hypocrisy; but still endeavored to show Job, that he had not displayed sufficient humility of spirit, nor a becoming reverence towards God.

Our text contains a portion of his address to Job. He refers to what Job had improperly said about himself; ver. 9 ; and still more so against God ; ver. 10, 11; and then follows the words of the text, "Behold in this," &c.

Observe,

I. *That even saints may entertain unjust views of God.*

II. *That God's greatness should silence our objections to his proceedings.*

And,

III. *That it is foolish and vain to strive against him.*

I. *That even saints may entertain unjust views of God.*

Now this may arise as in Job's case,

1. *From too high a view of ourselves.*

Job had said, "I am clean," &c., ver. 9.

Now Job, in defending himself against his three friends, had said more in his own favor than he ought. Had reasoned, perhaps, as one who was perfectly holy. The conduct of God must be different to perfectly holy and to imperfect beings; and if we do not judge of God thus, we shall infer falsely. God never disciplines absolutely holy beings; it is unnecessary. But he does this with his own children; for their spiritual improvement, &c.

We entertain unjust views of God,

2. *When we suppose that he is anxious to observe our failings.*

Verse 10.

Now in this Job erred greatly. God, so far from this, is gracious, forbearing, long-suffering, &c. See Psalm ciii. 8, 9, 10; Ps. cxxx. 3, 4. This is the very opposite view of God, and is really the true and just one. Satan may look for the halting of good men; and bad men may do it; but God *never* does so.

We entertain unjust views of God,

3. *When we conclude that God treateth us as enemies.*

If God did so, he would at once consume us. We should not have probation lengthened out, &c. No: God treats us as erring children. Hear what he said of backsliding Israel, &c. Hosea xi. 7, &c.; chap. xiv. 4.

Just as the father felt for the prodigal, and hailed him with joy—so God with his people. God never treats his people with wrath, as enemies; but with pity, as erring children, &c.

Observe,

II. *That God's greatness should silence our objections to his proceedings.*

"God is greater," &c.

1. *He is so in his dominion.*

God's dominion includes all things—all creatures—all worlds ; he has to govern all, and to arrange for all. We are but fragments, as it were, and therefore cannot judge God accurately, not being able to survey the whole. "And he giveth not account," &c. ; ver. 13.

2. *In his knowledge and wisdom.*

"We know next to nothing," &c. God thus speaks to Job at the end of the controversy. Chapter xxxviii., &c.

What would a child do in judging of the astronomer, in his mathematical calculations ?—of the man of science, in his wonderful achievements ?—of the learned man, in his profound studies ? Yet there is infinitely more resemblance in the faculties of the child and the philosopher, than in the highest creature and God. If the child could not be just in its conclusions, how can we ?

3. *God is greater than man in power and resources.*

There is a definite limit to the power of man. His resources are circumscribed, &c. But not so with God. Job knew what God had done. He knew his losses, his griefs, &c. All beyond man's power to repair. So far as man was concerned, utterly irreparable. Not so with God, &c. He can do every thing right and fit to be done. See the end of Job's history. How God turned his captivity, &c.; and restored his mercies and blessings, &c.

Notice, then,

III. *That it must be foolish and vain to strive against God.*

"Why dost thou strive," &c.

1. *It is foolish.*

He knows what is best—we do not. He sees all from the beginning, and to the end —we do not. How extremely absurd, then, to oppose we know not what. The wheel, we think, is moving in the wrong direction, but it is a wheel within a wheel, and it causes others to go rightly, &c.

But to strive is not only foolish,

2. *But it must be vain.*

For man cannot effectually resist him. If you dislike God's plans, &c., how will you frustrate them?

Think of the moth and the tempest!

Think of the insect and the lightning! &c. What can man do against God? See Isaiah xlv. 9; Amos ix. 1 to 6.

Learn,

1. To cultivate lowly views of yourselves.

2. Cherish august views of God,—his greatness and majesty, &c.

3. Rely on his goodness and grace. He is man's true and best friend, &c.

4. Be resigned to his providential arrangements. They are always wise and kind, &c. Submission is alike our duty and privilege.

CCI.—JOB'S PENITENTIAL CONFESSION.

[NO. XII.]

" Behold, I am vile," &c.—*Job* xl. 4.

THE character, sufferings, and trials of Job, form one of the most interesting and instructive subjects of Old Testament history. Here was a good man—one perfect in his generation, &c., reduced from the highest prosperity and happiness, to the deepest state of abasement and suffering. In the midst of his unparalleled afflictions, his friends come to visit him. They are intellectual, godly men. But they mistake the true principles of the Divine government. They conclude that God ever punishes sin, and rewards righteousness, in this life; and hence they surmise evil of Job,—conclude that he has been guilty of some heinous sins and deep hypocrisy. This goads and overwhelms the sufferer. His patience fails—he utters hard things of God, and even seeks that God should destroy him. God, the wise arbiter, steps in and decides the controversy. He admonishes Job—reproves his friends—and then, mercifully heals and restores his servant.

Now Job is humbled in the dust. His self-complacency is gone, and he exclaims—" Behold, I am vile."

Observe,

I. *The text is strikingly applicable to unrenewed human nature.*

The tree became bad—the fountain corrupt, &c.; therefore the stream defiled.

Hence God, in describing the state of the antediluvians, &c. Gen. vi. 5. Hence, also, that declaration: " The heart is deceitful," &c. What phases of wickedness! In indescribable forms of sensuality—in awful exhibitions of pride, &c. In concentrated forms of selfishness—in terrible forms of cruelty and blood. No tongue can describe—no mind conceive the intense, deep depravity of the human heart! Yet in the midst of the vilest there may be some remains of his primeval excellency—some features of the original image, &c.

II. *The text is not inappropriate to the renewed people of God.*

Case of Job. The best of men have felt it. Abraham—David—Isaiah—and Paul. See Gal. v. 17, &c. " If we say that we have no sin," &c. What awful thoughts! what strange feelings! what vile desires! what fearful folly!—have characterized even the good and excellent. And this sense of vileness is heightened,

(1.) Just as persons see the extent of the divine law.

(2.) Just as they feel the great claims God has upon them.

(3.) And as they discern the odiousness of all sin.

(4.) And the necessity of perfect holiness to enjoy God and heaven, &c. Forget these things, and you may easily be self-satisfied and self-righteous—or by comparing yourselves with others, or your former selves. But the true feeling is that of the text—" Behold, I am vile!"

III. *The text should lead to humiliation and contrition before God.*

If true, and really felt, there will be self-renunciation, self-loathing, self-distrust. There will be great modesty in speaking of ourselves,—great charity in speaking of others. Constant confession—repentance and prayer.

IV. *The text will lead to the right appreciation of the person and sacrifice of Christ.*

Here is the *malady*, and where is the remedy? " the fountain opened," &c. Here is the *sin*, and where is the salvation?—in the cross of Christ. Here is the *peril*, where is the deliverer?—Jesus who gave himself, that he might redeem unto himself, &c. Here is the *enemy*, where is the power for the victory?—Christ and his Holy Spirit, and efficient grace. A low sense of ourselves will produce a high sense of Christ,—so in the opposite case, &c. Christ will just be precious. as sin is felt, deplored, &c.

Oh, yes, Christ will be infinitely precious to the believer!

V. *The text is no plea for indifference to the divine commands.*

Not to sin that grace may abound. But mourn for sin, and strive against it. Seek entire deliverance from it. "We that are in this tabernacle groan," &c. Labor for the moral triumph over sin. Press after entire holiness, &c.

VI. *The text has no signification in the heavenly state.*

In the full redemption, all sin will be destroyed.—All depravity removed.—Hearts transparent.—Souls spotless.—Spirits immortal.

"Sin our worst enemy before," &c.

Washed their robes, &c. Without spot or wrinkle, &c. Don't suppose that death does this for the Christian, but the grace of God during life,—making meet for the inheritance, &c.

Let the subject,—

1. Lead the sinner to repentance.

2. The believer to lie in the depths of humility.

3. And all to prize and trust in the great Redeemer, and to abhor the folly of self-righteousness.

CCII.—THE CRISIS AND RESTORATION OF JOB.

[NO. XIII.]

"Then Job answered the Lord, and said, I know that thou canst do every thing, and that no thought can be withholden from thee."—*Job* xlii. 1, &c.

IN addition to the addresses of Job's three friends—Eliphaz, Bildad, and Zophar—a young man of extraordinary powers, stepped forth, and delivered a series of observations in the most lofty, sublime strains of sacred eloquence. His address occupies six chapters, from 32d to 38th, inclusive. He dwells chiefly on the grandeur, power, and wisdom of God. On the greatness of his works, and the illimitable extent of his dominion. Jehovah then steps forth and speaks out of the whirlwind, and the discourse of God is presented in the 38th, 39th, 40th, and 41st chapters.

During the delivering of God's righteous will, Job is humbled, and exclaims, "Behold, I am vile," chapter xl. 4. When God ceaseth to speak, Job answered, "I know thou canst do every thing," &c.

Now observe,

Job's sincere humiliation.

God's vindication of him.

His mediatorship on behalf of his friends; and,

His return to prosperity and happiness.

I. *His sincere humiliation.*

Observe, he had not fallen into the snare of the devil. He had not been guilty of secret sins against the Most High. But he had spoken rashly and irreverently—he exhibited too much of the spirit of self-exaltation—he had also indulged in a spirit of recrimination, &c.

Observe, in his humiliation,

1. *His declaration concerning the divine power and omniscience.*

Verse 2.

Almightiness is God's attribute, by which he can do all that he ought to do. Omniscience, by which he is not only cognizant of the actions and words, but thoughts. All desires and purposes are open to God. The heart is uncovered before him. How great and glorious is the Lord God! Who would not fear and stand in awe of him? Notice,

2. *His acknowledgment of his ignorance and presumption.*

Verse 3.

God had thus charged Job; chap. xxxviii.

2. He acknowledges, and evidently laments it. Yet how greatly elevated was Job above most men, in his religious knowledge. But there are regions inaccessible to all, &c. Too deep,—too high! &c. Much may be known, but the unknowable, how vast! How we should pause in our researches after divine knowledge, lest we act irreverently and with presumption. I think the 4th verse might be rendered so as to be a citation from his own presumptive irreverent exclamations. See chap. xiii. 1–3. Now he is abased, and docile as a little child.

3. *He expresses an important change in his views of the divine character.*

Verse 5. "I have heard of thee," &c.; and he had attained much knowledge of God; but now, having come in closer contact, so as to be placed in the divine presence, and hear from God's immediate lips, —he had higher, holier, and clearer views of his infinite majesty. "Mine eye seeth;" not literally, but the eye of the mind, &c.

4. *He utters the language of self-abhor-rence and true contrition.*

Verse 6. "Wherefore, I abhor," &c. I am ashamed. I despise and loathe myself. I feel my own vileness and pollution, and I repent, *i. e.*, change my views and feelings, in deep humility, &c. What a striking picture of a good man filled with the true spirit of genuine humility, and godly sorrow. Observe,

II. *God's vindication of the character of Job.*

Verse 7.

God was evidently displeased with the evil surmisings of Job's friends.

And with their hard sayings, and bitter reflections.

Job had said and done amiss, but his condition was peculiar—in deep waters, &c. God will remember all our circumstances, and we shall be judged according to them, &c. Job, on the whole, had a most correct view of the Almighty; and God gives the verdict in his favor.

How important to the good man, that God knows his ways! How desirable to fall into the arms of God!

Observe,

III. *His appointed mediatorship on behalf of his three friends.*

Verse 8.

Now observe in this,

1. *A recognition of the law of sacrifices.*

Of this we spoke at length, in our second discourse.

2. *We see an exhibition of mediatorial influence.*

They are told what to do. Job was to act and mediate between them and God. His intercessions were to arise, &c. Sacrifice and prayer united; ver. 9: God accepted the offerings and prayers, &c. Wherefore this arrangement in reference to Job's friends?

(1.) To point to the great sacrifice and mediator. In this, Job seems a type of the Saviour. He prayed for his accusers. Jesus for his murderers. Job's friends were accepted through sacrifice, and his intercession; so sinners with God, through Christ.

(2.) To humble Job's friends. They had exalted themselves—now God abases them. From accusers they must become suppliants.

(3.) To produce a spirit of reconciliation. They ask Job's prayers, and Job forgets his wrongs, and intercedes; and doubtless, this was the surest basis of future friendship.

How often could we easily settle our disputes and difference on our knees. But, alas! men have more of the spirit of controversy than of prayer.

Notice,

IV. *Job's restoration to prosperity and happiness.*

Verse 10. Observe,

(1.) The adverse stream is driven back.

(2.) The tide of prosperity sets in twofold.

(3.) He enjoys the society and affection of his friends. How often God employs friends as his instruments of comfort. This is good for both giver and receiver.

(4.) He has a family raised up to share his felicity; verses 13, 14. His daughters were celebrated for their beauty and loveliness; and his sons and daughters for the abundance of their possessions.

(5.) He had many years of peace and enjoyment; verse 16. He at length died, full of years, riches, and honor; verse 17.

APPLICATION.

Learn,

1. *The necessity of cultivating a spirit of humble penitence before God.*

Only safe while we are low. Seek not, aim not, at high things, &c.

2. *The importance of entire submission to God.*

God must have all the glory, as he has all the power and the might, &c.

3. *How needful to hold fast our hope.*

The Christian's motto should be, "Never despair!"

4. *A right state of heart towards God will lead to a spirit of love and reconciliation to our fellow-men.*

CCIII.—LESSONS TAUGHT BY JOB'S HISTORY.

[NO. XIV.]

"So Job died, being old and full of days."—*Job* xlii. 17.

IN our last discourse we saw the tide of Job's suffering and adversity rolled back, and we beheld the stream of prosperity filling him with joy and gladness.

Our design this morning, is a review, or practical application of the whole. What are the great lessons which Job's astonishing history teaches us.

I. *We see the mutability of earthly greatness and prosperity.*

When we view Job in the midst of affluence. The greatest man in all the East. On the summit of prosperity. With all that heart could wish. The sunshine of happiness gilding and beautifying all he had. We marvel not that he should say, "I shall die in my nest." What was to hinder? Surely his mountain would stand firm, and never be moved.

But observe, like a moving panorama, while you gaze, the scene changes—like a dissolving view, the representation is reversed,—the light and the beauty, and the abundance, are exchanged for darkness, and sadness, and adversity. One good fails after another. His possessions—his servants—his family—his health—his social enjoyments, &c. Life in a flickering state, and hope ready to expire—are all that remain, &c.

His magnificent vessel strikes upon the breakers—the sea rolls over it and destroys the cargo—the crew and the vessel,—himself and wife on planks and boards, reach the shore of dreariness and desolation. How true—"The fashion of this world passeth away," &c. Earthly titles, earthly grandeur and magnificence, — earthly power, pomp, and riches! certainty belongs to none of them. They recede as the ebbing tide, —they are effaced as characters written on the sand,—they vanish as the mists of the morning,—they fade as the flowers in autumn,—and they wither as the leaves in winter.

How exhibited in Cardinal Wolsey, and thousands of others! We see,

II. *The malevolence and power of Satan.*

He is Apollyon—the destroyer. It is true his wrath is restrained, and his energy limited : yet he is often permitted to exercise great and direful influence. He is called, "The god of this world, the prince of the power of the air," &c. He is the monarch of evil. Darkness is the region in which he dwells. Cruelty the element of his being. He binds in hellish fetters. He afflicts with misery,—he gloats in the tortures of his victims. Their tears are the joy of his spirit—and their sighs and groans, the music of his fallen soul! It is evident that he exerts his influence on the minds of men ; as in the case of the Sabeans and Chaldeans—on the elements of nature, as in the fire and lightning which he brought down—on the air, as in the whirlwind, &c. : on the body, as in the foul and loathsome affliction of Job.

In the Redeemer's time, his hellish power on earth seems to have reached a fearful ascendency. Hence, the numerous possessions, &c. That was, indeed, the hour of this world, and the hour of darkness. Against him we are solemnly warned. "Above all things, taking the shield of faith," &c. "Resist the Devil," &c.

III. *We see what an amazing series of afflictions may be borne, through the sustaining help of God.*

The saint is most feeble and impotent ; yet most powerful and elastic. Can do nothing, and bear nothing ; and yet can do all things and bear all things.

We should not have marvelled if Job had been overwhelmed with melancholy, enveloped in despair, or expired in anguish. A tithe of his sorrow, has often produced death. Such sudden reverses have made countless maniacs, and often peopled an early tomb. How did Job patiently endure? By the strength of the grace of God—by the power of religious principle. He reposed on God's bosom— he reclined on God's arm — he trusted to the divine help. Thus when he was weak, he was strong, &c. The life of God within, was the grand sustaining principle. So it has been to thousands.

IV. *We see the unfailing character of God's goodness and promises.*

The promises of God are exceedingly great and precious. He is the unchanging friend of his people. He will never leave nor forsake, &c. His goodness cannot fail, nor his pity falter. His tender mercy endureth forever. Had he forsaken Job, he would have perished, &c. Hence, the triumphant boast of the Apostle : "If God be for us," &c. "Who is he that can harm us?" &c. He hath assured us of this, in the emphatic language : "I will never leave thee, nor forsake thee." In the original there are five negatives employed : and it might read thus :—"I will not leave thee, I will never, never, never, forsake thee." Hence the paraphrase of the Poet—

"The soul that on Jesus hath lean'd for repose,
I will not—I will not, desert to his foes.
That soul, though all hell should endeavor to shake,
I'll never—no never—no never forsake."

V. *The best of men are weak and fallible.*

Job's friends were of the illustrious of the day ; doubtless, the most intelligent and holy of that age. Yet we see, even with the best intentions, how greatly they erred, and how they failed to be a solace to Job. The best of men are but men at best. Let us not expect too much from the creature. The arm of man is the arm of flesh. The mind of man is environed by darkness and error. The heart of man not only deceives others, but often itself. Who would go to the cistern, which may or may not contain water, and leave the fountain ? "Cease ye from man," &c. "Cursed is the man who maketh an arm of flesh his truth ; but blessed is the man who trusteth in the Lord," &c.

VI. *The severest afflictions of this life are necessarily light and evanescent.*

"Wherefore should a living man complain," &c. All men are sinners, even the best. All sin deserves perdition, even the least. Therefore, all suffering in this life, is as nothing, compared with our desert. Then how transitory ! At longest, it is but for a night. The Apostle says, " Our light afflictions which are but for a moment." The furnace of affliction, however hot, &c., is not hell ; and the sufferings of the saints, are not as the anguish of the lost.

VII. *How essential is the exercise of patience in suffering.*

To recognize God's hand. To rely on God's heart. To wait God's time. Job said, "I will wait," &c.

VIII. *God will more than recompense his suffering people.*

Are you surprised at Job's sufferings ? Do you feel inclined to suspect God of cruelty ? &c. Wait the issue. Job sows in tears, &c.; but reaps in joy. He has a dark night, &c.; but behold the light of day, &c. Often in this world God's people have a reward,—most certainly they shall have hereafter, "For I reckon that the sufferings of this present time," &c. Sufferings make the joys doubly rapturous. "These are they that came out of great tribulation," &c.

IX. *The last days of the godly, shall be their best.*

The journey may be tedious, but they shall come with joy, &c., to Zion. The voyage rough, but an abundant entrance shall be given, &c. The valley dark, but they shall emerge into the cloudless rays of eternal day.

Four advantages arise from Job's trials.— We see,

1. The reality of true religion.

2. The glory of God in his character, and government.

3. The experience Job improved.

4. An example of patience, left for the imitation of the Church, for all after ages, &c.

————◆————

CCIV. — JEREMIAH'S DISCOURAGEMENT, AND RETURN TO HIS ONEROUS DUTY.

"Then I said, I will not make mention of him, nor speak any more in his name. But his word was in mine heart as a burning fire shut up in my bones, and I was weary with forbearing, and I could not stay."—*Jer.* xx. 9.

JEREMIAH was one of the most distinguished of the Old Testament worthies. He entered on the service of God in early life, and therefore knew what it was to bear the yoke in his youth.

He began to prophesy in the thirteenth year of the reign of Josiah, about seventy years after the death of Isaiah ; and he continued in his work for at least forty years.

As a prophet, he was distinguished for great love to his nation, and a holy, burning zeal for God. He was also very much signalized for the tender and pathetic character of his spirit; and hence, is appropriately styled, "The Weeping Prophet."

He lived in very bad times—had many things to discourage him—suffered much in carrying out his sacred calling. My text has to do with his experience on one of these depressing occasions.

Observe,

I. *His rash and sinful determination.*

And,

II. *The course which he was constrained, notwithstanding, to adopt.*

I. *His rash and sinful determination.*

We say his determination was,

1. *Rash.*

Evidently not the habitual state of his mind. He had toiled and labored for upwards of twenty years. He had entered on his work from a conscientious conviction of duty and principle. His heart and soul were in the work. It was the great burden of his life, so that his exclamation was one of precipitate rashness—the outburst of haste and passion.

We find the best of men showing their infirmities, under peculiar circumstances.

Job, cursing the day of his birth.

The Psalmist, pronouncing all men to be liars.

Jonah, angry even at the gracious dispensations of God.

James and John, desiring that they might bring fire down to consume the Samaritans. But,

2. *It was sinful.*

Not mere excusable rashness. It was more than weakness. Just look at the language. What did he say? "I will not speak," &c. This was direct rebellion—daring presumption! Then, of whom did he speak? I will not make mention of "Him," that is, God. What had Jehovah done? Was he not great, and glorious, and blessed? "Nor speak any more in his name," &c. How irreverent and wrong! How unworthy of good, yet frail Jeremiah! How remarkable from the lips of one so pious, so faithful, so persevering! What an hour of weakness and sin!

Yet observe,

3. *The temptations to this sin were very great.*

We will only glance at the immediate and direct causes of that which, doubtless, affected the mind of the prophet.

He had been smitten by the sons of the Priest; ver. 2.

He had been put into the stocks, as a vile person; ver. 3.

Then he was a derision to the people, &c.; ver. 7.

They were also constantly looking for his overthrow and falling; ver. 10.

Now these were very trying scenes. A sad ordeal.—A distressing test. Think of his noble nature! Dignified spirit—high-toned generousness—his devotedness to God; and then, the sad return he received.

We now proceed to,

II. *The course which he was constrained, notwithstanding, to adopt.*

This moral aberration of mind was only very transitory. It was a cloud which passed away, &c. Now observe how, and to what extent, his resolution was changed.

1. *It was by the Word of the Lord.*

What God had said to him. What God had commanded him to do.

Now the "Word of God" contains the ideas, thoughts, determinations and emotions of the Lord. Some speak disparagingly of the *Word* of the Lord. Without something annexed to it, they describe it as a dead letter, &c. It is, however, the very reflection of God's mind and heart. It is most powerful and blessed. God has magnified his Word above all his name. By it, he created the world, &c. "He spake," &c. See Gen. i. 3, 6, 9, 11. By it he caused Sinai to tremble, &c. Ps. lxviii. 7–11, &c. By it he produces or stills the storms and tempests of nature. Ps. cxlviii. 5–7. The Word of the Lord is searching and quickening. The power of God is conveyed in it, and by it.

2. *It was the Word of God in him, as fire.*

See the same idea in the language of Elihu. Job xxxii. 18. See Ps. xxxix. 2, 3. So God describes it as fire: Jer. xxiii. 29.

(1.) It enlightens. It dispels the gloom, when kindled in the dark night. It has ever done so. In all countries, &c. Germany, Britain. In the dark mind of the sinner.

(2.) It purifies. The silver ore is thrown into it, &c.; and the dross is removed, &c. So it sanctifies the heart, &c.

(3.) It consumes the stubble and chaff, or wood. Its threats will burn up the sinner, &c., who abides in impenitence.

Now it was in the heart of the Prophet as fire.

3. *As fire, it burned out the precipitate rebellion of his spirit.*

"He was weary of forbearing. He could not stay." It inflamed him afresh with,

Zeal for God.

Love to souls.

A sense of his official duty. And he could not "stay."

What can withstand these all-powerful elements? What resist the influences of an enlightened conscience—a deep-toned pity and melting compassion, for the perishing? "The love of Christ constraineth," &c. "I count not my life dear," saith the Apostle, &c. He says, "I have become all things to all men, that by all means, I might save some," &c.

When the heart is sanctified to God's work, it is its misery not to be acting, and living, and serving him, &c. So the Prophet's heart loosened his tongue, and he continued to live, and toil, and suffer, in the cause of God and truth.

Learn,—

1. *The onerous and solemn work of the minister of God.*

In Jeremiah's time. Now, always, everywhere, &c.

2. *The discouragements to which they are exposed.*

See Jeremiah. See even Jesus, and his Disciples. See the Apostle of the Gentiles.

3. *The great necessity of Christian sympathy and co-operation.*

"Brethren, pray for us," &c. See Moses, and the elders of Israel standing and holding up his hands. I ask,

4. *What influence the Word of God has had on you.*

Are you receivers or rejecters—lovers or haters? Oh receive it in faith and love, that it may be the power of God to your soul's present and everlasting salvation.

CCV.—DANIEL'S EXCELLENT SPIRIT.

"Then this Daniel was preferred above the presidents and princes, because an excellent spirit was in him ; and the king thought to set him over the whole realm."—*Dan.* vi. 3.

THE Bible is full of condensed truths. A mighty event is often described in a paragraph. A few verses detail the creation of the world. A few chapters, its history for nearly two thousand years. A few sentences give an account of the Deluge. The Bible is a book of seeds ; from these a rich harvest of knowledge is to be realized.

Human compositions, at best, are as gold in the leaf, and thus a small quantity is spread over a great surface.

In the Bible we have it in ingots and precious bars, one of which will make a man rich for both worlds.

How true these remarks are in reference to Scripture Biography. A few words tell the history of Enoch, Melchisedek, and other illustrious worthies. The records of the life of Daniel are to be found in a few words, scattered through a book of only twelve short chapters.

Our text gives us a view of his moral excellences,—" An excellent spirit was in him."

Let us consider,

The characteristics of an excellent spirit ; and,

The importance of an excellent spirit.

I. *The characteristics of an excellent spirit.*

Now three preliminary observations may be necessary.

(1.) The spirit and dispositions of men naturally, are very diversified. A great and striking difference exists in men constitutionally.

(2.) An excellent spirit in a religious and spiritual sense, can only belong to man, as he has been renewed by the grace and spirit of God.

(3.) As to the features of an excellent spirit, we must be governed by the Word of God, and not by the maxims or opinions of men.

Laying down these great landmarks, we cannot err in our future conclusions. Now of the features or characteristics of an excellent spirit, we notice the following :—

1. *It is modest and humble, in opposition to a proud and arrogant spirit.*

Self-exaltation seems to be identical with human nature in its unregenerated condition. Hence, how common self-complacency — self-confidence—self-boasting. Divine grace dethrones self, and enthrones Christ. Then there is conviction of sin, self-loathing and abhorrence. Now the soul is clothed with humility. Now glorying in nothing, save the cross of the Lord Jesus Christ. What numerous reasons for this spirit! Our origin the dust. Our dependence on God for every thing. Our nothingness and vanity ; especially our sinfulness before the Lord. This spirit is often recommended and urged. "Put on humbleness." "Walk humbly." "Though the Lord be high," &c.

2. *It will be intelligent and wise, in opposition to an ignorant and uninformed spirit.*

One of the grand elements of Christianity is light—heavenly, divine, and spiritual knowledge. To know ourselves. To know God, as he is revealed in his works and word, and Jesus Christ whom he hath sent. To cherish such a spirit,—To grow in grace, and in the knowledge of the Lord Jesus Christ,—To inquire after knowledge,—To be fraught with the spirit of wisdom, &c. See the testimony given of Daniel, v. 11. Now divine knowledge is the excellency of knowledge. It is soul-saving ; yea, life eternal.

3. *It will be self-denying, in opposition to a self-seeking spirit.*

Now selfishness has an endless variety of manifestations : In luxuries—in flesh pampering—in rioting and wantonness—in love of ease, &c. Now, an excellent spirit is the opposite of this. "It is *crucifying* the flesh," &c. "It is denying ungodliness and worldly lusts," &c. It is taking up the cross, and following Christ Jesus. We see this also exhibited in Daniel, chap. i. 8.

4. *It is benevolent and generous, in opposition to a sordid and illiberal spirit.*

Goodness or benevolence is the very spirit and essence of religion. "God is love, and he · that dwelleth," &c. The Christian is called to do good, &c. To do good to all, &c. "To do good and communicate," &c. He has shed abroad in his heart, the love of Christ. The principle of his love is, Christ's love in him. "Ye know the grace of the Lord," &c.

A sordid worldly spirit is the opposite of God and godliness. It is odious in itself. It blights the mind; and must be annihilated, before we can be meet for a heaven of love.

5. *It is charitable and candid, in opposition to a bigoted and prejudiced spirit.*

Prejudice decides without evidence, and bigotry carries it out into dislike and exclusion. It was these which put prophets to death,—rejected the Redeemer, and crucified him, &c. It is these which have formed the spirit of persecution and intolerance in all ages. These are the two pillars of sectarianism of the present day. Charity and candor rejoice in truth and goodness, wherever they see them.

An excellent spirit delights in the lovely features of men, and not in their defects. Bigotry and prejudice say: "Master, we saw one casting out devils in thy name, and we forbade him," &c. But charity and candor reiterate the words of Jesus: "Forbid him not; for he that is not against us, is on our side," &c. How truly lovely is this feature in the Christian character! How it shone in Jesus! How it is perfected in heaven!

6. *It is decided and magnanimous, in opposition to a tame and compromising spirit.*

In religion, decision is essential. Magnanimity often indispensable. Religion must not only be enjoyed, but confessed and professed.

There must be the visible putting on of Christ—receiving Christ—and walking in him. Not to be ashamed of Christ, and his cause, and people. "We must go without the camp," &c. We must be ready to venture all for Christ, and trust all with him. See this in Daniel vi. 7, 10.

Decision and magnanimity are often required, even now, &c.

7. *It is reverential and praying, in opposition to a thoughtless and prayerless spirit.*

An excellent spirit reverences God's name —word—day, house, &c. It cherishes holy fear. Is in the fear of the Lord all day, &c. It also dwells in the atmosphere of prayer— regards prayer as a duty, and fulfils it;—as a privilege, and delights in it. It seeks the grace of prayer, and cultivates the gift of prayer. It links prayer with all other things. "Is anxious for nothing," &c. Thus keeps up hallowed communion with God, and daily intercourse with heaven.

Such are the leading characteristics of an excellent spirit. See Daniel ix. 16.

II. *The importance of an excellent spirit.*

1. *It is important to our religious character.*

By this we know that we are of God. "If any man have not the spirit of Christ," &c. Other tests may deceive us—as mere profession; general morality of conduct. The question after all is, What is our spirit?

2. *It is important to our enjoyments.*

This spirit carries its own atmosphere with it. It makes man blessed. Is a pure air— holy sunshine — perpetual feast. Secures peace and joy, &c. Heaven within us on earth, &c.

3. *It is important to our usefulness.*

It will give us the best of all kinds of influence. It will sanctify talent,—bless our labors to do good,—bear down opposition.

4. *It will recommend religion.*

Here, the religion of the Christian will be in harmony with the religion of the word of God. This will carry conviction to the hearts of skeptics and gainsayers. Thus we are epistles of Christ—thus true witnesses. Men will be constrained to behold, and admire, and take knowledge of us. Christ will be honored, &c. "We will go with you," &c.

Let the subject,

1. *Lead to self-examination.*

See what spirit you are of. Is it like Christ's? Does it respond to his?

2. *Seek after an excellent spirit.*

Strive for it—pray for it. Look with an eye of faith on the Redeemer. Let that mind be also in you, which was in Christ Jesus.

3. *Our future condition will be that which will be congenial to our spirits.*

Ignorant, proud, polluted, there will be no

place in God's dominions, suited to us, except hell—utterly unfit for heaven—could not enjoy it. Oh, then seek the renewal of your hearts. Pray as David did—"Create in me a clean heart," &c. Hear the words of eternal life in the gospel, and believe with your hearts, &c.

CCVI.—THE CHARACTER GIVEN OF DANIEL BY HIS ENEMIES.

"Then said these men, We shall not find any occasion against this Daniel, except we find it against him concerning the law of his God."—*Dan.* vi. 5.

Of all the encomiums ever passed on man by his enemies, our text contains one of the most striking and illustrious.

Daniel was one of the lineal descendants of David, and one of the most eminent godly men of the Jewish dispensation. His character, as presented in the Scriptures, is not marred by one instance of conduct unworthy of his holy profession. He shines in Scripture as a brilliant holy star of the very first magnitude; yet his excellences did not exempt him from envy, hatred, and persecution. Exalted by God, and favored by men, we see how a base attempt is devised, if possible, to effect his ruin; ver. 1 to the text.

I do not now enter on the subsequent parts of his life.

Let us look at him in the light in which his enemies portray him; and,

Then let me show you the excellences of such a character; and,

Urge you to its attainment.

I. *Let us look at Daniel in the light in which his enemies portray him.*

And here let me notice, that the basis of his character was,

1. *Sound religious principle.*

He knew God—adored him—loved him. Gave him the faithful homage of his heart, and the consecrated energies of his life. Not a cold profession, not half-hearted, &c.; but fully devoted to God. Here was the foundation on which his excellent character rested. As the result of this, he was celebrated,

2. *For the excellency of his spirit.*

Verse 3. His spirit was in unison with his religious principles. A noble, elevated spirit. Much depends on our spirit. An intelligent, kind, candid, and moderate spirit. Now Daniel had this. A spirit that com-

mended itself to all who knew him. He was distinguished,

3. *For his conscientious self-denial.*

Not a man of appetite—not a flesh pamperer. A beautiful instance is given of this: see chap. i. 3, 4, and 8.

Now here was an erect, hardy, self-denying servant of God, who could keep from his lips the sparkling wine-cup—and deny himself the luxurious viands, &c.

Then observe,

4. *His devoted patriotism.*

His self-denial was grounded on this. He would not be rejoicing and feasting, while his countrymen were in exile and adversity. And during all the changes of his eventful life, he never forgat his nation, his people, and his God. An intelligent, moral, religious love of country, is the only true patriotism. With this, observe,

5. *He was faithful in all his offices and duties.*

He did not deceive those who had placed confidence in him. His high station he honorably fulfilled. Faithful to God, he was not less so to man; verses 4, 5.

He was prompt, constant, careful, and faithful. Such, then, was Daniel, even as conceded by his enemies.

Let me,

II. *Show you the excellences of such a character.*

Here, my task is most easy and light; for observe,

1. *It is in harmony both with the laws of God and man.*

God requires this to meet his claims,—obedience and love to him. Then it is equally demanded as the essential element of morality between man and man.

2. *It is the highest recommendation of religion.*

Better than discussing the polemics of religion. Better than modes of worship. Here is holy principle—here is unblamable practice. Here religious forms and its actings are in harmony. Faith is exhibited by the works, — exemplification of Christ's command,—"Let your light so shine," &c. May I not add,

3. *It is the only true source of solid peace and enjoyment to the mind.*

Such a religion as Daniel's we must possess, if we are to be really happy. Nothing else will suffice. With this righteousness, there will be peace and joy in the Holy Ghost. Then it only remains,

III. *That I urge it on your attainment.*

An unblamable conduct like this, we urge,

1. *For its own sake.*

Like its Author, it is all *light*—all lovely —all benevolent! This is the pearl of great price,—The highest standard of excellence— the true glory of man.

I urge it,

2. *For the influence it will give you.*

In your family—shop—neighborhood— intercourse with the world, &c. In the church, and in fact, everywhere. It will give you moral power everywhere.

3. *For the final felicity it will secure.*

I do not overlook the present adversities, and opposition of ungodly men. See it in Daniel's history, &c. Yet, hear Christ's address—" Seek ye first," &c. Hear the apostle, " Godliness is profitable," &c. And there are the rewards of eternity,—the unfading crown of eternal life! &c.

In conclusion,

1. *I urge this religious excellency on those who are not religious at present.*

2. *Its close imitation by all God's people.*

3. *The provisions for its attainment are full and complete.*

The word, the Spirit, and the means of grace.

CCVII.—DANIEL PRAYING AS USUAL.

" Now when Daniel knew that the writing was signed, he went into his house; and his windows being open in his chamber towards Jerusalem, he kneeled upon his knees three times a day, and prayed, and gave thanks before his God, as he did aforetime."—*Dan.* vi. 10.

How often has it been verified that they who will live godly, shall suffer persecution! The way to the crown has been ever by the cross. In all ages, truth has had to be bought. A long train of facts fully illustrate and confirm this. We might begin with Abel, and come down to the end of the Acts of the Apostles.

Our text contains one very striking instance of the moral integrity, and self-denial, and holy courage, of an eminently wise and good man.

Observe,

I. *The writing referred to.*

II. *The course Daniel pursued.*

And,

III, *The principles on which he acted.*

I. *The writing referred to.*

Now here are several things that must be noticed.

1. *The envy of the presidents and princes.* Verses 1, 2, 3, 4.

But Daniel's integrity thwarted them in their purposes of hatred. At length they are constrained to testify this; verse 5. What a testimony! How honorable to Daniel, and the religion he avowed!

Notice,

2. *The conspiracy formed.*

They are determined to bring even the excellences of Daniel to bear on his overthrow; ver. 6, 7. Here was the result of their diabolical plot. The king was against their design. And Daniel was walking on in the integrity of his heart.

3. *The decree ratified.*

Having persuaded Darius to assent to the decree being signed, they saw their whole scheme ready to effect their diabolical purpose. The signing of it rendered it irrevocable; ver. 12, last clause.

Here, then, Daniel was at once within the drag of their malevolent and ruinous net. It was soon revealed to Daniel, and he saw at once the perilous condition in which he was placed. He perceived the whole matter. Fidelity to God and conscience would necessarily involve the violation of the decree that had been signed.

Observe,

II. *The course Daniel pursued.*

Now, here let us just consider what he might have done.

(1.) He might have given up his religious profession altogether. How many have done this, rather than brave persecution, or lose worldly advantages! Or,

(2.) He might have satisfied himself with secret religious services. Cherished the inward spirit of piety. Prayed in private, &c. Or,

(3.) He might have used means to avoid detection. Closed his window; or got a thick blind before it; or prayed during the night season.

But notice what he did do.

1. *He prayed, and gave thanks as before.*

No religion without these. One the breath of the soul, the other the fragrant incense of the spirit. Prayer and thanks. The one before the other. The two in company. Neither to be neglected,—kept up, and on together.

2. *He regarded these services as often as before.*

Three times a day. Probably at sunrise, and noon, and sunset. Many pious Jews observed these seasons of devotion. Ps. lv. 17.

Now, constancy and frequency of prayer are most important. We need it. It is the time of spiritual refreshment. If the body requires three meals a day, should not we feed the soul as often? But the spirit of constant prayer is the main thing. "Praying always," &c. "Pray without ceasing," &c. Daniel attended to his devotional exercises as often as before, and at the usual seasons.

3. *He regarded these services in the same place, and under the same circumstances as before.*

He went into his house, and his windows being opened, &c., he directed his face towards Jerusalem, the Holy City, the once far favored residence of Deity. The place to which the Messiah should come, &c. See also 2 Chron. vi. 36–38. His window was opened—not for ostentation—but, that there might be no intervening object between his eyes and the land of his love and religious devotedness. He "kneeled." A posture of body exceeding appropriate for devotional exercises; especially in the domestic circle, or in the secret chamber. And he did all this just as had been his wont and custom to do. Notice,

III. *The principles on which he acted.*

He exhibited,

1. *An unfaltering, pre-eminent attachment to religious duty.*

All duties are involved in religion. Duty to parents—masters—kings, &c. But if they come between God and us, God's claims must be first. He must be obeyed, at all risks. Religion can yield nothing—knows no compromise, &c.

He exhibited,

2. *Unwavering faith in God.*

He knew God was supreme, and all-sufficient! He knew he was above all earthly creatures. Therefore he believed in God, and cast all his care upon him.—Ventured to trust all he was, and all he had, to him. Oh, yes! it was strong living faith that operated and raised Daniel to this state of heroic resolution and constancy.

He exhibited,

3. *A readiness to risk all for his soul's salvation.*

He feared not the disgrace of an earthly king. He feared not bodily suffering. He feared not a violent and cruel death. But he feared to grieve God—to forsake the Most High—to risk his soul's salvation, by compromise, timidity, and submission to human authority, in matters of religion.

Learn,—

1. The true and noble spirit of real piety.

2. The trials the godly may experience.

3. The course, by the Divine grace, they should pursue.

CCVIII.—DANIEL'S PERIL AND DELIVERANCE.

"Then said Daniel unto the king, O king, live forever. My God hath sent his angel, and hath shut the lions' mouths, that they have not hurt me: forasmuch as before him innocency was found in me; and also before thee, O king, have I done no hurt."—*Dan.* vi. 21, 22.

WE have seen the holy noble course Daniel pursued. How he adhered, without the least varying, to his godly principles and practice. How he honored God, by the most uncompromising steadfastness, in the midst of imminent peril. No instance of noble-minded magnanimity is, or can be, superior to this. It is religion in its mightiest triumphs! and though Daniel had perished, as to this body and this life, he would have remained an immortal instance of true greatness, real goodness. But let us now enter on the narrative of his peril and deliverance.

Observe,

I. *The occasion of his peril.*

It was his steadfast piety; ver. 10.

Now his enemies knew him so well, that they were sure that they could ensnare him. Hence they assembled, and found Daniel praying as before; ver. 11. Never had he prayed under such circumstances before.

Then they refer it to the king.

Accuse Daniel; ver. 12, 13.

The king is sore displeased. He sees the plot. Loves the excellent Daniel. Sincerely endeavors to save him; ver. 14. No doubt he wished to do this according to the laws. He reasoned, doubtless, with his accusers, &c. Surely he regretted the hasty edict he had issued. Daniel's enemies demanded the fulfilment of the penalty—being fully set on his ruin; ver. 15.

Then observe,

II. *The peril itself.*

It was the imminent exposure of his life. Look at verse 7. To be cast into a den of lions—hungry, roaring lions.

This was one of the cruel and barbarous modes of putting criminals to death. The godly were often thus destroyed. From this danger they had no way of escape. In the mighty amphitheatre, the victim, sometimes by his heroism and strength, so excited sympathy among the cruel spectators, that he might be released. But here was a deep, dark den: the raging lions waiting for their prey; and the poor victim was let down or cast into their midst, and was in a few minutes torn to pieces, and devoured.

To this danger Daniel was exposed. The decree had gone forth. Repeal was impossible. And the king at length yielded, and Daniel was cast into it.

Two things are to be noted here,—

(1.) The king's faith in Daniel's deliverance; ver. 16.

(2.) And the process of security against human help, adopted; ver. 17.

The king retires to his palace fasting, and spent the night in sleepless anxiety; ver. 18. Early he arises, and hastens to the den of lions; ver. 19. He cries out with intense distress and fear; for though he had exhibited remarkable faith, yet fears rushed across his mind,—" O Daniel, servant of the living God," &c.; ver. 20.

This leads us to consider,

III. *Daniel's deliverance from peril.*

Here is the king at the den of the lions, crying to Daniel, and immediately the well-known voice is heard; ver. 22. " My God hath sent his angel," &c.

The deliverance of Daniel,

1. *Was evidently supernatural.*

It was God's work—miraculous! Not according to the course of nature, but in direct opposition to it. Nothing but God's power could restrain the lions, and preserve Daniel.

It is stated that an angel was the instrument of it. He often employed these shining ones to deliver his saints. What a strange association in the lion's den, the hungry, raging lions—Daniel their intended victim—and the shining angel in his brightness, and with the commission of God, to close the mouths of the wild beasts.

But Daniel's deliverance,

2. *Was complete.*

Not injured at all. Wild beasts around; but the angel of God with him, so that even his heart failed not; but God kept both body and soul in perfect peace.

But notice,

IV. *The subsequent results of the deliverance of Daniel.*

1. *Daniel's piety is signally honored.*

Verse 22.

Daniel had honored God, and God fulfils his own word, and honors Daniel. Attests the value of godliness, and the truth of that religion which Daniel had professed.

2. *Wickedness was publicly and awfully punished.*

The enemies of religion and Daniel, were now offered in sacrifice to the furious wild beasts. Their own envy and sinful devices, now brought destruction on themselves; verse 24. Skepticism may protest against the justice of the sentence, in reference to their wives and children. I only reply, that that which so appals us in a case like this, is taking place daily, in the events of the world's history. The plague—the pestilence—the earthquake, just do the same with children and with parents. We are connected so closely, that in a thousand respects, the innocent child has to bear the effects of the crimes of his guilty parents.

3. *The majesty and glory of God were proclaimed.*

Verse 25. The character and glory of the true God were thus proclaimed. God elicited good from evil; and made the wrath of man to praise him.

Learn from the whole,—

1. *The importance of religious decision.*

A good faith must be professed, and maintained at all hazards.

2. *The advantages of true godliness.*

It is profitable unto all things, &c. But even if men suffer and die for religion, it is everlasting gain.

3. *Who will consecrate themselves now to the Lord.*

CCIX.—DANIEL'S PRAYER FOR JERUSALEM.

" O my God, incline thine ear, and hear; open thine eyes, and behold our desolations, and the city which is called by thy name; for we do not present our supplications before thee for our righteousness, but for thy great mercies. O Lord, hear; O Lord, forgive; O Lord, hearken and do; defer not, for thine own sake, O my God: for thy

city and thy people are called by thy name."—
Dan. ix. 18, 19.

DANIEL was signally eminent in three respects :—

As a man of personal holiness.

As a distinguished patriot,—a true lover
of his country.

As an ardent lover of the Jewish faith,
and the public services of religion.

We might long expatiate on the various
striking traits of excellency, which were so
beautifully exhibited in each and all of these
great departments of his pre-eminent piety.

My text contains the mournful, yet fervent supplications of his soul, for the holy
city ; and contains just those emotions which
should ever characterize our prayers, on behalf of the church of God.   Now Jerusalem
of old,

Typified the social character of the church.

It typified the visibility of the church.

It typified the religious public exercises of
the church.

It typified the security and permanency
of the church.

It typified the afflictions of the church.

It typified God's interest in the church.

But I pass over all these points, and consider the prayer of Daniel as a beautiful
model, well worthy of our imitation, when
seeking the prosperity of Zion.

Observe,

I. *The desolations asserted.*

II. *The supplications presented.*   And,

III. *The grounds or reasons assigned.*

I. *The desolations asserted.*

Jerusalem in ruins. Temple destroyed.
The people of God in captivity.

Our present causes of mourning in reference to the church of God, may include,

1. *The spirit of prevailing formality.*

So many at ease. So many indifferent.
So many inactive. So few living for Zion's
weal, &c.

2. *The signs of evident weakness.*

Want of moral power and spiritual energy. Not telling on the masses at home.
Not making rapid progress on the heathen
abroad. Often apparently behind the spirit
of the age, and the movements of the times.
Her position often suspicious.

3. *The prevailing spirit of partyism and
denominationalism.*

More zeal for this, than for primitive
Christianity.   Proselytism more common
than conversion, &c.   Greater love and
union wanted.   More of Christ, and less of
men—more of the Bible, and less of creeds.
The original weapons are only mighty—the
word of God and prayer.   The original fire
essential,—fire of celestial zeal and love.
The original spirit of true Christian simplicity, and not a worldly religion.   Zion's
sins have thus eclipsed her, degraded her,
polluted her.   Notice,

II. *The supplications presented.*

1. *The gracious attention of God is entreated.*

"O my God, incline thine ear," &c. Ver.
19.   O Lord, hear, &c.   "O thou that hearest prayer," &c.   God is supposed to be offended, and to have departed.   He is now
implored to return, &c.   All in vain unless
God hear.   Yet how condescending, gracious, and long-suffering, &c., for God to do
so.

2. *His merciful inspection is sought.*

"Open thine eyes and behold," &c.   Are
we prepared for this active searching ordeal ?
Eyes of purity, as flames, &c.   If so, who
could stand ?   Are we that preach ready for
this ?   As to our subjects, studies, motives,
objects ? &c.   Are the officers of the church ?
Members of the church ?   As to our services, duties ? &c.   Unless in mercy, it
would be our undoing, our ruin, &c.   But
if humbled, abased, penitential, reforming,
it would be our salvation !

3. *God's interfering help is solicited.*

"O Lord, hearken and do."   Not what
we ought to do, or can do : God never does
this,

(1.) But do all *for* us, we cannot do, &c.

(2.) Do all *in* us, we need.   Work thine
own work, &c.   Fill us with thyself—thy
spirit—thy zeal, &c.

(3.) Do *by* us what thy church ought to
do in the world.   Use us, &c.   Qualify, and
then employ us, &c.

4. *The instant aid of the Lord is entreated.*

"Defer not."   Our state has been too
long sad and doleful, and we are waxing
worse.   Our sorrow and wretchedness are
great.   Souls are perishing in crowds—the
night of death is coming ; O Lord, defer
not, &c.   We should ever expect present
blessings,—a present salvation,—present reviving,—present comfort, &c.   Then consider,

III. *The grounds or reasons assigned.*

Here Daniel proves himself a successful
pleader.

1. *He repudiates all self-righteousness.*

"Not for our righteousness," &c.   How

essential to be sound here. All must be renounced, &c. Self-crucified, &c. "God forbid," &c.

2. *He appeals to God's name.*

"Called by thy name," &c. Name of God on his cause, and in it. God identified with it. God's honor, fidelity, &c. Its origin and progress, &c. How applicable to God's church.

3. *He pleads God's great mercies.*

How great! Who can tell? In magnitude—in number—in extent—in duration—in height, breadth, length, &c. We have this especially exhibited in the face of Jesus Christ—in the gospel, &c.

4. *He pleads God's own sake.*

His cause and his purposes.—His cause and his dispensations.—His cause and his promises.—His cause and his glory; all connected, &c. The great end of all God's doings, &c.

APPLICATION.

1. *Do we thus pray for the church?*

We ought. It needs it. It should have it.

2. *Let such prayers be accompanied with right action.*

Consecration to God's cause. Activity, labor, self-denial.

3. *Love to the cause of Christ and personal religious prosperity are inseparable.*

They that love thee *shall* prosper; not *may*, but shall.

4. *Urge upon sinners to pray for themselves, and to begin now.*

CCX.—JONAH AND THE STORM.

"But the Lord sent out a great wind into the sea, and there was a mighty tempest in the sea, so that the ship was like to be broken. Then the mariners were afraid, and cried every man unto his god, and cast forth the wares that were in the ship into the sea, to lighten it of them. But Jonah was gone down into the sides of the ship; and he lay, and was fast asleep."—*Jonah* i. 4, 5.

THE life of Jonah is a remarkable proof of the infirmity of good men, and the impartiality of the sacred writers.

Jonah's character stands out in all its points of weakness and moral unloveliness. Petulant, wayward, disobedient, he endeavors to run from the task of duty, and way of self-denial. Mortified by what should have yielded him pleasure, and that of the highest kind, he expresses his anger that the judgments of God were not developed; and yet this is the book that skeptics say is a false and spurious production of priests, for the sustaining of priestcraft, which so distinctly and fairly reveals all the sad blemishes of this ancient Prophet.

But our subject is the "storm," which Jonah experienced on this occasion, and its moral lessons.

I. *Man is exposed both to natural and moral storms.*

Tempests at sea, most sublime and awful. None more so than the sudden and fierce storms of the Mediterranean. There are land storms, as well as those by sea. The desolating tornado. The hot sand tempests of the desert, &c.

But there are moral tempests—storms within. When the lightnings of the divine truth, and thunders of the divine wrath, roll terribly over the region of the mind—arousing fears, scaring the conscience, &c. Sometimes the two come together, as in the case of Belshazzar, jailer, &c. Sudden visitations, &c.; so the text.

II. *How impotent is man amid the storms to which he is exposed.*

What can he do against the commotions and tempests of nature? His skill, or his power, what is it? As in the text. So in moral storms, the difficulties are equally formidable. What can he do? Where go? What means use? How little—weak—and helpless is man at best.

III. *In storms and dangers men flee instinctively to their gods.*

There is an immediate rush to the spiritual depths of the religious nature, for relief, &c. There is such a part of man's nature. It is seen and heard in the supplications, glances, mutterings, &c., of pagan tribes—ferocious hordes—intellectual metaphysical Hindoos or Chinese. It is like the winds; it blows on every shore, island, continent, sea, forest, &c. It has been exhibited by intelligent men of infidel sects, when in peril. So now, the mariners in the text.

Now this appeal to their gods, seems to settle the universal feeling of men, in reference to guilt and peril—helplessness and desire for safety.

IV. *To escape destruction men will make the greatest sacrifice.*

In the text—"Cast their wares into the sea." The one supreme object now was deliverance; at any rate—at any cost. Now this is seen in reference to the soul. As in duties, rites, penances, reformations, &c. Large sums left for the repose of their souls, &c. Men in religion may do all this, and do it in vain. This is not God's way of saving men. So it was in this case; the storm abated not. Deliverance is not by human might, &c. All meritorious acts on the part of men in vain,—can efface no sin, &c.; atone for no evil, &c.

V. *Men only can be saved through atoning blood.*

This impression is almost as universal as the world. Hence the victims, human and divine, that have been offered. Hence the sailors desire to throw overboard the sinner. Hence, too, Jonah's statement; vers. 11, 12. Now it was so. So in reference to the deliverance of men from sin and death. It behooved Christ to suffer, &c. He bare our sins, &c. He is the Lamb of God, &c.; the great atoning sacrifice. We are saved entirely through him. "Be it known unto you," &c.

VI. *The personal realization of this truth brings peace to the soul.*

As it brought a calm: ver. 15. So if I believe in Christ, as the surety, I am no longer anxious, tortured, &c. I no longer tremble, &c. The sentence is repealed, &c.

"Believing, we rejoice,
To see the curse remove," &c.

VII. *A believing realization of deliverance will produce a right state of heart and life towards God.*

Ver. 16. Love, gratitude, reverence, obedience, must follow precious faith, &c. Not as the root of religion, but the branches. Here is the great mistake—Satan's lie, as to the way of the soul's deliverance. No salvation, but by the sacrifice of Christ. All the wares may be thrown over in vain—ship may be lightened—but the storm rages. Nothing will do in place of Christ, and faith in him.

APPLICATION.

Let us ascertain our true state and condition, while God's wrath is revealed against sin.

1. *Who are asleep?*

Careless,—self-secure, &c. How many here? Let the mariners arouse us: "What meanest thou, O sleeper!" v. 6.

2. *Who are anxious for safety?*

Praying, crying, seeking, &c. Here is

deliverance! the atonement has been made, &c.: Matt. i. 38.

CCXI.—GOOD OLD SIMEON.

"And, behold, there was a man in Jerusalem, whose name was Simeon; and the same man was just and devout, waiting for the consolation of Israel; and the Holy Ghost was upon him. And it was revealed unto him by the Holy Ghost, that he should not see death, before he had seen the Lord's Christ."—*Luke* ii. 25-30.

THERE are two or three scenes most beautiful and interesting in nature—

The setting sun, going down in a clear sky, in all his magnificence and glory. He then appears larger; and the whole horizon is lit up with his declining beams, and setting grandeur.

The field ripe for the sickle. The golden waving corn, with its teeming abundance, inviting the active hand of the reaper.

The ship in full sail, within sight of her destined port. The sea crossed, the toils and perils of the voyage over, and friends on shore, ready to hail the crew and passengers to their native shores.

In the death of the aged Christian, all these interesting features are beautifully exhibited. As a moral sun: he now sets on earth, to arise and shine in the sphere of glory. As a shock of corn: he is ripe and ready for the garner of eternal life. As a gallant vessel: he has neared the shores of immortality; and an abundant entrance is about to be ministered into the haven of celestial blessedness.

Such was the character and circumstances of good old Simeon, as exhibited in the text. Let us consider,

His religious character.

His distinguished privileges; and,

His spiritual rapture.

I. *His religious character.*

Here observe,

1. *His evangelical faith.*

"Waiting for the consolation of Israel," that is, for the Messiah—the Saviour. He believed in the Prophecies—Promises—Types, &c., relating to the Messiah. It excited his desires and hopes, and influenced his character. "He waited."

2. *He was righteous in life.*

"Just." A man of integrity and uprightness. No religion without this. "Do ye unto others," &c. Thus before God and with men he was unblamable.

3. *He was of a devout spirit.*

A man of religious emotion—of worship and prayer.

These three are ever essential to true saving piety. Here is right principle—upright conduct—and spiritual emotion.

Observe,

II. *His distinguished privileges.*

1. *His supernatural gift.*

"The Holy Ghost was upon him." As formerly on the prophets. It had ceased for nearly 400 years, but was now specially imparted to Simeon.

2. *His express revelation.*

It was revealed that before he saw death, he should see the Saviour—Jehovah's Christ; the anointed—the Lord.

3. *His delightful interview.*

The period had now arrived. Simeon was led by the Spirit into the temple, &c. Then the holy child, Jesus, was brought in. Oh, think of the place, and the meeting! and how God brought it about!

4. *His reception of Jesus.*

"Saw him." "Took him in his arms," &c. Thus faith and love receive Christ. It is not Christ in the manger, or on the cross, or in heaven; but in the arms of faith and love, that can save us, and make us happy. This leads us, then,

III. *To his holy rapture.*

Observe the particulars of it:

1. *Gratitude to God.*

"Blessed God." Godly joy is ever grateful joy. His soul rose in holy exultation to the fountain of his privileges and blessings.

2. *His desired severance from the world.*

"Lord, now lettest," &c. All the ends of life he felt to be accomplished. World's attraction gone. Often persons wish to live for this and that end. The warrior—the statesman—the philosopher—the merchant —the parent. How imbecile, in general, these desires!

3. *His hallowed desires for glory.*

He longed now for the rest, and the bliss, of a better world. He had attained,

4. *The consummation of all his hopes.*

"For mine eyes have seen thy salvation," &c. Abraham saw Christ's day afar off.— Jacob died waiting for it.—David singing of it.—Good old Simeon realized it.

Observe in Simeon's history,—

1. *How lovely piety is in old age.*

2. *What a blissful conclusion of life.*

3. *What a meetness for eternity.*

4. *What a model for imitation.*

Seek the anointing of the Spirit.—Hold fast the Saviour by faith and love.—And be found ever waiting and hoping for the eternal state.

CCXII.—JOHN THE BAPTIST.

"Verily I say unto you, Among them that are born of women, there hath not risen a greater than John the Baptist: notwithstanding, he that is least in the kingdom of heaven is greater than he."—*Matt.* xi. 11.

THE life of the Baptist was full of striking incident, and therefore is well adapted, both to furnish instruction and edification to our minds. It will not be possible, however, in one discourse, to do more than give a rapid view of the main features of his history and character. Observe, then,

I. *That he was the subject of inspired prediction.*

See Malachi iii. 1. Now here he is predicted of under the title of "Jehovah's Messenger"—especially sent forth to be the harbinger of the Messiah. As such, he was to prepare the way of the Lord, and act as a herald to the world's Messiah!

II. *His birth was extraordinary and supernatural.*

His parents were the godly Zacharias and Elizabeth. Both were aged, and his mother past the time of bearing children. Luke i. 5–7. God sent a special messenger to announce the designed event. Hence, as Zacharias ministered before the Lord, &c., "an angel of the Lord appeared," &c. Verse 8–17. It will be seen, by reading the inspired narrative, that he was the cousin of our blessed Lord.

His name was given him, evidently, under supernatural direction. The name John signifies—"the gift," or "the grace," or "the mercy of the Lord;" and was exceedingly appropriate, as applied to John. Observe,

III. *The spiritual excellences of his character.*

These we may fully learn from the prediction given of him by the angel—"He was to be filled with the Holy Ghost;" Luke i. 15. Sanctified by God from the womb.

Hence he was eminently holy in his own person. A pure vessel for the Master's special use.

(1.) It was evident that he was to be particularly distinguished for seriousness of spirit. The fear of God was to be the great predominant feature of his moral character.

(2.) He was characterized for great self-denial. His dress—his style of living—his abstinence from wine and luxuries ; verse 15.

(3.) He was to be also eminently humble. He was to be the servant. Not to affect pomp,—not to glorify himself. Hence the striking evidence of his modesty, in hesitating to baptize the Redeemer ; and confessing that he was but the voice, sent to prepare the way of the Lord. John i. 19. Notice,

IV. *The characteristics of his work and ministry.*

Look at him,

1. *As a preacher.*

He stands forth eminently in this office. His subjects were,

(1.) Repentance. His ministry said,—Awake to the great concerns of religion,—turn from the world to God,—hear Jehovah's voice,—change your minds, and with it, your lives ;—for so the word repentance signifies.

(2.) Faith in the coming kingdom. "For the kingdom of heaven," &c. The reign of God by the advent of the Lord's anointed is at hand. Prepare for it. Prepare to welcome it. To be blessed by it.

"Hark the glad sound, the Saviour comes,
    The Saviour promised long ;
Let every heart prepare a throne,
    And every voice a song."

As a preacher,

(1.) He chiefly carried on his ministry in the open air. In the wilderness of Judea. Here, with the arch of heaven for the dome of his temple, and the wild scenery of nature around him, he published the will of God to the people.

(2.) His ministry was most faithful. He dealt faithfully with the souls of his hearers: Matt. iii. 7, 8.

(3.) His ministry was earnest and devoted. He is described as one " crying." Acting as a herald—lifting up his voice. Dwelling with life and ardor on the great subjects of his ministry. He spared not, but cried out

and caused the people to know their sins, and Jerusalem her iniquities.

2. *As a baptizer.*

He not only preached, but he received, and formed into a distinct class, those who received his doctrine and repented of their sins. Hence the disciples of John were baptized in the Jordan, as a token of their repentance and faith in the coming Messiah. It seems that multitudes thus professed their change of heart, and their expectation of the coming of the Messiah. Matt. iii. 5, 6. Observe,

5. *The circumstances of his eventful death.*

1. *His ministry was short.*

He labored ardently, and earnestly, and devotedly ; but the whole was probably little, if any more, than three years.

2. *His death was connected with the fidelity of his office.*

He was held in general and profound esteem and reverence by the people. Herod, the Tetrarch of Judea, had heard him, and perhaps more than once. Mark vi. 20. It is clear, too, that he had consulted him in reference to his purpose of marrying Herodias, his brother Philip's wife ; and John's faithful testimony is recorded, when the preacher said, "It is not lawful for thee to have her," &c. This was the direct link connected with his death.

3. *He died a martyr's violent death.*

See Matt. xiv. 6, &c. There was the festive scene in Herod's palace—a birth-day banquet. The company of the lords, high captains, &c. The dancing of Herodias' daughter. Herod's infatuated delight.—His absurd engagement, and imbecile oath.—And then the rankling revenge of the odious Herodias. At length the king's demand for the Baptist's head—and its immediate execution.

Thus died the holy, devoted servant of God—the herald of the Saviour, and one of the greatest among those born of women.

APPLICATION.

1. *Let the theme lead us to meditate on the occasion of John's death.*

Matt. xiv. 12, 13. Here is matter for solemn reflection—for grave consideration.

2. *Learn the connection oftentimes between duties and sacrifices.*

John might have evaded, and saved his head. He lost his life, and saved the truth, his conscience, his religion, and his soul. "He that loseth his life," &c.

3. *Learn to imitate John in his noble and godly excellences.*

4. *Christians may rejoice in the pre-eminency of their privileges, even over his.*

CCXIII.—HISTORY OF PETER.

[NO. I.]

"He first findeth his own brother Simon, and saith unto him, We have found the Messias, which is, being interpreted, the Christ. And he brought him to Jesus. And when Jesus beheld him, he said, Thou art Simon the son of Jona: thou shalt be called Cephas, which is by interpretation, A stone."—*John* i. 41, 42.

PETER's life and character occupy a large portion of the narrative and historical parts of the New Testament. His character stands forth very prominently, both as a devoted Christian, and a distinguished laborer in the kingdom of Jesus. In taking a brief sketch of his life, we may notice,

I. *His introduction to Jesus.*

It is supposed that he had been one of John's disciples, and was therefore waiting, in ardent hope, for the coming of the Messiah. It is evident this was the case with his brother Andrew; see ver. 35. Andrew having received Christ, as the expected Saviour, immediately findeth his brother, and communicates the glad tidings to him; ver. 14. How much is comprehended in those words! Here was indeed the pearl of peerless price. God's unspeakable gift. He not only relates the joyous tidings, but takes Peter to Christ. Ver. 42. "Brought him to Jesus." From love to both. How excellent the conduct of Andrew! how worthy of imitation! Should not all brethren, parents, friends, do the same?

Observe,

II. *Christ's recognition of Peter.*

Thou art Simon, or Symeon. A very common Jewish name. And he mentions his parentage—the son of Jona. Here Jesus showed his knowledge of Peter. He then adds, thou shalt be called Cephas; the Syriac name for Peter; and both signifying "Rock;" doubtless by this intending to show the energy, firmness, and perseverance he should display, as one of his most illustrious disciples.

It is scarcely necessary that I should remind you of Peter's original condition and calling. He was a fisherman, and probably a native of Bethsaida. No illustrious origin —no worldly glory or influence—no learning or intellectual distinction! A plain, humble, laborious fisherman. It has been supposed that he was one of the oldest of the disciples; and that he was born, at least, seventeen years before our blessed Lord. Observe, when called to the discipleship, he was engaged in his worldly pursuit: Matt. iv. 18. He and his brother are called by Christ, and they at once left all, and followed him. The terms of the call were striking —"Follow me, and I will make you fishers of men." The same calling spiritualized. The world, the sea. The gospel, the net. Souls, the fish. Their salvation, the end. Both labors of toil, and self-denial, and peril. Consider Peter,

III. *As elevated to the apostolic office.*

Matt. x. 1, 2. Here we find the precedence given to Peter. He is not only one of the highest officers in the church of Christ, but the very first of them; and this supremacy is exhibited in several striking events in his life. Not as having power over the other apostles, but being distinguished above them. As an apostle, he was to bear witness for Christ. He was to learn of the Saviour, concerning the laws, &c., of his kingdom. He was to preach the gospel of the kingdom. He was endowed with extraordinary gifts and miraculous powers. Moreover, as the first apostle, he was to be the *rock* and basis of the Christian kingdom.

This leads us,

IV. *To his good confession, and the distinction conferred upon him by Christ.*

See the account of this, Matt. xvi. 13. A more clear and full confession of Christ could not be made. How striking the terms employed: "Christ"—the anointed of Heaven—"Son of the living God," &c. Christ eulogizes the confession, and immediately distinguishes Peter; ver. 18. Now, we all know the perversion of this passage by Romanists. But have not Protestants gone to the other extreme? They have made the confession, the rock. Christ says it of Peter —not of his confession. The meaning is obvious. The Divine kingdom must have a beginning. Peter was the first stone, laid at the base. The first preacher of it. Had the keys to open the door and admit the

Jews, and afterwards opened the door to the Gentiles,—in the case of Cornelius.

Thus Peter was the rock—not meritoriously or efficiently—but in being the first agent in the new kingdom. Here is nothing to support Romish superstition; and nothing to produce Protestant anxiety for the truth. How distinguished does this servant of Jesus now appear—how excellent his character— how glorious his office—how high his commendation! But as the highest hills are often surrounded by the deepest valleys, we are now called to see Peter,

V. *As exhibiting very imperfect views of Christ and his kingdom.*

How good was his confession, &c.; yet doubtless, with the rest of his countrymen, he anticipated a kingdom visible, powerful; and arrayed in earthly magnificence and splendor. He did not see the traits by which it should be distinguished. Hence, when Jesus began to unfold his humiliation and sufferings, and to predict his death, &c., we see the ignorance and infirmities of Peter elicited. Matt. xvi. 21.

Now, observe the personal peculiarities of Peter's mind and temper :—ardent, earnest, impetuous, hasty. No doubt love and zeal had much to do with it. But it was irreverent in Peter to rebuke Christ. It was daring to say that Christ's own declaration should not be fulfilled. It drew upon Peter the severe reproof of the Saviour. Christ styles him "Satan," or adversary. Thou now speakest as an adversary. "Get thee behind me ;" desist from thy remarks ; thou art an offence, &c. "Thou savorest not"— hast not drank into the true spirit of my religion ; yet ignorant and earthly.

Here, for the present, we will leave this distinguished servant of Jesus, having witnessed both his exaltation and depression. Having seen his noble spirit, and heard his good confession, and observed also his infirmity as a man. We have seen already in Peter,

1. *Much to admire and imitate.*

2. *And something to blame and pity.*

Let us copy the one, and avoid the other.

CCXIV.—HISTORY OF PETER.

[NO. II.]

"Then Simon Peter answered him, Lord, to whom shall we go ? thou hast the words of eternal life."—*John* vi. 68.

WE parted with Peter at a time when he had brought on himself the severe reproof of our divine Lord. But like the sun under the cloud, we see him soon come forth again, with increased light and beauty.

Christ had been very faithfully discoursing on his own character, and the mysteries of his kingdom. Many who had followed him now abandoned him, and ceased to walk with his disciples. "Then said Jesus, Will ye also go away ?" To which Peter replied in the text : "Lord, to whom," &c.

Let us on this occasion notice,

I. *Some of the peculiar traits in the religious character of Peter.*

Of these we cannot fail to see,

1. *His marked humility.*

Two instances are on record, where this self-abasement of spirit was peculiarly displayed. On the miraculous draught of fishes, as given by Luke, v. 1–8. And when Christ washed his disciples' feet ; John xiii. 3, &c. Hence he evinced the most profound reverence for the Saviour, and the deepest self-humiliation.

2. *His couragcous faith.*

See Matt. xiv. 25. We see a similar act after Christ's resurrection : John xxi. 3, &c. He was evidently distinguished for holy boldness, and believing determination. A similar display he gave, though it was rash and unadvised, when he drew forth his sword to defend the person of his Lord, on the night of his arrestment in the garden.

Observe,

3. *His entire heartedness in the cause of Jesus.*

His whole career shows this. No one can read the sacred pages of divine history, and doubt it. And how worthy is Christ's cause of this, and what honor it confers on those who evince it ! Christ and his kingdom absorbed the thoughts and emotions of this distinguished disciple.

Consider,

II. *The striking privileges of which he was the favored subject.*

It is probable that he witnessed all Christ's miracles. That he was one of the personal and most favored friends of Jesus. Christ addresses him in terms of marked familiarity, and conferred special favors. See Matth. xvii. 24, &c. Also, remember that he was one of the favored three, who only were present at the transfiguration—at the raising of the ruler's daughter—and when Christ endured the agony in the garden. But consider Peter,

III. *In his personal and spiritual defects.*

He was not distinguished for prudence and self-control. Much the subject of impulse,—with powerful passions,—easily excited,—not vigilant, &c. This weakness led him into the sin which formed the great blot on his religious character. Eager, enthusiastic, he had averred his readiness to die with Christ. He had been admonished as to the coming storm: Matth. xxvi. 31, &c. He had reiterated his resolution after this admonition; ver. 33. Christ then directly forewarned him, and predicted his fall, ver. 34; and Peter again affirmed his courage and constancy. He afterwards appeared ready to vindicate this resolution, in drawing his sword for Christ. But Jesus is apprehended. The disciples flee. Peter most likely with them. Then he rallies,—follows afar off,—witnessed Christ hurried before the high priest, &c.,—sat to see the end of the matter in the hall of the palace. Is interrupted, not publicly by the officers, but by a servant, and denies his Lord. Is asked again by another maid, and again denies Christ. And a third time by those who stand by; and then he curses and swears, that he knows not the man. How marvellous! how wicked! how weak is man! how deceitful the heart, &c.

Then notice Peter,

IV. *In his recovery, and reinstalment in his office.*

He had sinned basely, ungratefully, heinously. But it was precipitately. Not from an unsound affection, or insincere principles; but rashly and immediately.

(1.) But see, his heart is broken. Luke xxii. 61, &c. Christ looked on Peter. What that look implied! What it said, in condemnation! in pity! how effectual it was!

(2.) He seeks Christ at the sepulchre. Ran with John. But the young disciple first reaches the spot. John only looks in,—Peter descends into it; just like Peter's ardor: John xx. 1–6.

(3.) He is favorably included in the message of the angel, concerning Christ's resurrection. The angel said to the women, "Go tell his disciples, and tell Peter," &c. Mark xvi. 1–7.

(4.) He is positively restored to his Lord's favor, and the apostolic work. The manner of his recovery was instructive and affecting. "So when they had dined," John xxi. 15, &c.

Here then again we must pause, in the history of Peter.

1. *Let us earnestly seek to copy his excellences.*

These were many. His humility, ardor, zeal, faith, &c.

2. *Let us guard against his errors and sins.*

His rashness and impetuosity,—his presumption,—his unwatchfulness.

3. *Let the backslider be cheered by his recovery.*

What hope there is for all who have gone from the fold, &c. Finally we would say to all,—

"Beware of Peter's word,
Nor confidently say,
I never will deny thee, Lord;
But grant—I never may."

CCXV.—HISTORY OF PETER.

[NO. III.]

"Verily, verily, I say unto thee, When thou wast young, thou girdedst thyself, and walkedst whither thou wouldst; but when thou shalt be old, thou shalt stretch forth thy hands, and another shall gird thee, and carry thee whither thou wouldst not. This spake he, signifying by what death he should glorify God. And when he had spoken this, he saith unto him, Follow me."—*John* xxi. 18, 19.

WE now enter on that part of the history of Peter, subsequent to the resurrection of our blessed Lord. We have had him reinstated in his office and work. His commission is renewed, and he is called upon by Christ, to "feed both his sheep and lambs." It is not certain whether Christ intended more by the commission he gave Peter, than that he should supply the flock of believers with spiritual aliment, or whether he was specially designated as the apostle to the Jews, as Paul afterwards was to the Gentiles, or uncircumcision. But we purpose in this lecture to consider the apostle Peter, in the various striking spheres in which Divine providence placed him, in connection with his labors in the cause of Jesus.

Observe him, then,

I. *As acting ecclesiastically in calling the brethren to fill up the number of the apostleship.*

By the apostasy and awful end of Judas, a deficiency was made in the number of the apostles; Acts i. 15, &c. Here the qualifications of the apostle are distinctly stated; verses 21 and 22. We then find that by lot, in connection with solemn prayer, this important matter was settled.

Observe Peter,

II. *As opening the kingdom of heaven to the Jews on the day of pentecost, and also to the Gentiles.*

Pentecost signifies "fifty;" and this day was the fiftieth from the passover, and also from the death of Jesus.

Now Christ's promise of the Holy Spirit is ratified; Acts i. 4 to 8. Now for the first time was the gospel emphatically proclaimed. Now the declaration of Jesus is fulfilled. "Thus it was written," &c.: Luke xiv. 46, 47. Also the predictions of the Psalmist; 110th Ps. The preacher was Peter. The substance of his sermon is recorded in the 2d of Acts. The sermon was most powerful and convincing. It excited in their hearts a deep sense of guilt, remorse, and intense anxiety, what they should do. Peter then proclaimed Christ; ver. 37, 38. The door of the kingdom of heaven was now thrown wide open, and three thousand were the first-fruits gathered into it on this occasion.

Shortly after this we see Peter confirming his ministry by restoring, in connection with John, the lame man at the gate of the temple; Acts iii. 1–6, &c.; and in connection with the miracle, again preaching Christ to the people, from the 8th verse to the end of the chapter. See the opening of the Divine kingdom to the Gentiles, by Peter: Acts x. 44.

Observe Peter,

III. *In the presence of the high priest, and when nobly vindicating the character and work of Jesus.*

He had as yet been preaching to the mass; but now the ecclesiastical powers became aroused, and Peter and John were seized, and confined, and brought before them; Acts iv. 1, &c. Peter arises to defend himself, the brethren, and the work in which they were engaged: chap. iv. 7, 8, &c. How truthful, plain, searching, and telling, the address of Peter on this occasion. Observe Peter,

IV. *As pronouncing the divine sentence upon two avaricious professors.*

The grace of God was so mighty and constraining in its effects, that men became indifferent to their worldly goods and riches. Hence the account given; Acts iv. 33 to the end. There were two who desired to act thus with the rest, but whom love of lucre evidently rendered incapable of doing so. They only brought, therefore, a part of the produce, and kept back the rest. Here was gross and wicked hypocrisy, and lying to the Holy Ghost; Acts v. 1, &c. Peter, therefore, had to deliver the will of God, and pronounce the Divine malediction upon the guilty parties—first on Ananias, and then on Sapphira, who were both smitten with death, on this solemn and affecting occasion. Thus Peter, while proclaiming the blessings of salvation to the most guilty and atrocious sinners on their repentance and faith in Christ—had to declare the just displeasure of heaven, on the avarice and hypocrisy of vain professors. Observe Peter,

V. *Again, twice imprisoned for his master and the gospel's sake.*

There is one especial circumstance connected with these imprisonments. In each case the angel of the Lord delivered the apostles; Acts v. 17, &c. Hence Peter and his brethren were set at liberty, and were found early in the morning preaching the words of eternal life; ver. 19, &c. Peter's defence, on this occasion, presents a wondrous specimen of sound and truthful eloquence; and again he preached to the rulers, the doctrines of life and salvation, through Jesus Christ; ver. 29, &c.

The second imprisonment was effected by Herod, and refers to Peter alone. James the brother of John, and one of the most favored of the apostles, he had slain with the sword; and now Peter's death was determined upon also; Acts xii. 1, &c. But God had still more work for Peter to do. He put the state of Peter into the hearts of the saints, and prayer was made for him continually. The next day, was resolved upon as the day of his execution. Peter is bound with two chains, &c., yet observe, he is sleeping. Acts xii. 6. The angel of the Lord awoke him, &c. He is led out of prison, and conducted in safety to the house of Mary, the mother of John Mark, where many were gathered together praying; ver. 12, &c. We now contemplate Peter,

VI. *In his final labors and death.*

Peter labored in the gospel in most of the provinces of lesser Asia, and at length reached Babylon; and there wrote his first epistle to the converted Jews, who had been scattered abroad by persecution. It is supposed in the year 64 or 65, Peter wrote his second epistle—a short time only before his death. As our text seemed to indicate, Peter was to die a violent death. Hence it is generally supposed Peter was cast into prison by Nero, at Rome; and that he was put to death in the year 67, by crucifixion. It is said when the executioner came to fulfil his work, that Peter desired to be crucified with his head downwards; as not being worthy to die in the same manner with his blessed Lord. It is also generally taught that Peter and Paul died by the same sentence, and at the same time—only Paul being a Roman citizen, was beheaded. Peter must have been upwards of eighty years of age when he sealed the doctrines of the gospel with his blood—having been a disciple and apostle thirty-seven years.

APPLICATION.

His diligence, devotedness, zeal, magnanimity, all deserve our admiration and imitation.

His infirmities and errors were, like his Christian virtues and excellences, of a marked and distinguished character. But he was greatly honored of the Saviour, and one of the greatest teachers and benefactors the world ever had. He lived—he labored—he died, to the honor of divine grace, and the glory of his Lord. Just behold the aged believer in prison! awaiting a public and ignominious execution—writing his second Epistle to the saints of Jesus, and thus concluding his dying testimony; 2 Peter iii. 18.

CCXVI.—THE APOSTLE JOHN.

" That disciple whom Jesus loved."—*John* xxi. 7.

A FULL and minute history of the apostles of Jesus, is not given to us in the sacred writings. By carefully observing the details of the Scriptures, we may gather up, however, the leading events in their history. The subject of our present discourse was one of the most eminent apostles of Jesus, and one of the most remarkable men of New Testament history. May a review of his life be instructive and edifying to our souls.

Observe then, in the history of John, that he is,

I. *Presented to us as a fisherman.*

A Galilean fisherman. Hence, one of the sons of toil—most likely uneducated and illiterate. He had spent his youth under the care of his father, and had been trained to his employment. Far from the metropolitan city of their country, he toiled from day to day, on the lake of Galilee, as an unpretending laborious fisherman. How striking the contrast between this station, and the sublime and glorious sphere God intended that he should afterwards occupy. Up to this period he had no other prospect before him but that of continuing his usual plain occupation, and was actually employed in mending nets, when Jesus called him. No honest station or employment is degrading to man, and from no class, however low—have not men been raised to high and exalted stations in society. In every sphere let us faithfully discharge the duties connected with them. We see him,

II. *As a disciple of Jesus.*

He went to work as usual on the morning of the momentous day that Christ called him. Only thinking of nets and fishing. Jesus, however, now had begun his great ministry. He had been baptized, anointed, and had passed through the temptations of the desert. He was now selecting those who should be the administrators of his kingdom, and the apostles of the world. He went not to courts, nor colleges, nor temples; but to the vessels of fishermen. He first called Peter: Matth. iv. 18, 30. And then he calls John, "He called them." And how prompt, direct, unquestioning their obedience. "And they immediately left their ship and their father, and followed him." It is supposed that John now was quite a young man; perhaps about twenty or twenty-two years of age. How blessed to be a disciple; still more so, to be a "young disciple." As a disciple of Christ, he was to abandon his worldly calling, and follow Jesus,—learning his will—studying his character—and doing his commands; and John was a humble, sincere, and whole-hearted disciple. As a disciple of Christ's, he was ardent, affectionate, faithful, constant and persevering. There is only one instance even of a defective spirit, when he and his brother desired that they might call for fire from heaven, to consume the Samaritans, for rejecting Christ.

Consider him,

III. *As one of the elected apostles of the Redeemer.*

All apostles were disciples, but all disciples not apostles. Jesus had only twelve apostles; see Matth. x. 1, &c. Hence, you see John just in the same position, in which we first find him. He and James following Peter and Andrew. The apostles were to be witnesses of Christ's teaching, miracles, and resurrection; and as such, they had to testify what they had seen. The highest office ever appointed in the church of the Redeemer. They were invested, too, with prodigious gifts and powers, and in fact, they were the prime ministers of Christ's kingdom. Of the apostles, John was one of the chief. Three of these were more favored than the rest :—Peter, James, and John.

They only were present at Christ's transfiguration; Matt. ix. 2. At the restoring to life of the ruler's daughter; Mark v. 57. When Christ endured his agony in the garden; Matth. xxvi. 37. But John, in connection with his devotion to Christ, was the only one of the three, who saw the pierced side of Christ; and therefore, the actual evidence of his death. John xix. 34, 35; and 1 John v. 5–7, &c.

There was no interesting event in the life of Jesus, with which John was not personally conversant.

Consider John,

IV. *As the bosom friend of the adorable Saviour.*

He evidently was the most familiar of all Christ's disciples. No title ever so illustrious as this—"The disciple whom Jesus loved;" that is, loved pre-eminently and specially. See the evidences of this :—

(1.) At the last supper he reclined on the bosom of his Lord.

(2.) He received from Christ's dying lips, his widowed mother as the object of his kind care.

(3.) He was strikingly exempted from a violent death.

(4.) He was favored with the most illustrious revelations of the divine will, in the visions of the Apocalypse.

The reasons of this might be,—he was the youngest disciple ; or more probably, he was the most loving, and therefore the most lovable of the disciples ; and yet his was not a tame effeminate character; for he and James were surnamed by Jesus—Boanerges,

i. e., Sons of Thunder. He evidently had a large generous heart, and his expanded soul was overflowing with goodness, gentleness, meekness, and love, and in these most resembled his blessed Lord.

Consider John,

V. *As one of the most distinguished writers of the New Testament scriptures.*

1. *His gospel.*

Which, while it contains fewer accounts of the miracles of Christ, is more replete with his doctrines and teachings than any of the other evangelists.

2. *There are also his three epistles.*

Full of the most important truths. Overflowing with the treasures of the gospel; and especially teeming with the spirit of the writer's pure and tender love.

3. *There are, too, the sublime revelations of the Apocalypse.*

The marvellous scenes of earth, and heaven, and hell—the events of time—and the array of judgment—and the decisions of eternity. The history of the world, and consummation of the church. The conflagration of earth, and the glories of heaven. Of all books, the most marvellous and sublime, that ever God gave to man ; and the conclusion of the canon of revealed truth.

Behold John,

VI. *As pre-eminently distinguished for the highest traits of elevated piety.*

His, was not merely official rank and glory ; but personal spiritual holiness. Observe,

1. *His consistent and persevering course of personal piety.*

From a youth to a very aged man. Probably for nearly eighty years did he profess and possess genuine and growing religion. He never halted—never turned aside. If he did desert Christ when he was arrested, he soon rallied, for he was the only man of Christ's disciples, who stood with the illustrious band of female heroines, around the tree of the Redeemer's execution. Yes, love took him there. Bound him there, &c.

He was afterwards persecuted ; and it is said, cast into a cauldron of boiling oil—at any rate he was banished, and became an exile in Patmos for Christ's sake.

2. *His end was specially illustrious and triumphant.*

A living witness for Christ for nearly eighty years. He died in Ephesus, in the reign of Trajan, about the year of our Lord, 100. It is said, before his death, when he was too feeble to walk to the Christian assembly, he was carried to deliver his favorite exhortation—his condensed sermon—" Little children, love one another."

Observe,—

1. *What a character for study and contemplation !*

2. *What an example to us.*

Especially to the young. If the servant was so excellent and lovely—how much more so the master—the Saviour Jesus. Yes, " He is the fairest among ten thousand," &c.

3. *John owed all to divine grace, which is freely offered to you.*

4. *We shall, doubtless, see John amongst the highest of the redeemed in heaven.*

CCXVII.—NATHANAEL.

" Philip findeth Nathanael, and saith unto him, We have found him, of whom Moses in the law, and the prophets, did write, Jesus of Nazareth, the son of Joseph," &c.—*John* i. 45.

VERY little is said of Nathanael in the New Testament history. It is generally supposed that he had two names ; and that he is the same with Bartholomew. As strong conjectural evidence of this, it is remarkable that no account is given of Bartholomew's call, unless this be it.

That the Evangelists who mention Nathanael, do not mention Bartholomew ; and those who refer to Bartholomew, do not name Nathanael. So also we find Philip and Bartholomew mentioned together by Matthew, as Philip and Nathanael are in the text; Matth. x. 3. But it is of little consequence who or what he might be as to name, &c., as compared with the moral and gracious excellences, for which he was so pre-eminently distinguished.

Let us then look at his religious character as presented to us in the Divine word.

Observe,

I. *How Nathanael was directed to the Saviour.*

1. *Philip, the apostle, was the honored instrument.*

Philip of Bethsaida, is to be distinguished from the excellent Philip, the deacon and evangelist. Philip was one of the apostles of Jesus, and was called by the Saviour to be his disciple ; ver. 43. Philip was a neighbor of Andrew and Peter. All of whom dwelt at Bethsaida. Interesting place to furnish so many of the illustrious apostles of Christ. Philip having found Jesus, and been called of him, becomes anxious to make him known to others—the necessary effect of the grace of God in the soul.

Observe,

2. *The manner in which Nathanael is directed to Christ.*

Verse 45. " We have found him," &c. They knew the law and the prophets. Had read to practical purpose. Had observed the signs of the Messiah's character and appearance. Had doubtless read the law and prophets expressly to find the Messiah. Philip had seen in Christ the evidences of the Messiahship.

Now, he states this to Nathanael—" We have found him," &c. Observe,

3. *The state of Nathanael's mind when he was first directed to Christ.*

Verse 46. This is evidenced when he replied—" Can any good thing," &c. Here we see the power of prejudice ! Prejudice as to place—prejudice in a good man !

The character of Nazareth was bad. To be a Galilean or a Nazarene was to be exposed to contempt. We see it will never do to judge of places or men in the mass ; and how necessary to guard against this evil influence in all matters, especially in those of a religious character.

Observe,

4. *How Nathanael yielded to the advice of Philip.*

Philip said to him—" Come and see." Better this, than reasoning with him about Nazareth. He wished him to be brought into contact with the Master. He relied more on the Saviour's loveliness, wisdom, and grace, than on his own powers of reasoning. How excellent the advice ! " Come and see." Don't decide without evidence ! Don't refuse the means of evidence ! But come, and let the evidence decide your mind. Nathanael acted on this advice ; and then we notice,

II. *His interview with the Saviour.*

Observe,

1. *Christ's eulogistic declaration.*

Verse 47. Jesus saw him, and said, " Behold ! an Israelite indeed," &c. In nature, as well as name. In reality, as well as profession. One who had sincere respect to the law of God. A real servant of the true

God—"in whom is no guile." Observe: he does not say, in whom is no weakness, or infirmity, or even sin—but no guile! Without the least vestige of deceit and hypocrisy of heart and life. Word and principle all in harmony. Walking alike before men and God. No pretence—no show—no ostentation! but upright and righteous before God. How excellent, how rare this character: Christ's exclamation proves this. In the midst of the pernicious errors of the Sadducees, and self-outward righteousness of the Pharisees—in the midst of the general apostasy—here is an Israelite indeed! Observe,

2. *Nathanael's interrogation.*

"Whence knowest thou me?" verse 48.

This was the first interview. He was surprised, &c.; and to know his heart, this was the wonder. Yes, Christ knows all things. Then observe,

3. *Christ's declaration of Nathanael's devotional character.*

"Jesus answered, before that Philip called thee, when thou wast under the fig-tree," &c. Verse 48.

Here Christ declares his own omniscience. Nathanael had retired—knew not that any one saw him; but Christ did, even there. He refers to the place. Under the fig-tree's thick foliage. No doubt, Nathanael retired to meditate and pray. Here secretly, silently, devoutly, he communed with God. Here, perhaps, he exercised faith and hope, in reference to the long expected Messiah. And there the eyes of the Messiah were upon him.

Notice,

III. *Nathanael's good confession.*

His eyes were now opened—his soul rejoiced in the Saviour—and he exclaimed, "Rabbi," &c. Here was a full and hearty confession.

"Son of God."—As such, having the attributes and glory of the Father.

"King of Israel."—Sent to rule and reign according to the ancient predictions. "Thou art." No doubt—no hesitation, prejudice, &c., all gone; and Jesus is honored and confessed by an Israelite indeed, &c.

Notice, then,

IV. *The enlarged privileges of which Jesus assured him.*

"Because," &c. Ver. 50.

1. *The general promise.*

"Greater things." It was yet only dawn. He was yet only a child. First lesson of the kingdom of God expounded to his soul.

2. *The particular statement.*

"Heaven opened." So it was, see John xii. 27, &c. So also at Christ's ascension; Luke xxiv. 50; Acts i. 9, &c. Thus, literally. He might intend also to intimate, that heaven should be open to him in its blessings, communion, and angelic protection.

Nathanael is supposed to have been put to a cruel death, after preaching the gospel in Judea and Persia—by the brother of the king of Armenia.

Learn,

1. Our duty to the unconverted. Like Philip, to bring them to Christ.

2. The great value of integrity of character. To be without guile.

3. The importance of private devotion.

4. The necessity of a public profession.

5. The gracious privileges of the people of God.

CCXVIII.—NICODEMUS.

"There was a man of the Pharisees, named Nicodemus, a ruler of the Jews."—*John* iii. 1.

JOHN is the only Evangelist who takes notice of Nicodemus, or of his interview with the Redeemer; and yet to that interview we owe one of the most interesting and important lessons on spiritual religion, that the divine word furnishes. But it is not the many and weighty doctrines comprised in this chapter, on which we can so much dwell, as on the peculiar characteristics of Nicodemus, whose history furnishes our subject on this occasion.

As such, notice,

I. *His general character as noticed in the text.*

This is distinctly specified, as to,

1. *His religious profession.*

He was a Pharisee. The Pharisees were one of the leading sects of the Jews, and were so called, because they professed to be separated from the rest of the Jews, and to be more fully devoted to the spiritual purposes of religion. Their views and doctrines contained several weighty truths, with many grave errors. They believed the world was governed by fate, or by a fixed predestinating decree of God. That the Jews were the especial favorites of God, and that he was obligated to distinguish them as the seed of Abraham. Their religion was ostentatious and vain. It sought publicity and the praise of men. It was exceedingly ceremonial: and deficient in integrity, sincerity, and spirituality. The Saviour dealt most faithfully with their deceits and hypocrisies. I may add, that they were the wealthy religionists of the day, and are well represented by the Tractarians of the present time.

No doubt, there were some excellent persons of this sect; but they were so in spite of a bad system, and were the exceptions to the general rule. Nicodemus is described,

2. *By his official station.*

"A ruler of the Jews;" that is, one of the great Sanhedrim, or council of the Jews. This was an office of an ecclesiastical kind—one of honor and influence, and possessed only by those of rank and power in the community.

Notice,

II. *His interview with Jesus.*

Here several particulars crowd on our attention.

1. *The season of this interview.*

It was by "night;" ver. 2. We know not the occasion of this period being selected. Was it to have a more calm and quiet opportunity for conversation? or was it from timidity, and want of moral courage? We fear it was the latter. His mind, however, was not fully, perhaps, certified as to the path of duty. Better, however, to come to Jesus by night, than not at all.

Observe at this interview,

2. *His views of Christ were pleasingly expressed.*

"We know that thou art a teacher," &c. Thus he not only expresses his own views, but those of many of his own class. He here acknowledges Christ as a great religious teacher. As a teacher confirming his doctrines, by the most surprising miracles. As thus giving the most satisfactory evidence of the divinity of his mission. Now these were enlightened just views, and they were clearly and well expressed.

It is evident, however,

3. *That his ideas of real religion were very defective.*

Jesus at once entered on the subject of experimental godliness; ver. 3. "Verily, verily, I say," &c. And then the ignorance of Nicodemus is made very apparent. "How can a man when he is old," &c. He seemed

to have a totally dark mind on the subject of inward piety—a new heart—spiritual religion. His religion had never recognized this. Jesus, therefore, enlarged on this subject—illustrated it—and proceeded to deliver his most rich and beautiful discourse on the redeeming love of God, towards our lost and perishing world; ver. 12 to 21.

The effect of this address is not stated—the two separate. And we have then a considerable interval in the history of this distinguished Pharisee.

Consider Nicodemus in connection with the history of Jesus,

III. *As a public advocate of truth and equity.*

Two years have probably passed since Nicodemus had heard Christ's marvellous discourse, when he went to him by night. The opposition towards Christ by the Jews, and especially by the Pharisees, had greatly increased. They were venturing even to arrest him. Hence, officers were deputed to perform this act; John vii. 31, &c. They return, however, without him. They had heard a part of that address, on the great day of the feast; chap. vii. 37–46. This led to a discourse among the Pharisees concerning him; ver. 47, &c. And now Nicodemus appears to advantage; ver. 50, 51. His remarks did honor both to his head and heart.

Nothing could be more reasonable and excellent than this. The season too was most appropriate. It was, too, unanswerable, except in the language of blind prejudice. It brake up the assembly for the time being. Nicodemus here displayed much moral courage, and evident improvement as a secret disciple of the Saviour. Notice,

IV. *The last connective link between Nicodemus and the Saviour.*

The burning envy and hatred of the Jews towards Christ increased; and at length his hour came, and the hour of darkness. Judas betrays him. The council condemn him. Herod mocks him; and Pilate signs his death-warrant, and delivers him to be put to death. He is crucified between two malefactors, and expires on the accursed tree. The bodies of malefactors were often cast into some pit, or allowed to go entirely without burial. Not so with the sacred remains of Jesus; John xix. 39, &c.

Here once more we meet with Nicodemus. He honors Christ's remains,—does it publicly,—at a considerable expense,—and in the face of his enemies,—and while the tide of popular fury was running against him. Surely this was honorable to Nicodemus, both as it respects his judgment, his heart, and his conduct. And here we part with Nicodemus. No more is recorded of him in the sacred page. We find it difficult to pass judgment, as to his real character. There is confessedly much to admire. His character is more favorable every time we see him; and yet, alas! there are some of Christ's own sayings which compel us to conclude unfavorably respecting him. "If any man will be my disciple," &c. Matt. xvi. 24, &c.; also chap. x. 32, 33.

It seems to me, that these passages speak out distinctly against the spirit of timidity —time serving—and unholy compromise, which appear to be the great defects in the character of Nicodemus.

Learn,—

1. *The necessity of whole-heartedness and decision.*

2. *The importance of a public profession of Christian principles.*

3. *The necessity of self-denial for conscience sake.*

Buying the truth at any rate, &c.

CCXIX.—STEPHEN'S CHARACTER AND DEATH.

"And they stoned Stephen, calling upon God, and saying, Lord Jesus, receive my spirit. And he kneeled down, and cried with a loud voice, Lord, lay not this sin to their charge. And when he had said this, he fell asleep."—*Acts* vii. 59, 60.

Our text records the death-scene of one of the earliest martyrs of the Christian church. Stephen had been chosen, on account of his eminent piety, to be one of the first deacons; chap. vi. 5. But now we find him delivering a most learned and elaborate address and defence of the Christian system, before the Sanhedrim, in reply to a charge that had been made against him; ver. 8, &c., of the previous chapter. This address concluded with the most faithful and searching application; ver. 51. This excited them to the greatest rage; ver. 54. God publicly honored Stephen by giving him a vision of the heavenly glory; ver. 55. This he attested to the people, and then followed the tragedy of his death, &c.; ver. 57.

Let us consider,

I. *The character of Stephen.*

And,

II. *The circumstances of his death.*

I. *The character of Stephen.*

Not much is said of him in the sacred volume. But that little is the highest testimony that can be given.

He is described,

1. *As full of faith and power.*

Chapter vi. 7. A man of earnest strong faith. A believer with all his heart. Unbelief, and doubting, and wavering excluded. Spiritual power and pious energy followed.

2. *He was filled also with the Holy Ghost.*

Of the Holy Spirit we have as we ask, and as we believe. He had large faith, and therefore, power with God; and was filled with the Holy Spirit. In all his illumining influences.—In all his sanctifying influences. —In all his comforting influences.—In all his strengthening influences.

3. *He was invested with miraculous powers.*

"Did great wonders," &c. Had the Spirit both in his ordinary and extraordinary operations.

4. *He was one of the first deacons of the church.*

The origin of the office is described: chap. vi. 1, &c. He filled it with honor and fidelity.

5. *He was a faithful witness for Christ.*

Read his powerful address, and see its conclusion. How direct and earnest, &c., in this. He ran all risks.—He dared all consequences.—He lost sight of every thing but his duty. His life and work ended together.

Such was Stephen. We might just advert to the reference made to his personal appearance: chap. vi. 15. So it is said of Moses: Exod. xxxiv. 30. Character and emotions often break through the veil of the body, both as to the vile and the holy. Some bad men have looked like demons. Some holy men like angels. The mind has much to do with the countenance, &c.

Notice,

II. *The circumstances of his death.*

His death,

1. *Was violent.*

He was martyred for Christ's sake. Dragged out of the city by a rude and lawless mob; then stoned to death. Hear the yells of the infuriated population,—how they clamor for his blood. See them stripped for the horrid deed! Look at the spectacle, and you see a young man standing by and assenting to his death! He cheerfully guards the clothes of those who stoned him. Ah! that is Saul: we shall shortly meet him again, &c.

2. *He died in the spirit of Christian clemency.*

Does he revile his revilers? Does he even reason with them—or implore their mercy? No. But he becomes their intercessor. Collected, calm, Christ-like, he kneels down—supplicates, with his dying breath, favor from Christ—"Lord, lay not this sin," &c. How supernatural! How divine!

3. *He commends his immortal spirit into the hands of Christ.*

He was favored with a vision of the heavenly glory; ver. 55, &c. He saw his blessed Lord standing as his Advocate and Friend. To him, therefore, he commends his deathless soul—"Lord Jesus," &c.

Here is worship paid to Christ. Prayer, the highest act of devotion. To whom could he go? &c.

4. *He then falls asleep in Jesus.*

Christ received the deposit. The spirit is impalpable—cannot be stoned or killed. It is unhurt. Christ opens his arms. Angels are sent, and the spirit soars on high, to dwell with Jesus forever, &c.

"Asleep;" such is the general description given of the death of the godly. It is,

A state of repose after toil. Work of the day done, &c.

A state of unconsciousness. The senses sealed till the day of the resurrection. No pain, &c. Yet only a state of temporary suspense. He shall awake again. It is but for a night.

A state of peace and tranquillity. No strife, &c.

Such was the death of the illustrious Stephen.

Learn from it,—

1. The connection often between fidelity and suffering.

2. The glorious results of a holy life. Vision of God. His presence in death, &c.

3. The benevolence of Christianity. It is a system of blessing, and not of cursing, &c.

4. The immediate entrance of the dying saint to glory.

5. The great event we should ever keep in view. The dying day.

CCXX.—PHILIP AND THE GOSPEL IN SAMARIA.

"Then Philip went down to the city of Samaria, and preached Christ unto them. And the people with one accord gave heed unto those things which Philip spake, hearing and seeing the miracles which he did."—*Acts* viii. 5-13.

OUR text contains an historical account of the introduction of the gospel into Samaria. That account is very clear, distinct and satisfactory. It contains a number of points that cannot fail to be interesting and edifying.

Perhaps we cannot do better, for the sake of order, than to look at

The preacher.

The sphere of his labor.

The message proclaimed; and,

The success by which it was attended.

I. *The preacher.*

Verse 5. Philip is introduced to us in two other passages of God's word.

1. *As a deacon.*

Chap. vi. 5. As a deacon, he was to take charge, with his brethren, of the tables; ver. 2. It was a secular work. A kind of stewardship in the church. Philip did not preach as a deacon; for that is distinguished from it; ver. 4. But a deacon might be more. So Philip is brought before us,

2. *As an evangelist:*

Acts xxi. 8. Now an evangelist differed both from an apostle, and a bishop, or pastor. An apostle must have *seen* Christ, and have been especially called by him. A bishop was the pastor of one flock—a resident in one place. An evangelist was one gifted with preaching attributes; and who went anywhere to lift up the cross, as Providence might direct. Such was the preacher on this occasion.

Observe,

II. *His sphere of labor.*

"Samaria." It does not mean any city of that name, but to the district of country so called. It might be in the district near to Sychar, where Christ had met with the woman at Jacob's well. Every place inhabited by human beings, is a fit sphere for ministerial effort. For, everywhere man is guilty—ignorant—helpless—perishing—and needs a Saviour. And there is a gospel for the whole world, and a Saviour for every creature.

Notice, then,

III. *The message he proclaimed.*

"He preached Christ unto them," ver. 5. What a great and comprehensive subject!

Christ is the sum of the gospel; yea, the sum of the whole Bible. He did not preach himself,—he did not preach human philosophy,—he did not preach the law,—he did not preach mere morality. He preached Christ.

1. *Christ as the predicted and promised Messiah.*

Of whom Moses in the law, &c. Universally expected. The desire of all nations.

2. *He preached Christ the anointed of God, to save the world.*

Redeemer sent by God,—anointed for this purpose, &c. Who had effected the great work of God. As an example—as a teacher—as a philanthropist—as a sacrifice—as Lord and King—as the only Saviour of perishing sinners.

3. *He preached Christ, i. e., expounded, taught, offered, urged, &c.*

This was the message—and this alone is the gospel. Every thing else is infinitely inferior, and should be at all times subordinate. Christ should be the centre, where all discourses should verge, &c.

Then observe,

IV. *The success which attended his ministry.*

1. *He obtained the attention of the people.*

This is the first step in success. To get the people to hear,—to give heed,—hearken with interest,—with careful and personal solicitude, &c.

(1.) This heed was very general. The "people," &c.

(2.) It was unanimous. "With one accord."

(3.) It was admiring attention. "For they beheld the miracles Philip did." These miracles were of the most striking description; ver. 7.

(4.) Joyful attention; ver. 8.

2. *They believed the message Philip preached.*

Attention—wonder, &c., will not save. This is not real success. But they believed the discourses he delivered, &c. Verse 12.

3. *They were baptized on the profession of their faith.*

Evidenced the reality of their faith, by being enrolled among Christ's disciples. Putting Christ on by baptism, into his death. Just literally carrying out Christ's commission, "Go ye into all the world," &c.

4. *Among the converts was a very distinguished person.*

Ver. 9. A great many conjectural things are said about him. We will abide by the statements of the text.

He was a magician, or sorcerer. Probably an astrologer, and one who professed to divine and tell future events. Lived on the credulity of the people. Warn the young against fortune-tellers. He had great influence, &c.

(1.) He believed, and was baptized.

(2.) He continued with Philip, &c.

(3.) But his soul had long been under one master vice—the vice of covetousness. He had lived on the credulity of the people. He therefore wished to obtain the Holy Ghost for miraculous purposes. He sought this of the apostles; ver. 14. He was rejected; ver. 20, 21. He was exhorted and threatened; ver. 22, 23. He was alarmed; ver. 24. We fear this was all, &c.

APPLICATION.

1. Men need the gospel now, as did the people of Samaria.

2. Preaching Christ is alone preaching that gospel.

It is only efficient, when heard with attention, faith, and obedience.

CCXXI.—SAUL OF TARSUS.

[NO. I.]

"And the witnesses laid down their clothes at a young man's feet, whose name was Saul."—*Acts* vii. 58.

OUR text contains the first reference in the sacred writings to Saul of Tarsus, a man who was destined to be one of the most illustrious of Christian apostles. Yet here he is introduced to us under circumstances most unfavorable to his moral and religious character.

A mob of infuriated bigots are stoning to death one of the most eminent of Christ's disciples—the holy Stephen—whose discourse had convicted them of rejecting the word of God, and hardening their hearts against the Holy Ghost. "When they heard these things, they were cut to the heart," &c.; verse 54, &c. The subject of our text consented to this cruel atrocity, and held the clothes of those who actually stoned Stephen to death.

Let us, at present, look at the history of Saul, up to the period of his conversion.

Notice,

I. *His parentage and birthplace.*

His parents were Jews, by lineage and profession. Hence he styles himself, "a Hebrew of the Hebrews." Neither of them were proselytes. They belonged to the tribe of Benjamin. Some of the learned fathers think the ancient prophecy of Benjamin is especially fulfilled in Saul of Tarsus. Gen. xlix. 27. His birthplace was Tarsus, the metropolis of Cilicia. A wealthy and flourishing city. Celebrated also for its proficiency in the arts and literature. It is said that both Athens and Rome were beholden to it for many of their illustrious scholars. It was a Roman municipal or free corporation, to which both Julius Cæsar and Augustus granted many distinguished immunities and privileges. Observe,

II. *His early life and education.*

As a native of Tarsus, he was favored with many distinguished privileges. Yet according to the great maxim of the Jews, he was trained to a lawful trade, that he might have the means of earning his own livelihood. Saul was a tent-maker. It was a proverb with the Jews, that, "he who teaches not his son a trade, teaches him to be a thief." Hence a manual trade was an essential part of education. Labor should ever be respected and dignified. Parents should consult especially three things in giving their children a trade :—

(1.) That it should be in accordance with the genius and powers of the child.

(2.) That it should be honest; and not likely to injure our fellow-men in body, soul, or estate.

(3.) That it should not be unfavorable to piety; but one on which God's blessing could be sought.

At that trade Saul worked, even after he had been installed in the apostle's office.

His education was evidently liberal. Having obtained all the instruction that his native city could confer, he was sent to Jerusalem to study the law, under one of the great Rabbins of the day. Acts xxii. 3.

Gamaliel was the president of the Sanhedrim—an illustrious teacher—and eminently celebrated for his wisdom and prudence. He it was that made that excellent speech in favor of the apostles. See Acts v. 33, &c. Here Saul became perfected in the principles of the moral laws of his religion, and an expert casuist in all the technicalities thereof.

Observe,

III. *The moral and religious character of Saul.*

1. *He was a Pharisee.*

The Pharisees were the strictest sect of the Jews. Exact in maintaining all the points of orthodox belief, and in fulfilling the minutiæ of the law. Regular in all observances. Exceeding the legitimate demand in tithes, &c. Scrupulous in their intercourse with society. Punctual in religious services. But their religion was adulterated with the most pernicious elements of pride, ostentation, and parade. It was chiefly external. It was not inward, and spiritual, and real. It lacked sincerity, humility, and mercy. It was awfully mingled with deceit, avarice, and hypocrisy; yet, bad and corrupt as it was, it was the best religion of the times; and, doubtless, there were many truly godly persons identified with it. Saul's account of his religious character as a Pharisee, is very minute. Philip. iii. 4, &c.

But observe, with all this, he was,

2. *A cruel bigot.*

Persecuting the followers of Christ. Acts xxii. 1–5. He refers to it also, 1 Tim. i. 12, &c. So it is described by Luke; Acts ix. 1, &c.

What a combination of elements! Light and darkness—religion and impiety—zeal for God, and hatred to men. What earnestness in a bad cause! What devotedness to cruelty! &c. How odious such a state of mind! and all this while he was young. A ravening wolf, &c. Here we see Saul in his original, unchanged character,—the enemy of Christ, and the persecutor of his people.

Consider,

IV. *His extraordinary conversion.*

Here several things can only just be glanced at. Observe,

1. *His actual engagements at the time.*

He was on a mission of persecution and cruelty. See Acts viii. 1; ix. 1. In the very midst of his mad opposition to Jesus and his cause.

2. *His conversion was miraculous.*

In the prints of the old masters, Saul is generally described as on horseback, with the extraordinary light bursting on his path, and a voice addressing him—"Saul, Saul," ix. 3.

Now this was not an illusion. For those with Saul heard the voice, and were speechless with astonishment; ver. 7.

Saul is overwhelmed—falls to the earth —hears the voice, and asks, "Who art thou, Lord," &c. And then the reply is given, "I am Jesus," &c.; ver. 5. Saul now is convinced. Becomes an inquiring penitent. And he trembling, said, "Lord, what wilt thou," &c.; ver. 6. Divine direction is given; ver. 6. He is affected powerfully in body and mind; ver. 9. Ananias, as a preacher of consolation, is sent to him; ver. 10, &c.

3. *The reality of his conversion is evident.*

Observe what God says of him, ver. 11: "Behold, he prayeth!" Prayer is the certain sign of the new life, &c. Before, he hated, blasphemed. Now, mark the change! "He prayeth." God vindicates this work, and thus shows,

4. *The special end his conversion is to answer.*

Verse 13, &c.

And now observe,

5. *The profession of his conversion is made.*

In connection with the visit of Ananias, he receives his sight—is filled with the Holy Ghost—and is immediately baptized. See his own account. Acts xxii. 12, &c.

Here we pause in the history of Saul of Tarsus.

Learn,—

1. *The power of religious prejudice and bigotry.*

It can hate, blaspheme, and put to death.

2. *The superior power of Divine grace.*

It can arrest, convict, and humble, and save.

3. *The transforming influence of religion on the soul.*

Now Saul will be a light to the world—a friend to man—and a brother of all the disciples—a consecrated servant of Jesus. Such are the effects of true religion, always, on the heart and life.

CCXXII.—THE APOSTLE PAUL.

[NO. II.]

"And when he had received meat, he was strengthened. Then was Saul certain days with the disciples which were at Damascus. And straightway he preached Christ in the synagogues, that he is the Son of God."—*Acts* ix. 19–30.

In our last discourse we followed the history of Saul of Tarsus to his conversion; and having seen him make a good profession of his faith in Christ Jesus, we left him, to derive certain useful lessons from it.

We now have to witness the first step which he takes in that glorious course of apostleship, by which he becomes so eminently useful to the church, and so great a benefactor—especially to the Gentile world.

Our text brings before us a variety of striking incidents, relative to the beginning of his ministry. By looking at it carefully, you will observe,

I. *That he associated now with the friends of Jesus.*

Verse 19. The grace that unites the soul to Jesus, also unites the heart and spirit to his followers. Now, he is a shepherd of the flock, not a destroying wolf. Now a friend—not an enemy. Now with Christ—not against him.

Here we see him a personal adherent and disciple of the Lord Jesus.

II. *He immediately entered on the ministerial work.*

Verse 20. He was very young in grace, —had not had much Christian experience. No church-meeting had been held. No council of ministers. But then he had been converted in a most extraordinary manner. Most probably Ananias had told him of his heavenly commission; ver. 15, &c. He refers to this, Gal. i. 15, &c.

Immediately then did Paul become a preacher of that gospel which he had labored to destroy.

Observe,

III. *The subject of his ministry was the Lord Jesus Christ.*

Verse 20. "Preached Christ." He began with this,—he ever held fast to this,— he ended his theme only with his life. He made his boast of this. See 1 Cor. i. 20; 2 Cor. iv. 5; Col. i. 27. He says of this to the Romans, "I am not ashamed," &c. "To the Philippians, iii. 8, "Yea, doubtless," &c. To the Galatians, "God forbid," &c. He studied, prayed, toiled, suffered, lived and died, to preach Christ. The one great object of his being, &c. In preaching Christ, he had especially one object to establish, and that was, his true Messiahship,—"that he was the Son of God." He did this in the synagogue of Damascus, —he did this before the crowds of astonished hearers, &c.

Observe, he did this most successfully; ver. 22. The Jews intended to gainsay and oppose; but Paul increased in strength, in much power, in divine knowledge—and proved the truth, that Jesus was the Christ.

Observe,

IV. *The persecution to which he was immediately exposed.*

Verse 23, &c. Here we see the seed of the serpent rising to bruise the heel of the woman's seed. Argument fails. Paul triumphs in that; so then they resort to persecution. Seek to take his life. These too were Jews, not barbarians, not infidels. Of all rancor and hate, that which has assumed the religious phase, has ever been most fierce and deadly. This spirit has been fearfully exhibited in the Church of Rome. Multitudes have been persecuted to death. How soon, in Paul's case, is a complete reverse of conduct exhibited! The persecutor a few days ago, is now the persecuted. Observe how his life was in imminent jeopardy, ver. 24. At length, means are adopted for his escape. The disciples of the Redeemer unite for his rescue. The gates are watched; and therefore, they go to a part of the wall distant from these, and let Paul down, under the cover of the night, in a basket; ver. 25.

Thus, Paul is delivered, and that life extended, which was to be so honorably employed in the cause of Jesus.

We are now directed,

V. *To the apostle's union with the church of Jesus, at Jerusalem.*

He now returns to Jerusalem, with the purpose of uniting with the disciples there. But he was only known in the city as a bitter enemy. They feared now that he designed to injure them, by treachery. They doubted the genuineness of his conversion; and hence, they were all afraid of him. But God raised up a friend for Paul in this emergency. This was the excellent Barnabas. He took the new convert by the hand, and brought him before the apostles, &c.; ver. 27. Explained how Christ had met him by the way—how he had preached at Damascus, &c. Thus he was received by the apostles—had communion with the church—enjoying all the freedom of the other disciples. "Coming in," &c.; ver. 28. Here also he labored in the ministry; ver. 29. He spake boldly in the name of Jesus. Disputing with the Grecians, that

is, the class of Jews who came from the provinces, and used the Greek language.

Thus the apostle went earnestly on, in his great and blessed work, to exalt the Redeemer, and save souls.

Observe,

VI. *The second persecution to which he is exposed.*

Here again his life is exposed and attempted. They go about to slay him. And again the brethren have to interpose to save him. This they do, by conveying him to Cæsarea; and from thence to Tarsus, his native city.

Here the chain of history breaks off. We know not how long he continued at Tarsus. We next find him, after the lapse of four or five years, sought by Barnabas, to take him with him to Antioch, where they spent a whole year—and taught much people; Acts xi. 25, &c. It is probable that Paul, during the interval, had been preaching the gospel, in Cilicia and Syria.

APPLICATION.

1. *Learn the connection between decided and elevated piety, and persecution.*

It is through much persecution, &c. In the world we must have tribulation, &c.

2. *The advantages of Christian fellowship.*

We see how at Tarsus, and again in Jerusalem, Paul was comforted and aided by the brethren. This is one of the grand designs of a Christian church.

3. *That the voice of duty and God must be regarded at all consequences.*

So did Paul obey God, and persevere in the way of duty. "We are to endure hardness," &c. "In patience possess our souls," &c. "Not cast away our confidence," &c.

CCXXIII.—HISTORY OF PAUL.

[NO. III.]

AS A PREACHER AND WRITER.

"In labors more abundant."—2 *Cor.* xi. 22.

In our last discourse, we traced the life of the apostle, from the period of his conversion, to the time that Barnabas sought him, and took him with him to Antioch, where they labored together in that city, for a whole year. Now, for the next twenty-five years, the Apostle Paul was fully devoted to the great work of the apostleship, and stayed not in his illustrious course, until he laid down his neck to the stroke of the executioner, in the imperial city of Rome.

But on this occasion, we wish to call your attention to two features in the apostle's life and labors.

His preaching; and,

His writings.

I. *The Apostle Paul's preaching.*

Now, it has generally been believed, that while the apostle possessed every mental, and spiritual, and supernatural qualification for the work—that, physically, he was not adapted to impress. Just read 1 Cor. ii. 4; and also Gal. iv. 13; 2 Cor. x. 10. It has hence been supposed that the apostle was low in stature. For Chrysostom says, "This man of three cubits height, was tall enough to touch the heavens." In that case, he was not more than four feet and a half high. Then, (2). It is supposed he had occasional hesitation, or difficulty of speaking. That his eloquence was that of matter, and not of enunciation; and that (3). He was subject to some physical disease, which caused him great suffering. His thorn in the flesh, was perhaps something of this kind.

But his profound learning—his highly cultivated intellect—his knowledge of the Scriptures—his ardent mind—his devotedness of spirit—with all the endowments of the Holy Ghost, made him a most eminent minister of the Lord Jesus Christ. Let us just listen to the apostle on four occasions.

He is a prisoner for Christ's sake. He is brought forth to be examined before Felix. His defence is most noble (Acts xxiv. 10–22). And afterwards, when the wife of Felix was with him; ver. 24, 25.

See the apostle also before Agrippa; Acts xxvi. 1–26; and then his direct application to the heart of the monarch; verse 27 to 29. Let us look at the apostle, when publicly laboring in the gospel at Athens; Acts xvii. 16, &c. And at Ephesus; Acts xix. 1–7 to 12; 18 to 20.

Now, we see the apostle in these cases, under circumstances of most extraordinary interest; and the course of noble and effective conduct he pursued, and the striking features which distinguished him as a preacher of the Lord Jesus. But let us next contemplate the Apostle Paul,

II. *As a writer.*

Here he stands forth most conspicuously to view. Here all his learning and mental qualities and endowments, are brought into the most effective operation. The speaker has many advantages over the writer, for the time being. Words spoken, are spirit and life. Hence the most extraordinary effects are produced. Hence Cicero and Demosthenes wrought upon the people, and moved them, as the winds agitate the leaves of the forest, or bend the waving corn.

But the advantages of the writer, are these,—

(1.) His own personal defects, as in the case of the Apostle Paul, are not known or observed.

(2.) The production can be more carefully drawn up, and more entirely finished.

(3.) The whole subject can be better brought under review.

(4.) The writer possesses a kind of ubiquity; and can teach and edify thousands of millions.

(5.) It has the advantage of perpetuity, the press gives permanency; so that its influences may last to the end of time. So, happily for the world, the epistles of Paul.

Paul's writings form more than one-fourth of the New Testament Scriptures. His epistles are fourteen in number.

They are distinguished,

(1.) For strong and logical argumentation.

(2.) Great vigor and energy.

(3.) Display much emotion and ardor in the writer.

(4.) Are very bold and faithful.

(5.) Often most tender and pathetic. Embrace,

(6.) All the great doctrines of Christianity.

(7.) Are also eminently characterized by experimental religion : and,

Finally. Display a most earnest zeal for practical holiness—and the loftiest virtues of benevolence and mercy.

His Epistle to the Romans is mainly occupied in illustrating the great doctrine of the sinner's justification by faith, in the Lord Jesus Christ; and the righteousness of God, in casting off incorrigible Jews, and electing Gentile nations to the privileges of the gospel.

His Epistle to the Hebrews was written anonymously, and designed to reconcile his countrymen to the Christian faith, by showing that the New Testament faith had been prefigured by the types and sacrifices of the old economy, and that Jesus was the end, and the sum of the law, and the prophets. His Epistle to the Philippians is most tender and affectionate. To the Colossians, most sublime and powerful. To the Corinthians and Ephesians, most searching and faithful. But all were appropriate, excellent, and divine. There was one golden thread running through all: " Christ crucified." Christ all in all.

In conclusion, consider,

1. *Paul was an example for ministers.*

Laborious, constant, diligent, evangelical, and faithful.

2. *As a pattern for religious writers.*

His research—his candor—his fidelity! We should rejoice,

3. *That Paul's labors remain for our benefit.*

CCXXIV.—THE TRIALS AND SUFFERINGS OF THE APOSTLE PAUL.

[NO. IV.]

"Are ye ministers of Christ! (I speak as a fool) I am more; in labors more abundant, in stripes above measure, in prisons more frequent, in deaths oft. Of the Jews five times received I forty stripes save one," &c.—2 *Cor.* xi. 23—29.

PAUL, though so remarkably converted, and fully devoted to the apostolic work, yet suffered through the jealousy of true, and the opposition of false teachers. In Corinth, a state of great confusion had risen, through the effects of the false principles they had received. Church discipline was neglected, party spirit was cherished; and even some of the converts of the apostle had begun to undervalue his character, and think lightly of his labors. He therefore had to vindicate himself; and in doing so, he was constrained to refer to his trials and sufferings, in the cause of the blessed Saviour. Some of these particular instances are only mentioned in this passage, and, therefore, we cannot state either the places or times where they occurred. Observe the particular things which are included in the apostle's affecting enumeration. He adverts, however,

I. *To his eminency as a minister of Christ.*

As if he had said, Are those who object to me, ministers of Christ? yet, "I am more." Doubtless he is alluding here to the very remarkable manner he was called and installed into the great work.

Apostles or churches might call other Christians to the ministry, seeing their piety and fitness; but he was called by the Lord Jesus himself. Distinctly, &c. The Lord had stated this to Ananias. Acts ix. 13–16. Paul often referred to the fact of his being called of the Lord, directly and immediately. See Gal. i. 1; also ver. 11 and 12. And then as to devotedness to the work,—no man ever excelled him, as to his fields of labor: See Gal. i. 15, &c. Rom xv. 19. This included a very large circuit, in which were comprised—Syria, Phenicia, Arabia, Cilicia, Pamphylia, Galatia, Asia, Thracia, Macedonia, Thessaly, Achaia, and many other provinces and countries. He also refers, not only to his labors, but also,

II. *To his numerous personal sufferings.*

He does this first, generally: ver. 23.

(1.) In stripes above measure. Exceeding the usual inflictions, &c. And also much more than the other brethren had endured.

(2.) In prisons more frequent. Often deprived of his personal liberty, and dragged to the dungeon, for Christ's sake.

(3.) In deaths oft. That is, often exposed to death. In very imminent peril of death —and that oft. 2 Cor. i. 8, 9. He then enumerates, more particularly, his sufferings and trials in, and for the gospel of Christ.

(1.) Scourged five times. It was a Jewish punishment, and was not allowed to exceed thirty-nine strokes. Generally with a whip with three thongs; so that thirteen blows would inflict the number of stripes.

(2.) Thrice he was punished with rods; ver. 25. We have an account of one of these instances of cruel persecution. Acts xvi. 22, &c.

(3.) He was once stoned. This account is given to us, as it occurred at Lystra. Acts xiv. 19.

(4.) Thrice he endured the privations and perils of shipwreck, &c. In his constant and extended labors, he often had to go by sea; and thus the dangers to which he was exposed. He mentions, that on one occasion, for a whole day and night, he had been in the deep. Probably resting on some plank, or clinging to the vessel, when submerged in the sea. Observe,

(5.) He refers to the variety of his labors. Perils from without. Repeated journeys in preaching the gospel. Perils by water—robbers, &c. Some of those parts in which he travelled, are still dangerous to travellers. Perils from his own countrymen—they often labored to destroy him. Hence the horrid covenant mentioned, Acts xxiii. 12. By the heathen—who were incensed at his preaching the one living and true God, &c. In the city, at Derbe, Lystra, Philippi, Jerusalem, Ephesus, &c. In the wilderness—from wild beasts. In the sea—as he had stated. Also from false brethren. Those who professed the same faith—labored in the same work, &c.; yet treacherously tried to undermine his reputation—injure his usefulness. See Gal. iv. 13, &c.; v. 9, &c. He adverts,

(6.) To his physical sufferings; ver. 27. What a train of sad and painful experiences. How he was the subject of outward wretchedness! How distressing and painful to flesh and blood! But he adds to the list,

(7.) By referring to his spiritual anxieties and responsibilities; ver. 28. "The care of all the churches;" that is, of the churches he had planted. His solicitude for their growth and prosperity. His distress at their schisms and apostasies. His often being required to advise, and counsel, and direct them. His heart was thus oppressed with the solemn weight, &c., respecting them. He concludes the sum of the whole,

(8.) By declaring his sympathy with all the suffering disciples of Jesus; ver. 29. "Who is weak?" &c. He felt no one could suffer, without his heart's sympathy, &c. No one could be offended, but his soul burned with holy indignation against the offenders; and with fervent emotion for the sufferer. How disinterested—unselfish—devoted, and Christ-like, the spirit and experience of the apostle Paul.

Learn,

1. *The greatness of the ministerial work.* Great in its theme—object—ends—and responsibilities.

2. *The need such have of the sympathy of the people.*

Hence the apostle urges—"Brethren, pray for us," &c. After all, they are but men; and need courtesy, kindness, and affection, &c. Their hands should be held up, &c.

3. *How we should rejoice in the privileges of our times, &c.*

And yet, the offence of the Cross has not entirely ceased, &c. Surely, after the apostle's history, we shall never complain of our persecutions and trials.

4. *The grace of God is sufficient for all our states and circumstances.*

CCXXV.—PAUL'S WAITING FOR MARTYRDOM.

[NO. V.]

"For I am now ready to be offered, and the time of my departure is at hand. I have fought a good fight, I have finished my course, I have kept the faith: Henceforth there is laid up for me a crown of righteousness, which the Lord, the righteous judge, shall give me at that day," &c.—2 *Tim.* iv. 6–9.

DURING Paul's first visit to Rome, as a prisoner, he was allowed to dwell in his own hired house, in which he received whom he would—and where he labored diligently in his holy calling. This residence extended to two years. From this peril, &c., he was delivered by the hand of the Lord. After this, he was again a prisoner in Rome, and it is to this period the text clearly refers. It is evident, too, that he now felt that his work was finished, and his end near.

Nero was at this time emperor of Rome; and severe persecution had been endured by the Christian Church in that city. Many had, doubtless, been put to death. So terror-stricken were the other Christians, that Paul had to record his standing alone before the imperial tribunal; ver. 16. Yet then he realized the presence of his unchanging Lord, &c.; ver. 17.

Observe, in the text,

I. *Paul's triumphant retrospect.*

II. *His present experience.*

III. *His future anticipation.*

I. *Paul's triumphant retrospect.*

He magnanimously affirms three things. Observe,

1. *His victorious warfare.*

"I have fought," &c. He had been a soldier under Christ. He had been a general under the great Captain. His warfare he calls "a good fight."

(1.) As a fight against evil. The moral evil of sin, and its attendant miseries and woes.

(2.) As a fight with hallowed weapons. The sword, the shield, &c.; but see, they are all spiritual. "The weapons of our warfare," &c. No instrument of pain, or misery, or death.

(3.) As a fight for a good object. The rights of Jesus, and the well-being of men. For truth, righteousness, benevolence, &c. Present and eternal salvation of the human race.

(4.) As a fight under a good Captain, the

Lord Jesus Christ. He is so designated; Heb. ii. 10.

Now, this fight Paul had fought. He had begun—he had entered on the service—he had never yielded—never given it up. Had won many battles, &c. Had trophies in every part of the then known world. His campaign and service were now ending. He affirms,

2. *That he had won the race.*

"Finished his course." Here is a reference to the Olympic racer, and the attainment of the goal, &c. Well Paul had finished, &c. He had obeyed all the laws of the course—he had kept in it—he had agonized—he now saw the goal before him. It had been a course of toil, suffering, and self-denial; but had been constant and persevering.

He affirms,

3. *His fidelity to the solemn trust the Lord Jesus had reposed on him.*

"I have kept the faith." He had once labored to destroy it—had been converted to it—had received it as an apostle, from Christ. To protect, guard, and vindicate it; and he had *kept it:* inviolably, faithfully. He had kept it pure, entire, prominent—to the end.

Notice,

II. *His present experience.*

"I am now ready to be offered up." How important to be ready for death! &c. He represents himself as a sacrifice—a sacrifice for the gospel and Christ's sake. He was awaiting the order; and had nothing to do, but to go to the scaffold, &c. Now his readiness consisted,

1. *In an assurance of his conversion and acceptance with Christ.*

No readiness without these. Paul knew this—never doubted it. "I know whom I have believed," &c. This readiness consisted,

2. *In having done his Lord's work.*

He had been Christ's servant, and Christ had used him for his own will; and in his cause for many years. His work now was finished; and therefore he was ready. He could say—as the Saviour had done—"I have finished the work," &c. The Christian's life is one of holy activity—serving God and our generation. Paul had done both. This readiness consisted,

3. *In being meet for heaven.*

Readiness for death and meetness for heaven, must be identical. Paul had it. It consisted in a heart in conformity with the will of God—that is, holiness—likeness to the Lord. Paul had been fully given up to Christ. He had lived, preached, and given up all for Christ. He was, therefore, ready to die, and be with Christ, which would be infinitely better. Paul's readiness was entirely owing to the rich grace of God, as the original cause, and as the sustaining principle of religion within the soul.

Observe,

III. *His future anticipation.*

"Henceforth there is laid up for me," &c.

1. *He anticipated a crown.*

Not that he had ever merited one; but he had fulfilled the gracious commands of his Lord, who had, in rich love, promised one. The Cross and Crown were connected with his Master, so with his followers. "If we suffer," &c.

Now this crown was symbolical of dignity, favor, riches, dominion. He had been a prince, and he was now coming to his kingdom.

2. *This crown was one of righteousness.*

Given in virtue of the righteous life and sacrifice of the Lord Jesus Christ—the purchase of his precious blood. Given to the righteous. Not to hereditary princes—not to the ambitious and the vile, but the righteous, &c. "Blessed are the poor in spirit, for theirs is the kingdom," &c. Not a crown, or wreath of olive, or laurel, but of righteousness.

3. *He expected Christ to bestow it.*

"Which the Lord the righteous Judge," &c. He had preached Christ as the great Judge of all, to the Athenians: Acts xvii. 31. Christ had said he would confess his disciples. He had said, "I give unto you a kingdom," &c. He had solemnly prayed that they might be with him, &c. Now Paul knew all this, and believed it, and hoped for it.

4. *He expected the crown in the day of Christ's appearing.*

He anticipated heaven immediately after death; but the final confession and reward he expected at the last day—the day of the Lord. Of his second advent, in power and glory. See Christ's own words: Matt. xxv. 31, &c.

5. *He anticipated that others would share with him in his glory.*

"Not to me only," &c. No narrow limitarian was Paul—no monopolist of the word of life. No believer would delight in enjoying felicity alone. The more, the happier and better, &c. Yet only one class would share—"Who love his appearing." Believe in it. Prepare for it. Expect it. Desire it.

Such are the precious parts of this important dying testimony, for Christ. He soon realized it. He was summoned to his destiny—became a spectacle to the world; and was beheaded for the word and testimony of the Lord.

Learn,—

1. How illustrious the history of Paul.
2. How useful, and like his master.
3. How triumphant his death.
4. How worthy of emulation, &c. Let us seek to be of the number who love Christ's appearing.

CCXXVI.—PHEBE.

"I commend unto you Phebe our sister, who is a servant of the church which is at Cenchrea: That ye receive her in the Lord, as becometh saints, and that ye assist her in whatsoever business she hath need of you; for she hath been a succorer of many, and of myself also."—*Rom.* xvi. 1, 2.

This chapter is one of Christian salutations. It is probable that most of the persons here referred to were those the apostle had met with in various places in his labors, and who had gone to reside in, or visit the imperial city. While Christianity condemns all adulation and flattery, yet it not only gives honor to whom honor is due, but also it is eminently courteous and polite. It exhibits the kind, considerate, and gentle spirit of goodness on all occasions. What is said of charity by the apostle, may, with equal truth, be said of Christianity, as a whole. "It suffereth long and is kind," &c. 1 Cor. xiii. 4–7.

This spirit was eminently displayed by the apostle Paul, and nowhere is it more beautifully seen than in this closing letter to the Christian Church at Rome.

These salutations he introduces by commending to their Christian courtesy Phebe, by whom it is very probable that this epistle was sent.

Observe respecting Phebe,

I. *What is said of her Christian character.*
II. *Of her Christian excellences.*

And,

III. *The demands the apostle makes on her behalf.*

Observe in reference to Phebe,

I. *What is said of her Christian character.*

She was a sister of the saints. "Our sister." And therefore, of necessity, a converted spiritual person. The church of the Saviour is one great family. God is Father and Head. Jesus is the elder brother, and all believers are brethren and sisters in Christ. Here is a fraternity—not like the isolated families of man—nor the local associations of countries, but a spiritual fraternity, composed of all regenerated persons, on the face of the earth.

To this holy sanctified family Phebe belonged. She was a Christian in heart, and life, and in profession; and was recognized as such by the apostle Paul.

Observe what is said of,

II. *Her Christian excellences.*

1. *She was a servant of the Church of Christ.*

"The church at Cenchrea." This was one of the ports or harbors of Corinth, and here a Christian church had been erected. Of this church she was a servant. The word rendered "servant" probably signifies deaconess — an office which doubtless obtained in the earliest ages of Christianity. Pliny speaks of this office when writing to Trajan, and says, "he had put two maid-servants to the torture, who were called ministræ." This class of persons evidently were appointed to be organs of communication with female inquirers, and also probably to visit and minister to the sisterhood in the church who might be poor or afflicted. Doubtless, in choosing such persons, they would be influenced by Christian intelligence, decision of character, and superior spirituality of mind. To be chosen, therefore, was a sign of the church's estimation and confidence in them. There is evidently as much need for this office now as ever; and no persons can be more useful, than intelligent, devoted women in the church of Christ. Now we think it is clear that Phebe was a deaconess of the church at Cenchrea.

2. *She was distinguished for Christian kindness and hospitality.*

"A succorer of many," &c. It is not unlikely that she was at the head of her domestic establishment, and as such, could make her dwelling the seat of Christian goodness and beneficence. Here was a little sanctuary for the disciples of Jesus. A peaceful retreat from a hating and persecuting world. Here was Christian principle living and acting according to Christ's own command, and in his spirit—in deeds of generous love and tender sympathy.

Many had been cheered by her benignant spirit. Many relieved by her timely hospitality. Many blessed by her spiritual communications. Of these the apostle refers to himself: "And of myself also." There is a reference to Paul's visit, Acts xviii. 18. But as Cenchrea was so near Corinth, it is likely that the apostle had often enjoyed the refreshings of kindly hospitality from the hands of Phebe.

It would seem from Paul's first letter to Timothy, v. 9, &c., that the church probably provided for the sustenance of this class of the servants of Christ; and he gives orders as to the features by which such should be distinguished.

Then notice,

III. *The demands the apostle makes on her behalf.*

"I commend," &c. He demands for her,

1. *Christian reception.*

"That ye receive her, &c., as becometh saints." Here is one of your own spiritual family—a sister to me and to you—let her have a cordial, kind welcome. Now a Christian reception would involve the idea,

(1.) Of thanks to God for her—for her Christianity—for her mercies, for her being brought to them. It would include also,

(2.) Prayer for her. That they would receive her in a devout spirit—seeking the divine blessing to rest upon her, and bless her.

(3.) Genuine love. Show her the affection worthy of the disciples of Christ. The love which is not in word, but in deed. Love unfeigned. The pure good-will and genuine complacency which the Spirit of God inspires.

He demands for her,

2. *Christian communion or fellowship.*

I think this is distinctly included in the phrase, receive her "in the Lord." As one of his dear children. And let her share with you in all your religious services and privileges. Enjoy your society—share in all the means of grace you possess. Now I hesitate not to affirm, that a real Christian should have a free passport to every Christian church in the world, and that by virtue of his common Christianity. He demands for her,

3. *Christian sympathy and assistance.*

Enter with her on the object of her visit.

Make her business yours. Give her counsel and help in any way she needs, and in any way you can. Let her feel that she has your confidence and affection, and then necessarily your kind co-operation.

Learn,—

1. *The exalting influence of Christianity on the female character and station.*

In Christ there is neither bond nor free—male nor female, &c.

2. *The generous spirit it breathes.*

A religion of goodness and love.

3. *The great claims it makes on all who possess it.*

CCXXVII.—PRISCILLA AND AQUILA.

"Greet Priscilla and Aquila, my helpers in Christ Jesus: who for my life laid down their own necks; unto whom not only I give thanks, but also all the churches of the Gentiles."—*Rom.* xvi. 3, 4.

HAPPY is the sight, when we see persons united in the bonds of natural relationship also fellow-heirs of the grace of life. Our text regards an instance of this kind. Priscilla and Aquila, husband and wife, were both of one heart and one mind in reference to religion. They had both heard the gospel, and experienced its saving power. As Christian disciples, they were distinguished for all that holy simplicity and zeal, which was so strikingly displayed by the early followers of Jesus. To these truly excellent persons, the apostle sends his Christian salutation. He says, "Greet Priscilla," &c.

Let us,

I. *Glance at their history, as recorded in the Scriptures.*

And,

II. *At the special references made to them in the text.*

I. *Glance at their history, as recorded in the Scriptures.*

We first meet with them,

(1.) After having been banished from Rome—residents at Corinth: Acts xviii. 2. It would appear at this time that they were Jews; and as such, had been persecuted and banished from Rome. It is highly probable that they were devout persons. In this connection we observe,

(2.) That they were laboring industrious persons. Their occupation was that of tent-makers. At that period, travellers depended chiefly on these, instead of inns; and hence both itinerant merchants, pilgrims, soldiers, and shepherds were often required to dwell in tents. The Apostle Paul, though he had received a liberal education, was also of this trade. The Jews thought it desirable to dignify labor, by giving their sons some lawful active occupation.

(3.) That they received the Apostle into their family and workshop. "He abode with them, and wrought." No small honor to receive a disciple; but here was a minister, an Apostle—yea, the chief of the Apostles—one of the most learned and useful of the whole. It is probable that the influence of his holy life and Christian conversation and discourses converted them to Christianity. This is not stated; but, I think, may be reasonably presumed; for, doubtless, they would accompany Paul to the Synagogue, &c. Ver. 4 and 5.

(4.) We find them next accompanying the Apostle to Ephesus. Acts xviii. 18, 19. It is clear that at this time, they were not only Christians, but well-instructed in the doctrines of the Gospel; and soon an opportunity of evidencing this was given them. The eloquent Apollos came to Ephesus, and Priscilla and Aquila heard him—discovered his deficiency in Christian knowledge; and they took him unto them, that is, into their house, or dwelling, and expounded to him the way of God more perfectly. An account of these results is described in verses 24–28.

There is only one reference to them more in the Divine word, when they united with the Apostle Paul, and sent their salutation to the saints in Corinth, with whom they formerly lived and communed. See 1 Cor. xvi. 19.

As this Epistle was written from Philippi, it is not unlikely that they were then residents of that city.

Notice,

II. *The special references made to them in the text.*

1. *They were fellow-helpers of the Apostle.*

In how many forms and modes they did this, is not stated. Indeed, these must always vary with circumstances. The main thing is, to feel the responsibility for laboring in Christ's cause; and then to have a heart and will to carry it out, as God may give opportunity.

Not only did they contribute to the Apostle's personal comfort, but it is evident they worked with him spiritually. He calls them,

"Helpers in Christ Jesus." Helpers in his spiritual calling. Acting with him for the exaltation of Christ, and the salvation of souls.

2. *They were self-denying and magnanimous disciples of Jesus.*

They were not ease lovers. Not Christians courting flowery paths and sunny scenes. Not merely professors when the church was peaceful and prosperous; but they walked in the thorny paths of self-denial—they hazarded their ease, property, and even lives, for the Apostle's sake, and for the gospel's sake—they stood fast, and firm, and prominent, in the day of peril. Ventured all for Christ. Left all to be disposed of by his providence, and relied on his efficient grace.

In this way they strengthened the Apostle, cheered him, and in this way contributed to the success of all the Gentile churches: last clause, ver. 4.

3. *They maintained the ordinances of religion in their own family.*

Ver. 5. Hence we read of the church that is in their house. At this time Christians had no distinct edifices for worship, so they met in private dwellings, or in rooms; and in the dwelling of Aquila and Priscilla, they had a church, that is, a Christian congregation, regularly assembling with them.

Now, at this time, they were in Rome; but it is evident from 1 Cor. xiv. 19, that when they were in Philippi, they also had a church in their house. They aimed at this. They labored for this. They attained this; and it is recorded as an evidence of the heartiness and activity of their piety.

Learn,—

1. *How useful Christians may be in the ordinary walks of life.*

Aquila and Priscilla had no extraordinary gifts and endowments, or sphere; but they had good common sense, real piety, and a holy zeal for Christ and his cause; and, hence, see the happy results of their efforts. All the churches of the Gentiles were indebted to them.

2. *See the social character of true religion.*

It makes the family a church—and the dwelling, a meeting-house for God's people.

3. *That Christianity has spheres of usefulness for each sex, and for every believer.*

———◆———

CCXXVIII.—HISTORY OF TIMOTHY.

"To Timothy, my dearly beloved son: Grace, mercy, and peace from God the Father and Christ Jesus our Lord. I thank God, whom I serve from my forefathers with pure conscience, that without ceasing I have remembrance of thee in my prayers night and day," &c.—2 *Tim.* i. 2–5.

AMONG the excellent New Testament worthies, whose character and history are particularly interesting and instructive, we may name Timothy, to whom two of the Epistles of Paul are addressed. Yet, it is only from a very few references in the inspired history of the Christian church, that we can obtain any satisfactory account of his life or labors. Let us then, on this occasion, just glance at those particulars, and ascertain what information and practical lessons, may be derived from them.

It is evident,

I. *That Timothy was a convert of the Apostle Paul.*

Neither the time, the place, or manner of his conversion, is stated; but we reasonably infer the truth of this from certain statements and corroborative incidents.

It would appear that Timothy was a native of Lystra, that his father was a Greek, but his mother a Jewess: Acts xvi. 1, &c. He was at this time a disciple, and of excellent reputation; ver. 2. Now, if you will go back to the 14th of Acts, you will find, that when Paul and Barnabas were persecuted in Jerusalem, that they fled to Derbe and Lystra. Ver. 6 and 7.

It seems most probable, that Timothy at this time heard the gospel from Paul, and was converted to the faith of the Lord Jesus Christ. That he was Paul's convert is evident, from the terms employed by the Apostle. 1 Tim. i. 2, and the text. We remark,

II. *That Timothy was a disciple of Christ in early life.*

This is quite clear from the first account given of him, and especially from the address of the Apostle, thirteen years after his conversion: 1 Tim. iv. 12. It is likely that Timothy was not more than sixteen at his conversion; for that would make him twenty-nine at this time. As a young disciple he had the honorable and happy opportunity to devote his whole life to the cause of Jesus. How important is this! How lovely is piety always; but especially in the period of youth! It is still more so in reference to those who are to be actively employed in the service of Jesus. Few men, compara-

tively, have risen to eminence as preachers and laborers, who have not become decidedly pious in their youth. And of young disciples, how admirable a model is exhibited in the piety and devotedness of Timothy.

We remark,

III. *That Timothy had been highly favored with pious ancestry and a religious education.*

His grandmother, Lois, was a believer in the Jewish Scriptures and an expectant of the promised Messiah. His mother, Eunice, had also embraced the same divine faith; and she lived in the holy believing hope of the appearing of the Lord's Christ. Hence, the stream of piety was seen flowing down from one to another, and the result of this was—Timothy had before him the pious example of both of these—especially the latter—who, also, added to it her utmost endeavor to train her son for God and immortality. Hence Paul reminds him—"And that from a child thou hast known the Holy Scriptures," &c. 2 Tim. iii. 15. Hence, then, Timothy had been early initiated in the truths of the word of God. He had read the law and the prophets, and thus his mind would be prepared to hear the Apostle proving from those Scriptures, that Jesus was the very Christ, of whom Moses in the law, and the Prophets did write. Happy parent! so to train her son; and blessed child—so to honor and reward the labors and anxieties of maternal piety and love.

We remark,

IV. *Timothy was distinguished for the genuine and decided evidences of religion which he gave.*

"The unfeigned faith that is in thee." This is, pure, unmixed faith. The real, and not merely pretended faith. The strong, lively, and austere faith. Now this faith was visible. Not in its essence, but in its operations and results. Paul saw it; and no doubt the church saw it, and the world saw it. Faith, in its fruits and influences, cannot be hid. The Apostle James states this most distinctly: chap. ii. 19. We read of the work of faith; and where there is unfeigned faith, there will be fervent love—and burning zeal—cheerful self-denial—and devout constancy. I only add on this—in religion, every thing should be unfeigned. No mere pretence,—nothing in the form of guise, &c.

V. *Timothy was a distinguished minister and laborer in the cause of Jesus.*

No case has been more perplexing to ecclesiastical writers, than that of Timothy—especially when they have had sectarian principles to maintain. It is quite clear that Timothy acted and labored as a general minister or Evangelist, as the Lord opened a door of usefulness for him. Paul thus speaks of him when writing to the Corinthians: "Now, if Timothy come," &c. 1 Cor. xvi. 10. Yet it is clear also, that afterwards he was Bishop of Ephesus, and said to be its first Bishop; yet, at the time he was Bishop, Paul writes and counsels him as to his personal conduct and ministerial conduct. 1 Tim. iv. 11, &c. And more than this, he tells him at the time of his bishopric labors, to "do the work of an Evangelist." 2 Tim. iv. 1–5. It is clear then, that though a Bishop, he was a hard-working preacher—and, as opportunity served, went abroad evangelizing the world, by preaching the gospel of Christ. To this sort of primitive episcopacy, who can object?

VI. *Timothy was distinguished for his self-denial, and fidelity to the cause of Jesus.*

It would seem that either he had naturally a delicate constitution, or that his labors had enfeebled his health. Hence it became essential that the Apostle should urge him to cease drinking water alone, and that he should take a little wine, &c. 1 Tim. v. 23. What a strange injunction to give to a bishop! He had drank water, and water only. Continued to do so in the midst of declining health, and it required apostolical authority to induce him to change his mode of life. Then he was only to take a *little*, and not as a *beverage*, but purely as medicine—for "his often infirmities." One of the most favorable passages, in the whole Word of God, against the daily use of intoxicating drinks.

But I add finally, that Timothy held on his course—lived and died in the cause of Jesus—and, it is generally believed, sealed the doctrines of the Cross with a martyr's blood.

In conclusion—

1. Let his character be studied.
2. The grace of God admired in him.
3. And let his excellent example be imitated—

By private Christians, and especially By the ministers of the Lord Jesus Christ.

CCXXIX.—THE NATURE OF ACCEPTABLE WORSHIP.*

[NO. I.]

"God is a spirit; and they that worship him must worship him in spirit and in truth."—*John* iv. 24.

THE text is a part of the conversation which Jesus had with the Samaritan woman. This conversation related to the place of public worship, the Samaritans contending that they ought to worship God in Mount Gerizim, a little way from Sychar, while the Jews demanded that Jehovah should alone be worshipped in the temple at Jerusalem, which had been expressly erected by his command, and for his glory. Jesus having admonished the woman of the darkness of their worship, and that the Jews were right in this controversy, he then observes, that the period of the new dispensation had arrived, when all material buildings and local places would be of no avail with God; that the spiritual reign of the Messiah was commencing, when God could only be acceptably worshipped by those who worshipped him in spirit and in truth. Our subject is the nature of acceptable worship.

I. *Let us offer some general remarks on public worship.*

II. *Show the nature and importance of the direction given in the text.*

I. *Let us offer some general remarks on public worship.*

1. *All places are alike acceptable with God.*

Once Jerusalem was the city of Jewish ordinances and festivals. Since then, God has given no such distinctions. Judaism was the national religion, and Jerusalem the metropolis. Christianity is a religion for the world, and every part is hallowed ground to the true worshipper of the living God. The mountain top, the deep glen, the secluded grove, the dreary desert, or the bosom of the ocean, are alike with God. The cathedral or the chapel, the room, the barn, or the house, are alike, and equally consecrated by scriptural and spiritual worship. "Wherever two or three," &c.

2. *Public worship should be conducted according to the word of God.*

It is not what men may deem instructive or impressive, but it is what is clearly found in the word of God. This we have in two

* *Series* 1.—For opening and anniversaries of chapels.

forms—positive direction, and clear precedents. Now it will easily be seen that the public worship of the New Testament comprises the reading of the scriptures, preaching the gospel, singing hymns or psalms, public prayer, and fellowship in the holy supper. See Acts ii. 41.

Now these are the only public ordinances we read of in the New Testament as connected with the believing, baptized followers of Jesus Christ. All more than these is will-worship, neither pleasing to God, nor useful to the worshipper.

3. *Public worship is the duty and privilege of all believers.*

Without it, God would have no monument to his grace in the world. No visible church. No visible army. No visible family. Without it, Christians would have no fellowship, and the ordinances would sink speedily into oblivion. Without it, there would be no profession of Christ before men. But imperative as the duty is, the privilege, &c., is still greater. To be allowed to have interviews with God, to have audience with the King of kings. To go to his holy place, and bend before his glorious throne, and in his sacred presence. We may well exclaim, Will God indeed dwell with man—will the high and lofty one condescend to behold what is done upon the earth? Oh yes, God has said, "To that man will I look," &c.

4. *Public worship requires due preparation, and right feelings in entering upon it.*

Preparation is always requisite before we enter upon any thing of great importance. The student before his examination. The orator before his address. The subject before he attends the levee of his sovereign. How much more here. If possible, services of the Saturday evening should have reference to it. Always the devotions of the Lord's day morning. Watchfulness and prayer in our way to the sanctuary. Serious self-examination as to our motives and feelings. Conversation and reading should be of a spiritual character.

5. *Public worship should be constant and regular.*

(1.) Constant as to the occasions of worship. Not once a day. Not mere fair-weather worshippers.

(2.) Regular as to time. Allow me to refer to the most common, notorious evil of late attendance. Many apologies, most of them exceedingly weak. Great toil on the preceding day. Family cares, &c. Would these prevent attention to your worldly business? No; the very person who speaks of toil, rises early six days. but cannot attend at eleven o'clock to worship God. Now, late attendance manifests lukewarmness of heart. It is a breach of the common rules of decency. It is injurious to others, and prevents them enjoying the services of God's house. Such can only render a maimed sacrifice to God. A little care and resolution would prevent this great evil.

"Lord, how delightful 'tis to see
A *whole* assembly worship thee;
At once they sing, at once they pray,
They hear of Heaven and learn the way."

6. *Public worship should be followed by reflection and prayer.*

The instructions must be treasured up. The emotions must be cherished. The seed received must be watered by our fervent prayers. All gossiping and idle conversation must be avoided, or Satan will easily steal away the seed out of our hearts. In this way only can our worship prove eminently useful. But we must now show,

II. *The nature and importance of the directions contained in the text.*

"God is a spirit," &c. That is, he is not a corporeal being, therefore not confined to any locality, &c.

1. *God is a spirit, therefore he requires the worship of the mind.*

The body may be brought before God, while the soul is far from his house and his service. God demands the soul, the intellect, the spiritual part of man. The tongue, the eye, the ear, will not please God, without the understanding, the judgment, the will, the affections, &c. "For God is a spirit," &c.

2. *God is an invisible spirit, and therefore he must be worshipped in the spirit of faith.*

"We walk by faith, and not by sight." The Jews had the cloud of the divine presence. We have his solemn word of promise, "Wherever two or three are met together in my name," &c. Now faith must realize this and act upon it.

3. *God is a great and glorious spirit, and therefore we must worship him in the spirit of reverence and fear.*

"God is greatly to be feared in the assembly of his saints," &c. Ps. lxxxix. 1. See Isa. viii. 13, "Sanctify the Lord of Hosts himself, and let him be your fear, and let him be your dread."

4. *God is a holy spirit, therefore we must worship him with contrition and prayer.*

"O come, let us worship and bow down, and kneel before the Lord," &c. Ps. xcv. 6, &c. Should we not feel and pray, "Lord, enter not into judgment," &c.

5. *God is a merciful and gracious spirit, and therefore we should worship him in the spirit of confidence and hope.* "Let us come bodily," &c. "Having therefore boldness to enter," &c.

6. *God is a spirit of infinite benevolence and love, and therefore we should worship him in the spirit of affection and delight.* "Lord, I have loved," &c. How "amiable are thy tabernacles, O Lord of hosts." "One thing have I desired of the Lord, and that will I seek after," &c.

7. *God is an omniscient spirit, and therefore we must worship him in sincerity and truth.* "Behold, thou desirest truth in the inward parts," &c., Ps. li. 6. "O Lord, thou hast searched me and known me," &c. Ps. cxxxix. 1–6.

APPLICATION.

1. Remember your constant unworthiness and need. Therefore draw nigh to God with reverence, lowliness, and godly fear.

2. Christ's preciousness and merit. And in the exercise of confidence approach his footstool.

3. And the Spirit's willingness to aid you, if you seek his influences.

CCXXX.†—THE CHRISTIAN CHURCH THE BODY OF CHRIST.

"The body of Christ."—*Ephesians* iv. 12.

The apostle is evidently referring in the text to the Church of God, which he denominates the body of Christ. This phrase he often uses in the same sense, Col. i. 18; Rom. xii. 4, and this is largely carried out in his epistle to the Corinthians, 1 Cor. xii. 12, 31. Now this is a very striking, instructive, and beautiful similitude.

Christ in his body of flesh has passed into the heavens. He is no longer visible to the eye of sense, but the Church is now his representative body in the world; and

† The Sketches marked thus (†) are original, and are now added into this edition.

the Church is responsible to Christ the Head for carrying out all his gracious purposes and designs. I need not enlarge on the nature of the Church the body of Christ, which confessedly includes all those who are spiritually united to him by living faith. But I wish to observe some points of importance connected with the Church as the body of the Redeemer. Observe,

I. *Its visibility.*

A body is visible. So was Christ's body. Men beheld it; it sojourned with mankind, &c. Now the essence of religion is unseen by the eye of mortals. But the evidences of its existence are ever palpable and manifest. So with the true Church of Christ, it is the visible body of Christ. Described as an elevated city,—a public light—a distinguished building—a glorious kingdom. To show forth the praises, &c. Separated and distinguished from the world and yet in it. Visible to God, to angels, to devils, and to men.

II. *It is a living body.*

Not an effigy or corpse, but the living body of Christ. Now the life of the body is the spirit of Christ. The spirit which formed Christ the Living Redeemer, that anointed him, that dwelt in him without measure, that raised him from the dead, which he poured out on the day of Pentecost. This spirit he has given to be the life of the body—the Church; John xiv., xvi., &c.: so also chap. xvi. 7. As the spirit quickeneth and is the life of every believer, personally, so also of the whole Church, collectively.

III. *As the body—the Church must exhibit Christ's mind and character.*

The body of flesh Christ had was under the control and hallowed influence of the Holy Spirit. It was the residence of the Deity. Now just so also his body the Church. It is to receive celestial influences and impressions from Christ and then to show them forth.

(1.) Was Christ meek and lowly? So must be his Church.

(2.) Spiritual and holy? So must be his Church.

(3.) Self-denying and forbearing? So must be his Church.

(4.) Devoted and obedient? So must be his Church.

(5.) Compassionate and merciful? So must be his Church.

The mind, and spirit, and life of Christ,

must be reflected by the Church the body of Christ.

IV. *As the body of Christ, it must carry out the purposes and will of Christ.*

Christ came into the world to do the will of the Father, Heb. x. 4. In that body passively he suffered, and actively he did God's will. Now the will of Christ must be carried out by his body the Church. He has taught his people to pray for this, " Thy will be done." God's will is to be done by the Church, and his kingdom is to be consummated by it. See this hinted at, Ephesians iv. 8–13. Now this involves,

1. *That the Church must be a teaching body.*

Christ taught men. His lips diffused knowledge. He was the great teacher. The teacher of righteousness, &c. He bare witness of the truth. Revealed his Father: opened the kingdom of God. Now so must the Church do also. Holding forth the word of life and exhibiting the cross. Unfolding the Scriptures. Being the pillar and ground of truth, the Church is to reflect the light and knowledge of the Lord Jesus Christ. Many of her disciples are to run to and fro, &c.

To maintain and diffuse the truth is the province of the Church. The body of Christ must contend earnestly for the faith once delivered to the saints.

2. *The Church must be a sympathizing body.*

How tender and delicate were the sympathies of Christ! How he felt for human suffering and woe! How he sympathized with the poor—how he felt for the unfortunate—how he relieved the sick—how he wept with the sorrowing—how he saved the penitent. Now these must all be carried out by the Church : he demands it. He observes : he will reward. A cup of cold water, &c.

3. *The Church must be an active body.*

How he journeyed, and travelled, and toiled. He never was diverted from his great work. He steadily labored until he could say, " I have finished the work."

What diligence and devotedness! What earnestness and zeal! What patience and perseverance! Now the Church must be Christ's active body. Hearkening to God's commands, delighting to do the Father's will, seeking the divine glory in all things.

4. *The Church must be a liberal and benevolent body.*

Christ was an embodiment of both. He was incarnate love, " Ye know the grace of the Lord Jesus," &c. What could exceed this ! He gave himself, his sacred life, precious blood! Not one selfish action in all his life. It was all generosity from his birth to his crucifixion. Now such must be the Church his body. Full of love; glowing with generosity; rich in goodness; diffusing her streams of liberty everywhere. Blessing all within her influence.

5. *It must be a heavenly body.*

It is of heavenly formation. It has a heavenly aspect, often called the kingdom of heaven. It has heavenly blessings and privileges, and it is heavenly in its destination. Christ was often communing with heaven. He had heaven in his spirit, and words, and life, so must the Church his body. Christ's body after suffering was exalted to heaven. It is now on the right hand of God : such is the destiny of the Church called with a heavenly calling to God's eternal kingdom and glory, destined in its completed character to the celestial temple of Jehovah in the heavens.

APPLICATION.

1. *Are we members of the body the Church?*

And do we count it our greatest privilege and honor?

2. *Are we deeply solicitous for the happiness and well-being of the body?*

Do we live for Christ and for the extension of his kingdom in the world?

3. *Do we rightly estimate the design of the Church?*

To bless and save the world.

4. *Do we rely on the communications of our divine head?*

His desires, his honors, his joys, his triumphs. Are they our greatest concern?

Oh, reflect on these, and whether you live, live to him, &c.

Make his interests yours, &c.

Do all Christ's will in his spirit and by the help of his grace, &c.

CCXXXI.—THE SUCCESSFUL WILLING WORKERS.

"So built we the wall; and all the wall was joined together unto the half thereof: for the people had a mind to work."—*Neh.* iv. 6.

NEHEMIAH was eminently distinguished for his fear of God, his patriotism, and zeal for the welfare of his nation. Under God he was instrumental in obtaining permission to build the desolated walls of Jerusalem. In this arduous work he made constant intercession to God, and employed all the energy he possessed to effect this praiseworthy and pious object. It was a very great undertaking. A very difficult one. One of much opposition; yet prudence, prayer, and devoted perseverance brought it to a satisfactory conclusion. Our text refers to the co-operation of the people with him, which was one great means of its speedy accomplishment. "So built we the wall," &c. We desire to ground three propositions on the text.

I. *The cause of Jesus must be built up.*

II. *It can only be done by the working of his people.*

III. *That his disciples should cheerfully devote themselves to the work.*

I. *The cause of Jesus must be built up.*

Notwithstanding the lapse of almost 2000 years, yet Christianity resembles to a great extent the dilapidated wall of ancient Jerusalem. The cause of Christ has been marred and despoiled. Many of the cities where it once flourished have crumbled into ruins. Mahommedanism reigns, and the crescent waves where the cross once triumphed. Spiritual Christianity became deteriorated by her alliance with earthly states and her participation of worldly glory. The great number of those denominated Christians, and have it associated with much that is carnal and superstitious. In Christian nations the majority are strangers to practical godliness: so that there is a pressing necessity for the cause of Jesus being built up. This state of things will not be perpetuated. Spiritual Christianity must be revived and extended. The prophecies clearly predict this. God has distinctly promised it. Jesus suffered in the joyful expectation that the whole earth should be filled with his glory. Our own views, feelings, and prayers establish this as the conviction of our hearts. We believe that the ordinances of religion are to be perpet-uated, and become universal. That the gospel is to be conveyed and preached to every creature. That the kingdom of Christ will come. That universal righteousness and peace shall bless the world, and that the waters of life shall give holy verdure and fruitfulness to the whole earth. Yes, the cause of Jesus must and will be built up. Of Christ it is said, "He shall live," &c., Ps. lxxii. 15, 16. But of this building up of the cause of Christ we observe,

II. *It can only be done by the working of his people.*

We do not mean that God could not do it in any other way. By angels or by the agency of miracles. But we mean that God has settled upon the plan, and he has fixed upon the instrumentality of the Church for effecting it. And therefore as the Great Architect is he whose design is perfect and cannot be improved, that it will not be changed, and that he will build up his cause by the working of his people. This labor, which devolves therefore on his disciples, is exceedingly varied in its form and character. As all the members and parts of the body,— muscles, nerves, tendons, the internal organs, &c., the minute and the large, the hands and the feet, all work, and all differently,— so this work of building up the Church presents endless diversity to the attention, &c., of the people of God. Observe,

1. *He calls the Church to this.*

"Arise, shine," &c. "Let your light so shine before men," &c. Go, "work to-day," &c. Hence they are the Lord's husbandry. God's fellow-laborers. His army. His witnesses, &c.

2. *He gives them ability and talents for this.*

See this beautifully exhibited, Rom. xii. 4–8. The parable of the talents also illustrates this. Every one has some peculiar talent and sphere of usefulness,—schools,— the sick,—the intemperate, &c.

3. *In every age he has thus employed his faithful people.*

In the Jewish Church. In the first age of the Christian era. We see apostles, evangelists, deacons, and members, all laboring and working for God. We find counsellors, military men, and fishermen, all working for God. We find women helping the apostles, and all striving for the success of the gospel. We see knowledge and eloquence, wealth and influence, all consecrated to the cause of the Lord. In no case did the cause of

Christ flourish when the people were cold, lethargic, or indifferent. Theoretical speculations will not do. Learning will not do. Gorgeous services will not do. Personal self-mortification will not do. Alone, even prayer itself will be unavailing. The work must be done. We proceed to notice, then,

III. *That Christ's disciples should cheerfully devote themselves to the work.*

Not only work according to their ability and talents, but be devoted, solemnly consecrated as the men of old, and that this devotion should be cheerful. "Had a mind." What meaning and emphasis there is in this, "a mind." We ask,

1. *Should not the love of Christ produce this mind?*

"Let that mind," &c. Did he not work? "Wist ye not," &c. He could say, "The zeal of thine house hath eaten me up." "I must work," &c. His soul was straitened till he could say, "I have finished the work," &c. "If any man have not the spirit," &c.

2. *Should not compassion to souls produce this mind?*

Look at the quarry of nature. See the materials. Precious, deathless,—redeemed, —yet perishing. Do you not feel and long for their salvation? Do you not pray—

"Oh, that the world might taste and see,
    The riches of his grace."

3. *Should not gratitude inspire us with love to the work?*

"I beseech you by the mercies of God," &c. By the precious blood that redeemed. The Spirit who sanctified. The promises applied. The peace produced. The joy excited. The hope which illumines, &c.

4. *Should not the reward?*

God will recompense you: read Matt. xix. 29. Then, my dear brethren, be faithful and diligent, and abounding in the work of the Lord, &c.

APPLICATION.

1. *To those who work not.* The indolent servant will have the same doom as the wicked enemy. The duty is imperative to work for God. Many are willing to enjoy, to receive, but not to work.

2. *To those who work half-heartedly.* Is this your love to Christ? In this way you cannot have comfort, &c. Look at the slaves of sin and Satan, how they work.

3. *To those who cheerfully work for God.* Be firm and constant. Look to God for his blessing, &c.

4. *Our opportunities of working for God are rapidly passing away.* Soon our bodies and charge must be laid down together. "Whatsoever thy hand findeth to do," &c. After all, how unprofitable! Let us,

5. *Be anxious for the work of grace to be carried on within us.*

"Carry on thy new creation,
    Pure and holy may we be,
Let us see our whole salvation
    Perfectly secured by thee.
Chang'd from glory into glory,
    Till in heaven we take our place,
Till we cast our crowns before thee,
    Lost in wonder, love, and praise."

CCXXXII.—REVERENCE FOR THE SANCTUARY.

"Keep thy foot when thou goest to the house of God, and be more ready to hear than to give the sacrifice of fools: for they consider not that they do evil."—*Eccles.* v. 1.

In public worship it is of great importance to avoid superstition on the one hand, and irreverence on the other. The Christian dispensation is eminently spiritual; it is not enfettered by numerous rites, or expensive ceremonies. No longer are we to regard any place as possessed of peculiar sanctity: the time now is, when all who are sincere worshippers may do it anywhere, if they worship him in spirit and in truth. Let this be ever kept in mind, and it will tend to preserve us from the dark and ghostly shadows of a pernicious superstition. But we should guard against the opposite extreme. We should avoid every appearance which may be construed into the indecorous or irreverent. We need not venerate the building as such—we need not attach sanctity to walls and benches; but the design of the place, the services of the place, the great Being whom we assemble to worship, require that "we keep our foot," &c. Let us advert,

I. *To the place specified, the house of God.*

All places are such where God is publicly worshipped and served. Jacob called Bethel such. The tabernacle, the temple, and the synagogue were such. Wherever two or three are met together, that place is such. Large or small, splendid or plain. Every such place is,

1. *The depository of the divine word.*

Here the lively oracles are preserved and read, and expounded from time to time. In this way the house of God becomes the pillar and ground of truth. The reading of the holy scriptures is an important part of Christian worship. Thus the Lord speaks, and we grow in the knowledge of his will. The house of God,

2. *Is the scene of divine manifestations.*

He filled the ancient temple with his glory. He fills his house with the overflowing streams of love and mercy. He reveals himself as the Lord merciful and gracious. He awakens, he softens, he converts, he pardons, he sanctifies, he establishes, he comforts, he prepares for the services of the skies.

3. *The place of holy exercises.*

There are three especial exercises of spiritual worship. Praise for all the Divine bounties and blessings. See 100th psalm. Meditation and holy communion with God, whereby we raise our thoughts and desires to the skies, and sit in heavenly places with Christ Jesus. Prayer for Divine mercy, for all needful blessings, for body and soul, for ourselves, the Church, and the whole world.

II. *The attendance referred to.*

" When thou goest." Here it is supposed that you do attend the house of God. Now, on this subject we shall see great diversity of spirit and character. There is great diversity,

1. *In the principles of attendance.*

With many it is a matter of custom,— the result of habit and education. With many a matter of taste, the exercises are agreeable, it is a change, or they fancy the manners of the minister, or the talent of the singers, or the sweetness of the music. With many it is a matter of conscientious superstition : they do not love and serve God, but they dread his wrath, and they attend the services of his house to appease the terrors of an alarmed conscience. We trust a goodly number have regard to the holy claims of God, and the true benefit of their undying souls. We shall see great diversity,

2. *In the periods and frequency of attendance.*

Many are once-a-day worshippers. Two hours in the evening is all they devote to religious things. Others are only morning worshippers, and then the remainder of the day is spent in visiting and conversation. Many are entirely fine-weather worshippers; they calculate and conclude as the horticulturist regulates his hot-house for his plants. Many are entirely Lord's-day worshippers, but they cannot spare a moment of the week for the services of the Lord's house. Under the old dispensation, they had their daily morning and evening sacrifices. Others, again, embrace every opportunity ; they are glad when it is said unto them, " Let us go up to the house of the Lord."

3. *We see great diversity in the spirit exhibited by those who attend.* Some exhibit a trifling spirit, some a dull and lethargic spirit, can scarcely keep awake. How different they are at home, and in their business, or if they went to pay homage to an earthly monarch. Some exhibit a wearisome spirit, they tire, and it is evidently a burden. Many are attentive, serious, and devout.

4. *We see great diversity in the results of attendance.*

How many attend, and yet are in the gall of bitterness—enemies to God, rejecters of Christ, guilty, perhaps avaricious, proud, profane, triflers, &c. Or others at best formal, " a name to live," &c. With others, delightful results. Enlightened, convinced, saved, meetened for the skies.

III. *The course recommended.*

" Keep thy foot." That is,

1. *Go with serious consideration.*

Remember your errand and object. A fool sports with serious and solemn things.

2. *Go with sincere intentions.*

Awaken your souls. Stir up every holy feeling, &c. God must have a living sacrifice. In an acceptable sacrifice the heart must be engaged ; whatever else there is, without that, it is a sacrifice of fools.

3. *Go with devout and humble prostration of spirit.*

" The sacrifice of God is a broken spirit," &c. " Bow down before the Lord, thy Maker." Avoid self-esteem and complacency, for such is the sacrifice of fools.

4. *Go and labor to profit by your attendance.*

In knowledge and understanding, in fear and love, in faith and obedience.

APPLICATION.

1. Which class of worshippers do you belong to?

2. In what spirit have you heard on this occasion?

3. What are your desires and resolutions?

CCXXXIII.—PAUL'S NOBLE AVOWAL.

"For I am not ashamed of the gospel of Christ; for it is the power of God unto salvation, to every one that believeth; to the Jew first, and also to the Greek."—*Rom.* i. 16.

THERE is no subject so truly interesting to man as the gospel. On the truth or fallacy of it rest all his hopes,—hopes in this life, and in the world to come. Liberty is of all things most desired by the slave and captive. Food is most anxiously sought by the hungry and famishing. Health is most eagerly looked for by the sick, and life is that for which a man will part with all he possesses, to retain. Now the gospel is the announcement of freedom to the bound; of food to the starving; of health to the afflicted; and of life, yea, eternal life to the condemned and perishing children of men. And there is this additional value to the blessings of the gospel, that they are spiritual and everlasting. Now this gospel is variously designated; as the gospel of the kingdom; the gospel of God; the gospel of salvation; and the glorious gospel of the blessed God. In our text it is represented as the gospel of Christ. It is the production of Christ's infinite wisdom and boundless love. It is the exhibition of Christ's person, work, and glory. Viewed as a system, Christ is the centre and the glory. As a superstructure, Christ is the foundation, and the headstone of the corner. Viewed in connection with the New Testament dispensation, it is the proclamation of blessings obtained by Christ; privileges conferred by Christ; ordinances and laws enforced by Christ, and designed to subjugate the world to the love and obedience of Christ. Let us then consider,

I. *The feelings the apostle avowed.*

II. *The reasons on which they were grounded.*

I. *The feelings the apostle avowed.*

Now here much more is included than what is expressed. So far from being ashamed, the apostle delighted, gloried in the gospel. It was the solace of his heart, the joy of his soul; to exhibit it, and diffuse it, the great end of his life. "Yea, doubtless, and I count all things but loss, for the excellency," &c. Yet there are many who are ashamed of the gospel of Christ. Many evidence this by not reading it, many by never hearing it; some who do hear, are ashamed to profess it. Many admire certain portions of it, but do not like the whole. But the whole must be received and avowed, or of the whole God will consider us ashamed.

1. *Some are ashamed of its mysteries.*

And the gospel has its profound secrets and mysteries. "Great is the mystery of godliness, God manifest in the flesh." Yet what a puerile objection! What would you think of a professed astronomer, who, because he did not know every particular of the solar system, should be ashamed of the sun, &c.? Or, of the naturalist, who, because he did not understand all connected with vegetation, should be ashamed of the fruitful earth? Or the linguist, because he could not decipher the characters of every tongue, being ashamed of learning? Nay, let such be ashamed of their own wonderful bodies and souls, because they are mysterious, and which no anatomist or metaphysician perfectly understands.

2. *Some are ashamed of the doctrines of the gospel.*

Many proud-hearted Pharisees dislike the gratuitous and the universal offer of it. They cling to their superiority of character; to their moral goodness, &c. Now the doctrines of the gospel prostrate the sinner, strip him of all his assumed excellency, abase him at the foot of the cross, and confer all the glory and merit on Christ, who loved him, and gave himself for him, &c.: and when these doctrines are established in the soul, man will be nothing, and Christ all and in all.

3. *Some are ashamed of the ordinances of the gospel.*

They like the precepts or doctrines, but they see no value or importance in the ordinances. How would such have sustained a godly character under the Mosaic dispensation? Besides, what a reflection on the wisdom of the head of the Church. Would the all-wise and all-gracious Saviour institute puerile and trifling ordinances in his Church? Those who undervalue ordinances, should read the history of those who despised the positive institutions and commands of God, in past ages,—Eve, Lot's wife, Uzziah, &c.

4. *Some are ashamed of the public profession of the gospel.*

They are internally in favor of the Christian system, they know Christ was a teacher sent from God, &c., but they view profession as a yoke, and as involving responsibilities. First of all, we should inquire, Is it right and essential to profess it? Now Christ demands a profession, a public and unflinching profession. This Christ calls his yoke. But is it not reasonable? Is it not delightful? Is it not dignifying? It will be so, where the love of Christ is experienced in the soul. Love is not, cannot be, ashamed of the object of its affection and delight. The apostle was not ashamed of its mysterious doctrines, of its ordinances, or to profess it before the world. A philanthropist ought not to be ashamed of the gospel of Christ. It is the best inheritance our species possess. Poor man's treasure, sick man's consolation, dying man's hope. A patriot ought not; it exalteth a nation, favors its mental improvement, smiles on industry, and is at once its glory and defence. A moralist ought not to be ashamed of it; no code of laws so just, so pure, yet so benevolent. A godly man cannot be ashamed of it; it will be his song, his joy, his delight. Notice,

II. *The reasons on which those feelings were grounded.*

1. *On the principle of its divine energy.*

"It is the power of God." God exerts two kinds of power, physical and moral. By the one he made the heavens and the earth, and still upholds them. By the other he ruleth over his intelligent and responsible creatures. The exertion of divine physical power would destroy our accountability; by the other it is established. In the gospel God reveals his mind, opens his benevolent heart to man, shows man his duty and his happiness are united. Allures by rewards held out, and awes by threatenings suspended. Higher, deeper, more striking motives cannot be brought to bear on man.

(1.) The gospel is full of the power of love. A man may resist tyranny or even justice, but to do violence to goodness, and love, and mercy, is unspeakably more difficult, and hence more criminal. "The love of Christ constraineth," &c.

(2.) The gospel is full of the power of truth. Like light it makes manifest; it comes home to the conscience; it bears its own evidence; and, like light, it exhibits its blessed author, the Sun of righteousness, to world. He was not ashamed of it, on the principle of,

2. *Its saving influence.*

"Power of God to salvation." It exhibits the only Saviour; it tenders salvation; when received by faith, salvation is enjoyed. It saves from the power of sin; dominion of Satan; curse of the law; the wrath of God; and from eternal death. It is the message of remission of sins, and the instrument of regeneration and holiness; and it builds up its recipients for eternal glory. Not ashamed of it,

3. *On account of its gracious universality.*

"To every one that believeth." Believing is actually embracing it. To all such it is saving in its power. It distinguishes not between rich and poor, learned or illiterate, black or white, moral or profane, Jew or Greek. It encompasses the world in its embrace, only excepting the unbeliever, because he excepts and excludes himself.

APPLICATION.

1. This gospel has long been proclaimed to you. How do you stand towards it? Many who are ashamed of it, the gospel would be ashamed to acknowledge as its disciples. Many are totally indifferent to it. Many hate and revile it. Many feel its importance, but defer giving it their cordial reception.

2. Believers of the gospel, give prominent evidence that you are not ashamed of it, that you rejoice in it, glory in it, love it, diffuse it. Be zealous for its promulgation.

————◆————

CCXXXIV.—RESOLUTIONS RESPECTING PUBLIC WORSHIP.

"But as for me, I will come into thy house in the multitude of thy mercy: and in thy fear will I worship toward thy holy temple."—*Ps.* v. 7.

IT has been said, and with very great propriety, that man is eminently a religious being. He has within him feelings and sentiments which tend to awe and veneration. Wherever we see men, and become intimate with their character, we discover the truth of this. The wild, untutored savage Indians of America, have their religious rites and superstitious fears. The intellectual Hindoos, their countless idols and forms of worship. In Egypt, amid all their learning, they deified almost every living thing. At Athens they erected countless altars, and at last one to the unknown God. The knowledge of the true and blessed God was committed to Abraham and his seed, and while the Gentiles were sunk in crime and darkness, they had the oracles of truth, and worshipped God in the beauty of holiness. Of all the sincere and devoted worshippers of the true God, David was one of the chiefs. In this he was celebrated in his own times, and he still stands forth as a model for Christian imitation. Observe,

I. *The place specified.*

"Thy house." Doubtless the tabernacle erected by divine command, and after his own mind. Set up for the congregation together of his people. That tabernacle has passed away, and the temple which succeeded it. Now all places are such, where his people meet in his name, and celebrate his worship. Wherever there is the spirit of true devotion, &c. So Jesus has taught us, John iv. 21, &c. "Wherever two or three," &c. It is desirable to avoid superstitious veneration for places. Just in proportion to this is there a want of enlightened piety. Contrast cathedral towns and cities, &c. Yet the other extreme is dangerous. Indifference and levity ought to be avoided for the sake of the exercises, and for the sake of the Great Being, &c. Observe,

II. *The resolution expressed.*

"But as for me," &c. In this he evidenced,

1. *His affection for the place.*

"I will," &c. Why? Because I love thy house, &c. Because thy tabernacles are so amiable. Oh, yes, I had rather be a door-keeper, &c.

2. *The constancy of his regards.*

I will come, not as a traveller or a guest, but like a child at home. I will not forget or neglect it, ver. 1–3. This resolution expressed,

3. *His personal decision.*

"I will." He could not answer for others, but for himself. He would not depend on, or follow the course of others. Not be influenced, &c. "I will come," &c. How necessary is this. For none can take our responsibility. A regard to the opinions and views of others is extremely foolish, and often pernicious.

III. *The purpose formed.*

"I will worship." The worship of God is the design. How often forgotten. Some worship the minister; others the place; others the service; some, we fear, themselves. Three things are especially included in worship.

1. *Praise.*

"Enter his courts," &c., Ps. c. 4. "Oh, sing unto the Lord," &c., Ps. xcii. 1; xcv. 1, 2.

2. *Prayer.*

House of prayer, &c.

3. *Meditation and communion with God.*

Mind and spirit lifted up to the Lord.

IV. *The spirit he would cultivate.*

1. *Confidence in God's mercy.*

"In the multitude of thy mercy." Sparing many to have the opportunity of mercy. In the remembrance of past mercies. To obtain mercy, &c.

2. *In the spirit of holy veneration.*

"And in thy fear," &c. Not presumptuously. Not self-complacently. Not lightly, but seriously. With solemnity—awe. Not as a person going to a house of amusement, hall of science, &c. Place of business, or scene of social friendship, but THE HOUSE OF GOD.

3. *In the spirit of expectation.*

"Towards thy holy temple," or rather "holy place." Place where thou dwellest, between the mercy-seat. Where thou hast engaged to be gracious. Here we must look to the holiest place of all, whither Christ the forerunner has for us entered. Look for all through Christ. Pardon, grace, comfort, &c. These desire, seek, and expect in faith, hope, and prayer.

APPLICATION.

1. Do we delight in the worship of God's house ?

2. Do we cultivate the right spirit ? Are we not as a congregation deficient in several things ? We should aim at order and composure, and avoid confusion. Let us aim at punctuality. Avoid lightness and levity. Guard against lethargy, &c. Should not these lead us,

3. To think of the worship of heaven ?

CCXXXV.—THE GLORY CONNECTED WITH MESSIAH'S APPEARING.

"And I will shake all nations, and the Desire of all nations shall come; and I will fill this house with glory, saith the Lord of hosts."—*Hag.* ii. 7.

THE text is a clear prophecy of the Redeemer. To no other person can it be appropriately applied. As it refers to Jesus it also refers to the second temple, which was now in course of erection, and which was to be filled with glory, in connection with the advent of the Messiah. Observe then in the prophecy,

I. *The distinguished title of the Saviour.*
"The Desire of all nations."
II. *His predicted advent.*
"The Desire of all nations shall come."
III. *The striking events which should distinguish his appearance.*
"I will shake all nations, and will fill this house with glory."

I. *The distinguished title of the Saviour.* "The Desire of all nations." The Hebrew prophets, under the inspiring influence of the Spirit, selected every significant term, and employed every striking metaphor, to set forth the glories and excellences of the Redeemer. None are more expressive than that of the text. "The desire of the world —the admiration of all men—the praise of universal being." Something parallel is that prophecy of the psalmist, "All people shall be blessed in him." "The fairest among ten thousand," &c. Christ may be styled the "Desire," &c.

1. *Because of his compassion and kindredness to all nations.*

The unity of the human species is an interesting doctrine. "God has made of one blood all the families of the earth." All nations are compacted into one brotherhood. Now, Jesus is the kinsman of the whole. He is allied, by the assumption of our flesh, to every child of man. He was of the nation of the Jews—of the seed of Abraham —the offspring of David—but he is the brother of every child of man. Every man on the face of the earth has in Christ a kinsman, and not only so, but a Saviour. The design of his assuming our nature was the lasting well-being of all nations. He is "the Desire of all nations."

2. *As the good and pious of all ages have pre-eminently desired him.*

Abel had especial respect to him in the sacrifice he presented. Noah looked beyond the ark for the body, to that ark for the salvation of his soul. Abraham rested all his soul upon him, and looked through the vista of succeeding ages, and saw his day and was glad. Jacob beheld him as the coming Shiloh, when the sceptre was departing from Judah, and the lawgiver, &c. Moses clearly announced him as the prophet, of whom he was the honored type.

David never sang so sweetly as when his inspired muse had respect to the King of Zion, he who was fairer than the children of men. Isaiah had respect to him when he prophesied of his sufferings and the glory which should follow. To him gave all the prophets witness. We find, too, that among the Gentile nations, when they had not the light of revealed truth, or the lively oracles, that for ages an expectation of some illustrious teacher and philanthropist existed. Socrates, the wisest and best of the heathen philosophers, expressed his desire and hope that God would send an instructor, to teach men how to express their prayers with acceptance. Suetonius and Tacitus both affirmed that the book of the fates declared that out of Judea an illustrious personage should come, who should have universal empire. It is evident, too, that at Christ's advent the great and the wise were intently looking for the appearing of some distinguished and dignified person. So that both among waiting, believing Jews, and the heathen Gentiles, the expectation of a coming deliverer existed. He is "the Desire of all nations."

3. *As he alone possesses those blessings which all nations require.*

Human nature everywhere without Christ is dark, guilty, polluted, and miserable; and for these diseases there is no remedy but that which Christ possesses. He is the light of the world. He is the mediator between God and the guilty. He is the regenerator of polluted nature. "The fountain opened," &c. He is the author of freedom, and happiness, and rest. In him is a balsam for our every wound; "all, all we want is there." "Come unto me, all ye that labor and are heavy laden," &c. "If any man thirst," &c. He is "the Desire of all nations."

4. *Because all nations shall ultimately delight and be made happy in him.*

He shall have dominion, &c. His reign is to be that of righteousness, peace, and joy, and it is to be universal. The whole earth is to be filled with his glory. The song of universal joy is to be "Hallelujah, for the kingdoms of this world," &c.

II. *His predicted advent.*

"The Desire, &c., shall come." This was long predicted,—long promised, even for 4000 years. Long expected and desired. Long hoped for and prayed for. At length the predictions were realized, and the promise fulfilled. He came,

1. *At the time specified.*

Daniel's weeks ending—the sceptre departing. At the fulness of the times.

2. *In the manner predicted.*

Of a virgin. In Bethlehem. In a lowly form. In circumstances of humiliation, yet with attendant displays of power and glory.

3. *For the work beforehand testified.*

To teach mankind. To exhibit a perfect model of holiness. To suffer for sin, and to offer the blessings of salvation.

III. *The striking events which were to distinguish his appearance.*

1. *Shake all nations.*

See also ver. 6. The passage evidently refers to a general convulsion of the chief empires and nations of the earth. Between the uttering of this prophecy and the coming of Jesus, the Assyrian empire was transferred to the Persians. The Persian empire was conquered by the Grecian, which extended its power everywhere under Alexander the Great. But after his death it was broken to pieces, and the Roman empire spread over all the then known world. But when Christ appeared there was universal peace, so that his gospel could be preached in every nation.

2. *To fill the temple with his glory.*

In several things that temple was inferior to the first. In size and external magnificence. In the loss of its vessels of gold and silver. It had not the ark, the tables of the law, the pot of manna, and Aaron's rod. Neither the Schechinah, the Urim and Thummim, the breast-plate, nor yet the sacred fires which came from heaven, and had burnt for ages on its altar—but its superiority arose from Christ's connection with it. Here he was presented, when good old Simeon took him in his arms, and said, "Lord, now lettest thou thy servant depart in peace, for mine eyes have seen thy salvation." In this temple the youthful Jesus reasoned with the teachers and doctors, asking them questions and giving answers. Here he often met the worshipping crowds

of Israel, and taught them the way of salvation. Here he manifested his zeal for his Father's glory, when he expelled the buyers and sellers. "Get ye hence," &c. In the temple appeared not the symbol, not the type, but the substance, and the great antitype. He was the real ark, the true manna. Not the cloud of the divine glory, but the glory itself.

APPLICATION.

1. Mark the pre-eminent glory and excellency of Christ. In all his offices, and titles, and works, he is the Desire of all nations. He is the sun of heaven, the glory and light of the world. How do you stand connected with Christ? Is he your riches, your beauty, your all in all?

2. We urge the sinner to reflect on the desirableness of an interest in Jesus. No substitute for him. You cannot do without him and be happy and safe.

3. The inquirer may now see his face, and live. He dwells in his church. He is in the midst of his worshipping people. Hear his gospel, and now believe in him to the salvation of your own souls.

CCXXXVI.—PAUL'S EVANGELICAL DETERMINATION.

"And I am sure that, when I come unto you, I shall come in the fulness of the blessing of the gospel of Christ."—*Rom.* xv. 29.

OUR text is one of pre-eminent importance. It relates to a subject of all others the most precious and interesting. But besides the intrinsic value of this portion of divine truth, there are a variety of incidental particulars connected with it, which should command our especial consideration. The speaker in the text was the great apostle of the Gentiles. One who had been so miraculously converted to the Christian faith, and put into the work of the ministry of reconciliation. His distinguished reputation as a zealous Pharisee, his ardent zeal for the religion of his fathers, with the sudden and marvellous transformation of his character, are points deeply interesting to the Christian's contemplation, and redound greatly to the glory of the Messiah. Then there was the peculiar honor bestowed upon him in exalting him to the apostleship, with the enlarged sphere of the whole Gentile world, to which he was devoted. Among other things connected with the text, is the church to whom it was directed, the church of Christ at Rome. Rome, the imperial city, the mistress of the world. A city famed for her philosophers, legislators, warriors, and poets. Now it cannot but be interesting to know how the apostle felt, and what he desired in reference to such a place. He expressed his earnest desire to visit them, that in Rome, as elsewhere, he might make known, among the pagan inhabitants of that city, " the unsearchable riches of Christ." He resolves, after the discharge of certain duties, to appear among them, and he avows the spirit and feeling with which he designed to fulfil his work among them. "And I am sure, that when I come unto you," &c. Four topics seem to arise out of the text.

I. *The gospel.*
II. *The gospel of Christ.*
III. *Its blessing.* And
IV. *The abundant measure thereof.*

I. *The gospel.*

Now the subject of the gospel is one so frequently brought before you, that two or three observations may suffice. We may view it,

1. *As the annunciation of joyous tidings.*

This is the express signification of the term, and as such Isaiah and Nahum both spake of it : Isa. lii. 7. " How beautiful upon the mountains are the feet of him who bringeth good tidings," &c.—Nah. i. 15, and both are quoted by the apostle Paul, " For whosoever shall call upon the name of the Lord shall be saved," &c., Rom. x. 13-15. Now these tidings are concentrated in one point, the redemption of the world by Jesus Christ. Tidings of salvation for a fallen, perishing race.

2. *As a revelation of divine knowledge.*

Now the gospel is called " the wisdom of God in a mystery." And here the gospel surpasses, in its revelations, all the discoveries of the philosophers and wise men of the world. It reveals the true character of God. And " the world by wisdom knew not God." It reveals the original condition of man, his fall, his depravity, the mode of his restoration, the purity of his renewed condition ; and the glories of time and eternity to which he is destined in the mercy and love of God. The immortality of the soul, the resurrection, and the certainty and nature of eternal life, are the revelations of the gospel.

3. *As a system of moral transformation.*

The overflowings of wickedness and crime had been lamented, &c. Remedies had been proposed, systems tried. Now all these failed ; none went to the root of the evil, none recognized man's inability, none possessed power of motive, and hence all failed. Not a country, a city, a village, was renovated ; they could not restrain their vices, much less produce purity of spirit and rectitude of character. Besides, they knew not man's real elevation ; they taught men to be proud and revengeful ; they scorned humility, they taught men to be ambitious and arrogant, and never recommended forbearance and mercy. Now the gospel is God's own system for cleansing the stream of human existence, for dignifying debased humanity, and arraying the defiled children of depravity with the robe of salvation, and the habiliments of holiness. In making men pure, it secures their real well-being both in time and eternity. Hence the transforming power of the gospel was especially seen in its influences on the polluted inhabitants of Corinth, and is described by the apostle, 1 Cor. vi. 9, 10, 11. " The grace of God that bringeth salvation," &c.

II. *This gospel is the gospel of Christ.*

1. *Christ is its author.*

It originated in him. It is the result of his wisdom, power, and grace. He is the fountain-head of its living waters. The foundation of its splendid structure. He saw the misery, he surveyed the impediments, he knew the demands. He undertook the work, and his arm alone effected salvation.

2. *Christ is the substance of the gospel.*

As he is the light of heaven, the life of the universe, so he is the substance of the gospel. All its doctrines emanate from him, and yet concentrate in him, as the concentrated rays of light in a focus. All duties of the gospel are transcripts of his holy life. All its privileges are the chartered immunities of his kingdom, the acts of his gracious legislation. All its blessings are the free gifts of his overflowing compassion and grace. Its highest enjoyment is in participating of his own love, and joy, and peace. Its final consummation is expressed in that promise. " Where I am, there shall ye be also," &c.

3. *Christ is the end of the gospel.*

His kingdom finished, his satisfaction complete, his glory redounding to him in the praises of the beatified forever and ever.

Observe,

III. *The blessings of the gospel.*

Now this includes numerous mercies. One of these is justification and acceptance with God; adoption into God's family—sonship with all its privileges, riches, and enjoyments. A third is holiness of nature, by which we have fellowship with God, and meetness for eternal life. With these there is peace and joy in the Holy Ghost, the experience of faith, and the delights of hope. "Whom having not seen ye love," &c. 1 Pet. i. 8. Then the great and final blessing of eternal glory. "This is the record," &c. Such are briefly the blessings of the gospel of Christ.

Notice,

IV. *The abundant measure.*

Now the abundance of the blessing,

1. *Includes abundant variety to meet all the wants of the miserable sinner.*

Regard him in his compound character, body and soul, the gospel has respect to both. Blesses and sanctifies both, elevates and saves both. Look at his diversified faculties—understanding, judgment, affections, conscience, imagination. For these it provides knowledge, truth, love, peace, and the exhaustless range of celestial enjoyment. Look at the varied stations and classes of men. Royal or abased, wise or ignorant, polished or savage. It suits Rome and Greenland, Athens, and the wilds of the uncultivated desert. Look at men in all circumstances, health or sickness, life or death, in time or in eternity.

2. *It includes a sufficiency for all ages and individuals.*

Light, air, water, have never failed. Population makes no difference. Not only unfailing, but undiminishable. So with the gospel.

3. *It will amply meet all the vast and ceaseless desires of its recipients through all eternity.*

Eternity of light, and joy, and glory. Everlasting life. Eternal salvation. So abundant as to last forever and ever.

APPLICATION.

1. Sinner, accept this gospel now. Only one way. Open thy heart, and freely receive it.

2. Believers, rejoice in it, &c.

3. It is the great work of ministers to diffuse it.

CCXXXVII.—THE IMPORTANT QUESTION.

"What do ye more than others?"—*Matt.* v. 47.

ALL the requirements of Heaven are based on the essential principles of justice and equity. God never exacts beyond our ability to perform. He calls to no duty for which he does not impart adequate opportunity and strength. Now God deals with all men on this principle. He deals thus with sinners. He requires nothing from them but what they can render to him. He calls upon them to "hear his gospel," and they can do this. He calls upon them to consider, to abandon their evil ways, to seek his grace, and to believe in his Son. Now, you will clearly perceive that equity to all his creatures will require from saints much more than from sinners. He requires from them what sinners are not expected to render, indeed, what they cannot render. Now this is the appeal of the text. After Christ had been inculcating the highest order of Christian morality, ver. 44, "But I say unto you, Love your enemies, bless them that curse you, do good to them which hate you," &c. Now we wish to impress the spirit of the text upon you, and to apply it with Christian energy, and benevolence. Let us see, then, how this can be responded to by our own hearts. "What do we more than others?"

I. *That there is much to be done which can only be rightly done by the church of Christ.*

Some things of importance men of the world may do. Things relating to commerce and industry, to politics and civil rights, to the arts and sciences, to literature and philosophy, to learning and mental education; yea, more, they may act usefully in reference to objects connected with humanity, such as compassion to the poor and afflicted of society. Now Christians can do all these things as well as worldly men, and besides, they can go onwards where none but renewed hearts and hallowed feet can move. Now this may be summed up in one sentence—benevolent effort for the spiritual welfare of mankind. Is it not clear that that sphere belongs to the church? Ungodly men cannot understand the spiritual miseries of their fellow-men, cannot feel for them, have no ability to help them. They who never wept over their own sins, who never prayed for themselves, who never looked to the cross for salvation, how can they be expected to weep over, and to pray for others? No! this is the province of the church. None but the godly can be instrumental in diffusing godliness abroad. The spiritual necessities of the world must be met by the church. The ordinances of religion must be perpetuated by the church. The gospel must be diffused by the church. The rising age must be educated in Christian principles by the church. The church must enlighten the world: "Ye are the light of the world." The church must evangelize the world: "Ye are the salt of the earth." Now it must be manifest that the church alone can do this, and if not done by the church, it will not, it cannot be done at all.

II. *Christians have the means and facilities of doing more than others.*

1. *They have knowledge to impart which others have not.*

Knowledge of the true God, of Jesus Christ, his only Son, the Saviour of the world. Knowledge of the way of salvation, of the experience and happiness of religion, soul-knowledge, and knowledge which relates to the all-momentous concerns of eternity.

2. *They have an example to exhibit which others have not.*

Now this in ancient times had a mighty effect on the pagan world. Whilst others were malevolent and revengeful, they were compelled to exclaim, See how these Christians love! So of their patience, resignation, and self-denial, and fortitude. Now these things often produced conviction where sermons had failed. Here they saw the truth which was preached, embodied. They beheld Christianity alive, speaking, and acting. It was to this Jesus adverted. "So let your light shine," &c.

3. *They have an influence to exert which others have not.*

Read the history of the godly as presented in the divine word. See what amazing power they have exerted at various times and seasons. They are pillars of the earth, the conservators of the world. Ten righteous persons would have preserved Sodom and Gomorrah from the destructive judgments of heaven. The prayers of one made the heavens as brass, and again made them soft as the tender fleece, and brought showers of rain upon the famished earth. Every Christian has influence with heaven, every Christian has power with God. Like Moses, they have often averted judgments. Like Elijah,

their prayers have often been effectual, and have prevailed. Oh, yes, that poor man who is generally unknown and accounted as nothing, he has influence in heaven, and in his closet he can lay hold of the strength of God, and, as another Jacob, become a prevailing prince, and move the hand that moves all things.

III. *Christians, therefore, are solemnly responsible for doing more than others.*

1. *There is the responsibility of profession.*

You profess more than others. You profess to be Christians, disciples of Jesus, followers of the Lamb. What did he do? Is there any resemblance? In your zeal for the divine glory, in your compassion for the souls of your fellow-men. In your acts of self-denial, in your active efforts of benevolence. You profess to be born again, to possess the Holy Spirit, to bear the image of the heavenly. But what is profession, if you do not more than others?

2. *There is the responsibility of superior blessings received.*

You have received more than others; much has been done for you, much forgiven. Then you ought to love much, and much love will be evinced in grateful returns to the Lord for all his benefits towards you. Who can estimate the blessings bestowed upon you? Heavenly blessings, blessings obtained by the blood of the cross, blessings worth more than the globe itself. Blessings unsearchable, unspeakable, and that pass all understanding.

3. *There is responsibility arising from the recompense of reward.*

Of Moses it is said that "he had respect to the recompense," &c. Now future rewards are exhibited to you in the glorious promises of the gospel. But as the promise is made to you and not to others, it is because you are to do what others do not. The promise is to character. The persevering racer is to have the crown. The successful warrior who overcomes the enemy is to sit down with Christ, "who also overcame," &c. The "well done" is to be pronounced to the good and faithful servant. The sheep are to be placed on the right hand, and they are to be commended and rewarded, because they did more than others. There will be an inseparable connection between what we do and what we shall receive.

4. *There is responsibility arising from the possibility of the unprofitable servant's doom.*

To do or not to do more than others is not an optional matter, a concern of trifling moment. Neglect will be productive of the most awful consequences. God will assuredly deal with you as that awful parable teaches. The matter will not be passed over. He will judge every man according to his works. Now this you believe. What a solemn incentive, then, to do what will insure his favor, and obtain the blissful reward. Let us now apply the subject. Mark the phraseology of the text:

1. *What* DO *you?*

Not what think, or say, or purpose, or profess—but do.

2. *What do* YOU?

It is personal, let conscience reply, and reply each man for himself, and to God.

3. WHAT *do you?*

What is the amount, in what way, for what object?

4. *What* MORE *than others?*

Are there not in the world people as generous, as compassionate as you? Are there not mere professors who do as much? Ought this to be so? Are there not persons with less ability that vastly surpass you?

5. *I now alter the question, What do you* LESS *than others?*

You have heard of the three Hebrews, and of a Daniel, who denied themselves of the luxuries of the king's table, and who offered their lives to God. You have heard of the penitent sinner who anointed the Saviour with precious ointment, which cost a princely sum. You have heard of the widow who threw all she had into the treasury. You have heard of the first churches, where believers sold all they had, and laid the price at the apostles' feet. You have heard of a Howard, who visited the prisons and hospitals of the world, &c. Are we not confounded?

6. *Are there any who are not the decided disciples of Christ?*

Do you say, What shall we do? Give yourselves to God. He must have your hearts first, then give yourselves to his Church, and devote all you are and have to the divine glory.

————◆————

CCXXXVIII.—PETER'S ECSTASY ON THE MOUNT.

"Then answered Peter, and said unto Jesus, Lord, it is good for us to be here."—*Matt.* xvii. 4.

THERE are many striking incidents presented to our notice in the holy scriptures. That was a magnificent scene when God displayed his glory to Moses and the elders of Israel. So when the glory of the Lord filled the consecrated temple of Solomon. Isaiah had an overwhelming vision of the divine majesty, when he beheld Jehovah of hosts, whose train filled the celestial, the heavenly temple. But none of these equalled, in all particulars, the sublime yet gracious scene associated with the transfiguration of Jesus, on the holy mountain. It is of that our text speaks, and to that we desire your earnest and prayerful attention. Three things will obviously claim our notice.

I. *The place.*

II. *The advantages.*

And,

III. *The spirit which it should produce.*

I. *The place.*

Literally the summit of Tabor, the mount of transfiguration. This mountain we shall especially contemplate, as emblematical of the sanctuary of the Lord's house, every place where God's name is recorded, and where his honor dwelleth. In this view several interesting points of resemblance will present themselves to our consideration. Let us view the place,

1. *As distinctly separate from the world.*

See ver. 1. Left the busy scenes of the world at a distance. They were now removed from the noisy confusion of earth, and sublunary employments. "Apart." Raised above its anxieties and engagements. Many of these are lawful and necessary, but they are all temporary and perishing. They toil for the bread that endures not, for the enjoyments which in their realization cannot satisfy; but the Christian in the house of the Lord has bread to eat which endures forever, and has a foretaste of the joys which ever flow at God's right hand. How absorbed and injured would all our spiritual powers become, if we did not turn aside, and ascend the mount of the Lord of hosts. We view it,

2. *As the place of happy intercourse with kindred minds.*

There were three of the disciples of Jesus, engaged in the same cause, possessing the same spirit, and partakers of the same grace, holding distinguished intercourse with each other. Man is a social being; it is not good for him to be alone. Our bliss is rendered much sweeter when we share it with others.

> "Our souls by love together knit,
>   Cemented, mixed in one;
> One heart, one soul, one mind, one voice,
>   'Tis heaven on earth begun."

But on the mount were also Moses and Elias. These sainted spirits came down, and united with the disciples in holding intercourse with the world's Redeemer, and the Lord of glory. It is not at all improbable that glorified spirits are intimately acquainted with the scenes on earth, and the affairs of the Church. It is affirmed of angels, that there is "joy in their presence over one sinner that repenteth." But then they must know and be acquainted with the event, &c. Why may they not then be present in our religious assemblies, seeing that they are "all ministering spirits sent forth," &c.? We view it,

3. *As a place of hallowed instruction.*

There never was on earth a more glorious convention than on the mount of transfiguration. Moses, Elias, Peter, James, John, and the Lord of glory. But how were the disciples instructed by the conversation of Moses, Elias, and Jesus? Luke states the nature and subject of the conversation, ch. ix. 30, &c. The subject was Christ's decease; that which in all the symbols and sacrifices of the law had typified the passion and death of Jesus. That to which all the prophets had testified — the sufferings of Christ, and the glory which should follow. That which was to be the great theme of the gospel ministry to the end of the world. Of all subjects, the most interesting, most important, and most precious; and to hear and read of Christ crucified is the great end contemplated in our religious assemblies. "That men may know him, and the power of his resurrection," &c.

4. *As a place of glorious manifestation.*

Here they beheld the Redeemer's glory, the glory of the only-begotten of the Father, &c. They saw his radiant countenance, his glittering raiment, his effulgent brightness! And when do we see Jesus so clearly, so beauteously, as in his house? David desired to dwell there, that he might behold his beauty. Hence the poet exclaims—

> "I've seen thy glory and thy power,
>   Through all thy temple shine,
> May God repeat that heavenly hour,
>   That vision so divine."

Yes, the glory of God is seen by spiritual persons in his sanctuary, and Christ manifests himself as he does not unto the world. From the place we proceed to consider,

II. *The advantages.*

"It is good to be here."

1. *It is good, as it is acceptable to God.*

The Lord demands the public homage of his saints.

> "He likes the tents of Jacob well,
>   But still in Zion loves to dwell."

And whoso goes up to the mount to praise and serve him, glorifieth God. With such exercises God is well pleased. It is morally good, to walk pleasing to God.

2. *It is good, as it is elevating to the mind.*

It exalts the Christian to an equality with angels. It ranks him by the side of seraphim and cherubim. It unites him with them in their services and offices—

> "They sing the Lamb in hymns above,
>   And we in hymns below."

Look at the Christian in prayer, bowed down at God's feet, laying hold of God's strength. Look at him in his praises and meditations, soaring on high,

> "Daring to approach the eternal throne,
>   And calling heavenly bliss his own."

3. *It is good, as it is joyous to the heart.*

"Blessed are they whom thou causest to approach unto thee; they shall be still praising thee." Our happiest feelings are those of the sanctuary; our sweetest joys are there, often, too, like a little heaven below. Who has not exclaimed—

> "My willing soul would stay,
>   In such a frame as this,
> And gladly sing herself away,
>   To everlasting bliss."

4. *It is good, as it is truly profitable to the soul.*

Here the Lord prepares the banquet of his love for those who wait upon him. By waiting upon the Lord, spiritual strength is renewed, &c. Holy desires are excited, power imparted, celestial blessings bestowed, heavenly peace, &c. "I will bless the provisions of thy house, and satisfy thy poor with bread." "They that wait on the Lord shall not want any good thing." What unnumbered blessings we have received in the house of the Lord. We have had cause to exclaim, "He anointed my head with oil," &c.

5. *It is good, as it prepares us for the services of heaven.*

The house of God beneath, is a striking emblem of the heavenly temple. It is the gate of heaven, near to heaven, like heaven, through which we pass to heaven. The hours of heaven upon earth are those we spend in the holy services of his house. A day in the Lord's courts is better than a thousand. Consider, then,

III. *The spirit which it should produce.*

1. *A spirit of diligence in rightly using the means of grace.*

How we should husband, and make the best of our opportunities. Days of adversity and sickness may come, when we cannot go up to the house of the Lord. Oh, then, let our souls cultivate living activity, giving heed to our mercies, that they may not rise in judgment against us. "Giving all diligence to make our calling and election sure." "Fervent in spirit, saith the Lord."

2. *A spirit of love and zeal for the prosperity of Zion.*

The Jews evinced this in the days of Moses, when they brought more than was required for the erection of the tabernacle. Nehemiah and his fellows, how they labored for the re-erection of the temple. David, too, how ardently attached he was to the courts of the Lord. "If I forget thee, Jerusalem," &c. "Pray for the prosperity of Jerusalem." "Peace be within thy walls." "For my brethren and companions' sake," &c.

3. *A spirit of ardent longing for the perfected scenes of heaven.*

If communion on earth is so sweet, what will it be in heaven? The fountain-head of bliss. The throne, not the footstool. Day, not dawn.

"Where the congregation ne'er breaks up,
And sabbaths never end."

"Fulness of joy, and pleasures for evermore."

APPLICATION.

1. How many can experimentally employ

the language of the text? It is the will of God it should be so. Seek heavenly influences, &c. It is necessary even to the happiness of this life. Then we are fortified against trouble, &c. We must descend from these mountains, &c.

2. Seek the end of these ordinances. Grace of God, &c. To behold, and enjoy God's favor, &c.

CCXXXIX.—PAUL AT CORINTH.

"Then spake the Lord to Paul in the night by a vision, Be not afraid, but speak, and hold not thy peace: for I am with thee, and no man shall set on thee to hurt thee: for I have much people in this city. And he continued there a year and six months, teaching the word of God among them."—*Acts* xviii. 6–11.

THIS evening we have to contemplate the history of the introduction of the gospel to the celebrated city of Corinth. You will remember the event of Paul preaching at Athens, and the treatment the gospel met with there. A few disciples of Christianity, and some of them persons of considerable importance, were left by Paul at Athens, but his success was very limited there. From Athens he came to Corinth. Corinth was a splendid city of Achaia, and the most wealthy of all Greece. It was distinguished for its seminaries of learning, its palaces, theatres, and temples. One of these temples was dedicated to Venus, where a thousand harlots contributed to the licentiousness of the city. About the year 53, the apostle, as the ambassador of mercy and salvation, entered the city, to make known among these lascivious Gentiles the unsearchable riches of Christ.

I. *Let us notice the course the apostle adopted.*

Here he met with two Christian Jews, Aquila and Priscilla, and with them he dwelt, working with them at his trade, for they, as well as Paul, were tent-makers. In his ministerial labors he went unto the Jews, v. 4, "and he reasoned in the synagogue every Sabbath, and persuaded the Jews and the Greeks." This seems to have been the invariable custom of the apostles. First they went to the lost sheep of the house of Israel. "He persuaded," and did this constantly. Silas and Timothy came, and this greatly animated the apostle, and he was so excited with vehement zeal for Christ, and to souls, that he "testified," &c., that Jesus was the Christ. This faithful preaching roused the opposition of the Jews. They were exceedingly opposed to the truth. They blasphemed, doubtless, the name and character of Christ and his gospel. Paul now expressed his faithfulness, before he left them, by a sign, by a declaration—"Your blood be upon your own heads," &c. ; by self-justification—"I am clean." My duty is discharged, the responsibility and guilt is at your own door. But here the apostle had some measure of success, v. 8. "And Crispus, the chief ruler of the synagogue, believed on the Lord with all his house ; and many of the Corinthians hearing, believed, and were baptized."

II. *The encouragement and direction the apostle received.*

See v. 9. No doubt the mind of Paul was depressed.

(1.) He was depressed, doubtless, by the smallness of his success. He longed for the salvation of souls. He travailed in birth for his prejudiced, unbelieving countrymen, the Jews. Yet the mass were incorrigible.

(2.) He was depressed by the signs of opposition which were manifested. Not that he was faint-hearted, not that he dreaded suffering for Christ's sake, but he saw the signs of a storm which was likely to throw the city into commotion, and prevent the success of his great mission among the people. To sustain and support the apostle, he was favored with a vision, see v. 9. By night, perhaps after a day of toil and anxiety, &c. God addresses his fears—"Fear not;" "Be not afraid." Now, when God commands, he gives power to perform. He addresses him as to his duty. "But speak, and hold not thy peace." "Weary not, faint not, continue, persevere ; be instant in season," &c. Success is not the rule of duty, nor opposition. God's work must be done, whether men receive or oppose. No compromise, &c. He assures him as to his safety—"For I am with thee," &c. Christ gave this promise originally—"And lo I am with you," &c. It is now renewed. We often seem to forget, or the impression is feeble. What can we need more ? God's presence. It includes every thing else. He guarantees his personal safety, v. 10. A Christian is immortal until his work is done. Neither fires nor floods can kill, if the Lord

preserves alive. He refers to his ultimate success. "I have much people in this city." It was very populous, many souls in it. But many, too, who would not be of the saved. God sees all things. He beheld in this city many proud, abandoned, perishing souls, who would be converted, sanctified, and eternally happy. He saw that by preaching many would hear, believe, and be saved. Here then he spoke to the hopes of the apostle, and doubtless this would act as a powerful impetus to him in his course.

III. *The perseverance of the apostle exhibited.*

"He continued there a year and six months," &c. The word of God was what he taught. And he persevered for eighteen months, diligently discharging his apostolical duty. It was during this time the Corinthian Church was formed and established. Observe,

IV. *The opposition he encountered.*

Now mark, this was the work of the Jews. The charge was, that he persuaded the people to "worship God contrary to the law," &c. Their spirit was bitter, &c. "This fellow." The judge to whom they appealed was Gallio. No person has ever suffered more from the ignorant and careless reader than Gallio. His name and conduct have been strangely misrepresented. He was the brother of the celebrated philosopher Seneca. He was distinguished for his mild and amiable temper and disposition. He is referred to by historians as a model of excellency, &c. His conduct to Paul deserves the highest possible praise. The office of Gallio was that of proconsul, a civil office ; he had to see the civil laws enforced ; he possessed no authority in matters of religion, and therefore we observe the decision was wise and righteous; see verse 14, 15. He refused to interfere in matters of religion and conscience. He refused to leave his own province of duty and power. He therefore rejected the clamorous Jews, drove them from the judgment-seat; "for he cared not," &c.

APPLICATION.

Learn,

1. The gracious character of the gospel. It excludes none. No: not the debased Corinthians. What mercy !

2. The vilest often receive it, while the more moral reject it.

3. The Christian minister must proclaim it to all, and under all circumstances.

CCXL.—THE PRIMITIVE DISCIPLES.

"These all continued with one accord in prayer and supplication."—*Acts* i. 14.

THE preceding verses relate to the interesting and glorious circumstance of Christ's ascension. It will be seen that the Redeemer, before he was taken from his disciples, gave them much instruction, for he was seen of them, and conversed with them, for forty days. His last address is contained in the paragraph from the fourth verse. Having given them his parting advice, while their eyes were fixed upon him, "He was taken up, and a cloud received him out of their sight." Filled with wonder and admiration, they continued to gaze upwards, until two celestial messengers thus addressed them: "Ye men of Galilee, why stand ye gazing up into heaven?" ver. 11. Then they returned to Jerusalem, &c. Let us consider,

I. *The assembly referred to.*

"These all," &c.

Now you will see at once, that the persons were disciples of Jesus. The apostles, evangelists, and friends of the Messiah, both men and women. Among them were the natural kindred and mother of the Redeemer. But there were three things connected with this assembly which will apply to congregations of believers in the present day.

1. *They assembled under divine command.*

Ver. 4. It was not the result of their own views and spirit, it was in obedience to the will of their divine Lord. Such authority have we in reference to the public assemblies of believers. "Forsake not the assembling of yourselves together," &c. Every idea given us of the Church is eminently social. A fold, a kingdom, &c. We are not to be isolated and separate, but united and compacted together. Thus there is a necessity for our meeting together.

2. *They assembled under divine promise.*

The promise was the outpouring of the Holy Spirit. The promise related to the presence of the Comforter, their guide,—the Spirit who was to supply the lack of Christ's personal presence. Under such promises do the disciples of Christ now meet: "Wherever two or three meet together in my name," &c. He is eminently present by his Spirit, in the congregation of the saints, to bless, to guide, to assist, to comfort, &c. &c.

3. *They assembled, expecting the realization of the promised blessing.*

And is not this equally important to us? Nothing else can render the sanctuary edifying. All other motives must be secondary. We should feel thus:—Christ has commanded, I will obey; he has promised, I will expect; and obeying, and expecting, I will look for the blessing. I will go for it, go believing, go trusting, go until I obtain it. Need we wonder that we have not, if we do not desire, or expect? Observe,

II. *The exercises in which they engaged.*

"In prayer and supplication," &c. The terms are often used for the same thing, often synonymous, and interchangeable.— But here it is probable that there is a distinction. They continued,

1. *In prayer.*

Asking for blessings, seeking for good to their souls, most probably pleading for the fulfilment of the promises. This must be our great object in the assembly of the saints,—to pray. "My house shall be called a house of prayer." It should be the first, last, and chief exercise. Nothing so important as this. Only think of your wants, of your dependence, and of the goodness of your heavenly Father.

2. *In supplication.*

Prayer against evil. Prayer for deliverance from danger; against the evil of our hearts; against the evils of the world; against the evils of the adversary. "Deliver us from evil." What a necessary and comprehensive request! Notice,

III. *The spirit in which their exercises were conducted.*

1. *There was unanimity.*

"With one accord." With one spirit, one subject. How was it? They had one head, one command, one spirit. Is it not so with us? Christ is every Christian's head, or legislator; obedience is essentially necessary in each. Religion produces the same spirit in all, the spirit of loyal obedience to Jesus Christ. Have we ever as an entire Church exhibited one instance of this external and internal obedience? You say some are sick, some necessarily detained; well, then, take the rest, and must we not feel ashamed? "These all," &c.

2. *There was constancy.*

"They continued." This was a part of the command. So it is to us. Besides, our wants, sins, and dangers continue. Our Lord's graciousness and goodness continue. Oh yes, this work of prayer is our business, our comfort, our life, &c.

1. *Let us regard three things when we meet together.*
(1.) The errand, prayer.
(2.) The spirit, unanimity.
(3.) The end, to be blessed, and to receive the promise.
2. *Let us meet together as often as possible.*
Our opportunities are golden, but they are passing away, &c.
3. *Let us often think of the meeting in heaven.*

CCXLI.—THE HERALDS OF MERCY.

"Behold upon the mountains, the feet of him that bringeth glad tidings, that publisheth peace! O Judah, keep thy solemn feasts, perform thy vows; for the wicked shall no more pass through thee; he is utterly cut off."—*Nahum* i. 15.

OUR text is very similar, both in spirit and letter, to a very striking passage in the prophecy of Isaiah, and which is quoted by the apostle Paul in his Epistle to the Romans. However the prophet may have designed the text to refer to the condition of the Jews in his day, we cannot fail to recognize a delightful and appropriate reference to the glorious gospel of the blessed God. It is in this light that we shall consider it on the present occasion. Observe,
I. *A beautiful representation of the gospel.*
II. *Of its ministry.*
III. *Of the obligation of its recipients.*
And,
IV. *Of the final and glorious triumphs it shall effect for the church.*
I. *A beautiful representation of the gospel.*
Indeed, the text contains a correct definition and analysis of the gospel, for the word itself signifies good news, or glad tidings. Two expressions are given to the gospel in the text.
1. *Glad tidings, or tidings of good.*
Now the gospel does not announce that which is ordinarily good. It loses sight of the inferior blessings which relate to the body and time, although these are generally found in its train, and refers us to that which is pre-eminently good, supremely good, eternally good. Now the good the gospel announces includes,
(1.) The enjoyment of God's favor and

love. By sin this is forfeited. In guilt, we are heirs only of wrath, and are condemned already. Sin exposes to death, the gospel reveals to us the divine mediation, by which it may be blotted out. It announces remission of sins in the name of Jesus Christ. "Be it known," &c. It calls the sinner. "Repent ye, and be converted, that your sins may be forgiven." It points to Jesus, and his atoning death, and says, "We have redemption in his blood." With the forgiveness of sin is connected God's favor, and the rich communications of his love.
(2.) The restoration of the divine image. Sin defiles the soul, it mars its beauty, impairs its health and vigor. It perverts its powers, and deranges all its dignified energies and attributes. The gospel directs to the means of purity. It refers to the blood of Jesus, which cleanseth from all sin. To the Spirit of God, which renews the mind, and by which the sinfulness of the heart is subdued, &c. To the divine word, by which the mind is led to the sanctifying knowledge of the truth as it is in Jesus. Hence the gospel is both the charter of mercy and the renovator of the heart, for it both brings salvation and teaches men to deny ungodliness, &c.
(3.) The offer of eternal life. Man is destined for endless being. His guilt exposes to endless punishment. "The wages of sin is death." But the gift of God is eternal life. It opens to men the gates of everlasting felicity.
2. *It publishes peace.*
The cessation of hostilities on the part of God towards the sinner, and the gracious terms on which he makes peace with him. Now this comports with the essential character of the gospel, which delivers from the power and works of the devil, and which brings into holy harmony with the will of God all the passions and feelings of the soul. This peace is the peace of God in us, as well as towards us, and our hearts are swayed by his word and Spirit into absolute obedience and love. But peace often signifies every good, and with the acceptance of the gospel every good is received and enjoyed: all the graces of the Spirit; all the plenitude of divine love; all the regards of a benign providence; all spiritual blessings in heavenly places in Christ Jesus. "If God spared not his own Son," &c. Our text refers,
II. *To the gospel ministry.*

"Behold the feet of him," &c. Now several ideas are here included.

1. *This ministry is human.*

Not angelic. Angels are deeply interested; they hailed the advent of the Messiah, and rejoice in its success, &c., but do not constitute its ministry. This celestial treasure is put into earthen vessels, &c. God sanctifies and calls men to go forth on this embassy of mercy and love.

2. *This ministry is benevolent.*

It is emphatically an offer of goodness. A message of mercy. Exhibition of love. The subject is the benevolence of God; the design is benevolent,—human happiness; the spirit is to be such. Love of Christ, and love to souls constrain. A messenger will produce little effect unless his heart overflows with it. He longs and prays, and exclaims,

> "Oh that the world would taste and see
> The riches of his grace," &c.

3. *This ministry is active and diligent.*

"Feet upon the mountains," &c. Following the benighted wanderers. Seeking the lost. Oh, see the field of effort, and the extent of labor. "Go ye into all the world," &c. "Instant in season and out of season."

4. *A ministry which should command attention.*

"Behold," &c. Here are depths of love. Here are subjects of sublime grandeur. Here are concerns of great importance. Here are facts and truths in which we are eternally interested. To attention to this we are called, and for it we are responsible; and what shall the end of those be who obey not the gospel? "If any man have ears to hear, let him hear."

III. *The obligation of its recipients.*

1. *Religious homage.*

"Solemn feasts." These were numerous under the law. Few and simple under the gospel. Religious service to be fervent. Not to be slighted or neglected, but valued and regarded. "Forsake not the assembling of yourselves together," &c. The first Christians continued steadfastly, &c. Keep them in the spirit of constancy, and with,

2. *Practical obedience.*

"Perform thy vows." Vows made when repenting, vows to the church, vows at the Lord's table, must be performed. That God may have fruit; the church evidence; and the world, conviction of the reality of religion. "Let your light so shine before men," &c.

IV. *The final and glorious triumph it shall effect for the church.*

The church shall be perpetuated and enlarged, her interests maintained, her glory increased, until Zion shall become a universal praise in the earth. Her conquests shall be peaceful, happy, and glorious.

APPLICATION.

1. *Rejoice in the tidings of the gospel.*

Make it your boast, &c. Glory in it. Secure its consolations.

2. *Value and support its ministry.*

To you it is committed. Do so with your influence, your prayers, and your lives.

3. *Be solicitous for its consummation.*

CCXLII.—THE GOSPEL ACCELERATED.

"The furtherance of the gospel."—*Phil.* i. 12.

PAUL, when he wrote this epistle, was a prisoner at Rome. A prisoner for preaching the glad tidings of salvation. Who does not feel regret, on two accounts, that Paul should be in bonds? On his own account; he was a holy man, his moral reputation was spotless. He was a good man, he loved his own countrymen, he loved the world. He was a useful man, wherever he went he was a distinguished blessing, he was the bearer of the best news mortals ever heard. But it was matter of regret on the gospel's account, and those to whom it was sent, that a herald of mercy should be stayed on his course—a messenger of life to condemned sinners, to be in bonds. Yet so it was, and Paul rejoiced even when a prisoner; because, said he, "I would ye should understand, brethren, that," &c. Three things we shall notice: The gospel, its furtherance, and our obligations to promote it.

I. *The gospel.*

Glad tidings of a Saviour to lost sinners. The angels sang on the plains of Bethlehem to the astonished shepherds, "We bring you good tidings of joy," &c.

Now there is,

1. *The history of the gospel.*

That is, the account of Christ and his work as presented by the four evangelists. Here we have the Son of God exhibited to our view. In his conception, birth, and life; in his offices and work; in his doctrines and miracles; in his love and mercy; in his sufferings and death, resurrection, and ascension to glory.

2. *There is the system of the gospel.*

That is, the comprehensive and harmonious doctrines and principles which are embodied in it. Now the gospel-system has Christ as its sun, its centre, and glory. The basis of this system is the twofold nature of Christ's person, the God-man, and his sacrificial death as an atonement for sin. We have both these in one splendid passage in this epistle, chap. ii. 6, &c. "Who being in the form of God, thought it not robbery to be equal with God, but made himself of no reputation," &c. In that passage also, "Ye know the grace of our Lord Jesus Christ," &c.

3. *There is the dispensation of the gospel.*

That is, the period designed for the gospel, meeting the purposes of God's mercy. There was previously the legal dispensation which came by Moses, and this existed until the coming of the Messiah : then were introduced the grace and truth of the gospel. The gospel dispensation is called " the last days," " the last times," and " the day of Christ." It was prefaced by the life and death of Christ, but really began with the outpouring of the Holy Spirit. Thus the gospel kingdom was really opened when Peter preached on the day of Pentecost. Before then the great facts of the gospel could not be proclaimed—the death, resurrection, and exaltation of Jesus Christ.

Notice,

II. *The furtherance of the gospel.*

1. *The gospel is designed for universal diffusion.*

Read Christ's authoritative commission. "Go ye into all the world, and preach the gospel to every creature." Glance at the statements and visions of prophecy and promise. His name, &c. " This gospel of the kingdom," &c. " And I saw another angel flying in the midst," &c. " The knowledge of the Lord shall cover the earth," &c.

2. *This gospel is powerfully opposed and variously impeded.*

It is opposed by paganism, Mohammedanism, skepticism, and Judaism. By blasphemers and profligates. This opposition has been maintained from the beginning, is so now, and will be so till Christ conquers every foe. It is impeded as well as opposed ;— by uniting it to worldly associations, and investing it w th human splendor. For ages

this has been the curse of Christianity. It has suffered much more from this than from all its open adversaries.

3. *Under all circumstances God will secure its furtherance.*

(1.) Directly. By raising up men to proclaim it—laborers for the vineyard. By raising up institutions as valuable auxiliaries. By blessing the means employed by the Church. By pouring down his Holy Spirit, &c.

(2.) Indirectly. By overruling all events to this end. Persecution scattered Christians over all the then known world. The flames of the martyrs made their religion known everywhere, their dying sayings were wafted on the wings of the wind, and bore everywhere a strong recommendation of the gospel. Even the divisions, &c., of the early churches were overruled. Paul and Barnabas could not agree as to who should accompany them, Acts xv. 26.

4. *In securing the furtherance of the gospel God employs the instrumentality of his Church.*

Not only the pastors of the Church, and the officers of the Church, but also the members. Every one who has heard and received the gospel may, and ought, to tell his family and neighbors. He that hears is to say, "Come." God says to every Christian, " Go, work in my vineyard." Each must lay out his talent, each one pray, and strive for the extension of the gospel. Let us then notice,

III. *Our obligations to promote it.*

1. *The obligation of duty.*

God demands it—enforces it. We are to publish, not conceal. Confess, not secrete, &c.

2. *The obligation of gratitude.*

Gratitude to those who brought the gospel to us, but especially gratitude to God. He requires that we exhibit our thankfulness by testifying of his grace, and making known to others his mercy and love. " Go home to thy friends, and show what great things," &c.

3. *The obligation of love.*

The love of Christ constraineth us to speak, and labor, and suffer, so that we may promote the furtherance of the gospel. This gives zeal to the spirit, energy to the character, swiftness to the feet, and liberality to the soul, so that the gospel may be extended. This will give steadfastness and perseverance to exertion.

1. Are we anxious for the furtherance of the gospel? Is it in our heart? When in the closet, the family, the sanctuary, &c. Do we exhibit our anxiety, &c.

2. Let every unbeliever forward its furtherance by receiving it into his heart. And at this time. For now is the accepted time, &c.

CCXLIII.—CHRIST'S VOLUNTEERS.

PREACHED BEFORE AN ASSOCIATION OF MINISTERS AND OTHERS AT SPALDING, JULY 1, 1840.

"Thy people shall be willing in the day of thy power, in the beauties of holiness from the womb of the morning; thou hast the dew of thy youth." —*Ps.* cx. 3.

THIS psalm contains one beautiful and continuous prophecy of the person, work, and kingdom of the Messiah. The Redeemer has given us the clear application of it to himself in the observations he made to the Pharisee, Matt. xxii. 40, &c. The apostle Paul also quotes the verse, when treating of the priestly office of the Saviour.

The psalm evidently refers to Christ subsequent to his resurrection. It begins with the authoritative yet gracious mandate of Jehovah, "Sit thou on my right hand, until I make thine enemies thy footstool." This seems to be a direct reply to Christ's sacerdotal prayer. "Jesus lifted up his eyes to heaven, and said, Father, the hour is come; glorify thy Son, that thy Son also may glorify thee," John xvii. 1. "I have glorified thee on the earth," &c., ver. 4, God replies to the prayers of his Son; thy engagements have been faithfully executed, thy humiliation is past, thy sufferings are over, thou hast redeemed a fallen world to thyself, thou hast a right to reign. The prophecy then reveals the means by which his kingdom is to be set up, and his triumph effected: "The Lord shall send the rod of his strength." Here is a manifest reference to the gospel. It coincides with the apostle's description, "The power of God unto salvation." It is to be sent "out of Zion." The gospel was to be first preached at Jerusalem, and to go forth from it to all the nations, "Thus it was written, and thus it behooved Christ to suffer," &c. Then the immediate results of preaching the gospel are brought before us. "Rule thou," or thou shalt rule, "in the midst of thine enemies." And so it was in the city of Christ's death, his kingdom was set up. In the city where dwelt Pilate, the high-priests, the council, the soldiers, and the people, he began his gracious triumphs. Then follows the passage we have chosen as a text. "Thy people," those who are subjugated by the power of thy gospel, who bow down before the sceptre of thy grace, they shall be "willing," or they shall be volunteers, or, as in the margin of some Bibles, "a people of willingness." They shall devote themselves to thy cause. They shall be thy cheerful, and faithful, and uncompromising followers and friends, and "in the beauties of holiness," or arrayed in holy vestments, they shall appear as a "holy nation," a "royal priesthood;" clothed in the garments of salvation, they shall adorn their profession, and show forth thy praise. Also in point of number, they shall appear as the dew-drops of the morning, and that too in thy youth, or in the beginning of thy conquests, or so soon as thy dominion is established in the world. How literally was all this accomplished. The first converts, clothed in the habiliments of gospel purity, gave themselves fully to the Lord; and by two sermons of the apostle Peter on the opening of the kingdom of heaven, five thousand souls were converted, and everywhere the word of the Lord ran, and was glorified. Such we conceive to be the spirit and meaning of the text. Now we cannot dwell on all the points which the text contains. For instance, in fully elucidating the text, we might dwell on the beauty and propriety of the figure, wherein the gospel dispensation is likened to a "day." "To Christ's day." The day of "Christ's power." That is, of his royal authority, of his right to reign and rule, and sway over all the earth the sceptre of his truth and love. But we wish to confine ourselves to two things:

I. *To the devotedness of the Church.*

II. *The connection between such devotedness, and the spread of the gospel and kingdom of Christ.*

I. *To the devotedness of the Church.*

I do not pass over the holy vestments of the people of God as of minor importance, but because we are now speaking only of the spiritual members of Christ's body, we only design our remarks to bear on those who are renewed in their minds, and who are professedly partakers of the divine nature, and in heart and in conversation are holy to the Lord. Such in reality are the Church of Christ, and such only. These are "Christ's people," and these are the cheerful volunteers, and consecrated followers of the Lamb. Observe, then,

1. *The extent of the willingness, or the devotedness of the Church.*

It clearly involves the devotedness of "themselves," their hearts, souls, minds, and bodies. "I beseech you, brethren, by the mercies of God," &c. It is to give our approbation, our esteem, and our love to Christ. It is to give him our desires, our joys, and our delights. Our thoughts, our admiration, and our praise. Our conversation, and loyal obedience to his commands. It is to place his interests and claims first and highest. It is to give every other thing a subordinate place. It is to speak and act, to eat and drink, to move and live, so as to glorify him. It is to recognize his will as our only rule,—his commands as our one directory. Now is this beyond Christ's claims? And when this, all this, is yielded, can any thing else be withheld? Can talents, however splendid? Can power, however mighty? Can influence, however extensive? Can wealth, however ample? If we have given Christ our souls, our entire selves, without reservation, shall we not be ready for health or sickness, for riches or poverty, for freedom or bonds, for life or death, for any thing to suffer or do, which he requireth of us? We see devotedness to this extent, yea, and beyond all we can say or even conjecture, was yielded by the early disciples, the first churches of Christ. Consider,

2. *The principle of such devotedness.*

This is one simple element, not miraculous influences, or gifts, but the indwelling operative love of Christ. The language of the apostle was the language of every disciple.

Wherefore do we abandon the faith of our fathers? Wherefore become the followers of the slandered malefactor? &c., &c. Wherefore give up ease, and wealth, and liberty, and life? "The love of Christ constraineth us." It has claims which these have not, and bears us away above all these things. It fills, it captivates, it absorbs our souls. Love so divine, so heavenly, so expensive to its author, so inexpressibly precious, constrains us. It expands, it causeth us to appear as fools to the world, as beside ourselves. Oh yes, this is the principle of true devotedness. Nothing else will accomplish this, this has done it, it cannot fail to do it. This is the hallowed fire which burns up the dross of selfishness; this, the hallowed flame which changes all into its own nature and element. This is the deep and rapid stream which fills the channel of the soul, and sweeps all before it, and bears the man onward to the ocean of eternal love. The Christian exclaims, I love him, I love his cause, and his gospel, his people, and the whole world, because he first loved me, and because his love is shed abroad in my heart, &c. Consider,

3. *How this devotedness is to be sustained.*

I need not say it will be tried. Our hearts will try, and resist, or be indolent. The world will try it, by its fascinations, its maxims, &c. Satan too will try it, and if possible suspend or weaken it. Formalists, too, will say, Be not righteous overmuch; be moderate, be prudent: all these will try it. How is it to be sustained? By faith and hope in the glories of a blissful immortality. Was it not that which sustained the devotedness of Moses, of the prophets, of the apostles, of the early Christians? The apostle while looking on the retrospect exclaimed, "I have fought a good fight, I have finished my course, I have kept the faith: henceforth there is laid up for me a crown of righteousness," &c. The primitive saints were so indifferent to the world, because they were seeking a better country; to their homes, because they had titles to heavenly mansions; to their friends, because they had their chief friend in heaven; to riches, because of the grandeur of their estate in glory; to life, because of the better resurrection to immortality beyond the grave. Oh! this devotedness may and will be sustained by keeping the eye of faith on the goal, on the prize, on heaven, and walking as on the precincts of eternity every day. But we pass on to notice,

II. *The connection between such devotedness, and the spread of the gospel and the kingdom of Christ.*

1. *The instrumentality for spreading the gospel, and extending the kingdom of Christ, is committed to the church.*

The world can only be evangelized by the truth. The original commission must still be regarded. The gospel must be preached in all the world, and to every creature: see Rom. x. 13. "For whosoever shall call upon the name of the Lord shall be saved." Now the church has the gospel in trust for the benefit of the world, and, bearing this standard, they are to extend Christ's domains, and give to him a people out of every nation. This is the work of the church in her collective capacity, and of each member. "Ye are the light," &c. "Ye are the salt of the earth," &c.

2. *In proportion to the church's devotedness will the cause of Christ prevail.*

Look at the apostolic age. Look at the three earliest centuries. Look at the reformation, in our land, in the days of Wesley and Whitefield. Look at churches where there is this devotedness in our own day, and the results are invariably the same. Means are established in the kingdom of grace, as in the kingdom of nature. If our brethren had not gone to India, &c., we should not have had converted Brahmins now preaching, &c.; and if the churches had not felt, and devoted their property too, the missionaries had not gone. Look at the dark ages, when the church was corrupt and faithless, and see the results. Look at churches where there is coldness, and avarice, and self, and see what is their condition.

3. *This devotedness of the church is indispensably necessary to this end, and nothing else is so necessary as this.*

When we look at the world, and see what is requisite for its salvation, where do we begin? With God; with the sacrifice of Christ; with the Holy Spirit; with the gospel. Can you believe any supposable blame rests here? Is there as much piety in our churches, as much zeal, as much love, as much liberality, as God demands? Is the talent and wealth of Christ's professing people given to him? No, not a tithe of it; not so much as God demanded for the the Jewish priesthood. Oh, how unlike the first disciples! We are not willing, not fully, not cheerfully, not entirely. If the church be not faithful in this matter, who shall accomplish this end? Eminent holiness is all-important, but can it exist without this devotedness?

CONCLUSION.

1. *Let the unwillingness of the church be the subject of solemn reflection.*

I do not say prayer so much, because the great defect is not there. Christians pray (I do not say enough), but much better than they act. Do not pray less, but act more in accordance with your prayers. Pray not less, but differently, so as not to lay the blame with God. Do not speak and pray as though you wanted souls to be saved, but that God was reluctant; that you desired the gospel to be sent everywhere, but God did not. Do not pray as if you would arouse Jehovah, but yourselves. "Be willing," and every thing shall be effected. "Be willing," and every church shall thrust out her sons into the harvest. "Be willing," beloved brethren and sisters, and from the smallest and the least, you may become the largest and most flourishing. "Be willing," and the converts of our churches shall be as the dew-drops of the morning.

2. *To the unconverted the gospel of the kingdom of Jesus is now come.*

Jesus seeks your return to loyal allegiance. He asks your hearts' affection, your spirits' devotedness, and your lives' obedience. He asks all on the ground of his love to you. Will you bow to the sceptre of his grace? His arms and heart are both open to receive you.

> "Oh that my Jesus' heavenly charms
> Might every bosom move:
> Fly, sinners, fly into those arms
> Of everlasting love."

CCXLIV.—PAUL PREACHING AT ATHENS.[*]

PART 1.

"Now while Paul waited for them at Athens, his spirit was stirred in him, when he saw the city wholly given to idolatry," &c.—*Acts* xvii. 16–23.

PAUL had been driven out of Thessalonica by a rude mob of the baser sort, and from thence he had repaired to Berea, where the people gave him a fair and candid hearing. "For these were more noble," &c. The result was, many believed, &c., ver. 12. But the persecuting Jews of Thessalonica pursued the apostle to Berea, and there also stirred up the people. It was deemed prudent, therefore, for Paul to leave Berea; and the brethren conducted him to Athens: here he waited until he should be joined by Silas and Timothy. Thus waiting, our text refers to the feelings and conduct of the apostle,

[*] *Series* 2.—For missionary occasions, &c.

"Now while Paul waited for them," &c. Observe,

I. *The description given of the city of Athens.*

It may not be amiss briefly to refer to its history. Athens was the most celebrated city of Greece. It was distinguished for the military talent, the learning, the eloquence, the luxury, and the politeness of its inhabitants. It was founded about 1600 years before the Christian era. It was called Athens in honor of Minerva, who was chiefly worshipped there, and to whom the city was dedicated. No city of antiquity was so celebrated for its warriors, statesmen, philosophers, sculptors, and poets. Here was the celebrated Acropolis, the glory of Grecian art. Within this was deposited all that was most interesting in painting, sculpture, and architecture. Here also was the Parthenon, or Virgin Temple of Minerva, 217 feet in length, and 98 in breadth. Within was a statue of Minerva, a master-piece of art, of ivory, 39 feet in height, and entirely covered with pure gold, to the value of £120,000 sterling. Besides these, outside the walls, were the temples of Theseus and Jupiter Olympius. Three-quarters of a mile to the north of the town was the academy where Plato taught. Here also was the Lyceum, where Aristotle diffused the light of science. In addition to these was the Areopagus. This was an open building on an eminence, in the centre of the city. Now this was the court of the supreme judges of Athens, where they met to dispense justice and enforce laws. Here the judges held their court at midnight, that they might be less liable to distraction from surrounding objects. Now within this highly-educated city the people were wholly given up to idolatry—full of idols. On every side there were victims, temples, and altars. Among these there was one peculiar monument or altar, which bore this strange inscription, "To the Unknown God." It is affirmed, on good historical testimony, that 600 years before Christ, the city was afflicted with a grievous pestilence. Epimenides took a number of sheep to the Areopagus, and then let them go whither they would; at the place where they halted, they were sacrificed, and the altar was erected to "the Unknown God." Such, then, is a brief description of this celebrated city.

Notice,

II. *The feelings which a survey of this city produced on the mind of the apostle.*

"His spirit was stirred in him." His soul was agitated, greatly excited.

1. *It was stirred in him with jealousy for the divine glory.*

Every idol and altar was a public dishonor to the true God. Here senseless statues had possession, and received the homage of the thousands of this celebrated city.

2. *It was stirred in him with compassionate indignation for human nature.*

The feelings of compassion and indignation are quite in accordance with each other; indignation against the evil, and compassion for the sinner. Here human nature presented a singular appearance; intellectual, yet ignorant; civilized, yea, polished, yet immersed in the senseless stupidity of idolatry. Behold those lofty minds of Athens, those master-spirits of their times and country, yet bowing to idols.

3. *It was stirred up with intense anxiety for their welfare and salvation.*

Athens, after all, was the seat of Satan. Its people were spell-bound. As an idolatrous city it was exposed to the displeasure and indignation of heaven. The soul of the apostle was filled with deepest solicitude for this dark, wicked, and infatuated people. See Deut. v. 7, &c.; xxvii. 15; Ps. xcvii. 7, "Confounded be all they that serve graven images, that boast themselves of idols," &c. Notice,

III. *The course which the apostle adopted.*

"He disputed in the synagogue with the Jews." That is, he reasoned, &c. Endeavored by statement and argument to convince the people they were wrong. He did this with the Jews, who had a synagogue, and he did it with devout or religious people, in the market-place, and he did this daily. Observe,

(1.) The apostle stood alone as a Christian minister, an apostle of the Nazarene. The people were all idolatrous, except a few Jewish proselytes.

(2.) The apostle grappled with the established errors of the place. He did not say, I will be passive, and allow all to do as they please: he could not do this. Then we see all controversies and disputations are not wrong. Christ disputed and argued with the Jews, &c. So also the apostles, and so must we with all the God-dishonoring enemies of truth.

(3.) He made this his occupation, it was his daily work. He was to be the light of Athens during his residence in it.

(4.) He did this publicly. In the synagogue, and also in the market-place. Wherever he could meet with a concourse of people he felt for them, and argued with them, &c., concerning idolatry, and concerning the true God. Notice, then,

IV. *The opponents the apostle had to encounter.*

We have previously referred to the intellectual celebrity of Athens, and therefore he had not to contend with a rude and maddened rabble, or bigoted Jews, but with highly cultivated minds, men of profound philosophical research. Certain of these philosophers, of two of the leading sects, encountered him.

(1.) The Epicureans. Epicurus, the founder of that sect, flourished about 300 years before Christ. He represented the world as being formed by a fortuitous concourse of atoms, which met and united, and formed all things. He denied the doctrine of providence, or that the gods exercise any care about human beings. His principal sentiment was, that pleasure was the chief good. He evidently intended more the pleasures of the mind than of the body. His followers, however, were given to indolence, effeminacy, and voluptuousness. Epicurus was a wonderful man for the age and country in which he lived, and was greatly admired for his endowments and virtues. He died in the 72d year of his age.

(2.) The Stoics. This was a sect of philosophers, of whom Zeno was the founder. They were so called, because he taught his disciples in an open portico, where he used to walk and deliver his instructions. He taught that there was only one supreme Being, and that all things happened by *fatal necessity.* He held that happiness consisted in obtaining a total insensibility to pain, and that a good man is always alike joyful, even under the greatest torture. Zeno lived until he was 96 years old, and died 264 years before Christ. Now, philosophers of these sects encountered Paul, because he preached unto them "Jesus and the resurrection." How great a contrast between the Master of Paul and the founders of these sects! How different his spirit, his maxims, his gospel, his life, his benefits! How strange to them the doctrine of the resurrection. In the soul's immortality many of the heathen philosophers believed, but a single conjecture is not to be found in the writings of all the pagans in the world, on the subject of the resurrec-

tion. This is one of the grand and glorious truths confined to the volume of eternal truth, and fully brought to light in the gospel.

CCXLV.—PAUL PREACHING AT ATHENS.

PART 2.

"Now while Paul waited for them at Athens, his spirit was stirred in him, when he saw the city wholly given to idolatry," &c.—*Acts* xvii. 16-23.

IN our former discourse we considered the description given of the city of Athens; the feelings which a survey of this city produced on the mind of the apostle; the course which the apostle adopted; the opponents the apostle had to encounter. We now proceed to notice,

V. *The spirit which the Athenians evinced.*

And here there is every thing to commend, for although Paul had come in direct collision with the tenets and the opinions of their distinguished philosophers, yet with candor and respect they gave the apostle an opportunity of stating fully and clearly the doctrines which he held. "May we know what this new doctrine whereof thou speakest is?" So they took him to the Areopagus, the seat of judicature, the highest and most dignified place within the city, and where thousands might hearken to the statements the apostle might make. Here, within one of the most celebrated tribunals of the world, had the apostle Paul to stand, to declare among these Gentiles the unsearchable riches of Christ. Observe,

VI. *The discourse which the apostle delivered.*

Doubtless we have but the analysis presented to our view.

1. *He refers to their superstitious veneration for idols.*

"I perceive," &c. Surely they could not be denominated an irreligious people, a reckless people; no, they carried their superstitious regards to the greatest possible extent. The city was full of temples, of idols, and altars. To these they added one to the "unknown God." How truly did this exhibit their true and real character and condition. To them the true God was unknown. They had learning, art, science, philosophy, &c., yet they were without God.

2. *The apostle gave a striking representation of the true Jehovah.*

" Whom, therefore, ye ignorantly worship, him declare I unto you."

(1.) He declares him as the Creator of all things.

(2.) He declares his universal dominion and authority. " Lord of heaven and earth."

(3.) He declares the immensity of his nature. " Dwelleth not in temples made with hands." That is, cannot be confined, not limited.

(4.) He declares his self-existence, and sufficiency. He is not to be served or worshipped " with men's hands," see Ps. l. 7.

(5.) He declares him the fountain and author of all life. " Giveth to all life," &c. Holds in his hands the breath of lives.

(6.) He declares him the universal parent of all men. " Hath made of one blood," &c.

(7.) He declares him to be the disposer and ruler of all events. " Hath determined the times before," &c.

(8.) He declares unto them his omnipresence. " He is not far from any one of us."

(9.) He declares him the source of all our bounties. " In him we live, and move, and have our being."

(10.) He declares his spirituality, ver. 29.

(11.) He declares the forbearance and long-suffering of God, ver. 30. Did not punish, &c.

(12.) He declared the necessity of universal repentance. " But now commandeth all men everywhere to repent."

(13.) He declared the righteous judgment of all by Christ Jesus. " Whom God hath raised up," &c.

Notice,

VII. *The effects which were produced.*

1. *Some mocked.*

Derided, as though he had spoken folly.

2. *Some deferred judgment, and agreed to hear again.*

3. *Some were converted.*

" Howbeit certain men clave unto him, and believed"—one of the judges, several men, and Damaris.

APPLICATION.

Learn,

1. *The corruption and blindness of the human mind.*

To give honor, &c., to stocks and stones— to idols.

2. *The insufficiency of the light of nature in matters of religion.*

What can any nation or people have that they had not? They had sun, moon, and stars. All the works of Deity were around them, &c. Yet by wisdom they knew not God; nay, all their science and literature were ineffectual here. Their poets and philosophers were all strangers to God. So it is with the heathen nations to this day.

3. *There is idolatry of heart as well as of worship.*

If Paul visited this metropolis, no such statues would arrest his eye, &c. But every one who refuses God's authority has a something enthroned, and that is his idol, and the love and service of that is idolatry.

4. *God demands the supreme homage of the mind, and affections of the heart.*

" Thou shalt have no other gods," &c. " Thou shalt love the Lord thy God with all thy heart," &c.

5. *How thankful we should be for the gospel.*

How precious, how invaluable. It will make you wise, holy, and happy. Receive it cordially.

CCXLVI.—THE GOSPEL SPHERE.

" The field is the world."—*Matt.* xiii. 38.

THE Redeemer had been illustrating the nature of the gospel dispensation, by a series of beautiful and interesting parables. Our text is part of the one on the tares and the wheat, which his disciples anxiously desired him to explain unto them, ver. 36. The sphere of labor for the gospel ministry is thus specified. " It is the world." Hence when he gave the great commission to his disciples, he said, " Go ye into all the world," &c. Let us then contemplate this field in the following forms.

I. *In its geographical and statistical extent.*

The greatness of God is seen in his works. Our world is as nothing when presented in contrast with other parts of the universe— but as a letter to a volume, a grain of sand, a drop. But when we view our world abstractedly in itself, it rises into true magnificence and greatness before our eyes. And in speaking of our own world, we can make our affirmations on the grounds of mathematical certainty. Our earth is eight thousand miles in diameter, twenty-five thousand in circumference, and its surface contains two hundred millions of square miles. Now, all this is soon said in words, but, to aid our views of this, let me suppose you placed on some eminence above the earth, and the whole should pass before you in scenes of ten miles, in every direction, one hundred and sixty thousand of these would have to pass, before you had seen, or even taken a survey of, our world. One of these every hour, twelve times a day, would take forty years. But look at this field statistically. Its population is at least eight hundred millions. While I speak, eight hundred millions are living and breathing, the accountable creatures of God, all pressing towards the gates of death and the judgment-seat. Every thirty years this tide of deathless beings passes into eternity, and other eight hundred millions flow into accountable existence. Just remember, too, that *one* of these has been pronounced by the great Redeemer as more valuable than the material globe!

II. *Look at this field in its moral condition.*

1. *One extended scene of moral darkness.*

"Darkness hath covered the earth," &c. Six hundred millions literally so! Not all in a state of brutal ignorance. Many may be learned and intellectual, &c., but ignorant of God, themselves, and Jesus Christ. Strangers to the saving truths of the gospel.

2. *Deeply involved in moral turpitude and guilt.*

The whole world is guilty before God. "All have sinned," &c. All wandered from God, under the power of Satan! At home the scene is heart-sickening! Yet here we have the gospel, wholesome laws, religious influence, Christian knowledge; but in many parts crimes are legalized, &c.; sensual rites, cruel sacrifices, forsaken children, debased and insulted womanhood. Lust, pride, hatred, inhumanity, blood, &c., all reigning with ferocious force, unchecked power, and triumph.

3. *Totally sunk in wretchedness and woe.*

Heathenism is one mass of misery. Go to the public shrines of idol worship, the way is marked by the bleached bones of those who have perished; there the sick languish, the infirm lie stretched across the sandy desert, and the voracious vulture often begins his attack before death has executed his commission. Go to the domestic hearth; it is an unmeaning sound among pagans. Children are exposed, daughters murdered, the aged neglected, the sick left to perish.

With all this, guilt and fear within. All around, the dark shadows of a gloomy and horrid superstition. With this, too, connect the peril, the fearful peril of eternal woe. The heathen are not accountable for the gospel, until they have it, but for the light they have, Rom. ii. 11.

III. *In its redeemed character.*

The compassion of Deity has visited it. God has pitied, loved, and redeemed it. "He so loved the world," &c. "Sent his Son," &c. Not one soul excluded, for he gave him to be a ransom for all. To taste death for every man. Not merely the church, but the rebellious world. "He is the propitiation," &c. Just as the light of the sun shines on all, the atmosphere is breathed by all, the fluid of life flows to all, so God's redeeming grace encompasses every creature. As such the gospel of the kingdom is to be preached to all, nationally and individually.

IV. *In its glorious destination.*

A grand destiny awaits it.

1. *A destiny of universal knowledge.*

"All flesh," &c. "The knowledge of the Lord shall cover the earth," &c. No need to say, "Know ye the Lord." This will be the glorious day of God.

2. *A destiny of universal righteousness.*

The desert be as the garden of the Lord. All men shall be righteous. Every heart, lip, life, &c., devoted to God.

3. *A destiny of universal peace.*

Weapons of war shall become implements of agriculture, and the nations shall not learn war any more.

4. *A destiny of universal felicity.*

"Nothing shall hurt, or destroy," &c. No accursed slavery. No tyrannical despotism. No domestic wailing. No personal misery. The curse rolled away. All men blessed in Christ, and all uniting to call him blessed. The travail of Christ fulfilled, and his soul satisfied. All this is certain, it is ratified, covenanted for, promised, therefore sure, for the mouth of the Lord hath spoken it. Let us contemplate,

V. *This field in its commanding claims upon us.*

1. *We are identified with it on the ground of humanity.*

All human beings are our brethren, only one family. On the ground,

2. *Of our exalted position.* We are lifted up. Retrospect of our country's history. We can survey in our deliverance, and the

instrumentality, clearly our duty to the rest of the world. On the ground,

3. *Of our profession as Christians.*

Like-minded with Christ. Love as he did, labor for God, &c. Tread in his steps, be zealous for his glory.

4. *Upon our resources.* We have what the world wants,—the bread of life, the balsam of salvation, glad tidings of eternal life. We have the word, the ministry, the ordinances, &c. Shall we withhold them? If so, the guilt and misery of the world will lie at our door.

APPLICATION.

1. Much has been effected. Great things have been achieved. Nations which once sat in darkness, &c. South Seas, Greenland, West Indies.

2. Much is now doing. The sun never sets on our missionary stations. In the regions of ice and cold, they are there; in the torrid zone, they are there; in the howling desert, in the crowded eastern city, they are there also. But,

3. Much has yet to be done, very much. Laborers must be increased ten thousand fold.* Our sphere of labor is the headquarters of the wicked one, the most benighted part of India, Juggernaut's temple, &c.

Will you reflect, sympathize, pray, and give your aid to this cause of God and man, of holiness and mercy?

———◆———

CCXLVII.—MESSIAH'S CONQUESTS.

"Gird thy sword upon thy thigh, O most mighty, with thy glory and thy majesty. And in thy majesty ride prosperously, because of truth and meekness and righteousness; and thy right hand shall teach thee terrible things. Thine arrows are sharp in the heart of the king's enemies; whereby the people fall under thee."—*Ps.* xlv. 3–5.

THIS striking and beautiful psalm evidently refers to the Messiah. It is impossible, without doing the greatest violence to the glorious truths it contains, to apply it either to Solomon or to any other earthly sovereign. This is evidently a poetical epi-

* Preached on behalf of the Baptist missions in Orissa.

thalami n, or song of congratulation, before the marriage of some celebrated monarch. The strain exactly agrees with such compositions. Three subjects are introduced: the splendor of the bridegroom—the beauty of the bride—and the happy results arising from the union. The glory of the bridegroom occupies the chief part of the psalm. He is praised for the comeliness of his person—the gracefulness of his address—his triumphant military exploits—his righteous administration—the lustre of his renown—and the magnificence of his court. The bride is celebrated for her high birth, her transcendent beauty, her splendid and costly apparel, and her dignified attendants. The results arising from the union are these:—The marriage is to produce a race of princes, who are to possess authority and dominion to the ends of the earth. The name, too, of the king is to live through posterity, and his renown to be lasting as time itself. Such is the beauty and richness of the psalm before us. It can apply to none but Jesus, who is King of kings and Lord of lords, and to whom the apostle applies the sixth verse, where he says, "But unto the Son he saith, Thy throne, O God, is forever and ever," &c., Heb. i. 8. The psalmist was doubtless inspired to set forth the marriage of the Son of God with his redeemed Church, a subject largely illustrated in the parables of the New Testament, and sustained in every part of the Divine word. That part which we have selected for our present contemplation, relates to the character of the bridegroom as a kingly conqueror, and shows the ardent interest the Church takes in his triumphant career. Thus she says, "Gird thy sword," &c. Consider the person, the cause, the weapons, and the triumphs of the Saviour.

I. *The person of the Messiah.*

"He is a king." Distinguished for his glory, majesty, and might. (1.) His glory is that of supreme Deity. The glory of the only begotten, &c. Glory underived—supreme—universal—everlasting. As the sun is the glory of the solar system, so Christ is the glory of the heaven of heavens. (2.) His majesty is that which involves the highest degree of royal authority. Hence his throne is above every other. By him all principalities exist. By him kings reign, and princes decree justice. King of kings. King of the whole earth; of the whole universe. (3.) Most mighty. Powerful in the highest degree. Yet this is but a feeble illustration of his boundless power. One in whom power is concentrated; who has it in all its infinite and uncontrollable plenitude; so much so, that what is impossible to the most powerful of the angelic hosts, yea, impossible to all created powers, is easily effected by the mere volition of his almighty mind. In creation he spake, and it was done. In the days of his flesh his word cured diseases—hushed tempests—expelled devils—and raised the dead.

II. *The cause of Messiah.*

His cause or kingdom is the very transcript of his own personal attributes and glory. His spiritual empire is based on the moral perfections of his own holy and blessed mind. Hence the great end of redemption is to bring our fallen world to reflect the glory of his moral excellence.

1. *It is the cause of truth.*

Sin began in falsehood; the whole empire of Satan is based upon this. Departure from the truth was the ruin of our world. Our first parents abode not in the truth. Hence Christ, in destroying the works of the devil, razes his fallacies, annihilates that which is tinsel, and presents God's truth for the reception of his lapsed and wretched creatures. Truth here, however, may be taken in its largest latitude: for reality—substance—knowledge. Christ is the truth of the gospel system. Truth, as it respects God, and man, and eternity.

2. *It is the cause of meekness.*

And here we see its resemblance to its author. Christ was eminently the meek one. " Meek and lowly of heart." But the term meekness is to be taken in its more enlarged sense, for lowliness and humility. The cause of sin is the cause of pride and self-exaltation. To this Satan aspired. To this the first human transgressors aspired. This fills the carnal heart. It is the mental delusion of every sinner. Christ's kingdom is essentially connected with human abasement; prostration of the sinner. It covers the contrite with the garment of humility; brings man to a right estimate of himself and his deserts, and thus fits him to be a vessel of mercy.

3. *The cause of righteousness.*

Christ is the Lord our righteousness. He came to set up a righteous dominion. Sin is unrighteousness—robs God—it is the refusal of Jehovah's claims, &c. This is the depravity of the spirit of man in its natural state. Christ's kingdom is a righteous king-

dom. He came to turn men from their iniquities. He came to fulfil the prophecy and promises. To put God's laws into their hearts, &c. To give a right spirit—so that they should walk in his statutes and ordinances to do them. By the gospel men are made righteous, and they work righteousness. Every kind of righteousness is included in the essential constitution of the kingdom of Christ. A right heart and life towards God, and also towards all mankind.

III. *The weapons which, as a warrior, he wields.*

These are the sword and bow. In the sublime visions of the Apocalypse, Christ is represented with both of these weapons, Rev. i. 16, " And out of his mouth went a sharp two-edged sword." See also Rev. vii. 2, " And I saw, and behold a white horse, and he that sat on him had a bow and a crown." The divine word is fitly represented by these weapons. Our text supposes Christ in a chariot of war, going forth into the midst of his enemies, using his two-edged sword, and directing his arrows in every direction. The word or gospel of Christ is both the sword and arrow. It slays, it pierces, it severs in two; or, like the arrow, it enters the vital part, produces anguish, bitterness, and death to sin. See Heb. iv. 12, " For the word of God is quick and powerful, and sharper than any two-edged sword, piercing even to the dividing asunder of soul and spirit," &c. Two ends have to be effected:

1. *Conviction of sin.*

A sense of it,—a desire for its removal, &c.

2. *The soul healed.*

Comforted and filled with joy and peace. Messiah's weapons produce both these effects, " The power of God to salvation." Every way effectual. " Mighty through God to the pulling down of the strongholds of sin and Satan." Mark,

IV. *The triumphs which Messiah achieves.*

In the phraseology of the text,

1. *He rides prosperously.*

As a man of war, he advances in his course. His holy crusade is successful: this is the promise, that " the pleasure of the Lord shall prosper in his hand." God has pronounced the mandate and fixed the decree, " that to him every knee should bow." He therefore says, " Sit thou on my right hand until I make thine enemies thy footstool."

2. *His right hand accomplishes wonderful things.*

For so the word was originally rendered in our old Bibles. The history of Christianity is a history of the wonderful things which the right hand of Jesus has accomplished. It was wonderful that his cause lived in the midst of the opposition of earth and hell. Jews and pagans all labored at exterminating it; but Christ's right hand sustained it, and, like the vessel on the lake of Galilee, it survived the storm; or, like the burning bush on Horeb's summit, it lived in the midst of flame. But it was more wonderful that this stone cut out of the mountain should overthrow all its opponents—silence all adversaries—triumph over all opposition—and succeed everywhere—in spite of earth and hell. His right hand effected wondrous things everywhere where the gospel chariot won its widening way.

3. *His enemies, subjugated, fell under him.*

Not by their destruction—not as the victims of wrath and vengeance—but as subdued in heart and converted in life, so as to be the devoted disciples of the Nazarene. Look at the 3,000 Jews—at Saul of Tarsus—the jailer, &c. Look to your own personal history, you who have felt his conquering love—resisted no longer, hated no longer—but were compelled, by the force of truth and the power of grace, to exclaim, in the words of the poet,

"I yield, I yield, I can hold out no more,
But sink, by dying love compelled,
And own thee conqueror."

Such are the triumphs the conquering Jesus obtains.

We ask by way of

APPLICATION.

1. Do you thus personally know the Saviour? Have you felt the power, the saving power of the gospel? Are you numbered with his loyal subjects, his devoted friends?

2. Are you fully committed to his cause? Do you consider his cause yours? Is his glory your first consideration? Do you pray for this—live for this—labor for this? Will this apply to each and all of you? Let us consider the text,

3. As God's voice. He speaks and looks with intense interest and delight on the church. Oh yes, and the bride too longs for the blissful consummation. Do we, all and each? This, then, be our prayer: "Blessed be the Lord God of Israel, who only doeth wondrous things," &c.

CCXLVIII.—MESSIAH'S FINAL TRIUMPH.

"I will overturn, overturn, overturn it; and it shall be no more, until he come whose right it is; and I will give it him."—*Ezek.* xxi. 27.

The prophecy of the text has reference to the removal of the crown from the head of Zedekiah, and the vacancy in the royal line of David, which should not be filled up until the sceptre should be given into Christ's hands, whose true right it should be to reign. Now, all this was literally fulfilled, for the kingdom of Judah ceased not until Christ appeared, who was the root and offspring of David, and King of kings and Lord of lords. But there is another version of the text which may be taken, and which is in perfect unison with the spirit of prophecy—that Jehovah has given universal empire to Jesus, that it is Christ's right to reign, and that God will overturn every obstacle and impediment until it be accomplished. Let these three topics, then, now engage our attention.

I. *Jehovah has given universal empire to Jesus.*

A few citations from the oracles of truth will establish this. Ps. lxxii. 1–11, ii. 8, lxxxix. 27; Dan. vii. 14; Zech. ix. 10; Phil. ii. 10; Acts ii. 32, &c. It is evident from these truths that Christ's dominion is to embrace the whole world—every empire, kingdom, continent, and island. All people of every language, and color, and tongue. His kingdom is to swallow up every other; and the kingdom that will not serve him is to utterly perish. This blissful consummation was beheld in prophetic vision by John, Rev. xi. 15. With this state of things will be associated universal righteousness, universal knowledge, universal peace, universal bliss. We notice,

II. *That it is Christ's right thus to reign.*

"Whose right it is." Now, this right of Jesus to reign supremely and universally, is founded,

1. *On his creative property in all things.*

The apostle says, Col. i. 16, "All things were made by him and for him." By his power, and for his glory. Satan is a usurper—the world is alienated from its rightful

Lord. But the right of Christ remains unaffected, and that right he will demand and obtain.

2. *On his supreme authority as universal Lord.*

He is Lord of all, King of kings, &c. His majesty and glory fill the heavens. His claims are as great as the universe. As such, he has a right surely to the earth—to the whole earth. This authority is seen in controlling all events, in upholding all things, &c. In his infinite out-goings of benevolence and love.

3. *He has a redeeming right.*

He became incarnate, he descended into the world, he brought the light of heaven into it, he gave his own life for it, he is the proprietor, &c. Here then is a right, ratified with his precious blood. And he redeemed it expressly that he might reign over it. That he might be King, and King alone, that the diadem might encircle his own brow. And thus in the extension of his kingdom he is receiving his joy and reward. He was willingly lifted up that he "might draw all men unto him."

III. *God will overturn every obstacle until this be effected.*

"I will overturn," &c. Now, in effecting this glorious purpose the works of the devil must be destroyed, and the empire of sin totally overthrown. Ignorance must give place to light, error to truth, sin to holiness. Satan must be driven from his strongholds, and thus Jesus will enlarge his empire, and extend his domains. There are, however, four mighty impediments, which must be overthrown, entirely overturned.

1. *Paganism, and all its multifarious rites.*

The idolatry of paganism, the superstitions of paganism, the cruelty of paganism. The very atmosphere of paganism is the smoke of the bottomless pit. Paganism, whether of the intellectual and metaphysical kind of the Hindoos, or of the rude and illiterate kind of the untutored tribes, must be overturned. Every pagan idol must be cast to the moles and the bats, &c. Every altar razed, and every temple desolated, Isa. ii. 18.

2. *Mohammedanism in all its earthly gratifications.*

Mohammedanism is a splendid admixture of adulterated truth and vulgar error. Now this must be overturned. The false prophet must be denounced and forsaken, the crescent must wane and retire into oblivion before the power of the cross.

3. *Judaism, with its obsolete rights.*

A system originally of God, but which consisted of types and shadows, which have long ago been ratified in Jesus, the great substitute and antitype. Eighteen hundred years ago that system lost its vitality; and Ichabod has been for ages written upon its rites, and services, and people—the glory has departed. The Jews are like persons who at eventide are looking for the rising of the sun; but every vestige of that shadowy economy must pass away, and all the relics of the scattered tribes be collected into the fold of the Nazarene, Rom. xi. 25.

4. *Antichristian Rome.*

The papal hierarchy is evidently that Man of Sin to which the apostle alludes, who must be destroyed. This is evidently the mystical Babylon, whose overthrow is certain. This is to be as a millstone thrown into the depths of the sea, Rev. xviii. 20. Every thing that exalteth itself against God, or attempts the division of Christ's merits, must be consumed before the brightness of Messiah's countenance, and the power of his truth. But you ask, How will God overturn, &c.? Doubtless his providence will subserve the purposes of his grace. He may cause science and commerce to open a passage for the message of truth. He may even overrule war, and may allow the military hero to pioneer the ambassador of peace. But he will do it by the power of the gospel of truth. The doctrines of the cross are to effect it. "We preach Christ crucified," &c. "Not by might, nor by power," &c. The spiritual sword is the word of God. He did this by the gospel in primitive times. In bigoted Jerusalem, in idolatrous Athens, in lascivious Corinth, in imperial Rome, and in these, then rude islands of the sea. He is doing so now. Look at the islands of the South Sea, look at Central Africa, look on the shores of continental India, look into the interior of Burmah; in one word, that which converts a blaspheming Briton will save a Hindoo idolater, or savage American Indian.

APPLICATION.

1. Are your sympathies and affections on the side of Jesus? Does the subject inspire, inspirit you? Has it your affections, prayers, influence, and help?

2. How necessary is devoted, concentra-

ted effort. What has to be achieved? make the calculation. We spoke of Pagans—write down 482 millions; Mohammedans, 140 millions; Jews, 3 millions; then add, as disciples of Papal Rome, 80 millions; total, 705 millions. Is it not hopeless? No—read the text. God has spoken it.

3. Secure a personal interest in the gracious administration of Jesus.

CCXLIX.—THE ENEMIES AND FRIENDS OF JEHOVAH.

"So let all thine enemies perish, O Lord; but let them that love him be as the sun, when he goeth forth in his might."—*Judges* v. 31.

GOD has often employed holy and devout women to effect his purposes, and carry on his cause. The Scriptures contain many biographical sketches of female piety and excellency. The name of Sarah is mentioned, and Ruth, Manoah's wife the mother of Samson, and Hannah; Esther was not half so illustrious in all her royal splendor, as when we view her pleading for her countrymen, and risking her life to save them from the Persian edict. In the New Testament we have a galaxy of pious women, who shone in the hemisphere of the church with bright effulgency, as the milky way in the midst of the heavens. There was Anna, the prophetess; Elizabeth, the mother of the Baptist; the amiable sisters of Bethany; Dorcas, the friend of the poor; Lydia, the first European convert; and, at the head of the illustrious list, the virgin mother of Jesus, of whom it was properly said, "Blessed is the womb," &c. But we must refer for a moment to the writer of the celebrated song, of which the text is the sublime conclusion. Deborah, the wife of Lapidoth, was raised up as a prophetess, and to be a judge in Israel. In connection with Barak, she roused the armies of Israel, encountered the powerful hosts of Sisera, and the Lord made them victorious; and she then recounts the whole in this song of triumph, and concludes, "So let all," &c. We may appropriately apply the text to the cause of Jesus, the Bozrah conqueror, who is going forth from conquering to conquer. Similar passage to the first clause, Ps. lxviii. 1, "Let God arise, let his enemies be scattered," &c. Let us rather read them as predictory declarations. Thus we shall consider the text,

I. *As descriptive of the true character and certain doom of the ungodly.* And,

II. *As giving an illustrious representation of the friends of Jesus.*

I. *As descriptive of the true character and certain doom of the ungodly.*

The term "enemies" will apply to all the unrenewed portions of mankind. The heart is positively hostile, &c. "Carnal mind is enmity against God," &c. Christ died for us when we were enemies. Not all enemies in the same way, or to the same degree.

1. *There are the daring enemies of God.*

Who skeptically treat his revelation, yea, deny his being. "The fool, who says in his heart, There is no God." They attack his rule—despise his word—rail at his servants—try to subvert his cause.

2. *There are the profane and reckless enemies of God.*

Who defy, contemn the Most High—Pharaoh, Belshazzar, Herod.

3. *There are those who are wickedly neutral, and who temporize in religion.*

Not professedly on the side of Satan. They admire, consent, are considerate, yet they are not decided, not changed, &c., see Matt. xii. 30. "He that is not with me is against me," &c. Now as to the doom of the enemies of God, they will all perish, except they repent; all have one condemnation, sentence, woeful abode. It will include,

(1.) *Utter shame and confusion.*

Now they boast and exalt themselves. Now they scoff, &c. Then they will be abased, and howl, and weep. "Many shall awake," &c. "Speechless," &c. "So will all," &c.

(2.) *Total wretchedness and misery.*

Now occasionally miserable, but have many subterfuges. Many awful statements. "Thou shalt break them," &c., Ps. xi. 6. "Upon the wicked he shall rain snares, fire, and brimstone, and a horrible tempest; this shall be the portion of their cup." He shall say, "Take these mine enemies," &c.

(3.) *Eternal ruin and despair.*

They shall perish irreparably. Beyond the reach of mercy, all felicity and hope expire, all misery concentrated. "So will all thine," &c. Let us now turn to the bright and glorious side of the text, and notice,

II. *The illustrious representation given of the friends of Jesus.*

"Them that love him." In the enemy we look for hate; in the friend, love. Now love to Jesus is,

1. *A divine principle.*

It is of God, and from God. The result of regeneration. "Love of God shed abroad in our hearts."

2. *It is a pre-eminent principle.*

Not inconsistent with other love, &c. But above all, it has the centre, it reigns, it subordinates, &c. "Lovest thou me more than these?"

3. *It is manifest.*

Not hidden. It lives, and breathes, and speaks, and acts. It moves all the springs of the heart. Affects all the machinery of the life. It loosens the tongue, employs the hands and feet. Now this is the character. Mark the representation—"Let them that love him be as the sun," &c. Now the metaphor will apply,

(1.) *To the exalted station which they occupy.*

Sin debases, sinks, &c. Religion exalts, raises the slave to be a prince, &c. "He shall dwell on high."

(2.) *To the spiritual rays they diffuse abroad.*

"Ye were once darkness," &c. Now lights, &c. "Arise, shine," &c. "Ye are the lights of the world," &c.

(3.) *As fertilizing and beautifying all around.*

When summer rays are gone, nature languishes, sterility reigns, &c. But as these rays return, every thing is softened and mellowed, the wilderness is gladdened. His rays, as the source of beauty, impart to every plant and flower its various hues and shades. Now believers shed moral beauty all around. Holy virtues, heavenly graces, Christ-like feelings, all tend to expel the winter of moral evil and misery, like the sun.

(4.) *Irresistibly advancing in their glorious career.*

Numerous foes and difficulties; but these cannot impede their course. Hell may be moved from beneath, tempests roar, &c. "Yet if God," &c. "In all these things," &c. "The path of the just shines brighter and brighter, until the perfect day." All efforts fruitless to subvert the cause of God. Those who have loved him have been as the sun, &c.

(5.) *Like the sun setting in celestial radiance, and moral splendor.*

However bright the career, it must cease on earth. See the young convert, as the rising orb. See the matured Christian shining in his meridian glory. See the aged Christian declining, &c.; at last it sets—but watch the scene. No stormy sky, no threatening tempest, no cloud; all still, and tranquil, and clear; the whole horizon mellowed with the golden glory. No wonder that Balaam exclaimed, "Let me die the death of the righteous," &c. "Mark the perfect man, and behold the upright; the end of that man is peace."

(6.) *As the sun rising in another hemisphere, and shining in fairer worlds.*

Is that setting sun annihilated? Is he no more? He rises in another land, as he sets in this. He exists and shines, &c. So with those who once shone here, &c. They are lost to us, but they still live, and are more radiant, shine brighter, &c. They now indeed shine forth in the kingdom of their Father, as the brightness of the sun, &c.

APPLICATION.

1. Let the subject be the test of character. Are we enemies, &c.

2. Learn the supreme excellence of true religion. Godliness leads to honor, usefulness, blessedness, and glory.

3. Let the enemies of God consider. Now pause, reflect, weigh the matter. Read the history of the enemies of God. Think of your adversary. What will you do? Now trembling, draw near, Christ is the way to God's favor. He is ready to pardon. "Let the wicked man turn from his wickedness." "Kiss the Son, lest he be angry," &c.

4. Let the professed friends of Jesus exemplify their principles. You are to diffuse knowledge, to communicate the warm beams of benevolence and mercy.

———◆———

CCL.—PERPETUITY OF CHRIST'S NAME AND PRAISE.

"I will make thy name to be remembered in all generations: therefore shall the people praise thee forever and ever."—*Ps.* xlv. 17.

WHATEVER original reference there may be in this psalm to David's son and successor, it is clear to the spiritually-minded reader that a greater than Solomon is here. The psalm contains a chain of clear and beautiful predictions of the Messiah and his kingdom. The text is the climax of the passage, and contains the declaration of Jehovah, that the name of the Redeemer shall be handed down to the latest posterity. "I will make," &c. Observe,

I. *The nature of the prediction.*

II. *The certainty of its realization.* And,

III. *The means of its accomplishment.*

I. *The nature of the prediction.*

The prediction consists of two parts—the perpetuation of the Saviour's name, and the celebration of his praise. Observe, then,

1. *The perpetuation of the Redeemer's name.*

"I will make thy name," &c. The name.

(1.) It is said of Christ that he had on his head many crowns, so he is distinguished by many titles. Like the stars of the firmament they bestud the oracles of truth : Jacob spake of him as the Shiloh ; Job as the Redeemer ; Isaiah as the child born, Immanuel. But the especial and pre-eminent name of the Redeemer is *Jesus*—" They shall call his name *Jesus*," &c. In connection with this " Christ" the anointed. The anointed Jesus. Now as the anointed Saviour he stands pre-eminent. His name belongs especially to his person and work. A name above every name ; sweeter and more precious than any other. A name which God put upon him, and in which he delights. A name which angels adore and worship. A name full of consolation to a lost world. A name before which *devils* fear and tremble. A name to be identified with all the interesting events of time, and to be remembered in all generations.

(2.) The remembrance of this name. It is not to be blotted out. It is not to be lost in the vast assemblage of great and distinguished names. Not as a star in the milky way, but as the sun, the orb of day, he is to stand forth, above every other, moving in his own glorious orbit, in all things having the supremacy. But few names live through posterity. Few are the subjects of general remembrance, and among these some are remembered on account of wicked and monstrous crimes, as Nero. Some on account of warlike achievements, as Alexander and Hannibal, Napoleon, &c. Some on account of their discoveries in science or art. Some on account of their literary productions, or their philosophy, &c. Some on account of their virtues. And some few on account of their goodness and philanthropy. Christ will be remembered on account of his personal purity—his holy doctrines—his astonishing miracles—his unbounded love—his unexampled sufferings—his mysterious passion—his marvellous death—his glorious

triumphs over men and devils, over earth and hell. He will be remembered as the Great Teacher—the priest of the universe—the founder of Christianity—and the Redeemer of the world. Observe,

(3.) This remembrance of the Redeemer's name is to be to the latest posterity, "through all generations." See a parallel passage, Ps. lxxii. 17. The last generation of human probationers shall remember it. It shall not perish with the conflagration of the earth, for it shall be the glory of the new heavens and of the new earth, wherein dwelleth righteousness. And it shall be the burden of the song of all the hosts of glory, through the rolling ages of eternity. But we are anticipating the prediction, for it also refers,

2. *To the celebration of his praise.*

" The people shall praise thee," &c. Now the idea is clearly this, that all the people shall praise him. That " all nations shall call him blessed." They shall praise him from the rising to the setting of the sun. Now although Christ has been remembered in all ages, yet the people, the majority, have not known his name. Myriads have never heard it. Myriads of Mohammedans degrade it. Myriads of Jews hate and blaspheme it. Myriads of skeptics revile it, and myriads care nothing about it. But then all people, of all climes, and colors, and tongues, shall know it, and love it, and adoring, present their incense of praise unto it. What a delightful period, when Christ's name shall be sung in every nation, on every hill, in every vale, on the mountain-top, and on the sea-shore, and when those who go in ships shall bear it across the waves of the ocean, when earth, and sea, and skies will resound with Immanuel's praise. Such, brethren, is the prediction. Let us consider,

II. *The certainty of its realization.*

It is not a doubtful matter. It is written in the volume of inviolable and eternal truth, of which not one jot or tittle can possibly fail. This certainty rests not only on its being a portion of the word of truth, but we may conclude as to its realization,

1. *From the claims of Christ.*

In the covenant made with the Saviour, it was stipulated that he should be rewarded for his toils, and be amply recompensed for all his sufferings and shame. This is beautifully and fully expressed by the prophet Isaiah, see liii. 10. Christ's prayer referred to the same subject, John xvii. 45 The apostle, too, refers to it, Phil. ii. 6, &c.

Now, shall the claims of Christ be disregarded? Assuredly not. He has entered upon his reward. He is receiving the joy. He is extending his kingdom, and assuredly "He shall reign until," &c. "His name shall," &c.

2. From the ability of the Father.

It is the engagement of the Father. Jehovah says, "I will," and upon what principle shall it fail? He is not fallible. He does not change. He will not break his word. He will not disregard his son's hard-earned claims. His power is sufficient. His resources exhaustless. His means ample. He hath said, and it must come to pass. Heaven and earth may pass away, but not one word of his can ever fail.

3. The history of the past, and the survey of the present, clearly indicate the certainty of its realization.

Before Messiah's advent his name and work were the subject of grateful contemplation through all generations. As the seed of the woman he was received by our first parents. As the Shiloh, &c., by the patriarchs. Abraham desired to see his day, &c.; the prophets all testified of Christ, of the sufferings he should endure, and the glory which should follow. The Baptist acted as his herald. Good old Simeon clasped him to his bosom. And the apostles and disciples preached him through the then known kingdoms of the world, &c. Even one apostle, Paul, preached him from Jerusalem to Illyricum. And from that period to the present, his name has been remembered. Then remember that earth and hell have conspired to blot out his name. The kings and rulers have covenanted against him. Learning and philosophy, power and wealth, influence and arms, have all been employed, but all in vain. His name has been perpetuated, and is still celebrated in the praises of countless thousands. And who, that surveys the present influence and extent of Christianity, can doubt its being continued to the latest posterity? Who can doubt its final triumphs and universal diffusion? It has lived in all ages, and in all countries, and now the sun never sets upon the disciples of the Lamb. But let us glance,

III. *At the means of its accomplishment.*

The dispensation is a dispensation of means. Christ's name is to be perpetuated by means.

1. There must be the diffusion of the scriptures.

As long as the Bible lasts, Christ's name will endure. Wherever that book is received, Christ's name will be prized and praised.

2. The gospel must be proclaimed.

It is the gospel of Christ. To preach the gospel is to exalt Christ. It is the express work of the ministers of the gospel.

> "'Tis all their business here below,
>   To cry, Behold the Lamb!"

3. The ordinances of religion must be maintained.

Where Christian worship is celebrated, and the ordinances administered, Christ's name must be remembered. Look at a Christian congregation. The place is palpably a Christian erection. The people are professed Christians. The word read is Christ's word. The gospel is the gospel of Christ. The prayer is based upon his merit, and presented in his name. The praise is to Christ. He is the subject of our songs. The church is Christ's. Baptism is being baptized into his death. The sacrament is the Lord's supper. The life of the Christian is to magnify Christ; and the death of the Christian glorifies the Lord. Now these are the means, and shall I ask, by way of

APPLICATION.

1. Are not we responsible for their employment?

Oh yes, it devolves on me, on you, on every Christian in the world.

2. Should we not feel intensely interested in them?

Shall we not identify ourselves? And,

3. Let our profession be embodied.

Let the love of Christ constrain us.

4. Oh, that Christ might be precious to some waiting soul for the first time.

What think ye of Christ? Oh, receive him. Let his name be engraven on your hearts.

5. Christ's name shall be remembered.

It must be. Nothing can prevent it. Think what it would require to erase it. Every Bible annihilated—every meeting-house thrown down—every Christian martyred—and all the angels must be silenced. Nay, more—the sceptre must be wrested from Jehovah's grasp, and his exalted throne levelled with the dust. Oh, rejoice, rejoice! "Christ's name shall be remembered in all generations, and the people shall praise him forever and ever!"

"Let every kindred, every tribe,
On this terrestrial ball,
To him all majesty ascribe,
And crown him Lord of all."

CCLI.—THE SIX MORNINGS.

"The morning cometh."—*Isa.* xxi. 12.

THE various portions of the day are often employed in the way of figure by the sacred writers. Day is the emblem of joy and gladness; night, of sorrow and trouble. Thus, too, evening is the sign of approaching distress or affliction, and morning is the token of happiness and prosperity. There are two or three things necessarily connected with morning. Night must precede, and day must follow. A few hours have passed away since darkness overcast the whole of our horizon; and now, since morning has shed its cheering beams, we are enjoying the gladsome light of day. How right and proper that every morning should bear witness to our gratitude to God for the mercies of the night, and our supplications for the needful blessings of the succeeding day. Every pious heart knows experimentally the meaning of these words, "My voice shalt thou hear in the morning." Our subject is the morning, and we design to lead your contemplations,

I. *To the morning of our world's existence.*

Ere that morning arose the earth was without form, and void; one dark, chaotic mass presented itself before the mind of the Eternal. Silent darkness reigned undisturbed. The Son of God had long anticipated the formation of our world. He had fixed his delights upon it before the mountains were settled, before the hills were brought forth, yea, long before the depths of the sea were formed, or its boundaries decreed. He was rejoicing in the habitable parts of the earth, and his delights were with the sons of men. At length the day of our world's existence dawned. The great Fountain of light, by his only-begotten Son, formed the worlds. The slumbers of night were broken by the voice of God. His spirit brooded o'er the mighty void; and he said, "Let there be light, and there was light." That was the first morning our world ever beheld—a morning which exhibited the almighty power of Jehovah, and gave a transcendently glorious manifestation of his benevolence and love. Now "the morning stars sang together," &c. The day which followed was one of purity and bliss. Every thing displayed the wisdom and goodness of the great Artificer; and God smiled with infinite complacency when he took a survey of the whole, and pronounced it very good. Eden was the sphere of man's labors, dominion, and enjoyment. But mark, the heavens darken, nature is convulsed, tempestuous clouds of an awfully threatening character streak the horizon. Sin has entered our world; pollution has defiled the noblest workmanship of God; hell has triumphed over wretched, apostate man; night, darkness, and death, in all their sable blackness, now surround our world. Mercy intervenes, compassion triumphs, and a ray of light indicates the coming of another day. Stars now irradiate the heavens; types, sacrifices, and promises lead Old Testament believers to expect the dawning of the day of mercy and salvation. Notice, then,

II. *The morning of our world's redemption.*

Before the breaking of the day the darkness is more dense and palpable. So before this day prophecy had ceased, and the oracles of heaven had been silent for ages. But at length the glad jubal morning arrived, the typical stars disappear, sacrificial mists pass away, and the Son of God appears in our world, and is manifest in our flesh. Angels introduced this morning with songs, as they did the morning of the world's existence—the anthem falls on the ears of the astonished shepherds, "Glory to God in the highest, peace on earth, and good-will to men." This morning was followed by the day of Christ's tabernacling among us. A day "when life and immortality were brought to light," &c. A day of mercy to the wretched and sinful of our race. Jesus went forth as the Sun of Righteousness, with healing beneath his wings. He stood as the sun in his lofty orbit, and exclaimed, "I am the light of the world." But this day ended in the night of Christ's sufferings and death. By the persecution of the Son of God, his rejection by his own people, by conspiracy, by cruel arrest, by Gethsemane's woes, and the ignominious death of the cross. That Sun, which rose in such beautiful and heavenly radiance in Bethlehem, now set in blood, on the summit of Calvary. There was the burial, and the silent darkness of the sepulchre. But this was a short night—it soon passed away; for behold, "the morning cometh."

III. *The morning of Christ's glorious resurrection.*

With this morning revived the hopes of the disciples of Christ. The salvation of the world seemed to be sepulchred with him. With this morning the hopes of the deathless myriads of our race were placed on a glorious and sure foundation. His resurrection declared him to be the Son of God, with power; it became the key-stone to the whole edifice of his church, and one of the leading doctrines of his blessed gospel.

> " Welcome, sweet day of rest,
> That saw the Lord arise,
> Welcome to this reviving breast,
> And these rejoicing eyes."

Yes, every Lord's day should remind us of this morning. The resurrection of Christ was the morning of the Christian's day of holy rest, and spiritual communion. At the close of the week it ought to gladden us that the morning cometh; and it ought to be introduced with the joyful lines of the poet—

> "Another six days' work is done,
> Another Sabbath is begun," &c.

And this introduced the gospel day—the day of Christ's spiritual reign on earth. In his day the kingdom of heaven was at hand; but he must suffer and rise again before its foundation could be laid. His spiritual empire was introduced on the day of pentecost, when the Spirit was poured out from on high. This was the beginning of the reign of the Holy Spirit of God, that to which Christ referred when he said, "If I go away, the Comforter will come," and to this he directed the attention of his disciples, just before he left them, Acts i. 4, &c. See its realization, Acts ii. 1, &c. Now began the progress of light and truth, the diffusion of the gospel, and the commencement of the New Testament dispensation among men. Observe,

IV. *The morning of the soul's conversion to God.*

It is darkness and night with all unbelievers. But when the gospel comes, light comes; and if received, the soul is illumined, and the beams of a holy morning dawn upon the soul—the life of the Christian is the day —a season of light, and joy, and holiness. His path begins with the morning, and "shines more and more unto the perfect day." Happy that soul on whom the Sun

of Righteousness has arisen! But this must be followed by the night of death. There is yet another day before the church of God.

V. *The morning of Christ's millennial kingdom and glory.*

Then will Christ shine forth in all his meridian brightness; his appearance will usher in his heavenly administration. Then will be the days of heaven upon earth. Then will God's tabernacle be with men, &c. Then Zion will arise and shine, her light having come, &c. The light of the moon will then be as the light of the sun, &c. "The Gentiles shall come to their light, and kings to the brightness of their rising." Behold the enrapturing vision, as beheld through the medium of prophecy, Isa. lx. 18 to end.

VI. *The morning of a glorious eternity.*

The saints shall now have dominion and glory—dwell in regions of celestial light. Jesus the Sun of the eternal world. No night to succeed this. One day of effulgent brightness and everlasting blessedness, Rev. xxi. 22. Now observe,

1. *Christ is essentially connected with each of these mornings.*

Creation, redemption, resurrection, spiritual reign, conversion, millennium.

2. *Each morning is identified with the happiness of man.* Look at his primeval dignity—redemption; raised in his resurrection; means for his transformation in the gift of the Spirit. Personally saved in the morning of conversion. That salvation consummated in the day of Christ's personal reign and glory.

3. *How many are the children of the morning of the day?*

If believers, "ye are not of the night, and of darkness." "Light is sown for the righteous, and joy for the upright."

4. *To the unbelieving, we observe, the night also is coming.*

Of death, and eternal misery.

———————

CCLII.—THE GOSPEL STANDARD.

" Lift up a standard for the people."—*Isa.* lxii. 10.

THE text forms a part of a prediction supposed to refer primarily to the deliverance of the Jews from Babylon, but a part of the prophecy clearly points to the Messiah, to the proclamation of his gospel, and the diffusion of his glory. It is in this evangelical sense that we consider that portion we have selected for our present meditation. Let us then consider,

I. *The state of the people.*

II. *The standard which must be elevated.*

III. *The duty of the Church, to lift the standard up.*

1. *The state of the people.*

By the people we must include the great mass of human beings. All nations, climes, colors, kindred, and tongues; Jews and Gentiles, barbarian and Scythian, bond and free. But more especially let us consider the state of the people without God, and ignorant of the gospel of his Son. In this light, there are four views in which the people may be contemplated.

1. *As wandering in the regions of ignorance and superstition.*

The pagan world is the valley and shadow of death. "Darkness hath covered," &c. The people dwell in darkness. Dark as to their nature and state; as to the supreme God; as to the blessed Messiah, and the way of life; as to heaven, eternity, and hell. Superstitious as they are ignorant. Gloomy shadows overspread their path. Horrific fears haunt their spirits.

2. *As the victims of Satanic vassalage.*

They are the captives of Satan. Enfettered with chains of guilt. Degraded and enslaved, he drags them at his infernal chariot wheels. Their vassalage is that of the soul. It is mental as well as bodily. It is a vassalage in which all is sunken and debased.

3. *As in a state of utter defilement.*

We say nothing of the common evidences of depravity. Their vice is that which has become more deep through the habits and customs of ages upon ages. Vice where the whole person is leprous—which enters into all their movements—which pollutes their literature—which infects their recreations—which spoils their domestic comforts—which is the glory of their religion, and perpetuated in the presence and under the patronage of their gods. Pollution stalking abroad—improved by the artist—composed in their poetry—sung in their songs—and identified with their being.

4. *As strangers to solid happiness.*

How can they be happy? Nature deranged and diseased throughout—without God—without hope—without peace. Their horrid rites tell you they are not happy, &c. And with all their guilt and depravity, are they meet for happiness in the world to come? Observe,

II. *The standard which must be elevated.*

Now this standard is that of the gospel. A standard bearing on it the form of the cross, on which is written in characters of blood, "Behold the Lamb of God," &c. See ver. 11. Now in the elevation of this standard we have a full and perfect remedy for the perishing condition of the people. The gospel standard,

1. *Communicates light.*

It reveals the knowledge, for the lack of which the people perish; it publishes the great salvation which they need—brings life and immortality to light—it is the harbinger of day to the people: and when it comes, "the people which sat in darkness," &c. The gospel standard is connected,

2. *With the publication of freedom.*

It gives "liberty to the captives, and the opening of the prison," &c.; it attacks and beats down the bulwarks of Satan's empire; it pulls to the dust his strongholds; it combats and overthrows the despotical powers of darkness, and opens a way of escape for the redeemed prisoners of hope. The people know the gospel truth, and it makes them free.

3. *It presents a remedy for human pollution.*

"It is a fountain open for sin," &c.; the grand catholicon remedy for all the moral maladies of the soul; nothing too complicated, too inveterate, &c. It can bring down to the humility of the child, the proud metaphysician, self-deified Brahmin. It even tames the savage—it turns the raven, &c.

4. *It imparts abiding peace to the miserable and perishing.*

Gives the favor of God to men—implants his kindness in the soul—gives the spirit the chief good, attracts it to the centre of bliss, and causes it to revolve in the light of purity and blessedness forever and ever. "Standard of salvation," the power of God to the eternal life of all who behold it.

III. *The duty of the Church to lift the standard up.*

We shall now speak to the members of the Church of Christ, and of the Church in her collective character.

1. *The standard is in our possession.* It

is intrusted to us—we must therefore be responsible; we have it not for monopoly, but diffusion; the people need it, and will die without it—and we have it. Christ expects us to lift it up to the people in the regions far off. The very spirit of

2. *Our religion involves this great principle.*

Our religion is love—it is having Christ's spirit—zealous for Christ's glory—to be Christ's conscientious property. Then that religion will inspire the missionary spirit, and consecrate us to the missionary cause.

3. *The grand commission requires it.*

Two views. At any rate, the gospel must be proposed to all. "If I be lifted up," &c. If we do not, God will give it others who will, &c.

APPLICATION.

1. Have you all been savingly interested in the standard of the gospel? You must look, and feel, and live. Be drawn and united.

2. The standard-bearers must be supported. By prayer, and help.

3. More laborers must be sent forth. "The harvest is great," &c.

CCLIII.—LIGHT AND DARKNESS; OR THE CHURCH AND THE WORLD.

"And there was a thick darkness in all the land of Egypt three days: they saw not one another, neither rose any from his place for three days; but all the children of Israel had light in their dwellings."—*Exod.* x. 22, 23.

NOTHING affects so much as contrast, and much of divine truth is presented to us in this form. In this way we are deeply struck with the condition of our first parents, before and after the fall, in the enjoyment and loss of paradise. Thus, too, the different characters of the righteous and wicked are more striking. See Cain and Abel: a murderer and a martyr: a child of Beelzebub and an heir of glory. Look, too, at Jacob and Esau. One ardently engaged in the pleasures of the chase, the other earnestly seeking "the favor and blessing of God." Sometimes this contrast is seen on a larger scale. Look at the families of Noah and his sons, and the whole world. See the one floating safely on the billows of that flood which involved the

other in utter ruin. Our text leads us to consider one of these striking contrasts. The ninth plague is now afflicting the land of Egypt. Thick darkness is covering the whole land, ver. 23. Universal horror is filling the minds of the Egyptians. But at this very time all the children of Israel had light in their dwellings. In this God made a miraculous and striking difference, and in this we have presented before us the contrast between the world and the Church; between the families of the wicked and the families of the pious; between the carnal and the renewed heart. Let us confine ourselves to this contrast, as existing between the world and the Church. We notice, then,

I. *Egypt, in its darkness, was a type of the world.* It was so also in other particulars. In its tyrannical dominion by the despotical Pharaoh; in its diversified idolatry; but particularly in the darkness which enshrouded it. But a question arises, *What do we mean by the world?* We mean all the intelligent responsible beings who are living without the fear of God, and strangers to his saving grace. They may greatly differ from each other. But those who constitute what in scripture is signified by the world, resemble each other in this: they are under the dominion of Satan, and not the servants of the Lord Jesus Christ. Now each such individual is a child of the world, and the whole, in their collective capacity, are in darkness.

1. *Darkness is an emblem of ignorance and error, and the world is involved in these.* In worldly matters there may be intelligence. Wise, as it regards literature and science; but with respect to God, their souls, salvation, and religion, they are in darkness—their understandings are blinded and their judgments perverted. "This darkness hath covered the earth, and gross darkness," &c.

2. *Darkness is an emblem of guilt, and the world is involved in this.* Sin is the work of darkness. Hence the apostle says, "Have no fellowship," &c. Now, the whole world is guilty before God. Every man is a transgressor. "There is not one righteous—no, not one."

3. *Darkness is an emblem of peril, and in this the world is involved.* As the world is guilty, so it is condemned. God's judgment of it is recorded. God's displeasure is announced. God's wrath is threatened. It is to be the scene of the divine vengeance. It is to be renovated by fire, 2 Peter iii. 10.

4. *Darkness is the emblem of misery, and in this the world is involved.* Now, the misery of the men of the world arises from *three things:*

(1.) From the accusations of guilt, the cause of their condemnation. As a fever it burns up their spirits, and this feeling they cannot extinguish.

(2.) From the unsatisfying nature of their portion. They want happiness, but cannot find it. They go to the briny flood which only adds to their thirst; or they sink into wretchedness as the prodigal, and have not even husks to eat.

(3.) From gloomy fears as to the future. Bad as the portion of the world is, it is their best—their good things. But it cannot be retained. Age advances,—infirmities encompass,—death stalks forth,—the grave opens,—and then there is the unknown world, the judgment, eternity. And they have no *light*—no *hope.* Surely, then, this is enough to account for the misery of the wicked. Let us then turn our attention to the Church of God.

II. *The Israelites with light in their dwellings were a type of the Church.*

Who constitute the Church? The spiritual seed of Abraham. Those who have left the world, and become the spiritual followers of Jesus. They are in the world as Israel in Egypt, but they are distinct and separate from it. They are not of it, even as their Lord was not of it, and like the Israelites of old they have light in their dwellings.

1. *They have the light of saving knowledge.*

They may be far inferior to the world in rank, station, wealth, and learning; but they possess the true knowledge of God and of his Son Jesus Christ. They know Christ as the true Messiah. They know him experimentally,—they know him in his power to save. Once they were in darkness, but now are they light, &c. They have been translated, &c.

2. *They have the light of the divine approbation.*

They know they are of God. They know their love to God. Also his love to them. The word of God assures them that they are beloved of God; the Holy Spirit bears witness, and hence their conscience testifies by its pacific voice, that "being justified by faith they have peace," &c.

3. *They have the light of holiness.*

Sin is darkness; holiness, light. They wear the robe of light. They are obedient to the statutes of light. They walk in the paths of light, and it shineth more and more, &c. Ye are the children of the light and of the day.

4. *They have the light of a joyful hope.*

Christ in them the hope of glory. See 1 Peter i. 4; Titus ii. 13. Now this hope cheers and sustains the believer, and fills him with joy unspeakable.

5. *They have the light of the divine presence.*

The Lord is ever with his people. He is their sun, making their day. He guides by his glorious presence through the whole pilgrimage of life. He was thus the light of Abraham, of Jacob, and Israel in the desert. Thus by his Spirit he leads his people into all truth, and conducts them to eternal glory.

In applying this subject we behold the contrast between those who are of the world and the people of God, in several conditions of life.

(1.) See them in adversity. The wicked have an addition of darkness. No solace,—no ray to cheer them; hence how often they sink into despair and rush into eternity. The Christian feels, but he recognizes God's hand. He bows down, bears the rod, and kisses the chastising hand, and God's blissful countenance enables him to rejoice in tribulation.

(2.) See them in sickness. No light. Painful, restless, and an overwhelming anxiety. The sick chamber is as dark as Egypt. But the righteous have light in their dwellings. The serene countenance, the pious resignation, the cheering hope, show the difference. It is all right, says the pious soul; to live is Christ. God is my portion.

(3.) See them in death. With the wicked it is a leap in the dark—a plunge into the horrid black abyss. Oh, how terrific!—how appalling! But the righteous have light in death—often the celestial beams of glory.

APPLICATION.

1. Believers, shine in your dwellings, &c.

2. Sinners, come to the light, &c.

———

CCLIV.*—THE CHRISTIAN MINISTRY.

"And every one had four faces; the first face was the face of a cherub, and the second face was the face of a man, and the third the face of a lion, and the fourth the face of an eagle."—*Ezek.* x. 14.

In this chapter the providence and government of God are set forth in mysterious and sublime hieroglyphics, a mode of writing particularly common to Ezekiel, and which is presented in awful grandeur in the book of the Apocalypse. The text seems to have a decided reference to the angelic hosts,—those ministers of God who do his pleasure. They are brought before us as the active instruments of the divine government, and the executors of his wondrous purposes. To resemble these should be the great desire of every Christian, that God's will may be done on earth even as it is done in heaven. But especially should this be the case with the Christian minister: his office greatly resembles that of the holy intelligences above; he is a messenger of God to mankind, an angel of the Church, and therefore well does it become him to study the character, and emulate the holiness of cherubim and seraphim in heaven.

To show you, dear brother, the particular points of resemblance, and urge their importance, will be the design of this address. The different likenesses of these holy beings are designed to exhibit their various attributes and characteristics. Observe the first face,

I. *Was that of a cherub.*

We shall consider this as the symbol,

1. *Of exalted dignity.*

Dwelling around the throne of Deity. In his immediate presence. His especial ambassadors, &c. No office can be more exalted than that of the Christian ministry. It is that to which Jehovah appointed his own Son. One writer quaintly remarks, "God had only one Son, and he made a preacher of him." "Workers together with God," &c.

2. *Of elevated devotion.*

They are represented as holding great intimacy and close fellowship with God. They are ever praising him, serving him day and night, &c. Crying one to another, "Holy, holy," &c. How indispensable that the ministers of Christ live near to the Lord, hold close communion with the skies. Thus, to be

like Abraham, and Moses, and Samuel, imbued with the spirit of devotion.

3. *Of distinguished holiness.*

Ye that bear the vessels of the Lord, &c., as the priests of old. "Holiness unto the Lord" must be on the breastplate of the Christian minister. Not only partakers of the ordinary graces of the Spirit, but adorned with the mature fruits of holiness to the glory of God. How the apostle urged upon Timothy, "Keep thyself pure," &c. Observe,

II. *The second symbol is that of a man.*

With the sanctity of the cherub is to be united the sympathy of sanctified humanity. Jesus, that he might be a faithful and sympathetic high-priest, was made in all points like unto us. As men, Christian ministers

1. *Are to be influenced by their relationship to Jesus as head of the Church.*

They should have his meekness, humility, lowliness, desire to labor, &c. Readiness to suffer, &c. As men, they are

2. *To feel for their fellow-sinners peculiar compassion.*

They are their brethren, of one blood, spirit, and destiny. Hearts are to feel, bowels to yearn, &c. Such long for their salvation. As men,

3. *They are to know their own insufficiency and entire dependence on God's blessing.*

This treasure in earthen vessels, &c. We preach not ourselves, &c. Who is sufficient for these things, &c. Paul planteth, &c.

III. *The third emblem was the face of a lion.*

By this we are to understand the strength and magnanimity, which are necessary to the ministerial office. The Christian minister must be strong in the grace which is in Christ Jesus. He must be strong to resist evil, to stand firm in the conflict, and to conduct himself as a man of God. Whoso quails, he must not fear. Whoso flies, he must be at his post. Whoso apostatizes, he must hold fast the faith. Whoso tires, he must run to the glorious goal. He must have fortitude to brave dangers, to withstand gainsayers, to fear not the face of men; and, if necessary, to lay down his life in the cause of Jesus. There are especial seasons, trying circumstances, and dangerous periods, when the minister cannot vindicate his official character, or fulfil his duty, unless he have the heart and face of the lion.

IV. *The fourth symbol is that of the eagle.*

By this,

1. *The true character of the minister's work is portrayed.*

He has to do with spiritual things. His business is not "of the earth, earthy," but his message, his powers, his designs, are all heavenly. He teaches not philosophy, science, economy, legislation, but the truths of the kingdom of God, the knowledge of the way of salvation. "These men are the servants of the living God," &c.

2. The symbol of the eagle may be designed also to be expressive of their *ardor and zeal.* And these are of the utmost importance to the minister of Jesus. With these his soul must burn with unabating fervency. He is to be instant, earnest, energetic, zealously affected in every good thing.

3. *His soul is to yearn with intense anxiety over perishing sinners.*

He is to devote all his powers to the exalting of his Lord, and the saving of souls. Such, then, are the symbolical features which should distinguish the ministers of Jesus Christ; and these peculiar excellences should be united. With the exalted dignity, elevated devotion, and distinguished holiness of the cherub, must be allied the lowliness, the human affection, and conscious self-insufficiency of man; and these are to be found in connection with an heroic and magnanimous spirit, and a fervent quenchless zeal in the cause of Jesus.

APPLICATION.

1. Let the solemn character of the office ever be cherished, and a lively sense of its importance be maintained from day to day.

2. Let the glorious results of faithfulness in the Saviour's service animate to constancy and perseverance.

The divine word will give abundant directions, and supply ample materials for the formation of the exalted ministerial character. The Holy Spirit will impart every necessary influence and gift; and Jesus, the head of the Church, will communicate a plenitude of grace from his unbounded fulness.

CCLV.—A MINISTERIAL CHARGE.

"Take heed to the ministry which thou hast received in the Lord that thou fulfil it."—*Col.* iv. 17.

OUR text refers solely to the work of the ministry. It is the apostle Paul's counsel to Archippus, that he "take heed," &c. On this occasion we shall presume that you are not a stranger to vital experimental religion. We assume it as a matter which is obvious to the members of this Church and your Christian brethren, that you are in spirit, profession, and practice, a disciple of Jesus Christ. Personal religion is of essential importance to every one, but pre-eminently so to the preacher of the gospel; otherwise his life is one scene of deception upon the Church and the world, and his addresses the mere soulless harangues of a hireling. But the profession of religion is not enough. In the pastor it should be lively, striking, decided, and influential. In the vestments of purity he is to be clad, and "Holiness to the Lord" is to be written on his breastplate, so that the light of his purity is to be manifest to all. On these momentous topics, however, we shall not now dwell, but devote all our attention to the truths expressly presented to us in the text. Consider,

I. *What duty the Christian ministry involves.*

And,

II. *The spirit in which it should be fulfilled.*

The Christian ministry presents four spheres of labor.

1. *The study.*

It is desirable that the Christian minister have such a place; that it should be a place adapted to usefulness and comfort; that it should be well ventilated, quiet, and well furnished with a choice selection of useful books. The study must be the place,

(1.) *Of reading.*

"Give thyself to reading," &c. Philosophy, science, history, poetry, general literature, may engage our occasional time. But theology is the direct course of reading which should engage your especial attention. The writings of the puritans and non-conformists present a deep rich mine of precious truth, in which you cannot dig without possessing invaluable treasure. But the holy Scriptures must be the great book of ministerial consultation. Here you have the great doctrines and truths which are to supply you with all the materials for your work. With patriarchs, prophets, and evangelists you must be on the most intimate terms. With their writings you are to be minutely conversant. Nothing can make up for a deficiency here. You must be so deeply read in biblical knowledge, that it shall impart its peculiar and divine savoriness to all your pastoral and ministerial discourses. Read much, read with distinct arrangement, and with a special object to your ministerial work. Reading must be followed by

(2.) *Meditation.*

By meditation, the food reading supplies is digested, and so incorporated as to become a part of our mental self. Meditation is urged by the apostle in connection with reading. By meditation we view subjects in all their bearings and tendencies. By meditation we avoid loading the mind with mere phantoms and useless crudities. To meditate in the law of the Lord is the duty of the private Christian; how much more necessary, therefore, is it to the Christian teacher. A good memory may store up words by reading, but meditation is essential to the extraction of the essences and the thoughts of subjects. From reading and meditation we pass on to notice,

(3.) *Composition.*

The selection and preparation of your pulpit discourses. The exact manner of doing this must greatly depend on your own peculiar characteristics of mind. As to the amount of writing, that must be left greatly to your own judgment. But in most cases some writing is essentially necessary; in many cases it should be rather extended in degree. But a few words here shall suffice. Select subjects adapted to the persons and circumstances of your congregation, especially those bearing on the great truths of religion. Never aim merely at pleasing,— seek not high things, but consult perspicuity of style, and great plainness of expression. But in all cases have both your ideas and phraseology so arranged, that without fear you may stand up to explain with clearness and ability, the topics which you have chosen. Do not go empty-handed to the hungry sheep of your pastoral care; and go not with bare disjointed thoughts or meager sketches, but laden with the good things of the gospel, having a portion of meat for all in due season. Lead the people into the rich verdant pastures of the divine word, and let not leanness be upon them through your negligent and incompetent provision. Prepare for them the finest of the wheat, and present them with the richest clusters of the refreshing grapes of Canaan. Let your study have a large proportion of your time, and cherish for it an affection which all the attractions of society cannot shake. The next sphere of ministerial usefulness is in,

2. *The pulpit.*

Here you are to stand with the message of God, and to proclaim it to the people. The great subject of your ministerings must be Jesus Christ. You are to teach and preach Jesus Christ. Christ, in his person, offices, obedience, sufferings, death, and resurrection, and glory. Christ as the sacrifice for human guilt. As the only Saviour possessing unbounded willingness, and illimitable power. Christ, in his full, free, and everlasting gospel, and that gospel in all its doctrines, ordinances, precepts, promises, privileges, and blessings. Enter the pulpit in the spirit of prayer, and seek God's Holy Spirit to aid you in your awfully responsible duties. In preaching the gospel to immortal souls,

(1.) *Be plain.*

Both as it regards a clear style, and the adoption of familiar, not vulgar, expressions. Never adopt words of rare use ; seldom interlard Greek and Latin, and never French quotations. The people cannot be edified unless they understand you, but the great majority cannot understand, unless you use great plainness of speech.

(2.) *Be earnest.*

Your message is one which demands this. You will effect little without it. A lethargic, formal preacher is a disgrace to the office, and brings insult to the gospel. If your heart glows with the love of Christ, you will preach with celestial fervor and burning zeal.

(3.) *Be faithful.*

Use not enticing words of human wisdom. Be not a trimmer, at your soul's peril. Declare the whole counsel of God. Keep no part of the truth back. Teach every man, warn every man, and let fidelity distinguish all your addresses as one who must give an account. Be faithful to your own conscience, to souls, to the Church, and to God, whose responsible servant you are. With fidelity,

(4.) *Be affectionate.*

Let love imbue your spirit, and it will breathe in your discourses. Have bowels of mercy. Cherish the tenderest sympathies. Often weep over perishing souls. Travail in anxious pangs of solicitude, till Christ is formed in your hearers.

(5.) *Be evangelical.*

Exalt Christ as the centre and glory of your system. Let him be alpha and omega. Ever seek his glory, and cause all truths to revolve around him, and be irradiated with the beams of his divine splendor. Remember—

> "'Tis all your business here below,
> To cry, Behold the Lamb!"

Threatenings and duties, ordinances and precepts, law and gospel, facts and prophecies, may all be preached evangelically. Leave the pulpit in the spirit of devotion, seeking the sanctifying blessing of God upon your labors. Your third sphere of labor is,

3. *The Church.*

Over this you have to preside, and in Christ's name and with the voice of the brethren to enforce the statutes of his kingdom. In the Church,

(1.) *Maintain discipline.*

In receiving members, in treating cases of offence, and in excluding from Church fellowship. Do not swerve from the precepts and precedents of the New Testament. Heed not mere usages, mere customs; conform to the infallible directions of the word of God.

(2.) *Administer the ordinances.*

Faithfully, with rigid, scriptural exactness; with due solemnity and with much prayer.

(3.) *Visit your flock.*

As often as you prudently can. With impartiality. Without ostentatious or priestly assumption. With a view to their edification. In the spirit of kindness and love. The last sphere of labor is,

4. *The world.*

You may claim, as Wesley did, the world for your parish. Wherever there is an opening for usefulness, and you have the means, labor to do good. Labor to enlarge the bonds of the Church. Seek for the extension of the gospel in your locality. Around you souls are perishing. Give your countenance and influence to the humane and benevolent institutions of the day. Plead for the poor; befriend the destitute; visit the wretched; open your mouth for the dumb. Enter earnestly on the work of the religious instruction of the young. Diffuse the Scriptures. Speak for the benighted heathen. Oh! cherish an enlarged, glowing, restless spirit of liberality and exertion. In one word, be ready for every good work. Notice,

II. *The spirit in which your ministry should be fulfilled.*

With,

1. *Great circumspection.*

"Take heed." Be not rash or precipitate, but prudent. Wise as a serpent. Seek heavenly wisdom. Be vigilant, watchful. Deeply ponder your work; intimately examine your spirit; prove yourself.

2. *Constantly cherish a sense of your responsibility.*

Your ministry has been received from the Lord. He has put you into the office. You work for God. The steward's account will be demanded. The results are of tremendous magnitude. This will lead to lowliness, to constant prayer and continual dependence on divine grace. The text has respect,

3. *To a spirit of perseverance.*

"Fulfil it." Be not only instant in season and out of season, but endure hardness. Hold on and out to the end. The course is to extend with your life, and both must end together. Be faithful unto death. Go not, nay look not back. "Be steadfast," &c. In

CONCLUSION.

1. You will have much to try you. Much to oppose you. Enemies without and fears within. It may be reviling scoffers and false brethren.

2. But you have every thing to encourage you. God is your helper. Christ is the unfailing source of your sufficiency. The Spirit in all his plenitude is promised. Angels are interested in your work. The holy and benevolent are around you to lift up your hands, and to pray down blessings upon you. And there is a glittering crown sparkling with celestial brightness before you; then "take heed to the ministry which thou hast received in the Lord, that thou fulfil it."

CCLVI.—THE DUTY OF CHURCHES TO THEIR PASTORS.

DELIVERED AT AN ORDINATION SERVICE AT BURTON-ON-TRENT, SEPT. 9, 1840.

"Now if Timotheus come, see that he may be with you without fear: for he worketh the work of the Lord, as I also do."—1 Cor. xvi. 10.

THE word of God is a perfect rule of faith and practice. It is not only profitable for doctrine, and reproof, and correction, but for perfect instruction in righteousness, that the man of God may be thoroughly furnished unto all good works. Every station and office has its corresponding duties. For instance, there are parental, which devolve upon parents; and filial, upon children. There are pastoral duties, which devolve upon ministers of Jesus Christ; to these our dear brother has been this day fully and specifically directed; but there are necessary corresponding duties which devolve upon Christian churches. To call your attention particularly to these is the object of the present occasion. Numerous are the passages which present this subject before you. In writing to the Hebrews, the apostle says, "Obey them that have the rule over you," &c., Heb. xiii. 17. To the Philippians the same apostle says, "Receive him therefore in the Lord with all gladness; and hold such in reputation." And to the Thessalonians he is still more explicit: "And we beseech you, brethren, to know them which labor among you, and are over you in the Lord, and admonish you," &c. The same spirit and design is evidently expressed in reference to Timothy in the text, when he wrote to them and said, "See that he be with you without fear," &c. In the text we have,

I. *A reference to the nature and design of the ministerial office.*

"He worketh the work of," &c.

II. *The obvious duty of the Church to see that such are with them without fear.*

I. *A reference to the nature and design of the ministerial office.*

"He worketh the work of the Lord." The Christian minister is called to his office by the Lord. He is qualified by the Lord. He is employed in doing the Lord's work. The means and instrumentality of doing it are laid down by the Lord. His great object is to glorify the Lord, and diffuse abroad the true knowledge and glory of God. His success is from the Lord, and his final reward the Lord, the righteous Judge, confers upon him. These important topics we must pass over, but we briefly call your attention to three views of his work.

1. *It is solemn.*

It is work connected with mind, and with spirit; with the undying souls of men. It is work which comprises, within its own legitimate sphere, all that is momentous in time and eternity. It is inseparably connected with the eternal glory or the everlasting misery of our fellow-beings.

2. *It is arduous.*

It is work which requires the outlay of the whole man—all the energies of the body—all the capacities of the mind—and all the emotions of the spirit. It is arduous from the lofty sublimity of its theme—from the array of its opponents with whom it has to contend. It is arduous, as it requires all the devotion of time, means, energies, and resources, which the most highly favored human being may possess. A Christian minister must devote all he has to God and the requirements of his office. It is a work pertaining to every day, every season, and every place where he lives or moves. Well might the apostle exclaim, "Who is sufficient for these things?"

3. *It is responsible.*

The Christian minister is but a servant or steward, and he must render a clear, minute, and complete account of himself and work to God. God will reckon with him, and reward or condemn, according to the employment of talents he has had committed to his trust. That responsibility is connected with the eternal destiny of those under his charge. The blood of souls, if he should be faithless, will be required at his hands. Such is the office and work of the Christian minister. Consider, then,

II. *The obvious duty of the Church with respect to him.*

He is to be with you without fear. In order to this,

1. *Supply his pecuniary need, and let him not fear as to his temporal support.*

If he is fully engaged in providing for you spiritual things, how reasonable that you should supply him with needful temporal things. I do not state the amount—to judge of this I must again refer you to his responsibility. A writer in the "Times," recently referred to the paltry sum of six or seven shillings per day being given to men who conduct the engines on the railways of our country; and observed, that a sum three times that amount should be given to those to whom the care of human life is committed. But surely the charge and care of souls is vastly more momentous, and deserving of much higher remuneration. But on this point, two principles should decide : the necessities of your pastor, and the ability you possess. If you cannot remunerate him adequately, you must do all you can; and this he has an equitable right to expect. Let this be done respectfully, with great courtesy, and in the spirit of promptitude and love.

2. *Give him your confidential and affectionate countenance, and let him be without fear as to the position he occupies in your esteem.*

Show him that he has favor in your eyes; that he is planted deeply in your regards; that you receive him as from God, and honor and love him as such.

3. *Be regular in your attendance on the means of grace, and let him not fear the acceptance of his ministry among you.*

This he has a right to expect. If he must study and preach, it is yours to be present, and hear what has been prepared for you. Be not guilty of religious vagrancy, and telling the world of the poverty of your own homes, by being found seeking a morsel here and everywhere. "Forsake not the assembling of yourselves together," &c.

4. *Unite with him in every holy enterprise, and let him not fear desertion in his efforts to do good.*

He may do a little single-handed. So did Moses during Israel's engagement with Amalek. But he may, like Moses, fail, unless you are near him, and with him, to encourage his heart and hold up his hands. I trust it will be said of him, "And there went with him a chosen band," &c.

5. *Pray fervently and continually for him, and let him not fear devotional neglect.*

How anxious Paul was for this, "Brethren, pray for us," &c. Do this in your closet, in your families, as well as in the social meetings of the church.

6. *Exhibit the holy fruit of his labors, and let him not fear losing his reward in the great day.*

See Phil. iv. 1; 1 Cor. iii. 13, &c. Live his sermons. See that the ends of preaching, and ordinances, and pastoral duties, are answered in your holy lives. Be living epistles, &c. Be the joy of his heart by your holy fruitfulness, and good works, and Christ-like spirit.

Let me conclude, by just naming a few motives why he should be with you without fear.

(1.) *His own comfort.*

If he is with you in fear, he cannot be happy. He will be your slave; his sufferings will be excruciating in the extreme. Would you have him happy and cheerful, "then see," &c.

(2.) *Your own profit.* He cannot do you good without having your confidence, affection, and esteem. Otherwise, he will be paralyzed. You will seek to be profited in vain.

(3.) *The Church's welfare.* A happy, comfortable pastor is indispensable. Without it, the Church will have no attractions to those without, and no joy for those within. If you are to have peace within your walls, you must have a happy pastor. Then see to it, &c.

(4.) *Your accountableness to God.* God will require you to answer for your treatment of our brother. Act as in God's sight, and for his glory, so that you may meet him in the presence of the Lord Jesus with exceeding great joy. "And now, may the Lord God of your fathers bless you," &c.

CCLVII.—EARLY AND PERSEVERING CULTURE RECOMMENDED.*

"In the morning sow thy seed, and in the evening withhold not thine hand; for thou knowest not whether shall prosper either this or that, or whether they both shall be alike good."—*Eccl.* xi. 6.

THE wise man, in this chapter, is inculcating benevolence — large, comprehensive benevolence, see ver. 1, "Cast thy bread upon the waters; for thou shalt find it after many days." Ver. 2, Do good largely and liberally. Do good under all circumstances, laboring actively, whatever may be the aspect of the times, ver. 4. Let active benevolence begin early, and be continued late, &c.— Text. Our subject would properly comprehend all useful exertions. The text would apply to the Christian preacher—to the parent—to the teacher of youth—to the dis-

* Series IV.—For school anniversaries, &c.

tributer of tracts, &c. We shall apply the subject, and restrict it on this occasion to the training of the rising generation for God's service and glory. Let us look, then,

I. *At the ground we design for cultivation.*

The minds and hearts of young people. We remark, the human soul,

1. *Is naturally barren of that which is good.*

There may be observable that which is intelligent, ingenuous, and even amiable. But where is the fear and love of God—a devotional spirit, and those virtues and graces which constitute acceptable piety? How very soon, too, briers, thorns, and weeds are exhibited! How soon the minds of children manifest a bearing towards things which are sinful! Look at the tempers they manifest, the expressions they utter, and the actions they display! The mind will not continue vacant, the ground entirely unoccupied, the heart will not mend itself, nor good grow out of evil; there never was an instance of this kind.

2. *The minds of children are capable of spiritual cultivation.* So soon as they can understand, they may be taught; they may be impressed, they may be convinced of evil, they may be converted to God. The Church of Christ has had many delightful instances of very early conversions, which have been followed by a life of piety and usefulness. The Holy Scriptures exhibit this frequently. Behold the lovely child, &c., 1 Sam. iii. 1, &c. Look at the pious Josiah, 2 Chron. xxxiv. 3 : "For in the eighth year of his reign, while he was yet young, he began to seek after the God of David his father," &c. Look also at Timothy, 2 Tim. iii. 15 : "And that from a child thou hast known the holy Scriptures," &c.

3. *Religious cultivation is much easier in childhood than afterwards.* The conscience is more tender—the will less perverse—the habits of sin less deeply rooted. Prejudices against religion not imbibed. According to the laws of the human mind, it is of the utmost importance to begin early. "Train up a child," &c. "A child left to himself," &c. "Ye fathers, bring up your children in the nurture and admonition of the Lord." Let us contemplate,

II. *The seed which must be cast into this ground.*

Now we do not attempt to dictate how or in what manner you shall govern your chil-

dren; but if you desire their salvation, if you train them up for God's service, then the seed sown must be the word of the living God. Word of God, is the good seed.

1. *The word of God appropriately selected.*

The plainer, simpler, and more striking parts of it,—parts which lead to right views of God, his goodness, &c. To sin, its evil, &c. To Jesus, in his life, &c. God has made religious subjects particularly plain. The New Testament as a whole, and especially the gospels, is the plainest book in the world.

2. *The word of God explained.*

And the best mode is by interrogation. Asking questions and giving answers. Thus was the youthful Jesus found in the temple.

3. *The word of God deposited.*

Seed must be sown,—hid in the earth,—treasured up. Not merely the words, but the sense, the meaning. " Thy word have I hid in my heart."

III. *The manner in which this cultivation must be carried on.*

1. *We must begin early.*

"In the morning." How important is the morning. The morning of the day,—the morning of life. Let not every thing else be first, and religion last. Let not briers have overgrown the whole soul. Let not the stem be stout and unyielding. Oh, begin early!

It must be continued late.

Until the evening. Parental authority never ceases, so long as they are beneath your roof. Don't give it up. Don't yield the ground to the enemy. Your work must be continuous; you cannot tell which lesson, which entreaty, which admonition, which effort is to prosper. Constancy, perseverance, and patience, must carry on the work.

3. *It must be associated with judicious discipline.*

After the seed is sown, care and attention are required to preserve it, &c. Christian discipline is indispensable. Children require the exercise of guardian care. Restraint is often necessary, and sometimes correction. This was Eli's sin, which brought ruin on himself and family, that his sons made themselves vile, &c.

4. *It must be connected with constant prayer.*

We may sow and labor, but God must bless. Look at the dying Jacob. "The angel who redeemed me from all evil, bless the lads." Look at the royal David, he returned to bless his household. We should pray that we may be able to do our duty, and to be examples, &c.; and that God would bless our work. God has given us great encouragement in the right and conscientious discharge of our duty. Observe,

IV. *The motives by which we should be induced to attempt the cultivation of the minds of the young.*

1. *It is a duty.*

To neglect it is sin. Sin against the children,—against society,—against the church, —against God.

2. *We have good reason to hope that our efforts will succeed.*

It is likely, possible, yea probable, that it will prosper. Thousands have rejoiced over pious children. What a delightful scene is a pious family. Parents and children walking in the fear of God.

3. *We shall avoid condemnation though we should entirely fail.*

Let every means be employed faithfully, prayerfully, and perseveringly, and then God will not condemn us, and our conscience will be clear when we meet them before the bar of God.

APPLICATION.

1. Many children are left without Christian instruction. They have parents who do not fear God. Others must care for them and teach them. Sabbath-schools meet these cases, and they are very numerous. Besides, many parents cannot do all that is requisite, and Sunday-schools may assist and carry out their good desires, &c., towards them.

2. In these schools the seed of the divine word is sown. We meet now to arrange for the continuance of these efforts for another year. Let all, then, assist.

CCLVIII.—JACOB'S PRAYER FOR THE SONS OF JOSEPH.

"The angel who redeemed me from all evil, bless the lads."—*Gen.* xlviii. 16.

THE text places before us a very interesting and striking scene,—it is the dying chamber of a man of God. A man laden with years, bending with holy fruit, like a shock of corn quite ripe for the garner of glory. The tabernacle is beginning to be taken down,—the vessel it about to be moored in the haven of rest,—the gates of heaven are opening,—kindred spirits are waiting; and the dying Jacob has only two things to do, and the consummation of his blessedness is realized. He has to bless his posterity, and to commend his spirit into the hands of God. His sons and grandchildren are summoned, the room is thronged, the dying patriarch is raised in his bed, and then filled with prophetic influence, he announces the intentions of heaven concerning them. The sons of Joseph are presented, he lifts up his soul to God, and says, in reference to them, "The angel who redeemed me," &c. Notice,

I. *The glorious personage addressed.*

"The angel," &c. Now, here we have two things: the title and achievements of this glorious personage.

1. *The angel.*

It cannot refer to that order of created intelligences who worship before the throne, &c. There are no instances of adoration and prayer being presented to them, &c. The text refers to the same person, as ver. 15. Now this is none other than the Son of God. It is highly probable that God never did hold any intercourse with our world but by his Son,—he created all things by and for Christ, and he rules it, &c. Angel signifies a messenger. As such he appeared to Hagar, Gen. xxi. 17; to Abraham, on Mount Moriah, Gen. xxii. 12; to Jacob, when he wrestled, &c.; to Moses in the bush, Exod. viii. 2, and xxxii. 28; to Joshua, v. 13. These passages will show how appropriate is this title to Jesus. Jesus is the head—the Lord of angels. Angels are *wise;* Christ is the wisdom of God. *Holy;* Christ is the fountain of holiness. *Benevolent;* love is the essence of Christ's nature. *Powerful;* Christ is almighty. They are *sons;* Christ is the Son of God. "From everlasting to everlasting," &c. "The same yesterday, to-day, and forever." "God over all," &c.

2. *The achievements of this angel.*

"Redeemed me from all evil."

(1.) Let us look at this literally. Jacob had to flee from the face of Esau; and the angel had to guide and protect him. When he returned, pursued by Laban, the angel appeared to Laban, and said, "Speak not to Jacob either good or bad." When Esau came forth to meet him, the angel interfered, and Esau is pacified, &c. When famine had spread its sable mantle, and Joseph was not, Simeon was not, &c.; and when concentrated evil was hanging over his aged head, at eventide, it was light, &c.; the angel was now redeeming him, &c.; all possible good was at hand. Yes! he was redeemed from all evil. Full of years he died, leaving a numerous posterity; and full of faith and hope he expired, saying, " I have waited for thy salvation, O Lord!" Jesus is still the Lord of providence. He has redeemed us in numberless instances from the temporal evils of the present life. Let us look at this,

2. *Spiritually.*

The redemption of man's body and soul. *How?* By assuming our nature, by becoming our surety, by magnifying the law, by shedding his blood. *From what?* From evil,—the evil of sin, its power, love, defilement, the evil of the curse of the law. From the power of the devil, from the evil of death, the evil of the grave, and from the evil—the extreme evil of the wrath to come. Yes! from all evil, internal and external; present and future. Redeemed to God, to his reconciled favor, to the possibility of receiving the offer of pardon, grace, and eternal glory.

Now this redemption is to be remembered. It ought to be gratifying and consolatory to our souls; it ought also to inspire faith and hope. This leads us then to notice, in the second place,

II. *The interesting prayer presented.*

"Bless the lads." Now Jacob's prayer had particular respect to the sons of Joseph. It may with propriety include both sexes. Man is generally addressed, woman included. We ask,

1. *What is sought?*

"Bless," &c. This expression is very comprehensive. The outline we may fill up according to circumstances, &c. Three things we should especially seek on their behalf.

(1.) Knowledge and wisdom. Knowledge is power. "For the soul to be without knowledge," &c. Science, literature, &c., important; knowledge of Christ, the most important. The wisdom that cometh from above. Knowledge and wisdom combined. There are many intellectual profligates, skeptics; devils are intellectual; they know God and tremble, &c. That they may be wise to salvation.

(2.) Genuine religion. It begins with knowledge evidenced by fruits of piety; it must be the religion of the heart, and of the life.

(3.) That God may make them extensively useful. The world is to be evangelized. These are to be the instruments. We labor and die. The millennial temple is to be reared by these hands.

2. *Who should thus pray?*

(1.) Those who profess to be lovers of their species. If you want man to be free, happy, and great, kneel down and adopt this prayer.

(2.) Those who are called patriots,—lovers of their country. What can exalt a nation more than this, &c. Bend before the God of nations, and thus pray. These are to fill our civil offices, &c.

(3.) Parents. You love your children, show it by your example. Take them with you to the throne of grace, and pray as in the language of the text.

(4.) Sunday-school teachers. Teach and impress divine truth upon your scholars; but, after all, pray for them in the spirit of the text.

(5.) Fellow-Christians,—all who love Jesus Christ,—Christ says to each of us, and to all, "Suffer little children to come unto me," &c. "Feed my lambs."

3. *The manner of presenting this supplication.*

This must be done under a consciousness,

(1.) Of the necessity of the divine blessing. "The watchman may keep the city," &c. "The builder may build the house," &c. "Paul may plant, and Apollos may water, but Christ alone can cause to grow."

(2.) In strong faith. We have promises and examples: Abraham for Ishmael; the father for his dumb child; the nobleman for his daughter.

(3.) In connection with our own efforts; God's blessing with, and following the employment of right means; God's blessing with our own exertions. Observe,

The obvious bearing of the text on Sabbath-school institutions.

CCLIX.—CHRISTIAN ZEAL.

"But it is good to be zealously affected always in a good thing."—*Gal.* iv. 18.

WE here see the relapsed state of the Christians in Galatia. They had received the gospel joyfully. So attached were they to the apostle, that they would have given themselves to have served him. But judaizing teachers diverted them from the simplicity of the gospel truth. The design of this epistle was to restore them to their former purity of belief and practice. The apostle shows that the old economy had passed away; that they could not be the disciples of both. Either they must be the groaning bondmen of the old, or the free children of the new dispensation. He applies his subject pointedly, and yet affectionately, ver. 10, &c. Our immediate subject is Christian zeal. Let us consider its nature, its object, its excellency, and its importance.

I. *The nature of Christian zeal.*

Zeal is an enlivened and impassioned ardor of mind, the opposite of coldness and apathy. It is the intense employment of means to acquire some real or imaginary object. It is from a word which signifies to boil. Hence it is obviously a warm and burning temperature of mind. I need not say it is an affection of the mind which may be applied either to good or bad. Our subject is Christian zeal; which,

1. *Is a spiritual principle, and therefore divine in its origin.*

A man may be zealous in sin; as Manasseh, as Saul. A man may be a zealous bigot or sectarian; but no man can be spiritually zealous, until he is a spiritual man. "The carnal mind is enmity against God," &c. "They that live after the flesh," &c., they cannot please God. A man may be zealous for forms. He may be a zealous Catholic, Protestant, Churchman, Dissenter; but not a zealous Christian.

2. *Christian zeal is an intellectual principle, and therefore the result of knowledge.*

We are to know why and wherefore we are zealous. The Jews had a zeal, Rom. x. 2. So had Saul, but it was a blind one. Christian zeal not only warms, but it illumines. It is based on eternal truth. Like the sun, bright, clear, and glorious. To be able to give a reason, &c.

3. *Christian zeal is a modest and humble principle.*

False zeal is ostentatious. It desires to be seen and distinguished. Come, see my zeal, &c. A pharisaical zeal seeks to gain human applause. Peter had too much of this before his fall. "Though all men forsake thee," &c. Afterwards he learned by experience. "Simon, son of Jonas, lovest thou me," &c. How changed, how different; yet how sincere! "Lord, thou knowest all things," &c.

4. *Christian zeal is a constant, enduring principle.*

Not like the Galatians; "Ye did run well." Not a flaming meteor, or startling comet; but like the rising orb of day shining more and more. Not the feverish heat of a diseased body, but regular constitutional warmth; the sign of health and life, and which only expires at death. "O Ephraim, what shall I do unto thee," &c.

5. *Christian zeal is an active, vigorous principle.*

Not merely a zeal of words, of professions, of desires, of resolvings, of wishes, &c. It loosens the tongue, opens the hand, swiftens the feet. It prays, as well as believes; it labors, as well as hopes. It is embodied. Not a metaphysical something. Not like the wind; you see, hear, and feel it. And without this practical body it is a mere spectre, and can be of no use in our material world.

6. *Christian zeal is an affectionate principle, and is always connected with fervent love.*

No anathemas; no shibboleths. It is not suspicious, but open; not narrow, but broad, and liberal, and generous. It dwells not on the dark and terrific mount of Sinai, but on the light, serene, and peaceful mount of Zion. It is not the furious demon from beneath, but the bright and celestial angel from above. It has the eagle's eye and wing, but it has the gentleness of a dove. It has the power of the ox, the energy of the lion; but the nature of the lamb, and the face of man. Brethren, this is an important distinction. Christian zeal is the zeal of love. Indignant at sin, but loves the sinner; hates heresy, but prays for the heretic. See it in Moses. He is grieved for the rebellion of the Israelites, yet he prays, &c. See it in Paul while warning the Galatians, &c. Especially in Christ. He pronounced all the woes against the Pharisees, &c., and then burst into tears, &c. While dying on the cross, his zeal was yet undamped, yet on behalf of his murderers, prayed, "Father, forgive them," &c.

II. *The object of Christian zeal.*

"In a good thing," &c. Now there is a two-fold sphere for the exercise of Christian zeal.

1. *In securing the greatest possible amount of good to ourselves.*

Zealous in seeking extensive knowledge. Zealously laboring after more of the spirit of Christ. Dying daily to the world; rising into the divine life; advancing in all the graces of the Spirit; abounding in every good word and work. Now this must be first. Our own soul's welfare first, &c.

2. *In communicating all the good in our power to those around us.*

What an enlarged sphere! The world itself is our field. But especially there are those immediately surrounding you. The perishing, starving, afflicted, dying poor. The ignorant, the vile, those going down to the pit. The church of Christ, with her blessed institutions, schools, tracts, sending the word abroad. Now Christ's honor and glory are identified with all these, &c.

III. *The excellency of Christian zeal.*

"It is good, always to be zealously affected."

1. *It is good to the soul which is under its influence.*

The same as exercise to the body. No health or strength without it. It produces energy, buoyancy, safety, and happiness. Without it coldness, gloom, and paralyzation.

2. *It is good for the church.*

Can you estimate the amount of good conferred upon the church by Moses; by Caleb, Josiah, the spies, &c.; by Nehemiah, by Ezra, by Zerubbabel, by the apostles, by the fathers and martyrs, by the reformers of our own country? Had it not been for these, the volume of British Martyrology never would have been written. It was this that caused the Erskines of Scotland, Wesley and Whitefield and others in England, to be such distinguished blessings to the cause of the Redeemer.

3. *It is good to the world at large.*

The zeal of the Christian church in our own country has already spread its happy influence to most parts of the habitable globe. I appeal to those moral wastes in our own nation which have been fertilized. I appeal to the thousands in the islands of the west, who have been doubly emancipated by the zeal of their Christian brethren, from the fetters of the tyrant and the curse of sin. Behold our missionary stations scattered over the wide surface of the globe.

4. *It is good, as it associates us with the highest intelligences of the heavenly world.*

The happy angels are distinguished for knowledge, power, holiness, and goodness. But especially, too, are they distinguished for zeal. So zealous, that they are called "flames of fire." So zealous, that they burn night and day before the throne of the Eternal, waiting to execute the divine commands. Allow me to ascend yet higher. To remind you of one who has obtained a more eminent name than they; "who is exalted a prince and a Saviour," &c. How intensely he felt this holy affection. It induced him to sign the *bond of the new covenant;* it induced him to enter upon its fulfilment with eagerness and delight; it induced him to make it his meat and drink. How intensely and constantly it burned within him. "The zeal of thy house hath eaten me up." "I have a baptism to be baptized with, and how am I straitened till it be accomplished."

IV. *The importance of Christian zeal.*

This must in a great measure appear from what has already been advanced. We rather wish to say something of its present importance in certain matters, and under certain circumstances.

1. *It is pre-eminently important when the object contemplated is great and glorious.*

Christian zeal contemplates the eternal salvation of deathless spirits—to save blood-bought and precious souls from everlasting burnings.

2. *It is pre-eminently important when difficulties are numerous.*

What can be done with startling and formidable opposition without zeal? Combination of earth and hell, wicked men and fallen spirits, the opposition of black ignorance, hardness, infatuation, satanic power, &c.

3. *It is pre-eminently important when the time of action is limited.*

This affected Christ himself; "I must work," &c. Time is hastening. We are exposed to the arrows of death—the opening of the grave. Our fathers, where are they? or the prophets, where are they? Another generation is already treading upon our heels. How solemnly precious and important the thought.

4. *When the responsibilities are momentous.*

It is not a secondary concern. Not optional. It is imperative that we be zealously affected in every good work. Our destiny awaits us according to the spirit and practice we have pursued on earth.

APPLICATION.

1. Let Christians cherish this holy principle.

2. Let unpardoned sinners zealously seek the salvation of their souls.

3. Let the church be zealous for the instruction of the rising age.

CCLX.—THE SUBLIME PRAYER OF MOSES.

"And he said, I beseech thee show me thy glory."—*Exod.* xxxiii. 18.

WHAT astounding facts are associated with the biography of the word of God! Those who are interested in the marvellous, need not pass by the records of inspiration. Besides, the wonders of God's word are true, they are fair and faithful likenesses, and they are adapted to improve the heart as well as to astonish and interest the mind. The biography of Moses occupies a full place in the Old Testament scriptures, and his life is crowded with wonders. The child of obscurity, yet the adopted of the princess of Egypt. The shepherd of Midian, and then the ambassador of heaven to the court of Pharaoh. He appears as the high servant of Jehovah, the leader, lawgiver, and mediator to the nation of Israel. He was distinguished as a man of devotion; his prayers were lofty, fervent, powerful, and prevailing. Of all the occasions wherein his supplications are recorded, none equal that which the text records. Oh, that we might drink into the same spirit, while we meditate on the subject!

I. *The immediate circumstances which preceded the prayer.*

II. *The prayer itself.*

III. *The answer returned.*

(1.) Moses had been receiving the law from the mouth of Jehovah on the summit of Sinai. Here the moral law was pronounced by the mouth of the Lord.

(2.) After this, Moses again ascended, and God gave a resplendent exhibition of his majesty, &c., and with this revelation, Aaron, Nadab, and Abihu, with seventy of the elders of the children of Israel, were favored. Exod. xxiv. 10, 11.

(3.) Moses was invited to ascend the mount, and there alone he was surrounded by the glory of the Lord. "And Moses went up into the mount, and a cloud covered the mount. And the glory of the Lord abode on Mount Sinai, and the cloud covered it six days, and the seventh day he called unto Moses out of the midst of the cloud. And the sight of the glory of the Lord was like devouring fire on the top of the mount, in the eyes of the children of Israel; and Moses went into the midst of the cloud, and gat him up into the mount, and Moses was in the cloud forty days and forty nights." Ver. 14–18. On this occasion the whole ritual was given, and every minutiæ which had respect to the tabernacle, sacrifices, and worship.

(4.) Moses is dismayed on account of the idolatry of the people. See xxxii. 1. "And when the people saw that Moses delayed to come down out of the mount, the people gathered themselves together unto Aaron, and said unto him, Up, make us gods, which shall go before us; for as for this Moses, the man that brought us up out of the land of Egypt, we wot not what has become of him." God's wrath was enkindled, &c. Moses intercedes, and his prayer is heard. He then descends to the camp,—burns the golden calf, grinds it to powder, &c. The people are punished, and three thousand are put to death by the sword.

(5.) Moses again ascends the mount, and again affectionately intercedes for the people. It was on this occasion that he chose rather to perish than that Israel should be blotted out of God's book, xxxii. 32. God now engages to send his angel, xxxiii. 1, &c. Moses now causes the people to put aside their ornaments and to assemble in the tabernacle of the congregation. Moses doubtless went into the holy place, and thus prayed with the Lord. See ver. 12, 13. He obtains his suit, God engages his presence, &c., ver. 17. Then, strengthened and encouraged, Moses prayed, "I beseech thee, show me thy glory." Such were the immediate circumstances, &c. Notice,

II. *The prayer itself.*

"Show me thy glory." It is clear from the context that he meant, Unveil thyself to my vision; let me see thy essential majesty and splendor; remove every veil from my eyes, all obscurity from my vision. Such was doubtless the desire of Moses. We have to observe here,

1. *The imperfection of the best saints.*

Imperfect in knowledge and judgment; fallible in our desires and devotions. Moses a man of prayer, yet knew not how he prayed on this occasion. Peter prayed in like manner,—"Let us build three tabernacles," &c. Paul, that the thorn in the flesh might be removed.

2. *The beneficence and care of God for his people.*

Not only in giving, but in withholding. Well has the poet expressed it:

> "Good when he gives, supremely good,
> Nor less when he denies;
> E'en crosses from his sov'reign hand,
> Are blessings in disguise."

How important to ask according to his will. To refer all to his wisdom and love, and in every thing to be able to say, "He hath done all things well." Observe,

III. *The answer returned.*

1. *The literal request was mercifully refused.*

And he said, "Thou canst not see my face and live," ver. 20. We need not wonder at this. The sun in the heavens, a feeble emblem of Deity, can overwhelm and destroy both vision and life. Even the moon, which shines with subdued brightness, yet in certain latitudes, by a single stroke, can produce paralysis and death. The brightness of celestial beings has often dazzled almost to destruction those favored by the vision. See the account given of Daniel, viii. 15. John when he had the vision of the Redeemer, on whose bosom he had formerly rested, "fell down at his feet as dead." Rev. i. 1. Was it not then merciful in the Lord refusing the literal desire of Moses?

2. *The spirit of the prayer was graciously answered.*

The Lord pitied his servant's weakness. He did not chide; he was not grieved: and, in the fulness of his grace, granted the spirit of his request. "I will make all my goodness pass before," &c. As much as the sight could bear was granted. But the chief revelation was to the ear. "And the Lord passed by," &c. God's goodness is his glory. And his glory the transcript of his goodness. But how can we see the glory of God? It is presented broadly and fully in four scenes, for our contemplation and improvement.

(1.) *The first scene is that of the divine works.*

All the works of God praise him. "The heavens declare the glory of God, and the firmament," &c. We see in the mountain and the plain,—in the brook and in the ocean,—in the vastness and in the minuteness of his works and ways, "How marvellous are thy works, O Lord God Almighty!"

(2.) *The second scene is that of the divine word.*

The word of the Lord is full of the glory of the divine mind. Here we have the beams of the divine wisdom and goodness, opening the way to life and immortality.

> "Father of mercies, in thy word
> What endless glory shines!
> Forever be thy name ador'd,
> For these celestial lines."

(3.) *The third scene is that in which the Deity tabernacled in human flesh.*

Of him John wrote, "We beheld his glory," &c.—he was the brightness of the Father's glory, &c. All the attributes of Deity are resplendent in him. If the goodness of God be his glory, then Christ was the embodiment of that goodness. That goodness made palpable;—that goodness clothed in our flesh,—living,—speaking, suffering,—dying,—ascending; and then diffusing itself, by the Holy Spirit, to all the members of his body, the church.

(4.) *The fourth scene is reserved for heaven and eternity to disclose.*

The pure in heart shall see God. How, in what medium, to what extent, we know not. The oracles respond not to these inquiries; but it is written that the visions of heaven will be satisfying: "I shall be satisfied," &c. Transforming: "We shall be like him," &c.

APPLICATION.

1. Learn the lofty eminence to which true piety exalts a man. Intercourse with heaven. Communion with God. Friendship with Deity.

2. The true breathings of the devout soul. "Show me thy glory." Every thing else is tinsel. Let me see thy glory, especially in extending thy kingdom, and saving souls; see it in the sanctuary, &c.

3. A perfect acquaintance with God's goodness is offered us in the gospel. "Oh, taste and see," &c. "God is love," &c.

CCLXI.—THE PROMISED INCREASE PLEADED.

"The Lord God of your fathers make you a thousand times so many more as ye are, and bless you, as he hath promised you."—*Deut.* i. 11.

In calling your attention to this striking prayer, we shall consider,

I. *The glorious Being addressed.*
" The Lord God of your fathers."
II. *The comprehensive petition presented.*
" Make you a thousand," &c.
III. *The ground of encouragement adduced.*
" As he hath promised," &c.

I. *The glorious Being addressed.*
" The Lord God of your fathers." He is addressed,

1. *In his essential character as Lord God.*
All the titles connected with the blessed God are important, and full of glorious meaning. *Lord* or *Jehovah* relates to his dominion. A dominion extending to all creatures and all worlds. Lord of earth, angels, heaven, and hell. *God* is one of Jehovah's titles, which has more especial reference to the benevolence of the Deity. It signifies the good Being, the fountain of happiness, &c. A Lord may possess power, and yet be an object of terror. In Jehovah power and goodness are united. Goodness is not so much an attribute, as the essence of God. His name and nature. God is good: God is love. We see the combination of Lord and God in all his works.

(1.) Creation is the work of Jehovah, Lord of power, wisdom, &c., yet all connected with goodness, and expressive of his love.

(2.) In the providence and the works of God. Yes. The Lord reigneth. He holds the reign of universal dominion. Yet we see God in all and through all, opening his hand and supplying all creatures with good.

(3.) In redemption, almighty power and infinite wisdom were requisite for the restoration of an apostate world. But here especially was goodness manifested. " God so loved the world"—a love which passeth understanding. This view of the Supreme Being is highly consolatory. A being of illimitable authority and power, yet

" Whose love is as great as his power,
And neither knows measure nor end."

2. *In his relative character.*
" Lord God of your fathers." He is often spoken of as the God of Abraham, Isaac, and Jacob. God of Israel. In this way his name is associated with various events and manifestations of himself. Let us consider the term,

1. *Literally in its application to Israel.*
The Lord God, who called Abraham, blessed Isaac, and blessed and surnamed Jacob; who delivered his people from the proud yoke of Pharaoh; brought them through the Red Sea; guided, guarded, and supplied them in the wilderness; gave them the rich land of promise. Surely Israel might well sing, " There is no God like unto the God of Jeshurun." Then let us apply it,

2. *To many of our fathers after the flesh.*
Many of our fathers served and trusted in the living God. We remember how they loved his word; how they took us with them to his house; how they sung his praises; how often they kneeled at the family altar; how often they prayed, " Oh, that my son, my daughter might live," &c. How generally happy. We remember when they sickened, how cheerfully resigned before they died. How anxious for our welfare. How they spake of God; " Behold I die, but serve God, and he will be with you. Oh, do not cast off God, but serve him, and he will again unite us in the indissoluble bonds of a glorious immortality." Is not their memory still sweet; their sleeping dust still precious; and do you not feel something endearing in the term, " The Lord God of your fathers?"

3. *The subject has a general application to our spiritual predecessors.*
Those who preceded us in the vineyard of the Lord; those early *Christian fathers*, who had to witness before the pagan world, and who passed through the horrid afflictions of ten persecutions, and yet were supported, and made successful in spreading the gospel through the whole world. *Those early British and German reformers*, who snatched the torch of truth, and lighted up the doctrines of the Protestant faith, which all the might of the Romish power could not extinguish. *The fathers of dissent*, those spiritual giants of the sixteenth, seventeenth, and eighteenth centuries, who were bold enough, holy enough, and disinterested enough, to despise the pompous ceremonies of a state hierarchy, and who, to the number of *two thousand* abandoned their livings from love to the "*faith once delivered to the saints.*" Notice,

II. *The comprehensive petition presented.*
" Make you," &c. In the petition are two parts,—multiplication of numbers and the divine blessing.

1. *Multiplication of numbers.*
" Make you a thousand times," &c.
(1.) There is nothing in this impossible. The Lord God had already blessed them.

Now in reference to the *Christian cause* equally possible. *Ample scope.* The field is the world. The world is peopled with souls. The whole world is lying in wickedness. *Ample materials.* The gospel of the Lord God. It is God's work. The soul of Jesus is travelling with it. The spirit is poured out for this end, &c. Therefore our text is not hyperbolical, but literal.

(2.) Something in the prayer truly desirable. *On God's account:*—that he may be pre-eminently loved and adored. "Thy will be done," &c. That earth, and air, and seas, may be vocal with his praise. On *Messiah's account.* Who can contemplate the extent of his sorrows, the depths of his humiliation, the intensity of his agonies, the bitterness of the cup ? &c. And wherefore did he drink it ? That he might see his seed, prolong his days, and see of the travail of his soul, until he should be satisfied. On the *world's account.* When men are added to God's family,—what is it? Of civilization, education, we hear much, &c. But this is conversion from darkness, &c. It is the regeneration of the soul. It is adoption into the household of faith. It is salvation. Heaven on earth and heaven forever. *On our own account.* Christianity is not a selfish monopoly. No patents to restrict it to ourselves. When others join the festival the banquet is sweeter. The joy of each adds to the whole. In one of the miracles of the loaves, 4000 partook of five loaves and several fishes, and only seven baskets remained. But in the other, 5000 partook of five loaves and two fishes, and twelve baskets remained! Yes, by increase the felicity of the church is greatly augmented. Prayer for the peace of Jerusalem. They that love her shall prosper. Another part of this prayer is,

2. *The divine blessing.*

"Bless you."

(1.) With what is necessary to this increase. The spirit of humility, prayer, zeal, are all produced by divine influence. "Not by might," &c. "Prove me now," &c.

(2.) With what will render an increase a *blessing.* Not mere increase should satisfy; but an increase of stones squared and polished, and laid on the true foundation, of those who are true lights, or the real glory of the church will not be increased. Of those who savor of holiness; of those who possess the stern principles of truth and integrity; or the church will not withstand the floods of error, &c. Those who possess the spirit of holy enterprise, of divine philanthropy, or all the nations of the earth will not hear the doctrines of the cross. Oh yes! While we seek an increase, let us not forget the blessing necessary to effect and also to sanctify it.

III. *The ground of encouragement adduced.*

"As he hath promised." Now God did promise Abraham and Jacob, &c., and he hath promised equal prosperity to us. Observe some of the traits of these promises. They are,

1. *Absolute in their nature.*

He has not said he will multiply the church if,

(1.) Her friends are active and willing. No. But he will make his people willing in the day of his power. They shall be volunteers in the day when Christ puts forth his authoritative claims, &c. He has not said he will prosper his church,

(2.) If the governments of the world and the great of the earth are favorable; but it is written, "They *shall* bring the gold of Sheba," &c. He shall overturn and overturn until all things shall be subdued to himself. The purposes of God and his promises are absolute in their nature.

2. *They are numerous.*

Not one isolated promise, not merely the text, but they are countless like the stars which shine in the milky way. These promises are scattered over the whole extent of revelation.

3. *They have been principally made to Christ.*

The reward of his covenant engagements not only pledged to the church, but also to the Saviour. The stipulated price has been paid. He did not fail, &c. Ask of me, &c., Isa. xxi. 22, liii. 10, lx. 4, 5.

4. *Partially fulfilled.*

We appeal to apostolic ages; we appeal to the Reformation; we appeal to the revival of religion during the past and present century; we appeal to the exertions of all denominations of Christians at the present period; and we appeal to the prospects connected with missionary enterprises.

APPLICATION.

Three inferences:

1. *The divinity of our religion.*

Our God is the Lord God of Sabaoth.

2. *The benevolence of our religion.*

It embraces a world. True benevolence is love to souls.

3. *The final triumphs of our religion.*

God shall speak, &c., to the north and to the south. "The kingdoms of this world shall become the kingdoms of our God and of his Christ," &c.

4. *The bearing of our subject on the religious instruction of the rising generation.*

How all-important to train up our youth for the service and glory of God. Here chiefly is our hope of a speedy realization of the prayer of the text.

———————

CCLXII.—A DISCOURSE TO CHILDREN.

"I love them that love me; and those that seek me early shall find me."—*Prov.* viii. 17.

My young hearers will perceive that our text is represented as being the language of wisdom. See ver. 12. Now it is generally agreed that Jesus Christ, the Son of God, and redeemer of the world, is here described by the term Wisdom. This is clearly established by the truths contained in the twenty-second to the thirty-first verse. As such, then, we will now consider it. But what does Jesus say? He addresses two kinds of children.

1. Those who love him.

2. Those who seek him; and he promises gracious things to both of them. "I love them," &c. "Those that seek me early shall," &c. Now, we will consider these characters separately. And we inquire,

I. *What is it to love Christ?*

You all know what love signifies. You can tell the difference between that and dislike,—between that and indifference. I place three persons before you : one whose character is very bad ; he is said to hate and be cruel to children ; his countenance is very dark, and he has some deadly weapon in his hand. Why, if you knew all this you would not wish to be near him ; you would feel dislike to him, and dread him. Well, there is a second, and he is a stranger ; you never heard either good or evil of him, never saw him before,—why, you would feel indifferent to him, you would not however feel towards him as to the other. Well, now, your father or mother, or some very kind friend draws near—oh, how differently you now feel ; you do not dislike, neither are you indifferent. Your heart loves this person. Now, to love is to esteem, to value, to approve of, and to delight in the person beloved. Do you thus love God? Do you often think of God? Do you often speak to God in prayer? Do you try to obey God? Do you fear to grieve God? Do you love his day, his house, his people, his word? I am sure you ought to love him ; for he made you, gave you life, gave you all your senses, all your faculties ; gave you kind parents, health,—all things. You have nothing but what he gives you. He gave you himself ; he came from heaven to show his love, and to die for you ; and he did die, even on the cross, for you children's salvation. He sent you the blessed Bible, and he tells you there that he has prepared heaven for all pious children when they die. Besides, he says, "he loves them," &c. You rejoice because your parents love you ; but how much better that God loves you. He can help you when they cannot ; he never dies, but your parents die. He will guide you, keep you, bless you, and make you happy forever and ever.

II. *What he says to those who seek him.*

But let me just ask two or three questions here.

1. *Are some children living far from him —living without him?*

Oh yes! we grieve to say that many are wandering by sin far from God. All who do wickedly, all who are profane, all who break the Sabbath, all who disobey parents, all who never pray, or who say their prayers without thought—all who do not fear God, all who have not given him their hearts.

2. *But in what way are children to seek Jesus Christ?*

Why, they should seek him in the scriptures. Here you will learn all concerning Christ ; what he has done for you ; and how you may enjoy the blessings provided. Of Timothy, it is said, "From a child," &c. You should seek him by earnest prayer. Prayer is calling upon him. It is going to his throne. Of Saul of Tarsus, it was said, "Behold he prayeth." Religion begins with prayer.

3. *You must seek him by turning away from evil.*

The prodigal would never have found

his father had he not turned back. So you must return to God; give up all that you know is evil.

4. You must seek him by believing what he has said.

"Without faith," &c. God has said the sinner shall die. If you believe that, you will feel afraid and tremble. He has said that he does not wish the sinner to die, thus you will begin to hope. He has said that if you will trust in Christ with all your hearts, he will forgive you all your sins, and love you. This believing on Christ, is gratefully depending on what Christ has suffered for you, for acceptance with God. Now, in this seeking God, your whole heart and soul must be in earnest. If you seek him with all your hearts. But he refers us in the text to early seeking,—that is, very soon in life. You cannot seek him too early; many children have sought him when only four or five years old.

(1.) You cannot seek him too early, because you cannot be happy too soon. He will make you really and truly happy.

(2.) Because you cannot be safe too soon. If you know good from evil, then you are accountable to God; and if you die disliking God, you cannot go to heaven; and you may die very early. I feel persuaded some of you will die while you are children. Have you not known some who have died? If you seek the Lord, then if you die young you will go to heaven,—have the crown and the white robe.

(3.) It is much easier to find the Lord early; you have not gone so far from him; your evil habits are not now so strong and deep-rooted. Look at that little plant, you could pull it up; not so in a year or two. A little stream.

(4.) If you find the Lord when young, God may employ you in his service, and make you very useful in the world. Who can tell what God has for you to do? Many of you may be teachers, preachers, missionaries—do much good in the world. Have you not heard of Luther, of Wesley, Cecil? and then there was the apostle John, who "leaned on Christ's bosom," &c.

APPLICATION.

1. How many of you love the Lord?
2. How many will engage to seek him from this morning?

CCLXIII.—THE CONSECRATED BAND.

"And there went with him a band of men whose hearts God had touched."—1 Sam. x. 26.

THE text is literally connected with the desire of Israel to have a king, and the setting apart of Saul to that high and dignified office. In this desire they exhibited discontent with the form of government which God had set over them, and incurred his holy and just disapprobation. Samuel was directed to expostulate with them, and to state the evils which their choice would bring upon them. Still they persisted, and God allowed them to see their hearts' desire. God often refuses our requests, in mercy. How important that prayer should be according to the will of the Lord! Well, Saul was anointed king, and some of the factious of the people were displeased with him on account of his humble station and his rural mode of life, and said, contemptuously, "How shall this man save us?" &c. Saul, however, returned home to Gibeah, and "there went with him a chosen band," &c. We desire not to occupy your attention with the character and history of Saul, but we have chosen the passage to refer you to another king, even Jesus, and to the character of his loyal and obedient servants. Observe,

I. *The characters described.*

"A band," &c. An appropriate representation of the disciples of Jesus, the followers of the Lamb. Now here we observe, that the heart of man is naturally sinful and disloyal; not subject to Christ, nor obedient to his authority. Now in the transformation of the soul we notice,

1. *Divine influence is essentially necessary.*

Nothing but this can renew the soul. Education cannot. Human authority or influence cannot. It is the Spirit's peculiar province to take away the heart of stone, &c.; to implant the new nature, &c. That which is spiritual in man, must be moderated by the Spirit.

2. *Divine influence in the heart will be evident.*

The mode and process may not be evident. "The wind bloweth," &c. As the rain, &c., in vegetation, operates effectually, yet invisibly and silently; so divine influences on the soul. But still the effects will be manifest, the evidences will be clear and palpable. When the Spirit of God touches the heart,

(1.) *It will become tender and affectionate.*

It will lose its hardness and be melted down—its callousness, and be susceptible of holy feelings, &c.—its malevolence, and become kind, and benevolent, and merciful. It will be the seat of love to God, and love to man. He that is of God loveth, &c.

(2.) *It will become contrite and humble.*

The high look, the towering imagination, the lofty spirit, will all be brought down into the depths of self-abasement; clothed, as it were, in sackcloth; sin will be mourned over, and confessed; and God will be praised and extolled. The divinely touched heart is always lowly and humble.

(3.) *It will become spiritual and devout.*

Until spiritually moved, we do not know the things of the Spirit, not being spiritually discerned. As spiritual, the desires and feelings will be such, the thoughts and meditations such. And with these will be united the spirit of devotion. The heart that has been touched, moves towards God in prayer. Prayer is the atmosphere it breathes, &c.; the language of the renewed soul.

(4.) *It will be self-denying and zealous.*

The natural mind is earthly and selfish; loves ease; under the incubus of sloth and indifference. God's glory and man's welfare never enter into his designs, &c. The opposite of this is the heart touched by the finger of God : self is mortified, and goodness and zeal actively cherished. The love of Christ constrains ; the Spirit of Christ excites; the power of grace impels to holy and devoted activity for the good of souls, and for the glory of Christ. Observe the hearts God hath touched are,

(5.) *United and associated together.*

"A band." Not isolated beings; not cold, unsocial beings; but collected together, enrolled and united in the bonds of the truth, and in the service of Christ. Grace unites man to man. The Church is a flock, an army, a family, "a band," united, not by ties of relationship, of learning, rank, or color; but cemented in the love and faith of the gospel.

II. *The statement made.*

"And there went with him," &c. Now Christ's disciples go with him. They may not go with the learned and philosophical; not with politicians; not with earthly warriors, &c. No, they are followers of Christ; his attendants ; they hear his voice, &c.; they go with him,

1. *To confess him as the trophies of his grace.*

Christ's living witnesses; monuments of divine mercy; the fruit of his crimson labors. As such, they testify of Christ, and confess him before men.

2. *To obey his commands, as his loyal subjects.*

In this they act consistently with their profession. In this they prove their love to Jesus. In this they recommend Christ's religion to the world. "Have their fruit unto holiness," &c.

3. *To extend his kingdom, as his devoted friends.*

They live to Christ, and for him. They are identified with Christ—seek his glory pre-eminently. They are not their own, &c.; Christ is all and in all. Give up all to Christ.

APPLICATION.

1. *Are we the characters?*

Has the heart been set right? Have we the signs upon us? &c.

2. *Are we going forth with Christ?*

Is this the chief end of life? our meat, our delight, our highest aim? &c. If so, how pleasing the prospect, how blessed the cause, how glorious the reward !

3. *Urge others to unite.* Who is for Christ? who will love, serve, and glorify the Redeemer? &c.

4. *Are not our chief hopes in reference to this band to be found associated with our Sabbath-schools?*

Here the talent of our churches is to be expended, and from these the army of the Saviour is chiefly to be replenished. Many of our future ministers and deacons are to be reared in these hallowed seminaries of Bible education and Sabbath training.

CCLXIV. — HONORING GOD, DIVINELY HONORED.*

"For them that honor me I will honor, and they that despise me shall be lightly esteemed."— 1 *Sam.* ii. 30.

God has inseparably connected holiness with happiness—religion with our best interests. Sin is a service which produceth

* *Series* v.—Designed especially for young persons.

the fruit of shame and misery. Piety is productive of joy unspeakable and full of glory. "Godliness," saith the apostle, "is profitable unto all things," &c. "The way of transgressors is hard," and "the wages of sin, death;" but "the ways of wisdom are ways of pleasantness, and all her paths are peace." Such is the spirit of the text. God says, "Them that honor me, I will honor," &c. In what way, we inquire,

I. *Can we honor God?*

To honor is to respect, to revere, to worship, exalt, or serve. Now we should honor God,

1. *By sacred reverence for his most holy name.*

"Hallowed be thy name." It is a glorious name—a great and terrible name; never to be used lightly; not to be intermixed with common conversation—not pronounced without awe. Sir Isaac Newton never, it is said, pronounced it without a solemn pause. Angels pronounce it with sublime emotions of veneration.

2. *By a constant regard to his sacred laws.*

God is our lawgiver; he has revealed his will, and his will is obligatory and binding. These laws are wise, just, and good. The basis of all acceptable obedience is faith in his Son. See John vi. 29. God's great commandment to us is, to receive his Son as our Saviour and hope, and to honor him even as we honor the Father. Thus only do we obtain grace, by which we can serve God acceptably, with reverence and godly fear. Now just as a child honors its parents by obedient regard to their commands; and as the subject, the sovereign by loyal obedience—so we honor God by having respect to all his commandments.

3. *By a regular attendance on his public worship.*

God is exalted in his sanctuary; here his glory is proclaimed—his praises sung—his word revered. God delighteth in these assemblies. "He loveth the gates of Zion better than all the dwellings of Jacob." Now a devoted attachment, evinced by regular attendance, honors God.

4. *By an avowal of religion before men.*

"If any man will be my disciple," &c. Thus did Moses. Thus did Daniel, and the three Hebrews; and thus did the apostles. Not to attempt secrecy, like Nicodemus, either from shame or fear.

5. *By an entire consecration of all we are and have to his glory.*

The glory of God is the great end of the Christian's life. It was so in Christ's life, and must be so in ours. Hence he requires that we consecrate ourselves—our persons—our talents—our wealth—our influence—in one word, our all.

6. *By unswerving adherence to the truth and service of God.*

Not to swerve in prosperity, nor in poverty; in health or sickness—in life or death. Enduring to the end—being faithful unto death, &c. We now ask,

II. *How will God honor us?*

He will do so: he has said it, explicitly and clearly.

1. *By conferring the most distinguished titles.*

In this way monarchs express their approbation, &c. Now when the sinner yields himself to God, he loses all the appellations of sin and misery which were upon him. Once a sinner, now a saint; a rebel, now a loyal subject; an enemy, now a child—they are princes and priests unto God.

2. *By bestowing especial marks of his favor.*

He will give evidence of his love, John xiv. 23. Confer peace and joy, &c. Allow access to him at all times.

3. *He will make you a blessing to others.*

"I will bless," &c. See how he honored Joseph in every station. Daniel. The three Hebrews. He will bless the work of our hands.

4. *By giving comfort and support in affliction and death.*

To exult in prospect of dissolution. Then to have his rod and staff in the dark valley. Visions of glory, as Stephen. His arms upholding while the tabernacle is being taken down. When flesh and heart fail, and when death appears, to send a convoy of angels, as to Lazarus.

5. *By publicly confessing and rewarding you at the last day.*

Christ, the judge, has said that he will confess such before his Father and the holy angels. Pronounce the "Well done, good and faithful servants," &c. Place the sparkling diadem on the brow of his faithful servants, and give them a glorious admission into his everlasting kingdom.

APPLICATION.

1. How many present live to honor God? Do you so entirely, devotedly, fully? Is it

your meat and drink to do his will ? Public, domestic, and private labors. In all things.

2. Let such rejoice in the truth the text expresses. Well may you bear present adversity, scorn, persecution, suffering, &c. "The suffering of the present time is not worthy to be compared with," &c.

3. How many dishonor God! Despise him in his Son, gospel, day, ordinances, &c.! Think of the consequences! What might they have been now, but for his mercy and long-suffering. Oh, think—pause—consider—repent—and seek his grace.

———————◆———————

CCLXV.—VALUELESS PHYSICIANS.

"All physicians of no value."—*Job* xiii. 4.

JOB, who uttered the language of the text, was called to pass through the deep waters of sorrow. He is justly represented before us in holy writ, as an example of what the godly may suffer, and the patience which divine grace can impart in seasons of severest distress. The apostle James thus practically refers to the suffering pious Job : "Behold, we count them happy which endure. Ye have heard of the patience of Job," &c., v. 11. The anguish of his wounded spirit was greatly increased by the unkind, suspicious, and ungenerous reflections of his professed friends. Persons who quite mistook his case, and greatly aggravated his sufferings ; no wonder that he exclaimed, "All physicians of no value."

I. *The human heart often stands in need of a physician.*

II. *That most are physicians of no value.* Yet,

III. *There is one Physician of incomparable worth.*

I. *The human heart often stands in need of a physician.*

It does so,

1. *When awakened to a sense of its true condition.*

There is a great difference between our imaginary and real state. Most think they are whole, or at worst but very partially afflicted with moral evil. The human heart is a proud, ignorant, and boasting heart. Many go about establishing their own righteousness ; but when light flashes across the mind, and the sword pierces the spirit, and the arrow of conviction is fastened in the heart—then earnest anxiety is the result, the real diseased, condemned soul is filled with alarm, disquietude, and prayer. Then the leprous sinner cries, Lord, heal me ; the blind sinner, Lord, that I might receive my sight ; the sinking, perishing sinner, Lord, save, or I perish. Oh, yes, in that day a physician is earnestly desired.

2. *When mourning over the unsubdued evils of our nature.*

Sin is forgiven, and the love and dominion destroyed, but it is not annihilated—crucified, but not dead ; there is a warfare carried on between the flesh and the spirit—between the new and the old man. This is the great affliction of the Christian. How he feels, and laments, and contends against the evils and plague of his own heart! He often exclaims, "Oh, wretched man that I am, who shall deliver me," &c. He needs none to upbraid him ; he daily feels and confesses the weaknesses and infirmities of his soul.

3. *When passing through painful and distressing visitations.*

Often they are heavily laden with sorrow and accumulated troubles. Wave after wave, billow after billow, loss after loss, bereavements, &c., trials, tempests, &c. The spirit wounded, heart sad, soul cast down. Oh, how necessary divine healing and comfort is! How desirable is joy and gladness! How valuable a physician with some healing potion for the broken heart! We notice,

II. *That most are physicians of no value.*

1. *Such are all worldly advisers.*

Men of the world naturally recommend worldly remedies. The various scenes of gayety, the assembly-room, the card-table, the fashionable party, &c. What valueless physicians ! Who ever found peace, or obtained a good hope, or cast aside their sorrows, by the aid of these ? Oh, no, they are all physicians of no value.

2. *Such also are all teachers of mere morality.*

That is, morality instead of Christianity. True religion will ever produce morality ; but to recommend morality to a sin-sick soul, is like cautioning the dying patient against taking cold. Even perfect righteousness would not blot out the stains of sin. There must be pardon and sanctifying grace. Good works are indispensable as the fruits, but utterly valueless as the root and basis of happiness.

3. *We may include also all who elevate particular doctrines as specifics for the human heart.*

Right sentiments are of the utmost value, the doctrines of the cross essential.

But the admission or credence of the most essential doctrine is not sufficient for the true health and peace of the soul. A man's theology may be good, and his soul still in the bonds of sin; his views clear, but his heart sad; his doctrines evangelical, and his spirit joyless. Yet with some this is the alpha, &c. How futile all this to the penitent or struggling Christian, or the sorrowing disciple of Jesus.

4. *All created sources are as physicians of no value.*

No one can pardon, or save, or bind up, or heal the spirit of his fellow. Not an angel in heaven, &c. How distressed the apostles were, when the people of Lystra would have paid them divine honors! Acts xiv. 11, &c. No, all created intelligences are, to the sin-afflicted and troubled soul of the believer, physicians of no value. We add,

III. *There is one physician of incomparable worth.*

This is Job's Redeemer, to whom he looked and in whom he trusted. "Christ is the great and infallible physician," &c.

1. *He pardons and heals the soul.*

He is exalted to do this. He often did it. It is his prerogative and delight. "They shall call his name Jesus." A wonderful method of healing he hath, &c.

2. *He sanctifies and perfects the work of grace in the heart.* "He is the author," &c. "He that hath begun the good work," &c. He says, "My grace is sufficient for thee." He perfects what is lacking, and conforms to his own likeness, &c.

3. *He consoles in all the troubles of life.*

Is the consolation of Israel, the tender shepherd, the unfailing friend. "Let not your heart be troubled," &c. He is our sympathizing high priest.

APPLICATION.

1. Let other physicians be abandoned. They are all valueless.

2. Let Jesus be consulted and obeyed. Trust in him. He will save, and to the uttermost, all who come unto God by him.

CCLXVI.—THE REAL AND THE ALMOST CHRISTIAN.

"Then Agrippa said unto Paul, Almost thou persuadest me to be a Christian."—*Acts* xxvi. 28.

OUR object leads us to contemplate the apostle Paul in one of the most striking events of his wonderful life and holy mission. He was now a prisoner for the gospel's sake, and was called to stand before the tribunal of Agrippa. Paul had previously vindicated himself before Felix and Festus. King Agrippa and Bernice, being on a visit to Festus, and hearing of Paul, desired to see him; and therefore the apostle delivered before him that eloquent address, of which our text is both the conclusion and application. The power and truth of that appeal constrained the monarch to exclaim, "Almost thou persuadest me," &c. Let us consider,

I. *What it is to be a Christian.*

II. *What to be almost persuaded.*

III. *The importance of being altogether such.*

I. *What it is to be a Christian.*

1. *A clear knowledge of the Christian Scriptures.*

Not a learned, critical, or perfect knowledge of them. Not a knowledge of the nature of its mysteries, &c.; but a clear knowledge of the great truths of the gospel—the doctrines and laws of Jesus Christ's kingdom. It is this knowledge which dispels the mists of darkness from the soul, so that unto those who dwell in the regions of darkness and death, light springs up. The way of salvation is only revealed here. "Life and immortality brought to light by the gospel." Now this knowledge may be attained either by reading or hearing. "Search the scriptures." "Blessed are the people that know the joyful sound," &c. There may be fanaticism; but there cannot be true religion without a knowledge of the Christian scriptures.

2. *A cordial faith in the person and work of Christ.*

Now, under this head there are four particulars. There must be faith in Christ—credence in the testimony of the gospel—a firm persuasion of its veracity; and this faith must be that of the heart—an affectionate, willing reception of the truth: "For with the heart man believeth," &c. "If thou believest with all thine heart," &c. Then it must be faith in Christ's person, as the Son of God—the true Messiah, the Saviour of the world. "Dost thou believe on the Son of God?" But it must also rest on Christ's work. Christ, as the sacrifice offered, the victim which bore our guilt, conquered our adversaries, and who is now within the holy place, exalted to give repentance and remission of sins.

3. *Conformity to the mind of Christ.*

"Let the same mind be in you," &c. There must be a measure of this to constitute the Christian character. A disciple is one who learns of Christ. "If any man have not the Spirit of Christ, he is none of his." Like-minded with Christ is the true representation of the Christian.

4. *Loyal obedience to Christ.*

"Ye are my friends," &c. "Whoso doeth the will of my Father, the same is my mother, and sister, and brother." Allegiance to Christ, reverential regard to his authority, and a desire to please him, are indispensable to the Christian character. "His sheep hear his voice, and follow him," &c.

5. *An uncompromising profession of Christ.*

Knowledge, faith, and resemblance, must be seen in our profession. We are not to be ashamed of Christ and his words. We are to confess him, &c.; we are to come out of the world, and be separate from it, to be his living epistles. It was for the profession of Christ that men have suffered the reproaches, &c., of the world, and the loss of life itself. A Christian exclaims, "I am not ashamed of the gospel of Christ," &c.

II. *What to be almost persuaded.*

Such are different to the unbelieving skeptic, the reviling opposer, or those who refuse all attention to divine things. Agrippa may well be our type of those who are only almost persuaded to be Christians.

1. *He heard the apostle with attention.*

And hearing is an essential prerequisite to faith and salvation. Thus many feel it right, yea, take a pleasure in hearing Christ preached. They cannot live in open neglect of the ordinances of the gospel—they go up regularly to the house of the Lord; and pay every possible respect to the message of salvation; yet, they are only "almost persuaded," &c.

2. *He admired, and seemed to admit the truths Paul declared.*

Hence Paul, in an eloquent, yet abrupt interrogation, said, "King Agrippa, believest thou the prophets? Yea, I know that thou believest," &c. It is evident that the royal hearer felt no ordinary interest in the apostle's discourse. Now, there are many who thus feel, and thus admire—they have no doubt as to the authenticity of the scriptures—as to the reality of religion—as to the preciousness of the gospel; but here they rest, and are satisfied with being almost persuaded to become Christians.

3. *He expressed his convictions, and testified to the power of the truth on his mind.*

"Then Agrippa said," &c.; "he felt, and not only thought, but spake, and that, too, openly. Now this was noble and candid. How many do the same!—they speak well of the gospel—they speak to their friends—to their consciences, to God, and this is all; here they rest.

III. *The importance of being altogether such.*

"Then Paul said, I would to God, that not only thou, but also all that hear me this day, were both almost," &c. Now, this will evidently appear,

1. *If we consider the necessity of decision of character to the improvement of the mind.*

A state of vacillation is unfriendly to the mental enlargement of the faculties. In arts and sciences, it is desirable to have a mature judgment and express views. But surely, in religion, it is vastly more so.

2. *Consider it in connection with real comfort and enjoyment.*

There is no peace in being almost persuaded, no joy, no abiding consolation.

3. *Consider it in connection with salvation.*

Only the Christian will be saved; the almost Christian will be almost saved; but then that will be more awful than if he had been afar off. Almost at the ark, but the door will be closed; almost within heaven, but the gate will be shut; almost at the city of refuge, but the avenger has overtaken; almost at the joyous banquet, but oil is wanting; and while they go to buy, they that are ready enter in.

APPLICATION.

1. It is the will of God that you should be altogether Christians, in heart and life; in profession and reality; in time and eternity. There is no necessity for your going from this house ere you give yourselves wholly to the Lord.

2. Let almost Christians endeavor to ascertain the cause of their decision. It is said

that Agrippa lived with his sister Bernice as his wife; if so, we can easily account for his being only almost, &c. Find out the impediment, the hindrance; and let it be what it may, weigh it with the value of the soul, the preciousness of Christ, and the glories of heaven. What is your reply? How will you decide? "I beseech you, brethren, by the mercies of God, be ye reconciled," &c.

CCLXVII.—CONSECRATION TO THE LORD.

" And this they did, not as we hoped, but first gave their own selves to the Lord, and unto us by the will of God."—2 *Cor.* viii. 5.

THE apostle is describing the benevolent conduct of the churches of Macedonia. They were afflicted and poor, but they were pious and liberal, ver. 2 ; and their liberality was not only to the utmost of their ability, but beyond, see ver. 3. They were deeply anxious to assist their suffering brethren, and therefore they prayed and urged the apostles, &c., ver. 4 : " Praying us, with much entreaty, that we would receive the gift." In the text we have the great mainspring of this goodness and generosity brought out, for they had given themselves to the Lord, and united with the churches of the apostles by the will of God. Our reading is somewhat ambiguous, for it would appear that the apostles had hoped that they would have adopted a different course—a better course. But if we read it thus, we have the clear sense, as well as the power of the text expressed : " Yea, and beyond our expectation, for they first gave themselves to the Lord, and to us through the will of God." Our text leads us to consider,

I. *The subject of personal consecration to God.*

II. *Devotion to his Church.*

III. *The principles on which such a course is grounded.* We are,

I. To consider the subject of personal consecration to God.

1. *Something always precedes the consecration of the soul to God.*

The mind must be awakened ; consideration must be produced ; a sense of our sin and danger must be felt ; a knowledge of the way of salvation must be possessed.

Now, in effecting this preparatory process, both the events of Providence and the means of grace are employed. Thus in the jailer at Philippi.

2. *The act of consecrating ourselves* includes,

(1.) The surrender of heart and soul to God. We will be the Lord's; he shall be our God ; he shall have our supreme love ; all idols shall be cast down ; he shall reign over us, and within us.

(2.) This surrender must be our own personal act. "Gave their own selves." Friends may instruct and counsel ; they may allure by their kind spirit and example ; they may influence by sweet persuasion ; they may give efficiency to the whole by their fervent prayers—but religion must be our own personal act. None gave others, but each one himself, to the Lord.

(3.) It must be a willing surrender. Religion is not to be the production of dread and terror, but of cheerfulness and love. This is beautifully expressed by the prophet Isaiah, xliv. 5 : " One shall say, I am the Lord's ; and another shall call himself by the name of Jacob ; and another shall subscribe with his hand unto the Lord, and surname himself by the name of Israel."

(4.) It must be a surrender in and through the mediation of Christ. We cannot come to God but by Christ Jesus. He will only receive us in and through him. Every plea, every name, every object of trust renounced ; and in Christ's name, righteousness, and merits must be all our trust. Under the law, the worshipper brought his gift and laid it on God's altar. Christ is the altar. On this altar alone God will accept us.

(5.) This must be an entire and unreserved surrender of ourselves. God will have all as his right and due. The hand and heart— the mind and life—talents and influence. The surrender must be entire, and not in part ; and this is what the penitent believer is ready to give. The love of Christ causes the soul to exclaim,

"Were the whole realm of nature mine,
    That were a present far too small ;
Love so amazing, so divine,
    Demands my soul, my life, my all."

(6.) This surrender must be given with earnestness and solemnity. The most momentous act to which our spirit can be called. It cannot be performed with halfheartedness, with apathy, or in the spirit of frivolity. Its weight impresses the whole spirit—fills the whole mind.

(7.) This surrender must be made publicly. Real religion, that which is genuine, is in the heart; none but God can see it; but this must be accompanied by a visible and outward profession of Christ before men. Now this is most clearly insisted upon. "My sheep hear my voice, and follow me." " If any man will be my disciple," &c. "Whosoever is ashamed of me before men," &c. This leads us to notice the other branch of the text.

II. *Devotion to the Church of Christ.*
" And unto us," &c.

1. *Consider the propriety of this.*
Kindred spirits associating together. " I am a companion," &c. " We will go with you," &c. " This people shall be my," &c.

2. *Consider the necessity for this.*
We are only partially instructed—liable to err—weak. Counsel is necessary. Mutual sympathy, help, and comfort. Without this, how could ordinances be observed; Christianity diffused; Christian graces exhibited; or duties discharged?

3. *Consider the advantages of this.*
Union is both strength and comfort. Pilgrims go in company; soldiers unite in armies; individuals constitute themselves into families, &c. We notice,

III. *The principles on which such a course is grounded.*
Why should you give yourselves to the Lord and his people?

1. *There is the high authority of God.*
God demands it. He issues his mandate; he claims this; he does so in justice to himself, and in mercy to you.

2. *Your own present well-being.*
Religion will make you happy. No peace elsewhere. It is well with all who fear God.

3. *The salvation of your immortal souls.*
No other way to heaven; no other escape from hell. Then all, now and forever, give yourselves to the Lord.

CCLXVIII.—PERSONAL RELIGION.

" One shall say, I am the Lord's; and another shall call himself by the name of Jacob; and another shall subscribe with his hand unto the Lord, and surname himself by the name of Israel."—*Isa.* xliv. 5.

It appears evident that the prophecy of the text relates to the conversion of the Gentiles to God. And the day of Pentecost seems to be the realization of the visions of the prophet. Then God indeed poured down his Holy Spirit in copious and miraculous effusion; and then it was that persons assembled from every part of the then known world, heard Peter publish the word of life, and there was added to the Church a great multitude of repenting, believing souls. And after the gospel was preached to the Gentile nations, vast accessions were everywhere made to the kingdom of the Messiah. " One said, I am the Lord's," &c. Our subject is the nature, characteristics, and importance of religion.

I. *The nature of true religion.*

1. *It is a surrender of ourselves to God.*
" I am the Lord's." (1.) He has an original right. He formed us for himself. (2.) He has a reasonable right. I am made for him, he is the end of my being. (3.) He has a redeeming right. He hath ransomed me from death and hell. He says, " I have redeemed thee, not with corruptible things, &c., but with the precious blood of Christ." Now it is to acknowledge all this—to feel all this—to act upon the principle of all this. Many give themselves up to sin, many to the world, many to self and their own ways. But in the day of conversion God's right is felt, and conceded, and the soul says, " I am the Lord's."

" Take my body, spirit, soul,
Only thou possess the whole."

2. *It is an avowed acknowledgment of God.*
" Another shall call himself," &c. Profession is demanded by the Lord. We are to bear his name, be his witnesses, confess him before men. Then hold fast that profession; thus did Jesus, thus did the apostles and early Christians. Now in the ordinance of baptism we are immersed into Christ's name and visibly put him on.

3. *It includes union and fellowship with his people.*
" Call themselves by the name of Jacob, and surname themselves," &c. " We will go with you," &c. " This people shall be my people, and their God my God." The apostle says of some converts, " They gave themselves to the Lord, and then to us." They that believed and were baptized were to-

gether. Religion unites the heart to God, and the spirits of the saints to one another. Building all on one foundation and cemented together; all believers are one spiritual building, or house of God. "Ye are all one in Christ Jesus." Observe,

II. *The characteristics of religion as presented in our text.*

1. *It is personal.*

"One shall say, I am," &c. This cannot be said by one for another; no, not by the parent for the child—not by the wife for her husband, &c. It is expressly individual, between God and the soul. Men are not saved in masses or groups. Each understanding must be enlightened, every conscience convinced, every heart impressed, &c. No such thing as religious or Christian countries, tribes, or congregations. It is lamentably otherwise.

2. *It is voluntary.*

As we cannot be pious by proxy, neither can we by constraint (I mean force). There is, indeed, a constraint, the constraining love of Jesus—the constraining power of truth. But these do no violence to the will. Yet responsible. This is clear from the many references to the will. " Why will ye die ?" " Ye will not come unto me," &c. " I would have gathered you as a hen gathereth her chickens under her wings, but ye would not." "I beseech you, brethren, that ye present yourselves a willing sacrifice," &c. Just as the worshippers brought the gift freely, &c.

3. *It is deliberate.*

"And another shall subscribe himself," &c. This supposes the utmost coolness and reflection. Convictions may be sudden, impressions vivid and instantaneous; but the surrendering of the heart must be serious and deliberate; they are to abide. Here is the court of mercy, the declaration of God's love, the offer of eternal life. The terms are all published, the deed is before you, the appeal is made, and the enlightened soul, influenced by the truth and glory of the gospel, takes the pen, affixes his name, ratifies the contract, and makes it valid as his own act and deed.

4. *It is determinate.*

That is, the full decided act of the mind. A resolution firmly made and taken. See the whole phraseology of the text. Determination is necessary, or our own wavering hearts would produce constant vacillation. Determination is ne-

cessary, or the influence of others would shake our purposes, &c. See it in the case of the man who wanted to bid adieu to his friends; another to bury his father. You will never serve Christ until you are determined fully resolved to do so. Now let us consider,

III. *The importance of such a spirit of religion.*

1. *It is intensely important to Jesus.*

For this he dwelt in your flesh, lived, suffered, was abased, and died. Sent his gospel, his Spirit, opened a way to heaven. He invites you to do this, woos, urges, entreats. It is the travail of his soul. Every such case of decision is the reward of his toil, and the satisfaction of his heart.

2. *It is of great importance to the pious members of the church.*

They pray for this; keep open the sanctuary; invite you. It fills them with joy. The man who does not rejoice in it is not a Christian. He cannot be.

3. *It is supremely important to yourselves.*

It is no vain thing, it is your life. All that is sacred and precious is involved in it. The favor of God. Peace of conscience,—eternal glory. It is the one thing needful, of everlasting consequence. The soul, heaven, hell, eternity, are all solemnly connected with it, and with your happiness forever and ever.

APPLICATION.

1. The text is the experience of many here. Do you not rejoice in it? You continue to this day,—hold fast.

2. Are not many inquiring? Decide, be prompt.

3. Who refuses? Oh, reconsider. "Be wise," &c.

CCLXIX.—SEEKING THE LORD, AND ITS ADVANTAGES.

"The hand of our God is upon all them for good that seek him, but his power and his wrath is against all them that forsake him."—*Ezra* viii. 22.

OUR text contains a great scriptural truth, applicable to all ages, countries, and persons. It is a truth which is corroborated by many parallel passages, and therefore expresses a subject of more than ordinary importance. There are two things clearly expressed in the text,—man's responsibility, and the different results of piety and sin. God's hand shall be upon all those who seek him, and that for good, and his wrath is against those who forsake him. Observe, we are directed,

I. *To seeking God and its advantages.*

Seeking God denotes,

1. *A consciousness of our need of him.*

Men in general do not regard God,—he is not in all their thoughts. Many feel as Pharaoh did, when he exclaimed, "Who is the Lord," &c. But the enlightened, convicted sinner, and the true Christian, feel that God is the fountain of their existence, and the only source of their peace and happiness. "Whom have I in heaven, but thee," &c. God is all and in all to the pious mind, and their need of him is every moment's experience.

2. *Earnest and fervent prayer to God.*

Ver. 23. Seeking and praying are synonymous. Thus Christ taught his disciples. Ask, seek, knock, &c. Thus, too, Job says, xxiii. 3, "Oh that I knew where I could find him," &c. We cannot find God but by earnest prayer and supplication, and he is ever near to all who call upon him. "Whosoever shall call upon the name of the Lord."

3. *To seek the Lord is to come to him in the way of his appointment.*

We may seek anxiously and fervently, but what will it avail if we seek in the wrong way? Thus heathen philosophers labored to know the true God. Thus, too, many anxious pagans. Many are like the devotional eunuch, they read, &c., but understand not. The word of God is, however, explicit and full on this subject. "Christ is the way, the truth, and the life." One God, and one mediator, &c. "No man cometh to the Father but by Christ."

4. *To labor in all things to have his approbation.*

To commit all to him,—to refer all to him,—to acknowledge him in all,—and seek his blessing upon all our steps. To set the Lord always before us, and to labor to walk well-pleasing in his sight. Notice the advantages arising to those who thus seek him. "The hand of the Lord is upon all," &c.

1. *The hand of his pardoning mercy.*

To those who thus seek him, he says, "I, even I, am he who blotteth out your iniquities." "Seek ye the Lord," &c. Then it follows, "Let the wicked forsake his ways, and the unrighteous man his thoughts," &c.

2. *The hand of his delivering power.*

He delivers the souls of his people,— raises them from the horrible pit, &c. Translates them from the kingdom of darkness,—brings their spirits out of the prison of sin, and from the dominion of Satan. Rescues from the gall of bitterness, and the bonds, &c.

3. *The hand of his providing goodness.*

They that seek the Lord shall not want any good thing. He is their shepherd, and they shall not want. He leads them into green pastures, &c. "My God shall supply all you need," &c.

4. *The hand of his heavenly guidance.*

The Lord leads and guides his people. "He led them by the right way," &c. "The Lord shall lead thee continually," &c. "Thou shalt guide me by thy counsel, and afterwards receive me to glory."

5. *The hand of his sustaining grace.*

The Christian is weak and feeble; of himself insufficient; exposed to many enemies and perils. The saints of the Lord are therefore only absolutely secure in his hand. He keeps them by his mighty power,—he preserves them for his kingdom and glory. We notice, there is often

6. *The hand of his manifest providence.*

How clearly do we see this in the history of his church and people. It is said of one, "So long as he sought the Lord, the Lord made him to prosper." How many thousands have experienced that "godliness is profitable to all things," &c. Notice,

II. *Forsaking God, and its attendant evils.*

To forsake God is the opposite course to that we have described in seeking the Lord. It is refusing him homage and veneration. It is to disobey him, to live without his fear; to turn from the way of righteousness; to withdraw our hand from the gospel plough, &c. To draw back, to make shipwreck, &c. Now against these, his power and wrath are declared. See text. Power to punish, wrath to inflict a fearful and eternal doom. Power and wrath of God to cast both body and soul into hell fire. See Heb. x. 22, &c. "A certain fearful looking for of judgment and fiery indignation, which shall devour the adversaries."

APPLICATION.

We learn,

1. The value of true religion. The good hand of the Lord upon us.

2. The awfulness of apostasy from the Lord.

3. The necessity of both vigilance and perseverance. See Heb. iii. 12 ; iv. 10–13.

4. Urge the unconverted to seek the Lord, and live.

————◆————

CCLXX.—READING THE SCRIPTURES.

"Understandest thou what thou readest."— *Acts* viii. 30.

OUR text relates to a distinguished individual, a Jewish proselyte, who was the prime minister of the Queen of Ethiopia ; and was now returning to his own country, after observing the Jewish festivals at Jerusalem. Reading in his chariot, his mind was occupied in perusing a portion of the Old Testament scriptures. How dignified and profitable an employment, how exactly fulfilling the command of the Lord to his ancient people. Deut. vi. 6, "And these words which I command thee this day shall be in thine heart; and thou shalt teach them diligently unto thy children, and shalt talk of them when thou sittest in thine house, and when thou walkest by the way, and when thou liest down, and when thou risest up," &c. Philip was directed by the Lord to join himself to this illustrious traveller.

I. *Let us notice the book.*

He was reading the scriptures. The revelation of God's mind, the word of eternal truth, the only book wherein God has made known his will. But the eunuch had only access to the Old Testament scriptures,— the law, the psalms, the narratives, and the prophets. We have the completed volume, —all they possessed, and much more ; the gospels, the epistles, the vision of the apocalypse. We have this book, too, in our own tongue. Originally it was a sealed book, except to the learned. How different now, and how grateful we should be for it. In 1420, the Bible would have cost about £2 16s., a sum equal to £25 of the present currency. Portions of the Scriptures were translated into the languages of the British islanders in the eighth century ; but the oldest translation was by Wycliffe, about 1390.

II. *The exercise.*

He was reading. Now, let us view this in three lights.

1. *As a human right.*

It was thought for centuries that none but the priests should read it. The most awful curses were pronounced upon those who dared to do so. Now this doctrine was the chief pillar of the Romish church for ages, and gave to the priests a wicked monopoly of the word of life. I need not remind you that such a prohibition is contrary to God's express will, and tramples upon the rights of human conscience.

2. *This exercise is more than a right,—it is an express duty.*

I not only may, but ought to do so. If I do not, I am guilty of breaking God's positive precepts. He says, " Search ye out of the book of the Lord, and read." "Search the Scriptures, for in them ye think ye have eternal life, and they are they which testify of me." But it is more than a duty, it is,

3. *A distinguished privilege.*

And so all the godly in every age have felt it. Listen to Job. "I have esteemed the words of thy mouth more than my necessary food." David says, "The law of thy mouth," &c. Does not the poor man count it a privilege to have access to a rich treasury,—the sick man to a laboratory of healing medicines,—the warrior to an armory of every kind of weapon,—the famishing man to a feast ? Such is the word of God to the Christian. There too he peruses the bequest of his future inheritance. Our subject relates,

III. *To the manner.*

"How readest thou," &c. Now, this is a very important question. We know of few more so. The right manner of doing this is what we wish chiefly to impress on your notice.

1. *We should do so with an unwavering belief of its divinity and truth.*

If we read in doubt we cannot profit. If doubts exist, they must first of all be removed by a candid consideration of the style and the subjects of revelation. Its prophecies, its miracles, &c. Its morality, its external and internal influence, on its disciples, &c.

2. *With solemn reverence for its author.*

With what reverence it should be perused. This is God's book. God speaking on the most momentous subject in the universe.

3. *With a spirit of candid discrimination.*

Every word of God is pure. That is, of the original scriptures. In the languages in which they were written. But always difficulty in translating,—many things could not be expressed in the exact words of the original. What could we do with the words ice, snow, and frost, in a language spoken where these are not known. Now, the truths are divine. God's words; but not the peculiarities of our translation, not the divisions of the chapters and the verses, not the words in italics, not the head lines to the chapters, &c. Bibles are most useful with marginal readings, references, &c.

4. *With a view to understand the sense and meaning.*

Not to bring our meaning to be supported, but to take God's meaning, and be satisfied with it. Now, we must have the meaning, and not merely the sound, if we profit. The ideas, the thoughts, &c.

5. *With a sincere desire to practise and enjoy its blessings.*

Not to speculate; not as a form; but to be made wiser, better, happier, and more meet for eternal glory. Let me press the question, "Understandest thou," &c.

(1.) So as to have clear views of the way of salvation. Of sin, and grace; your ruin, and redemption; your danger, and help.

(2.) So as to derive internal enjoyment from it. A sense of God's love and favor.

(3.) So as to regulate your entire selves by it.

APPLICATION.

Let me, in applying this subject, observe,

1. The criminality of total negligence.

2. The inefficiency of an indifferent perusal of it. It is a mine, and we must dig; an ocean, and we must dive for its pearls; a field, and we must search and labor in it.

3. The necessity of greater regard and attention to it. Who is not deficient? In reading, in laboring to understand it, in practising it. With humility and prayer let us treat this book as we never did before.

CCLXXI.—THE OFFERING AND SACRIFICE OF CHRIST.*

"Be ye therefore followers of God, as dear children: and walk in love, as Christ also hath loved us, and hath given himself for us, an offering and a sacrifice to God for a sweet-smelling savour."—*Eph.* v. 1, 2.

* *Series* vi.—For services connected with the Lord's Supper, Good Friday, &c.

THE text contains a glorious exhibition of both doctrine and practice,—of theory and duty united; we have announced the exceeding love and graciousness of God to us, and the influence it should have on our hearts and lives. The love of Christ produces love in the soul of the believer, not only love to Christ, but love to one another. And where such mighty motives fail, as those produced in the text, all other reasons must be futile and powerless. Let us consider the text in the two leading points, in which it so prominently stands out. Observe,

I. *The sublime doctrine which the text reveals.*

II. *The practical course the text enjoins.*

I. *The sublime doctrine which the text reveals.*

"Christ loved us," &c. The text refers,

1. *To the priestly office of the Saviour.*

Christ presented an offering and sacrifice to God. To this office the scriptures repeatedly refer. He is the great high-priest of our profession;—a priest not of Aaron's order,—but after the order of Melchisedec. Of this, the high-priest also under the law was a type. Thus Zechariah spake, "He shall be a priest upon his throne." "The Lord hath sworn," &c. See Heb. ii. 17. As the priest had to present the offerings and sacrifices to Jehovah. Then, observe, the text refers,

2. *To the offering and sacrifice Christ presented to God.*

"Himself." Not a lamb, goat, or bullock, but himself. Here is a great mystery, the priest and the victim meet in the same person. To this the apostle refers when quoting an ancient prophecy, Heb. x. 5–10. Now this offering he voluntarily laid on God's altar. He had power to do this, &c. He had a right to do this; it was his own life which he assumed for this end. His whole existence on earth was the offering. It began with his birth, carried on in his circumcision, baptism, ministry, suffering, &c. His death was the sacrifice,—the sacrifice of himself. Including the anguish of bitterest sorrow in Gethsemane, and his expiring on the cross. We are referred in the text,

3. *To the persons on whose behalf this sacrifice was presented.*

"For us." Clearly here the saints at Ephesus and the apostle. Yet to this limitation who would wish to confine it? That Christ died for all saints, for all believers, is a great truth. Observe in scripture we have this gradacion; Paul says, Christ died for him, Gal. iii. 20; for the church, Eph. v. 25; for the world, 1 John ii. 2. One of these is as much a truth as the other; and they are all true, and do not contradict each other, as some imagine. The ruin and the remedy in scripture are both universal. See Isaiah liii. 6; also Rom. v. 18. "Therefore as by the offence of one, judgment came upon all men to condemnation," &c. The text directs us,

4. *To the acceptance of this sacrifice by God.*

"For a sweet-smelling savour." That is, grateful and pleasing to Jehovah. Thus, as the ancient sacrifices were sprinkled with precious perfumes, and by these had a grateful odor, so the sacrifice of Christ was acceptable to God. The evidence of this was given in Christ's resurrection from the dead, and his ascension to the right hand of the majesty on high. See Phil. ii. 6; also Heb. x. 12. Notice, the text directs us,

5. *To the great moving principle, which actuated Christ to present this sacrifice to God for us.*

"Christ loved us," &c. To this the redemption of our lost race is invariably attributed. To what else could we trace it? Not to the moral excellence of the redeemed. Not to any traces of amiability or loveliness. Not to any claim or merit. Not to any moving appeals, or entreaties. Not to any expectations of return, &c. Oh no, it was love, infinite, wondrous, surpassing knowledge. "God so loved the world," &c. Christ loved us, &c.; how much, the loftiest seraph cannot tell. Such is the sublime doctrine the text reveals. Let us observe,

II. *The practical course the text enjoins.*

1. *God is to be the great object of our imitation.*

"Followers of God." Religion is designed especially to renew man into the likeness of God. This was his original glory. This by the fall was lost. This in regeneration is partially restored,—restored in a degree. We again become his children,—partake of the divine nature. Now this is to be cultivated, matured, &c. We are to set the Lord always before us; to contemplate his character as seen in his works and word, and especially in his Son, and in the gospel. We are to seek conformity to his spirit and likeness, and to pray for the influences of the Holy Ghost.

2. *We are to cherish the filial and fraternal affection of "dear children."*

"As dear children, walk in love." These affections are to respect God as our heavenly Father. As children dearly beloved of God; sensible of it; influenced by it, and who return it in the most ardent manner. And this is to be fraternal, as well as filial. It is to embrace every member of the divine family. We are to love all the holy brethren, with pure hearts fervently. This affectionate state of heart is the essential element of true piety. "God is love, and he that dwelleth," &c.

3. *In these holy and affectionate exercises we are to make constant advancement.*

"Be ye followers." "Walk in love." These things are to be in us, and abide. These things to be matured, and increased. Religion is to be progressive; we are to go from strength to strength; faith must be stronger, hope brighter,—love more ardent, —humility more deep,—zeal more intense; and the features of the divine likeness more full and distinct. The Christian must go forward, until he reaches the celestial Canaan, and is fully meet for the inheritance of the saints in light.

APPLICATION.

Learn,

1. *The connection between grace and holiness.*

Salvation is of the free grace and love of God, but nevertheless it requires the renovation of the heart, and the affectionate devotedness of the life to God and his service.

2. *God has made ample provision for promoting the holiness of the Christian character.*

His wisdom enlightens,—his Spirit and truth sanctifies,—his grace supports,—and the blood of Jesus Christ cleanseth from all sin.

3. *Christian activity is not superseded by the work of the Spirit within us.*

"Work out your own salvation." "For it is God worketh in you," &c.

4. *Love is the glory and perfection of the Christian religion.*

Supreme love to God, and sincere love to one another. "Then be ye followers of God, as dear children," &c.

CCLXXII.—THE AWAKENED SWORD.

"Awake, O sword, against my shepherd, and against the man that is my fellow, saith the Lord of Hosts; smite the shepherd, and the sheep shall be scattered: and I will turn mine hand upon the little ones."—*Zech.* xiii. 7.

OUR text contains a most solemn and affecting prophecy of the Saviour's sufferings. We cannot misunderstand it, inasmuch as Jesus distinctly applied it to himself, when he received with his disciples the sacramental emblems of his death. "And when they had sung a hymn, they went out into the mount of Olives. Then saith Jesus unto them, All ye shall be offended because of me this night, for it is written, I will smite the shepherd, and the sheep of the flock shall be scattered abroad," Matt. xxvi. 3, &c. Our text refers,

I. *To the personal divinity and glory of the Saviour.*

God speaks of him as "his fellow." Such language is never applied to the most distinguished saints. Moses was God's exalted servant, and Abraham was styled the "friend of God." David was a man after God's own heart, but nothing is ever said of the loftiest saints at all equal to this. Such language is never applied to angels, or the highest orders of the celestial hierarchy. It is never applied to any but Christ, "the anointed of God."

(1.) In the psalms and prophets we meet with the like phraseology. In the forty-fifth psalm, the Son is thus addressed, "Thy throne, O God, is forever and ever," &c. So again in 93d and 110th. "The Lord said unto my Lord, Sit thou at my right hand until I make thine enemies thy footstool." Isaiah in two very sublime prophecies refers to the deity of the Redeemer: "And a virgin shall conceive," &c. And again, "Unto us a child is born," &c.

(2.) The Saviour taught the same truths concerning himself, John x. 30, &c., "I and my Father are one," &c. So also to Philip he said, "He that hath seen me, hath seen the Father," &c., John xiv. 9.

(3.) The apostles clearly made known the Godhead of Christ. "Who being in the form of God, thought it not robbery to be equal with God," &c., Phil. ii. 6. So Rom. ix. 5, "Who is God over all, blessed for evermore." So also the apostle John, i. 1 : "In the beginning was the Word, and the Word was with God, and the Word was God."

And in the First Epistle of John, v. 20, he describes the mission of the Son of God, and then says, "This is the true God and eternal life," &c. It is clear, therefore, that Christ in his divine nature claims a perfect equality with the Father. He assumes the eternity of the Father ;—the power, the glory, the majesty, the dominion, and the immutability of Deity, as his own. And God requires that all men should honor the Son, even in the same manner, and to the same extent, as they honor the Father. Notice in the text,

II. *The perfect humanity of the Saviour in connection with his Godhead.*

"The man that is my fellow." The manhood of Jesus is too manifest to need proof. The first prediction describes him as the "seed of the woman." He was to be both "the root and offspring of David." As a man, the place and time of his birth were predicted. And thus the apostle, " In the fulness of the times God sent forth his Son," &c. We often see both the evidences of his divinity and humanity in the course of his life and mission. As a man, you see him in the weakness of infancy lying in a manger. As a God, he receives the homage of the Eastern sages. As a man, he was weary and hungry. As a God, he multiplied the loaves, and fed the thousands in the desert. As a man, he endures reproach ; as a God, he awed the multitudes, so that they were astonished at his doctrine. As a man, he drank the deep cup of grief, and was tempted and buffeted by the evil one ; as a God, he was transfigured on the mount, performed miracles of the highest grandeur, expelled demons, stilled the tempest, and raised the dead. As a man, he was betrayed and arrested by the rude soldiery ; as a God, he overwhelmed them by his voice ; and when he said, "Whom seek ye ?" they fell as dead men at his feet, John xviii. 6. As a man, you see him suffering and dying on the cross ; but his deity is attested by the rending of the veil, the quaking of the earth, the tearing of the rocks, and the darkening of the sun, so that the centurion exclaimed, "Surely this was the Son of God." As a man, his mangled remains were interred in the prepared sepulchre, where they rested in the gloomy region of the king of terrors ; but as a God, he dismantled himself of his burial clothes, rolled away the stone, and rose in glorious triumph over death and the grave. As a man, we see him conversing with his disciples, and eating with them ; as a God, he ascends in the angelic cloud, and is received back to the throne of his glory, where he sits exalted to exercise his reign and rule, until his enemies become his footstool.

III. *Our subject refers to the mediatorial office and work of Christ.*

"God's shepherd."

(1.) As a shepherd, he was sent to collect together the wandering and lost sheep of the human race. Men had wandered from God,—wandered on the mountains of darkness, unbelief, and peril of endless death. He came, therefore, "to seek and to save that which was lost."

(2.) As a shepherd, he came to provide a fold for his gathered people. He came that men might have restored unto them the enjoyment of God's grace, and the blessings of holiness and love. And in effecting this he designed to establish a church in the world over which the celestial motto might be written, " Glory to God in the highest, peace on earth, and good-will towards men."

(3.) As a shepherd he came to redeem his sheep, and obtain for them eternal life. See John x. 11, 15, " I am the good shepherd : the good shepherd giveth his life for the sheep." Christ is the great shepherd, the head and ruler of the church. But this will lead us to notice,

IV. *The sufferings by which his mediatorial work was effected.*

"Awake, O sword," &c.

(1.) The instrument of his sufferings was the sword. The infliction of just punishment,—righteous suffering. Now Christ suffered unrighteously as a holy person, or righteously as a guilty person, or substitutionally as a righteous person on behalf of others. Now this is the scriptural view ; he freely gave himself for our sins, and cheerfully took our iniquities upon him, so that with his stripes we might be healed. Hence as the surety, he suffered that the claims of God's violated law might be honorably and fully met. " He suffered the just for the unjust, that he might bring us to God."

(2.) It is implied that the sword had long slumbered. Now this was literally the case. Sin had existed in its wrath-deserving guilt for *four* thousand years. One dispensation after another had passed away, until, at length, the crisis of solemn retribution arrived, when Christ was to present his own body as an offering for transgression, and thus magnify the law, and make it honorable.

(3.) The mandate to the slumbering sword was given by Jehovah. He said, " Awake," &c. So that the sufferings inflicted by the Jews, and by the powers of darkness were permitted. He allowed them to have their own hour of darkness and triumph. But especially does this refer to those agonies which Christ endured immediately from God. When alone in the garden, he was seized with horror, and uttered the awful exclamation, " My soul is exceeding sorrowful," &c. Oh, yes, then did Christ feel the sword sheathed in his own soul. " Then his soul was made an offering for sin," &c., Isai. liii. 10.

V. *Observe the circumstances predicted concerning the sheep of Christ during the Messiah's sufferings.*

1. *The disciples of Christ were to forsake him.*

" The sheep were to be scattered." Now this was minutely fulfilled, for all Christ's disciples forsook him and fled, so that he literally trod the wine-press alone. None assisted him in his mediatorial work.

2. *His timid and fearful followers were again to be restored.*

The term " little ones" is that which Christ gave to his disciples, Matt. xviii. 10, &c. Now these little ones, though frail, weak, and erring, were remembered by their Lord. To the most guilty the tidings of his resurrection were sent, for the angel said, " Go, tell his disciples and Peter," Mark xvi. 7. He afterwards breathed his own peace upon them ; he gave them many assurances of his love, and finally imbued them with the Holy Ghost for their great work. Thus did he turn his hand, in restoring mercy upon the little ones.

APPLICATION.

Learn,

1. The extreme evil of sin. It is not seen so vividly in the torments of the lost, as in the agonies of Christ.

2. The preciousness of redemption. " Redeemed not with corruptible things, such as silver and gold, but with the precious blood of Christ."

3. The individual interest we should seek in the mediatorial office and work of Christ. Are we his sheep; saved in him; loving and following him ?

4. The only hope for the sinner. Rejecters of Christ must bear the awful weight of the sword in their own persons forever and ever.

CCLXXIII.—THE NECESSARY REMEMBRANCE.

"But thou shalt remember that thou wast a bondman in Egypt; and the Lord thy God redeemed thee thence."—*Deut.* xxiv. 18.

It is said of the Israelites, that they greatly multiplied in the land of Egypt, so that they became exceedingly mighty, and the land was filled with them. Joseph, the friend and shield of his kindred, was now dead, and his bones were resting in the land of promise. The Pharaoh of Joseph's time had gone the way of all flesh, and another king reigned over Egypt, who knew not Joseph. Under the dominion of this king the people were greatly oppressed. See Exod. i. 9, &c., "The cry of the people came up before the Lord;" and it is said, Exod. ii. 24, &c., "God heard their groaning," &c. Finally, God effected their deliverance; he brake the yoke from their neck, and by his mighty hand he led them forth to the land of promise. On the borders of that land they were now assembled, when Moses addressed to them the language of the text. The text may with great propriety be applied to the redemption of the soul from the power of sin and death; and in this light we shall consider it on the present occasion. Observe,

I. *The Christian's original state.*

"A bondman in Egypt." The apostle, when writing to the Ephesians, reminds them of their former state, and says, Eph. ii. 11, &c., "Wherefore, remember, that ye being in times past gentiles in the flesh," &c. Now the bondage of the Israelites in Egypt typified the state of the sinner,

1. *In its degradation.*

Slavery is an insult to our species; it is utterly repulsive to every emotion of the soul. A man may be poor, afflicted, in the lowest walks of life; but if he be free, however miserable, he feels no degradation. But the slave is lowered to the level of the brute, and is robbed of all his dignity as a man. This is the natural condition of every sinner; the sinner is the captive of sin, the slave of the devil. Robbed of his original glory, his crown in the dust, the whole soul is debased. See the prodigal feeding swine, and you have the true picture of the sinner's state.

2. *In its oppression.*

A bondman is one who is oppressed, one devoted to a servile and painful occupation. The work of sin is oppressive; the load of sin is oppressive; the guilt of sin is oppressive. The fears and alarms of sin are oppressive. The wicked have no peace,—no rest, like the troubled sea, &c.

3. *In its helplessness.*

The Israelites must have remained burdened and wretched had not God interposed. They had no power or might against their oppressors. Slavery enfeebles, enervates, prostrates both the powers of mind and body. This is the sinner's state. In himself he is without strength. Blinded, enfettered, in the region of death; his deliverance by his own power is impossible. So far as his own energies are concerned he is without hope.

II. *The Christian's happy deliverance.*

"Redeemed." That is, emancipated, disenthralled, made free. Now in reference to the Israelites, God redeemed them by his mighty arm. He exerted his stupendous power, and set the hosts of Israel free. Our redemption, like theirs,

1. *Originated in God's free compassion.*

"He saw, and oh, amazing love, he ran," &c. Without claim or merit. He saw our self-procured ruin, and exercised his infinite mercy towards us. Oh, the wonderful love of God, the marvellous mercy of the Lord. "He helped us in our low estate, for his mercy endureth forever." Our redemption,

2. *Was effected by the mission and work of his Son.*

For Israel he raised up Moses his servant. He went to the people and to Pharaoh. He wrought by the power of God the miracles in Egypt. He led the people forth, and was with them until they came to the borders of the goodly land. For our redemption God sent forth his Son, made of a woman; made under the law, &c. The Son of God was manifested that he might destroy the works of the devil. He came "to proclaim liberty to the captive, and the opening of the prison doors," &c. But Jesus redeemed us not only by the exertion of his mighty power, but by the price of his precious blood. The Israelites were redeemed by power alone,—but Jesus had to pay the penalty of sin which guilty beings had incurred, and then by his all-powerful arm to deliver us from our enemies. Our redemption,

3. *Is connected with faith and obedience to our great deliverer.*

The means of deliverance were for all the thousands of Israel; none were excluded. It was for all the seed of Abraham; and they were all actually led out of the land of oppression. But the final advantages were only to be enjoyed by exercising faith in God, and obeying his word. Hence the great majority of them entered not into the land of promise. The apostle reminds us of this and cause thereof. See Heb. iii. 7–11 and 17–19. Also iv. 1, 2. Now it is a glorious truth that the whole world is redeemed, "For God so loved the world that he gave his," &c. Yet the blessings of that redemption can only be enjoyed by faith in Christ, and obedience to his gospel. Christ must be received, and he must be loved and obeyed. Therefore, says the apostle, "Let us labor therefore to enter into that rest, lest any man fall after the same example of unbelief." Heb. vi. 11.

III. *The Christian's obligation to remember his redemption.*

But can we forget? Is it possible? Why, the Israelites did. It is said of them, that they forgat God; they even made a calf and honored it as a deity. Our own hearts are prone to forget; the cares of the world choke the soul, and cause us to forget God. Satan, by his temptations, would seduce us from this remembrance.

1. *We should remember it with intentness of soul and gratitude of heart.*

Such love and goodness,—such mercy and compassion should never be obliterated. A lively remembrance will keep the flame of gratitude burning on the altar of our hearts.

2. *We should remember it with feelings of humility and contrition.*

If self-righteousness would spring up; if we look upon those around with feelings of self-importance and superiority; if we would glory at all in ourselves,—this remembrance will lead us back to our original state, and then all boasting will be slain, and we shall say, "Not I, but the grace of God that was in me;" "Not unto me, but unto the Redeemer be all the glory."

3. *We should remember that we may feel for those around who are still in the gall of bitterness and the bonds of iniquity.*

The love of Christ to us should fill us with love to our fellow-men. It should excite us to tell to all around,

"What a dear Saviour we have found."

4. *We should especially remember, when in the means of grace, and at the table of the Lord.*

When cold, lethargic, and dull. When the service is a load, &c. The remembrance of our lost state,—of God's love,—of Christ's redeeming grace,—should stir up every feeling, and kindle the flame of ardent love and glowing zeal. This remembrance should begin and end every Lord's day,—and all the services of his house. To the redeemed, yet unsaved sinner, we say, God invites thee to return to him. He says, "Return, for I have redeemed thee." "Oh, *come* unto him that you may have life, and that you may have it more abundantly."

CCLXXIV.—AFFECTIONATE OBEDIENCE.

"If ye love me, keep my commandments."— *John* xiv. 15.

OUR text is a part of the Saviour's address to his disciples before he left them. Every word therefore has a peculiar weight and solemnity connected with it. He designed each sentence to be treasured up, that after his decease they might be remembered, and carried out in their feelings and practice. In our text he gives them the true and infallible test of their love to him; and therefore of the genuineness of their profession, "If ye love me," &c. Our text directs us,

I. *To the important principle of love to Jesus Christ.*

II. *To consider the evidence of its possession.*

"Keep my commandments."

I. *The important principle of love to Jesus Christ.*

Consider this principle,

1. *As to its nature.*

Love to Christ implies several things.

(1.) A knowledge of Christ. We cannot love an unknown object, we may love one whom we have never seen. In reading the history of the good you feel an affection for them. Now love to Christ must be preceded by a knowledge of him. This is presented in this blessed book. The scriptures testify of Christ, reveal his nature, perfections, offices, work, and glory. It implies,

(2.) Satisfaction with Christ. We may know, and not feel interested,—not entirely approve of the object known. But in Christ there is every thing to satisfy the soul. He is, as to purity, clear light without a spot. He is, as to goodness, love embodied. The love of God, living, breathing, and speaking in our flesh. Then, his dignity and glory are those of Deity. "The brightness of the Father's glory." Whoso contemplates Christ's character must exclaim,— "Thou art fairer than the sons of men, grace is poured into thy lips," &c. "Thou art the desire of all nations." "The fairest among ten thousand," &c. It implies,

(3.) Esteem for Christ, and delight in him. To real love these are essential. The spiritually minded feel for Christ the highest reverential esteem, and with this the greatest degree of delight. The breathings of the heart, the thoughts of the mind, and the desires of the soul, will all bear witness to this delight. This esteem and delight will place us at his feet, like the devoted Mary. It will lead us to desire his presence everywhere, and to prefer him to every other object. "To whom shall we go," &c. It will discover us in the ordinances of his grace, seated near him, and reclining our heads on his compassionate bosom. Consider love to Christ,

2. *In its causes.*

Now, it is not a natural feeling, nor the result of education, nor an accidental principle. It is the result of his love to us, and our apprehension and application of it to our souls. We love him because he first loved us. But why did we not love him sooner? because we did not apprehend; we did not consider, and believe, and apply it to our souls.

" E'er since by faith I saw the stream,
    Thy flowing wounds supply,
  Redeeming love has been my theme,
    And shall be till I die."

But in connection with our apprehension and application of Christ's love to our hearts, the love of God must be shed abroad in the soul, by the Holy Spirit given unto us.

3. *Consider this love in its characteristics.*

What should be the features of this love?

(1.) It should be ardent. A flame burning intensely on the altar of the heart.

(2.) It should be progressive. Increase daily. It cannot be stationary. It must advance or decline. But especially,

(3.) It should be pre-eminent. More than we love what ought to be beloved;

more than we love friends, or the brethren; more than our own ease and enjoyment. It must be the highest, the deepest, and the most comprehensive subject, occupying our thoughts and hearts. Consider this love,

4. *In its importance.*

Without it we cannot be loved of God— without it there can be no piety, no peace of mind, no enjoyment of heaven; nay, more, listen to the fearful denunciation, "If any man love not the Lord Jesus Christ, let him be anathema maranatha." If so, then is it not clear that love to Christ should be an evident principle, that of which we feel fully and satisfactorily assured? How are we to be certain that we love Christ? A delight to think of him, and converse respecting him; a love to his gospel and ordinances; a love to his people; all these are good evidences. But there is one of Christ's own application,—one which he has set up, and it is supplied in our text. Hence, in reference to love to Christ, consider,

II. *The evidence of its possession.*

"If ye love me keep my commandments." Obedience is the essential fruit of a renewed heart.

" 'Tis love which makes our cheerful feet
  In swift obedience move."

Christ's commandments,

1. *Are revealed.*

They are left on the pages of holy writ. "To the law and the testimony." Never mysteriously conveyed; nothing ambiguous.

2. *They are sometimes difficult.*

Hence self-denial and cross-bearing are always so. To be spiritually-minded, meek, forgiving, &c. To bear reproach, act singularly, &c. To crucify self, &c.

3. *They are always practicable.*

Who is sufficient? not the carnal man, not the formalist, not the supine; but the humble Christian, seeking and depending on the graciousness of Christ. "I can do all things through Christ strengthening me."

4. *They are indispensable.*

Not to be despised or neglected. Essential to Christ's favor, and our own comfort. "If ye love me," &c. Nothing will make up for disobedience. The friend says, If you love me, consult my mind and pleasure; do not grieve me. The parent says, If you love me, let me have filial respect and obedience. The monarch says, Ye are my loyal subjects, if ye regard my laws and statutes to do them. What wonder then that Christ says, "If ye love me," &c.

APPLICATION.

1. Right obedience to Christ is humble, universal, and hearty. It does not question, or choose, or obey reluctantly.

2. Christ's order seems this:—Hear, repent, believe, be baptized, and then do whatsoever else I command you.

CCLXXV.—THE SPIRIT OF GRACE AND SUPPLICATIONS.

"And I will pour upon the house of David, and upon the inhabitants of Jerusalem, the spirit of grace and of supplications: and they shall look upon me whom they have pierced, and they shall mourn for him as one mourneth for his only son, and shall be in bitterness for him as one that is in bitterness for his first-born."—*Zech.* xii. 10.

THIS is a very striking prophecy, and was delivered many centuries before its accomplishment. Its fulfilment was fully and minutely realized in the penitence and conversion of the three thousand on the day of pentecost. It has, however, been supposed that the complete accomplishment of this prediction is yet future; when the whole Jewish people shall own their long rejected Messiah, and return to him with believing minds and penitent hearts. How glorious will that day be! How we should rejoice to see the long despised and persecuted children of Abraham, gathered out of all nations to worship and adore the Saviour of sinners. We think, however, this passage may be spiritually instructive and edifying in its application to sinners generally, who are brought to an acknowledgment of Christ Jesus. It is to this view of the text we therefore invite your attention. Let us then consider,

I. *The characters specified.*
II. *The promise given.* And,
III. *The results affirmed.*

I. *The characters specified.*

Literally the Jewish people,—the house of David, &c. But we just refer to what is said concerning them in that portion of the text. "Him whom they have pierced." No doubt exists as to the signification of this. It refers to Christ and his sufferings on the cross. See John xix. 30, &c. But

you say this will only apply to the soldiers, or, at the most, to the Jews who put him to death. We observe that they acted according to the evil of the human heart; and all sinners who reject Jesus imitate their conduct, and are guilty of their sin. The *self-righteous* now treat Christ as the Pharisees did. The *despisers* of Christ now treat him as the chief of the Jews did. The *skeptics* now treat Christ as the scribes and Pharisees did. The *worldlings* now as those who were bidden to the Jewish gospel feast, but who all began with one consent to make excuse. The *timid* and *half-hearted* now desert Christ as his friends and disciples did at his apprehension, &c. *Backsliders* now follow Christ at a distance, and deny him as Peter did. And all *haters of Christ and the gospel* have the same spirit that could crucify him, yea, that mocked him and pierced him on the cross. Let us observe that all sinners who reject the gospel pierce him,

1. *By their unbelief.*

To despise the testimony, and treat what is said as false, is the greatest possible indignity that you can offer to another. Unbelief thus treats Christ. It rejects as false, or as of no importance, the truths of his holy gospel. It thus reflects on his purity and truth, and pierces the immaculate soul of God's Son.

2. *By ungratefulness.*

The advent of Jesus into our world was on an errand of mercy. He came to enlighten the ignorant, heal the diseased, emancipate the enslaved, and deliver the wretched from sin, misery, and eternal death. He came to do all this by substituting himself, and enduring the deserved punishment of the guilty. But Jesus in these striking manifestations of his love is forgotten and ungratefully neglected by the unconverted sinner, and the height of this ingratitude is in proportion to the dignity of the person, and the preciousness of the blessings which are iniquitously despised.

3. *By carnal hostility.*

Sin is not only ungratefulness, but hostility to Jesus. It was sin that brought him down from his throne, &c. Sin is an attack on his *love*, on his goodness, on his purity, on his kindness. He came to destroy the works of the devil, &c. Sin upholds them. Sin is leagued with Satan and the world to oppose Christ, to betray him, to sell him, and put him to death. Then *we are* the characters specified in the text. Notice, then,

II. *The promise given.*

"I will pour," &c. The gospel dispensation is the dispensation of the Holy Spirit. Christ engaged to send the Holy Ghost, &c. He was poured out on the day of pentecost, &c. Now the gospel contains the mind of the Spirit. The love of the Spirit. And it is the power of the Spirit and sword of the Spirit. Wherever it comes, the Holy Spirit of God comes. For it is the great instrument of the Spirit in extending the kingdom of Jesus Christ. The gospel and the Spirit go together, and the reception of the gospel is the reception of the Spirit. See Acts ii. 37. "Our gospel came to you, not in word only," &c. Now this gospel is full,

1. *Of the spirit of grace.*

It makes known God's grace; hence it is called the grace of God that brought salvation, &c. It announces the favor of God. It offers pardon and eternal life.

2. *It produces in the soul of its recipients the spirit of supplication.*

The converted Jews cried out, "Men and brethren," &c. It leads the mind to see the evil and peril of its state, and excites a deep longing for deliverance. As the gospel is addressed and received, one cries out, "Lord, save me, or I perish;" "Lord, help me;" "Lord, that I may receive my sight;" "Son of David, have mercy upon me;" "Lord, if thou canst do any thing for us," &c.

III. *The results affirmed.*

1. *Christ shall be the object of their supreme attention.*

For this purpose Christ is lifted up. "Look unto me," &c. "Behold the Lamb of God," &c. "As Moses lifted up," &c.

2. *Deep humiliation and contrition shall be expressed.*

They shall mourn, &c. Observe this mourning,

(1.) *Shall be chiefly for Christ,* i. e., on his account.

There may be many other grounds of mourning, but this will be the chief. My sin abased the condition, and crucified the holy and blessed Jesus.

(2.) *It shall be very pungent and intense.*

Heavy heart. The spirit bowed down. Worldly comforts rejected. Mourn as for an only son,—for the first-born, &c.

(3.) *Allow me to add, this mourning shall be turned into ecstasy and joy.*

"Blessed are they that mourn," &c. "Go in peace," &c. One *look* to the cross breaks the *heart,*—another heals it. One *look* condemns,—another *justifies.* One pierces,—another solaces. One beholds the wrath of God against sin, and the other the mercy of God to the worthless sinner.

APPLICATION.

1. How many have felt this godly sorrow, &c.? Now glory, &c., in the cross of Christ.

2. Urge all to look on Jesus, &c.

3. The whole world will at last behold him.

CCLXXVI.—THE SUFFERINGS OF JESUS.

"Christ also suffered for us."—1 *Pet.* ii. 21.

EVERY word in the text is important. The person spoken of is Christ; God's anointed Son; the Messiah of Israel; the salvation of the Gentiles; the joy of the earth; and the glory of heaven. That to which the text refers is deeply interesting: "He suffered." Christ's sufferings were unparalleled, and in every respect extraordinary and marvellous. Those for whom those sufferings were borne: "For us;" us men; us sinners: but especially in their efficacious and saving power—us believers. The whole of these particulars is too comprehensive for one discourse; we shall therefore just glance at the sufferings of Christ, as presenting a mirror in which we may see our natural desert, and thus be led to view those sufferings as especially vicarious, i. e., as endured for us. In these sufferings,

I. *There was the advent of Christ from a world of glory to our earth of sin and sorrow.*

In this first step Jesus must have been very painfully exercised. Behold him possessing the glory of the Father,—the glory of regal pomp and splendor,—the glory of angelic adoration and worship,—the glory of heaven's palace and temple, all elevated and pure, arrayed in his holy nature and perfections. Behold, then, the scene of his visitation: the earth, his original footstool; but not only so, but a world of pollution, guilt, blighted, cursed, &c. Think of an oriental monarch dwelling in the filthy hut of a New Zealand cannibal: yet this is nothing in comparison to the humiliation of Christ's advent into our world. He thus suffered to open a way for *us* to heaven, that men might ascend to the realms of light and glory.

II. *There was the assumption of our nature, and its eternal union with his divine glory.*

We can never fathom the depths of this mystery. Deity clad in human flesh; God tabernacling in humanity; "God manifest in the flesh," &c. Had the loftiest seraph assumed the form of a worm, &c., this would have been the transition of a creature into the form of another creature. The abasement would be great; but with Jesus the abasement was infinite, immeasurable, &c. This he suffered that we might be partakers of the divine nature, and attain the adoption of sons.

III. *There was the life of adversity and humiliation which Jesus lived during his sojourning in our world.*

Invested with the reins of the universe, he became "poor." The child of a poor virgin; the son of a poor hard laboring family. Poor throughout life,—more poor than the fowls of the air, than the beasts of the field. The fowls had their nests, the sheep their fold, the foxes their holes, the fierce tiger its lair; but Christ had not where to lay his head. He borrowed his first residence and couch from the animal creation; and his sepulchre was not his own, but the property of another. If he crossed the lakes it was in other men's boats; if he entered Jerusalem as a king, the colt on which he rode was another's; and the last meal he had, was in a room borrowed by his disciples from a friend. In this we see again the insolvency in which sin had involved our world. By the treason of our transgressions we had forfeited every thing, and God might justly have withholden every bounty from us. But Christ's poverty was designed to open the treasury of the eternal riches of God's love and grace.

IV. *There was the shame, and scorn, and insults, to which Jesus submitted.*

His reputation maligned; his motives, his acts all misrepresented; his person insulted; his life hunted with hellish ferocity, &c.; his arrest; his mock trial; his being clothed in the attire of a madman; blindfolded; spit upon; the hair plucked from his cheek; long furrows ploughed upon his back. Now in all this we see the degradation and ruin which sin had brought upon man. Here

we see into what depravity transgression can plunge its victims. Besides, in this we see how our spiritual and celestial glory was obtained. Man was to be raised, elevated, glorified, and therefore Christ suffered thus that we might be kings and priests unto God and the Lamb.

V. *There was the descent of God's glittering sword into the bosom of Christ, when he agonized in the garden.*

These sufferings were entirely mental and spiritual. Now he was retired from the calumniating world. Now no human hand was upon him. As yet he had not endured those corporeal inflictions to which we have referred. Yet, behold his fear. See how he trembles. His soul was seized with horror. Thick mists of darkness settle on his spirit. He falls prostrate to the ground. His agony causes him to sweat, as it were, great drops of blood. We feel assured these were his deepest and most intense sufferings. It was now his soul was offered up: and wherefore? That the spirits of guilty sinners might not suffer the anguish and despair of eternal woe! Oh, yes! now it was he expiated and procured our deliverance from all the black horror of those doomed to the everlasting prison of the second death.

VI. *There was his ignominious and painful death upon the cross.*

Sin and death were united in the first threatenings: "The wages of sin is death." Sin produced spiritual death; opened the grave for the dying body, and the regions of eternal death for the soul. Christ therefore suffered death for us, and this in connection with his agony in the garden, constituted the atonement for sin. Thus he was the great sacrifice for transgression, and obtained eternal redemption for mankind. By his death the river of life was opened, so that its saving streams might resuscitate our guilty world. Thus, my dear friends, we have seen in several striking points wherein "Christ also hath suffered for us."

APPLICATION.

1. *Have you right views of these truths?*
He suffered not for himself; not for angels; not for devils; not that wicked man might be saved in sin, but that the guilty might have in him a way of approach to God's mercy and eternal life.

2. *Are you personally interested?* Do

you feel that you are resting your all here, —body, soul, &c.

3. *Be ready to suffer for and with Christ.*

"If we suffer," &c. There must be conformity between the members and the head, between the soldiers and the captain of our salvation.

CCLXXVII.—THE EXPIRING SAVIOUR.

"Jesus, when he had cried again with a loud voice, yielded up the ghost."—*Matt.* xxvii. 50.

DEATH, under any circumstance, is indeed a solemn and affecting thing. To be removed out of the present world ;—to be severed from all our friends and associates ;—to leave all the scenes of sense, and go into another state of existence,—a world unknown ; beyond our sight and hearing, and from whence no traveller ever returned. Then there is the agony of the separation, in the dissolving of the connection between matter and spirit, body and soul. What more truly serious than a mortal being struggling with the king of terrors, until, at length, the terrific enemy conquers, and nothing remains to the view but the cold and inanimate corpse? But there are cases where all these things become more striking from the dignity of the sufferer, or the peculiar manner of his death. Thus *Socrates*, whose life and talents had blessed the Grecian empire, received the cup, not of the people's gratitude, but of poison, and died the death of a criminal. But a greater than Socrates is here. We meet to meditate upon the death of Jesus Christ, the Redeemer of the world. Consider,

I. *The person to whom the text refers.*

Let us view Jesus,

1. *In his transcendent greatness.*

There are grades and classifications among men ; but Jesus was the greatest man, most dignified of any of the human race. Greater than Solomon ; higher than the princes of the earth ; higher than the angels ; the beloved and only begotten Son of God. Isaiah thus describes him, "Unto us a child is born," &c. Zechariah represents him as the "fellow of Jehovah." He himself claimed equality with God.

2. *In his supreme and unrivalled excellences.*

In him concentrated righteousness and truth. Every virtue, every grace and goodness embodied. Love,—living, speaking, acting, and dying. Without spot. Angels chargeable with folly before him,—the heavens unclean in his sight. The fountain of all blessedness.

3. *In his substitutionary character.*

Wherefore does such purity suffer?—such excellency die? How is it that men should persecute him to death? How that God left him to be torn by the bulls of Bashan? To allow the sea of sorrow to dash its terrific waves over his head? How that his feelings should be so lacerated,—his heart so torn,—his soul so heavy,—his spirit so overwhelmed,—his body so mangled? The substitutionary character of Christ is the key to the whole. He was acting as the representative of a guilty world. He was now sustaining a public character. He was now filling up the distance between God and the sinner. He suffered and died for the ungodly. He poured out his soul an offering for sin. "By the grace of God, he was tasting death for every man," Isa. liii. 5–11. Notice,

II. *Some circumstances connected with his death.*

We cannot now dwell on the sufferings which preceded it ; on the ignominy associated with the manner of it ; on all the aggravations connected with it. Let us look at what the text involves.

1. *Observe what he had previously uttered, while enduring the agonies of the cross.*

Mark! Not one word of reprehension,—not one accusation against his enemies,—not one word of regret for aught he had committed. He had commended his mother to the care of the beloved John. He had given the thief a passport to glory. He had expressed his horror at the withdrawal of the divine presence. "My God! my God! why hast thou forsaken me!" He had uttered the pain he felt from the scorching heat which affected his body. "I thirst." He now commended his soul into his Father's hand. The moment of death had now arrived, and he surrenders his spirit up to God.

2. *What his last expression involved.*

(1.) That he had still strength to retain his life. In ordinary cases such suffering produced extreme and scorching fever, delirium, exhaustion, and gradually death. Not so with Christ. All his pains and agonies had not subdued the power which he possessed. He had power to retain his life.

(2.) That his death was voluntary. He gave himself. He came freely to suffer and die. He was to be a willing sacrifice. He redeemed us by the blood of his own heart, which he freely shed for our salvation. He had long anticipated this event. He had predicted it. He had longed for it. "I have a baptism," &c. And now having finished all his work, he cried with a loud voice, &c.

APPLICATION.

1. Meditate on the design of Christ's death; especially as an amazing display both of justice and grace.

2. See that you realize the benefits it obtained for us—pardon, holiness, and eternal life.

3. Interested in this, and influenced by it, we shall both living and dying glorify Jesus with our body and spirit, which are his.

CCLXXVIII.—THE GARDEN SEPULCHRE.

"Now in the place where he was crucified there was a garden; and in the garden a new sepulchre wherein was man never yet laid."—John xix. 41.

THE goldsmith is careful of the very dust of the precious metal on which he employs his care and skill. The holy word of God is far more precious than thousands of gold and silver. Every word of God is both pure and precious. Even the incidental passages of the scriptures would well repay our careful and serious meditation. Our text is a part of the evangelist's account of the death and burial of the Saviour. Surely every word of such events deserves to be read with devout feelings and holy attention. There is nothing trifling in the history of the life and sufferings of the Son of God. But Jesus has now given up his life. He has uttered the last exclamation: he has surrendered his spirit into his Father's hand; and now is fulfilled a remarkable prophecy,—"He made his grave with the rich in his death." How unlikely was this. He was a poor man. He was despised and rejected of men. He died as a malefactor. Yet "he made his grave with the rich." Two rich men, his secret disciples, were the instruments of this. One was the celebrated ruler, Nicodemus; he

bought myrrh and aloes to give a kind of embalmment to the body of the Saviour. The other was Joseph of Arimathea; he begged the body, and laid it in his own tomb,—"Now in this place," &c. Now we shall consider the text,

I. *Literally, and see the instruction that it contains.*

And,

II. *We shall accommodate the passage as suggesting several subjects worthy of our serious reflection.*

Let us look at the TEXT LITERALLY, and

I. *See the instruction it contains.*

Several things are referred to in the account of the Redeemer's burial. It was

1. *A new sepulchre.*

No corpse had ever been deposited there before. How fit to be the temporary residence of the Redeemer's holy body. He neither saw nor mingled with corruption. Observe,

2. *It was a private sepulchre.*

Not one of the public cemeteries of the city; and for this he was indebted to the voluntary kindness of a friend. He seemed to own nothing in our world. When born he had to borrow his infantile residence from the cattle. He had no wealth,—"The foxes," &c. He had not the tribute-money, &c. He had no grave for his remains. Who so poor?

3. *It was a sepulchre in a rock.*

In this way it was the more easily secured. Only one entrance. The stone rolled to the mouth and sealed, a small guard could easily protect it.

4. *It was in a garden.*

The body of man is of too dignified a character to be treated with contempt, even after the spirit has fled. It was usual for criminals to have ignominious interments, as harmonizing with their crimes and death. Rich individuals were particular about their family sepulchres. The crowded burial yards of our cities are utterly disgusting. Jesus was sepulchred in a garden, of all the places the most desirable for the resting of the body in hope of a resurrection to eternal life. We just remark that it was in a *garden* where sin entered our world. In a *garden* where Christ endured the inexplicable agony. And in a *garden* rest the remains of the Messiah, who by his death and resurrection opened the gates of the celestial paradise to all believers.

II. *We shall accommodate the passage as*

suggesting several subjects worthy of our serious reflection.

1. *The family is likened to a garden, and in that there is a sepulchre.*

David refers to our children being as olive plants round about our tables. A very sweet and striking representation. The varied ages and dispositions resembling the numerous flowers and plants of the garden. Such a scene, when in the enjoyment of health and happiness, when visited with the genial rays of a smiling sun, and the refreshing dews of a benign Providence, is a delightful object of contemplation. But in this garden there is a *sepulchre.* How family ties are dissolved. How soon some bloom and die. Ezekiel is mourning for the death of his wife ; Rachel, her children ; others, their friends, &c. If so, then let us view them *as mutable.* Let the family altar *be reared,* and Christ's presence solicited, who is the resurrection and the life.

2. *The church of Christ is a garden, but there is a sepulchre in that.* Here are the trees of the Lord. Here are the verdant cedars, and flowers of holy loveliness. Here the Lord dwells in all his beautifying and fertilizing influences. But there is a sepulchre in this garden. "The prophets, do they live ?" &c. Where are the worthies of the church ? Where Christ's saints ? After serving God and their generation, they fell asleep by the will of God. Both these views of the church should excite to diligence and fervor. Jesus felt this, and said, "I must work while it is called to-day," &c.

3. *We have two distinguished gardens where there are no sepulchres.*

(1.) *The Eden on earth.*

Not a spot for death's possession. Sin expelled man from that, and thrust him out into a wilderness of sorrow and death.

(2.) *In the paradise above.*

We read of the *tree of life,*—rivers of *life,*—region of life. No sin, therefore no death. No mourning in that family. No separations, &c. No bereavements in that heavenly church. Because Christ lives, we shall live also.

APPLICATION.

1. Sin is the cause of all kinds of death. Body and soul.

2. Christ is the fountain of all life. Soul, —body,—eternity. Christ is the surety. He came to give the world life. "Life and immortality," &c.

3. Christ has hallowed the grave by his own presence. Thus he has sanctified every condition and circumstance of life. He has hallowed the periods of childhood and youth and maturity. Poverty, sufferings, death, and also the tomb. He has illumined the dreary sepulchre.

4. He was but the temporary resident of the sepulchre. As it had been written, "On the third day," &c. He is the first-fruits of them who slept. If we die with him, we shall rise and live with him, &c. Faith in him removes the sting of death, and gives victory over the grave.

CCLXXIX.—THE TEMPLE OF CHRIST'S BODY.*

" Jesus answered and said unto them, Destroy this temple, and in three days I will raise it up. Then said the Jews, Forty and six years was this temple in building, and wilt thou rear it up in three days ? But he spake of the temple of his body."—*John* ii. 19–21.

The Christian structure rests principally on two great facts,—the death and resurrection of Christ. These are the two leading truths of the gospel,—that Christ died for us according to the Scriptures, and rose again according to the Scriptures. Remove either of these and the Christian edifice is involved in ruin, and the hopes of a sinful world are blighted forever. These facts were both typified and predicted thousands of years before they were accomplished. When the ancient priests offered one goat in sacrifice, and sent the scapegoat into the wilderness, both the death and the resurrection of the Saviour were clearly prefigured. Both David and Isaiah had foretold Messiah's resurrection, "Thou wilt not leave my soul in hell," &c. "Thy dead men shall live ; together with my dead body shall they rise." Jesus, in referring to the events of his own future history, often spoke of his death and resurrection. He referred on one occasion to Jonah ; and in the text, under a striking figure, he teaches the same important truth. "Destroy this temple," &c. Notice,

I. *The figurative description Jesus gives of himself.*

"This temple." "The temple of his

body." The apostle employs the same metaphor when speaking of believers. " Your bodies are the temples of the Holy Ghost." What then is the resemblance between the ancient temple and Christ's body?

1. *In their divine construction.*

The plans of construction both of the tabernacle and temple were of God. All things were made by the divine authority and pattern; and the temple was formed of the most precious and costly materials. How beautifully all this applies to the Saviour. His body, while it was really and truly human, yet it was different to all others. Think of its mysterious conception. A virgin the mother. Think of its purity and perfection. Without taint or spot, or any such thing.

2. *In their especial design and use.*

The temple was the dwelling-place of God; his earthly palace. Here he displayed both his grace and glory; here, too, he communed with man; gave audience to the sinner; heard prayer; received praise, &c. See how this applies to Jesus. God was in Christ. "God manifest in the flesh." "The Word was made flesh and dwelt among us," &c. Here heaven and earth met; Deity and man united. Here it is, too, that we can come to God. Christ is the way. He is in the Father, and the Father in him. "The one *mediator*," &c.

3. *The ends of the services and furniture of the temple are answered in Christ.*

In the temple was the *oracle*, from whence God spake to the people; the *mercy-seat*, whence mercy was obtained. How illustrated are these in Christ. He is the *living oracle*. God says, "Hear ye him." He is the last great prophet; the immediate mouth of God; the great teacher, &c. He is our only *mercy-seat*. In him we have remission of sin, and acceptance with God. In the temple was the altar, and Christ is our altar. In the temple was the *shew-bread*, and he is our living bread. The *incense*, and his intercession renders us acceptable to God. Notice,

II. *The prediction he delivered concerning it.*

"Destroy this temple," &c. Now, both particulars of this may be considered as predictive; for he knew they would destroy that temple, and hence the text embraces both the event of his death and resurrection. Thus, in due time they did accomplish the first part by crucifying the Lord of life and glory; and he effected the second part by his own eternal power, in raising himself from the tomb. Now, observe here, he predicts that this shall be accomplished,

1. *By his own power.*

"I will," &c. Hence he said, "I have power to lay down my life, and I have power to take it up again." Now, in previous ages God had employed instruments, as in the instances of Elijah and Elisha. Jesus, too, had raised several from the dead; but this was the most stupendous of all his miracles,—to raise himself. None could do this without possessing divine and changeless life in himself. This is indeed the demonstration of the divinity of Jesus.

2. *The identical body.*

"I will raise IT up," &c. This was fully proved by the exhibition of his hands and feet to Thomas. And before the throne he still bears the imprints of the nails and spear. With that body he ate and conversed. Those very hands he stretched over his disciples when he was taken up to heaven. Yet, how *changed*,—how radiant and beautiful,—how refulgent and glorious.

3. *The time is specified.*

"In three days," or on the third day. Thus he was laid in the tomb on Friday evening, and there he reposed on Saturday; and on the first day of the week, the third day, he arose with power and great glory. Thus the first day of the week has become the Lord's day—the day of the Christian institution—the day of triumph and rejoicing to the church of God to the end of the world.

APPLICATION.

1. *See the connection and resemblance between Christ and his people.*

You are the temples of God,—a spiritual house,—an habitation for the Lord.

2. *Your earthly edifices must be destroyed.*

Death will cast them to the dust. You must have fellowship with Christ in death. The tomb must encircle you. But it is now illuminated and fragrant,—it is now the vestibule of heaven.

3. *Christ will raise you up.*

By his own power,—in his own likeness, —to his own glory. From dust and loathsomeness to unfading beauty; from death to endless life; from earth to heaven; from the clods of the valley to the throne of paradise. O ye disciples of Jesus, rejoice in hope of the glory to be revealed. "Behold, now are we the sons of God," &c. Urge all to secure by faith in Jesus an interest in these everlasting blessings.

CCLXXX.—TRUE BENEFICENCE.*

"When the ear heard me then it blessed me; and when the eye saw me it gave witness to me: because I delivered the poor that cried, and the fatherless, and him that had none to help him," &c.—*Job* xxiv. 11–16.

FEW histories are so eventful and interesting as that of Job. His career opens upon us as peculiarly bright; the morning of his life was serene, cloudless, and happy. The sun of prosperity shone upon his path, and heaven and earth harmonized in promoting his prosperity. No wonder that he should exclaim, "I shall die in my nest." But it pleased God to visit him with a total reverse of circumstances. His flocks and herds are taken; his servants are slain; his sons suddenly cut off. These calamities are followed by a disease in his own person of the most afflictive kind; his friends write bitter things against him, and the wife of his bosom suggests to him, that he had better "curse God and die." How rapidly and totally did his earthly comforts flee away. Two things, however, did not fail him. A firm hope in the predicted Saviour, and a comfortable remembrance of the course of life he had pursued. His faith, even in the darkest hour, recognized his living Redeemer. "I know that my Redeemer liveth." And as to his life, he could remember how he had labored not only to enjoy the blessing of God, but also to be a blessing to those around him. "When the ear heard me," &c. Let us notice,

I. *The benevolent course he had pursued.* And,

II. *The reason why we should adopt and imitate it.*

Let us notice,

I. *The benevolent course he had pursued.*

He had mercifully regarded the sufferings of those around him. He specifies several classes of suffering which it had been his solicitude to alleviate.

1. *The poor that cried.*

Poverty is one of the afflictions of life,

* *Series* viii.—Designed for Benevolent Institutions.

and one that is necessarily associated with pain and sorrow. Especially is this true of abject poverty. Poverty that compels its victims to cry for relief. It is difficult for the affluent to form correct ideas of the miseries of this condition. To be hungry, and have no food; to be cold, and have uncomfortable clothing; to have a cheerless dwelling, &c. And this, too, often in the midst of plenty. To see around us the rich, the joyous, the affluent rolling in profusion. It is obvious that some degree of poverty has affected the world in all ages. There are occasions, however, when it is more severe and more general. He refers,

2. *To the fatherless children.*

The father is expected to provide for his household. To him the children have a right to look up. But we see that fathers are sometimes taken away, and the support of dependent children therefore fails. Have not such helpless little ones a claim upon our help? Ought we not to compassionate their condition, and stretch out the hand of kindness towards them? They have not only temporal wants, but they have minds to be cultivated, and souls to be trained up in the nurture and admonition of the Lord.

3. *To the disconsolate widow.*

The case of the widow is always mentioned with tenderness in the holy Scriptures. It is often with the widow as with the fatherless, that her earthly support is taken away, her means of livelihood removed, and she is left to stand against the storms of life solitary and single-handed. Often, too, the necessities of such are aggravated by the wicked and unprincipled conduct of persons, who will even rob the fatherless, and devour the portion of the widow. He refers,

4. *To those afflicted in person.*

The blind and lame are expressly mentioned in the text. In health, persons may struggle with poverty. But when lame they lose their energy; or when darkness beclouds their vision, what then can they do? How greatly poverty is deepened and embittered by affliction. Personal affliction, with every comfort and with the utmost attention, is only just bearable. What is it then when wedded to poverty and want? He refers,

5. *To those ready to perish.*

It is truly distressing to think of our fellow-creatures perishing for want. Yet we know that this is sometimes the case. Persons do perish with hunger,—with cold,—in

their afflictions,—through want of relief
Die neglected, unpitied, and unknown.

6. *To such as had none to help them.*

Some poor afflicted persons meet with
kind friends. Others have relatives or neighbors who assist them. But there are cases
where there are none to help. Persons who
in their afflictions depend on the compassion
of the benevolent. Often strangers who are
suddenly afflicted, and who require immediate aid or they perish, "having none to
help them." Let us just notice how these
varied cases were treated by the godly Job.

(1.) *He exercised compassion of heart
towards them.*

He did not shut his ears or close his eyes
to the miseries of those around him. He
did not wrap himself in the mantle of selfish
indifference. He saw, and heard, and pitied
the miseries of those around him.

(2.) *He administered effectual relief.*

"Delivered the poor." "Caused the
widow's heart," &c. "Eyes to the blind."
&c. He labored from this fulness to supply
the need of the wretched. He did not
merely say, Be fed, be clothed, be warmed.
But he administered the bread and the raiment, &c. His feelings were embodied in
actions of goodness and mercy.

(3.) *He assiduously devoted himself to
works of beneficence.*

"The cause which I knew not," &c. He
did not exercise his benevolence occasionally,
or just as they came across his path, but he
searched for objects of misery. This was
one part of his duty, and with diligence he
fervently attended to it. It is clear,

(4.) *That he exercised mercy and goodness
with cheerful affection.*

The whole passage breathes the gentle
and the tender. His was not harsh-wrought
and upbraiding charity; but the soft affection, the courteous and kind overflowings
of his heart. He acted willingly; not of
constraint, but of a ready mind. Now let
us consider,

II. *The reasons why we should adopt the
same course and imitate his example.*

1. *There are the sympathies of our common humanity.*

God has formed us for the exercise of
kindness and compassion. He has planted
these feelings in our hearts. He has so constituted us that the sight or hearing of suffering produces an immediate effect on our
souls. This is common to man as man; to
the savage as well as the philosopher. To
shut up our bowels of compassion is to do
violence to the principles of our humanity.

2. *There are the laws of righteousness.*

One of the commandments of God is, that
we are to love our neighbor, &c. And Christ
has taught us the extent of that love in the
parable of the Good Samaritan. Jehovah
demands this from us. It is a moral exac-
tion. Disobedience is therefore spiritual immorality.

3. *There are the higher claims of Christian goodness.*

We are under the dispensation of mercy.
Ours is a religion of love. Christ is our
teacher and example. Under the law, God
made great provision for the poor and the
stranger. Jesus embodied goodness and
mercy, and exhibited them in every part of
his life. He was the friend of the poor and
the solace of the distressed.

4. *There are the dignities and pleasures
arising from it.*

The text speaks of it as a *robe* and a *diadem.* It is the most beautiful and dignified
garment in which we can be clothed. It is
the celestial garment of love, and the diadem of mercy. But it is also essentially
connected with pleasure. True pleasure.
The loftiest and finest of our nature. That
which angels have, &c. That which God
enjoys. The richest and sweetest felicity we
can have on earth. It is so often, too, in the
retrospect. Was it not so to Job? He
could look back and remember this with
pleasure.

5. *There are connected with it many great
and precious promises.*

Let us look at two or three,—Psalm xli.
1–3; Isaiah lviii. 16, &c. "Blessed are the
merciful," &c. Christ will acknowledge
every act of goodness to the poor as though
done to himself. He has said, "The poor
cannot recompense you, but ye shall be
recompensed in the resurrection of the just."

APPLICATION.

1. *Have we exhibited any of the Spirit
of Job?*

Do we in the least degree experimentally
know the meaning of the text?

2. *Let our beneficence be wisely and prudently administered.*

3. *Remember our need of God's constant
goodness to us.*

Both in body and soul.

4. *Goodness is the fruit, not the basis of
piety.*

CCLXXXI.—THE BENEVOLENCE OF JESUS

"Who went about doing good."—*Acts* x. 38.

In whatever light we contemplate the Saviour, we are constrained to exclaim, "Thou art the fairest," &c. If we witness his spotless life, we feel that we contemplate a holy being, one who was "harmless, undefiled, and separate from sinners." If we listen to his teaching, with the officers who were sent to arrest him, we exclaim, with admiration, "Never man spake," &c. If we behold his wondrous miracles, with astonishment we ask, "What manner of man is this," &c. "We know that thou art a teacher sent from God," &c. If we are called to read the evangelical history of his blessed life, what is the conclusive impression with which we sum up the whole? Let our text be the reply, "Who went about doing good." Observe,

I. *The mission of Christ to our world was expressly one of mercy and beneficence.*

Our world was benighted, and he came to illumine it; miserable, and he came to bless it; enslaved, and he came to emancipate it; accursed, and he came to redeem it; lost, and he came to save it. "Ye know the grace," &c. "I am come that ye might have life," &c. "This is a faithful saying," &c.

II. *Mercy and beneficence distinguished his whole life.*

His first great work after he entered on his public ministry. Read Matt. iv. 23, &c. From this period to his death, he labored incessantly in doing good. When arrested in the garden, he healed the ear of Malchus, which had been smitten by the sword of Peter.

III. *The mercy and beneficence of Christ respected both the bodies and souls of men.*

It is said of him that he healed all manner of diseases. Let us look at a few. He restored the lame to soundness; he unstopped the ears of the deaf; he loosed the tongues of the dumb; he gave eyesight to the blind; he cured those diseased with dropsies and fevers; he gave vigor to the paralyzed; and loathsome lepers were cleansed. He also removed lunacy, and expelled demons from the possessed. But he regarded the *souls* of mankind. He taught them the doctrines of the gospel. He forgave sins and healed their spiritual diseases. He transformed men from darkness to light, &c. He gave

them peace, and joy, and hope, through believing. He had respect also to the *circumstances* of mankind. Several thousands had so listened to his discourses, that they had neglected due attention to their bodily necessities: they were ready to faint. For these he multiplied the loaves, &c. His disciples were exposed to the terrific tempest on the lake of Galilee. He rises from his slumber, and rebukes the sea, &c. A beloved family, where he had often been a welcome guest, were bereaved of an only brother. He repairs to Bethany, and weeps with the afflicted sisters. Then groaning in spirit, he commands Lazarus to come forth, and he came forth from the dead.

IV. *The mercy and beneficence of Jesus had respect to all classes and grades of suffering humanity.*

A *military officer* seeks his aid; and he freely restores the centurion's servant. A *ruler* applies on behalf of his daughter, and he raises her to life. A *nobleman* pleads in behalf of his son, and he replies, — "Go thy way, thy son liveth." These were persons of distinction. But behold, a *poor Syrophenician woman* seeks his merciful help for her daughter; and having tried her faith, exclaims, "Be it unto thee," &c. Two *blind beggars* moan their piteous cry, "Jesus, thou Son of David," &c. Jesus at once had compassion and touched their eyes, and immediately they received their sight.

V. *Jesus went forth from place to place in the exercise of his mercy and beneficence.*

He sought out the wretched. His journeys were designed to scatter blessings on the miserable and perishing. At Capernaum and throughout all Galilee. Just look at one day's labor of the blessed Jesus, Matt. viii. He delivers his sermon on the mount. He descends and heals a leper; restores the centurion's servant, ver. 14. Heals Peter's wife's mother. In the evening, see ver. 17, &c. Then he enters on a voyage of mercy, and seeks repose amid the howlings of the storm.

VI. *In performing acts of mercy and beneficence Jesus displayed the most tender sympathy and affection.*

He ever displayed the good and tender shepherd. He did not reproach or upbraid the guilty. He had merciful respect even to the woman taken in adultery. "Neither do I condemn thee," &c. He did not break the bruised reed, nor quench the smoking flax. Contrast with the beneficent life of Jesus,

1. The work of the prince of darkness. He is the poisonous serpent. The destroying lion. "He goeth about seeking whom he may devour."

2. Contrast it with the conduct of some of the distinguished heroes of our world. Men who sought glory and distinction by the desolations of war, and by the edge of the sword. Look at depopulated districts,—burned cities,—streams of blood. Hear the groans of the dying,—the sighs of the widow and the fatherless.

3. Contrast it with the excellences of the best of men. How narrow and limited is human kindness and generosity. How seldom extended to the worst of men, or to enemies. But the arms of Jesus embraced the vilest of the vile, and provided eternal life for those who shed his blood.

4. Christians present, contrast it with your own course of beneficence and goodness. Alas! how feeble, worthless, &c. Yet is it not our *model?* Shall we not seek to imitate it, &c. We have numerous objects around us both temporal and spiritual. We have certain talents. We have opportunities. Have we not then the responsibility? Then whatever our hand findeth, &c. Let us not be weary, &c. Finally, we recommend this merciful Saviour to every miserable sinner. He still lives to do good. Do you not remember the beautiful hymn?—

"Where high the heavenly temple stands,
The house of God not made with hands,
A great high-priest our nature wears,
The guardian of mankind appears.

He who for men their surety stood,
And poured on earth his precious blood,
Pursues in heaven his mighty plan,
The Saviour and the friend of man," &c., &c.

CCLXXXII.—THE REWARDS OF BENEVOLENCE.

" And if thou draw out thy soul to the hungry, and satisfy the afflicted soul, then shall thy light rise in obscurity, and thy darkness be as the noon-day: and the Lord shall guide thee continually, and satisfy thy soul in drought, and make fat thy bones: and thou shalt be as a well-watered garden, and like a spring of water whose waters fail not."—*Isa.* lviii. 11, 12.

THE Bible has one grand and peculiar character,—it is the book of goodness; it everywhere recommends and extols the principle of benevolence; its two grand precepts are love to God and love to man. It never dispenses with either; it will allow of no enthroned idol. "Thou shalt love, &c., and *him only* shalt thou serve." And it will allow of no substitute for goodness or benevolence to man. Knowledge, gifts of tongues, and even faith without works is dead. Of all the striking exhibitions of the beauty and value of this cardinal quality, none can excel the one given by the evangelical prophet in the text, "If thou draw out thy soul," &c. Notice in the text,

I. *The objects of benevolent regard.*

These are described in two forms:

1. *The hungry.*

Those who have craving appetites, and no means to satisfy them. Such is indeed a pitiable condition, yet not by any means rare. Often occurring. Many, very many are called occasionally to feel it. Sometimes our fellow-creatures perish of it. This state, painful in itself, is often aggravated by *surrounding plenty.* It is difficult to hunger in time of famine; but where there is enough, what a temptation to steal. So thought Agur, Prov. xxx. 8, 9. The text directs us,

2. *To the afflicted.*

This is much worse than poverty alone. Health gone; strength gone; resources dried up; thrown upon the bed of languishing; wearisome days and nights, &c. What wretched scenes are often discovered; dismal apartments, comfortless beds, cold, miserable, &c. Oh, how many pallid distressing forms are there to be seen when the abodes of misery are explored. Often, too, this state is the *reverse* of their former condition in life. *Often too, poor, friendless* children have to suffer; and often there is a *worse* disease than that of the body,—a guilty spirit, a defiled conscience, and dreadful fears of a future state. Dwell upon such objects of misery. Think that it may be your lot, and then you will appreciate the next division of our subject, viz.,

II. *The nature of benevolent regards.*

Now, we are to exercise,

1. *Tender compassion and sympathy.*

"Draw out thy soul." Not be heedless and careless of such; not neglect; not be callous; but "Draw out thy soul." Investigate, inquire, excite our best feelings, cherish soft and benevolent passions; annihilate sel-

fishness; crucify self; labor after generosity, and true charity. In all this we are
to be active. Not wait for opportunities of
doing good. Now, there may be many
things having a tendency to close our hearts.
The improvidence of the poor, and ingratitude; cases of imposition. But, we must
not forget how miserable we should be if
God gave us our deserts, &c. To this we
must add,

2. *Kind and suitable aid.*

We must "satisfy the hungry," &c. Not
profess to feel, and leave them to starve, or
pine away; but give them help, &c. Sympathy without this is mockery. God deems
it an insult to himself, and to his image, which
man bears.

(1.) It is also obvious our assistance must
be in proportion to our means.

(2.) It should be timely,—in season.

(3.) It should be with kindness of manner.

(4.) With prayer for God's blessing to
accompany it.

(5.) From purity of motive,—not for show
and ostentation; but out of love, &c., to the
glory of God. Notice,

III. *The rewards of benevolent attention
to the poor and afflicted.*

1. *It shall be followed by a dignified
reputation.*

"Then shall thy light," &c. No title or
distinction equal to that of goodness. What
is valor? or learning? knowledge? or even
righteousness? or equity of life? A *good
man* is the highest style, &c. "For a good
man some would even dare to die," &c.
Such,

2. *Shall have the gracious guidance of
God.*

"And the Lord shall guide them," &c.
How necessary is this,—how desirable,—
how pre-eminently precious, to have the
providential interpositions of God, and the
guiding influences of the Spirit. Guide
them rightly and graciously to the end, even
to a city of habitation.

3. *They shall have internal happiness and
satisfaction.*

When others are lean and comfortless,
they shall be prosperous and happy. "The
blessing of God maketh rich," &c. Their
goodness shall return, and bless their own
souls, especially when afflicted, Ps. xli.
1–3.

3. *They shall have abundant spiritual
prosperity.*

"Like a watered garden,"—green, fertile,
fruitful, fragrant. And this shall be perpetuated. Comforts, &c., shall not fail.
God is the fountain; and as such, he never
changes, &c., &c. Now this reward is often
the consolation of the benevolent in this life.
It was Job's solace, &c., in his adversity, &c.,
Job xxix. 11–16.

5. *The full recompense shall be given at
the last day.*

Christ says, that those who provide for
the poor, the halt, the blind, &c., shall be
blessed, and be recompensed at the resurrection of the just, Luke xiv. 14. At the last,
Christ shall deem it as done to himself. "I
was imprisoned," &c.

APPLICATION.

1. Put not benevolence in the place of
experimental piety. It is the first, &c.
Yet,

2. That is not genuine which does not
produce benevolence.

———◆———

CCLXXXIII.—REMEMBRANCE OF THE
POOR ENJOINED.

"We should remember the poor."—*Gal.* ii. 10.

ONE part of religion consists in yielding
cheerful homage, reverential fear, and sincere and affectionate obedience to God.
Another part of true religion consists in the
right regulation of our own faculties and
powers, and in the progressive sanctification
of our hearts. Inward, experimental piety
is having the kingdom of God within us.
That kingdom which is righteousness, peace,
and joy in the Holy Ghost. But there is a
third branch of acceptable religion, which
consists in our conduct towards our fellow-
men. Equity, love, and mercy are indispensable to this part of practical piety. We
are to honor all men; to do unto all men
as we would they should do unto us. We
are to love all men. And finally, we are to
show mercy unto all. Our text relates to a
specific duty we owe to one class of our fellow-creatures. Observe,

I. *To whom the text refers.*

II. *The duty the text specifies.*

III. *The motives by which it may be enforced.*

I. *To whom the text refers.*

"The poor." The poor need no description. We are acquainted with them. It is not necessary to go to their comfortless dwellings, or to describe their insufficient clothing, or to speak of their necessities and sufferings. Let us take two or three views of the poor.

1. *Many are so evidently through the righteous appointment of God.*

In every age of the world, &c. In the earliest period to which revelation refers. Book of Job. In all countries, &c. We see everywhere this diversity of condition; and it is written, "The poor shall never cease in the land." There are myriads who never could have been otherwise. Their lot has thus fallen. It is their heritage, &c.

2. *Many are poor through their own imprudence.*

Poor in spite of God's bounty. How many are poor through extravagance, and riot, and waste. Look at the prodigal. He spent his portion, and then he was in want. The improvident involve others,—the anxious care-worn wife, the helpless dependent children. Of all vices intemperance has made the greatest number of poor; yea, more than all other sources put together.

3. *There are the pious poor.*

Those whose poverty has been sanctified. Those who gladly heard the gospel of salvation. Those who have godliness and contentment, which is great gain. There was a Lazarus. There was the liberal widow. There are tens of thousands who are poor in the temporal sense of the word, yet are heirs of the kingdom. Notice,

II. *The duty the text specifies.*

"We should remember," &c. Now the text means more than recollection or memory. This remembrance is unavoidable. But our remembrance,

1. *Should be devotional.*

We should remember them in our prayers. " I will that prayer and supplication should be made for all men," &c. We should bear them up in our arms of intercession, and supplicate God's kindness on their behalf. Our remembrance,

2. *Should be kind and benevolent.*

We should cherish feelings of love and compassion. Our speech, and temper, and disposition should all breathe good-will, pure benevolence. Our remembrance,

3. *Should be sympathetic and practical.*

We cannot love them without sympathizing with them in their sorrows. We are commanded to "weep with those who weep," &c. And where this sympathy is genuine, it will lead us to give our aid to alleviate their sorrows, and remove their distresses. Without helping, our pity is mere fiction, and our sympathy worthless. Our love and sympathy are to be made tangible, imbodied. See James ii. 15, 16.

4. *It should be constant.*

So long as the poor exist, and so long as we possess the ability, so long are we to " remember the poor." It ought not to be a remembrance of constraint, irksome, or unpleasant; but the cheerful and ready service of the heart. Notice, then,

III. *The motives by which it may be enforced.*

" We should remember," &c.

1. *Because of the indissoluble affinity which subsists between us.*

That is a striking and sublime passage, Acts xvii. 21. Noble blood, royal blood, &c., are foolish and absurd, if not wicked distinctions. Roam through the world, descend in the scale of society, find the most abject, the most distressed and wretched, whatever may be his color or language, &c., he is thy brother. He has thy nature, &c. Not to remember the poor is to insult the claims of humanity.

2. *Because of our mutual connection and dependence.*

The rich and the poor all meet, &c. Now the rich are dependent on the poor, if not to the same extent as the poor are dependent on the rich. Look how numerous the classes who have to labor for the comfort of the rich. Some have to build our houses; make our furniture, clothes, &c. Many of these, through their large families and contingencies, &c., are ever poor—but particularly so in sickness.

3. *Because God has strictly enforced it in every age and dispensation.*

If we go back to the Levitical dispensation, one passage shall suffice, Deut. xv. 7, &c. Hear what God says by the prophets, Isa. iii. 13, &c.; Ezek. xxii. 29; Dan. iv. 27. Hear what the apostles taught, Rom. xii. 10, 15; Heb. xiii. 16. Now as we are but stewards, if we refuse to obey God we rob both him and the poor. One intention of our pecuniary talents is, that we may remember the poor.

4. *Because of that true pleasure and of those real benefits which a remembrance of the poor will produce.*

It is the soul's highest pleasure and dignity. To share with angels. To feel and act as God himself acts. Many promises, Ps. xli. 1, 3.

5. *In this way we honor the blessed Redeemer.*

Not only by obeying and imitating him, but by regarding those whose condition he honored. Think of the condition of Jesus. "He was poor." Perhaps you never knew a person so poor as Christ. Indifference to the poor is indignity to Christ; Christ deems it done to himself.

6. *Because of that common level to which all classes are hastening.*

We brought nothing into this world, &c. Soon all distinctions will cease. Go to the grave. Go to the judgment-seat, &c.

APPLICATION.

1. Let this duty have the serious consideration of all.

2. Let not duty be the basis of your hope, but the evidence of your piety.

3. Let the rich seek after poverty of spirit.

4. The poor after the riches of eternal life.

CCLXXXIV.—THE BIRTH OF JESUS.*

"And the angel said unto them, Fear not: for behold, I bring you good tidings of great joy, which shall be to all people. For unto you is born this day, in the city of David, a Saviour, which is Christ the Lord."—*Luke* ii. 10, 11.

THE subject of the text is the nativity of the world's Redeemer; an event of a most astonishing and glorious description; an unprecedented event; an event which only occurred once within the history of the world. Every thing concerning Jesus is matter of delightful contemplation to the Christian. His name is as precious ointment poured forth. Let us, then, with humble views of grateful delight, direct our meditations to the nativity of the Son of God. In doing this, we shall confine our thoughts to the text. We have,

I. *The messenger employed.*

"The angel of the Lord." More probably one of the most exalted of all the cherubic hosts. One of the dignified sons of light. One of those who witnessed the creation of our world, and who, with his holy com-

* *Series* ix.—Intended for Christmas day.

panions, as morning stars, sang together, when all the sons of God shouted for joy. An ambassador from heaven to earth; from God to man. A service of unrivalled glory and benevolence; calculated to excite wonder and abundant praise. By the redemption which is in Christ, angels become our brethren, our friends, and our companions forever. It is probable their joys and honors are greatly advanced by the work of the Messiah.

II. *The persons addressed.*

Jewish shepherds, v. 8, 9. This is decisive evidence that the incarnation did not take place in December, but rather in September or October. After the beginning of October the weather was too cold for the flocks in the mountainous region of Bethlehem. What a contrast between the ambassador and those to whom he appeared! How different, too, to the doings of men, and human expectations! It would have been supposed, the tidings should have been given to kings, or philosophers, or assuredly to the priests, &c. "But God's ways," &c. In all the works and life of Christ, God poured contempt upon worldly glory and distinctions. In his parentage, &c.; in his condition of life; in his disciples, &c.; in his chief followers. God has especially honored the calling of shepherds: Abel, Jacob, Moses, David, and many of the prophets. Notice,

III. *The message communicated.*

Now the angel not only stated this, but affixed to it, "I bring you," &c. These tidings are the birth of the Saviour.

1. *He describes his person.*

(1.) Saviour; Christ; Lord. His errand, work, and object, was to save; to redeem men; to ransom the lost world. He was typified, predicted, promised, &c., as a Saviour. Not a temporal, but spiritual; not a Saviour of men from earthly bondage, &c., but a Saviour of souls from eternal death to eternal glory.

(2.) Christ. The same with Messias: that is, the Anointed One. One sent, commissioned, and qualified by Jehovah. The ancient kings and priests were anointed with oil, &c. Christ with the Holy Ghost, without measure.

(3.) The Lord. Here is the dignity, power, and glory of this Saviour. "A virgin shall conceive," &c. "Unto us a child is born," &c. "God manifest in the flesh," &c.

2. *He announces his birth.*

"Is born," &c. Not promised; not prophesied afresh. Prophecies had ceased, &c. The scene of types has ended. Now the event. The long prayed and longed-for event. The years accomplished. The fulness of the times. The place, too, according to prediction. Micah v. 2.

3. *He affirms this to be an event of good tidings, &c.*

Tidings of divine grace and salvation. All other tidings insignificant. A physician for a sick world. A Redeemer. Tidings of light, of life, of happiness and of eternal glory. "*Good* tidings of great joy."

4. *He notices the universal application of these good tidings.*

"You." The Jews, &c., first. Yes; Christ was emphatically their Saviour; he was of their seed: he lived, &c., with them. But "*all people.*" How cheering to the Gentiles! All the Gentiles! "All people." How vast the comprehension—how universal! Wherever we find even a horde of wandering savages, Christ is born for them. All people. All classes, countries, ages, &c.

APPLICATION.

1. *Is the end of Christ's birth answered in you?*

Is he yours indeed?

2. *If so, rejoice.*

Let it be spiritual, holy, constant, and then it will be eternal.

3. *Caution against the evils of the season.*

CCLXXXV.—THE PROMISED SHILOH.

"The sceptre shall not depart from Judah, nor a lawgiver from between his feet, until Shiloh come, and unto him shall the gathering of the people be."—*Gen.* xlix. 10.

OUR text is one of the predictions of the dying Jacob. It is evidently a prophecy concerning the promised Messiah. It is a prophecy which has greatly perplexed the Jews; and in some cases has led them to believe that Christ was he who should come; and in embracing him they have not looked for another. Perhaps there is no part of the Old Testament scriptures which they find so difficult to reconcile with their unbelief in Jesus as this. As a very graphic and explicit prophecy of the Redeemer, it stands forth to the Christian as one of those solid proofs

of the authority and divinity of our holy religion; 1700 years before the Saviour's incarnation was that event so fully and yet minutely declared. Thus did holy men, inspired by the Holy Ghost, testify of Jesus, of the work he should accomplish, and the glory which should follow. Let us consider the title, the appearing, and the work of the Messiah, as exhibited in the text.

I. *The title of the Saviour.*

He is here predicted of as the Shiloh. The term appears to have a threefold signification. It is interpreted to mean,

1. *A messenger, or one who is sent.*

Now Jesus was the sent of the Father— the messenger of God's love and mercy to our lost world. "For this we know, and testify, that the Father sent the Son," &c. Christ also particularly refers to his own character as the sent of the Father, in the following scriptures: "This is the will of God, that ye believe on him whom he hath sent," John vi. 29; "For I came down from heaven not to do mine own will, but the will of him that sent me," ver. 38. See also ver. 57, ch. vii. 16, xxviii. 9–33. Now, as the messenger, or sent of God, he covenanted with the Father for the redemption of the world. In the fulness of time God sent him forth, &c. Then he was anointed to the great work by the descent of the Holy Ghost. Afterwards he entered on his public ministry by saying, "The Spirit of the Lord is upon me," &c., Luke iv. 18. Shiloh signifies,

2. *Peace-maker.*

This strikingly agrees with the prophecy of Isaiah, "Prince of peace." And with the song of angels, "Peace on earth," &c. Earth had rebelled against heaven; man against his God. Sin exposed our guilty race to the wrath of Deity. Jesus came to set up an honorable system of mediation. He undertook to render perfect satisfaction to the insulted justice and holiness of God; "to magnify the law," &c., Eph. ii. 13; Col. i. 20. Through him all believers have peace with God. The gospel of peace is freely procured, and a spiritual empire of peace and holiness set up in our world. Shiloh also signifies,

3. *Prosperous Saviour.*

He was the sent of God to be the Saviour. He became a Saviour through making peace for us. But as a Saviour he is to be prosperous. As such, he possesses every qualification for saving souls. "He is mighty to save." "He can save to the uttermost," &c. As a Saviour, the covenant, too, ran thus :—"He shall see his seed, he shall prolong his days, and the pleasure of the Lord shall prosper in his hands." His kingdom is to be an everlasting kingdom, and his dominion forever and ever. His reign of mercy is to be universal,—to encompass every nation, people, and tongue. "Until the kingdoms of this world," &c. His arm of subjugating grace he will make bare in the sight of all nations; and the people shall praise him forever and ever. Does not every pious heart exclaim,

"O Jesus, ride on till all are subdued,
    Thy kingdom make known, and sprinkle thy
        blood,
Display thy salvation, and teach the new song,
To every nation, and people, and tongue."

II. *To the appearing of the Messiah.*

"Until Shiloh come." This "Sent of God,"—this blessed peace-maker, and prosperous Saviour, was to come. Our world was to be the scene of his wondrous works and glorious achievements.

In the coming of the Shiloh *two* things are especially to be observed.

1. *He was to be of the tribe of Judah.*

Hence this is specified in the genealogy of Christ, as given by both Matthew and Luke. But,

2. *He was to come before the rule and authority of, the tribe of Judah should cease.*

Now, observe, authority and power are especially predicted in reference to this tribe, ver. 8. As the priestly office pertained to the tribe of Levi, so the royal line was that of Judah. Now, it is very remarkable that legislative power and authority pertained to the Jews until the appearing of the Saviour. In the time of Augustus, the Roman emperor, they became a conquered nation, and afterwards a Roman province. The Jewish senate were struggling for their departing power at the time of Christ's birth; and in the twelfth year of the life of Christ, a Roman procurator was appointed, and the power of life and death was taken out of their hands. We see that the Jewish sanhedrim had not power to put Christ to death. Forty years after the death of God's Son the city was seized, the temple razed, and the people scattered; and never since have the Jews possessed legislative power and authority in any nation under heaven. How manifest, then, that either the prophe-

cy of Jacob was false, or that the Shiloh must have truly appeared. Now, notice,

III. *The work of the Messiah.*

"Unto him shall the gathering of the people be." There is a very striking passage in the Epistle to the Ephesians, ch. i. 10. Now, by the people we are probably to understand the Gentile nations, as they are often thus designated. Messiah's administrations were to extend to the people who sat in darkness, and in the region of the shadow of death. Or, perhaps, by the people, mankind in general, without distinction as to Jew or Gentile, were to be collected by the promulgation of the gospel of Christ. Now this was strikingly ratified in the setting up of the administration of Christ's spiritual kingdom. His death was to be the great moral *attractor.* "If I be lifted up," &c. Thus Peter lifted him up on the day of Pentecost, and drew 3,000 Jews to his standard. Afterwards the apostles went forth everywhere through the then known world, and gathered out of all nations a people to the Redeemer's praise. So in every age, wherever the gospel has been preached, souls have been gathered to Christ. So it is now—the heralds of mercy have gone forth into all the accessible lands of our world, expressly to gather men to Christ. They are gathered,

(1.) To his cross as the source of salvation.

(2.) To his cause as his devoted followers.

(3.) To his church as the visible friends of his kingdom.

(4.) To his royal standard as his loyal and obedient subjects; and,

(5.) To his glorious kingdom as the trophies of his grace, to shine forth in the lustre of purity and blessedness forever and ever.

CONCLUSION.

Learn,

1. *The true character of the Lord Jesus.*

He is the promised Shiloh. His name, and work, and glory, are peculiarly his own. He claims the homage, and the praise, and the love of our redeemed race.

2. *Have we been brought to a saving experimental knowledge of his grace?*

Salvation is being gathered to him, as wandering sheep brought to his fold,—as outcasts, &c., brought nigh. O sinner, let his arms of love embrace thee.

"Fly, sinner, fly into those arms
  Of everlasting love."

3. *The full accomplishment of the text is yet to come.*

His scattered people are to be collected. He is to set up his kingdom from the rivers, &c. "Blessed be the Lord God of Israel," &c.

———

CCLXXXVI.—ADMONITORY COUNSELS FOR THE CONCLUDING YEAR.*

"See then that ye walk circumspectly, not as fools, but as wise," &c.—*Eph.* v. 15.

[PART 1.]

THE text is an exhortation of the apostle Paul to the members of the Ephesian church. It is an exhortation relative to practical Christianity, and is equally necessary and important to us as it was to them. It relates to that which is ever seasonable, but which is still more particularly so on certain occasions. To young converts the admonition is especially important. To all Christians, who are more exposed to the influence and example of the world, this is also exceedingly necessary. At certain seasons also, the admonition seems to be requisite and appropriate. We conclude, then, the services of the sanctuary, by considering the admonition of the apostle. In which we have,

I. *The course against which we are cautioned.*

"Not as fools." That is, not to walk as fools. Now the word seems to signify persons who are idiotic or insane; and the conduct of the mass of mankind is of this description. Hence sin is called folly, and sinners fools. Now the ungodly walk as fools or madmen,

1. *As they have no rule of conduct.*

No principle by which they are governed. No certified mode of action. You do not find wicked men at all agreed. Every one chooses his own way. All at variance as to what is best. The ancient philosophers could not agree,—nor the modern skeptics. All darkness and confusion. Wicked men walk as fools,

* *Series* x.—For the commencement and end of the year.

2. *As they have no direct or distinct object in view.*

A maniac wanders both in speech and walk. Now surely there must be some great object worthy of a rational and immortal being's ambition. Now they do not all agree to seek mental dignity, or intellectual pleasure, or the riches of this world. But some have one thing in view, and some another, and in the pursuit of all, there is confusion, dissatisfaction, and vexation. See Eccles. i. 12 to end.

3. *As they walk often presumptuously and without fear of danger.*

Maniacs have been known to do astonishing feats of peril,—foolhardiness. Now see wicked men doing acts of daring; trifling with the most terrific subjects; sporting with danger and eternal death.

4. *They often act without regard to their real welfare.*

Hence on this ground persons of weak minds have guardians to transact their affairs, &c. Often degrade and debase themselves. Now wicked men are pre-eminently guilty of this. They barter solid riches for the stubble of earth,—the gratification of the body for the joys and solid blessings of the mind. This world's fleeting vanities they prefer to eternal treasure, and everlasting bliss.

II. *The course which is recommended for our adoption.*

"To walk circumspectly, as wise." Now this is just the opposite of the walk of fools. In doing this,

1. *We must walk by a wise rule.*

The scriptures are the records both of wisdom and goodness. Here are solid principles of wisdom, precepts of wisdom, &c. Not an attainment of true politeness or excellency, but it is to be found in the Bible. Humility in taking the lowest seat. Not to exalt ourselves, &c. Kindness to the poor, —compassion to the wicked,—veneration and respect for age,—courtesy to all men,— equity and purity, benevolence and mercy, love and holiness, are all set before us.

2. *We must possess the spirit of wisdom.*

Now this must come from above. See James iii. 17. "The wisdom that is from above is first pure, then peaceable, gentle, and easy to be entreated, full of mercy and good fruits, without partiality, and without hypocrisy." This wisdom is to be obtained by prayer. See this exemplified in the case of Solomon, 2 Chron. i. 7, &c. "If any

man lack wisdom, let him ask of God,"
&c.

3. *We must imitate the divinely recorded
examples of wisdom.*

Was not Noah wise? Moses, &c. But
wisdom was resplendent in one, even in Jesus. He was filled with it. Now he is our
model in all things. We are to "look unto
Jesus." See the estimate he put upon various things. He ever kept in view the final
close of his life, and of his work. Let us
therefore often meditate and reflect, &c.

4. *We must walk and keep company with
the wise.*

The companion of fools will become one,
and be destroyed. Nothing is of greater
importance than the society we keep. It
will influence our principles,—our spirit,—
our conversation,—and our practice. In
connection with this, let us think of the society we expect to join in, in a future state.
Heaven is the palace of the God of wisdom.
Angels are all distinguished for wisdom and
knowledge, &c. There the wise shine forth,
&c.

APPLICATION.

1. Exhort all to abandon the paths of
folly. Do not walk as fools. Think of the
dignity of your souls,—your awful destination.

2. Exhort all believers to persevere in the
ways of wisdom and life; Prov. iii. 13, &c.,
"Happy is the man that findeth wisdom,
and the man that getteth understanding.
For the merchandise of it is better than the
merchandise of silver, and the gain thereof
than fine gold," &c.

CCLXXXVII.—ADMONITORY COUNSELS
FOR THE CONCLUDING YEAR.

[PART 2.]

"Redeeming the time because the days are
evil."—*Eph.* v. 16.

In discoursing on the former verse, we
considered both the course prohibited, and
the course recommended for our adoption
by the apostle. Our present subject is intimately connected with it. One of the highest evidences of wisdom is redeeming the
time. One of the most palpable proofs of
folly is trifling and whiling it away. We
consider the subject as more especially appropriate at the conclusion of the year. Let

the text then be considered as addressed to
us, especially on the last Sabbath evening of
the expiring year, "Redeeming the time,"
&c. Consider,

I. *The subject to which we are directed.*

That is to "time." It is measured duration. It is thus distinguished from eternity,
as eternity is without limits and immeasurable. No signs by which eternity is distinguished. On the other hand, with time,
we have it divided into several portions, as
years, months, weeks, days, hours, and minutes. Now this measurement is of great
importance to short-lived man. It assists
us in the distribution and arrangement of
our affairs. Now let us just dwell a little
upon the subject of time.

1. *Consider its true character.*

It is the material of life. The measure of
our earthly existence,—the stream which
bears all our race to the ocean of eternity.
It often appears very different from the position which we occupy. If we are anxious
to obtain some future good, or if we are suffering pain, it creeps with the pace of the
snail. If we dread some evil, or fear the removal of some good, it flies, yea, darts forth
with irresistible rapidity. But these are extreme views. Viewed under calm and collected feelings it is even in its course, and
regular in its flight.

2. *Consider its value.*

And here we are at an utter loss. Consider there is no substitute for it. Consider
its real scarcity. One moment is measured
out at once. Consider how some would
have purchased it. Many would have given
a kingdom for a day; thousands for one
hour. Consider there is no mart where it
is to be had.

3. *Consider the brief portion which is allotted for our service.*

Now no even regular amount is guaranteed. But we will take a long life,—threescore years and ten. What are they? A
dream, a vapor, a thing of naught, a span,
&c. But few enjoy so large a portion.
Most do not reach half that period. Then
strike off the necessary deductions; ten
years of childhood and folly; one-third
passes over in sleep, making twenty more;
so that forty years is the utmost that can
be calculated in the long life of threescore
years and ten.

4. *Consider the right application of time.*

Now there are the temporal claims of the
body. Avocations of business, &c. These

things must draw largely, &c., particularly upon the poor, &c. The improvement of the mind. Increase of mental capacity, &c. Then the welfare of the soul, and a preparation for the eternity before us. Life is the period of our stewardship, the time of our probation. All guilt must be removed,—all holiness attained,—all duties discharged, —all graces matured, and all disposed for the heavenly state. Surely this is the chief end of man, the grand employment of time. Consider,

II. *The course recommended.*

"Redeeming the time," &c. This signifies to recover, to buy back. Now we cannot do this literally, but in a certain sense we may. The traveller who has loitered in the early part of the day, &c., may hasten swiftly onwards. The workman who has lost his morning opportunity, may by diligence and extensive exertions do much to make it up. Just so we may redeem the time, by keeping the great end of our existence in view. We may do so then,

1. *By saving all the time we can.*

Much time is lost in unnecessary sleep,—much in frivolity,—in trifling,—in folly. Most may save one hour in the day from these. This will add half a day to each week. Much may be accomplished in that period.

2. *By cherishing activity and diligence.*

Indolence is the bane of the body,—of the mind,—of society. Soul is capable of wonderful exertion. Formed with faculties, &c., for it. How necessary this diligence. "Whatsoever thy hand findeth," &c.

3. *By regarding first the most momentous subjects.*

Attend to these; secure these; then all will be well. The rich fool did the opposite. Soul first. Labor for eternity. Oh yes, the time is truly redeemed which is devoted to prayer and heavenly purposes.

III. *The motives assigned.*

"Because the days are evil."

1. *They are uncertain in their number.*

You may have few left. Glass nearly run out. "Verily there is but a step," &c.

2. *They are days of temptation and sin.*

Much will oppose you. Many snares and attractions. Many things to draw you aside, &c. Without vigilance you will make little out.

3. *They are liable to be interrupted by infirmity and sickness.*

Then your opportunities, and means, and powers of exertion will be unavailable. Then you will be called to suffer, not fight; to bear, not to do the will of God.

APPLICATION.

1. Our subject is of universal and individual importance. It addresses each of us. The young and the aged, &c. The sinner and the saint.

2. With some much time has been wasted, yea murdered. Years upon years. Life nearly ended, yet its work not begun. Yea, you have been only making work for repentance. Oh, think of this. Do not longer barricade the door against yourselves. Do not render your salvation more difficult.

3. Our subject is connected with eternity. What a word! How truly solemn! Yes, the acting time and the realities of eternity are inseparably connected.

4. Exhort all to repentance. Do not procrastinate or defer. Not merely resolve. Let your watchword be NOW. The present. Now is all I can call my own, &c. All I am sure of, &c.

CCLXXXVIII.—A NEW YEAR'S PERSONAL INQUIRY.

"What lack I yet?"—*Matt.* xix. 20.

THE case of the ruler, to which the text calls our attention, is one of very great interest and importance. The inquirer was a man possessing extensive moral qualities,—one of general consistent demeanor,—one who was earnest in his application,—reverent towards Christ, and who called forth the affectionate regards of the Saviour towards him. See Mark x. 21. His errand was of vast, yea, of eternal moment. It related to eternal life,—to the eternal life of his own soul. The glorious person to whom the application was made, "Jesus Christ,"—the Great Teacher, the infallible guide of men into all truth, the only way to Father, &c. The conversation is given in full, ver. 16, "Good Master, what good thing shall I do, that I may have eternal life?" The text is the second interrogation of the ruler to Jesus, "What lack I yet?" We remark,

I. *There may be many excellences, and much that is amiable in man, without true religion.*

Let us look at some of these particulars.

1. There may be general and extensive morality of character.

It was so with this ruler, and it is so in many cases. Equity in pecuniary transactions; truth and honor in the various movements of life; freedom from the gross vices of the times; general uprightness of character, &c. And all this is to be admired and commended, but yet it is not religion.

2. There may be exhibited many of the benevolent and social virtues.

Great paternal affection, conjugal fidelity, filial love and reverence. Men may be frank and generous, hospitable and beneficent, liberal and kind-hearted; and yet all this is not religion.

3. There may be correct knowledge and orthodoxy of creed.

Men by reading, and hearing, and studying theology, may be familiar with the great principles of Christian truth and doctrine. The mind may be tutored into an acquaintance with the glorious subjects of divine revelation; there may be no heterodoxy in the views and sentiments they hold with respect to the gospel; and yet this is not religion.

4. There may be respect for divine things, and reverence for divine ordinances.

How many there are who value the scriptures; fear an oath; respect God's day; attend his sanctuary; and labor to maintain the institutions of divine worship. How many listen to the reading of the oracles of the living God, hear with interest the gospel, join in the praises, and assent to the prayer offered up; and yet all these do not constitute religion. Nicodemus doubtless went so far; Saul of Tarsus too; and thousands of the Pharisees. Is it not so with many of you?

II. *There are various evils which keep men from being entirely the Saviour's.* With some,

1. There is self-complacency.

They are satisfied with themselves. They compare themselves with the wicked, or with inconsistent professors, or with backsliders from Christianity. They are ignorant of the extensive claims of the law, and their own hearts.

2. There is the esteem, and honor, and favor of the world.

Many live and toil to possess the world's good name, and its breeze of fame and favor. Now this is the very antipodes of piety; this is the opposite of God's favor; cannot pay court to the world and the

church. How thousands are bound by the silken cords; yet, though silken, the cords of death. The man who rests his head on the lap of Delilah shall like Samson be shorn of moral strength, and be unfit for the service of God.

3. There is a fond craving and attachment to riches.

How many, like the inquirer of the text, allow riches to separate between them and Christ. Hence see Christ's application of this case in the context. Ver. 23. "Verily, I say unto you, that a rich man shall hardly enter into the kingdom of heaven." Some love riches for their own sake,—to hoard them; a sordid spirit which sinks its victims lower than the fallen condition of demons. Others for the purpose of self-elation, authority, and power; others for vanity and display; some to gratify their desires for the sensual pleasures of life. The love of riches and the love of God cannot dwell together. The love of riches and the love of our fellowmen are the opposite of each other. What a fearful snare! How many they have shipwrecked! How many drowned in perdition! How many shut out of heaven, and shut up in hell!

4. There is unwillingness to take up the cross and exercise self-denial.

Christ must be followed, ver. 21. But how can this be done, if we will not confess him or suffer reproach for his name? As Christ was despised and hated, and persecuted, how can we expect to escape? Then there is self-denial; mortify self, only seeking to please Christ, &c. "Lay aside every weight," &c. Taking up the cross and yoke of Jesus. We must "count all things but loss for the excellency," &c.

III. *The inquiry of the text is one which is worthy of personal consideration.*

"What lack I yet?" In order that the inquiry may be useful to you,

1. Ask the question as in Christ's presence.

He is the searcher of hearts. "His eyes are as a flame of fire." He knoweth all things. You cannot, therefore, act deceitfully before the Lord.

2. Ask the question with all possible seriousness.

It is indeed a very solemn matter, it has reference to eternal things. Eternal life and death are concerned. There can be no religion without deep seriousness.

3. Ask the question with perfect deference to God's word.

No voice will speak; no spirit will appear; no miraculous reply. But God's word will tell you what to do, and how to do it. It is the word of salvation. Let the word speak fully, and it alone. Repent and be converted, &c. Repent and believe the gospel, &c.

4. *Confine the question to yourselves.*

What do I lack? Avoid curiosity about others; judge no man; leave every case to the righteous Lord. Religion is entirely personal in its essence.

5. *Ask in a spirit of prayer and with a resolution to obey the answer.*

Ask for the old paths and walk therein; hear and do the will; hearken and believe; learn and obey,—and pray that you may have grace to do so.

APPLICATION.

1. This question is suitable in all stages of the Christian life.

2. To all classes in the church of Christ.

3. It is the will of Christ that we should be perfect, lacking nothing.

CCLXXXIX.—A NEW YEAR'S FRIENDLY INTERROGATION.

"Is it well with thee? Is it well with thy husband? Is it well with the child? And she answered, It is well."—2 *Kings* iv. 26.

OUR subject takes us back to the time of the prophet Elisha. The holy prophet of God often had to pass in his journeys through a place called Shunem. In this place dwelt a distinguished woman, doubtless a true servant of the God of Israel. Observing the prophet, she made him welcome to the hospitalities of her house. The prophet's journeys being frequent, she at length said to her husband, "Behold, now I perceive," &c., ver. 9. Think of a prophet's accommodation, &c. Elisha, grateful for the kindness proposed, said to Gehazi, his servant, &c., ver. 12. Her noble answer exhibited satisfaction and contentment with her lot. How worthy of our imitation. " Godliness with contentment is great gain." God favored this good woman, who had been childless, with a son. This son was the object of peculiar affection. He must have lived at least for some years. At length, however, the child died,—died suddenly, ver. 18. Her affliction was great, —the blessing given, suddenly snatched away. Observe the course she adopted, ver. 22. Elisha witnesses her approach, and sends Gehazi to meet her with the interrogation of the text. The text exhibits resignation and submission under a very dark and trying dispensation. God's government must be always well; his dispensations are all mercy and truth. But to feel this and confess it, and act accordingly, is difficult, if not impossible. But we leave the original occurrences of the text to dwell on the interrogation, "Is it well with thee?" We apply the text to the soul,—to that thinking principle which is endowed with consciousness, and which bears the impress of immortality. Is it well with your soul?

I. *Let me assist you to answer the question.* "Is it well with thee?"

1. *If so, it is different with you now, to what it once was.*

It cannot be well with the person who is in his natural unconverted state. It cannot be well for the soul to be in darkness, in disease, in guilt, in fetters, under sentence of death, exposed to everlasting ruin. Now, this is the state of every person who is not changed by the grace of God. This was the state of every believer before he knew the grace of God in truth. Have you passed from death unto life? Have you been brought up out of the horrible pit, &c.? Have you been plucked as a brand, &c.? Can you say, I, even I have obtained mercy? If it is well with you,

2. *You are the children of God's family.*

Look at the prodigal famishing, ready to perish; look at him then clothed, with the ring of reconciliation, at the festive board. Every believer is a child of God. He resembles God. He loves God. He fears God. He serves God. If it is well with you,

3. *You have an interest in the precious promises.*

Word of God full of these; for body and soul, time and eternity; they refer to every possible condition, and insure every blessing we can possibly need. "Hereby are given unto us great and precious promises," &c. With these we are rich and ought to be happy—without them we are wretched and poor. If it is well with you,

4. *You have a sure title, and a bright hope of a better world.*

Some persons never think of another world,—care not, &c. Death is a step in the dark. The Christian knows by the conviction of faith in God's word that there is a better world. He acts upon the direction of the gospel; embraces the offer of God's grace; and confidently hopes and looks. Looking for the blessed hope, &c. "Rejoice not in this, that the devils are subject," &c. "I know whom I have believed," &c. "For we know if this earthly house," &c. If it is well with you,

5. *You are glorifying God in the world.*

It cannot be well with the misanthrope, such an one as Cain. With the slothful, who labor not in their vocation, &c. With those who do no good; shed no influence abroad; remove no sorrow; diffuse no bliss. It is well with the active, useful, liberal Christian.

II. *Let me urge the question upon a variety of characters present.*

1. *Professors, is it well with you?*

Is your profession the title-page to the contents of your hearts? Have you the root of the matter? Have you a pacified conscience? Are you bearing fruit? Is it increasingly well with you? Are you truly the better for your religion, and is religion greatly bettered by you?

2. *Young persons, is it well with you?*

Do you fear God in youth? Do you cleanse your way, by taking heed unto God's word? Do you avoid evil company? Do you flee the scenes of folly and dissipation? Have you given your hearts to God? Do you daily pray, "My Father, be thou the guide of my youth?"

3. *Parents, is it well with you?*

Have you a strong impregnable wall around your families? Is the God of Israel your defence? Have you his blessing on your substance? Is God supreme ruler? Have you an altar,—is the voice of prayer heard?

4. *My aged friends, is it well with you?*

As the outward man decays, &c. Do you bring forth fruit to old age? What is your conversation, experience, influence? Are you ripening for heaven? Are you sailing close to the shores of glory?

5. *Inquirers, is it well with you?*

Oh, you say, we wish it were,—you are mourning, distressed, &c. Well, it is well with you,—God says so. "Blessed are they that mourn," &c. "To that man will I look," &c. Was it not well with the publican, the woman who was a sinner, &c.?

6. *Careless sinner, is it well with you?*

It cannot be, "Say unto the wicked it shall be ill," &c. It is not now, and it must

be worse and worse. But it may be well with you. "If you repent," &c.

IN CONCLUSION,

1. Let each ask the question, Is it well with my soul? Well in real experience? Well for the next world?

2. We cannot settle this question with absolute certainty for others. We are not called to judge. Examine thyself. Prove thyself, &c. Carnal people cannot judge.

3. Let our course be to please God, and then it must be well with us forever.

———————

CCXC.—TEMPORAL AND ETERNAL THINGS.

"While we look not at the things which are seen, but at the things which are not seen: for the things which are seen are temporal; but the things which are not seen are eternal."—2 *Cor.* iv. 18.

OUR subject embraces all that is comprehensive and important to man. It relates both to this world, and to that which is to come. It refers us both to temporal and to eternal things; and it shows us the chief objects which engage the Christian's attention. He looks not on the things which are seen, &c. Consider,

I. *The things which are temporal, and how we should treat them.*

And,

II. *The things which are eternal, and what influence they should have upon us.*

I. *The things which are temporal, and how we should treat them.*

Now temporal things are those which are visible or palpable,—"things which are seen." Things which come under the observation of our senses. Now of temporal things there are two distinct classes.

1. *Lawful temporal things, and these are to be used.*

The bounties of God's providence—the blessings of this life, food and raiment, and other natural enjoyments. Now these things are to be obtained by industry and labor; they are to be used and sanctified to us by prayer and thanksgiving. In these temporal bodies we shall daily stand in need of these things. Two evils ought to be avoided: extravagance and waste, avarice and parsimony.

2. *There are sinful temporal things, and these should be avoided or renounced.*

The pleasures and fashions of the world—the pomps and vanities of sinful life—those things which tend to pride, or vanity. I need not stay to explain what they are. Worldliness is not so like religion, that it is difficult to draw the line. Now how should we treat temporal things? According to their true nature. Not forget their vanity and emptiness; not forget their unsuitability to the soul; not forget how transient they are. Look at that title: how many have had it, but where are they? That crown: how many have worn it, and where are they? That estate: how many have enjoyed it, but where are they? Alas! alas! not only do the fashions of this world pass away, but things which are temporal and lawful must only be used as the traveller does his conveyance, or the mariner his vessel. The Christian should feel as the poet describes the pilgrim:

> " Nothing on earth I call my own;
> A stranger to the world unknown,
> I all their goods despise:
> I trample on their whole delight,
> And seek a country out of sight,
> A country in the skies."

II. *The things which are eternal, and what influence they should have upon us.*

Eternal!—what a word! Properly speaking, only one being so—God. The high and lofty One, &c. Ever existing, without origin or end. But the word is used for things which will be everlasting. Now of these,

1. *There is heaven.*

A house not made with hands, eternal in the heavens. No flood, or fire, or earthquake, ever affected it. A changeless and endless world. A world of eternal light, and health, and life. The riches, the titles, the pleasures, are all eternal. Pleasures infinite and everlasting. Now this world is not seen—literally out of sight. Revelation and faith alone enable us to discover it.

2. *The soul is eternal.*

A spark never to be extinguished; a ray of light never to be blotted out; an intellectual, thinking existence, that will never die. The longest life, therefore, is but as a moment of its duration. When we think of one continued series of links, forming an eternal chain of being, the mind is overwhelmed; yet this is a sober reality. The soul, immortal as its sire, will never die. We mention only one thing more, and that is,

3. *Eternal salvation.*

And this is what Christ has effected on behalf of every believer. This is the heaven enjoyed by the soul forever and ever. Everlasting purity and joy—everlasting dignity and bliss. All that the soul shall enjoy will be eternal. Worship and adore the eternal God; bow down before the eternal throne; engage in eternal acts of devotion and praise; partake of the eternal streams of life; and be eternally secure from sin, sickness, and death. All this is hidden from the eye of sense, and the eye of learning, and the eye of philosophy; it is only discernible by the eye of faith in God's holy and blessed word. Now what influence should these have upon us?

1. *Should they not have our deepest solicitudes?*

These eternal realities are worth all our souls' thoughts and desires and anxieties. We may be careful indeed about these—we may covet these—aspire after these.

2. *Should they not be the objects of our first concern and labor?*

First in importance—first in the week—first in the day. If toil is demanded, or self-denial, or mortification, or trouble, or affliction, is not the end sufficient to animate, &c.? " I press," said the apostle, " towards the mark," &c. Should we not,

3. *Be joyful in the blessed hope of these things?*

> " Yea, and before we rise
> To that immortal state,
> Thoughts of such amazing bliss
> Should constant joys create."

The way-worn traveller sees his home at a distance, and is cheered. The mariner looks to the distant haven, and in the buffetings of the storm he is cheered. The racer perceives the goal, and stretches every nerve, and is cheered; and the Christian looks at eternal things, and is filled with rapture and delight. He says, in his poverty and sorrows,

> " I would not change my blest estate
> For all the world calls good and great;
> And while my faith can keep her hold,
> I envy not the sinner's gold."

APPLICATION.

We address,

1. *Those who are absorbed with temporal things.*

How poor, meager, &c. Are you satisfied? But if you are, we call you to behold,

2. *Eternal things.*

Think of the eternal things you forfeit. Loss of heaven—loss of eternal life. But there are eternal things of another description. A hell which is eternal. Lake of fire—chains—darkness—weeping and wailing. Now weigh the two—look at the contrast, and stop, consider, repent. Escape for your life. Trample temporal things under foot.

3. *Christians, this is your duty and privilege.*

Look at eternal things, and live loose to time and earth; be ready for heaven and eternity.

———◆———

CCXCI.—IMMEDIATE DEVOTEDNESS TO GOD.

"Consecrate yourselves to-day to the Lord."— *Exod.* xxxii. 29.

THE literal history of the text is gathered from the preceding part, of which the text is the conclusion. Israel had grievously sinned; the wrath of God waxed hot against them. The sons of Levi were to be the messengers of his vengeance. And by the edge of the sword there fell 3,000 men. Our text had been the address of Moses to the sons of Levi on this awful occasion. We take the text, however, and apply it to a very different purpose. We design to rest upon it the great necessity and importance of immediate personal piety, and the desirableness that this act of consecration should take place. Thus applying our subject, and accommodating it to our present audience, we shall consider, by divine assistance,

I. *The nature of this consecration.*

To consecrate is to devote to divine purposes. Hence the vessels of the tabernacle. Also the victims for sacrifices. Likewise the priests and Levites to their official services. Now personal consecration to God is the entire surrendering of ourselves to serve and live to the glory of God. A state and life of sin is against God—against his laws and authority, &c. Now, consecration to the Lord is the contrast of this—the very opposite. In this there are several things involved.

1. *We must recognize the claims of Jehovah.*

He demands our hearts, souls, and lives.

Are these claims just and reasonable? Do we dispute any of the grounds on which the claims of Jehovah rest? His supremacy, his creatorship, his preserving goodness, his redeeming right. Our own powers adapted to this exalted station. Now, these claims must be conceded, and fully recognized.

2. *We must concur as to the manner of our consecration.*

Every thing in religion must have God for its author, or it is spurious and counterfeit. Now God has not left this to our opinion or taste. We must be consecrated by water and blood. So were the priests of old. The blood of Christ is the only medium of our salvation. The sacrifice of Christ is the only foundation of our hopes. In it we have pardon, peace, and sanctification. In it our robes must be washed, &c. It cleanses from all sin. By *baptism in water* the external act of consecration is to take place. By the gospel men are to be brought to Jesus Christ. In his blood they find redemption, and then Christ is to be put on by baptism into his death. Neither of these will do alone. There must be faith and profession: profession and faith.

3. *We must be deeply anxious respecting this consecration.*

The course of a religious life cannot be entered upon with indifference. The change is too great, and the matter too momentous, to be effected by a cold formality. The three thousand were pricked in their hearts, and cried earnestly, "Men and brethren," &c. So did Saul of Tarsus. So did the jailer at Philippi. A man's soul must be impressed, and deeply wrought upon, and he must see this as the most important act in the world, and on which pend eternal consequences.

4. *We must earnestly and believingly give ourselves up to the Lord.*

Renounce our own imaginary right. Throw off the despotic yoke of the devil; come fully out of the world and prostrate our hearts, and souls, and bodies, at the footstool of God's mercy.

" Take my body, spirit, soul,
  Only thou possess the whole."

5. *This act of consecration must be entire and forever.*

No reservation, no half-heartedness; not the assumption of the form only, but the power; not only the blessings, but the crosses of Christ must be taken. This consecration must be for all places, and seasons, and circumstances; for life and death, and forever.

6. *This act must be our own individual act.*

We may teach, invite, exhort, warn, and pray for others, but we can only consecrate ourselves. Religion, from first to last, is personal. My own mind, and heart, and life, are to be influenced by it.

7. *This act must be effected and sustained by divine grace.*

Hence the necessity of prayer and full dependence on the grace of God. Our convictions will be slight, our resolutions evanescent, our goodness transient, without this. We shall give up our purposes and break our vows without this. We must lay hold of God's strength, cast ourselves entirely on his merciful aid, or we shall not consummate this great and essential work. I only add,

8. *That this act must be immediate.*

"To-day." To-day we have life, and the means, and the promises. To-morrow all may be lost, and forever. Now God stoops and entreats; now the gates of paradise are widely opened; now the Holy Spirit hovers, ready to descend; now angels wait, ready to strike their harps afresh:

" All heaven is ready to resound,
The dead's alive—the lost is found."

Now, let us urge you to this immediate consecration,

II. *By several important considerations and motives.*

1. *It is rational.*

Equally so, nay, more so, with allegiance to rulers, and obedience to parents. Every thing in religion dignifies its subjects. It tends to enlarge and refine the mind; it produces self-government; it enforces the various duties of life, propriety of speech and temper. Now, to say the least. all this is rational.

2. *It is improving.*

It makes men better—better in all the relationships of life—better hearted—better parents, friends, neighbors, &c. The lion is now a lamb; the raven a dove; the curse a blessing. By your own dignity, then, I urge you to consecrate yourselves to-day to the Lord.

3. *It is felicitous.*

Produces real happiness, solid pleasure, internal joy. So striking is this, that the very features are affected by it. Now no terror, no remorse, no writhing, gnawing worm within. Now there is peace and joy in the Holy Ghost, &c. Some have said, this is only imaginary and delusive. Be it so : what have you in its stead? Why do not deists provide their votaries imaginary felicity too?

4. *It is consolatory.*

We often require consolation. Trials of life, troubles of the world, afflictions, bereavements, &c. Now, in these times how sweet is consolation! As bread to the hungry—as water to the fainting—as rest to the weary—so is consolation to the spirit. It makes happy in adversity and distress. It cheers and supports, and sanctifies our afflictions.

5. *It is saving.*

No salvation without personal consecration. This is salvation—to be the Lord's. To say really and experimentally, The Lord is my salvation; his favor is life; his love is heaven; his wrath is hell. All who remain unconverted are cast as briers, and thorns, and chaff, into the burning lake. Enemies are dashed in pieces; unprofitable servants cast into outer darkness. But the saints, the devoted children of God, are confessed, and exalted, and glorified, with Christ forever and ever.

APPLICATION.

1. Let me urge the text on all classes, the *young especially.* Oh, I long to see a host of young persons, who will join a juvenile band to serve and fear the Lord. Oh, decide, all and every one.

2. Let me urge all now. "To-day." This first Sabbath of the new year. From this time resolve—this very night.

3. I urge by a countless number of considerations. By the majesty and glory of the God who seeks your salvation, and not death. By the grandeur of his majesty—the greatness of his power, and the fierceness of his wrath. By the *spirit* within you. That thinking, eternal, conscious soul, that pants for happiness : oh, consecrate it to the Lord. By the flight of time. The years, and months, and days are flying. Our opportunities are passing away. Remember, when time is wasted, more than blood is spilt. By the solemnities of death. You must die, and perhaps this year. By a heaven of glory—to this you are called. There is a throne, a crown, offered you. An ocean of bliss may be yours. By a hell of

horror, and wailing, and woe. Oh, flee from the wrath to come! Oh, straightway flee from the brink of blackness and the regions of despair. Now, who will consecrate *himself* this day to the Lord?

CCXCII. — HEAVEN THE COUNTRY OF THE CHRISTIAN'S DESIRE.*

"But now they desire a better country; that is, an heavenly."—*Heb.* xi. 16.

THE apostle, having referred to the heroic faith and holy lives of several of the Old Testament saints, then pronounces the manner in which they finished their earthly course. "These all died in faith." This had been their mode of life: they lived by faith, and when they came to the close of life, still they had not received the promise, neither the entire possession of Canaan, nor the promised Messiah, but they were unshaken in their belief in death. As the troubles of life could not move them from the foundation on which they rested, neither could the waters of death. "They died in faith." And as to the influence of faith on the general tenor of spirit and conversation, it is said they considered "themselves strangers." For had they sought to return to their native land, the country of Mesopotamia, they might easily have done so. But they preferred being strangers and pilgrims, because "they desired a better country," &c. Let us take a brief survey,

I. *Of the revelation concerning heaven.*
II. *In what respects it is a better country.*
III. *The desire which all true believers have for its possession.*

I. *Of the revelation concerning heaven.*

We wish to dwell emphatically on the word revelation, because what can we know of a future state except what is revealed? Human imagination may sketch a heaven, but then it is only ideal, and therefore not that which hope can appropriate to itself. Mahomet has promised his followers a heaven, but such an one as he knew would fascinate the oriental sensualist. Now the scriptures reveal,

1. *A heavenly place.*

This place they call by a variety of significant appellations. Habitation of God.

* *Series* xi. — Designed for funeral services, &c.

God's right hand. Glory. Our Father's house. The New Jerusalem. The City of God. Paradise. We presume not to say where it is, but it is doubtless in the most exalted and glorious part of God's universe. It is represented as being upward; Christ ascended to it. Paul was caught up into the third heavens. Now in this place God has his palace—his throne—his temple—his servants—his worshippers. But mark, the scriptures reveal it chiefly,

2. *As a state.*

As the state of the glorified spirits who dwell with God; worship him incessantly; enjoy the rivers of pleasure which are at his right hand for evermore. It is represented as a state of rest from toil; of triumph after warfare; of glory after suffering; of life after death; of honor, and immortality, and endless bliss. But these points will be more appropriate when we view the subject comparatively.

II. *In what respects is it a better country than this?*

1. *It is a sinless country.*

How beautiful and fair was this earth when God expressed his perfect approbation, and pronounced it very good! Sin defaced and marred it. Sin converted it into the region of woe, and the shadow of death. Sin diffused ruin through every part of it. Now, that better country is sinless; the plague-spot of sin is not within all its borders. The streams are all pure; the sky is cloudless and radiant; the air unimpregnated with pollution. In all that country God has his own bright image reflected. Not one spirit devoted to the service of the evil one. The refulgent rays of the divine holiness spread through all the extent of that better land. How different to this world!

2. *It is a healthful country.*

Sickness is the fruit of sin. Pain the offspring of iniquity. Could we be borne on the wings of some heavenly intelligence to every hospital, infirmary, and afflicted chamber, what should we see and hear? Afflictions abound among all classes of men—in the palace of the monarch as well as in the cottage of the peasant. The wasting consumption, the burning inflammation, the raging fever, the suffocating asthma, with a fearful train of ills and pains, storming every part of the citadel of man. The heavenly atmosphere is untainted. Not a disease is incidental to that better world. The air is salubrious; the enjoyments without peril;

the food incorruptible; and therefore sickness is unknown.

3. *It is a country inhabited by perfect beings.*

The perfect and blessed God. The perfect and blessed Mediator. The perfect and holy angels. The spirits of the perfected saints. Not one imperfect being within the celestial range. Now, to speak more especially of the redeemed saints—they are all entirely holy. How different that country to this!

(1.) Let us look without the church, and there is the ungodly world. Hating God and hating his people. Persecuting, bitter, malignant tongues. Devouring spirits, ravenous as wild beasts; hateful and hating as demons. Not an envious person—not a detractor, or evil speaker—not a calumniator—not one person with an evil heart or evil tongue.

(2.) No imperfect brethren. Here we are often distressed through the infirmities of our fellow-disciples : one is possessed of an uninformed understanding; another, an unsound judgment; a third, a stubborn disposition ; a fourth, a wayward or hasty temper; and in many things we all offend. There the inhabitants will have clear, unclouded understandings; true, and righteous, and hallowed judgments; hearts full of celestial love, and spirits of courtesy, gentleness, and meekness. Then, that which is imperfect shall be done away, and every inhabitant contribute to the peace and happiness of the whole. Nothing shall hurt or vex in all God's holy mountain.

4. *It is a country of better enjoyments.*

This world is full of God's goodness, but the richer blessings are above. Besides, there our enjoyments,

(1.) Will be overflowing. Here, only a sip, a gleam, a taste ; there, an ocean, noonday light, and an eternal banquet.

(2.) Will be incessant. Here, interrupted; there, ever joyous; here, like angels' visits, &c.; there, continuous; a rolling sea of glory; pleasures which have no interruption.

(3.) Eternal. Perpetuity of bliss, is bliss. Death terminates all earthly enjoyments : but the terms, age, infirmity, suffering, death, are nowhere to be found in the vocabulary of heaven. There, time is not; that is, duration measured; all is eternity; no night, but endless day; no death, but eternal life. What a country! How it should attract us! &c.

III. *The desire which all true believers have for its possession.*

Others may wish, but the true Christian really desires it. This desire,

1. *Is formed in regeneration.*

Born for and from above. New nature tends upwards.

2. *Is cultivated by sanctifying grace.*

Growing in grace is growing in meetness, &c.

3. *Is heightened by spiritual visits to it.*

He ascends in prayer—in faith—in hope. " Oh that I had wings like a dove," &c.

4. *Is exhibited in holy diligence to obtain it.*

He labors to enter; he gives all diligence.

APPLICATION.

1. This better country is offered to all who will set out on the heavenly pilgrimage. Who then will begin the holy journey ?

2. How truly blest are all the children of the heavenly Zion. Now on their way to the land of rest—to their Father's house—to endless glory. How cheerful they should be ! " Yea, and before we rise to that immortal state," &c.

3. There is a worse country, the world of woe, of darkness, of despair, of endless death. Flee from it, and now.

CCXCIII.—DEATH IN THE MIDST OF LIFE.

" Her sun is gone down while it was yet day."
—*Jer.* xv. 9.

OUR text we select irrespective of the literal application of it when uttered by the prophet. The word of God contains a great amount of metaphorical representations. In this figurative style of speech most of the prophets abounded, and every subject of revelation is more or less illustrated in the form of allegory or metaphor. The metaphor of the sun is often thus borrowed by the sacred penman. " The Lord God," &c. " Unto you that fear," &c. There is one passage where the prophetess Deborah uses it, when she sang, " Let them that love thee be as the sun when he goeth forth in his might," Judges v. 31. In accommodating the text to the present solemn occasion, let us consider,

I. *The sun as an emblem of the saints of God.*

II. *And its setting, or going down, as representing their mortality.*

I. *The sun as an emblem of the saints of God.*

When we contemplate the great orb of day, we are impressed,

1. *With his greatness and elevation.*

The centre of the solar system exalted above our globe ninety-five millions of miles, and supposed to be a million times larger than the earth. From its size, it stands forth as one of the most sublime of all the works of Deity. We wonder not that nations without revelation should have given it divine honor and worship. This greatness and elevation fitly represent the true character of the Christian, contrasted with what he was, with what others are around him. Knowledge makes a man great. Grace of God elevates and lifts up to heaven. "I will set him on high," &c.

2. *Natural glory and magnificence.*

The most glorious of all the heavenly bodies. Now in this we are directed to the moral glory and excellence with which believers are adorned. "The king's daughter," &c., Psal. xlv. 13. See this strikingly set forth, 2 Cor. iii. 18.

3. *As the great diffuser of light and beauty.*

How dreary without his rays! He lights up and gilds, with his beams, universal nature. The Christian is first the recipient of light, and then he is called to shine. "Arise, shine," &c. "Ye are the lights of the world," &c. "So let your light shine," &c.

4. *As the chief source of fertility and fruitfulness.*

Cold, and ice, and sterility, reign in the absence of his rays. He makes the desert to rejoice. He revives and fructifies the earth, and this is the great cause of vegetable fruitfulness. Such is every spot where Christians do not dwell. There, is ignorance and cruelty, wretchedness and death. Where Christians live there is knowledge, benevolence, happiness, and life. Look at all our institutions of temporal and moral goodness. We now proceed to consider,

II. *The setting of the sun as a striking representation of the mortality of the Christian.*

1. *The going down of the sun is a usual, and therefore expected event.*

So sure as he arises, we know he will go down. How equally true of the sun of life! Man is born to die, &c. "I know that thou wilt bring me to death," &c. "The living know," &c.

2. *The period of the going down of the sun is very diversified.*

Look at the short winter's day and the long summer's day. So in life—every age is alike mortal, &c. But the text speaks of the sun going down while it is yet day—prematurely. How often is this the case! The eye is not dim; the ear is not dull; the almond-tree has not blossomed; the strong men do not bow themselves; bones are full of marrow—and yet disease assails, and the tabernacle is levelled with the dust.

3. *The going down of the sun is often peculiarly splendid and beautiful.*

His appearance is then often larger, his beams softened down into radiant mellowness, and the whole horizon is gilded with his golden glory. How characteristic of the good man's death! Then truly greater, mellowed in the fruitfulness of Christian graces and goodness. His dying room lit up with the beams of celestial glory, until every visitor feels it to be the ante-chamber of heaven. No wonder that Balaam exclaimed, "Let me die the death of the righteous," &c.

4. *The sun goes down, to arise and shine upon another horizon.*

Thus, as the curtains of evening are drawn around us, they are opening with the dawn of day in another hemisphere. Just so is it with the saints of God. To die, is to be with Christ. To dwell in the holier and happier abodes of bliss. To shine forth in the kingdom of our Father forever and ever. Not blotted out. Not in sleep or stupor, but shining forth in the celestial world, to the glory of God and the honor of his grace.

APPLICATION.

1. Are we spiritual suns, illuminated and elevated, &c.?

2. Let us not forget the going down. Live holily—usefully—anticipating the shades of evening.

CCXCIV.—DILIGENT WORKING.

"I must work the works of him that sent me while it is day; the night cometh when no man can work."—*John* ix. 4.

THESE are the words of the Lord Jesus, in reference to his own personal ministry and work. The Lord Jesus was not only an example of holiness, goodness, and benevolence—but also of diligence, activity, and perseverance. He had a divine and perfect mind. He had all miraculous influences at his command. All resources were to him available, yet he felt the pressure of duties so much upon him, that he had no time to trifle away, but exclaimed, "I must work," &c. How completely was the spirit of these lines exemplified in his arduous and suffering life! He went about doing good; he never wearied, but with ceaseless zeal and diligence accomplished all that his Father had given him to do. His life and work ended together, when he cried with a loud voice, "It is finished! and gave up the ghost." Now, brethren, let us apply these words to you, and to the great duties which devolve upon you. Let us consider,

I. *The work which God has given you to perform.*

It is the work which God calls you to do; the work which you must do, if you answer the end of your creation, and if the designs of redeeming love are answered with respect to you. Now this work is not the pursuit of the things of this world; not the pursuit of its riches or honors ; and not the pursuit of learning or mere mental improvement. And yet all these are proper when they are considered as subordinate things. God is willing that you should be diligent in business ; he is willing that you should enjoy the esteem and approbation of the great and good; he is willing that you increase in all knowledge, &c. None of these are despicable things, but they are secondary ; and you may succeed in all these, and yet neither glorify God, be happy in this life, or be fit for a future state. This is a direct and specific work, which God calls upon you to perform ; in one word, this is the work of religion. The work of personal, scriptural, and relative religion. The work of which Christ is the blessed and perfect example. Now let me direct you to four distinct yet united branches of this work.

1. *There is the work of repentance.*

If sin is an evil thing, deserving of punishment, and we are personally guilty, it must be repented of. We ought to feel extreme sorrow for it ; we ought to confess and deplore it; we ought to renounce and forsake it. Repentance is a necessary, essential work; God enjoins it upon all people. "Except ye repent," &c.

2. *There is the work of faith in Jesus Christ.*

1 John iii. 23, "And this is his commandment, that we should believe on the name of his Son, Jesus Christ." Now it is this faith in Christ which brings us to the enjoyment of forgiveness of all past sin. "Be it known unto you men," &c. Here is God's grace, that he does not require merit or price, but faith in Christ, the one blessed Mediator between himself and us.

3. *Work of obedience to the Lord.*

If ye have received the Lord Jesus Christ, so walk in him, &c. "This is the love of God, that we keep his commandments," &c. We are to serve the Lord Jesus Christ—living according to the rule he has given.

4. *The work of benevolence to our fellow-men.*

Man is not to live only for himself; not to seek entirely his own things, but the good of others. Society is connected by the links of mutual dependence. We are to love our neighbors, &c. To do good to all. This was Christ's chief work. This is the noblest and happiest work of the Christian. No Christian can possibly be exempt from this work; all have gifts and means to lay out. Time, wealth, influence, all must be expended for God. Look at the world—what ignorance, depravity, misery, &c.; what poverty, affliction, and distress! Think of the widow and the fatherless. Look either at home or abroad. Look at the Church—what is to be done there ? Work for every Christian; every good man should have his heart full, his hands full, his life full. Such, then, is the work. Consider,

II. *The period specified for its accomplishment.*

"While it is called to-day."

1. *The day is a period of manifestation.*

The sun is risen—all things are manifest. Such is our day. The Sun of righteousness has arisen upon our world. Not in pagan gloom, &c. You know your duty. The days of ignorance are fled, &c.

2. *A day is a very circumscribed period.*

A few hours bound it ; dissimilar in length ; some very short. They vary from a midsummer's day to the short day of winter. So the difference of human life.

3. *A day speedily passes over.*

So the day of life. What is your life ? There is the morning, how quickly that flies !

and midday—afternoon—and evening soon arrives.

4. *The day is succeeded by the darkness of night.*

"The night cometh," &c. It may be,

(1.) The night of bodily affliction. Or,

(2.) The night of infirm old age. Or,

(3.) The night of death. The night cometh; every hour it draws nearer.

APPLICATION.

1. Who are fully living in the spirit of the text? Go on.

2. Who only partially? Bestir yourselves, &c.

3. Who entirely neglecting it? Oh! awake.

4. Let the groans of the afflicted and languishing arouse us to the spirit of diligent working.

5. From the sepulchres of our deceased friends, the voice of admonition is heard: "Work," &c.

CCXCV.—HUMAN FRAILTY AND PERPETUITY OF THE DIVINE WORD.

"The voice said, Cry. And he said, What shall I cry? All flesh is grass, and all the goodliness thereof is as the flower of the field," &c.—*Isa.* xl. 6–8.

In this sublime chapter the prophet is commissioned to proclaim comfort to God's ancient people. This consolation is evidently connected with the atoning work of the Messiah, ver. 2. The third verse clearly relates to the Baptist, who should act as the herald of the Saviour. "The voice of him," &c. The blessed results of the Redeemer's advent are then declared, ver. 4. "Every valley," &c. Then the glorious permanency of the gospel dispensation, as contrasted with the changeableness of human nature, is forcibly described: "The voice said, Cry," &c. ver. 6–8. In this subject two things demand our attention.

I. *The mutability of human nature.*

And,

II. *The immutability of the divine word.*

I. *The mutability of human nature.*

Now in this description there are several things requiring our notice.

1. *The true character of human nature.*

"All flesh is grass." Of course the whole description refers to the body; to the material corruptible part of our nature. The *origin* of the human body is the earth. In this we are formed of the same materials precisely with the grass of the field. The *supplies* for the human body are also from the earth; so that which nourishes the grass provides man with his daily sustenance. The destination of the human body is the earth. "Dust thou art," &c. In this also we see our kindredness with the grass of the field. We see in this description,

2. *The superficial evanescence of human nature.*

"The grass withereth," &c. Man is not likened to iron or to stone, or to oak, for these remain for generations, for centuries. Some of the ancient monuments have stood for thousands of years. But man "cometh forth like a flower, and is cut down." What more fragile than the grass? What more mutable than the flower of the field? Yet these are the true emblems of human nature. The life of man is as nothing. At his best estate he is vanity. Threescore years and ten pass swiftly away, and are but as "a tale that is told." But how few reach that period of life! The grass and the flower of the field have a natural tendency to decay; but this is oftentimes hastened by the withering wind and scorching sun. So we see this in the ravages of death, on all the varied conditions and ages of human beings. There is,

(1.) That *infant flower*, the joy of its parents, the very image of loveliness. Yet how often does it fade and perish, to the grief of all who beheld and admired it. We are often called to condole with Rachel, &c.

(2.) There is that *intellectual flower*, where the child has risen into youth, and where youth has been beautified with knowledge and intelligence. But in many cases like the morning star, they set in the very opening of the day. I have known many such cases. The student,—the youthful preacher, —the active Christian. There is,

(3.) That flower of *purity*, where eminent piety adorns the character; where the graces are continually displayed; where their conversation, spirit, and tempers, all adorn the Christian profession. But for flowers of piety there is no exemption from the ravages of death and the stroke of mortality. We are directed,

3. *To the divine influence by which mortality is produced.*

The clothing of the grass, the decking of the flower, is the work of God, and by his agency it perishes. So it is with human life. Our breath is in his hands; our health and strength come and go at his bidding. He gives power, or produces weakness. He protracts life, or "changes man's countenance, and sendeth him away." With God are the issues of life and death. "The spirit of the Lord bloweth upon it," &c. All resistance to this is puerile and vain. "As the grass he withereth," &c. Observe,

4. *The solemn attention which our frailty demands.*

"The voice said, Cry." People forget this; often live as though they disbelieved it; will not reflect upon it. Hence the lamentation of Moses—"Oh that they were wise," &c. Now this apathy, the foolish banishment of this theme, renders it necessary that we remind mankind that "it is appointed unto men once to die." And this subject claims our serious consideration, our solemn reflection. Let us then turn to the other part of the text,

II. *The immutability of the divine word.*

"But the word," &c. We do not explain this of the word of God in general, so much as of the gospel in particular. For many of the ordinances and feasts of the Jewish dispensation have passed away; but the gospel is destined to abide forever and ever. Now let us look at several things to which this is peculiarly applicable.

1. *The great doctrines of the word of God are immutable.*

All these are essential, infallible truths. Jehovah's greatness, purity, and goodness. The Saviour's divinity, power, and glory. Man's guilt, pollution, and helplessness. Christ's atoning sacrifice, resurrection, and intercession. Faith's vital power in the truth effectually to save and make men free from sin, and holy in heart and life. These, with all the other doctrines of the gospel, abide forever. They are the verities of every age—of the world to the end of time.

2. *The promises of God's word are immutable.*

These, like the divine gifts, are without repentance. They are all yea and amen. The promises to the repenting penitent,—to the humble believer, — to the persevering saint. Not one is erased from the book of God's covenant. As sure to us as to the primitive saints of God. "For the word of the Lord," &c.

3. *The warnings and threatenings of the divine word are immutable.*

These rest on the purity and justice of God; and are, like those attributes, unchangeable. Hence all the denunciations of God's threatened wrath are now equally applicable to persons of the same guilt with those to whom they were first made known. The warnings to the old world are adapted to all inconsiderate persons. The warning to Lot's wife equally applies to the penitent, escaping from the city of destruction, &c. So all the warnings and threatenings endure forever.

4. *The word of God is immortal, as our only guide to a blissful immortality.*

Jesus said, "Search the scriptures," &c. Peter said, "We have a more sure word of prophecy," &c. Paul said, "Let the word of Christ dwell in you richly," &c. It has been the guide of millions, and it has conducted every sincere inquirer to eternal glory. It is yet the one infallible guide to eternal and everlasting bliss. Now this word of the Lord abideth forever. This is marvellous. It might have been lost. It might, humanly speaking, have been destroyed. But it has survived the lapse of *eighteen centuries*, and is not only preserved, but is in the probable way of being circulated to the ends of the earth, and published in every language and tongue of the human race.

APPLICATION.

1. In both departments of the subject we are all individually concerned. All fragile, dying creatures. All hastening to the tomb. Let us not forget this. Improve it, and by repentance and faith in Christ, prepare for it. "Set thine house in order," &c. For our *comfort* we all have this word of the Lord, this gospel of salvation. This remedy for the evils of life, and the darkness of death.

2. Negligence and impenitence will not exempt us from the portion of mortal beings, and the misery of the wicked in a future world.

CCXCVI.—THE SINNER'S DAY.

"And when he was come near he beheld the city, and wept over it, saying, If thou hadst known, even thou, at least in this thy day, the things which belong unto thy peace! but now they are hid from thine eyes."—*Luke* xix. 41, 42.

Of Jesus it was predicted that he should be "a man of sorrows," &c. This was fully borne out in his suffering life. Never were any sorrows like unto his; for never did any heart feel such tender susceptibilities as that of the Saviour. On three occasions did these feelings burst forth into tears. At the grave of Lazarus, when he saw the ravages of death as the curse of human transgression. When he was taking the cup from the hand of his Father, that cup in which was the unmixed anguish due to sin, and which, as our surety and Redeemer, he tasted for every man. Of the affecting scene in Gethsemane the apostle speaks thus : " Who in the days of his flesh, when he had offered up prayer and supplication, with strong crying and tears," Heb. v. 7. What those tears meant, and all that they involved, none will ever know, but he by whom they were shed, and the Eternal Father, on whose hallowed shrine they were presented. The third instance is that of our text, when the Redeemer wept over Jerusalem, and said, " If thou hadst known," &c. We clearly see the force and beauty of the text in reference to Jerusalem. For centuries they had been favored with the immunities and privileges of the people of God. They had the temple, and the priesthood, and the sacrifices. They had the prophets, and holy men, as pastors and teachers. They had the oracles of truth, the promises of mercy, and the ordinances of religion. And, last of all, they had Elijah's antitype, the faithful Baptist, as the herald of the Messiah ; and whose proclamations were followed by the glorious appearance of the Messiah himself. Jesus had taught in their streets, and had filled their country with the fame of his miracles. But, alas ! they hated instruction, they rejected the anointed one of God; and the omniscient Jesus beheld the glory departing from them, and the shadows of a long dark night stretching over them. Hence, when he came near the city, " he wept over it," &c. Forty years after, this destruction came upon it, their nation was taken from them, their city destroyed, and their temple razed and burnt to its foundation. But we desire to give this passage a personal application. Hence we remark,

I. *That the sinner has his day of mercy and hope.*

II. *That this day is accompanied with things which belong to his peace.*

III. *That if these things are not known during the day that is afforded, they will be forever hidden from his eyes.* We notice, then,

I. *That the sinner has his day of mercy and hope.*

This is, generally, the period of human life. We say generally, for sometimes the mind becomes deranged, and reason dethroned, long before death performs its solemn and fatal office. But the life of the sinner is, properly speaking, his day. As such,

1. *It is a period of light.*

Night is the season of darkness. The sinner has a threefold light. The light of nature—the evidences of God's power and wisdom in the works of creation. The light of conscience—the internal impression of his accountability to God. The light of revelation—the light of the glorious gospel of the blessed God. Christ is the sun of the moral world. "I am the light of the world." Now, with the beams of this threefold light we are all favored. Unto us, who sat in the region of the shadow of death, has this blessed and gracious light sprung up. As a day,

2. *It is a period of activity.* "I must work while it is called to-day," &c. With the opening morning man riseth and goeth forth to labor; with the ending day he returns, and retires to rest. So it is in the day of the sinner's life. All that work which relates to the soul and eternity must now be performed. Hence the wise man urges, "Whatsoever thy hand findeth to do," &c.

3. *It is a period exceedingly limited.*

"A day." How swiftly it passes over—how soon it is gone ! The longest day, what is it ? Just so with life. What is your life ? ask the inspired writers. It is a vapor—a thing of naught—an arrow that is swiftly shot to its destination—a cloud that passes away—a flower that fadeth. It is as nothing before God ; so affectingly short that, though the wise man says, "There is a time to be born, and a time to die," he makes no mention of a time to live. But a step from the cradle to the tomb !

4. *The present period is our day.*

The patriarchs and the ancient Jews had their day ; the apostles and early Christians had their day ; our forefathers had their day ; and, now, the present is ours. This, says God to each of us, is "thy day." Let conscience re-echo the solemn truth. With many around me it is far spent. With others of us, if we live to old age, it is half past, and how quickly does the afternoon of life pass away! With the youngest here, let it be remembered and pondered over, that life is one short day, and this is yours.

II. *This day is accompanied with things which belong to the sinner's peace.*

By peace, here, we understand the welfare, the salvation of the sinner. The peace of God is the pledge and earnest of every blessing. Now in this day we have,

1. *The gracious provisions of peace.*

Christ has made peace by his cross, and before us is the cross lifted up. There is no peace for the guilty but through his blood; and this fountain is opened to us, and accessible to the vilest of the vile. Then there is the proclamation of peace in the gospel. The gospel trumpet announces peace. "How beautiful are the feet of them that preach the gospel of peace!" The doors of the Saviour's Church are open, and before him are placed the inviting ordinances of religion.

2. *The invitations and promises of peace belong to this day.*

"To-day, if ye will hear his voice." "Seek the Lord while he may be found," &c. Now he is only near to us in mercy in this life. He can only be found now. Neither mercy nor pardon are offered to the sinful dead, but to those only whose day of probation is not ended.

3. *The means of obtaining peace belong to this day.*

There must be genuine repentance—God commands all men now, everywhere, to repent. There must be earnest prayer—now only can prayer be availing. No throne of grace for the lost—the rich man in hell was refused a drop of water. There must be faith in Christ Jesus—but here only is he preached. Not a messenger of mercy will ever visit the damned. Our mercies and opportunities all relate to this life, and this life is our day in which we have the things which belong to our peace. We notice,

III. *That if these things are not known now, in this our day, they will be forever hidden from our eyes.*

Now observe,

1. *The future state of the sinner is one of night.*

As such, it is a period of darkness. No sun to illuminate—no moon to dispel the darkness—no stars to bespangle the firmament of hell. It is night only—darkness only—the blackness of darkness—thick darkness—mists of darkness: not one ray of light shall ever streak the horizon of the lost. Then men will be anxious for the breaking of the morning—but no morning shall ever cheer their eyes. For observe,

2. *This state of night will be everlasting.*

Of the exclusion from Christ's presence, it is said, "These shall go away into everlasting punishment." It is also said, such shall be "punished with everlasting destruction from the presence of the Lord, and from the glory of his power." "Take these mine enemies, and bind them hand and foot, and cast them into outer darkness," &c.

APPLICATION.

We learn,

1. That the sinner's present state is one of probation and mercy. There is an eternal connection between your present and everlasting state. Whatsoever a man soweth now, then shall he reap. Now God evidences his long-suffering, and patience, and mercy.

2. That God sincerely desires the salvation of souls. "Oh, that thou hadst known," &c. He has solemnly declared it. He has done all he can consistently with his own glory to effect it.

3. That all who lose their souls do so by their own impenitency. "I would have gathered thee, and ye would not." See Prov. i. 24.

4. Let all now attend to the things which belong to their peace; and to these chiefly, heartily, immediately, &c.

———◆———

CCXCVII.—THE TALE OF LIFE.

"We spend our years as a tale that is told."—*Psa.* xc. 9.

It is very probable that this psalm is one of the oldest compositions in the world; it was written by Moses at least three thousand three hundred years ago. It is a psalm in which there is a striking representation of the eternal immutability of Jehovah, ver. 1, 2. With this is given a most affecting representation of the brevity and vanity of human life, ver. 3, and to the text. Numerous are the figures employed by the sacred penman to make this subject striking and affecting. Man is a hireling or servant, who goes to labor in the morning and returns to rest in the evening. His days are as a weaver's shuttle—as a shadow, &c. He cometh forth as the flower, &c. And in the affecting imagery of our text, "We spend our years as a tale that is told." Our text presents two important ideas for our reflection.

I. *Life in its responsibilities.*
II. *Life in its evanescence and vanity.*
I. *Life in its responsibility.*

"Our years." Life is that period which God has given us ; it is ours as an evidence of his goodness and long-suffering. We may look at our years in several respects.

1. *In their design.*

The design of them is, that by their wise improvement we may secure a blessed eternity. Our years are to be spent in reference to the future. We are now to labor for the bread of eternal life. *Now* to build a structure which is to last forever. *Now* to form a character and acquire the prerequisites for an endless state of being. *Now* sin must be blotted out. Regeneration of heart and a title to heaven secured. We waste and pervert our years, if objects inferior to these engross our energies and lives. Consider our years,

2. *As distinguished by many mercies.*

Very varied, indeed, are the circumstances of mankind ; very diversified are those of the same individual. But there is one characteristic which follows us all the days of our life, and that is *mercy.* The mercy of a just and holy God towards us sinners. Mercies which are seen flowing to us in temporal bounties, supplying all the need of our dying bodies. Mercies which regard our health and strength of body, our reason, &c. ; our domestic blessings, &c. Mercies which relate to the means of grace, &c.—to the provisions of holiness—and to all our opportunities of salvation. Our years may be regarded,

3. *As to our responsibility for them.*

We must give an account both of them and for them. They are all recorded in God's book. They will all stand before us in the last day. Not one year, nor even one day will be forgotten. They will be presented to us just as we spent them, whether wisely or foolishly—whether religiously or profanely—whether usefully or as perverted by us. Our years, as the pages of a volume, will be filled up by our actions, words, and thoughts ; and not one incident in our lives,

whether good or bad, left out. Our years then will fix our state and decide our everlasting destiny. How we should value them ; how we should be affected by their removal ; how we should examine and see whether our years are spent so that we shall not be ashamed or terrified when they meet us again at the last day. But let us notice,

II. *Their evanescence and vanity.*

"We spend our years as a tale is told." This part of our text is variously rendered. By some it is thought to mean, as a meditation or rapid thought of the mind ; or, as a word that is quickly spoken ; or, according to the literal reading of the text, as a story or tale that is told. Let us look for the illustration of the text, in a number of persons assembled round the domestic hearth, and when the evening is spent in the telling and hearing of stories or tales. Now we see,

I. *All the variety of tales or stories in the lives of mankind.*

The history of some persons is made up of levities and foolishness, and resemble the idle or ludicrous story. The history of others is associated with mere pleasures, like the story which just amuses. In the lives of others we see link after link of striking incidents, like a highly-wrought and affecting tale. Others seem born for adversity and cradled for sorrow, as the calamitous or tragic tale. But most interesting tales are distinguished for variety of incident ; and are rendered more striking by the light and shade, the prosperous and the adverse, which in succession are presented to the reader. Now this best accords with human life. Like an affecting tale, it is made up of changes and reverses, of joy and grief, of health and sickness, of births and funerals, of the gay and grave. In this, how life resembles the day, bright, cloudy, calm, stormy, &c. Or the ocean, still and serene, or boisterous and tempest-tossed.

2. *Our lives are often spent as idly and vainly as a tale is told.*

The telling and hearing of a mere story is at best but amusing, and is not attended by profit. Just so, to a great extent, with our years. We may not neglect our temporal concerns ; our pecuniary affairs ; indeed, we may be very diligent in these : but is this the end of life ; will this do for us in a dying hour and in the day of judgment ? If we live without self-improvement ; if we live without glorifying God ; if we live without doing good to those around us : in other words, if we are not wiser, and holier, and more useful—then do we spend our years as a tale that is told. All else but these are mere trifles, and so we shall consider them at the last day.

3. *We spend our years as imperceptibly and rapidly as a tale is told.*

An amusing or striking tale beguiles time, and we are often amazed how quickly the hours have flown. Just so is it with life. Let any person look back for any given number of years; the youth upon the last few years; the mature upon twenty years of the past; the aged on the threescore years which they remember—and what is the feeling—the solemn impression? How short, how rapid, how evanescent, one and all would exclaim : " We spend our years as a tale is told." We remember when we were surrounded by the companions of our childhood; the play-fellows of our youth; the friends of our riper years : and we stand amazed at the years we have lived, and exclaim, " We spend our years," &c.

4. *Our years resemble a tale that is told, in the certainty of their termination.*

The tale or story has its finis as well as its beginning. So our years must come to a conclusion. Every year is a chapter in the volume of life; every month is a paragraph, every week a sentence, every day a word, every moment a letter, and the sum and finish of the whole must come. Every thing around us proclaims the certainty of this. Our friends, of whom we have been bereaved; our habiliments of mourning; our funeral processions; our newly-made sepulchres : all remind us that the tale of life will certainly come to an end. And it may be that our lives may only be an episode, or a brief narrative, or a mere fragment; but, however protracted, it must conclude; and that period cannot be far off, " for we spend our years," &c. Let us learn,

1. *To form a true and sober estimate of human life.*

Let us not deceive ourselves in this matter. The scriptures will aid us in these meditations, and they are adapted greatly to improve and profit us.

2. *Let us take a review of the past.*

Have we not spent much of the past idly, vainly, and to no really good end or purpose? For this we should mourn before the Lord, and seek the forgiving mercy of God. But should we not resolve as to the future, and

redeem the time?—not only because the days are evil, but so many have been spent as a tale, &c.

3. *To a wise and satisfactory employment of life, several things are necessary.*

(1.) A good foundation. A saving knowledge of Christ and the power of the gospel. A new heart and right spirit.

(2.) A good rule of action. To regulate our lives by God's holy word. To take this for our guide and directory.

(3.) A diligent spirit in matters of religion. To be ready to every good work. To be fervent in spirit, &c.

(4.) A good end in view. Keeping the approbation of God before our eyes. Looking not at the things which are seen, &c. Let me entreat you to regard these things. Oh, that we all and each might be awakened from a tale-telling mode of existence—that we might give all diligence to make our calling and election sure !

CCXCVIII.—THE SALVATION OF THE CHURCH.*

" O Lord, save thy people."—*Jer.* xxxi. 7.

OUR text is found in the midst of a cluster of precious declarations and gracious promises respecting God's ancient Israel. It is quite clear, in looking over this series of predictions and promises, that their accomplishment has not yet been realized. The whole passage, of which our text is a brief sentence, refers to a glory which yet awaits that interesting, and, originally, devoted people of God.

It is impossible for the Christian to feel indifferent to the best interests of the Jewish nation. Who does not desire that they may be brought to acknowledge Him whom they have despised; to believe in Him whom they have rejected; and to be saved in Him who, to the present period, has been a stumbling-block to them? We ought to desire this for their sakes, and for our sakes; for the interests of the Gentile world are interwoven with their restoration.

In the eleventh chapter of Romans, where the apostle is speaking of the casting off of the Jews and their final restoration, he states, " I would not, brethren, that ye should be

* *Series* xii.—On revivals of religion, &c.

ignorant of this mystery, lest ye should be wise in your own conceits; that blindness in part is happened to Israel, until the fulness of the Gentiles is come in." Therefore on their own account, and because of the happy influences which their restoration shall exert on the rest of mankind, we ought earnestly to supplicate God's gracious throne, that he would "save his people." Such is the natural interpretation of the text; but we have not selected it that we may dwell on the restoration of the Jews to their native land; but rather that we may refer it to the Church of God, and especially to the churches of our times. We wish the text to be considered in its appropriateness to the state of the Church; and that, while we are anxious for the salvation of the world—that transgressors should be turned from unbelief and disobedience—that while we are deeply concerned for the miserable condition of the heathen—while we are devoutly praying that the crescent should wane and the cross be erected in all lands, idolatry perish and Antichrist be overthrown, and the knowledge of the gospel spread from the rivers to the ends of the earth—we should also be deeply solicitous for the welfare of God's people, and that in reference to them we should offer up the prayer of our text. No person doubts the propriety of praying for the conversion of the world: I beg to submit the propriety of a re-conversion of the Church. I believe, better and richer influences would descend upon the world, conversions be more frequent, revivals be more extensive, and that there would be a greater in-gathering into the fold of Christ, if a salvation of a higher, holier, deeper, and more spiritual character, distinguished the Church. I therefore deem the prayer of the prophet as peculiarly appropriate to the churches of Christ at the present time, and I would wish, therefore, that every person present should exclaim with fervor, and with burning and glowing zeal, "O Lord, save thy people!" We inquire,

I. *What does the prayer of the text involve?*

It obviously includes the *idea of peril.* If the Church is in no danger, then the prayer of the text would not be appropriate; but if, on the contrary, she is in the midst of perils, then it is directly and distinctly appropriate, and should be the language of every sincere believer.

The history of the Church is the history of her perils and deliverances. She has always been in circumstances of peril. Her enemies have ever labored to destroy her; and against these, there have been the providence and promises of God. God has been the support and the bulwark of his people. He has been in the midst of his Church to preserve it; to extend its interests, and increase its glory. But the greatest peril of the Church of Christ arises from within. She has been assailed by powerful earthly adversaries; but she is impregnable and invulnerable, so long as she continues faithful to God. Her real danger lies in her own moral weakness and spiritual unfaithfulness. What injured Israel in the wilderness? Not her numerous adversaries, but her sins. Her sins weakened her, and brought upon her the Divine displeasure, causing tens of thousands of that professing Church to perish, whose remains lay scattered in the desert as monuments of God's righteous anger. Her own sins were also her weakness in the times of the Judges and the Kings. The public enemies of the Church have never been really injurious to her interests, for the opposition and persecution of foes have often been blessed to the furtherance of the Divine glory.

The interests of Dissenters, Wesleyan Methodists, and Evangelical Churchmen in this country, have never been more depressed, or more deeply involved in a state of apathy, than at the present time. We inquire, then, is not the prayer of the text singularly appropriate to the Churches of Christ at this crisis? Is it not desirable that our God should interfere for us—that we should be delivered from that sterile condition in which we are placed—that religion should be revived, and our churches increased?

Some persons consider the Church in peril from the spread of Popery and Puseyism; but Popery was never more rampant than at the commencement of the last century, and Popery was what it is now in the time of Wesley and Whitefield, and yet the Church was never more prosperous than it was then. No: the chief perils of the Church are from within, and these should constrain us to pray, "O Lord, save thy people." Allow me to refer to several things fraught with peculiar danger to the Church's best interests, and which are within the Church itself.

1. *The peril of worldly conformity.*

The Church is to be distinct from the world. If we would understand the nature of this distinctness, the Redeemer explains it clearly. He says, his people are not of the world, *even as he is not of the world.* Jesus then is the model of our separation from the world, and he has left us an example that we should follow his steps. And is there not fearful danger arising from attachment to worldly honors and riches—to worldly maxims, luxuries, customs, and conversation? Do you not believe that a grand line of demarcation between the Church of God and the world ought to exist? And if so, how can we expect the Church to be in a healthy condition—how can we expect the divine influences to rest upon it—if we maintain not our adherence to God, and spiritual religion?

2. *The peril of spiritual apathy.*

Are there those spiritual traits of life among professors which ought to distinguish the followers of the Lamb? Is it not clear, that in many instances there is the presence of spiritual death, and the abounding of nominal Christianity, where there was once glowing zeal and devotedness to God? Alas! alas! in many cases it is quite evident, that we have lost our first love. There is lukewarmness and a mere attention to the routine of religious services; but life, pathos, and spirituality are wanting. I ask you, if this condition is not to be deprecated and lamented? Ought we not to mourn over the formality which prevails in our churches? Surely the cause of Jesus and the interests of the cross ought not to sink down into mere formalism and nominalism; and on account of the prevalence of these we should pray, "O Lord, save thy people."

3. *The peril of sordid selfishness.*

Even the apostle, during his time, had to lament, that "all men sought their own, and not the things of Jesus Christ." And is not that exclamation peculiarly applicable to the times in which we live? £53,000,000 are annually laid upon the altar of Bacchus, the idol of Britain; and places of amusement and pleasure are everywhere well supported. Is it not then melancholy to reflect upon the money expended in the pleasures and vanities of this dying world, and the attention bestowed on the expenses of life and family concerns, while the interests of religion are so poorly supported, and that too by men who are ever ready to confess, that they owe to God "their hearts, their souls, their all?" What a niggardly spirit is oftentimes displayed in supporting our great benevolent institutions which are designed to bless the world! While this continues, the Church will always be weak: it is only when she becomes liberal that she shall also become fertile, and beautiful, and prosperous. And remember, when the Jews withheld from God those tithes which he demanded for the support of the interests of his own cause, he said, "Prove me now, and see if I will not open the windows of heaven, and pour out such a blessing that there will not be room enough to receive it." While then it is right to be careful about those things which pertain to the body, and which have respect to our families and friends, it is of the highest moment that we be delivered from a spirit of avarice and selfishness, and neglect not those great concerns which brought the Saviour from his throne to die upon the cross.

4. *The Church is in peril from her sectarian divisions.*

There is in many instances a great amount of activity and zeal manifested by the various branches of the Church; but we must take care to discriminate between that which is mere sectarian zeal, and fire, and that which is pure glowing zeal for the gospel. A man may be a very devoted and zealous friend of the Wesleyan or Baptist connection, and not be a very ardent and spiritual Christian. A man may be deeply concerned for the perpetuity of his own denomination, and yet absolutely indifferent to the world's conversion and the Church's true prosperity. There is plenty of zeal and devotedness to our particular section, just because it is our own, and this principle of sectarian seclusiveness tends greatly to impede the promotion of piety, to provoke the displeasure of God, and to prevent his blessing resting upon us. I am not supposing that we ought not to feel a greater interest in our own churches than in the churches of other denominations—that we ought not to devote our chief energies, and prayers, and contributions to the support of our own body of Christians, respecting whom we have said, "This people shall be my people, and their God shall be my God!" But let us not be influenced by zeal for party, when we should be zealous for the glory of God and the conversion of the world. Believe me, our zeal, however high, our energies however active, our influence, however important and extensive, will not be rightly directed, and will not bear the immediate stamp of the Redeemer's approbation, unless—however ardently attached we may be to our particular churches—we can spread out our arms and open our extended bosoms to embrace with sincere and unfeigned love the whole family of Jesus, and say, "Grace and peace be multiplied to all them that love our Lord Jesus Christ in sincerity and in truth." All true Christians are anxious that a revival of religion should take place, not only in their own connection, but in all the connections of the catholic Church. Who would restrict the blessings of heaven to their own small section? Oh, let us see that we cherish charity, which is the bond of perfectness. The prayer of the Redeemer is peculiarly expressive of the unity of his visible Church. He prays that "his people may be one, even as the Father and He are one." Oh! think of the intimacy, the sweetness, the purity, and the blessedness of that union. And Jesus adds, "that the world may believe that thou hast sent me." As though he had said, "A divided Church will prevent the conversion of the world—will prove a stumbling-block to the world—will prevent consideration and reflection, and shut out conviction. Oh, may my people therefore be one, that the world may be constrained, by the traits of love and affection it shall behold in them, to believe that thou hast sent me."

Never forget, then, that the union of the Church and the conversion of the world hang or fall together; and therefore in reference to the spirit of sectarianism, we may devoutly pray, "O Lord, save thy people." Let us ascertain,

II. *What the text includes.*

1. *A conviction of our perilous state.*

If we are satisfied with the Church's low state;—if we are crying "Peace! Peace!" if we say, "Zion prospers as much as we expect, and almost as much as we can desire!" if we can look upon the Church's sterility without alarm, and entertain the strange fancy that all is well—then the prayer of the text cannot be the prayer of our hearts; for if it be the prayer of our hearts, then it is evident that we do not possess a self-complacent spirit, and that we are not among those who say they are rich and increased in goods and stand in need of nothing. Is it not desirable that we should know the worst of the Church's

condition? Some persons, although they suspect something is wrong in their affairs, will not look the matter fairly in the face till ruin overtakes them. Often when individuals are suffering under the disease of consumption, they will delay applying the proper remedies until suddenly they are surprised by the stroke of mortality. This is not the way we ought to judge of the Church's condition. We should inquire, are our conversations as numerous as they ought to be? Are souls saved in such abundance as God would have them? God is anxious to make the Church as a beautiful and fertile garden, abounding in plants of righteousness to the honor of his name. Our God wants his Church to rejoice, and to increase in the number of those who are saved by the power of his truth; and if her condition were such as God desires, it would be as prosperous as now it is adverse, as fertile as now it is barren, and as glorious and interesting as now it is beclouded and darkened. Let us then have a deep and thorough conviction of this truth; and our prayer will be proportionably earnest and intense, "O Lord, save thy people!"

2. *An earnest longing for the Church's revival and prosperity.*

A wish to know the worst and desire the best. I am inclined to think, a spiritual man would not give utterance to the text in a formal manner. He would not in the public congregation, or at the family altar, or in his closet, utter in feeble and apathetic accents, "O Lord, save thy people." No! he would drink of the well of which the prophet drank, and would utter it with earnest and intense solicitude. Preferring Jerusalem above his chief good, he would not be ashamed to say, "If I forget thee, O Jerusalem, may my right hand forget her cunning." In this spirit, and greatly concerned for the prosperity of the truth, the Christian exclaims, with ardor of soul, "O Lord, save thy people!"

3. *A confident persuasion that God will hear us.*

You remember that astonishing and interesting saying of Jesus to the man who asked that his child might be freed from Satan's agency—"All things are possible to him that believeth." The prayer of our text is of God's own inspiring; it is written by the finger of the Almighty, and though contained within a sentence, is so comprehensive that it includes the highest destinies of the Church and of unnumbered myriads of mankind. Can we present it then without having confidence in God? Has it not an intimate connection with prophecies and promises? And has he spoken, and will he not do it? Has he not predicted the prosperity of his cause, and will he not realize it? Will he disappoint the hopes of those who trust in him? Will he refuse to hear the prayers of his people? Our God, thanks to his eternal name, is a prayer hearing God, and he delights to answer. It is the glory of God to give; it is his glory to bless. He is far readier to give than we are to receive. There is nothing contracted with him, and can you imagine that he is indifferent about the interests of his own glory, the concerns of his Son, and the destinies of millions of those for whom the Redeemer died? Oh, no! Let then this thought of God's willingness to hear and to answer inspire us with confidence to approach his throne, and with the most intense earnestness to exclaim, "O Lord, save thy people."

III. *The grounds on which we should earnestly present this prayer.*

1. *From a deep concern for the glory of Christ.*

Jesus says in reference to his people, "I am glorified in them." "What the Church is, I am; what it endures, I endure—I am glorified in it." But, beloved, is God glorified in a formal church? Is the Redeemer glorified in a selfish and apathetic church? —in a sectarian church? These interrogations answer themselves. The Redeemer cannot be glorified where there are formality, apathy, and selfishness, and where men are more anxious in diffusing their own peculiarities than they are in seeking to diffuse the great evangelical truths of saving religion. Do I then desire the glory of Christ? Do I wish his fame to be celebrated all over the world? Do I wish the Saviour to be exalted above all the gods of the heathen? Do I wish the Redeemer's name to be sung from the rising to the setting of the sun? If so, then must I pray for the prosperity of the Church, by which alone Christ can be glorified. "O Lord, save thy people."

2. *From a deep concern for the well-being of mankind.*

Not only will a low condition of the Church affect itself, but other important interests will suffer. If the Church has lost her spiritual power, she has lost her influence of doing good; and if she loses her influence, what is to become of the myriads who are perishing in the world? If the Church does not enlighten this country, what shall? If the Church does not save this country from Puseyism, Popery, and Infidelity, what shall? What is it can preserve our beloved nation in her elevated position in the scale of nations if the Church sink?—become dispossessed of her spiritual power and celestial purity? That very low state of the Church is then the death and the ruin of thousands of immortal souls. For the sake of our families and friends, for the sake of our rural villages, and for the sake of our densely populated towns where iniquity is awfully prevalent, for the sake of our country and the world at large, may we present this prayer, "O Lord, save thy people."

3. *Our own spiritual prosperity is intimately and inseparably connected with it.*

Our own interests are inseparably connected with those of the Church, our happiness with hers; our prosperity with hers. We have identified ourselves with her, and thus consecrated ourselves, body and soul and spirit, to the service of God. How can we rejoice when Zion languishes? Are not her interests engraven on our hearts? If rich blessings descend upon her shall we not share them? Were our expressions of attachment to her the result of mere enthusiasm? Was it not rather godly sympathy, the influence of divine truth, and therefore came immediately from the throne of God? And are we not anxious for our own souls' prosperity? Are we not desirous of growing in grace? If God arises and shines upon the Church, how will our holiness be increased, and our bliss enlarged! Should we not therefore pray, "O Lord, save thy people?"

IN CONCLUSION.

1. *Let the prayer be the true and fervent breathing of each soul present.*

O Lord, thy people need saving; they are exposed to adverse influences. They are not what thou wouldst have them to be, nor are they so holy as thy grace might make them. O God, save thy people into closer conformity with thy own blessed likeness, that thou mayest see thy face and character in thy people. Oh, save thy people, that they may witness for thee everywhere: that all who look upon them may be interested and say, "Surely God is with them of a truth." Oh, save thy people, that even ungodly men may be constrained like the false prophet of old to say, "Let me die the death of the righteous, and let my last end be like his." "O Lord, save thy people," that they may be a kind of magnet, drawing souls to thee. Oh, save thy people, that thy Church may no longer be a word of reproach and derision to worldly men, but that even they may be compelled to admire her. Oh, save thy people, that they may propagate thy truth, extend thy cause, further thy gospel, until the earth itself shall be full of the knowledge of the glory of God. Oh, may this prayer be the prayer of those who minister in holy things, and of those who hear. May it be our prayer in the house of God—our prayer at the family altar, and our prayer in the closet. May this short sentence, this comprehensive text, this important passage, have a constant place in all our supplications— "O Lord, save thy people."

2. *Let the means be employed corresponding with the prayer offered.*

We need prayer, but we want prayer and exertion together. We want prayer to be associated with holy activity—with burning unquenchable zeal—with self-denial, generosity, and liberality. Let our prayers be identified with these, and then the Church will prosper and religion be revived, and God himself will honor those who honor him.

3. *There may be some persons here who are not yet saved at all;* who are yet in the gall of bitterness and in the bonds of iniquity; who have rejected the counsel of God against themselves; and who have never yet believed to the saving of their souls. To such we say, you may have caught some of the spirit of excitement; you may desire religion to flourish and Zion to prosper, and in this we rejoice. But this should succeed and not precede the conversion of your own souls to God. Give your adherence to the truth, no longer rebel against Christ, throw down your weapons and humbly confess in the language of the poet,

"I yield—I yield, I can hold out no more,
  I sink by dying love compelled,
  And own thee conqueror."

I now leave this subject to your anxious and devout consideration. If we honor God by humble prayer, by believing his word, by seeking his glory—by desiring spiritually and faithfully to live in his service, the win-

dows of heaven will be opened and abundant blessings showered down upon us. May then the text be sealed upon our hearts, may it impregnate our spirits, burn within our bosoms, and be the utterance—the daily, constant utterance, of our souls, "O Lord, save thy people."

———————

CCXCIX.—HOPE FOR THE CHURCH.

"Thou shalt arise and have mercy upon Zion: for the time to favor her, yea the set time is come."—*Psalm* cii. 13.

There is considerable doubt as to the writer of this psalm. Some attribute it to Daniel, others to Nehemiah, others to Ezra. It is generally thought to have respect to the time of the Babylonish captivity; and to express the distress and affliction of the inspired writer on that account. There are those, however, who apply it to the Gospel Church; and the Syriac version entitles it,—" A prophecy concerning the New People," viz.— the Gentiles in the faith. Others apply the psalm to a period still more remote, and refer it to the times in which we live; and suppose the restoration of the Jews to their own land, and the final conversion of that people to Christianity, with the rebuilding of their ancient city, are intended. Zion of old was clearly typical of the Church of Christ, and in that sense we shall apply the subject of the text on the present occasion. Let us then inquire,—

I. *What the text involves.*
II. *What the text affirms.* And
III. *The reasons on which this affirmation is grounded.*

I. *What the text involves.*

The idea involved in the text is the low state of Zion. This is the burden of the psalm; the deep shades of the picture before us. It was evidently this that so oppressed the writer. He was afflicted on Zion's account. Now, Zion, or the Church of God, may

1. *Be numerically low.*

Her friends may be few in number. Elijah thought at one time, that he alone was left of the servants of the true God, but it appeared that 7000 had not bowed the knee to Baal: yet how few were 7000! Even in the nineteenth century of the Christian era, how true is this of Zion.

(1.) Those bearing the Christian name are

few compared with the millions of Pagans, Mohammedans, and Jews.

(2.) Those holding the truth in purity, are few compared with those who adhere to the corrupt forms of Christianity in the Romish, Greek, and other eastern churches.

(3.) Spiritual persons in any church, are evidently few compared with the nominal professors of Christianity. In our villages and towns, how few are entirely consecrated to the cause of Christ.

2. *Zion may be low doctrinally.*

Truth is not only the ornament, but the very atmosphere of life to the children of Zion. Error is the blight, the plague-spot of the church. A century ago, the doctrines of the cross—pure, evangelical truth, were almost exiled from our land. The *Church of the State*, through her thousands of clergy, was giving utterance to dry, lifeless essays on the externals of morality.

The *venerable meeting-houses* of the land, where the holy Nonconformists had preached a crucified Saviour, now echoed forth another gospel, in which Jesus was undeified, and the atoning blood of the cross never preached. Thanks be to God for the revival of evangelical religion through the labors of Wesley, Whitfield, and others. But still, have the great truths of the gospel, even now, the pre-eminence which they ought to have? Have we not just witnessed the attempt to revive a superstitious reverence for rites and ceremonies? Have we not witnessed a desperate effort to elevate the priesthood, and invest it with almost saving power? And where pure doctrines are held and maintained, have they always the ascendency? Is it Christ crucified, first, last, and always? Have not rich sermons of evangelical savor given way to metaphysical essays and rhetorical harangues? Is there that godly simplicity, that heartiness of affection to the glorious gospel which so distinguished the primitive fathers?

3. *Zion may be low spiritually and experimentally.*

There may be both numbers and orthodoxy, and yet spiritual sterility and barrenness. Professed Christians may become mere religious effigies, instead of burning holy witnesses for God. There may be the form without the power—the name without the life. "Lord! Lord!" may be on the lips, and the spirit of experimental piety absent from the heart. I fear this lamentably applies to our day. There is much profes-sion; but elevated, doctrinal religion is evidently rare. What a lack of fervor in prayer! What a lack of zeal, of self-denial,—of generous liberality in the cause of God! What a lack of spiritual activity and enterprise!

4. *Zion or the church may be low influentially.*

The church is to be God's instrument for operating mightily on the world;—the light of the world—the salt of the world—the bulwark of the world—the blessing of the world. Now, is the church of Christ exerting this influence? Is it checking the world's vice and profligacy? Is it holding enormous wickedness in abeyance? Is it restraining the iniquity of the masses? Is it lessening the world's power of evil? Is it decreasing the world's misery? Is it telling decidedly on any great classes in the world? On the youth; on parents; on the poor: on the rich; on rulers; on kings, &c.? Is it gaining on the world — extending Christ's territory—enlarging his kingdom—adding to his followers? Spoiling satan,—robbing hell? Now, what is the answer? Why, the converts in heathen countries bear no comparison to the increase of Pagans by birth. In this country, all Christian denominations together, are not increasing in any thing like the ratio of the population: so that the world and not the church is increasing and flourishing. How distressing and almost overwhelming is this idea! But observe,

II. *What the text affirms.*

"That God shall arise," &c.

(1.) The ability of God to do this is indisputable. Oh yes! he can do it. He can do it easily—at any time, and efficiently.

(2.) God's arising must be an act of mercy. Judgment would overwhelm, yea, ruin the church—blot it out, for its unfaithfulness and apostasies. The church requires mercy, and nothing but mercy can save it. Now, the affirmation of the text may seem well grounded, when you contemplate,

1. *The relationship of God to the church.* It is his. He is the God of Zion; its founder, its keeper, its glory. He is the owner of the vineyard—the father of the family. It is graven on his hands—dwells in his heart—the object of his incessant and intense love.

2. *The engagements he has made in reference to it.*

Look at the predicted engagements. One roll of prophecy after another—one splendid promise after another—one rapturous vision and scene after another, &c., all yea and amen. Not one can fail. He is a promise-keeping God. But there is also the engagement made with his own Son, and ratified with the blood of the cross. Isaiah liii. 10, &c., Philippians ii. 6, &c.

3. *His past providential interpositions on behalf of his church.*

He heard the groanings, &c., in Egypt. He wrought a series of magnificent miracles in the wilderness. He rebuked kings, &c. He raised up Cyrus, &c. He has in no instance forsaken it. He preserved it amid the valleys and the mountains of the Waldenses. He raised up Luther and Wyckliffe, &c. He gave the power and the unction to the Puritans. To the founders of Methodism, &c. And all this may cause us to hope, &c. But observe in the text,

III. *The reasons on which the affirmation is grounded.*

One of these relates to the church, and the other to God.

1. *The divine mercy.*

He will arise, &c. The purposing of a church originated in mercy—the redeeming, calling, the preserving, &c. The temple of the church is a temple of mercy—inexhaustible, everlasting. He delights in it. He will surely have mercy, &c. The other reason is found,

2. *In the church itself.*

"Thy servants take pleasure," &c. Now this has ever been the case in the worst times of apostasy. Look at Nehemiah, David, Jeremiah. There are some now in the church who do so, who can exclaim, "If we forget," &c. "Lord, we have loved," &c. "One thing," &c., who daily pray—"Peace be within thy walls," &c. "For our brethren and companions' sake," &c. Now, these live, and pray, and toil for this object: and if ten righteous men would have saved Sodom, rely upon it, the presence of the pious and spiritual shall save the church. God will honor them—their prayers shall prevail; for "the effectual, fervent prayer," &c. "The Lord shall arise," &c. Finally, we are referred to,

3. *" The set time."*

The set time must come. Not for us to know the times and seasons: but to wait in prayer, in the spirit of humiliation and self-denial.

APPLICATION.

1. *How deeply concerned should all the followers of Christ be on this subject.*

For our several churches, and for the universal church of the Redeemer.

2. *Do we exemplify the character in the text?*

Have we a burning love to the cause of Jesus? Do we adorn it by our exemplary lives? Do we pray for it—labor for it, and support it? Do we cheerfully give our substance? How happy such are, &c.

3. *Where this spirit exists there will be joy and delight in the erection of places of worship, &c.*

There will be a desire for the multiplication of Christian sanctuaries. The future history of this building, who can tell? May it be the birth-place of hundreds! May it be the spiritual residence of a flourishing family for Christ! May it be the depository of divine truth! May it be the house of God! &c.

CCC.—CHRISTIAN CATHOLICITY.

"Grace be with all them that love our Lord Jesus Christ in sincerity. Amen."—*Eph.* vi. 24.

THE human mind is prone to extremes. Hence we see men running into superstition on the one hand, or formality on the other; rising to a sort of fanatical enthusiasm, or sinking into indifferent listlessness. So also in reference to our estimate of other Christians, either there is cherished a spirit of exclusive bigotry and intolerance, or a spirit of extravagant liberalism, and indifference to the essentials of divine truth. Now surely there is a happy medium to be found between these wide extremes—a medium wherein truth will not be compromised nor love destroyed. A reference to the infallible truths of revelation will lead us into this radiant path of purity and peace. Our text is an epitome of it. "Grace," &c. Observe,

I. *The characters specified.*

And,

II. *The affectionate prayer expressed.*

I. *The characters specified.*

They are not described by any peculiar distinction—by any creed which they held —by any form of worship they adopted—by any locality in which they dwelt; but by their uncorrupted love to the Lord Jesus Christ. Here are three things,

1. *The object of their love.*

"The Lord Jesus Christ." This description of the Saviour gives a full view of his excellences and glory. He is,

(1.) Lord. Said to be "Lord of all." Possessed of all possible power, authority, and glory. Lord of angels—Lord of all worlds. Hence the address of the Father, "Thy throne, O God, is forever," &c.

(2.) Jesus. This signifies "Saviour," and it was given to him on account of his mission and work. "They shall call his name," &c. Hence the appropriateness of this name —its sweetness—its saving power.

(3.) Christ. Signifies "Anointed." The anointed Saviour. The Christ predicted, promised, expected, at length revealed; dedicated to God at his baptism by the Holy Ghost; attested by Jehovah as his Son, for whom he demanded the reverential attention of mankind. "This is," &c. "Hear," &c.

2. *The nature of their love.*

"Love our Lord Jesus Christ in sincerity." Here is the affection and the kind of affection. Now, love to Christ,

(1.) Is always the result of faith in his love to us. We never love him till we know, and believe, and feel his love to us. His love kindles ours; is its reason and cause. "We love," &c. "The love of Christ constraineth us," &c.

(2.) Love to Christ is always an evident emotion. We easily see the affection of the mother,—of the friend, &c. Love to Christ delights in him, rejoices in him, extols him, obeys him, converses with and of him. Observe, this love,

(3.) Is sincere. It may be rendered "uncorrupted,"—without alloy. It means real, in opposition to pretended love—intense, in opposition to languid—constant, in opposition to vacillating—a love of Christ which is supreme; greater than any other,—higher, more powerful, &c., a love which trials do not quench; which is not deteriorated by intercourse with the world; which glows and burns in the soul; which fills with holy jealousy for his glory; which assimilates to Christ's likeness; which delights in union and communion with him. This is loving Christ in sincerity. Alas! how many love in mere word, in pretence, in profession, &c. Observe,

3. *The extent of the prayer in reference to the characters specified.*

"All them." Now, this is true New Testament catholicity. How different to the catholicity of Rome! The Romish church breathes peace and good-will only to all Romanists; and by the Catholic church they mean all Roman Catholics in the world, and exclude and anathematize all else. What hypocrisy and delusion! Now, New Testament catholicity extends to the true disciples of Jesus everywhere. "All them." It does not say, "Prosperity to all their notions and opinions—to all their forms and ceremonies;" but "Grace to the persons who love," &c. Corrupt as the Romish church is, there are, doubtless, many Christians within her pale, &c. So in every form and section of the Church of Christ; and the text includes each and every one of these dwelling upon the face of the earth.

II. *The affectionate prayer expressed.*

"Grace," &c. It does not mean that they may become the subjects of grace, for all who love, &c., are so. But it signifies, that grace may be supplied. All the grace they require. For all seasons and circumstances. In all its variety. In all its plenitude. Now observe here,

1. *All the saints of the Lord Jesus require this grace.*

None independent of it. None can be happy, or safe, or useful without it.

2. *This grace is provided for all the disciples of Jesus.*

It is common stock. "Out of his fulness have we all," &c. It is for all the family; no exclusiveness with the Redeemer.

3. *We should seek sincerely in prayer that all may possess it.*

And that for the following reasons:

(1.) All who love, &c., are loved of God and chosen of him.

(2.) They are all our brethren and sisters in Christ.

(3.) We are in circumstances of common need and dependence. We require their prayers for grace, &c. All saints are exposed to common perils, &c.

(4.) We have all one Spirit. All who love the Lord Jesus Christ have his Spirit.

(5.) We are destined to one common inheritance. There will be no sectarian niches above: Romanists, *i. e.*, those who are pious, will not have one; nor church people; nor Wesleyans; nor Independents; nor Baptists. One grand temple; one commingling multitude; one united service; one affectionate congregation; all extolling divine love—all reflecting it—all filled with it —all adding to it. One region of perfect happy love, with the grandeur and impress of eternity upon it. "Grace be with all them," &c.

APPLICATION.

1. *We see the true nature of apostolical Christianity.*

A religion of love.

2. *We perceive the unhappy influences of sectarianism.*

The divisions—the strifes; coldness, persecutions, &c. This is one stumbling-block to the conversion of the world. Let us abhor it—avoid it—return to the primitive spirit, &c.

3. *The text does not annihilate essential distinctions.*

It includes only the uncorrupted, &c. Men may pretend to love—men may loudly profess; but is it borne out? Is it in sincerity? &c. &c.

CCCI.—CHRISTIAN CATHOLICITY.

II.

"Truth and love."—2 *John* 3.

EACH of these is an essential principle of true religion. There cannot be acceptable worship when either is wanted. There is no substitute for either. It is desirable that they should be found working harmoniously together. Where they both exist, and are cherished, spiritual health and prosperity must be the blessed result. Let us just notice briefly the definition we should give to these when considering them in their utmost religious latitude and extent. *Truth* in the ordinary sense of the term signifies *veracity;* but it also includes fidelity, sincerity, and correctness. Veracity in opposition to falsehood; fidelity in opposition to inconstancy; sincerity in opposition to deceit; and correctness in opposition to error. *Love* includes affection, goodness, mercy, and kindness. Now in this extensive sense shall we consider the words of the text. We remark,

I. *We see these strikingly exhibited in the divine character.*

They are both leading characters in the Godhead. Both stand prominently out; and in both is the godly man deeply concerned and interested. God is truth. God

is love. David says of Jehovah, that all his ways are truth. "Just and true are thy ways, O thou king of saints." "He is a God of truth, without iniquity; just and righteous is he." "All his works are truth, and his ways judgment." Truth is the basis of the divine throne. Truth is the girdle of all the divine perfections. Truth is the honor of the divine nature, the glory of the divine government, and the very essence of the divine law. We could have no esteem for, or confidence in, Jehovah, unless his ways and works were true and righteous altogether. But truth might subsist with stern severity or inexorable wrath. It might be associated with the awful and terrific only. But in Jehovah it is in glorious harmony with *love.* God is love. His essential nature is goodness. "Oh, taste and see that the Lord is good." The whole earth is full of his goodness. Goodness or love is the glory of all the attributes. Moses prayed, "I beseech thee show me thy glory;" and he said, "I will make all my goodness," &c. Now the love of God is represented in scripture as encompassing the world in the provisions of redemption. "God so loved the world," &c. But this love is exercised only in all its tender and complacent exercises on holy beings. It is the saint's peculiar prerogative; the believer's present bliss, and the foretaste of his future heaven. The Lord loveth the righteous, &c. His love is shed abroad in our hearts, &c. In this the people of God dwell: "He that dwelleth in God," &c. As a God of truth we reverence, adore, and trust in him. As a God of love we delight in him, and love him. "We love him because he first loved us." Both truth and love were,

II. *Eminently displayed in the economy of human redemption.*

God had a two-fold design in the redemption of our world. The first was to vindicate his truth and to magnify his righteousness. The other, to exhibit his love, and exercise his mercy. In the holy life and sacrificial death of Christ, the truth of Jehovah was rendered especially illustrious. He magnified the law and made it honorable. He ratified both the threatening and the promise. In his death the penalty was extorted, and yet in that death by the woman's seed was the serpent bruised. Redemption is full of truth. Truth as well as grace came by Jesus Christ. But how gloriously did the love of God appear. "Herein is love,"

&c. A love which provided so great a gift, and made such an amazing sacrifice. Redemption seems to exhaust the merciful resources of God's infinite love. It will be the song of the redeemed forever and ever. Even then it will never be fully told.

"Angels, assist our mighty joys,
    Strike all your harps of gold;
But when you raise your highest notes,
    His love can ne'er be told."

Both truth and love were,

III. *Fully embodied in the life and mission of Jesus.*

He said, "I am the truth." He was the reality of the types and shadows,—the end of all the sacrifices, &c. He was the preacher of truth. He came to proclaim truth in all its fulness and purity. He was the prince of truth. His lips poured forth streams of celestial truth. Then he lived the truth. He was the model of perfect truth. He was holy, harmless, &c. No guile was ever found in his mouth. But see also *Jesus* as *incarnate love.* Love moved him to the great work. Love brought him from heaven. Love distinguished all his acts. Love beamed in his eyes; spake in all his discourses; ministered in his hand; caused him to traverse Judea, &c., on journeys of beneficence. "He went about doing good." His miracles were all miracles of love. His sorrows, sufferings, and death, were all the effects of his love to us. But truth and love were always seen in harmony. He never sacrificed either. He ever exhibited the majesty of truth, and the tenderness of love.

IV. *Both truth and love are essential to the existence of true religion.*

(1.) We become religious by a saving knowledge of the truth. (2.) We walk in truth. (3.) Love the truth. (4.) Obey the truth. (5.) We must have our loins girt about with truth. (6.) Witness for the truth. (7.) Worship God in truth. (8.) Labor to diffuse the truth. Now these points show us the essentiality of truth to the existence of vital religion. Ignorance, insincerity, and unfaithfulness are the marks of the children of the devil; but the disciples of Jesus are of the truth. "They are the true circumcision who worship God in the spirit," &c. But *love* is equally essential to the Christian character. He that dwells in God dwells in love. Love is our best evidence of real piety. "Whoso loveth is born of God." Now the love of the Christian is the love of holiness to a holy being, —the supreme love of God,—the ardent love of Jesus Christ,—the sincere love of the believer. (1.) This is to be the *spirit* of the Christian. (2.) The *conversation* of the Christian—speaking in love. And (3.) The *perfection* of the Christian—to dwell in perfect love. (4.) The *badge* of the Christian—"By this shall all men know," &c. (5.) The *watchword* of the Christian. "Little children, love one another." But truth and love are to be maintained in harmony. Truth dignifies and hallows love; and love sweetens and sanctifies truth. *Truth and love* are to resemble the beams of the sun; bright and warm; not like the lava of the volcano, hot and destructive. Truth must irradiate the mind, and love influence the heart. One is the perfection of holiness, and the other the essence of goodness. Now the influence of these on the Christian character deserves our attention. *Truth* will be seen in our sincerity; in our fidelity to God and one another; in our exactness of speech; in the ingenuousness of our demeanor; in the candid guileless movements of the life. Love will be seen in the cultivation of goodness, and beneficence, and mercy, and kindness. Love will destroy selfishness of heart. Love will soften, and fill us with gentleness. Love will keep up the sympathies of our best feelings, and the ardor of our finest sensibilities. Love seems to affect all the senses of the body. It gives the ear acuteness, the eye sensible tenderness, the hand gentle softness, and the heart a glowing goodness.

V. *Truth and love are perfected in the spirits of the glorified.*

Heaven is the region of truth and love. There is the throne which rests on eternal invincible truth, and there is the sceptre of grace and love. Just so it is with the inhabitants. Perhaps no mere human being ever possessed pure truth without any mixture of darkness or error; or *pure love,* without any dross of selfish alloy. But the saints in heaven are all as *crystal,* clear, transparent, bright, reflecting the purity of God. And there too, are they as *seraphim,* flames of holy, disinterested love. There are the perfections of holiness and fulness of bliss. Nothing else is necessary to the high honor and felicity of intellectual beings.

APPLICATION.

Now let *us apply this subject.*

1. *Are we under the influence of both?*

Do we know the truth, and love it, and live it? Are we the subjects of spiritual love? Love to God, and to our fellow-men, &c.

2. *Let these be cherished.*

They are associated with our real welfare, prosperity, and usefulness.

3. *Let us labor to diffuse them.*

O Lord, send out thy light and thy truth.

4. Earth will resemble heaven when they become universal.

CCCII.—SINLESSNESS,—SELF-DECEPTION.*

"If we say we have no sin, we deceive ourselves, and the truth is not in us."—1 *John* i. 8.

SIN is the transgression of the law. To constitute sin there must therefore be a law, —a law with which we may be acquainted, and that, with the knowledge of its requirements, we wilfully violate its enactments. Now, with sin all men are chargeable. God has pronounced the whole world guilty, "There is none righteous, no, not one." To know and feel this is one important step towards salvation. A knowledge of the disease of our hearts is nearly half the cure. Ignorance or unbelief of this must necessarily preclude the possibility of cure. On this the text is explicit, "If we say that we have no sin," &c. Now, the text is not only true of unregenerated persons, but even of the children of God. For in these the body of sin is mortified, but not exterminated; and there is a severe conflict between the flesh and the spirit,—between the remains of the carnal mind and the new man. We lay down two propositions :

I. *All men are chargeable with sin.*

II. *A denial of this is manifest self-deception.*

I. *We are all chargeable with sin.*

"If we say," &c.

1. *We have all sinned against God.*

Against his holy laws; against his government; against his goodness, mercy, and long-suffering.

2. *Our sins have been both of commission and omission.*

* Miscellaneous.

Omitted to perform divinely instituted duties. Take one case, "Thou shalt love the Lord thy God with all thy heart," &c. Who is not guilty? Committed positive transgression. Take the first commandment, or the second, or the last. Have we not served other Lords? Have we not taken his name in vain? Have we never been guilty of covetousness?

3. *We have all sinned against our fellow-men.*

"Thou shalt love thy neighbor as thyself." As parents, and children ; servants, and masters. Against the law of goodness and mercy to all men. Who has not transgressed?

4. *We have all sinned against our own souls.*

Have we improved our faculties, attended to self-cultivation, self-government, &c.? Have not our sins withholden good things from us?

5. *We have all sinned, both in thought, expression, and practice.*

Remember your imaginations, your desires, your resolvings; and then say, has not your heart sinned? Remember your conversation,—what has been the fruit of your lips? Your communications, have they not been vain, and foolish, and often extremely wicked? Remember your lives,—review all your conduct, and see if it has been wise and upright, holy and good.

6. *We have all sinned in numberless instances.*

I mean, beyond our computation. Count the drops of the dew,—count the falling leaves of autumn, or the stars of heaven.

7. *Our sins have justly exposed us to God's displeasure.*

"The soul that sinneth shall die." Every sin is against his purity, his authority, his government, his throne. Every sin gives power to Satan, and upholds the kingdom of darkness.

8. *Our sins must be forgiven or punished.*

God will not be, cannot be, indifferent. The divine veracity and holiness demand it. To each one, then, this is a matter of the deepest moment,—of eternal consequence.

II. *A denial of our sinfulness is manifest self-deception.*

"If we say we have no sin, we deceive," &c.

1. *Some deny their sinfulness by excluding the existence or government of God from the world.*

Some men reject the first great truth of religion, and say there is no God. Others say, that he takes no concern in human actions; and, therefore, that our conduct only affects our circumstances in this life. Need I attempt to show the wickedness and infatuation of such reasoning? Do not your consciences speak, and rebuke such infidelity and madness? Have you not an internal impression that you are responsible to the Great Being who made you, and whose power and glory is displayed through all the works of nature around us? The effects of those views were fearfully felt in France.

2. *Others deny their sinfulness by contrasting themselves with the more debased of mankind around them.*

Hence they refer to some of the monsters of cruelty, or to some of those abandoned to viciousness. They have not moved in the pre-eminent rank of transgressors; and, withal, they may be considered respectable members of society. Now, all this may be true; but this does not meet the claims of Deity, the demands of Jehovah. It is true there are degrees of guilt, but because men are not thousand pence debtors, it does not prove that they are not hundred, or fifty pence debtors. Instead of contrasting ourselves with the worst, let us compare ourselves with the best and holiest. Do we walk with God as Enoch did? Fear and obey him with Noah; honor and trust in him as Abraham did; love and delight in him as David; or with Paul count all things but loss for the excellency of the knowledge of Christ Jesus the Lord?

3. *Some again deny their sinfulness by evincing a self-righteous spirit.*

They have exalted views of their own goodness. Full of self-love and complacency, they rejoice in their own superiority over the rest of mankind. "I fast twice in the week, I pay tithes," &c. "I thank thee I am no extortioner," &c. With these the external is every thing. Religious show and parade, a name for sanctity. How ignorant they must be of their own hearts; what strangers to the extensive purity of God's law. Many, we notice,

4. *Deny their sinfulness through a persuasion that they have attained absolute perfection.*

That we are called and exhorted to perfection, is clear from the divine word. But the attainment of this is never given in the history of even the most illustrious saints. Look at Job; and yet in his generation he was a perfect man. Let us look at the great apostle of the Gentiles, Phil. iii. 12. There may and ought to be sincerity and decision; and it is desirable to aim at elevated holiness; "but if we say we have no sin, we deceive ourselves." We fear that those who lay claim to entire perfection are peculiarly deficient in one of the most essential graces, viz., humility, and are not really and spiritually in the most prosperous and safe condition. Oh, let us beware of pride, especially that which has to do with religion. Let us rather be clothed with humility, knowing that "all who exalt themselves," &c.

APPLICATION.

1. Aim at a true knowledge of your state. Prove yourselves, &c.

2. Having obtained it, be abased. What need of daily contrition and prayer before God. Seek the sanctifying influences of the Spirit. "Grow in grace," &c.

3. For all sin, and every sinner, there is salvation. Contemplate the latter part of the text.

CCCIII.—CONFESSION AND PARDON.

"If we confess our sins, he is faithful and just to forgive us our sins, and to cleanse us from all unrighteousness."—1 *John* i. 9.

THE preceding verse affirms the positive sinfulness of the best of men, and the danger of self-deception, from a supposition of our perfect holiness. To these topics we have called your attention already. Our present subject leads us to the remedy and means by which our sins may be forgiven, and by which our souls may be cleansed from iniquity. The eighth verse should check presumption,—our text prevent despair. It is a truth that all are guilty; but it is also a truth that all may be forgiven. Our text leads to the consideration of confession and pardon, and the grounds of certainty that the one shall follow the other. Notice, then,

I. *The confession required.*

"If we confess," &c. Now confession is something more than mere admission, more than a repetition of a form of words. Scriptural confession implies,

1. *A conscious knowledge of our sins.*

And this supposes that we know what God has legislated; for by the knowledge of the law and word of God comes a conviction of sin. We cannot confess that of which we are unconscious and ignorant. It is a great mercy to know our real state before God. Many say they are rich, &c.; while God sees them as poor, and blind, and wretched.

2. *This confession must be associated with sincere sorrow and contrition for sin.*

"I will declare my iniquity, I will be sorry for my sin," Psalm xxxviii. 18; see, also, Joel ii. 12; and 2 Cor. vii. 10. "The sacrifices of God are a broken spirit; a broken and contrite heart," &c., Psalm li. 17. Confession must be united,

3. *With fervent supplication.*

"Whosoever calleth upon the name of the Lord," &c. Sin known and felt. Sin producing sorrow and contrition must excite to prayer. Thus David, Psalm li. 1, 3, 7. The publican, "God be merciful," &c. Thus the dying thief, "Lord, remember me," &c. Confession must be connected,

4. *With faith in Jesus Christ.*

"With the heart," &c. A knowledge of sin leads to consideration; consideration to conviction; conviction to contrition; and contrition places the soul in the dust;—then the cry is, Lord, help me, Lord, save me, &c. Christ is then presented in the gospel as "the way, the truth, and the life;" as the great sacrifice, &c. Faith exercised in him brings peace and joy into the soul. True scriptural confession is followed,

5. *By newness of life.*

Now the conversation becometh the gospel; now they walk after the Spirit; walk in Christ; delight in his statutes and ordinances to do them. Sin is loathed, abhorred, forsaken. The wicked forsake their way and the unrighteous man his thoughts, &c. There are two points often overlooked. God often requires confession to our fellowmen, and as far as possible restitution or reparation, Matt. v. 23, &c. Thus God treated with Job's friends, xlii. 8. As to restitution, see Ezekiel xxxiii. 15. Zaccheus thus acted, &c., Luke xix. 8. Notice,

II. *The blessings promised.*

"To forgive," &c. Right confession insures, according to the spirit of the text,

1. *Pardon.*

To forgive us our sins. Now it will be clear that this forgiveness will be,

(1.) A *gracious* act. As confession of a crime can never entitle a culprit to mercy. God pardons for his name's sake; for his mercy's sake: but especially in respect of the sacrifice and merits of his Son, Jesus Christ.

(2.) A *full* and *free* act. He pardons readily, freely; without restriction as to the number or aggravations of guilt. He abundantly pardons. "Though your sins be as scarlet," &c. It is likened to the blotting out of a cloud; or, the casting a stone into the depths of the sea. He remembers their iniquities no more.

(3.) It is a *present* act. When confession is made he does not defer or postpone; he waits to forgive. Time present is with God the time in which he delights to exercise his clemency and love. To-day, if ye will hear and confess, he will say, "Thy sins which are many are all forgiven," &c. He will enable you to sing, "I will praise thee, for though thou wast angry," &c. The other blessing promised, is,

2. *Sanctification.*

"And to cleanse us from all unrighteousness." A change of our nature is as essential as a change in our state. This formed one of the chief Old Testament promises, Ezekiel xxxvi. 25–28, "Then will I sprinkle clean water upon you, and ye shall be clean: from all your filthiness and from all your idols will I cleanse you. A new heart also will I give you, and a new spirit will I put within you; and I will take away the stony heart out of your flesh, and I will give you a heart of flesh. And I will put my spirit within you, and cause you to walk in my statutes, and ye shall keep my judgments and do them. And ye shall dwell in the land that I gave to your fathers, and ye shall be my people and I will be your God." This was the great end of Christ's death, for he "gave himself for us, that he might redeem us from all iniquity, and purify," &c., Titus ii. 11. Now this renewal is alike essential to our happiness and salvation. "There is now, therefore, no condemnation," &c. "If any man be in Christ he is a new creature," &c., Titus iii. 5–7. Observe,

III. *The certainty that these blessings shall follow confession.*

Two words in the text fully guarantee this.

1. *God's fidelity.*

"He is faithful." God has engaged to

do so. His promises are full and explicit. Some of these are made to Christ, and others to the sinner. God cannot lie; besides, he has sworn it, Heb. vi. 16, &c.

2. *God's justice.*

"And just." God can forgive sin justly. With Christ, and the satisfaction Christ has yielded, the sinner can be justly forgiven, and every sinner's pardon is as just as it is merciful. Just to the Mediator and merciful to the sinner, Rom. iii. 24, &c.

APPLICATION.

1. Urge immediate evangelical confession on every sinner in God's presence.

2. Call upon Christians to bless and magnify the grace of God.

3. Remind the impenitent of the awful consequences of sin in the eternal world.

CCCIV.—THE MISERY OF A SINFUL STATE.

PREACHED ON THE EXECUTION OF A MURDERER.

"The way of transgressors is hard."—*Prov.* xiii. 15.

ONE of the most common figures of speech employed in the Bible is to exhibit the course of a man's life under the similitude of a way. Here we read of the way of wisdom, and the way of folly; the way of life, and the way of death; the way of shame, and the way of honor; the way of holiness which leads to heaven, and the way of darkness which leads to hell. Jesus, the Great Teacher, adopts the same metaphor, "Enter ye in at the strait gate; for wide is the gate and broad is the way," &c., Matt. vii. 15. Now, in these two ways the whole of mankind are travelling. Only two classes before God where there is a real distinction. The righteous and the wicked; the sinner and the saint; the Christian journeying heavenward, and the transgressor urging his course to ruin and death. Our subject relates to "the way of the transgressor," &c. Let us then,

I. *Define the character.*

"The transgressor."

It is clear that all who violate the law of God, and break the divine commandments, are included in this term. If so, then the text involves all men who are in their natural and unconverted state. "All have sinned," &c. But the grades of guilt are almost endless.

1. *There are those who may be denominated impious transgressors.*

Who deny God's being, reject revelation, and deride all religion. Who give themselves up to unbelief, &c. It is awful to see the daring and effrontery of these.

2. *There are those who are abandoned and open transgressors.*

Men who give themselves up to work wickedness; who drink it in, &c.; who glory in their shame; who are champions of vice; sit in the seat of the scorner; who mock at sin; reckless and daringly vile.

3. *There are those who are the victims of particular vices.*

(1.) The *swearer,* who wantonly profanes God's name, and presumptuously prays for vengeance on himself and those around him.

(2.) The *victims of lust,* who mind only earthly things.

(3.) The *eager worldling,* who cares not how he gets riches, so that he may get them. Who makes gold his confidence, and fine gold his god.

(4.) The *slave of intemperance,* who drowns his reflection, dethrones his reason, and ruins his health and soul in the intoxicating cup.

4. *All those who disobey the gospel, and neglect the great salvation.*

"How shall we escape," &c. What shall the end be of those who obey not the gospel; who refuse to believe in the mercy and love of God, and neglect their best and eternal concerns? To which of these classes do you belong? In one or the other you are, each and all, who do not love Christ and serve him, included. Having defined the character,

II. *Let us describe the way.*

"The way of transgressors is hard."

1. *This way is broad, and adapted to the desires of the corrupt mind.*

It is a downward path, and therefore can be traversed without great effort. It is a flowing stream; and the person who ventures on it is readily borne onwards. Our own evil hearts love it: it suits our carnal desires.

2. *It is a way of infatuated delusion.*

Its own victims tell us it is the way of pleasure,—of enjoyment,—of life; but of what kind? Its flowers are those of sickness; its fruit like the apples of Sodom, &c.; its enjoyments those of delirium; its salutations are deceit, and its caresses the embraces of death; its festivals, like those of Belshazzar; its songs and mirth, like those of a carnival, where the soul of the sinner is the victim sacrificed to the god of this world—the price of hell.

3. *It is a way which is thickly peopled with immortal beings.*

The crowd is in it. The majority—the majority of all classes. Of the rich, and of the poor. Of the young, and of the old. Of the learned, and of the illiterate. In this way it is that they strengthen each other's hands, and keep each other in countenance. It is truly an awful consideration. Go into any kingdom, or neighborhood, or rank of life, or profession, or trade, or circle, and the majority are in this way.

4. *Yet it is a way manifestly evil.*

Not the right way,—not the way of peace. Ask the consciences of its travellers, and they will tell you, they feel they are sinners. Many do not attempt to deny it. Where the gospel shines it exposes it as the way of death. Wherever there is a church, or chapel, it is a silent beacon. Every Christian who acts and walks differently shows that the other is the way of evil and ruin. Let us then,

III. *Establish the affirmation.*

" The way of transgressors is hard."

1. *It often produces bitter adversity.*

Most of the temporal suffering is the result of transgression. Vice, idleness, and improvidence, are generally united. Many have expended their whole substance in support of vice. Large estates have been wasted; bright prospects blighted; nakedness and starvation are often the direct results of sin. Indeed, the way of transgressors is hard.

2. *It often involves its victims in utter disgrace.*

Some vices may be passed over by the mass, but there are others at which even the vile profess disgust. How many has transgression chased out of respectable society! How many have fled across seas, or retired into obscurity, on account of the loathsomeness of their character and reputation!

3. *It often tends to extreme suffering and anguish.*

Go to the *gloomy prison,* and see the toiling criminal shut out from society, &c. Go

to the *penal settlements,* and see men exiled for life in degraded raiment and clanking chains. Go to the *hospital,* and see how many are groaning with pain and disease immediately brought on by iniquity. Go to *asylums for the insane,* and remember by far the greater number of maniacs have prostituted their reason to sin. Is not the way of transgressors, then, hard?

4. *It often leads to premature and awful deaths.*

The wicked do not live out half their days. The impious Pharaoh,—the covetous Achan,—the suicide Saul,—the slain Belshazzar,—the traitor Judas,—the lying Ananias and Sapphira. But need we refer to ancient times? Go to the daily records of our own times and city. Our river, our canals, our coroner's inquests, our ignominious brutal executions, all establish the text, &c.

5. *It plunges its victims into eternal sorrows.*

The wages of sin is death—eternal death. The wicked shall be turned into hell, &c. All the sufferings of this world are just as a drop to the ocean of divine wrath in the world to come.

APPLICATION.

1. View the way of transgressors with deep alarm and solemn dread. Let the sinner stand and pause before he advances another step.

2. Let the alarmed and convicted flee instantly from it. Escape for your life, and fly to the hope set before you in the gospel.

3. Let the believer travel in the royal highway of holiness, with joy and gladness, until he reaches the heavenly Zion, where sin and sorrow shall forever be unknown.

CCCV.—FAITH AND ITS PREREQUISITES.

" Therefore, whether it were I or they, so we preach, and so ye believed."—1 *Cor.* xv. 11.

In this chapter the apostle gives us a full and clear account of the gospel which he preached. He also states the saving character of this gospel to believers, ver. 2, &c. He relates the evidences of the resurrection of Christ, from ver. 5 to 7. He then refers to his own vision of the Redeemer, ver. 8. Afterwards he speaks of his own unworthiness, and the triumphs of divine grace to him and in him, ver. 10. He modestly refers to his abundant labors in the gospel, and its success, &c., see the text. Now the text evidently refers to saving faith, and the way in which it was produced. This agrees exactly with Rom. x. 17, "So faith cometh by hearing," &c. Let us then notice,

I. *The things which are essentially requisite to faith.*

1. *There must be a testimony or declaration.* There must be something to be believed. Now this testimony is the gospel of Jesus Christ. This record of God concerning his Son. This record presents to us God's Son in *human flesh*, as the mediator between God and man. Thus the apostles called upon men to believe in the Lord Jesus Christ. Here the titles refer to his divinity,—to his work; and to his being anointed for its execution. God's testimony also exhibits the death of Jesus as a sacrifice for sin. That he is the Lamb of God, &c.; that he died, &c.; that he bare our sins, &c. And thus that all who come to God by Christ, shall not perish, &c. This, then, briefly is the testimony, and which is the first great essential requisite to faith.

2. *This testimony must be published and made known.* Men must hear it or read it. Hence Christ sent his disciples with it to all the world, and to every creature. "So we preach," &c. Men cannot be accountable for the gospel until they possess it. Wherever it comes, it is the imperative duty of mankind to hear it. To refuse to hear it is sin; to neglect it is to insure condemnation. "I called, but ye refused," &c.

3. *There must be capacity in those who hear it, to understand it.* Now we know that a peculiar cast of mind is necessary to understand some branches of science, &c. Also with respect to metaphysics. Hence had the gospel been a series of mathematical problems, or metaphysical essays, only a very few could have understood it. But the gospel refers to two great facts in the history of Jesus Christ, and demands the belief of these, on the ground of the truth of the gospel. Every person, therefore, of sane mind, however small in mental capacity, or unlearned, may understand this testimony, without which faith could not be exercised. Here, then, we see that it is essential to faith that there be a testimony, brought and presented to minds capable of understanding it. Consider,

II. *The nature of saving faith.*

Now, from what has been said, it is clear that where the gospel testimony is preached, it may be treated by some with *indifference.* Others may treat it with *idle speculation,* form peculiar opinions about it, and thus leave it. Others may listen with interest, and cordially believe it. Now saving faith is the cordial belief of the gospel. It is the belief of the heart; the act of the *will* and the *affections.* "With the heart man believeth unto righteousness," &c. Now a cordial belief of any great truth will be influential; it will operate on the mind and life. That faith which is real and saving is thus distinguished, and made manifest from all that is counterfeit. But we shall see this more fully if we look at the scriptural representation of faith.

(1.) Man is far off. He has wandered towards the regions of death. Faith in this case is coming to Christ. Returning to the Lord. Drawing near on the ground of his invitations and promises. "Him that cometh," &c. "Come unto me all ye that labor," &c. "Seek my face and live." "Thy face, O Lord, will I seek."

(2.) Man is guilty. Under sentence of death, and pursued by the avenger of blood. God has provided a city of refuge, &c. To this he is urged to flee. He is assured the gates are wide open, and he has the word and oath of God to rely upon, that if he flies and enters he shall live. Believing this, the passions of the soul are excited, and his whole heart moves swiftly to the hope set before him. He exclaims,

"Hide me, O my Saviour, hide,
    Till the storm of wrath is past,
Safe into the haven guide,
    Oh, receive my soul at last."

(3.) Man is diseased with the serpent sting of sin. He is on the verge of death. His drooping spirit is fainting within him. But the antidote is proclaimed. Christ is lifted up, and he is told to look,—to look to the cross of Christ, to see the Lamb of God; and he does so, and exclaims,

"See there my Lord upon the tree,
    I hear, I feel, he died for me."

(4.) Man is a moral wreck, floating on the ocean of life, ready to sink into perdition. Jesus in the life-boat of mercy, comes near to him, and throws out the rope of deliverance. He is urged to lay hold of it; and with the earnest grasp of a person conscious of perishing, he does so, and is thus rescued from eternal misery.

(5.) Man is lost. Wandering in darkness on the mountain of ruin. He is exhorted by one he meets to call out for help, and that Jesus is not far from him. He does so. He utters in loud exclamations of fear, "Lost, lost, lost!" and he unites with it, "Save, Lord, or I perish;" Jesus hears and delivers him from the destruction to which he was exposed. Now in each of these instances you see how faith is the soul and spring of the movement of the sinner towards Christ. To show the workings of the opposite principles of presumption or indifference, the person exhorted to flee to the city of refuge with the avenger of blood in pursuit, if he presumes on his safety, he lingers, and is overtaken; or, if he is indifferent, he is involved in the same ruin. So thousands presume instead of exercising present faith; and thousands intend to do so at another period, and thus perish in their unbelief. We ask,

III. *What are the evidences of saving faith?* Now these evidences are of two kinds.

1. *Those of which the believer only is conscious, and which we shall call internal evidences of faith.*

(1.) Faith produces *hope*. Fear and terror are annihilated. No longer dread and dismay is felt hanging over the soul.

"Now I have found the ground wherein
Sure my soul's anchor may remain:
The wounds of Jesus for my sin,
Before the world's foundation slain;
Whose mercy shall unshaken stay,
When heaven and earth shall flee away."

(2.) Faith produces *peace and joy*. Being justified, &c. "I will praise thee," &c.

(3.) Faith produces *love*. "Works by love." Christ is now the chief among ten thousand, &c. The heart is set on fire with it. "The love of God is shed abroad," &c. "We love him," &c. "Unto him who hath loved us," &c. The other kind of evidences are,

2. *Those which are visible to all men, and which we denominated external.*

(1.) Faith produces humility and contrition. Soul now in the dust. No self-exaltation. No self-vindication. Faith prostrates the mind before God, and real abasement will be visible to those around.

(2.) Faith leads to a profession of Christ. Christ will be honored by the lips, and by the assumption of his name and cross. Not

ashamed to own him and to follow him before men. Hence in the Acts we ever read that when faith was exercised, the exhibition of it, was being baptized into the Lord Jesus Christ. The 3000 at Jerusalem; the Samaritans, Paul, the eunuch, &c.

(3.) Faith leads to practical godliness. It is seen in obedience to Jesus Christ. Evidenced in good works; walking in Christ, and treading in his steps. Hence faith is a holy principle. Brings men out of the world, and out of the way of sin, into the church and the way of salvation.

APPLICATION.

1. Let our faith be tested by these evidences. Examine, &c. Prove yourselves, &c.

2. Learn the importance of faith. No salvation without it. You may be saved without learning, or wealth, or great gifts, but not without *faith*. He that believeth not, &c. We see the cause of this essentiality of faith, as *unbelief rejects* God's provision of mercy—shuts the opened gates of salvation.

3. Now receive the gospel message, and live.

CCCVI.—MINISTERIAL SOLICITUDE.

"Therefore, my brethren, dearly beloved and longed for, my joy and crown, so stand fast in the Lord, my dearly beloved."—*Phil.* iv. 1.

THE church of Christ at Philippi could trace its origin, and the beginning of the gospel among them, to the labors of the apostle Paul. Of course there would be mutual recollections of love, and endearing sympathy between them. It appears, too, that the disciples in Philippi were distinguished for their sincerity in the truth, and for a greater regard both to the primitive doctrines and practical duties of Christianity, than most of the other churches. So that this epistle is free from reprehension; and the most unqualified tokens of confidence and approbation are reiterated by the apostle. But the very best Christians stand in need of caution, admonition, and exhortation; and with these the epistle abounds. He exhorts them to a consistent walk and conversation. "Only let your conversation," &c. ii. 27. To lowliness and humility of spirit, ii. 3. "Let nothing be done through strife or vain-glory," &c. To great diligence in attending to the interests of personal religion. "Work out," &c., ii. 12. The third chapter refs very greatly to his own experience, and the glorious hope the saints possessed of a blissful resurrection to eternal life. "For our conversation," &c., iii. 20. Then follows the affectionate exhortation of the text, "Therefore," &c.

I. *The endearing appellations by which the saints at Philippi are designated.* And,

II. *The important exhortation which is addressed to them.*

I. *The endearing appellations by which the saints at Philippi are designated.*

1. *The first term exhibits the spiritual affinity which exists among Christians.*

"My brethren." There is a human brotherhood which is based on the one blood of which God has made all the families of the earth. There is a relative brotherhood existing among the immediate kindred of the same domestic circle. But there is a spiritual brotherhood, in which all believers are allied by the gracious ties of a spiritual nature one to another. In this they are all the children of God by regeneration, adoption, and grace. This affinity extends to all offices, ages, &c., of the Christian character. All are brethren,—one is your Master, &c. The second term exhibits,

2. *The reciprocated affection which should be manifested among the disciples of Christ.*

"Dearly beloved." Believers are dearly beloved of the Father, of the Son, of the Holy Spirit. But they are called to love one another with pure hearts fervently. All Christians are under the law of Christian love. This is Christ's new, and last, and greatest commandment, "That ye love one another." Beloved, if so God loved us, we ought also to love one another. This is the sign of our renewed state, &c.

3. *The third term denotes the anxious solicitude of the Christian minister for his people.*

"And longed for." The faithful minister when absent longs for fellowship with his flock; and when present he longs for their spiritual welfare, improvement, and happiness. As a *faithful shepherd* he longs for the security and comfort of his flock. As a conscientious *instructor* or teacher, he longs for their progress in the truth, and all spiritual understanding. As a *father* in the gospel, he longs to see his children rising up in spiritual health and vigor, and becoming young men and mature Christians in all the graces and virtues of the gospel. In his *study* they are his "longed for," and he

reads, and meditates, and prepares his discourses for their edification and profit. In his *closet* they are his "longed for." Here he bears them on his arms of faith and prayer, and entreats the richest blessings of heaven to descend upon them. In his *public labors* they are his "longed for;" and when he appears before them, it is to seek their profit; and hence he comes unto them in the fulness of the blessings of the gospel of Christ. See Col. i. 28. "Whom we preach," &c. Observe,

4. The fourth class of expressions denote *the satisfaction and felicity the faithful minister derives from his charge.*

"My joy and crown." Now a people are only the joy and crown of the minister, when, like the Philippians, they are united in the faith and hope of the gospel, and are bearing the fruit of righteousness to the glory of the divine name. The backsliding and Judaizing Galatians caused great grief and distress of mind in the apostle. No joy can arise to Christian ministers from wavering, from the formal members of their churches. But they are both their joy and crown, the cause both of honor and satisfaction to their ministers, when they are living to show forth the praises of him who hath called them out of darkness to light, &c. It is the joy of benevolence arising from success. The crown of honor as the attainment of the minister's holy ambition. Look at the *fisherman*, toiling hard and taking nothing. How depressed, &c. But when the net is cast on the right side of the vessel, and bears its fulness to the shore, it is then he exults and evinces the joy of his heart. Look at the *builder*, who designs the erection of a superb and costly structure. As he beholds its walls rising in symmetry and beauty, his heart rejoices; and when the whole is finished, it reflects the honor of the builder, as it regards both his wisdom and perseverance. Look at that *ambassador* sent to treat with a rebellious colony. His mission is successful; revolt subsides; order and loyalty is effected. Is it not both his joy and crown? So when the Christian minister sees around him those who, though once afar off, are now nigh to God, and loyal in heart and life to King Jesus, they become his joy and crown. In the people being the joy and crown of ministers, we see,

(1.) What is the end the true servants of Christ set before them. They seek the good of the people, not theirs. They aim at the salvation of their hearers. They labor for souls as those who must give an account.

(2.) We see in this how the ministers of Christ are identified with Christ. Christ lived and died that he might see of the travail of his soul. Converted souls are the joy of Jesus,—the crown of the Saviour.

(3.) The full joy and honor of the Saviour and his servants will not be completed until the last day. Then will Christ have seen all the desire of his heart, and he will be *satisfied*. Then, too, shall every pastor of the Lord Jesus present his charge, and say, "Here, Lord, am I, and the children thou hast given me." Then they that have turned many to righteousness, shall shine as the brightness of the firmament, &c. This leads us to consider,

II. *The important exhortation which is addressed to them.*

"Stand fast in the Lord." Christian stability is that which is urged. It is important,

1. *That you stand fast in the truth of Christian doctrines.*

The faith of the gospel. Not to be borne away by every wind of doctrine. In all ages the church has been exposed to heretical teachers. Thus the Galatians went back to half Judaism. How needful for Christians to hold fast the truth. To abide by the voice of the lively oracles. "To the law," &c.

2. *That you stand fast in the enjoyment of experimental religion.*

Not to dwindle down into formality, but to have the grace of God within us of a truth. To know and feel it, and not to abandon the happy conscious possessions of joy and peace in the Holy Ghost, &c.; the assurance that all is committed into Christ's hands, &c.

3. *Stand fast in the exercise of practical godliness.*

As ye have received the Lord Jesus Christ, so walk in him. Having Christ's mind, and walking in his steps. Let your light so shine, ver. 8, 9.

4. *That you can stand fast only in the Lord.*

Now two remarks here. Our steadfastness depends on our abiding in Christ. See John xv. 4. Also our steadfastness must be secured by the grace and blessings which he communicates. Our attainments, and experience, and resolutions, are worth nothing without him. "My grace," &c. Here is

our security. "Kept by the power of God."

APPLICATION.

1. *Learn the peril to which the best of Christians are exposed.*

From their own weaknesses, temptations, &c. "Let him that thinketh he standeth," &c. "Take heed lest there be in any of you an evil heart," &c.

2. *How comforted and encouraged we should be that all sufficient comfort and strength are provided.*

Our resources are ample, infinite, and exhaustless.

3. *How desirable that minister and people should be a mutual joy to each other.*

Your joy is closely connected with the labors of the word. Thus feel, and pray for, and encourage those who labor, &c.

CCCVII.—THE APOSTOLIC BENEDICTION.

"The grace of our Lord Jesus Christ be with you all."—2. *Thess.* iii. 18.

It has been customary in all ages for the religious services of the sanctuary to conclude with an appropriate benediction. The benediction or blessing the Jewish priests pronounced was this,—"The Lord bless thee and keep thee; the Lord make his face to shine upon thee and be gracious unto thee; the Lord lift up his countenance upon thee and give thee peace." The benediction of the apostles seems to have been generally of the construction of our text, with a little variation,—and thus Paul concludes the chief of his epistles. At this season of the year, friends are in the habit of exchanging their friendly wishes; and as this will conclude the services of the sanctuary for the present year, let the text express our warmest and best desires on your behalf. Notice, then,

I. *The blessing itself.*

"The grace of our Lord Jesus Christ." Grace signifies favor, good-will. May you have the favor of Christ. All the blessings of this life are blessings of grace; we merit nothing,—have a right to nothing. Then all our temporal and spiritual blessings are of grace. But how are the blessings of the Lord Jesus Christ? In three respects.

1. *He meritoriously obtained them all by his death.*

We had forfeited all things, even life, by sin. Blocked up the way to heaven, opened the passage to perdition. Now he became our surety, and paid the penalty, so that in Christ God is reconciled. We owe all to his work, &c. "Ye know the grace of our Lord Jesus Christ," &c.

2. *He came to publish and offer grace.*

The law came by Moses, but grace and truth by Jesus Christ. "God sent not his Son into the world to condemn the world," &c.—"I am come that ye might have life."

3. *He bestows grace.*

In him it dwells—all fulness of it; and it is his, to confer it. "Whosoever thirsts let him come unto me and drink." All power is given to him. He is the sun of grace,—the ocean of grace. Notice,

II. *The benevolent desire expressed.*

"The grace of our Lord Jesus Christ be with you all."

1. *May the gospel of grace be the charter of liberty and hope.*

Men are naturally captives—bound—prisoners, &c. The gospel proclaims liberty to the captive. "Ye shall know the truth, and the truth shall make you free." This frees the mind from guilt and fear, and it is the basis of hope. "Christ has loved me, and given himself for me." May this be the case with you. It has come to you in word, may it dwell with you in power. May you receive it by faith.

2. *May the Spirit of grace fill your hearts with peace and joy.*

The Spirit, Christ has promised and sent. If ye believe ye shall receive the Holy Ghost. He dwelleth in all the hearts of his saints. Ye have received, says the apostle, the spirit of adoption, &c. "The Spirit itself beareth witness with our spirits," &c. Now the Holy Spirit produces peace—the peace of God which passeth all understanding,—and it also lights up in the soul heavenly joy,—joy unspeakable and full of glory.

3. *May the blessings of grace enrich your experience, and make you fruitful in every good work.*

The Christian is called to work out his own salvation; to grow, to bear fruit, to shine, to do good. Who is sufficient for these things? Christ says, "Without me, ye can do nothing."—"My grace is sufficient." Now this is as the rain or dew to the garden, or the food to the child,—essential.

4. *May the power of his grace be seen in your preservation and deliverance from all evil.*

We walk in a world of peril,—in the region of death,—exposed to countless ills and woes. In this forest there is the tiger's lair and the serpent's path. How are we to escape? Christ's grace will shield and preserve, keep and sustain. No weapon, &c.

5. *May the designs of Christ's grace be answered in your everlasting salvation.*

Christ's grace is to save our souls,—to fit us for his will on earth; for a happy death, and a blissful eternity. May you realize it in all your sorrows and afflictions,—in every movement of life; and thus be prepared for eternal glory. Notice,

III. *The extent to which this desire is offered.*

"Be with you all." The original signification was the Thessalonian church. With all the disciples of Jesus. "Grace be with all," &c. To every child of God on earth. But we remark,

1. *That all present stand in need of it.*

Essentially so. It is indispensable to every one of you. You who are unconverted need restraining grace, sparing grace, converting grace.

2. *There is no barrier to all of you receiving it.*

God's grace in Christ is offered to every one. No limitation, or respect of persons with God. If you desire it, seek it, and believe it,—it is yours.

3. *That a period will come when the possession of this grace will make the most momentous and everlasting difference.*

Death will be such a period, and that will come. The judgment will be such a period, and that will follow. What a contrast will then be presented between the gracious and the graceless: those who have it, and those who have it not. Then let me, in applying the subject,

1. Urge it upon your immediate acceptance. Now receive the grace of God in truth. Now live for it, earnestly pray, "God be merciful to me a sinner."

2. Christians, improve it. Grow in grace. Let it be seen in and upon you. Lay it out: diffuse it.

3. Let gratitude be expressed for the grace of God displayed towards you during your past lives.

4. Exercise hope for the future. And now, to each and all, "May the grace of the Lord Jesus Christ be with you. Amen."

SERMONS

DESIGNED FOR THE

SICK-ROOM, FAMILY READING, AND VILLAGE WORSHIP.

I.—THE SHORT BED; OR AN INEFFICIENT RELIGION.

"For the bed is shorter than that a *man* can stretch himself *on it*: and the covering narrower than that he can wrap himself in it."—*Isaiah* xxviii. 20.

AMIDST the striking representations of the Prophets, we often meet with beautiful maxims and telling sentences, sayings and proverbs, which illustrate general or particular truths. Now, this remark will apply to the text under consideration. The chapter refers probably to the wars of Israel with the Assyrians, and to the distress in which they would be involved. And then that their efforts at comfort should utterly fail them: "For the bed," &c. Just as a weary traveller lies down to get refreshing repose, but he has not space to stretch out his fatigued limbs, nor a sufficiency of covering to preserve him from the night cold, so should it be to Israel in their calamities. Now we wish to use the text as strikingly portraying the characteristics of an insufficient religion.

Now, I remark,

I. *That men in general seem to feel the need of some kind of a religion.*

This we need not wonder at, when we remember that man has a moral, as well as a physical and mental nature. His conscience appeals to him on moral duties, and urges him to the attainment of moral blessings. It chastises moral delinquency, and smiles on moral obedience. Hence it is not in the power of mere physical or mental resources, to make man satisfied and happy. Then the history of the world establishes the same truth. The great majority of mankind seek after religious influences. Ignorant of the true God, the wild Indian listens to the winds and storm,—the Persian gazes on the bright sun,—the Hindoo on his idol representations.

Where divine revelation exists, men generally seem anxious to adopt some mode of religion. They resort to some form of worship or creed, to meet the longings of their moral nature.

Hence, the superstitious find Romanism just adapted to their feelings. The less superstitious, but ostentatious, find it in the pomp and ceremonies of a splendid hierarchy. The metaphysical look for it in abstruse theories and profound subtleties. The less profound and less superstitious labor after what they term a more rational form; but nearly all evince a desire to have a religion of some kind. Those who have rejected all religious beliefs and all modes of worship, have ever been the very small minorities of the people. For as a rule, the irreligious and ungodly do not deny, so much as they neglect, the great teachings of Nature, Conscience, and Revelation, on the subject. There are few who would not admit the inward cravings of their moral nature, after religious enjoyment and satisfaction.

Let us then notice,

II. *What are the obvious signs of an inefficient religion;* or, when is "the bed shorter than that a man can stretch himself on it?"

That religion is inefficient which does not,

1. *Secure conscious pardon of sin.*

Every man unquestionably is a sinner. As such, he absolutely needs forgiveness; and without it, he must be callous or wretched.

It is of little moment to the establishment of this point what views we may entertain of the doctrines of the gospel; for whatever may be the standard of moral right they may set up, what man can appeal to his whole life, and say, that by such a standard he is innocent, free from all guilt and from all blame; both as it regards God and man? As to personal iniquity, every mouth is stopped, and every soul stands guilty before God. However varied the shades of guilt and the hues of pollution, there is no heart clean, no conscience righteous before Him whose eyes search the very inmost recesses of the human soul.

Does it not then follow that the religion that does not meet man's guilt and condemnation with an entire and full pardon, is inefficient? Man's recovery and blessedness must be based on the entire remission of all his sins.

That religion is inefficient which does not,

2. *Give real permanent peace.*

Now, dread and anguish and torment are the result of guilt. It is guilt that brings gloom and terror over the soul. It is this which produces the restlessness that is compared to the ever agitated and roaring sea, and which is ever casting up mire and dirt. Just as in the physical system disease produces pain and derangement, so does the plague of sin lead to the distraction and misery of the soul. There is no peace to the wicked, so says revelation—so says the conscience—so says that wandering anxious eye—so says that sinking soul—so say the despairing and wretched everywhere.

If religion does not hush the storm, still the tempest, and give perfect peace, it is ineffectual. It is equally inefficient,

3. *If it does not purify the heart and life.*

Holiness bears its own divine recommendation on it; and to make us holy should be the very tendency of religion. Not merely externally moral, but inwardly pure. To subordinate the passions to reason—the will to God—the heart in all its confidence and affection to the Saviour. And from this renewed heart, the good stream of practical religion must flow. Now, if religion leaves a man just as he was—polluted, vile, and wicked, it is manifestly inefficient. It is worthy of reflection, that no religion, except that revealed in the Holy Scriptures, ever contemplated purifying the heart, and sanctifying alike the thoughts and emotions of the soul.

It is inefficient,

4. *If it does not give a well-grounded hope for the future.*

We are in every respect much more connected and dependent on the future than the present. This is true both as to pleasure and pain. Real enjoyment, therefore, has much to do with our hopes and fears. If the light of hope illumines the horizon before us, we are happy. If not, nothing can make us truly so. How true the words—

> "Man never is,
> But always to be blest."

Present satisfaction must essentially arise from future prospects. And as this world is not our continued · place of abode, the great inquiry arises—where am I going—what will my future lot be—what will be that state which will immediately succeed this life—will it be a blessed one of rest, of purity, of joy, and of celestial dignity—will it be glory, immortality, eternal life? Now the religion that does not irradiate the future with the light of heavenly hope, cannot be satisfactory. Where there is not a clear hope of glory and immortality, that religion is inefficient. It is indeed as the bed that is too short, and as the covering that is too narrow. Then observe,

III. *What kinds of religion come under this appellation.*

And here I might say—in one sentence— *all* kinds, but that of evangelical faith in the Lord Jesus Christ. But observe more particularly,

1. *That it applies to what is styled Natural religion.*

This "bed is shorter," &c. Now the religion of Nature, or that which is produced by a contemplation of the works of God, or attending to the light of reason only, is inefficient; as it leaves the most momentous problems unresolved, and the most weighty interrogatories unanswered. It does not reveal what I need to know. The first elementary question—what is virtue, goodness, religion—is not distinctly met. What is moral evil—what does God will—what does he require from me as a reasonable accountable being—what mode of worship shall I adopt—what offerings shall I present? In what does my accountability consist—shall an investigation of my conduct ever take place—and where, and when, and for what end—will he forgive the guilty— and if so, on what principle—and what means must I adopt to secure it? Now all these, and ten thousand other great questions, natural religion does not meet,—and yet, I ought to have satisfactory responses to them, or the "Bed is too short, and the covering too narrow," for my comfort and well-being. We add, too, that natural religion cannot bestow what I so deeply require. It utters no pardon—bestows no peace—imparts no holiness—nor gives a sure hope of immortality.

It applies equally,

2. *To a mere Ceremonial religion.*

Ceremonials, even at best, are but signs. They may be the alphabet of divine words and ideas; but they cannot renew the polluted soul, nor give a reasonable hope of eternal blessedness. Surely it is self-evident that animal sacrifices are but types and shadowings forth of the atonement. Neither the blood of goats nor calves can put away sin. No external rite, irrespective of a believing state of heart, can avail to our peace or satisfaction. And equally inefficient are all divine ordinances, if trusted to, if relied on, as the basis of acceptance with God. Baptism, without faith in the atonement, is a mere outward washing of the body. The Lord's Supper, without a spiritual reception of Christ and feeding on him by faith, is a mere valueless ceremonial. It cannot be that outward things should affect savingly the inward man, and convey vital power and holiness to the conscience. And however devout may be the feelings, and however exact the observance, a ceremonial religion is like "the bed shorter than a man can stretch himself on it."

It equally applies,

3. *To a self-righteous religion.*

This, however satisfactory to the carnal heart, is especially offensive to God. Self-abasement and humility must be cardinal virtues in all true and acceptable religion. Besides, we may well ask, what can self do —what are its fruits—of what has it to boast? The experience of wise pagans, as well as the efforts of the anxious heart of man in all ages, ought to show that true religion must be of heavenly origin; and thus holy and divine in its nature.

It is not for darkness to produce light. It is not in pollution to produce purity. It is not in entire moral impotence to produce moral energy and spiritual power. It is not in a bad fountain to send forth sweet streams; or for thorns to yield figs. The experience of our race has been, that man cannot illumine, renew, and save himself. Now, if he cannot do this, he must be indebted entirely to a higher power, if he becomes renewed at all. Thus, all self-righteousness, and all human vaunting, is at once overthrown. How fully and explicitly is this revealed to us in the word of God. "For as many as are of the works of the law are under the curse : for it is written, Cursed is every one that continueth not in all things which are written in the book of the law to do them. But that no man is justified by the law in the sight of God, it is evident : for, the just shall live by faith."—Galatians iii. 10, 11. "For what the law could not do, in that it was weak through the flesh, God sending his own Son in the likeness of sinful flesh, and for sin, condemned sin in the flesh : that the righteousness of the law might be fulfilled in us, who walk not after the flesh, but after the Spirit."—Romans viii. 3, 4. "Not by works of righteousness which we have done, but according to his mercy he saved us, by the washing of regeneration, and renewing of the Holy Ghost; which he shed on us abundantly through Jesus Christ our Saviour : that being justified by his grace, we should be made heirs according to the hope of eternal life."—Titus iii. 5–7. "For by grace are ye saved through faith; and that not of yourselves : it is the gift of God : Not of works, lest any man should boast."—Ephesians ii. 8, 9.

APPLICATION.

Then we learn from this subject,

1. That the religion of Christ contains all that we need. Here is pardon, repose, comfort, purity, and hope. This in reality contemplates us in all our guilt and moral pollution, and misery; and brings near to us a full and complete salvation. Here there is,

> "A balm for every wound—
> All, all we want, is here."

We ask,

2. Have you this religion in possession? We may understand what religions are false and inefficient—we may know, too, the way of life as revealed in the gospel—but the grand inquiry should be—Do we possess it? In our heart's experience do we realize it? and are its fruits evidenced in our life and conversation?

3. If not, earnestly now seek it, and secure it. Do you inquire what you shall do to be saved,—how you shall enjoy the pardoning love of God,—how receive Divine

peace and comfort into your souls? then hear what the commissioned Prophet says —" Ho, every one that thirsteth, come ye to the waters, and he that hath no money; come ye, buy, and eat; yea, come, buy wine and milk without money and without price."—Isaiah lv. 1. Hear what your gracious Saviour says—" Come unto me, all ye that labor and are heavy laden, and I will give you rest. Take my yoke upon you, and learn of me; for I am meek and lowly in heart; and ye shall find rest unto your souls."—Matthew xii. 28, 29. Hear what the Holy Spirit says, amidst the concluding words of the Apocalypse—" And the Spirit and the bride say, Come. And let him that heareth say, Come. And let him that is athirst come. And whosoever will, let him take the water of life freely."—Revelation xxii. 17. Then you need not err, for here is truth and light. You need not despair, for here is mercy and grace. You need not even delay, for, " Behold now is the accepted time, and behold now is the day of salvation." " But the righteousness which is of faith speaketh on this wise, Say not in thine heart, Who shall ascend into heaven: (that is, to bring Christ down from above:) Or, who shall descend into the deep? (that is, to bring up Christ again from the dead.) But what saith it? The word is nigh thee, even in thy mouth, and in thy heart: that is, the word of faith, which we preach. That if thou shalt confess with thy mouth the Lord Jesus, and shalt believe in thine heart that God hath raised him from the dead, thou shalt be saved. For with the heart man believeth unto righteousness; and with the mouth confession is made unto salvation."—Romans x. 6–10.

II.—A BEACON TO YOUNG MEN.

" A young man void of understanding."—Proverbs vii. 7.

To be void of understanding, is to act as one who is insane or mad. To do violence to reason—to despise wisdom, and to be reckless as to the results of our conduct.

Now, reason is the glory of man. It is a light within the soul, by which he is exalted above the brutes that perish. And yet God often charges men with displaying less judgment, than the mere animal creatures.

Hence, " The ox knoweth his owner, and the ass his master's crib: but Israel doth not know, my people doth not consider."—Isa. i. 3. The birds of the air and the fish of the sea know their time; and guided by their respective instincts, migrate at their proper seasons. But men often do not know, and will not consider. Our text, however, relates to one class of mankind. To young men, who display this want of reason and a sound mind, and of whom Solomon says, I discerned among the youths, " A young man, void of understanding."

Let us consider,

I. *The evidences of this state.*

II. *Its evil results.*

And,

III. *The only remedy.*

I. *The evidences of this state.*

How can we know and discern with certainty the young, who are void of understanding?

We remark, those are so,

1. *Who throw off the restraints and counsels of their parents and friends.*

Honor thy father and mother—is the first commandment, with promise. One of the kind arrangements of a beneficent Providence is, the parental relationship, by which the wisdom, and power, and affection of others, secure to us the blessings we need. Now to despise this arrangement, or to neglect it, is folly. Nothing can be more important to the young, than the parental oversight and care. How myriads have been ruined by casting it off. The ignorant and inexperienced have relied upon their sufficiency, and that too at the most critical period of life; and have thus made utter shipwreck of themselves. See that haughty self-complacent youth, defying parental authority, and casting off its restraints! Look at the prodigal son demanding his portion, and treating his father with base ingratitude. How heinous the sin! How mad the course! What misery and ruin the result! When counsel and supervision are most needed, they are rejected—when the benefits of a wise experience are so all-important, they are despised, and that too, when a guide is so indispensable,—and who so fit to guide and counsel as the parent? Did you ever see such a wayward rebellious son? then you beheld " A young man void of understanding." I refer,

2. *To those who become the companions of the foolish and wicked.*

Nothing will influence us more, than the company we keep. A serious youth keeping company with triflers. A religiously disposed youth with skeptics. A modest youth with the impudent and daring. A youth of regular habits with the dissipated. In all such cases, the most disastrous results must follow. No other influence will be so disastrous on our highest interests, as that of evil companionship. It will insidiously undermine every good principle—root out every moral purpose, and destroy all virtuous sensibility, and all modest excellence. It will eat out every thing that is pure and lovely, and of good report. " A companion of fools shall be destroyed." I refer,

3. *To those who disregard the opinions of the wise and good around them.*

A regard to the estimation of others, is one of the most useful influences of society. Hence, we read of the value of a good name as being better than riches. A respectable character is of more real worth than gold. When a youth begins to say, " I don't care what people think and say," he gives evidence that he is far gone in the way of degradation, and is void of understanding. In such a case, one of the main bulwarks of virtue and excellency is manifestly broken down. We should ever hold in highest respect and favor the opinions of the wise and good. One of the luxuries of this life, is to have the esteem of the excellent of the earth, and to enjoy fellowship with the wise and holy of mankind.

The text will include,

4. *Those who neglect the institutions of religion.*

The atmosphere of religious ordinances is that of health and life to every virtue and grace of the soul. Here every genial and righteous emotion will bloom and flourish. How important the private reading of God's holy word,—a regular regard to closet meditation and prayer,—an open and avowed attachment to public religious service,—a sacred and reverential esteem of the Christian Sabbath. Negligence of these will produce moral darkness, and lethargy, and supineness of spirit. Thus tenderness of conscience will be lost, and spiritual ossification of the heart will follow.

By neglecting Divine ordinances and services, the heart and mind run fallow; and instead of holy fruit being raised to the honor of God, nothing but weeds, and briers, and thorns, will be produced. How soon will reflection and seriousness be entirely banished, and vanity, and emptiness, and foolish display, be all for which that youth will be distinguished. Sabbath profligacy alone, how it destroys the holy affections of the soul—exposes to countless temptations—and has ruined myriads upon myriads of the young.

5. *To those who yield themselves up to sensual gratifications.*

Now, the name of these gratifications, is legion. I refer to,

(1.) The use of tobacco, in any form, as most pernicious. Think of the habits it engenders—the money it wastes—the stupor it produces—the time it destroys. And above all, its connection with dissipated company, and evil places of resort.

(2.) The young man who indulges in intoxicating drinks. This is often the attendant of the last habit. Here the snares are countless. The places, the society, are evil in every sense. It is the open broad-way of moral deterioration and wretchedness. Not only is the habitual use of intoxicating drinks perilous in itself, but it begets a habit which it is most difficult to break off; and a love of unnatural excitement, extremely unfavorable to true seriousness of spirit. The cautions of the divine word on this subject are most powerful and graphic. " Wine is a mocker, strong drink is raging : and whosoever is deceived thereby is not wise."—Prov. xx. 1. " Look not thou upon the wine when it is red, when it giveth his color in the cup, when it moveth itself aright. At the last it biteth like a serpent, and stingeth like an adder."—Prov. xxiii. 31–2. And the inspired record declares, that it is perilous even for the lofty and the great to indulge in these ensnaring liquors. " It is not for kings, O Lemuel, it is not for kings to drink wine ; nor for princes strong drink : lest they drink, and forget the law, and pervert the judgment of any of the afflicted."—Prov. xxxi. 4, 5. Besides, the intoxicating glass is the panderer to other sins, and evil courses of life. It is often linked with *gambling*, and its awful and ruinous effects—with the theatre, which may be pronounced, beyond a doubt, the very way to the pit of destruction. Here men go down with rapid strides to the gulf of woe. Look at the neighborhoods surrounding such places, how defiled and profligate : children trained to theft —women to prostitution, &c. The very atmosphere is one of moral pestilence and death.

The text refers,

(3.) To the ensnaring woman. "For at the window of my house I looked through my casement, and beheld among the simple ones, I discerned among the youths a young man void of understanding, passing through the street near her corner; and he went the way to her house, in the twilight, in the evening, in the black and dark night. And behold, there met him a woman with the attire of an harlot, and subtil of heart. (She is loud and stubborn; her feet abide not in her house: Now is she without, now in the streets, and lieth in wait at every corner.) So she caught him, and kissed him, and with an impudent face said unto him," &c. Prov. vii. 6–13. " With her much fair speech she caused him to yield, with the flattering of her lips she forced him. He goeth after her straightway, as an ox goeth to the slaughter, or as a fool to the correction of the stocks: Till a dart strike through his liver; as a bird hasteth to the snare, and knoweth not that it is for his life."—Ver. 21–23. How fearful the result! Money, reputation, health, mind, morals, life, and the soul, all sacrificed! Look at this horrible picture! See him tempted by some polluted, filthy, miserable creature. He yields: then shame, remorse, and ruin, are the result. His means are drained—his health suffers—his constitution is broken—his soul is blighted. Hear his groans in the hospital. See him literally one mass of corruption. Friends are horrified! An early death closes the scene on earth, and the tortures and agonies of the lost perpetuate the dire tragedy through eternity.

Observe, in reference to this character,

II. *Its evil results.*

And consider,

1. *The morally evil condition of the youth themselves.*

Here are powers perverted—talents prostituted—sin and misery increased—an immortal being withering beneath the influence of evil. How sad the state! how truly deplorable! A gem of peerless price is forfeited—an intellectual spirit blighted—an undying soul lost!

2. *The pernicious influence they exert on others.*

Every such youth has his young friends and relations, all of whom may be corrupted by his conduct. He spreads abroad the bad atmosphere of his own corrupt mind. His example is deadly to all those within the range of his influence. He diffuses everywhere he goes the evil contagion of his corrupt spirit, and his conversation and example act as a blight and a mildew on other hearts and minds. How often an elder brother leads younger branches of the family, in the same way of dissipation and ruin! So many young men, by their wit, or talents, or mental power, are daring ringleaders in vice. They act on all who associate with them, and form the centre power of the terrible whirlpool which involves the ruin of many with themselves.

But consider especially,

3. *The eternal misery to which they are hastening.*

Supposing it possible that God should withhold his anger and wrath, their doom must, notwithstanding, be one of sorrow, and woe, and despair. They have no fitness for a heaven of holy knowledge—a heaven of holy emotions—of holy society—of holy exercises. Polluted and guilty; darkness, remorse, and destruction, must be their final portion—their end is certain eternal death.

And how great the number of young men who thus perish, without God and without hope. How many who are sent from rural districts, and from moral homes, to great towns and cities, die every year! How intensely solicitous, then, should parents and guardians, and ministers be, to watch over the rising youth, that they may not be numbered with those who are "void of understanding." But observe, in reference to such,

III. *The only remedy.*

How are they to be rescued? We reply, by the adoption of personal religion. There must be,

1. *Immediate and genuine repentance.*

Prompt consideration. Wise reflection, as to what has been the cause of this state. A conviction of the evil of it. To this must be added, intense hatred of it; and then turning away from it at once. Ceasing to do evil, and learning to do well. There must be no parleying, no hesitancy, no delay. At once, and with full earnestness, there must be a stand made, in the downward way of death. The resolution must be, I will go no further, not one step more, in the dark road to perdition. Just as the prodigal stood still, and then said, "I will arise and go to my father."

2. *There must be the yielding of the heart to Christ.*

Christ alone can open the blind eyes—

expel the foul spirit—renew the heart—save from folly and sin. Faith in him will extract the healing virtue of his grace, and restore the soul. Now, as repentance towards God involves all the consideration and turning from evil we have spoken of; so it must be ever connected, and that most directly, with coming to Christ.

A knowledge of our ruin, a sense of our guilt, and a desire to be delivered from it, are all really essential; but they must terminate in looking to Christ, the only Saviour. In resting on his atoning sacrifice for acceptance with God, and in washing in that only precious fountain which has been opened for sin, and for uncleanness. Thus the spirit will be disburdened—the conscience renewed—and the whole moral nature be sanctified and made fit for the divine service and glory.

Then this must be succeeded,

3. *By the regulation of the life by the Word of God.*

" Wherewithal shall a young man cleanse his way? By taking heed according to thy Word." The Word of God must be taken as the one and only infallible guide. This is the clear directory to a holy, useful life, and to a blessed immortality. This book makes wise the simple—counsels the inexperienced—establishes the wavering—is a shield to the imperilled—and produces moral growth and vigor in all those in whom it dwells richly. How needful that all, but especially the young, should read it regularly, and with prayer and much meditation, become intimate with its revelations, both of doctrine, precept, and promise. An early knowledge of Scripture had made Timothy wise to salvation, and, no doubt, eminently qualified him to be so great an ornament, as well as so instrumentally useful in the churches of Jesus. Then there must be,

4. *Union to, and fellowship with, God's people.*

They that walk with wise men shall be wiser. The Church is God's kingdom, into which all his subjects are to be introduced; for their own safety, improvement, and comfort. Here they are to honor Christ—labor for souls—and grow in meetness for heaven. By religious associations, the young will be encouraged and aided amid the difficulties and perils incident to early piety. Here, too, they will find a sphere for the development of their powers, and the employment of their talents and

time. Here they will dwell as in a holy fortress, and by divine grace be preserved from worldly pollution and the attacks of the devil. Here they will have companionship and union with the wise and good of earth; and, by a diligent and devout use of the privileges and ordinances of the Church, be fitted for their bright and eternal calling in the heavenly state. Oh yes, the Church of Christ is the fold for his flock—the family for his children—and the garrison for those who are engaged in the good warfare.

APPLICATION.

Learn, in conclusion,

How truly important is our subject. How all Christians should feel it to be such. The young are, manifestly, to be lights to the Church and the world. We appeal to all young men. We ask, what is your moral state, character, and prospects? Have you thought of yourselves, the great ends of your being, and your fitness for accomplishing those ends? Are you so living, that your conduct will tend to your moral reputation and usefulness; and are you so living, that you may reasonably expect your youthful state to terminate in an honorable maturity; and when life itself shall end, in a safe and joyous eternity? Oh, ponder these momentous questions; and if conscience does not respond satisfactorily, at once give God your heart, and resolve to devote your whole being to glorify him.

We remark, finally, that our text need not be confined to young men, young women are equally interested. Divine wisdom is as needful for them as for young men. Folly is as ruinous in them as in young men. Indeed, vice of any kind appears more odious in them, than in the other sex. Religion is every thing to the young woman, for both worlds. Oh, think of the godly women of Scripture, and emulate their spirit, and follow their example. Remember Mary's wise and holy choice, and secure the one thing needful, the good part, that which shall not be taken from you. So shall you enjoy the love of the Saviour—adorn the gospel of God—and eventually be crowned with glory, immortality, and eternal life.

III.—BIGOTRY'S PASSWORD.

"Then said they unto him, say now Shibboleth; and he said Sibboleth: for he could not frame to pronounce it aright."—*Judges* xii. 6.

THE ancient history of the Jews is little better than one fearful exhibition of malevolence and slaughter. It is painful to read of their incessant wars with other nations. But it is still more melancholy to observe their civil contentions, and intestine revolutions, and cruelties. The text is found in connection with one of the most diabolical of these.

At this time the renowned Jephthah was ruler in Israel. He had gone to war against the Amorites, and had not invited the Ephraimites to unite with him. They were incensed against Jephthah on this account, and threatened to burn his house. "And the men of Ephraim gathered themselves together, and went northward, and said unto Jephthah, Wherefore passedst thou over to fight against the children of Ammon, and didst not call us to go with thee? we will burn thy house upon thee with fire:" ver. 1. He assigns his reason for this: "And Jephthah said unto them, I and my people were at great strife with the children of Ammon; and when I called you, ye delivered me not out of their hands. And when I saw that ye delivered *me* not, I put my life in my hands, and passed over against the children of Ammon, and the Lord delivered them into my hand: wherefore then are ye come unto me this day, to fight against me?" ver. 2, 3.

This led to a war between the men of Gilead and the Ephraimites. "Then Jephthah gathered together all the men of Gilead, and fought with Ephraim; and the men of Gilead smote Ephraim, because they said, Ye Gileadites are fugitives of Ephraim among the Ephraimites, and among the Manassites:" ver. 4. In the conflict, the Gileadites first passed over the ford of Jordan, and here they adopted a plan to cut off the Ephraimites (ver. 5, 6).

It is singular that there should be different dialects and pronunciations of the same people. The Ephraimites could not sound the H, but said Sibboleth; and by this they were distinguished, and slain at the passages of Jordan. But there was the evil of envy, malignity, and murder in the test, to which the text refers. Happy had it been if the history of Shibboleths had ended here! But

its pernicious influence is felt in various forms, to the present day. Look at our country; how often distracted with political shibboleths. Often there is the district or parochial shibboleth. But the worst of all, is the religious shibboleth. To this we shall now more fully call your attention. In doing so, the subject must be carefully guarded. There are two perils—one the sectarian prescribed shibboleth; the other, the vague irresponsible one of latitudinaranism.

Observe,

I. *What is essential to a true church of Christ; and which does not involve a sectarian Shibboleth.*

II. *The things which are non-essentials, but which are identified with sectarian Shibboleths.*

And,

III. *The evils of sectarian Shibboleths.*

Notice,

I. *What is essential to a true church of Christ; and which does not involve a sectarian Shibboleth.*

And I refer,

1. *To Christian doctrine.*

The essential doctrines of Christianity, are those which are vitally connected with the purity and efficacy of the gospel. What assails these, imperils the whole system. Now, of course, there will be different views as to these essential doctrines. But it appears from apostolic teaching, that there are, at least, three cardinal truths which are indispensably so.

(1.) Christ's supreme Divinity. It cannot possibly be a matter of secondary moment, whether my Saviour is a man or God, whether he is to be worshipped or not. We think this truth stands forth as the prominent truth of the gospel. That Christ, while he is the son of man, is also the Son of God; and that in a Divine sense, he has given to him not only superiority over angels, but absolute equality with the Father, that he is one in essence, and power, and glory, and authority with God. So that the rejection of this truth, appears to strike at the very foundation on which the whole superstructure of Christianity rests. So we also consider,

(2.) The doctrine of the atonement. Whether Jesus has offered a sacrifice for sin or not, must be a most important question. Next to the divinity of Christ's person, is the grand consideration of his work. What did he come to do—what has he done for man's salvation? He has taught the will of God—he has revealed new and grand doctrines—he has given new precepts—established new ordinances—and set up a new dispensation. Besides, he has given a perfect example of holiness and benevolence to mankind. But has he not also offered up a sacrifice for human transgression? Is he not the victim for sin, typified by the ancient beast slain and presented on Jewish altars? If not, then both prophecy and declarations are alike involved in impenetrable obscurity. It is said, that he was "wounded for our transgressions"—that the "iniquity of us all was laid on him"—that "his soul was made an offering for sin"—that he is the "Lamb of God which taketh away the sin of the world"—that he "tasted death for every man"—that he "died for the ungodly" —that "he bare our sins in his own body on the tree."

Now, not only in this view is Christ's death constantly exhibited, but to it sinners are directed to look, in this they are to trust. So that a rejection of the atonement thus scripturally given, must involve the setting up of another gospel, and remove at once the solid basis of the sinner's hope.

We refer,

(3.) To the doctrine of justification by faith. Whether God's mercy in Christ is to save us on our believing, or whether we are to be saved on the ground of our own good works. This doctrine is vitally connected with the last,—because it follows, if there is no atonement for sin, our salvation must be the result of God's mercy, on the ground and for the consideration of our repentance, and future obedience to him. But this is distinctly opposite to being saved by grace, through faith in the Lord Jesus, and not for any righteousness we have, or can present. So that this is the grand and divine fingerpost set up in our world, to direct the wandering and lost in the true way of life, and on which is written—"Believe on the Lord Jesus Christ, and thou shalt be saved." But reject this doctrine, and then another way of salvation is proposed, which is the repentance and obedience of the sinner, and which renders Christ's work utterly unnecessary and worthless. So that, if Christ's church and kingdom is to maintain essential truth, we cannot conceive their unyielding adhesion to these as displaying the spirit of party, or bigotry. Now these doctrines appear to be vital.

Then we notice, as essential to the Christian church, and which is not sectarian,

2. *Spiritual experience.*

Now, the church of God is for certain classes of characters—not for disbelievers, nor unbelievers; but it is to be formed entirely of believers; therefore, there is nothing sectarian in requiring evidences of faith in those who unite with Christ's church. That they are manifestly spiritual persons, whose faith works by love, and purifies the heart; who have Christ in their hearts the hope of glory. Then there must be,

3. *Christian practice.*

The church of Christ must have members of a specific course of life. This course of life is expressed in one word—obedience to Christ's moral precepts. Such as labor to exhibit his spirit, and walk in his steps.

Now, we have here the right place for good works, as the fruit of divine grace, and as the real evidence of the life of God in the soul. So, that whilst we must never allow good works to form the basis of the Christian superstructure, they must ever be demanded as the consecrated walls of the spiritual temple, and as the only evidence that we love Christ, and are his disciples and friends. And that no orthodoxy of creed, or zeal for services, can in the least compensate for an unholy life. So that it is in no wise sectarian to demand from those who wish for fellowship with Christ's church, that they give unquestionable proofs of a spiritual state of heart, by a conversation becoming the gospel of Christ.

Now these three things are essential to the spiritual constitution and prosperity of the church, and are not, in any sense, sectarian.

Notice,

II. *The things which are non-essentials, but which are identified with sectarian Shibboleths.*

And here we mention,

1. *Human notions on various points of belief.*

Of these, we may instance, peculiar ideas as to the secret will and predestinating purposes of God.

As to the precise mode of Divine operations on the soul.

As to the nature of the relationships of the Divine persons in the Godhead.

As to the way by which belief is produced in the mind and heart.

Now, these we give, only as so many instances in which men may not only differ in sentiment, but differ without their views affecting, in the least, the great truths of salvation. And to this small list we might add numberless other items, which fastidious men have, in all ages, been anxious to place as essentials of Christian belief; and, therefore, as essential for communion with the Christian church; and he who did not pronounce these metaphysical, in many instances doctrinal Shibboleths, was ecclesiastically put to death, and cast beyond the pale of the divine mercy.

We notice, also, as other sectarian Shibboleths,

2. *Views as to the precise character, and importance of Christian ordinances.*

With respect to baptism—its subjects, mode, and efficacy, and design.

The Lord's Supper—its express object, and manner, and frequency of communion; also its specific efficacy on the heart.

Then we might add, that not only have certain views of divine ordinances been made Shibboleths, but, also, mere human rites, and ecclesiastical institutions. As sponsorship, youthful confirmation, in one church; in another, a weekly attendance on a meeting for Christian experience; while in a third, it has been a regard to certain fasts and observances, of times and seasons. And in such things, sectarianism has wielded its sceptre—uttered its denunciations—and decided the exact pronunciation of these ordinances, as expressed by the various parties holding them, on penalty of exclusion from their fellowship.

Then there have been Shibboleths, also, in matters relating,

3. *To ecclesiastical polity and Church government.*

Whether it is to be an Episcopate, with its bishops and multifarious rites—or Presbyterian, with its synods and assemblies—or Congregational, giving to the whole church a religious democracy.

Then, again, whether it is to be identified with the civil power, or to be left under spiritual authority only, and maintained by the voluntary liberality of its members.

Now, these, when carried out and explained, almost cover the whole ground of sectarian Shibboleths as manifested, at least, in Protestant lands. Notice, then,

III. *The evil of these Shibboleths.*

They are so,

1. *As they interfere with Christ's authority.*

In religion, he is the only King, Lawgiver, Master. We must not add to, or take from, what he requires in order to discipleship.

Now, the only one condition to this, is clearly faith in himself, with its legitimate fruit. He never proposed either a greater or less number of articles of belief. He did not insist on a round of ceremonial observances. He did not even demand submission to his own ordinance of baptism, in many of the instances where he healed diseases and forgave sins. So that we can have no right to add to the one evangelical condition of simple faith; which was the only one he ever required in order to the bestowment of the richest blessings of his goodness and grace.

2. *It tramples on the rights of conscience.*

Men are accountable to God. They must think, and judge, and conclude for themselves. To their own master they stand or fall. Who are we, that we should demand they should pronounce our Shibboleth?

If we deem our fellow-Christians, or those inquiring after religion, to be in error, we may, and ought, to teach them. But beyond the employment of divine truth and moral suasion, we have no right to use any other means whatever. And it is not within our province to insist that our views of what Scripture says, shall be taken as infallible; if so, in what do we differ from the Romish church? And if so, how have we attained to so infallible a power of judgment? In nothing should we exhibit more delicate care and tender susceptibility, than in intruding our views on the consciences of men who are equally enfranchised with the liberty to judge, and to decide as to the meaning of the word of God, with ourselves.

3. *It attempts to set up a worthless uniformity.*

If a man will say "Shibboleth," it is enough. He may be extensively ignorant —spiritually defective—or, often he may be practically unworthy; yet, let him be a violent sectarian, and it will cover a multitude of faults. But what thinking intelligent minds will demand uniformity? What is it worth—or how can it be really effected?

(1.) In order to such a consummation, all minds would require to be of the same quality and capacity.

(2.) They should have had the same kind and degree of cultivation.

(3.) Then they should occupy the same point of observation in looking at all Christian subjects.

Now as all this is impossible, then uniformity is futile and absurd;—and yet all this ought to be realized, if one uniform and exact Shibboleth is to be pronounced.

4. *It leads to a bad spirit, which dishonors our common Christianity.*

Sectarian points of belief are magnified above the essentials of religion. Thus men become isolated from, and bitterly opposed to, one another. They exhibit their energies against the professed friends of religion, instead of against the enemies of Christ. The consequences are, that we see one regiment of God's host, furiously combating another regiment in the same professed army; which is not only a perversion of their energies and time, but which makes evil men to rejoice, and weakens, beyond description, the Christian cause. This, for ages, has been the blight and mildew of the religion of Jesus. Hence, Pagans, Mohammedans, and Jews; avowed Atheists, bitter Romanists, and Free Thinkers, of all grades, as they call themselves—hold up this divided and torn robe of our Christian profession, to the scorn and ridicule of the world. Nothing has been so disastrous to New Testament religion, as the dividing its friends into petty parties and numerous divisions, and multiplying almost beyond number their several sectarian Shibboleths.

APPLICATION.

1. We address all seekers of religion. To such we say, be sure and obtain your religion from the Holy Scriptures. Here you will have it not only pure and undiluted, but also in all its divine and blessed simplicity. The waters of truth are not dark and turbid, but transparent as crystal. There is not a saving doctrine, nor a holy precept of Christ's religion, but what has been presented in such unmistakable plainness, that a child may comprehend it; and the wayfaring man, though a fool, need not err therein. We say to all,

2. Seek to have the life and spirit, as well as the form of religion. You may have a creed most orthodox and correct, and the outward exhibition of your religion may be beautifully developed; but all this may be like the chiselling of statuary, or the casting of a model—where there is neither breath nor life. Remember, religion is a vitality—a living reality in the soul; and without this spiritual pervading power, every thing else is utterly in vain.

3. Cherish a kind and forbearing spirit towards all the avowed friends of Jesus. It may be long before the churches of Christ may come to the important conclusion to abolish every thing from their various sections of it, which may not be absolutely essential; but in the mean while, every Christian may exhibit a catholic spirit, and a loving disposition and temper, towards every believer of every name.

Sectarianism is more likely to be destroyed by the genial atmosphere within the church, than by any associations from without. But in every way, let true Christians unite to remove this foul thing from the religion of him, who has declared, that love only is the badge of loyal obedience: and that by this shall all men know who are really his disciples.

4. Maintain Christian independence, and honor it in others. Remember how easy it is to take up a creed made ready to our hands; and how difficult often to be hard readers, and devotional explorers of the Scriptures—the only mine where divine and saving truth is to be found. Not only be valiant for the truth yourselves, but honor all who have moral courage, and persevering effort, and self-denial, to obtain it for themselves. Yet, in every noble-minded effort to obtain truth, do not be deceived by supposing that truth only dwells in the region of novelty,—rather remember that you are to "Stand in the ways and see, and ask for the old paths—where is the good way?" and having found that, then you must "walk therein;" and the gracious promise is, that in so doing, "ye shall find rest to your souls."

IV.—THE TWOFOLD SONG OF THE BELIEVER.

"I will sing of mercy and judgment: unto thee, O Lord, will I sing."—*Psalm* ci. 1.

SINGING seems to involve the elevation of the heart and the utterance of the lips, by which some theme or topic is proclaimed aloud, and exultingly, before others. The angels are represented as singing the praises of Jehovah. This seems to be a department of their constant service. They behold his face, and praise God in adoring songs continually. We have also a reference to two of these songs, in regard to our earth.

At the creation, the "Morning Star sang together, and all the sons of God shouted for joy."

At the incarnation of the Redeemer, "suddenly there was with the angel a multitude of the heavenly host praising God, and saying, Glory to God in the highest, and on earth peace, good-will towards men."—Luke ii. 13, 14. The godly in all ages have been accustomed to sing. Hence we have the highly-wrought poetical song of Moses and Miriam, on the overthrow of Pharaoh. Sacred singing was part of the service of the Tabernacle and the Temple. The writer of the text was the great sacred song writer of Israel. We have also the rich, luxurious, and oriental song of songs, which was Solomon's. Many of the prophets interspersed songs with their predictions. There is one beautiful specimen—"And in that day thou shalt say, O Lord, I will praise thee; though thou wast angry with me, thine anger is turned away, and thou comfortedst me."—Isa. xii. 1. Even Christ our Lord, on the last night of his sorrowful abode on earth, concluded the eucharistic supper with a holy song. It is said "they sang a hymn, and then went out." This service of song is also inculcated by the apostle: "Let the word of Christ dwell in you richly in all wisdom; teaching and admonishing one another in psalms and hymns and spiritual songs, singing with grace in your hearts to the Lord."—Col. iii. 16.

Then let the text dictate suitable subjects for our humble, yet heartfelt, exultation. If we carry out its spirit,

I. *We shall sing of mercy.*

Now you will remember, David was often singing of this. "I will sing of the mercies of the Lord forever: with my mouth will I make known thy faithfulness to all generations."—Psa. lxxxix. 1. And the rich repeated offering is fully given in Psalm 136. So in the hundred and third psalm. Now we ask,

1. *What is mercy?*

It is something more than goodness. It is goodness and kindness to the undeserving. It is the commiserating of the unworthy, and acting even graciously towards the guilty. God is good to angels—good to all the inferior creatures—good to all! But he is merciful to the human family. It is probable, that mercy was first exhibited to our guilty fallen race.

It is obvious, that holy angels did not stand in need of mercy, and for the fallen angels we have no record that mercy has ever been offered. So that this glorious perfection of Deity, so far as we know, has been confined to our worthless apostate world. Surely then, man, so remembered, so distinguished, ought to sing of mercy.

But we may inquire,

2. *What is there in mercy, of which we ought to sing?*

(1.) Of the marvellousness of its origin. Where did mercy take its rise, and how? There seems to have been a wise and perfect harmony in the perfections of the Godhead before. There was righteousness and purity. Goodness and love for the excellent,—equity and justice for all—and wrath for the disobedient. Now, what more was needful in the moral government of God? Well, guilt and unworthiness appear in the new-formed race, and then another modified perfection of the Godhead is seen. It pities—it compassionates—it smiles—and its name is *mercy*. But yet the *how* and wherefore of this mercy is still an unsearchable mystery. We should sing,

(2.) Of the expensiveness of its sacrifices. Mercy, not merely in feeling, or speaking, or acting; but in suffering for us. Mercy flowing through the channel of the humiliation, self-denial, sorrow, anguish, and death of God's Son. The moral principle was ever known and recognized by Jehovah, that guilt must be punished, and that without shedding of blood there could be no remission. We should sing,

(3.) Of mercy, in the abundance of its blessings. Every thing a sinner has, or enjoys, must flow from mercy. His continued being—his daily food and raiment—his health—his reason—his friends—his privileges, and means of improvement—his soul's illumination, conviction, conversion, pardon, adoption, heirship to glory. He is blessed with merciful providences, promises, enjoyments, present salvation, and the good hope of eternal life. "Looking for the mercy of the Lord Jesus Christ to eternal life!" We should sing,

(4.) Of its universality and freeness. Not a few rays of merciful light, but the bound-

less sun, full orbed in noontide glory. Not
a few drops, but rivers and oceans of mercy.
Not exhibited to a few, but to all our fallen
race, and to all God's works. It is the horizon of every land. It is the belt of the
earth. It is the air of life to every man.
Free, free, free! to each, to all, to every
child of man. We should sing,

(5.) As to other special distinctions of
mercy. Its length—from eternity to eternity. Its height—higher than the heavens,
and above the clouds. Its perpetuity—it
endureth forever. Besides, it is said to be
strong, rich, tender, faithful; and above all,
God himself delighteth in it. What a theme
then for holy contemplation and joyous
song! What a subject for rapturous exultation, to proclaim the wondrous subject to the
moral universe! We may well exclaim in
reference to this—

"Let rocks and hills,
Their lasting silence break."

Every rightly regulated mind, every sanctified heart, every grateful spirit, must sing of
mercy.

But under the influence of the text,

II. *We will sing also of Judgment.*

Now judgment might mean God's righteousness, or his law, or word, or his inflicted punishments on the impenitent. And all
of these are well worthy of song.

(1.) God's righteousness is his glory.
This is the basis of his moral government.
Without this, he would inspire no confidence, command no veneration, nor possess
any exalted affection from his intelligent
creatures. "Say among the heathen that
the Lord reigneth: the world also shall be
established that it shall not be moved: he
shall judge the people righteously."—Ps.
xcvi. 10. "The Lord reigneth; let the earth
rejoice; let the multitude of isles be glad
thereof. Clouds and darkness are round
about him: righteousness and judgment are
the habitation of his throne."—Psa. xcvii.
1, 2.

(2.) God's law. His law and word are
holy, just, and good; and worthy of him.
"I will praise thee with uprightness of
heart, when I shall have learned thy righteous judgments. With my lips have I declared all the judgments of thy mouth. Thy
statutes have been my songs in the house of
my pilgrimage. Accept, I beseech thee,
the freewill offerings of my mouth, O Lord,
and teach me thy judgments."—Psa. cxix.

7, 13, 54, 108. So also the Apostle: "Let
the word of Christ dwell in you richly in all
wisdom; teaching and admonishing one another in psalms and hymns and spiritual
songs, singing with grace in your hearts to
the Lord."—Col. iii. 16.

(3.) His wrath. Now, his wrath is ever
just. It is ever put forth after the sinner's
long probation. It is God's strange work.
It never exceeds the desert of the culprit.
There is no despotism, nor tyranny, nor
what we call revenge, in it.

God's wrath is the wise and equitable infliction of punishment on the guilty; and as
such, however terrible, it may be celebrated
in holy and reverend song, as was the overthrow and utter ruin of Pharaoh and his
host in the waters of the Red Sea.

But, in the text, we may consider judgment to mean God's chastening dispensations—the afflictive cup he gives his people
to drink. Now this is the common portion
of man. Man that is born of a woman, is
born to trouble. But there are corrective
afflictions sent to his own children, for their
spiritual profit and eternal well-being. It is
through much tribulation that believers enter the kingdom. Well, what in judgments
of this kind is there to sing of? We may
sing,

(1.) Of their wise administration. He
never sends them but when there is a needs-
be for their employment. Never too soon.
He is always guided by infallible skill. He
ever acts as our wise and best friend. No
accident nor chance in them. They do not
spring out of the dust. Not contingent occurrences, but events under the control of
infallible knowledge and never-failing goodness.

Then there is,

(2.) The tenderness of their application.
Look at the parent correcting the child! he
forgets not that he is correcting his own nature. Look at the mother giving the cup of
bitter medicine! she does it feelingly. So
God in his dealings infinitely transcends the
tenderness of both. "He knoweth our frame,
he remembereth we are dust." He does
not afflict the children of men willingly.
His pity never forsakes the subjects of his
chastisements; and his love is never more
tender than when he wields the corrective
rod. Especially when we contemplate God
in Christ Jesus, we may well sing,

"His heart is made of tenderness,
His bowels melt with love."

Then consider,

(3.) The supports he gives with them. He ever strengthens the shoulder for the cross. He tempers the blast to the shorn lamb. He gives grace to suffer, as well as to live and labor. And this grace, in kind and degree, is ever sufficient. He sends no pain, nor allows any trial which they are not able to bear. And he says to each of his sorrowing ones—"As thy day is, so shall thy strength be." He too never allows his people to be in the lion's den, or in the fiery furnace, or in the gloomy dungeon, or on the sick-bed, alone. He is ever there to give might, and support, and consolation; to sustain or deliver.

Then we may sing, when we reflect,

(4.) On the great ends his judgments are to accomplish. Now these unquestionably are,—Our benefit, our real, present, and permanent good. Our good for both worlds. The gale is not to wreck the vessel, but to drive it more rapidly into the desired haven. The fire is not to consume, but to purify. The medicine is not to kill, but to heal. The rod is not to injure, but to sanctify and bless. Hence the Apostle dwells on this most beautifully—"My son, despise not thou the chastening of the Lord, nor faint when thou art rebuked of him. For whom the Lord loveth he chasteneth, and scourgeth every son whom he receiveth. If ye endure chastening, God dealeth with you as with sons; for what son is he whom the father chasteneth not? But if ye be without chastisement, whereof all are partakers, then are ye bastards, and not sons. Furthermore, we have had fathers of our flesh which corrected us, and we gave them reverence: shall we not much rather be in subjection unto the Father of spirits, and live? For they, verily, for a few days chastened us after their own pleasure; but he for our profit, that we might be partakers of his holiness."—Heb. xii. 5–10. So he avers—"And we know that all things work together for good to them that love God, to them who are the called according to his purpose."—Rom. viii. 28. And to this he adds—"For our light affliction, which is but for a moment, worketh for us a far more exceeding and eternal weight of glory; while we look not at the things which are seen, but at the things which are not seen: for the things which are seen are temporal; but the things which are not seen are eternal."—2 Cor. iv. 17, 18. And he reasons on the blessed process of af-

flictions, thus—"And not only so, but we glory in tribulations also: knowing that tribulation worketh patience; and patience, experience; and experience, hope; and hope maketh not ashamed; because the love of God is shed abroad in our hearts by the Holy Ghost which is given unto us."—Rom. v. 3–5. Hence, then, what ample matter for grateful meditation and exulting joy. And though nature may not see the same reason to sing in affliction as in prosperity; yet grace will ever unite in its holy anthems both mercy and judgment. Now we ask,

1. Have we not given a key-note which ought to suit every heart and voice? Who will excuse himself from the exercise of holy song? Who has not mercies to celebrate, and afflictions to be thankful for? Just take a retrospect of all the way the Lord has led you,—just read a few pages either in the volume of providence, or God's word; and then you will be constrained to say, "I will sing of mercy and judgment; unto thee, O Lord, will I sing." And do not forget either of these topics; they are both worthy of heartfelt grateful remembrance.

2. The advantages of this joyous course will be many. It will lighten the load of sorrow. It will sweeten the bitter potion. It will while away the dreary hour. It will elevate the dormant spirit. It will exhilarate the oppressed and fainting heart. It will, by a kind of divine chemistry, bring new elements of health and comfort out of nauseous medicines. It will cheer the soul, honor religion, glorify your Father, and aid greatly in your spiritual and upward flight to the land of eternal joy and everlasting glory. O sorrowing child of earth, sing on thy way to the land of Beulah, which is before thee! Remember what the prophet has said—"And the ransomed of the Lord shall return, and come to Zion with songs and everlasting joy upon their heads: they shall obtain joy and gladness, and sorrow and sighing shall flee away."—Isa. xxxv. 10.

3. May some now learn to sing the Lord's song in a strange land. Have you been heedless of God's mercies? how criminal—how ungrateful! Have you never blessed the hand that has chastened you? how insensible and unwise! Now, let these be the themes of your serious reflection. See if your own well-being is not bound up in acknowledging God, and singing of mercy and judgment. Finally,

4. Sing on the way to heaven, in the expectation of singing there, forever and ever. Many of the services of earth will cease in heaven. Probably all watchings, and conflicts, and prayers—all toil and all temptation, and all suffering. But praise will only there be presented in exalted purity,—only there ascend from spotless hearts, and unfaltering lips. Cherish then this service here, that you may join with Seraphim and Cherubim, and all the shining hosts of the blessed, in singing the wondrous praises of God and the Lamb forever.

V.—JOSEPH'S EGYPTIAN NAME.

"And Pharaoh called Joseph's name Zaphnath-paaneah."—*Gen.* xli. 45.

There is no narrative, either sacred or profane, more deeply interesting than that of the life of Joseph. It is inimitably simple—beautifully interwoven with a great variety of changing events. It strikingly develops not only his own character, but that of his affectionate parent, and of each and all of his brethren. It forms an essential link in the chain of Israel's history, and introduces us to a familiar acquaintance with one of the celebrated monarchs of Egypt.

But in the midst of a rich variety of thought, our text leads us to consider a circumstance in Joseph's history, which to many may appear of no importance. It was the name given to him by Pharaoh. Names were often changed, or given under peculiar circumstances. Abram, which signified a high father, was altered to Abraham, which signified father of a great multitude. So Jacob to Israel. So Saul to Paul. So the name of Joseph, which signifies Increase, to Zaphnath-paaneah; which may be rendered—The man to whom secrets are revealed; or, a revealer of secrets.

Now let us see,

I. *The appropriateness of the name to Joseph in his own person.*

And then under that appellation, let us notice him,

II. *As an illustrious type of the world's Redeemer.*

Let us consider,

I. *The appropriateness of the name to Joseph in his own person.*

"Zaphnath-paaneah."

Now in both senses of its interpretation, it was very applicable to Joseph. God revealed his mind specially to him, both by the dreams he had, and by the spirit of interpretation which rested on him.

1. *By his own dreams.*

"And Joseph dreamed a dream, and he told it his brethren: and they hated him yet the more. And he said unto them, Hear, I pray you, this dream which I have dreamed: for, behold, we were binding sheaves in the field, and, lo, my sheaf arose, and also stood upright; and, behold, your sheaves stood round about, and made obeisance to my sheaf. And his brethren said unto him, Shalt thou indeed reign over us? or shalt thou indeed have dominion over us? And they hated him yet the more for his dreams, and for his words. And he dreamed yet another dream, and told it his brethren, and said, Behold, I have dreamed a dream more: and, behold, the sun and the moon and the eleven stars made obeisance to me. And he told it to his father, and to his brethren; and his father rebuked him, and said unto him, What is this dream that thou hast dreamed? Shall I and thy mother and thy brethren indeed come to bow down ourselves to thee to the earth? And his brethren envied him; but his father observed the saying."—Gen. xxxvii. 5–11. You know how exactly the spirit of these dreams came to pass. "And Joseph was the governor over the land, and he it was that sold to all the people of the land: and Joseph's brethren came, and bowed down themselves before him with their faces to the earth."—Gen. xlii. 6.

Here then how fully and minutely was the predictive vision realized; and that without any plan or contrivance on the part of any concerned in it. Nothing but God's prescience could have detailed it so graphically, so many years before. But we see the appropriateness of the name to Joseph,

2. *By the spirit of interpretation which rested on him.*

He is in prison, falsely and wickedly accused. Two prisoners of note are with him. "And it came to pass after these things, that the butler of the king of Egypt and his baker had offended their lord the king of Egypt. And Pharaoh was wroth against two of his officers, against the chief of the butlers, and against the chief of the bakers. And he put them in ward in the house of the captain of the guard, into the prison, the place where Joseph was bound. And the captain of the guard charged Joseph with them, and he served them: and they continued a season in the ward. And they dreamed a dream both of them, each man his dream in one night, each man according to the interpretation of his dream, the butler and the baker of the king of Egypt, which were bound in the prison. And Joseph came in unto them in the morning, and looked upon them, and, behold, they were sad. And he asked Pharaoh's officers that were with him in the ward of his lord's house, saying, Wherefore look ye so sadly to-day? And they said unto him, We have dreamed a dream, and there is no interpreter of it. And Joseph said unto them, Do not interpretations belong to God? tell me them, I pray you. And the chief butler told his dream to Joseph, and said to him, In my dream, behold, a vine was before me; and in the vine were three branches: and it was as though it budded, and her blossoms shot forth; and the clusters thereof brought forth ripe grapes: and Pharaoh's cup was in my hand; and I took the grapes, and pressed them into Pharaoh's cup, and I gave the cup into Pharaoh's hand. And Joseph said unto him, This is the interpretation of it: The three branches are three days: Yet within three days shall Pharaoh lift up thine head, and restore thee unto thy place; and thou shalt deliver Pharaoh's cup into his hand, after the former manner when thou wast his butler."—Gen. xl. 1–13; see also v. 16 to 19.

The events literally occurred as he had intimated. For the chief butler was restored to office and favor again; but the wretched baker was hanged, as Joseph had predicted. So, that, here God had revealed events that no human sagacity could have foretold to Joseph; and he had expressly stated the secrets to the men, so deeply concerned in the revelation. But notwithstanding the affecting appeal of Joseph to the butler, "But think on me when it shall be well with thee, and show kindness, I pray thee, unto me, and make mention of me unto Pharaoh, and bring me out of this house; for indeed I was stolen away out of the land of the Hebrews: and here also have I done nothing that they should put me into the dungeon:" ver. 14, 15: it is recorded—"Yet did not the chief butler remember Joseph, but forgat him;" ver 23.

Having been forgotten by the chief butler for two years, Pharaoh dreamed; and his dream is very striking and comprehensive. "And it came to pass at the end of two full years, that Pharaoh dreamed: and, behold, he stood by the river. And, behold, there came up out of the river seven well-favored kine and fat-fleshed; and they fed in a meadow. And, behold, seven other kine came up after them out of the river, ill-favored and lean-fleshed; and stood by the other kine upon the brink of the river. And the ill-favored and lean-fleshed kine did eat up the seven well-favored and fat kine. So Pharaoh awoke. And he slept and dreamed the second time: and, behold, seven ears of corn came up upon one stalk, rank and good. And, behold, seven thin ears and blasted with the east wind sprung up after them. And the seven thin ears devoured the seven rank and full ears. And Pharaoh awoke, and, behold, it was a dream."—Gen. xli. 1–7. To interpret this dream, the magicians were called in. "And it came to pass in the morning that his spirit was troubled; and he sent and called for all the magicians of Egypt, and all the wise men thereof: and Pharaoh told them his dreams; but there was none that could interpret them unto Pharaoh,"—ver. 8. Then the chief butler remembered Joseph. "Then spake the chief butler unto Pharaoh, saying, I do remember my faults this day:" ver. 9. Joseph is called in, is interrogated. "Then Pharaoh sent and called Joseph, and they brought him hastily out of the dungeon: and he shaved himself, and changed his raiment, and came in unto Pharaoh;" ver. 14. He modestly and piously honors God. "And Pharaoh said unto Joseph, I have dreamed a dream, and there is none that can interpret it: and I have heard say of thee, that thou canst understand a dream to interpret it;" ver. 15. And he interprets the dream,—gives him advice,—and then came Joseph's release, advancement, and honor. "And Pharaoh said unto Joseph, Forasmuch as God hath showed thee all this, there is none so discreet and wise as thou art: thou shalt be over my house, and according unto thy word shall all my people be ruled; only in the throne will I be greater than thou. And Pharaoh said unto Joseph, See, I have set thee over all the land of Egypt. And Pharaoh took off his ring from his hand, and put it upon Joseph's hand, and arrayed him in vestures of fine linen, and put a gold chain about his neck; and he made him to ride in the second chariot which he had; and they cried before him, Bow the knee; and he made him ruler over all the land of Egypt. And Pharaoh said unto Joseph, I am Pharaoh, and without thee shall no man lift up his hand or foot in all the land of Egypt. And Pharaoh called Joseph's name Zaphnath-paaneah; and he gave him to wife Asenath the daughter of Poti-pherah, priest of On. And Joseph went out over all the land of Egypt;" ver. 39–45.

Now here is seen the appropriateness of the name as applied to Joseph. But let us look at it in its application to Joseph,

II. *As an illustrious type of the world's Redeemer.*

Of all Old Testament typical persons or events, none more specially prefigured Christ than Joseph. In some forty particulars, it has been shown, by ingenious writers, how these points of resemblance were exhibited. We here advert to a few.

His original name, Joseph. His father's extreme affection for him. His wonderful wisdom in his youth. His being envied of his brethren. His being sent on a message of kindness to them. The conspiracy formed against him. His being sold. His being falsely accused. His imprisonment. His exaltation. His power and authority. His clemency to his brethren. His being the saviour of his father's house. But we shall confine ourselves to the text—Joseph a type of Jesus, as a revealer of secrets. And as such, observe,

1. *What he revealed.*

There had been revelations before. " God, who at sundry times and in divers manners spake in time past unto the fathers by the prophets, hath in these last days spoken unto us by his Son, whom he hath appointed heir of all things, by whom also he made the worlds."—Heb. i. 1, 2. But he revealed truths more fully; and he revealed new truths to mankind. He revealed,

(1.) The character of God. "No man hath seen God at any time; the only begotten Son, which is in the bosom of the Father, he hath declared him."—John i. 18.

Previous revelations had been brief, and in a kind of oracular sentences. Christ came and made the Father more fully known; and he did so especially as a God of grace and mercy, pitying and loving his guilty children; and also, as one essentially with him-self. "Philip saith unto him, Lord, show us the Father, and it sufficeth us. Jesus saith unto him, Have I been so long time with you, and yet hast thou not known me, Philip? he that hath seen me hath seen the Father; and how sayest thou then, Show us the Father? Believest thou not that I am in the Father, and the Father in me? the words that I speak unto you I speak not of myself; but the Father that dwelleth in me, he doeth the works."—John xiv. 8, 9, 10.

(2.) He revealed the way of the sinner's restoration and acceptance with God. How fully he did this in his discourse with Nicodemus, when he said—" And as Moses lifted up the serpent in the wilderness, even so must the Son of man be lifted up; that whosoever believeth in him should not perish, but have eternal life. For God so loved the world, that he gave his only begotten Son, that whosoever believeth in him should not perish, but have everlasting life. For God sent not his Son into the world to condemn the world; but that the world through him might be saved."—John iii. 14–17.

And how in his divine and inimitable parables of the lost sheep and the prodigal son, did he most beautifully show God's rich and compassionate heart to his fallen and perishing creatures; and also, all his teaching and miracles presented the power and simplicity of faith; and its essentiality to the attainment of pardon, blessedness, and salvation.

(3.) He revealed the doctrine of the resurrection of the dead, and of eternal life. "Verily, verily I say unto you, he that heareth my word, and believeth on him that sent me, hath everlasting life, and shall not come into condemnation; but is passed from death unto life. Verily, verily, I say unto you, The hour is coming, and now is, when the dead shall hear the voice of the Son of God: and they that hear shall live. For as the Father hath life in himself; so hath he given to the Son to have life in himself; and hath given him authority to execute judgment also, because he is the Son of man. Marvel not at this; for the hour is coming, in the which all that are in their graves shall hear his voice, and shall come forth; they that have done good, unto the resurrection of life; and they that have done evil, to the resurrection of damnation."—John v. 24–29.

Now, here were truths which had only been most faintly taught before. But Christ opens the dreary tomb, and exhibits eternal life to his believing followers. How truly did he bring life and immortality to light, by the gospel. And how appropriate the declaration as to him—" God hath given to us eternal life, and this life is in his Son." So that he that " hath the Son hath life."

Now, these were some of the great subjects of the revelations of the Lord Jesus Christ to our world. It is worthy of our particular observation,

2. *How he revealed these things.*

Not figuratively ; by shadows, and types, and sacrifices, but literally. Not metaphysically, but clearly. Not learnedly, but simply. So as to be adapted to the capacity of all. Not partially, but fully.

All previous revelations had been gradual and progressive ; but those of Christ were full and complete. He appeared as the sun of righteousness to give perfect day ; while, previously, only stars had given their twinkling rays. And the revelations of Jesus meet the whole moral exigency of our benighted world. Nothing more is needed to man's spiritual elevation, holiness, blessedness, and to his complete and eternal salvation.

Then also consider,

3. *The supreme importance of the revelations he made.*

In the case of Joseph, his revelations were of the highest importance to his father's house, and in some sort to the whole world. So Christ's revelations particularly had special reference to his people the Jews, as whose Shepherd and King he came. But his advent and revelations had respect also to the best interests of the whole human race. Joseph's revelations related to the preservation of life—Jesus, to the life of the soul and eternal felicity. None but Joseph could reveal what was necessary to those ends; and none but Christ could manifest the love of God, and open the gates of the kingdom of heaven. If the name of Zaphnath-paaneah exactly expressed the character of Joseph—how much more fully is it embodied in him of whom, after all, Joseph was a feeble and imperfect type.

Then in conclusion, we demand for Jesus,

1. Holy and devout veneration. He is to be honored and worshipped even with the highest kind of homage and adoration, of which we are capable. He is not to be placed among prophets and illustrious men only ; but he is to be exalted above angels, principalities, and powers ; yea men are to honor him, even as they honor the Father. Hence when God brought his Son into our world, the mandate went forth—" Let all the angels of God worship him." He also should have,

2. Our high and ardent praise. He should be exalted and praised from the rising to the setting of the sun. For his whole work was for our benefit and salvation. His humiliation, self-denial, sufferings and death, were all endured that we might not perish, but have everlasting life. He became, in himself, the bread of life for a dying world. No marvel that every harp in heaven is employed to celebrate his worthy praise. We should give him,

3. Supreme love and confidence. Every view of Jesus is adapted to win our esteem—command our admiration—and elicit our confidence and love.

Well has the poet said—

" No theme is like redeeming love,
No Saviour is like ours."

" Let then, with elevated voice,
Harmonious anthems raise ;
Be thou the spring of all our joys,
The life of all our praise.

Be thou exalted in the heavens,
And o'er this earthly ball ;
Let creatures into nothing sink,
And Christ be all in all."

We should feel the importance,

4. Of a personal application of his gracious revelations to our own souls. These revelations are not merely for exciting our wonder and admiration, but Christ has made known to us what we must understand and feel, and realize in our experience, in order to our salvation. So that we must hear the blessed Saviour, that our souls may live—receive his words that we may know how to escape the righteous displeasure of God, and attain the remission of sin, and finally enjoy everlasting blessedness. See to it then that you come to Christ, that you may know him, and that your knowledge is experimental and saving. And forget not, that he alone stands forth to give to the anxious inquiring soul, the words of Eternal Life !

VI.—JOY AND BENEFICENCE.

"I know that there is no good in them, but for a man to rejoice, and to do good in his life."— *Eccles.* iii. 12.

THERE are two views which may be taken of this world—one bright, the other dark. In the dark view, we may see in it, sorrow, affliction, misery, and death. It seems one dreary valley of dry bones—one gloomy sepulchre.

Now this view seems to present to our mind certain portions of divine truth with peculiar effect; for instance, the peculiar admonition of Micah,—"Arise ye, and depart; for this is not your rest: because it is polluted, it shall destroy you, even with a sore destruction;" ii. 10. See also Job xiv. 1, 2; and Heb. xi. 13–16.

The other view regards this world as the production of infinite wisdom and goodness; and also as full of the evidences of his love, and gracious regards to man. Hence we behold it replete with divine beauty—overflowing with streams of mercy; and we see the great Parent of all opening his liberal hand, and supplying all his creatures with good. Now it is this view of God's goodness to us, in this life, which should lead to the wise and pious conclusion of the text—that the end of all is, that men should rejoice and do good in this life.

Observe, then,

1. *The nature and the characteristics of the joy we should cherish.*

Now this joy is evidently to be an emotion of the soul—the very opposite,

1. *Of desponding gloom.*

We are to behold God's world; and to gaze, and admire, and adore! We are to contemplate God in his marvellous works with enlightened eyes, and not with superstitious terror. We are to behold his goodness with confidence, and with a holy, trusting spirit. Not to seek out the dreary and the dark; but look for, and dwell on, the manifest goodness of God.

An intelligent survey of the divine works is eminently calculated to fill the soul with feelings of lofty exultation and joy. And the Christian should cherish this, and endeavor to delight himself, not only in God's character and relationship to him, but in the Divine government and works. The consideration that every thing in this wondrous world, is the work of his heavenly Father, should fill him with holy admiration and delight.

Then this joy is to be the opposite,

2. *Of ungrateful discontent.*

It is true, there is much to make us grave and serious—much to produce consideration and reflection; but how much to fill us with the spirit of grateful satisfaction? Just think, that the God of love rules the world. That he is so forbearing to his frail creatures. That he is so beneficent to all his dependent creatures. That even crosses are sent as medicine to heal us. That we enjoy so very much, and really suffer so little. That we absolutely deserve nothing. That by reason of sin, we have forfeited all right to any enjoyment whatever.

Now, under a government so gracious as this, shall we murmur and complain? Shall we fret ourselves against God, and find fault with him? Shall we be discontented and unhappy? A course like this would involve base ingratitude towards God, a spirit of arrogance in ourselves; and could only be productive of inward wretchedness and misery. See Psalm ciii. 10 to 14.

Now, let these things be considered; and content will reign in the soul, and praise flow from the lips. Then this spirit of joy is the opposite,

3. *Of unbelieving alarm.*

We need not constantly be looking out for evil or grief. We may trust God, and hope in him: there is no real joy in which trust and hope do not meet. They are essential to its being. Unbelief and terror destroy it. Well, see then the great beneficence of God, as exhibited in the world. There is no good in them, but for a man to rejoice. Let this supply the Morning hymn of praise; the Evening song of thanksgiving; the continued gratitude and gladness of the whole day, and of the whole life. And how fully are we furnished with the essential material for inspiring this joyous life and confidence in God; and for expressing it in thoughts and words, appropriate to the moral grandeur of the subject. See Psalms lxxxix. 1; cv. 1–3; cvi. 1, 2; cvii. 1; cxiii. 1–3; and cxlv. 1, 2, &c.

Observe,

II. *The practice of goodness we should exhibit.*

Not only to rejoice, but "to do good."

Now, we must not only rejoice in God's goodness, but we must also imitate it. See Matt. v. 43–8. Not enjoy it selfishly, nay, we cannot do this. As the Israelites could not hoard up the manna in the wilderness without it becoming putrescent—so all self-ishness defeats its aim, inasmuch as what we hoard can confer no real enjoyment on ourselves. In such cases we rob others, and are not enriched thereby. If others are not allowed to partake with us, then will it become unfit even for our own use.

Now, selfishness sins not only against man, but against God. It is contrary to his goodness and benevolent laws. He has demanded that we shall love him supremely, then our neighbor as ourselves. And we cannot keep either of these commandments separately. If we really love God with all our hearts, we shall delight to obey the law of love in reference to our fellow-men. And the real unselfish love of men will ever be accompanied with true love to God. This love, in both cases, is the same holy principle and emotion; but diverging into the two directions of God and our fellow-creatures. We are to rejoice in God's goodness, and to imitate it as dear children.

Now in reference to this practice of beneficence, observe,

1. *The sphere of goodness is large.*

It includes the wide world. Everywhere there is sin, misery, and death. And everywhere are demands on Christian piety and mercy. No clime, or people, or tongue, forms an exception. No object can be too near or too distant. One suffering man on the utmost verge of the globe, would have a right to our compassion and mercy. Love of kindred, and friends, and objects close at hand—may well first engage our beneficent regards. Love of country may next occupy our loving purposes and actions. But true Christian goodness, like the love of God, is to clasp the world in its merciful embraces, and seek the real happiness, as far as possible, of every creature. Hence the enlarged command—" to do good unto all men, especially to such as are of the household of faith."

2. *The objects of goodness are numerous and diversified.*

There are few who could not be benefited by Christian goodness. See that crowd of the poor, evidently in deep adversity ! Behold those widows, orphans, and fatherless children ! See that crowd of the ignorant, morally benighted, and observe that mass of the profligate and perishing ! Millions of heathen, both at home and abroad. How manifold the forms of wretchedness that stand out before us ! None need go far to find those whom his goodness may not bless, and whom his beneficence may not relieve ; so that you will not require to go far, or wait long, to carry out the text ; but the difficulty will be rather to select the most wretched and miserable from among the almost infinite variety of the suffering around you. Observe,

3. *The means of goodness are ample and various.*

Who can doubt, but that the Church of God possesses a plenitude of moral and benignant power, almost sufficient to dry up the griefs of the world. There is the wealth of the Church of Christ, which, if collected and wisely expended, would do immense good to the poor and the afflicted. If Christ's disciples were trained in his own school of self-denial, and all worldly luxuries and fashion eschewed, what provision might be made for the wants of the wretched ! Not only would the resources of the Church be sufficient for all spiritual work—whether at home or abroad—but it might imitate its gracious and loving Lord, in going out everywhere to bless and relieve the temporal miseries of mankind. Now along with the means possessed, there is the spirit of goodness in the hearts of God's people—the promise of the divine blessing ; and in addition to all these, all kinds of talents, and gifts, and opportunities.

Observe,

4. *Neglecting practical goodness, we cannot please God.*

We have shown you, that the first table of the law requires—homage, and love, and obedience to God. The second—love and goodness to our fellow-men. If this is true of the law, still more so is it of the gospel. This is emphatically a dispensation of tender love and mercy. Now, to neglect the exercise of goodness, is to violate the express commands of God—to oppose the spirit within our hearts—to run counter to Christ's blessed example—and to sin against our fellow-men.

Hence, how fully and distinctly we are taught this in the divine word. Jas. i. 27 ; 1 John iii. 17 ; Heb. xiii. 16.

5. *Disregarding goodness, we cannot enjoy the highest order of happiness.*

(1.) Our human nature cannot. The eye, the ear, the heart, are all made in connection with the whole nervous system, for pity and sympathy ; so that the exercise of goodness is really a source of pleasure to our wonderfully made physical system. It adds enjoyment to the tender sensitive nervous system of our material frame and animal nature.

(2.) Our spiritual nature. Now, if the natural man receives enjoyment from the active outgoings of goodness—how much more our new and moral nature, that which has been born from above. The divine within us must be exalted and blessed, as it is in unison with God, its source and exemplar. So, that to follow him, as dear children, is to give scope to the new man, and enjoyment to our spiritual and sanctified emotions. So that we are blessed, as we bless. Happy, as we make others happy. Full, as others are satisfied. Exalted, as others are lifted up. Hence the exercise of goodness is the very law of spiritual life—the very blessedness of the new man.

6. *The opportunity of goodness is specifically circumscribed.*

The text says—" To do good in his life." And who can tell how long it will last ? A few years, or only another day ! How clear that it will be a span at most! Hence Christ said—" I must work while it is day, for the night cometh when no man can work." See Eccl. ix. 10. So that this life presents the only sphere for beneficent actions. Neglect this, and our opportunity of doing good is gone forever. Our probation relates to this life—our facilities of usefulness are in this life—our money and talents are to be employed in this life. Here we are to labor, to sow the good seed—to imitate the Saviour—to carry out the design of our stewardship—to honor religion—to bless man, and glorify God. Now, each and every claim must be met—or never ! No giving— no teaching—no pitying—no helping in the grave, or the eternal world. Then how forcible the text—" I know that there is no good in them, but for a man to rejoice and to do good in his life."

APPLICATION.

From this subject,

1. See the great ends of life. Joy and usefulness. Not gloom and indolence—not melancholy and isolation—not murmuring and misanthropy ! No, but grateful joy towards God—and true and unfeigned goodness towards men. Observe also,

2. The connection of the two. Beneficence will make the eye bright, and heart glad. And joy in God will produce a tender and loving spirit towards the sorrowing and suffering around us. In this sense, the joy of the Lord will be our strength to do good, and to honor his holy name. We perceive the reason,

3. Why so few enjoy the bliss of elevated piety. They yield themselves to gloom, and murmuring, and despondency. They fret themselves against God. And often, in addition to this, they neglect active beneficence. How strange, if such had much real enjoyment.

4. How all should labor to rise to the dignity of the spirit of the text. This is the great privilege of all the children of God. The text belongs to no order or class of God's people; but it is to be received and exemplified by all. Every converted soul is called to rejoice in God ; and according to their means, to do good in this life.

———

VII.—CHRISTIAN SYMPATHY.

" Rejoice with them that do rejoice, and weep with them that weep."—*Romans* xii. 15.

CHRISTIANITY embraces within its range all conceivable good. In many cases, it does so in detail. Hence, in reference to the duties we owe to our fellow-men, we have often the very minutiæ presented to us. As in relative duties, those between parents and children, husbands and wives, masters and servants, rulers and subjects. Then there are also great principles developed, which lead us out into the spirit to be cherished, and the actions to be performed towards all men. Now among these we notice, that involved in the text, namely, Sympathy. Rejoicing with the happy, weeping with the sorrowful.

Now, this law is one of those in which the benevolence of Deity is conspicuously displayed. For constituted as we are, much of our enjoyment depends on it. Under both aspects, whether the sympathy of joy in their felicity, or of sorrow in their afflictions, it is alike precious and important. Let us then look at it in its general bearings and importance. We will,

I. *Endeavor to comprehend its true nature.*

And,

II. *Urge to its constant and universal exercise.*

Let us, then,

I. *Endeavor to comprehend its true nature.*

Now, sympathy may be defined—kindredness of feeling, oneness of emotion. Now, in physics, we see something like this in the law of attraction. Hence, certain things attract each other, as is observed in the loadstone, and particular bodies, how it draws and unites them. So, also, other electrical substances. Now we see this further developed in the animal economy. Mere animals sympathize with each other. Hence they enjoy food and recreation in each others' company. They flee together in peril, and warn one another of danger. They suffer also, if their mates are in distress and agony. Now, this sympathy of animal instinct is beautiful; and it is interesting to observe its development. But the highest description of sympathy, is that to which the text urgeth us, as intelligent and moral beings, to feel with, and for one another; so that, if one weeps, we weep; or if one rejoiceth, we also rejoice. Now this element of sympathy is implanted within us, and is, therefore, natural to us. For instance: if you were on a river by night, and heard the cry of one apparently drowning, you are acted upon at once; and the first impulse would be, to make every effort to rescue the object in danger. Or, if you see one suffering, you intensely feel desirous of administering relief. A person enveloped in flames, or a person on the verge of a precipice, would instantly excite you to sympathy. And this feeling can even come upon you, without seeing or hearing the object of sympathy; for if you read of a person in keen suffering, it at once acts on your emotions; and you are excited with commiseration.

Now, this sympathetic feeling, religion is to cultivate; and we are to cherish it in the highest possible degree. Religion opens fresh views of human misery, and gives scope to the emotions which mere humanity would never recognize. It enters into the spiritual region. It regards the souls of men. It feels for those who feel not for themselves. It blushes for those who have no shame. It weeps for those who weep not on their own behalf. It fears for those who fear not. It desires the eternal welfare of those who desire it not at all. Now this high-toned tender spiritual sensibility, is to be cherished by the Christian. Let us, then,

II. *Urge to its constant and universal exercise.*

Christians should thus sympathize on every possible ground; but, especially,

1. *Because it is in harmony with the law of our being.*

Its ordinary exercise, we have shown you, mere animals exhibit. So our fellow-men, without religion, often strongly display it; therefore the Christian, to be indifferent to it, is to sink his religious character below that of the brute instinct; and thus descend into the lowest kind of debasement. To exercise the emotions rightly, is to answer the end of our wondrous conformation. For this, the sensitive nervous system was placed within us. The heart made soft—the eye quick to observe—and the ear to catch the sounds vibrating on it. And, therefore, we repeat, as you are defective here, you are below the standard of manhood and humanity. In this way, you sin against the very elements and constitution of your being; and so far you defeat the noble purposes for which you were destined.

We should exhibit this spirit of sympathy,

2. *Because of its magnificent embodiment in the life and spirit of Jesus.*

The law demands this, as expressed, and thus written—" Thou shalt love thy neighbor as thyself." Every man loves himself; and the result is, every part of the body sympathizes with every other part; and so the body with the head and heart, and the mind with the body, hand, or the foot. Now this the law of God demands from us, as it was first written, on the table of stone, by the finger of Jehovah. But, see, to make it more expressive, God constitutes his Son a human being—a perfect man—one made like unto us in all things; and he calls on the whole intellectual universe to behold the law of sympathy, living and acting in Christ. It brought him from his throne, into this debased world. It made him a man of sorrows and griefs. It filled his lips with blessings, and his hands with mercies. It caused him to travel about, seeking objects of pity, and compassionate help. It arrested him whenever sorrow's moans were heard. Hence, the cry of the blind men fastened him to the spot,—he stood still, stayed in his course, till he had responded to their piteous appeal. It knew no distinction of objects—a ruler's daughter or a blind beggar, were alike regarded. It healed the righteous and the wicked. It rejected none, and welcomed all who cried for help. It never wearied, and never gave up. When Jesus was arrested, it felt and pleaded for the disciples who were in peril. When ascending the hill of Calvary, and when women's plaints rent the air, Christ was so touched, that he seemed to forget all his own sorrows. When dying, it sympathized with the victims of misery, and ignorance, and sin; and pleaded for divine forgiveness. A world's guilt, brought a world's curse and condemnation; and Christ sympathized with the perishing race of men, and had both transferred to himself. Hence, " He bore our sins in his own body on the tree." Here was the law of sympathy in all its moral grandeur—without the least selfish alloy; and it was in constant exercise, and extended to all mankind. Well might angels wonder, and God delight in his Son; and say in reply to his prayer— " I have glorified thee, and will glorify thee again."

3. *Because all the influences of religion tend to this end.*

True religion draws the heart to God; and, at the same time, extends its tender regards to men. The love of God fills it with love to man; and love to man, too, is the evidence of our love to God.

Religion softens the heart, and enlarges it. Religion without sympathy is a by-word—a delusion—and an impossibility. Religion, if it is efficient, destroys that which is antagonistical to sympathy—selfishness. It cherishes that from which sympathy springs and flows—love. Thus it will be manifest, that all the influences of religion must tend to this good and benevolent end. No law of nature is more certain than this divine law of God in the soul. And as water flows downward, and as sparks fly upward, so the grace of God softens and expands the soul, destroying coldness and isolation, and filling it with the genial and lovely impulses of pity and compassion. But more, we should cherish this spirit of sympathy,

4. *Because the exercise of this, more than any thing else, tends to promote true religion.*

Now, just see how it does this.

(1.) It does it within our own hearts. As we cherish this spirit, we grow in likeness to Jesus, we rise in assimilation to the nature of our heavenly Father; for God is love; and they who dwell in love, dwell in God. This is the domain of the greatest of the graces. It is the operation of divine love in the soul. Besides, this will insure the smile of God, and the bestowal of all the other graces of the Spirit. God delights to see the reflection of his moral likeness; and we never please God more, than when we thus follow him as dear children. For God is not only love, but he dwells in this benignant moral atmosphere, so that, when filled with this spirit, we are nearest and dearest to our Father in heaven.

(2.) It will promote religion with others. " By this shall all men know that ye are my disciples, if ye love one another." Men ought to see a religion full of Christ's spirit and character—a religion full of his life. Metaphysical disquisitions may amuse, and even interest the learned—systems of wire-drawn doctrines gratify sects; but the world wishes to see a religion with a heart, with a soul in it; and let this grand law be seen in full operation in the Christian church, and infidelity would stand abashed, the world would be constrained to admire; and the result would be, that multitudes would say, —" we will go with you, for surely God is with you, of a truth; and you are the seed, which he hath blessed."

We do not undervalue the manifestation of truth, or its defence, by talent or scholarship,—neither do we question for a moment the importance of maintaining the gospel in all its glorious purity; but with these, and along with the influence thus put forth, we want the goodness of religion to be seen, its deep-toned sympathies exhibited. The benevolent heart of religion to be seen, as well as its intellectual head. Religion, like its founder, must be an incarnation; and that must be an incarnation like his—of love and mercy to the world. And there is a potency in this, which no abstract doctrines possess —which no creed can suffice for—and for which no flaming profession can be a sufficient apology. We must have the soul endowed with the pure love of God, and the life flowing with tender susceptibilities. Prove that your religion is unselfish and full of love, and then even skeptics to your creed will do homage to your life.

Then, in conclusion, we see,

1. What is so greatly wanted. It is the constant and universal exercise of this principle. Like light and air, it should permeate and surround the world. It should be to the world of mind, what the law of gravi-

tation is to the physical universe,—it should bind all together, and keep all in beautiful harmony, and moral loveliness.

How blessed will be our earth, when all the abodes of men shall be hallowed by this law of sympathy. When all the relationships of life shall be sanctified by it. When it shall hold in holy union all classes of society. When it shall make all colors and nations of men shake hands with each other. Then, neither fleets nor armies will be needful. Cruelty and oppression will cease to exist; and the world will be one vast Paradise regained. Then will be realized what John saw in vision. See Revelations xxi. 1–3.

2. We see what is the great element of opposition to this. It is—selfishness. The carnal heart, cold, isolated, unfeeling. And while this is the soul's great evil, it is also its greatest curse. As there can be no moral culture in that condition, so there can be no real enjoyment. This is the essential law of the moral world—that the most loving are the most happy; just as God is the most happy and blessed, because he is the most benevolent.

Now this moral law in its character and results must ever hold, unless God could cease to be good, and thus cease to be the benevolent legislator of the world; and the great example for the holy imitation of all his moral offspring.

To enjoy—as God enjoys, to be happy as he is—of course, in our finite degree, then we must be the subjects of his love, and show forth the spirit of the text in "rejoicing with those that rejoice, and weeping with those that weep." And the great hindrance to this, our natural sinful selfishness, is as operative in preventing the joyous, as it is in preventing the sorrowful aspects of the text. It in the one case leads to envy, and in the other it tends to indifference. So that this selfish weed must be plucked up by the roots, or we cannot exhibit true Christian sympathy, under either of its aspects. A loving heart will only rejoice with the happy, or weep with the distressed.

Finally,—How great the sphere for its exercise in this world; and how adapted to dispose us for the next.

What scenes of varied and accumulated distress surround us! what objects of pity! what scenes of sadness! what abodes of wretchedness! what physical destitution— mental misery—and moral peril! what a field for compassion, and effort, and self-denial, does the world present! Then let the spirit of the text be cherished to the utmost, and ever be freely developed, as means and opportunity be afforded to us. Thus carrying out the precept of the apostle—doing good unto all men, but especially remembering the household of faith.

––––––––

VIII.—THE LIFE OF SIN LONG ENOUGH.

"For the time past of our life may suffice us to have wrought the will of the Gentiles, when we walked in lasciviousness, lusts, excess of wine, revellings, banquetings, and abominable idolatries."—1 *Peter* iv. 3.

THE Apostle Peter is showing in the text, that a life of iniquity had not been abandoned too early—that the time spent in ungodliness had been sufficiently long; and, therefore, that a wiser and better course could not begin too soon. Now this simple, clear, and powerful process of reasoning, I wish to apply to all, in order to show the great importance of immediately seeking saving religion. What thoughtful mind will not agree with the apostle, that the time past may well be sufficient to have wrought the will of the Gentiles? By the will of the Gentiles, we understand an irreligious life—a life of ungodliness—a life of sin and rebellion against God.

And I ask, in reference to such a life,

I. *Did you not live in that state sufficiently long, when you reflect on the rebellion, and ingratitude, that life involved?*

Every day and hour was a life in opposition to God. Sin, daring, open sin,—of aggravated evil, positive evil—of ingratitude to God. You sinned against your heavenly Father, your Divine Benefactor, your continual Preserver—against a patient, long-suffering Friend. How base then the sinfulness of that state! how evil the whole life! And, therefore, surely it could not terminate too soon. How merciful on the part of God, that it was not ended, so far as your probation was concerned, by the stroke of his righteous wrath, and severe displeasure. A life involving every element of folly and baseness, could not be brought to a conclusion too early. Did you not live in that state long enough, when you reflect,

II. *On the prostitution and continued perversion of your own powers?*

From the course pursued, let us glance at the character and condition you occupied as

God's accountable creatures. Let it be observed that you were men, and not brutes—rational intellectual men, possessing an understanding, a judgment, a will, and moral affections formed for high and noble purposes and objects—destined to be wise and holy—to be in rank, only a little lower than the angels. Yet how low did you sink in the scale of excellency—how debased and degraded was your condition. The lord had become a vassal, a menial, a slave! The child, a wretched wanderer and outcast! The heir of immortality, a criminal, exposed to endless infamy and death! Surely, in that state, you had lived long enough.

How true the text,

III. *When you remember the enjoyments of which you deprived yourselves.*

A life of sin is evil; but it is also bitter. For it not to be bitter, the conscience must be destroyed; or at least, so seared, as to be utterly obdurate. Think of the self-accusation you felt—of the self-loathing endured —of the mental pain you experienced—of the remorse you had to bear; you might have had peace, comfort, calm, sunshine, hope! but your soul was like the agitated lake—the restless sea; and you had within the gnawing worm. Oh, surely, this state was long enough.

But it was so, when you reflect,

IV. *On the pernicious influence your conduct exerted on others.*

We do not, and cannot live and stand alone; nor sin, nor fall, nor perish alone. When you wrought the will of the Gentiles, you had kindred, perhaps children—a wife and relatives. What did you teach them— what example present before them—what influence exert upon them? Do you know the mischief you did? Where are all your evil associates now? How many in the grave—how many perhaps in perdition! If they could address you—what would they say—allured, fascinated, destroyed, and by you! How true the declaration,—One sinner destroyeth much good. So it was with you, when you wrought the will of the Gentiles. These evils you cannot now fully repair. But at any rate, is it not certain that the time of such a course ought to suffice, yea, even be more than sufficient? Would you not now rejoice if your career of vice had ended long before; and if, instead of being a ringleader in sin, you had been an instrument to warn souls of the error of their ways?

But the text is true, when you think of the,

V. *Talents, influence, and blessings of which it deprived you.*

How different might have been your Christian character, if you had served God earlier—had you begun in youth. How improved would have been your talents—how telling your influence. The weakness sin has left, perhaps will never be entirely removed. The hours of the short day of life were worse than wasted. Talents worse than idle. Opportunities most precious, are now forever gone. And all that rich series of blessings connected with those favorable seasons, have fled with them. The seed-time of spring, and the glowing beams of summer have passed away, and to you will never more return. Then the retrospect, so dark and so dreary—must establish the truth of the text, —that the life of iniquity was vastly too long.

If one year of accountable existence is spent in wrong-doing, in debasing sensuality, in "lascivious lusts," which sink men to a level with brutes; in "excess of wine," which induces drunkenness; wherein man descends to a state lower than beastly degradation,— "revellings, banquetings, and abominable idolatries," by which the intellect and moral powers become utterly polluted. Surely to that solitary year, the true and forcible language of the text may be applied,—"That the time past of your life may well suffice, wherein you wrought the will of Gentiles." Then, if the text is so manifestly true, should you not learn,

(1.) That the present time ought to be highly valued. How needful to estimate the period still allotted to you as increasing in value, from the time that has been so fearfully wasted. In reality you only have begun to live, since you abandoned the former course of your sinful being. You only entered on the happier, holier period of your moral existence, when you began to glorify God with your body and soul, which are his. When you gave to him a confiding heart, and an obedient subjection to his will.

(2.) Your deliverance should be gratefully remembered. Bless God that at length he saved you,—that his mercy and long-suffering endured so long,—that his patience waited for your repentance and penitential return. That rescue, you must never forget. It was the bright spot in your history. The crisis of your immortal being; and on which was suspended all real blessedness here, and all hope in reference to the future world. It was then, that you were brought out of the mire and clay, and your feet set upon a rock, and that a new song of praise to God was put into your mouths. Never forget the hand that raised you—never cease to exult in the grace that delivered you.

> "The theme demands an angel's song,
> And an eternal day."

(3.) Your time and powers should be most fully occupied in God's service. You should make up in some measure, if possible, for past folly, by doing good in God's work. Activity, diligence, devotedness to the divine glory, should now absorb your whole being. Oh, yes! are you not under the most solemn of all obligations to do all you can for Christ—for souls—for the church —for the world at large? Yes; ask how you can best exhibit a devoted heart, and employ a sanctified life, to the praise of God and the good of men. And let your religion be one bright flame of Christian philanthropy and usefulness.

Finally,—Let the subject influence the young to decision. Now is the best time for commencing a religious course. Perhaps the only time you may have. Besides, it is now much easier for you to begin. Evil habits are not yet established. The fetters of iniquity are not forged so fast and firm around your moral powers. The roots of the evil tree are not so deeply imbedded in depravity and guilt. Oh, how all-important to avoid the destructive evils which abound in the world! To rise, at once, in life and holiness. To grow up from youth in God's fear, that the whole man may be his.

But one word, in conclusion, to the mature in life, and to the aged. To you we say, no longer delay. Should not the time past more than suffice? And in reference to sin, what have you gained by it—what are the benefits you really derived—what can you expect to reap in the great harvest? Must not the end be death, everlasting death! And to that state of woe and ruin you are rapidly approaching. The Judge may be at the door. Perhaps only a few days, or weeks, will be allotted you for consideration, repentance, and for fleeing from the wrath to come to the Lord Jesus, the only Saviour of the wretched and the lost. Be wise, then, and hesitate not for a moment, but flee for safety to the shelter of Christ's cross. And do it now, to-day, while the Holy Spirit strives with you; lest the door of mercy be closed, and you perish without remedy and without hope.

IX.—RELIGION, TRUE WISDOM.

(A SERMON TO THE YOUNG.)

"My son, if thine heart be wise, my heart shall rejoice, even mine."—*Prov.* xxiii. 15.

THE entire of religion is often in Scripture represented under one or two of its more prominent attributes. It is described as the fear of God—as the knowledge of God—as the love of God—as obedience to God. So both in the Old and New Testament scriptures, it is frequently described as wisdom. It is so in Job xxviii. 12: and this idea runs entirely through the book of Proverbs. So Christ, in reference to the virgins who were ready for the bridegroom. So the apostle James describes religion, as wisdom from above. Jas. iii. 17.

Now the idea of the text is, the extreme desirableness of the young being wise, that is—really religious. To be wise, is more than being learned or intellectual. It may be defined as the practical application of the knowledge we have of God and his will.

Let us then ascertain,

I. *Why religion may be described as wisdom.*

II. *The importance of this to young people.*

And,

III. *The certain means for its attainment.*

I. *Why may religion be described as wisdom?*

Now it may be so,

1. *As it involves the possession and right application of knowledge.*

There can be no religion without knowledge. A knowledge of God as revealed in his blessed word—as exhibited in Christ, his beloved Son. A spiritual apprehension of the way of salvation, as published in the gospel. We must know God, before we can return to him, and be saved by his grace. But we may know theoretically his will, and refuse, or neglect to do it. So to be wise, is earnestly to follow the light we have, to apply the knowledge we possess.

In this way we obtain, and exhibit, *heart* wisdom; without which, head knowledge cannot benefit, but will rather add to our condemnation.

Religion may be described as wisdom,

2. *As it gives the first attention to the most momentous concerns.*

This is a primary sign of true wisdom. Now, is not the soul the most precious—the most exalted of the divine-made creatures? Formed to resemble, to serve, and enjoy God. Made for the reflection of the divine perfections and glory. Can the man be wise who undervalues and neglects his most precious soul? Then this soul is enveloped in depravity and pollution. It is ignorant, defiled, guilty; and as such, is in a perishing state. A right and wise appreciation of the soul, will lead to the employment of means for securing its pardon—its regeneration—and its restoration to the divine favor and family. It is of the utmost moment for the soul to be at peace with God —to enjoy his favor—and thus a good hope of eternal life.

Hence, then, religion appears to be the wisest of all pursuits. All else, with this neglected, is complete folly. Religion may be described as wisdom,

3. *As it adopts the most likely means for securing these great ends.*

It first of all is wise to pursue the most important ends. But inseparably connected with this is, the way and means we labor to secure them. Now, the way to render certain the soul's salvation, is revealed in the divine word; therefore it must be sought for there. God's word only makes wise the simple. God's word gives light to the understanding, and truth to the judgment; and leads the whole moral nature into an element of safety and blessedness. With this complete, yet portable, volume of mercy within our reach, it would be folly of the most melancholy kind, to seek for the way of life elsewhere.

And then, wisdom as to the time of doing this, declares it should be first. First in life —first in preference—first in earnestness. Wisdom will ever put things in their due and fitting place. The body will have its right amount of attention. Secular things will be placed where they will receive due attention. Mental pursuits will have an exalted position; but religion will be pre-eminent, and hold the highest rank both in our affections and desires. It will ever be chief.

At all times and in all places, be in the ascendant.

Religion is wisdom,

4. *As it secures the greatest amount of good both for the present and the future.*

Now, we may meet the rejector of this proposition, thus:—Man has a soul, immortal—to prepare for death and eternity; and to give attention to this, is the course wisdom would suggest. But if this be denied, well, we say, is it not wise to adopt the best means, at any rate, to attain the highest ends!—Eternal blessedness is the highest end man can aim at. But we add, irrespective of the future—Religion is best for the body and this life. It favors the carrying out the great conditions of health. It promotes industry, honesty, and providence. Hence the two declarations—" Seek ye first the kingdom of God, and his righteousness; and all these things shall be added unto you."—Matt. vi. 33. " Godliness is profitable unto all things, having promise of the life that now is, and of that which is to come."—1 Tim. iv. 8. Is not religion, then, the highest wisdom?

Then consider,

II. *The importance of this to young people.*

It is so to all, but especially to the young.

1. *Because of their necessary inexperience.*

From their youthful condition, they must be inexperienced. If so, how much they stand in need of this wisdom! If inexperienced, and foolish, or reckless, the result must be disastrous. Apply it to the case of a traveller, who is journeying through unknown regions. Or, to a mariner who is traversing strange seas. How great the peril in both cases! And the ways of life, —the strange and unknown by-ways and intricate scenes, often surrounded by the most deadly perils, to the young, renders this wisdom absolutely essential to perfect security. The young, too, are generally confident, and unsuspicious. All that glitters, they are ready to presume, is fine gold. They have not encountered the disappointments of older persons. Nor have they been betrayed and deceived by the wiles and deceits of the vicious; and, therefore, they are in constant danger from their inexperience, as to these matters. How all-important to their security is the guidance of God, and the possession of heavenly wisdom.

2. *Because of the countless perils which surround them.*

In addition to the dangers which surround all men, there are the peculiar perils of the young. There have been perils to the young in all ages. Hence the numerous admonitions of the word of God. But never were perils more numerous than now; especially in the large cities and towns of our land. Look at the multifarious baits and snares of dissipation and pleasure, which everywhere abound! Look at the fascinating evil books, which teem from the press! Look at the gay and frivolous classes of society, ever waiting to hail to their ranks the uninitiated youth around them!

Now, many of these evils are such, if not avoided altogether, they will destroy reputation, health, life—and, finally, the soul itself.

3. *Because the future circumstances of life depend much on the course adopted in youth.*

This is so self-evident, that I need scarcely dwell on it at all. A careless youth, rarely becomes a wise and good man. A prudent, godly, early life — on the other hand—lays the foundation for every kind of excellence and happiness. Almost every illustrious man in the church of God has been distinguished for early piety. So that, if this foundation be early laid, the most magnificent structure may be reared upon it.

On the other hand, if youth be negligent, and given up to vicious courses, a future change of life is extremely doubtful. The days and opportunities of early life cannot be re-called,—the tender emotions of the heart restored,—the page of their personal history is not now fair, to write on what you please; but it is already filled with inscriptions of moral degradation and woe. And what erasures will be requisite before that page can have printed on it—the records of wisdom and godliness. The enemy has sown evil; and that seed has not only preoccupied the ground, but has made it fertile in evil fruits,—as briers and thorns, rejected of God; and nigh unto cursing, whose end is to be burned. Heb. vi. 8. Hence the importance of religion to young people, that the good seed of the kingdom may have the precedence; and that the result may be, a life of holy fruitfulness to the glory of Divine grace.

But notice,

III. *The certain means of its attainment.*

Now in order to the attainment of this wisdom,

1. *There must be a deep conviction of its need and value.*

There can be nothing done, till this conviction is wrought in the heart,—that you need it. Self-sufficiency is often the bane of the young and inexperienced; and this must be displaced, by distrust, and a deep personal sense of need of Divine wisdom, to insure happiness and security. And just as this impression is deep and vivid, will there be a high appreciation of the Divine aid, which the word of God reveals. Then no chart will be more welcome to the mariner, no guide more esteemed by the traveller, than will the wisdom from above be valued and sought for, that moral peril and misery may be avoided. Let the young be conscious that a higher intelligence must direct them, a superior power control them, and a more secure shield protect them from danger and ruin. And these are just what religion provides for all who seek God in early life.

2. *There must be the hearty and simple application of faith, for its realization.*

God desires you to be early pious. He says—"Remember now thy Creator in the days of thy youth, while the evil days come not, nor the years draw nigh, when thou shalt say, I have no pleasure in them."— Ecc. xii. 1. He expostulates—"Wilt thou not from this time cry unto me, Be thou the guide of my youth." And he tells you to seek him; and he assures you, "That they that seek him early, shall find him."

Now, you must believe God in these his statements of love and mercy; and come to him through Christ Jesus, just as you are— weak, ignorant, guilty; and obtain an interest in his love and mercy. Give God your heart, and devote your life to him; and rely on it, that he will in nowise cast you out. His goodness towards you in providence— but especially his riches of mercy and grace in Christ Jesus—present the most certain guarantee, that he will give you a hearty welcome to his loving heart, and blessed family. Then, let this resolution, and application of devout earnestness and faith,

3. *Be adopted now.*

The great evil, in most cases, is procrastination; and especially with the young. But there can be no good ground of hope, unless you now resolve thus to seek God. It cannot be too early. Life is uncertain, even with you. If you postpone, the feeling of indifference will grow; and the difficulty of coming to God, be increasingly greater. Besides, duty is an ever present responsibility. Safety should first of all be realized. None can be too early wise, and good, and happy. Who will presume that even youthful vigor may not be invaded by sudden, fatal affliction; or, that the early conscientious desires of the heart after God may not depart, and return no more. On no ground of reason, or propriety, can delay be vindicated. It should be now, and it may indeed be now —or never.

Then, let me in conclusion, present the subject to your serious attention. (1.) By the evils of neglecting religion. Look at that ignorant profligate youth—that hardened impenitent youth—that young man wandering in a distant land—that outcast—that diseased, dying youth—that criminal! And only reflect, what guilt would have been avoided, if they had early yielded their hearts to the love and service of Jesus.

(2.) Look at the opposite scene of moral loveliness and excellency. See that group of young men rising into life, how they are distinguished for dignity and usefulness. How they stand out in society, as its ornaments and pillars, and how they bid fair to attain honor and blessedness here, and glory and celestial life in the world to come. Shall not their choice be yours—their God yours —their portion yours? Oh, then, hearken— ponder—and now decide! and from this day act, as believing that wisdom is the principal thing, and that only is wisdom which leads to the service of God, and to the entire consecration of the whole man to his glory.

X.—FAITH IN CHRIST, THE WORK GOD DEMANDS.

"Then said they unto him, What shall we do, that we might work the works of God? Jesus answered and said unto them, This is the work of God, that ye believe on him whom he hath sent."—*John* vi. 28, 29.

CHRIST was surrounded by a multitude of persons, most likely influenced by various feelings and desires. Some, doubtless, were actuated by idle curiosity. Some to see his wondrous works,—others, we presume, out of an ardent concern to obtain real good to their souls,—others were entirely sordid. See ver. 26. Jesus urges on them the supreme importance of laboring for the imperishable bread of everlasting life. See v. 27.

Then, they ask, in the words of the text— "What shall we do, that we might work the works of God?" To which Christ answers, that faith in the sent of God, is what the Father demands.

Observe, the text presents,

I. *An important inquiry.*

And,

II. *A Divine direction.*

The text presents,

I. *An important question.*

Let us carefully examine the question, and it will be requisite,

1. *To define it.*

It evidently signifies what they should do, to do those works pleasing and acceptable to God. How shall we live and act, so as to please God? Thus, it was a proper, clear, and simple question. One which all reasonable beings should present, and one to which they should labor to have a full and satisfying answer.

It was a question,

2. *Of the greatest importance.*

It is of essential consequence, to know the will of God concerning us; for without this, it is not possible to present to him an intelligent and acceptable service. And this question is at the basis of all divine knowledge and moral excellence. Now, whether you look upon the intrinsic value of the soul—the supreme importance of religion— or the inconceivable grandeur of eternal life, this question stands forth as the most vital that man can present. Others may inquire about the world, about riches, pleasures, and fame; but the serious spirit will ask—"What shall I do, that I may work the works of God?" This question relates to the whole of man, and to both worlds; and, therefore, is the highest of all inquiries. Every thing else is secondary and minor.

3. *It was a personal question.*

Not about others. Not about secret or hidden things, as divine purposes; the times and the seasons, which he has not revealed to man. But what shall we do? We shall never be truly religious, until our interrogatories relate to ourselves, to our own hearts and lives.

Idle curiosity may ask, What God would

that this or that man should do! But the answer of Jesus will ever be, as it was to Peter,—" What is that to thee, follow thou me." First of all—chief of all, we must exhibit a pure concern for our own personal salvation.

It was a question proposed,

4. *To the most proper person, for obtaining a satisfactory reply.*

Thus the Jews often appealed to Abraham, to Moses, to their Priests and Rabbis. But on this occasion, they appealed to Christ, —to the great, divine, infallible, and gracious Teacher. He who came from heaven expressly to impart light and knowledge to the world,—to instruct the ignorant, and lead men in the way of peace.

God has put his broad seal on Jesus, both at his Baptism and Transfiguration; and he averred, that he was his beloved Son, in whom he was well pleased; and has authoritatively affixed to it the divine mandate—" Hear ye him !" So that in the whole universe, there was not one to whom they could have proposed the question, so wisely and appropriately, as to Jesus. So when we ask the same question in reference to ourselves, shall we go to the historian, or the philosopher, or the mere moralist? Surely not. Who can instruct us in Christian doctrines, principles, and precepts, but Jesus ? He is our Lord and Master, our Lawgiver and Ruler. Both officially, and in his person and work, he is " The way, the truth, and the life." Yes, let us learn the Christian religion, at any rate, from Christ. To whom should we go, but to him; for he has the words of eternal life.

Observe, to this question,

II. *A divine direction given.*

Now observe, he did not say the work of God was to offer sacrifices, or attend to ceremonial institutions—nor to perform penances—nor to seek God's favor by self-righteous preparations of outward duties— nor to abide indolently waiting for the divine aid. But, he demands at once, and most explicitly, that the soul should exercise faith in himself (ver. 29). Now thus to believe in the Lord Jesus as the sent of God, would involve the following particulars :

(1.) To believe in him, and to receive him, as testified of—predicted—promised, in the Holy Scriptures. Christ often appealed to these, as evidences of his Messiahship. Hence the comprehensive reasoning on this subject, as given by the Evangelist, in the 5th of John, and which thus concluded :—" And the Father himself, which hath sent me, hath borne witness of me. Ye have neither heard his voice at any time, nor seen his shape. And ye have not his word abiding in you : for whom he hath sent, him ye believe not. Search the Scriptures ; for in them ye think ye have eternal life ; and they are they which testify of me. And ye will not come to me, that ye might have life ;" ver. 37–40.

(2.) To hear the truth of salvation from his lips, and to welcome those truths into the heart.

(3.) So to believe in Christ, as divine and true, that the soul's salvation be entirely committed to him. This, and not less than this, is included in believing on him whom God hath sent. It is clearly the yielding of mind and soul up to him—resting only on him, as the one elect and sure foundation of mercy and hope. Now, observe, this believing on Christ,

2. *He declares this to be the work of God.*

It is so efficiently : that is, it is his work, which he by truth and grace produces in us. Christ was sent that men should believe in him. He preached and taught that they might believe. And hence, faith was thus the production of God; as he thus wrought it in the hearts of its happy subjects. But this is God's work, objectively, that which he demands from the sinner. And the propriety and importance of this is seen on several accounts.

(1.) Nothing before this can be acceptable to God, even the moral works of an unbeliever cannot please God. Because, while the heart is carnal, and the character that of a rebel, no deeds, however relatively good, or lovely, can be esteemed by God. There is wanting the purity of motive, and the right principle of all holy action; without which, God cannot be pleased. Hence it is written, as one of the grand yet elementary truths of Christianity—" But without faith, it is impossible to please him : for he that cometh to God must believe that he is, and that he is a rewarder of them that diligently seek him."—Heb. xi. 6. Here, then, is the first lesson that the anxious inquirer after God's favor must learn.

(2.) As to merit, Christ's work is all-sufficient. We need no other righteousness. He is the Lord our righteousness. Spotless in his nature, and perfect in his obedience. He fully magnified the law, and made it honorable. We need no other sacrifice—for he has offered up himself; and his blood possesses infinite efficacy. Hence the conclusive reasoning of the Apostle, Heb. ix. 11, 12. So also is the decisive statement of the Apostle Peter, 1 Pet. ii. 24. We do not require to pacify God, for God is reconciled to us in Jesus Christ. All is done, therefore, that our guilt and misery need. Faith in Christ, therefore, secures us a present and complete interest in his finished work. It brings us to the enjoyment of pardon, justification, and adoption. His spirit and word regenerate. And he gives to all his sheep, who hear his voice, eternal life. To attempt, by human merit, to render our salvation more complete or certain, must, therefore, be unnecessary; and if attempted, utterly fallacious.

(4.) Faith will procure us the grace, by which we shall do all things to God's glory. When the fountain of the heart is cleansed, then the stream of life will be pure. If the tree is made good, so will be the fruit presented to God. Let the soul be brought under the dominion of Jesus; and obedience to Jesus will be cheerful and complete. Faith works by love; and love gives all to Christ. Faith gives existence to all Christian graces and virtues, and thus adorns the whole man. See how the ancient heroes acted by faith—as given in the eleventh of Hebrews. Noah's faith works, and he builds the ark. Abraham's faith works, and he goes out and obeys God. Moses, by faith, consecrates his life to God. And the comprehensive, yet concisely stated summary, is well worthy of our attention, where the apostle adds—"And what shall I say more? for the time would fail me to tell of Gedeon, and of Barak, and of Samson, and of Jephtha; of David also, and Samuel, and of the prophets: who through faith subdued kingdoms, wrought righteousness, obtained promises, stopped the mouths of lions, quenched the violence of fire, escaped the edge of the sword, out of weakness were made strong, waxed valiant in fight, turned to flight the armies of the aliens. Women received their dead raised to life again; and others were tortured, not accepting deliverance, that they might obtain a better resurrection; and others had trial of cruel mockings and scourgings: yea, moreover, of bonds and imprisonment; they were stoned, they were sawn asunder, were tempted, were slain with the sword; they wander about in sheepskins and goatskins; being destitute, afflicted, tormented; (of whom the world was not worthy;) they wandered in deserts, and in mountains, and in dens and caves of the earth."—Heb. xi. 32–38.

Now faith is the main-spring of the moral machinery, and when acting, sets it to work, and puts all the wheels in motion; and then, as the result, God is glorified.

In conclusion, let this subject,

1. Be pondered by you. Are you anxious to do God's works? Do you feel as rational moral beings you ought to do them—that your peace and well-being depend thereon? That God's claims are just and right, and therefore, your obedience should be, both in spirit and extent, what he requires? That his will is law; and his word reveals that law for your guidance and safety? If so, then,

2. See the simplicity of the Gospel system. There must be faith, and not works first. This just suits man's condition. You cannot work, but you can believe. You cannot present a righteousness which God will accept; but you may avail yourself of the obedience of the Son of God. The sinner can will to be healed. He can look up to the Cross. He can rely on Jesus. He can plead for mercy as a sinner, and plead it on the ground of Christ's sacrifice. Blessed, gracious system! Who can fail to admire and adore the manifest wisdom and grace of God? And who will not rejoice that "this is the work of God"—the work God demands—the only work you can give—and the work that will secure every other—and finally, eternal life! "That ye believe on him whom he hath sent."

And as at the beginning of the Christian life, so during all its progress, to its final consummation, faith must work in the soul, and by the soul, to the doing of God's holy will, and the glorifying of his blessed name. So that, well is it said, that we live and walk by faith; that the life we live in the flesh, is a life by the faith of the Son of God. Gal. ii. 20. And the whole warfare of the Christian is one conflict of faith, which is to be kept up and sustained, till the good fight is fought, and the wreath of imperishable glory and eternal life be placed on the victor's brow, by the hand of the great Captain of our salvation.

Then, so live—so work—so fight—and so die in the faith of the Lord Jesus Christ. Amen.

XI.—ADVANTAGES OF COMMUNION WITH GOD.

"But it is good for me to draw near to God."— *Psalm* lxx. 28.

VARIOUS are the representations given of that communion, which the soul is privileged to have with God. It is often represented as waiting on the Lord—coming to God—calling upon him—meditating on him. The expression of the text is very striking; it is, drawing near to God. The mind is apt to wander, and to tarry at a distance—to attach itself to worldly things—to cleave to the dust—to forget God. The varied pursuits of life easily absorb all our time, and engross all our thoughts; so that a life of ungodliness is necessarily the result. And how melancholy is such an exhibition! Man, with all his lofty powers and moral emotions, wandering from the centre of all blessedness, and being satisfied with the worthless husks that earthly things afford. Often this state of mind is evident, where there is much that is naturally lovely and pleasing—where there is the absence of direct profligacy, or skeptical rejection of God, or his claims. But the influence of the carnal mind is ever directed to estrange the thoughts and desires from God, and to employ them with an entire devotedness to inferior things; and even where the grace of God has renewed the soul, there is the tendency to depart from God, and not to cleave fully to him with full purpose of heart; so that the Christian must use all spiritual appliances to keep the heart fixed in its regards and attention to divine things. There is, therefore, an indispensable necessity for drawing near to God; that is, cherishing close and frequent communion with him; and all who do so will realize the truth of the text—That "it is good" thus "to draw near to God."

We ask, then,

I. *What is included in drawing near to God ?*

And,

II. *The advantages derivable therefrom.*

Notice,

I. *What is included in drawing near to God ?*

Now it is evident, that certain states of mind are necessary to this.

(1.) There must be a scriptural knowledge of God. We cannot draw near to an un-known object. We must know God, as his word reveals him to us. We must know him as our God, in Christ Jesus. Without a spiritual knowledge of God, we shall have no desire for fellowship and communion with him; and it is in Christ Jesus that he appears to us as the Father of mercy, and God of all grace. It is thus that he attracts us to himself, and that he comes near to us. He is thus, God reconciling the world to himself—God commiserating our misery, pitying our wretchedness, and extending to us the means of restoration—both to his image and favor. Yes, God must be evangelically known, or we cannot acceptably draw near to him.

(2.) There must be faith in God. "He that cometh to God must believe that he is, and that he is the rewarder of those who diligently seek him." Now, in order to this faith in God, the mind must rest on his gracious character, and on his divine promises of mercy and salvation. Faith must have a warrant for its exercise; and God's good word is that warrant. Hence, we may inquire, What has God declared, and what has he engaged to do for those who come to him in the way of his gracious appointment? And to these inquiries, the most ample replies of affectionate solicitude may be returned. He will hear the voice of the contrite suppliant; he will raise the oppressed and downcast soul; he will forgive all sin—blot out all iniquity—remove all defilement—renew the heart—and adopt the recipients of his mercy into his divine kingdom, and make them heirs of righteousness and eternal life.

Now faith in God builds the soul's hope of everlasting blessedness, on the person and mediation of the Lord Jesus Christ; and the answer of faith is, the formation of Christ in the soul, as the hope of glory.

(3.) There must be an explicit apprehension of the only medium of drawing nigh to God, and of access, whether it be by prayer, meditation, or communion with him. Christ, he is the only medium, "the way." "No man cometh to the Father, but by him." And all our fellowship with God must be by his Son. Every desire and aspiration—every act of praise and thanksgiving—must ascend to him through Jesus, the one blessed and only mediator. How prone we are to rely on our own ability and powers, especially if we are more than ordinarily excited, or happy in religious exercises; if we have fluency in prayer, elevation of heart in praise, pleasure in hearing, or delight in meditation. And yet, even in our best and happiest seasons of religious enjoyment, we must cherish the great evangelical truth, that our holiest exercises must be presented to God, through the intercessory work of our Great High Priest, without which, it cannot possibly be acceptable to him. So that Christ's work must be interwoven with all our Christian experience, and with all the exercises of a godly life.

(4.) There must be humble, yet confident dependence on the aids of the divine grace. "Without me," Christ has said, "ye can do nothing." We need, at the outset, the inward sense of the importance of holy things; we need the heartfelt desire; we need the spiritual power—the antecedent hungering and thirsting for righteousness—the gracious expressions of our desires before God—the spirit of pleading and believing supplication, his blessed Spirit must supply. Yea, and God waits to bestow these blessings. He waits to confer the qualifications by which we can come to him and attain with moral certainty the good things our souls may need. How important then to seek, that he may "teach us to pray"—increase our faith; and enable us with all confidence and hope to wait upon, and to repose our trust entirely in him. All these God supplies by his rich and gracious Spirit, to those who ask him.

Now these things being understood and premised, then we proceed to consider what it is to draw near to God. It is,

1. *To have a deep sense of his presence.*

It is true that he is everywhere. We may associate the idea of God's presence with the ancient temple and its rites. But now the time is, when God may be approached everywhere. In the house of prayer he has specially engaged to be with his people. But he is no less present when the domestic altar is reared, or in the retired closet. We may behold God, and enjoy communion with him, when contemplating his power, and wisdom, and goodness, in the manifold works of his hand. And so, in all places and at all times, the devotional spirit will recognize an ever-present God. God above us, around us, leading us; whose vigilant eye is never closed, and whose gracious ear is ever bending over us, to hear our plaints, and receive our supplications.

We never need either to ascend to find him, or to traverse the earth to come to him, or seek for an earthly temple where he may be found; but everywhere God is near to those who worship him in truth, and call upon him with a lowly heart and contrite spirit.

To draw near to God—

2. *It is to lift up the heart and soul to him.*

We must rise in thought and contemplation. We must meditate on his goodness and love to us. We must dismiss other subjects and things, and compel them to make room, and give place to God, our Maker and Redeemer. We must exclaim, intelligently and devoutly: "Whom have we in heaven but thee?" "Lord, on thee we would wait all the day long." To the Divine exhortation, "Seek ye my face," we must respond, "Lord, thy face will we seek."

3. *It is to attend to religious exercises in a spiritual manner.*

In reading or hearing the Divine word. In public, social, or private prayer. In holy reflection and meditation. In ardent and grateful song. In all these acts, the soul must be spiritualized, in order to our drawing near to God. So, also, when we endeavor to set God before us in the duties and engagements of life, we must seek after spirituality of mind. Our moral perceptions and emotions must be spiritually alive and fervent. All mere forms must be disclaimed, and all resting on nominalism discarded. However needful the letter may be, in that we must not rest; but attain to a spiritual frame, and a fervent intensity, in all God's service; and without this, we do not wait on God, really at all. We may go to his house, and wait on his ministers. We may wait on external services. We may wait on the written word, and on outward forms of worship; but the heart must rise to God, and the soul become spiritually elevated above earthly things, in order to our truly drawing near to him.

Notice then,

II. THE ADVANTAGES DERIVABLE THEREFROM.

"It is good," says the Psalmist, "to draw near to God." It tends—

1. *To the intellectual elevation of the soul.*

It is the highest pursuit of an intelligent mind; the most opposite to that which is low, and earthly, and degrading, and grovelling. It is mind in contact with infinite light—judgment in contact with infinite truth—emotions in harmony with boundless goodness—conscience in peaceful concord with unspotted purity. This is the climax of exaltation! It is the man on the earth, raised to the kingdom and throne of heaven. Nowhere is he so great, or so highly exalted, as when drawing near to God. It is essentially adapted,

2. *To man's spiritual improvement.*

How is the earthly and carnal to be destroyed, and how the spiritual and holy to be cherished, but by drawing near to God. Communion with God, essentially produces God-likeness—a resemblance to his moral character. This is thus beautifully set forth: "Beholding as in a glass the glory of the Lord, we are changed into the same image from glory to glory, even as by the Spirit of the Lord."—2 Cor. iii. 18. Like Moses, whose communion with God caused his face to shine with a celestial radiance and glory. It is so even with human beings. Communion always produces assimilation. So we grow in likeness to God, as we draw and live near to him. It is,

3. *The source of man's highest blessedness.*

"Blessed are they that dwell in thy house, for they will be still praising thee." Now, in drawing near to God, the soul enjoys the Divine favor—the chief good. As the eye delights in the light, and what the light reveals; as the ear in sounds, and the varied results of musical harmony; as the tongue is gratified by the different varieties of taste— so the whole soul is blessed and happy in the highest degree, in holding fellowship with God. Hence the Psalmist exclaims: "O God, thou art my God; early will I seek thee; my soul thirsteth for thee, my flesh longeth for thee in a dry and thirsty land, where no water is: to see thy power and thy glory, so as I have seen thee in the sanctuary. Because thy loving-kindness is better than life, my lips shall praise thee. Thus will I bless thee while I live; I will lift up my hands in thy name. My soul shall be satisfied as with marrow and fatness; and my mouth shall praise thee with joyful lips: when I remember thee upon my bed, and meditate on thee in the nightwatches. Because thou hast been my help, therefore in the shadow of thy wings will I rejoice. My soul followeth hard after thee; thy right hand upholdeth me."—Psalm lxiii. 1–8. God is the soul's rest, the soul's portion, and the soul's unspeakable joy.

It is good,

4. *As connected with our absolute safety.*

Man is but as vanity. Exposed to a thousand perils. His body, frail and dying; vulnerable in his reputation and in his peace; and surrounded by dangers unnumbered; while a thousand enemies are ready to assault him. Besides, he is insufficient in himself, either for his own guidance or defence.

Now, to draw nigh to God, is to place ourselves in absolute security. "Who shall harm you, if ye be followers of that which is good?" "The Lord is a sun and a shield" to all his people. If we draw near to him, we have an interest in his all-benignant providence, and in all the blessings of his grace. All our interests are thus committed to him, and they will be infallibly secure, whether for time or for eternity. Hence God said to Abraham, "Fear not, I am thy shield." See this treated on, at full length, in the ninety-first Psalm.

We add, finally,

5. *It is an essential preparation for the glory of heaven.*

Heaven is the scene of perfect, uninterrupted communion with God. It is being absolutely near to him;—in his immediate presence. To be with God, and to enjoy him forever. To this state of consummate bliss however, there must be previous meetness. Adaptation of mind and heart for it. And this necessarily and mainly consists in, communion with God here—drawing near to God, is the direct way to glory. It is the education of the soul for infinite blessedness. Then how sublimely true is the declaration of the text,—That it is "good to draw near to God."

We ask, in conclusion,

1. Are you experimentally acquainted with this exercise? Do you know the experience the text brings before us; and do you know the blessedness it affirms? If you do, we say, cherish this experience;—be often thus in communion with God; guard against all lets and hindrances to it. Let this service be constant, close, and uninterrupted.

2. We invite the sinner to draw near, by faith in Jesus. God says to you by Christ —"Come unto me, all ye that labor and are heavy laden, and I will give you rest."—Matt. xi. 29. "Come now, and let us reason together, saith the Lord: though your sins be as scarlet, they shall be white as snow; though they be red like crimson, they shall be as wool."—Isa. i. 18.

3. We urge on the formal, the importance of spiritual exercise and communion with

thing else can please God, or benefit souls. As well seek warmth without fire—or physical nutrition without food or repose and vigor without refreshing sleep; as to seek for moral and holy strength, and spiritual excellence, without drawing near to God. Our spiritual being can only live and grow, by constant communion with the one Divine fountain of life and salvation. And drawing near to God, is essential to that communion; so that the text, like a celestial link, unites man to God, and allies earth itself with heaven.

XII.—ICHABOD,—THE DEPARTFD GLORY.

"And she named the child Ichabod, saying, The glory is departed."—1 *Sam.* iv. 21.

AMONG the godly Israelites there was an intense regard manifested for the glory of God, and the honor of his name. This they preferred to all earthly considerations of any and every kind. It alike glowed in the bosoms of the women, as well as in the men of Israel.

The chapter in which the text is found, records a fearful conflict between the Israelites and the Philistines. On this occasion the results were most disastrous. The ark was taken—the sons of Eli slain; and Eli also, the venerable prophet of God, fell down and died at the tidings conveyed to him. The wife of Phineas was near the hour of maternity; and when she was told the whole series of distresses, she was seized with the pangs of travail; and though she heard from the attendant women that a son was born, yet it availed not; but on this melancholy occasion, and in the bitterness of her grief, she gave to her offspring a name expressive of Israel's disasters and woes; for she named the child "Ichabod!" saying, "The glory is departed." Such is the literal history of the text.

We design, however, to give it a general application; and to look at it as,

I. *Expressive of the consequences of the first transgression.*

As applicable,

II. *To the aspects of the visible church of God in various ages.*

Let us look at it,

I. *As expressive of the consequences of the first transgression.*

I do not take into account at this time, the whole physical and moral grandeur which distinguished the world before the entrance of sin; but I confine our views to man, the most noble and exalted of God's works.

Now, first contemplate him in the tremendous reverses which characterized his history, in connection with his moral fall. Look,

1. *At his exclusion from the peaceful abode of Eden.*

His first dwelling was Paradise. A place of abounding blessings. Here he had every luxury for all the senses of the body—for the exercise of the mental faculties, and for the realization of perfect bliss. Doubtless, angels looked on with delight and joy. There was not one ingredient of earthly blessings lacking. With this, too, he had dominion over the inferior creatures. "And God said, let us make man in our own image, after our likeness: and let them have dominion over the fish of the sea, and over the fowl of the air, and over the cattle, and over all the earth, and over every creeping thing that creepeth upon the earth."—Gen. i. 26. How peaceful, dignified, and blessed was man! But, behold the effects of his transgression! He is arraigned at the Divine bar —convicted of transgression—and doomed to toil, and sorrow, and death. And at length, he is driven out from Eden's peaceful scenes into the wide world, to earn his bread by the sweat of his brow; until he should return to his native earth. "So he drove out the man;" and Ichabod was written over the gates of Paradise,—The glory is departed! We write the inscription,

2. *On the bodies of the human pair.*

The human body was marvellously formed. God was its artificer. Its erect form—wonderful parts—intellectual head—the face divine, were worthy of God as his last and best work. So in the body, originally, there was no pain—no disease—no fatigue,—he had perfect physical enjoyment. But see the effects of sin on the human physical constitution.

(1.) To Eve, and women. They were to bear the dreadful unutterable sorrows of travail and child-bearing; and both were subject to disease and death, as the general result of sin. Go to the slave, toiling under a burning sun,—to the patient, racked with pain,—to the death-bed of a fellow-being struggling with the agonies of mortality,—to the corpse, the earthly remains of a human creature—to the grave, the loathsome charnel-house of the dead. On each scene, may we not write—Ichabod! The glory is departed. We inscribe it also,

3. *On the immortal soul of man.*

See the brief description of the soul's pristine grandeur. "So God created man in his own image. in the image of God created he him; male and female created he them."—Gen. i. 27. Now, look at man in his intellectual and moral nature. His understanding is the sun of the soul. His judgment the assayer, or tester of truth. The affections, like flaming cherubim, ascending in pure and holy love to God. The conscience, exercising its control as God's vicegerent on the throne, and whispering peace. The will, swaying an undisputed authority, in harmony with God's mind and law.

And then, look, at the results of transgression! See the effects of the fall! Ignorance and darkness of the mind—the sun of the understanding eclipsed. Error and delusion perverting the judgment. The affections earthly and sensual. The conscience perverted and false. The will disloyal and rebellious. How striking God's account of the antediluvians. "And God saw that the wickedness of man was great in the earth, and that every imagination of the thoughts of his heart was only evil continually."—Gen. vi. 5. (And Pslam xlix. verses 12 and 20.) "The heart is deceitful above all things, and desperately wicked : who can know it ?"—Jer. xvii. 9. So the whole of the first part of the epistle to the Romans, is confirmatory of this.

It may be inscribed,

4. *On man's spiritual state.*

Originally, he had a place in God's family—he enjoyed God's favor—he had communion with God; and, therefore, was a partaker of Divine blessedness. But now, as fallen, he is an alien—outcast—wanderer—rebel—and an heir of wrath and perdition! How fearful the change that has come over his spiritual condition! How deplorably altered his position as a moral being! The crown fallen from his head—the sceptre snatched from his hand—and the inheritance of honor and glory forfeited by his treason against the royal authority of heaven. He had occupied a station but a little lower than the angels ; and had possessed a pre-eminence over all the other works of God's hands,—but see his miserable and low estate, by reason of his transgression! He is now inwardly blighted in his moral powers—he has the trembling appearance of a wretched culprit; and instead of being God's vicegerent on earth, and the monarch of this lower world—he becomes an exile from his original blissful domain, is doomed to toil, sorrow, affliction, and death. No greater contrast can be conceived, than our first parents in innocence, and honor, and blessedness; and then viewed in their estate of apostasy and moral woe.

How truly Ichabod may be inscribed upon it,—" The glory is departed."

But, we apply the text,

II. *To the aspects of the visible church of God, in different ages of the world.*

1. *In reference to the Jewish church.*

See it in its original constitution and glory; and then behold it when it had only the external rites, and ceremonies, and symbols left,—as it was in truth, in the days of the Redeemer. Hear what he says of the temple, of the Priests, the Scribes, the Pharisees, and of the services. How all was changed. The nation was apostate, and the ecclesiastical powers corrupt; and deceit and hypocrisy, like a leprosy, defiled the whole body of the professing people.

Let it be remembered in proof of this that the Pharisees had more sound doctrine, and were more exact in their religious services, than any other class among the Jews. Yet, hear Christ's denunciations of their gross infatuations and self-delusions. Professing to be God's temple, he declares them to be " whited sepulchres." Professing to be God's people, he declares that they are " a generation of vipers." Professing to delight in prayer and beneficence, he declares them to be ostentatious " hypocrites and devourers of widows' houses." Professing to be zealous to proselyte others to their faith, Jesus declares that their converts only became more manifold the children of darkness. How fearful this picture, thus drawn by him who could not err ! ·

Alas, the glory was departed! Then apply it,

2. *To the Christian church, and that very soon after its establishment.*

See it at first in its regenerated character; its members born from above—partakers of the Divine nature—their spirituality, how prominent and striking—their unity, how entire—their love, how fervent and beautiful—their zeal for Christ, how intense and self-denying !

Then see the lamentable change : the

awful errors in doctrine—their early corrupt practices—their carnal dissensions—their indifference to the Scripture rule of faith and order—their neglect of Christ's glory !

The deterioration of the first Christian churches was most rapid and extensive. The account of the gross evils that crept into the church at Corinth, soon after it was founded, is quite appalling. A careful perusal of the third, fifth, and eleventh chapters of Paul's first epistle to that church, will most amply corroborate the truthfulness of these statements. And these, and similar evils, spread among the other churches, so that a century scarcely passed over before the Christian church was torn with schism, marred with unsound doctrines, and polluted with heathen practices. It is thus that we read the rebukes and admonitions which pervade the Divine letters to the seven Asiatic churches, as given to us in the Revelations of John. Alas, how soon upon Christ's heavenly kingdom on earth, to a great extent, was the inscription of the text applicable—" Ichabod, the glory is departed !"

We apply the text,

3. *Very extensively to the visible Christian church now.*

Is there one section of the church of God with much of the primitive spiritual glory left? Is it the Romish Church, that harlot of abominations? Is it the Greek Church, with its tawdry vestments, and pompous yet unmeaning ceremonies and puerilities? Is it the ancient Nestorian Church, where with much that is ancient and simple, there is the silence and formalism of death? Is it the Reformed Churches of Germany and France? The Lutheran, or any other, where Neologian sentiments and mixtures of doctrinal corruptions, have left only a cold ecclesiastical system, instead of a vital power? Is it the Episcopal Church of England, in its state hierarchical pomp, and having within its bosom every error—from the lowest Socinianism to the worst and most superstitious dogmas of Rome? Is it the Wesleyan Church, with their primitive power and spirituality exchanged for priestly assumptions, and lordly exhibitions of ecclesiastical tyranny? Is it the Congregational Church—whether Baptists or Pædo-Baptists—where often, beyond the maintenance of a cold routine of services, there is scarcely a pulse beating in sympathy with the sorrows of our suffering humanity, where there may be doctrinal truth, and church membership rights, but where the benevolent outgoings of a true Christian spirit are feeble and languishing?

It was surely designed that in the church of Jesus, not only should truth be preserved and holiness exhibited, but that the mind and heart of the Saviour should be found so dwelling in his followers, that they should be blessings to all around them. As he went about doing good, so should they. As he was the friend of the poor and the wretched, so should they be. As he mixed with the masses of the people to bless them, so should they. As his spirit sympathized with all the neglected and oppressed, and down-trodden of mankind, so should theirs. But in our day we often see mere worldly men, and oftentimes infidels, more acutely sensitive to the sufferings of the people than Christian churches are. In great movements of real unmistakable philanthropy and self-denial, the churches of the day are most wofully deficient—most disastrously in the rear—instead of having the front position in every cause that can bless man and glorify God. Hence, men of the world, of generous hearts, look, as they well may, with distrust on Christian teachers and professors. Alas! there is not one church in christendom to which, to some extent, the inscription may not be affixed—the glory is departed !

The entire church of God requires to be aroused from its slumbers—stirred up from its apathy—and quickened afresh for its great work of saving men, and glorifying God.

APPLICATION.

But Ichabod need not be the abiding inscription on man—on our world—or on the church of our Redeemer ; for,

1. The gospel brings back the glory of redemption to man. He need not perish ; but, by faith in the Lord Jesus, he may be restored to the divine image and favor, and eventually to eternal life.

It is most clear that the departed glory would never have returned, but for the gracious intervention of God. God became man's help in his low estate—his compassionate Friend when exposed to ruin and woe. He therefore revealed to the guilty culprits, when arraigned before him, the blessed intimation that the woman's seed should bruise the serpent's head. This was the first ray of hope that gleamed upon our benighted and sin-smitten world. And this light gradually increased : it grew brighter and brighter, until at length the day-star arose, and the fields of Bethlehem resounded with the angelic anthem, sung at the birth of man's Redeemer. Christ came as the orb of day to enlighten the world. He came to bring back the forfeited glory; and he effected his great work. He redeemed man from the condemnation of the law, and the power of death. He opened back for him a way to the holiest of all. He suffered the just for the unjust, to bring man again to God. And now the blessed gospel not only reveals these truths, but offers to man the restoration of the departed glory. By faith, Christ, the glorious Saviour, is received into the soul, and thus men again become the happy and dignified sons of God. John i. 11, 12.

2. The New Testament is sufficient to restore the glory to the church. Nothing has so tended to impair, and weaken, and carnalize the church of God as the admission of human authority, and the setting up of human ceremonials, for the guidance and observance of Christ's disciples. Jesus designed his religion to be eminently simple, and free from all glare and show. He designed the clear exhibition of faith in himself with its necessary fruit, as all-sufficient to discipleship. But how melancholy is the exhibition now presented; the church of Jesus divided into fractions! All sorts of creeds, and forms, and ceremonies introduced. Human authority riding rampant over the precepts of Jesus; and pure, simple Christianity almost lost in the tawdry vestments in which she has been robed. What is to be done to bring the church again to her pristine purity, that she may shine forth in all her original glory?

Let the whole church of Jesus return to a prayerful study of the divine word, and to a faithful imitation of the churches' first order and spirit; and thus Zion may arise and become a universal praise in all the earth.

3. The Holy Spirit waits to confer the glory, both on man, by his renewal and sanctification, and on the Church, by investing it with all heavenly graces—and thus making it as a fruitful garden of the Lord.

It can never be admitted that God desires the church to remain thus distracted, divided, feeble, and almost uninfluential. On the contrary he waits to pour the Spirit out from on high. He waits to visit his vineyard with all the reviving influences of his grace. He waits to convert the dreary arid desert into a fruitful field. Now these displays of heavenly love and power should be sought in earnest and importunate prayer. If he gives his Holy Spirit to individual believers when they ask him, how much more would he send abundant and copious showers of his divine and fructifying influences on the Church, if his people unitedly sought it by believing prayer. But it must be sought before God will send it; for without the earnest desire for the blessing it would be unvalued, and bestowed extensively in vain.

Finally—Remember that the desires and travail of Christ's soul are connected with the glorifying of his church. And as his reward is most certain, and his expectations cannot possibly fail, then so surely shall Zion be redeemed, and she shall yet arise arrayed in all the glory of her Head and Lord. The Redeemer's final triumphs shall beautify his church, and fill the whole earth with his glory.

" Sovereign of worlds, display thy power ;
Be this thy Zion's favored hour:
Bid the bright morning Star arise,
And point the nations to the skies.

Set up thy throne where Satan reigns,
On Afric's shore, on India's plains,
On wilds and continents unknown;
And be the universe thine own.

Speak, and the world shall hear thy voice;
Speak, and the world shall rejoice;
Scatter the gloom of heathen night,
And bid all nations hail the light."

XIII.—DESPISERS OF CHRIST ADDRESSED.

" Behold, ye despisers, and wonder, and perish: for I work a work in your days, a work which ye shall in no wise believe, though a man declare it unto you."—*Acts* xiii. 41.

THE text is connected with a most solemn warning given to the Jews, in reference to their rejection of the Messiah. " Beware, therefore, lest that come upon you, which is spoken of in the prophets:" verse 40. The results of such a course had been declared by Moses, in the most terrible threatenings. By various of the prophets, in the most awful predictions. And the apostle entreats them to beware, lest these denunciations should be realized in their history. And he concludes this affectionate warning in language most striking—" Behold, ye despisers, and wonder, and perish : for I work a work in your days, a work which ye shall in no wise believe, though a man declare it unto you." Most likely the apostle had before him the destruction of their city and temple, and the ruin of their nation, as one of the calamities which would arise from their unbelief and contempt of God.

We, however, shall apply the text to the peril of every unbelieving and incorrigible sinner ; and the certain consequences of obstinate impenitence and sin.

Notice, then,

I. *The characters addressed.*

II. *The results intimated.*

And,

III. *The lessons suggested.*

I. *The characters addressed.*

" Ye despisers."

In the text, despisers of Christ are intended. We may retain the same exact idea, and inquire, who are despisers of the Lord Jesus ? To this we reply,

1. *Disbelievers in his work and mission.*

Of such were many of the Jews. They did not give credit to his mission. Would not own him as the Messiah. " He came unto his own, but his own received him not." They railed at him—reviled him—scorned him—treated him as an impostor—as one in league with devils.

In this sense, they were a type of the Deists and Rationalists of our own times, who reject revelation, who, if they admit that Jesus Christ existed and taught—yet say he was but a virtuous man—a harmless Jew—but not the Son of God—not specially sent to save. They deny his teaching to be infallible. Treat his miracles as mere sleight of hand exhibitions.

Then the text will apply,

2. *To unbelievers in his word and message.*

There is a great difference between disbelievers and unbelievers. The former reject his official character—the latter do not receive his message. Many of the Jews, as to Christ, were skeptics : the mass of them, however, merely did not believe. So, now, the crowds of men are in unbelief—do not hearken to the gospel, so as to understand it. Do not consider it, so as to decide on its acceptance. This is often the result of a sinful apathy in reference to all truly religious concerns.

Now, all unbelief is despising of Christ. For, think of the glorious Messenger, and the gracious message ! And then to put it away by unbelief. How great the affront to God ! How glaring the contempt it exhibits ! How heinous the sin which is involved in it !

The text applies,

3. *To all who are so engrossed with other things, as to neglect Christ.*

Now this is a class of unbelievers of a peculiar kind. They may in their minds and judgments be rather favorable to Christ—feel interested in his work—often disposed to become disciples ;—but they are so occupied—so fully engaged with other things and pursuits, that they excuse themselves for the present. The farm—the merchandise—domestic duties, and other things, fill their hearts and absorb their whole time. It is not only easy to lose the soul by following forbidden objects, but also by giving up the mind and heart totally to things lawful in themselves, but which should only engage our secondary attention. Christ's kingdom and his righteousness should surely be first, as well as pre-eminent in our esteem and attention. Hence, a man may make science, or philosophy, or literature, the main end of his life, to the neglect of his moral welfare, and of Christ the only Saviour, from the wrath to come. Nay, a man may yield himself up to humane pursuits, and generous lines of actions, and yet live in the neglect of spiritual religion ; and thus, in reality, be a despiser of the Lord Jesus Christ. Yet, surely, this must involve the charge in the text of despising the Redeemer. But what multitudes are included in the one or the other of these classes ! Disbelieving Christian truth, or remaining in unbelief, or preferring other things to the Lord Jesus Christ. But in each and every case,—how heinous the sin,—how infatuated the course pursued,—and how fearful must be its consequences !

Notice, then,

II. *The results intimated.*

Now these results may be comprehended in the three terms employed.

1. *Such shall behold.*

They shall see the threatenings of the Lord Jesus fulfilled. Just as the Jews saw the Roman armies, and the burning temple, and the sacked desolate city. Unbelief will not render null and void the word of God. So all despisers of Christ shall see, or behold the fulfilment of the sentence of the Lord's displeasure.

They often do so in this life. How frequently is bitterness, and sorrow, and woe, even in this life, the result of neglecting the soul, and despising the Saviour! On the bed of sickness;—what self-reproach—what dolorous regrets—and what horrible forebodings! In a dying hour;—what overwhelming terrors—what anguish and despair, when they realize the misery and woe of a Christless condition! " And thou mourn at the last, when thy flesh and thy body are consumed."—Prov. v. 11. They shall behold, in the day of judgment. "Behold, he cometh with clouds; and every eye shall see him, and they also which pierced him: and all kindreds of the earth shall wail because of him. Even so, Amen."—Rev. i. 7. " And then shall appear the sign of the Son of man in heaven: and then shall all the tribes of the earth mourn, and they shall see the Son of man coming in the clouds of heaven with power and great glory."—Matt. xxiv. 30.

This conscious beholding, or realizing, shall be their state forever. They shall behold the Saviour they have rejected—the heaven they have despised—the saints they hated. Just as the rich man saw Lazarus and the world of bliss in the fearful unapproachable distance.

2. *They shall wonder.*

They shall be filled with astonishment. It shall come upon them with surprise and astonishment,—as the tempest on the traveller—as the storm on the mariner—as the calamity on Belshazzar—as the Roman army on Jerusalem, while enwrapped in carnal security. They shall be singing of peace; when, suddenly, destruction shall come upon them. They must see, and behold; and will no longer have power to put the vision of wrath away from their eyes.

But this wonder shall only be the precursor of their final and inevitable ruin. For observe,

3. *They shall perish.*

For their sins, and in them. By the righteous wrath of heaven. According to the threatenings of God's word. Now to perish, in the scriptural sense of the word, implies,

(1.) That they are now in circumstances where all means of safety have fled, and gone forever. Christian institutions, ordinances, mercies, ministers, Sabbaths, &c.

(2.) That the day of probation is over. That man's natural and rational life is the limit of his probation, is most evident from the word of God. The night of death is the period of darkness and inactivity, when no man can work. The harvest then is past, the summer then is ended.

(3.) That all their hopes are annihilated. Not only real hopes, but even false hopes, are all destroyed—their ruin having become inevitable and irremediable. It is only necessary to read the Saviour's awful descriptions of the state of the lost, to feel how intensely dreadful is the condition of those who perish. Exclusion from God's presence, from the society of the holy, and the joys of the blessed; with banishment into outer darkness, where there is weeping and wailing and gnashing of teeth, is the fearful doom of those who die in their sins.

Such, then, are the certain results of unbelief and despising Christ. Observe, then, from the subject,

III. *The lessons suggested.*

1. *That despising Christ must be a sin most heinous.*

It is the climax of transgression, the completion of guilt. The filling up of iniquity. If the dignity, graciousness, and sacrifice of Jesus be considered, then this sin must stand out as one of indescribable enormity. No baseness can exceed it. No act, in point of moral turpitude, can surpass it. To reject Christ—refuse Christ—and to put him, as it were, to open shame again, and, as far as possible, to treat with gross indignity his pity, his tears, and his dying love. We learn,

2. *That a believing reception of Christ is the sinner's duty.*

That it is so, is manifest from the following considerations:—This is God's command. This is what Christ himself urges. This is what is evidently and clearly the design of the gospel being sent to you. For this the spirit of God calls and strives. We ought to do it, without further evasion, or neglect, or delay.

We ought to give the message of reconciliation the most earnest, immediate, and hearty welcome. And say not that you cannot do this, until you have made the effort, and sought the help of the freely-offered grace of God. God would not demand it, nor could unbelief be any sin, unless the ability and means of faith were within your reach, and available, even now, to your salvation.

To despise Christ, and plead a necessity for doing so, is to add blasphemy to iniquity. For would God call men to repentance, and demand their faith, and neglect to provide them with the means of either; and then would he add to this, a most terrible punishment for neglecting that course of action which they had no ability to pursue? That a natural man cannot perform spiritual actions is most manifest. But the question is, can he receive the offered grace of God, and so become spiritual? Of course he can: and herein is manifestly exhibited his moral free agency, and accountability to God.

The subject suggests,

3. *That the sinner's ruin is self-procured.* Is it not manifestly so? for the guilt is the sinner's own. The rejection of the remedy is their own willing act. If so, this is soul murder. Suicide of the immortal spirit. Well may we solemnly ask, Whom do you intend to blame, if you go down into the pit? God, the Father? who so loved the world as to send his Son to redeem it. The Son? who gave himself up to agony and death; and who tasted that death for every man. The Holy Spirit? who is emphatically the spirit of grace; and who waits to renew and sanctify every believing sinner. Angels? who are loving ones; and who are ready to rejoice over every repenting sinner. Ministers? who have preached, and warned, and invited, and wept, and prayed for your conversion. Circumstances? has God in his decrees or providence shut you up to ruin, or out of the possibility of salvation? His solemn oath—in which he declares his having no pleasure in the death of the sinner—renders this impossible. You can have been placed in no condition, in which you were shut up to abide in unbelief, and thus to perish.

Oh, no! like the man without the wedding garment, you will be speechless; except in self-reproaches. Oh! think of this now—in time; while it will avail you.

I urge this course on all, and every man. But if ye will not consider, and believe, and obey; then I repeat the text—and forget not, that the sound will again fall upon your ears. Yes, you may hear it on the bed of languishing and death, when calm reflection and earnest prayer may be impossible; or if not then, in that solemn day when Christ shall come to judge, and not to save,—to pronounce the sinner's doom, and not to invite him to his heart and arms of mercy.

"Behold, ye despisers, and wonder, and perish!"

"Sinner, oh why so thoughtless grown?
Why in such dreadful haste to die?
Daring to leap to worlds unknown,
Heedless against thy God to fly.

Wilt thou despise eternal fate,
Urg'd on by sin's fantastic dreams,
Madly attempt th' infernal gate,
And force thy passage to the flames?

Stay, sinner, on the gospel plains,
Behold the God of love unfold
The glories of his dying pains,
Forever telling—yet untold."

XIV.—THE PROFITS OF AFFLICTION.

"It is good for me that I have been afflicted; that I might learn thy statutes."—*Psalm* cxix. 71.

"MAN is born to trouble as the sparks fly upward." No state, or condition of life, is exempted. The history of all people, in all ages, establishes it. This equally applies to the best and holiest of mankind. We may presume that if God loves his people, he will only appoint what is for their real good. He does appoint them afflictions; and therefore, it is most evident that it is really good for them to be afflicted.

Our subject then is the salutary, or profitable tendency of afflictions. Two remarks must preface our illustrations.

(1.) That only *sanctified* afflictions are salutary. And that afflictions can only be sanctified by prayer, and by the blessing of God. Fire can both consume and purify. It melts the lead, but purifies the gold. It burns up the chaff, but refines the silver.

(2.) That afflictions are only so far profitable, as they are thus sanctified. So that it is the grace of God in affliction that makes them at any time profitable; and without this grace, no believer ever experienced the beneficial results, as expressed by the Psalmist, in the text.

Let us see then how good it is for the people of God to be afflicted. It is so,

I. *By the lessons afflictions teach.*

It is when afflicted that we are led to feel our own nothingness and unworthiness. It is then that our sinfulness is made self-evident. In affliction, there is a tendency to reflection; and this brings our iniquities before us. Our omissions of duty, our imperfect services, and our manifold sins. Prosperity and health are often found connected with thoughtlessness and inattention to the state of our own souls; but when confined to the silent chamber and the couch of pain, then reflection and consideration are inevitable; and by this moral process, our afflictions oftentimes become really and most truly our best teachers. But they also show us our utter dependence on God. When in health and vigor, we are apt to lean on our own sufficiency, and may conclude that we have resources within ourselves for securing our well-being and happiness. But afflictions show us, how all our enjoyments and blessings depend on God's will. How desirable his favor is to our real happiness; and that his friendship and help are essential to our blessedness and security.

Afflictions also impress our hearts and minds, as to the certainty of our mortality. Have you not often experienced what a stroke of pain can do? How speedily the most vigorous constitution is made to shake and tremble as the oak, smitten by the tempest! How soon we are brought to the verge of the tomb; and how we feel we must certainly come to be its inhabitants.

Now, it might be supposed that a survey of the afflictions of others would teach this. That general observation would produce a solemn estimate of our dying state. But universal experience proves, that "men think all men mortal, but themselves." And it is needful that the king of terrors should knock at our own door, before we are sufficiently awakened to the reality of his coming.

Afflictions thus teach us our true condition, our sinful character, our utter helplessness, and our dying estate. And well is it, that these lessons should be indelibly engraven on the tablet of our wayward and frivolous hearts. It is on the sick-bed that we feel the force of those graphic lines,—

" Let others boast how strong they be,
    Nor death nor danger fear;
But we'll confess, O Lord, to thee,
    What feeble things we are.

Our life contains a thousand springs,
    And dies if one be gone;
Strange! that a harp of thousand strings
    Should keep in tune so long."

And it is well, when the devout impression leads us to add,—

"But 'tis our God supports our frame,
    The God that built us first;
Salvation to the almighty name
    That rear'd us from the dust.

While we have breath, or use our tongues,
    Our Maker we'll adore;
His spirit moves our heaving lungs,
    Or they would breathe no more."

Afflictions do us good,

II. *By the feelings which they produce.*

They tend to produce tenderness of spirit. They give sensibility, acuteness, and sharpness to the conscience. They remove moral stupor and apathy. They tend also to humility of spirit. Health and prosperity lift up the mind, lead to self-satisfaction and elation. Afflictions bring down the haughty spirit—bend it—prostrate it before God, make us to feel that we are poor and frail; and at best, but as vanity; and that all boasting and vaunting must be put away. That in the dust before God is our fitting place. They also often remove coldness and indifference to the sufferings of others. We then feel tender humanity and kindness to the suffering, and our need of the sympathy of our fellow-creatures, and also our mutual dependence on one another.

It is almost impossible for those ever healthy and vigorous, to feel rightly for the delicate and the weak; or, for the prosperous man to feel rightly for the poor, and those born for adversity. But in the furnace this dross, this callousness, this want of susceptibility is often consumed, and our hearts are made soft.

We are often brought, in affliction, also to feel deadness to the world. Mid the showers and sunshine the roots sink deeper into the soil. The winds of affliction loosen them, and show us that this is not our resting-place. That speedily the tree will fall, and return to its native elements in the dust. Thus affliction places the world in its true light, showing us that worldly honors are a mere breath, worldly pleasures a delusion, worldly riches are as dross, and all worldly scenes a passing panorama. We can then apply the words of the poet, in a most experimental manner, and say,—

" Vain delusive world, adieu,
    With all of creature good;
Only Jesus I pursue,
    Who bought me with his blood.
All thy pleasures I forego;
    I trample on thy wealth and pride;
Only Jesus will I know,
    And Jesus crucified."

In addition to the weaning influences of afflictions, they also often produce *a greater love to Divine things*.

To the *Bible*—as the solace of this life, and the only guide to immortality. Yes, it is in perplexity that the chart is incomparably precious. In sorrow—that the promises are so sweet. In darkness—that the rays of celestial light are so cheering.

To *Prayer*—as the only exercise which can bring relief to the spirit; and peace and hope to the mind. Is any man afflicted? let him pray. And the humble Christian will both submit and pray—be resigned, and yet solicitous for relief.

This is well expressed in a very plaintive, yet spiritual manner, in the following lines:

> " Why should a living man complain
>   Of deep distress within,
> Since every sigh and every pain,
>   Is but the fruit of sin?
>
> No, Lord, I'll patiently submit,
>   Nor ever dare rebel;
> Yet sure I may, here at thy feet,
>   My painful feelings tell.
>
> Thou seest what floods of sorrow rise,
>   And beat upon my soul;
> One trouble to another cries,
>   Billows on billows roll.
>
> From fear to hope and hope to fear,
>   My shipwrecked soul is toss'd;
> 'Till I am tempted in despair
>   To give up all for lost.
>
> Yet thro' the stormy clouds I'll look
>   Once more to thee, my God:
> Oh, fix my feet upon a rock,
>   Beyond the gaping flood.
>
> One look of mercy from thy face
>   Will set my heart at ease;
> One all-commanding word of grace
>   Will make the tempest cease."

To *Meditation*—by which our soul's experience is connected with Divine communion, and consolation, and joy.

To *Praise*—for how sweet our mercies are then. How precious is Christ then. How great the promises; and how unspeakably good is God, our heavenly Father.

Afflictions also lead us to a *higher appreciation of Divine mercies and heavenly realities*. When is pardon so sweet, as when realized on the bed of languishing? When is the inward peace so serene—the joy so bright—the hope so cheering, as in the night of sorrow, and sickness, and suffering! Then, too, it is, that heaven rises in value; and that we feel a closer acquaintance, and a more endearing union with the spirits of the just, and the glories of the skies.

As the Christian nears the better land, he catches its fragrant perfumes; and often receives clusters of its rich grapes, as the first fruits of the eternal plenty, which is before him. He may may too, on the bed of affliction, be favored with spiritual seasons of ascending Pisgah's top; and from thence catch enrapturing glances of the good land before him;—so that death may be welcomed, that Canaan may be enjoyed.

APPLICATION.

1. Have you experienced these benefits from affliction? If so, seek that they may permanently abide with you. Guard against the flight of these lessons and emotions with returning health. Seek often to repeat the lessons you learned, and to feel over again the experience you then enjoyed. Learn,

2. How entirely and fully we should be resigned to God and his will. He knows what is best for us. He will do that which will eventually tend most to our abiding blessedness. Then seek the spirit that can cheerfully say,—" Not our will, but thine be done!" Oh, yes, say to your heart—

> " Be still, my heart! these anxious cares
>   To thee are burdens, thorns, and snares;
> They cast dishonor on thy Lord,
>   And contradict his gracious word.
>
> When first before his mercy-seat,
>   Thou didst to him thy all commit;
> He gave thee warrant, from that hour,
>   To trust his wisdom, love, and power.
>
> Did ever trouble yet befall,
>   And he refuse to hear thy call?
> And has he not his promise pass'd,
>   That thou shalt overcome at last?
>
> He who has help'd me hitherto,
>   Will help me all my journey thro';
> And give me daily cause to raise
>   New Ebenezers to his praise.
>
> Tho' rough and thorny be the road,
>   It leads thee home, apace, to God:
> Then count thy present trials small,
>   For heaven will make amends for all."

Man's safety and blessedness is to be so given up to God's gracious providence, as to welcome in the spirit of grateful submission all his dispensations. Yes, all his dispensations. For when you surrendered yourself to Christ, did you not say,—

> " Jesus, I my cross have taken,
>   All to leave and follow thee;

Naked, poor, despised, forsaken,
  Thou, from hence, my all shalt be.
Perish ev'ry fond ambition,
  All I've sought, or hop'd, or known;
Yet how rich is my condition!
  God and heav'n are still my own.

Go, then, earthly fame and treasure,
  Come, disasters, scorn, and pain;
In thy service, pain is pleasure,
  With thy favor, loss is gain.
I have call'd thee Abba, Father,
  I have set my heart on thee;
Storms may howl, and clouds may gather,
  All must work for good to me."

3. Have afflictions been of no service to you? How fearful that state! And if not, don't forget that if tenderness of heart and purity of spirit are not produced—if they do not make us wiser and better—they will increase our obduracy, and make us more meet for the unmitigable sorrows and anguish of eternity.

XV.—INFATUATED HEARERS.

"Speak unto us smooth things."—*Isaiah* xxx. 10.

It seems unaccountable that intelligent beings should become so foolishly infatuated, that they should prefer deceit to sincerity, and falsehood to truth. And yet men do so, not in reference to temporal things, which are only of secondary moment; but in reference to the soul and the great realities of the eternal world. The more important the subject, and the more valuable is the truth relating to it; and the more needful to avoid error. So that to be willingly deceived in the highest of all concerns, amounts to nothing short of moral insanity. Yet of this worst form of madness, men are most extensively guilty. The context exhibits the character of such. "That this is a rebellious people, lying children, children that will not hear the law of the Lord:" ver. 9: and then follows the text itself. Surely such may be accounted infatuated hearers indeed.

Let us then notice,

I. *What it is to speak smooth things.*

II. *Why people desire it.*

III. *Its final results.*

I. *What it is to speak smooth things.*

(1.) Now we are not to confound this with speaking kind and affectionate things. A great portion of God's word is occupied in declarations of Divine kindness, and in promises of a gracious character.

Now the minister may not only dwell on these things, but give them a holy prominence in his teaching. The Saviour did this, and so did the Apostles. Their chief theme was God's love to a perishing world, and the universal mercifulness of the Gospel economy.

(2.) Nor with a prudent presentation of truth, so as to avoid as much as possible the prejudices of those we address. We are to be wise as serpents in these things. The utmost prudence may be used in order to disarm prejudice, and obtain a welcome for the truth. And a minister may go great lengths in accommodating himself to the condition and circumstances of his hearers, with a view to secure their eternal salvation.

So Paul acted: "For though I be free from all men, yet have I made myself servant unto all, that I might gain the more. And unto the Jews I became as a Jew, that I might gain the Jews; to them that are under the law, as under the law, that I might gain them that are under the law; to them that are without law, as without law (being not without law to God, but under the law to Christ), that I might gain them that are without law. To the weak became I as weak, that I might gain the weak: I am made all things to all men, that I might by all means save some."—1 Cor. ix. 19–22.

(3.) Nor is it to appeal to the generosity or candor of men. Paul often did this as before Felix and Agrippa; and also, when he called the Jews at Rome together, to hear his message, (Acts xxviii. 17, &c.)

Now let these distinctions be kept in view, To speak smooth things, is not necessarily,

(4.) To teach error; nor yet to adulterate the truth. A man may declare truth all his life, and yet may so garnish it, and soften down its forcible style—and so avoid directness of aim—that he shall be really guilty of the evil of speaking smooth things. So that false teaching is not absolutely essential to smooth speaking. But it is to keep back every thing which is disagreeable to our hearers. It is to avoid,

1. *A too searching process with the consciences of men.*

Not to offend the covetous by declaring the mind of Christ on worldliness. Not to offend the pleasure-taker, by showing its utter incompatibility with holy things. Not to offend the formalist, by urging spiritual religion. Not to offend the latitudinarian, by declaring the woes of the Gospel, on those who teach or believe another Gospel; not to mortify the pride of the assuming; not to assail the vanity of the ostentatious; not to arouse the solicitudes of the apathetic; not to humble the spirit of the self-righteous; not to denounce the baseness of hypocrisy; not to expose the heartlessness of the selfish. Now these are examples in which ministers are in danger of speaking smooth things.

2. *This is done by a generalizing way of speaking the truth.*

So speaking, as if you were referring to persons out of the congregation. As though those present did not require to be aroused, threatened, condemned! A sort of loose style of address, which never takes effect—because it has no point, no force. A sword—very bright it may be, and beautiful to look upon, but without edge. The hammer of truth may be heavy, but it may descend so gradually that there shall be no effect produced—no signs of power visible—and, in reality, no execution done by it.

3. *This is done by neglecting to enforce the threatenings of God's word.*

Dwelling ever on the sunny side of subjects, and avoiding what would alarm or disturb the hearer. Balak wanted just such a prophet to gratify his wicked malevolence, by prophesying evil of the children of Israel. Ahab, the king of Israel, wanted such a prophet. Herod, and his unlawful wife, would have been delighted with such a preacher. The Jews would never have rejected the Saviour, had he not unveiled their hypocrisy, and declared to them the righteous wrath of God. So Stephen might have died in peace, had he not declared to the incorrigible multitude that they were stiff-necked and uncircumcised in heart, and the murderers of the Just one. By avoiding the denunciations of God's holy displeasure, men fulfil the request of the text; and, in fact, prophesy smooth things.

Let us inquire,

II. *Why people desire it.*

1. *It is in harmony with the delusions of the carnal heart.*

It suits man's fallen, corrupt nature. Here is no violence done to principles or habits. It is respectable and courteous to be rocked in the cradle of self-esteem and self-gratulation. While this is agreeable to man's innate love of self, and ease, and applause, it is especially the snare of certain temperaments, who never consider fidelity in any

other light than that of rudeness and insult. But men desire this, because,

2. *It effects an agreeable compromise with a sort of religion, and with their sins.*

People have no objection generally to religion, if they can have one to suit them. One which is convenient, agreeable, and which gives full and undisturbed scope to their evil nature. Indeed, man feels his need of religion—and one of this sort is as a sweet morsel to the mouth, and as an opiate to their moral nature.

Now, that people do desire smooth things declared to them, is evident,

(1.) Because such teaching secures a large attendance of approving persons. There is the papal religion, of ceremonies and priestly influences—smooth to the heart's content of the sinner. So others are delighted with a national state religion, in which they are to be saved according to ecclesiastical canons, and by duly appointed and consecrated priestly authority and influence. There is the Antinomian religion, by which men are saved independently of their own choice and of their own conduct; and where they have only to wait and be acted upon by influences they cannot resist, and be rendered eternally blessed as the result of a purpose before all worlds.

Now, when there is any talent in exhibiting these human dogmas and vain deceits, the rule will be, that multitudes will crowd to hear and receive these smooth things.

(2.) Persons will freely support such a religion. Hence costly erections, magnificently decorated edifices, and hired singing men and singing women, distinguish such places. All these expensive modes of worship are cheerfully met, if the priest will only speak smooth things.

(3.) They will unite in publicly professing such a religion. It is the artificial carpeted way to heaven. No thorns in the way, no self-denial to be experienced, no moral cross to be borne, and no inconvenience felt. Here unsanctified human nature, the world, and a deceived conscience shake hands, in this miserable and delusive compromise.

Let us look,

III. *At its final results.*

To speak smooth things,

1. *Will grieve the Holy Spirit of God.*

Here what God says by the prophet: "Son of man, I have made thee a watchman unto the house of Israel: therefore hear the word at my mouth, and give them warning from me. When I say unto the wicked, Thou shalt surely die; and thou givest him not warning, nor speakest to warn the wicked from his wicked way, to save his life; the same wicked man shall die in his iniquity; but his blood will I require at thine hand."—Ezek. iii. 17, 18. So also, the prophet is commanded at all risks to deal faithfully with the people. "And thou, son of man, be not afraid of them, neither be afraid of their words, though briers and thorns be with thee, and thou dost dwell among scorpions: be not afraid of their words, nor be dismayed at their looks, though they be a rebellious house. And thou shalt speak my words unto them, whether they will hear, or whether they will forbear; for they are most rebellious."—Ezek. ii. 6, 7. And what a fearful picture the prophet Isaiah draws of such as are guilty of the fearful sin of infidelity to their solemn charge. "His watchmen are blind: they are all ignorant, they are all dumb dogs, they cannot bark; sleeping, lying down, loving to slumber. Yea, they are greedy dogs which can never have enough, and they are shepherds that cannot understand: they all look to their own way, every one for his gain, from his quarter."—Isaiah lvi. 10, 11.

2. *It is opposed to the conduct of the faithful servants of God, in all ages.*

What illustrious instances are given! Look at Moses in the presence of Pharaoh. Nathan in the presence of David. Elijah in conversation with Ahab (1 Kings xxi. 17). The Baptist and Herod, in reference to his having his brother's wife. But the Great Teacher, Jesus, whose spirit was grace itself, and who manifested it to all, and showed compassion to the vilest. Yet hear him, in his address to the religionists of his day, (Matt. xxiii. 1, &c.) And so also Paul (Acts xx. 26, 27), the good and the faithful servant of Jesus, said, I have declared the whole counsel of God.

3. *It is fraught with ruin to souls.*

Under such teaching, men trifle and slumber on in their sins, until their desolation and overthrow is complete. Thus priest and people—the deceiver and the deceived—perish together. One for his infidelity to God and souls, and the other through yielding to the spirit of delusion. The blind leading the blind, they both fall into the ditch. How unspeakably terrible must be the eternal condition of such teachers! And how awful will be the meeting between the destroyers and the ruined, in the great day of God.

Of all trusts, that of the Christian minister is most solemn and momentous; and how needful is it that hearers of the word should feel their own individual responsibility, and test all teaching, by bringing it to the law and to the testimony. Instead of this, however, multitudes utter the language of the text, and dare all consequences, if the prophet will only declare to them smooth things.

APPLICATION.

Learn—

1. The true interests of hearers. To place yourselves beneath the teaching of faithful watchmen. Better have truth plainly and sometimes even roughly conveyed, than be the victims of error and smooth things. In a clerk for your business—a teacher for your children—a physician for your bodies, you would desire fidelity. How much more should you seek it in the servant of Christ, who ministers to your soul!

2. Speaking and hearing have each their inevitable results. False teaching, and prophesying smooth things, must be as poison to the soul. It must tend to the most fearful of all catastrophes—the death of those who receive it. So hearing should not only have respect to the truth, but the mind should be directed to hear with discrimination, with solicitude, with prayer, with an earnest desire to obtain present and everlasting good. And a right hearing of true things will effect this; for God has said to those who hear his gracious word, "Hear, and your souls shall live."

XVI.—SALVATION THE WORK OF GOD AND MAN.

"Work out our own salvation with fear and trembling. For it is God which worketh in you both to will and to do of his good pleasure."—*Philippians* ii. 12, 13.

Two rules are essential to a right understanding of the divine word. First: that we understand the persons to whom the passages are addressed. For it must make all the difference, whether they be believers or disbelievers—converted or unconverted—disciples of Christ, or backsliders from him. Then it is essential, secondly, that we always take the words in their clear and obvious connection, for disjointed portions of the Bible may be made to teach the most idle, gross, and absurd fictions.

With these two points ever in view, we ought to be ready to throw aside every sectarian prepossession, and allow the word of eternal life to speak out fully and freely for itself. I am led to these remarks by the peculiar character of the text. I suppose two persons of opposite theological systems to come to its consideration. Ah, says the first, religion is a matter left to our own efforts—it devolves totally on ourselves; for it is written—" Work out your own salvation." No, says the person of the opposite religious creed, salvation is entirely of God; for it is written—" God worketh in you to will and to do of his good pleasure."

Now both take a part of the truth—both are to some extent right; yet both are to a greater extent wrong. Both see through the colored medium of their peculiar creed; and hence neither of them see the pure light of truth in all its colorless beauty.

Let us then honestly and prayerfully look at this momentous passage, and ascertain the mind of the Holy Spirit thereon. Observe,

I. *The object set before us.*
Our " own salvation."
II. *The means for its attainment.*
" Work out."
III. *The ability supplied.*
" For it is God," &c.

Notice, then,

I. *The object set before us.*
Our " own salvation."

Observe carefully what this is. It is not our own *atonement*—nor our own *pardon*—nor our own *adoption* or *regeneration ;* but, our own *salvation.* It is obviously the completion of that inward work which God has commenced. The text is addressed to Christians. Salvation consists of knowledge and holiness. The germs of these are in every believing heart. But they must be wrought out—there must be growth—advancement—completion. The race is begun, but it is to be finished. The warfare is going on, but the victory is not won; therefore it must be carried on and out—so running, till we obtain. Fighting the good fight, till we lay hold of eternal life. So that there must be the maintenance of the life of God in the soul. Perseverance in the good old way. Steadfastness in the faith, and holy progression, till we obtain the meetness requisite to the enjoyment of eternal life ; for a holy meetness must necessarily precede its enjoyment.

Observe, this salvation is our *own.* Not that we are to be indifferent to the salvation of others, but this must be *first,* and regarded *chiefly ;* and then, that of others. In all other matters we do think of ourselves first, and often we may add, chiefly. As in reference to our physical health. In reference to personal safety. To the enjoyment of pleasure. In the pursuit of wealth or honor. A starving man does not forget his own perishing condition, though hundreds of like perishing ones may surround him. A drowning man would seek first to escape the impending danger, before he could attempt to aid those in similar danger. So evidently ought it to be in reference to the soul's salvation. We must surely act in like manner, or we evince a spirit of the sheerest folly and inconsistency.

It is perfidy to ourselves, if we are absorbed with the eternal interests of others, and neglect our own ! Oh, that we felt this as we ought to do, and that the words were written on our hearts :—" Our own salvation."

Then notice,

II. *The means for its attainment.*
" Work out your own salvation."

Observe, it is to be a matter,

1. *Of labor—of work.*

Not self-righteous work, but spiritual labor. Hence all the passages of God's word on Christian diligence. On striving—contending. Observe, too, that this is much more than talking—purposing—or even professing. It is working : and it is described as a work of faith, and a labor of love. And it is not every sort of effort that may be thus described, but it must be specified working—working by Christ's authority, and Christ's rule—and by his grace. Working with all the renewed powers we possess. And this work includes—self-government, self-denial, and self-devotedness to God and his glory.

In one word—it involves the whole of what we understand by practical godliness. All that God demands in reference to his own, special and supreme claims on our veneration, love, and obedience. All the duties we owe to mankind—whether of equity, goodness, or compassion and mercy. And all those personal duties which include the elevation of the mind—the sanctity of the heart—and the demeanor of the life. Forget not, that religious work must enter into all the concerns of life; and give a tone to all our engagements, whether secular or spiritual.

This working is to be the constant movement of the moral machinery within us; and which was started into action when we were quickened and renewed by the Spirit and grace of God. See how frequently it is urged, and powerfully enforced. "And besides this, giving all diligence, add to your faith virtue; and to virtue knowledge; and to knowledge temperance; and to temperance patience; and to patience godliness; and to godliness brotherly kindness; and to brotherly kindness charity. For if these things be in you, and abound, they make you that ye shall neither be barren nor unfruitful in the knowledge of our Lord Jesus Christ."—2 Pet. i. 5–8. And how the apostle prays for this: "Now the God of peace, that brought again from the dead our Lord Jesus, that great Shepherd of the sheep, through the blood of the everlasting covenant, make you perfect in every good work to do his will, working in you that which is well-pleasing in his sight, through Jesus Christ, to whom be glory forever and ever. Amen."—Heb. xiii. 20, 21. And constant progression is enforced, when he says:— "Therefore leaving the principles of the doctrine of Christ, let us go on unto perfection; not laying again the foundation of repentance from dead works, and of faith towards God."—Heb. vi. 1. And to excite to this, he reminds them: "For God is not unrighteous to forget your work and labor of love, which ye have showed towards his name, in that ye have ministered to the saints, and do minister; and we desire that every one of you do show the same diligence, to the full assurance of hope unto the end; that ye be not slothful, but followers of them who through faith and patience inherit the promises."—Heb. vi. 10–12.

Notice,

2. *It is continuous labor.*

For we must "Work out." Begin and continue in well-doing. Enter the vineyard, and remain in it till the day ends. Religion is to be our constant exercise—our established habit—our daily life. In this work the various virtues must be worked out and matured. So the graces must work, that they may be strong and vigorous. So

our talents must be expended faithfully in the divine service. And all our means must be fully employed and improved. Observe,

3. *It is labor connected with earnest and ardent solicitude.*

"With fear and trembling." We must work in the spirit of holy fear. This is the beginning of wisdom. We are to have this before our eyes, and to be in it all the day long. We must cherish a fear of offending and grieving God. So needful is this, that it is often put for the whole of religion. That man is pronounced happy, who feareth always. This will be both an incentive to Christian diligence, and a preservative against apostasy. Then to this fear of God we are exhorted, also, to work out our salvation with "trembling." This trembling, or deep solicitude, is to have particular respect to ourselves. And what abundant occasion there will be for this,

(1.) When we reflect on our spiritual enemies and perils.

(2.) When we consider our weaknesses and infirmities.

(3.) When we think of the number of apostates around us.

(4.) When we think on what is at stake— our soul's present weal, and eternal salvation. But lest this fear and trembling should degenerate into despondency, there is added in the text, that which may well give us confidence and hope.

For observe, then, in reference to this labor,

III. *The ability supplied.*

"For it is God that worketh in you."

In contemplating God's gracious provision, you will see that it is just what we need.

1. *We require motives to influence us, and God supplies these.*

He worketh in us "to will." The highest and most glorious motives are urged on us. God gives us great and bright prospects; including—dignity, most exalted—joy, most elevated—and blessedness, most enduring! And by a regard to these, he gently and sweetly acts on the will, and it bends before his holy influences, as the willows before the winds that pass over them. How needful it is to have the will in entire subjection to God's mind; and only determining, and choosing, and resolving—as he graciously directs and disposes.

2. *We require strength.*

There can be nothing effected without

strength. Well, he supplies this; for he worketh in us " to do," as well as " to will." He strengthens with all might the inward man. He gives moral power and ability for doing all he commands. His grace is ever suitable, and ever sufficient. He empowers for action—for conflict—and for suffering. He upholds, and sustains, and endows with spiritual vigor; so that as the day is, so will the strength be. And observe, that he worketh not only in us, but he does this freely, of his own good pleasure—that is, God delights to work thus in us. He will, therefore, never fail to do this. We need not dread his forsaking us, or neglecting us; for he worketh in us both to will and to do of " his good pleasure."

Now, see then in the text,

(1.) The connection between Divine influence and human activity. He presents truth, and gives us power to see it; and we are called to behold—and understand—and believe it. The Cross is to us, as the brazen serpent was to the dying Israelites. God provided the remedy, and sent the message of his mercy to the perishing, to look and live; and just so, Christ has been offered a sin-atoning sacrifice; and the message of God's love to us in Christ is sent, that we may " Behold the Lamb of God, who taketh away the sin of the world."

He gives us the spirit of prayer, but we are to pray. He gives us gracious power, and we are to work.

Observe, there are,

(2.) Some things God must do for us, and in us; or they cannot be done at all. We could not make our own atonement. We could not obtain justification by any act of our own. We could not change our depraved hearts. We could not renew, or sanctify our own souls. God must do these for us, and in us;—and he does so by his Divine Son—by his Holy Spirit—and by the Word of his grace.

But observe also, there are,

(3.) Some things we must do, or the end will not be attained. The text refers to both of these. We must work out our own salvation. We must hear God's voice. Submit to God's righteousness. Believe in his Divine Son. Yield our hearts up to the Holy Spirit, and his gracious aid. We must serve God—be vigilant,—devout,—faithful, —constant,—and persevering, even to death. We must stir up the good gift within us; and by reading, meditation, and faith, let the word of Christ dwell richly in us. We must use the grace imparted, that it may be increased; and by a cheerful, believing, and humble spirit, earnestly labor for the soul's present well-being, and also for the final attainment of glory, immortality, and eternal life.

How very appropriate the verses of the devoted Wesley,—

" Be it my only wisdom here
    To serve the Lord with filial fear,
        With loving gratitude:
    Superior sense may I display,
    By shunning every evil way,
        And walking in the good.

Oh may I still from sin depart;
    A wise and understanding heart,
        Jesus, to me be giv'n:
    And let me through thy Spirit know
    To glorify my God below,
        And find the way to heaven."

XVII.—JEHOVAH-JIREH.

" And Abraham called the name of that place Jehovah-jireh: as it is said to this day, in the mount of the Lord it shall be seen."—*Gen.* xxii. 14.

THE text is connected with one of the most striking events in patriarchal times. God had called Abraham to be his servant. Given him illustrious promises. The fulfilment of these promises is long deferred. These promises related to a numberless nation springing from his loins; one of whom should be the Messiah—the Redeemer of mankind.

Ishmael is born; but the promise was not to be fulfilled in him, or through his posterity. At length—under the most unlikely circumstances—Isaac is born of Sarah, when she was past age. He now had grown up to man's estate,—was at least twenty-five years of age. Abraham's hope, therefore, would be bright and gladdening. Just at this time God resolves to tempt, or to try him. He gives forth the mandate for the sacrifice of Isaac, and that by his father's hands. Abraham hears—believes—obeys. Preparation is made. The journey begun. The spot nearly reached. Isaac interrogates his beloved parent, as to the sacrifice to be offered up (ver. 8). The altar is reared— Isaac bound (ver. 9). Now the arm of Abraham is lifted up, and God arrests the fatal blow (ver. 11, 12). Then Abraham beheld a ram caught, which he offered up to the Lord. The place was then piously designated, "Jehovah-jireh;" which signifies, the Lord will see, or provide.

Let us then consider the text as it is applicable,

I. *To the provisions of grace.*

And,

II. *As to the arrangements of Divine providence.*

Look at the text as it applies,

I. *To the provisions of grace.*

Here the text seems to have its greatest significancy. Man, by guilt and rebellion, was exposed to peril and death. His doom was just and righteous. His condemnation was hopeless. He could not save himself, nor could any created hand rescue him. At this crisis, Jehovah saw, and felt, and provided the means of salvation. The provision God made for man was most extraordinary.

1. *It was the innocent for the guilty.*

As in the ram caught, which typified the offering of the Lord Jesus. So Christ the just, suffered for us the unjust. He had no sin. No real charge could be brought against him. He was holy, harmless, and separate from sinners. He was perfect purity. There was not even guile found in his mouth.

It is most obvious, if Christ had not been holy, he must have first offered up a sacrifice for himself, as the priests under the law did. Hence says the Apostle of him—"Who needeth not daily, as those high priests, to offer up sacrifice, first for his own sins, and then for the people's: for this he did once, when he offered up himself. For the law maketh men high priests which have infirmity; but the word of the oath, which was since the law, maketh the Son, who is consecrated for evermore."—Heb. vii. 27, 28. Notice,

2. *It was of God's providing.*

Not of man's seeking, or obtaining; but God saw—remembered us in our low estate. He sent his only-begotten Son to be the victim for sin. None but he could do it,—none but he would do it. He only saw the depth of our misery,—the extremity of our peril,—and he only could send forth one, every way able to save to the uttermost our guilty and perishing world. Besides, it required the exercise of infinite grace to make such a provision for the vile, the worthless, and the self-ruined. Especially, too, when man had no desire to return to his original

state of primeval purity. How needful that this view of God's graciousness towards us should never be forgotten. For not only will it prevent all self-righteous boasting, but it will exhibit Jehovah, both as the source and final end of the sinner's salvation. The apostle speaks of God, as the being "for whom are all things, and by whom are all things;" and while this will apply to all his works, it will more especially do so in reference to the provisions of mercy for our dying world.

3. *By this offering, salvation was obtained for us.*

It was so in the case of Isaac. He is released. Lives, and God is honored. So through Christ, we also have life. He stipulated that he only should die, and the rest be free. Our salvation is through the Lord Jesus Christ. But it differs from the case of Isaac, as it is the soul's salvation; and not the mere rescue of the body from death. It is also eternal salvation. Besides, it includes the salvability not of one person only, but of the whole world. "For God so loved the world, that he gave his only-begotten Son, that whosoever believeth in him should not perish, but have everlasting life."—John iii. 16. How delightful is the view thus given of God's universal love and compassion! It was joyous to Abraham's anxious heart, to have a substitute for Isaac—but how much more joyous to the Father of mercy, to provide a propitiation for countless myriads of the human race. Notice,

4. *The offering, in both cases, was in the land of Moriah.*

Jerusalem was built in this land, and Christ died there; and probably on the very spot where Isaac had been typically and intentionally offered nineteen hundred years before. How interesting to observe how type and antitype agree. How the shadow is followed by the substance—the prediction by the realization—and the promise by the fulfilment. God did provide himself with an offering to take the place of Isaac; and Christ was thus typified, and strikingly set forth. God also signalized the same place, as being the scene of both events.

5. *The place and offering should be had in perpetual remembrance.*

Abraham signalized it. He gave it a special and appropriate name. How much more should Calvary and its victim be had in grateful perpetual remembrance. The cross and the sacrifice of Jesus is to be our grand theme of reflection and glorying. We are to remember and know nothing, in comparison of Christ, and him crucified. So great is this subject, that it is to be preached to the whole world, and to every creature;—and eventually it is to attract the attention of all men. For Jesus said—"And I if I be lifted up, I will draw all men unto me." The Lord's Supper is to be the perpetual outward memorial of that great transaction on the tree. It is at his hallowed table that we are to keep before us the wondrous mystery of the passion and death of the Lord Jesus Christ.

So much, then, for the text, in its application to the provisions of grace.

Look at it,

II. *In its application to the arrangements of Divine Providence.*

Now here we may behold the golden link between the sacrifice of Christ, and all needful good for God's people. "He that spared not his own Son, but delivered him up for us all, how shall he not with him also freely give us all things."—Rom. viii. 32. God in Christ will see to it, and provide for all the need and exigencies of his people. "My God shall supply all your need, according to his riches in glory, by Christ Jesus."

We must never disassociate Christ as Lord of providence, because he is king of grace. For not only is he Mediator and Lord in his spiritual kingdom, but all things are given into his hand. And his government is universal, and his power and authority are over all. He who died for his people; also lives, and reigns, and makes all events and circumstances subservient to their welfare in both worlds. Hence we may remark,

1. *In times of peril, he will provide deliverance.*

So Paul experienced—"For we would not, brethren, have you ignorant of our trouble which came to us in Asia, that we were pressed out of measure, above strength, insomuch that we despaired even of life: but we had the sentence of death in ourselves, that we should not trust in ourselves, but in God which raised the dead: who delivered us from so great a death, and doth deliver: in whom we trust that he will yet deliver us." —2 Cor. i. 8–10. So it is promised— "There hath no temptation taken you but such as is common to man: but God is faithful, who will not suffer you to be tempted above that ye are able; but will with the temptation also make a way to escape, that ye may be able to bear it."—1 Cor. x. 13. The apostle triumphantly asks—Who shall harm us, if we be the followers of that which is good?

2. *He will provide a supply of all needful blessings.*

Blessings of grace,—for duty, for ordinary and special services for God. He will also give strength in suffering, and abounding consolation. He will not withhold any good thing. The whole man—body and soul— he will care for; and this care shall be so special and complete, that Christ declares to his disciples,—the very hairs of their head are all numbered. It is on this principle that the apostle admonishes us :—"Be careful for nothing; but in every thing by prayer and supplication with thanksgiving let your requests be made known unto God. And the peace of God, which passeth all understanding, shall keep your hearts and minds through Christ Jesus."—Philip. iv. 6, 7. So the Apostle Peter urges—"Casting all your care upon him; for he careth for you."—1 Peter v. 7.

3. *He will provide an everlasting home for his people, when they die.*

Now this consoling truth is most beautifully set forth in various forms, by the sacred writers. The Psalmist says, "Precious in the sight of the Lord is the death of his saints." Hence, Jesus also said to his sorrowing disciples—"Let not your heart be troubled : ye believe in God, believe also in me. In my Father's house are many mansions : if it were not so, I would have told you. I go to prepare a place for you. And if I go and prepare a place for you, I will come again, and receive you unto myself; that where I am, there ye may be also." John xiv. 1–3. So Paul felt, that to live was Christ, but to die would be gain; as by death, he would depart and be with Christ, which would be far better. "For we know that if our earthly house of this tabernacle were dissolved, we have a building of God, a house not made with hands, eternal in the heavens."—2 Cor. v. 1. So that most sublime prayer of Jesus, just before his death, fully teaches,—"Father, I will that they also, whom thou hast given me, be with me where I am; that they may behold my glory, which thou hast given me : for thou lovedst me before the foundation of the world."—John xvii. 24. Now the arrangements of Divine Providence, in reference to all the concerns and interests of God's people, will always be exact, sufficient, and sure.

Learn, then,

1. The claims of a providing God on your love, obedience, and devotedness! If you can depend on the Divine goodness, how you should feel obligated to him; and how by praise and thanksgiving, you should daily bless and magnify his name.

2. See what is the interest and happiness of man to obtain. An interest in the gracious promises made. If God provides mercy, we must seek and obtain it. If he offers salvation, we must willingly accept it. If he never fails in merciful care, we must never cease to avail ourselves of it, by faith and constant prayer. For if we have not, it is because we ask not; or, because we ask amiss.

Learn,

3. The consolation of God's people. To remember his name—"Jehovah-jireh;" and to use it in times of sorrow and peril. His name is a strong tower, and the righteous runneth into it, and are safe.

Well may the believer exultingly sing,—

"This is the God we adore,
  Our faithful unchangeable Friend ;
 Whose love is as great as his power,
  Which neither knows measure nor end.

'Tis Jesus, the first and the last,
  Whose spirit shall guide us safe home ;
 We'll praise him for all that is past,
  And trust him for all that's to come."

XVIII.—A DECLARATION OF RELIGIOUS EXPERIENCE.

"Come and hear, all ye that fear God, and I will declare what he hath done for my soul."— *Psalm* lxvi. 16.

TRUE religion involves two things. An inward realization of divine grace, and an external profession and evidence of that grace in our lives.

David had both. He was not a cold nominalist, nor a timid believer. He had the experimental enjoyment of God's favor in his heart. Nor was he ashamed to be known as a godly man,—he made an honorable outward profession. His, was a conscientious emotional religion,—his lips often sang of it; and in the text, he desires a universal convocation of the good and pious, that he might tell them his experience, and

what God had done for his soul. Do we understand religion of this kind? Do we thus feel it? And are we willing to declare it to God's people?

Observe in the text, three things,

I. *The nature of religious experience.*

II. *The publication of religious experience.* And,

III. *The grounds on which that publication may be justified.*

I. *The nature of religious experience.*

"What God hath done for my soul."

The text limits our subject to the personal experience of God's gracious operations. Not what he has done for the world, by the redemption through Christ Jesus. Not what he has done for the church in all ages, by wonderful interpositions and signal providences! Not what he has done for special individual cases—as Noah, Enoch, Lot, and the celebrated worthies;—but what he has done for my soul! Verses 17, 19, and 20 of the psalm, would seem to apply the text specially in reference to answered prayer. Well, all God's people can thus unite with the Psalmist,

1. *In God answering penitential prayers, for his forgiving mercy.*

When conviction of sin had been produced. Alarm for safety excited. Desires for salvation imparted. When you prayed like the publican, or the woman of Canaan, or the Philippian jailer, how he dispersed the clouds—lifted up his reconciled countenance upon you—spoke the pardoning word of grace and peace to your souls. You cried for mercy, and he had mercy upon you. You asked for pardon, and he remitted all your sins, and blotted out all your iniquities. He gave you the blessedness of the man to whom iniquity is not imputed, and whose transgressions are forgiven. You looked with the eye of self-condemnation, and yet with the look of deep solicitude; and you felt that the uplifted sacrifice on the cross, had taken away all your sins; so that you could sing—"I will praise thee, for though thou wast angry with me, thine anger is turned away, and behold thou comfortedst me."

How often have we realized the text,

2. *In God answering our prayers, for guidance in perplexity.*

The people of God sometimes appear shut up in perplexity, and shut out of the Divine supervision; and know not what to do, or whither to go. But prayer is presented—

then a way of deliverance is opened : a plain, often a joyous way, and always a right way.

This door of hope is often opened to God's people, in the valley of Achar. This way of escape is often given, when they are perplexed and well-nigh sinking in despair. Thus the Lord's servants are led on and upwards, towards the city of their habitation;—and they find that in going out—and knowing not whither—that faith in God's gracious leadings is all that is needful, both for their comfort and safety. How important to feel the leading hand of our heavenly Father, in the dark night of spiritual perplexity ; or to be assured that in performing the celestial voyage to the better land, that though neither sun, nor moon, nor stars, may shine for many days, that our vessel is under the control of infinite skill, fidelity, and love! And that amid the unseen trackless deep, God is steering the vessel towards the much longed-for haven of eternal day, and uninterrupted repose.

The text is experienced,

3. *In God answering our prayers, for deliverance and protection.*

The godly are often in straits and difficulties—in afflictions and troubles. They have to pass through deep waters, and endure fiery trials. Often they are cast into the heated furnace, and the lion's den. Yet how surely prayer prevails, and deliverance is given. It is in these seasons that God becomes the shield and help of his people. It is now that he is the hiding-place to his saints—their rock, and fortress, and strong tower. It is now that he blunts the barbed weapon, turns aside the deadly missile, and so environs his trusting people, that no weapon formed against them prospers—that no malevolent attack succeeds. Hence, he has often brought his saints through floods and through flames, and through marshalled hosts of foes; and not allowing a hair of their head to perish, or any evil counsel or stratagem to succeed. He delivers them from all their enemies, and brings them out of all their distresses. And this equally applies to the malice of wicked men, or to the assaults of hell. And if, as in the case of the ancient martyrs, God should allow their enemies to spoil them of their goods—or deprive them of their liberty—or sacrifice their lives, yet, even then, God so sustained and strengthened them, that the fiery chariot was ascended with delight, that they might obtain a better resurrection. And though it were by the door of flame, yet God did deliver, and received them to his presence and glory. In their experience, to die was present and everlasting gain.

We see the text realized,

4. *In God answering prayer for the bestowment of especial blessings.*

There are not only the ordinary seasons of constant need, but there are sometimes special seasons of extraordinary need. Sometimes there has been required a supply of heavenly wisdom—special energy—and holy might and moral courage. Sometimes peculiar displays of Divine love and communion,—a brighter hope, and a more celestial joy. The day of some trials have need of a spring-tide of grace, an overflowing of Divine tenderness. Well, even then, prayer prevails. The desired good is sent. He is God all-sufficient to his people, and grants them the full desire of their souls. Yes, while ordinary grace is afforded for the daily avail of God's people, extraordinary and special mercies are given, in seasons of peculiar need. But in all seasons, and under all providences, God never fails to honor prayer, and meet all the exigencies of his dependent children. And this is the blessed experience which Christ promised his disciples. "And whatsoever ye shall ask in my name, that will I do, that the Father may be glorified in the Son. If ye shall ask any thing in my name, I will do it."—John xiv. 13, 14. "Hitherto have ye asked nothing in my name : ask, and ye shall receive, that your joy may be full."—John xvi. 24. Now, is not the experience of answered prayer, in all our earthly sojournings, the utmost that any spiritual mind can desire ? So that the Psalmist might well exult and exclaim, in the language of the text—" Come and hear, all ye that fear God, and I will declare what he hath done for my soul."

Thus, then, we learn what God has often done for them. It will be easily seen, how this department of the subject is capable of the most extensive amplification; but enough has been stated to show the blessedness of such a religious experience.

Observe,

II. *The publication of this experience.*

We see,

1. *The character of those to whom he would publish it.*

" Come and hear, all ye that fear God." All such,

(1.) Could understand his experience. Others could not. The carnal mind does not discern spiritual things. And religious conversation often appears to them as airy visions, or idle tales.

(2.) They would sympathize as fellow-members of the same body. Others would not. It is evident that God's people agree most in matters of religious experience. In doctrines, and systems, and names, and forms they extensively differ; but in inward experience they all agree. The experience of one—as to God's love—and the value of prayer, is the experience of all.

Then notice,

2. *The declaration he would make.*

"What God had done for his soul." His declarations would relate to God's doings, not his own. It requires great modesty, simplicity, and sincerity, in making known our religious experience. Not only should we exalt God, and his love and mercy, but should we not ever abase ourselves? However much we may extol the Lord and his gracious operations, we can have no good thing to say of ourselves. How needful to guard against spiritual pride and all self-estimation, in detailing the work of God in the soul! "God forbid that we should glory, save in the Cross of our Lord Jesus Christ." The child must exalt the parent —the patient the physician—the pardoned criminal the gracious monarch—and the believer must testify of the goodness and love of God.

It is often quite melancholy to hear people relate dreams, fancies, impulses, or their own doings; and then designate all this as their religious experience. The Psalmist's experience was the constant enjoyment of God's mercy and favor in answer to prayer. And this experience is that which we should most highly value, and most constantly extol.

Now let us see,

III. *If the publication of religious experience can be justified.*

Shall we speak, or be silent? We think there are many reasons for declaring it. Surely there is,

1. *A reason connected with God.*

Gratitude to God—a desire to honor him. Should we not extol the Lord, and speak well of his holy name? How base to hide the gift of God within us,—how base to be healed of the leprosy, and not return and give thanks,—how base to be delivered from death and hell, and not magnify our great deliverer,—how base to be saved by precious blood, and not exult in him who loved and gave himself for us! Not to declare what God has done for our souls, would be the essence of all cold-hearted ingratitude.

Then is there not,

2. *A reason connected with those we address?*

Our experience may do them good. It may instruct, encourage, and edify. We are all interested alike in this great subject of religious experience. Who can tell the advantages we have derived from the experience of patriarchs, and prophets, and holy men of old? Who is not indebted to Noah, and Abraham, and Jacob, and David, and the prophets? We read of their sorrows, and perils, and deliverances; and we are thereby encouraged and strengthened, even to this day. Then, so should we also cheer and edify one another.

Then there is,

3. *A reason connected with ourselves.*

It is good for our own souls. It will greatly enliven and quicken us. It will revive our experience, and make it vivid and fresh to us again. Cause us to live it over in joy afresh. How much better, too, is this, than foolish talking, or worldly conversation! One of the best means of avoiding evil conversation, is to have the tongue consecrated always to that which is holy and good.

But there is,

4. *A reason connected with religion itself.*

We thus show that our religion is one of goodness—of deliverances—of mercies—of enjoyments and gladness. We thus cast back the aspersion that religion is necessarily gloomy and sad, and that it tends to melancholy. So that the wise and cheerful declaration of religious experience honors our spiritual calling, and renders the life of the child of God manifestly one of holy and increasing light, and joy, and blessedness.

APPLICATION.

1. Every child of God has much to say of God's gracious dealings with their souls. I suppose a volume might be written of the experience of every spiritual person.

2. How dumb we often are on these best subjects. Can we be so, without being criminal before God, and grieving his Holy Spirit?

3. How desirable to speak for God! To

tread on diffidence, and the fear of man. For it is generally these that prevent seasonable Christian communications one with another.

4. What have the servants of Satan and the world to say, in behalf of their service? Is not their experience dark, hard, profitless? and the end thereof is death!

We invite all such to abandon the works of sin—to cast off the yoke of Satan—and to yield themselves up to him, whose yoke is easy, whose burden is light; and whose service is inseparably connected with righteousness, peace, and joy in the Holy Ghost; and whose gift to all his people—is eternal life.

XIX.—ON PROFANING THE SABBATH.

"Then I contended with the nobles of Judah, and said unto them, What evil thing is this that ye do, and profane the Sabbath-day? Did not your fathers thus, and did not our God bring all this evil upon us, and upon this city? yet ye bring more wrath upon Israel by profaning the Sabbath."—*Nehemiah* xiii. 17, 18.

FEW subjects have been more discussed of late than that of the question of the Sabbath, or Lord's day. Various views of this important subject are taken by different parties. Some would put all distinction of days down entirely, and leave men to act as they pleased. Others would enforce a Jewish strictness of Sabbath observance. While others look at the Sabbath as a question both involving duties and privileges; but take a medium course between the letter of Jewish strictness and continental laxity. We contend for an observance of the Lord's day, which shall include two grand points:—Cessation from all secular labor and toil; and the devotion of its hours to our moral and religious improvement.

Observe, then,

I. *For what we contend, in reference to the Lord's day.*

Now, we contend,

1. *For a cessation from all secular labor and toil.*

We do this on three grounds.

(1.) The facts stated in reference to the institution of the first Sabbath. "Thus the heavens and the earth were finished, and all the host of them. And on the seventh day God ended his work which he had made; and he rested on the seventh day from all his work which he had made. And God blessed the seventh day and sanctified it: because that in it he had rested from all his works which God created and made."—Gen. ii. 1–3. Here was the divine Architect setting the illustrious example to his intelligent creatures. He distinguished the seventh day. He blessed it specially. He devoted it to peculiar purposes. Rest was one. "He sanctified it,"—set it apart for holy exercises. And as God made the world extensively for man, so precisely for him did he make the Sabbath.

Then we ground it,

(2.) On its introduction into the moral code, as given on Sinai. "Remember the Sabbath-day, to keep it holy. Six days shalt thou labor and do all thy work. But the seventh day is the Sabbath of the Lord thy God: in it thou shalt not do any work, thou, nor thy son, nor thy daughter, thy manservant, nor thy maid-servant, nor thy cattle, nor thy stranger that is within thy gates. For in six days the Lord made heaven and earth, the sea, and all that in them is, and rested the seventh day; wherefore the Lord blessed the Sabbath-day, and hallowed it." —Exod. xx. 8–11. How definite, exact, full, clear, and unequivocal is the whole language! Here it became part and parcel of the moral law.

Now, those who call it Jewish, forget it existed, by divine precedent, two thousand years before Abraham, the father of the Jewish nation, was born. It became a part of the code which still stands entire. Not one jot or tittle of the moral law has, or ever will, pass away. Now, are not these arguments, when fairly considered, unanswerable?

Then we ground it, also,

(3.) On the essential fitness of things. Because it was so, evidently, when God ordered it. To dispute this is to assail the infinite wisdom of God. He deemed the Sabbath's rest necessary to man's constitution and state. But if it was so to unfallen beings, how much more to those who are fallen. If holy beings required a Sabbath, how much more sinful and polluted ones. If in innocency—before Satan erected his throne on the earth—how much more now amid the perils of sense, the world, and the devil. It is alike needful to man's body, mind, and spirit, that he should have a weekly Sabbath. It has been demonstrated, that real physical health, and mental vigor, can only be permanently sustained by intervals of repose and quietude; and there can be no doubt but many constitutions have prematurely become feeble, and many minds imbecile, by the continuous straining of incessant toil; without the intervening relief of the Sabbath. But,

2. *We contend for the Sabbath, as a day of moral and spiritual improvement.*

Now, the reasons for this must be manifest if we consider,

(1.) That the mind and the moral nature of man require improvement.

(2.) That it is awfully criminal to neglect them.

(3.) That the body and secular toils engross the greater part of the week; therefore the Lord's day should be fully devoted to mental and moral services. Among these we include, profitable reading, private meditation, public worship, and works of benevolence, and charity, and religion. It is right and proper to do good on the Lord's day.

Now, thus in brief we exhibit a chart of Lord's-day duties and exercises. Such as are alike in harmony with man's moral nature, and the obvious demand of God's holy word. Here we leave plenty of margin for other things to be introduced, if they are only lovely and of good report.

Let us consider,

II. *How the Sabbath may be profaned.*

I need not dwell on profaning it by attendance on our usual secular business. But it may be profaned,

1. *By devoting it to indolence.*

Whiling, or sleeping, or lounging its hours away. While it is evidently for physical rest, it is not for mental or moral lethargy. We have the example of the pious Jews in their services; and also the conduct of Jesus and the Apostles—afterwards the mode of life on this day of the early Christians. So that indolence is a profanation of the Lord's day.

No scene is more disgusting, than to see a family in disorder—its members unwashed —and all in confusion, through the prevailing spirit of sloth, on God's day.

2. *By yielding its hours to foolishness and frivolity.*

Now there are many things which tend to this kind of profanation. Frivolous reading will do it. Frivolous society and parties still more effectively. Mere sight-seeing, and rambling abroad for what is falsely called—pleasure. Worldly pleasure is ever enfeebling to the moral powers, as well as being unfavorable to all pious influences; but how much more is it so when the day given especially for holy pursuits is thus prostituted to trifling and folly.

3. *By neglecting the services of religion.*

I don't pretend to say how many we should attend. Our circumstances and opportunities must decide this. There needs no law on this point for those who love God and divine things. Such will ever exclaim, in reference to the house of God:

"I have been there, and oft would go; 'Tis like a little heaven below."

It is a heinous sin to despise God's house, and to refuse him our public homage and worship. Not only is public worship demanded on the ground of God's claims to our reverence and praise; but it is exhilarating and refreshing, often both to body and mind. When rightly regarded, it is a feast of fat things to the soul,—a season of spiritual banqueting to the devout spirit.

4. *By mixing the world and the Sabbath together.*

By giving God and worship the forenoon, and the world and pleasure the afternoon and evening; by giving God certain external duties, and giving the world vain and secular conversation; by trying thus to serve both God and mammon. This mixture defeats the service of both.

No doubt, a worldly man, who lives entirely in a worldly atmosphere, may afford much gratification to his carnal desires; but bring in this religious element, and it will destroy this earthly enjoyment. So the good man will have spiritual enjoyment in God's service; but bring in the worldly element, and it will neutralize it altogether. Yet, how this is extensively done, by the attempt to divide or compromise the Lord's day.

Then,

III. *Let us offer some suggestions why we should not profane the Sabbath.*

We should neither profane nor neglect the Sabbath,

I. *For it is God's favorite day.*

He has distinguished it, and so should we: he loves it, and so should we. If there were no other reason than this, it should suffice; for if we love God, our hearts and minds should be in harmony with his.

2. *It is our day. A part of our patrimony as God's children.*

As such, we should make the most it, and

also the best of it,—use it in reference to our inward moral necessities—use it in reference to God's claims upon us. It is too good to be neglected or perverted. There are but three gifts to be compared in value to it—Jesus, the Spirit, and the Word; and these and the Sabbath are all in unison with each other.

3. *On account of its typical character.*

Now there are two other Sabbaths, of which this is the external sign. One of these is the Christian's rest in Christ. "We who have believed, have entered into rest." Believing in Christ gives the soul an inward spiritual Sabbath. Then it also points to the eternal rest of heaven. The apostle adds—"There remaineth therefore a rest to the people of God." So that the salvation we have now in Christ, and the eternal consummation of that in the glory of heaven, are both typified by the Sabbath which God has given us.

On account,

4. *Of its connection with the Divine blessing.*

Let us hear the evangelical prophet—" If thou turn away thy foot from the Sabbath, from doing thy pleasure on my holy day; and call the Sabbath a delight, the holy of the Lord, honorable; and shall honor him, not doing thine own ways, nor finding thine own pleasure, nor speaking thine own words: then shalt thou delight thyself in the Lord; and I will cause thee to ride upon the high places of the earth, and feed thee with the heritage of Jacob thy father: for the mouth of the Lord hath spoken it."—Isa. lviii. 13, 14. " Blessed is the man that doeth this, and the son of man that layeth hold on it; that keepeth the Sabbath from polluting it, and keepeth his hand from doing any evil."—Isa. lvi. 2. Now, don't suppose that these passages must have a Jewish exposition, and be confined only to that people, and to that dispensation.

The universal history of nations and countries shows, that the Divine blessing accompanies the honoring and keeping the Sabbath. While laxity, as to the Lord's day, invariably produces dissipation—dissoluteness—open profligacy—contempt of religion—despising the written or preached word; with all the moral train of evils, arising therefrom. On the other hand—with a due observance of the Sabbath, there will be national intelligence—national propriety of moral and manners—a regard to Divine worship; as the moral result, the accompanying smile and blessing of God.

Then let us,

1. Have, and hold right views of the Sabbath. A false impression on this subject will lead to a bad use of it. Let us,

2. Rightly use the Sabbath. Apply it to its true and legitimate purposes. Give it to God, and the soul's intellectual and spiritual improvement.

Let us,

3. Not withhold the Sabbath from those connected with us. Remembering the Sabbath is precious to us; it is, or ought to be so, also to our domestics and servants. Let us not, for the sake of any comfort—imaginary or real—deprive our dependents of the privileges and blessings of this day. And let us not countenance its profanation in others. Let us not avail ourselves of the toil of any class of men on this day.

Finally,—Devote it to a devout preparation for the sabbath of heaven. That it may tend to that,—begin it with prayer. Be conscientious in the application of its hours to spiritual and religious objects; and conclude it in God's fear, and in the expectation of his blessing.

Thus, this day will be as a green and verdant spot in this wilderness world. Here will be fruit found for the soul. Here vigor and strength will be renewed; and all the duties of the coming week, whether secular or moral, will be discharged with greater promptness and efficiency. The spiritual mind would rather add to the number of his Sabbaths, than diminish them. He would lengthen them out, and extend their hallowed hours, rather than abridge them. And such know, by an experience the most blessed, that a Sabbath's emotions, and desires, and delights, lead to the devout longing for that eternal Sabbath-keeping, in the celestial state, which remains for all the children of God. Blessed are the dead, who die in the Lord; for they shall rest from their labors. Their future being is one sabbatical service, devoted to Him who loved them, and washed them from their sins, in his own blood; to whom be ascribed all praise, and honor, and glory, forever and ever. Amen.

———◆———

XX.—THE TWO YOKES.

"The yoke of my transgressions is bound by his hand: they are wreathed, and come upon my neck."—*Lam.* i. 14.

"For my yoke is easy, and my burden is light." —*Matt.* xi. 30.

WE are generally most powerfully struck and most deeply impressed, by viewing things in contrast. Thus, the value of light is most evident, when contrasted with darkness,—health, when contrasted with sickness,—pleasure, when contrasted with pain,—hope, when contrasted with despair.

Now, we wish to place, in direct and striking contrast, the two yokes:—The yoke of sin, and the yoke of Jesus. But, we premise,

(1.) That all men bear the one or the other of these yokes. All men are under the power of Satan, or God—of evil, or of holiness. We further premise,

(2.) That the yoke of sin assumes various aspects. In one, it is bold infidelity. In another, daring profanity. In a third, public profligacy; while in others, it may be reckless indifference—inconsideration—worldliness. We further add,

(3.) By the yoke of Christ: we mean spiritual, experimental, and practical godliness. Not the name, or mere form; but the inward kingdom of his grace in the soul. These things being understood, observe the contrast in the two yokes,—

I. *In their influence on the body.*

The yoke of sin often leads to habits which injure the health—destroy the constitution—and shorten life. "The wicked do not live out half their days." Go to the hospital, and see how many are there, incurable and hopeless, directly through the influence of their sins. How true the text, that the yoke of transgression is bound by his hand; they are wreathed and come upon the neck; irritating, and galling, and destroying all comfort and enjoyment. Many of the maladies which shorten life, are the results of special sins—such as gluttony, intemperance, sensuality. The slave of sin, who turns night into day, and gives up the wonderfully wrought system of the body, to the drudgery of iniquity—no wonder that his course is quickly run, and that he soon enters the house appointed for all living.

But Christ's yoke tendeth to health and long life. Hence how the wise man, in proverbs of truth and godliness, dwells on this view of the subject. He says of wisdom; by which true religion is intended—"It shall be health to thy navel, and marrow to thy bones. Length of days is in her right hand; and in her left hand riches and honor."—Prov. iii. 8 and 16. "For they are life unto those that find them, and health to all their flesh."—Prov. iv. 22. Religion saves from the habits and customs which destroy health and shorten life. It favors order, sobriety, and prudence. The man who values his soul, will not neglect the temple of the body, in which it dwells. And hence, in all ages and countries, it is the virtuous and godly, as a rule, who attain to old age and long life. Hence it may be said to the wise and God-fearing man—"Thou shalt come to thy grave in a full age, like as a shock of corn cometh in, in his season." "The fear of the Lord is the beginning of wisdom; and the knowledge of the holy is understanding. For by me thy days shall be multiplied, and the years of thy life shall be increased."—Prov. ix. 10, 11. "The fear of the Lord prolongeth days: but the years of the wicked shall be shortened."—Prov. x. 27. Then as to these yokes,

II. *Contrast them in their influence on reputation.*

There are great moral principles which men of the world respect; and some of which are absolutely essential to a good standing, even in common society. Of these, we may mention, truth and probity, integrity and faithfulness, and to which may be added, prudence and diligence.

Now the yoke of sin leads to habits which have a tendency to lower the reputation. We name only two or three:—Profanity of speech,—general dissipation,—extravagance,—evil companionship. Now, which of these would be a recommendation to a young man, seeking a situation? Do not all these lower and degrade? Do they not expose to suspicion? Are they not all disreputable? No employer would welcome such to an office of trust and responsibility. No parent could desire such to be united to any member of his family.

But look at those who bear the yoke of Christ. Here will be purity of conversation—orderly habits—prudential conduct—good company—honesty—sobriety. Such will have been taught by the grace of God, "To deny ungodliness and worldly lusts, and to live soberly and godly." Would not these traits of moral character, anywhere, or to any man, be points of great importance in regard to reputation. Let me quote again— "Exalt her, and she shall promote thee: she shall bring thee to honor, when thou dost embrace her. She shall give to thine head an ornament of grace: a crown of glory shall she deliver to thee."—Prov. iv. 8, 9. Religion adorns the character, and clothes its possessor with dignity and worth. Contrast them,

III. *In their influence on the mental powers.*

Two things must here be conceded. Many wicked persons are intelligent and learned. Many of the pious are illiterate, and even ignorant. But this often arises from the circumstances in which both have been placed, in early life. All other things being equal, this anomaly would not exist; for godliness would never willingly dwell with illiteracy or ignorance, but would ever select as her votaries the men of knowledge and wisdom. But after all, what does learning or knowledge do for the man who neglects his soul's spiritual elevation?

What are the loftiest objects of mere mental pursuit? The things of time, and not of eternity. The things of men, and not of God. Can it be doubted then, that after all, that man must be most mentally exalted, who pursues the knowledge of Divine things, —the true knowledge of God, in his works and his word. The man, whose knowledge includes the soul's salvation, and his best interests in both worlds. The yoke of sin tends to pervert the powers. To blight and poison them. Religion to expand, spiritualize, and exalt. Religion sanctifies talent and learning, and makes them infinitely more valuable and important. Contrast their influence,

IV. *On man's true peace and happiness.*

The yoke of sin is heavy—tyrannical—goading. It frets and wreathes the spirit; so says the text. As poisons by their acrid influence create pain and agony, so does sin to the man wearing its yoke. What harassing fears! What perplexing restlessness! Like the troubled sea, they cannot rest. What horrid forebodings! What self-procured agonies and misery! It is the gloomy region of sadness, wretchedness, and despair. A yoke often too intolerable to be borne. Hence how many, like Saul and Judas, rush with frantic madness out of life, unable any longer to endure so unbearable an existence! Christ's yoke is easy and light. So soon as assumed, it brings rest—spiritual inward rest. It is ever united with confidence, and peace, and hope. There is the calm and the sunshine of heaven within, and a happy prospect before. It is the region of true blessedness. Great peace have they who love God's law. Observe again the declarations of the wise man: "My son, forget not my law; but let thine heart keep my commandments. For length of days, and long life, and peace, shall they add to thee. Happy is the man that findeth wisdom, and the man that getteth understanding. Her ways are ways of pleasantness, and all her paths are peace. When thou liest down, thou shalt not be afraid; yea, thou shalt lie down, and thy sleep shall be sweet."—Prov. iii. 1, 2, 13, 17, 24.

Contrast them,

V. *In their connection with the future world.*

What is the end of both? The yoke of sin is connected with the darkness, and the fetters and chains of the second death. "He who being often reproved, hardeneth his neck, shall suddenly be destroyed, and that without remedy." "The wicked shall be driven away in his wickedness." The end of those things is death—the second, the everlasting death. How great the contrast of this, with the man who bears the yoke of Jesus. His path is that of the just, which shineth more and more unto the perfect day. His course tends to increasing peace, and to real joy, and then to endless glory. It is and ever shall be well, in all respects, with the righteous. His last end is linked with promises of blessedness and joy that shall never fail, nor never end. You will observe, too, that in respect of these two characters, there is fitness in both for their future destiny. For sin tends to death, and holiness to life everlasting. He who has borne the galling yoke of sin and rebellion to death, would be unfit for the services and enjoyments of heaven; and he who has followed Christ in the regeneration, is equally unfit for the society or the woes of the hopelessly lost in perdition.

Then we ask, in conclusion, which yoke,

1. Are you wearing? Be particular in your reply. Don't mistake in answering this question. And surely it is not difficult to ascertain this. The contrast is so striking, that a knowledge of your present condition is most obviously within your power. If you feel the yoke of sin is upon your neck, then,

2. I urge you to throw it off. It may be difficult; but it can be done. But it can only be done in one way; and that is, by humble faith in the grace of the Lord Jesus Christ. Cry then to Christ for help. Say, Lord, save me! Plead his own love to you, and the rich invitation of his mercy, as proclaimed in the text.

Finally,—Let the people of God rejoice in their emancipated and happy condition. Let them gratefully bless God for his saving mercy; and let them feel, and earnestly labor to bring those who now wear the yoke of rebellion and sin, to Jesus, that they may take his yoke, and then find rest to their souls. It should ever be felt both to be a duty and a privilege to speak to weary and heavy-laden sinners, and, if possible, to bring them to Christ. This work of holy mercy neither requires profound learning, splendid talents, nor oratorical powers. Have you found the blessedness of Christ's yoke by experience—and learned of him? Then, simply and affectionately,

> "Tell to sinners round,
> What a dear Saviour you have found."

And thus re-echo Christ's blessed invitation, and illustrate its sincerity and effectiveness, by showing the great things he has done for you. If this kind of plain, social experimental preaching was adopted by Christians generally, the results could not fail to be most cheering. It is just what is wanted in the Church; and it is just what would extensively meet the moral exigences of the world around us. And say not that the preacher only should do this; remember the restored demoniac, who published the tidings of Jesus in Decapolis; and the woman of Samaria, who told her neighbors of the Messiah; and let love to the Saviour and pity for souls constrain you to go and do likewise.

How beautifully the poet urges this course, on distressed and heavy-laden souls!

> "Come! said Jesu's sacred voice,
> Come and make my paths your choice;
> I will guide you to your home:
> Weary pilgrim, hither come!
>
> Thou who, destitute, forlorn,
> Long hast borne the proud world's scorn,
> Long hast roamed the barren waste,
> Weary pilgrim, hither haste!
>
> Ye who, toss'd on beds of pain,
> Seek for ease, but seek in vain—
> Ye whose swoln and sleepless eyes
> Watch to see the morning rise—

> Ye, by fiercer anguish torn,
> Who for guilt sincerely mourn,
> Here repose your heavy care:
> Wounded spirit, welcome here!
>
> Sinner, come! for here is found
> Balm that flows for every wound;
> Peace that ever shall endure,
> Rest, eternal, sacred, sure."

XXI.—OUR BREATH IN GOD'S HAND, &c.

"But hast lifted up thyself against the Lord of heaven; and they have brought the vessels of his house before thee, and thou, and thy lords, thy wives, and thy concubines, have drunk wine in them; and thou hast praised the gods of silver, and gold, of brass, iron, wood, and stone, which see not, nor hear, nor know; and the God in whose hand thy breath is, and whose are all thy ways, hast thou not glorified."—*Daniel* v. 23.

THE circumstances connected with the text are awfully sublime. Daniel is called to interpret the ominous inscription on the wall of Belshazzar's palace, whilst he and his princes and nobles were engaged in banqueting. "Belshazzar the king made a great feast to a thousand of his lords, and drank wine before the thousand. Belshazzar, whilst he tasted the wine, commanded to bring the golden and silver vessels which his father Nebuchadnezzar had taken out of the temple which was in Jerusalem; that the king, and his princes, his wives, and his concubines might drink therein."—Ver. 1, 2. You will see, too, that at this festive scene, the sacred vessels of the Lord's house were desecrated. "Then they brought the golden vessels that were taken out the temple of the house of God which was at Jerusalem; and the king, and his princes, his wives, and his concubines, drank in them. They drank wine, and praised the gods of gold, and of silver, of brass, of iron, of wood, and of stone."—Ver. 3, 4. Then follows the account of the man's hand: "In the same hour came forth fingers of a man's hand, and wrote over against the candlestick, upon the plaster of the wall of the king's palace; and the king saw the part of the hand that wrote."—Ver. 5. We see the startling effect produced on the king, and the calling in of the astrologers. "Then the king's countenance was changed, and his thoughts troubled him, so that the joints of his loins were loosed, and his knees smote one against another. The king cried aloud to bring in the astrologers, the Chaldeans, and the sooth-sayers. And the king spake, and said to the wise men of Babylon, Whosoever shall read this writing, and show me the interpretation thereof, shall be clothed with scarlet, and have a chain of gold about his neck, and shall be the third ruler in the kingdom. Then came in all the king's wise men; but they could not read the writing, nor make known to the king the interpretation thereof."—Ver. 6, 7, and 8. Finally—Notice the invitation to Daniel, to whom rich presents and honors were offered. "Then was Daniel brought in before the king. And the king spake and said unto Daniel, Art thou that Daniel, which art of the children of the captivity of Judah, whom the king my father brought out of Jewry? I have even heard of thee, that the spirit of the gods is in thee, and that light and understanding and excellent wisdom is found in thee. And now the wise men, the astrologers, have been brought in before me, that they should read this writing, and make known unto me the interpretation thereof: but they could not show the interpretation of the thing: and I have heard of thee, that thou canst make interpretations, and dissolve doubts; now, if thou canst read the writing, and make known to me the interpretation thereof, thou shalt be clothed with scarlet, and have a chain of gold about thy neck, and shalt be the third ruler in the kingdom."—Ver. 13 to 16. We have then Daniel's reply: "Then Daniel answered and said before the king, Let thy gifts be to thyself, and give thy rewards to another; yet I will read the writing unto the king, and make known to him the interpretation. O thou king, the most high God gave Nebuchadnezzar thy father a kingdom, and majesty, and glory, and honor; and for the majesty that he gave him, all people, nations, and languages trembled and feared before him: whom he would he slew; and whom he would he kept alive; and whom he would he set up; and whom he would he put down. But when his heart was lifted up, and his mind hardened in pride, he was deposed from his kingly throne, and they took his glory from him: and he was driven from the sons of men; and his heart was made like the beasts, and his dwelling was with the wild asses: they fed him with grass like oxen, and his body was wet with the dew of heaven—till he knew that the most high God ruled in the kingdom of men, and that he appointeth over it whomsoever he

will."—Verses 17 to 21. And then the application of the subject to Belshazzar. "And thou his son, O Belshazzar, hast not humbled thine heart, though thou knewest all this: but hast lifted up thyself against the Lord of heaven; and they have brought the vessels of his house before thee, and thou, and thy lords, thy wives, and thy concubines, have drunk wine in them; and thou hast praised the gods of silver, and gold, of brass, iron, wood, and stone, which see not, nor hear, nor know: and the God in whose hand thy breath is, and whose are all thy ways, hast thou not glorified."—Ver. 22, 23.

Such are the events identified with the text. Our subject in both its parts, is equally applicable to multitudes of mankind—perhaps to many here.

Observe, in the text,

I. *Man's dependence on God.*

And,

II. *Man's neglect to glorify him.*

I. *Man's dependence on God.*

Here the language of the text is very graphic and figurative. The text speaks of God's hand; that power by which God sustains, directs, and rules. God's hand is a fashioning hand; for it has made and modelled all things. A supporting hand; for it upholds all creatures and all worlds. A providing hand; for it supplies the wants of every living thing. A preserving hand; for it is the hand that protects and preserves his needy dependent creatures. This hand is sometimes employed, too, to chasten, and sometimes even to destroy. Observe in the text,

1. *Man's breath is described as being in it.*

The breath is the evidence of life. The exhalation of the lungs, so to speak; so long as the lungs heave, there will be breath; so long as breath, life. Man's first existence is thus described: "And the Lord God formed man of the dust of the ground, and breathed into his nostrils the breath of life; and man became a living soul."—Gen. ii. 7. It is afterwards used as the symbol of life. "And, behold, I, even I, do bring a flood of waters upon the earth, to destroy all flesh, wherein is breath of life from under heaven; and every thing that is in the earth shall die."—Gen. vi. 17. "Seeing he giveth to all life, and breath, and all things."—Acts xvii. 25. The cessation of this is death. "Thou hidest thy face, they are troubled: thou takest away their breath, they die, and return to their dust."—Ps. civ. 29. Now this breath is in God's hand—at his disposal; so says the text; so says Job: "In whose hand is the soul of every living thing, and the breath of all mankind."—Job xii. 10. All the means of life or of death are with God.

Now, reason and observation alike confirm this. So that life in its commencement, progress, and termination, is under the divine control. In whose hands, supremely and constantly, is man's breath. Then notice,

2. *Our ways are under the divine government.*

"And whose are all thy ways." Some people speak of chance—of fortune—of luck —of man's skill. The truth is, there is no chance, or mere accident, or luck. No man that breathes can direct his *own* steps, or say this or that will be secured. Our ways are under the regulation of God's providence. This will apply to poverty or riches; for he makes rich, or brings low. Success or dejection: he exalts or debases. Prosperity or adversity: he gives sunshine or sorrow —health or sickness. "The lot is cast into the lap, and the whole disposing thereof is of the Lord." See how this is stated: "The Lord killeth, and maketh alive: he bringeth down to the grave, and bringeth up. The Lord maketh poor, and maketh rich: he bringeth low and lifteth up. He raiseth up the poor out of the dust, and lifteth up the beggar from the dunghill, to set them among princes, and to make them inherit the throne of glory: for the pillars of the earth are the Lord's, and he hath set the world upon them. He will keep the feet of his saints, and the wicked shall be silent in darkness; for by strength shall no man prevail. The adversaries of the Lord shall be broken to pieces; out of heaven shall he thunder upon them: the Lord shall judge the ends of the earth; and he shall give strength unto his king, and exalt the horn of his anointed." —1 Samuel ii. 6-10. "For promotion cometh neither from the east, nor from the west, nor from the south. But God is the judge: he putteth down one, and setteth up another."—Ps. lxxv. 6, 7. Now the history of Abraham, Jacob, Joseph, Moses, David, Mordecai and others, all establish this. Yes, the ways of men are seen by the eyes of God. He weighs human actions. He decides human affairs. This should never be forgotten. And we should practically act on it. See Psalm xxxvii. 5, and xxxiv.

But observe,

II. *Man's neglect to glorify God.*

"Hast thou not glorified?"

In the case of the text, Belshazzar had not profited by the afflictions of his father (ver. 18–22). He had praised his senseless idols. He had profaned the vessels of the Lord. He had lifted himself up against God; and therefore God's wrath was stirred up against him. Now, have not many here just neglected to glorify God, by a similar course of conduct towards him?

1. *Have you profited by the divine dispensations?*

With respect to those around you? His judgments—his destruction of the profane and reckless,—their sudden death; or by visitations in your families, perhaps relatives and friends; or by your own bodily afflictions and trials. Have God's dispensations been pondered—his hand acknowledged— his corrections been received with humility and submission? Then we ask,

2. *Have not you exalted and praised other things rather than God?*

Belshazzar did so of idols. You, perhaps, have done the same of science, philosophy, fame, wealth. Have you not given your chief attention to inferior things? Have not other things had the place of God—and is not this the essence of idolatry? However lawful the things may be, or however secondarily excellent; yet, if it usurps God's throne, and have the homage he demands, then is God not glorified.

3. *Have you not been guilty of profanity?*

Belshazzar profaned the vessels of the Lord's house. I ask you in reference to the divine word, is it not true that God has written to you the great things of his law, and yet you have esteemed them as a strange thing? So the divine ordinances of religion. Have they not been neglected or perverted? So the divine name. Have you not profaned it by swearing, or by using it lightly, and without reverence and awe? So the divine day. Have you not profaned the day of God, by giving it up to secular pleasure or trifling pursuits? Alas, how few are exempted from the charge of some kind of profanity! Then we ask,

4. *Have you not lifted up your hearts against God?*

Belshazzar did this. "And thou his son, O Belshazzar, hast not humbled thine heart, though thou knewest all this; but hast lifted up thyself against the Lord of heaven:" ver. 22, 23. This is done by the opposition of heart and life to God. By rejecting the voice of God in his word, and conscience, and providences. By refusing the only way of acceptance with him, which involves penitence, faith, and prayer. To many, is not the charge in the text literally true? You have not glorified God; but by a life of practical infidelity, or wicked idolatry—of spiritual, or manifest profanity, and by lifting up your hearts in pride against God, the charge is equally true as it was of Belshazzar of old; only with this additional aggravating clause—that your light and means of moral elevation have been much greater than those the infatuated monarch possessed.

Now, this not glorifying God is heinously wicked. All the holy intellectual hosts of heaven glorify God. All the pious on earth, in all ages, have done it. All the irrational inferior creatures do it, by obeying their respective instincts, and answering the end of their existence. All the works of God do it. The heavens and the earth—day and night—all the seasons and operations of God's hand. And observe, God will have it even from his enemies. Though unwillingly, he had it from the awful wonders of the destructive deluge. From the overthrow of Pharaoh and his hosts. From the destruction of Belshazzar. So in the Judgment-day, and in the dark pit of perdition, both from fallen angels and lost souls, he will have it.

Then suffer the word of exhortation,—

1. To the unconverted. "Give glory to God" before he cause darkness,—before he overwhelms with ruin,—before it is too late. Honor God by repentance and faith in the Lord Jesus Christ.

Pray in the language of the hymn—

> " O God, mine inmost soul convert,
> And deeply on my thoughtful heart
>   Eternal things impress!
> Give me to feel their solemn weight,
> And tremble on the brink of fate,
>   And 'wake to righteousness.
> Be this my one great business here,
> With serious industry and fear
>   My future bliss t' insure:
> Thine utmost counsel to fulfil,
> And suffer all thy righteous will,
>   And to the end endure."

2. To the Christian. Remember he demands, that whether you eat or drink, you do all to his glory. You are to glorify God in your bodies and souls, which are his.

3. To all. We exhort to think of the two parts of the text—our dependence on God; and then, the glory we should render. He is thy God, worship thou him. Seek his glory in all things. Let this object be the one absorbing aim of your being—the great end of your existence; and then life shall be holy and happy, and eternity one of dignity, uninterrupted joy, and blessedness.

XXII.—BELIEVERS COMPLETE IN CHRIST.

" And ye are complete in him."—*Col.* ii. 10.

THE apostles had to contend with two main difficulties in establishing the religion of the Lord Jesus Christ. With the Jews, they had to contend with the prejudices in favor of the rites and ceremonies of the Mosaic dispensation. And the converted Jews were prone to cling to these, and often desired to mix them with the ordinances of Christianity. Paul's epistle to the Galatians shows the difficulties of this kind, which obstructed the progress of pure religion.

With the Gentiles, there were prejudices arising out of their various systems of philosophy. Hence, false notions of the Divine character and government were liable to be introduced. Hence, Paul avows his resolution to maintain the gospel in its purity, in opposition to both these. " Where is the wise? where is the scribe? where is the disputer of this world? hath not God made foolish the wisdom of this world? For after that in the wisdom of God the world by wisdom knew not God, it pleased God by the foolishness of preaching to save them that believe. For the Jews require a sign, and the Greeks seek after wisdom; but we preach Christ crucified, unto the Jews a stumbling-block, and unto the Greeks foolishness; but unto them which are called, both Jews and Greeks, Christ the power of God, and the wisdom of God."—1 Cor. i. 20–24. So also he exhorts the Colossians in this chapter: " As ye have therefore received Christ Jesus the Lord, so walk ye in him: rooted and built up in him, and stablished in the faith, as ye have been taught, abounding therein with thanksgiving. Beware lest any man spoil you through philosophy and vain deceit, after the tradition of men, after the rudiments of the world, and not after Christ. For in him dwelleth all the fulness of the Godhead bodily. And ye are complete in him, which is the head of all principality and power :" ver. 6–10.

Now the truth of the text is this, that the Christian is complete in Christ, irrespective of Moses or of heathen philosophy. Now, in confirmation and illustration of this, observe,

I. *In Christ we have a complete system of revealed truth.*

Lay aside all the volumes of ancient philosophy, yea, even close the volume of the Old Testament scriptures, though Divine and precious, yet we do not lose one great truth. The Divine existence, character, attributes, and government, are all written in the New Testament as with a sunbeam.—Man's state of depravity, guilt, and helplessness.—His imminent and eternal peril.—His redemption, as the result of the Divine love. The whole system of mediation, on behalf of our guilty race, is clearly, fully, and explicitly presented to us in Christ Jesus,—perfectly revealed in his wondrous ministry and life. Here, then, all the great principles of the system of Divine truth are unfolded to us by Jesus Christ.

It will not be thought that we seek to undervalue the writings of Moses and the prophets, much less to dispense with their use; but while they exhibit great and momentous truths, yet they most fully testify of Christ. He is the centre, in which the lines of Old Testament revelation meet and converge. " To him gave all the prophets witness." So that in and by Christ Jesus, we have presented to us a complete system of Divine truth. And now God refers to him as the GREAT ORACLE, and issues the imperative mandate—" Hear ye him !"

II. *In Christ we have a complete system of Christian doctrines.*

The former head of our discourse, in some sense, comprehended this. But I wish us to look at the grand leading doctrines of Christianity, and to see how they are all connected with the Lord Jesus.

The justification of the sinner is by faith in Christ. " Be it known unto you, therefore, men and brethren, that through this man is preached unto you the forgiveness of sins : and by him all that believe are justified from all things, from which ye could not be justified by the law of Moses."—Acts xiii. 38, 39.

The regeneration and sanctification of the sinner is by the word and spirit, and through the blood of the Lord Jesus. " He came unto his own, and his own received him not. But as many as received him, to them gave he power to become the sons of God, even to them that believe on his name. Which were born, not of blood, nor of the will of the flesh, nor of the will of man, but of God."—John i. 11, 12, 13. " Whosoever believeth that Jesus is the Christ, is born of God."—1 John v. 1. " Being born again, not of corruptible seed, but of incorruptible, by the word of God, which liveth and abideth forever."—1 Peter i. 23.

The preservation of the believer by the power of Divine grace to perfect salvation, is complete in Christ; together with the gift of eternal life. " My sheep hear my voice, and I know them, and they follow me : and I give unto them eternal life; and they shall never perish, neither shall any man pluck them out of my hand."—John x. 27, 28. So also Christ teaches this in his solemn prayer—" And now I am no more in the world, but these are in the world, and I come to thee. Holy Father, keep through thine own name those whom thou hast given me, that they may be one, as we are. While I was with them in the world, I kept them in thy name : those that thou gavest me I have kept, and none of them is lost, but the son of perdition; that the scripture might be fulfilled."—John xvii. 11, 12.

The resurrection of the body, and the glorification of body and soul in heaven forever, are the direct work of Jesus, and are complete in him. " For our conversation is in heaven ; from whence also we look for the Saviour, the Lord Jesus Christ : who shall change our vile body, that it may be fashioned like unto his glorious body, according to the working whereby he is able even to subdue all things unto himself."—Philip. iii. 20, 21.

Now, these are the grand distinctive doctrines of the gospel ; and we see how fully, with respect to all these, we are complete in Christ.

III. *In Christ we are complete, as we have a perfect rule of life.*

The laws of the New Testament are perfect. Nothing more can be added to them. It is one holy temple ; perfect from the base to the head-stone.

Our relationship to God, and the exact duties we owe him, are supreme love—hearty belief—and cheerful obedience. Now these

Christ not only fully taught, but completely exemplified. We see in him the most exalted love to his Father, the most entire confidence in him, and the most absolute and cheerful obedience to his will. His law was his delight. It was written on his heart.

Our relationship to the Lord Jesus as Mediator, and the great duties we owe him, of unfeigned love and confidence. Jesus ever insisted on the faith of his disciples, and on their most explicit dependence on him. He ever showed the essential connection between himself and people; and that without his mediation and grace, they could do nothing. John xv. 5–7.

Our relationship to all believers, and the duties we owe them. Of love, sympathy, communion, help; were taught and exhibited by him. Hear how pathetically he enforces this love, and service, and sympathy, towards one another,—"So after he had washed their feet, and had taken his garments, and was set down again, he said unto them, Know ye what I have done to you? Ye call me Master and Lord; and ye say well; for so I am. If I, then, your Lord and Master, have washed your feet, ye also ought to wash one another's feet. For I have given you an example, that ye should do as I have done to you. Verily, verily, I say unto you, the servant is not greater than his lord; neither he that is sent greater than he that sent him. If ye know these things, happy are ye if ye do them. A new commandment I give unto you, That ye love one another; as I have loved you, that ye also love one another. By this shall all men know that ye are my disciples, if ye have love one to another."—John xiii. 12–17; 34, 35.

So also he showed the duties we owe to mankind in general. Such as universal equity, goodness, and mercy. It is worthy of note, how Jesus laid the foundation of all his moral teaching, in enforcing rigid equity, and general goodness to mankind. "Think not that I am come to destroy the law or the prophets; I am not come to destroy, but to fulfil."—Matt. v. 17. "Therefore all things whatsoever ye would that men should do to you, do ye even so to them: for this is the law and the prophets."—Matt. vii. 12. "Ye have heard that it hath been said, Thou shalt love thy neighbor, and hate thine enemy. But I say unto you, Love your enemies, bless them that curse you, do good to them that hate you, and pray for them who despitefully use you, and persecute you. That ye may be the children of your Father who is in heaven: for he maketh his sun to rise on the evil and on the good, and sendeth rain on the just and on the unjust."—Matt. v. 43–45.

Now as in these, so in all the peculiar states of life, the word of Jesus has provided for. As the duties of parents and children, masters and servants, rulers and subjects, &c.

IV. *In Christ we are complete, as we have a complete model of purity for our imitation.*

In this, all the great teachers of philosophy were deficient. So also were Moses and the prophets. Here Jesus shines forth in all the glories of perfect holiness. I have left you an example, he says, that ye follow my steps. An example palpable, clear, full, perfect. His life is a perfect copy for our contemplation and imitation. His conversation —his conduct—his spirit, were all perfect. No flaw—no defect—no admixture of evil.

How we ought to seek, that Christ's holy life should be transferred to us, that we might exhibit its lovely features.

"Be thou my pattern; make me bear
More of thy gracious image here;
Then God, the Judge, shall own my name,
Amongst the followers of the Lamb."

V. *In Christ we have complete blessedness.*
As spiritual knowledge. A knowledge of the true God, and of eternal life.

Spiritual liberty. From all moral bondage and slavery. "And ye shall know the truth, and the truth shall make you free." John viii. 32.

Spiritual peace. That peace which passes all understanding. The peace of God, which Jesus brought from heaven to earth; and which he left, as his best and most gracious legacy to his disciples, when he said,— "Peace I leave with you, my peace I give unto you; not as the world giveth, give I unto you. Let not your heart be troubled, neither let it be afraid." John xiv. 27. And also unspeakable joy, and a hope of eternal glory.

Peace is the soul's solace and rest; but Christ gives holy joy—an elevation of mind —an ecstasy, kindred to that which the blest have in heaven; for it is said to be not only "unspeakable," but full of glory. And this joy is essentially allied with an inward assured hope of eternal life. This hope is inexpressibly precious; and as such, it is likened to an anchor, by which the vessel safely rides, amidst the howling tempest, and terrible storm. And it is the helmet, by which the head is both adorned and protected in time of battle.

Now this good and precious hope, is the confident anticipation of the glory that shall be revealed; and is represented as "looking for the mercy of our Lord Jesus Christ unto eternal life."

Now we have all these blessings in relation to this life. Thus is present blessedness complete in Christ. But the future is equally complete in him. We have an everlasting home in his Father's house, which he has gone to prepare; and to which he will receive his faithful followers. An eternal inheritance, which he will bestow. An unfading crown, which he will place on the victor's head. And fulness of joy, and pleasures forevermore, at his right hand. Hence, eternity is inscribed on the blessedness to come. We see the charter of the Christian's blessedness is summed up thus, "All are yours, ye are Christ's, and Christ is God's."

Now observe three things, in conclusion,—

1. This completeness is "in Christ" only. He is the author, and source, and bestower, of all our blessings. God the Father hath given all things into his hands. In him all fulness dwells. He is all and in all. And of his fulness have all we received.

Observe the characters addressed.

2. "Ye," are complete. Not all men. Who then? See verses 5 and 6. Not unbelievers. Not the mere formalist. No; believers in Christ; and those only.

Yet notice, the gospel,

3. Offers Christ, and this complete salvation, to all men. "For God so loved the world, that he gave his only-begotten Son, that whosoever believeth in him should not perish, but have everlasting life."—John iii. 16. "For I am not ashamed of the gospel of Christ; for it is the power of God unto salvation to every one that believeth; to the Jew first, and also to the Greek."—Rom. i. 16. Therefore, the apostle adds, "Whosoever shall call upon the name of the Lord, shall be saved."—Rom. x. 13.

XXIII.—DAVID'S SONG OF TRIUMPH.

"Thou hast also given me the shield of thy salvation; and thy gentleness hath made me great."
—2 Sam. xxii. 36.

OUR text is found in the midst of one of David's most joyous songs. It exhibits the Psalmist under the various trying and distressing sorrows and troubles of life; and in the deliverances and mercies with which God had so signally blessed him. He commences with the language of holy exultation. "And he said, The Lord is my rock, and my fortress, and my deliverer; the God of my rock; in him will I trust: he is my shield, and the horn of my salvation, my high tower, and my refuge, my saviour; thou savest me from violence;" ver. 2, 3. He then avers his resolution to consecrate himself by prayer, to the Lord. "I will call on the Lord, who is worthy to be praised: so shall I be saved from mine enemies:" ver. 4. And he rests his resolution on the past interpositions of the Divine mercy. "The sorrows of hell compassed me about; the snares of death prevented me; in my distress I called upon the Lord, and cried to my God; and he did hear my voice out of his temple, and my cry did enter into his ears:" ver. 6, 7. Our text repeats what God had been to him, and had done for him in the midst of all his sorrows. "Thou hast also given me the shield of thy salvation: and thy gentleness hath made me great."

Observe,

I. *The dangers implied.*

II. *The salvation afforded.*

And,

III. *The greatness conferred.*

I. *The dangers implied.*

David's dangers had been personal, both as to body and soul, and also domestic and national. His life had been one series of perils. He had in early life been exposed to the terrible lion and bear,—to the boasting Goliath,—to the envious and malevolent Saul,—to the hazards of war,—to the sorrows of domestic conspiracy and national rebellion.

We too are exposed to dangers, and like David's they are,

1. *Personal.*

And include those both of body and soul. Life is in danger from disease. Soul in peril from the power of sin, and the attacks of the devil. Most can testify to both these. For all men, while in the body, are liable to sickness and death; and while in the world must encounter the countless attacks of spiritual adversaries. So that life is one scene of personal tribulation and conflict. Our dangers too, like those of David,

2. *Arise from various sources.*

Perils of the world—alike from its frowns and smiles. For in either case, its influence is deadly to genuine piety. Its favors are alike deadly with its hostile spirit, and often indeed its flattery is more to be dreaded, than its bitterest hate.

Perils from the powers of darkness. And the name of these is—legion.

Perils from our own hearts, which are so partially sanctified at best, and so prone to wander from God, and yield to the temptations of evil. Yes, all around are foes to assail us, and within the very citadel is the weak vacillating heart, which may, through fear, or indolence, or lethargy, yield up all to the enemy of our peace and salvation.

3. *These perils might have been most disastrous in their results.*

Yes, had we fallen by them, loss of peace —loss of hope, would have been the result. No calamity can be really greater, than to make shipwreck of faith and of a good conscience. Yet all would have been thus lost, had our spiritual foes prevailed. And following that, as the necessary result, would have been the loss of the soul. A ruin, extending its terrible results throughout a black and hopeless eternity. Let no Christian then think lightly of his spiritual foes and perils; they are too formidable to be despised, too deadly to be neglected.

Then notice, in David's experience,

II. *The salvation afforded.*

Now, observe, God did not exempt him from dangers, but he delivered and saved him out of them. God's delivering presence was David's shield. So he sang,—"The Lord is a sun and shield." God had said to Abraham—"Fear not, for I am thy shield."

Now the salvation thus afforded, was,

1. *Divine.*

"Thy salvation." Not mine—not an angel's—not of men. A salvation effected by God's wisdom, power, and presence. God's graciousness produced the deliverance and the safety. "Salvation is of the Lord," &c. "There is no king saved by the multitude of a host; a mighty man is not delivered by much strength. A horse is a vain thing for safety : neither shall he deliver any by his great strength. Behold, the eye of the Lord is upon them that fear him, upon them that hope in his mercy"—Ps. xxxiii. 16–18. "For I will not trust in my bow, neither shall my sword save me. But thou hast saved us from our enemies, and hast put them to shame that hated us."—Ps. xliv. 6, 7.

This salvation,

2. *Was seasonable.*

At the hour of critical peril. In the season of greatest extremity. In the day of most imminent danger. Just at the right and momentous crisis. So it is ever with God's people in their deliverances. The Lord is the shield of their salvation, when they most need him; and when there is a season of greatest danger, he usually selects that for the rescue of his people. He did so with Israel of old, as they approached the waters of the Red Sea. Hostile foes were close in the rear—precipitous mountains on either side—the deep waters immediately before them; but then God appeared, and the waters clave asunder and stood on heaps, that his people might pass through as on dry ground.

This salvation,

3. *Was efficient.*

Always a complete salvation. "For by thee I have run through a troop; by my God have I leaped over a wall. As for God, his way is perfect; the word of the Lord is tried : he is a buckler to all them that trust in him. For who is God, save the Lord ? and who is a rock, save our God ? God is my strength and power, and he maketh my way perfect. He maketh my feet like hinds' feet, and setteth me upon my high places," ver. 30–34. His achievements were complete. Goliath did not flee, but was slain. Just as the three Hebrews were effectually saved from the fire—and Daniel from the lions—and Peter from prison. So David's deliverances were ever efficient and complete. So God entirely and fully delivers his feeble and trusting people.

But observe, this salvation,

4. *Was ever connected with the use of means.*

God did not deliver David by supernatural agency or miraculous interposition, but by the use of means, which he blessed and rendered effective. God gave him the wisdom, and might, and magnanimity, so needful in his perilous career. Now so it is still : God preserves and delivers his people by the use of means. Prayer—which lays hold of God's strength. The Word—which is the two-edged sword. Faith—which is the shield of defence against fiery darts. Hope—which is the helmet. Now all these are to be spiritually employed against our spiritual adversaries. See Eph. vi. 11–18. And so with regard to the troubles and sorrows of life, means are to be employed; and the spirit of prudence, vigilance, and activity, cultivated; and then on these, and with them, the divine blessing is to be sought, and trusted in for safety and for triumph.

Notice,

III. *The greatness conferred.*

" Thy gentleness hath made me great."

Now here there are two things to be carefully observed :

1. *The greatness itself.*

(1.) There is physical greatness; and God gave this to David : for he was strong and vigorous in his bodily powers.

(2.) There is mental greatness, and he also bestowed this. Hence the wonderful display of thought and intellect his powerful addresses and songs exhibit.

(3.) There is also moral greatness. The love of right—the earnest desire to be holy—the deep-toned love of God and his law, by which sin is resisted, and temptation overcome, and purity of character attained; and David had this. Hence his devotion—his fortitude—his self-denial—his uprightness—his spirituality, &c. All these were signs of moral greatness.

He especially gave two striking evidences of lofty moral dignity, on two remarkable occasions. When he might have rid himself of his mortal enemy, Saul, from whom he had so often to flee for his life ; but when the life of that infatuated monarch was in his hand, hear his address to him : " And David said to Saul, Wherefore hearest thou men's words, saying, Behold, David seeketh thy hurt ? Behold, this day thine eyes have seen how that the Lord had delivered thee to-day into mine hand in the cave ; and some bade me kill thee : but mine eye spared thee ; and I said, I will not put forth mine hand against my lord ; for he is the Lord's anointed."—1 Sam. xxiv. 9, 10.

The other case was, when he was exposed to the curses of the wretched Shimei. " And when king David came to Bahurim, behold, thence came out a man of the family of the house of Saul, whose name was Shimei, the son of Gera : he came forth, and cursed still as he came. And he cast stones at David, and at all the servants of king David : and all the people and all the mighty men were on his right hand and on his left." " Then said Abishai the son of Zeruiah unto the king, Why should this dead dog curse my lord the king ? let me go over, I pray thee, and take off his head. And the king said, What have I to do with you, ye sons of Zeruiah ? So let him curse, because the Lord hath said unto him, Curse David. Who shall then say, Wherefore hast thou done so ? And David said to Abishai, and to all his servants, Behold, my son, which came forth of my bowels, seeketh my life : how much more now may this Benjamite do it ! Let him alone, and let him curse, for the Lord hath bidden him. It may be that the Lord will look on mine affliction, and that the Lord will requite me good for his cursing this day."—2 Sam. xiv. 5, 6 ; 9–12. Here was exhibited the greatest possible manifestation of self-control and submission to God. This was the loftiest moral heroism indeed, and of a truth ! And God abundantly prospered and increased the house and kingdom of David ; so that his reign was illustrious, magnificent, and great.

Then observe,

2. *How the greatness was bestowed.*

" By God's gentleness."

Now the idea is this, that God's great love, as evidenced in kindness, and forbearance, and tenderness towards him, had made him great.

(1.) Look at the ideas suggested in reference to God's treatment of Israel. " For the Lord's portion is his people ; Jacob is the lot of his inheritance. He found him in a desert land, and in the waste howling wilderness ; he led him about, he instructed him, he kept him as the apple of his eye. As an eagle stirreth up her nest, fluttereth over her young, spreadeth abroad her wings, taketh them, beareth them on her wings." Deut. xxxii. 9–11. The eaglets are to be made great in valor and flight. Then they must be forced from the nest to attempt the hazardous flight; but not at once — not roughly—not fiercely ; but gently and affectionately. " Ye have seen what I did unto the Egyptians, and how I bare you on eagles' wings, and brought you unto myself."—Exod. xix. 4. " In all their affliction he was afflicted, and the angel of his presence saved them ; in his love and in his pity he redeemed them; and he bare them, and carried them, all the days of old."—Isa. lxiii. 9.

(2.) Look at the trainer of youth. He wishes to educate his mind and spirit. Well, he does it gently; by elementary efforts first; by gradual steps; by leading the pupil on from lesson to lesson. So God did by David. His paternal goodness and gentle care had made him great. So he does by all his people. Hence he represents himself as standing in connection with them, as a pitiful Father; more loving and faithful than the devoted mother; careful as the watchful nurse; and by the dispensations of his infinite compassion and loving kindness, he trains his people for service, and warfare, and perils, and greatness. Any thing else would crush, and dispirit, and destroy them.

APPLICATION.

Then observe from the text,

1. The security of God's people. God being their shield and their salvation, who, or what, can harm them?

2. What should be the great object of our desire? "Greatness." Moral, spiritual greatness. To be eminently good—singularly pious—publicly self-denying—unceasingly useful. Notice,

3. The example God presents to us, in the gentleness of his training. Parents, teachers, and ministers may learn from it how they may best succeed in making favorable impressions, and imparting the loftiest principles, to those committed to their care. Of this the Apostle Paul gives us an eminent example, 2 Thess. ii. 7–9.

———————◆———————

XXIV.—EBENEZER.

"Then Samuel took a stone, and set it between Mizpeh and Shen, and called the name of it Ebenezer, saying, Hitherto hath the Lord helped us."—1 *Sam*. vii. 12.

THE chapter in which the text is found, contains an affecting history of the ark of the Lord. It had been brought from the Philistines by the men of Kirjath-jearim (ver. 1) to the house of Abinadab. It had been there twenty years (v. 2). The people mourned over it. Samuel called for the humiliation and sanctification of the people (ver. 3). They obeyed, and put away their gods (v. 4). Then Samuel gathered the people to Mizpeh (ver. 5 and 6). They were afraid of the Philistines (ver. 7). Samuel directed them to pray (ver 8). Sacrifice was offered (ver. 9). God was gracious (ver. 9). The artillery of heaven was employed (ver. 10). The Philistines fled; Israel pursued until they came to Bethcar (ver. 11). Then Samuel took the monumental pillar, and inscribed on it Ebenezer—"The stone of help," &c.

Observe from this subject,

I. *God's people have often been in circumstances of conflict and peril.*

It has been so from the time of the fall to this hour. We see it in the envy and hate of Cain against Abel. We see it in the spirit of Ishmael towards Isaac. We see it in the history of the Israelites oppressed by the Egyptians; then by the Canaanitish nations. So it has been in reference to the New Testament church. Christ distinctly taught it. "In the world," he said, "ye shall have tribulation." "If the world hated me, it will hate you." Often God's people are hated and persecuted on account of their religion; often on account of that, but under other feigned causes. Hence Christ was said to be a wine-bibber, and friend of publicans and sinners; also a stirrer up of sedition; also a blasphemer. So the apostles were persecuted as factionists, political agitators, infidels, profaners of temples. So now, persecution is often presented under false colors, and thus all manner of evil is spoken against those who fear God, But in this way the reputation, peace, civil rights, and often the lives of Christ's disciples, are placed in jeopardy.

Now, observe, neither wisdom, nor piety, nor peaceableness, can always exempt from this kind of peril.

But we notice,

II. *In times of peril, help should be sought of the Lord.*

Now, so did Samuel pray unto the Lord. And there are four things to be observed and imitated in the course he adopted:

(1.) The reformation by which the prayers were preceded. Prayer, however earnest, must be preceded by a turning from evil, and a putting away of our transgressions. If iniquity is retained, God will not hear; and if sin is cherished, all devotional exercises will be rejected of him. It was thus that God heard the Ninevites. "And God saw their works, that they turned from their evil way; and God repented of the evil, that he had said he would do unto them; and he did it not."—Jonah iii. 10. It was thus that God reasoned with Israel of old—"And when ye spread forth your hands, I will hide mine eyes from you: yea, when ye make many prayers, I will not hear: your hands are full of blood."—Isa. i. 15. And then God demands the needful reformation—"Wash you, make you clean; put away the evil of your doings from before mine eyes; cease to do evil; learn to do well; seek judgment; relieve the oppressed; judge the fatherless; plead for the widow."—Isa. i. 16, 17. Observe, the prayer for help was preceded,

(2.) By the offering of sacrifice. "And Samuel took a sucking lamb, and offered it for a burnt-offering wholly unto the Lord; and Samuel cried unto the Lord for Israel; and the Lord heard him."—1 Sam. iii. 9. Now, Christ is our sacrificial offering, by whom we are to come to God with our prayers and supplications. "But Christ being come an high-priest of good things to come, by a greater and more perfect tabernacle, not made with hands, that is to say, not of this building; neither by the blood of goats and calves, but by his own blood he entered in once into the holy place, having obtained eternal redemption for us. For if the blood of bulls and of goats, and the ashes of an heifer sprinkling the unclean, sanctifieth to the purifying of the flesh."—Heb. ix. 11, 12, 13. "Let us therefore come boldly unto the throne of grace that we may obtain mercy, and find grace to help in time of need."—Heb. iv. 16.

But look,

(3.) At the prayer itself. It was fervent. There was intense feeling, and ardent pleading with God. It was thoroughly earnest, and therefore it is said, "The Lord heard Samuel." In vain we offer mere formal service, or cold lifeless supplication. In peril we must cry unto the Lord, that God may hear and save us. "And Samuel cried unto the Lord for Israel; and the Lord heard him:" verse 9.

And then all this was accompanied,

(4.) By the use of prudent means. They were prepared for the combat, and it is added that, "The men of Israel went out of Mizpeh, and pursued the Philistines, and smote them, until they came unto Bethcar:" verse 11.

Now, in difficulties and troubles, we are not so to rely on God as to neglect means; but in the use of means, and for the rendering of means effectual, we are to call upon the Lord, and to confide in his all-sufficient and gracious aid. But observe,

III. *God will hear and deliver his people in time of need.*

1. *He is pledged to do so.*

The sacred Scriptures are full of these precious promises and blessed engagements. The Bible is liberally stored with them. Let us just look at a few. "And call upon me in the day of trouble: I will deliver thee, and thou shalt glorify me." "Thou shalt not be afraid for the terror by night; nor for the arrow that flieth by day; nor for the pestilence that walketh in darkness; nor for the destruction that wasteth at noonday. A thousand shall fall at thy side, and ten thousand at thy right hand; but it shall not come nigh thee. Because he hath set his love upon me, therefore will I deliver him: I will set him on high, because he hath known my name."—Psalm l. 15; xci. 5-7, and 14. "No weapon that is formed against thee shall prosper; and every tongue that shall rise against thee in judgment thou shalt condemn. This is the heritage of the servants of the Lord, and their righteousness is of me, saith the Lord."—Isaiah liv. 17. "There hath no temptation taken you but such as is common to man: but God is faithful, who will not suffer you to be tempted above that ye are able; but will with the temptation also make a way of escape, that ye may be able to bear it."—1 Cor. x. 13.

2. *He loves to do so.*

God delights in his people; and, therefore, he takes infinite pleasure in delivering them. To this, all the experience of God's people will bear testimony. "I sought the Lord, and he heard me, and delivered me from my fears." "As for me, I will call upon God: and the Lord shall save me. Evening, and morning, and at noon, will I pray, and cry aloud; and he shall hear my voice. He hath delivered my soul in peace from the battle that was against me; for there were many with me." "Ye that love the Lord, hate evil; he preserveth the souls of his saints: he delivereth them out of the hand of the wicked."—Psalm xxxiv. 4; lv. 16, 17, 18; xcvii. 10.

3. *He ever has done so.*

God has never forsaken his people in their difficulties and straits, but he has ever been their shield and their help. Abraham found it so; and the mount of trial was the mount of deliverance. So Jacob experienced it during a long life; so Joseph, in the midst of severe adversities and sorrows; so Moses, so Samuel, so David, so Daniel and the three worthies, so all his people, in every age and country; so many of you have oftentimes experienced it.

IV. *God's delivering interpositions should be commemorated.*

They should be recognized at the time, and gratefully acknowledged in songs, celebrating our deliverance.

They should be piously recognized. We should devoutly observe God's hand, and in a humble frame of mind glorify him. Hence, of old, the pious marked God's favors by days and festivals of holy remembrance. Thus Jacob did at Bethel. How often Israel did this in the desert. So how beautifully it was done in the text. So all nations have agreed to erect their monuments of victory and deliverances—though these are often done to exalt man. Many of these, too, perpetuate the remembrance only of scenes of blood and misery. But piety gives glory to God—honors his name, and power, and grace. Hence it was so in the text, in reference to rearing the Stone of Help.

APPLICATION.

Let the subject have a personal bearing on all.

Will it not apply to your conviction on account of sin, when God brought you to see your peril? To your conversion, when he turned your feet into the way of life? To spiritual deliverances from temptation, in your religious experience? To remarkable interpositions, in your providential course? And should not all these blessed recollections inspire you with a grateful love to God?—with believing confidence in his holy word? And should these not lead you, in every trial, to devout prayer and entire dependence on his seasonable help?

Both a thanksgiving and devotional spirit, should be promoted by a remembrance of God's providential and gracious interpositions. How richly and appropriately this has been expressed by the poet:

"Come, thou fount of every blessing!
  Tune my heart to sing thy grace!
 Streams of mercy never ceasing,
  Call for songs of loudest praise.

Teach me some melodious sonnet,
  Sung by flaming tongues above;
 Praise the mount—O fix me on it,
  Mount of God's unchanging love!

Here I raise my Ebenezer,
  Hither by thy help I'm come;
 And I hope, by thy good pleasure,
  Safely to arrive at home.

Jesus sought me when a stranger,
  Wandering from the fold of God;
 He, to rescue me from danger,
  Interposed his precious blood."

See to it that such shall be the sentiments of your hearts; then will your deliverances and timely help be double blessings; for not only will they be so in themselves, but in their grateful celebration you will enjoy them over again; and often the second experience of them will be the sweetest and the best.

Our greatest mercies, like the hoarded manna in the desert, will become totally perverted; and finally, most loudly condemn us, if they have not been acknowledged in praise, and if they have not led us to cherish a more humble, trusting, and prayerful spirit towards our heavenly Father.

———◆———

XXV.—ON PRAYING, &c., FOR ALL MEN.

"I exhort therefore, that, first of all supplications, prayers, intercessions, and giving of thanks, be made for all men; for kings, and for all that are in authority; that we may lead a quiet and peaceable life in all godliness and honesty. For this is good and acceptable in the sight of God our Saviour; who will have all men to be saved, and to come unto the knowledge of the truth."—1 *Tim.* ii. 1–4.

THE benign influence of Christianity is seen in all its doctrines and precepts. It is most evidently a religion of love and good-will to men. It condemns all intolerance, and breathes forth sympathy, charity, and pity to all. In this, it is a perfect transcript of the Divine goodness, which is the glory of God; and which is so fully displayed in all his works.

Now among the varied expressions of goodness, we are to exhibit towards our fellow-men, we may notice—sympathy, kindness, and mercy; and these are to be accompanied by an earnest spirit of prayer and thanksgiving, on their behalf. How evidently these views are exhibited in the text: "I exhort," &c.

Let us then look,

I. *At the course we are exhorted to adopt.* And,

II. *The reasons on which this course is grounded.*

The *what* we are to do, and the *why* we are to do it, will be the divisions of the text.

Notice then,

I. *The course we are exhorted to adopt.*

1. *It is a course of prayer.*

This is one of the great essentials of religion. Prayer is the breath of the soul. We cannot live, or enjoy a religious life, without it. But the devotional spirit must not be confined to ourselves only, but it is to be like the smoke of the incense, and fill as it were the whole temple of our world with its fragrant odor.

A devotional selfish spirit is a manifest contradiction in terms. He whose heart does not expand with love to man, will not be rightly affected with the spirit of that worship which will be acceptable to God.

Hence notice,

2. *This spirit of prayer is to inclose all men in its solicitudes.*

All nations, tribes, and colors,—all conditions; physical, mental, or moral,—all classes, from the highest and most exalted, to the lowest and most obscure,—all moral grades, from the most excellent and holy, to the most defiled and worthless. "All men:" we are not to exclude one human being. Our arms are to be lifted up in prayer, and extended over the whole family of man. No national prejudices—no personal antipathies—no isolating influences are to be exerted, so that any shall be forgotten, disregarded, or despised. But when we come to the loving Father of all men, we are to breathe forth the spirit of supplication for all his dependent and needy children.

But observe,

3. *We are to make special reference to certain orders of society.*

When the Apostle has spoken of the whole race, he then makes more special reference to "kings, and for all that are in authority:" verse 2.

Now this class of persons occupy very exalted stations; places of great trust and responsibility; their influence also extends to all other classes. They too are but men, like others. How needful then to seek for them the blessings of Divine providence, and the riches of God's grace. Often the great and the dignified of the earth are the objects of men's envy; but if their perils are duly considered, such a feeling will be exchanged for pity, and a tender solicitude for their welfare. And though the text does not distinctly name the poor and the unfortunate, the widow and the orphan, the afflicted and the tried, the prisoner and the captive; yet, these may well be kept in our compassionate remembrance, when we go to God in prayer. These form the other extreme of society; and while we pray that God may mercifully bestow the spirit of wisdom and grace to preserve kings and rulers from infatuation and ruin, so may we seek that he would sustain the poor, deliver the tried, and be the friend and deliverer of those who have no helper.

4. *Prayer in its different kinds and variety is inculcated.*

Observe, we are to pray for all, that is, ask God on the behalf of all. We are to supplicate; that is, humbly implore; to stand forth entreating on behalf of them; or, as some think the word indicates—to deprecate the evils to which men are exposed, and seek God's preventing mercy and preserving care on their behalf. We are to intercede; that is, employ our influence, as a royal priesthood. As Abraham did on behalf of Sodom; and imitate the great High Priest of our profession. This is prolonged prayer, extended supplication.

We are also to give thanks—rejoice in the happiness of others—and give the glory to God. Thank God for the general blessings, both of his providence and grace, to mankind.

Here then is the course to which we are exhorted.

Notice,

II. *The reasons on which it is grounded.*

Or, why should we thus pray for all men?

1. *It may rest on the universal brotherhood of mankind.*

All men are of one family. Hence, only one species. We ought to feel this, and recognize it before the one Father of the whole human race. Hence our blessed Lord has taught us to address God, as "Our Father;" that is, the Father of our race. In reference to rulers,

2. *We should do it that their influence may tend to civil and religious liberty, and peace.*

That we may lead a "quiet" unmolested

life. Have our civil rights unimpaired, and also that we may not be interrupted in religious exercises and privileges; that we may lead a quiet and peaceable life; to which the Apostle adds—"In all godliness and honesty."

Now, much depends on the spirit and laws of those in authority, as to these things; and it is our duty to seek God's blessing on their behalf, that they may rule in his fear, and administer wise, and good, and wholesome laws. We are to pray for all,

3. *Because it is pleasing to God.*

"For this is good and acceptable in the sight of God our Saviour:" verse 3. He delights in it. It is a reflection of his own mind. It is the echo of his voice. It is the response to his heart's pity and love of his own children. "God is love:" and he delights in its manifestation in others. Such are his children—partakers of his mind and nature—none else are so; for he who loveth not, is not of God. Hear the testimony of the apostle John :—" We know that we have passed from death unto life, because we love the brethren. He that loveth not his brother abideth in death. Whosoever hateth his brother is a murderer: and ye know that no murderer hath eternal life abiding in him." —1 John iii. 14, 15. "Beloved, let us love one another: for love is of God; and every one that loveth is born of God, and knoweth God. He that loveth not knoweth not God; for God is love. Beloved, if God so loved us, we ought also to love one another. No man hath seen God at any time. If we love one another, God dwelleth in us, and his love is perfected in us."—1 John iv. 7, 8, 11, 12.

It is in harmony,

4. *With God's will respecting the salvation of mankind.*

"Who will have all men to be saved, and come unto the knowledge of the truth:" verse 4. Now if it be true that God does not love all men, that he has reprobated any, then it would be inconsistent, that he should require us to pray for all. But if God's mercy reaches to all, if he wills the salvation of all, and if he has provided for the restoration of every perishing sinner, in the gift of the Lord Jesus Christ; then how beautifully is the text in harmony with that; and how forcible and entirely conclusive the reason given—" Who will have all men to be saved." He hates none—has reprobated none—sealed the ruin of none; but on the other hand, seeks the salvation of all and

every soul. Just according to his solemn oath—"Say unto them, As I live, saith the Lord God, I have no pleasure in the death of the wicked; but that the wicked turn from his way and live: turn ye, turn ye from your evil ways; for why will ye die, O house of Israel !"—Ezek. xxxiii. 11.

Now this reason for prayer, &c., for all men, is of the highest and sublimest kind. All men have erred and gone astray from God,—all men are rebels by nature and practice,—all men are justly exposed to everlasting death; but God has pitied and loved all men, and desires the salvation of every wandering sinner; and he therefore demands that we have a similar spirit of compassion towards all mankind. Now this provision of mercy for all, in the work and mediation of Christ, is presented to us in every conceivable variety of form. The apostle Paul says of him—" Who gave himself a ransom for all, to be testified in due time."—1 Tim. ii. 6. So again—" But we see Jesus, who was made a little lower than the angels for the suffering of death, crowned with glory and honor; that he by the grace of God should taste death for every man." —Heb. ii. 9. And John distinctly avers in reference to Christ's sacrificial work,—" And he is the propitiation for our sins; and not for ours only, but also for the sins of the whole world."—1 John ii. 2. And the design of universal mercy is most forcibly expressed,—" And we have seen and do testify that the Father sent the Son to be the Saviour of the world."—1 John iv. 14.

Now we see at once, how beautiful and appropriate it is that the love of God in our hearts, should make us earnest intercessors on behalf of all our fellow-men.

" Would Jesus have the sinner die ?
  Why hangs he then on yonder tree ?
What means that strange expiring cry ?
  (Sinners, he prays for you and me ;)
' Forgive them, Father, O forgive :
They know not that by me they live !'
Oh, let thy love my heart constrain,
  Thy love for every sinner free ;
That every fallen soul of man
  May taste the grace that found out me,
That all mankind with me may prove,
Thy sovereign, everlasting love.'

Then learn from the text,

1. The comprehensiveness of Christian prayer. "All men." We may pray more for some persons than others, and more intensely. Dear friends and kindred nearest

our hearts, may occupy the warmest place in our affectionate remembrances; but they are not to absorb all our devotional solicitudes. Just as a stone thrown into the centre of a lake makes its greatest as well as its first circles, where it strikes the water, then other circles more distant; but at length acts on the whole, till the most outward ones kiss the margin on every side: so in prayer for all men, we are to pray for those nearest to us, and most beloved; but we are not to cease our intercessions until we have sought from God his rich blessing for the whole wide world, and for every creature.

2. See the powerful motives to cherish universal prayer. One reason is in ourselves. It is for "men"—our family—our species—our brethren. The other is in God, who is so universally good, and so benignant to all. While all men are our brethren, God is the Father and Saviour of all.

3. There are crises when prayer for special persons and objects is most important. Such as the present time, when all the nations of Europe are excited, and preparing for war! Do you believe in God—in prayer—in providence? Then let it be offered with supplication and intercession at this momentous juncture, for the rulers and administrators of the nations of Europe, that God may lead them to see the value of peace, and dispose all their hearts to justice, goodness, and mercy; and that the period may be hastened when the nations of the earth shall not learn, or practice, war any more.

Finally: Do you all live in the habit and spirit of prayer? Do you enjoy communion with God—and are you thus in friendship with him? If so, continue in prayer and thanksgiving; and seek constantly, that the spirit of prayer and supplication may be richly poured into your hearts. And if you have never really, humbly, penitently prayed to God, now bend the knee, and lift up your souls to him, who is rich in mercy to all that call upon his name. Remember that the work and mediation of Jesus opens a way for you to the Father; and whosoever comes to God by him, shall in no wise be cast out. Then with penitent hearts, and lowly souls, wait upon him, and seek his forgiving mercy and renewing grace, that so you may enjoy his blessed favor here, and in the world to come, life everlasting. Amen.

XXVI.—FORMAL AND UNPROFITABLE WORSHIPPERS.

"And they come unto thee as the people cometh, and they sit before thee as my people, and they hear thy words, but they will not do them: for with their mouth they show much love, but their heart goeth after their covetousness. And, lo, thou art unto them as a very lovely song of one that hath a pleasant voice, and can play well on an instrument: for they hear thy words, but they do them not."—*Ezekiel* xxx. 31, 32.

HUMAN nature is the same in all ages. Hence the very follies and sins of the ancients we see developed around us every day. Were there skeptical men then, like Pharoah? So there are now. Were there daring blasphemers? so now. Degraded profligates? so now. Frivolous and thoughtless persons? so now. Were there others observing the proprieties and decencies of life? so are there now. Were there also then formalists, men who had only the name and externals of religion? so there are now. Who will not perceive that the prophet's description is just as close, and searching, and true, in reference to multitudes now, as it was when he uttered it in reference to Israel of old? Now it is in this way that God's word becomes not only a true record of past events, and a faithful describer of human conduct, but it is a clear transparent mirror of the human heart and character. Every man may thus see his own likeness reflected, in the spirit and doings of some order or class of persons who lived in past ages. And the chief value of this department of God's word arises from its vivid portraitures of the human heart. Now, a considerable portion of the masses who give external attendance to outward worship, we fear, may see their true state in the picture our text presents. Happy, if thus seeing it, they may be led to feel the great importance of becoming spiritual worshippers; as God can only accept and be pleased with such.

Let us then notice, in the description,

I. *What is commendable.*

II. *What blameworthy.*

And,

III. *The cause assigned for it.*

In the description, notice,

I. *What is commendable.*

Observe,

1. *There is attention to Divine things.*

They come to God, that is, to his house. They do not neglect religious observances.

They regard the Sabbath—they regard the sanctuary; and, therefore, were not rejecters nor despisers of Divine things. How proper and right is all this! God ought to be worshipped, and his holy ordinances regarded. He demands this; and it is alike our duty and privilege to be obedient to his commands. How beautiful and hopeful is this course, when contrasted with those in whose thoughts God and Divine things have no place! Who ask, "Who is the Lord that I should serve him; or, what profit will there be in calling upon him?" A man who neglects yielding homage and worship to the Most High, is both guilty of great impiety and practical atheism. Let all men thus act, and God would have no intellectual recognition in his own world. But our text describes a class who do acknowledge God, who do honor his name, and attend to his worship and ordinances.

But observe,

2. *Their spirit and demeanor are serious and reverential.*

They are not light and trifling,—they are not slumberers,—they are not charged with forgetting what they heard;—but they are serious, and grave, and reverential as God's people. No human eye can discern any difference. They come to God, says the prophet, "As thy people." Hear with the same apparent interest and concern. How proper and pleasing is all this! A becoming demeanor in the sanctuary is most important. For where should there be lowliness of spirit, and veneration of soul, if not in the presence of Jehovah? And how reprehensible the conduct of those who, in the sanctuary, seem as thoughtless and giddy as though they were in the ball-room, or some place of worldly display! Where it is evident to gaze abroad, and attract the observation of others, is the chief end in view. But those brought before us in the text are distinguished for the utmost external decorum; and they come, and hear, and sit, even as God's people.

But still more, observe,

3. *They appear to love Divine things.*

"With their mouth they show much love;" that is, much love to God and to his service—to his house—to his people. Speak kindly and affectionately of religious things. How encouraging this is! How really gratifying to minister and people! It is not unusual, however, for us to come in contact with this warm and ardent approbation of public religious services—where there is the complete absence of spirituality of mind. Men love music, and they enjoy the service of song.—They love eloquence, and they are delighted with the addresses of the preacher.—They are eminently social, and they love to mingle in the assembly of God's people. But, alas! after all, they are only outward court worshippers, and never venture into the holiest of all, or hold communion of heart with the living God.

But, in the text, they go even beyond this, for,

4. *They enjoy, and are delighted with Divine things.*

"And, lo, thou art unto them as a very lovely song," &c. They praise the preacher. What a wise man! they exclaim. What an excellent man! How eloquent! how original! how edifying! what a treat to hear him! There is, in fact, no end to their eulogies. And we have no reason to suspect their sincerity. They, no doubt, in some sense feel and mean what they say. Such receive the word with manifest joy. It acts upon them as an intellectual or emotional stimulant. It tells upon their lively imaginations, or nervous temperaments; or it accords with their theological predilections, or religious convictions. Now these things are all commendable, so far as they go; but they are all the while at an immeasurable distance from true and saving piety; and the root of the matter is not in them. However cheering it may be to witness the conduct they exhibit, yet, observe, the serious defalcations related in the text; and this leads us to notice, in their spirit and conduct,

II. *What is blameworthy.*

We have seen what is right so far;—but the first charge against them is, that they are not practical hearers. "They hear thy words, but they will not do them." They hear and they understand, and know their duty; but will not do it. Not that they cannot do them; for then it would be their misfortune. Duty always conveys to us the idea of ability possessed, or attainable; and where there is neither, there can be no moral obligation. But they *can*, and *ought* to do them; but *will not*. It is our wills that are at fault. Ye *will* not come unto me, said Christ. They are awed by threatenings, but do not flee from their sins. They are moved by expostulations, but do not yield their hearts to God. They are affected by invitations, but they do not come and return to the Lord with repentant minds and penitent hearts. They are pleased with Divine things, and wish to be counted God's people; but will not in heart and life serve him. They may have good desires, good resolutions, and good purposes; but they do not obey God's word. A grave and fatal deficiency! Remember the necessity of being not hearers only, but doers of God's work; that ye may be blessed in your deed. So while there is much to admire—how much more to censure and condemn! How melancholy is this exhibition! yet is it not the state of multitudes who go to God's house and worship as his people? If such be the fearful condition of many who go up to the services of God's house, how needful is it that we should cherish the spirit of faithful self-examination, lest we should deceive ourselves; and, like the foolish virgins, find at last the door of hope closed against us. And in the sanctuary we may well present the following thoughts to God, in earnest prayer:—

"Now, mighty God, thine arm reveal,
  And make thy glory known;
Now let us all thy presence feel,
  And soften hearts of stone.

Send down thy Spirit from above,
  That saints may love thee more;
And sinners now may learn to love,
  Who never loved before.

Furnish us all with light and powers
  To walk in Wisdom's ways;
So shall the benefit be ours,
  And thou shalt have the praise."

Then let us consider,
III. *The cause assigned.*
Now, various are the hindrances to the acceptable and profitable worship of God. There is no one cause that operates upon all. With one, it may be unsettledness and dissipation of mind. With another, it may be listlessness and apathy of spirit. With a third, it may be want of self-application, and serious reflection; or inattention and forgetfulness. (See James i. 22–24.) But the text speaks of one prevailing evil in the days of the Prophet, an evil which we fear is yet very common, and very fatal to profitable worship. "Their heart goeth after covetousness." See this illustrated in the parable of the sower,—" He also that received seed among the thorns is he that heareth the word; and the care of this world, and the deceitfulness

of riches choke the word, and he becometh unfruitful."—Matt. xiii. 22.

See it in the young ruler to whom Christ said—" If thou wilt be perfect, go and sell that thou hast, and give to the poor, and thou shalt have treasure in heaven, and come and follow me. But when the young man heard that saying, he went away sorrowful; for he had great possessions."—Matt. xix. 21, 22. See it in the cause, producing the apostasy of Demas; who loved the present world, and forsook Christ and his people. See it in those, who when invited to the feast, excused themselves on the ground, that their farms, and oxen, and merchandise, must occupy their attention; and, therefore, they could not come. How fallacious this! for a proper regard to the things of this world is quite compatible with a godly life.

Now, observe, diligence, prudence, frugality, are all in unison with Christian virtues. But covetousness is the inordinate desire of the heart, for some earthly attainment; it may be for riches. If so, they that will be rich, fall into divers temptations. The love of mammon and the love of God are opposites. It may be an inordinate desire for worldly fame—the honor and approbation of men. If so, we cannot supremely desire God's favor, and seek intensely the approbation of men. In all cases a covetous spirit, whether it goes after riches or fame, hardens the heart. It is the moral ossification of the soul. It destroys sympathy, tenderness, and generosity. Any class of men are more easily impressible, than the covetous. It closes the heart against God's good Spirit, and his supreme claims. There cannot be two on the throne of the affections—gold and God. If covetous, then God is excluded. We may further add, that this inordinate earthly spirit, tends to moral darkness of soul. It deceives the heart. It is a respectable vice. Other sins are generally disreputable,—seldom is covetousness so. Persons reason thus: I seek to improve my condition. My conduct and pursuits injure no one. To which we reply: Covetousness robs the whole world, and your own soul also. It is a deceiving vice. It hoodwinks the moral perceptive powers, and darkens the mind to its own destruction. Every thing that hardens the heart, must do so. So that, if covetousness could exist alone, and have no companion sin, it would effectually exclude all acceptable religion; and finally, sink the soul into endless perdition. No covetous person can enter into the kingdom of God.

In conclusion, then, learn,

How necessary is self-inspection. Examine your hearts, and know yourselves fully and honestly. How needful is real earnestness in religion, experimental piety ; that which gives the whole heart and soul to God. To withhold our intellect, or affections, or profession, or practise of holiness from God, is to rob him of his righteous and just claims. We say to those who are desirous of possessing what is truly good and precious, covet earnestly the best gifts. There are things really worth having—intrinsically valuable ; and the possession of which it is right, yea most laudable, to desire, and that with all your hearts.

There is the divine favor, which is better than life, the holy influences of the Divine Spirit, and a full plenitude of that grace which is treasured up in Christ, for all his people. Be careful not to be content with being *as* his people, but be of the number who truly are his children. And see to it, that while attendant on the outward forms of piety, that thou seek and attain to its inward, spiritual, and vital power. And thus God himself will be the rich portion, and everlasting joy of your souls.

XXVII.—JEHOVAH-SHALOM.

"Then Gideon built an altar there unto the Lord, and called it Jehovah-shalom."—*Judges* vi. 24.

THE chapter in which the text is found relates the sin of Israel, and their consequent oppression by Midian : "And the children of Israel did evil in the sight of the Lord ; and the Lord delivered them unto the hand of Midian seven years :" verse 1. When their oppression was extremely severe and distressingly great, the children of Israel cried unto the Lord—" And Israel was greatly impoverished because of the Midianites ; and the children of Israel cried unto the Lord :" ver. 6. The Lord sends a message to them, in which they are reminded of his great goodness to them and their fathers ; and the disobedience of which they had been guilty : "And it came to pass, when the children of Israel cried unto the Lord because of the Midianites, that the Lord sent

a prophet unto the children of Israel which said unto them, Thus saith the Lord God of Israel, I brought you up from Egypt, and brought you forth out of the house of bondage : and I delivered you out of the hand of the Egyptians, and out of the hand of all that oppressed you, and drave them out from before you, and gave you their land ; and I said unto you, I am the Lord your God ; fear not the gods of the Amorites, in whose land ye dwell ; but ye have not obeyed my voice :" ver. 7–10. Then Gideon is selected to be the leader against the Midianites. The uncreated angel of the Lord called Gideon to the work when at his daily occupation : "And there came an angel of the Lord, and sat under an oak which was in Ophrah that pertained to Joash the Abiezrite : and his son Gideon threshed wheat by the winepress, to hide it from the Midianites. And the angel of the Lord appeared unto him, and said unto him, The Lord is with thee, thou mighty man of valor :" ver. 11, 12. Gideon's modesty and diffidence are beautifully expressed—" And he said unto him, O my Lord, wherewith shall I save Israel ? behold, my family is poor in Manasseh, and I am the least in my father's house :" ver. 15. God assures him of his divine presence : "And the Lord said unto him, Surely I will be with thee, and thou shalt smite the Midianites as one man :" ver. 16. He also seeks a sign of the Lord : "And he said unto him, If now I have found grace in thy sight then shew me a sign that thou talkest with me. Depart not hence, I pray thee, until I come unto thee, and bring forth my present, and set it before thee. And he said, I will tarry until thou come again :" ver. 17, 18. The significant sign is given. "And Gideon went in, and made ready a kid, and unleavened cakes of an ephah of flour : the flesh he put in a basket, and he put the broth in a pot, and brought it out unto him under the oak and presented it. And the angel of God said unto him, Take the flesh and the unleavened cakes, and lay them upon this rock, and pour out the broth. And he did so. Then the angel of the Lord put forth the end of the staff that was in his hand, and touched the flesh and the unleavened cakes ; and there rose up fire out of the rock, and consumed the flesh and the unleavened cakes. Then the angel of the Lord departed out of his sight :" ver. 19.–21. But now Gideon's fear is excited, because he had seen the angel of the

Lord. "And when Gideon perceived that he was an angel of the Lord, Gideon said, Alas, O Lord God! for because I have seen an angel of the Lord face to face :" ver. 22. Then God reassures him of his favor, and blesses him with peace. And then Gideon built an altar to the Lord, and called it Jehovah-shalom: "And the Lord said unto him, Peace be unto thee; fear not; thou shalt not die. Then Gideon built an altar there unto the Lord, and called it Jehovah-shalom: unto this day it is yet in Ophrah of the Abi-ezrites :" ver. 23, 24.

Such are the historical circumstances of the text. The word signifies, "the Lord send peace."

Then let us consider,

I. *The text, as involving an important admission.* Man needs peace.

II. *As revealing a great truth.*

That God only can give it. And,

III. *As elucidating the mode of its bestowment.*

Look,

I. *At the text, as involving an important admission.* Man needs peace.

Now you may look at peace, as it respects,

1. *Man and God.*

Sin has produced contrariety, conflicts, and collision, and warfare. Man is against God, and wars against his holy law,—strives with God,—rebels against his authority. God's anger is therefore justly kindled against him. God can, and as a righteous governor must, punish the rebel who remains impenitent. How obvious, then, that reconciliation and peace with God are most important. Wretchedness must be the result without it ; and ultimately, final ruin.

But observe,

2. *He needs peace with conscience.*

Conscience is God's vicegerent in the soul. It has not all its original clearness and power. It has been weakened and defiled with sin. It still, however, can scourge or smile on the sinner, and bless or curse him.

Now, it is said, "The wicked are like the troubled sea," when it cannot rest ; whose waters cast up mire and dirt. "There is no peace, saith my God, to the wicked."—Isaiah lvii. 20.

3. *He needs the spirit of peace towards his fellow-men.*

No marvel if men hate God, that they should hate one another. The carnal mind is not only enmity towards God, but also often evil and malevolent towards men. Hear the apostle James—"From whence come wars and fightings among you ? come they not hence, even of your lusts that war in your members ?"—James iv. 1. And the apostle Paul adds, that the fruits of the flesh are—"Idolatry, witchcraft, hatred, variance, emulations, wrath, strife, seditions, heresies, envyings, murders, drunkenness, revellings, and such like."—Gal. v. 20, 21. Peace with God, and concord with mankind, are essentially united. Now it is self-evident, that man with God—man in himself—and man with men, needs peace ; and without it there is no real blessedness.

Notice in the text,

II. *A great truth revealed.*

That God alone can give peace. Hence his name—"Jehovah-shalom." Hence also his designation—"The God of peace." Observe, he has set up,

1. *A covenant of peace.*

This is beautifully described by Isaiah the prophet, when God offers to make an everlasting covenant with his transgressing people, even the sure mercies of David (lv. 3) ; and also the permanency and graciousness of this covenant is described by the same prophet (liv. 10) ; and the experimental and practical result of this covenant is given by Ezekiel, where God has provided not only for man's restoration to favor, but also to holiness and blessedness. "Then will I sprinkle clean water upon you, and ye shall be clean : from all your filthiness, and from all your idols, will I cleanse you. A new heart also will I give you, and a new spirit will I put within you : and I will take away the stony heart out of your flesh, and I will give you a heart of flesh. And I will put my spirit within you, and cause you to walk in my statutes, and ye shall keep my judgments, and do them."—Ezekiel xxxvi. 25–27.

Now God can give both pardon and peace. Bring the sinner into a right state, and give the right spirit.

Then observe,

2. *He has published and offered peace.*

He sent his son—the Prince of Peace. The gospel—the message of peace. His apostles—to preach peace. (See Isa. lii. 7 ; lvii. 19.) "In his days shall the righteous flourish ; and abundance of peace so long as the moon endureth."—Ps. lxxii. 7. See this also in the language of the apostle—"And all things are of God, who hath reconciled us to himself by Jesus Christ, and hath given to us the ministry of reconciliation."— 2 Cor. v. 18. Ministers therefore are ambassadors of peace.

3. *He imparts to his people the Holy Spirit of peace.*

"Being justified by faith, they have peace with God." The fruit of the Spirit within them is given. "But the fruit of the Spirit is love, joy, peace, long-suffering, gentleness, goodness, faith, meekness, temperance; against such there is no law."—Gal. v. 22, 23. Then, when experimental religion is embodied under the idea of wisdom; it is not only pure, but peaceable. Thus we see that God giveth peace.

But, observe, he only can do it. It is his prerogative. Hence it is said emphatically of him—"He blesseth his people with peace." And the present peace he confers, is the emblem of blessedness and peace forever. His people, when they die, enter into peace. The wicked there cease from troubling. In the celestial Canaan, all is calm, and joy, and peace.

But consider,

III. *The text, as elucidating the mode of its bestowal.*

How did God send peace to Gideon?

1. *By the angel of the covenant.*

Now, observe, Christ is the peace-maker and bestower. Hence the Apostles went forth preaching peace, by Jesus Christ. He is the Prince of Peace. He came to bring peace to earth and good-will to men. So that without Christ, there is no peace; and so long as men are aliens to him, there is no peace.

To the obtaining of peace,

2. *There must be personal consecration.*

The angel required an offering of Gideon; and hence the kid and the unleavened cake were laid on the rock, and consumed by fire (verse 19).

Now Christ requires the unfeigned offering of the whole man, as the Apostle indicates. "I beseech you therefore, brethren, by the mercies of God, that ye present your bodies a living sacrifice, acceptable unto God, which is your reasonable service."— Rom. xii. 1. We have nothing to do to make God peaceful towards us. But the peace Christ has obtained, must be received by us in the way of the Divine appointment. And that way is by yielding ourselves up to God. By repentance and godly contrition

and real faith—receiving his grace and mercy into our souls. We cannot be benefited by Christ's work, except we surrender to him the body and soul he has bought with his own blood.

We remark, when this peace is received,

3. *It insures all needful good.*

Deliverance from guilt, oppression, wrath, and death. It insures all the blessings of a good providence—the precious promises— and the enjoyment in our hearts of the Holy Spirit of God. And the Spirit dwells in our hearts as the pledge of God's peace; and as the fruitful and blessed source of all peacefulness of heart both towards God and men. And the peace that rules in the soul, prepares for, and terminates in, all the joys and glories of eternal life.

But we add,

4. *This peace should be kept in grateful remembrance.*

The altar should be built, and the name given to it—"Jehovah-shalom." We should remember God's mercies and loving kindnesses.—We should have them engraven on our hearts.—We should often refer to this all-important subject, and with love and gratefulness celebrate it. Our daily motto and song should be in harmony with the language of the text.

APPLICATION.

We ask,

1. Do you know God as Jehovah-shalom? That is, as the sender of peace? If not, your condition is one of heinous guilt and fearful peril! To be at war with God, and rebel against him, must end in your certain and everlasting ruin. And if you do not thus know God, what is the reason? The hindrance is not with God; for he has taken all difficulties out of the way. He has, by a process the most costly, brought peace to you by the Lord Jesus Christ. Be at once concerned then to seek this peace by faith, in his precious blood.

2. Let the Christian cherish, and expect this peace. The peace of God must be daily, prayerfully sought. It will grow in the humble, and contrite, and devout soul. We should desire its overflowing influence, that it may be as a river of comfort to our souls. And as we possess it, we should exhibit it to all around,—to the disciples of Jesus, first and chiefly; but also, as far as is possible, to all men. We are to be manifestly the disciples of the Prince of Peace;

and must do honor, both to our Divine master and his peaceful kingdom, which we profess to have been set up within our hearts. And in this we shall find both comfort and dignity; and we shall realize the fulfilment of that promise, that God will keep in perfect peace, those whose hearts are stayed on him, because they place their trust in him.

XXVIII.—CHRISTIANS ALL ONE IN CHRIST JESUS.

"There is neither Jew nor Greek, there is neither bond nor free, there is neither male nor female; for ye are all one in Christ Jesus."—*Gal.* iii. 28.

UNDER the law, the Jews were the special and favored people of the Lord. Their advantages were of the most distinguished kind. They had the oracles—covenants—tabernacle—priesthood, and finally, as the grand blessing of heaven to that nation, the Messiah came; "who is God over all, blessed forever." But Christianity was designed to destroy that separating line between Jew and Greek—between Israel and the other nations of the earth. So that the apostle remarks—"Where there is neither Greek nor Jew, circumcision nor uncircumcision, Barbarian, Scythian, bond nor free; but Christ is all, and in all."—Col. iii. 11.

But, observe, the text is more comprehensive still. "There is neither male nor female." All inferiority of sex is repudiated by Christianity. Woman was much honored under the law—still more under the gospel. Not like some false religions which made woman a mere soulless slave; Christianity knows no distinction; but elevates her in the scale of moral dignity, and places her not lower, nor yet higher, but side by side with man, and says—"There is neither Greek nor Jew, there is neither bond nor free, there is neither male nor female; for ye are all one in Christ Jesus."

Our subject is the oneness of all believers. Observe then,

I. *In what the oneness of believers consists.*

II. *Where it is realized.*

And,

III. *The influence it should exert.*

1. *In what the oneness of believers consists.*

Now we remark, that it is evident that this is not *oneness* of creed, or oneness of forms, or in denominational distinctions. Nor oneness of religious experience, either as to exact likeness, or degree of religious knowledge, —or oneness as to the state of the emotions. In these there is evidently a great diversity. And it is clear this diversity neither destroys nor impairs the oneness of true Christians.— "For ye are all one in Christ Jesus."

This oneness, however,

1. *Regards faith.*

They are one in a saving belief of the truth. Not in opinions, or modes of illustration; but in the act and exercise of faith in the Lord Jesus Christ. There is but one faith that justifies, and brings the soul into a state of acceptance with God.

Now in an experimental belief of the gospel of Christ, all Christians are one. As there are not two Saviours or two gospels, so there is only one faith, by which Christ is received into the soul, and all the saving benefits of the gospel enjoyed. Hence it is declared that all believers are the children of God, by faith. So, the apostle says, when speaking of the essential unities of the gospel, "there is one faith."

Then, as to this oneness,

2. *It regards spirituality of nature.*

All Christians have one renewed holy nature. Born again from above—born of God —born of incorruptible seed, and thereby partakers of the Divine nature. All such have the new heart and the right spirit. Just as all men have one human nature, so all Christians have one Divine and spiritual nature.

3. *This oneness regards relative affinities.*

God is the Father of all—Jesus the Saviour and elder brother of all—the Spirit the sanctifier and comforter of all—the Church the mother of all. Hence it follows, each Christian is brother of all. There is but one family of God—one household of faith, and all spiritual persons, of every color, and country, or language, belong to it.

Observe, as to this oneness,

4. *It regards the privileges of Christians on earth.*

All are one in the privileges of the children of God; they all have one holy catholic church—they all have one fold. There is one glorious gospel for all—one true covenant for all—one series of precious promises for all—one throne of mercy for all. The rich and infinite plenitude of grace in Christ the Mediator, is for all. There is no partiality nor respect of persons, as it respects those who are in Christ Jesus; for they are all essentially and declaratively one in him.

5. *It regards the destiny of Christians in a future state.*

They are all called to God's eternal kingdom and glory. All begotten again to a lively hope of the resurrection from the dead —all have their names written in the Lamb's book of life—all shall finally sit down together with the whole company of the redeemed in the heavenly kingdom. They shall form one united, pure, and holy assembly around the eternal throne of God forever; for heaven is but one house, with numerous mansions: all shall have the glory with Christ which he had with the Father before the world was. Thus are all Christians truly and essentially one.

We ask,

II. *Where this oneness is realized?*

The text responds, "in Christ Jesus."

All Christians are one in Christ as the common meeting place between God and man. All come to God through Christ, and all are accepted in Christ. Here they meet, and here they become one.

Every believer is such through the sacrifice and work of the Mediator; and the Mediator is one, so that in him all Christians must meet. The grace then that unites the soul to Christ, binds all believers together. So all Christians, as living stones, are united by Christ the corner-stone. He holds and connects the Jewish with the Gentile believers, and so all others unite and adhere by and through him. So, as all members of the body are united by the head, Jesus is the head of his body, and all Christians are members of him, and therefore members one of another. By these figures there is no difficulty in seeing that all Christians are one in Christ Jesus.

Then Jesus refers us also,

To the vine. He is the vine, believers are the branches, and as all the branches are connected with the one vine, so all believers are one in Christ Jesus.

Now, thus you see in every case, how all Christians are one, and also how they are all one in Christ Jesus.

It is equally obvious, that in no other will Christians ever be really one. Not in the Fathers—not in the Protestant Reformers— neither in Wickliffe, nor Luther, nor Calvin —not in any of the glorious martyrs—nor puritans—nor founders of religious sects or parties—not in Baxter, nor Whitfield, nor Wesley. It is equally clear that all Christians will never unite and be openly one in Episcopalianism, however reformed — nor Presbyterianism, however strict—nor Congregationalism, however liberal — nor in Methodism, however practical. Diversity will characterize God's people in many things, probably to the end of time; but Jesus, the one blessed and only mediator, will be the centre of attraction to each and every one. And how desirable that this real unity should be cherished, honored, and exhibited. As the various regiments of our national army honor the same laws, and are enlisted under one monarch, so, all the host of God's elect have Jesus as the one and only captain of their salvation.

Then observe,

III. *The influence which this subject should exert on all the people of God.*

It should lead,

1. *To mutual Christian recognition.*

There should be a distinct, generous acknowledgment of one another. Instead of excluding one another, there should be a reception of each other. The Christianity of each should be cheerfully admitted, and this admission should be followed by a hearty recognition, and by a holy and lofty esteem of one another in Christ Jesus. Instead of suspicion, there should be a generous confidence; instead of coldness, there should be a frank, warm spirit of brotherly union.

2. *There should be mutual Christian love.*

There may, and will be preferences. We may innocently be specially attached to our own band, and select our own company, with whom we shall fraternize most intimately; but there should be universal charity to the whole family of Christ. This should reach to all, and embrace all. To love persons for their likeness to us, or for their creed or sectarian character, may exist without one particle of real Christian affection. Christian love is the love of the Christian character; and the love of the Christian character for its own sake, and for its reflecting the likeness of our blessed Lord. And in proportion to this Christ likeness and Christ mindedness, ought our affection to be intense and enlarged.

No attachment to others deserves to be called Christian, unless it is grounded on the foregoing principle of resemblance to our divine and blessed Lord. And this should be very superior to any mere party or denominational attachment.

3. *There should be mutual Christian forbearance.*

There may sometimes be a need for controversy, for expressing difference of views, for taking different actions in ecclesiastical matters; but there should be ever prominently exhibited with all this, the spirit of the Christian. It should be done with Christian dignity and forbearance, and not with bitterness and wrath. And the differences of the Church can never be adjusted till believers approach each other in the spirit of brotherly love; and till they are as eager for the interests of charity, as they are for the interests of truth itself.

Truth is never promoted when love is either undervalued, or made to hold a secondary position; for of all the graces, this is the chiefest and the best.

4. *There should be mutual Christian co-operation.*

As far as circumstances will admit, and in all things, when conscience will allow, let there be fraternal intercourse and united effort to glorify God and to save souls. Christianity has to conflict with ignorance, depravity, and ungodliness, in all its forms and phases, and the aggressive energies of the church should embrace the power of every Christian; and that power in a united form. No petty difference should divide the army of Christ—separate the friends of Christ—or prevent the whole spiritual church from living, loving, and laboring together.

Such a blessed union and combination would be the brightest star of hope, in reference to our world's millennial glory. And it is utterly utopian ever to think of a golden age of Christian glory on earth, until all God's children shall have one heart and one way.

This united co-operation to exalt Jesus and save souls, would do more in any one year for religious progress, than sectarian zeal could effect in a whole century.

" Christ, from whom all blessings flow,
Perfecting the saints below,
Hear us, who thy nature share,
Who thy mystic body are.

Join us, in one spirit join,
Let us still receive of thine ;
Still for more on thee we call,
Thou who fillest all in all.

Closer knit to thee, our head ;
Nourish us, O Christ, and feed ;

Let us daily growth receive,
More and more in Jesus live.

Sweetly may we all agree,
Touched with softest sympathy ;
Kindly for each other care,
Every member feel its share.

Wounded by the grief of one,
Now let all the members groan :
Honored if one member is,
All partake the common bliss.

Many are we now and one,
We who Jesus have put on ;
There is neither bond nor free,
Male nor female, Lord, in thee !

Love, like death, hath all destroyed,
Rendered our distinctions void !
Names, and sects, and parties fall—
Thou, O Christ, art all in all !"

Then, in conclusion, let us see how fitly the spirit of oneness and love is eulogized and enforced in the divine word. Hear the devout exclamation of the Psalmist ! " Behold how good and how pleasant it is for brethren to dwell together in unity ! It is like the precious ointment upon the head, that ran down upon the beard, even Aaron's beard ; that went down to the skirts of his garments ; as the dew of Hermon, and as the dew that descended upon the mountains of Zion : for there the Lord commanded the blessing, even life for evermore."--Ps. cxxxiii.

And still more let us hear the declaration of Jesus before his death : " A new commandment I give unto you, That ye love one another ; as I have loved you, that ye also love one another. By this shall all men know that ye are my disciples, if ye have love one to another."—John xiii. 34, 35.

And which was ratified by his sacerdotal prayer—"Neither pray I for these alone, but for them also which shall believe on me through their word ; that they may all be one ; as thou, Father, art in me, and I in thee, that they also may be one in us : that the world may believe that thou hast sent me."—John xvii. 20, 21.

And now suffer the word of apostolic exhortation : " If there be therefore any consolation in Christ, if any comfort of love, if any fellowship of the Spirit, if any bowels and mercies, fulfil ye my love, that ye be like-minded, having the same love, being of one accord, of one mind. Let nothing be done through strife or vain glory ; but in lowliness of mind let each esteem other better than themselves."—Phil. ii. 1-3. " Put on, therefore, as the elect of God, holy and beloved, bowels of mercies, kindness, humbleness of mind, meekness, long-suffering; forbearing one another, and forgiving one another, if any man have a quarrel against any; even as Christ forgave you, so also do ye. And above all these things, put on charity, which is the bond of perfectness."—Col. ii. 12–14.

XXIX.—ARGUMENTS AGAINST BEING WEARY IN CHRIST'S CAUSE.

"For consider him that endured such contradiction of sinners against himself, lest ye be wearied and faint in your minds."—*Heb.* xii. 3.

THE Apostle has been speaking of the Christian race, and giving directions for its successful accomplishment. Having urged to it by the most weighty considerations, he then follows it up by presenting to the mind the example of the Redeemer, in order to prevent Christians from being wearied and faint in their minds.

Christ is to be our exemplar and model in all things. In the spirit of devotion we are to cherish towards God; in the spirit of self-government as it respects ourselves; in the spirit of goodness we are to cherish towards our fellow-men. And we are to keep him before our eyes, that we may be constant in duty, persevering in our course, and faithful to all the claims of conscience and God.

As all the followers of Jesus are liable to discouragement, and may tire and even faint in their heavenly course, it is important that they should fortify their minds by the considerations the text presents.

Observe then,

I. *The evil deprecated*—

Being "wearied and faint in your minds."

II. *The remedy suggested*—

"Consider him that endured such contradiction of sinners against himself."

I. *The evil deprecated.*

"Lest ye be wearied and faint in your minds."

The text supposes the Christian course may be long and trying, and often be connected with various discouragements and opposition. There are various things which may produce this weariness.

It may arise,

1. *From a partially sanctified nature being engaged in the service.*

Not so angels and glorified spirits; their nature and service are in continual harmony. It is their very life and joy to serve God. How different it is with us! We have to contend with the remains of the carnal heart, that is selfish, proud, indolent, and earthly. Often when we would do good, evil is present with us, and our moral nature, through its frailties and weaknesses, has to be impelled and constrained by various influences in the way of obedience and devotedness to God. How often do we cleave to the dust! How often is the mind dark, the heart cold, and the spirit lethargic; and thus we are in danger of wearying, and being faint in our minds.

In addition,

2. *Then there are the inevitable duties which appertain to this life.*

Toil for the bread that perisheth—family cares—business anxieties. Now these secular things are in themselves lawful, and they must be diligently attended to. But often it is difficult to give them their proper place, and their due proportion of solicitude and time. It is not easy always to keep the world out of the heart.

And yet these earthly tendencies clog the soul—keep it in an unhealthy atmosphere—produce weariness of spirit—choke the good seed, and not unfrequently lead to an open renunciation of the way of life. Demas forsook Christ, having loved the present evil world; and myriads have thus made shipwreck of faith and a good conscience.

What need there is of vigilance and devotedness to spiritual exercises, to keep the soul in a right and healthy state! And lawful things address us so plausibly, and they can present so many apparently reasonable claims.

3. *Then there are the various temptations to which we are exposed.*

Some of these from the world; some from Satan. All kinds of attractions, and at all seasons. An incessant moral warfare is thus kept up. Our spiritual enemies are legion, and we are ever exposed to their malignant opposition.

Hence, the warnings and admonitions of the divine word. Hence, also, the numerous directions given to vigilance, to heroism, and to the use of the whole armor of God. "Wherefore take unto you the whole armor of God, that ye may be able to withstand in the evil day, and having done all, to stand. Stand, therefore, having your loins girt about with truth, and having on the breastplate of righteousness; and your feet shod with the preparation of the gospel of peace; above all, taking the shield of faith, wherewith ye shall be able to quench all the fiery darts of the wicked. And take the helmet of salvation, and the sword of the Spirit, which is the word of God. Praying always with all prayer and supplication in the Spirit, and watching thereunto with all perseverance and supplication for all saints."—Eph. vi. 13–18.

4. *Then there are often the reproaches and persecutions of men.*

Hence the offence of the cross still continues. Evil men are yet haters of spiritual religion, and sometimes these are found among our friends and relations.

Jesus most fully warned his disciples on this subject. He distinctly averred, that parents should betray and persecute their children, and children their parents; and that often a man's foes would be those of his own household. And it has been so in all ages, and in all countries of the world. The spiritual and the devoutly pious must endure in some form the oppression and hatred of the world. Hence Christ stated, " they shall lay their hands on you, and persecute you, delivering you up to the synagogues, and into prisons, being brought before kings and rulers for my name's sake. And it shall turn to you for a testimony. Settle it therefore in your hearts, not to meditate before what ye shall answer : for I will give you a mouth and wisdom, which all your adversaries shall not be able to gainsay nor resist. And ye shall be betrayed both by parents, and brethren, and kinsfolks, and friends; and some of you shall they cause to be put to death. And ye shall be hated of all men for my name's sake."—Luke xxi. 12–17.

Now, human nature instinctively shrinks from pain, and distress, and suffering; and therefore, when these become the allotment of Christians, they are often tempted to be weary in the Saviour's cause.

5. *Then there are also the troubles and afflictions of life.*

Bodily infirmities and maladies. "Many are the afflictions of the righteous." Jacob, Job, David, Asaph, Hezekiah, and many others have left their experience in the sacred pages, showing us that " man is born to trouble as the sparks fly upward."

And the connection between body and mind is so close, and the influence of one upon the other so powerful, that depression of spirits, and even despondency, is often the result of physical maladies.

Happy will it be for Christians thus suffering, when they shall view this subject calmly and philosophically. For it would be as reasonable to expect melody from a bruised musical reed or pipe, as to expect joy and hope, in many instances, when the whole frame is prostrated by physical disease and mental suffering. Here are natural causes producing natural results, and to the prevention of which miraculous interposition will be essential.

Many of God's most spiritual children have suffered thus in their heavenward pilgrimage in the desert, and have been in danger of wearying and becoming faint in their minds. To these we add,

6. *Gloomy forebodings of the future.*

Fears within; often as to the things of this life; gloomy fears concerning death, judgment, eternity. Fears about the reality of their conversion and acceptance with God. Fears that they would perish by their enemies, or be swallowed up in the swellings of Jordan.

It is unnecessary to show how these things tend to make the mind weary and faint. Of Israel it is said, " The soul of the people was discouraged because of the way." So Paul speaks, when describing their trials and sorrows, " For we would not, brethren, have you ignorant of our trouble which came to us in Asia, that we were pressed out of measure, above strength, insomuch that we despaired even of life : but we had the sentence of death in ourselves, that we should not trust in ourselves, but in God, which raiseth the dead."—2 Cor. i. 8, 9. " We are troubled on every side, yet not distressed; we are perplexed, but not in despair; persecuted, but not forsaken; cast down, but not destroyed; always bearing about in the body the dying of the Lord Jesus, that the life also of Jesus might be made manifest in our mortal flesh. So then death worketh in us, but life in you."—2 Cor. iv. 8–12.

Now, having looked at the dark side of the cloud—the evil deprecated—let us consider,

II. *The remedy suggested.*

That is the consideration of Jesus. In verse 2, we are called to look to Jesus. But the text urges more than that; it is consideration, and the pondering over the circumstances of Christ's life.

1. *Consider what Christ endured.*

"The contradiction of sinners." Their opposition to his person, mission, and work; and this opposition was general, continued, vile, bitter, &c. Think of the names they called him, and the aspersions they cast on him. How they leagued him with devils, and how they scorned, reviled, and treated him with every indignity, and at last with wicked hands took him and put him to death. Well may we exclaim:

> "O Lamb of God, was ever grief,
> Was ever pain like thine!"

The bitter opposition Jesus encountered began with his ministry; for in the chapter that records his entering the synagogue, and reading the Messianic declarations of Isaiah, and applying them to himself, there we also read, that the Jews were filled with wrath, "and rose up, and thrust him out of the city, and led him unto the brow of the hill whereon their city was built, that they might cast him down headlong. But he, passing through the midst of them, went his way."—Luke iv. 29, 30.

And this bitter enmity to Christ followed him during the whole course of his work and life on earth, and even assailed him in base and vile invectives as he was expiring on the cross.

2. *Consider the dignity and excellence of Him who endured all this.*

It was God's Son, the Messiah, the Holy One, the lovely Jesus, the Friend of sinners, the embodiment of goodness, pity, and love to our world. Remember, too, his delicacy of sense and feeling, and the rude and vile insults he bore. For just in proportion to this holy sensitiveness must Christ have felt the most inexpressible agony in the midst of the sorrows and griefs which he endured.

3. *Think of the spirit and temper in which he endured it.*

Well may we inquire how did he bear it? And we then have to request your attention to his meekness and gentleness, his resignation, patience, fortitude, and perseverance. He wearied not, fainted not; held on his course. He finished the work he came to do; and in his deep agony in the garden, he feared, and prayed, and was delivered from that fear. "Who, in the days of his flesh, when he had offered up prayers and supplications with strong crying and tears unto him that was able to save him from death, and was heard in that he feared."—Heb. v. 7.

He fully justified the predictions of Isaiah the prophet, who had intimated seven hundred years before, that the Messiah should be oppressed and afflicted, yet he should not open his mouth, but be "brought as a lamb to the slaughter; and as a sheep before her shearers is dumb, so he opened not his mouth." And so Peter speaks of the Saviour's gracious spirit, and gentle disposition, and says, "who, when he was reviled, reviled not again; when he suffered, he threatened not; but committed himself to him that judgeth righteously."—1 Peter ii. 23.

4. *Consider the ends for which Christ suffered all this.*

No doubt his chief aim was to glorify his Father, and to save the world. But in the troubles of his life he came to be an example to his afflicted people. He has thus left his own patient life as a model for our imitation. Now observe this is the great point of the text. Consider Jesus, and imitate him; possess his spirit, and follow his steps. When poor and in adversity, consider Jesus, hungry and weary, and having nowhere to lay his head. When despised and persecuted, consider Jesus as assailed and vilified. When tempted, think of his terrible conflict with the powers of darkness, both in the desert and on the cross.

Now, as Christians we are bound to consider Jesus, who is our avowed master, and to labor to possess his blessed spirit, and walk in the course which he has left for all who would be participants of his eternal joy and glory.

Let these considerations,

(1.) Lead you to humility of spirit. What are you compared to Jesus? What your sufferings, and what your trials compared to his?

Let it,

(2.) Lead you to cheerful resignation. There is a needs be for these things; and the very letter of the contract is, we must suffer with Christ if we would reign with him.

Let it lead,

(3.) To fortitude. Not to grow weary; not to become faint. What will that do for you? You will lose all you have gained, and all you have expected. You must be faithful unto death, if you would receive the crown of life.

Let it lead,

(4.) To prayer. Thus Jesus sanctified his own lot of trials and afflictions; the deeper the anguish, and he prayed the more earnestly.

Then consider,

Finally, the glorious results. "But we see Jesus, who was made a little lower than the angels for the suffering of death, crowned with glory and honor."—Heb. ii. 9. And so shall it be with his faithful servants.

> "Who suffer with our Master here,
> We shall before his face appear,
> And by his side sit down;
> To patient faith the prize is sure;
> And all that to the end endure
> The cross, shall wear the crown.
>
> Thrice blessed, bliss-inspiring hope!
> It lifts the fainting spirit up;
> Itbrings to life the dead;
> Our conflicts here shall soon be past,
> And you and I ascend at last,
> Triumphant with our Head."

Then, in conclusion,

Let the text reconcile us to the crosses and sorrows of this life.

Let it cheer us on our way to the better land.

Sinners ought to weary and faint. They have a bad service—dark prospects; and the wages of sin will be everlasting death.

XXX.—THE UNCERTAINTY OF THE FUTURE.

" Go to now, ye that say, To-day or to-morrow we will go into such a city, and continue there a year, and buy and sell, and get gain; whereas ye know not what shall be on the morrow. For what is your life? It is even a vapor, that appeareth for a little time, and then vanisheth away. For that ye ought to say, If the Lord will, we shall live, and do this, or that."—*Jas.* iv. 13-15.

MAN, in many respects, is a paradoxical being. His powers are capable of an almost infinite expansion. There are no limits to the range of his knowledge, or the imagery and of the ideal within him. He can contemplate things material and immaterial, past or present. Earth in its deepest strata, the numberless things on its surface, the air we breathe, and the heavens above us, are all open to his investigation. He can chronicle the history of all past ages, form his system of Ethics or Philosophy, detail the rise, pro-

gress, and ruin of dynasties, the foundation and fall of empires. More than this, he can analyze distinctly the laws of life, and can show in the aggregate the principles of longevity. How great and marvellous are the powers of man! Yet as it respects one all-important subject, he knows nothing: That one subject is the Future. This God reserves to himself. It is one of the secret things which he has never given, except by direct predictive inspiration, to mortals. It is likely that all created beings are equally ignorant of the future with ourselves.

To this subject the text refers.

Observe,

I. *A reprehensible course, which is commonly adopted.*

To say, "To-day or to-morrow we will go into such a city, and continue there a year, and buy and sell, and get gain."

II. *A solemn truth, too generally neglected.*

"Whereas ye know not what shall be on the morrow."

III. *A godly principle, which should direct our conduct.*

"For that ye ought to say, if the Lord will, we shall live, and do this, or that."

Notice, then,

I. *A reprehensible course, which is commonly adopted.*

To say, "To-day or to-morrow we will go into such a city, and continue there a year, and buy and sell, and get gain."

It can scarcely be necessary to say much,

1. *To establish the truth of this charge.*

That men are in the habit of doing so, is most evident. It is unhappily the rule, and not the exception. Most men do this; the buyer, the seller, the merchant, the politician, and the traveller, in fact all classes and orders of men do it. We see this in the domestic circle in reference to children. Parents often speak as if the destiny of their children was in their own hands. Hence they speak of disposing of, and establishing them, as if they could infallibly do it. Everywhere, with regard to plans and arrangements for the future, do men act thus.

2. *The chief causes of this state of mind.*

Worldly absorption—want of reflection—inconsiderate levity of spirit; then as the results—established presumption. But the line of demarcation is confessedly very fine between the right and wrong. It is proper in a thousand things to act as if we expected to live to-morrow, and for many years. In business—indeed in every thing—this must in one sense be recognized. Now, this necessary prudence becomes an evil, when at length it takes away the remembrance of the mutability of every thing around us. We often do so from the experience of the past. We have acted thus for years with impunity; and therefore we conclude, as it has been, it will still continue; forgetting that every year narrows the margin of life, and renders the things we calculate on in the future less certain.

But notice,

3. *The evils of this state are manifold.*

We may just hint at a few.

Dependence on God is withdrawn—our reason and intellectual powers abused—for, if consulted, they would teach us better the claims of the soul neglected, or a general spirit of procrastination cherished. In addition to these, eternity is mostly forgotten. Therefore this evil is most fearfully fatal to the highest interests of our deathless souls. We ought to live, and think, and act, in reference to our highest interests, and our everlasting well-being. But just as the future is shut out of our thoughts, is this impossible.

Now such is the evil reprehended. But observe, in the text,

II. *A solemn truth too generally neglected.*

"Whereas ye know not what shall be on the morrow." To-morrow is a period near at hand. Yet it is beyond the ken of the most sagacious mortal, as to how it will dawn, progress, conclude! Indeed, though so near, yet it is as really concealed as the most distant period of time.

Its incidents with respect to ourselves are utterly unknown. We cannot even, with any probability, guess what these will be. Whether health or sickness—safety or peril —joy or sorrow. It may be a day of unequalled felicity, or of unexampled misery. It may be fraught with all that can bless us, or connected with all that can distress us. Its hours and moments may all bear witness to the liveliest enjoyment, or the most poignant grief. For observe, life itself is held on a tenure the most uncertain. "For what is your life? it is even a vapor." Human life is not as oak, but as the grass, yea, the flower of the grass. Is it not like rock or iron? No, it is a vapor, a thin misty exhalation. A breath of wind scatters it, and it is gone.

Now this is the case with all men; not only with the delicate, but the robust; not only with the old, but the young; not only with the sickly, but the hale, the vigorous, and the strong. Man, like the vapor, appeareth but a little while, and then vanisheth away. The longest life is as a short drama. Man appeareth on the stage of life, acts a few parts for good or evil, and then retires, and is seen no more.

How this truth has been admitted, and pondered, and illustrated, and expressed by philosophers, moralists and politicians of all ages! How it is presented to us in the proverbs and maxims of all nations, and of every age of our world's history! Yet, alas! how feeble the impression it makes on our hearts and lives!

Observe, then, in the text,

III. *A godly principle which should direct our conduct.*

"For that ye ought to say, if the Lord will, we shall live, and do this or that."

Observe,

1. *Our lives are contingent on God's will.*

He can sustain the weak and ailing, or cast down the strongest. His will alone decides the momentous question. But do not imagine that the divine will is capricious, much less ever despotical. No, it is the will of your infinitely wise, and holy, and good God; but still he, as the Governor of the universe, decides the condition and tenure of our lives. He abridges or lengthens, extends or concludes, our probationary state.

2. *This truth we should constantly cherish.*

To forget it, is so absurd as to be irrational. Even nature would teach it. All the mutations of earth, the varying seasons, the falling leaves, the withering flowers, the ending day, the impress of death we see on every thing; all, all, should teach us this solemn truth. And moreover, it ought to be confessed in our phraseology: ye ought to say, "If the Lord will."

How wise and proper to use a phraseology which may remind both ourselves and others of our transitory and uncertain state. There can be no affectation in this—no sickly cant; for it is just matter-of-fact truth; and, as such, should be remembered and uttered.

Then we remark,

3. *This principle would exert a most beneficial influence upon us.*

It would produce moderation in all our worldly affairs. See how this is urged by the apostle : " But this I say, brethren, the time is short : it remaineth, that both they that have wives be as though they had none ; and they that weep, as though they wept not ; and they that rejoice, as though they rejoiced not ; and they that buy, as though they possessed not ; and they that use this world, as not abusing it ; for the fashion of this world passeth away."—1 Cor. vii. 29-31.

It would most assuredly lead to seriousness of mind ; and this would be favorable to the habitual preparation for death, and thus sanctify life itself. For there can be no right and wise application of life, where the probable approach and the final certainty of death are not realized. Pride, ambition, hate, worldliness, and vanity, would not thrive in such an atmosphere.

Then let the text lead all classes of persons to solemn reflection.

The unconverted should not delay immediate repentance, and should trifle no longer with the soul and eternity.

The true Christian should beware of a presumptuous self-confident spirit. They should feel and act as strangers and pilgrims on the earth.

This is not their rest, it is polluted. Life is just a journey towards the eternal world. Every day abridges it, and brings it nearer to a termination. Our forefathers, and many of our friends, have finished it ; they have reached the city of habitation. But we are still sojourners, pitching our tents here to-day, and elsewhere to-morrow. But speedily we shall be gathered to those who are gone before ; to the same mother earth our remains will be committed. Let it be our daily desire and unswerving purpose, to make the most of life, by a wise and pious employment of it, in glorifying God, cultivating our moral powers, and doing good to our fellow-men. And that we may do so, let our probationary and responsible state be ever remembered. How beautifully did the pious ancients think of these things !

Hear Moses, the man of God. Psa. xc. 8-9. Psa. xc. 12. Hear Job, vii. 6 ; xiv. 1-2. Hear the evangelical prophet. Isa. xl. 6-8.

But this is the consolation of God's people, that amidst all the mutations of earth, " the word of our God abideth forever."

———◆———

XXXI.—INCREASING IN THE KNOWLEDGE OF GOD.

" And increasing in the knowledge of God."— *Col.* i. 10.

RELIGION is often presented to our notice under some one of its special attributes. As a system of faith—as the exhibition of love —as true wisdom—and oftentimes as consisting of divine knowledge. To know God, is often synonymous with godliness. Hence irreligion is represented as not having the knowledge of God. So the reverse is, " this is life eternal, to know the true God." And the apostle deemed this his greatest boast : " Yea doubtless, and I count all things but loss for the excellency of the knowledge of Christ Jesus my Lord : for whom I have suffered the loss of all things, and do count them but dung, that I may win Christ."— Phil. iii. 1.

Now, the true knowledge of God is that saving apprehension of him, by which we are brought to his favor and likeness and enjoyment.

Now, where this is possessed, the individual is godly—one of the Lord's disciples ; and it is to such the exhortation of the text applies, and to such only : " and increasing in the knowledge of God."

Let us consider,

I. *The knowledge spoken of.*

II. *The increase to be desired.*

III. *The means by which it may be obtained.*

I. *The knowledge spoken of.*

Now, the knowledge spoken of may include,

1. *A knowledge of God's nature and perfections.*

We may ask with profound reverence, What is God? And the response from the oracles of truth is, " God is a spirit." A spirit possessed of every perfection, and essentially self-existing, and underived. Eternal, without a beginning,—infinite, without limits,—Almighty, all-wise, ubiquitous,—all-seeing, or omniscient,—supreme over all. In his moral character, holy, without spot,— just, without iniquity,—good, without malevolence ; and in connection and in harmony with all, merciful, gracious, pitiful, and of tender compassion. Such is the Bible portrait of God ; to which may be added, He is absolutely unchangeable, " The same yesterday, to-day, and forever." He says, " I am the Lord, and I change not."

Is it not marvellous that a Being so great, so perfect, so glorious, so benignant, should be denied by the skeptical atheist; should be hated by the wilful transgressor; and should be feared with horrible dread by the superstitious devotee. Arrayed in all his goodness, and clemency, and love, he should be adored, and served, and praised by all his intelligent creatures.

It should include,

2. *A knowledge of his works.*

These meet us everywhere—above, below, around,—the vast and the minute. It includes creation in all its grandeur—providence, or the government of the world, with all its perfection—and redemption with all its infinite glories. In the first, we see God forming all; in the second, ruling over all; in the third, redeeming all the fallen of our perishing race.

Each of these topics would open an ample theme for a volume; for God in any compartment of his works, presents endless variety and beauty to charm and delight the mind. Hence, hear the Psalmist: "The works of the Lord are great, sought out of all them that have pleasure therein."—Psa. cxi. 2. And, "Great is the Lord, and greatly to be praised; and his greatness is unsearchable. One generation shall praise thy works to another, and shall declare thy mighty acts. I will speak of the glorious honor of thy majesty, and of thy wondrous works. And men shall speak of the might of thy terrible acts; and I will declare thy greatness. They shall abundantly utter the memory of thy great goodness, and shall sing of thy righteousness."—Psa. cxlv. 3–7.

The work of redemption in its moral grandeur, far surpasses the development of the divine power in the physical universe. It is here, the moral attributes of Deity are displayed in all their illustrious brightness and harmony.

> "Here the whole Deity is known,
>   Nor dares a creature guess,
>   Which of the glories brightest shone,
>   The justice or the grace."

It would include,

3. *A knowledge of his will.*

What is the mind of God concerning man? What does he love and hate? What does he desire us to be, and to do, and to enjoy?

Now, these are all momentous questions to those who are the subjects of his rule, and who are in a state of probation and accountability. How shall I act wisely, and safely, without a correct knowledge of the right rule of conduct, without a clear perception of God's holy will and law? Now this revelation of God's will is furnished in the Holy Scriptures. "All scripture is given by inspiration of God, and is profitable for doctrine, for reproof, for correction, for instruction in righteousness: that the man of God may be perfect, thoroughly furnished unto all good works."—2 Tim. iii. 16, 17. There is no case of duty, personal or relative, which is not here plainly marked by the finger of God.

The Bible contains the only holy code of moral and saving laws, and which in every particular is clear, perfect, and complete.

It should include,

4. *A knowledge of his favor.*

To know God especially, in all his reconciled love in Jesus—as a God of pardoning mercy—as a God loving and gracious—as a God of tender pity. To be able to say, he is mine, and I am his. To call him "Abba," that is, Father, and enjoying as the result, the divine life by the indwelling of his Holy Spirit.

Now, this inward spiritual knowledge is essential. There can be no peace, no hope, no solid joy without it; and though we know all the rest, without this we must inevitably perish. This is what Paul so longed for. "That I may know him, and the power of his resurrection, and the fellowship of his sufferings, being made conformable unto his death."—Phil. iii. 10. And it is this which he so solemnly sets before the believing Ephesians. "That the God of our Lord Jesus Christ, the Father of glory, may give unto you the spirit of wisdom and revelation in the knowledge of him; the eyes of your understanding being enlightened; that ye may know what is the hope of his calling, and what the riches of the glory of his inheritance in the saints, and what is the exceeding greatness of his power to us-ward who believe, according to the working of his mighty power, which he wrought in Christ, when he raised him from the dead, and set him at his own right hand in the heavenly places, far above all principality, and power, and might, and dominion, and every name that is named, not only in this world, but also in that which is to come: and hath put all things under his feet, and gave him to be the head over all things to the church, which is his body, the fulness of him that filleth all in all."—Eph. i. 17–23. And it was this knowledge that so distinguished the apostle as a preacher, as an apostle, and as an inspired writer of heavenly truths.

This then is the knowledge of God the text includes. Observe,

II. *The increase to be desired.*

"Increasing in the knowledge of God."

Now, observe, in reference to this increase,

1. *It is possible.*

We do not know all at the first stage of Christian experience. Nay, we know little; we have just a gleam; just know the first letters of the Christian alphabet; just understand the first elements of divine truth. The region beyond is infinite; eternity itself will never exhaust the subject. Besides, our minds are constituted for intellectual progress; the seeds of knowledge will germinate within us, and thus the mind will expand, and the powers of the soul be enlarged.

Look at Newton when a child, pondering over his lessons, and then in the midst of his philosophical greatness and mental glory.

We notice also,

2. *This increase is most desirable.*

It adds to, and constitutes our dignity; it also adds to our strength; "they that know their God shall be strong." It adds to our moral confidence and magnanimity; it adds to our happiness and solid comfort. It is our duty, equally with our privilege, to increase in it.

3. *This increase may be viewed in several aspects.*

We may increase, for instance, in the clearness of our knowledge; seeing more distinctly and lucidly every part of holy truth. In the abundance of our knowledge; knowing additional things of God, and of his works and ways. In extensiveness; knowing the same truths in a very enlarged degree, observing them in their results and consequences. In the harmony of our knowledge; seeing the various parts of the divine character in combination, forming one beautiful symmetrical whole. In the experience and practical bearings of the knowledge possessed; seeing how it may be better applied to our moral elevation and enjoyment, and security. In all these ways may we increase in the knowledge of God.

Observe,

4. *Of this increase there will be no termination.*

We shall never know all on any one sub-

ject, in the utmost degree. "Who by searching can find out God?" Glorified saints cannot—angels cannot—cherubim and seraphim cannot know God fully and perfectly. Thus the increase of the knowledge of God may be progressive, through all time, and through all eternity.

Then consider,

III. *The means by which it may be attained.*

Now this increase must be in connection with means: means God in his wisdom and love has provided. We may increase in the knowledge of God,

1. *By reading and hearing of God.*

The study of the Bible, and attendance on the ministry of the word. Here are two inlets to knowledge—the ear and the eye, and by both the materials of knowledge may be conveyed into the soul. The one we may use in the closet and in the family, the other meets us in society. Hence the priest's lips are to convey knowledge. The Christian pastor is to feed his sheep with knowledge and understanding. And as a rule, that must be a meager discourse indeed, which does not add to our means of increasing in the knowledge of God.

By a diligent perusal of the Holy Scriptures, and by a regular attendance on the ministry of reconciliation, we must increase in the knowledge of God.

It will be effected,

2. *By observation and reflection.*

God's works, creation and providence, are ever before us, and they are spread out before us for our study and reflection. We are to behold, and contemplate, and learn how the ancients did this as it is exhibited in the Book of Job—and the Psalmist, how he did this. "The heavens declare the glory of God; and the firmament showeth his handiwork. Day unto day uttereth speech, and night unto night showeth knowledge. There is no speech nor language, where their voice is not heard."—Ps. xix. 1–3. "O Lord our Lord, how excellent is thy name in all the earth! who hast set thy glory above the heavens. Out of the mouth of babes and sucklings hast thou ordained strength because of thine enemies, that thou mightest still the enemy and the avenger. When I consider the heavens, the work of thy fingers, the moon and the stars, which thou hast ordained; what is man, that thou art mindful of him? and the son of man, that thou visitest him?"—Psa. viii. 1–4.

His works and doings should be pondered by his intelligent creatures, especially by those who profess to be his loving and obedient children.

3. *By prayer and communion.*

In the one case asking for wisdom and knowledge, as the wise man teaches us. " My son, if thou wilt receive my words, and hide my commandments with thee, so that thou incline thine ear unto wisdom, and apply thine heart to understanding ; yea, if thou criest after knowledge, and liftest up thy voice for understanding ; if thou seekest her as silver, and searchest for her as for hid treasures ; then shalt thou understand the fear of the Lord, and find the knowledge of God. For the Lord giveth wisdom : out of his mouth cometh knowledge and understanding."—Prov. ii. 1–6. So also, as urged by the Apostle : " If any of you lack wisdom, let him ask of God, that giveth to all men liberally, and upbraideth not; and it shall be given him."—Jas. i. 5.

Then by communion we know and experience God's spirit and love. Here is intimacy; here he reveals himself to those who love him, as he does not to the world. See this taught by our divine Lord : " Judas saith unto him, not Iscariot, Lord, how is it that thou wilt manifest thyself unto us, and not unto the world ? Jesus answered and said unto him, If a man love me he will keep my words ; and my Father will love him, and we will come unto him, and make our abode with him."—John xiv. 22–23.

Here then are the appointed means for increasing in the knowledge of God.

Let the subject,

1. Lead to personal inquiry.

Are we increasing in the knowledge of God ? Is it more clear, full, harmonious, satisfying, and consoling.

2. Are we earnestly desirous that this increasing should be more and more ? Are we diligent in the use of the means ? Can we distinctly assure ourselves that we have made progress ; and that we still desire to do so, day by day ?

3. Are there any who know not God ? Of such speaks the Apostle ; " some men have not the knowledge of God ;" he adds, " I speak this to your shame." How reproachful is this state ! How fraught with evil ! How finally disastrous must it be !

Well, we reveal God to you this day, by the proclamation of his truth. We call on you to view the great revelation he has given of himself in his works and ways. We ask you to seek his favor and live. Obey him—love him—enjoy him, as offered to you in Christ Jesus his Son. He who believes in Christ, thus comes to the saving knowledge of God. And unbelief is necessarily associated with spiritual ignorance of God ; and must terminate in the blackness of darkness forever.

———————

XXXII.—THE OFFICE AND WORK OF A DAYSMAN.

" Neither is there any daysman betwixt us, that might lay his hand upon us both."—*Job* ix. 33.

In all cases where two constructions are possible, it is the line of charity to give it that which is favorable to the party in question.

Now Job has been speaking of himself in strong language, and it may be interpreted either greatly to his disparagement, or may be so considered as to give a meaning rather honorable to his godly sincerity. We feel, therefore, that the latter course of interpretation is the one we ought to take. He had to clear himself against a gross charge of hypocrisy brought against him by his mistaken friends; but he had also to stand before God, and to contemplate the divine character and goodness in the sufferings he was called to endure. He seems to represent the impossibility of his attaining a purity which would meet the divine requirements. " If I wash myself with snow-water, and make my hands never so clean ; yet shalt thou plunge me in the ditch, and mine own clothes shall abhor me :" ver. 30, 31. He assigns as reasons for this conclusion. " For he is not a man, as I am, that I should answer him, and we should come together in judgment :" ver. 32. He then laments that there is no daysman, one who might bring the matter to a complete and satisfactory termination.

Now, what Job did not seem to realize at this period of his sorrow, we have in the person of the Lord Jesus Christ ;—and such is the application we shall give the subject. Notice then,

I. *What the office of a daysman involves.*

II. *What it includes.*

And,

III. *The end to be realized.*

I. *What the office of a daysman involves.*

It involves,

(1.) The idea of two parties, for whom he is to act.

(2.) That the two parties are at difference, and not in agreement with each other.

Now this is the case between God and man.

GOD has claims and demands on us. These claims are righteous and just. They are reasonable and good; and, therefore, ought to be met.

MAN has rejected these claims,—has set himself up in defiance of God; and is, therefore, exposed to the divine displeasure.

(3.) A daysman involves the idea that one or the other of the parties, or both, are willing to have the matter set at rest, by the interposition of a third person.

Now, God is thus willing to appeal to another. He has appealed to the heavens and the earth. He has declared his holiness, and truth, and goodness. But, as the sinner is a man—weak, and ignorant, and impotent—God, in mercy to him, has referred the whole to a daysman. He has called and sent forth one, who should, in the language of the text, lay his hand upon both.

Now, notice in reference to a daysman,

II. *What it includes.*

1. *As it regards the person of the daysman.*

He should not be inferior to either party; if so, his decision would not be likely to be satisfactory. He should be equal to both in authority, in dignity, and in wisdom. Now, such is the Lord Jesus Christ—a holy, wise, and perfect man; but also one in power, dignity, majesty, and glory with the Father. The loved and honored of the Father; possessing the divine nature, and the divine perfections; one infallible in judgment; and essentially righteous in his decisions.

2. *The work of the daysman.*

(1.) He must hear both parties, and know all the grounds of the differences existing. This he must know clearly and fully.

(2.) He must judge between both, weighing the whole, for and against, and so do this that every existing point of difference shall be examined, and have its due place and importance in the settlement to be made.

(3.) He must have a right to decide the matter in dispute; both must yield the matter implicitly to him, and abide by his conclusion.

Now, the Lord Jesus occupies this position. He perfectly knows the whole subject. He can infallibly and impartially judge it. He has in fact decided the matter in dispute. In this decision,

(1.) He has vindicated the divine character as righteous and perfect.

(2.) He has pronounced the divine law as holy, just, and good.

(3.) He has convicted man of sin and rebellion against God. His decision is, that God is in the right, and man in the wrong.

He has therefore condemned sin, and justified the interests of holiness. He has honored the Father in his moral government, and thrown the whole blame on man, the delinquent transgressor of the laws of heaven. Nay, he has even shown how conspicuously the divine goodness has been exhibited to man, so that the sinner has not one good pretext for his hostility to God; not one reasonable pretext for the state of opposition and rebellion which he occupies. Oh how glorious and good, how grand and merciful is God, as revealed to us in the teachings of the Lord Jesus; and especially, as revealed to us in the benignant and gracious mission of the world's Redeemer!

But then consider,

III. *The end to be realized.*

That is, if possible to reunite, so to adjudge that reconciliation shall be effected. Now Christ has just done this.

(1.) He demanded for God's law perfect obedience.

(2.) He demanded that the full penalty of transgression be paid.

Man could not do the first, and the second would involve his eternal condemnation. Well, to meet this extreme exigency, the Daysman engages to do both for man—to be the law magnifier and repairer—to bear its curse, and thus he relieved man from the consequences of his guilt and rebellion. It is in this light that we see the full meaning of those striking passages which relate to the atoning work of Christ. Hence the apostle says, "For as many as are of the works of the law are under the curse: for it is written, cursed is every one that continueth not in all things which are written in the book of the law to do them. But that no man is justified by the law in the sight of God is evident: for, the just shall live by faith. And the law is not of faith : but the man that doeth them shall live in them. Christ hath redeemed us from the curse of the law, being made a curse for us : for it is written, cursed is every one that hangeth on a tree."—Gal. iii. 10–13. And again, "For what the law could not do, in that it was weak through the flesh, God sending his own Son in the likeness of sinful flesh, and for sin condemned sin in the flesh."—Rom. viii. 3. And still more explicitly, "For when we were yet without strength, in due time Christ died for the ungodly."—Rom. v. 6. And the extent of this gracious propitiatory interposition the apostle states in the summary of a lengthy paragraph, thus : "Therefore, as by the offence of one, judgment came upon all men to condemnation ; even so by the righteousness of one, the free gift came upon all men unto justification of life. For as by one man's disobedience many were made sinners, so by the obedience of one shall many be made righteous. Moreover the law entered, that the offence might abound. But where sin abounded, grace did much more abound ; that as sin hath reigned unto death, even so might grace reign through righteousness unto eternal life by Jesus Christ our Lord."—Rom. v. 18–21.

Here then the great work to be done, that which was essential to the restoration of the sinner to the favor of God, Jesus Christ undertook and fully accomplished. Thus every impediment in the way of our salvation was removed, and now full justification might be preached to the unworthy delinquent, and he can be entirely absolved from all the consequences of his transgression.

You will easily perceive that the Daysman by his work,

1. Enables God honorably to be reconciled to the sinner. "Whom God hath set forth to be a propitiation through faith in his blood, to declare his righteousness for the remission of sins that are past, through the forbearance of God ; to declare, I say, at this time his righteousness : that he might be just, and the justifier of him which believeth in Jesus."—Rom. iii. 25, 26. So that God in releasing the sinner from the penalty of his sins, has not relaxed his claims, nor compromised his holiness, nor sacrificed his justice, nor weakened his holy law ; but he has rather given a fresh and grander expression to his character as a moral governor, by giving his Son to be the penalty bearer of man's transgression.

2. The Daysman now enables the sinner to return again to God. He has laid his hand on both. God appeals to the work of Jesus and pardons the sinner. The sinner appeals to the work of Jesus and receives pardon. So that in Christ there is perfect reconciliation between God and man. So the apostle avers, "And all things are of God, who hath reconciled us to himself by Jesus Christ, and hath given to us the ministry of reconciliation ; to wit, that God was in Christ, reconciling the world unto himself, not imputing their trespasses unto them ; and hath committed unto us the word of reconciliation."—2 Cor. v. 18, 19.

We see then, so far as God is concerned the matter is settled. An everlasting righteousness has been brought in ; and he can be merciful to every transgressor. But the sinner must sue for the benefits of righteousness, and seek it by and in Christ Jesus. He must become a willing, consenting party, or he loses all the advantages of the work of Christ the Daysman. And if he stubbornly and wickedly holds out, so far as his salvation is concerned, Christ has lived and died in vain.

Here then we remark,

1. The grand doctrine of the gospel is brought before us. For the very essence of the gospel is this, that we have pardon, holiness, and eternal life, in and by Christ Jesus. That Jesus is the way to the Father ; the one and only Mediator between God and man, and that in his name remission of sins may now be freely offered to all people.

2. The faith demanded of the sinner. The deed of reconcilement hath the signature of God to it. God declares he wants no more in the way of sacrifice or merit to secure his favor. He is well pleased in the finished work of his Son.

But the sinner must append his signature too, by expressing his satisfaction with Christ's mediation, and he must rely on it entirely as the ground of his acceptance with God. Nothing else will do but this. All things else needful to the reconciliation have been done.

3. Unbelief thus becomes the most heinous of all sins ; for unbelief decides on resisting the divine claims—on treating the work of Christ with avowed contempt—and on persisting in an open course of enmity towards God.

So that the unbeliever necessarily exposes himself to the wrath of God and eternal death. See how this is expressed: "He that believeth on the Son hath everlasting life: and he that believeth not the Son shall not see life; but the wrath of God abideth on him."—John iii. 36.

To such we reveal the doctrine of God's mercy in Christ Jesus, and urge an instant and earnest attention to his sacrificial work.

"From the cross uplifted high,
  Where the Saviour deigns to die,
  What melodious sounds I hear!
  Bursting on my ravish'd ear:
  Love's redeeming work is done,
  Come and welcome, sinner, come.

Sprinkled now with blood the throne,
  Why beneath thy burden groan?
  On my pierced body laid,
  Justice owns the ransom paid;
  Bow the knee, and kiss the Son,
  Come and welcome, sinner, come."

XXXIII.—THE BLISS OF THE PARDONED.

"Saying, Blessed are they whose iniquities are forgiven, and whose sins are covered. Blessed is the man to whom the Lord will not impute sin."—Rom. iv. 7, 8.

The text stands in connection with the Apostle's reasoning, in reference to the free justification of the sinner by faith, without the deeds of the law. But we do not intend to take up that argument, as it would involve the necessity to go through the greater part of the preceding chapter, and the whole of this. But we just wish to look at the text, as it stands alone; for it contains a complete and most interesting theme in itself; and is one in which every soul of man is deeply and eternally interested. You will see too, that it is a quotation from the thirty-second Psalm. So that it had been uttered by divine inspiration, more than a thousand years before Paul quotes it, by David, the sweet singer of Israel.

It will be seen also from this that the real essence of religion has been the same in all ages. Just as men have always been sinners, and always unable to deliver themselves from guilt and its consequences; so God from the beginning has been rich in mercy to all who have believed in his revealed will of grace and compassion towards our perishing world.

Doubtless, Abel experienced this pardoning grace, as he offered his sacrifice in the exercise of faith in the promised Messiah. So Abraham and the devout patriarchs, and prophets, and godly men of all ages, up to the period of Christ's manifestation in the flesh. Let us then look at this all-important subject as presented in the text. And in doing so,

Observe then,

I. *The state described.*

And,

II. *The blessedness declared.*

Notice,

I. *The state described.*

Now this state most obviously implies,

1. *Previous guilt.*

When there is no guilt, there can be no pardon. So that it is clear from the text, that the divine law had been violated—that sin had been committed—that iniquity had marked the heart and life. Now these remarks apply to all mankind. "As it is written, There is none righteous, no, not one. There is none that understandeth, there is none that seeketh after God. They are all gone out of the way, they are together become unprofitable; there is none that doeth good, no, not one."—Rom. iii. 10-12. All our race are guilty, depraved, and condemned before God; and on this ground of man's pollution and misery, is the great scheme of divine mercy and salvation revealed, and its blessings offered to him. The text refers,

2. *To Divine pardon.*

"Whose iniquities are forgiven."

Now, on this point, observe the momentous truths involved. That God alone can forgive sin—he has expressed himself as a forgiving God, as delighting to pardon. He forgives sin, however, only through the medium of sacrifice. "Without shedding of blood there can be no remission." That sacrifice is the Lord Jesus Christ in whose blood we have redemption, even the remission of sin. He forgives only in connection with repentance and faith,—a change of mind and life in reference to sin and faith in God's gracious word as waiting in plenteous love to pardon. Now, each of these points deserves our most serious consideration; for our pardon must flow from God's rich mercy, through Christ's sacrifice, and be received by repentance and faith on the part of the sinner. Hence the urgent exhortation—"Repent ye therefore, and be converted, that your sins may be blotted out when the times of refreshing shall come from the presence of the Lord."—Acts iii. 19.

Observe in the text, a reference,

3. *To the entire removal of sin.*

"Whose sins are covered." No longer visible. No longer in the book—but effaced. "Blotted out as a cloud." "Cast as a stone into the depths of the sea." Put away into everlasting oblivion.

Now, here the full and everlasting character of pardon is presented. So far as it can be, the sin, if thus forgiven, is annihilated—it shall be remembered no more. However diligently sought for, it shall not be found. God remembers our pardoned sins no more. His pardon is a complete and final act.

The text refers,

4. *To the righteous acceptance of the pardoned, with God.*

"To whom the Lord will not impute sin." God has now no charge against him. (See Romans viii. 1, &c.) He treats him as though he had never sinned; deals with him as a righteous person. Thus all such are with God accepted, sanctified, and justified before him. It may also refer to the great truth, that though the obedience of such is not perfect, yet the heart being renewed, and the spirit upright, and the soul resting on the Lord Jesus, God constantly accepts their persons and services in him, and imputes not sin unto them—though rigidly he might do so; for, if he marked iniquity who could stand?

Such then is the state described in the text. And this state was not peculiar to David, or to the early Christians, but is the happy state of all who have believed on the Lord Jesus. For all such enjoy the full and entire remission of sins; all such are accepted and beloved of God, and are holy and approved of him. Every child of God has been brought into this most gracious state of pardon and favor.

Observe then,

II. *The blessedness declared.*

"Blessed are they whose iniquities are forgiven." You see the same is repeated in the text—"Blessed is the man to whom the Lord will not impute sin."

1. *He is blessed with a personal interest in redeeming love.*

The love of God has been predicted published, embodied in Christ, and preached in the gospel. But the person in the text re-

alizes it. It comes home to his heart and conscience; he feels it—knows it—can declare it. For the love of God is shed abroad in his heart by the Holy Ghost given to him. He exclaims with delightful transport, "I love him because he first loved me." He can sing experimentally—

"My God is reconciled,
His pardoning voice I hear;
He owns me for his child,
I can no longer fear:
With confidence I now draw nigh,
And 'Father, Abba, Father!' cry."

2. *He is blessed with all the results of the Saviour's work.*

It is a truth that Christ has come from heaven—lived—suffered—died—risen and ascended to heaven. But the pardoned sinner knows and enjoys this in his experience. He can say, He loved me and gave himself for me; and Christ dwells in his heart the hope of glory. He is Christ's, and Christ is his. He has found the peerless pearl. All that Christ is, and has, and has done, and is doing, and will forever do, belong to him; and how unspeakable the treasure—to possess a whole Christ in all his glorious fulness, and in all his comprehensive work.

3. *He is blessed with the peaceful enjoyment of the divine Spirit.*

The result of the forgiveness of sins is the gift of the Holy Spirit. So Peter preached on the day of Pentecost. "Then Peter said unto them, Repent, and be baptized every one of you in the name of Jesus Christ for the remission of sins, and ye shall receive the gift of the Holy Ghost."—Acts. ii. 38. So the apostle avers: "But if the Spirit of him that raised up Jesus from the dead dwell in you, he that raised up Christ from the dead shall also quicken your mortal bodies by his Spirit that dwelleth in you. Therefore, brethren, we are debtors, not to the flesh, to live after the flesh. For if ye live after the flesh, ye shall die: but if ye through the Spirit do mortify the deeds of the body, ye shall live. For as many as are led by the Spirit of God, they are the sons of God. For ye have not received the spirit of bondage again to fear; but ye have received the Spirit of adoption, whereby we cry, Abba, Father. The Spirit itself beareth witness with our spirit, that we are the children of God."—Rom. viii. 11–16. Now it is evident the Holy Spirit is God's great gift under the New Testament dispensation; that which Christ pronounced as the climax of the divine munificence; and is designed to be the source of holiness, peace, light and joy to the Christian. Hence Christ said, "And I will pray the Father, and he shall give you another Comforter, that he may abide with you forever; even the Spirit of truth; whom the world cannot receive, because it seeth him not, neither knoweth him: but ye know him; for he dwelleth with you, and shall be in you. I will not leave you comfortless: I will come to you."—John xiv. 16–18.

4. *They are favored with an interest in all the blessings of the new Covenant.*

Look at its rich blessings; beginning with pardon, and terminating in eternal glory. Its glorious privileges—sonship and friendship with Christ—"Heirs of God." Its countless promises, like the brilliant stars of the firmament. Its heavenly enjoyments—fellowship with God, and with his Son Jesus Christ, and blessed communion with all his people. Its eternal glories—a crown—a kingdom—a throne; and all inseparably connected with everlasting felicity, and pleasures for evermore.

Now, such is the blessedness of the man whose sin is forgiven. And, observe also, it is present blessedness. Not past, or only future, but present; he is now the blessed man. It is real blessedness; yea, superlatively higher than any thing earth can give. Not mere show, but that which is solid and satisfactory. It is also a blessedness which shall endure forever.

It is impossible to do more than merely paint in feeble outline, the rich course of mercies which they are called to enjoy, who have experienced the pardoning love of God. For with this stupendous act of the divine clemency, there is given to the happy believer a chain of promises, the highest link of which unites him to Christ's throne and joy in heaven.

We ask then in conclusion, as to this blessedness,

(1.) Is it yours? Do you enjoy it? Do you exhibit its results? If so, rejoice in it, and remember everywhere and in every state, that you are God's blessed people. And let this remembrance be grateful and obedient; by this spirit and life, show forth Christ's praise, and the riches and sanctifying power of his grace.

Observe of this pardon,

(2.) It is the offer of God in the gospel to all men. "Be it known unto you there-fore, men and brethren, that through this man is preached unto you the forgiveness of sins: and by him all that believe are justified from all things, from which ye could not be justified by the law of Moses. Beware, therefore, lest that come upon you, which is spoken of by the prophets: Behold, ye despisers, and wonder and perish: for I work a work in your days, a work which ye shall in no wise believe, though a man declare it unto you."—Acts xiii. 39–40.

God who is most blessed, and whose blessedness is the source of all blessings to his creatures, waits to confer this favor through Christ his son, on all who repent and believe on his name.

For this the gospel is preached—invitations of mercy sent out—expostulations of divine pity uttered; so that the most depraved and guilty need not remain ignorant, guilty, and perishing, but if he will come to God by faith in Jesus, he shall be freely received, graciously pardoned, fully blessed, and finally and eternally saved into the enjoyment of glory, immortality, and eternal life.

How sweetly appropriate the hymn of the devout Doddridge—

"Hark how the gospel trumpet sounds!
  'Tis a delightful voice:
' Prisoners of death, no longer groan:
  Ye broken hearts, rejoice.'

Pardon to sinners is proclaimed
  By their affronted God;
'Tis God beseeches to accept
  Peace made by Jesus' blood.

When vengeance might have crushed to death
  The poor rebellious worms,
The God of love proposes peace
  In most alluring forms.

What heart such kindness can resist,
  Or spurn such wondrous grace?
Come, sinners, hear your Maker's voice,
  And take in heaven your place."

XXXIV.—THE WONDERS OF CHRIST'S LOVE.

"May be able to comprehend with all saints what is the breadth, and length, and depth, and height; and to know the love of Christ, which passeth knowledge."—*Eph.* iii. 18, 19.

EVERY word of the concluding part of the text might well furnish enough of matter for a profitable discourse.

" Christ !"—what discourse could exhaust that theme ! When should we have done with all the great essential particulars connected with him ? His various offices—work—sufferings—and glory. Then the " love of Christ,"—the great spring—the eternal fountain—the active cause and source of every blessing—the glory and blessedness of Christ's nature. Then, " to know,"—clearly to discern and perceive the nature, peculiarities, excellences, and value, of this " love."

How rich, then, is the text before us ! We can only take a few feeble glances at some of the all-important truths contained in it.

We request your consideration, then,

I. *To the love of Christ.*

II. *To some of its dimensions.*

III. *To our experimental knowledge of it.*

IV. *To a few of its unknowable features.*

Let us advert, then,

I. *To the love of Christ.*

Now the love of Christ to our sinful race, was a love,

1. *Of rich mercy and pure compassion.*

Not an admiring love of excellences; for we were vile and polluted. Not a complacent affection of delight. But a feeling of commiserating pity and compassion, where there was every thing to condemn, abhor, and hate; for there was no trait of loveliness in us.

Consider,

2. *The general and self-denying character of the love of Christ.*

Not mere pity; not a powerful emotion only; but it was love embodied in his nature—undertaking humiliation, suffering, and death. He became a man of sorrows and griefs, to effect our redemption. " For ye know the grace of our Lord Jesus Christ, that, though he was rich, yet for your sakes he became poor, that ye through his poverty might be rich."—2 Cor. viii. 8, 9. He loved us and gave himself for us—Gethsemane and the cross—how they attest it !

Notice,

3. *The grand objects contemplated by its manifestation.*

Christ, in his love to us, contemplated our delivery from guilt—from moral defilement—the curse of the divine law—and from eternal death. Then its positive design was, our salvation from all evil, and to the enjoyment of peace, holiness, and eternal life—that we might " not perish, but have everlasting life." These are the three grand features of the love of Christ to our dying world.

Notice, then,

II. *Some of its dimensions.*

The text directs us,

1. *To its breadth.*

Now this idea may refer to the extent and multitude of its objects. Did he love all men, or merely some ? Did he die for all, or only for a few ? If only for a very few, I do not see how its breadth can be matter for wondrous admiration. But his love did extend to the whole world, and to every creature. Our entire species are all inclosed in it ; not one soul left out. All were guilty—all were miserable—all were condemned—all were perishing—and he took upon himself the " iniquity of us all."

The rejection of this love by some, and their ruin thereby, does not affect the love itself.

2. *Its length.*

Or the durability of this love. A love preceding the world's existence, and lasting beyond the end of time. Properly and essentially eternal; coeval with Christ's own being. It was in his heart before he had formed the world, or created one responsible being; and runs parallel with all time, and to the eternal ages to come.

Then there is,

3. *Its depth.*

This may well refer to the condition of its objects, to which we have already referred. It stooped down to earth—to its rebels, hateful haters of God and of one another. The poet has well said—

" At hell's dark door we lay."

On the very verge of the pit. The Bible says " we were children of wrath,"—" ungodly." How fully this was established in the treatment Christ received ! He came to his own, but his own rejected him, and put him to death, and preferred Barabbas, who was a murderer.

But notice, also,

4. *Its height.*

This is seen in what this love confers ; the celestial blessings it bestows, and the dignities and glories it reveals. It raises fallen men to Christ's favor—likeness—sonship—heirship of God, and of his eternal kingdom and glory. Hence, we see what it comprehends, in the prayer of the Lord Jesus, offered on behalf of his ransomed people—

"And the glory which thou gavest me, I have given them; that they may be one, even as we are one; I in them, and thou in me, that they may be made perfect in one; and that the world may know that thou hast sent me, and hast loved them, as thou hast loved me. Father, I will that they also, whom thou hast given me, be with me where I am; that they may behold my glory, which thou hast given me: for thou lovedst me before the foundation of the world."—John xvii. 22–24. And the final sublime exaltation of the beatified saint is expressed in that rich promise—"To him that overcometh will I grant to sit with me in my throne, even as I also overcame, and am set down with my Father in his throne." —Rev. iii. 21.

Such, then, are the glorious dimensions of the Saviour's love. But notice in the text a reference,

III. *To the experimental knowledge of it.*

"To know the love of Christ, which passeth knowledge."

To know it,

1. *As revealed to us in the divine word.*

The Holy Spirit has inspired a blessed revelation of it. This is in fact the very heart and life of the gospel. It should be heard, and read, and meditated on, so that the word of Christ may dwell in us richly. Now it is by seeing it in the sacred pages of the divine book, and from them bringing it to bear on ourselves by faith, that we attain to a spiritual apprehension of it. And the word of God, while it is precious to us on every possible account, yet it is pre-eminently so, as it contains the striking record of the Saviour's love. Christ is to the word what the pearl is to the casket, or the Shekinah to the temple. The Scriptures in themselves would be beautiful, marvellous, and interesting, but they are also saving, as revealing to us the love and work of the Lord Jesus Christ.

To know it,

2. *As experienced in our hearts.*

To know it by its being shed abroad in our souls by the Holy Ghost. To know it thus really, and for ourselves. To feel its melting and renewing power: to be saved by it from the love of sin, and to the love of holiness. This is the inward assurance and personal result of faith in the revelation of it, as given in the gospel.

To know it,

3. *In its transforming influence.*

Christ's love transforms the heart and life —subordinates the emotions to God, and enables the believer to exclaim, "We love him because he first loved us!"

It produces in us the mind of Christ—it gives tenderness and affection to the heart— spirituality to the mind—obedience to the life, and holiness to the character. This is to know the love of Christ in demonstration and in power: and we should know this more and more; we should grow in it, until like fire it has consumed every evil element within us, and transmuted our whole being into Christ's holy and divine nature. "But we all, with open face beholding as in a glass the glory of the Lord, are changed into the same image from glory to glory, even as by the Spirit of the Lord."—2 Cor. iii. 18.

"Whereby are given unto us exceeding great and precious promises: that by these ye might be partakers of the divine nature, having escaped the corruption that is in the world through lust."—2 Pet. i. 4.

Yet observe the text refers,

IV. *To the unknowable features of this love.*

"Which passeth knowledge." Now, much as we may know of Christ's love—and we may know all that is essential to salvation, and be eternally increasing in it—yet in many particulars it is beyond our comprehension, and "passeth knowledge."

It does so,

1. *In its rise.*

We cannot trace it to its springing forth; nor assign an adequate reason for it. All we can say is, that he "so loved us."

It does so,

2. *In its fulness.*

Men may compute the dimensions of the ocean, and its contents; and the sun, and its light; but this ocean of love—this source of light and grace, passeth knowledge.

It is so,

3. *In its results.*

We have said something of them, but there is a vast, infinite, and eternal, beyond, that we cannot record. For if eye hath not seen, nor ear heard, nor heart conceived, of the blessings this love has provided for us here—how can we judge fully, and completely, of the unending bliss and glory it has laid up for us in the future world? Eternity alone will unfold to us the joy and felicity procured for us by the love of Jesus.

Then, in conclusion, learn,

(1.) That the gospel message makes known this love to our perishing race. And thus it is, that the sound of the gospel should be music to our ears, and melody to our hearts. Oh, hear the gospel with joy, and receive it into your hearts with gladness!

(2.) The knowledge of this love is the great experimental privilege of the believer. He who receives the gospel by faith, receives this love into his soul, and thus he knows of a truth the love of Christ towards him.

(3.) This love should ever fill our hearts with spiritual transport and delight.

Oh yes, this is the theme of that adoring song which the celestial hosts sing in heaven; and which is described as a new song. "And they sung a new song, saying, Thou art worthy to take the book, and to open the seals thereof: for thou wast slain, and hast redeemed us to God by thy blood out of every kindred, and tongue, and people, and nation; and hast made us unto our God, kings and priests; and we shall reign on the earth. And I beheld, and I heard the voice of many angels round about the throne and the beasts and the elders; and the number of them was ten thousand times ten thousand, and thousands of thousands; saying with a loud voice, Worthy is the Lamb that was slain, to receive power, and riches, and wisdom, and strength, and honor, and glory, and blessing."—Rev. v. 9–12.

(4.) This love will command our loftiest and closest contemplations through all eternity. We may study it, and praise it here; and we may long with the poet—

"That the music of his name,
Refresh our souls in death."

Yea, more, we may resolve,

" This will we sing, till nature fail,
Till sense and language die;"

And, in the language of a blissful hope, expect

"Then to resume the pleasing theme,
In happier worlds on high."

Amen.

XXXV.—THE OVERTHROW OF BABYLON.

"Prepare the table, watch in the watch-tower, eat and drink; arise, ye princes, and anoint the shield."—*Isa.* xxi. 5.

Our text is a part of a vision which Isaiah had in reference to Babylon. The language he employs is energetic and poetical. He describes the effect the vision had upon himself: "Therefore are my loins filled with pain: pangs have taken hold upon me, as the pangs of a woman that travaileth: I was bowed down at the hearing of it; I was dismayed at the seeing of it. My heart panted, fearfulness affrighted me: the night of my pleasure hath he turned into fear unto me."—Isa. xxi. 3–4. He saw Babylon apparently secure, and filled with pleasure and feasts. Suddenly its invasion and overthrow are brought before his mind; and our text, in one short sentence, states the rapid change from feasting to ruin—from joy to desolation—which that city experienced.

Let it be remembered that this vision of Isaiah's was at least one hundred and twenty years before the events so graphically portrayed occurred.

In the further consideration of the subject, we will,

I. *Take a rapid view of the destined city.*

II. *The particulars of the vision Isaiah had, and its literal fulfilment.*

And,

III. *The practical lessons which it suggests.*

Let us,

I. *Take a rapid view of the destined city.*

The city of Babylon is supposed to have been built by the first descendants of Noah, two thousand two hundred and thirty-four years before Christ. It was enlarged by Nimrod, about two thousand years before Christ; and almost rebuilt by the Assyrian queen, Semiramis, twelve hundred years before Christ. It was afterwards enlarged and beautified to a great degree of splendor and magnificence, by Nebuchadnezzar.

Babylon stood in the midst of an immense plain, and was divided into two parts, by the river Euphrates. The city formed a complete square, and extended to four hundred and eighty furlongs in compass. Each of the four sides of the city had twenty-five gates of solid brass; and at every corner was a strong watch-tower. The city was composed of fifty streets, fifteen miles long, and one hundred and fifty feet wide. It contained six hundred and seventy-six squares. The walls were eighty-seven feet broad, and three hundred and fifty feet high. It contained two magnificent palaces, united by a long subterraneous passage. In connection with one of them, there were hanging gardens and elevated terraces. In this city also,

THE OVERTHROW OF BABYLON

was the celebrated Temple of Belus, six hundred feet high; and which had eight towers at equal distances from each other. In this temple, it is said, was a golden image, forty feet in height, and equal in value to three and a half millions sterling; besides other sacred Trias, said to be worth forty-two millions of pounds sterling.

It may be that some of these statements are exaggerated; but making allowance for these, no doubt Babylon was at least six times larger than London and its suburbs. Enriched with the spoils of the East, it seemed to be the queen city of the world, and was known for its luxury, revelry, pride, and oppression.

Let us just look at two or three descriptions of it, as given in the Scriptures.

"And Babylon, the glory of kingdoms, the beauty of the Chaldees' excellency, shall be as when God overthrew Sodom and Gomorrah."—Isa. xiii. 19. "For thou hast said in thine heart, I will ascend into heaven, I will exalt my throne above the stars of God: I will sit also upon the mount of the congregation, in the sides of the north: I will ascend above the heights of the clouds; I will be like the Most High."—Isa. xiv. 13–14.

Such was Babylon; the city destined to entire and irrevocable ruin.

Observe,

II. *The particulars of the vision Isaiah had, and its literal fulfilment.*

Our text has reference to one exact period in the history of Babylon. For two years Cyrus had been besieging it; he had tried all sorts of methods to enter it, and to starve its inhabitants. At length he learned that there was to be a great feast in the city, and he resolved that night, by diverting the stream of the river, to enter it by its channels.

Now, it was at this time that the infatuated monarch, Belshazzar, is supposed to have used the language of the text. He issues an edict,

1. *For the festival.*

"Prepare the table." See the account of this: "Belshazzar the king made a great feast to a thousand of his lords, and drank wine before the thousand. Belshazzar, whiles he tasted the wine, commanded to bring the golden and silver vessels which his father Nebuchadnezzar had taken out of the temple which was in Jerusalem; that the king, and his princes, his wives, and his concubines might drink therein. Then they brought the golden vessels that were taken out of the temple of the house of God which was at Jerusalem; and the king, and his princes, his wives, and his concubines, drank in them. They drank wine, and praised the gods of gold, and of silver, of brass, of iron, of wood, and of stone."—Dan. v. 1–4.

He adds to this,

2. *That vigilance should be maintained.*

"Watch in the watch-tower." While we feast, let the guard be on the alert: let not the tower be deserted. This was prudent in itself; but the example now set of universal revelry, would quite counteract it.

3. *He now invites to the banquet.*

"Eat, drink;" dismiss care, enjoy life. Now let the music, and feasting, and the dance begin. But observe the semicolon in the text. Almost immediately—even before the feast is ended—the alarm is given; and the excited and affrighted monarch utters,

4. *The signal of war.*

"Arise, ye princes, anoint the shield." Peril is around us; the enemy is at the door. Fly from the banquet; let the trumpet sound for battle; anoint the shield, that the weapons might not take effect. The ancient shield was made of the skin of the rhinoceros, or leather rubbed over with oil, that it might be slippery to the pointed dart or javelin.

Now Cyrus is represented by Xenophon as saying on that eventful night: "Now," says he, "let us go against them. Many of them are asleep—many of them intoxicated—and all of them are unfit for battle."

His army entered the city, and imitated in their cries the revelry of the intoxicated, and forced their way into the banqueting hall, while Daniel is interpreting the writing on the wall.

"And this is the writing that was written, MENE, MENE, TEKEL, UPHARSIN. This is the interpretation of the thing: MENE—God hath numbered thy kingdom, and finished it. TEKEL—thou art weighed in the balances, and art found wanting, PERES—thy kingdom is divided, and given to the Medes and Persians. Then commanded Belshazzar, and they clothed Daniel with scarlet, and put a chain of gold about his neck, and made a proclamation concerning him, that he should be the third ruler in the kingdom. In that night was Belshazzar the king of the Chaldeans slain."—Dan. v. 25–30.

Now such was the prediction of Isaiah,

and most exact and literal was its fulfilment.

Consider then,

III. *The practical lessons which it suggests.*

Notice,

1. *The inevitable certainty of the divine purposes.*

God had doomed the wicked city, and nothing could save it. How sublimely true the confession of Nebuchadnezzar: "And at the end of the days, I Nebuchadnezzar lifted up mine eyes unto heaven, and mine understanding returned unto me, and I blessed the Most High, and I praised and honored him that liveth forever, whose dominion is an everlasting dominion, and his kingdom is from generation to generation: and all the inhabitants of the earth are reputed as nothing: and he doeth according to his will in the army of heaven, and among the inhabitants of the earth: and none can stay his hand, or say unto him, What doest thou?"—Dan. iv. 34–35.

How true too that passage,—

"When he giveth quietness, who then can make trouble? and when he hideth his face, who then can behold him? whether it be done against a nation, or against a man only."—Job xxxiv. 29. Power, wealth, armies, avail not when he pleases. God's foreknowledge of all events is absolute, clear, and infallibly unerring. And his holy purposes, grounded on that foreknowledge, are in every case inevitable. There is no contingency, no peradventure with him, whose infinite mind at one glance, sees all from the beginning to the end.

Learn,

2. *The destructive influence of worldly pleasure.*

How infatuated the condition of Belshazzar, and the princes of Babylon, with a formidable army at the gates, to yield themselves up to feasting and revelry. How in this instance, the banquet became the carnival of death. Is it not equally so in individual cases? Is not the path of dissipation the way of death? The sensual banquet and perdition, are closely connected with each other.

3. *The manifest truth of God's word.*

Here was the prophecy of Belshazzar's ruin, distinctly stated one hundred and seventy years before, and it came literally to pass, and by the person named by the prophet.

None of the persons were living who should act their part in this fearful drama, neither Belshazzar nor Cyrus, nor the Captains, nor the soldiery. But time rolls on. The era arrives—the men appear—the crisis comes, and the city of cities is utterly demolished. How true is God's word! how surely what he has spoken shall come to pass, whether of threatening or promise: the language uttered by Jehovah to Isaiah is most forcible:—"For as the rain cometh down, and the snow from heaven, and returneth not thither, but watereth the earth, and maketh it bring forth and bud, that it may give seed to the sower, and bread to the eater: so shall my word be that goeth forth out of my mouth: it shall not return unto me void, but it shall accomplish that which I please, and it shall prosper in the thing whereto I sent it."—Isa. lv. 10–11.

Let not the admonition of the apostle Peter be forgotten—"But, beloved, be not ignorant of this one thing, that one day is with the Lord as a thousand years, and a thousand years as one day. The Lord is not slack concerning his promise, as some men count slackness; but is long-suffering to us-ward, not willing that any should perish, but that all should come to repentance. But the day of the Lord will come as a thief in the night: in the which the heavens shall pass away with a great noise, and the elements shall melt with fervent heat, the earth also, and the works that are therein shall be burned up."—2 Peter iii. 8, 9, 10.

4. *In Babylon's overthrow we have a type of the ruin of mystical Babylon—Papal Rome.*

In how many things do the two cities resemble each other? In pomp, magnificence, riches, antiquity, and self-security. As Babylon too, had been the persecutor of God's Israel, so Rome of the saints. And God's word avers, that Rome's destruction shall be as certain, sudden, entire, and as universal, perpetual, and irrevocable, as that of Babylon.

See John's vision—

(1.) Of mystical Babylon, and its splendor.—"How much she hath glorified herself, and lived deliciously, so much torment and sorrow give her; for she saith in her heart, I sit a queen, and am no widow, and shall see no sorrow."—Rev. xviii. 7.

(2.) Of its destruction—"And after these things I saw another angel come down from heaven, having great power; and the earth was lightened with his glory. And he cried mightily with a strong voice, saying, Babylon the great is fallen, is fallen, and is become the habitation of devils, and the hold of every foul spirit, and a cage of every unclean and hateful bird."—Ver. 1, 2.

(3.) Of the suddenness of her overthrow—"Therefore shall her plagues come in one day, death, and mourning, and famine; and she shall be utterly burned with fire: for strong is the Lord God who judgeth her."—Ver. 8.

(4.) The consequence of it—"And a mighty angel took up a stone, like a great millstone, and cast it into the sea, saying, Thus with violence shall that great city Babylon be thrown down, and shall be found no more at all."—Ver. 21.

(5.) The joy this shall be to heaven and earth—"Rejoice over her, thou heaven, and ye holy apostles and prophets; for God hath avenged you on her."—Ver. 20. "And after these things I heard a great voice of much people in heaven, saying, Alleluia; salvation, and glory, and honor, and power, unto the Lord our God: for true and righteous are his judgments: for he hath judged the great whore, which did corrupt the earth with her fornication, and hath avenged the blood of his servants at her hand. And again they said, Alleluia. And her smoke rose up forever and ever."—Rev. xix. 1–3.

5. *In Babylon's overthrow we see the imminent peril of personal carnal security.*

This is true of all men at ease in sin. Men asleep under the sentence of the divine wrath. Wicked men, infatuated and thoughtless. Formal professors at ease in Zion. And what is the evident duty and safety of all such?

To awake—consider—repent. To fly to God, as a God of mercy in Christ Jesus, and thus escape his righteous displeasure, and final wrath.

XXXVI.—"IMMANUEL."

"Therefore the Lord himself shall give you a sign; Behold a virgin shall conceive, and bear a son, and shall call his name Immanuel."—*Isa.* vii. 14.

To Christ, it is said, all the prophets gave witness; but none so clearly, fully, and evangelically, as Isaiah. He dwells largely on Christ's person, offices, work and sufferings, and also on the glory that should follow. He points to his righteous kingdom, his gracious conquests, and final supremacy. From his prophecy, it would not be difficult to give an outline of Christ's ministry, and of the world's redemption.

But the text gives one view of Christ. It is the name most befitting his character—"Immanuel"—which being interpreted, signifies "God with us."

Now there are three leading ideas in the text,

I. *Christ's deity.*

He is God.

II. *Christ's gracious nearness to us.*

He is "God with us."

And,

III. *Christ's claims arising from these views of his character.*

I. *Christ's deity.*

He is Immanuel, "God." Now as to Christ's deity, we inquire,

1. *As to its clear signification.*

By it we mean that he is more than a messenger from God; more than a prophet; higher than the loftiest angel or seraph. That he is indeed in truth, in essence and nature, God. That he is essentially one with the Father; that he is God in the most supreme sense of the word. That his divine titles, attributes, and glory, are not those of a subordinate being, not merely official, but involve his real true Godhead.

Then consider,

2. *As to the possibility of the doctrine.*

Why should not God dwell in the tabernacle of the Redeemer's humanity? He did give the manifestation of his presence and glory in the cloud over the mercy-seat; and in the fiery pillar and cloud that went before Israel; and as possessing all resources, there is nothing incompatible with his power, to dwell in all his fulness in the manhood of Jesus bodily. To dispute the possibility of this, is to limit the Holy one of Israel. If God is Almighty, and can do every thing wise and just to be done, then he can most confessedly, tabernacle in our flesh, and be Immanuel, "God with us."

3. *As to the apparent probability of the doctrine.*

Look at Christ's attributes, and what he assumed. For instance, he was invested with all power. "All power," said he, "is given to me both in heaven and on earth." He was to impart all blessings. To give repentance to the sinner; pardon and regeneration to the believer; and eternal life to all his faithful disciples.

He was also to judge all men. All judgment, he said, was committed to him. He is to raise the dead; sit on the great tribunal; pass sentence on all intelligences—men and angels.

Now, do these seem offices likely to be delegated to a mere creature? Rather are they not the prerogatives of the supreme and ever blessed God?

Then note,

4. *As to the absolute certainty of the doctrine.*

The prophets say Christ is God. "How beautiful upon the mountain are the feet of him that bringeth good tidings, that publisheth peace; that bringeth good tidings of good, that publisheth salvation; that saith unto Zion, thy God reigneth."—Isa. liii. 7. Now it is clear that Christ is the glorious being here to be beheld, for he alone is King in Zion. Then nothing can be more direct than the anticipatory exclamation of the same Prophet—"For unto us a child is born, unto us a son is given: and the government shall be upon his shoulder: and his name shall be called Wonderful, Counsellor, the mighty God, the everlasting Father, the Prince of Peace."—Isa. viii. 6. So Jeremiah, in a prediction more expressly directed to Jesus, says—"Behold, the days come, saith the Lord, that I will raise unto David a righteous Branch, and a King shall reign and prosper, and shall execute judgment and justice in the earth. In his days Judah shall be saved, and Israel shall dwell safely: and this is his name whereby he shall be called, the Lord our righteousness."—Jer. xxiii. 5–6.

Evangelists and apostles say he is God. If the introduction to St. John's gospel is a revelation, and not a mystification, then Christ is truly God." "In the beginning was the Word, and the Word was with God, and the Word was God." "And the Word was made flesh, and dwelt among us (and we beheld his glory, the glory as of the only-begotten of the Father), full of grace and truth."—John i. 1 and 14. This plain testimony is corroborated in every particular by the apostle Paul. "Who is the image of the invisible God, the first-born of every creature. And he is before all things, and by him all things consist."—Col. i. 15 and 17. "Whose are the fathers, and of whom as concerning the flesh Christ came, who is over all, God blessed forever."—Rom. ix. 5. "Who, being in the form of God, thought it not robbery to be equal with God."—Phil. ii. 6.

So Peter concludes one of his epistles in the following ascriptions to Jesus—"But grow in grace, and in the knowledge of our Lord and Saviour Jesus Christ. To him be glory both now and forever. Amen."—2 Peter iii. 18.

Christ professed to be God. Hear his own testimony: "I and my Father are one."—John x. 30. And again, "Jesus saith unto him, Have I been so long time with you, and yet hast thou not known me, Philip? He that hath seen me hath seen the Father; and how sayest thou, then, show us the Father."—John xiv. 9. And once more—"And now, O Father, glorify thou me with thine own self, with the glory which I had with thee before the world was."—John xvii. 5.

So the Jews understood Christ, and therefore they charged him with blasphemy. The Father also declared Christ to be God. "For unto which of the angels said he at any time, thou art my Son, this day have I begotten thee? And again, I will be to him a Father, and he shall be to me a Son. And again, when he bringeth in the first-begotten into the world, he saith, and let all the angels of God worship him. And of the angels he saith, he maketh his angels spirits, and his ministers a flame of fire. But unto the Son he saith, thy throne, O God, is forever and ever: a sceptre of righteousness is the sceptre of thy kingdom."—Heb. i. 5–8.

And as such the hosts of heaven understand it; and hence they worship Christ as God. For John, in his celestial vision, bears witness thus—"And I beheld, and I heard the voice of many angels round about the throne and the beasts and the elders; and the number of them was ten thousand times ten thousand, and thousands of thousands; saying with a loud voice, worthy is the Lamb that was slain to receive power, and riches, and wisdom, and strength, and honor, and glory, and blessing. And every creature which is in heaven, and on the earth, and under the earth, and such as are in the sea, and all that are in them, heard I saying, blessing, and honor, and glory, and power, be unto him that sitteth upon the throne, and unto the Lamb orever and ever."—Rev. v. 11–14.

Here, then, the doctrine of the Redeemer's godhead is most clearly and fully established.

But notice,

II. *Christ's gracious nearness to us.*

"God with us." In his own essence—He is God above us, beyond our ken, or means of finding out. As the Governor of the world, he is God around us ; and, therefore, everywhere present.

As the holy Legislator of the moral creation, he is God justly displeased with us on account of our iniquities. As Immanuel, he is God " with us."

1. *God in our humanity.*

The son given, and the child born—the creator, and the creature—the eternal, and the one sent forth in the fulness of the times —the perfect, and the finite. He assumed our nature—took it upon him—was clothed with it—made of a woman, and was in all respects a man. Not only arrayed in our flesh, but also having a reasonable soul, and thus a perfect man—one of our common species, and brother of the whole race. Thus he was God " with us."

But he was,

2. *God our Saviour.*

With us—to feel as we feel ; to pity and commiserate our condition of guilt ; to show mercy to us and love us. With us—to do for us what is needful for our recovery, holiness, and salvation. With us—in our sins, by the voluntary assumption of our iniquity. With us—in our obligation to the whole law of God, by becoming obedient to that law. With us—in our sorrows, by sympathy and tenderest pity. With us—in our condemnation, by the substitution of himself to bear our sins in his own body on the tree.

With us—in all the stages and conditions of life. With us in the helplessness of infancy, in the growth of childhood, in the maturity of manhood. With us—in temptation, and affliction, in death, and in the grave. With us—as our deliverer and redeemer. "God with us," to bless and deliver us from all our iniquities and woes.

Then consider,

III. *Christ's claims arising from his being God with us.*

He claims our profound attention and regard. Here is the greatest wonder that the universe presents—God dwelling in our manhood. But he also claims our grateful love and confidence.

He comes near to us, to win our confidence and our love, as a man and as a brother—the God-man and the Saviour. Ought he not to have our most intense love, and loftiest praise ?

He claims our homage and obedience. In his wondrous character as God-man, he is our " Lord," and we are to obey him. He is to rule in us, and over us. We are to bow to him, and serve him with reverence and fear.

But he is to have our worship and self-devotion. We are to be his—his ransomed people, his loyal subjects, his cheerful disciples —to love, and praise, and adore, and serve him forever. " For none of us liveth to himself, and no man dieth to himself. For whether we live, we live unto the Lord ; and whether we die, we die unto the Lord : whether we live, therefore, or die, we are the Lord's."—Rom. xiv. 7, 8.

Now, such are Christ's claims as Immanuel, God " with us."

APPLICATION.

1. The subject should lead to the immediate subjection of all his enemies. Who can resist him ?

2. To the increased joy and ardent praise of his followers. What a glorious object for admiration, wonder, love, and praise !

3. To a firm confidence as to all the events of the future. None of his purposes can perish, none of his schemes can be frustrated, none of his gracious engagements can fail. The Christian is not called to depend on a finite arm, or on a created intelligence ; but to trust his body, soul, and spirit for all time, and for all eternity, to a Saviour whose glorious title is—IMMANUEL, GOD WITH US !

XXXVII.—SELFISHNESS.

" For none of us liveth to himself, and no man dieth to himself. For whether we live, we live unto the Lord ; and whether we die, we die unto the Lord : whether we live, therefore, or die, we are the Lord's."—*Rom.* xiv. 7, 8.

OUR text is meant to show the benevolent and spiritual character of true religion. The converted man lives to Jesus Christ; indeed Christ is his life—the source, the strength, the model, and the end of the Christian's life. Therefore it follows that the terms sel-fish and Christian mean opposite things : that no man can compound the two.

A Christian selfish man! A selfish Christian! How strange the very sound. No; the apostle avers, that "none of us liveth to himself;" but, "whether we live, we live unto the Lord ; and whether we die, we die unto the Lord." However naturally and practically selfish the heart may be, yet, when softened and renewed by the grace of God, it becomes soft, and tender, and benig-nant; and its emotions become spiritual, benevolent, and Christ-like.

We design, however, in this discourse, to try ourselves, and see whether self or Christ be the end and object of our life.

We ask, then,

I. *When do men live to self, and not to Christ ?*

Observe,

1. *Some live in direct opposition to Christ.*

They oppose his spiritual authority, and despise his gospel and salvation; give them-selves up to despisers of his grace, and to work iniquity. These are the open enemies of the cross—the avowed servants of Belial, —men who bear the mark of rebellion on their foreheads, who glory in their shame, and only mind earthly things.

2. *Others are absorbed in their own things, and neglect Christ.*

These are not profane, skeptical, vile ; but they are occupied solely with their own worldly pursuits—never take into account Christ's divine claims. They cannot come to Christ's feast, because their farms, and their merchandise, and their secular pur-suits, demand their whole time and attention.

Now, these industrious worldlings, from their respectable position in society, and their freedom from gross vices, are in ex-treme peril of concluding that all is well with them.

But selfishness is the very atmosphere of their being. Christ and his claims are to-tally neglected, and therefore they have no interest in true and saving religion. It is possible to be in the world, and attend to its concerns with attention and diligence, and yet to honor Jesus by giving him al-ways, and in all things, the pre-eminence. His kingdom being sought first, other things may have their legitimate place, and time, and attention. But the lovers of the world exclude Christ altogether, and live entirely to themselves.

3. *Others seek their own things chiefly, and more than Christ's.*

Christ has some of their thoughts, and their time, and their influence ; but he is not first and chief. The fragments are given to Christ. They invert the spirit of the text, and seek first the things of the body and time, and hope that Christ's things will be added to them ; but they will not, they cannot. For the soul must be cared for first, or not truly at all. Christ must have the throne of the heart, or he will not dwell in the soul at all. He must have our pre-eminent love, or he will not accept what affection may be saved from other objects. Now, this is a modified form of selfishness; but still it has all the fatal evil within itself, that will destroy the soul. Hear Christ's searching declaration on the subject. " And there went great multitudes with him : and he turned, and said unto them, If any man come to me, and hate not his father, and mother, and wife, and chil-dren, and brethren, and sisters, yea, and his own life also, he cannot be my disciple. And whosoever doth not bear his cross, and come after me, cannot be my disciple. For which of you, intending to build a tower, sitteth not down first, and counteth the cost, whether he have sufficient to finish it. Lest haply, after he hath laid the foundation, and is not able to finish it, all that behold it begin to mock him, saying, This man be-gan to build, and was not able to finish. Or what king, going to make war with another king, sitteth not down first, and consulteth whether he be able with ten thousand to meet him that cometh against him with twenty thousand ? Or else, while the other is yet a great way off, he sendeth an ambassage, and desireth conditions of peace. So, likewise, whosoever he be of you that forsaketh not all that he hath, he cannot be my disciple."—Luke xiv. 25–33.

4. *Others make their own happiness the end of living to Christ.*

This point requires careful attention. There is, indeed, a right, virtuous, honora-ble, and important self-love. To seek our real and spiritual good for body and soul, and for both worlds. To this we are often directed, especially in the Proverbs, and in the Psalms ; where religion and health, and long life, and honor, and happiness, are ex-hibited as being inseparably connected.

Now to keep this connection in view is most right and proper. But this, our own happiness, is not the sole end of religion. It is only one part, that which we receive—"I will bless thee." But we live to ourselves if we leave out the other part—"thou shalt be a blessing."

We much fear this is the crying sin of the Church—making our own so-called happiness the sole end of living to Christ. Now, this is not the meaning of the text. No man can live to Christ solely for his own good. Now to this last modification of selfishness—being religious for the sole sake of being comfortable, and eventually happy—the rest of our discourse will be directed. Let me, then,

II. *Show you the evil of this state.*

That is making ourselves the end of our religion.

1. *It is utterly discordant with the character of God.*

God is love; essential, infinite, exhaustless, eternal love. Most blessed and happy in himself; but he is the source of blessing to all the various creatures of his hands. The heavens, the earth, and the vast universe is full of his goodness; and he "is good to all, and his tender mercies are over all his works."

Now, our moral nature must be in harmony with his, if we are to be truly religious. Except we are partakers of his love, and his mercy, and goodness, and benignity, we cannot be acceptable to him. Hence Jesus laid the utmost stress on this in his divine teaching. He showed his disciples that they were ever to imitate God in his patience and long-suffering, to the vilest and most unworthy. "Ye have heard that it hath been said, thou shalt love thy neighbor, and hate thine enemy. But I say unto you, love your enemies, bless them that curse you, do good to them that hate you, and pray for them which despitefully use you, and persecute you; that ye may be the children of your Father which is in heaven: for he maketh his sun to rise on the evil and on the good, and sendeth rain on the just and on the unjust. For if ye love them which love you, what reward have ye? do not even the publicans the same? And if ye salute your brethren only, what do ye more than others? do not even the publicans so? Be ye therefore perfect, even as your Father which is in heaven is perfect."—Matt. v. 43–48.

2. *It is entirely unlike the spirit and conduct of Jesus.*

He was perfectly holy and devout, and was filled with the love of the Father; but he was practically and constantly benevolent. Indeed, the very constitution of his person, and his whole work, rested on the outgoings of the most elevated love and mercy to our world. Hear what the apostle says of the motives and ends of his great mission. "For ye know the grace of our Lord Jesus Christ, that, though he was rich, yet for your sakes he became poor, that ye through his poverty might be rich."—2 Cor. viii. 9. Hear what he himself averred on the same subject:—"Even as the Son of man came not to be ministered unto, but to minister, and to give his life a ransom for many."—Matt. xx. 28. He lived not to himself, or he had never left heaven; never become human; never had been born of a virgin; never lived in poverty, affliction, sorrow, and grief; would never have gone about doing good. His life of goodness, and works of love, were only suspended by his death for a few transitory hours, for they revived with him, and burst forth with renewed ardor, when he rose from the dead, and his last act on earth was the gracious outpouring of his blessing and grace, on the disciples who surrounded him, on the mount of ascension.

He still possesses the same spirit, and is engaged in the same gracious work, now that he is seated at the right hand of the Majesty on high.

How opposed to this is the professed Christian who lives to himself!

3. *It is completely counter to the principles of the gospel.*

Let me inquire, as it regards the believer, for what is he regenerated, if he is still under the dominion of the old selfish nature? Blessed with the spirit of Christ for what? Replenished with grace, for what purpose or end?

Is not love the atmosphere of true religion? Not a mere sentimental feeling, but a living, glowing emotion, put forth in practices of goodness and generosity. And if the gospel has not softened and enlarged the heart, what has it really done?

4. *It is contrary to all the works of God, and laws of the divine government.*

Throughout the universe, so far as we know, he makes one thing a blessing to another. Angels to each other, and to us. Men also, one to another. All the pious were so in the early ages of the world's history. Nothing was ever designed to terminate in itself. Not the sun, with its exhilarating beams; nor the sea, with its liquid resources; nor the air, with its vitalizing power; nor the earth, with its fertile and producing energy; nor flowers, with their fragrances and beauties. Sin only is the great element of selfishness, and equally of destruction to its victims. Selfishness is subversive of that happiness which it seeks.

No man who lives to himself enjoys what he seeks, even though he should possess it. Take the beautiful flower from its native soil, and how soon it begins to wither and die.

Selfish persons are generally morose and discontented. God's laws are violated, and wretchedness is the consequence. We get out of the light and the sunshine, and all is dark and dreary. Goodness is the very atmosphere of enjoyment and blessedness.

Then what is the application of the text?

(1.) That true religion consists in living to Christ; living to him as our model to study. Him as the Lord we should please in all things; him as the end of our lives; so that, whether we live or die, Christ may be magnified. Now to this end has he redeemed us, that we may be always his; his—body, soul, and spirit, for time and eternity.

(2.) The means of this life—is the grace he supplies. The roots of selfishness are deep and spreading, and difficult to be rooted up; yet his grace is sufficient to effect it. Let our hearts be fairly laid open to the silent yet omnific energy of divine grace, and it will become soft and fruitful; and instead of the briers and thorns of selfishness, it will produce abundantly all the fruits of goodness to the glory of God.

(3.) How we should examine and prove ourselves as to the state of our hearts. Has the native selfishness of our hearts been destroyed? Do we respond fully and feelingly to the word of truth and the spirit of Christ? Do we delight in goodness, and cherish a spirit of kindness and benignity to our fellow-men? And is this state of heart one we seek to cultivate by prayer and communion with God?

Finally, we urge the claims of Christ on the unconverted. Mark what he has done for you, and the infinite claims he has on all you are and have. You belong to him, and not to yourselves; and living in sin and open rebellion is just one course of wicked robbery of God. A robbery, however, which, while it grieves God's spirit, will prove most disastrous to your best interests for both worlds. Oh, think that, to live to Christ, and for Christ, is just that life which every intelligent spirit should aspire after, and which is alike dignified, secure, and happy.

XXXVIII.—SELF-LOATHING.

" Then shall ye remember your own evil ways, and your doings that were not good, and shall loathe yourselves in your own sight for your iniquities and for your abominations."—*Ezek.* xxxvi. 31.

THE text is to be understood only by looking at the connection in which it stands with verses 25 to 27. "Then will I sprinkle clean water upon you, and ye shall be clean : from all your filthiness, and from all your idols, will I cleanse you. A new heart also will I give you, and a new spirit will I put within you : and I will take away the stony heart out of your flesh, and I will give you an heart of flesh. And I will put my Spirit within you, and cause you to walk in my statutes, and ye shall keep my judgments and do them."

Now, the work of the Spirit of God, so far from producing self-complacency and satisfaction, just produces the opposite effects. How different the mind of God, and the mind of his renewed people! He pardons, and their sins are never more remembered; he upbraideth not. But though the godly man is forgiven, yet he often remembers with grief his evil doings, and loathes himself before God. Self-loathing is one of the genuine effects of the converting and renewing grace of God.

No one can remember his former evil life, and not feel deep regret and shame on account thereof. So says the Apostle in regard to the believers who had been made free in Christ Jesus from the bondage of sin. "For when ye were the servants of sin, ye were free from righteousness. What fruit had ye then in those things whereof ye are now ashamed? For the end of those things is death."—Rom. vi. 20–21. And it is this feeling of penitential sorrow, and holy shame, which is expressed so graphically in the text.

Let us then consider,

I. *The spirit the text describes.*

And,

II. *Why it should be cherished?*

I. *The spirit the text describes.*

Now, the spirit of the text is described under three particulars.

1. *A remembrance of the past.*

The past ought to be remembered. It is alike connected with the present and the future. Life is one whole. And as the days or seasons of the year, its events are all linked together. Many live entirely without reflection; they consider neither the dispensations of God towards them, nor yet their own conduct with regard to the Most High. This want of thought and consideration, is most detrimental to the mind, and is often the main hindrance to a knowledge of ourselves.

The traveller often takes a retrospect of his journey. The mariner attends to the log, to know the latitude in which he is sailing, and notes down the daily events of the voyage. The philosopher does this, and keeps a record of his intellectual discoveries, and advances in knowledge. So should the Christian do this, and his real self-improvement and moral elevation are absolutely connected with it. This remembrance was continually enforced on the Israelites of old. "And thou shalt remember all the way which the Lord thy God led thee, these forty years in the wilderness, to humble thee, and to prove thee, to know what was in thine heart, whether thou wouldest keep his commandments, or no. And he humbled thee, and suffered thee to hunger, and fed thee with manna, which thou knowest not, neither did thy fathers know; that he might make thee know that man doth not live by bread only, but by every word that proceedeth out of the mouth of the Lord, doth man live."— Deut. viii. 2–3.

The spirit in the text is,

2. *A remembrance of our past evil doings.*

Many only remember what they deem the good they have done, while their sins are forgotten. Now this ought not so to be. It is well to keep up the remembrance both of the omissions of good, and the commissions of evil; and true piety will ever do so. How late, says one, before I gave my heart to God! How deadly my example and influence, says another, before I became renewed in my mind! How base, and vile, and brutish, says another, was I while carnal and sold under sin! How profitless my existence, and perverted my powers, before God

had my heart, says the abased follower of Jesus.

God says, he will produce this remembrance in his people. "And I will establish my covenant with thee; and thou shalt know that I am the Lord; that thou mayest remember, and be confounded, and never open thy mouth any more because of thy shame, when I am pacified towards thee for all that thou hast done, saith the Lord God." —Ezek. xvi. 62–3. So Paul remembered his former state, and says—"And I thank Christ Jesus our Lord, who hath enabled me, for that he counted me faithful, putting me into the ministry; who was before a blasphemer, and a persecutor, and injurious: but I obtained mercy, because I did it ignorantly in unbelief. And the grace of our Lord was exceeding abundant with faith and love which is in Christ Jesus."—1 Tim. i. 12–14.

Three things should never be forgotten as to our past sins—First, the Being against whom we did this evil—our Creator, Benefactor, Preserver, Redeemer,—the greatest and best of beings. Second, the voluntariness of our sins. They were the free acts of our own wickedness. We might have temptations, but the sins were our own. Third, often the aggravated circumstances of our sins. Favored as we were with light, and means, and mercies, friends and influences for good; yet despite all, we sinned against God.

The spirit of the text includes,

3. *A deep abhorrence in connection with the remembrance of the past.*

"Loathe" yourselves, as a person loathes that which is foul; or as a person would loathe a plague: the feeling is one of distaste, disapprobation, and disgust; holy indignation against our hearts, and spirits, and lives.

God infinitely abhors evil, and as we have his spirit so shall we. We shall behold sin as the abominable thing God hates; as the defiler of man, the destroyer of the soul, and the peopler of perdition. Would that this spirit were more often directed against ourselves! How ready we are to indulge in it against others! Even as David, when the parable of Nathan was delivered to him, immediately pronounced sentence against the oppressive and unjust evil-doer; so we never find it difficult to express indignation against the sins of men around us; but how indulgent we are in general with regard to ourselves. We loathe that pride, and that vanity, that avarice, that sensuality, that unbelief, and that cruelty in others, but how many of these may dwell and ramble in our own souls! Ah! we might often look nearer home, and let our censures tell on ourselves with much profit.

How needful to keep to the spirit of the text, and cherish self-abasing views and feelings with respect to our own hearts. Let us survey the foul imagery there, condemn the treason there, and mourn over the fearful defilement there; and thus carry out fully the sentiments of the text, and loathe ourselves in our own sight, for our iniquities and our abominations.

Let us then notice,

II. *Why the spirit of the text should be cherished.*

And here many reasons might be assigned. But we notice,

1. *This is in accordance with the renewed state of our mind.*

This spirit is the necessary result of divine grace in the soul. We now see and think and feel differently, yea oppositely, to what we formerly did. Then we saw no evil in sin, and therefore felt none ; but now being new creatures, old things have passed away, and all things have become new. When in darkness, we could not discern the fearful and polluted condition of the chambers of our souls. But when God gave both light, and eyes to see, then did we perceive that all within was vile, and were led to exclaim, as Isaiah did—"Woe is me! for I am undone; because I am a man of unclean lips." Hence how the best and holiest have thus expressed themselves, as Abraham, Job, David, Daniel, Paul.

2. *Gratitude to God should produce it.*

It is only by recognizing the deep-seated character of the disease that the skill of the physician is displayed. In the heinousness of sin, is exhibited the richness and grace and mercy of God.

Now this remembrance and self-loathing honors God, as it shows the wondrous compassion he has shown to objects so utterly unworthy of his regards, as is essential to true and unfeigned gratitude for the mercy we have received.

3. *It is necessary to our own safety.*

We ought not to forget past sins, that we may never rise from the depths of true humility. How Paul felt this, even thirty years after his conversion! he writes to Timothy and describes himself as the chief of sin-ners. Besides, these past evil events of our lives should be beacons—there is that hidden shoal, that sunken rock, that perilous current, that terrible Maelstrom. Now how clear it is, that this state of mind is essential to our safety. Forgetfulness may be fraught with imminent danger to our best interests. How the Psalmist and the prophets, and Stephen and Paul, reminded the Jews of the sins of their nation, and of their evil doings, which had justly brought on them calamities and woe. But how much better if Israel had remembered, and been admonished, and avoided the danger into which they so repeatedly fell. Now just so it is with ourselves ; we must remember and keep up the self-loathing, if we are to be spiritually safe. The inferior creatures often by dint of their instincts, avoid the snares which are laid for them, and escape. How much more circumspect should rational beings act, especially when they have been blessed with supplies of that wisdom which cometh from above.

4. *It will ever lead us to rely on the provisions of the divine mercy.*

With this spirit we shall never dream of trusting to ourselves ; of taking matters into our own hands. Divine grace alone will ever be our hope and refuge. The love and mercy of God in Christ will be our abiding trust. His precious blood, his efficient grace our daily resource. No hand can safely lead us but the hand of our heavenly Father; no power protect but his; no mercy bear with us, and save us but his. His abiding covenant—the all-prevailing sacrifice and intercession of Jesus our Lord, will set before us the only ark of safety, the only path to purest blessedness and eternal life.

5. *It should lead us to pity, and be compassionate to others.*

Hear what is said of Christ's sympathy and compassion as our great High Priest— "For every high priest taken from among men is ordained for men in things pertaining to God, that he may offer both gifts and sacrifices for sins ; who can have compassion on the ignorant, and on them that are out of the way; for that he himself also is compassed with infirmity."—Heb. v. 1, 2. Then if we have his spirit, and loathe ourselves, we shall be quite ready to hearken to the injunction—"Brethren, if a man be overtaken in a fault, ye which are spiritual restore such an one in the spirit of meekness; considering thyself, lest thou also be tempted."—Gal. vi. 1. And to do this, let the words of the apostle James never be forgotten:—"Brethren, if any of you do err from the truth and one convert him, let him know that he which converteth the sinner from the error of his way shall save a soul from death, and shall hide a multitude of sins."—Jas. v. 19, 20.

In conclusion:

(1.) We urge the spirit of the text on all God's people. Persons often used to set apart days for humiliation and prayer; whether we do so or not, we should labor to keep up a deep sense of our unworthiness, and this will lead to the self-loathing the text enforces.

(2.) We would address the unrenewed sinner. The subject is of the utmost importance to you. Have you ever looked at the extreme evil of sin—looked at it through the medium of God's word—of his holy law —as that which is utterly opposed to his purity? Have you thought of it, as crushing the Saviour to the ground in Gethsemane, and nailing him to the rugged tree? Have you thought of it as opening the pit of blackness and woe for all the finally incorrigible and impenitent? Oh! if not, now think, and ponder, and pray, that you may be delivered from its guilt, indwelling, and power; especially that you may be led to hate and loathe it with all your hearts.

(3.) How odious is self-righteousness! No marvel that Jesus who was so compassionate to the vilest, so tender-hearted towards the worst, was so fearfully faithful to the self-righteous scribes and Pharisees. And how he exposed their self-complacency and base hypocrisy:—"Woe unto you, scribes and Pharisees, hypocrites! for ye make clean the outside of the cup and the platter, but within they are full of extortion and excess. Thou blind Pharisee, cleanse first that which is within the cup and platter, that the outside of them may be clean also. Woe unto you, scribes and Pharisees, hypocrites! for ye are like unto whited sepulchres, which indeed appear beautiful outward, but are within full of dead men's bones, and of all uncleanness. Even so ye also outwardly appear righteous unto men, but within ye are full of hypocrisy and iniquity."—Matt. xxiii. 25–28.

How we should guard against being partakers of such a spirit; and the effectual way to do it will be to allow the truth of the text ever to dwell in our hearts, so that it may produce within us all lowliness and humility to the honor of God and the glory of his grace.

XXXIX.—SELF-EXAMINATION.

"Examine yourselves, whether ye be in the faith."—2 Cor. xiii. 5.

Our subject is one of the greatest possible importance. It is the ascertaining of our true state and character before God. It is seeing whether the tree has been made good —whether the coin bears Christ's superscription—whether we are in the church or in the world—whether we are converted or unconverted. Now these are momentous questions, essentially connected with our happiness in both worlds.

It is, however, matter of great satisfaction that we can ascertain our true condition, and be delivered from all possibility of error on this subject. It is not needful that we should be in any doubt; for the process recommended will most assuredly lead to a clear and definite conclusion.

It is worthy of note that the apostles ever speak of the Christian state as one of conscious knowledge and evident assurance. To be in Christ—in the faith—in the body of the true church—are ever spoken of as matters of spiritual consciousness; yet indifference to the question can never bring us to a satisfactory conclusion. To know ourselves, and see clearly how we stand before God, it is needful to adopt the course the text recommends:—"Examine yourselves whether ye be in the faith." Let then the subject have our grave and serious consideration.

Observe,

I. *What is premised in the text.*

We are exhorted to examine ourselves. It clearly supposes that we may be in error on this subject. We may err in supposing,

1. *Educational influence as synonymous with the faith.*

Christian training exerts a mighty power, especially when followed by good and pious example; persons are thus enlightened in religious doctrines, and restrained in their daily practice and life. Now all this may be, without being in the faith, and yet may be mistaken for it.

We may err also,

2. *In confounding a regard for, and an*

attendance on religious services, with being in the faith.

Multitudes evidence this every day. This regard to worship often arises from religious training, and the force of habit; from the power of natural conscience ; from a mental pleasure in religious services—for such there is in hearing the word eloquently spoken; singing, and the attendant musical engagements. Or it may arise from a conviction of the good influence which worship has on the character and mind. There are multitudes of persons who have sensible enjoyment in religious duties, and they would on no account relinquish them; yet they are unrenewed, and without a knowledge of God. Self-deception is very easy under these otherwise pleasing circumstances.

We may err,

3. *In mistaking inward emotions with being in the faith.*

The passions may be moved; as of fear— as in the case of Felix who trembled when Paul preached of righteousness, temperance, and a judgment to come. Of desire—as in the case of the young man who asked with evident desire what he should do to inherit eternal life. And also as in the case of Agrippa, who was almost persuaded to become a Christian. There may be the transient grief and sorrow; or sudden joy—as in those who received the word with gladness, but who after all were but stony-ground hearers.

It is good to have the heart excited. Religious impressions must produce emotions; but all this may be, without being in the faith. It may go so far as to lead to church fellowship, and union with God's people. The lamp of profession may be taken, and like others we may be avowedly waiting for the bridegroom.

Now, as mistakes may arise from any or all these grounds, how needful the admonition to examine ourselves.

Observe,

II. *To what the text distinctly refers.*

"Being in the faith,"—evidently, having the true faith of a disciple of Christ. There is a kingdom, spiritual and divine, and the very atmosphere of this kingdom is faith. Are we then in it? There is a holy brotherhood, all bound together by faith. Are we of it? Now if we are in the faith, then manifestly,

1. *The faith of the Gospel will be in us.*

We shall have believed with our hearts unto righteousness; we shall have believed to the saving of our souls. Thus we shall have come to Christ, looked to Christ, rested on Christ, and have obtained saving virtue, and holy power out of Christ. Now nothing can be more evident than that our being in the faith must be ever in unison with the faith being in us; there cannot be the one without the other. Now if the faith is in us, we are consequently in the faith; if so, we are relying on the Lord Jesus Christ, and by that confiding dependence have peace, and hope, and joy, through believing. So that to answer the question, whether you are in the faith, we must propose another—"Dost thou believe on the Son of God?" And if you can say that you do really believe on him, then are you most obviously in the faith.

If you are in the faith,

2. *The experience of faith will be in us.*

Faith worketh by love. "Whom having not seen, ye love; in whom, though now ye see him not, yet believing, ye rejoice with joy unspeakable and full of glory : receiving the end of your faith, even the salvation of your souls."—1 Pet. i. 8, 9. So also the apostle speaks of the results of faith thus— "Therefore being justified by faith, we have peace with God through our Lord Jesus Christ : by whom also we have access by faith into this grace wherein we stand, and rejoice in hope of the glory of God. And not only so, but we glory in tribulation also, knowing that tribulation also worketh patience," &c.—Rom. v. 1–3. Now such are the experimental results of faith : the fruit faith always bears, the consequences that ever follow its existence in our hearts. And if such holy results are the experience of your hearts, then are you manifestly in the faith.

3. *The signs of faith will be upon us.*

The mouth will glorify God. Is it possible for the tongue to be silent, if Christ has been believed on to the saving of the soul ? The soul will be filled with emotions, that must be expressed :—

"Brightness of the Father's glory—
  Shall thy praise unuttered lie ?
  Fly, my tongue, such guilty silence !
  Sing the Lord who came to die."

The life will show forth his praise. Faith in the heart purifies the life; it spreads over the whole man a hallowed influence and sanctifying power; hence there will be self-abasement, self-denial, and obedience. This is Christ's own test—keeping his words, doing as he has commanded, and walking in his steps. Faith ever produces these results, ever exhibits this practical fruit.

Observe,

III. *The course the text enjoins.*

"Examine yourselves, whether ye be in the faith."

And,

I. *Do this with earnestness of spirit.*

It is a weighty, solemn thing, worthy of care, and not to be passed over carelessly or formally, when the favor of God, the glory of Christ, and the salvation of the soul, are all concerned—then there cannot be too much intensity of thought and earnestness of spirit. Apathy in the performance of this duty would be moral insanity. It should be done with all the awakened powers of your soul.

2. *Do this with the word of God as your rule.*

Not examine and compare yourself with yourself, for you are not to make yourselves, at any period, the standard of spiritual examination. Nor yet with others, for God has given you no directions that you are to aim at being like this or that person. Nor with human tests and human standards, for these are all defective, and not to be relied upon:—but with the word of God. This is the true mirror, the real touchstone, the only infallible standard of true holiness. It is a Bible question, and that book only can settle it. Besides, how foolish to test yourselves by other means, when the true ordeal is at hand, and within your power. In this matter it is ever to be kept in view, that we appeal to the "law and to the testimony;" and if our views, and convictions, and belief, will stand justified here, then are we truly and savingly in the faith.

3. *Do it in the spirit of prayer.*

It is needful to make it an object of prayer, that God may open your eyes to discern clearly and correctly; make you faithful, that you may not flatter yourselves; aid you by his Spirit, that you may not be led astray by natural feelings, which will be against this exercise. Grace only will conquer human nature, and give you power for this necessary duty.

4. *Do it from time to time.*

It is an exercise often to be repeated. We may suffer loss—we may be ensnared—religion may be neglected and die out—we may relapse into sin, or go back into the world, and turn aside from God. Then it should be done often. Some godly persons have made this a daily exercise; and if prayer and praise should be constantly regarded, so would it be well for examination to accompany them—in fact, we cannot regard and attend to it too often.

Then let us note,

IV. *Some motives by which this course may be enjoined.*

We should regard it,

1. *As a duty.*

God commands it; he knows its vast importance; he sees its essentiality. It is absolute, and binding on all Christians.

We should regard it in reference,

2. *To our comfort.*

It is for the comfort of the traveller to know he is in the right way; for the mariner to know his course of sailing is correct; for the heir to be sure that his title is unquestionably valid. How much more that we know the soul is right for eternity! Hence the poet sings:

> " When I can read my title clear
>   To mansions in the skies,
> I'll bid farewell to every fear,
>   And wipe my weeping eyes."

3. *It is connected with our safety.*

If, on examination, matters are not right, all may be made so. Now is the time to get the mistake rectified; now only can it be done—it may indeed be perhaps now, or never.

Then we urge the admonition of the text,

(1.) On the consideration of all. On the young Christian, and on the aged believer; on Christians of every grade, and of every order; for it is alike needful to each and every one.

We would,

(2.) Exhort the seeker of true religion to attend to self-examination; see what hinders you from coming to the truth as it is in Jesus. What is the stumbling-block in your way to true peace?

(3.) Let the subject be strictly remembered, and be personally carried out by all. It is ourselves who are to be examined—not others. We are not to be busy in testing and proving those around us. Alas! we fear this is often much pleasanter and easier than self-examination. But before you do this, have counsel and command from God to do it. And here we may be instructed from the conduct of impetuous Peter, who was anxious to know what should happen to the disciple John : "Then Peter, turning about, seeth the disciple whom Jesus loved following; which also leaned on his breast at supper, and said, Lord, which is he that betrayeth thee ? Peter seeing him, saith to Jesus, Lord, and what shall this man do ? Jesus saith unto him, if I will that he tarry till I come, what is that to thee ? follow thou me."—John xxi. 20–22.

Reader! examine thine own heart; and in that solemn work there will be so much to do, so much to repent of, so much to amend, so much to claim thy whole attention, that prying curiously into the state of others, will meet with no disposition or opportunity to be indulged.

XL.—WHAT CHRIST IS MADE TO BE-LIEVERS.

"But of him are ye in Christ Jesus, who of God is made unto us wisdom, and righteousness, and sanctification, and redemption."—1 *Cor.* i. 30,

OUR text contains a very rich and striking view of the happy state and privileges of the Christian. The apostle has been dwelling on the insufficiency of the wisdom of this world to lead men to the attainment of saving knowledge. He is also showing how God set at naught earthly grandeur and philosophy in the establishment of his kingdom, and how he resolved to pour contempt on earthly science and greatness. Hear the interesting questions of the apostle : "Where is the wise? where is the scribe? where is the disputer of this world? hath not God made foolish the wisdom of this world?"—Ver. 20. Then he shows God's own expedient for making the world wise and happy : "For after that in the wisdom of God the world by wisdom knew not God, it pleased God by the foolishness of preaching to save them that believe. For the Jews require a sign, and the Greeks seek after wisdom ; but we preach Christ crucified, unto the Jews a stumbling-block, and unto the Greeks foolishness ; but unto them which are called, both Jews and Greeks, Christ the power of God, and the wisdom of God. Because the foolishness of God is wiser than men; and the weakness of God is stronger than men. For ye see your calling, brethren, how that not many wise men

after the flesh, not many mighty, not many noble, are called ; but God hath chosen the foolish things of the world to confound the wise ; and God hath chosen the weak things of the world to confound the things which are mighty ; and base things of the world, and things which are despised, hath God chosen, yea, and the things which are not, to bring to naught things that are : that no flesh should glory in his presence."—Ver. 21–29.

Then he turns to the direct and glorious privileges of his people : "But of Him are ye in Christ Jesus, who of God is made unto us, wisdom, and righteousness, and sanctification, and redemption."

Observe,

I. *The union of believers with Christ.*

"But of Him are ye in Christ Jesus." "If any man be in Christ," says the apostle, "he is a new creature." "I knew a man in Christ," he says in another place. Now the believer is in Christ—as the branch is in the vine—as the stone is in the building—as the members are in the body. Several Old Testament symbols illustrate this idea : as Noah in the ark, and the manslayer in the city of refuge.

This union, also, must be mutual; Christ in us, and we in Christ. We may know Christ—come to Christ—be near to Christ; but religion also includes being in Christ; virtually, really, and vitally so in him, that he is our head, our life, and our all in all. So in him, that we are one with Christ ; so in him, that we are baptized into his death, participators of his resurrection, and are co-sharers of his glory.

Observe in the text,

II. *That this union is ascribed to God.*

"Who of God is made unto us," &c. In every sense this is true. God gave and sent his Son ; God revealed his Son ; God brought us nigh to Christ ; God by his Holy Spirit united us to Christ. The work is the Lord's; yet man is not passive, and merely acted upon. He must hear of Christ, as proclaimed in the Gospel ; he must believe in Christ, and receive him into the soul. "To as many as received him, he gave power to become the sons of God." Now in this we see exemplified the amazing mercy and love of God, and the gracious power of the Spirit. For it is a work both of love and power. It is a new creation, in which both the might, and wisdom, and power of God are put forth and glorified—" that according as it is written, he that glorieth, let him glory in the Lord."

Our text shows us,

III. *The advantages of this union with Christ.*

"Who of God is made unto us wisdom, and righteousness, and sanctification, and redemption." Now it is well to observe, how Christ, in his gracious fulness, is just the adapted good, the wretched helpless sinner needs. Just look at our fallen estate, and our moral exigencies :

1. *As we are dark and ignorant, Christ is made unto us wisdom.*

He is the light of the world—the true light that lighteth every man. He came to reveal that which the world could not find out—the true God, and the eternal life. He opens up the way of reconciliation. Hence he illumines the understanding, and gives the knowledge of salvation. He makes known the way of peace, and by him we become the children of light, and of the day.

See Saul ignorant of the scheme of mercy, and see him when God had revealed his Son in him;—then he exclaims—" Yea, doubtless, and I count all things but loss for the excellency of the knowledge of Jesus Christ my Lord ; for whom I have suffered the loss of all things, and do count them but dung, that I may win Christ."—Phil. iii. 8. Now this is true, saving wisdom.

2. *As sinners, we are guilty and condemned ; and Christ is made unto us righteousness, or justification.*

For by him alone can the sinner be justified. His person, and obedience unto death, form the great moral ground of our pardon, and acceptance with God. See this clearly attested in Paul's address at Antioch :—" Be it known unto you therefore, men and brethren, that through this man is preached unto you the forgiveness of sins ; and by him all that believe are justified from all things, from which ye could not be justified by the law of Moses."—Acts xiii. 38–39. See also the reasoning of the apostle in his letter to the Romans :—" For if by one man's offence death reigned by one ; much more they which receive abundance of grace and of the gift of righteousness shall reign in life by one, Jesus Christ. Therefore, as by the offence of one, judgment came upon all men to condemnation ; even so by the righteousness of one the free gift came upon all men unto justification of life. For as by one man's disobedience many were made sinners, so by the obedience of one shall many be made righteous."—Rom. v. 17–19. And the result of this justification, he states— "Therefore being justified by faith, we have peace with God through our Lord Jesus Christ."—V. 1. How beautifully this agrees with the prediction of Jeremiah the prophet! " And this is the name whereby he shall be called—the Lord our Righteousness." It is also stated that—" He was made sin for us who knew no sin." He hath fully met all the claims of the law. In him, we are not under its condemnation.

3. *As defiled in heart and life, he is made unto us sanctification.*

Now justification is a work of grace done for us ; sanctification is a work of grace done in us. Justification affects our state as sinners ; sanctification affects our character as defiled. Justification is effected at once; sanctification is a progressive work, which begins with our regeneration, and only ends in glory.

Now Christ is made unto us sanctification by the Holy Spirit which he promised, and sent down from heaven ; who by the truth renews, and carries on the work of holiness in the soul of the believer ; thus he sets up within us a kingdom of righteousness, and peace, and joy in the Holy Ghost. "Who gave himself for us, that he might redeem us from all iniquity, and purify unto himself a peculiar people, zealous of good works."—Titus ii. 14. And, "But after that the kindness and love of God our Saviour towards man appeared, not by works of righteousness which we have done, but according to his mercy he saved us, by the washing of regeneration, and renewing of the Holy Ghost."—iii. 4–5.

The atoning blood which he shed is not only the ground of our pardon, but is the medium of our purification. This was the fountain opened for sin and uncleanness. This blood, says the apostle John, "cleanseth us from all sin."—1 John i. 7. So also the powerful statement of Paul,—" For if the blood of bulls and of goats, and the ashes of an heifer sprinkling the unclean, sanctifieth to the purifying of the flesh : how much more shall the blood of Christ, who through the eternal Spirit offered himself without spot to God, purge your conscience from dead works to serve the living God ?"—Heb. ix. 13, 14. And the description of the redeemed, as beheld in the vision of John— " And I said unto him, Sir, thou knowest.

And he said to me, These are they which came out of great tribulation, and have washed their robes, and made them white in the blood of the Lamb."—Rev. vii. 14.

4. *We are mortal creatures, and must become the captives of death and the grave; therefore Christ is made unto us redemption.*

This most evidently refers to something beyond, and subsequent to sanctification. Now this obviously relates to the resurrection of the body, and the glorification of body and soul in heaven. "For we know that the whole creation groaneth and travaileth in pain together until now. And not only they, but ourselves also, which have the first-fruits of the Spirit, even we ourselves groan within ourselves, waiting for the adoption, to wit, the redemption of our body." —Rom. viii. 22, 23. "And grieve not the Holy Spirit of God, whereby ye are sealed unto the day of redemption."—Eph. iv. 30.

Now Christ is the resurrection, or redemption of his people. He is so in every conceivable sense of the term. Not only will he raise the dead, but his indissoluble union with the Christian, will constitute the everlasting life to which he has been called. His resurrection, also, is both the pledge and pattern of theirs. "For our conversation is in heaven; from whence also we look for the Saviour, the Lord Jesus Christ: who shall change our vile body, that it may be fashioned like unto his glorious body, according to the working whereby he is able even to subdue all things unto himself."—Phil. iii. 20, 21. This will be the grand consummation —the end of the work of Christ in us, and for us. Beyond this, there will be the blessedness of complete and eternal glorification.

Such then is the Lord Jesus made to all his people. He is their wisdom, righteousness, sanctification, and redemption.

Learn then,

(1.) Man's natural deplorable condition— ignorant, guilty, defiled; the victim of death; and in himself without merit or help. See,

(2.) The preciousness of the Lord Jesus. He is all our need; all our desires and salvation are completed in him. None of these blessings can we have without Christ; but with Christ, God will freely give us all things.

(3.) The necessity of union to Christ— personal, spiritual union—a union of heart and soul.

(4.) We see why Christ should ever be the subject of preaching, and the object of faith—because there is salvation in no other. Here is the one rock of perfect hope and blessedness, and nowhere else is there a foundation sufficiently strong to bear up the boundless interests of immortal souls. In Christ, God's glory has been revealed, and man's help found; so that the apostle may well add,—" He that glorieth, let him glory in the Lord."

Now learn also,

Finally. That our union to Christ should be the chief end of our solicitude. It may be well and profitable to be associated with some department of Christ's church; and to be honorably identified as public professors of Christ's religion; but this will really avail nothing, without we are spiritually united to Jesus, and unless he is our wisdom, righteousness, sanctification and redemption. This is the essential reality, after which we should aspire—and without which we should not be satisfied—and strangers to which we cannot finally be saved.

The experimental enjoyment of this spiritual union to Christ, with the emotions it should excite, are beautifully versified by Dr. Doddridge:

"My God, assist me while I raise
An anthem of harmonious praise!
My heart thy wonders shall proclaim,
And spread its banners to thy name.

In Christ I view a store divine:
My Father, all that store is thine;
By thee prepared, by thee bestowed;
Hail to my Saviour, and my God!

Condemned, thy criminal I stood,
And awful Justice asked my blood;
That welcome Saviour, from thy throne
Brought righteousness and pardon down.

My soul was all o'erspread with sin,
And lo! his grace hath made me clean:
He rescues from the infernal foe,
And full redemption will bestow.

Ye saints, assist my grateful tongue;
Ye angels, warble back my song;
For love like this demands the praise
Of heavenly harps and endless days."

XLI.—GOD'S UNWILLINGNESS TO AF-
FLICT HIS PEOPLE.

"For the Lord will not cast off forever: but though he cause grief, yet will he have compassion according to the multitude of his mercies.

For he doth not afflict willingly nor grieve the children of men."—*Lam.* iii. 31–33.

THIS world is a scene of trouble, and sorrow, and death. Man that is born of woman is evidently subject to them, as the sparks fly upward. There is no escape for any class or condition of men from the afflictions of life. But often these troubles are the direct result of our iniquities. God often chastises, that he may not destroy,—purifies, that he may not utterly consume.

The text was uttered when severe judgments had overtaken the Jewish nation. How affecting the recital of their miseries as recorded in this book—chap. i. 1–6. Yet even in this dreary scene the prophet affirms the mercy of God:—"It is of the Lord's mercies that we are not consumed, because his compassions fail not. They are new every morning: great is thy faithfulness. The Lord is my portion, saith my soul; therefore will I hope in him. The Lord is good unto them that wait for him, to the soul that seeketh him."—Lam. iii. 22–25. He then avers God's unwillingness to grieve the children of men.

The subject may justly lead us to consider the afflictions of God's people in general.

Notice then,

I. *The Author.*

II. *The character.*

And,

III. *The design of our afflictions.*

By afflictions I mean all those events which affect man's person, condition, and enjoyments,—poverty, trials, temptations, bereavements, sickness, &c. Our text indirectly informs us of their origin—"Though he cause grief." Afflictions do not spring from chance; nor are they directly the work of Satan—but the work of God. All events are immediately of him, or permitted by him. We often only go to the palpable cause of our sorrows; but above all is the great cause. "I form the light, and create darkness: I make peace and create evil: I the Lord do all these things."—Isa. xlv. 7. "Shall a trumpet be blown in the city, and the people not be afraid? shall there be evil in a city, and the Lord hath not done it?"—Amos iii. 6.

Let not this view lead you to suppose, that men do not often injure themselves, and plunge themselves into many needless sorrows; yet even here God's permissive providence must be acknowledged. And if

men are to be free and accountable beings, God must permit these things; but in tender mercy he often sends the counteracting remedy—the antidote to the sorrow; knowing their infirmities, and remembering that they are dust.

Observe,

II. *The character of our afflictions.*

God doth not "afflict willingly," or from his heart; they are disciplinary, and are ever mixed with mercy and compassion. Unmixed affliction is only the lot of the lost. Now this view of our trouble is clearly established, if you consider,

1. *The superabounding blessings we enjoy.*

For one cup of sorrow, how many have we of enjoyment! For one hour of pain, how many weeks and months of ease and rest! Affliction in drops—blessings in showers.

It is amazing how years even of health and prosperity are enjoyed without special note; while a fit of sickness, or a day's trouble, becomes the theme of morbid remembrance, or mourning discontent.

This is also evident,

2. *From the ameliorating circumstances in our afflictions.*

In our deepest afflictions how many blessings are retained! What a multitude of good things are left to us! If health fails—friends abound; if the body is in pain—the mind is very often unattacked. If in the world we have sorrow—in Christ we have peace; if bereavements distress us—yet how many beloved objects are continued to us. And best of all, afflictions and troubles do not affect our relationship to God—to the covenant—and to the Saviour; the promises too are all ours, and are as free, rich, and overflowing as ever.

We may often see this,

3. *When we compare our afflictions with those of others.*

Look around! see the bitter cup others have to drink. We often think and say our lot is the worst—but is it so? Look at our first parents—see Abel is murdered, and by Cain his brother. Look at Jacob's family—what changes and disasters in his family and condition. Remember the degradation of Dinah—the pollution of his sons—the loss of Joseph—the unexpected death of Rachel. Then in old age a threatening famine, that seemed to expose his whole family to desolation. Look at David's household—where strife, and rebellion, and lust, and want of conjugal confidence and esteem, were united with a nation often in arms and confusion. Look at Job—cast down from a high eminency of worldly greatness and richness into poverty—bereaved of his sons and daughters—afflicted in his own person with a distressing and loathsome disease—tempted to rail presumptuously by his wife—suspected by his friends; until he appears like a monument of misery, with every possible inscription of distress engraven upon him. Look at the writer of the text—the weeping prophet—the bard of personal and national sorrow! How few and light are your griefs compared with others.

4. *Then think of your deserts.*

If God meted out pure justice—what you deserve, what would be the fearful result? How awful the consequences! Every stream of joy would be dried up, and every conceivable agony would be inflicted. Despair would settle on your wretched and doomed spirit forever and ever. " It is of the Lord's mercies that we are not consumed; because his compassions fail not."

Notice then,

III. *The design of our afflictions.*

One word expresses it—our real and ultimate good. " For whom the Lord loveth he chasteneth, and scourgeth every son whom he receiveth. If ye endure chastening, God dealeth with you as with sons; for what son is he whom the Father chasteneth not ?"—Heb. xii. 6, 7. " Now no chastening for the present seemeth to be joyous, but grievous; nevertheless afterwards it yieldeth the peaceable fruit of righteousness unto them which are exercised thereby."—V. 11. This is most distinctly affirmed in various parts of God's revealed word, especially by the apostle Paul—" For our light affliction which is but for a moment, worketh for us a far more exceeding and eternal weight of glory."—2 Cor. iv. 17. The apostle Peter also shows the sanctifying influence of our trials and sorrows :—" Wherein ye greatly rejoice, though now for a season, if need be, ye are in heaviness through manifold temptations: that the trial of your faith, being much more precious than of gold that perisheth, though it be tried with fire, might be found unto praise and honor and glory at the appearing of Jesus Christ."—1 Pet. i. 6, 7. Besides, these trials are needful to our conformity to Jesus. The promise runs—" If so be that we suffer with him, that we may also be glorified together."—Rom. viii. 17.

Besides, all nature furnishes us with striking illustrations of the salutary influence of affliction. Hear that terrific tempest of wind, and thunder, and lightning. How awful! Trees levelled—houses destroyed—persons killed. Yet observe—the district has been suffering by disease; the air has been impregnated with death. The storm purifies it, and makes it balmy with health and life.

Look forth and see the sterile scene of winter! The hard nipping frost—nature appears dead—not a bird or flower—no sound of joy. Yet the frost is essential to the resuscitation of the earth. It is the precursor of spring; and generally as is the keenness of winter, so are the bloom of spring, and the fruits of summer.

See that intensely heated furnace! The refiner takes the silver ore which is incrusted with dross, he places it in the crucible, on a burning fire, and it melts; the dross falls—the pure silver becomes clear, and at length the refiner sees reflected his own likeness, and the silver is purified.

Look at that sickly person, in pain and weariness. Well, the physician prescribes; but the potion is bitter, nauseous—yea, and it produces still more pain for a time. But its effects are the relief and health of the sufferer.

I need not dwell at much length on figures of this kind, you will see their application at once.

(1.) There is listlessness and apathy—and God sends the storm to awaken—to excite to action and spirituality of soul.

(2.) There is worldliness—and God sends the winter and frost, to destroy the weeds of covetousness in the soul.

(3.) There is the dross of sin still in the heart—and God puts his people into the furnace, and brings them forth hating iniquity, and purified for his own body service.

(4.) There is still moral weakness in the system—and God mixes the medicine to give soundness and vigor to the inward man.

Now God's mercies are strikingly seen in all these; and often, when affliction is unto death, in pity he takes his saints away from the evil to come.

APPLICATION.

Learn the importance of acquiescence and resignation. You can gain no advantage by murmuring and discontent. Ascertain if your afflictions have been sanctified. Have they led you closer to God, and made you more spiritual by cherishing unfeigned and devout gratitude to him? Bless him even when his strokes are upon you; for all his strokes are regulated by wisdom, tenderness, and love. Anticipate a state of future, yet certain, and unmixed joy. But that is to be in eternity—not in time; in heaven—not on earth.

Let the unconverted ask why the end of God's chastening dealings with them has not been attained. God seeks your restoration to himself. He wishes you as prodigal children to feel your misery, and come to his home, and heart, and salvation.

Backslider! God says to you—"Therefore, behold, I will hedge up thy way with thorns, and make a wall, that she shall not find her paths. And she shall follow after her lovers, but she shall not overtake them; and she shall seek them, but shall not find them; then shall she say, I will go and return to my first husband; for then was it better with me than now."—Hos. ii. 6, 7.

XLII.—FAMILY WORSHIP.

"And upon the families that call not on thy name."—*Jer.* x. 25.

THE text contains a divinely inspired imprecation on those who are involved in the sin of neglecting to call upon God in their families. And though we cannot seek the wrath of God on any class of sinners, yet the subject shows, in most forcible words, the awful condition of all such. We may look at the text as a prediction that God will pour out his fury on prayerless families; and as such it surely claims our solemn consideration. There can be no doubt that the social character of a people will be the best index to their true moral condition. Where the people are ignorant, the families will be so many circles of darkness and evil. Where irreligion prevails, the families will be without any recognition of God, or regard to the exercises of piety. And where sin and profligacy abound, there the families will be so many centres of vice, pollution, and blasphemy. On the other hand, where there is Christian intelligence, and moral order, and religious power, there the families of the people will be peaceful, and be the abodes of the Christian virtues, where all the social graces will be seen in all their genial influence, and transcendent loveliness. O yes! it is piety that gives home its loftiest charms, and its sweetest blessedness!

But where piety abides, will there not be the acknowledgment and worship of the living God? Will not the altar of prayer be reared? And will not holy praise and thanksgiving ascend from thence to the great Source of all our blessing?

Let us then consider,

I. *The grounds of family worship.*

II. *The nature of acceptable family worship.*

III. *The advantages of family worship.*

And,

IV. *Reply to some objections.*

Notice then,

I. *The grounds of family worship.*

And here we would observe,

1. *The moral exigencies of families.*

All the members of every family are fallen, depraved, guilty, and therefore stand in need of divine mercy. The state of one family is the state of each and all. Each, therefore, requires the divine knowledge, the divine favor, and the divine image; and their mutual moral exigencies should lead to mutual prayer. Much diversity of moral condition will be seen in the family groups of the land; but as every family—the most educated, the most moral, and the most orderly—is composed of fallen, sinful beings, then each family requires to be brought into direct contact with God's great remedy for our depravity and sin. Here, then, is seen most clearly one essential ground for the family worship of the living God.

2. *Family necessities and dependency should be a reason for family worship.*

No man is independent of God for any blessing; so truly, the families of mankind are dependent on him. Daily existence, food, health, and every comfort, proceed from God, and he must give them, or we must be miserable and perish. And if God is the author of all our good gifts, especially is he so of the more elevated or perfect blessings which relate to the mind, and the soul's present and immortal welfare. Every peaceful enjoyment, every joyful emotion, every spiritual desire, every holy longing, every heavenly aspiration, must he bestow, or we must remain strangers to them. Now this entire dependency on God should be acknowledged and honored in the exercise of family worship.

3. *The conduct of pagans should excite us to this.*

They have their household gods, and their family offerings. Laban had his family gods. How the heathen shame thousands of professedly Christian families! The recognition of God, and providence, religiously, seems to be taught, even by nature. For it is observable that almost all classes of idolaters regard social religious acts as essential to their domestic well-being and security. But how much more should the rearing of our offspring amid the light of divine religion, ever be regarded in connection with the daily worship of the true Jehovah. If home is to be the sanctuary of every thing most lovely and precious, especially should it be so of those invaluable things which are immortal and divine.

We may well ground it,

4. *On the examples of the godly families of all ages.*

Abraham, wherever he went, reared his family altar to the Lord; and hear God's testimony of him: "For I know him, that he will command his children and his household after him, and they shall keep the way of the Lord, to do justice and judgment; that the Lord may bring upon Abraham that thing which he hath spoken of him."—Gen. xviii. 19.

Joshua resolved to make this, one special object of his life: "Now therefore fear the Lord, and serve him in sincerity and in truth; and put away the gods which your fathers served on the other side of the flood, and in Egypt; and serve ye the Lord. And if it seem evil unto you to serve the Lord, choose you this day whom ye will serve; whether the gods which your fathers served that were on the other side of the flood, or the gods of the Amorites, in whose land ye dwell: but as for me and my house, we will serve the Lord."—Jos. xxiv. 14, 15.

So of David. Amidst all the heavy duties and magnificent attractions of a palace and a court, it is said, "Then David returned to bless his household."—2 Sam. vi. 20.

How delightful is the account given of Cornelius: "There was a certain man in Cæsarea called Cornelius, a centurion of the band called the Italian band. A devout man, and one that feared God, with all his house, which gave much alms to the people, and prayed to God alway."—Acts x. 1, 2.

Now let these instances suffice as brief examples of social piety; and there can be no doubt that the truly religious heads of families, in all ages and all countries, have delighted to honor God around the family altar,

Observe,

II. *The nature of acceptable family worship.*

Our text refers,

1. *To prayer.*

The solemn and comprehensive duty of prayer must ever be one essential of all true worship. Prayer for divine pardon—for divine grace—for spiritual wisdom and understanding. Prayer for providential direction, and all daily temporal blessings. Prayer for all needful aid—for protection from enemies, deliverance from evil, and guidance into all truth. Prayer for the sanctification of all sorrows and afflictions. Prayer, in one word, for our present and everlasting well-being. Prayer for others; for connections, and kindred, and friends; for the church of Christ, and for a perishing world. With the exercise of prayer, we should cherish the spirit and grace of prayer, and also labor to improve the gift of prayer. We should also aim at earnestness; and remember that without faith no kind of prayer can be acceptable to God; and that Jesus the Mediator, must be the way of our approach, at all times, to the throne of grace. For this is an essential condition of successful prayer— "That we ask the Father in Christ's name." With prayer should be united,

2. *Thanksgiving.*

All prayer should be united to this. The apostle unites them—"Be careful for nothing; but in every thing by prayer and supplication with thanksgiving let your requests be made known unto God."—Phil. iv, 6. "Rejoice evermore. Pray without ceasing. In every thing give thanks; for this is the will of God in Christ Jesus concerning you." —1 Thess. v. 16–18. "Speaking to yourselves in psalms and hymns and spiritual songs, singing and making melody in your heart to the Lord. Giving thanks always for all things unto God and the Father in the name of our Lord Jesus Christ."—Eph. v. 19, 20. If this holy thank-offering can be embodied in the sacred hymn or psalm, it will enliven family worship, and also teach holy melody to the young persons of our household. How sweet to hear the united voice of praise arising to God from the domestic hearth!—when, with one voice, parents and children, masters and servants, and often visitors of the household, all glorify God together.

3. *There should be the reading of the word of God.*

Observe the divine command by Moses to the Israelites: "And these words, which I command thee this day, shall be in thine heart: and thou shalt teach them diligently unto thy children, and shalt talk of them when thou sittest in thine house, and when thou walkest by the way, and when thou liest down, and when thou risest up. And thou shalt bind them for a sign upon thine hand, and they shall be as frontlets between thine eyes. And thou shalt write them upon the posts of thy house, and on thy gates."— Deut. vi. 6–9. Now, here is a direction most explicit and clear; and it is manifest that only thus can our families become spiritually and minutely intimate with the holy records of eternal life. Thus, however, they will know the Scriptures, which are able to make them wise unto salvation. And the exhortation of the apostle is most applicable to family worship, where he says—"Let the word of Christ dwell in you richly in all wisdom; teaching and admonishing one another in psalms and hymns and spiritual songs, singing with grace in your hearts to the Lord."—Col. iii. 16.

We may refer,

4. *To the frequency of family worship.*

Some really pious families regard it three times a day—morning, noon, and evening. Most, however, attend to it morning and evening. It seems natural, with the beginning and end of the day, to honor God. With some, it can only be regarded once; the head of the household has to leave early, or other circumstances render twice impossible. If the principle be regarded, and the service loved, then the frequency may be left to the consciences of God's people.

We may refer also,

5. *To the persons who should have the privilege of family worship.*

To this we reply, the entire family; children, servants, visitors—all. All beneath the family roof should be kindly and cordially invited.

Let a few minor directions on the subject here be added.

(1.) Family worship should not be long and tedious at any time, but especially in the evening; thus it becomes a burden, and an unpleasant task, especially to young persons. It may thus disgust them, and give a distaste for divine things.

(2.) The reading of the word should be appropriate. All the word of God is precious, but not equally so. Much of the Old Testament, especially its histories, and the Levitical rites, may be omitted with advantage. The book of Job, the Psalms, and some of the Prophets, however, should occupy a chief place. But the new Testament should be read through and through, except the latter chapters of the visions of the Apocalypse—unless the parent possesses wisdom enough to elucidate them. It will be well always, when needful, to add short expository remarks, and explain difficult words.

(3.) It should be varied and lively. Monotony should be carefully avoided. Some families have certain objects of prayer for each day in the week; as, missions, Christian unity, conversion of the Jews, salvation of the world, &c. Whether this method be adopted or not, if the same ideas, in the same stereotyped phrases, be constantly employed, the service will cease to be edifying, if not absolutely oppressive to those attending it.

How needful to seek the quickening grace of God; and thus to keep the fire of true devotion burning on the altar of the heart!

III. *The advantages of family worship.*

1. *It will be profitable to our own souls.*

By waiting on the Lord, we shall renew our strength; and God will draw nigh to us and bless us. He will answer our prayers, and send us tokens for good. It is not a vain thing; and never can be profitless to worship God.

2. *It may be saving to our families.*

In the use of the means, may we not expect the special blessing of God? At any rate, our children and dependents expect to see consistency; and whether they are benefited savingly or not, they will be left without excuse.

3. *It will certainly secure the Divine approbation.*

It will please God; and forget not, his favor is life, his smile is bliss. If we have God's favor may we not hope that he will be the defence of our families?—sanctifying our states of prosperity or adversity, of health and affliction; and thus all that is really best in providence and grace will be secured.

4. *It will be honorable to religion.*

It will be a family testimony for God—a social manifestation for Bible religion—a rebuke to the families of profligacy, worldliness, and sin around us. It is of great importance to maintain an open and public profession of godliness before the world. And even the ungodly around us will secretly respect the moral consistency of those who are not afraid or ashamed to give religion a place in their family arrangements.

But let us reply,

IV. *To some of the usual objections.*

Some persons object on the ground of,

1. *Personal timidity, and the fear of man.*

This, if allowed to prevail, is sinful: seek grace to overcome it; strive against it. This fear of man, indeed, brings a snare.

2. *Want of talent.*

This is often the excuse of pride. Do it as you have ability; you can do no more; God requires no more. It is not fine prayer that pleases him; and your talents will be increased by using them. "To him that hath shall be given." Begin, and your ability will improve. Better read prayers than neglect the service altogether.

Persons often plead,

3. *Want of time.*

Perhaps for twice a day; but not for once, surely. Not ten minutes a day for family worship! How deplorable such a plea! Time for every thing but the soul, and for the souls of your families. You may have plenty of time to be pent up in the chamber of affliction; and you will have time to die. Then, surely, you should seek time really to live, and to honor God, and seek his blessing. The real inward reason, however, I fear is, want of disposition—want of love to spiritual things—want of the fear of God—want of a deep concern for eternal realities.

Let God's demands, consistency of piety, and the claims of those around you, decide the question. No one will insult God in the great day, by saying they had no time for his worship and service.

I have just three counsels to give in reference to family worship.

(1.) Arrange for it; and be punctual and constant. Do nothing indifferently that pertains to God and religion. Avoid previous confusion, and bustle, and unseeming haste.

(2.) Avoid formality. Labor to be in the spirit, or there will be no profit to any one. There may be the altar, but it will avail nothing without the hallowed fire.

(3.) Expect God's blessing. Do it in humble, simple faith—look to Christ always—avoid self-righteousness.

Finally,

(4.) A word to prayerless families. You cannot, of course, expect God's blessing; but forget not, his curse may rest on your dwellings. He can send blighting influences, and wither every joy, embitter every good, and dissipate every hope. And more, he will demand an account at the last day. Think, then, of your own souls; and also forget not the souls and deathless interests of those committed to your care. Then be persuaded to seek personal religion; give your hearts up to God; and having done so, by faith in Jesus Christ, the only Mediator, then set up the altar of worship in your dwellings, to the honor and glory of his grace.

"Father of all! thy care we bless,
  Which crowns our families with peace:
From thee they sprang, and by thy hand
  They have been, and are still sustained.

To God, most worthy to be praised,
  Be our domestic altars raised;
Who, Lord of heaven, scorns not to dwell
  With saints in their obscurest cell.

To thee may each united house,
  Morning and night, present its vows;
Our servants there, and rising race,
  Be taught thy precepts and thy grace.

Oh, may each future age proclaim
  The honors of thy glorious name!
While pleased and thankful we remove
  To join the family above."

XLIII.—DELIGHT IN DIVINE ORDINANCES.

"And the whole assembly took counsel to keep other seven days: and they kept other seven days with gladness."—2 Chron. xxx. 23.

OUR text refers to a very interesting public religious service, convened by the good king Hezekiah. Apostasy and profanity had fearfully ravaged the nation. A work of reformation was now attempted; and a public service for confession of sin, and a reverential regard to divine ordinances, was convened. "So the posts went with the letters from the king and his princes throughout all Israel and Judah, and according to the commandment of the king, saying, Ye children of Israel, turn again unto the Lord God of Abraham, Isaac, and Israel, and he will return unto the remnant of you that are escaped out of the hand of the kings of Assyria. And be not like your fathers, and like your brethren, which trespassed against the Lord God of their fathers, who therefore gave them up to desolation, as ye see. Now, be ye not stiff-necked, as your fathers were, but yield yourselves unto the Lord, and enter into his sanctuary, which he hath sanctified forever: and serve the Lord your God, that the fierceness of his wrath may turn away from you. For if ye turn again unto the Lord, your brethren and your children shall find compassion before them that lead them captive, so that they shall come again into this land; for the Lord your God is gracious and merciful, and will not turn away his face from you, if ye return unto him."—Verses 6–9. The service was duly held. "And the children of Israel that were present at Jerusalem kept the feast of unleavened bread seven days with great gladness: and the Levites and priests praised the Lord day by day, singing with loud instruments unto the Lord. And Hezekiah spake comfortably unto all the Levites that taught the good knowledge of the Lord: and they did eat throughout the feast seven days, offering peace-offerings, and making confession to the Lord God of their fathers."—Verses 21, 22.

After this protracted service of seven days, the whole assembly took counsel, and they resolved to keep other seven days; and they did so with gladness. This, then, is the subject of our discourse.

We wish to ground two propositions on the text.

I. *Why the people of God should delight in religious worship.*

And,

II. *How they will evince it.*

Notice, then,

I. *Why the people of God should delight in religious worship.*

They should do so on account,

1. *Of its divine authority.*

God demands it. "Thou shalt worship the Lord thy God" is his great command. He has expressly appointed it; sanctioned it with promised rewards; and disobedience to it he has connected with severe threatenings. The intelligences of heaven worship him; and even inanimate nature is called

upon to join in the hallowed service. Hence the Psalmist exclaims—"Praise ye the Lord. Praise ye the Lord from the heavens: praise him in the heights. Praise ye him, all his angels: praise ye him, all his hosts. Praise ye him, sun and moon: praise him, all ye stars of light. Praise him, ye heavens of heavens, and ye waters that be above the heavens. Let them praise the name of the Lord: for he commanded, and they were created."—Ps. cxlviii. 1–5. And, "Bless the Lord, ye his angels, that excel in strength, that do his commandments, hearkening unto the voice of his word. Bless ye the Lord, all ye his hosts; ye ministers of his that do his pleasure. Bless the Lord, all his works in all places of his dominion: bless the Lord, O my soul."—Psalm ciii. 20–22.

They do so because,

2. *Of its adaptation to man's nature and powers.*

A contemplation of the great, and glorious, and good, produces emotions of pleasure. Nearly all the tribes of men worship something. One nation adores the glorious orb of day—another the wind—and another the invisible spirit. Others make idols to represent their imaginary deities. It is obvious that man was destined for religious homage—reverence—prayer—faith—and adoration. To worship God, is to direct the powers of the mind to the right and only object, worthy of it. Man is thus lifted up into holy contact with his Creator; he comes into spiritual connection with the high and lofty One who inhabiteth eternity; and this is the summit of human greatness, and the perfection of man's blessedness and glory.

3. *Because public worship harmonizes with the social constitution of man.*

Secret prayer and meditation are necessary, and truly precious; but man was destined to sympathize most with his fellowmen. Thus they minister to each other's delight; thus they excite and provoke one another to higher and holier exercises. The holy emotion goes from eye to eye, and from heart to heart. The sorrowful lose their griefs amid the sunshine of the service—the joyous have their ecstasies chastened and sanctified, by their communing with the distresses of the sad. The poet has sweetly sung—

"Lo, what an entertaining sight
Are brethren that agree;
Brethren, whose cheerful hearts unite
In bands of piety.

When streams of love, from Christ the spring,
  Descend to every soul;
And heavenly peace, with balmy wing,
  Shades and bedews the whole."

The atmosphere of worship is evidently adapted to produce social affection, and sympathy, and benignity. Hence, all ranks, and classes, and conditions, are the better for their union and communion in the hallowed services of God's house; and the constant attendant on divine services feels, as he sings—

"Peace be within this sacred place,
  And joy a constant guest!
With holy gifts and heavenly grace
  Be her attendants blest.

My soul shall pray for Zion still,
  While life or breath remains;
There my best friends, my kindred dwell,
  There God my Saviour reigns."

4. *Divine worship involves the most interesting and sacred exercises.*

(1.) The attainment of the highest knowledge. Here they hearken to the oracles of truth and life, and obtain supplies of celestial wisdom.

(2.) The offering of sweet and hallowed praise. Returning God thanks for all his mercies—blessing and exalting his holy and glorious name. Praise for life and being—for health and strength—for mental faculties and moral powers—for food and raiment —for prolonged probation, and for renewed mercies—for the chief of gifts, the Lord Jesus Christ—the precious gospel—the throne of mercy, and the bright hope of a boundless bliss in the world to come. How extensive the sphere of praise! How multiplied the benefits to be acknowledged! And how ardent the heart should be, that is thus employed! How exultingly the pious heart bursts forth—

"Praise ye the Lord! my heart shall join
In work so pleasant, so divine,
Now, while the flesh is my abode,
And when my soul ascends to God.

Praise shall employ my noblest powers
While immortality endures;
My days of praise shall ne'er be past,
While life and thought and being last."

(3.) Humble prostration, a sense of unworthiness before God, and devout supplication for mercy and grace. What subject for enlargement! The ignorant seeking knowledge—the guilty seeking pardon—the polluted seeking holiness—the weak seeking strength—the mortal man seeking eternal life, and everlasting glory; besides, all earnestly uniting in prayer, and intercession, and thanksgiving, for all mankind. Oh yes! these services are good and pleasant, and profitable to the soul. No wonder our sacred national bard should portray it so beautiful, when he sings—

"Lord, how delightful 'tis to see
  A whole assembly worship thee!
At once they sing, at once they pray;
  They hear of heaven, and learn the way."

And when he avers—

"I have been there, and still would go;
  'Tis like a little heaven below."

We should delight in it, because,

5. *Divine worship is connected with the greatest of all blessings.*

Divine and spiritual illumination of soul— conviction of conscience, and sorrow for sin —repentance and reform of life—production of faith, and acceptance with God—sanctification of the soul, and its conformity to the divine likeness—obedience to the divine authority—delight in the divine government —resignation under adverse dispensations— elevation of the soul to heavenly things— and withal an increasing meetness for endless glory.

The house of God is the school of celestial training for the service of the skies. It is the palace of present joy, and the very gate to Jehovah's exalted temple in heaven. No marvel that the Psalmist should exclaim —"One thing have I desired of the Lord, that will I seek after; that I may dwell in the house of the Lord all the days of my life, to behold the beauty of the Lord, and to inquire in his temple."—Ps. xxvii. 4. Surely these are ample reasons for delighting in the worship of God.

We proceed then to show,

II. *How this delight will be evinced.*

It will be manifested,

1. *By the holy cheerfulness which will distinguish our attendance.*

"I was glad when they said unto me, let us go into the house of the Lord."—Psa. xxii. 1. "How amiable are thy tabernacles, O Lord of hosts! My soul longeth, yea even fainteth for the courts of the Lord: my heart and my flesh crieth out for the living God. For a day in thy courts is better than a thousand. I had rather be a doorkeeper in the house of my God, than to dwell in the tents of wickedness."—Psa. lxxxiv.

1, 2, 10. The attendance will not be reluctant, or late, or irregular; but cheerful, willing, and constant. They will feel, and sing—

"Sweet is the work, my God and King,
    To praise thy name, give thanks and sing;
To show thy love by morning light,
    And talk of all thy truth by night."

2. *By the spirit which will characterize the worship itself.*

It will be reverential and humble—not self-laudatory, and pharisaical. Adoring and grateful; the soul's highest and sweetest emotions will be excited, and presented to God. Spiritual and heavenly—not bodily service merely—not earthly homage; but the employment of the mind and soul, in which heavenly aspirations, desires, and associations, will be cherished and cultivated. It will be enjoyed as a privilege, and not considered as a duty only. The heart will be really in it, and it will not be wearisome; but there will rather be sorrow and regret when it is over. And as in the text, the worshippers would fain prolong the service, and continue the hallowed exercises; each one exclaiming—

"My willing soul would stay
    In such a frame as this,
And gladly sing herself away,
    To everlasting bliss."

3. *By the moral fruits of worship which we shall exhibit.*

We shall show that it makes us wiser, holier, more heavenly-minded—that it exalts and dignifies the soul—gives moral beauty and celestial loveliness to the spirit—that we carry a sense of God's presence with us, so that the world will take knowledge of us, that we have been with Jesus. Just as things bear away the fragrant odor of the boxes in which they have been placed; so God's people will carry with them, from the house and services of God, the sweet fragrances of divine things; and they will appear to others as the seed which God has blessed.

4. *By giving the interests of divine worship our cordial and liberal support.*

How the Israelites did this in reference to the erection of the tabernacle! How most modern instances of liberality are thrown into the shade, by the accounts given to us of the holy zeal and devotedness which they exhibited! "The children of Israel brought a willing offering unto the Lord, every man and woman, whose heart made them willing to bring for all manner of work, which the Lord had commanded to be made by the hand of Moses."—Exod. xxxv. 29. "And they received of Moses all the offering, which the children of Israel had brought for the work of the service of the sanctuary, to make it withal. And they brought yet unto him free offerings every morning. And all the wise men, that wrought all the work of the sanctuary, came every man from his work which they made; and they spake unto Moses, saying, The people bring much more than enough for the service of the work, which the Lord commanded to make. And Moses gave commandment, and they caused it to be proclaimed throughout the camp, saying, Let neither man nor woman make any more work for the offering of the sanctuary. So the people were restrained from bringing."—Exod. xxxvi. 3–6.

So David, and the nobles, and the people, in reference to the temple. It is worthy of remark, how all orders and classes assisted most cheerfully in the great work. It is said of the king, besides the costly materials he had provided, that he said—"Moreover, because I have set my affection to the house of my God, I have of mine own proper good, of gold and silver, which I have given to the house of my God, over and above all that I have prepared for the holy house, even three thousand talents of gold, of the gold of Ophir, and seven thousand talents of refined silver, to overlay the walls of the house withal."—1 Chron. xxix. 3, 4. And of the nobles, and chiefs of the people—"Then the chief of the fathers and princes of the tribes of Israel, and the captains of thousands and of hundreds, with the rulers of the king's work, offered willingly, and gave for the service of the house of God, of gold five thousand talents and ten thousand drams, and of silver ten thousand talents, and of brass eighteen thousand talents, and one hundred thousand talents of iron. And they with whom precious stones were found, gave them to the treasure of the house of the Lord, by the hand of Jehiel the Gershonite."—Ver. 6–8. And all this was followed by the general offerings of the people —"Then the people rejoiced, for that they offered willingly, because with perfect heart they offered willingly to the Lord: and David the king also rejoiced with great joy." —Ver. 9.

If we love divine worship, we shall freely and liberally support it, as God gives us the means; and we shall ever recognize the pious sentiments of the king of Israel, who devoutly said—"Both riches and honor come of thee, and thou reignest over all; and in thine hand is power and might; and in thine hand it is to make great, and to give strength unto all. Now, therefore, our God, we thank thee, and praise thy glorious name. But who am I, and what is my people, that we should be able to offer so willingly after this sort? For all things come of thee, and of thine own have we given thee."—Ver. 12–14.

Now in proportion to our delight in divine worship, our support will be cheerfully given. This support will also include our time, our influence, and our prayers to God for his blessing. We shall labor, and give, and pray; and do all with a single eye to the glory of God.

Such will be the evidences of ardent attachment to divine worship.

APPLICATION.

(1.) Let the subject lead us to self-examination. Do we thus love God's house and ordinances? Do we eagerly anticipate them—spiritually enjoy them—and would we most gladly prolong them? Would we, as in the text, "keep other seven days with gladness?"

(2.) Let it excite us to greater attachment. Are we not liable to cool in our ardor—to slacken in our service? And do not earthly things often take away the holy relish for spiritual services? If so, let the subject stir us up, and lead us to a more entire consecration to God's service.

(3.) Let it connect the worship of earth with that of heaven. Soon we shall be present in earthly ordinances for the last time. Every service lessens the number of those exalted privileges, and others will be called to occupy our places, both of responsibility and enjoyment. But let the sanctuary, with its blissful exercises, be spiritually regarded, and then their termination here will be followed by the temple services of glory—by the enjoyment of the grand and endless Sabbath above—and by the ravishing delights and pleasures, which are at God's right hand, for evermore. Oh! realize then the sentiments—

"Ours, Saviour, may these glories be,
  When earthly joys are past;

And having lived on earth to thee,
  May we exchange, at last,
This house—these hours of praise and prayer,
For holier—happier worship there."

XLIV.—DOING GOD'S WORK FROM RIGHT PRINCIPLES AND WITH ALL THE HEART.

" And thus did Hezekiah throughout all Judah, and wrought that which was good and right and truth before the Lord his God. And in every work that he began in the service of the house of God, and in the law, and in the commandments, to seek his God, he did it with all his heart, and prospered."—2 Chron. xxxi. 20, 21.

The character of good Hezekiah is beautifully drawn in the Holy Scriptures. God has strikingly exhibited in his history the declaration that those who honor him he will honor; so that while many of the kings of Judah and Israel only appear on the record of Holy Scripture, covered with shame and infamy—Hezekiah, the servant of God, has his name, and an honorable reputation preserved, and handed down for the admiration of future generations.

Hezekiah was a great national and religious reformer; and this chapter abounds with the pleasing details of his labors. But it is not so needful for our purpose, that we enter minutely into the consideration of these, as that we look at the great principles on which he acted. Thus, his spirit and conduct will be found well worthy of our imitation. And they were such as ought to distinguish all God's people in their efforts to extend the cause of Christ in the world.

Let us contemplate,

I. *The great principles by which he was governed.*

II. *His zeal and devotedness to the cause of God.*

And,

III. *The Divine prosperity with which he was favored.*

Observe, then,

I. *The great principles by which he was governed.*

Reversing the order, a little, of the text, we shall observe that he was actuated,

1. *By equity.*

In the text it is said, he wrought that which was "right." Avoided all injustice, —all wrong. Acted equitably in all he did. Did not consult his own pecuniary interests, or the law of expediency, but the claims of justice. This is the only true basis of solid excellency. What does the Lord require of his people? "To do justly." This is one of the essential principles of Divine morality and true godliness. However we may seek to honor God, or advance religion in the world, we must have as the basis of all our operations an unswerving regard to equity and righteousness. God will not have robbery for a burnt-offering. He will not accept of the fruits of oppression, or of the gains of avarice. He will not be pleased even with the most costly sacrifices, if the claims of justice are either disregarded or neglected. Hezekiah's good work rested, in the first instance, on doing that which was "right"—right towards God and towards man.

Another of these principles was that,

2. *Of benevolence.*

In the text called "good." This is the very spirit of the Divine law.—"Thou shalt love thy neighbor as thyself." To do that which is for the real good of others, and that from a good feeling of kindness. There is a difference between a mere righteous and a good man. In both, we are assimilated to the Divine character; but goodness is the glory of God, and the highest perfection of the godly man.

To be righteous, is the demand of the law. To be good, is the end both of the law and the gospel. A righteous king or a righteous reformer must be a blessing to a community; but he is also still more exalted, and more lovely, when all is done in the spirit of benevolence and love. Right doing must be perfected by kind and benignant doing. Hezekiah did that which was "right," and also "good," before the Lord his God.

His conduct also was distinguished,

3. *For fidelity.*

Described as "truth." Fidelity in regarding God's covenants. Sincerity and uprightness of character. For it is added, "before the Lord"—he acted as accountable to God—as in his sight, with reference to his glory. Fidelity involves purity of motive, and simpleness of eye. Having no mixed designs, but acting from an enlightened conscientious desire to honor God. And it also involves constancy in opposition to vacillation; and perseverance in well-doing, in opposition to wearying, or turning aside.

Now, here are the grand essential pillars of religious reformation—equity, goodness, and fidelity; or, as in the text, they are expressed as "right," and "good," and "truth."

Now these were Hezekiah's principles of action, in doing God's work.

How essential these principles are to all true excellency! Notice then,

II. *His zeal and devotedness to the cause of God.*

"And in every work that he began in the service of the house of God, and in the law and in the commandments." Observe,

1. *His labors were numerous.*

"In every work," &c. Not merely one work, but "many." The great workers for God and souls will have many claims on their labors. The friends and donors of one great object are often so, in reference to several and many. The friends of education, are also the friends of peace and liberty. With care and order, a man may do much for many good and useful objects. No man should excuse himself because he is already engaged in one work. Look at the claims made on God's ancient servants! on Moses, on Joshua, on David, on Nehemiah, on Daniel, and on the Apostles of Jesus; also on the Protestant reformers. Think of what Luther had to do! What Calvin had to do! What Knox, and Whitfield, and Wesley had to do! Look at the engagements of Wilberforce—of the missionaries Williams, and Moffat, and Knibb, and others! So Hezekiah threw himself fully into varied and numerous services.

2. *His labors had special respect to the house of God.*

He recognized this as connected with the Divine glory—the Divine favor—and the Divine blessing. He saw too, its intimate bearings on man's elevation, happiness, and salvation. So it is now, and must ever be. Christian sanctuaries are the bulwarks of a nation. Its turrets of honor. Its temples of purity and of peace.

He who would truly bless his country and benefit his species, cannot do so in any way so effectual, as by directing his zeal and liberality to the house of God. The house of God becomes the centre of light to the benighted neighborhood—the school of religious education for the young. It acts as salt, in staying the moral putrescence of the district. It tends to intellectualize the people around. It rears massive barriers against the tide of profligacy. It essentially purifies manners, blesses and exalts the social hearth; and above all, it brings perishing men within the range of life and salvation. Here man is blessed, and blessed in all respects; and here God is most honored and glorified.

3. *His labors were done with entire earnestness and sincerity.*

"With all his heart." This was the main-spring; and gave an impetus to all his efforts. With all his heart—with all its affection for the work. Not coldly—not languidly; but with all the fervor and power of his heart.

The things of religion demand this. God, the soul, and eternity, should ever be identified with this right and whole-heartedness. Religion deserves it—ought to have it. This is according to true wisdom; to give the best to the best objects. Who can fail to admire the full service of the whole heart! And God is pleased with this. It is just in harmony with his claims and demands. We may give attention, and time, and labor, and even diligence to secular duties; but the fervor of the soul God must have for his service. He will not accept the work of the hands without the heart—nor will he accept of half the heart; but he must have the whole heart given to him, and devoted to his work.

Such then was the zeal and devotedness of Hezekiah in the work of the Lord.

Notice,

III. *The Divine prosperity with which he was favored.*

He did God's work with all his heart, "and prospered." Prospered both personally, as a godly man; and publicly, as a king. Those who are fully devoted to God, prosper,

1. *As they are the especial subjects of Divine Providence.*

God cares for them—will undertake for them—keep them—and often signally delivers them. Look at Joseph, and the moral heroes we have mentioned—Moses—David —Daniel! Look at the apostles of Jesus— the great Protestant reformers, and Puritans, and revivalists of all ages and countries! As a rule, they have prospered; they have carried out their plans of piety— succeeded in their works of usefulness; and have alike been victorious for the truth, and blessings to the world. God's providence has been signally displayed in their history; in silencing opposition—beating down their enemies—overruling apparent evil for real good, and delivering them from the most deadly perils. Often, the stones of the street, and the beasts of the field, have been in league with them, and all things have worked together for their good.

But they have also prospered,

2. *As they have been the objects of precious promises.*

God's declarations and engagements of love and mercy towards them, are varied, rich, and numerous—they are both temporal, and spiritual, and eternal. God's blessing is with, and upon them. It maketh rich, and addeth no sorrow therewith.

Now, these conveyances of God's love, cheered his people in all ages. These animated them to duty, and made them happy in it. These were their present support, and a full realization of them, their future reward.

Such also shall prosper,

3. *As their final recompense shall be great and eternal.*

Every thing favorable to eternal life is prosperity. Even poverty, troubles, affliction, in the end, yield a perfectly satisfying reward. Every good act shall be rewarded. Even a cup of water, given to any and every one, in the name of a disciple. Besides, the good God's people do, by the gracious help of God, shall last and abide; and this in itself shall be more than a full return for the toil, and pain, and sacrifice, they have given, or endured, in God's service. To witness the triumph of truth over error—of holiness over sin—of happiness over wretchedness. To behold brands plucked from the burning. To witness in the day of eternity, the fruits of righteous effort, and to be permitted to say to the benignant Judge upon the throne —"Here are the children thou hast given me." Here are the sheaves of the blessed harvest—here are the triumphs of thy cross; and as such, the crown and rejoicing of our souls. Oh, yes! this is prosperity, alike beyond all our present utterance, or conception.

Hezekiah's success in God's work was an ample reward, both of honor and joy to his godly spirit.

Then learn,—

1. That true religion has its distinct recognized principles. Righteousness—goodness—fidelity. We can do nothing without these; and these must never be compromised or superseded.

2. That true religion involves the consecration of ourselves to God. "I beseech you therefore, brethren, by the mercies of God, that ye present your bodies a living sacrifice, holy, acceptable unto God, which is your reasonable service."—Rom. xii. 1. How we should seek to obtain this entire heartedness in the service of God. How we should labor in God's work, and for his glory; so that the sentiments of the poet should be written on our inmost souls:

"I would the precious time redeem,
And longer live for this alone:
To spend, and to be spent, for them
Who have not yet my Saviour known;
Fully on these my mission prove,
And only breathe, to breathe thy love.

My talents, gifts, and graces, Lord,
Into thy blessed hands receive;
And let me live to spread thy word;
And let me to thy glory live;
My every sacred moment spend
In publishing the sinner's Friend."

3. That God's favor will ever secure real prosperity. Yes, prosperity is here—and nowhere else. That is true prosperity which will abide the test of time—the ordeal of a dying hour—and the scrutiny of the judgment-day. Let us so live and labor, that we may anticipate in hearing Christ say— "Well done, good and faithful servant; thou hast been faithful over a few things, I will make thee ruler over many things: enter thou into the joy of thy Lord."—Matt. xxv. 23.

———

XLV.—FELLOWSHIP WITH CHRIST.

"It is a faithful saying: for if we be dead with him, we shall also live with him: if we suffer, we shall also reign with him; if we deny him, he also will deny us: if we believe not, yet he abideth faithful. He cannot deny himself."—2 *Tim.* ii. 11–13.

THE whole system of the Christian religion is one of conditional arrangements. There are great blessings and privileges independent of us, and without our concurrence—such as, the love of God to our lost world—such as, the sacrifice of Jesus for sin—such as, the sending forth of the gospel to all men; but even here, in these revelations of the divine grace, no saving benefit can be derived by man without his concurrence—without the act and exercise of his

own mind. God's love must be the object of our faith—Christ's sacrifice the foundation of our hope—the gospel be received with joy—or those great gifts, so far as we are concerned, are in vain.

Now the same continuous system of mutual considerations runs through the experience and life of the Christian; and the text exhibits them to our view. Let it not be thought that these conditions involve the idea of human merit; or, that they detract from the infinite and sovereign love, and mercy, of God in Christ Jesus; for without the provisions of grace, we should have had no means of returning to God. Without his love to us, we should have had no incentive to love him. Without Christ's atoning sacrifice, there would have been no way of access to the Father. But full redemption having been provided for—then the terms of our acceptance are proposed, and the conditions of discipleship laid down. The text contains these; and we shall take them in the exact order they are placed before us.

Observe,

I. *Dying with Christ, is essential to living with him.*

This subject is treated at large by the apostle Paul—"For if we have been planted together in the likeness of his death, we shall be also in the likeness of his resurrection. Knowing this, that our old man is crucified with him, that the body of sin might be destroyed, that henceforth we should not serve sin. For he that is dead is freed from sin. Now if we be dead with Christ, we believe that we shall also live with him: knowing that Christ being raised from the dead, dieth no more; death hath no more dominion over him. For in that he died, he died unto sin once; but in that he liveth, he liveth unto God."—Rom. vi. 5–10.

Observe: in our carnal state we are alive to sin; we live in sin, to sin; and sin lives and works in us.

Observe: Christ died on account of sin; not on account of his own sin—for he was holy; but on account of ours. Without shedding of blood there could be no remission. He died to put away sin, by the sacrifice of himself.

Then observe: we must enter into this work of his by faith. We must be crucified with Christ, and thus die to sin. By virtue of his atoning blood, the power of sin must be destroyed, and we must become dead to it. Further: Christ having died for sin—

lived again. He died once; but he rose—and now liveth evermore. Now it is just so with the believer. "Likewise reckon ye also yourselves to be dead indeed unto sin, but alive unto God through Jesus Christ our Lord."—Rom. vi. 11. We have life through faith in Christ; we experience a spiritual resurrection from the dead—"You hath he quickened, who were dead in trespasses and sins." Now the link of connection here is, that—unless we die to sin, we cannot live with him—"Jesus said unto her, I am the resurrection, and the life: he that believeth in me, though he were dead, yet shall he live."—John xi. 25.

Then observe,

II. *Suffering with Christ, is essential to reigning with him.*

Now Christ led a suffering life; he was poor—a child of sorrows and griefs. He was tempted, tried, despised, persecuted, and vilely treated. Now observe, he distinctly stated, that his people would have to tread in his steps—partake of his suffering—drink of his cup. Hear what he says—"If the world hate you, ye know that it hated me before it hated you. If ye were of the world, the world would love his own; but because ye are not of the world, but I have chosen you out of the world, therefore the world hateth you. Remember the word that I said unto you, the servant is not greater than his lord. If they have persecuted me, they will also persecute you; if they have kept my saying, they will keep yours also. But all these things will they do unto you for my name's sake, because they know not him that sent me."—John xv. 18–21.

Now to suffer with Christ, is to suffer in the same cause—in the service of holiness and God. To suffer on his account—for being his disciples—for owning him as our head and Lord, and being found among his faithful and spiritual followers. To suffer in his spirit—with resignation towards God, and meekness towards men. To bear scorn and contempt, and injuries for Christ's sake; in the spirit of patience, and prayerful submission. And instead of hating our persecutors, and reviling in return for reviling—to pity them, and pray for them, and bless them; thus showing to the world the mind and temper of the Lord Jesus.

But mark, after Christ had suffered, he reigned; his cross and crown were connected. Christ's deepest humiliation was the stepping-stone to his highest glory; Calvary was united to heaven, and his cross was the ladder to his eternal throne. "And being found in fashion as a man, he humbled himself, and became obedient unto death, even the death of the cross. Wherefore God also hath highly exalted him, and given him a name which is above every name: that at the name of Jesus every knee should bow, of things in heaven, and things in earth, and things under the earth; and that every tongue should confess that Jesus Christ is Lord, to the glory of God the Father."—Phil. ii. 8–11. "But we see Jesus, who was made a little lower than the angels for the suffering of death, crowned with glory and honor; that he by the grace of God should taste death for every man." In his sacerdotal prayer, he connected his finishing the Father's work, with the Father's glorifying him at his right hand. His suffering servants shall in like manner reign with him. He does not wish to reign alone; all his saints are co-heirs with him. "And if children, then heirs; heirs of God, and joint heirs with Christ; if so be that we suffer with him, that we may be also glorified together."—Rom. viii. 17.

Now in reference to his saints reigning with him, and partaking of his glory, hear what he says to his disciples—"Ye are they which have continued with me in my temptations. And I appoint unto you a kingdom, as my Father hath appointed unto me." —Luke xxii. 28, 29. Hearken to his solemn prayer—"Neither pray I for these alone, but for them also which shall believe on me through their word; that they all may be one; as thou, Father, art in me, and I in thee, that they also may be one in us: that the world may believe that thou hast sent me. And the glory which thou gavest me I have given them; that they may be one, even as we are one: I in them, and thou in me, that they may be made perfect in one; and that the world may know that thou hast sent me, and hast loved them, as thou hast loved me. Father, I will that they also, whom thou hast given me, be with me where I am; that they may behold my glory, which thou hast given me: for thou lovedst me before the foundation of the world."—John xvii. 20–24.

Hear also, what the Spirit said to the churches—"He that overcometh, the same shall be clothed in white raiment; and I will not blot out his name out of the book of life, but I will confess his name before my Father, and before his angels. To him that overcometh will I grant to sit with me in my throne, even as I also overcame, and am set down with my Father in his throne."—Rev. iii. 5, 21.

Thus Christian discipleship, as it is in antagonism to the world, is likely in some way, to demand from the Christian, sacrifice, and self-denial, and willingness to bear the cross. And the condition of reigning with Christ, is, that we do cheerfully bear the cross, endure shame, reproach, loss, afflictions, or imprisonment, and even yield up life, if his cause and the interests of truth should demand it, rather than abandon our profession, and make shipwreck of faith. As suffering and reigning were linked together in Christ's history and work, so, they may also be with us; and to this item in the claims of Jesus, a cheerful submission must be given.

Then notice,

III. *Denying Christ will be followed by Christ denying us.*

One of the Saviour's addresses refers to this subject, and distincly conveys this truth to our minds :—"But whosoever shall deny me before men, him will I also deny before my Father which is in heaven."—Matt. x. 33. Now to deny Christ is to cast off the profession of him before men; or it is to unite with his enemies, and relapse into worldliness; to go back into a course of irreligion, settled sin, and rebellion, Now this is alike base and ungrateful. It is a heinous sin; a flagrant act of perfidy and treason against the Son of God. And the text supposes that this denial of Christ is persisted in; for Peter denied him, and repented, and was pardoned. But the text involves the idea, that the denial of Christ, is not the result of sudden temptation sincerely repented of; but is a virtual and continued denial of Christ— a taking off his costume—casting away his yoke—a renunciation of his name—separation from his people; and the abandonment of his authority.

Now this apostasy persevered in, will result in Christ denying them. He will disown them as his followers—reject them as his disciples—cease to recognize them as his friends. He will say,—"I know you not." "I do not approve of you, ye workers of iniquity."

Now, this principle God maintained with Israel of old. "When I shall say to the righteous, that he shall surely live; if he trust to his own righteousness, and commit iniquity, all his righteousness shall not be remembered; but for his iniquity that he hath committed, he shall die for it."—Ezek. xxxiii. 13. And on this equitable principle, he will deal with all his people in the last day. Holiness, truth, and the honor of his cause, alike demand it. Hence a denial of Christ, and apostasy from him, will expose its miserable victims to "a certain looking for of judgment and fiery indignation, which shall devour the adversaries."—Heb. x. 26–30.

Then, observe, the declaration,

IV. *That however men may vacillate, Christ is unchanging.*

"He abideth faithful: he cannot deny himself."

Now Jesus says—"These are the terms I propose,—these are the principles I establish,—from these I will never swerve." Faithfulness is essential to Christ's honor and glory. He cannot deny himself, any more than the sun can produce darkness. It is an eternal impossibility. Any want of fidelity in Christ, in any respect, would throw his moral kingdom into dire and irreparable confusion. His unchangeable truthfulness— his unswerving fidelity, are the very pillars of his throne, the very basis on which his empire rests. What a ground of joy is this! No circumstances can affect Christ, so as to make his sayings and promises uncertain. He cannot deny himself,—he never has done so,—he never will do so. So, if we apostatize, he will be faithful. He, in that case, must disown us. The one is just as true and essential to Christ, as the other. He is the word of God—the truth of God; and therefore, he cannot lie : he abideth faithful, and cannot deny himself.

Observe : our unbelief does not affect him, because his promise is made to faith,—his rejection of men, to their unbelief. Faith will realize the blessing; apostasy incurs the curse. So that his purity and truth, in either case, remains unaffected.

Learn, then,

1. The terms of Christian discipleship. These are—deadness to the world; living to Christ and to righteousness; confession of Jesus before men; readiness to suffer for his sake ; and fidelity in the use of the appointed means of salvation. All these are indispensable; and they are all reasonable in themselves. Nothing is demanded, which is not in perfect harmony with our moral elevation,—spiritual happiness,—and eternal safety.

2. Remember that Jesus provides grace for all his people, and which is ever sufficient for them. Self-reliance will not be effectual, but entire dependence on Jesus. "I can do all things," said Paul, "through Christ who strengtheneth me." And so it will be with every humble trusting Christian. The promises of Christ are all that we need. They insure the grace that will establish us—that will fortify us—that will give endurance and patience, and render fidelity easy and joyous to us. So that while so much is demanded from us, yet sufficient ability is guaranteed. On this, then, must we devoutly rely, and seek the supplies needful for every exigency and trial.

3. It should surely be enough to be co-sharers with Christ. The highest dignity God can bestow on us, is to make us co-heirs with his beloved Son. To be sons of God with him. To be beloved with him. To have a place in his Father's house—and a share in his kingdom—and a part of his throne. And then at length to participate of his glory and ineffable joy forever. But with his joy—his crown, his glory, are his sufferings. And how reasonable, too, that we have fellowship with these, in order to our exaltation and blessedness with Christ for evermore. Never forget the terms and the glorious end as expressed in the lines—

"To patient faith the prize is sure,
 And all who to the end endure
 The cross, shall wear the crown."

XLVI.—HELP IN TROUBLE.

"Give us help from trouble; for vain is the help of man."—*Psa.* cviii. 12.

OUR text contains a very striking and affecting prayer. It is one, too, that all will be called on to offer at one time or another. Happy is it when sorrow leads to prayer, and affliction to a more devoted and spiritual life. Trouble is sometimes borne in sullen moroseness, and with a rebellious spirit towards God. Sometimes it is accompanied with fretfulness, and impatience. Sometimes persons contend with it in a spirit of self-sufficiency, and rely on their own arm. Sometimes in trouble human aid is chiefly sought; but how much better to cherish the spirit of the text, and go at once to the divine throne, and say—"Give us help in trouble." Besides, trouble—whether sanctified or not—will often be our portion; whether willing or not, we must bear it; and whether we go to finite sources or not, it will often baffle all our efforts for its removal, except by the divine aid. So that reason as well as piety unites in the sentiments of the text. Then, instead of being turbulent and unresigned—instead of leaning on our own strength, and instead of seeking the aid of fallible beings like ourselves—let us at once invoke the gracious help of God our Father, who can sustain in troubles, or deliver us out of them; or so overrule them, that they shall be placed first in the inventory of our choicest blessings.

Observe then in our subject,

I. *A very common experience.*
"Trouble."

II. *A very certain resource.*
Prayer to God. "Give us help," &c.

III. *A very evident truth.*
"For vain is the help of man."

Observe then,

I. *A very common experience.*
"Trouble."

Now the word is very comprehensive. It may include,

1. *Bodily trouble.*

Sin has sown the seeds of disease in the human system; and the result is a fearful harvest of pains and maladies, and physical suffering. Every part of the body is now vulnerable and frail, and liable to disorder, derangement, and disease. Sometimes these bodily troubles are severe, accumulated, and continued; often they are incurable by human agency. The Psalmist speaks of troubles of this kind which bore heavily upon him:—"In the day of my trouble I sought the Lord; my sore ran in the night, and ceased not; my soul refused to be comforted. I remembered God, and was troubled; I complained, and my spirit was overwhelmed. Thou holdest mine eyes waking: I am so troubled that I cannot speak."—Psa. lxxvii. 2–4.

How melancholy the condition of the patient Job! "So am I made to possess months of vanity, and wearisome nights are appointed to me. When I lie down, I say, when shall I arise, and the night be gone? And I am full of tossings to and fro unto the dawning of the day. My flesh is clothed with worms and clods of dust; my skin is broken, and become loathsome. My days are swifter than a weaver's shuttle, and are spent without hope."—Job vii. 3–6.

Then there is,

2. *Family trouble.*

Family enjoyments are all fragile and mutable. Change is written on every aspect of the social circle. Parents, children, and friends, are all liable to affliction and death. They are all depraved. Often enemies of God and rejecters of the gospel. How great and trying may be the troubles arising from these sources! Bereavements often darken the dwellings of the righteous. How Job felt this, in reference to the storm that swept over his dwelling, and left him childless in an hour! How Abraham mourned over Sarah—Jacob over Rachel—David over Absalom; and others who were removed from the family circle! See the sisters at Bethany, overwhelmed with distress, at the death of Lazarus, their brother! But bitter as this cup of family trouble is, yet is it not more distressing to have rebellion against God in our families? To see displayed the workings of religious contempt,—the bitter hate of carnal hostility to God and to his service. Yet the best of men, and the most devoted of parents, have thus suffered. So did our first parents when their first-born was an envious hater and murderer of his brother. So did Abraham suffer. So Jacob most severely. So Eli and David, and many others. And so it may be with you; for this is still a very general experience, even of godly parents. Besides,

3. *There is church trouble.*

The ark of God may be in exile. The house of God in ruins. The cause of God in adversity. The church may be low spiritually, or be persecuted, or abandoned by its former friends. And hence, how great and intense a trouble this is to the pious children of God. How most deeply did David make God's cause his own. God's house, and ordinances, and people, were his delight. He says—"I was glad when they said unto me, let us go into the house of the Lord. Our feet shall stand within thy gates, O Jerusalem." He declares how he is concerned for its peace. "Pray for the peace of Jerusalem: they shall prosper that love thee. Peace be within thy walls, and prosperity within thy palaces. For my brethren and companions' sake, I will now say, Peace be within thee. Because of the house of the Lord our God I will seek thy good:" ver. 6–9.

And how feelingly and devotedly did good Nehemiah feel for the city and temple of God. Hear the tender plaints of his soul; and hearken to his earnest supplications to God. "And it came to pass when I heard these words, that I sat down and wept, and mourned certain days, and fasted, and prayed before the God of heaven. And said, I beseech thee, O Lord God of heaven, the great and terrible God, that keepeth covenant and mercy for them that love him and observe his commandments: let thine ear now be attentive, and thine eyes open, that thou mayest hear the prayer of thy servant which I pray before thee now, day and night, for the children of Israel thy servants, and confess the sins of the children of Israel which we have sinned against thee: both I and my father's house have sinned." —Neh. i. 4–6. And how his grief affected his health and countenance as he attended to his official duties as cup-bearer to the king. "Wherefore the king said unto me, Why is thy countenance sad, seeing thou art not sick? this is nothing else but sorrow of heart. Then I was very sore afraid, and said unto the king, Let the king live forever; why should not my countenance be sad when the city, the place of my fathers' sepulchres, lieth waste, and the gates thereof are consumed with fire?"—Neh. ii. 2, 3.

So also did Jeremiah pour out his soul in reference to God's cause. "Zion spreadeth forth her hands, and there is none to comfort her: the Lord hath commanded concerning Jacob that his adversaries should be round about him: Jerusalem is as a menstruous woman among them. Behold, O Lord, for I am in distress; my bowels are troubled, mine heart is turned within me; for I have grievously rebelled: abroad the sword bereaveth, at home there is as death." —Lam. i. 17, and ver. 20. And again, how he weeps and prays. "Mine eye runneth down with rivers of water for the destruction of the daughter of my people. Mine eye trickleth down, and ceaseth not, without any intermission, till the Lord look down and behold."—Lam. iii. 48–50.

Now such an experience is not uncommon to those who are laboring to extend religion, and where sterility and deadness pervade the visible kingdom of Jesus.

We notice,

4. *That there is heart-trouble.*

Religion begins with it. For weeping for sin, and brokenness of heart, precede the comforts and joys of salvation. It is often the result of our negligence and formality, and relapses into sin. How much mental anxiety and spiritual distress is caused by our backslidings and moral aberrations. Often doubts and fears cause us trouble: often alarm and anxieties as to perils do this.

Now, these mental and moral troubles of heart are often most painful. So the godly in all ages have acknowledged it. Other troubles can be borne when the mind is serene, and the heart strong, and the graces vigorous; but a depressed soul, languid emotions, feeble graces, moral dreariness and winter withering all things, must be most painful to the devout servant of God. Hence the forcibleness of the lines:

> " O that I new the secret place
>   Where I might find my God!
> I'd spread my wants before his face,
>   And pour my woes abroad.
>
> I'd tell him how my sins arise,
>   What sorrows I sustain:
> How joys decay, and comfort dies,
>   And leave my heart in pain."

So all joy seems fled, and all hope ready to expire under heart-trouble:

> "But O! when gloomy doubts prevail,
>   I fear to call thee mine;
> The springs of comfort seem to fail,
>   And all my hopes decline."

How true the proposition grounded on the text, that trouble of some kind or another is the Christian's common experience.

But notice, our subject reveals,

II. *A very certain resource.*

That is, betaking ourselves to God in prayer.

Observe here,

1. *The resource itself.* God.

Now, just remember, that he knows all our troubles. Then, that he can deliver from them; or he can sustain us under them; or he can make trouble a blessing of the very greatest magnitude. He also is a resource at hand, and not afar off. He is ever graciously disposed to help and comfort his people. Moreover, he has invited us to come to him in every trial and time of sorrow; and he has given us great and precious promises, adapted to every season of affliction and suffering.

But notice,

2. *How the resource is available.*

By prayer. As in the text—"Give us help from trouble."

Now, the prayer need not be lengthy, or arranged, or fine, as the text proves; but it may be very short—a mere fragment. But it must be the prayer of conscious need. We must feel our troubles, and implore relief by earnest prayer. We must long for the help we ask for, and fervently pant after it. And it must be the prayer of believing supplication. Not mere asking, but we must supplicate, and that in faith—faith in both God's ability and willingness—faith, too, in the appointed medium of all our mercies—the Lord Jesus Christ, our living Advocate and Intercessor. And our prayer must be that of humble hope. We must expect the deliverance,—lift up our eyes and hearts to God, and wait for the deliverance. We must look for it as a watchman looks for the morning. And withal, our prayer must be the prayer of patient submission. Not to dictate to God about the way or the period, or the instruments of our deliverance; but be passive, and leave all the processes of the help to God alone.

Observe, such is the resource of mercy for the soul in trouble. Now, while God is our help in trouble, he will be inquired of, and sought after; and hence prayer is the medium of our success. For he has said— " And call upon me in the day of trouble: I will deliver thee, and thou shalt glorify me."—Ps. l. 15. "He shall call upon me, and I will answer him: I will be with him in trouble; I will deliver him, and honor him."—Ps. xci. 15. So he has expressly assured us by his servant. "But now thus saith the Lord that created thee, O Jacob, and he that formed thee, O Israel, fear not: for I have redeemed thee, I have called thee by thy name; thou art mine. When thou passest through the waters, I will be with thee; and through the rivers, they shall not overflow thee: when thou walkest through the fire, thou shalt not be burned; neither shall the flame kindle upon thee."—Isa. xliii. 1, 2. And he has given us the most solemn assurance of his presence and delivering mercy. "For he hath said, I will never leave thee, nor forsake thee. So that we may boldly say, the Lord is my helper, and I will not fear what man shall do unto me."—Heb. xiii. 5, 6.

But notice in our subject,

III. *A very evident truth.*

" For vain is the help of man."

Now, good men may give us wise counsel, and they may sympathize sincerely and tenderly, and they may pray for us, and thus be instrumental of good to our souls; but they can neither sustain us in trouble, nor sanctify our sorrows, nor deliver us out of our afflictions.

Observe,

1. *They cannot control our circumstances.* But God can: he alone disposes of the conditions of men—raiseth up or casteth down, enriches or impoverishes, sends prosperity or adversity, joy or grief. All events are at his disposal; so confessed Nebuchadnezzar. "And at the end of the days, I Nebuchadnezzar lifted up mine eyes unto heaven, and mine understanding returned unto me, and I blessed the Most High, and I praised and honored him that liveth forever, whose dominion is an everlasting dominion, and his kingdom is from generation to generation : and all the inhabitants of the earth are reputed as nothing : and he doeth according to his will in the army of heaven, and among the inhabitants of the earth; and none can stay his hand, or say unto him, What doest thou?"—Dan. iv. 34, 35.

2. *They cannot drive back our enemies.*

Either those in the world, or our spiritual ones; but God can; he can enable us effectually to resist both, and to triumph over them. Hence sang David—"Blessed be the Lord, who daily loadeth us with benefits, even the God of our salvation. He that is our God is the God of salvation; and unto God the Lord belong the issues from death. But God shall wound the head of his enemies, and the hairy scalp of such an one as goeth on still in his trespasses."—Psalm lxviii. 19–21.

3. *They cannot turn our afflictions into a blessing.*

But God can: he is able "out of the eater to bring forth meat, and out of the strong to bring forth sweetness." He can make the fire to purify and not consume; he can cause the winds to scatter the chaff, while the grain abides, and is preserved. Hence the apostle shows the experimental profitableness of affliction : "And not only so, but we glory in tribulations also; knowing that tribulation worketh patience; and patience, experience; and experience, hope; and hope maketh not asham-

ed: because the love of God is shed abroad in our hearts by the Holy Ghost which is given unto us."—Rom. v. 3–5.

4. *They cannot deliver us from our troubles.*

Look at Abraham on the mount with Isaac! Look at Jacob meeting Esau! Look at the Israelites on the way to the Red Sea! Look at Daniel in the den of lions! Look at the Hebrews in the fiery furnace! Look at Peter in prison—at Paul in the stocks! Now, in all these cases vain would have been the skill and power of man; but God did deliver each and all of them; and he will deliver those who put their trust in him. Then how complete and conclusive is the text, and how we should rejoice in the solace it affords!

APPLICATION.

Then we call upon all in trouble to adopt it.

(1.) It is your duty to do so, because God has enjoined it—commanded it over and over again. But it is your privilege to do so; and what a privilege! How great, how blessed, how unspeakable! In adopting it, especially seek to realize it by faith—to trust to it without the shadow of doubting.

(2.) How miserable the prayerless in trouble! What a sad and dreary spectacle! How mournful—how pitiable are these indeed! And then how great the advantages which religion presents, not only as to futurity, but even in the present life.

(3.) Be thankful for the help experienced. Let mouth, and heart, and life praise the Lord. Let your whole being magnify his name.

> "I 'midst ten thousand dangers stand,
> Supported by his guardian hand;
> And see, when I survey my ways,
> Ten thousand monuments of praise.
>
> Thus far his arm hath led me on;
> Thus far I make his mercy known;
> And while I tread this desert land,
> New mercies shall new songs demand.
>
> My grateful soul on Jordan's shore
> Shall raise one sacred pillar more;
> Then bear in his bright courts above
> Inscriptions of immortal love."

XLVII.—CHRIST OUR GREAT AND WONDERFUL SAVIOUR.

"And he saw that there was no man, and wondered that there was no intercessor: therefore his arm brought salvation unto him; and his righteousness, it sustained him. For he put on righteousness as a breastplate, and as an helmet of salvation upon his head; and he put on the garments of vengeance for clothing, and was clad with zeal as a cloak."—*Isaiah* lix. 16, 17.

In the commencement of this chapter there is a fearful description of the moral degradation and misery of the Jewish nation. The prophet denies the surmise that Jehovah could not save them. "Behold, the Lord's hand is not shortened, that he cannot save; neither his ear heavy, that it cannot hear:" verse 1. But he shows how iniquities had separated between them and God. "But your iniquities have separated between you and your God, and your sins have hid his face from you, that he will not hear. For your hands are defiled with blood, and your fingers with iniquity: your lips have spoken lies, your tongue hath muttered perverseness. None calleth for justice, nor any pleadeth for truth: they trust in vanity, and speak lies; they conceive mischief, and bring forth iniquity:" verses 2, 3, and 4. Having shown the character of their natural vices, he then also exhibits the infatuation and vanity arising therefrom (ver. 5 & 6). He then adds the list of their most heinous and aggravated sins (ver. 7 & 8). Then the consequence of this is given in a most fearfully graphic manner (ver. 9 to 13). In the midst of all this moral evil—judgment, and equity, and truth, had apparently failed (ver. 14 & 15). In considering this moral misery, he then introduces one to plead for them, and save them.

It is quite clear that the passage points to the blessed Messiah who came emphatically to save his people from their sins. But the text is equally applicable to Jesus, as the Saviour of mankind in general; and in this extended sense we shall apply it in this discourse.

Observe,

I. *Man's miserable and hopeless condition.*

"He saw there was no man," v. 16.

(1.) Now here there is something implied, and that is, the moral ruin of the people, and their wretchedness, as the result of their woeful guilt and rebellion against God. This guilt was followed by the most extreme moral debasement, and consequent misery. Now this description applies to all mankind, for all have sinned against God. Not one human being is righteous, no, not one; all have gone astray from God, and his holy commandments; and thus all are guilty and defiled before him.

(2.) Something more also is stated—there was no deliverer—no man; perhaps, literally, no brother to redeem—no mediator to interpose, or advocate to plead for them. Now this was literally the fact in reference to mankind. In all the millions of our race, there was no suitable one to interpose, to redeem, to deliver us. Now the want of such a Saviour arose partly from the universal depravity of all mankind; for the Redeemer, or Mediator, must not be involved in the guilt or condemnation, or he would not be able to deliver or ransom others. As every man was involved in the common condemnation and misery, there was none to intercede—not one in the whole family of man. Such, then, was the condition of our apostate, perishing world. Such was our ruin, helplessness, and desperate estate, by reason of our transgression against God. But how delightful the consideration, that when thus involved in moral darkness, and apparent hopelessness, God remembered us in our low estate—for his mercy endureth forever!

Observe, then,

II. *The divine and gracious provision made on our behalf.*

"Therefore his arm brought salvation unto him; and his righteousness, it sustained him."

Now notice here,

1. *Salvation originated with God.*

"His arm." Now here, both the skill to devise, and the power to effect our salvation, seem included. God saw the means by which man might yet be delivered; he therefore planned the great achievement—arranged the wondrous scheme. Then he also executed it; for as no created mind could devise, so, no created power could effect it. He therefore undertook the whole, and by his almighty energy he brought salvation. Now our salvation is often represented as a work of Almighty power; hence the poet has said:

"'Twas great to speak a world from naught,
But greater to redeem."

Now in bringing salvation, notice,

2. *He did it in connection with our nature.*

As "there was no man," he formed himself into a man, for this object and this work. He put on our humanity. He took on him the nature of the culprit to be redeemed. He tabernacled in the flesh—was "made of a woman." Hence he became emphatically "the man"—"the Son of man." And it was in this vestment of our nature, that he put forth his own arm to bring salvation. By the assumption of our nature, he became our brother, on whom devolved the right to redeem back his enslaved kinsmen; so that it behooved him to be made in all things like unto his brethren.

Observe, in effecting our salvation,

3. *The various and illustrious characteristics he displayed.*

(1.) He was sustained by righteousness. Now, his object was a righteous one. The display of God's unsullied and perfect righteousness. So he put on the holiness which appertained to him, as the only-begotten Son of God, to manifest his Father; and in his pure and sinless nature, and spotless spirit and example, and work, it shone forth.

Besides, it was his object to open a way for the restoration of man to righteousness. For there could not be a salvation which did not include this principal idea, of man being brought again to bear a moral likeness to God.

Now this holy purpose sustained him. It was the energetic element of his being, in all his work. And this perfect righteousness of his own nature, was to him as a breastplate. It protected his heart against the rude and wicked assaults of those who treated him as an impostor, a deceiver, and wicked person. Hence he inquired, "Which of you convinceth me of sin?" So when they charged him with being in league with Satan, and the works of darkness—he had inward conscious purity, and a righteous holy spirit; and this he put on as his breastplate.

(2.) He had on his head the helmet of salvation. He came to save. He was, so to speak, the great hero of mercy—the Deliverer of the slave—the Friend of the perishing. He was announced as "mighty to save." How he displayed his saving power, in the days of his flesh! He saved persons of all nations, and conditions, and degrees of guilt. The extortionate Zaccheus—the tax-collecting Matthew—the impure woman, denominated "a sinner;" "the dying thief," &c.

He went forth to save; and he met with no case too difficult for his saving energy. However wretched, or humanly hopeless, or deeply possessed by the powers of darkness; his word delivered, his grace redeemed. At his merciful bidding, all manner of diseases, of miseries, and woes, forsook their wretched victims, and fled.

(3.) He wore the "garments of vengeance." By the assumption of these, he seems to be prepared for aggressive movements. Now, his vengeance was displayed against the hypocrisy and soul-destroying practices of the Scribes and Pharisees and Rulers. How he exposed and denounced these! Hear his withering and condemning appeals! "Woe unto you, Scribes and Pharisees, hypocrites! for ye devour widows' houses, and for a pretence make long prayer: therefore ye shall receive the greater damnation. Woe unto you, Scribes and Pharisees, hypocrites! for ye are like unto whited sepulchres, which indeed appear beautiful outward, but are within full of dead men's bones, and of all uncleanness. Even so ye also outwardly appear righteous unto men, but within ye are full of hypocrisy and iniquity."—Matt. xxiii. 14, 27, 28.

He also exhibited this vengeance against all forms of sin and moral evil. He especially manifested it against the powers of darkness; hence his expulsion of demons, and their trembling, and their confessing and flying before him. He also exerted this vengeance over death and the grave: hence he uttered in majestic effect, the language of the ancient prophecy: "I will ransom them from the power of the grave; I will redeem them from death; O death, I will be thy plagues; O grave, I will be thy destruction; repentance shall be hid from mine eyes."—Hosea xiii. 14.

Now his vengeance was displayed against that which had cursed and degraded man; and with this combination of evil he had to do battle, that we might be rescued from a condition of galling bondage and peril.

But observe,

(4.) He "was clad with zeal as with a cloak." An intense, burning spirit of zeal dwelt in him, and encompassed him as he went on to his great work. He was never formal, never supine, nor apathetic; he never wearied, nor turned aside; he never faltered, or hesitated ; his zeal covered him all over as a cloak. See him when twelve years of age, in the temple ; and hear his reply to his anxious mother : "And when they saw him, they were amazed : and his mother said unto him, Son, why hast thou thus dealt with us ? Behold, thy father and I have sought thee sorrowing. And he said unto them, How is it that ye sought me ? wist ye not that I must be about my Father's business ?" See him travelling to Jordan, ninety miles, to be baptized ! See him toiling and laboring all day, and praying all night. Hear his exclamation—"I have a baptism to be baptized with, and how I am straitened till it is accomplished !" Behold him in the garden, and hear his exclamation of sorrow and horror : "My soul is exceeding sorrowful, even unto death ; tarry ye here, and watch with me. And he went a little farther, and fell on his face, and prayed, saying, O my Father, if it be possible, let this cup pass from me : nevertheless, not as I will, but as thou wilt."—Matt. xxvi. 38, 39.

Behold him erect, in conscious dignity, before the Jewish Sanhedrim ! Hear how he vindicates his mission and character before Pilate ; and he never quailed during that dreary night of suffering and anguish. He makes the cause of the weeping daughters of Israel his own ; he instructs and saves the dying malefactor by his side ; he commends his heart-pierced mother to John, his beloved disciple ; he agonizes amidst the darkness of his apparently deserted spirit ; he rallies at the last moment, and shouts with a loud voice, as a dying Redeemer triumphing—"It is finished !"—then gave up the ghost.

Then learn from this subject,

1. The utter inadequacy of human means to save a sinful world. If earthly power had been sufficient, God could have raised up a great hero for the work ; he could have given wisdom, as he did to Solomon ; meekness and endurance, as to Moses ; courage, as to Joshua and David ; and physical might, as to Samson ; but all would have been mere feebleness, in regard to a work so stupendous as our redemption. No man, nor even angel, could achieve it.

Observe,

2. The fitness and perfect ability of Jesus to save us.

Yes, it is in Christ we see the power needed, the ability required ; so that God might well say of him—"In thy name shall they rejoice all the day : and in thy righteousness shall they be exalted. For thou art the glory of their strength : and in thy favor our horn shall be exalted. For the Lord is our defence ; and the Holy One of Israel is our king. Then thou spakest in vision to thy holy one, and saidst, I have laid help upon one that is mighty ; I have exalted one chosen out of the people."—Psalm lxxxix. 16–19.

Consider,

3. The confidence and gratitude he should inspire in our souls.

"Come, let us all unite to praise
    The Saviour of mankind ;
Our thankful hearts, in solemn lays,
    Be with our voices joined.

Worship and honor, thanks and love,
    Be to our Jesus given !
By men below, by hosts above,
    By all in earth and heaven !"

Notice,—

4. The folly and wickedness of despising the salvation he has brought. Where shall we look for deliverance if we despise Christ, and reject his gospel ? Besides, how heinous and base the state of heart that can treat his person and wondrous love with neglect, or disdain. How awful will be their condition in the great day of Christ's second advent, and when he shall sit upon his glorious throne of judgment.

"But sinners, filled with guilty fears,
    Behold his wrath prevailing ;
For they shall rise and find their tears
    And sighs are unavailing :
The day of grace is past and gone ;
Trembling they stand before the throne,
    All unprepared to meet him."

Learn,

5. The welcome Jesus waits to give to the vilest transgressor, who penitently and believingly seeks his saving grace. Oh, how marvellous, that despite our guilt, and impenitence, and unbelief, he still stands willing, yea, solicitous to bless us, and to make us the rich partakers of his pardoning and adopting love. How truly it is said even of the vilest—

"Jesus ready stands to save them,
    Full of pity, love, and power."

XLVIII.—CHRIST THE BELOVED, AND FRIEND OF HIS PEOPLE.

" Yea, he is altogether lovely. This is my beloved, and this is my friend, O daughters of Jerusalem."—*Cant.* v. 16.

UNLESS we understand this book in its allegorical application to Christ and his Church, we can see no spiritual object or end attained by its holding a place in the inspired canon. But when thus understood, it is not only gorgeous in its figures, but rich in impassioned sentiment, and every way adapted to excite a holy, ardent love to the Saviour. In this light we shall consider the passage on this occasion.

Observe,

I. *What Christ is in himself.*

II. *What he is to his people.*

III. *The profession they make of their attachment to him.*

I. *What Christ is in himself.*

" Altogether lovely." So sang the sweet singer of Israel in reference to him. " My heart is inditing a good matter : I speak of the things which I have made touching the king : my tongue is the pen of a ready writer. Thou art fairer than the children of men : grace is poured into thy lips ; therefore God hath blessed thee forever."—Psa. xlv. 1, 2.

We see the appropriateness of this,

1. *When applied to the spotlessness of his nature.*

He was without moral infirmity—pure—holy—separate from sinners—the perfect reflection of the divine holiness. As such, not only his soul, but his body was without taint of sin or evil. No doubt his countenance was the most lovely and benignant ever beheld ; so that body and soul displayed perfect purity. He was holy, even as God is holy ; for he was the very " brightness of his glory, and the express image of his person."

The description of the text is true,

2. *When applied to his unrivalled perfections.*

He had all the faculties and powers of man in a transcendent degree. But he had also all the illustrious perfections of the Deity. All the Father's attributes were in him, both natural and moral ;—eternity, almightiness, ubiquity, omniscience, immutability, infinite wisdom, boundless knowledge, unspotted purity, unchanging faithfulness, inflexible righteousness, unspotted truth, immeasurable goodness, boundless mercy, and tenderest pity. He was incarnate love—embodied compassion—grace living, speaking, acting, and suffering for the world's well-being and man's redemption. Such a combination of celestial and holy perfections, angels had never beheld before. For there was divine grandeur incorporated with human weakness—eternity linked to a new-born babe—immensity lodged in the contracted span of an earthly tabernacle. No marvel that the apostle John exclaims—" We beheld his glory, the glory as of the only-begotten of the Father, full of grace and truth."

Observe the appropriateness of the text,

3. *When applied to his varied offices.*

(1.) He was the most exalted Prophet, in whom all the treasures of wisdom and knowledge dwelt ; compared with all others, —the sun of the system of divine revelation.

(2.) The most sacred and exalted Priest. The priest of the human race, in whom the offices both of prophet and great high priest meet and are centred. The antitype of the whole sacerdotal order ; for his priesthood is not only universal, but perpetual. His sacrifice of real and infinite value ; his temple the holiest of all. The blessings he imparts involving pardon for all sin, entire holiness, and eternal life.

(3.) As the most magnificent Monarch. His kingdom is spiritual, righteous, benevolent, prosperous, and shall be universal and everlasting. No king so rich, so powerful, so gracious, so blessed as he. He is " King immortal, invisible, eternal," and on his vesture, and on his thigh, it is written, " King of kings, and Lord of lords."

See the truth of the text,

4. *When applied to his spirit and temper.*

Love, meekness, tenderness, benignity, are the graces which pre-eminently distinguish Jesus. In youth it is said, " he grew in favor with God and man." How he displayed this loveliness in his general conduct, discourses, miracles ! How many could have testified to the truth of the text ! Even the unworthy woman that was so notorious a sinner, Zaccheus, the woman of Samaria, the dying thief—the officers sent to arrest him, with multitudes of others, have borne witness of the graciousness of his spirit, and the loveliness of his mien and temper towards them.

How striking the description,

5. *When compared with the most renowned and excellent of men.*

Take Abraham the faithful, Moses the meek, David the generous, or John the ardent and affectionate; he had all their excellences in a perfect degree, and none of their frailties. He was "altogether lovely;" under all circumstances—during his whole life—in all he ever was, or said, or did. He was so to God—to angels—and to all holy men.

I do not dwell on his titles, though they are so beautiful, varied, and interesting. All nature is drawn upon to set him forth. The heavens—for he is the morning star, and the sun of righteousness. The earth—for he is the rose of Sharon—the plant of renown—the pearl of great price. Yea, " he is altogether lovely."

Observe,

II. *What Christ is to his people.*

"Their beloved and friend." As such, he is,

1. *The object of their ardent and supreme love.*

Loved really, sincerely, and pre-eminently. He must have our superlative affection; he must be loved more than wealth, or friends, or life. He must have the throne of the heart, or he will not reign within us; he must be preferred to all others. But never forget, that our love to him is ever the result and effect of his love to us. "We love him because he first loved us."

Now this love to Jesus is a conscious emotion. "Whom not having seen we love." With humility we can say, "Thou knowest all things, thou knowest that we love thee."

2. *He is their chief friend.*

He avers himself their friend, and he calls them his friends. Mutual love unites them; mutual communion is maintained; and mutual delight is exhibited. His friendship contains every element of excellency and preciousness. He is their real friend—their constant friend—their sufficient and efficient friend—for all places, and all times. He is their unchanging and everlasting friend. No one like him—he is their unrivalled friend. How honorable—how blessed—how sweet the friendship of Christ! Happy they who can say—" he is my beloved and friend."

Now the leading thoughts concerning Christ's friendship we have only just hinted at. The outline is given, so that the subject may be contemplated, and enlarged on, and be the theme of renewed meditation, with the greatest possible profit to the soul. Only just remember that he is the friend of friends—the friend of the friendless—the friend of the unworthy—even of sinners; but the especial and beloved friend of those who know him, and believe in him. Hence he says to them—"Greater love hath no man than this, that a man lay down his life for his friends. Ye are my friends if ye do whatsoever I command you. Henceforth I call you not servants; for the servant knoweth not what his lord doeth : but I have called you friends; for all things that I have heard of my Father I have made known unto you."—John xv. 13–15.

Then consider,

III. *The profession his people make of their attachment to him.*

"This is my friend, O daughters of Jerusalem."

We observe here,

1. *True love to Christ cannot be concealed.*

What the heart intensely feels, the mouth will utter. The heart is the main-spring of man; all will follow its powerful emotions. The miser talks of his gold—the pleasure-taker of his banquets—the literary man of his books; so, the Christian of the Saviour. Hence the holy affection must be expressed; it must be spoken and avowed to the daughters of Jerusalem. Christian conversation is never so profitable as when Jesus is the theme, and when our attachment to him is the subject of pious and ardent exultation.

2. *True love to Christ ought not to be concealed.*

It would violate Christian duty—Christ has enjoined it. It would be especially ungrateful. Think of his publicly attested love to us. To profess Christ is honorable both to the intellect and heart. This profession should be made to the church; the church has a right to demand this from us, that they may recognize us, as Christ's disciples. Much better that we show our love to Christ, as the fitness for communion, than any mere attachment to creeds, and names, and ceremonies.

This profession ought to be made before the world. We are to confess him before men—before all ranks and classes of men. Always be ready to give a reason for the hope that is within us. Never to be ashamed of Christ and his words.

3. *This profession should be exemplified in the life.*

It should be seen that we love Christ. Our spirit, and temper, and conduct should testify this. We are to be his epistles, his friends, his disciples; and thus to be like-minded with Christ. Having his spirit, wearing his costume, doing his work, keeping his commandments, seeking his glory,— in one word, "living to Christ," and showing forth his grace in our temper and demeanor, and conduct in general. It is most honorable to religion, and most pleasing to the Saviour, when all our actions point to him, and say—"he is our beloved and friend."

APPLICATION.

And now we ask,

(1.) What think ye of Christ? Do you admire and esteem and love him? Or are you his avowed enemies? or are you indifferent to Christ? or are you only nominally connected with him? These are momentous questions! And we should be faithful in examining our own hearts, that we may know precisely how we stand in relation to Jesus, the great and lovely Saviour of the world.

We would appeal,

(2.) To those who despise or neglect Christ. What baseness! What folly! And how ruinous must be the result! Despising him, where will you go for pardon, for holiness, for eternal salvation? Ponder well the words of Holy Scripture on this subject. "How shall we escape if we neglect so great salvation?"—Heb. ii. 3. "What shall the end be of them that obey not the gospel of Christ?"—1 Pet. iv. 17. And then remember that most terrible malediction,—"If any man love not the Lord Jesus Christ, let him be anathema maranatha."—1 Cor. xvi. 22.

(3.) To those who desire to love Christ, we say, contemplate his person and work. Consider him as revealed in the gospel. Come to him as sinners, and give him the faith of your hearts. Trust in him for salvation. Do it now—entirely, solemnly, and forever. He asks your faith and your hearts, give both to him, and then the experience of the text will be yours.

(4.) To the Saviour's friends we add, show forth his praise in all you do. Aim at this, and labor to do this. Often cherish in your hearts, and utter with your lips, the sentiments of the text—"He is altogether lovely." And be not satisfied unless you can truly sing—

"Yes, thou art precious to my soul—
  My transport and my trust;
Jewels to thee are gaudy toys,
  And gold is sordid dust.

All my capacious powers can wish
  In thee doth richly meet:
Nor to my eyes is light so dear,
  Nor friendship half so sweet.

Thy grace shall dwell upon my heart,
  And shed its fragrance there;
The noblest balm of all its wounds,
  The cordial of its care.

I'll speak the honors of thy name
  With my last laboring breath;
Then, speechless, clasp thee in mine arms,
  The antidote of death."

XLIX.—THE GREATEST DECEIVER.

"The heart is deceitful above all things, and desperately wicked: who can know it?"—*Jer.* xvii. 9.

ALL men profess to admire candor and truth, and hate guile and hypocrisy in others. An open foe is generally preferred to a deceitful friend. To be deceived is not only to be injured, but to be degraded. We feel that while our interests have been assailed, our judgment and acuteness have been over-reached. There are many things around us of a deceiving character. Circumstances often deceive us; appearances which promise much often leave us disappointed. Few have loved long who have not suffered by deceitful friends. The world is a great deceiver. How its myriads of vassals are every day involved in the meshes of its treachery! Satan began his evil reign on earth by treachery and guile; he is described as that old serpent—the devil. But we are now to consider the master spirit of treachery—the greatest of all deceivers—and that is the carnal human heart. So says the text—"the heart is deceitful above all things, and desperately wicked: who can know it?" Then let us endeavor to establish and illustrate the truth of the text.

The superlative deceitfulness of the heart is manifest,

I. *By its multifarious modes of operation.* The devices it employs are legion. It has its thousands of schemes and plans of action. It diversifies its measures according to the varied circumstances in which its victims are placed; and it suits its deception to the temperaments, constitutions and dispositions of its subjects. It deceives the sanguine by exhibiting false and delusive objects of hope. It deceives the desponding by foolish and superstitious claims. It deceives the impetuous by hurrying them on to rashness; it deceives the supine by encumbering them in the incrustations of lethargy. It deceives the self-willed by overweening confidence; and the timid by incessant fears. It would lead the moral into pharisaism; and the licentious into antinomian quagmires. It would deceive the prosperous by exciting them to arrogance and pride; and the unfortunate by sinking them into sullenness and despondency. It has its characteristic plans, and its appropriate modes, for all the endless varieties of human state and condition.

We see the truth of the text,

II. *In the universal sphere of its influence.*

Go where you will, you see the workings of the deceitful heart. Some nations are proverbially so; but the fact is, all are really so. It is seen in the cunning of the savage, and in the adroitness of the intelligent. It is alike observable in all latitudes and zones —amidst all people and tongues. It lives in all regions—and speaks and operates in all languages. It is never absent from the 'Change, or the busy scenes of merchandise. It is even present in the rural and retired hamlets of seclusion. It is the privileged guest of cabinets, and courts, and councils. It has laid under its ban trade and commerce, art and science, philosophy and literature, morals and religion. Like the atmosphere, it fills, and surrounds, and impregnates all regions and countries with its pestiferous influences.

III. *It subjects to its control all orders and classes of men.*

How soon it betrays the child into equivocation and falsehood! And how it involves the hoary head in the mists of duplicity! It debases the noble youth; and maiden purity is not proof against its assaults. It is seen often to throw its shadows over the manly brow, and over womanly excellency. There is no age nor period of life when men are free from its vassalage. It disturbs, and renders foul and turbid, the streams of knowledge; corrupts the principles of virtue; and cankerworms the very acts of philanthropy and goodness. The woman of fashion, and the demure nun—the man of pleasure, and the man of austere devotion—the downcast beggar and the exalted monarch—are each and all spell-bound by its deleterious machina-

tions. While it reigns rampantly in many places, it reigns insidiously everywhere; so that you cannot escape its miasmatic power. There is no region where it is not, and there are no classes absolutely exempted from its operations. It lives in all latitudes and climes; and no community of men, however small, has yet been discovered entirely strangers to it. It is the disease of our race —the plague-spot of the family of man.

But observe,

IV. *It deceives the whole man.*

It darkens the understanding and covers it with mists of error. It perverts the judgment, and makes its decisions false and valueless. It surrounds with felicitous glare the imagination, so that vanity is preferred to that which is real, and a lie to truth. It gives to the affections a corrupt influence, and excites with unhallowed desires and passions. It binds the will with its silken cords, or fastens it securely in its gaudy trappings. It pollutes the conscience, and bribes God's vicegerent to duplicity or silence. It betrays the memory into a tenacity for evil, and an oblivion-like fatuity as to good.

If the mind is thus entirely possessed, no marvel that the senses are led captive at its will. It enlists the eyes with treacherous gaze to go on voyages of evil discovery. It employs the ear as the recipient of external and evil communications; and it anoints the tongue with flattery, dissimulation, and falsehood. It makes the countenance to change its aspects as the chamelion its colors; and invests the whole man, both physical, mental, and moral, with hypocrisy and guile. Who then can know its depths, its wiles, and its deadly evils? How true of the soul of man, as of Israel of old!— "The whole head is sick, and the whole heart faint. From the soul of the foot even unto the head there is no soundness in it; but wounds, and bruises, and putrifying sores: they have not been closed, neither bound up, neither mollified with ointment." —Isa. i. 5, 6.

V. *It deceives the most distinguished and illustrious of our race.*

It not only deceives the masses, but also the *élite;* the worthless, but also the excellent of the earth; the profane of the world, but also the pious of the church. Look at Noah, the father of the postdiluvian world, deceived into drunkenness and shame! Look at Abraham, deceived into dissimulation and lying! Look at Lot, deceived into sensuality and incest! Look at Jacob, deceived into overreaching, duplicity, and fraud! Look at Moses, deceived into rashness and passion! Look at Elijah, deceived into petulance and discontent, and a longing for death! Look at David, deceived into pollution and bloodshed! Look at Solomon, deceived, even in old age, into voluptuousness and idolatry! Look at Jonah, deceived into misanthropy and anger! Look at the Disciples of our Lord, deceived into worldliness and ambition, and again into cowardice and temporary apostasy! See the chief of them, Peter, deceived into lying and perjury! What saith this illustrious galaxy of the earth's greatest and best men? "That the heart is deceitful above all things, and desperately wicked: who can know it?"

Now, the power of this moral illusion is specially proven, when the wise, and the good, and the great, and the godly, are among its victims—when it insidiously overcomes the prudent, and the strong, and the noble of mankind. And it is thus that the pre-eminent deceit of the heart is made manifest.

Then notice,

VI. *That its deceptions are often repeated.* We may suppose that all men might occasionally be deceived. At least once, or say twice; but the heart deceives over and over again. It holds men in its delusive enchantments for years, and often for the whole of life. And what is astounding, it makes men in love with their deceits. They prefer the ideal to the palpable—the shadow to the substance—the dross to the fine gold. No bird would be ensnared often, but the heart is. No animal instinct would be often deluded, but the heart is; and this is one of the peculiar traits of the depth of the deceit, in which the human heart is involved.

To advert more at length to some cases the word of God has handed down to us— Noah, whose piety kept him pure amidst the general depravity of the old world, fails to preserve him after the terrible scenes and judgments of the flood. Lot, who was holy in Sodom, becomes depraved in retirement. Solomon, who began his career with so much humility, prayer, and wisdom, renders his gray hairs despicable, by his open apostasy from sound knowledge and the way of godliness.

VII. *The heart deceives us in concerns of the greatest moment and importance.*

Thus, these heart-deceivings dishonor man,

and cover him with shame and reproach; and sink him lower than the beasts that perish. It impoverishes man, steals his true riches, and degrades him into mental and spiritual poverty,—clothes him with rags,— leaves him in a state of moral impotency.

It destroys man. Blinds his eyes—hardens his heart—poisons his spirit. It is the plague of the soul—the leprosy of the moral nature. It finally involves him in eternal death. It cheats the soul out of present peace and good; and abandons it to everlasting destruction. A deceitful heart is unfit for divine communion, and for the divine presence. It cannot enter through the gates of the holy city of God. It is now condemned, and under the divine wrath, and is exposed to eternal death. So that this deceitfulness of the heart is its undoing; there can be no moral health, nor purity, nor bliss, so long as we are under its deadly influence. The question then arises—is there any remedy? Or is the heart helplessly and hopelessly deceitful? Is there no cure? No power to break the delusion, to expel the poison, and to save the soul? To this we reply,

VIII. *That for the deceitfulness of the heart the gospel provides the only remedy.*

How ancient philosophers and moralists disputed, and wrangled, and taught, on the evils of the world, and means of moral deliverance! Epicurus, Zeno, Socrates, Plato, and Seneca—how they discoursed and reasoned in vain! How their best remedies were at most but slight palliatives, that left the disease untouched, and the malady as deep and inveterate as ever! But thanks be to God, the divine word announces the great specific! Hear it prophetically described by the ancient seer of Israel—"Then will I sprinkle clean water upon you, and ye shall be clean: from all your filthiness, and from all your idols, will I cleanse you. A new heart also will I give you, and a new spirit will I put within you: and I will take away the stony heart out of your flesh, and I will give you an heart of flesh. And I will put my spirit within you, and cause you to walk in my statutes, and ye shall keep my commandments, and do them."— Ezek. xxxvi. 25–27.

Hear Jesus asking the morally diseased if they would be made whole; and then exerting his divine power in forgiving sins, and healing their spiritual maladies. "Behold!"—says John, in reference to Christ—

"the Lamb of God which taketh away the sin of the world." Hear too what he attests as to this great remedy—"If we say that we have no sin, we deceive ourselves, and the truth is not in us. If we confess our sins, he is faithful and just to forgive us our sins, and to cleanse us from all unrighteousness."—1 John i. 8, 9. So the apostle Paul dwells on this one and only theme. "For if the blood of bulls and of goats, and the ashes of an heifer sprinkling the unclean, sanctifieth to the purifying of the flesh, how much more shall the blood of Christ, who through the eternal Spirit offered himself without spot to God, purge your conscience from dead works to serve the living God."—Heb. ix. 13, 14.

Now, the heart must be brought by humble and entire faith to rest on Christ's atoning sacrifice, and thus it experiences, "That the blood of Christ, God's Son, cleanseth from all sin." Then light takes the place of darkness—truth the place of deception—and sincerity the place of guile, in the human soul. God by his Spirit, through the atoning blood of the cross, and by the energy of his divine word, sanctifies the heart, and makes it his hallowed dwelling, his consecrated temple.

Oh, yes, it is matter of infinite joy, that there is truth to enlighten the heart—grace to renew it—and the Holy Spirit of God to dwell in it, and to keep it.

Then in conclusion,

1. Let the depravity and deceitfulness of the heart be acknowledged and confessed. Don't add to its deceivings by dreaming that it is not so deceitful. But rather humble yourselves before God, and seek that grace which alone can deliver and sanctify you.

2. The man, who by faith in Christ is a new creature, let him show forth, and recommend to others the great remedy which has been so efficacious to his own moral healing. And let all remember,

3. Despising Christ's cleansing blood and renewing grace, and we know of no other means for the real spiritual elevation of man. Education, and other useful influences, may preserve him from the loathsome aspects of vice; but only in the fountain opened for sin and uncleanness can he find an entire and abiding cure for the deep inwrought depravity of the soul.

———————

L.—PURE RELIGION.

"Pure religion, and undefiled before God and the Father, is this, to visit the fatherless and widows in their affliction, and to keep himself unspotted from the world."—*Jas.* i. 27.

MAN was evidently destined for religious purposes—by which we mean—for the belief of religious mysteries—the worship of the supreme God—the discharge of religious duties—and the cherishing of religious emotions. A careful examination of human beings, and the records of all nations, will confirm this declaration.

But it is not enough to be religious; but to have the right religion, which in the text is called "pure religion." It must be of the greatest moment to have truth instead of error—to know and serve the true God, instead of an imaginary deity—to yield the worship that is intelligent and dignifying, and not the blind ceremonials of ignorance and superstition—to live in the exercise of those duties that must please a Holy Being, and not be the victims of practices alike dishonorable to God and degrading to ourselves. No subject, then, can be more momentous than that of pure religion. The word religion signifies virtue, as arising from reverence for God. But in its more extensive and understood meaning, it may comprehend the faith, experience, and practice of the soul, as to sacred things.

Then let us proceed,

I. *To define pure religion.*

And here observe it is not to be confounded with,

1. *The religion of superstition.*

The Athenians had this; and hence their countless idols and altars. So that Paul said—"I perceive that in all things ye are too superstitious." Such is paganism. Now, whether in the refined and subtle forms of Hindooism, or the rude aspect it presents in the South Sea Islander or North American Indian, all these are composed of gross and ridiculous marvels—essentially the religions of terror, of deprecations, fancies, dreams, and fabulous narratives.

Pure religion dwells in the region of heaven's sunlight and divine truth. Its intellectuality is one of its essential elements of purity. It recognizes nothing grovelling, puerile, and vain. However it may rise above human reason, it never insults it, or degrades it.

Nor must it be confounded,

2. *With a religion of ceremonies.*

Here Mahometanism, Popery, and the Greek Church must be present to our minds. Perhaps with Popery we are most acquainted. With its gorgeous priesthood, and attractive rites; with its penance, and absolution, and masses. So that the little Christian truth Rome has, she does with it as Herod did with Christ—array it in mock apparel, and clothe it in the garb of buffoonery. Her rites merely gratify the eye and the imagination; and these are amused at the expense of conscience and sound sense.

Pure religion is adorned with simple drapery. Her institutes and ordinances are clear, and spiritual, and significant—while Romanism and the Greek Church have a patchwork external system of paganism and Judaism, with some few indistinct traits of Christianity.

Nor must we confound it,

3. *With the religion of mere rationalism.*

A religion without mysteries. Of cheerless speculations—abstract reasonings. That refuses to go beyond the region of the senses. That ridicules all it cannot understand. That brings every thing down to its own stunted capacity, and tests every thing by it. That explains away inspiration, miracles, Christ's divinity, the personality of the Spirit, Satan's existence; and rejects all that we call experimental piety.

This system of religion, or, rather, of non-religion, is the extremely opposite of that of superstition. That is the prolific region of all imaginative luxuriance; this the northern pole of cold, and ice, and sterility, and perpetual winter, where no lovely flower grows, no genial sunbeams play, no spiritual life is put forth.

But we must equally avoid confounding it,

4. *With the religion of fanaticism.*

A religion without intelligence, without moral evidence. A religion of entire excitement, impulse, fancies, and feeling. Sometimes of almost avowed predictions and miracles. A religion of presumptuous familiarity with God—of irreverent use of the divine name—and ignorant application of the Holy Scriptures.

In all ages there have been outbursts of this sort, alike degrading to man and in direct hostility to the Holy Word of God. Germany has been fruitful in both extremes of fanaticism and rationalism; so Russia; so the United States of America—especially in that most foul and polluted system of extravagance and immorality, called Mormonism.

It is essential that we do not confound it,

5. *With a religion of self-righteousness.*

Of human works, as the merits and ground of our salvation; of comfort, derived from our own doings, and which is incessantly boasting of self-reliance, self-satisfaction. Such as the Pharisees of old had, and such as myriads of our mere formalists have now. A religion in which there is no room for the cross of Christ—the fountain opened—or the riches of divine grace—or where these have only a secondary place—or are so mixed up with human merit, as to lose their virtue and value.

And I add, lastly, we must not confound it,

6. *With a religion of unrighteousness.*

Of mere doctrine, without practice; of antinomianism—that perverts all that is evangelical, under the pretence of not needing any thing that is practical. That is afraid of holiness, and makes the gospel and the grace of God minister to unrighteousness. That takes Christ as a priest, but not as a king. That says, Lord, Lord, but does not the things which he commands. That goes for its principles to eternal decrees, unknown purposes, secret councils, arbitrary—miscalled by them—sovereign authority. That makes God partial—Christ the redeemer of a few—the work of the Holy Spirit restrictive to the veriest fragments of the human race; and man from first to last entirely passive, without any power or responsibility, as to repentance, faith, or submission to the gospel of salvation.

Now, pure religion, in contrast with all these,

(1.) Rests on the pure truth of the divine word. It goes here for its doctrines—its principles, ordinances, precepts, motives, hopes. It most sacredly appeals to the law and to the testimony. It takes the Scriptures as its all-sufficient guide. It adds nothing thereto; it evades nothing—alters nothing. It asks, What has God spoken? and to that it bows with profound and unvarying respect. It values every grain of God's pure truth. It deems nothing he has commanded, to be of trivial moment; and it seeks to keep all his precepts. If we go to any other ordeal or test, there must be contradiction and confusion. There will be council against council—synod against synod; great and learned, and even godly men, set up one against the other. But

God's word is clear, full, and sufficient for faith, experience, and practice; and pure religion draws all its waters from this divine and living fountain.

(2.) It is essentially pure in its operations. Pure religion brings man into a state of relative purity, or a condition of righteousness, in which justification is enjoyed. A justification which saves us from all charges of guilt and condemnation; in which, by faith in Christ, we are righteous, and accepted of God. To this it superadds the inward renewal of the soul—an entire change of heart and life. It gives a new spirit—a holy nature and emotions—which delight in God, and truth, and obedience. So that when the inward man is thus made holy, the outward life is fruitful in all good works. Especially is love to God supreme; faith in Christ decided, vigorous; and benignity and goodness to men most strikingly manifest. But observe,

(3.) It is pure in its blessed conformity to the holy example of the Redeemer. Thus we see these invariable characteristics of pure religion—pure principles, purity of state and heart, purity of life; and these ever belong to the evangelical religion of the New Testament. But the text, in illustrating this purity, lays hold of beneficence to man, and non-conformity to the world—"To visit the fatherless and widows in their affliction, and to keep himself unspotted from the world." To do so in the spirit of tender sympathy and kindly aid; to do them good, as Christ did in his life of compassion and love. And then to avoid worldly influences and pollution—" to keep himself unspotted from the world." To live in the world, and yet in spirit and life to be separate from it; even as Christ did, who said—"I am not of the world." Not to be spotted with worldly avarice, or ambition, or vanity, or pleasure, or care; but to live above it, and be crucified to it. Such, then, is pure religion.

Now let me,

II. *Urge it on your adoption.*

And, in doing so, we may remind you,

1. *That you need it.*

Nothing else will suit your state of guilt and pollution, meet your necessities, or satisfy your desires for permanent and everlasting good. You need religion. You need the religion of the divine word; and this religion is in every sense adapted to your state and exigencies.

But it may be urged because,

2. *It will lead to your mental and moral elevation.*

It invariably exalts and dignifies its subjects. The pagan, the savage, or the Mahometan, it ennobles and blesses. It refines and purifies the taste and manners; and whether it finds its disciples in palaces, or in the mudwalled cottage, it gives them mental dignity and moral power. It will make you both wiser and better.

But more,

3. *It will fit you for a pure and blissful futurity.*

God is holy, and without holiness no man can see his face. Heaven is holy, and nothing that defileth can enter therein. Its services, engagements, society, are all pure; so that only pure religion can fit you for that state of existence which stretches into the eternity to come. The pure in heart shall see God. The undefiled shall ascend his holy hill. Those who are meet shall have the inheritance. So that pure religion is essential to future bliss and glory.

APPLICATION.

We ask,

(1.) Do you possess this pure religion? If so, rejoice in it; cultivate it. Seek daily growth, and increased conformity to the Lord Jesus Christ.

(2.) If you have it not—then reflect on its importance, and seek it by simple faith in Jesus Christ. Come to the fountain opened; come to the physician of souls; come to the gracious Redeemer—cast yourselves on his power and willingness to save you. And so come and seek this pure religion, that it may have a preference and pre-eminence in your thoughts, desires, and resolutions, over every other object and pursuit.

(3.) The Christian will pray and labor for the spread of this pure religion throughout the world. How blessed and glorious earth will be, when God's will shall be done in it, as it is done in heaven!

LI.—THE SOLEMN QUESTION.

"Have the gates of death been opened unto thee? or hast thou seen the doors of the shadow of death?"—*Job* xxxviii. 17.

OUR text is the address of Jehovah to Job. We do not intend to dwell on the occurrence which brought it forth; but the idea is that God observes all things, and that hades—the unseen world—is without a covering before him. Man—whatever be his talents, or learning, or skill—cannot penetrate the future; and without a revelation from God, all he can do is to guess and conjecture what is the condition of the eternal world. With God, the past, present, future—heaven, earth, hell, are easily explained; he observes all with perfect clearness and accuracy; and therefore he is most intimately conversant with all the events which happen to men. He not only sees the moment of our birth, but he sees the hour of our departure from this life. He witnesses our entrance into this world, and also he knows when the gates of death shall be opened to us. But that momentous crisis of our being he has wisely and in great goodness concealed from us. We know not what shall be even on the morrow; we cannot tell what a day will bring forth.

Let us consider the text then, with the light which revealed truth has shed upon it, and with a view to our individual edification.

Let us notice,

I. *A few things concerning the gates of death.*

Observe,

1. *The gates are the boundaries of certain dominions.*

Death is the boundary of life; it is placed between time and eternity to separate the living from the dead—probationers from those whose lot is irrevocably fixed. So that these gates let us out of life into the solemn and unknown region of the dead. Passing through them we cease to be creatures of this world and of time, and become the inhabitants of the eternal state.

Notice,

2. *Gates are under official jurisdiction.*

The king, or governor, or the ruling powers, set them up. So the gates of death are under the control of God. He is the arbiter of life; he has the keys of death and hades; he fixes the boundaries of our existence, and determines the point of our earthly being, beyond which we shall not pass. Death is not an accident, but the yielding up of life to God—at his pleasure, and by his indisputable authority.

Notice,

3. *Through these gates all men must pass.*

It is appointed unto men once to die. So in all times past this has been exemplified—except in the instances of Enoch and Elijah. So with reference to all living now—they know that they must die. There is no escape—no exception from the fatal stroke of mortality. However exalted by worldly glory and magnificence, however rich, however invested with power and authority, however magnanimous, however strong, however favored by God or men,—every living man must pass through the gates of death.

Life is a journey towards these gates. Some go with accelerated speed, and soon reach them. Others journey more slowly; but all are going towards that terminus of human existence on earth.

We note,

4. *Through these gates none shall repass to the present world.*

In some cases of miraculous interposition they have done so, both under the Old Testament dispensation and the New; but these are exceptions to the rule. Christ also did so, as "the resurrection and the life." But not so with mankind in general. Men will remain in the region beyond after death, until the second coming of the Lord Jesus Christ. There is no return from that land. So David said of his child—"Then said his servants unto him, What thing is this that thou hast done? thou didst fast and weep for the child while it was alive; but when the child was dead, thou didst rise and eat bread. And he said, While the child was yet alive, I fasted and wept; for I said, Who can tell whether God will be gracious to me that the child may live? But now he is dead wherefore should I fast? can I bring him back again? I shall go to him, but he shall not return to me."—2 Sam. xii. 21–23. So also Job most plaintively expresses the same truth—"My days are swifter than a weaver's shuttle, and are spent without hope. O remember that my life is wind: mine eye shall no more see good. The eye of him that hath seen me shall see me no more: thine eyes are upon me, and I am not. As the cloud is consumed and vanisheth away: so he that goeth down to the grave shall come up no more. He shall return no more to his house, neither shall his place know him any more."—Job vi. 7–10.

Observe,

II. *These gates have in a certain sense been opened to us.*

1. *Often to let through our beloved relatives and friends.*

Parents, children, kindred, have been called away from us to pass through them. You watched over them. The crisis came. The last breath. The gates were silently drawn back, and your friends escaped—they passed through, and then these gates were closed again. How solemn and affecting!

In this way we seem brought near to these gates of death ourselves. We are compelled to feel how close the living are to the regions of the dead; just one step between us and death. Our friends take that step, and cross beyond the gates of mortality, while we are left on earth's side of them to feel the stroke, and to weep on account of them. The gates of death have been in a certain sense open to us.

2. *When by affliction we have been brought near to them.*

There can be no doubt that the tendency of disease is to wean men from life and this world; and also to give a more keen and sensible impression of death and eternity. And in this way, how very often have we imagined the gates of death to be opening for our exit through them! Life's work seemed as if finished—earthly ties seemed dissolving—the mind was being made up for the last stage of the journey—the plans of the physician seemed vain—the hopes of relations were flickering; and then God in mercy restored to us the healing influence—added to our strength—renewed our vigor—and gave us again a supply of years of probationary being. He thus put into our souls the experience of the Psalmist—"Thy vows are upon me, O God: I will render praises unto thee. For thou hast delivered my soul from death: wilt not thou deliver my feet from falling that I may walk before God in the light of the living?"—Psa. lvi. 12, 13. "Return unto thy rest, O my soul; for the Lord hath dealt bountifully with thee. For thou hast delivered my soul from death, mine eyes from tears, and my feet from falling."—Psa. cxvi. 7, 8.

They have been opened,

3. *As revelation has shed light on what is beyond these gates.*

Take the prospect glass of divine truth and place the eye of faith to it, and thus look through; and life and immortality are then brought to light. Beyond are two distinct worlds. The one beneath is described as an abyss of darkness—a pit of despair—a fiery lake. It is hell—where are the multitudes of the impenitent, and the wicked; for "the wicked shall be turned into hell;"—all unbelievers—all idolaters, infidels, blasphemers, drunkards—all haters of God, and rejecters of Christ—all the worldly—all mere formalists. How terrible is this world of blackness, despair, and woe!

Then—above. Beyond the gates of death, there is a world of light, and peace, and glory. It is heaven. There is the radiant throne of God, the effulgent lustre of which is so overwhelming that the seraphim and cherubim cover their faces before it. There are angels and archangels, the holy patriarchs, prophets, apostles, martyrs, and all the good and holy men of every age and nation. Many of our friends, we trust, are mingling with that throng.

Such are the worlds beyond the gates of death. Paradise and perdition. The abode of the glorified and the happy, and the prison of the condemned and the lost. And to one of these worlds all men are hastening. This is the sphere of probation; and as we journey towards eternity we are daily becoming meet for the inheritance above the skies, or for the dark regions of misery and despair. Christ our blessed Saviour, constantly kept these worlds before those whom he addressed; and he describes in the most graphic manner, the last separation between the righteous and the wicked. "When the Son of man shall come in his glory, and all the holy angels with him, then shall he sit upon the throne of his glory: and before him shall be gathered all nations: and he shall separate them one from another, as a shepherd divideth his sheep from the goats. And he shall set the sheep on his right hand, but the goats on the left. Then shall the King say unto them on his right hand, Come, ye blessed of my Father, inherit the kingdom prepared for you from the foundation of the world."—Matt. xxv. 31–34. "Then shall he say also unto them on the left hand, Depart from me, ye cursed, into everlasting fire, prepared for the devil and his angels." v. 41. "And these shall go away into everlasting punishment; but the righteous into life eternal." v. 46.

Observe,

4. *The gospel provides a safe passport through the gates of death.*

This passport is acceptance with God through faith in the Lord Jesus Christ. By this we pass from death unto life; and the

Spirit of God is given to us, as the earnest of eternal glory. The possession of this delivers us from fear and torment now; it saves from despair in the dying hour; and it insures our everlasting salvation from hell, and a glorious entrance into Christ's heavenly kingdom. These gates of death shall thus become the gates of paradise. To die will be great and eternal gain. Such die in triumph, exclaiming—"O death, where is thy sting? O grave, where is thy victory? The sting of death is sin, and the strength of sin is the law. But thanks be to God which giveth us the victory through our Lord Jesus Christ."—1 Cor. xv. 55–57.

APPLICATION.

(1.) How solemn is the subject! How it deserves serious consideration! How it should be pondered, and form matter for daily reflection!

(2.) It is personal, as well as solemn. We must all have to do with these gates of death. We are born to die, and every hour of life is a nearer approach to that solemn event. To attempt to shut out the subject is worse than vain; it is madlike and wicked. It is our duty to "die daily;" and thus to be ready to pass through, whenever the gates of mortality shall be opened to us.

(3.) We cannot tell how soon we shall have to realize the meaning of the text. However relatively distant, it must in truth be really near; for a long life is just spent "as a tale that is told." We urge upon all to be evangelically ready for it—savingly in Christ. Then death is ours—not our enemy, but a friend; not a destroyer, but a servant of God, to tell us that he comes to bid us welcome to our Father's house; our everlasting and joyous home, where we shall be forever with the Lord.

Let the Christian contemplate with joy and hope the blessed results which will follow the passing through the gates of death. Beyond these gates will be the unending day of glory—immortality—eternal life! There is the better land—the land afar off—the inheritance of the saints—and the home of all the children of God.

The love of life is natural—one of the strongest innate feelings of the soul; but true religion sanctifies this feeling, and raises the mind to that which is beyond, even the higher life, for which this state of being is designed only to be preparatory. The Christian need not repine, or be cast down, that there are gates which let him out of a world of suffering and sin, and through which we shall pass to a world of perfect felicity and purity. To depart, and pass beyond this life, is far better; just as it is better for the traveller to be at home, and at rest within the holy city of habitation. And how delightful when the mind can so realize this by faith, without anxiety or dread; when the title to the better land is clear, and the meetness complete! The passage to the dying Christian between these gates and those of the celestial city, shall be inconceivably short; in a moment shall the transition be effected. So that the apostle speaks of being "absent from the body," and "present with the Lord." The one following the other immediately; and so the poet has caught the idea, when he says—

"In vain our fancy strives to paint
The moment after death;
The glories that surround the saints
When they resign their breath.

One gentle sigh their fetters breaks;
We scarce can say 'they're gone,'
Before the willing spirit takes
Her presence near the throne."

Now this glad thought has often sustained the dying Christian in the severest agonies of dying; and from the most excruciating pangs connected with dying, they have given one shout of victory—put their foot on the head of their last enemy—and soared at once into the high and transporting regions of the celestial world. The very hope of this should fill the mind with joy unspeakable and full of glory.

Then embody in your experience the thoughts of the holy Wesley—

"Be this my one great business here,
With holy trembling, holy fear,—
To make my calling sure!
Thine utmost counsel to fulfil,
And suffer all thy righteous will,
And to the end endure!

Then, Saviour, then, my soul receive,
Transported from this vale, to live,
And reign with thee above;
Where faith is sweetly lost in sight,
And hope in full, supreme delight,
And everlasting love."

LII.—THE CONCLUDING WORD.

"Amen."—1 *Cor.* xiv. 16.

OUR text is a word of very expressive and comprehensive signification, and which has occupied a place in the worship of the church of God for thousands of years. Now, we think the study of the text may be both instructive and edifying. It is ever worthy of the attention of intelligent worshippers of Jehovah, to know, clearly and distinctly, the meaning of the terms they use; so that with the mind, as well as with the heart, they may give homage to the living God. There can be no doubt, that the one signification of the word, Amen—involving both the assent and consent of those using it, is generally understood; but it will be seen that the word is rich in the variety of its meanings; and as such, opens a wide field for reflection and observation.

Now in reference to the word "Amen,"

I. *Let us consider the various modes of its application.*

II. *How we may intelligibly use it.*

I. *Consider the various modes of its application.*

The literal signification is "True," "Faithful," "Certain." But in the Scriptures, we meet,

1. *With the Amen of description.*

Where the word is applied to represent some object, or being.

(1.) It is a title applied to God. "That he who blesseth himself in the earth shall bless himself in the God of truth; and he that sweareth in the earth shall swear by the God of truth; because the former troubles are forgotten, and because they are hid from mine eyes."—Isaiah lxv. 16.

Now here it represents the Deity—God, as a God of truth. In the original, it is Amen. This term is one that is most expressly applied, and in perfect harmony with his holy nature. "He is the Rock, his work is perfect; for all his ways are judgment; a God of truth and without iniquity, just and right is he."—Deut. xxxii. 4. Now, truth is the basis of the divine government. This is expressly stated by the Psalmist—"For the word of the Lord is right; and all his works are done in truth."—Ps. xxx. 4. "The works of his hands are verity and judgment: all his commandments are sure. They stand fast forever and ever, and are done in truth and uprightness:" Ps. cxi. 7, 8. So truth is

the glory of the divine character. "Not unto us, O Lord, not unto us, but unto thy name give glory, for thy mercy, and for thy truth's sake."—Ps. cxv. 1.

(2.) It is applied also to the Redeemer. "And unto the angel of the church of the Laodiceans write: These things saith the Amen, the faithful and true witness, the beginning of the creation of God."—Rev. iii. 14. Now here it is designed to represent Christ as the Truth. He so styled himself, when he said—"I am the way, the truth, and the life." So it is said—"Grace and truth came by Jesus Christ." And we read —"Of the truth as it is in Jesus." Christ was "the Amen;" as in him was the "fulfilment of the prophecies," and the types of the Old Testament: and as he embodied and exemplified the end of all sacrifices and offerings for sin. So also as the witness for God. The one to verify God's word of promise—God's covenant of grace—and God's infinite love to the world. It is the glory of Christ to be the "Amen." As the personal representation of God he was "full of grace and truth."

2. *There is the Amen of affirmation.*

The declaration, that that which is spoken, is true. So it is used in Christ's address to Nicodemus, where the word may be rendered, instead of verily, "Amen." As if Christ had said, it is really, absolutely true, that a man must be born again, or he cannot enter into the kingdom of God. So it is used in reference to the promises—"For all the promises of God in him are yea, and in him Amen, unto the glory of God by us." —2 Cor. i. 20.

Here the divine engagements given in the declarations of his grace in Christ are said to be "Amen"—absolutely true, and infallibly certain.

Then there is,

3. *The Amen of assent and concurrence.*

Now, thus it is chiefly used in the Divine Word. It is so in reference to the divine curses. "Cursed be the man that maketh any graven or molten image, an abomination unto the Lord, the work of the hands of the craftsman, and putteth it in a secret place. And all the people shall answer and say, Amen."—Deut. xxvii. 15. We see this repeated by the people, in each and every succeeding verse to the end of the chapter. So Benaiah used it in reference to Solomon being king. "And Benaiah the son of Jehoiada answered the king, and said, Amen:

the Lord God of my lord the king say so too. As the Lord hath been with my lord the king, even so be he with Solomon, and make his throne greater than the throne of my lord the king."—1 Kings i. 36, 37. So it is used in reference to the divine praise and worship. "Blessed be the Lord God of Israel forever and ever. And all the people said, Amen, and praised the Lord."—1 Ch. xvi. 36.

4. *There is the Amen of desire and faith.*

In this way it is annexed to prayer, or thanksgiving. "Blessed be the Lord God of Israel from everlasting to everlasting. Amen and Amen."—Ps. xli. 13. "Even the prophet Jeremiah said, Amen: the Lord do so: the Lord perform thy words which thou hast prophesied, to bring again the vessels of the Lord's house, and all that is carried away captive, from Babylon into this place."—Jer. xxviii. 6. "And lead us not into temptation, but deliver us from evil; for thine is the kingdom, and the power, and the glory, forever. Amen."—Matt. vi. 13. So in the text. "Else when thou shalt bless with the spirit, how shall he that occupieth the room of the unlearned say Amen at thy giving of thanks, seeing he understandeth not what thou sayest."—1 Cor. xiv. 16. Now, so we use it in divine worship, when our hearts give a believing concurrence to the praise offered, or the prayer presented.

Then there is,

5. *The Amen of hope and anticipation.*

Where we believe, and expect, and desire some future good, in reference to ourselves or others. Now, thus it is used when David concluded his life and devotions—"Blessed be the Lord God, the God of Israel, who only doeth wondrous things. And blessed be his glorious name forever: and let the whole earth be filled with his glory. Amen, and Amen."—Psalm lxxii. 18, 19. And still more striking are the passages in the splendid visions of the Apocalypse, where the coming of our Lord is earnestly and prayerfully anticipated and desired: "Behold, he cometh with clouds; and every eye shall see him, and they also which pierced him; and all kindreds of the earth shall wail because of him. Even so, Amen. I am the Alpha and the Omega, the beginning and the end, saith the Lord, which is, and which was, and which is to come, the Almighty."—Rev. i. 7, 8. "He which testifieth these things, saith, Surely, I come quickly. Amen: even so, come, Lord Jesus." —Rev. xxii. 20.

Now, thus we see the scriptural history of this expressive and significant word.

Notice then,

II. *How we may intelligibly use it.*

Now, it will be manifest, as an appropriate expression in worship, that it cannot be used by the skeptical and disbelieving—nor by the profane and irreligious—nor by the thoughtless and irreverent—nor by the apathetic and formal. In all these cases it would be utterly out of place; and not only unmeaning, but insincere and hypocritical. It can only be rightly employed by the devout Christian and spiritual worshipper, who will enter into its spirit and significancy, and appropriately express it.

Now, it may be adopted either mentally, or be spoken out. The latter is, doubtless, the true mode. It would seem that it should be uttered—the people said, "Amen." So in the text—how shall "they say, Amen." In the early ages of the Christian church, the responses at the end of the prayers, it is said, were like distant thunder. But it must be said,

1. *Intelligibly.*

We must understand to what we affix it. This is the very essence of the text; so that all who lead in prayer should be clear, plain, and scriptural, that all may understand, and give their intelligible Amen.

2. *It must be said from the heart.*

Lip worship is easy, often gratifying to ostentation and self-righteousness. But if the heart be not in it, it is worthless and vain. How wretched to draw nigh with the mere person, and present only the utterance of the mouth. The tongue should only do the bidding of the spirit, and the inmost powers and emotions of the soul should unite, when to the praises or prayers of a Christian assembly we add our clear and audible—Amen.

3. *It must be said in faith.*

Faith in God, the hearer of prayer; faith in his promises, which we plead in prayer. Faith in the medium which is absolutely essential to the acceptance of our persons or services before God. Without faith it is impossible to please God; and we must ask in faith, saying Amen, to applications presented in faith.

4. *It must be said in ardent and earnest hope.*

Looking for the blessing sought—expecting its realization. Keeping the eye lifted up to heaven, and the heart extended towards

God, the fountain of grace. Waiting for the Lord, and the bestowment of his mercy. Now, thus will the Amen be an acceptable part of worship, and please God, and truly benefit our own souls.

APPLICATION.

In reference to the various significations of this word, we ask—

(1.) Do you contemplate God, and the Lord Jesus Christ, in their truth and faithfulness? For this view is essential to your confidence and hope. For just as you recognize the fidelity of God will your dependence upon him be entire; and in proportion to that dependence will be your peace and joy through believing. Think of God as a rock—as the eternal and immutable Jehovah—and then you will feel that in him is every moral element to command your complete repose, and unvarying trust.

(2.) Have you said Amen to Christ's overtures of the divine mercy? God's lovingkindness and saving grace are revealed in, and through, the person and work of Christ. Jesus is God's messenger of reconciliation, and he came expressly to restore you to God's favor and image. In virtue of that mission, by his word, and ministers, and Spirit, he has sought your faith, and love, and obedience. Have you yielded up your souls to him? And when he sought an entrance into your heart, did you, in the spirit of the Amen, say—

" Come quickly in, thou heavenly guest,
    Nor ever hence remove ;
But sup with me, and let the feast
    Be everlasting love."

(3.) Do you pray, and unite in the prayers of others in the spirit of the Amen? Resting, hoping, and desiring the blessings you need, and the general mercies which are sought? Without this, all services of devotion must be merely formal and vain. There must be the outgoings of our heart's fervent longings, and high aspirations, if either the prayers of others, or our own supplications, be acceptable and effective. What need of self-examination, lest we be cold, nominal worshippers, who have neither lot nor part in spiritual things!

4. Can you use it in reference to all events and dispensations? When Christ sends you trouble and affliction—when he appoints your lot in a land of sorrow and disappointment — can you say — " Amen ;

Lord, let it be so. Not my will, but thine be done."

How difficult to be able to say Amen to all God's doings and demands ; and to say it truly and cheerfully from the heart ! How needful to pray for grace to do this ! And yet true godliness involves the soul's perfect acquiescence in God's will and appointments. If we are not in this state of harmony with God in all things, are we really so in any thing? Is it not God's claim upon us, that we be unreservedly, for all uses, and at all times, and under every circumstance given up to him. To live, to labor, or to suffer, as it may be his supreme will to appoint. How sweetly has this Christian state of mind been set forth in the following lines :

" Renew my will from day to day ;
    Blend it with thine, and take away
    All that now makes it hard to say,
        'Thy will be done.'

Should pining sickness waste away
    My life in premature decay,
    In life, in death, teach me to say,
        'Thy will be done.'

And when on earth I breathe no more
    The prayer oft mixed with tears before,
    I'll sing upon a happier shore,
        'Thy will be done.' "

(5.) Is it expressive of your desires in reference to the coming of the Lord Jesus, and the enjoyment of eternal life? Whenever he shall come to you at death, and call you to himself, are you ready with the acquiescing and ready Amen? So that with Paul you can say, you had rather " depart and be with Christ, which is far better." How different is the state of mind of those who know not God—have no faith in Christ, nor any title to heaven ! How terrific is the aspect of death to the unbelieving and the impenitent ! And how dreadful will be the state of that vast and countless mass of beings, when Christ, in the day of judgment, shall pronounce that most awful sentence— " Depart, ye cursed !"—a sentence which will seal their doom ; and which will be followed by the multitudinous hosts of holy angels, and redeemed souls, uttering, with a sound like the roaring of many waters, " Amen, for thou, O Lord, art righteous and true, and faithful in all thy works, and just in all thy ways ; and thou art worthy to be adored and praised by all thy saints for evermore."

And how glorious will be that bright and innumerable throng which shall stand arrayed in vestments of celestial purity, on the right hand of the Judge; and who shall hear the public confession — the audible welcome; and who shall enter with ineffable gladness, and most joyous triumph, into the kingdom prepared for them from the foundation of the world. How all benevolent intelligences will yield their loving "Amen" to the Saviour's blissful benedictions in that day!

Reader! if a stranger to God's mercy, and the hope of salvation, deprecate having a portion with the unbelieving and incorrigible, thus excluded from the divine presence; and earnestly and promptly betake thyself to the Lord Jesus Christ, who alone can deliver thee from the wrath to come; and by the grace he freely waits to bestow, prepare thee for mansions of eternal light and glory. And what should be the solemn concern and earnest desire of every thoughtful, intelligent being of our race? but that when the probation of time shall have ended, and the opportunities of pardon and renewal of mind shall have passed away, that through the blood of the everlasting covenant they may have been made meet to be partakers of the inheritance of the saints in light. Will it not be the devout and daily prayer of such—

" Let me among thy saints be found,
  Whene'er the archangel's trump shall sound,
    To see thy smiling face;
  Then loudest of the crowd I'll sing,
  While heaven's resounding mansions ring
    With shouts of sovereign grace."

Amen.

THE END.

INDEX TO THE TEXTS

Alonzo Barbar Jr.
11/82